Financial Theory and Corporate Policy / THIRD EDITION

THOMAS E. COPELAND
Professor of Finance
University of California at Los Angeles

Firm Consultant, Finance
McKinsey & Company, Inc.

J. FRED WESTON
Cordner Professor of Managerial Economics and Finance
University of California at Los Angeles

ADDISON-WESLEY PUBLISHING COMPANY
Reading, Massachusetts · Menlo Park, California · New York
Don Mills, Ontario · Wokingham, England · Amsterdam
Bonn · Sydney · Singapore · Tokyo · Madrid · San Juan

This book is dedicated to our wives, Casey and June, who have provided their loving support; and to the pioneers in the development of the modern theory of finance: Hirshleifer, Arrow, Debreu, Miller, Modigliani, Markowitz, Sharpe, Lintner, Jensen, Fama, Roll, Black, Scholes, Merton, Ross, and others cited in the pages that follow. Without their intellectual leadership this text could not exist.

Library of Congress Cataloging-in-Publication Data

Copeland, Thomas E., 1946–
  Financial theory and corporate policy.

  Includes bibliographies and index.
  1. Corporations—Finance. I. Weston, J. Fred
(John Fred), 1916–   . II. Title.
HG4011.C833 1988   658.1'5   87–12595
ISBN 0–201–10648–5

Many of the designations used by manufacturers and sellers to distinguish their products are claimed as trademarks. Where those designations appear in this book, and Addison-Wesley was aware of a trademark claim, the designations have been printed in initial caps or all caps.

Reprinted with corrections, May 1992.

15 16 17 18 19 MA 95

Preface

In this third edition we seek to build on our experiences and the suggestions of users of the two previous editions. The feedback that we have received from all sources confirms our original judgment that there is a need for a book like *Financial Theory and Corporate Policy*. Therefore, we will continue to emphasize our original objectives for the book. Primarily, our aim is to provide a bridge to the more theoretical articles and treatises on finance theory. For doctoral students the book provides a framework of conceptual knowledge, enabling the students to understand what the literature on financial theory is trying to do and how it all fits together. For MBAs it provides an in-depth experience with the subject of finance. Our aim here is to equip the MBA for his or her future development as a practicing executive. We seek to prepare the MBA for reading the significant literature of the past, present, and future. This will help the practicing financial executive keep up to date with developments in finance theory, particularly as they affect the financial executive's own thinking processes in making financial decisions.

As before, our emphasis is on setting forth clearly and succinctly the most important concepts in finance theory. We have given particular attention to testable propositions and to the literature that has developed empirical tests of important elements of finance theory. In addition, we have emphasized applications so that the nature and uses of finance theory can be better understood.

A. PURPOSE AND ORGANIZATION

Over the past 30 years a branch of applied microeconomics has been developed and specialized into what is known as modern finance theory. The historical demarcation point was roughly 1958, when Markowitz and Tobin were working on the theory of portfolio selection and Modigliani and Miller were working on capital structure and valuation. Prior to 1958, finance was largely a descriptive field of endeavor. Since then major theoretical thrusts have transformed the field into a positive science. As evidence of the changes that have taken place we need only look at the types of people who teach in the schools of business. Fifty years ago the faculty were drawn from the ranks of business and government. They were respected and experienced statesmen within their fields. Today, finance faculty are predominantly academicians in the traditional sense of the word. The majority of them have no business experience except for consulting. Their interest and training is in developing theories to explain economic behavior, then testing them with the tools provided by statistics and econometrics. Anecdotal evidence and individual business experience have been superseded by the analytic approach of modern finance theory.

The rapid changes in the field of finance have profound implications for management education. As usual, the best students (and the best managers) possess rare intuition, initiative, common sense, strong reading and writing skills, and the ability to work well with others. But those with the greatest competitive advantage also have strong technical training in the analytical and quantitative skills of management. Modern finance theory emphasizes these skills. It is to the students and faculty who seek to employ them that this textbook is addressed.

The six seminal and internally consistent theories upon which modern finance is founded are: (1) utility theory, (2) state-preference theory, (3) mean-variance theory and the capital asset pricing model, (4) arbitrage pricing theory, (5) option pricing theory, and (6) the Modigliani-Miller theorems. They are discussed in Chapters 4 through 8 and in Chapter 13. Their common theme is "How do individuals and society allocate scarce resources through a price system based on the valuation of risky assets?" Utility theory establishes the basis of rational decision making in the face of risky alternatives. It focuses on the question "How do people make choices?" The objects of choice are described by state-preference theory, mean-variance portfolio theory, arbitrage pricing, and option pricing theory. When we combine the theory of choice with the objects of choice, we are able to determine how risky alternatives are valued. When correctly assigned, asset prices provide useful signals to the economy for the necessary task of resource allocation. Finally, the Modigliani-Miller theory asks the question "Does the method of financing have any effect on the value of assets, particularly the firm?" The answer to this question has important implications for the firm's choice of capital structure (debt-to-equity mix) and dividend policy.

It is important to keep in mind that what counts for a positive science is the development of theories that yield valid and meaningful predictions about observed phenomena. The critical first test is whether the hypothesis is consistent with the evidence at hand. Further testing involves deducing new facts capable of being observed but not previously known, then checking those deduced facts against additional empirical evidence. As students of finance, we must not only understand the theory, but also review the empirical evidence to determine which hypotheses have been validated. Consequently, every effort has been made to summarize the empirical evidence related to the theory of finance. Chapter 7 discusses empirical evidence on the capital asset pricing model and the arbitrage pricing theory. Chapter 8 includes studies of how alternative option pricing models perform. Chapter 9, newly added to this edition, discusses the theory and evidence on futures markets. Chapter 11 covers evidence on the efficient markets hypothesis. Chapter 14 reviews evidence on capital structure; Chapter 16 on dividend policy; Chapter 20 on mergers and acquisitions; and Chapter 22 on international finance.

Finally, in addition to the theory and empirical evidence there is always the practical question of how to apply the concepts to difficult and complex real-world problems. Toward this end, Chapters 2 and 3 are devoted to capital budgeting, Chapter 14 shows how to estimate the cost of capital for a large, publicly held corporation, and Chapter 16 determines the value of the same company. Chapter 18, another change in this edition, emphasizes the theory and evidence on topics of interest to chief financial officers: pension fund management, interest rate swaps, and leveraged buyouts. Throughout the text we attempt, wherever feasible, to give examples of how to apply the theory. Among other things we show how the reader can estimate his or her own utility function, calculate portfolio means and variances, set up a cross-hedge to reduce the variance of equity returns, value a call option, determine the terms of a merger or acquisition, use international exchange rate relationships.

In sum, we believe that a sound foundation in finance theory requires not only a complete presentation of the theoretical concepts, but also a review of the empirical evidence that either supports or refutes the theory as well as enough examples to allow the practitioner to apply the validated theory.

B. CHANGES IN THE THIRD EDITION

We have tried to move all the central paradigms of finance theory into the first half of the book. In the second edition this motivated our shifting the option pricing material into Chapter 8. In this third edition we decided to add a completely new chapter on futures markets—Chapter 9. It covers traditional material on pricing both commodity and financial futures, as well as newer issues: why futures markets exist, why there are price limits in some markets but not others, and empirical evidence on normal backwardation and contango.

In the materials on portfolio theory we have added a section on how to use T-bond futures contracts for cross-hedging. In Chapter 7 we have updated the literature review on the Capital Asset Pricing Model and the Arbitrage Pricing Model. Chapter 8 contains new evidence on option pricing. The materials on capital structure (Chapters 13 and 14) and on dividend policy (Chapters 15 and 16) have been completely rewritten to summarize the latest thinking in these rapidly changing areas of research.

Chapter 18 is completely new. Many topics of importance to chief financial officers are applications of finance theory. Pension fund management, interest rate swaps, and leveraged buyouts are the examples developed in this chapter.

Chapters 19 and 20 on mergers and acquisitions, restructuring, and corporate control represent up-to-date coverage of the burgeoning literature. Similarly, Chapters 21 and 22 reflect the latest thinking in the field of international financial management.

We made numerous other minor changes. In general, we sought to reflect all of the new important literature of finance theory—published articles and treatises as well as working papers. Our aim was to keep the book as close as possible to the frontiers of the "state-of-the-art" in the literature of finance theory.

C. SUGGESTED USE IN CURRICULUM

At UCLA we use the text as a second course in finance for MBA students and as the first finance course for doctoral students. We found that requiring all finance majors to take a theory-of-finance course before proceeding to upper-level courses eliminated a great deal of redundancy. For example, a portfolio theory course that uses the theory of finance as a prerequisite does not have to waste time with the fundamentals. Instead, after a brief review, most of the course can be devoted to more recent developments and applications.

Because finance theory has developed into a cohesive body of knowledge, it underlies almost all of what had formerly been thought of as disparate topics. The theory of finance, as presented in this text, is prerequisite to security analysis, portfolio theory, money and capital markets, commercial banking, speculative markets, investment banking, international finance, insurance, case courses in corporation finance, and quantitative methods of finance. The theory of finance can be, and is, applied in all of these courses. That is why, at UCLA at least, we have made it a prerequisite to all the aforementioned course offerings.

The basic building blocks that will lead to the most advantageous use of this text include algebra and elementary calculus; basic finance skills such as discounting, the use of cash flows, pro-forma income statements and balance sheets; elementary statistics; and an intermediate-level microeconomics course. Consequently, the book would be applicable as a second semester (or quarter) in finance. This could occur at the junior or senior undergraduate year, for MBAs during the end of their first year or beginning of their second year, or as an introductory course for Ph.D. students.

D. USE OF THE SOLUTIONS MANUAL

The end-of-chapter problems and questions ask the students not only to feed back what they have just learned, but also to take the concepts and extend them beyond the material covered directly in the body of the text. Consequently, we hope that the solutions manual will be employed almost as if it were a supplementary text. It should not be locked up in the faculty member's office, as so many instructor's manuals are. It is not an instructor's manual in a narrow sense. Rather, it is a solutions manual, intended for use by the students. Anyone (without restriction) can order it from the publisher. We order it, through our bookstore, as a recommended supplemental reading.

Understanding of the theory is increased by efforts to apply it. Consequently, most of the end-of-chapter problems are oriented toward applications of the theory. They require analytical thinking as well as a thorough understanding of the theory. If the solutions manual is used, as we hope it will be, then students who learn how to apply their understanding of the theory to the end-of-chapter problems will at the same time be learning how to apply the theory to real-world tasks.

E. ACKNOWLEDGMENTS

We have received help from many persons on the three editions of the book. We especially benefited from the insightful corrections, clarifications, and suggestions of Eugene Fama, Herb Johnson, and Kuldeep Shastri. Nai-fu Chen and Ronald Bibb wrote Appendixes B and D, respectively. Ron Masulis rewrote Chapter 5.

We also wish to acknowledge the help of the following: Ed Altman, Enrique Arzac, Dan Asquith, Warren Bailey, Gerry Bierwag, Diran Bodenhorn, Jim Brandon, Michael Brennan, William Carleton, Don Chance, Nai-fu Chen, Don Chew, Kwang S. Chung, Halimah Clark, Peter Clark, S. Kerry Cooper, Larry Dann, Harry and Linda E. DeAngelo, Dirk Davidson, David Eiteman, Chapman Findlay, Kenneth French, Dan Galai, Robert Geske, Mark Grinblatt, C. W. Haley, Ronald Hanoian, Iraj Heravi, David Hirshleifer, Tom Ho, Chi-Cheng Hsia, William C. Hunter, Ashok Korwar, Clement Krouse, Steven Lippman, Stephen Magee, Dubos Masson, Bill Margrabe, Charles Martin, Ronald Masulis, David Mayers, Guy Mercier, Edward Miller, Merton Miller, Timothy J. Nantell, Ron Necoechea, Jorgen Nielson, R. Richardson Pettit, Richard Pettway, Richard Roll, Shigeki Sakakibara, Eduardo Schwartz, Jim Scott, Jandhyala Sharma, Kilman Shin, Ron Shrieves, Keith Smith, Dennis Soter, Joel Stern, Sheridan Titman, Brett Trueman, Jim Wansley, Marty Weingartner, Richard West, Randy Westerfield, Robert Whaley, Stuart Wood, and Bill Ziemba.

For their considerable help in preparation of the text, we thank Susan Hoag and Marilyn McElroy. We also express appreciation for the cooperation of the Addison-Wesley staff: Steve Mautner, Herb Merritt, and their associates.

There are undoubtedly errors in the final product, both typographical and conceptual as well as differences of opinion. We invite readers to send suggestions, comments, criticisms, and corrections to the authors at the Anderson Graduate School of Management, University of California, Los Angeles, CA 90024. Any form of communication will be welcome.

Los Angeles, California   T.E.C.
                                                                               J.F.W.

Contents

ix

PART I

The Theory of Finance

P ART I OF THIS TEXT covers what has come to be the accepted theory of financial decision making. Its theme is an understanding of how individuals and their agents make choices among alternatives that have uncertain payoffs over multiple time periods. The theory that explains how and why these decisions are made has many applications in the various topic areas that traditionally make up the study of finance. The topics include security analysis, portfolio management, financial accounting, corporate financial policy, public finance, commercial banking, and international finance.

Chapter 1 shows why the existence of financial marketplaces is so important for economic development. Chapters 2 and 3 describe the appropriate investment criterion in the simplest of all possible worlds—a world where all outcomes are known with certainty. For many readers, they will represent a summary and extension of material covered in traditional texts on corporate finance. Chapter 4 covers utility theory. It provides a model of how individuals make choices among risky alternatives. An understanding of individual behavior in the face of uncertainty is fundamental to understanding how financial markets operate. Chapter 5 introduces the objects of investor choice under uncertainty in the most general theoretical framework—state-preference theory. Chapter 6 describes the objects of choice in a mean-variance partial equilibrium framework. In a world of uncertainty each combination of assets provides risky outcomes that are assumed to be described in terms of two parameters: mean and variance. Once the opportunity set of all possible choices has been described, we are able to combine Chapter 4, "The Theory of Choice," with Chapter 6, "Objects

1

of Choice," in order to predict exactly what combination of assets an individual will choose. Chapter 7 extends the study of choice into a market equilibrium framework, thereby closing the cycle of logic. Chapter 1 shows why capital markets exist and assumes that all outcomes are known with certainty. Chapter 7 extends the theory of capital markets to include equilibrium with uncertain outcomes and, even more important, describes the appropriate concept of risk and shows how it will be priced in equilibrium, including the very general arbitrage pricing theory. Chapter 8 on the option pricing model includes a treatment of the equilibrium prices of contingent claim assets that depend on the outcome of another risky asset. Therefore these materials provide a framework for decision making under uncertainty that can be applied by financial managers throughout the economy. Chapter 9 introduces commodity and financial futures contracts and how they are priced in equilibrium. Chapter 10, the last chapter in Part I, discusses the concept of efficient capital markets. It serves as a bridge between theory and reality. Most of the theory assumes that markets are perfectly frictionless, i.e., free of transactions costs and other "market imperfections" that cannot be easily modeled. The questions arise: What assumptions are needed to have efficient (but not necessarily frictionless) capital markets? How well does the theory fit reality?

The empirical evidence on these and other questions is left to Part II of the text. It focuses on applications of financial theory to corporate policy issues such as capital budgeting, the cost of capital, capital structure, dividend policy, leasing, mergers and acquisitions, and international finance. For almost every topic, there is material that covers the implications of theory for policy and the empirical evidence relevant to the theory, and that provides detailed examples of applications.

1

Through the alterations in the income streams provided by loans or sales, the marginal degrees of impatience for all individuals in the market are brought into equality with each other and with the market rate of interest.

Irving Fisher, *The Theory of Interest*, Macmillan, New York, 1930, 122

Introduction: Capital Markets, Consumption, and Investment

A. INTRODUCTION

The objective of this chapter is to study consumption and investment decisions made by individuals and firms. Logical development is facilitated if we begin with the simplest of all worlds, a one-person/one-good economy. The decision maker, Robinson Crusoe, must choose between consumption now and consumption in the future. Of course, the decision not to consume now is the same as investment. Thus Robinson Crusoe's decision is simultaneously one of consumption and investment. In order to decide, he needs two types of information. First, he needs to understand his own subjective trade-offs between consumption now and consumption in the future. This information is embodied in the utility and indifference curves depicted in Figs. 1.1 through 1.3. Second, he must know the feasible trade-offs between present and future consumption that are technologically possible. These are given in the investment and production opportunity sets of Figs. 1.4 and 1.5.

From the analysis of a Robinson Crusoe economy we will find that the optimal consumption/investment decision establishes a subjective interest rate for Robinson Crusoe. Shown in Fig. 1.5, it represents his (unique) optimal rate of exchange between consumption now and in the future. Thus interest rates are an integral part of consumption/investment decisions. One can think of the interest rate as the price of

3

deferred consumption or the rate of return on investment. After the Robinson Crusoe economy we will introduce opportunities to exchange consumption across time by borrowing or lending in a multiperson economy (shown in Fig. 1.7). The introduction of these exchange opportunities results in a single market interest rate that everyone can use as a signal for making optimal consumption/investment decisions (Fig. 1.8). Furthermore, no one is worse off in an exchange economy when compared with a Robinson Crusoe economy and almost everyone is better off (Fig. 1.9). Thus an exchange economy that uses market prices (interest rates) to allocate resources across time will be seen to be superior to an economy without the price mechanism.

The obvious extension to the introductory material in this chapter is the investment decision made by firms in a multiperiod context. Managers need optimal decision rules to help in selecting those projects that maximize the wealth of shareholders. We shall see that market-determined interest rates play an important role in the corporate investment and production decisions. This material will be discussed in depth in Chapters 2 and 3.

B. CONSUMPTION AND INVESTMENT WITHOUT CAPITAL MARKETS

The answer to the question "Do capital markets benefit society?" requires that we compare a world without capital markets to one with them and show that no one is worse off and that at least one individual is better off in a world with capital markets. To make things as simple as possible, we assume that all outcomes from investment are known with certainty, that there are no transactions costs or taxes, and that decisions are made in a one-period context. Individuals are endowed with income (manna from heaven) at the beginning of the period, y_0, and at the end of the period, y_1. They must decide how much to actually consume now, C_0, and how much to invest in productive opportunities in order to provide end-of-period consumption, C_1. Every individual is assumed to prefer more consumption to less. In other words, the marginal utility of consumption is always positive. Also, we assume that the marginal utility of consumption is decreasing. The total utility curve (Fig. 1.1) shows the utility of consumption at the beginning of the period, assuming that the second-period consumption is held constant. Changes in consumption have been marked off in equal increments along the horizontal axis. Note that equal increases in consumption cause total utility to increase (marginal utility is positive), but that the increments in utility become smaller and smaller (marginal utility is decreasing). We can easily construct a similar graph to represent the utility of end-of-period consumption, $U(C_1)$. When combined with Fig. 1.1, the result (the three-dimensional graph shown in Fig. 1.2) provides a description of trade-offs between consumption at the beginning of the period, C_0, and consumption at the end of the period, C_1. The dashed lines represent contours along the utility surface where various combinations of C_0 and C_1 provide the same total utility (measured along the vertical axis). Since all points along the same contour (e.g., points A and B) have equal total utility, the individual will be indifferent with respect to them. Therefore the contours are called *indifference curves*.

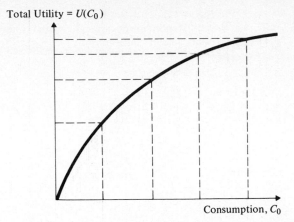

Total Utility = $U(C_0)$

Figure 1.1
Total utility of consumption.

Consumption, C_0

Looking at Fig. 1.2 from above, we can project the indifference curves onto the consumption argument plane (i.e., the plane formed by the C_0, C_1 axes in Fig. 1.3). To reiterate, all combinations of consumption today and consumption tomorrow that lie on the same indifference curve have the same total utility. The decision maker whose indifference curves are depicted in Fig. 1.3 would be indifferent as to point A with consumption (C_{0a}, C_{1a}) and point B with consumption (C_{0b}, C_{1b}). Point A has more consumption at the end of the period but less consumption at the beginning than point B does. Point D has more consumption in both periods than do either points A or B. Point D lies on an indifference curve with higher utility than points A and B; hence curves to the northeast have greater total utility.

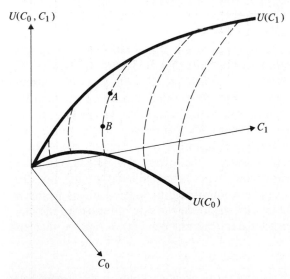

$U(C_0, C_1)$

$U(C_1)$

C_1

$U(C_0)$

C_0

Figure 1.2
Trade-offs between beginning and end-of-period consumption.

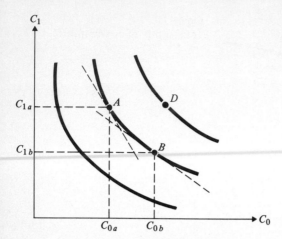

Figure 1.3
Indifference curves representing the time preference of consumption.

The slope of the straight line just tangent to the indifference curve at point B measures the rate of trade-off between C_0 and C_1 at point B. This trade-off is called the *marginal rate of substitution* (MRS) between consumption today and consumption tomorrow. It also reveals the decision maker's subjective rate of time preference, r_i, at point B. We can think of the subjective rate of time preference as an interest rate because it measures the rate of substitution between consumption bundles over time. It reveals how many extra units of consumption tomorrow must be received in order to give up one unit of consumption today and still have the same total utility. Mathematically, it is expressed as[1]

$$\mathrm{MRS}_{C_1}^{C_0} = \left.\frac{\partial C_1}{\partial C_0}\right|_{U = \mathrm{const.}} = -(1 + r_i). \tag{1.1}$$

Note that the subjective rate of time preference is greater at point A than at point B. The individual has less consumption today at point A and will therefore demand relatively more future consumption in order to have the same total utility.

Thus far we have described preference functions that tell us how individuals will make choices among consumption bundles over time. What happens if we introduce productive opportunities that allow a unit of current savings/investment to be turned into more than one unit of future consumption? We assume that each individual in the economy has a schedule of productive investment opportunities that can be arranged from the highest rate of return down to the lowest (Fig. 1.4). Although we have chosen to graph the investment opportunities schedule as a straight line, any decreasing function would do. This implies diminishing marginal returns to investment because the more an individual invests, the lower the rate of return on the marginal investment. Also, all investments are assumed independent of one another and perfectly divisible.

---

[1] Equation (1.1) can be read as follows: The marginal rate of substitution between consumption today and end-of-period consumption, $\mathrm{MRS}_{C_1}^{C_0}$, is equal to the slope of a line tangent to an indifference curve given constant total utility $\left[\partial C_1/\partial C_0\right]|_{U = \mathrm{const.}}$. This in turn is equal to the individual's subjective rate of time preference, $-(1 + r_i)$.

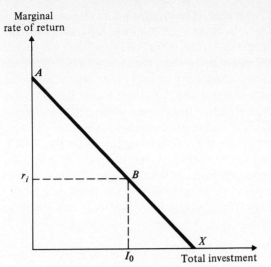

Figure 1.4
An individual's schedule of productive investment opportunities.

An individual will make all investments in productive opportunities that have rates of return higher than his or her subjective rate of time preference, r_i. This can be demonstrated if we transform the schedule of productive investment opportunities into the consumption argument plane (Fig. 1.5).[2] The slope of a line tangent to curve ABX in Fig. 1.5 is the rate at which a dollar of consumption foregone today is transformed by productive investment into a dollar of consumption tomorrow. It is the

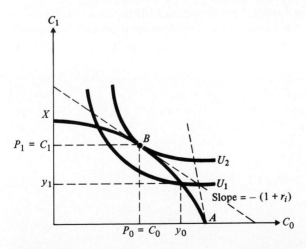

Figure 1.5
The production opportunity set.

<hr>

[2] See Problem 1.6 at the end of the chapter for an example of how to make the transition between the schedule of productive investment opportunities and the consumption argument plane.

marginal rate of transformation (MRT) offered by the production/investment opportunity set. The line tangent to point A has the highest slope in Fig. 1.5 and represents the highest rate of return at point A in Fig. 1.4. An individual endowed with a resource bundle (y_0, y_1) that has utility U_1 can move along the production opportunity set to point B, where the indifference curve is tangent to it and he or she receives the maximum attainable utility, U_2. Because current consumption, C_0, is less than the beginning-of-period endowment, y_0, the individual has chosen to invest. The amount of investment is $y_0 - C_0$. Of course, if $C_0 > y_0$, he or she will disinvest.

Note that the marginal rate of return on the last investment made (i.e., MRT, the slope of a line tangent to the investment opportunity set at point B) is exactly equal to the investor's subjective time preference (i.e., MRS, the slope of a line tangent to his or her indifference curve, also at point B). In other words, the investor's subjective marginal rate of substitution is equal to the marginal rate of transformation offered by the production opportunity set:

$$MRS = MRT.$$

This will always be true in a Robinson Crusoe world where there are no capital markets, i.e., no opportunities to exchange. The individual decision maker starts with an initial endowment (y_0, y_1) and compares the marginal rate of return on a dollar of productive investment (or disinvestment) with his or her subjective time preference. If the rate on investment is greater (as it is in Fig. 1.5), he or she will gain utility by making the investment. This process continues until the rate of return on the last dollar of productive investment just equals the rate of subjective time preference (at point B). Note that at point B the individual's consumption in each time period is exactly equal to the output from production, i.e., $P_0 = C_0$ and $P_1 = C_1$.

Without the existence of capital markets, individuals with the same endowment and the same investment opportunity set may choose completely different investments because they have different indifference curves. This is shown in Fig. 1.6. Individual

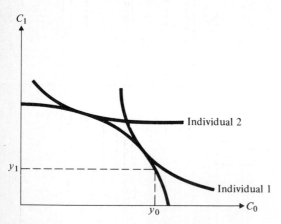

Figure 1.6
Individuals with different indifference curves choose
different production/consumption patterns.

2, who has a lower rate of time preference (Why?), will choose to invest more than individual 1.

C. CONSUMPTION AND INVESTMENT WITH CAPITAL MARKETS

A Robinson Crusoe economy is characterized by the fact that there are no opportunities to exchange intertemporal consumption among individuals. What happens if—instead of one person—many individuals are said to exist in the economy? Intertemporal exchange of consumption bundles will be represented by the opportunity to borrow or lend unlimited amounts at r, a market-determined rate of interest.[3]

Financial markets facilitate the transfer of funds between lenders and borrowers. Assuming that interest rates are positive, any amount of funds lent today will return interest plus principal at the end of the period. Ignoring production for the time being, we can graph borrowing and lending opportunities along the *capital market line* in Fig. 1.7 (line W_0ABW_1). With an initial endowment of (y_0, y_1) that has utility equal to U_1, we can reach any point along the market line by borrowing or lending at the market interest rate plus repaying the principal amount, X_0. If we designate the future value as X_1, we can write that the future value is equal to the principal amount plus interest earned,

$$X_1 = X_0 + rX_0, \qquad X_1 = (1 + r)X_0.$$

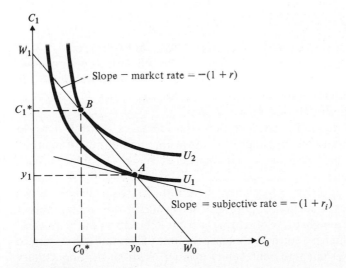

Figure 1.7
The capital market line.

---

[3] The market rate of interest is provided by the solution to a general equilibrium problem. For simplicity, we assume that the market rate of interest is a given.

Similarly, the present value, W_0, of our initial endowment, (y_0, y_1), is the sum of current income, y_0, and the present value of our end-of-period income, $y_1(1 + r)^{-1}$:

$$W_0 = y_0 + \frac{y_1}{(1 + r)}. \tag{1.2}$$

Referring to Fig. 1.7, we see that with endowment (y_0, y_1) we will maximize utility by moving along the market line to the point where our subjective time preference equals the market interest rate. Point B represents the consumption bundle (C_0^*, C_1^*) on the highest attainable indifference curve. At the initial endowment (point A), our subjective time preference, represented by the slope of a line tangent to the indifference curve at point A, is less than the market rate of return. Therefore we will desire to lend because the capital market offers a rate of return higher than what we subjectively require. Ultimately, we reach a consumption decision (C_0^*, C_1^*) where we maximize utility. The utility, U_2, at point B is greater than the utility, U_1, at our initial endowment, point A. The present value of this consumption bundle is also equal to our wealth, W_0:

$$W_0 = C_0^* + \frac{C_1^*}{1 + r}. \tag{1.3}$$

This can be rearranged to give the equation for the capital market line:

$$C_1^* = W_0(1 + r) - (1 + r)C_0^*, \tag{1.4}$$

and since $W_0(1 + r) = W_1$, we have

$$C_1^* = W_1 - (1 + r)C_0^*. \tag{1.5}$$

Thus the capital market line in Fig. 1.7 has an intercept at W_1 and a slope of $-(1 + r)$. Also note that by equating (1.2) and (1.3) we see that the present value of our endowment equals the present value of our consumption, and both are equal to our wealth, W_0. Moving along the capital market line does not change one's wealth, but it does offer a pattern of consumption that has higher utility.

What happens if the production/consumption decision takes place in a world where capital markets facilitate the exchange of funds at the market rate of interest? Figure 1.8 combines production possibilities with market exchange possibilities. With the family of indifference curves U_1, U_2, and U_3 and endowment (y_0, y_1) at point A, what actions will we take in order to maximize our utility? Starting at point A, we can move either along the production opportunity set or along the capital market line. Both alternatives offer a higher rate of return than our subjective time preference, but production offers the higher return, i.e., a steeper slope. Therefore we choose to invest and move along the production opportunity frontier. Without the opportunity to borrow or lend along the capital market line, we would stop investing at point D, where the marginal return on productive investment equals our subjective time preference. This was the result shown for consumption and investment in a Robinson Crusoe world without capital markets in Fig. 1.5. At this point, our level of utility

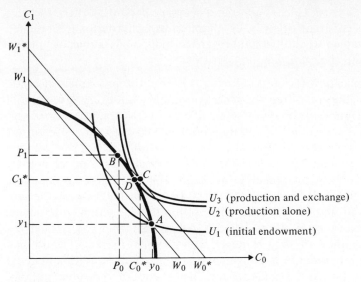

Figure 1.8
Production and consumption with capital markets.

has increased from U_1 to U_2. However, with the opportunity to borrow, we can actually do better. Note that at point D the borrowing rate, represented by the slope of the capital market line, is less than the rate of return on the marginal investment, which is the slope of the production opportunity set at point D. Since further investment returns more than the cost of borrowed funds, we will continue to invest until the marginal return on investment is equal to the borrowing rate at point B. At point B, we receive the output from production (P_0, P_1), and the present value of our wealth is W_0^* instead of W_0. Furthermore, we can now reach any point on the market line. Since our time preference at point B is greater than the market rate of return, we will consume more than P_0, which is the current payoff from production. By borrowing, we can reach point C on the capital market line. Our optimal consumption is found, as before, where our subjective time preference just equals the market rate of return. Our utility has increased from U_1 at point A (our initial endowment) to U_2 at point D (the Robinson Crusoe solution) to U_3 at point C (the exchange economy solution). We are clearly better off when capital markets exist since $U_3 > U_2$.

The decision process that takes place with production opportunities and capital market exchange opportunities occurs in two separate and distinct steps: (1) first, choose the optimal production decision by taking on projects until the marginal rate of return on investment equals the objective market rate; (2) then choose the optimal consumption pattern by borrowing or lending along the capital market line to equate your subjective time preference with the market rate of return. The separation of the investment (step 1) and consumption (step 2) decisions is known as the Fisher separation theorem.

Fisher separation theorem. Given perfect and complete capital markets, the production decision is governed solely by an objective market criterion (represented by maximizing attained wealth) without regard to individuals' subjective preferences that enter into their consumption decisions.

An important implication for corporate policy is that the investment decision can be delegated to managers. Given the same opportunity set, every investor will make the same production decision (P_0, P_1) regardless of the shape of his or her indifference curves. This is shown in Fig. 1.9. Both investor 1 and investor 2 will direct the manager of their firm to choose production combination (P_0, P_1). They can then take the output of the firm and adapt it to their own subjective time preferences by borrowing or lending in the capital market. Investor 1 will choose to consume more than his or her share of current production (point A) by borrowing today in the capital market and repaying out of his or her share of future production. Alternately, investor 2 will lend because he or she consumes less than his or her share of current production. Either way, they are both better off with a capital market. The optimal production decision is separated from individual utility preferences. Without capital market opportunities to borrow or lend, investor 1 would choose to produce at point Y, which has lower utility. Similarly, investor 2 would be worse off at point X.

In equilibrium, the marginal rate of substitution for all investors is equal to the market rate of interest, and this in turn is equal to the marginal rate of transformation for productive investment. Mathematically, the marginal rates of substitution for investors i and j are

$$MRS_i = MRS_j = -(1 + r) = MRT.$$

Thus all individuals use the same time value of money (i.e., the same market-determined objective interest rate) in making their production/investment decisions.

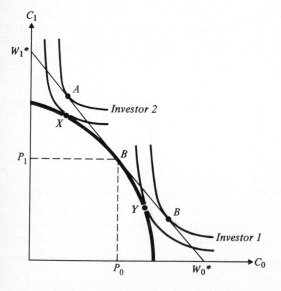

Figure 1.9
The investment decision is independent of individual preferences.

The importance of capital markets cannot be overstated. They allow the efficient transfer of funds between borrowers and lenders. Individuals who have insufficient wealth to take advantage of all their investment opportunities that yield rates of return higher than the market rate are able to borrow funds and invest more than they would without capital markets. In this way, funds can be efficiently allocated from individuals with few productive opportunities and great wealth to individuals with many opportunities and insufficient wealth. As a result, all (borrowers and lenders) are better off than they would have been without capital markets.

D. MARKETPLACES AND TRANSACTIONS COSTS

The foregoing discussion has demonstrated the advantages of capital markets for funds allocation in a world without transactions costs. In such a world, there is no need for a central location for exchange; that is, there is no need for a marketplace per se. But let us assume that we have a primitive economy with N producers, each making a specialized product and consuming a bundle of all N consumption goods. Given no marketplace, bilateral exchange is necessary. During a given time period, each visits the other in order to exchange goods. The cost of each leg of a trip is T dollars. If there are five individuals and five consumption goods in this economy, then individual 1 makes four trips, one to each of the other four producers. Individual 2 makes three trips, and so on. Altogether, there are $\lceil N(N-1) \rceil/2 = 10$ trips, at a total cost of $10T$ dollars. This is shown in Fig. 1.10. If an entrepreneur establishes a central marketplace and carries an inventory of each of the N products, as shown in Fig. 1.11, the total number of trips can be reduced to five, with a total cost of $5T$ dollars. Therefore if the entrepreneur has a total cost (including the cost of living) of less than $10T - 5T$ dollars, he or she can profitably establish a marketplace and everyone will be better off.[4]

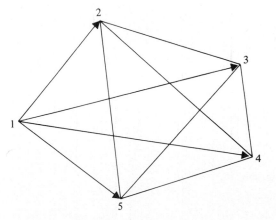

Figure 1.10
A primitive exchange economy with no central marketplace.

---

[4] In general, for N individuals making two-way exchanges, there are $\binom{N}{2} = N(N-1)/2$ trips. With a marketplace the number of trips is reduced to N. Therefore the savings is $[N(N-1)/2 - N]T$.

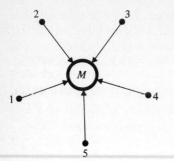

Figure 1.11
The productivity of a central marketplace.

This example provides a simple explanation for the productivity of marketplaces. Among other things, they serve to efficiently reduce transactions costs. Later on, we shall refer to this fact as the *operational efficiency* of capital markets. The lower the transactions costs are, the more operationally efficient a market can be.

E. TRANSACTIONS COSTS AND THE BREAKDOWN OF SEPARATION

If transactions costs are nontrivial, financial intermediaries and marketplaces will provide a useful service. In such a world, the borrowing rate will be greater than the lending rate. Financial institutions will pay the lending rate for money deposited with them and then issue funds at a higher rate to borrowers. The difference between the borrowing and lending rates represents their (competitively determined) fee for the economic service provided. Different borrowing and lending rates will have the effect

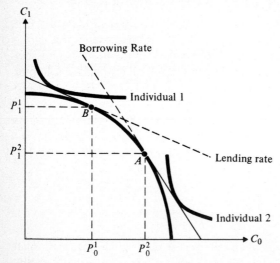

Figure 1.12
Markets with different borrowing and lending rates.

of invalidating the Fisher separation principle. As shown in Fig. 1.12, individuals with different indifference curves will now choose different levels of investment. Without a single market rate they will not be able to delegate the investment decision to the manager of their firm. Individual 1 would direct the manager to use the lending rate and invest at point B. Individual 2 would use the borrowing rate and choose point A. A third individual might choose investments between points A and B, where his or her indifference curve is directly tangent to the production opportunity set.

The theory of finance is greatly simplified if we assume that capital markets are perfect. Obviously they are not. The relevant question then is whether the theories that assume frictionless markets fit reality well enough to be useful or whether they need to be refined in order to provide greater insights. This is an empirical question that will be addressed later on in the text.

Throughout most of this text we shall adopt the convenient and simplifying assumption that capital markets are perfect. The only major imperfections to be considered in detail are the impact of corporate and personal taxes and information asymmetries. The effects of taxes and imperfect information are certainly nontrivial, and as we shall see, they do change the predictions of many models of financial policy.

SUMMARY

The rest of the text follows almost exactly the same logic as this chapter, except that from Chapter 4 onward it focuses on decision making under uncertainty. The first step is to develop indifference curves to model individual decision making in a world with uncertainty. Chapter 4 is analogous to Fig. 1.3. It will describe a theory of choice under uncertainty. Next, the portfolio opportunity set, which represents choices among combinations of risky assets, is developed. Chapters 5 and 6 are similar to Fig. 1.5. They describe the objects of choice—the portfolio opportunity set. The tangency between the indifference curves of a risk-averse investor and his or her opportunity set provides a theory of individual choice in a world without capital markets (this is discussed in Chapter 6). Finally, in Chapter 7, we introduce the opportunity to borrow and lend at a riskless rate and develop models of capital market equilibrium. Chapter 7 follows logic similar to Fig. 1.8. In fact, we show that a type of separation principle (two-fund separation) obtains, given uncertainty and perfect capital markets. Chapters 10 and 11 take a careful look at the meaning of efficient capital markets and at empirical evidence that relates to the question of how well the perfect capital market assumption fits reality. The remainder of the book, following Chapter 11, applies financial theory to corporate policy decisions.

PROBLEM SET

1.1 Graphically demonstrate the Fisher separation theorem for the case where an individual ends up lending in financial markets. Label the following points on the graph: initial wealth, W_0; optimal production/investment (P_0, P_1); optimal consumption (C_0^*, C_1^*); present value of final wealth, W_0^*.

1.2 Graphically analyze the effect of an exogenous decrease in the interest rate on (a) the utility of borrowers and lenders, (b) the present wealth of borrowers and lenders, and (c) the investment in real assets.

1.3 The interest rate cannot fall below the net rate from storage. True or false? Why?

1.4 Graphically illustrate the decision-making process faced by an individual in a Robinson Crusoe economy where (a) storage is the only investment opportunity and (b) there are no capital markets.

1.5 Suppose that the investment opportunity set has N projects, all of which have the same rate of return, R^*. Graph the investment set.

1.6 Suppose your production opportunity set in a world with perfect certainty consists of the following possibilities:

Project	Investment Outlay	Rate of Return
A	$1,000,000	8%
B	1,000,000	20
C	2,000,000	4
D	3,000,000	30

a) Graph the production opportunity set in a C_0, C_1 framework.

b) If the market rate of return is 10%, draw in the capital market line for the optimal investment decision.

REFERENCES

Alderson, W., "Factors Governing the Development of Marketing Channels," reprinted in Richard M. Clewett, *Marketing Channels for Manufactured Products*. Irwin, Homewood, Ill., 1954.

Fama, E. F., and M. H. Miller, *The Theory of Finance*. Holt, Rinehart and Winston, New York, 1972.

Fisher, I., *The Theory of Interest*. Macmillan, New York, 1930.

Hirshleifer, J., *Investment, Interest, and Capital*. Prentice-Hall, Englewood Cliffs, N.J., 1970.

2

When the first primitive man decided to use a bone for a club instead of eating its marrow, that was investment.

Anonymous

Investment Decisions: The Certainty Case

A. INTRODUCTION

The investment decision is essentially how much not to consume in the present in order that more can be consumed in the future. The optimal investment decision maximizes the expected satisfaction (expected utility) gained from consumption over the planning horizon of the decision maker. We assume that all economic decisions ultimately reduce to questions about consumption. Even more fundamentally, consumption is related to survival.

The consumption/investment decision is important to all sectors of the economy. An individual who saves does so because the expected benefit of future consumption provided by an extra dollar of saving exceeds the benefit of using it for consumption today. Managers of corporations, who act as agents for the owners (shareholders) of the firm, must decide between paying out earnings in the form of dividends, which may be used for present consumption, and retaining the earnings to invest in productive opportunities that are expected to yield future consumption. Managers of not-for-profit organizations try to maximize the expected utility of contributors—those individuals who provide external funds. And public sector managers attempt to maximize the expected utility of their constituencies.

The examples of investment decisions in this chapter are taken from the corporate sector of the economy, but the decision criterion, which is to maximize the present value of lifetime consumption, can be applied to any sector of the economy. For the time being, we assume that intertemporal decisions are based on knowledge of the market-determined time value of money—the interest rate. Furthermore, the interest rate is assumed to be known with certainty in all time periods. It is nonstochastic. That is, it may change over time, but each change is known with certainty. The interest rate is assumed not to be a random variable. In addition, all future payoffs from current investment decisions are known with certainty. And finally, there are no imperfections (e.g., transactions costs) in capital markets. These assumptions are obviously an oversimplification, but they are a good place to start. Most of the remainder of the text after this chapter is devoted to decision making under uncertainty. But for the time being it is useful to establish the fundamental criterion of economic decision making—the maximization of the net present value of wealth, assuming perfect certainty.

The most important theme of this chapter is that the objective of the firm is to maximize the wealth of its shareholders. This will be seen to be the same as maximizing the present value of shareholders' lifetime consumption and no different than maximizing the price per share of stock. Alternative issues such as agency costs are also discussed. Then the maximization of shareholder wealth is more carefully defined as the discounted value of future expected cash flows. Finally, techniques for project selection are reviewed, and the net present value criterion is shown to be consistent with shareholder wealth maximization.

B. FISHER SEPARATION: THE SEPARATION OF INDIVIDUAL UTILITY PREFERENCES FROM THE INVESTMENT DECISION

To say that the goal of the firm is the maximization of its shareholders' wealth is one thing, but the problem of how to do it is another. We know that interpersonal comparison of individuals' utility functions is not possible. For example, if we give individuals A and B $100 each, they will both be happy. However, no one, not even the two individuals, will be able to discern which person is happier. How then can a manager maximize shareholders' utility when individual utility functions cannot be compared or combined?

The answer to the question is provided if we turn to our understanding of the role of capital markets. If capital markets are perfect in the sense that they have no frictions that cause the borrowing rate to be different from the lending rate, then (as we saw in Chapter 1) Fisher separation obtains. This means that individuals can delegate investment decisions to the manager of the firm in which they are owners. Regardless of the shape of the shareholders' individual utility functions, the managers maximize the owners' individual (and collective) wealth positions by choosing to invest until the rate of return on the least favorable project is exactly equal to the market-determined rate of return. This result is shown in Fig. 2.1. The optimal production/investment decision, (P_0, P_1), is the one that maximizes the present value of the shareholders' wealth, W_0. The appropriate decision rule is the same, independent of the shareholders' time preferences for consumption. The manager will be directed, by all shareholders, to undertake all projects that earn more than the market rate of return.

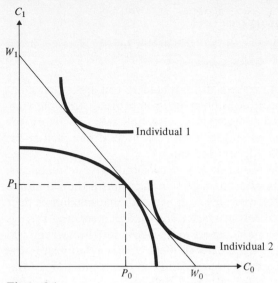

Figure 2.1
Separation of shareholder preferences from the
production/investment decision.

If the marginal return on investment equals the market-determined opportunity cost of capital, then the shareholders' wealth, W_0, is maximized. Individual shareholders can then take the optimal production decision (P_0, P_1) and borrow or lend along the capital market line in order to satisfy their time pattern for consumption. In other words, they can take the cash payouts from the firm and use them for current consumption or save them for future consumption, according to their individual desires.

The separation principle implies that the maximization of the shareholders' wealth is identical to maximizing the present value of their lifetime consumption. Mathematically, this was demonstrated in Eq. (1.3):

$$W_0 = C_0 + \frac{C_1}{1 + r}.$$

Even though the two individuals in Fig. 2.1 choose different levels of current and future consumption, they have the same current wealth, W_0. This follows from the fact that they receive the same income from productive investments (P_0, P_1).

Because exchange opportunities permit borrowing and lending at the same rate of interest, an individual's productive optimum is independent of his or her resources and tastes. Therefore if asked to vote on their preferred production decisions at a shareholders' meeting, different shareholders of the same firm will be unanimous in their preference. This is known as the *unanimity principle*. It implies that the managers of the firm, in their capacity as agents of the shareholders, need not worry about making decisions that reconcile differences of opinion among shareholders. All shareholders will have identical interests. In effect, the price system by which wealth is measured conveys the shareholders' unanimously preferred productive decisions to the firm.

C. THE AGENCY PROBLEM.
DO MANAGERS HAVE THE CORRECT
INCENTIVE TO MAXIMIZE
SHAREHOLDERS' WEALTH?

So far, we have shown that in perfect markets all shareholders will agree that managers should follow a simple investment decision rule: Take projects until the marginal rate of return equals the market-determined discount rate. Therefore the shareholders' wealth is seen to be the present value of cash flows discounted at the opportunity cost of capital (the market-determined rate).

Shareholders can agree on the decision rule that they should give to managers. But they must be able to costlessly monitor management decisions if they are to be sure that management really does make every decision in a way that maximizes their wealth. There is obviously a difference between ownership and control, and there is no reason to believe that the manager, who serves as an agent for the owners, will always act in the best interest of the shareholders. In most agency relationships the owner will incur nontrivial monitoring costs in order to keep the agent in line. Consequently, the owner faces a trade-off between monitoring costs and forms of compensation that will cause the agent to always act in the owner's interest. At one extreme, if the agent's compensation were all in the form of shares in the firm, then monitoring costs would be zero. Unfortunately, this type of scheme is practically impossible because the agent will always be able to receive some compensation in the form of nonpecuniary benefits such as larger office space, expensive lunches, an executive jet, etc. At the opposite extreme, the owner would have to incur inordinate monitoring costs in order to guarantee that the agent always makes the decision the owner would prefer. Somewhere between these two extremes lies an optimal solution. The reader who wishes to explore this classic problem in greater depth is referred to books by Williamson [1964], Marschak and Radner [1972], and Cyert and March [1963], and to articles by Jensen and Meckling [1976], Machlup [1967], Coase [1937], and Alchian and Demsetz [1972] as good references to an immense literature in this area. The issue is also explored in greater depth in Chapter 14 of this text.

In spite of the above discussion, we shall assume that managers always make decisions that maximize the wealth of the firm's shareholders. To do so, they must find and select the best set of investment projects to accomplish their objective.

D. MAXIMIZATION OF
SHAREHOLDERS' WEALTH

1. Dividends vs. Capital Gains

Assuming that managers behave as though they were maximizing the wealth of the shareholders, we need to establish a usable definition of what is meant by *shareholders' wealth.* We can say that shareholders' wealth is the discounted value of after-tax cash flows paid out by the firm.[1] After-tax cash flows available for consumption can be shown to be the same as the stream of dividends, Div_t, paid to shareholders. The discounted value of the stream of dividends is

$$S_0 = \sum_{t=0}^{\infty} \frac{\text{Div}_t}{(1 + k_s)^t}, \tag{2.1}$$

where S_0 is the present value of shareholders' wealth (in Fig. 2.1 it is W_0) and k_s is the market-determined rate of return on equity capital (common stock).

Equation (2.1) is a multiperiod formula that assumes that future cash flows paid to shareholders are known with certainty and that the market-determined discount rate is nonstochastic and constant over all time periods. These assumptions are maintained throughout this chapter because our main objective is to understand how the investment decision, shown graphically in Fig. 2.1 in a one-period context, can be extended to the more practical setting of many time periods in a manner consistent with the maximization of the shareholders' wealth. For the time being, we shall ignore the effect of personal taxes on dividends, and we shall assume that the discount rate, k_s, is the market-determined opportunity cost of capital for equivalent income streams. It is determined by the slope of the market line in Fig. 2.1.

One question that often arises is: What about capital gains? Surely shareholders receive both capital gains and dividends; why then do capital gains not appear in Eq. (2.1)? The answer to this question is that capital gains *do* appear in Eq. (2.1). This can be shown by use of a simple example. Suppose a firm pays a dividend, Div_1, of $1.00 at the end of this year and $1.00(1 + g)^t$ at the end of each year thereafter, where the growth rate of the dividend stream is g. If the growth rate in dividends, g, is 5% and the opportunity cost of investment, k_s, is 10%, how much will an investor pay today for the stock? Using the formula for the present value of a growing annuity stream, we get[2]

$$S_0 = \frac{\text{Div}_1}{k_s - g} = \frac{\$1.00}{.10 - .05} = \$20.00.$$

Next, suppose that an investor bought the stock today for $20 and held it for five years. What would it be worth at the end of the fifth year?

$$S_5 = \frac{\text{Div}_6}{k_s - g}.$$

The dividend, Div_6, at the end of the sixth year is

$$\text{Div}_6 = \text{Div}_1(1 + g)^5, \qquad \text{Div}_6 = \$1.00(1.05)^5 = \$1.2763.$$

---

[1] Since much of the rest of this chapter assumes familiarity with discounting, the reader is referred to Appendix A for a review.

[2] The formula used here, sometimes called the Gordon growth model, is derived in Appendix A. It assumes that the dividend grows forever at a constant rate, g, which is less than the discount rate, $g < k_s$.

Therefore the value of the stock at the end of the fifth year would be

$$S_5 = \frac{\$1.2763}{.10 - .05} = \$25.5256.$$

The value of the stock at the end of the fifth year is the discounted value of all dividends from that time on. Now we can compute the present value of the stream of income of an investor who holds the stock only five years. He or she gets five dividend payments plus the market price of the stock in the fifth year. The discounted value of these payments is S_0.

$$S_0 = \frac{\text{Div}_1}{1 + k_s} + \frac{\text{Div}_1(1 + g)}{(1 + k_s)^2} + \frac{\text{Div}_1(1 + g)^2}{(1 + k_s)^3} + \frac{\text{Div}_1(1 + g)^3}{(1 + k_s)^4} + \frac{\text{Div}_1(1 + g)^4}{(1 + k_s)^5} + \frac{S_5}{(1 + k_s)^5}$$

$$= \frac{1.00}{1.1} + \frac{1.05}{1.21} + \frac{1.10}{1.33} + \frac{1.16}{1.46} + \frac{1.22}{1.61} + \frac{25.52}{1.61}$$

$$= .91 + .87 + .83 + .79 + .76 + 15.85$$

$$= 20.01.$$

Except for a one-cent rounding difference, the present value of the stock is the same whether an investor holds it forever or for only, say, five years. Since the value of the stock in the fifth year is equal to the future dividends from that time on, the value of dividends for five years plus a capital gain is exactly the same as the value of an infinite stream of dividends. Therefore Eq. (2.1) is the discounted value of the stream of cash payments to shareholders and is equivalent to the shareholders' wealth. Because we are ignoring the taxable differences between dividends and capital gains (this will be discussed in Chapter 15, "Dividend Policy"), we can say that Eq. (2.1) incorporates all cash payments, both dividends and capital gains.

2. The Economic Definition of *Profit*

Frequently there is a great deal of confusion over what is meant by profits. An economist uses the word *profits* to mean rates of return in excess of the opportunity cost for funds employed in projects of equal risk. To estimate economic profits, one must know the exact time pattern of *cash flows* provided by a project and the opportunity cost of capital. As we shall see below, the pattern of cash flows is the same thing as the stream of dividends paid by the firm to its owners. Therefore the appropriate profits for managers to use when making decisions are the discounted stream of cash flows to shareholders—in other words, dividends. Note, however, that *dividends* should be interpreted very broadly. Our definition of dividends includes *any* cash payout to shareholders. In addition to what we ordinarily think of as dividends the general definition includes capital gains, spinoffs to shareholders, payments in liquidation or bankruptcy, repurchase of shares, awards in shareholders' lawsuits, and payoffs resulting from merger or acquisition. Stock dividends, which involve no cash flow, are *not* included in our definition of dividends.

We can use a very simple model to show the difference between the economic definition of profit and the accounting definition. Assume that we have an all-equity firm and that there are no taxes.[3] Then sources of funds are revenues, Rev, and sale of new equity (on m shares at S dollars per share). Uses of funds are wages, salaries, materials, and services, W&S; investment, I; and dividends, Div. For each time period, t, we can write the *equality between sources and uses of funds* as

$$\text{Rev}_t + m_t S_t = \text{Div}_t + (\text{W\&S})_t + I_t. \tag{2.2}$$

To simplify things even further, assume that the firm issues no new equity, i.e., $m_t S_t = 0$. Now we can write dividends as

$$\text{Div}_t = \text{Rev}_t - (\text{W\&S})_t - I_t, \tag{2.3}$$

which is the *simple cash flow definition of profit*. Dividends are the cash flow left over after costs of operations and new investment are deducted from revenues. Using Eq. (2.3) and the definition of shareholders' wealth [Eq. (2.1)], we can rewrite shareholders' wealth as

$$S_0 = \sum_{t=0}^{\infty} \frac{\text{Rev}_t - (\text{W\&S})_t - I_t}{(1 + k_s)^t}. \tag{2.4}$$

The accounting definition of profit does not deduct gross investment, I_t, as investment outlays are made. Instead, the book value of new investment is capitalized on the balance sheet and written off at some depreciation rate, dep. The *accounting definition of profit* is net income,

$$\text{NI}_t = \text{Rev}_t - (\text{W\&S})_t - \text{dep}_t. \tag{2.5}$$

Let ΔA_t be the net change in the book value of assets during a year. The net change will equal gross new investment during the year, I_t, less the change in accumulated depreciation during the year, dep_t:

$$\Delta A_t = I_t - \text{dep}_t. \tag{2.6}$$

We already know that the accounting definition of profit, NI_t, is different from the economic definition, Div_t. However, it can be adjusted by subtracting net investment. This is done in Eq. (2.7):

$$S_0 = \sum_{t=0}^{\infty} \frac{\text{Rev}_t - (\text{W\&S})_t - \text{dep}_t - (I_t - \text{dep}_t)}{(1 + k_s)^t}$$

$$= \sum_{t=0}^{\infty} \frac{\text{NI}_t - \Delta A_t}{(1 + k_s)^t}. \tag{2.7}$$

---

[3] The conclusions to be drawn from the model do not change if we add debt and taxes, but the arithmetic becomes more complex.

Table 2.1   LIFO vs. FIFO (numbers in dollars)

	LIFO	FIFO	Inventory at Cost
Revenue	100	100	4th item in 90 → LIFO
Cost of goods sold	−90	−25	3rd item in 60
Operating income	10	75	2nd item in 40
Taxes at 40%	−4	−30	1st term in 25 → FIFO
Net income	6	45	
Earnings per share (100 shs)	.06	.45	

The main difference between the accounting definition and the economic defini-tion of profit is that the former does not focus on cash flows when they occur, whereas the latter does. The economic definition of profit, for example, correctly deducts the entire expenditure for investment in plant and equipment at the time the cash outflow occurs.

Financial managers are frequently misled when they focus on the accounting definition of profit, or earnings per share. The objective of the firm is *not* to maximize earnings per share. The correct objective is to maximize shareholders' wealth, which is the price per share that in turn is equivalent to the discounted cash flows of the firm. There are two good examples that point out the difference between maximizing earnings per share and maximizing discounted cash flow. The first example is the difference between FIFO (first-in, first-out) and LIFO (last-in, first-out) inventory accounting during inflation. Earnings per share are higher if the firm adopts FIFO inventory accounting. The reason is that the cost of manufacturing the oldest items in inventory is less than the cost of producing the newest items. Consequently, if the cost of the oldest inventory (the inventory that was first in) is written off as expense against revenue, earnings per share will be higher than if the cost of the newest items (the inventory that was in last) is written off. A numerical example is given in Table 2.1. It is easy to see how managers might be tempted to use FIFO accounting tech-niques. Earnings per share are higher. However, FIFO is the wrong technique to use in an inflationary period because it minimizes cash flow by maximizing taxes. In our example, production has taken place during some previous time period, and we are trying to make the correct choice of inventory accounting in the present. The sale of an item from inventory in Table 2.1 provides $100 of cash inflow (revenue) regard-less of which accounting system we are using. Cost of goods sold involves no current cash flow, but taxes do. Therefore with FIFO, earnings per share are $0.45, but cash flow per share is ($100 − $30)/100 shares, which equals $0.70 per share. On the other hand, with LIFO inventory accounting, earnings per share are only $0.06, but cash flow is ($100 − $4)/100 shares, which equals $0.96 per share. Since shareholders care only about discounted cash flow, they will assign a higher value to the shares of the company using LIFO accounting. The reason is that LIFO provides higher cash flow because it pays lower taxes to the government.[4] This is a good example of the

---

[4] In 1979 the Internal Revenue Service estimated that if every firm that could have switched to LIFO had actually done so, approximately $18 billion less corporate taxes would have been paid.

difference between maximizing earnings per share and maximizing shareholders' wealth.[5]

A second example is the accounting treatment of goodwill in mergers. Since the accounting practices for merger are discussed in detail in Chapter 20, only the salient features will be mentioned here. There are two types of accounting treatment for merger: pooling and purchase. *Pooling* means that the income statements and balance sheets of the merging companies are simply added together. With *purchase*, the acquiring company adds two items to its balance sheet: (1) the book value of the assets of the acquired company and (2) the difference between the purchase price and the book value. This difference is an item called *goodwill*. Opinion 17 of the Accounting Principles Board (APB No. 17, effective October 31, 1970) of the American Institute of Certified Public Accountants requires that goodwill be written off as an expense against earnings *after* taxes over a period not to exceed 40 years. Obviously, earnings per share will be lower if the same merger takes place by purchase rather than pooling. There is empirical evidence, collected in a paper by Gagnon [1971], that indicates that managers choose to use pooling rather than purchase if the write-off of goodwill is substantial. Managers seem to behave as if they were trying to maximize earnings per share. The sad thing is that some mergers that are advantageous to the shareholders of acquiring firms may be rejected by management if substantial goodwill write-offs are required. This would be unfortunate because *there is no difference in the effect on cash flows between pooling and purchase.* The reason is that goodwill expense is not a cash flow and it has no effect on taxes because it is written off *after* taxes.[6]

It is often argued that maximization of earnings per share is appropriate if investors use earnings per share to value the stock. There is good empirical evidence to indicate that this is not the case. Shareholders do in fact value securities according to the present value of discounted cash flows. Evidence that substantiates this is presented in detail in Chapter 11.

E. TECHNIQUES FOR CAPITAL BUDGETING

Having argued that maximizing shareholders' wealth is equivalent to maximizing the discounted cash flows provided by investment projects, we now turn our attention to a discussion of investment decision rules. We assume, for the time being, that the stream of cash flows provided by a project can be estimated without error, and that the opportunity cost of funds provided to the firm (this is usually referred to as the *cost of capital*) is also known. We also assume that capital markets are frictionless, so that financial managers can separate investment decisions from individual shareholder preferences, and that monitoring costs are zero, so that managers will maximize shareholders' wealth. All that they need to know are cash flows and the required market rate of return for projects of equivalent risk.

---

[5] See Chapter 11 for a discussion of empirical research on this issue.

[6] See Chapter 11 for a discussion of empirical evidence relating to this issue.

Three major problems face managers when they make investment decisions. First, they have to search out new opportunities in the marketplace or new technologies. These are the basis of growth. Unfortunately, the Theory of Finance cannot help with this problem. Second, the expected cash flows from the projects have to be estimated. And finally, the projects have to be evaluated according to sound decision rules. These latter two problems are central topics of this text. In the remainder of this chapter we look at project evaluation techniques assuming that cash flows are known with certainty, and in Chapter 12 we will assume that cash flows are uncertain.

Investment decision rules are usually referred to as *capital budgeting techniques*. The best technique will possess the following essential property: It will maximize shareholders' wealth. This essential property can be broken down into separate criteria:

- All cash flows should be considered.
- The cash flows should be discounted at the opportunity cost of funds.
- The technique should select from a set of mutually exclusive projects the one that maximizes shareholders' wealth.
- Managers should be able to consider one project independently from all others (this is known as the *value-additivity principle*).

The last two criteria need some explanation. *Mutually exclusive projects* are a set from which only one project can be chosen. In other words, if a manager chooses to go ahead with one project from the set, he or she cannot choose to take on any of the others. For example, there may be three or four different types of bridges that could be constructed to cross a river at a given site. Choosing a wooden bridge excludes other types, e.g., steel. Projects are also categorized in other ways. *Independent projects* are those that permit the manager to choose to undertake any or all, and *contingent projects* are those that have to be carried out together or not at all. For example, if building a tunnel also requires a ventilation system, then the tunnel and ventilation system should be considered as a single, contingent project.

The fourth criterion, the *value-additivity principle*, implies that if we know the value of separate projects accepted by management, then simply adding their values, V_j, will give us the value of the firm, V. In mathematical terms, if there are N projects, then the value of the firm is

$$V = \sum_{j=1}^{N} V_j. \tag{2.8}$$

This is a particularly important point because it means that projects can be considered on their own merit without the necessity of looking at them in an infinite variety of combinations with other projects.

There are four widely used capital budgeting techniques: (1) the payback method, (2) the accounting rate of return, (3) the net present value, and (4) the internal rate of return. Our task is to choose the technique that best satisfies the four desirable properties discussed above. It will be demonstrated that only one technique—the net

Table 2.2 Four Mutually Exclusive Projects

	Cash Flows				
Year	A	B	C	D	PV Factor at 10%
0	− 1000	− 1000	− 1000	− 1000	1.000
1	100	0	100	200	.909
2	900	0	200	300	.826
3	100	300	300	500	.751
4	− 100	700	400	500	.683
5	− 400	1300	1250	600	.621

present value method—is correct. It is the only technique that is always consistent with shareholder wealth maximization.

To provide an example for discussion, Table 2.2 lists the estimates of cash flow for four projects, each of which has a five-year life. Since they are mutually exclusive, there is only one that will maximize the price of the firm's stock; i.e., there is only one that will maximize shareholders' wealth. We would normally assume at this point that all four projects are equally "risky." However, according to the assumption used throughout this chapter, their cash flows are known with certainty, therefore their risk is zero. The appropriate discount rate in a world with no risk is the risk-free rate (e.g., the Treasury Bill rate).

1. The Payback Method

The payback period for a project is simply the number of years it takes to recover the initial cash outlay on a project. The payback periods for the four projects in Table 2.2 are:

Project A,   2 years;

Project B,   4 years;

Project C,   4 years;

Project D,   3 years.

If management were adhering strictly to the payback method, it would choose project A, which has the shortest payback period. A casual inspection of the cash flows shows that this is clearly wrong. The difficulty with the payback method is that it does not consider all cash flows and it fails to discount them. Failure to consider all cash flows results in ignoring the large negative cash flows that occur in the last two years of project A.[7] Failure to discount them means that management would be indifferent

---

[7] It is not too hard to find real-world examples of projects that have negative future cash flows and cannot be abandoned. A good example is nuclear power plants; at the end of their useful life they must be decommissioned at considerable expense.

in its choice between project *A* and a second project that paid $900 in the first year and $100 in the second. Both projects would have the same payback period. We reject the payback method because it violates (at least) the first two of the four properties that are desirable in capital budgeting techniques.[8]

2. The Accounting Rate of Return

The *accounting rate of return* (ARR) is the average after-tax profit divided by the initial cash outlay. It is very similar to (and in some uses exactly the same as) the return on assets (ROA) or the return on investment (ROI), and they suffer from the same deficiencies. Assuming, for the sake of convenience, that the numbers in Table 2.2 are accounting profits, the average after-tax profit for project *A* is

$$\frac{-1000 + 100 + 900 + 100 - 100 - 400}{5} = -80,$$

and the ARR is

$$\text{ARR} = \frac{\text{Average after-tax profit}}{\text{Initial outlay}} = \frac{-80}{1000} = -8\%. \tag{2.9}$$

The ARRs for the four projects are:

Project *A*,   ARR $= -8\%$;
Project *B*,   ARR $= 26\%$;
Project *C*,   ARR $= 25\%$;
Project *D*,   ARR $= 22\%$.

If we were using the ARR, we would choose project *B* as the best. The problem with the ARR is that it uses accounting profits instead of cash flows and it does not consider the time value of money. The difference between accounting profits and cash flows has been discussed at length, and it is therefore unnecessary to repeat here why it is incorrect to use the accounting definition of profits. In fact, if the numbers in Table 2.2 were accounting profits, we would need to convert them to cash flows before using the ARR. A second deficiency of ARR is that failure to use the time value of money (i.e., failure to discount) means that managers would be indifferent in their choice between project *B* and a project with after-tax profits that occur in the opposite chronological order because both projects would have the same accounting rate of return.

3. Net Present Value

The *net present value* (NPV) criterion will accept projects that have an NPV greater than zero. The NPV is computed by discounting the cash flows at the firm's opportunity cost of capital. For the projects in Table 2.2, we assume that the cost

---

[8] See Problem 2.10 at the end of the chapter. It demonstrates that the payback technique also violates the value-additivity principle.

of capital is 10%. Therefore the present value of project A is[9]

(Cash Flow) × (PV Factor) =		PV
−1000	1.000	−1000.00
100	.909	90.90
900	.826	743.40
100	.751	75.10
−100	.683	−68.30
−400	.621	−248.40
	NPV =	−407.30

We have discounted each of the cash flows back to the present and summed them. Mathematically, this can be written as

$$NPV = \sum_{t=1}^{N} \frac{NCF_t}{(1+k)^t} - I_0, \qquad (2.10)$$

where NCF_t is the net cash flow in time period t, I_0 is the initial cash outlay, k is the firm's weighted average cost of capital, and N is the number of years in the project. The net present values of the four projects are:

Project A,   NPV = −407.30;

Project B,   NPV = 510.70;

Project C,   NPV = 530.85;

Project D,   NPV = 519.20.

If these projects were independent instead of mutually exclusive, we would reject A and accept B, C, and D. (Why?) Since they are mutually exclusive, we select the project with greatest NPV, project C. The NPV of a project is exactly the same as the increase in shareholders' wealth. This fact makes it the correct decision rule for capital budgeting purposes. More will be said about this when we compare the NPV rule with the internal rate of return.

4. Internal Rate of Return

The *internal rate of return* (IRR) on a project is defined as that rate which equates the present value of the cash outflows and inflows. In other words, it is the rate that makes the computed NPV exactly zero. Hence this is the rate of return on invested capital that the project is returning to the firm. Mathematically, we solve for the rate of return where the NPV equals zero:

$$NPV = 0 = \sum_{t=1}^{N} \frac{NCF_t}{(1+IRR)^t} - I_0. \qquad (2.11)$$

---

[9] The reader who wishes to brush up on the algebra of discounting is referred to Appendix A.

Table 2.3   IRR for Project *C*

Year	Cash Flow	PV at 10%		PV at 20%		PV at 25%		PV at 22.8%	
0	−1000	1.000	−1000.00	1.000	−1000.00	1.000	−1000.00	1.000	−1000.00
1	100	.909	90.90	.833	83.33	.800	80.00	.814	81.40
2	200	.826	165.20	.694	138.80	.640	128.00	.663	132.60
3	300	.751	225.30	.579	173.70	.512	153.60	.540	162.00
4	400	.683	273.20	.482	192.80	.410	163.84	.440	176.00
5	1250	.621	776.25	.402	502.50	.328	410.00	.358	447.50
			530.85		91.13		−64.56		−.50

We can solve for the IRR on project *C* by trial and error. (Most pocket calculators have programs that can quickly solve for the IRR by using similar iterative techniques.) This is done in Table 2.3 and graphed in Fig. 2.2.

Figure 2.2 shows that the NPV of the given set of cash flows decreases as the discount rate is increased. If the discount rate is zero, there is no time value of money, and the NPV of a project is simply the sum of its cash flows. For project *C*, the NPV equals $1250 when the discount rate is zero. At the opposite extreme, if the discount rate is infinite, then future cash flows are valueless, and the NPV of project *C* is its current cash flow, −$1000. Somewhere between these two extremes is a discount rate that makes the present value equal to zero. Called the IRR on the project, this rate equates the present value of cash inflows with the present value of cash outflows. The IRRs for the four projects are:

Project *A*,   IRR = −200%;
Project *B*,   IRR = 20.9%;
Project *C*,   IRR = 22.8%;
Project *D*,   IRR = 25.4%.

If we use the IRR criterion and the projects are independent, we accept any project that has an IRR greater than the opportunity cost of capital, which is 10%. Therefore

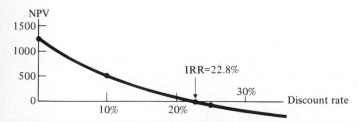

Figure 2.2
NPV of project *C* at different discount rates.

we would accept projects B, C, and D. However, since these projects are mutually exclusive, the IRR rule leads us to accept project D as the best.

F. COMPARISON OF NET PRESENT VALUE WITH INTERNAL RATE OF RETURN

As the example shows, the net present value and the internal rate of return can favor conflicting project choices. The net present value favors project C, whereas the IRR favors project D. Both techniques consider all cash flows and both use the concept of the time value of money in order to discount cash flows. However, we must choose from among the four mutually exclusive projects the one project that maximizes shareholders' wealth. Consequently, only one of the two techniques can be correct. We shall see that the NPV criterion is the only one that is necessarily consistent with maximizing shareholders' wealth.

Figure 2.3 compares projects B, C, and D. For very low discount rates, project B has the highest net present value; for intermediate discount rates, project C is best; and for high discount rates, project D is best. The NPV rule compares the three projects at the same discount rate. Remember, 10% was not arbitrarily chosen. It is the market-determined opportunity cost of capital. We saw earlier in the chapter that this market-determined discount rate is the one managers should use if they desire to maximize the wealth of all shareholders. Consequently, no other discount rate is appropriate. Project C is the best project because it gives the greatest NPV when the opportunity cost of funds invested is 10%.

The IRR rule does not discount at the opportunity cost of capital. Instead, it implicitly assumes that the time value of money is the IRR, since all cash flows are

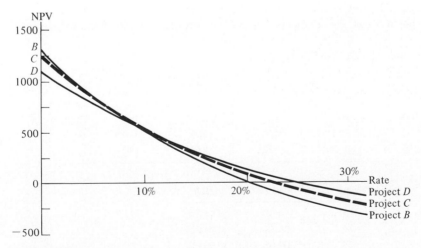

Figure 2.3
Comparison of three mutually exclusive projects.

discounted at that rate. This implicit assumption has come to be called the *reinvestment rate assumption.*

1. The Reinvestment Rate Assumption

The correct interpretation for the reinvestment rate is that it is really the same thing as the opportunity cost of capital. Both the NPV rule and the IRR rule make implicit assumptions about the reinvestment rate. The NPV rule assumes that shareholders can reinvest their money at the opportunity cost of capital, which in our example was 10%. Because 10% is the market-determined opportunity cost of funds, the NPV rule is making the correct reinvestment rate assumption. On the other hand, the IRR rule assumes that investors can reinvest their money at the IRR for each project. Therefore in our example, it assumes that shareholders can reinvest funds in project C at 22.8% and in project D at 25.4%. But we have been told that both projects have the same risk (namely, cash flows are known with certainty). Why should investors be able to reinvest at one rate for project C and at another rate for project D? Obviously, the implicit reinvestment rate assumption in the IRR rule defies logic. Although the IRR does discount cash flows, it does not discount them at the opportunity cost of capital. Therefore it violates the second of the four properties mentioned earlier. It also violates the Fisher separation theorem discussed in Chapter 1.

2. The Value-Additivity Principle

The fourth of the desirable properties of capital budgeting rules demands that managers be able to consider one project independently of all others. This is known as the *value-additivity principle,* and it implies that the value of the firm is equal to the sum of the values of each of its projects [Eq. (2.8)]. To demonstrate that the IRR rule can violate the value-additivity principle, consider the three projects whose cash flows are given in Table 2.4. Projects 1 and 2 are mutually exclusive, and project 3

Table 2.4 Example of Value Additivity

Year	Project 1	Project 2	Project 3	PV Factor at 10%	1 + 3	2 + 3
0	−100	−100	−100	1.000	−200	−200
1	0	225	450	.909	450	675
2	550	0	0	.826	550	0

Project	NPV at 10%	IRR
1	354.30	134.5%
2	104.53	125.0%
3	309.05	350.0%
1 + 3	663.35	212.8%
2 + 3	413.58	237.5%

**Table 2.5 Oil-Well Pump
Incremental Cash Flows**

Year	Estimated Cash Flow
0	−1,600
1	10,000
2	−10,000

is independent of them. If the value-additivity principle holds, we should be able to choose the better of the two mutually exclusive projects without having to consider the independent project. The NPVs of the three projects as well as their IRRs are also given in Table 2.4. If we use the IRR rule to choose between projects 1 and 2, we would select project 1. But if we consider combinations of projects, then the IRR rule would prefer projects 2 and 3 to projects 1 and 3. The IRR rule prefers project 1 in isolation but project 2 in combination with the independent project. In this example, the IRR rule does not obey the value-additivity principle. The implication for management is that it would have to consider all possible combinations of projects and choose the combination that has the greatest internal rate of return. If, for example, a firm had only five projects, it would need to consider 32 different combinations.[10]

The NPV rule always obeys the value-additivity principle. Given that the opportunity cost of capital is 10%, we would choose project 1 as being the best either by itself or in combination with project 3. Note that the combinations of 1 and 3 or 2 and 3 are simply the sums of the NPVs of the projects considered separately. Consequently, if we adopt the NPV rule, the value of the firm is the sum of the values of the separate projects. Later (in Chapter 7) we shall see that this result holds even in a world with uncertainty where the firm may be viewed as a portfolio of risky projects.

3. Multiple Rates of Return

Still another difficulty with the IRR rule is that it can result in multiple rates of return if the stream of estimated cash flows changes sign more than once. A classic example of this situation has come to be known as the *oil-well pump problem*. An oil company is trying to decide whether or not to install a high-speed pump on a well that is already in operation. The estimated incremental cash flows are given in Table 2.5. The pump will cost $1,600 to install. During its first year of operation it will produce $10,000 more oil than the pump that is currently in place. But during

[10] The number of combinations for five projects is

$$\binom{5}{0} + \binom{5}{1} + \binom{5}{2} + \binom{5}{3} + \binom{5}{4} + \binom{5}{5} = 32.$$

Imagine the number of combinations that would have to be considered if there were 50 projects.

the second year, the high-speed pump produces $10,000 less oil because the well has been depleted. The question is whether or not to accept the rapid pumping technique, which speeds up cash flows in the near term at the expense of cash flows in the long term. Figure 2.4 shows the NPV of the project for different discount rates. If the opportunity cost of capital is 10%, the NPV rule would reject the project because it has negative NPV at that rate. If we are using the IRR rule, the project has two IRRs, 25% and 400%. Since both exceed the opportunity cost of capital, the project would probably be accepted.

Mathematically, the multiple IRRs are a result of Descartes' rule of signs, which implies that every time the cash flows change signs, there may be a new (positive, real) root to the problem solution. For the above example, the signs of cash flows change twice. The IRR is the rate that causes the discounted value of the cash flows to equal zero. Hence we solve the following equation for IRR:

$$NPV = 0 = \frac{-1,600}{(1 + IRR)^0} + \frac{10,000}{(1 + IRR)^1} + \frac{-10,000}{(1 + IRR)^2},$$

$$0 = \frac{-1,600(1 + IRR)^2 + 10,000(1 + IRR) - 10,000}{(1 + IRR)^2},$$

$$0 = 1,600(1 + IRR)^2 - 10,000(1 + IRR) + 10,000.$$

This is clearly a quadratic equation and has two roots. It has the general form

$$ax^2 + bx + c = 0$$

and can be solved using the quadratic formula

$$x = \frac{-b \pm \sqrt{b^2 - 4ac}}{2a}.$$

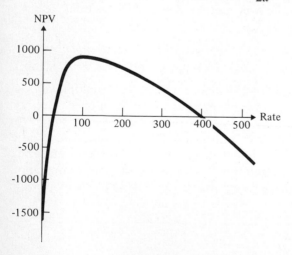

Figure 2.4
Multiple internal rates of return.

Therefore for our example the roots are

$$(1 + IRR) = x = \frac{10,000 \pm \sqrt{10,000^2 - 4(1,600)10,000}}{2(1,600)},$$

$$(1 + IRR) = \frac{10,000 \pm 6,000}{3,200},$$

$$IRR = 25\% \quad \text{or} \quad 400\%$$

An economic interpretation to the multiple root problem can be found in a textbook by Teichroew [1964]. We can think of the project as an investment, with the firm putting money into it twice: $-1,600$ at the time of the initial investment, and $-10,000$ in the second time period. The project can be thought of as lending $+10,000$ to the firm in the first time period. Let us assume that the positive cash flows provided by the project to the firm are lent at 10%, which is the opportunity cost of capital. This assumption makes sense because the $+10,000$ received by the firm cannot be invested in another oil-well pump (only one is available). Therefore it is appropriate to assume that the $+10,000$ received by the firm in the first period is reinvested at the opportunity cost of capital, namely, 10%. On the other hand, the firm expects to earn the IRR (whatever it is) on the cash flows it puts into the project. Therefore the firm invests $-1,600$ now and expects to earn the IRR at the end of the first time period. Mathematically, the value at the end of the first period should be

$$1,600(1 + IRR).$$

The difference between this result and the amount of money ($+10,000$) that the project lends to the firm at the opportunity cost of capital, 10%, in the second period is the amount borrowed at rate k. The net amount lent to the firm is given in brackets below. The future value of this amount in the second period is the net amount multiplied by $(1 + k)$:

$$[10,000 - 1,600(1 + IRR)](1 + k).$$

The firm then invests $-10,000$ at the end of the second period. This is set equal to the future value of the project that was given above. The result is

$$10,000 = [10,000 - 1,600(1 + IRR)](1 + k).$$

Recalling that the opportunity cost of capital, k, is 10%, we can solve for the rate of return on investment:

$$\frac{10,000 - 11,000}{-1,760} = 1 + IRR$$

$$-43.18\% = IRR.$$

This way of looking at the cash flows of the project solves the multiple root problem because positive cash flows lent to the firm are assumed to be provided at a known rate of return equal to the opportunity cost of capital. This makes it possible to isolate the rate of return on money invested in the project. This rate can be thought of as the IRR. For the example of the oil-well pump, we see that when it is viewed properly, the IRR gives the same answer as the NPV. We should reject the project because the internal rate of return is less than the opportunity cost of capital.

4. Summary of Comparison of IRR and NPV

The IRR rule errs in several ways. First, it does not obey the value-additivity principle, and consequently managers who use the IRR cannot consider projects. independently of each other. Second, the IRR rule assumes that funds invested in projects have opportunity costs equal to the IRR for the project. This implicit reinvestment rate assumption violates the requirement that cash flows be discounted at the market-determined opportunity cost of capital. Finally, the IRR rule can lead to multiple rates of return whenever the sign of cash flows changes more than once. However, we saw that this problem can be avoided by the simple expedient of assuming that all cash inflows are loaned to the firm by the project at the market opportunity cost, and that the rate of return on cash flows invested in the project is the IRR.

The NPV rule avoids all the problems the IRR is heir to. It obeys the value-additivity principle, it correctly discounts at the opportunity cost of funds, and most important, it is precisely the same thing as maximizing the shareholders' wealth.

G. CASH FLOWS FOR CAPITAL
BUDGETING PURPOSES

Up to this point we have made the implicit assumptions that the firm has no debt and that there are no corporate taxes. This section adds a note of realism by providing a definition of cash flows for capital budgeting purposes, given debt and taxes. In particular, we shall see that some cash flows, such as interest paid on debt and repayment of principal on debt, should not be considered cash flows *for capital budgeting purposes*. At the same time, we shall demonstrate, by using an example, that there is only one definition of cash flows that is consistent with shareholder wealth maximization.

To understand discounted cash flows it is also necessary to have a rudimentary understanding of the opportunity cost of capital of the firm. Chapter 13 discusses the cost of capital in great depth; however, the basics will be given here. The firm receives its investment funds from two classes of investors: creditors and shareholders. They provide debt and equity capital, respectively. Both groups expect to receive a rate of return that compensates them for the level of risk they accept.[11] Debt holders receive a stream of fixed payments and can force the firm into receivership or bankruptcy if they do not receive payment. On the other hand, shareholders receive the firm's

---

[11] The assumption that future cash flows are known with certainty must be relaxed at this point, in order to allow risk-free debt and risky equity. The reader who is interested in the related theoretical problems is referred to Chapters 13 and 14.

Table 2.6   Pro Forma Income Statement

Rev	Revenue	1300
$-VC$	Variable costs	-600
$-FCC$	Fixed cash costs	0
$-$dep.	Noncash charges (depreciation)	-200
EBIT	Earnings before interest and taxes	500
$-k_dD$	Interest expenses	-50
EBT	Earnings before taxes	450
$-T$	Taxes @ 50%	-225
NI	Net income	225

residual cash flows that remain after all other payments are made. Consequently, the interest rate paid to debt holders is less than the required rate of return on equity because debt is less risky.

It is important to understand that projects undertaken by the firm must earn enough cash flow to provide the required rate of return to creditors, repayment of the face amount of debt, and payment of expected dividends to shareholders. Only when cash flows exceed these amounts will there be any gain in shareholders' wealth. When we discount cash flows at the weighted average cost of capital, this is exactly what we are saying. A positive NPV is achieved only after creditors and shareholders receive their expected risk-adjusted rates of return.

In order to provide an example of this very important concept, consider the following (somewhat artificial) situation. A firm is going to be created from scratch. It will require an initial investment, I, of $1000 for equipment that will depreciate at the rate of $200 per year. Owners have decided to borrow $500 at 10% interest. In other words, the before-tax coupon rate on debt capital, k_d, is 10%. The expected annual cash flows for the project are implicit in the pro forma income statement given in Table 2.6. We shall assume that shareholders require a rate of return of 30% in order to compensate them for the riskiness of their position. Thus the cost of equity, k_s, is 30%.

To provide the simplest possible example, assume that all the cash flows are perpetual, i.e., the firm has no growth. This assumption has the effect of keeping the firm's market value debt-to-equity ratio constant through time.[12] Perpetual cash flows are obtained, first, by writing a consol bond that never matures and pays a coupon of $50 each year; and second, by investing $200 annually to replace the depreciation of the equipment.

Table 2.7 details the exact cash flows assuming that the project is held for five years. At the end of five years the firm will be sold for its market value. Shareholders will receive the cash, use some of it ($500) to pay off bondholders, and keep the remainder.

---

[12] Without a constant debt-to-equity ratio, the weighted average cost of capital would change through time, and the problem would become much more complex.

Table 2.7 Total Cash Flows for the Project

Year	Inflow	Outflow	Depre-ciation	Replacement Investment	Interest	Tax	Net Income	Residual Cash Flow
0	1000	−1000						
1	700		200	−200	−50	−225	225	225
2	700		200	−200	−50	−225	225	225
3	700		200	−200	−50	−225	225	225
4	700		200	−200	−50	−225	225	225
5	700	−500	200	−200	−50	−225	225	225 + 1250

Current cash flows are $500 provided by creditors and $500 from equity holders; outflows are $1000 paid for the equipment. In years 1 through 5 the project returns $700 in cash after the cash costs of production ($600) are subtracted from revenues ($1300). Then depreciation, a noncash charge ($200), is deducted, leaving $500 in earnings before interest and taxes. The deduction of $50 of interest expenses leaves taxable income of $450. After taxes, there is $225 in net income. To compute *free cash flows* available for payment to shareholders, depreciation ($200), a noncash charge, must be added back, and replacement investment ($200), a cash outflow, must be subtracted. Thus residual cash flow available to shareholders is $225 per year.

Shareholders' wealth, S, is the present value of their stream of residual cash flows, discounted at the cost of equity capital, $k_s = 30\%$. Recalling that their stream of residual cash flows continues forever, we can compute their wealth as shown below.[13]

$$S = \frac{\text{Residual cash flow}}{k_s} = \frac{\$225}{.3} = \$750.$$

The present value of bondholders' wealth, B, is the present value of their perpetual stream of coupon payments discounted at the market cost of debt, k_b:

$$B = \frac{\text{Interest payments}}{k_b} = \frac{\$50}{.10} = \$500.$$

Thus we see that the market value of the firm, V, is expected to be

$$V = B + S = \$500 + \$750 = \$1250.$$

Note that the present value of debt and equity are not affected by the fact that they will be sold at the end of year 5. The new bondholders and shareholders simply take over ownership of their streams of cash, paying $500 and $750, respectively. As shown in the last row of Table 2.7, the shareholders receive $1250 in year 5 for the firm but must pay $500 to bondholders. Note also that the present value of shareholders' wealth is $750, but they had put up $500 of the initial investment. Therefore their change in wealth, ΔS, is $750 minus $500, which equals $250. We shall see that this is exactly the same thing as the NPV of the project.

Instead of working through the complicated procedure given above, it will be

---

[13] This formula is exact for perpetual cash flows. See Appendix A.

easier to analyze capital budgeting projects by defining *cash flows for capital budgeting purposes* and discounting them at the firm's weighted average cost of capital. First, what is the weighted average cost of capital (k = WACC)? As shown in Eq. (2.12) below, it is the after-tax market cost of debt capital, $k_b(1 - \tau_c)$, multiplied by the percentage of the market value of the firm owned by creditors, $[B/(B + S)]$, plus the cost of equity, k_s, multiplied by the percentage of the firm's value owned by shareholders, $[S/(B + S)]$. Note that τ_c is the firm's marginal tax rate.

$$k = \text{WACC} = k_b(1 - \tau_c) \frac{B}{B + S} + k_s \frac{S}{B + S} \qquad (2.12)$$

$$= .10(1 - .5)(.4) + .30(.6) = 20\%.$$

In a world without any taxes, the cost of capital would simply be a weighted average of the costs of debt and equity. However, in the real world, the government allows corporations to deduct the interest paid on debt as an expense before paying taxes. This tax shield on debt payments makes the cost of debt even less expensive from the firm's point of view. The weighted average cost of capital is the same as the after-tax market-determined opportunity cost of funds provided to the firm.

After determining the after-tax weighted average cost of capital, we need to find a definition of cash flow for use in standard capital budgeting procedures that is consistent with maximizing shareholders' wealth. The appropriate definition of *net cash flow for capital budgeting purposes* is after-tax cash flows from operations, assuming that the firm has no debt and net of gross investment, ΔI. Marginal operating cash flows are the change in revenues, Rev, minus the change in the direct costs that include variable costs of operations, VC, and the change in fixed cash costs, FCC, such as property taxes and administrative salaries and wages:

Marginal operating cash flows = $\Delta\text{Rev} - \Delta\text{VC} - \Delta\text{FCC}$.

Operating cash flows net of investment, ΔI, are called *free operating cash flows*.

Free operating cash flows = $\Delta\text{Rev} - \Delta\text{VC} - \Delta\text{FCC} - \Delta I$.

Taxes on operating cash flows are the tax rate, τ_c, times the change in revenues minus the change in direct cash costs and depreciation (dep).[14]

Taxes on operating cash flows = $\tau_c(\Delta\text{Rev} - \Delta\text{VC} - \Delta\text{dep} - \Delta\text{FCC})$.

Therefore the correct definition of cash flows for capital budgeting purposes is free operating cash flows minus taxes on free operating cash flows.[15]

---

[14] Depreciation is a noncash charge against revenues. If there are other noncash charges, they should also be included here.

[15] An equivalent definition is

$$\text{NCF for cap. budgeting} = \Delta\text{NI} + \Delta\text{dep} + (1 - \tau_c)\Delta(k_dD) - \Delta I, \qquad (2.13a)$$

where ΔNI stands for the change in net income, the accounting definition of profit, and Δk_dD is the change in the coupon rate, k_d, on debt times the change in the face value of debt, D. Although sometimes easier to use, it obscures the difference between cash flows for capital budgeting purposes and the accounting definition of profit.

NCF for cap. budgeting $= (\Delta\text{Rev} - \Delta\text{VC} - \Delta\text{FCC})$

$$- \tau_c(\Delta\text{Rev} - \Delta\text{VC} - \Delta\text{FCC} - \Delta\text{dep}) - \Delta I$$

$$= (\Delta\text{Rev} - \Delta\text{VC} - \Delta\text{FCC})(1 - \tau_c) + \tau_c(\Delta\text{dep}) - \Delta I. \quad (2.13)$$

This definition is very different from the accounting definition of net income. Cash flows for capital budgeting purposes can be thought of as the after-tax cash flows the firm would have if it had no debt. Interest expenses and their tax shield are not included in the definition of cash flow for capital budgeting purposes. The reason is that when we discount at the weighted average cost of capital we are implicitly assuming that the project will return the expected interest payments to creditors and the expected dividends to shareholders. Hence inclusion of interest payments (or dividends) as a cash flow to be discounted would be double counting. Furthermore, the tax shield provided by depreciation, $\tau_c(\Delta\text{dep})$, is treated as if it were a cash inflow. Table 2.8 shows the appropriate cash flows for capital budgeting purposes using the numbers from the example we have been using. To demonstrate that these are the correct cash flows, we can discount them at the weighted average cost of capital. The resulting number should exactly equal the increment to the shareholders' wealth, i.e., $250 (see Table 2.9). It is no coincidence that this works out correctly. We are discounting the after-tax cash flows from operations at the weighted average cost of capital. Thus the NPV of the project is exactly the same thing as the increase in shareholders' wealth.

One of the advantages of discounting the firm's free cash flows at the after-tax weighted average cost of capital is that this technique separates the investment decisions of the firm from its financing decisions. The definition of free cash flows shows what the firm will earn after taxes, assuming that it has no debt capital. Thus changes in the firm's debt-to-equity ratio have no effect on the definition of cash flows for capital budgeting purposes. The effect of financial decisions (e.g., changes in the ratio of debt to equity) is reflected in the firm's weighted average cost of capital.

The theory of the firm's cost of capital is discussed in greater detail in Chapter 13. In most applications it is assumed that the firm has an optimal ratio of debt to equity, which is called the target capital structure. For the firm as a whole, the ratio of debt to equity is assumed to remain constant across time even though the financing for

Table 2.8   Cash Flows for Capital Budgeting

Year	Operating Cash Flow	Depreciation	Tax*	NCF = Cash Flow
0	− 1000			− 1000
1	700	200	250	250
2	700	200	250	250
3	700	200	250	250
4	700	200	250	250
5	700	200	250	250 + 1250

* The tax is the tax on operating income, i.e., .5(500).

Table 2.9   NPV of Cash Flows*

Year	Cash Flow	PV Factor at 20%	PV
0	− 1000	1.000	−1,000.00
1	250	.833	208.33
2	250	.694	173.61
3	250	.579	144.68
4	250	.482	120.56
5	250	.401	100.47
5	1250	.401	502.35
			250.00

* Recall that in year 5 the firm was sold for a market value of $1250. This amount is the present value of cash flows from year 5 on, i.e., $250 \div .20 = 1250$.

individual projects may require that debt be paid off over the life of the project. Without this assumption, the cost of capital would have to change each time period.

Another relevant issue worth pointing out is that the definition of cash flows for capital budgeting purposes includes all incremental cash flows attributable to a project. Too often, analysts forget that the total investment in a project includes working capital requirements as well as the cash outlays for buildings and equipment. Working capital includes any changes in short-term balance sheet items such as increases in inventories, accounts receivable, and accounts payable that are expected to result from undertaking a project. Net working capital requirements are the difference between changes in short-term assets and short-term liabilities.

SUMMARY AND CONCLUSION

The objective of the firm is assumed to be the maximization of shareholders' wealth. Toward this end, managers should take projects with positive NPVs down to the point where the NPV of the last acceptable project is zero. When cash flows are properly defined for capital budgeting purposes and are discounted at the weighted average cost of capital, the NPV of a project is exactly the same as the increase in shareholders' wealth. Given perfect capital markets, the owners of the firm will unanimously support the acceptance of all projects with positive NPV. Other decision criteria, such as the payback method, the accounting rate of return, and the IRR, do not necessarily guarantee undertaking projects that maximize shareholders' wealth.

PROBLEM SET

2.1 *Basic capital budgeting problem with straight-line depreciation.* The Roberts Company has cash inflows of $140,000 per year on project A and cash outflows of $100,000 per year. The investment outlay on the project is $100,000; its life is 10 years; the tax rate, τ_c, is 40%. The opportunity cost of capital is 12%.

a) Present two alternative formulations of the net cash flows adjusted for the depreciation tax shelter.

b) Calculate the net present value for project A, using straight-line depreciation for tax purposes.

2.2 *Basic capital budgeting problem with accelerated depreciation.* Assume the same facts as in Problem 2.1 except that the earnings before depreciation, interest, and taxes are $22,000 per year.

a) Calculate the net present value, using straight-line depreciation for tax purposes.

b) Calculate the net present value, using the sum-of-the-years digits method of accelerated depreciation, for tax purposes.

2.3 *Basic replacement problem.* The Virginia Company is considering replacing a riveting machine with a new design that will increase the earnings before depreciation from $20,000 per year to $51,000 per year. The new machine will cost $100,000 and have an estimated life of eight years, with no salvage value. The applicable corporate tax rate is 40%, and the firm's cost of capital is 12%. The old machine has been fully depreciated and has no salvage value. Should it be replaced by the new machine?

2.4 *Replacement problem when old machine has a positive book value.* Assume the same facts as in Problem 2.3 except that the new machine will have a salvage value of $12,000. Assume further that the old machine has a book value of $40,000, with a remaining life of eight years. If replaced, the old machine can, at present, be sold for $15,000. Should the machine replacement be made?

2.5 *Cash flows.* The Cary Company is considering a new investment that costs $10,000. It will last five years and have no salvage value. The project would save $3000 in salaries and wages each year and would be financed with a loan with interest costs of 15% per year and amortization costs (repayment of principal on the loan) of $2000 per year. If the firm's tax rate is 40% and its after-tax cost of capital is 20%, what is the net present value of the project? [Note: The annuity factor for five years at 20% is 2.991.]

2.6 Calculate the internal rate of return for the following set of cash flows.

$$
\begin{array}{ll}
t_1: & 400 \\
t_2: & 400 \\
t_3: & -1000
\end{array}
$$

If the opportunity cost of capital is 10%, should the project be accepted?

2.7 Calculate the internal rate of return on the following set of cash flows:

$$
\begin{array}{ll}
t_0: & -1000 \\
t_1: & 100 \\
t_2: & 900 \\
t_3: & 100 \\
t_4: & -100 \\
t_5: & -400
\end{array}
$$

2.8 The Ambergast Corporation is considering a project that has a three-year life and costs $1200. It would save $360 per year in operating costs and increase revenue by $200 per year. It would be financed with a three-year loan with the following payment schedule (the annual rate of interest is 5%).

Payment	Interest	*Repayment of* *Principal*	Balance
440.65	60.00	380.65	819.35
440.65	40.97	399.68	419.67
440.65	20.98	419.67	0
	121.95	1200.00	

If the company has a 10% after-tax weighted average cost of capital, has a 40% tax rate, and uses straight-line depreciation, what is the net present value of the project?

2.9 The treasurer of United Southern Capital Co. has submitted a proposal to the board of directors that, he argues, will increase profits for the all-equity company by a whopping 55%. It costs $900 and saves $290 in labor costs, providing a 3.1-year payback even though the equipment has an expected 5-year life (with no salvage value). If the firm has a 50% tax rate, uses straight-line depreciation, and has a 10% weighted average after-tax cost of capital, should the project be accepted? Income statements before and after the project are given in Tables Q2.9A and Q2.9B, respectively.

Table Q2.9A

Before	Year 1	Year 2	Year 3	Year 4	Year 5
Revenue	1000	1000	1000	1000	1000
Variable cost	500	500	500	500	500
Depreciation	300	300	300	300	300
Net operating income	200	200	200	200	200
Interest expense	0	0	0	0	0
Earnings before taxes	200	200	200	200	200
Taxes	−100	−100	−100	−100	−100
Net income	100	100	100	100	100

Table Q2.9B

After	Year 1	Year 2	Year 3	Year 4	Year 5
Revenue	1000	1000	1000	1000	1000
Variable cost	210	210	210	210	210
Depreciation	480	480	480	480	480
Net operating income	310	310	310	310	310
Interest expense	0	0	0	0	0
Earnings before taxes	310	310	310	310	310
Taxes	−155	−155	−155	−155	−155
Net income	155	155	155	155	155

2.10 The cash flow for projects A, B, and C are given below. Calculate the payback period and net present value for each project (assume a 10% discount rate). If A and B are mutually exclusive and C is independent, which project, or combination of projects, is preferred using (a) the payback method or (b) the net present value method? What do the results tell you about the value-additivity properties of the payback method?

		Project	
Year	*A*	*B*	*C*
0	−1	−1	−1
1	0	1	0
2	2	0	0
3	−1	1	3

2.11 Calculate the internal rate of return on the following set of cash flows, according to Teichroew's economic interpretation of internal rate of return. Assume that the opportunity cost of capital is 10%.

Year	*Cash Flow*
0	−5,000
1	10,000
2	−3,000

REFERENCES

Alchian, A., and H. Demsetz, "Production, Information Costs, and Economic Organization," *American Economic Review*, 1972, 777–795.

Bierman, H., Jr., and S. Smidt, *The Capital Budgeting Decision*, 4th ed. Macmillan, New York, 1975.

Bodenhorn, D., "A Cash-Flow Concept of Profit," *Journal of Finance*, March 1964, 16–31.

Coase, R. H., "The Nature of the Firm," *Economica*, 1937, 386–405.

Cyert, R. M., and J. G. March, *A Behavioral Theory of the Firm*. Prentice-Hall, Englewood Cliffs, N.J., 1963.

Gagnon, J.-M., "The Purchase-Pooling Choice: Some Empirical Evidence," *Journal of Accounting Research*, Spring 1971, 52–72.

Hirshleifer, J., *Investment, Interest, and Capital*. Prentice-Hall, Englewood Cliffs, N.J., 1970.

Hong, J.; R. S. Kaplan; and G. Mandelker, "Pooling vs. Purchase: The Effects of Accounting Mergers on Stock Prices," *Accounting Review*, January 1978, 31–47.

Jensen, M., and W. Meckling, "Theory of the Firm: Managerial Behavior, Agency Costs and Ownership Structure," *Journal of Financial Economics*, October 1976, 305–360.

Machlup, F., "Theories of the Firm: Marginalist, Behavior, Managerial," *American Economic Review*, March 1967, 1–33.

Marschak, J., and R. Radner, *Economic Theory of Teams* (Cowles Foundation Monograph 22). Yale University Press, New Haven, 1972.

Stern, J., "Earnings per Share Doesn't Count," *Financial Analysts Journal*, July–August 1974, 39–43.

Sunder, S., "Relationship between Accounting Changes and Stock Prices: Problems of Measurement and Some Empirical Evidence," *Empirical Research in Accounting: Selected Studies*, 1973, 1–45.

———, "Stock Price and Risk Related to Accounting Changes in Inventory Valuation," *Accounting Review*, April 1975, 305–315.

Teichroew, D., *An Introduction to Management Science: Deterministic Models*. Wiley, New York, 1964, 78–82.

Williamson, O. E., *The Economics of Discretionary Behavior: Managerial Objectives in a Theory of the Firm*. Prentice-Hall, Englewood Cliffs, N.J., 1964.

3

The basic problem of time valuation which Nature sets us is always that of translating the future into the present, that is, the problem of ascertaining the capital value of future income.
Irving Fisher, *The Theory of Interest*, Macmillan, New York, 1930, 14

More Advanced Capital Budgeting Topics

A. INTRODUCTION

Although Chapter 2 introduced the net present value (NPV) criterion, there were several implied assumptions that require further investigation. For example, all the illustrations in Chapter 2 assumed that mutually exclusive projects had the same life and scale. What happens when these assumptions are relaxed? This question is dealt with in the first part of this chapter.

Next, we will turn the usual capital budgeting problem around and attempt to determine the optimal life for a project with growing cash flows. For example, when should growing trees be harvested or aging whisky be bottled? Finally, let us suppose that the firm is operating under a fixed budget. How will this affect the project selection process?

The above topics are not usually covered in introductory finance texts. One reason is that they require more than an introductory level of mathematical sophistication. For example, the optimal harvest problem requires calculus optimization techniques (see Appendix D), and multiperiod constrained capital budgeting requires linear programming. The reader who is not interested in the mathematics need read only the introduction and conclusion to sections C.2 and D.2 of this chapter.

Section E discusses the problem of capital budgeting in an inflationary environment. Needless to say, there has been growing interest over the last decade in this important applied problem. The reader should be cautioned, however, that solution techniques assume that future rates of inflation are known with certainty. Therefore an important element of realism, namely uncertainty, is lacking. Capital budgeting under uncertainty is covered in Chapter 12.

The last topic covered is the term structure of interest rates. All the discounting procedures up to this point have assumed that the market interest rate is constant in every time period. What if it is expected to change to different levels each period? How does this problem affect capital budgeting analysis? How is the term structure of interest rates determined?

B. CAPITAL BUDGETING TECHNIQUES IN PRACTICE

Chapter 2 argued that the NPV and the internal rate of return (IRR) techniques of capital budgeting were the most sophisticated of the four commonly used criteria. They both consider cash flows (not earnings per share) and discount them in order to take into account the time value of money. Yet the question often arises: Do corporations actually employ these techniques?

A survey of large corporations conducted by Klammer [1972] and reported in the *Journal of Business* has provided an estimate of the actual usage of different capital budgeting techniques. His results are duplicated in Table 3.1.

Table 3.1   Project Evaluation Techniques

Technique	Percentage Using in*		
	1970	1964	1959
Profit contribution analysis required:			
For over 75% of projects	53	53	50
For 25%–75% of projects	41	40	34
For less than 25% of projects	6	7	16
Total	100	100	100
Minimum profitability standards required:			
For most projects	77	65	58
For some projects	13	23	20
For few projects	10	12	22
Total	100	100	100
Most sophisticated primary evaluation standard:			
Discounting (rate of return or present worth)	57	38	19
Accounting rate of return	26	30	34
Payback or payback reciprocal	12	24	34
Urgency	5	8	13
Total	100	100	100

* Percentages shown are yes divided by yes + no, multiplied by 100.

Klammer, T., "Empirical Evidence of the Adoption of Sophisticated Capital Budgeting Techniques," reprinted from *The Journal of Business*, July 1972, 393.

Approximately 180 firms responded in 1970, 150 in 1964, and 145 in 1959. For our purposes the most interesting statistic is the most sophisticated primary evaluation standard. Note the increased usage of discounted cash flow techniques such as the IRR or NPV and the simultaneous decrease in payback. With the advent of computer technology and pocket calculators it is very easy to use the more sophisticated, and more correct, discounted cash flow techniques. A study by Schall, Sundem, and Geijsbeek [1978] sampled 424 large firms (with a 46.4% response rate) and found that 86% use discounted cash flow methods, most of them combined with a payback or ARR analysis.

One of the interesting implications of capital budgeting is that the net present value of a project is equal to the expected increase in shareholders' wealth. This means that the moment a firm publicly reveals that it has undertaken a positive NPV project, the market price of the firm's stock should increase by the project's NPV, even though no cash inflows from the project have yet been received. Empirical confirmation of this idea is provided by McConnell and Muscarella [1985]. They studied the effect of the announcement of capital expenditure plans for a sample of 658 corporations over the interval 1975 through 1981. Capital expenditure announcements were separated into four categories: (1) an announcement of an annual capital budget that is an increase from the previous year's budget, (2) a decrease from the previous year's budget, (3) an announcement of an increase in the current year's previously announced budget and (4) a decrease in the current year's previously announced budget. Theory predicts that if managers accept positive NPV projects, any announcement of an increase in planned capital expenditures should result in an increase in the firm's stock price, whereas any announcement of a decrease will imply fewer positive NPV opportunities and result in a decline in the stock price. Table 3.2 summarizes the McConnell and Muscarella results. The two-day announcement period returns (i.e., the day the news appeared in the *Wall Street Journal* and the following day) were significantly positive for budget increases announced by industrial firms and significantly negative for budget decreases. These results confirm that the market reacts immediately to news about capital expenditure plans, at least for industrial firms.

Table 3.2   Common Stock Returns upon Capital Expenditure Announcements

	Sample Size	Announcement Period Return	Comparison Period Return	t-Statistic
Industrial firms				
All budget increases	273	1.30%	.18%	5.60
All budget decreases	76	−1.75	.18	−5.78
Public utility firms				
All budget increases	39	.14	.11	.07
All budget decreases	17	−.84	.22	−1.79

Adapted from McConnell, J. and C. Muscarella, "Corporate Capital Expenditure Decisions and the Market Value of the Firm," *Journal of Financial Economics*, September 1985, 399–422.

Public utilities, however, are a different story. They are regulated and earn only their weighted average cost of capital. Hence on average they have few positive NPV projects. The empirical evidence indicates no statistically significant market reaction to public utility announcements of capital expenditure changes.

C. PROJECTS WITH DIFFERENT LIVES

All examples used in Chapter 2 compared projects with the same life. Now we turn our attention toward methods of choosing among mutually exclusive projects with different lives. We begin by demonstrating the correct technique. It uses the NPV rule assuming that projects are replicated indefinitely at constant scale. A good example of a replicable project is the harvesting of trees. After the harvest the identical acreage is replanted, and the project is started anew at the same scale. Next we will borrow from Hirshleifer [1970] to show why the NPV criterion (when correctly formulated) is superior to the IRR criterion, given that projects have different lives and are replicable.

1. An NPV Technique for Evaluating Projects with Different Lives

Consider the cash flows estimated for the two projects in Table 3.3. If the opportunity cost of capital is 10%, the (simple) NPVs of the projects are

$$\text{NPV(project } A) = 41\cent, \qquad \text{NPV(project } B) = 50\cent.$$

However, if it makes sense that the projects can be replicated at constant scale, project A should be superior to project B because it recovers cash flow faster. To compare projects with different lives, we compute the NPV of an infinite stream of constant scale replications. Let $\text{NPV}(N, \infty)$ be the NPV of an N-year project with $\text{NPV}(N)$, replicated forever. This is exactly the same as an annuity paid at the beginning of the first period and at the end of every N years from that time on. The NPV of the annuity is

$$\text{NPV}(N, \infty) = \text{NPV}(N) + \frac{\text{NPV}(N)}{(1 + k)^N} + \frac{\text{NPV}(N)}{(1 + k)^{2N}} + \cdots. \qquad (3.1)$$

In order to obtain a closed-form formula, let

$$\frac{1}{(1 + k)^N} = U.$$

Table 3.3   Projects with Different Lives

Year	Project A	Project B
0	−10	−10
1	6	4
2	6	4
3		4.75

Then we have

$$\text{NPV}(N, \infty) = \text{NPV}(N)(1 + U + U^2 + \cdots + U^n). \tag{3.2}$$

Multiplying both sides by U, this becomes

$$U[\text{NPV}(N, \infty)] = \text{NPV}(N)(U + U^2 + \cdots + U^n + U^{n+1}). \tag{3.3}$$

Subtracting Eq. (3.3) from (3.2) gives

$$\text{NPV}(N, \infty) - U\text{NPV}(N, \infty) = \text{NPV}(N)(1 - U^{n+1}),$$

$$\text{NPV}(N, \infty) = \frac{\text{NPV}(N)(1 - U^{n+1})}{1 - U}.$$

And taking the limit as the number of replications, n, approaches infinity gives

$$\lim_{n \to \infty} \text{NPV}(N, \infty) = \frac{\text{NPV}(N)}{1 - U} = \text{NPV}(N)\left[\frac{1}{1 - [1/(1 + k)]^N}\right],$$

$$\text{NPV}(N, \infty) = \text{NPV}(N)\left[\frac{(1 + k)^N}{(1 + k)^N - 1}\right]. \tag{3.4}$$

Equation (3.4) is the NPV of an N-year project replicated at constant scale an infinite number of times. We can use it to compare projects with different lives because when their cash flow streams are replicated forever, it is as if they had the same (infinite) life. Furthermore, the NPV of an infinitely replicated project is the same as the value of shareholders' wealth. It is the present value of the entire stream of projects.

In our example the value of the two-year project, A, replicated at constant scale forever is

$$\text{NPV}(2, \infty) = \text{NPV}(2)\left[\frac{(1 + .10)^2}{(1 + .10)^2 - 1}\right]$$

$$= (\$.41)\left[\frac{1.21}{.21}\right]$$

$$= \$2.36.$$

And for project B, the three-year project, we have

$$\text{NPV}(3, \infty) = \text{NPV}(3)\left[\frac{(1 + .10)^3}{(1.10)^3 - 1}\right]$$

$$= (\$.50)\left[\frac{1.33}{.33}\right]$$

$$= \$2.02.$$

Consequently, we would choose to accept project A over project B because when the cash flows are adjusted for different project lives, A provides the greater wealth. Another way of comparing the projects is to multiply the NPVs of the infinitely replicated projects by the opportunity cost of capital to obtain what is called the *annual equivalent value*, which is given in Eq. (3.5).[1]

$$k\text{NPV}(N, \infty) = \text{NPV}(N)\left[\frac{k(1 + k)^N}{(1 + k)^N - 1}\right]. \tag{3.5}$$

This decision rule is equivalent to that provided by Eq. (3.4) as long as the projects being compared have equal risk. If they have different risk, the annual equivalent should not be used. For example, suppose that we were considering two projects with the same NPV as project A in the previous example but that they have different risk. The computation of $\text{NPV}(N, \infty)$ will tell us that the project with higher risk contributes less to the value of the firm because it will have a lower $\text{NPV}(N, \infty)$. Yet when the lower $\text{NPV}(N, \infty)$ of the higher risk project is multiplied by a higher risk-adjusted opportunity cost, k, it is possible to reach the opposite conclusion. For an example, work Problem 3.3.

2. The Duration Problem

We have just seen that when projects have different lives, the simple NPV rule, when misused, can lead to incorrect decisions. Correct use of the simple NPV rule depends on whether or not one can reasonably assume a project is replicable. If it is unique and cannot be repeated, then the simple NPV computes the increment to shareholders' wealth from a single undertaking. If it is replicable (and many projects are), then $\text{NPV}(N, \infty)$ gives the change in the value of the firm from a strategy of replicating at constant scale every N years. But why is constant scale replication the correct decision criterion for replicable projects? Why does it maximize the NPV of the shareholders' wealth when a simple comparison of NPVs or use of the IRR rule does not?

An interesting type of problem that highlights the differences between simple NPV, NPV with infinite replication at constant scale, and IRR is the determination of the optimal life, or duration, of a project. For example, when should growing trees be harvested, or when should aging whisky be bottled?

A. USING THE SIMPLE NPV RULE TO SOLVE THE DURATION PROBLEM.   Assume that we own a growing stand of trees. Let the revenue, Rev_t, that can be obtained from harvesting them at time t be represented by the expression

$$\text{Rev}_t = 10,000\sqrt{1 + t}.$$

Also, let the initial cost, c, be \$15,000 and let the opportunity cost of capital be 5%

---

[1] Note that Eq. (3.5) is equivalent to
$$k\text{NPV}(N, \infty) = \frac{\text{NPV}(N)}{\text{Annuity factor}}$$
where the annuity factor = $[1 - (1 + k)^{-N}]/k$.

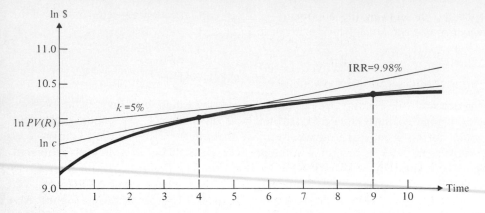

Figure 3.1
Tree-harvesting problem.

compounded continuously.[2] Figure 3.1 is a graph of the revenues as a function of time. Note that the vertical axis is a logarithmic scale, so that geometrically increasing functions—e.g., continuously compounded interest—appear as straight lines.

First, we shall determine the harvesting time that maximizes the simple NPV of the project. For a project with a life of t years,

$$\text{NPV} = \text{Rev}_t e^{-kt} - c.$$

To find the harvesting time, t, that maximizes the NPV, we take the first derivative of NPV with respect to t and set it equal to zero:

$$\frac{d\text{NPV}}{dt} = -k\text{Rev}_t e^{-kt} + \frac{d\text{Rev}_t}{dt} e^{-kt} = 0.$$

Solving for k, we have

$$k = \frac{d\text{Rev}_t/dt}{\text{Rev}_t},$$

which says that the NPV is maximized when the marginal rate of return, $(d\text{Rev}_t/dt)/\text{Rev}_t$, is equal to the opportunity cost of capital, k. Graphically, this is the point of tangency between the straight line whose slope is 5% and the revenue function. As shown in Fig. 3.1, tangency occurs at $t = 9$ years. The same result can be shown mathematically by using the revenue function to solve for marginal revenue per unit time and setting the result equal to $k = 5\%$. The revenue function is

$$\text{Rev}_t = 10{,}000(1 + t)^{1/2}.$$

Its derivative with respect to t is the marginal revenue

$$\frac{d\text{Rev}_t}{dt} = \frac{1}{2}(10{,}000)(1 + t)^{-1/2},$$

---

[2] Appendix A contains a complete reference to the mathematics of continuous compounding.

and the marginal rate of return is

$$\frac{d\text{Rev}_t/dt}{\text{Rev}_t} = \frac{5{,}000(1+t)^{-1/2}}{10{,}000(1+t)^{1/2}} = \frac{1}{2(1+t)}.$$

Setting this equal to the opportunity cost of capital, k, we get

$$\frac{1}{2(1+t)} = .05, \qquad t = 9 \text{ years.}$$

B. USING THE IRR RULE TO SOLVE THE DURATION PROBLEM. Next, we would like to compare the simple NPV result with the harvest time that maximizes the IRR of the project. The IRR is the rate that sets the NPV of the project equal to zero. Mathematically, this is

$$\text{NPV} = 0 = \text{Rev}_t e^{-(\text{IRR})t} - c.$$

Adding c to both sides and taking the natural logarithm, we have

$$\ln \text{Rev}_t - (\text{IRR})t = \ln c,$$

and solving for IRR, we have

$$\text{IRR} = \frac{1}{t} \ln \frac{\text{Rev}_t}{c}.$$

Substituting in the revenue function, we obtain

$$\text{IRR} = \frac{1}{t} \ln \left[\frac{10{,}000(1+t)^{1/2}}{15{,}000} \right].$$

If we try different values of t, the project life that maximizes the IRR at a value of 9.98% is four years.

We can find this result graphically in Fig. 3.1 by rotating a line that passes through an intercept of $\ln c$ (at $t = 0$, if the natural logarithm of the present value of revenue is equal to $\ln c$, then the NPV of the project is zero) until it is just tangent to the revenue curve. The point of tangency gives the optimal harvest time, four years, and the slope of the line is the maximum IRR, 9.98%.

It is frequently argued that the IRR rule gives the best solution to the simple duration problem. However, this is incorrect because the IRR rule implicitly assumes that the funds provided by the project can continuously be reinvested in projects with *proportional expansion of scale*. In other words, we started out in our example with an investment of $15,000. After four years, we would reinvest

$$\$15{,}000e^{\text{IRR}(t)} = \$22{,}359,$$

and so on, in ever increasing amounts. So long as the IRR is greater than the opportunity cost of capital (5% in our example), the present value of an infinite replication of a proportionately growing stream of projects is infinite. This is patently absurd.

C. USING THE NPV RULE WITH CONSTANT SCALE REPLICATION.   The correct formulation of the optimal duration problem is to assume that the project can be replicated indefinitely at *constant scale*. In the tree-harvesting problem this is equivalent to assuming that once the trees are harvested, the same acreage is replanted so that the project begins again at constant scale.

If the project is reformulated with constant scale replication, the NPV of an infinite stream of projects would be

$$\text{NPV} = -c + (\text{Rev}_t - c)e^{-kt} + (\text{Rev}_t - c)e^{-2kt} + \cdots .$$

The second term is the present value of the revenue received at the time of harvest less the cash outlay for replanting at constant scale. The third term is the present value of the cash flows at the time of the second harvest, and so on. The NPV of this stream is

$$\text{NPV} = -c + \frac{\text{Rev}_t - c}{e^{kt} - 1}.$$

To maximize, we set the derivative of the NPV with respect to project life, t, equal to zero.[3]

$$\frac{d\text{NPV}}{dt} = \frac{d\text{Rev}_t}{dt} - \frac{(\text{Rev}_t - c)k}{1 - e^{-kt}} = 0, \qquad \frac{d\text{Rev}_t}{dt} = \frac{(\text{Rev}_t - c)k}{1 - e^{-kt}}.$$

Using the numbers from our example, we get

$$\frac{5,000}{(1 + t)^{1/2}} = \frac{(10,000(1 + t)^{1/2} - 15,000).05}{1 - e^{-.05t}}.$$

Table 3.4 shows the values at the left- and right-hand sides of the solution for various values of t. The optimal duration is approximately 4.6 years. This answer lies between the solution for simple duration with the NPV rule (9 years) and replication with proportionately increasing scale using the IRR rule (4 years).

D. A COMPARISON OF THE THREE TECHNIQUES FOR SOLVING THE DURATION PROBLEM.   Table 3.5 compares the three project evaluation techniques (simple NPV, IRR, and NPV with constant scale replication) for projects of different lives. Given

---

[3]
$$\frac{d\text{NPV}}{dt} = \frac{d}{dt}[-c + (\text{Rev}_t - c)(e^{kt} - 1)^{-1}] = 0$$

$$= \frac{d\text{Rev}_t}{dt}(e^{kt} - 1)^{-1} + [(\text{Rev}_t - c)](-1)(e^{kt} - 1)^{-2}ke^{kt} = 0$$

$$= \frac{d\text{Rev}_t}{dt}(e^{kt} - 1) - (\text{Rev}_t - c)ke^{kt} = 0$$

$$\frac{d\text{Rev}_t}{dt} = \frac{k(\text{Rev}_t - c)}{1 - e^{-kt}}.$$

Table 3.4   Solution to the Duration Problem with Constant Scale Replication

t	Left-hand Side	Right-hand Side	Difference
4	2236.07	2033.31	202.76
4.5	2132.20	2097.76	34.44
4.6	2112.89	2108.81	4.08
5	2041.24	2146.38	− 105.14

Table 3.5   Comparison of Three Techniques

		A	B	C
Initial outlay		− 15,000	− 15,000	− 15,000
	4.0 years	22,361	0	0
Cash inflow at t years	4.6 years	0	23,664	0
	9.0 years	0	0	31,623
IRR		9.98%	9.91%	8.29%
Simple NPV		3,308	3,802	5,164
NPV with constant scale replication		18,246	18,505	14,249

the data from the tree-harvesting problem, recall that all three projects have the same scale because each requires an outlay of $15,000. However, their lives vary between 4 and 9 years. An important question is: How much would you pay to purchase the forestry operation, assuming that you harvest after t years, then replant, thereby replicating the project at constant scale every t years forever, and that the time value of money to you is 5%? The answer is $18,505. It is the current value of the forestry operation because it represents the present value of the cash stream provided by the operation into the indefinite future. It is the present value of a strategy of harvesting every 4.6 years.

The above example demonstrates that the correct procedure for comparing projects with different lives is the same as the correct solution to the optimal duration problem. Both require that NPV maximization be formulated as the maximization of the NPV of a stream of projects replicated at constant scale.

D. CONSTRAINED CAPITAL BUDGETING PROBLEMS

A capital budgeting constraint implies that the firm can obtain only N dollars of funding at a fixed cost of capital. Implicitly, the cost of capital in excess of N dollars is infinite. Therefore the firm is limited to a fixed budget. Most economists would agree that strict capital constraints simply do not exist in the real world. For example, consider a small firm with a "budget" of only a few thousand dollars of capital that suddenly acquires a new patent for economically converting garbage into gasoline.

Certainly the firm would not find it very difficult to raise large amounts of money even though its initial budget was quite limited. As long as capital markets are reasonably efficient, it will always be possible for a firm to raise an indefinite amount of money so long as the projects are expected to have a positive net present value.

Weingartner [1977] discusses capital rationing in terms of situations imposed from within the firm and those imposed by the capital market. Self-imposed expenditure limits may arise to preserve corporate control or reflect the view of owners of closely held firms that the sale of the firm as a whole at a future date will provide a greater present value of wealth than the piecemeal sale that may permit faster growth. Externally imposed capital rationing could result from an attitude of the capital markets that providing funds beyond a specific amount would lead to increased risks of high bankruptcy costs—so high that feasible interest rates would not be adequate compensation. An aspect of this is the "Penrose effect," which holds that the organizational problems of obtaining and training additional personnel are large. Hence growth that involves increasing the organization's size by more than some percentage, e.g., 50%, in one year is fraught with high risks of organizational inefficiencies, which increase risks of bankruptcy and give rise to high costs owing to the loss of efficiency of a previously effectively functioning organization system or firm.

Although it is hard to justify the assumption of limited capital, nevertheless we shall review various decision-making techniques, assuming that capital constraints do in fact exist.

1. Projects with Different Scale. The Present Value Index

Suppose we are comparing two mutually exclusive projects that have the same life. Furthermore they are the only projects available. Project A costs \$1,000,000 and has a net present value of \$1,000, whereas project B costs \$10 and has a net present value of \$500. It is very tempting to argue that project B is better because it returns more net present value per dollar of cost. However, the NPV rule is very clear. If these are mutually exclusive projects, the correct decision is to take the one that has the highest NPV, project A.

But let us assume that there is a meaningful capital constraint imposed on our firm. How should the NPV rule be modified to consider projects of different scale? Table 3.6 shows the present value of the cash inflows and outflows of four independent projects that have identical lives. If there were no capital constraints we would accept all four projects because they all have positive NPVs. Project 1 has the highest

Table 3.6   Present Value Index

Project	PV of Inflows	Current Outflows	PVI	NPV
1	230,000	200,000	1.15	30,000
2	141,250	125,000	1.13	16,250
3	194,250	175,000	1.11	19,250
4	162,000	150,000	1.08	12,000

NPV, followed by project 3, then 2, and finally 4. Suppose that there is a capital constraint that limits our spending to $300,000 or less. Now we would accept only projects 2 and 3 because they have the greatest NPV among those combinations of projects that use no more than $300,000. The logic leading to this decision is formalized by what is known as the *present value index* (PVI).

The PVI is defined as the present value of cash inflows divided by the present value of cash outflows:

$$PVI = \frac{\text{Present value of inflows}}{\text{Present value of outflows}}. \tag{3.6}$$

When used correctly, it is equivalent to maximizing the NPV of a set of projects subject to the constraint that project outlays be less than or equal to the firm's budget. The PVI for each project is given in Table 3.6. The PVI of excess funds, not invested in any of the projects, is always assumed to be equal to 1.0. (Why?)

The objective is to compare all sets of projects that meet the budget and find the one that maximizes the weighted average PVI. For example, if projects 2 and 3 are selected, the weighted average PVI is

$$PVI = \frac{125,000}{300,000} (1.13) + \frac{175,000}{300,000} (1.11) = 1.1183.$$

It is computed by multiplying the PVI of each project by the percentage of the total budget allocated to it. If project 1 is selected, no additional project can be undertaken; therefore the PVI for project 1 is

$$PVI = \frac{200,000}{300,000} (1.15) + \frac{100,000}{300,000} (1.00) = 1.1000.$$

Project 1 is not preferred to projects 2 and 3 because $100,000 must be invested in marketable securities that have a PVI of 1.0 (i.e., their cost is always equal to the present value of their cash inflows).

The PVI can be used to solve simple problems where there is a one-period capital constraint. It can also be used to compare mutually exclusive projects of different scale, although a simple comparison of NPVs provides the same result. For example, refer to projects A and B (at the beginning of this section). The first project cost $1,000,000 and had an NPV of $1,000, whereas the second cost only $10 and had an NPV of $500. If these are the only two projects available to the firm and if they are mutually exclusive, we can evaluate them by comparing their PVIs with the assumption that the firm has a $1,000,000 budget.[4]

The PVI of project A is

$$\frac{1,000,000}{1,000,000} \left(\frac{1,001,000}{1,000,000} \right) = 1.001,$$

---

[4] We could also assume any budget whatsoever as long as it is greater than $1,000,000 without changing the results. (Why?)

Table 3.7   Two-Period Capital Constraint

Project	Period-1 Outlay	Period-2 Outlay	NPV
1	12	3	14
2	54	7	17
3	6	6	17
4	6	2	15
5	30	35	40
6	6	6	12
7	48	4	14
8	36	3	10
9	18	3	12

and the PVI of project B is

$$\frac{10}{1,000,000}\left(\frac{510}{10}\right) + \frac{999,990}{1,000,000}(1.00) = 1.0005.$$

Because project A has a higher PVI, it is superior. The PVI solution is exactly the same as the NPV solution; i.e., we take the project with the highest NPV. The PVI merely helps to highlight the assumption that if the projects really are mutually exclusive, then the extra $999,990 that is not invested in project B must be invested in marketable securities with a PVI of 1.0.

Usually, the projects to be compared are not so exaggerated as the above example; however, it does help to illustrate the meaning of a capital constraint. If a strict budget exists, then the PVI should be used. Otherwise, the firm should accept all projects with a positive NPV.

2. Multiperiod Capital Constraints. Programming Solutions

The capital constraint problem can be extended to consider budget constraints $(C_0, C_1, \ldots C_t)$ in many future time periods. If we assume that it is possible to undertake fractions of projects, then the problem may be formulated using linear programming. If projects are indivisible, integer programming may be used. With binding capital constraints it is conceivable that a project with negative NPV may be accepted in the optimal solution if it supplies the funds needed during the later time period to undertake very profitable projects.

A great deal has been written on the topic of constrained capital budgeting.[5] However, because of space limitations, only the simplest model is presented here. Lorie and Savage [1955] posed the two-period problem given in Table 3.7.

Let us assume that cash flows cannot be transferred between time periods, that projects are infinitely divisible, and that the cash budget in period 1 is $50, whereas

---

[5] The interested reader is referred to Lorie and Savage [1955], Weingartner [1963], Baumol and Quandt [1965], Carleton [1969], Bernhard [1969], and Myers [1972] as an excellent set of references.

in period 2 it is \$20. The problem is to find the set of projects that maximizes NPV and satisfies the cash constraints. Weingartner [1963] solved the problem by using linear programming. If we designate b_j as the NPV of each project, X_j as the fraction of each project that is accepted, c_{tj} as the cash outlay used by the jth project in the tth time period, and C_t as the cash budget, the linear programming problem is written as

$$\text{MAX} \sum_j b_j X_j, \quad (Primal\ problem) \tag{3.7}$$

$$\text{subject to } \sum_j c_{tj} X_j \le C_t,$$

$$X_j \le 1.$$

If S_t and q_j are designated as slack variables, the primal problem can be rewritten as

$$\text{MAX} \sum_j b_j X_j, \tag{3.8}$$

$$\text{subject to } \sum_j c_{tj} X_j + S_t = C_t,$$

$$X_j + q_j = 1.$$

The objective is to choose the set of weights, X_j, that maximizes the combined NPV of all projects. The constraints require (1) that the set of projects undertaken use less cash than is budgeted and (2) that no more than 100% of any project be undertaken.

Every linear programming problem has a counterpart called the *dual problem* where the primal constraints appear in the dual objective function and the primal decision variables become dual constraints. The dual for this problem can be written as

$$\text{MIN} \sum_t \rho_t C_t + \mu_j \cdot 1, \quad (Dual\ problem) \tag{3.9}$$

$$\text{subject to } \sum_t \rho_t c_{tj} + \mu_j - \gamma_j - b_j,$$

$$\rho_t, \mu_j \ge 0.$$

The dual introduces three new variables, ρ_t, μ_j, and γ_j. The last, γ_j, is a slack variable. We can define μ_j by using the notion of complementary slackness. When one of the projects enters into the primal solution (i.e., $X_j > 0$), then the corresponding constraint in the dual is binding and therefore $\gamma_j = 0$. Thus the dual constraint can be written as an equality:

$$\sum_t \rho_t c_{tj} + \mu_j = b_j,$$

or, solving for μ_j, we have

$$\mu_j = b_j - \sum_t \rho_t c_{tj}. \tag{3.10}$$

Therefore μ_j may be thought of as the difference between the NPV of a project's cash flows, b_j, and the imputed value of the outlays needed to undertake the project, $\sum_t \rho_t c_{tj}$. Conceptually, it is similar to the PVI in the single-period problem because it is a measure of the benefit (NPV) minus the imputed cash cost of a project. Finally, ρ_t may be thought of as the implicit one-period discount rate caused by the cash constraints in the linear programming problem. It is the value of relaxing the cash constraint by \$1, the shadow price. This can be demonstrated by using (3.10) and noting that for fractionally accepted projects, where the constraint is binding, $\mu_j = 0$. Therefore (3.10) becomes

$$\sum_t \rho_t c_{tj} = b_j.$$

This says that the NPV of a project, b_j, equals the discounted value of its cash flows. Consequently, ρ_t is the one-period discount rate:

$$\rho_t = \frac{1}{1 + {}_t r_{t+1}}. \tag{3.11}$$

Table 3.8 shows the linear programming problem and solution to the Lorie-Savage problem. Projects 1, 3, 4, and 9 are accepted, and projects 6 and 7 are fractionally accepted into the optimal solution, which has an NPV of \$70.27. Cash constraints

Table 3.8   Linear Programming Model and Solution

Maximize:

$$14x_1 + 17x_2 + 17x_3 + 15x_4 + 40x_5 + 12x_6 + 14x_7 + 10x_8 + 12x_9$$

Subject to:

$$12x_1 + 54x_2 + 6x_3 + 6x_4 + 30x_5 + 6x_6 + 48x_7 + 36x_8 + 18x_9 + S_1 = 50$$
$$3x_1 + 7x_2 + 6x_3 + 2x_4 + 35x_5 + 6x_6 + 4x_7 + 3x_8 + 3x_9 + S_2 = 20$$

$x_1 + q_1 = 1$	$x_4 + q_4 = 1$	$x_7 + q_7 = 1$
$x_2 + q_2 = 1$	$x_5 + q_5 = 1$	$x_8 + q_8 = 1$
$x_3 + q_3 = 1$	$x_6 + q_6 = 1$	$x_9 + q_9 = 1$

Solution	Primal slack	Dual variable	Dual slacks
$x_1^* = 1.0$	$q_1^* = 0$	$\mu_1^* = 6.77$	$\gamma_1^* = 0$
$x_2^* = 0$	$q_2^* = 1.0$	$\mu_2^* = 0$	$\gamma_2^* = 3.41$
$x_3^* = 1.0$	$q_3^* = 0$	$\mu_3^* = 5.0$	$\gamma_3^* = 0$
$x_4^* = 1.0$	$q_4^* = 0$	$\mu_4^* = 10.45$	$\gamma_4^* = 0$
$x_5^* = 0$	$q_5^* = 1.0$	$\mu_5^* = 0$	$\gamma_5^* = 29.32$
$x_6^* = 0.970$	$q_6^* = 0.030$	$\mu_6^* = 0$	$\gamma_6^* = 0$
$x_7^* = 0.045$	$q_7^* = 0.955$	$\mu_7^* = 0$	$\gamma_7^* = 0$
$x_8^* = 0$	$q_8^* = 1.0$	$\mu_8^* = 0$	$\gamma_8^* = 0.5$
$x_9^* = 1.0$	$q_9^* = 0$	$\mu_9^* = 3.95$	$\gamma_9^* = 0$
$S_1^* = 0$	—primal slacks—		$S_2^* = 0$
$\rho_1^* = 0.136$	—dual variables—		$\rho_2^* = 1.864$

Total present value: \$70.27

Weingartner, H. M., reprinted from *Mathematical Programming and the Analysis of Capital Budgeting Problems*, Prentice-Hall, Englewood Cliffs, N.J., 1963 (reissued by Kershaw Publishing Co., London, 1974).

in both time periods are binding since the primal slacks, S_1 and S_2, are zero. The project with the greatest net "benefit" is project 4 with $\mu_4 = 10.45$. Although it has a smaller NPV than several of the other projects, it also uses less cash than the others. Finally, a comparison of the dual variables, ρ_1 and ρ_2, tells us that the value of relaxing the second-period constraint is greater. In other words, providing extra cash in the second period would increase the firm's NPV more than providing extra cash in the first time period. We can also use the values of ρ_t to calculate the one-period implicit interest rates:

$$_1r_2 = \frac{1 - \rho_1}{\rho_1} = 635\%,$$

$$_2r_3 = \frac{1 - \rho_2}{\rho_2} = -46.4\%.$$

Linear programming solutions to capital budgeting have great versatility and have been applied to many types of problems. However, it is difficult to justify the existence of capital constraints in the first place. Also, once uncertainty is introduced as a major consideration, linear programming models fail to handle it adequately. For these and other reasons, linear programming models have become less popular in recent years.

E. CAPITAL BUDGETING PROCEDURES UNDER INFLATION[6]

The United States has experienced persistent inflation since 1966 at levels exceeding the moderate price level changes of previous peacetime periods. What effects does this have on the results of capital budgeting analysis? We can analyze the impacts of inflation by using an illustrative example to clarify the new influences introduced.

Let us begin with the standard capital budgeting case in which inflation is absent. The expression for calculating the NPV of the investment is shown in Eq. (3.12):

$$\text{NPV} = \sum_{t=1}^{N} \frac{\text{NCF}_t}{(1 + k)^t} - I_0. \tag{3.12}$$

The symbols used have the following meanings and values:

NPV = net present value of the project,

NCF_t = net cash flows per year from the project = \$26,500,

k = cost of capital applicable to the project = 9%,

N = number of years the net cash flows are received = 5,

I_0 = required investment outlay for the project = \$100,000,

τ_c = applicable tax rate of 50%.

---

[6] For articles on this subject see Van Horne [1971] and Cooley, Roenfeldt, and Chew [1975]; also see their exchange with Findlay and Frankle [1976].

With the data provided, we can utilize (3.12) as follows:

$$NPV_0 = \sum_{t=1}^{N} \frac{\$26,500}{(1.09)^t} - \$100,000$$

$$= 26,500(3.8896) - 100,000$$

$$= 103,074 - 100,000$$

$$= \$3,074.$$

We find that the project has an expected NPV of \$3,074, and under the simple conditions assumed, we would accept the project. Now let us consider the effects of inflation. Suppose that inflation at an annual rate of 6% will take place during the five years of the project. Note that we assume that the future inflation rate is known with certainty, and that the rate of inflation is constant.

Since investment and security returns are based on expected future returns, the anticipated inflation rate will be reflected in the required rate of return on the project or the applicable cost of capital for the project. This relationship has long been recognized in financial economics and is known as the *Fisher effect*. In formal terms, we have

$$(1 + r)(1 + \eta) = (1 + k), \tag{3.13}$$

where k is the required rate of return in nominal terms, η is the anticipated annual inflation rate over the life of the project, and r is the real rate of return. For our example, Eq. (3.13) would be

$$(1 + .09)(1 + .06) = (1 + .09 + .06 + .0054).$$

When the cross-product term, .0054, is included, we have .1554 as the required rate of return in nominal terms.

It is at this point that some biases in capital budgeting under inflationary conditions may be introduced. The market data utilized in the estimated current capital costs will include a premium for anticipated inflation. But while the market remembers to include an adjustment for inflation in the discount factor, the cash flow estimates used by the firm in the capital budgeting analysis may fail to include an element to reflect future inflation. Given that the cost of capital (observed using market rates of return) already includes expected inflation, the decision maker can correct for inflation either (a) by adding an estimate of inflation to the cash flows in the numerator or (b) by expressing the numerator without including an adjustment for inflation and removing an inflationary factor from the market rate in the denominator.

It is more natural to utilize market data and to explicitly incorporate estimates of the anticipated inflation rate in the cash flows in the numerator. But either way, the difficult problem is how to estimate the expected future inflation rate. Some ideas on how to do this will be discussed in the next section of this chapter.

Sound analysis requires that the anticipated inflation rate be taken into account in the cash flow estimates. Initially, let us assume that an inflation rate of 6% is applicable to the net cash flows as well as to the discount rate. We take this step in setting forth the expression for the project NPV_1 as follows:

$$NPV_1 = \sum_{t=1}^{N} \frac{\$26,500(1.06)^t}{(1.09)^t(1.06)^t} - 100,000 = \sum_{t=1}^{N} \frac{\$26,500}{(1.09)^t} - \$100,000.$$

Since inflation factors are now in both the numerator and the denominator and are the same, they can be canceled. The result for the calculation of NPV_1 will therefore be the same as for NPV_0, which was a positive $3,074. Thus when anticipated inflation is properly reflected in both the cash flow estimates in the numerator and the required rate of return from market data in the denominator, the resulting NPV calculation will be in both real and nominal terms. This was noted by Findlay and Frankle [1976] as follows: "Any properly measured, market-determined wealth concept is, simultaneously, *both nominal and real.* NPV, or any other wealth measure, gives the amount for which one can 'cash out' now (nominal) and also the amount of today's goods that can be consumed at today's prices (real)" (p. 84). Thus if inflation is reflected in both the cash flow estimates and in the required rate of return, the resulting NPV estimate will be free of inflation bias.

To this point we have purposely kept the analysis simple to focus on the basic principles, since controversy has erupted over the issues involved. We may expect that the effect of the anticipated inflation on the required rate of return will differ from that on the cash flow estimates. Indeed, the components of the net cash flows— the cash outflows and the cash inflows—may themselves be influenced to different degrees by the anticipated inflation. These complications will not, however, change the basic method of analysis, only the specifics of the calculations. The nature of the more complex case is illustrated by Eq. (3.14):

$$NPV_0 = \sum_{t=1}^{N} \frac{[(\text{inflows})_t(1 + \eta_i)^t - (\text{outflows})_t(1 + \eta_0)^t](1 - \tau_c) + (\text{dep})_t(\tau_c)}{(1 + k)^t} - I_0.$$

(3.14)

The cash inflows may be subject to a rate of inflation η_i that is different from the rate of inflation in the cash outflows η_0. Both may differ from the anticipated rate of inflation reflected in the required rate of return in the denominator. Also, depreciation (dep) may be constant in nominal dollars, but the value of the depreciation tax shield will fall in real terms. Some illustrative data will demonstrate the application of (3.14).

Table 3.9 sets forth data for expected cash flows without inflation effects. The pattern is a constant $26,500 per year for five years, as in the original example. In Table 3.10 the estimates of expected net cash flows include inflation effects. The cash inflows are subject to a 6% inflation rate, whereas the cash outflows are subject to a 7% inflation rate. The resulting expected net cash flows are shown in the bottom line of the table. The required rate of return of 15.54% is assumed to reflect a 6% inflation rate, as before.

The calculation of the expected NPV ($\overline{NPV}_2$) is shown in Table 3.11. Taking all the inflation influences into account, we find that $\overline{NPV}_2$ is a negative $3,773. The project should be rejected. In this example, the inflationary forces on the cash outflows

Table 3.9 Expected Net Cash Flows without Inflation Effects

	Year 1	Year 2	Year 3	Year 4	Year 5
Expected cash inflows	$53,000	$53,000	$53,000	$53,000	$53,000
Expected cash outflows	20,000	20,000	20,000	20,000	20,000
Earnings before taxes	$33,000	$33,000	$33,000	$33,000	$33,000
Multiplied by τ_c	16,500	16,500	16,500	16,500	16,500
Earnings after taxes	$16,500	$16,500	$16,500	$16,500	$16,500
Depreciation tax shelter	10,000	10,000	10,000	10,000	10,000
Expected net cash flows	$26,500	$26,500	$26,500	$26,500	$26,500

Table 3.10 Expected Net Cash Flows Including Inflation Effects

	1	2	3	4	5
Expected cash inflows ($\eta_i = 6\%$)	$56,180	$59,551	$63,124	$66,912	$70,927
Expected cash outflows ($\eta_0 = 7\%$)	21,400	22,898	24,501	26,216	28,051
Earnings before taxes	$34,780	$36,653	$38,623	$40,696	$42,876
Multiplied by τ_c	17,390	18,327	19,312	20,348	21,438
Earnings after taxes	$17,390	$18,327	$19,312	$20,348	$21,438
Depreciation tax shelter	10,000	10,000	10,000	10,000	10,000
Expected net cash flows	$27,390	$28,327	$29,312	$30,348	$31,438

Table 3.11 Calculation of NPV$_2$

Year	Cash Flow (1)	Discount Factor 15.54% (2)	PV (1 × 2)
1	$27,390	.8655	$23,706
2	28,327	.7491	21,220
3	29,312	.6483	19,004
4	30,348	.5611	17,029
5	31,438	.4857	15,268

$$\text{NPV}_2 = \$96,227 - \$100,000 = -\$3,773$$

were greater than on the cash inflows. Some have suggested that this influence has been sufficiently widespread and that it accounts for the sluggish rate of capital investment in the United States during the late 1970's and early 1980's.

The situation we illustrated initially was that failure to take inflation into account in the expected cash flows resulted in an erroneous capital budgeting analysis. A project was accepted which, when measured correctly, produced a return below the required rate of return. The allocation of capital would be unsound if the bias in the analysis due to inflation had not been taken into account. In our second and more complex example, inflation caused the cash outflows to grow at a higher rate than the cash inflows. As a consequence, the expected NPV of the project was negative. Making the inflation adjustment does not always necessarily result in a negative NPV for the project, it simply results in a more accurate estimate of the net benefits from the project—positive or negative.

F. THE TERM STRUCTURE OF INTEREST RATES

Throughout Chapters 2 and 3 there has been the implicit assumption that interest rates are nonstochastic and constant in a multiperiod setting. This has been a convenient but misleading assumption. Interest rates are not constant through time. The yield on a particular financial instrument (a bond, for example) is a function of the length of time to maturity. The yield also depends on the risk of the security, but we shall continue to assume, for the time being, that there is no risk.

Figure 3.2 shows the term structure of interest rates for United States Treasury securities at three points in time, March 1976, August 1981, and May 1987. Each point on the graph gives the yield to maturity, $_0R_T$, on a bond that is bought today (at time zero) and that matures T years hence. The bond is assumed to be default free. *Default free* means that there is no uncertainty about the nominal payments promised by the bond. There are, however, other kinds of risk. For example, unexpected changes in future interest rates will induce risk because the market value of the bond will change when interest rate expectations do.

1. The Yield to Maturity

The yield to maturity, $_0R_T$, is computed in exactly the same way one would solve for the internal rate of return on a security. Consider the following hypothetical

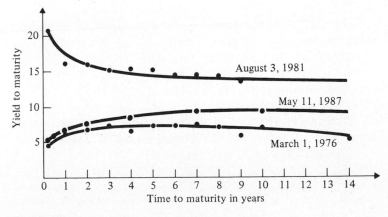

Figure 3.2
The yield to maturity on U.S. Treasury securities.

example: A bond promises to pay a 15% coupon at the end of each year for three years, then pay a face value of $1000. We observe the current market price, B_0, of the bond to be $977.54. The yield to maturity on the bond may be computed by solving for $_0R_T$ in the following present value formula:

$$B_0 = \sum_{t=1}^{T} \frac{\text{Coupon}_t}{(1 + {_0R_T})^t} + \frac{\text{Face value}}{(1 + {_0R_T})^T}, \tag{3.15}$$

$$977.54 = \sum_{t=1}^{T} \frac{150}{(1 + {_0R_T})^t} + \frac{1000}{(1 + {_0R_T})^T}.$$

Solving iteratively, we find that the yield to maturity, $_0R_T$, is 16%.

The term structure shows the yield to maturity for all bonds of all maturities. In March 1976 and May of 1987 the term structure was upward sloping. Long-term bonds paid higher yields than short-term bonds. In August 1981 the opposite pattern existed. The term structure was downward sloping. One thing that both term structure patterns have in common is that the interest rate is not constant. The yield on securities clearly depends on when they mature.

2. Forward Rates, Future Rates, and Unbiased Expectations

The term *structure* is said to be unbiased if the expected *future interest rates* are equivalent to the *forward rates* computed from observed bond prices. This is called the *unbiased expectations hypothesis*, which was first postulated by Irving Fisher [1896], then further developed by Friedrich Lutz [1940]. An example will help to clarify the meaning of forward rates and expected future rates.[7] Suppose we have three zero coupon bonds. They pay a face value of $1000 upon maturity; mature one, two, and three years hence; and are observed to have current market prices of $826.45, $718.18, and $640.66, respectively. The observed yield to maturity, $_0R_T$, is assumed to be the product of the one-period forward rates, $_tf_{t+1}$, as shown in Eq. (3.16):

$$[(1 + {_0R_T})]^T = (1 + {_0R_1})(1 + {_1f_2}) \cdots (1 + {_{T-1}f_T}). \tag{3.16}$$

The forward rate, $_1f_2$, is the one-period rate computed for a bond bought at the end of the first period and held to the end of the second period. Hence it is a one-period rate for the second period. Note that the forward rate for the first year can be observed directly. It is $_0R_1$.

To compute the implied forward rates, one would first compute the yields to maturity using Eq. (3.15).[8] For the three bonds in our example, the yields to maturity are 21%, 18%, and 16%, respectively. The term structure for this example is shown in Fig. 3.3. Suppose we want to know the forward rate implied for the third time period.

---

[7] To keep things simple, we assume that forward rates are one-period rates and that all prices and yields are observed at the present time. One could also discuss N-period forward rates observed at any time, t. For an excellent discussion of the term structure, the reader is referred to *Financial Rates and Flows* by James C. Van Horne [1978].

[8] Note that like the internal rate of return the yield to maturity implicitly assumes that funds are reinvested at the implied yield. This contrasts with the assumption of discounting at the market-determined rate to get a net present value.

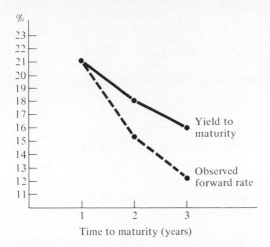

Figure 3.3
A simple term structure example.

It can be computed by taking the ratio of the (geometric product of the) yields to maturity on the three- and two-period bonds:

$$1 + {}_2f_3 = \frac{(1 + {}_0R_3)^3}{(1 + {}_0R_2)^2},$$

$$1 + {}_2f_3 - \frac{(1 + {}_0R_1)(1 + {}_1f_2)(1 + {}_2f_3)}{(1 + {}_0R_1)(1 + {}_1f_2)},$$

$$1 + {}_2f_3 = \frac{(1.16)^3}{(1.18)^2} = \frac{1.560895}{1.3924} = 1.121,$$

$${}_2f_3 = 12.10\%.$$

Similarly, one can compute the second-period forward rate as 15.07%, and of course the one-period rate is observed directly to be 21%. The pattern of forward rates in this example would be consistent with expectations that future inflation will be less than current inflation.

By itself, the forward rate is merely an algebraic computation from observed bond data. The unbiased expectations theory attempts to explain observed forward rates by saying that expected future rates, ${}_tr_{t+1}$, will, on average, be equal to the implied forward rates (1) if investors' expectations of future one-period rates are unbiased and (2) if bonds of different maturity are perfect substitutes for each other. Among other things, this second condition requires that the risk and transactions costs for a strategy of rolling over a one-period bond three times are the same as holding a three-period bond. If the two strategies are in fact perfect substitutes, investors will keep the rates in line with expectations by forming arbitrage positions whenever interest rates (and bond prices) are "out of line."

To show how arbitrage might work, suppose that we believe that the pattern of future rates in our example is out of line. Table 3.12 shows the actual prices and rates, along with our expectations. We believe that the implied forward rate in the second year is too low—that it should be 17% instead of 15.1%. What should we

Table 3.12 An Investor's Expectations

Time to Maturity	Bond Price	Yield	Observed Forward Rate	Investor's Forward Rate
1 year	$826.45	21%	21.0%	21.0%
2 years	718.18	18	15.1	17.0
3 years	640.66	16	12.1	12.1

do? The logical action would be to sell short the two-year bonds for $718.18. If we are right, interest rates in the second year will be higher than the market expects, and we will make a capital gain. If enough people believe the observed forward rate is too low, the decreased demand for two-year bonds will lower their prices until the implied forward rate rises to 17%. Then interest rates will be in line with revised expectations.

If there were no transactions costs and if there were no uncertainty, then there is every reason to believe that the unbiased expectations theory of the term structure would hold. Implied forward rates would be exact forecasts of expected future rates.[9]

3. A Liquidity Premium in the Term Structure

Future interest rates become more uncertain the further into the future one tries to predict. Attempts to deal with this fact have led to theories of a *liquidity premium* in the term structure of interest rates.[10] Hicks argues that a liquidity premium exists because a given change in interest rates will have a greater effect on the price of long-term bonds than on short-term bonds. Hence there is greater risk of loss (and, one should add, a greater probability of gain) with long-term bonds.[11] Consequently, risk-averse investors will require a higher yield in order to hold longer-term bonds. This extra yield is called a *liquidity premium.*

To illustrate the sensitivity of bond prices to changes in the interest rate, consider two bonds. They both pay $120 per year in coupons and have a $1000 face value, but one has 5 years to maturity and the other has 10. If current interest rates are 10%, the present value of the 5-year bond, B_5, is

$$B_5 = \sum_{t=1}^{5} \frac{\$120}{(1 + .10)^t} + \frac{\$1000}{(1 + .10)^5} = \$1075.82,$$

and the present value of the 10-year bond is

$$B_{10} = \sum_{t=1}^{10} \frac{\$120}{(1 + .10)^t} + \frac{\$1000}{(1 + .10)^{10}} = \$1122.89.$$

[9] Empirical evidence on the validity of the expectations hypothesis is discussed in Chapter 9.

[10] For example, see Hicks [1946], Keynes [1936], Kessel [1965], Hirshleifer [1972], and Woodward [1979].

[11] A more lengthy discussion of bond risk, including default risk and duration, can be found in the Appendix to Chapter 14.

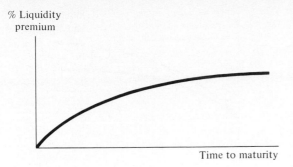

Figure 3.4
The liquidity premium.

What happens to the market prices of the bonds if the interest rate increases from 10% to 15%, a 50% increase? By similar calculations, we find that

$$B_5 = \$899.44 \quad \text{and} \quad B_{10} = \$849.44.$$

The market value of the 5-year bond has decreased 16.4%, whereas the 10-year bond has fallen by 24.4%. Clearly, the 10-year bond is more sensitive to the increase in interest rates. This is the risk Hicks had in mind when he described the liquidity premium.[12]
   Figure 3.4 shows how the liquidity premium is posited to change with the time to maturity on bonds. Note that the liquidity premium increases for bonds of longer maturity, but that it increases at a decreasing rate. Figure 3.5 shows how the liquidity premium is added to unbiased expectations in order to arrive at the observed term structure.
   Using monthly returns data on U.S. Treasury bills (1964–1982) and on portfolios of U.S. Government bonds (1953–1982), Fama [1984b] investigated term premiums in bond returns. He found statistically reliable evidence that expected returns on longer-term bills exceed the returns on one-month bills, but that the premium did not increase monotonically with maturity (as shown in Fig. 3.4, for example); rather, it tended to peak at around eight or nine months. The high variability of longer-term bond returns made it impossible to draw any conclusions about liquidity premia in their returns.

4. The Market Segmentation Hypothesis

   A third theory of the term structure, attributable to Culbertson [1957], Walker [1954], and Modigliani and Sutch [1966], is called the *market segmentation hypothesis*. It is argued that there is relatively little substitution between assets of different maturity because investors have preferred "habitats." For example, a firm that borrows to undertake an investment program will try to tailor its debt payments to the expected

---

[12] See the Appendix to Chapter 14 for an explanation of "duration," which measures the sensitivity (price elasticity) of bond prices to changes in interest rates.

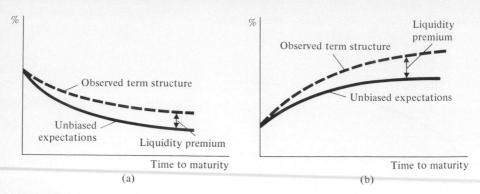

Figure 3.5
The liquidity premium added to a decreasing term structure (a) and to an increasing term structure (b).

cash flows from the project. Capital-intensive firms that construct long-term plant and equipment will prefer to issue long-term debt rather than rolling over short-term debt, and less capital-intensive firms will prefer to borrow short-term. Insurance companies with long-term liabilities (their life insurance policies) prefer to lend long term. Thus the market segmentation hypothesis argues that suppliers and users of funds have preferred habitats. Interest rates for a given maturity are explained mainly by the supply and demand for funds of that specific maturity.

While the market segmentation hypothesis can explain why implied forward and expected future rates may differ, the direction and magnitudes are not systematic. Recall that the Hicksian liquidity premium causes forward and future rates to differ systematically, depending on the maturity of the bonds.

5. Implications for Capital Budgeting

Regardless of which theory of the term structure is correct, the fact that one-year forward rates are not constant is relevant for the capital budgeting decision. The cash flows estimated for each year should be discounted to the present, using the information revealed in the term structure of interest rates. Let us use the hypothetical term structure example that was given earlier in the chapter to illustrate the relationship between the term structure and capital budgeting. Table 3.13 gives the yields to maturity, the implied forward rates, and cash flows for two projects. It is not uncommon for corporate treasurers to compute the NPV of these projects by discounting at the cost of capital for "three-year money," i.e., 16%. After all, both projects have a three-year life. When the cash flows are discounted at 16%, project A has a NPV of $8.55, whereas B has a lower NPV of $8.21. Project A appears to be superior. Unfortunately, this procedure does not account for the fact that the real opportunity cost of funds is 21% for cash flows received in the first year, 15.07% for second-year cash flows, and 12.1% for third-year cash flows. The correct discount rate for cash flows in each year is the yield to maturity for that year. Note that this is also equal to the product of the implied forward rates from year 1 up to the year of the cash flows. For example, the three-year

Table 3.13   The Term Structure and Capital Budgeting

Year	Yield to Maturity	Forward Rate	Cash Flow for A	Cash Flow for B	Discount Factor
0	—	—	$-100	$-100	1.0000
1	21%	21.00%	62	48	.8265
2	18	15.07	50	52	.7182
3	16	12.10	28	44	.6407

discount factor is

$$(1.16)^{-3} = [(1.21)(1.1507)(1.1210)]^{-1} = .6407.$$

The correct discount factors are given in the last column of Table 3.13. When the cash flows are appropriately discounted, the NPVs of projects A and B are $5.08 and $5.21, respectively. Now project B is preferred over A.

When the term structure is downward sloping, as in our simple example, a firm that uses the long-term rate (the three-year rate) to discount all cash flows will tend to overestimate the NPVs of projects. Of course, when the term structure is upward sloping, the opposite bias exists. In addition, as the example has shown, it is possible for the wrong project to be selected if the information given in the term structure is ignored.

It has been suggested that the term structure provides the best estimate of expected inflation.[13] If so, a downward-sloping term structure implies that investors expect near-term inflation to be higher than long-term. An upward-sloping term structure (removing the liquidity premium) implies the opposite. If the firm's capital budgeting procedure discounts nominal cash flows (cum inflation) at market rates, the cash flow estimates should reflect inflation on a year-by-year basis.

SUMMARY AND CONCLUSIONS

Perhaps the single most important decision faced by management is the selection of investment projects that maximize the present value of shareholders' wealth. Therefore it is hardly surprising that much of the literature in finance focuses on the capital budgeting problem. Both this chapter and its predecessor have emphasized capital budgeting techniques. However, the story is far from complete. Throughout we have maintained the assumption that future cash flows are known with certainty and can be estimated without error. In addition, we assumed that the opportunity cost of capital (the discount rate) was given.

Chapters 4 through 7 introduce the reader to a world where decisions must be made under the assumption of uncertainty. It is not until Chapter 12 that we return, for a second time, to the important capital budgeting decision. However, at that time

---

[13] For empirical evidence consistent with this point of view see Fama [1975].

we will be able to discuss the problem of project selection under uncertainty. Fortunately, the inclusion of uncertainty does not materially change the subject matter presented in Chapters 2 and 3. However, some important extensions to project selection techniques will be introduced. Finally, the logical cycle is completed in Chapter 13, when we discuss the determination of the appropriate opportunity cost of capital in a world of uncertainty. At that time all the necessary elements will have been covered under the assumption of uncertainty. They include the correct definition of cash flows for capital budgeting purposes, determination of the appropriate cost of capital, and a proof of why the NPV criterion is consistent with shareholder wealth maximization.

PROBLEM SET

3.1 The Johnson Company is considering the following mutually exclusive projects:

	Project J	*Project K*	*Project L*	*Project M*
Investment	$48,000	$60,000	$60,000	$36,000
Cash flow	20,000	12,000	16,000	10,000
N	5	15	10	15

The cost of capital used by the Johnson Company is 16%.

a) How should the fact that the projects have differences in scale be taken into consideration?

b) Rank the projects, assuming that they can be repeated with constant scale replication, and that the differences in scale are invested at the cost of capital.

3.2 If the opportunity cost of capital is 10%, which of the following three projects has the highest PVI? Which will increase shareholders' wealth the most?

Year	*Project A*	*Project B*	*Project C*
0	−1000	−2000	−3000
1	1000	1000	4000
2	1000	1000	
3		1000	

3.3 The cash flows for two mutually exclusive projects with different lives are given below:

Year	*Project A*	*Project B*
0	−10.00	−10.00
1	6.00	6.55
2	6.00	6.55
3		6.55

The opportunity cost of capital for project A is 10%, but project B is much riskier and has a 40% cost of capital.

a) What is the simple NPV of each project?

b) What is the NPV(N, ∞) of each project?

c) What is the annual equivalent value [see Eq. (3.5)] of each project?

d) Which project should be accepted? Why?

3.4 The Hansen Company is considering four mutually exclusive projects as follows:

	Project A	Project B	Project C	Project D
Investment	$40,000	$25,000	$40,000	$30,000
Cash Flow	12,000	8,000	8,000	6,500
N	5	5	10	10
k	12%	12%	12%	12%

a) Compute the NPV and IRR of each project and rank the investments from best to worst under each method. What factors are responsible for the differences in rankings between the two approaches?

b) Compute the PVI for each project and rank the alternatives. What are the implicit assumptions of the PVI method with respect to scale and duration of projects? When is it appropriate to use the PVI method?

c) If the projects are mutually exclusive, which should be accepted if they are independent? Why?

3.5 The Dandy Candy Company is considering two mutually exclusive projects. They are the only projects available. The risk-free rate is 5%. The cash flows from the projects are known with certainty and are given below:

Year	Project 1	Project 2
0	−10,000	−1,000
1	4,000	2,700
2	4,000	2,700
3	4,000	
4	4,000	

a) Which project has the higher net present value?

b) If the firm has no capital constraints, which project would you select?

c) If the firm has a capital constraint of $12,000, which project would you select? Why?

3.6 *Optimal duration.* Plaid Scotch Ltd. has just kegged its latest Scotch whisky at a cost of $50,000. The whisky's value will increase over the years according to the following formula:

$$V_t = \$100,000 \ln t.$$

What is the optimal time of bottling for the Scotch if the firm's cost of capital is 15% compounded continuously?

3.7 You are given the following information: The Dorkin Company has made an investment of $40,000, which is expected to yield benefits over a five-year period. Annual cash inflows of $90,000 and annual cash outflows of $75,000 are expected, excluding taxes and the depreciation tax shelter. The tax rate is 40%, and the cost of capital is 8%. Dorkin Company uses straight-line depreciation.

a) Compute the NPV of the investment.

b) On investigation, you discover that no adjustments have been made for inflation or price-level changes. The data for the first year are correct, but after that, inflows are expected to increase at 4% per year, outflows are expected to increase at 6% per year, and the annual rate of inflation is expected to be about 6%. Reevaluate the NPV of the project in light of this information.

3.8 The Baldwin Company is considering investing in a machine that produces bowling balls. The cost of the machine is $100,000. Production by year during the five-year life of the machine is expected to be as follows: 5,000 units, 8,000 units, 12,000 units, 10,000 units, and 6,000 units.

The interest in bowling is declining, and hence management believes that the price of bowling balls will increase at only 2% per year, compared with the general rate of inflation of 5%. The price of bowling balls in the first year will be $20.

On the other hand, plastic used to produce bowling balls is rapidly becoming more expensive. Because of this, production cash outflows are expected to grow at 10% per year. First-year production cost will be $10 per unit.

Depreciation of the machine will be straight-line for five years, after which time the salvage value will be zero. The company's tax rate is 40% and its cost of capital is 15%, based on the existing rate of inflation. Should the project be undertaken?

3.9 The yields to maturity on five zero coupon bonds are given below:

Years to Maturity	Yield
1	12.0%
2	14.0
3	15.0
4	15.5
5	15.7

a) What is the implied forward rate of interest for the third year?

b) What rate of interest would you receive if you bought a bond at the beginning of the second year and sold it at the beginning of the fourth year?

REFERENCES

Baumol, W. S., and R. E. Quandt, "Investment and Discount Rates under Capital Rationing," *Economic Journal*, June 1965, 317–329.

Bernhard, R. H., "Mathematical Programming Models for Capital Budgeting—A Survey, Generalization and Critique," *Journal of Financial and Quantitative Analysis*, June 1969, 111–158.

Bierman, H., Jr., and S. Smidt, *The Capital Budgeting Decision*, 4th ed. Macmillan, New York, 1975.

Carleton, W., "Linear Programming and Capital Budgeting Models: A New Interpretation," *Journal of Finance*, December 1969, 825–833.

Cooley, P. L.; R. L. Roenfeldt; and I. K. Chew, "Capital Budgeting Procedures under Inflation," *Financial Management*, Winter 1975, 18–27.

Cox, J. C.; J. Ingersoll, Jr.; and S. A. Ross, "A Theory of the Term Structure of Interest Rates." Unpublished working paper, Stanford University, 1980.

Culbertson, J. M., "The Term Structure of Interest Rates," *Quarterly Journal of Economics*, November 1957, 489–504.

Fama, E. F., "Short-term Interest Rates as Predictors of Inflation," *American Economic Review*, June 1975, 269–282.

———, "The Information in the Term Structure," *Journal of Financial Economics*, December 1984a, 509–528.

———, "Term Premiums in Bond Returns," *Journal of Financial Economics*, December 1984b, 529–546.

———, and G. W. Schwert, "Asset Returns and Inflation," *Journal of Financial Economics*, November 1977, 113–146.

Findlay, M. C., and A. W. Frankle, "Capital Budgeting Procedures under Inflation: Cooley, Roenfeldt and Chew vs. Findlay and Frankle," *Financial Management*, Autumn 1976, 83–90.

Fisher, I., "Appreciation and Interest," *Publications of the American Economic Association*, August 1896, 23–29, 91–92.

Hicks, J. R., *Value and Capital*, 2nd ed. Oxford University Press, London, 1946.

Hirshleifer, J., *Investment, Interest, and Capital*. Prentice-Hall, Englewood Cliffs, N.J., 1970.

———, "Liquidity, Uncertainty, and the Accumulation of Information," in Carter and Ford, eds., *Essays in Honor of G. L. S. Shackle*. Basil Blackwell, Oxford, 1972.

Kessel, R. A., *The Cyclical Behavior of the Term Structure of Interest Rates*. National Bureau of Economic Research, New York, 1965.

Keynes, J. M., *The General Theory of Employment, Interest and Money*. Harcourt, Brace and World Inc., 1936.

Klammer, T., "Empirical Evidence of the Adoption of Sophisticated Capital Budgeting Techniques," *Journal of Business*, July 1972, 387–397.

Lorie, J. H., and L. J. Savage, "Three Problems in Capital Rationing," *Journal of Business*, October 1955, 229–239.

Lutz, F. A., "The Structure of Interest Rates," *Quarterly Journal of Economics*, November 1940, 36–63.

Malkiel, B. G., "Expectations, Bond Prices, and the Term Structure of Interest Rates," *Quarterly Journal of Economics*, May 1962, 197–218.

McConnell, J., and C. Muscarella, "Corporate Capital Expenditure Decisions and the Market Value of the Firm," *Journal of Financial Economics*, September 1985, 399–422.

McCulloch, J. H., "An Estimate of the Liquidity Premium," *Journal of Political Economy*, January–February 1975, 95–119.

Meiselman, D., *The Term Structure of Interest Rates*. Princeton University Press, Princeton, N.J., 1966.

Modigliani, F., and R. Sutch, "Innovation and Interest Rate Policy," *American Economic Review*, May 1966, 178–197.

Myers, S. C., "A Note on Linear Programming and Capital Budgeting," *Journal of Finance*, March 1972, 89–92.

Nelson, C., *The Term Structure of Interest Rates*. Basic Books, New York, 1972.

Roll, R., *The Behavior of Interest Rates: An Application of the Efficient Market Model to U.S. Treasury Bills*. Basic Books, New York, 1970.

Sargent, T., "Rational Expectations and the Term Structure of Interest Rates," *Journal of Money, Credit and Banking*, February 1972, 74–97.

Schall, L.; G. Sundem; and W. Geijsbeek, Jr., "Survey and Analysis of Capital Budgeting References," *Journal of Finance*, March 1978, 281–287.

Van Horne, J. C., "A Note on Biases on Capital Budgeting Introduced by Inflation," *Journal of Financial and Quantitative Analysis*, January 1971, 653–658.

———, *Financial Rates and Flows*. Prentice Hall, Englewood Cliffs, N.J., 1978.

Walker, C. E., "Federal Reserve Policy and the Structure of Interest Rates on Government Securities," *Quarterly Journal of Economics*, February 1954, 22–23.

Weingartner, H. M., *Mathematical Programming and the Analysis of Capital Budgeting Problems*. Prentice-Hall, Englewood Cliffs, N.J., 1963.

———, "Capital Rationing: *N* Authors in Search of a Plot," *Journal of Finance*, December 1977, 1403–1432.

Wood, J. H., "Expectations, Error and the Term Structure of Interest Rates," *Journal of Political Economy*, April 1963, 160–171.

Woodward, S., "The Liquidity Premium and the Solidity Premium," *American Economic Review*, June 1983, 348–361.

4

We wish to find the mathematically complete principles which define "rational behavior" for the participants in a social economy, and derive from them the general characteristics of that behavior.

J. Von Neumann and O. Morgenstern, *Theory of Games and Economic Behavior,* Princeton University Press, Princeton, 1947, 31

The Theory of Choice: Utility Theory Given Uncertainty

Economics is the study of how people and societies choose to allocate scarce resources and distribute wealth among one another and over time. Therefore one must understand the objects of choice and the method of choice. The following two chapters (Chapters 5 and 6) are devoted to the objects of choice faced by an investor. Here, we focus on the theory of how people make choices when faced with uncertainty. Later on—once the theory of choice and the objects of choice are understood—we shall combine the two in order to produce a theory of optimal decision making under uncertainty. In particular, we shall study the allocation of resources in an economic society where prices provide a system of signals for optimal allocation. There are, however, other means of allocation. Instead of using prices, we might allow an individual or committee to make all the allocation decisions, or we might program allocational rules into an algorithm run by machine.

We shall begin with a discussion of the axioms of behavior used by economists. However, before rushing into them, we must recognize that there are other theories of behavior. Social sciences such as anthropology, psychology, political science, sociobiology, and sociology also provide great insight into the theory of choice. And very early in this chapter we shall be forced to recognize that individuals have different tastes for the time preference of consumption and different degrees of risk aversion.

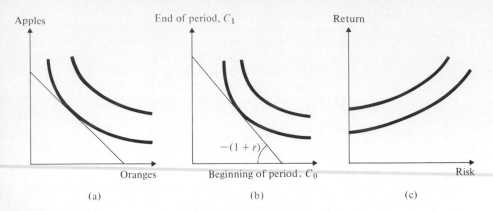

Figure 4.1
Indifference curves for various types of choices: (a) Choice between consumption goods under certainty; (b) choice between consumption and investment under certainty; (c) choice between risk and return.

Economic theory recognizes these differences but has little to say about why they exist or what causes them.[1] The other social sciences study these problems. However, as we shall see, there is much one can say about the theory of choice under uncertainty without, for example, understanding why a 70-year-old person is more or less risk averse than the same person at age 20, or why some people prefer meat, whereas others prefer vegetables.

The theory of investor choice is only one corner of what has come to be known as utility theory. Most students are already familiar with the microeconomic price theory treatment of choices among various bundles of perishable commodities such as apples and oranges at an instant in time. The indifference curves that result are shown in Fig. 4.1(a). Another type of choice available to individuals is whether to consume now or to save (invest) and consume more at a later date. This is the utility theory of choices over time, which is fundamental for understanding interest rates. This type of one-period consumption/investment decision was discussed in Chapter 1 and is illustrated in Fig. 4.1(b). Our main concern here is the choice between timeless risky alternatives, which we call the theory of investor choice. The theory begins with nothing more than five assumptions about the behavior of individuals when confronted with the task of ranking risky alternatives and the assumption of nonsatiation (i.e., greed). The theory ends by parameterizing the objects of choice as the mean and variance of return and by mapping trade-offs between them that provide equal utility to investors. These mappings are indifference curves for timeless (or one-period) choices under uncertainty. They are shown in Fig. 4.1(c), and are used extensively in Chapters 6 and 7.

---

[1] An interesting exception is an article by Rubin and Paul [1979] that suggests a theory of why people exhibit different attitudes toward risk at different stages in their lives.

A. FIVE AXIOMS OF CHOICE UNDER UNCERTAINTY

To develop a theory of rational decision making in the face of uncertainty, it is necessary to make some very precise assumptions about an individual's behavior. Known as the *axioms of cardinal utility*, these assumptions provide the minimum set of conditions for consistent and rational behavior. Once they are established, all the remaining theory must follow.[2]

Axiom 1   Comparability (sometimes called completeness). For the entire set, S, of uncertain alternatives, an individual can say either that outcome x is preferred to outcome y (we write this $x \succ y$) or y is preferred to x ($y \succ x$) or the individual is indifferent as to x and y ($x \sim y$).[3]

Axiom 2   Transitivity (sometimes called consistency). If an individual prefers x to y and y to z, then x is preferred to z. (If $x \succ y$ and $y \succ z$, then $x \succ z$.) If an individual is indifferent as to x and y and is also indifferent as to y and z, then he or she is indifferent as to x and z. (If $x \sim y$ and $y \sim z$, then $x \sim z$.)

Axiom 3   Strong independence. Suppose we construct a gamble where an individual has a probability α of receiving outcome x and a probability $(1 - \alpha)$ of receiving outcome z. We shall write this gamble as $G(x, z : \alpha)$. Strong independence says that if the individual is indifferent as to x and y, then he or she will also be indifferent as to a first gamble, set up between x with probability α and a mutually exclusive outcome z, and a second gamble, set up between y with probability α and the same mutually exclusive outcome, z.

$$\text{If } x \sim y, \text{ then } G(x, z : \alpha) \sim G(y, z : \alpha).$$

Axiom 4   Measurability. If outcome y is preferred less than x but more than z, then there is a *unique* α (a probability) such that the individual will be indifferent between y and a gamble between x with probability α and z with probability $(1 - \alpha)$.[4]

$$\text{If } x \succ y \geq z \text{ or } x \geq y \succ z, \text{ then there exists a unique } \alpha,$$
$$\text{such that } y \sim G(x, z : \alpha).$$

Axiom 5   Ranking. If alternatives y and u both lie somewhere between x and z and we can establish gambles such that an individual is indifferent between y and a gamble between x (with probability α_1) and z, while also indifferent between

---

[2] The notation and much of the conceptual outline follow the development found in Fama and Miller [1972].

[3] The symbol used to indicate preference ($\succ$) is not a mathematical inequality. It can rank only preferences. For example, an individual may prefer one Picasso to two Rembrandts, or vice versa.

[4] The reason for bounding y on only one side or the other is to eliminate the possibility of $x \sim y \sim z$, in which case any α would satisfy the indifference condition required by the gamble.

u and a second gamble, this time between x (with probability α_2) and z, then if α_1 is greater than α_2, y is preferred to u.

If $x \succeq y \succeq z$ and $x \succeq u \succeq z$, then if $y \sim G(x, z : \alpha_1)$ and $u \sim G(x, z : \alpha_2)$, it follows that if $\alpha_1 > \alpha_2$, then $y \succ u$, or if $\alpha_1 = \alpha_2$, then $y \sim u$.

These are known as the axioms of cardinal utility. They boil down to the following assumptions about behavior. First, all individuals are assumed to always make completely rational decisions. A statement that "I like Chevrolets more than Fords and Fords more than Toyotas but Toyotas more than Chevrolets" is not rational. Second, people are assumed to be able to make these rational choices among thousands of alternatives—not a very simple task.

The axiom of strong independence is usually the hardest to accept. To illustrate it, consider the following example. Let outcome x be winning a left shoe, let y be a right shoe, and let z also be a right shoe. Imagine two gambles. The first is a 50/50 chance of winning x or z, i.e., a left shoe or a right shoe. The second gamble is a 50/50 chance of winning y or z, i.e., a right shoe or a right shoe. If we were originally indifferent between the choice of a left shoe (by itself) or a right shoe (by itself), then strong independence implies that we will also be indifferent between the two gambles we constructed. Of course, left shoes and right shoes are complementary goods, and we would naturally prefer to have both if possible. The point of strong independence is that outcome z in the above examples is always mutually exclusive. In the first gamble, the payoffs are a left shoe *or* a right shoe but never both. And in the second gamble, the payoffs are a right shoe *or* a right shoe but never both. The mutual exclusiveness of the third alternative z is critical to the axiom of strong independence.

Having established the five axioms, we add to them the assumption that individuals always prefer more wealth to less. In other words, people are greedy. The marginal utility of wealth is always positive. This assumption, in conjunction with the other five, is all that is needed to provide a complete development of utility theory.

Next, we need to answer the question, How do individuals rank various combinations of risky alternatives? We can use the axioms of preference to show how preferences can be mapped into measurable utility. How do we establish a utility function that allows the assignment of a unit of measure (a number) to various alternatives so that we can look at the number and know that if, e.g., the utility of x is 35 and the utility of y is 27, then x is preferred to y? To do this we need to discuss two properties of utility functions.

B. DEVELOPING UTILITY FUNCTIONS

The utility function will have two properties. First, it will be order preserving. In other words, if we measure the utility of x as greater than the utility of y, $U(x) > U(y)$, it means that x is actually preferred to y, $x \succ y$. Second, expected utility can be used to rank combinations of risky alternatives. Mathematically, this means that

$$U[G(x, y : \alpha)] = \alpha U(x) + (1 - \alpha)U(y).$$

To prove that utility functions are order preserving, consider the set of risky outcomes, S, which is assumed to be bounded above by outcome a and below by outcome b. Next consider two intermediate outcomes x and y such that

$$a \succ x \succeq b \quad \text{or} \quad a \succeq x \succ b$$

and

$$a \succ y \succeq b \quad \text{or} \quad a \succeq y \succ b.$$

By using Axiom 4 (measurability), we can choose unique probabilities for x and y in order to construct the following gambles:

$$x \sim G(a, b : \alpha(x)), \qquad y \sim G(a, b : \alpha(y)).$$

Then we can use Axiom 5 (ranking) so that the probabilities $\alpha(x)$ and $\alpha(y)$ can be interpreted as numerical utilities that uniquely rank x and y. By Axiom 5,

$$\text{If } \alpha(x) > \alpha(y), \text{ then } x \succ y.$$

$$\text{If } \alpha(x) = \alpha(y), \text{ then } x \sim y.$$

$$\text{If } \alpha(x) < \alpha(y), \text{ then } x \prec y.$$

In this way, we have developed an order-preserving utility function. The maximum and minimum outcomes, a and b, may be assigned any number at all (e.g., let $a = 100$ and $b = 0$). Then by forming simple gambles, we can assign cardinal utility numbers to the intermediate outcomes x and y.

Next it is important to show that expected utility can be used to rank risky alternatives. This is the second property of utility functions. Let us begin by establishing the elementary gambles in exactly the same way as before. This is illustrated in Fig. 4.2. Next, consider a third alternative, z. Note that we can rely on Axiom 3 (strong independence) to say that the choice of z will not affect the relationship between x and y. Next, by Axiom 4, there must exist a unique probability, $\beta(z)$, that would make us indifferent as to outcome z and a gamble between x and y. (See Fig. 4.3.) Now we can relate z to the elemental prospects a and b. If we can trace the branches in the decision tree represented by Fig. 4.3, we will be indifferent between z and outcome a with probability $\gamma = \beta(z)\alpha(x) + (1 - \beta(z))\alpha(y)$ and outcome b with probability $(1 - \gamma)$.

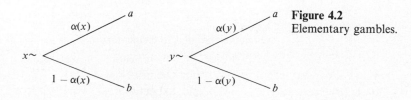

Figure 4.2
Elementary gambles.

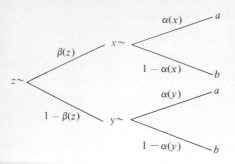

Figure 4.3
Outcome z compared with a gamble between outcomes x and y.

This is shown in Fig. 4.4. We can write the gamble as follows:

$$z \sim G[a, b : \beta(z)\alpha(x) + (1 - \beta(z))\alpha(y)].$$

Now, we have already established, by Axioms 4 and 5, that the utilities of x and y can be represented by their probabilities, i.e., $U(x) = \alpha(x)$ and $U(y) = \alpha(y)$. Therefore the above gamble can be rewritten as

$$z \sim G[a, b : \beta(z)U(x) + (1 - \beta(z))U(y)].$$

Finally, by using Axioms 4 and 5 a second time, it must be true that the unique probability of outcome z can be used as a cardinal measure of its utility relative to the elemental prospects of a and b. Therefore we have

$$U(z) = \beta(z)U(x) + (1 - \beta(z))U(y). \tag{4.1}$$

In this way we have shown that the correct ranking function for risky alternatives is *expected utility*. Equation (4.1) says that the utility of z is equal to the probability of x times its utility plus the probability of y times its utility. This is an expected utility that represents a linear combination of the utilities of outcomes.

In general, we can write the expected utility of wealth as follows:

$$E[U(W)] = \sum_i p_i U(W_i).$$

Given the five axioms of rational investor behavior and the additional assumption that all investors always prefer more wealth to less, we can say that investors will always seek to maximize their expected utility of wealth. In fact, the above equation is exactly what we mean by the theory of choice. All investors will use it as their objective function. In other words, they will seem to calculate the expected utility of wealth for all possible alternative choices and then choose the outcome that maximizes their expected utility of wealth.

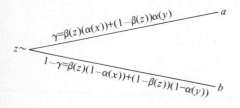

Figure 4.4
Outcome z related to elementary prospects a and b.

Table 4.1   Payoffs, Probabilities, and Utilities

Loss	Gain	Probability of Gain	Utility of Gain	Utility of Loss
−1000	1000	.60	6.7	−10.0
−1000	2000	.55	8.2	−10.0
−1000	3000	.50	10.0	−10.0
−1000	4000	.45	12.2	−10.0
−1000	5000	.40	15.0	−10.0
−1000	6000	.35	18.6	−10.0
−1000	7000	.30	23.3	−10.0
−2000	2000	.75	8.2	−24.6
−3000	3000	.80	10.0	−40.0
−4000	4000	.85	12.2	−69.2
−5000	5000	.90	15.0	−135.0

From *Dividend Policy and Enterprise Valuation*, by James E. Walter. © 1967 by Wadsworth Publishing Company, Inc., Belmont, Calif. Reprinted by permission of the publisher.

Now, we can use the properties of utility functions to demonstrate how our utility function might be constructed. Suppose we arbitrarily assign a utility of −10 utiles to a loss of $1000 and ask the following question: When we are faced with a gamble with probability α of winning $1000 and probability $(1 - \alpha)$ of losing $1000, what probability would make us indifferent between the gamble and $0.0 with certainty? Mathematically, this problem can be expressed as

$$0 \sim G(1000, -1000:\alpha)$$

or

$$U(0) = \alpha U(1000) + (1 - \alpha)U(-1000).$$

Suppose that the probability of winning $1000 must be .6 in order for us to be indifferent between the gamble and a sure $0.0. By assuming that the utility of $0.0 with certainty is zero and substituting $U(-1000) = -10$ and $\alpha = .6$ into the above equation, we can solve for the utility of $1000:

$$U(1000) = \frac{(1 - \alpha)U(-1000)}{\alpha}$$

$$= -\frac{(1 - .6)(-10)}{.6} = 6.7 \text{ utiles.}$$

By repeating this procedure for different payoffs it is possible to develop a utility function. Table 4.1 shows various gambles, their probabilities, and the utility of payoffs for a risk-averse investor. The cardinal utility function that obtains for the set of preferences indicated in Table 4.1 is given in Fig. 4.5.[5]

---

[5] This example can be found in Walter [1967].

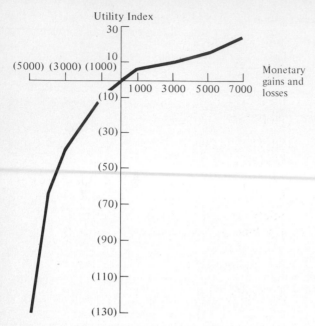

Figure 4.5
Cardinal utility function. (From *Dividend Policy and Enterprise Valuation*, by James E. Walter. Copyright © 1967 by Wadsworth Publishing Company, Inc., Belmont, Calif. Reprinted by permission of the publisher.)

An important thing to keep in mind is that utility functions are specific to individuals. There is no way to compare one individual's utility function to another's. For example, we could perform an experiment by giving two people $1000. We would see that they are both happy, having just experienced an increase in utility. But whose utility increased more? It is impossible to say! Interpersonal comparison of utility functions is impossible. If it were not, we could establish a social welfare function that would combine everyone's utility, and we could then use it to solve such problems as the optimal distribution of wealth. We could maximize society's utility by taking wealth from individual i and giving it to individual j. However, it is not possible to know how real-world utility functions for different individuals should be aggregated. It follows that group utility functions, such as the utility function of a firm, have no meaning.

Another important property of cardinal utility functions is that we can sensibly talk about increasing or decreasing marginal utility. This can best be illustrated with an example taken from the centigrade and Fahrenheit temperature scales. Consider two outcomes: the freezing point of water and its boiling point. Call them x and y, respectively. Each scale may be likened to a function that maps various degrees of heat into numbers. Utility functions do the same thing for risky alternatives. The difference between two outcomes is marginal utility. On the centigrade scale the difference between freezing and boiling is 100°C. On the Fahrenheit scale the difference is 180°F. The ratio of the "changes" is

$$\frac{212° - 32°}{100° - 0°} = 1.8.$$

If the two scales really do provide the same ranking for all prospects, then the ratio of changes should be the same for all prospects. Mathematically,

$$\frac{U(x) - U(y)}{\psi(x) - \psi(y)} = \text{constant},$$

where $U(\cdot)$ and $\psi(\cdot)$ are the two utility functions. Compare any two points on the two temperature scales and you will see that the ratio of changes between them is a constant, i.e., 1.8. Hence changes in utility between any two wealth levels have exactly the same meaning on the two utility functions, i.e., one utility function is just a "transformation" of the other.

C. ESTABLISHING A DEFINITION OF RISK AVERSION

Having established a way of converting the axioms of preference into a utility function, we can make use of the concept to establish definitions of risk premia and also precisely what is meant by *risk aversion*. A useful way to begin is to compare three simple utility functions (Fig. 4.6) which assume that more wealth is preferred to less—in other words, the marginal utility of wealth is positive—$MU(W) > 0$. Suppose that we establish a gamble between two prospects, a and b. Let the probability of receiving prospect a be α and the probability of b be $(1 - \alpha)$. The gamble can be written as before: $G(a, b: \alpha)$. Now the question is this: Will we prefer the actuarial value of the gamble (i.e., its expected or average outcome) with certainty—or the gamble itself? In other words, would we like to receive $10 for sure, or would we prefer to "roll the dice" in a gamble that pays off $100 with a 10% probability and $0 with a 90%

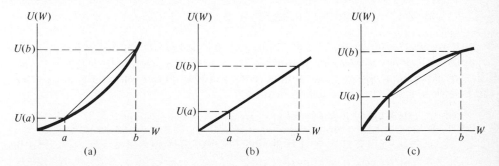

Figure 4.6
Three utility functions with positive marginal utility: (a) risk lover; (b) risk neutral; (c) risk averter.

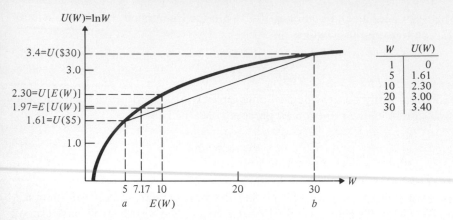

Figure 4.7
Logarithmic utility function.

probability? A person who prefers the gamble is a risk lover; one who is indifferent is risk neutral; and one who prefers the actuarial value with certainty is a risk averter. In Fig. 4.7, we have graphed a logarithmic utility function: $U(W) = \ln(W)$. The gamble is an 80% chance of a $5 outcome and a 20% chance of a $30 outcome. The *actuarial value of the gamble* is its expected outcome. In other words, the expected wealth is

$$E(W) = .8(\$5) + .2(\$30) = \$10.$$

The utility of the expected wealth can be read directly from the utility function: $U[E(W)] = 2.3$. That is, if an individual with a logarithmic utility function could receive $10 with certainty, it would provide him or her with 2.3 utiles. The other possibility is the utility of the gamble. We know from Eq. (4.1) that it is equal to the expected utility of wealth provided by the gamble.

$$E[U(W)] = .8U(\$5) + .2U(\$30)$$

$$= .8(1.61) + .2(3.40) = 1.97.$$

Because we receive more utility from the actuarial value of the gamble obtained with certainty than from taking the gamble itself, we are risk averse. In general, if the utility of expected wealth is greater than the expected utility of wealth, the individual will be risk averse. The three definitions are:[6]

If $U[E(W)] > E[U(W)]$, then we have risk aversion.   (4.2a)

If $U[E(W)] = E[U(W)]$, then we have risk neutrality.   (4.2b)

If $U[E(W)] < E[U(W)]$, then we have risk loving.   (4.2c)

---

[6] These definitions can be found in Markowitz [1959].

Note (see Fig. 4.6) that if our utility function is strictly concave, we will be risk averse; if it is linear, we will be risk neutral; and if it is convex, we will be risk lovers.

It is even possible to compute the maximum amount of wealth an individual would be willing to give up in order to avoid the gamble. This is called a *risk premium*. Suppose that Mr. Smith is faced with the gamble illustrated in Fig. 4.7, has a current level of wealth of $10, and has a logarithmic utility function. How much will he pay to avoid the gamble? If he does nothing, he has an 80% chance of ending up with $5 (a decline of $5) and a 20% chance of ending up with $30 (an increase of $20). The expected utility of the gamble has already been determined to be 1.97 utiles. From the logarithmic utility function in Fig. 4.7 we see that the level of wealth that provides 1.97 utiles is $7.17. On the other hand, Smith receives an expected level of wealth of $10 (equal to his current wealth) if he accepts the gamble. Therefore, given a logarithmic utility function, he will be willing to pay up to $2.83 in order to avoid the gamble. We shall call this the *Markowitz risk premium*. If Smith is offered insurance against the gamble that costs less than $2.83, he will buy it.

We shall adopt the convention of measuring the *risk premium* as the difference between an individual's expected wealth, given the gamble, and the level of wealth that individual would accept with certainty if the gamble were removed, i.e., his or her *certainty equivalent wealth*. There is another convention that might be called the *cost of the gamble*. It is defined as the difference between an individual's current wealth and his or her certainty equivalent wealth. Note that in the first example, given above, expected wealth and current wealth were identical because the expected change in wealth was zero. Thus there was no difference between the risk premium and the cost of the gamble. To illustrate the difference between the two definitions, consider the following example. A risk-averse individual has the same logarithmic utility function as in Fig. 4.7 and the same current wealth, i.e., $10, but the gamble is a 10% chance of winning $10 and a 90% chance of winning $100. We can compute the following numbers:

$$\text{Current wealth} = \$10,$$

$$\text{Expected wealth} = \$101,$$

$$\text{Certainty equivalent wealth} = \$92.76.$$

Our convention will be to define the risk premium as the difference between expected wealth and certainty equivalent wealth, i.e.:

$$\text{Risk premium} = \text{Expected wealth} - \text{certainty equivalent wealth}$$

$$= \$101 - \$92.76 = \$8.24.$$

This measures, in dollars, the risk premium associated with the gamble. Note, however, that since the gamble is favorable (we can only win if we take it), we would be willing to pay a positive amount to take the gamble. The cost of the gamble is

$$\text{Cost of the gamble} = \text{Current wealth} - \text{certainty equivalent}$$

$$= \$10 - \$92.76 = \$-82.76.$$

In other words, we would be willing to pay up to $82.76 in order to take a gamble that has a 10% chance of increasing our wealth from $10 to $20, and a 90% chance of increasing it from $10 to $110. We would pay even more if we were less risk averse. Note that for a risk averter the risk premium as defined above is always positive, whereas the cost of the gamble can be positive, negative, or zero, depending on the risk of the gamble and on how much it is expected to change one's current wealth.

Throughout the remainder of this text we shall assume that all individuals are risk averse. Their utility functions are assumed to be strictly concave and increasing. Mathematically, this implies two things: (1) they always prefer more wealth to less (the marginal utility of wealth is positive, $MU(W) > 0$), and (2) their marginal utility of wealth decreases as they have more and more wealth ($dMU(W)/dW < 0$).[7]

Now we know how to characterize a risk-averse utility function and how to measure a risk premium for a given gamble, but it is even more interesting to provide a specific definition of *risk aversion*. This was done by Pratt [1964] and Arrow [1971]. Take an individual, say Ms. Torres, with a current amount of wealth, W, and present her with an actuarially neutral gamble of $\tilde{Z}$ dollars (by *actuarially neutral* we mean that $E(\tilde{Z}) = 0$). What risk premium, $\pi(W, \tilde{Z})$, must be added to the gamble to make her indifferent between it and the actuarial value of the gamble? In Fig. 4.7, which illustrates our first example, the risk premium is analogous to the difference between $U[E(W)]$ and $E[U(W)]$ if it is measured in utiles, or the difference between $10 and $7.17 if measured in dollars. Presumably, the risk premium will be a function of the level of wealth, W, and the gamble $\tilde{Z}$. Mathematically, the risk premium, π, can be defined as the value that satisfies the following equality:

$$E[U(W + \tilde{Z})] = U[W + E(\tilde{Z}) - \pi(W, \tilde{Z})]. \tag{4.3}$$

The left-hand side is the expected utility of the current level of wealth, given the gamble. Its utility must equal the utility of the right-hand side, i.e., the current level of wealth, W, plus the utility of the actuarial value of the gamble, $E(\tilde{Z})$, minus the risk premium, $\pi(W, \tilde{Z})$. We can use a Taylor's series approximation to expand the utility function of wealth (whatever it might be) around both sides of Eq. (4.3).[8] Working with the right-hand side of (4.3), we have

$$U[W + E(\tilde{Z}) - \pi(W, \tilde{Z})] = U[W - \pi(W, \tilde{Z})].$$

Since $E(\tilde{Z}) \equiv 0$, an actuarially neutral risk, the Taylor's series expansion is[9]

$$U(W - \pi) = U(W) - \pi U'(W) + \text{terms of order at most } (\pi^2). \tag{4.4}$$

The Taylor's series expansion of the left-hand side of (4.3) is

$$E[U(W + \tilde{Z})] = E[U(W) + \tilde{Z}U'(W) + \tfrac{1}{2}\tilde{Z}^2 U''(W) + \text{terms of order at most } (\tilde{Z}^3)]$$

$$= U(W) + \tfrac{1}{2}\sigma_Z^2 U''(W) + \text{terms of smaller order than } \sigma_Z^2. \tag{4.5}$$

---

[7] Decreasing marginal utility is probably genetically coded because without it we would exhibit extreme impulsive behavior. We would engage in the activity with the highest marginal utility to the exclusion of all other choices. Addictive behavior would be the norm.

[8] Students not familiar with Taylor's series approximations are referred to Appendix D.

[9] We assume that the third absolute central moment of $\tilde{Z}$ is of smaller order than σ_Z^2 (normally it is of the order of σ_Z^3).

The above result may require a little explanation. It is true because

$$E[U(W)] = U(W), \qquad \text{current wealth is not random;}$$
$$E[\tilde{Z}] \equiv 0, \qquad \text{the risk is actuarially neutral;}$$
$$E[\tilde{Z}^2] = \sigma_Z^2, \qquad \text{because } \sigma_Z^2 \equiv E[\tilde{Z} - E(\tilde{Z})]^2.$$

Next we can equate (4.4) and (4.5):

$$U(W) - \pi U'(W) + \cdots = U(W) + \tfrac{1}{2}\sigma_Z^2 U''(W) + \cdots. \tag{4.6a}$$

Solving (4.6a) for the risk premium, we obtain

$$\pi = \tfrac{1}{2}\sigma_Z^2 \left(-\frac{U''(W)}{U'(W)} \right). \tag{4.6b}$$

This is the *Pratt-Arrow measure* of a local risk premium. Since $\tfrac{1}{2}\sigma_Z^2$ is always positive, the sign of the risk premium is always determined by the sign of the term in parentheses. We shall define the measure of *absolute risk aversion* (ARA) as

$$\text{ARA} = -\frac{U''(W)}{U'(W)}. \tag{4.7}$$

It is called absolute risk aversion because it measures risk aversion for a given level of wealth. The Pratt-Arrow definition of risk aversion is useful because it provides much more insight into people's behavior in the face of risk. For example, how does ARA change with one's wealth level? Casual empiricism tells us that ARA will probably decrease as our wealth increases. A $1000 gamble may seem trivial to a billionaire, but a pauper would probably be very risk averse toward it. On the other hand, we can multiply the measure of absolute risk aversion by the level of wealth to obtain what is known as *relative risk aversion* (RRA):

$$\text{RRA} = -W \frac{U''(W)}{U'(W)}. \tag{4.8}$$

Constant relative risk aversion implies that an individual will have constant risk aversion to a proportional loss of wealth even though the absolute loss increases as wealth does.

We can use these definitions of risk aversion to provide a more detailed examination of various types of utility functions to see whether or not they have decreasing ARA and constant RRA. The quadratic utility function has been used widely in academic literature. It can be written (for $W \le a/2b$)

Quadratic utility function,		$U(W) = aW - bW^2;$ (4.9)
First derivative, marginal utility,		$U'(W) = a - 2bW;$
Second derivative, change in MU with respect to changes in wealth,		$U''(W) = -2b.$

For the quadratic utility function, ARA and RRA are

$$\text{ARA} = -\frac{2b}{a - 2bW}, \qquad \frac{d(\text{ARA})}{dW} > 0,$$

$$\text{RRA} = \frac{2b}{(a/W) - 2b}, \qquad \frac{d(\text{RRA})}{dW} > 0.$$

Unfortunately, the quadratic utility function exhibits increasing ARA and increasing RRA. Neither of these properties makes sense intuitively. For example, an individual with increasing RRA would become more averse to a given percentage loss in wealth as wealth increases. A billionaire who loses half his wealth, leaving $500 million, would lose more utility than the same person who started with $20,000 and ended up with $10,000. This result is simply not intuitive.

Friend and Blume [1975] have used Internal Revenue Service data to replicate, from reported dividends, the portfolios held by individual investors. Sophisticated econometric techniques were used to estimate changes in ARA and RRA as a function of the wealth of investors. The results were consistent with decreasing ARA and constant RRA equal to 2.0. These properties are consistent with a power utility function with $a = -1$ (for $W > 0$). It can be written as

$$U(W) = -W^{-1}, \qquad U'(W) = W^{-2} > 0, \qquad U''(W) = -2W^{-3} < 0. \quad (4.10)$$

For this power utility function, ARA and RRA are

$$\text{ARA} = -\frac{-2W^{-3}}{W^{-2}} = \frac{2}{W}, \qquad \frac{d(\text{ARA})}{dW} < 0,$$

$$\text{RRA} = W\frac{2}{W} = 2, \qquad \frac{d(\text{RRA})}{dW} = 0.$$

The power function given by Eq. (4.10) is consistent with the empirical results of Friend and Blume and exhibits all the intuitively plausible properties: the marginal utility of wealth is positive, it decreases with increasing wealth, the measure of ARA decreases with increasing wealth, and RRA is constant.

D. COMPARISON OF RISK AVERSION
IN THE SMALL AND IN THE LARGE

The Pratt-Arrow definition of risk aversion provides useful insights into the properties of ARA and RRA, but it assumes that risks are small and actuarially neutral. The Markowitz concept, which simply compares $E[U(W)]$ with $U[E(W)]$, is not limited by these assumptions.

An interesting comparison of the two measures of risk premiums is offered in the following example. An individual with a logarithmic utility function and a level of wealth of $20,000 is exposed to two different risks: (1) a 50/50 chance of gaining or losing $10 and (2) an 80% chance of losing $1,000 and a 20% chance of losing

$10,000. What is the risk premium required by the individual faced with each of these risks? Note that the first risk is small and actuarially neutral, so that it approximates the assumptions that were used to derive the Pratt-Arrow risk premium. The second risk, however, is large and very asymmetric.

The first risk is a small, actuarially neutral gamble, so the Pratt-Arrow measure of the risk premium [Eq. (4.6b)] should yield a result almost identical to the Markowitz measure. The Pratt-Arrow measure is

$$\pi = -\tfrac{1}{2}\sigma_Z^2 \frac{U''(W)}{U'(W)}.$$

The variance of the first risk is

$$\sigma_Z^2 = \sum p_i(X_i - E(X))^2$$
$$= \tfrac{1}{2}(20{,}010 - 20{,}000)^2 + \tfrac{1}{2}(19{,}990 - 20{,}000)^2$$
$$= 100.$$

The ratio of the second and the first derivatives of a logarithmic utility function evaluated at a level of wealth of $20,000 is

$$U'(W) = \frac{1}{W}, \qquad U''(W) = -\frac{1}{W^2}, \qquad \frac{U''(W)}{U'(W)} = -\frac{1}{W} = -\frac{1}{20{,}000}.$$

Combining these results, we obtain an estimate of the Pratt-Arrow risk premium:

$$\pi = \frac{100}{2}\left(-\frac{1}{20{,}000}\right) = \$.0025.$$

The Markowitz approach requires computation of the expected utility of the gamble as follows:

$$E[U(W)] = \sum p_i U(W_i)$$

$$= \tfrac{1}{2}U(20{,}010) + \tfrac{1}{2}U(19{,}990)$$

$$= \tfrac{1}{2}\ln(20{,}010) + \tfrac{1}{2}\ln(19{,}990) = 9.903487428.$$

The certainty equivalent wealth level that would make us indifferent to our current level of wealth, given the gamble and a lower but certain level of wealth, is the level of wealth that has a utility of 9.903487428. This is

$$W = e^{\ln(W)} = \$19{,}999.9974998.$$

Therefore we would pay a risk premium as large as $.0025002. The difference between the Pratt-Arrow risk premium and that of Markowitz is negligible in this case.

If we repeat similar computations for the second risk in the above example, the Pratt-Arrow assumptions of a small, actuarially neutral risk are not closely approximated. Nevertheless, if we apply the Pratt-Arrow definition, the risk premium is calculated to be $324. The Markowitz risk premium for the same risk is the difference between expected wealth, $17,200, and the certainty equivalent wealth, $16,711, or $489. Now the dollar difference between the two risk premia is much larger.[10]

The above example illustrates the difference between risk aversion for small, actuarially neutral risks, where the Pratt-Arrow assumptions are closely approximated, and risk aversion in the large, where the magnitude of the gamble is large or where it is not actuarially neutral. In general, the Markowitz measure of a risk premium is superior for large or asymmetric risks. This does not mean that the Pratt-Arrow definition of risk aversion is not useful. As we have seen, the intuition provided by the definition of risk aversion was useful for distinguishing between various types of concave utility functions.

E. STOCHASTIC DOMINANCE

So far we have discussed the axioms of investor preference, then used them to develop cardinal utility functions, and finally employed the utility functions to measure risk premia and derive measures of risk aversion. Clearly, any investor, whether risk averse or not, will seek to maximize the expected utility of his or her wealth. The expected utility rule can be used to introduce the economics of choice under uncertainty. An asset (or portfolio) is said to be stochastically dominant over another if an individual receives greater wealth from it in every (ordered) state of nature. This definition is known as *first-order stochastic dominance*. Mathematically, asset x, with cumulative probability distribution $F_x(W)$, will be stochastically dominant over asset y, with cumulative probability distribution $G_y(W)$, for the set of all nondecreasing utility functions if

$$F_x(W) \le G_y(W) \qquad \text{for all } W,$$
$$F_x(W_i) < G_y(W_i) \qquad \text{for some } W_i. \qquad \textit{First-order stochastic dominance} \qquad (4.11)$$

In other words, the cumulative probability distribution (defined on wealth, W) for asset y always lies to the left of the cumulative distribution for x. If true, then x is said to dominate y. Figure 4.8 shows an example of first-order stochastic dominance assuming that the distribution of wealth provided by both assets is a (truncated) normal distribution. It is obvious from the figure that x dominates y because the cumulative distribution of y always lies to the left of x.

First-order stochastic dominance applies to all increasing utility functions. This means that individuals with any of the three utility functions in Fig. 4.6 would prefer asset x to asset y, because first-order stochastic dominance guarantees that the expected utility of wealth offered by x will be greater than that offered by y for all increasing utility functions. This fact can be illustrated by using Fig. 4.9 and the definition

---

[10] Had we calculated the cost of the gamble instead of the risk premium, we would have subtracted the certainty equivalent wealth, $16,711, from the individual's current wealth, $20,000, to find that the individual would have paid up to $3,289 to avoid the gamble.

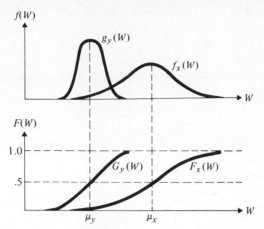

Figure 4.8
An example of first-order stochastic dominance.

of expected utility:

$$E[U(W)] \equiv \int_{-\infty}^{\infty} U(W)f(W)\,dW, \tag{4.12}$$

where

$U(W)$ = the utility function,

W = the level of wealth,

$f(W)$ = the frequency distribution of wealth.

The utility functions in Fig. 4.9 are linear, but they could just as easily be any of the set of increasing functions that we are comparing with any set of nonincreasing functions. Expected utility is the sum of the utilities of all possible levels of wealth weighted by their probability. For a given frequency of wealth, $f_i(W)$, in the top half of Fig. 4.9, the increasing utility function assigns higher utility to the level of wealth offered by asset x than by asset y. This is true for every frequency. Consequently, the expected utility of wealth from asset x is greater than that from asset y for the set of increasing utility functions (i.e., all utility functions that have a positive marginal utility of wealth). Of course, the opposite would be true for utility functions nonincreasing in wealth.

  Second-order stochastic dominance not only assumes utility functions where marginal utility of wealth is positive; it also assumes that total utility must increase at a decreasing rate. In other words, utility functions are nondecreasing and strictly concave. Thus individuals are assumed to be risk averse. Asset x will be stochastically dominant over asset y for all risk-averse investors if

$$\int_{-\infty}^{W_i} [G_y(W) - F_x(W)]\,dW \geq 0 \qquad \text{for all } W, \qquad \textit{Second-order stochastic} \tag{4.13}$$

$$G_y(W_i) \neq F_x(W_i) \qquad\qquad \text{for some } W_i. \qquad \textit{dominance}$$

This means that in order for asset x to dominate asset y for all risk-averse investors, the accumulated area under the cumulative probability distribution of y must be

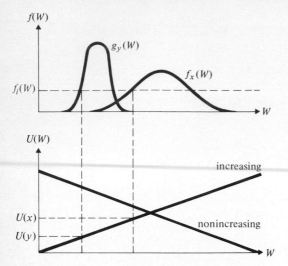

Figure 4.9
First-order stochastic dominance and expected
utility.

greater than the accumulated area for x, below any given level of wealth. This implies
that, unlike first-order stochastic dominance, the cumulative density functions can
cross. Figure 4.10 provides a graphic example, this time assuming normal distributions. Obviously, asset x will dominate asset y if an investor is risk averse because
they both offer the same expected level of wealth ($\mu_x = \mu_y$) and because y is riskier. It

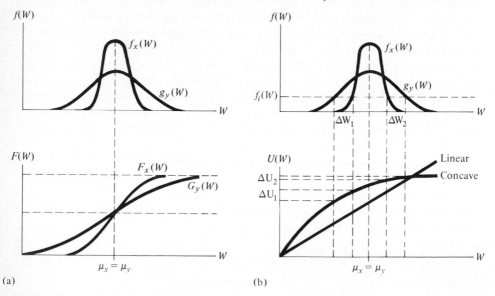

Figure 4.10
An example of second-order stochastic dominance.

$\int [G_y(W) - F_x(W)]\,dW$

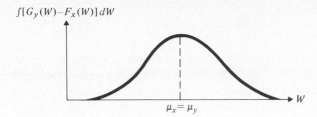

$\mu_x = \mu_y$

Figure 4.11
Graphical representation of the sum of the differences
in cumulative probabilities.

has greater variance. The second-order stochastic dominance criterion requires that the difference in areas under the cumulative density functions be positive below any level of wealth, W_i. Up to the mean, $G_y(W)$ is strictly greater than $F_x(W)$. Beyond the mean, the opposite is true. Figure 4.11 shows that the sum of the differences between the two cumulative density functions is always greater than or equal to zero; therefore x dominates y.

Figure 4.10(b) ties the concept of second-order stochastic dominance back to the notion of maximizing expected utility.[11] The concave utility function of a risk averter has the property that the increase in utility for constant changes in wealth declines as a function of wealth. Therefore if we select a given frequency of wealth such as $f_i(W)$, it maps out equal changes in wealth ΔW_1 and ΔW_2. The difference in utility between x and y below the mean is much greater than the difference in utility for the same change in wealth above the mean. Consequently, if we take the expected utility by pairing all such differences with equal probability, the expected utility of x is seen to be greater than the expected utility of y. If the individual were risk neutral, with a linear utility function, the differences in utility above and below the mean would always be equal. Hence a risk-neutral investor would be indifferent relative to x and y.

Stochastic dominance is an extremely important and powerful result. It is properly founded on the basis of expected utility maximization, and even more important, it applies to any probability distribution whatsoever. This is because it takes into account every point in the probability distribution. Furthermore, we can be sure that if an asset demonstrates second-order stochastic dominance, it will be preferred by all risk-averse investors, regardless of the specific shape of their utility functions. We could use stochastic dominance as the basis of a complete theory of how risk-averse investors choose among various risky alternatives. All we need to do is find the set of portfolios that is stochastically dominant and then select a portfolio from among those in the set.[12]

---

[11] The graphical presentation given here is intuitive and not meant to be a proof of the fact that second-order stochastic dominance maximizes expected utility for risk-averse investors. For proof, the reader is referred to Hanoch and Levy [1969].

[12] There is a growing body of literature that uses this concept. The interested reader is referred to Bawa [1975], Whitmore [1970], Porter, Wart, and Ferguson [1973], Levy and Kroll [1976], Vickson and Altman [1977], Jean [1975], and Kira and Ziemba [1977].

F. USING MEAN AND VARIANCE AS
CHOICE CRITERIA

If the distribution of returns offered by assets is jointly normal, then we can maximize expected utility simply by selecting the best combinations of mean and variance.[13] This is computationally much simpler than stochastic dominance but requires that we restrict ourselves to normal distributions. Every normal distribution can be completely described by two parameters: its mean and variance—return and risk. If we adopt utility functions that maximize expected utility of end-of-period wealth (assuming a single-period model), it is easy to show the relationship between wealth and return:

$$R_j = \frac{\tilde{W}_j - W_0}{W_0}.$$

If the end-of-period wealth from investing in asset j is normally distributed with mean $\bar{W}$ and variance σ_W^2, then the return on asset j will also be normally distributed with mean $E(R_j) = [(E(W_j)/W_0) - 1]$ and variance $\sigma_R^2 = (\sigma_W^2/W_0^2)$.

Assuming that the return on an asset is normally distributed with mean E and variance σ^2, we can write our utility function as[14]

$$U = U(R_j; E, \sigma).$$

Our expected utility is

$$E(U) = \int_{-\infty}^{\infty} U(R)f(R; E, \sigma)\,dR. \tag{4.14}$$

We would like to express the indifference curve of a risk-averse investor as a function of the mean and standard deviation of a distribution of returns. The indifference curve is a mapping of all combinations of risk and return (standard deviation or variance) that yield the same expected utility of wealth. Obviously, if the combinations offer identical expected utility, the investor will be indifferent between them. Figure 4.12 shows the end result of the following proofs, i.e., the indifference curves of a risk-averse investor.

We want to show that the marginal rate of substitution between return and risk is positive and that the indifference curves are convex. This can be done, first by converting the random return into a unit normal variable, Z, which has a mean of zero and variance of one.

$$\tilde{Z} = \frac{\tilde{R} - E}{\sigma}. \tag{4.15}$$

---

[13] By *jointly* normal we mean that all assets are individually normally distributed, and in addition, their interrelationships (covariances) obey the normal probability laws. This concept is developed further in Chapter 6.

[14] This proof can be found in Tobin [1958]. Also note that the proof applies equally well to any continuous, symmetric two-parameter distribution.

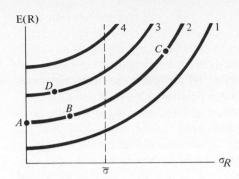

E(R)

Figure 4.12
Indifference curves for a risk-averse investor.

From this we see that

$$\tilde{R} = E + \sigma\tilde{Z}, \qquad \frac{dR}{dZ} = \sigma, \qquad dR = \sigma\,dZ,$$

and when $R = -\infty$, then $Z = -\infty$, and when $R = \infty$, then $Z = \infty$. Now, by using the change of variables technique from integral calculus, we can rewrite (4.14) as[15]

$$E(U) = \int_{-\infty}^{\infty} U(E + \sigma\tilde{Z})f(Z; 0, 1)\,dZ. \tag{4.16}$$

Next, we take the derivative of the expected utility with respect to a change in the standard deviation of return:[16]

$$\frac{dE(U)}{d\sigma} = \int_{-\infty}^{\infty} U'(E + \sigma\tilde{Z})\left(\frac{dE}{d\sigma} + \tilde{Z}\right)f(Z; 0, 1)\,dZ = 0. \tag{4.17}$$

An indifference curve is defined as the locus of points where the change in the expected utility is equal to zero. Therefore (4.17) has been set equal to zero, and the solution of the equation represents an indifference curve. Separating terms, we have

$$0 = \frac{dE}{d\sigma}\int_{-\infty}^{\infty} U'(E + \sigma\tilde{Z})f(Z; 0, 1)\,dZ + \int_{-\infty}^{\infty} U'(E + \sigma\tilde{Z})Zf(Z; 0, 1)\,dZ.$$

Therefore the slope of the indifference curve is

$$\frac{dE}{d\sigma} = -\frac{\int U'(E + \sigma\tilde{Z})Zf(Z; 0, 1)\,dZ}{\int U'(E + \sigma\tilde{Z})f(Z; 0, 1)\,dZ} > 0. \tag{4.18}$$

The denominator must be positive because of the assumption that marginal utility, $U'(E + \sigma\tilde{Z})$, must always be positive. People always prefer more return to less. The

---

[15] Since $f(R; E, \sigma) = (1/\sigma)f(Z; 0, 1)$, it follows that

$$E(U) = \int_{-\infty}^{\infty} U(E + \sigma\tilde{Z})f(Z; 0, 1)\frac{\sigma}{\sigma}\,dZ.$$

[16] $\partial f(Z)/\partial\sigma = 0.$

numerator will be negative (and therefore the entire ratio will be positive) only if we have a risk-averse investor with a strictly concave utility function. The marginal utility of every negative value of Z in Fig. 4.13 is greater than the marginal utility of an equally likely positive value of Z. Because this is true for every pair of outcomes $\pm Z$, the integral in the numerator of (4.18) is negative, and the (entire) numerator is positive. Consequently, the slope of a risk averter's indifference curve in Fig. 4.12, i.e., his or her marginal rate of substitution between mean and variance, is everywhere positive, excepting when $\sigma = 0$ where the slope is also zero.[17]

The indifference curves in Fig. 4.12 will be used throughout the remainder of the text to represent the theory of choice for risk-averse investors. Any points along a given indifference curve provide us with equal total utility. For example, we would not care whether we were at point A in Fig. 4.12, which has no risk, at point B with higher risk and return, or at point C. They all lie on the same indifference curve. Moving from right to left across the family of indifference curves provides us with increasing levels of expected utility. We would prefer point D on indifference curve 3 to point C on indifference curve 2, even though D has a lower return. The reason, of course, is that it has a much lower risk, which more than makes up for the lower return. The easiest way to see that expected utility increases from right to left is to fix the level of risk at $\bar{\sigma}$ and then note that the expected return increases as we move from curve 1 to curve 4. Although the indifference curves in Fig. 4.12 appear

---

[17] The convexity of the utility function can be shown as follows. Let (E_1, σ_1) and (E_2, σ_2) be two points on the same indifference curve so that they have the same expected utility. If a third point is constructed to be a weighted average of the first two, $(E_1 + E_2)/2$, $(\sigma_1 + \sigma_2)/2$, the indifference curve is convex, if for every Z,

$$\tfrac{1}{2}U(E_1 + \sigma_1 Z) + \tfrac{1}{2}U(E_2 + \sigma_2 Z) < U\left(\frac{E_1 + E_2}{2} + \frac{\sigma_1 + \sigma_2}{2} Z\right).$$

In the case of declining marginal utilities, this is obviously true because the utility of the second point, (E_2, σ_2), will be less than twice the utility of the first. Consequently,

$$E\left[U\left(\frac{E_1 + E_2}{2}, \frac{\sigma_1 + \sigma_2}{2}\right)\right] > E[U(E_1, \sigma_1)] = E[U(E_2, \sigma_2)],$$

and the third point, which is a weighted average of the first two, lies above the indifference curve. This is shown graphically in Fig. 4A.

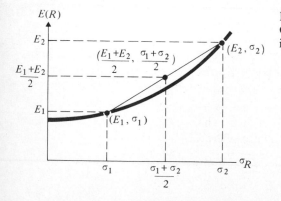

Figure 4A
Convexity of the risk averter's indifference curve.

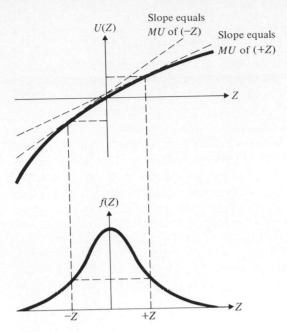

Figure 4.13
Graphic representation for
$\int U'(E + \sigma Z)Zf(Z; 0, 1)\,dZ < 0.$

to be parallel, they need not be. The only requirement is that they never touch or cross.

G. A MEAN VARIANCE PARADOX

Although it is convenient to characterize return and risk by the mean and variance of distributions of return offered by assets, it is not always correct. In fact, it is correct only when the returns have a normal distribution. Consider the following example. Two companies with equal total assets and exactly the same distribution of net operating income differ only with regard to their financial leverage. Table 4.2 shows their respective income statements in different, equally likely, states of nature.

The mean and standard deviation of earnings per share for firm A are $5 and $1.41, respectively. For firm B, they are $7 and $2.82. These alternatives are plotted in Fig. 4.14. According to the mean-variance criterion, individual I would be indifferent between the risk-return combinations offered by A and B. Individual II, who is less risk averse, would prefer alternative B, which has a greater return. Finally, individual III would prefer alternative A, which has lower risk. The paradox arises when we reexamine the earnings per share offered by the two firms. The earnings per share for firm B are equal to or greater than the earnings per share for firm A in every state of nature. Obviously, the mean-variance criterion provides misleading results. No investor with positive marginal utility would prefer firm A.

Table 4.2   Mean-Variance Paradox

	Economic State of Nature				
	Horrid	Bad	Average	Good	Great
Net operating income	$1200	$1600	$2000	$2400	$2800
Probability	.2	.2	.2	.2	.2
Firm A					
Interest expense	0	0	0	0	0
Earnings before tax	1200	1600	2000	2400	2800
Tax at 50%	−600	−800	−1000	−1200	−1400
Net income	$600	800	1000	1200	1400
Earnings per share (200 shares)	$3.00	$4.00	$5.00	$6.00	$7.00
Firm B					
Interest expense	−600	−600	−600	−600	−600
Earnings before tax	600	1000	1400	1800	2200
Tax at 50%	−300	−500	−700	−900	−1100
Net income	300	500	700	900	1100
Earnings per share (100 shares)	$3.00	$5.00	$7.00	$9.00	$11.00

Firm A			Firm B		
Assets	Liabilities		Assets	Liabilities	
	Debt	0		Debt	10,000
	Equity	20,000		Equity	10,000
$20,000		$20,000	$20,000		$20,000

   The trouble with trying to apply the mean-variance criterion to the above problem is that the distribution of outcomes is not normal. Instead, it is a rectangular
distribution with equal probabilities for each state of nature. However, we can use
second-order stochastic dominance regardless of the shape of the probability distri-

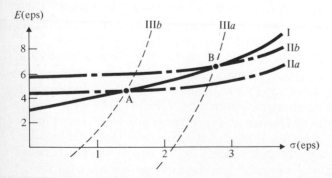

Figure 4.14
A mean-variance paradox.

Table 4.3   Using Second-Order Stochastic Dominance

Eps	Prob. (B)	Prob. (A)	F(B)	G(A)	F − G	∑ (F − G)
3.00	.2	.2	.2	.2	0	0
4.00	0	.2	.2	.4	−.2	−.2
5.00	.2	.2	.4	.6	−.2	−.4
6.00	0	.2	.4	.8	−.4	−.8
7.00	.2	.2	.6	1.0	−.4	−1.2
8.00	0	0	.6	1.0	−.4	−1.6
9.00	.2	0	.8	1.0	−.2	−1.8
10.00	0	0	.8	1.0	−.2	−2.0
11.00	.2	0	1.0	1.0	0	−2.0
	1.0	1.0				

bution.[18] This is done in Table 4.3. Because the accumulated area under the distribution of earnings per share offered by firm B is always less than or equal to the accumulated distribution for firm A, we can say that B clearly dominates A. The density functions and cumulative density functions are shown in Fig. 4.15.

This mean-variance paradox example demonstrates very clearly the shortcomings of a theory of choice that relies on the (somewhat heroic) assumption that returns

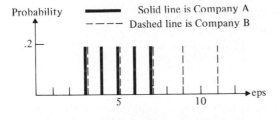

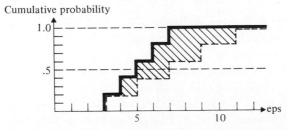

Figure 4.15
Stochastic dominance applied to the mean-variance paradox.

---

[18] First-order stochastic dominance also obtains in this example. We have used second-order dominance because we assume a risk-averse decision maker.

are normally distributed. Nevertheless, much of the remainder of this text will assume that returns are in fact normally distributed.

H. RECENT THINKING AND EMPIRICAL EVIDENCE

Utility theory is founded on the axioms of Von Neumann and Morgenstern [1947] and the elegant mathematics which follows logically from them. Furthermore, the basic results—increasing marginal utility, risk aversion, and decreasing absolute risk aversion—seem to conform to economists' casual empiricism. There has been almost no empirical testing of the axioms or of their implications, at least not by economists. Psychologists, however, have been busy testing the validity of the axioms. Do individuals actually behave as described by the axioms? The answer seems to be a resounding no—they do not.

Kahneman and Tversky [1979, 1986] point out that the way decisions are framed seems to matter for individual decision making. They give the following example where people are asked to decide between surgery and radiation therapy for cancer treatment.

Survival Frame

Surgery: Of 100 people having surgery, 90 live through the postoperative period, 68 are alive at the end of the first year, and 34 are alive at the end of five years.

Radiation Therapy: Of 100 people having radiation therapy, all live through the treatment, 77 are alive at the end of one year, and 22 are alive at the end of five years.

Mortality Frame

Surgery: Of 100 people having surgery, 10 die during surgery or the postoperative period, 32 die by the end of the first year, and 66 die by the end of five years.

Radiation Therapy: Of 100 people having radiation therapy, none die during treatment, 23 die by the end of one year, and 78 die by the end of five years.

The information in both frames is exactly the same, yet when presented with the survival frame, 18 percent preferred radiation, and when presented with the mortality frame, 44 percent preferred radiation—a significant difference. The framing effect was not smaller for experienced physicians or for statistically sophisticated business students.

If individual decision making is not adequately described by the Von Neumann and Morgenstern axioms, then it becomes necessary to rethink the descriptive validity of expected utility theory. No widely accepted answer to this problem has appeared, but it is safe to say that the foundations of mathematical utility theory have been shaken by the empirical evidence. Much work remains to be done.

SUMMARY

The logic of the theory of investor choice can best be summarized by listing the series of logical steps and assumptions necessary to derive the indifference curves of Fig. 4.12.

- First, the five axioms of rational behavior were described.
- The expected utility rule was derived from the axioms.
- Cardinal utility functions were derived from the axioms.
- We assumed positive marginal utility. This and the expected utility rule were used to argue that individuals will always maximize the expected utility of wealth.
- Risk premia were defined and a Pratt-Arrow measure of local risk aversion was developed.
- Stochastic dominance was shown to be a general theory of choice that maximizes expected utility for various classes of utility functions.
- Mean-variance indifference curves (which exhibit second-order stochastic dominance for normally distributed returns) were developed as a parametric theory of choice.

In Chapter 6 we shall use the mean-variance theory of choice as embodied in the mean-variance indifference curves to describe the manner in which investors actually choose optimal portfolios.

PROBLEM SET

4.1 State in your own words the minimum set of necessary conditions needed to obtain mean-variance indifference curves like those graphed in Fig. Q4.1.

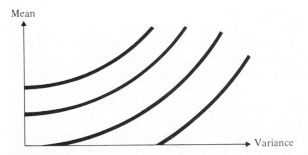

Figure Q4.1
Mean-variance indifference curves.

4.2 Figure 4.6 shows the utility curve of a risk lover. What does the indifference curve of a risk lover look like?

4.3 You have a logarithmic utility function $U(W) = \ln W$, and your current level of wealth is $5000.

a) Suppose you are exposed to a situation that results in a 50/50 chance of winning or losing $1000. If you can buy insurance that completely removes the risk for a fee of $125, will you buy it or take the gamble?

b) Suppose you accept the gamble outlined in (a) and lose, so that your wealth is reduced to $4000. If you are faced with the same gamble and have the same offer of insurance as before, will you buy the insurance the second time around?

4.4 Assume that you have a logarithmic utility function for wealth $U(W) = \ln(W)$ and that you are faced with a 50/50 chance of winning or losing $1,000. How much will you pay to avoid this risk if your current level of wealth is $10,000? How much would you pay if your level of wealth were $1,000,000?

4.5 Given the exponential utility function $U(W) = -e^{-aW}$.

a) Graph the function, assuming $a > 0$.

b) Does the function exhibit positive marginal utility and risk aversion?

c) Does the function have decreasing absolute risk aversion?

d) Does the function have constant relative risk aversion?

4.6 What kind of utility function of wealth might be consistent with an individual gambling and paying insurance at the same time?

4.7 Suppose that $A > B > C > D$ and that the utilities of these alternatives satisfy $U(A) + U(D) = U(B) + U(C)$. Is it true that $U(\frac{1}{2}B + \frac{1}{2}C)$ is greater than $U(\frac{1}{2}A + \frac{1}{2}D)$ because the former has a smaller variance? Why or why not?

4.8 A small businesswoman faces a 10% chance of having a fire that will reduce her net worth to $1.00, a 10% chance that fire will reduce it to $50,000, and an 80% chance that nothing detrimental will happen, so that her business will retain its worth of $100,000. What is the maximum amount she will pay for insurance if she has a logarithmic utility function? In other words, if $U(W) = \ln W$, compute the cost of the gamble. [*Note:* The insurance pays $99,999 in the first case; $50,000 in the second; and nothing in the third.]

4.9 If you are exposed to a 50/50 chance of gaining or losing $1000 and insurance that removes the risk costs $500, at what level of wealth will you be indifferent relative to taking the gamble or paying the insurance? That is, what is your certainty equivalent wealth? Assume your utility function is $U(W) = -W^{-1}$.

4.10 Consider a lottery that pays $2 if n consecutive heads turn up in $(n + 1)$ tosses of a fair coin (i.e., the sequence of coin flips ends with the first tail). If you have a logarithmic utility function, $U(W) = \ln W$, what is the utility of the expected payoff? What is the expected utility of the payoff?

4.11 (Our thanks to David Pyle, University of California, Berkeley, for providing this problem.) Mr. Casadesus's current wealth consists of his home, which is worth $50,000, and $20,000 in savings, which are earning 7% in a savings and loan account. His (one-year) homeowner's insurance is up for renewal, and he has the following estimates of the potential losses on his house owing to fire, storm, etc., during the period covered by the renewal:

Value of Loss, $	*Probability, %*
0	.98
5,000	.01
10,000	.005
50,000	.005

His insurance agent has quoted the following premiums:

Amount of Insurance, $	Premium, $
30,000	$30 + \text{AVL}_1^*$
40,000	$27 + \text{AVL}_2$
50,000	$24 + \text{AVL}_3$

* Actuarial value of loss = expected value of the *insurer's* loss.

Mr. Casadesus expects neither to save nor to dissave during the coming year, and he does not expect his home to change appreciably in value over this period. His utility for wealth at the end of the period covered by the renewal is logarithmic, i.e., $U(W) = \ln(W)$.

a) Given that the insurance company agrees with Mr. Casadesus's estimate of his losses, should he renew his policy (1) for the full value of his house, (2) for $40,000, or (3) for $30,000, or (4) should he cancel it?

b) Suppose that Mr. Casadesus had $320,000 in a savings account. Would this change his insurance decision?

c) If Mr. Casadesus has $20,000 in savings, and if his utility function is

$$U(W) = -200,000W^{-1},$$

should he renew his home insurance? And if so, for what amount of coverage?

[*Note:* Insurance covers the first x dollars of loss. For simplicity, assume that all losses occur at the end of the year and that the premium is paid at the beginning of the year.]

4.12 Assume that security returns are normally distributed. Compare portfolios A and B, using both first- and second-order stochastic dominance:

Case 1	Case 2	Case 3
$\sigma_A > \sigma_B$	$\sigma_A = \sigma_B$	$\sigma_A < \sigma_B$
$E_A = E_B$	$E_A > E_B$	$E_A < E_B$

4.13 Given the following probability distributions for risky assets X and Y:

Probability X_i	X_i	Probability Y_i	Y_i
.1	−10	.2	2
.4	5	.5	3
.3	10	.2	4
.2	12	.1	30

a) If the only available choice is 100% of your wealth in X or 100% in Y and you choose on the basis of mean and variance, which asset is preferred?

b) According to the second-order stochastic dominance criterion, how would you compare them?

4.14 You have estimated the following probabilities for earnings per share of companies A and B:

Probability	A	B
.1	0	−.50
.2	.50	−.25
.4	1.00	1.50
.2	2.00	3.00
.1	3.00	4.00

a) Calculate the mean and variance of the earnings per share for each company.

b) Explain how some investors might choose A and others might choose B if preferences are based on mean and variance.

c) Compare A and B, using the second-order stochastic dominance criterion.

4.15 Answer the following questions either true or false:

a) T _____ F _____ If asset A is stochastically dominant over asset B according to the second-order criterion, it is also dominant according to the first-order criterion.

b) T _____ F _____ If asset A has a higher mean and higher variance than asset B, it is stochastically dominant, according to the first-order criterion.

c) T _____ F _____ A risk-neutral investor will use second-order stochastic dominance as a decision criterion only if the returns of the underlying assets are normally distributed.

d) T _____ F _____ A second-order stochastic dominance criterion is consistent with utility functions that have positive marginal utility and risk aversion.

4.16 Consider the following two risky scenarios for future cash flows for a firm:

Project 1			*Project 2*	
Probability	Cash Flow, $		Probability	Cash Flow, $
.2	4,000		.4	0
.6	5,000		.2	5,000
.2	6,000		.4	10,000

Given that the firm has fixed debt payments of $8000, and limited liability, which scenario will shareholders choose and why? How would your answer change if there were not limited liability?

4.17 (Our thanks to Nils Hakansson, University of California, Berkeley, for providing this problem.) Two widows, each with $10,000 to invest, have been advised by a trusted friend to put their money into a one-year real estate trust which requires a minimum investment of $10,000. They have been offered a choice of six trusts with the following estimated yields:

Trust	*Probability That Yield Will Be*																	
	−2	−1	0	1	2	3	4	5	6	7	8	9	10	11	12	13	14
A							.4	.2	.2	.2							
B	.1		.1	.1		.1	.1				.1		.1	.1	.1	.1	
C							.2	.2	.2	.2	.2						
D		.2			.2					.1	.1		.1	.1			.2
E								.4		.6							
F		.2			.2					.1	.1		.1	.1		.1	.1

Before making up their minds, they have called on you for advice.

a) The first widow leaves you unsure as to whether she is risk averse. What advice can you give her?

b) The second widow shows definite risk aversion. What is your advice to her?

4.18

a) Reorder the six real estate trusts in Problem 4.17, using the mean-variance criterion.

b) Is the mean-variance ranking the same as that achieved by second-order stochastic dominance?

REFERENCES

Arrow, K. J., *Essays in the Theory of Risk-Bearing.* North-Holland, Amsterdam, 1971.

Bawa, V. J., "Optimal Rules for Ordering Uncertain Prospects," *Journal of Financial Economics,* March 1975, 95–121.

Fama, E. F., and M. H. Miller, *The Theory of Finance,* Chapter 5. Holt, Rinehart and Winston, New York, 1972.

Friedman, M., and L. J. Savage, "The Utility Analysis of Choices Involving Risk," *Journal of Political Economy,* August 1948, 279–304.

Friend, I., and M. Blume, "The Demand for Risky Assets," *American Economic Review,* December 1975, 900–922.

Hanoch, G., and H. Levy, "The Efficiency Analysis of Choices Involving Risk," *Review of Economic Studies,* 1969, 335–346.

Herstein, I. N., and J. Milnor, "An Axiomatic Approach to Expected Utility," *Econometrica,* April 1953, 291–297.

Jean, W., "Comparison of Moment and Stochastic Dominance Ranking Methods," *Journal of Financial and Quantitative Analysis,* March 1975, 151–162.

Kahneman, D., and A. Tversky, "Prospect Theory: An Analysis of Decision Under Risk," *Econometrica,* March 1979, 263–291.

Keeney, R. L., and H. Raiffa, *Decisions with Multiple Objectives: Preferences and Value Tradeoffs.* John Wiley and Sons, New York, 1976.

Kira, D., and W. T. Ziemba, "Equivalence among Alternative Portfolio Selection Criteria," in Levy and Sarnat, eds., *Financial Decision Making under Uncertainty.* Academic Press, New York, 1977, 151–161.

Levy, H., and Y. Kroll, "Stochastic Dominance with Riskless Assets," *Journal of Financial and Quantitative Analysis*, December 1976, 743–778.

Markowitz, H., *Portfolio Selection*. Yale University Press, New Haven, 1959.

Porter, R. B.; J. R. Wart; and D. L. Ferguson, "Efficient Algorithms for Conducting Stochastic Dominance Tests of Large Numbers of Portfolios," *Journal of Financial and Quantitative Analysis*, January 1973, 71–82.

Pratt, J. W., "Risk Aversion in the Small and in the Large," *Econometrica*, January–April, 1964, 122–136.

Rubin, P. H., and C. W. Paul II, "An Evolutionary Model of Taste for Risk," *Economic Inquiry*, October 1979, 585–596.

Tobin, J., "Liquidity Preference as a Behavior toward Risk," *Review of Economic Studies*, February 1958, 65–86.

Tversky, A., and D. Kahneman, "Rational Choice and the Framing of Decisions," *Journal of Business*, October 1986, S251–S278.

Vickson, R. G., "Stochastic Dominance for Decreasing Absolute Risk Aversion," *Journal of Financial and Quantitative Analysis*, December 1975, 799–812.

———, and M. Altman, "On the Relative Effectiveness of Stochastic Dominance Rules: Extension to Decreasingly Risk-Averse Utility Functions," *Journal of Financial and Quantitative Analysis*, March 1977, 73–84.

Von Neumann, J., and O. Morgenstern, *Theory of Games and Economic Behavior*. Princeton University Press, Princeton, N.J., 1947.

Walter, J. E., *Dividend Policy and Enterprise Valuation*. Wadsworth, Belmont, Calif., 1967.

Whitmore, G. A., "Third Degree Stochastic Dominance," *American Economic Review*, June 1970, 457–459.

———, and M. C. Findlay, *Stochastic Dominance*. Lexington Books, D.C. Heath and Co., Lexington, Mass., 1975.

Ziemba, W. T., and R. G. Vickson, eds., *Stochastic Optimization Models in Finance*. Academic Press, New York, 1975.

5

In this formulation the objects of choice are not derivative statistical measures of the probability distribution of consumption opportunities but rather the contingent consumption claims themselves set out in extensive form.

J. Hirshleifer, "Efficient Allocation of Capital in an Uncertain World," *American Economic Review*, May 1964, 80

State-Preference Theory[1]

Finance deals with investment decisions of individuals and firms linked through the supply and demand for securities in the capital market. Firms borrow capital for investment in real assets by *selling* securities; individuals obtain claims to firms' real assets by *investing* in securities. Thus securities present opportunities for intertemporal shifts of consumption through the financing of productive activities. Individual consumption/investment decisions that determine aggregate security demand, and firm investment decisions that determine aggregate security supply are both affected by security prices. By equating security supply and demand, security prices yield a consistent set of firm and individual investment decisions. In this chapter, we will analyze how optimal individual investment decisions and optimal firm investment decisions are determined under uncertainty for a given set of security prices.

In Chapter 4 we found that, under specified conditions, individual decision making under uncertainty is accomplished by maximizing *expected* utility of end-of-period wealth. This decision criterion was shown to be valid when individuals are rational, prefer more wealth to less, and follow the five axioms of choice under uncertainty. Implicitly, it was also assumed that individuals can assess a security's probability distribution of end-of-period payoffs. It was shown that the expected utility criterion is a very simple way of choosing among mutually exclusive investments having different probability distributions of end-of-period payoffs. By choosing the investment

---

[1] Ronald W. Masulis was the primary author of the chapter text and has benefited from lecture notes on this topic by Herbert Johnson.

with the highest expected utility, the optimal investment is determined, thus condensing a choice across N probability distributions of end-of-period payoffs into a comparison among N expected utility values.

In this and following chapters, we wish to move beyond the individual's choice problem of mutually exclusive investments to the more general problem of portfolio decision making, i.e., the optimal choice of investing in more than one risky security. This is equivalent to the problem of choosing an individual's probability distribution of end-of-period wealth that is consistent with the set of available risky securities and the individual's initial wealth. The individual's choice problem is to find that portfolio or linear combination of risky security quantities that is optimal, given his or her initial wealth and tastes. We assume a perfect capital market to ensure that there are no costs of portfolio construction.

A. UNCERTAINTY AND ALTERNATIVE FUTURE STATES

Securities inherently have a time dimension. The securities investment decisions of individuals are determined by their desired consumption over future time intervals. The passage of time involves uncertainty about the future and hence about the future value of a security investment. From the standpoint of the issuing firm and the individual investors the uncertain future value of a security can be represented as a vector of probable payoffs at some future date, and an individual's portfolio of investments is a matrix of possible payoffs on the different securities that compose the portfolio.

In the state-preference model, uncertainty takes the form of not knowing what the state of nature will be at some future date. To the investor a security is a set of possible payoffs, each one associated with a mutually exclusive state of nature. Once the uncertain state of the world is revealed, the payoff on the security is determined exactly. Thus a security represents a claim to a vector (or bundle) of state-contingent payoffs.

In the simplest case, there are two possible outcomes with probabilities π_1 and π_2 and therefore two mutually exclusive states of nature with probabilities π_1 and π_2. Take as an example an investment in a lottery ticket with outcomes ($10,000, $0). With probability π_1, state 1 is realized and the lottery ticket pays off $10,000; with probability $\pi_2 = 1 - \pi_1$, state 2 is realized and the lottery ticket pays off nothing (Fig. 5.1).

The probability of a state of nature occurring is thus equal to the probability of the associated end-of-period security payoff. The states of nature are assumed to capture the fundamental causes of economic uncertainty in the economy; e.g., state 1 could represent peace and state 2 could represent war, or state 1 could represent prosperity and state 2 could represent depression. Once the state of nature is known, the end-of-period payoff of each risky security is also known. By summing over individual security holdings and then over individuals, it follows that once the state of nature is known, individual and aggregate end-of-period wealth are also known.

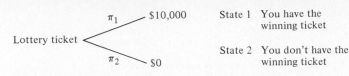

Figure 5.1
Elementary state–contingent claim.

In principle, there can be an infinite number of states of nature and thus an infinite number of end-of-period payoffs for a risky asset. This set of states must meet the critical properties of being mutually exclusive and exhaustive. That is to say, one and only one state of nature will be realized at the end of period, and the sum of the probabilities of the individual states of nature occurring equals one. It is also assumed that (1) individuals can associate an outcome from each security's probability distribution of its end-of-period payoff with each state of nature that could occur, and (2) individuals are only concerned about the amount of wealth they will have if a given state occurs; once their wealth is known they are otherwise indifferent as to which state of nature occurs (i.e., individuals have state-independent utility functions).[2]

B. DEFINITION OF PURE SECURITIES

Analytically, the generalization of the standard, timeless, microeconomic analysis under certainty to a multiperiod economy under uncertainty with securities markets is facilitated by the concept of a pure security. A *pure* or *primitive security* is defined as a security that pays $1 at the end of the period if a given state occurs and nothing if any other state occurs. The concept of the pure security allows the logical decomposition of market securities into portfolios of pure securities.[3] Thus every market security may be considered a combination of various pure securities.

In terms of state-preference theory, a security represents a position with regard to each possible future state of nature. In Fig. 5.2, market securities are defined with respect to the characteristics of their payoffs under each alternative future state. A market security thus consists of a set of payoff characteristics distributed over states of nature. The complexity of the security may range from numerous payoff characteristics in many states to no payoff at all in all but one state.

C. COMPLETE CAPITAL MARKET

In the state-preference framework, uncertainty about securities' future values is represented by a set of possible state-contingent payoffs. Linear combinations of this set of state-contingent *security* payoffs represent an individual's opportunity set of

---

[2] For example, if an individual's utility were a function of other individuals' wealth positions as well as one's own, then the utility function would generally be state dependent.

[3] Pure or primitive securities are often called Arrow-Debreu securities, since Arrow [1964] and Debreu [1959] set forth their original specification.

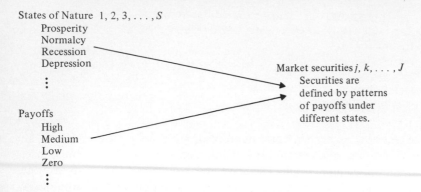

States of Nature 1, 2, 3, . . . , S
    Prosperity
    Normalcy
    Recession
    Depression
    ⋮

Market securities $j, k, . . . , J$
Securities are
defined by patterns
of payoffs under
different states.

Payoffs
    High
    Medium
    Low
    Zero
    ⋮

Figure 5.2
States, payoffs, and securities.

state-contingent *portfolio* payoffs. An important property of this opportunity set is determined by whether or not the capital market is complete. When the number of unique linearly independent securities is equal to the total number of alternative future states of nature, the market is said to be complete. For the case of three states of nature, suppose that a risk-free asset with payoff (1, 1, 1), an unemployment insurance contract with payoff (1, 0, 0), and risky debt with payoff (0, 1, 1) all exist, but no other securities can be traded. In this case we have three securities and three states of nature, but we do not have a complete market since the payoff on the risk-free asset is just the sum of the payoffs on the other two market securities; i.e., the three securities are not linearly independent. If, as in this example, the market is incomplete, then not every possible security payoff can be constructed from a portfolio of the existing securities. For example, the security payoff (0, 1, 0) cannot be obtained from (1, 1, 1), (1, 0, 0), and (0, 1, 1). The existing securities will, of course, have well-defined prices, but any possible new security not *spanned* by these securities (i.e., cannot be created from the existing securities) will not have a unique price.[4]

Suppose now that in addition to the security payoffs (1, 1, 1), (1, 0, 0), and (0, 1, 1), a stock with payoff (0, 1, 3) also exists. Then among these four securities there are three that are linearly independent state-contingent payoffs, and with three states the market is complete. Assuming the market is perfect, any pattern of returns can be created in a complete market. In particular, a complete set of pure securities with payoffs (1, 0, 0), (0, 1, 0), (0, 0, 1) can be created as linear combinations of existing securities. It takes some linear algebra to figure out how to obtain the pure securities from any arbitrary complete set of market securities, but once we know how to form them, it is easy to replicate any other security from a linear combination of the pure securities. For example: a security with payoff (a, b, c) can be replicated by buying (or short selling if a, b, or c is negative) a of (1, 0, 0), b of (0, 1, 0) and c of (0, 0, 1).[5]

---

[4] One person might think the security with payoff (0, 1, 0) is worth more than someone else does, but if the security cannot be formed from a portfolio of existing market securities, then these virtual prices that different people would assign to this hypothetical security need not be the same.

[5] See Appendix A to this chapter for a general method of determining whether a complete market exists.

Given a complete securities market, we could theoretically reduce the uncertainty about the value of our future wealth to zero. It does not make any difference which uncertain future state of nature will actually occur. That is, by dividing our wealth in a particular way among the available securities, we could, if we chose, construct a portfolio that was equivalent to holding equal amounts of all the pure securities. This portfolio would have the same payoff in every state even though the payoffs of individual securities varied over states.[6]

Without going through a complex solution process to attain the general equilibrium results that the concept of a pure security facilitates, we shall convey the role of the concept of a pure security in a more limited setting. We shall demonstrate how in a perfect and complete capital market the implicit price of a pure security can be derived from the prices of existing market securities and how the prices of other securities can then be developed from the implicit prices of pure securities.

D. DERIVATION OF PURE SECURITY PRICES

Given that we know the state-contingent payoff vectors of both the market securities and the pure securities, we wish to develop the relationship between the *prices* of the market securities and pure securities in a perfect and complete capital market.

The following notation will be used throughout this chapter:

p_s = prices of pure securities,

p_j = prices of market securities,

π_s = state probabilities—individuals' beliefs about the relative likelihoods
    of states occurring,

Q_s = number of pure securities.

Let us begin with an analogy. The Mistinback Company sells baskets of fruit, limiting its sales to only two types of baskets. Basket 1 is composed of 10 bananas and 20 apples and sells for $8. Basket 2 is composed of 30 bananas and 10 apples and sells for $9. The situation may be summarized by the payoffs set forth in Table 5.1.

Using the relationships in Table 5.1, we can solve for the prices of apples and bananas separately. Let us denote apples by A, bananas by B, the baskets of fruit by 1 and 2, and the quantity of apples and bananas in a basket by Q_{jA} and Q_{jB}, respectively. Using this notation, we can express the prices of the two baskets as follows:

$$p_1 = p_A Q_{1A} + p_B Q_{1B}, \qquad p_2 = p_A Q_{2A} + p_B Q_{2B}.$$

---

[6] While a complete market may appear to require an unreasonably large number of independent securities, Ross [1976] showed that in general if option contracts can be written on market securities and market securities have sufficiently variable payoffs across states, an infinite number of linearly independent security and option payoffs can be formed from a small number of securities.

Table 5.1   Payoffs in Relation to Prices of Baskets of Fruit

	Bananas	Apples	Prices*
Basket 1	10	20	$8
Basket 2	30	10	9

* The probabilities of the states are implicit in the prices.

Only p_A and p_B are unknown. Thus there are two equations and two unknowns, and the system is solvable as follows (substitute the known values in each equation):

$$\text{(1) } \$8 = p_A 20 + p_B 10, \qquad \text{(2) } \$9 = p_A 10 + p_B 30.$$

Subtract three times Eq. (1) from Eq. (2) to obtain p_A:

$$\$9 = p_A 10 + p_B 30$$
$$\underline{-\$24 = -p_A 60 - p_B 30}$$
$$-\$15 = -p_A 50$$

$$p_A = \$.30.$$

Then substituting the value of p_A into Eq. (1), we have

$$\$8 = (\$.30)20 + p_B 10 = \$6 + p_B 10,$$
$$\$2 = p_B 10,$$
$$p_B = \$.20.$$

Given that we know the prices of the market securities, we may now apply this same analysis to the problem of determining the implicit prices of the pure securities. Consider security j, which pays $10 if state 1 occurs and $20 if state 2 occurs; its price is $8. Security k pays $30 if state 1 occurs and $10 if state 2 occurs; its price is $9. Note that state 1 might be a gross national product (GNP) growth of 8% in real terms during the year, whereas state 2 might represent a GNP growth rate of only 1% in real terms. This information is summarized in Table 5.2.

Any individual security is similar to a mixed basket of goods with regard to alternative future states of nature. Recall that a pure security pays $1 if a specified state occurs and nothing if any other state occurs. We may proceed to determine the price of a pure security in a manner analogous to that employed for the fruit baskets.

Table 5.2   Payoff Table for Securities j and k

Security	State 1	State 2	
j	$10	$20	$p_j = \$8$
k	$30	$10	$p_k = \$9$

The equations for determining the price for two pure securities related to the situation described are

$$p_1 Q_{j1} + p_2 Q_{j2} = p_j,$$

$$p_1 Q_{k1} + p_2 Q_{k2} = p_k,$$

where Q_{j1} represents the quantity of pure securities paying \$1 in state 1 included in security j. Proceeding analogously to the situation for the fruit baskets, we insert values into the two equations. Substituting the respective payoffs for securities j and k, we obtain \$.20 as the price of pure security 1 and \$.30 as the price of pure security 2:

$$p_1 10 + p_2 20 = \$8,$$

$$p_1 30 + p_2 10 = \$9,$$

$$p_1 = \$.20, \qquad p_2 = \$.30.$$

It should be emphasized that the p_1 of \$.20 and the p_2 of \$.30 are the prices of the two pure securities and not the prices of the market securities j and k. Securities j and k represent portfolios of pure securities. Any actual security provides different payoffs for different future states. But under appropriately defined conditions, the prices of market securities permit us to determine the prices of pure securities. Thus our results indicate that for pure security 1 a \$.20 payment is required for a promise of a payoff of \$1 if state 1 occurs and nothing if any other states occur. The concept of pure security is useful for analytical purposes as well as for providing a simple description of uncertainty for financial analysis.

E. NO ARBITRAGE PROFIT CONDITION

Capital market equilibrium requires that market prices be set so that supply equals demand for each individual security. In the context of the state-preference framework, one condition necessary for market equilibrium requires that any two securities or portfolios with the same state-contingent payoff vectors must be priced identically.[7] Otherwise, everyone would want to buy the security or portfolio with the lower price and to sell the security or portfolio with the higher price. If both securities or portfolios are in positive supply, such prices cannot represent an equilibrium. This condition is often called the *single-price law of markets*.

If short selling is allowed in the capital market, we can obtain a second related necessary condition for market equilibrium, i.e., the absence of any riskless arbitrage profit opportunity. To short sell a security, an individual borrows the security from a current owner and then immediately sells the security in the capital market at the current price. Then, at a later date, the individual goes back to the capital market

---

[7] This condition implies the absence of any first-order stochastically dominated market securities. Otherwise the former payoff per dollar of investment would exceed the latter payoff per dollar of investment in every state. The latter security would be first-order stochastically dominated by the former security.

and repurchases the security at the then-current market price and immediately returns the security to the lender. If the security price fell over the period of the short sale, the individual makes a profit; if the security price rose, he or she takes a loss. In either case the short seller's gain or loss is always the negative of the owner's gain or loss over this same period.

When two portfolios, A and B, sell at different prices, where $p_A > p_B$, but have identical state-contingent payoff vectors, we could short sell the more expensive portfolio and realize a cash flow of p_A, then buy the less expensive portfolio, for a negative cash flow of p_B. We would realize a positive net cash flow of $(p_A - p_B)$, and at the end of the period, we could at no risk take our payoff from owning portfolio B to *exactly* repay our short position in portfolio A. Thus the positive net cash flow at the beginning of the period represents a riskless arbitrage profit opportunity. Since all investors are assumed to prefer more wealth to less, this arbitrage opportunity is inconsistent with market equilibrium.

In a perfect and complete capital market, any market security's payoff vector can be exactly replicated by a portfolio of pure securities. Thus it follows that when short selling is allowed, the no–arbitrage profit condition requires that the price of the market security be equal to the price of any linear combination of pure securities that replicates the market security's payoff vector.

F. ECONOMIC DETERMINANTS OF SECURITY PRICES

To gain an understanding of what determines the price of a market security, we will first consider what determines the price of individual pure securities. Since a market security can always be constructed from the set of pure securities in a complete market, we can then answer the first question as well.

The prices of the pure securities will be determined by trading among individuals. Even if these pure securities themselves are not directly traded, we can still infer prices for them in a complete market from the prices of the market securities that *are* traded. The prices of pure securities will be shown to depend on

1. Time preferences for consumption and the productivity of capital;
2. Expectations as to the probability that a particular state will occur;
3. Individuals' attitudes toward risk, given the variability across states of aggregate end-of-period wealth.

To understand how (1) affects security prices, we need to recognize that a riskless security can always be constructed in a complete capital market simply by forming a portfolio composed of one pure security for each state. Hence the payoff on this portfolio is riskless since a dollar will be paid regardless of what state is realized. In the case of three states the price of this riskless portfolio is the sum of the prices of the three individual pure securities—$p_1 + p_2 + p_3 = .8$, for example. The price of a riskless claim to a dollar at the end of the period is just the present value of a dollar discounted at the risk-free rate r, that is to say, $1/(1 + r) = p_1 + p_2 + p_3$; so for the above example $r = 25\%$. In general the risk-free interest rate is found from $1/(1 + r) = \sum p_s$. If there is positive time value of money, the riskless interest rate will be positive. The actual size of this interest rate will reflect individual time preferences for consumption and the productivity of capital, just as is the case in a simple world of certainty.[8] Thus one determinant of the price of a pure security paying a dollar if state s occurs is the market discounted rate on a certain end-of-period dollar payoff.

The second determinant of a pure security's price, and a cause for differences in security prices, is individuals' beliefs concerning the relative likelihood of different states occurring. These beliefs are often termed *state probabilities*, π_s. Individuals' subjective beliefs concerning state probabilities can differ in principle. However, the simplest case is one in which individuals agree on the relative likelihoods of states. This assumption is termed *homogeneous expectations* and implies that there is a well-defined set of state probabilities known to all individuals in the capital market. Under the assumption of homogeneous expectations the price of a pure (state-contingent) security, p_s, can be decomposed into the probability of the state, π_s, and the price, θ_s, of an expected dollar payoff contingent on state s occurring, $p_s = \pi_s \cdot \theta_s$. This follows from the fact that pure security s pays a dollar only when s is realized. Thus the expected end-of-period payoff on pure security s is a dollar multiplied by the probability of state s occurring. This implies that we can decompose the end-of-period expected payoff into an expected payoff of a dollar and the probability of state s. Even when prices of expected dollar payoffs contingent on a particular state s occurring are the same across states ($\theta_s = \theta_t$; for all s and t), the prices of pure securities will differ as long as the probabilities of states occurring are not all identical ($\pi_s \neq \pi_t$; for all s and t).

A useful alternative way to see this point is to recognize that the price of a pure security is equal to its *expected* end-of-period payoff discounted to the present at its expected rate of return

$$p_s = \frac{\$1 \cdot \pi_s}{1 + E(R_s)},$$

where $0 < p_s < 1$. Thus the pure security's expected rate of return is

$$E(R_s) = \frac{\$1 \cdot \pi_s}{p_s} - 1 = \frac{\$1}{\theta_s} - 1, \quad \text{where} \quad 0 < \theta_s < 1,$$

since $p_s = \pi_s\theta_s$ under the assumption of homogeneous expectations. So if the θ_s's were identical across states, the expected rates of return would be equal for all pure securities. But given that the probabilities across states differ, the expected payoffs across pure securities must also differ. If expected payoffs vary, expected rates of return can

---

[8] The property that individuals prefer to consume a dollar of resources today, rather than consume the same dollar of resources tomorrow, is called time preference for consumption. As discussed in Chapter 1, an individual's marginal rate of time preference for consumption is equal to his or her marginal rate of substitution of current consumption and *certain* end-of-period consumption. In a perfect capital market, it was also shown that the marginal rates of time preference for all individuals are equal to the market interest rate.

be the same only when the prices of the pure securities vary proportionally with the state probabilities.

The third determinant of security prices, and a second cause for differences in these prices, is individuals' attitudes toward risk when there is variability in aggregate wealth across states. Assuming that individuals are risk averse, they will diversify by investing in some of each pure security to ensure that they are not penniless regardless of what state is realized.[9] In fact, if the prices, θ_s's, of expected payoffs of a dollar contingent on a particular state occurring were the same for all states (and thus the expected rates of return of pure securities are all equal), then each risk-averse individual would want to invest in an equal number of each pure security so as to eliminate all uncertainty about his or her future wealth. Not everyone can do this, however, since aggregate wealth is not the same in every state; i.e., there is *nondiversifiable risk* in the economy and it must be borne by someone. Consider the following example. End-of-period aggregate wealth can be one, two, or three trillion dollars, depending on whether the depressed, normal, or prosperous state occurs; then the average investor must hold a portfolio with a payoff vector of the form $(X, 2X, 3X)$. Because individuals are risk averse, dollar payoffs are more valuable in states where they have relatively low wealth, which in this example is state 1. In order for people to be induced to bear the risk associated with a payoff vector of form $(X, 2X, 3X)$, pure security prices must be adjusted to make the state 1 security relatively expensive and the state 3 security relatively cheap. In other words, to increase demand for the relatively abundant state 3 securities, prices must adjust to lower the expected rate of return on state 1 securities and to raise the expected rate of return on state 3 securities.

If aggregate wealth were the same in some states, then risk-averse investors would want to hold the same number of pure securities for these states and there would be no reason for prices of expected dollar payoffs to be different in these states. Investors would not want to hold unequal numbers of claims to the states with the same aggregate wealth because this would mean bearing risk that could be diversified away, and there is no reason to expect a reward for bearing *diversifiable risk*. So it is the prospect of a higher portfolio expected return that induces the risk-averse investors to bear nondiversifiable risk. Thus risk aversion combined with variability in end-of-period aggregate wealth causes variation in the prices (θ_s's) of dollar expected payoffs across states, negatively related to the aggregate end-of-period wealth or aggregate payoffs across states. This in turn causes like variations in the pure security prices.

There is a very important condition implicit in the previous discussion. We found that when investors are risk averse, securities that pay off relatively more in states with low aggregate wealth have relatively low expected rates of return, whereas securities that pay off relatively more in states with high aggregate wealth have relatively high expected rates of return. Since aggregate wealth is equal to the sum of the payoffs on all market securities, it is also termed the payoff on the *market portfolio*. Securities with state-contingent payoffs positively related to the state-contingent payoffs on the market portfolio, and which therefore involve significant nondiversifiable risk bearing, have higher expected rates of return than securities that have payoffs nega-

---

[9] This also requires the utility function to exhibit infinite *marginal* utility at a zero wealth level.

tively or less positively related to the payoffs on the market portfolio, and which therefore involve little nondiversifiable risk bearing. We will return to this important condition in Chapter 7.

It follows from this analysis that a pure security price can be decomposed into three factors:

$$p_s = \pi_s \theta_s = \frac{\$1\pi_s}{1 + E(R_s)} = \frac{\$1}{1 + r}\,\pi_s\left[\frac{1 + r}{1 + E(R_s)}\right]$$

$$= \frac{\$1}{1 + r}\,\pi_s\left[1 - \frac{E(R_s) - r}{1 + E(R_s)}\right], \quad \text{where} \quad E(R_s) \geq r.$$

The first factor is an end-of-period dollar payoff discounted to the present at the riskless rate. It is multiplied by the second factor, which is the probability of payoff. The third factor, in brackets, is a risk adjustment factor. Note that if investors are all risk neutral, the expected rate of return on all securities will be equal to the riskless interest rate, in which case the above risk adjustment factor (i.e., the factor in brackets) becomes one. In summary, security prices are affected by (1) the time value of money, (2) the probability beliefs about state-contingent payoffs, and (3) individual preferences toward risk and the level of variability in aggregate state-contingent payoffs or wealth (i.e., the level of nondiversifiable risk in the economy).

G. OPTIMAL PORTFOLIO DECISIONS

Now that we have developed the basic structure of state-preference theory, we will return to the problem of optimal portfolio choice in a perfect and complete capital market. This will then be followed by an analysis of a firm's optimal investment problem, also in a perfect and complete capital market. Since any portfolio payoff pattern can be constructed from the existing market securities or from a full set of pure securities in a complete capital market, we can obtain the same optimal portfolio position whether we frame the analysis in terms of market securities or pure securities. Since pure securities are much simpler to analyze, we will phrase the optimal portfolio problem in terms of these securities. Thus we can write an individual's expected utility of end-of-period wealth as $\sum \pi_s U(Q_s)$, where $Q_s =$ number of pure securities paying a dollar if state s occurs. In this context Q_s represents the number of state s pure securities the individual buys as well as his or her end-of-period wealth if state s occurs.

Now consider the problem we face when we must decide how much of our initial wealth, W_0, to spend for current consumption, C, and what portfolio of securities to hold for the future. We wish to solve the problem[10]

$$\text{MAX}\left[u(C) + \sum_s \pi_s U(Q_s)\right] \tag{5.1}$$

---

[10] This formulation assumes that the utility function is separable into utility of current consumption and utility of end-of-period consumption. In principle, the utility functions, $u(C)$ and $U(Q_s)$, can be different functions.

subject to

$$\sum_s p_s Q_s + \$1C = W_0. \tag{5.2}$$

That is, we are maximizing our expected utility of current and future consumption subject to our wealth constraint. Our portfolio decision consists of the choices we make for Q_s, the number of pure securities we buy for each state s. Note that there is no explicit discounting of future utility, but any such discounting could be absorbed in the functional form for $U(Q_s)$. In addition, the p_s's include an implicit market discount rate. There is no need to take an expectation over $u(C)$, our utility of current consumption, since there is no uncertainty concerning the present.

There are two ways to maximize expected utility subject to a wealth constraint. We could solve (5.2) for one of the Q_s's, say Q_1, and then eliminate this variable from (5.1). Sometimes this is the easiest way, but more often it is easier to use the Lagrange multiplier method (see Appendix D at the end of the book):

$$L = u(C) + \sum_s \pi_s U(Q_s) - \lambda \left(\sum_s p_s Q_s + \$1C - W_0 \right), \tag{5.3}$$

where λ is called a Lagrange multiplier. The Lagrange multiplier λ is a measure of how much our utility would increase if our initial wealth were increased by \$1. To obtain the investor's optimal choice of C and Q_s's, we take the partial derivatives with respect to each of these variables and set them equal to zero. Taking the partial derivative with respect to C yields

$$\frac{\partial L}{\partial C} = u'(C) - \$1\lambda = 0, \tag{5.4}$$

where the prime denotes partial differentiation with respect to the argument of the function. Next, we take partial derivatives with respect to Q_1, Q_2, and so on. For each Q_t, we will pick up one term from the expected utility and one from the wealth constraint (all other terms vanish):

$$\frac{\partial L}{\partial Q_t} = \pi_t U'(Q_t) - \lambda p_t = 0, \tag{5.5}$$

where $\pi_t U'(Q_t)$ = expected marginal utility of an investment Q_t in pure security s. We also take the partial derivative with respect to λ:

$$\frac{\partial L}{\partial \lambda} = \left(\sum_s p_s Q_s + \$1C - W_0 \right) = 0. \tag{5.6}$$

This just gives us back the wealth constraint. These first-order conditions allow us to determine the individual's optimal consumption/investment choices.[11]

As an example, consider an investor with a logarithmic utility function of wealth and initial wealth of \$10,000. Assume a two-state world where the pure security prices

---

[11] We also are assuming that the second-order conditions for a maximum hold.

are .4 and .6 and the state probabilities are $\frac{1}{3}$ and $\frac{2}{3}$, respectively. The Lagrangian function is

$$L = \ln C + \tfrac{1}{3} \ln Q_1 + \tfrac{2}{3} \ln Q_2 - \lambda(.4Q_1 + .6Q_2 + C - 10{,}000),$$

and the first-order conditions are

(a) $\dfrac{\partial L}{\partial C} = \dfrac{1}{C} - \lambda = 0,$ which implies $C = \dfrac{1}{\lambda},$

(b) $\dfrac{\partial L}{\partial Q_1} = \dfrac{1}{3Q_1} - .4\lambda = 0,$ which implies $Q_1 = \dfrac{1}{1.2\lambda},$

(c) $\dfrac{\partial L}{\partial Q_2} = \dfrac{2}{3Q_2} - .6\lambda = 0,$ which implies $Q_2 = \dfrac{1}{.9\lambda},$

(d) $\dfrac{\partial L}{\partial \lambda} = 10{,}000 - C - .4Q_1 - .6Q_2 = 0.$

Substituting Eqs. (a), (b), and (c) into (d) yields

$$\text{(d')} \quad \frac{1}{\lambda} + \frac{.4}{1.2\lambda} + \frac{.6}{.9\lambda} = 10{,}000,$$

and multiplying by λ yields

$$\text{(d'')} \quad 1 + \tfrac{1}{3} + \tfrac{2}{3} = 10{,}000\lambda, \quad \text{which yields} \quad \lambda = \frac{1}{5{,}000}.$$

Now, substituting this value of λ back into Eqs. (a), (b), and (c) yields the optimal consumption and investment choices, $C = \$5{,}000$, $Q_1 = 4166.7$, and $Q_2 = 5555.5$. Substituting these quantities back into the wealth constraint verifies that this is indeed a feasible solution. The investor in this problem divides his or her wealth equally between current and future consumption, which is what we should expect since the risk-free interest rate is zero [i.e., $\sum p_s = 1 = 1/(1 + r)$] and there is no time preference for consumption in this logarithmic utility function. However, the investor does buy more of the state 2 pure security since the expected rate of return on the state 2 pure security is greater. Because the utility function exhibits risk aversion, the investor also invests some of his or her wealth in the state 1 pure security.

In this example we assumed that the investor is a price taker. In a general equilibrium framework, the prices of the pure securities would be determined as part of the problem; i.e., they would be *endogenous.* The prices would be determined as a result of individuals' constrained expected utility maximization (which determines the aggregate demands for securities), and firms' optimal investment decisions (which determine the aggregate supplies of securities). The critical condition required for equilibrium is that the supply of each market security equal its aggregate demand. In a complete capital market this equilibrium condition can be restated by saying that the aggregate supply of each pure security is equal to its aggregate demand.

H. PORTFOLIO OPTIMALITY CONDITIONS AND PORTFOLIO SEPARATION

In a complete capital market, we can obtain a number of important portfolio optimality conditions. These conditions hold for any risk-averse expected utility maximizer. Rewriting Eq. (5.4) and Eq. (5.5) in terms of λ and eliminating λ yields two sets of portfolio optimality conditions:

$$\frac{\pi_t U'(Q_t)}{u'(C)} = \frac{p_t}{\$1} \quad \text{for any state } t \tag{5.7}$$

and

$$\frac{\pi_t U'(Q_t)}{\pi_s U'(Q_s)} = \frac{p_t}{p_s} \quad \text{for any two states } s \text{ and } t. \tag{5.8}$$

In both cases, the optimal allocation of wealth represents choosing C and the Q_s's so that the ratio of expected marginal utilities equals the ratio of market prices for the C and the Q_s's. That is, the optimal consumption and investment choices involve choosing points on the various indifference curves (curves of constant *expected* utility) that are tangent to the associated market lines. This is equivalent to choosing consumption and investment weights so that the slopes of the indifference curves (which are defined as the negative of the marginal rates of substitution) representing current consumption and future consumption contingent on state t (as in Fig. 5.3) or representing future consumption contingent on state s and state t (as in Fig. 5.4) are equal to the slopes of the respective market lines (representing the market exchange rates, e.g., $-p_t/p_s$).

An alternative way of stating the optimality conditions of the above portfolio is that the expected marginal utilities of wealth in state s, divided by the price of the state s pure security, should be equal across all states, and this ratio should also be equal to the marginal utility of current consumption. This is a reasonable result; if expected marginal utility per pure security price were high in one state and low

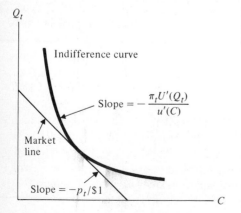

Figure 5.3
Optimal consumption/investment decisions.

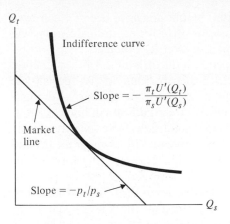

Figure 5.4
Optimal portfolio decisions.

in another, then we must not have maximized expected utility. We should increase investment in the high expected marginal utility security at the expense of the security yielding low expected marginal utility. But as we do that, we lower expected marginal utility where it is high and raise it where it is low, because a risk-averse investor's marginal utility decreases with wealth (his or her utility function has a positive but decreasing slope). Finally, when Eq. (5.8) is satisfied, there is no way left to increase expected utility.[12]

When investors' portfolio choices over risky securities are independent of their individual wealth positions, we have a condition known as *portfolio separation*. This condition requires that there are either additional restrictions on investor preferences or additional restrictions on security return distributions.[13] Under portfolio separation, investors choose among only a few basic portfolios of market securities. Thus the importance of having a complete market is greatly decreased. Recall that when capital markets are incomplete, individuals are limited in their choices of state-contingent payoff patterns to those payoff patterns that can be constructed as linear combinations of existing market securities. However, with portfolio separation, investors will

---

[12] This entire procedure will ordinarily not work if the investor is risk neutral instead of risk averse. A risk-neutral investor will plunge entirely into the security with the highest expected return. He or she would like to invest even more in this security but, being already fully invested in it, cannot do so. Equation (5.8) will not hold for risk neutrality.

[13] Cass and Stiglitz [1970] proved that for arbitrary security return distributions, utility functions with the property of linear risk tolerance yield portfolio separation. The risk tolerance of the utility function is the reciprocal of the Pratt-Arrow measure of absolute risk aversion discussed in Chapter 4. Thus a linear risk-tolerance utility function can be expressed as a *linear* function of wealth:

$$-U'(W)/U''(W) = a + bW. \tag{5.9}$$

If investors also have homogeneous expectations about state probabilities and all investors have the same b, then there is *two-fund separation* where all investors hold combinations of two basic portfolios.

Utility functions exhibiting linear risk tolerance include the quadratic, logarithmic, power, and exponential functions. Ross [1976] proved that for arbitrary risk-averse utility functions a number of classes of security return distributions (including the normal distribution, some stable Paretian distributions, and some distributions that are not stable Paretian, e.g., fat-tailed distributions with relatively more extreme values) yield portfolio separation.

often find that the infeasible payoff opportunities would not have been chosen even if they were available. Thus under portfolio separation, investor portfolio decisions will often be unaffected by whether or not the capital market is complete.

Portfolio separation has been shown to depend on the form of the utility function of individuals and the form of the security return distributions. In the special case where investor utility functions of wealth are quadratic, or security returns are joint-normally distributed, portfolio separation obtains. With the addition of homogeneous expectations, portfolio separation provides sufficient conditions for a security-pricing equation. This security-pricing relationship can be expressed in terms of means and variances and is called the *capital asset pricing model*.[14] The resulting form of the security-pricing equation is particularly convenient for formulating testable propositions and conducting empirical studies. As we shall discuss in the following chapters, many of the implications of portfolio separation in capital markets appear to be consistent with observed behavior and have been supported by empirical tests.

I. FIRM VALUATION, THE FISHER SEPARATION PRINCIPLE, AND OPTIMAL INVESTMENT DECISIONS[15]

In state-preference theory, individuals save by purchasing firm securities. Firms obtain resources for investment by issuing securities. Securities are precisely defined as conditional or unconditional payoffs in terms of alternative future states of nature. All individual and firm decisions are made, and all trading occurs at the beginning of the period. Consumers maximize their expected utility of present and future consumption and are characterized by their initial endowments (wealth) and their preferences. Firms are characterized by production functions that define the ability to transform current resources into state-contingent future consumption goods; e.g., where I_j is initial investment, $Q_{sj} = \phi_j(I_j, s)$. Total state-contingent output produced by a firm must equal the sum of the payoffs from all securities issued by a firm.

Firms maximize an objective function that, in its most general form, is maximization of the expected utility of its current shareholders. To do this it may appear that firms would need to know the utility functions of all their current shareholders. However, in Chapter 1 it was shown that in a perfect capital market (a frictionless and perfectly competitive market) under certainty, actions that maximize the price of the firm's shares maximize both the wealth and the utility of each current shareholder. So managers need not be concerned with the specific preferences of their shareholders but need only know the market discount rate and the cash flows of their investment projects to make optimal investment decisions. This separation of investment/operating decisions of firms from shareholder preferences or tastes is termed the *Fisher separation principle*.

---

[14] The capital asset pricing model is discussed in detail in Chapter 7.

[15] Hirshleifer [1964, 1965, 1966] and Myers [1968] were among the first papers to apply state-preference theory to corporate finance problems.

In shifting from firm decision making under certainty to decision making under uncertainty, it is important to know under what conditions, if any, Fisher separation continues to hold. It can be shown that firms that are maximizing the price of current shares are also maximizing current shareholders' *expected* utility when the capital market is (1) perfectly competitive and frictionless and (2) complete. The first condition ensures that firm actions will not be perceived to affect other firms' market security prices, whereas the second ensures that the state-space "spanned" by the existing set of linearly independent market securities (i.e., the set of risk opportunities) is unaffected by the firm's actions. Thus firm actions affect shareholders' expected utility only by affecting their wealth through changes in the firm's current share price. This is analogous to the certainty case in Chapter 1.

The two conditions of a perfect and complete capital market ensure that the prices of a full set of pure securities can be obtained from the prices of the market securities, and vice versa, given the state-contingent payoff vectors of the market securities. As a result the firm's objective function of maximizing current share price can be phrased in terms of a portfolio of pure securities that replicates its shares. The firm's objective function then becomes $\sum Q_{js}p_s$, where Q_{js} is defined as the state s–contingent end-of-period payoff on firm j's existing securities. In this formulation the price of a firm's current shares is determined by (1) the firm's state-contingent production function $Q_{js} = \phi_j(I_j, s)$, which transforms current resources into state-contingent future payoffs, and (2) the initial investment I_j, which represents the current cost to the firm of producing its state-contingent payoff. It follows that the price Y_j, for which the current owners could sell the firm prior to making the investment I_j, is

$$Y_j = \sum_s p_s Q_{js} - I_j, \tag{5.10}$$

where the firm's technological constraints are captured in its production function $Q_{js} = \phi_j(I_j, s)$.

For divisible investment projects, the production function is assumed to be a continuous differentiable function of I_j that exhibits diminishing returns to scale and has the property that zero investment yields zero output. The firm's optimal investment scale is determined by the first-order condition

$$\frac{dY_j}{dI_j} = \sum_s p_s \phi_j'(I_j, s) - 1 = 0. \tag{5.11}$$

For indivisible investment projects with finite scale the optimal investment rule is to accept all projects with positive net present value. In this context, (5.10) represents the net present value of the project's state-contingent net cash flow.

It is important to note that acceptance of positive NPV investments increases the price of the firm's current stock and therefore the wealth and expected utility of all current shareholders in a perfect and complete capital market. Since all shareholders are made better off by these investment decisions, these firm investment decisions are unanimously supported by all the firm's current shareholders. However, if the capital market is incomplete or imperfect, this is not necessarily true, because the firm's investment decisions may affect the price of other firms' shares or the feasible set of

**Table 5.3   Firm A's Stock and Investment
Project Payoffs**

States of Nature	State-Contingent Payoffs on Firm A's	
	Stock	Proposed Investment Project
State 1	100	10
State 2	30	12

Firm A's stock price = 62; initial investment cost
of its project = 10.

**Table 5.4   Firm B's Stock and Investment
Project Payoffs**

States of Nature	State-Contingent Payoffs on Firm B's	
	Stock	Proposed Investment Project
State 1	40	12
State 2	90	6

Firm B's stock price = 56; initial investment cost
of its project = 8.

state-contingent payoffs. As a result, increasing the price of a firm's shares may *not* increase the wealth of all current shareholders (since the prices of some of their other shareholdings may fall) and may not maximize shareholder expected utility (since the opportunity set of feasible end-of-period payoffs may have changed).[16]

Let us now consider an example of a firm investment decision problem in a two-state world of uncertainty. Assume that all investors are expected utility maximizers and exhibit positive marginal utility of wealth (i.e., more wealth is preferred to less). Consider the following two firms and their proposed investment projects described in Tables 5.3 and 5.4.

To determine whether either firm should undertake its proposed project, we need to first determine whether the capital market is complete. Since the state-contingent payoffs of the two firms' stocks are linearly independent, the capital market is complete. In a complete market, the Fisher separation principle holds, so that the firm need only maximize the price of current shares to maximize its current shareholders' expected utility. This requires that the firm invest only in positive net present value

---

[16] See DeAngelo [1981] for a critical analysis of the unanimity literature and a careful formulation of the conditions under which it holds in incomplete and complete capital markets.

investment projects, which requires knowing the pure security prices in the two states. These two prices can be obtained from the market prices of the two firms' stocks and their state-contingent payoffs by solving the two simultaneous equations

$$100p_1 + 30p_2 = 62,$$

$$40p_1 + 90p_2 = 56,$$

to obtain the solution $p_1 = .5$ and $p_2 = .4$. To calculate the net present value of the two projects, we use the NPV definition in (5.10):

$$NPV_A = 10p_1 + 12p_2 - I_0^A = 10(.5) + 12(.4) - 10 = -.2$$

and

$$NPV_B = 12p_1 + 6p_2 - I_0^B = 12(.5) + 6(.4) - 8 = .4.$$

Since firm A's project has a negative NPV, it should be rejected, whereas firm B's project should be accepted since it has a positive NPV.

In examining this optimal investment rule, it should be clear that the prices of the pure securities affect the firm's investment decisions. It follows that since these security prices are affected by (1) time preference for consumption and the productivity of capital, (2) the probability of state-contingent payoffs, and (3) individual preferences toward risk and the level of nondiversifiable risk in the economy, firm investment decisions are also affected by these factors.

We have applied state-preference theory to the firm's optimal investment decision while assuming that the firm has a simple capital structure represented by shares of stock. However, it is also possible to allow the firm to have more complicated capital structures, which include various debt, preferred stock, and warrant contracts. In doing this, state-preference theory can be used to address the important question of a firm's optimal financing decision.[17] For this purpose it has been found useful to order the payoffs under alternative states. One can think of the payoffs for future states as arranged in an ordered sequence from the lowest to the highest payoff. Keeping in mind the ordered payoffs for alternative future states, we can specify the conditions under which a security such as corporate debt will be risk free or risky.[18]

The state-preference model has also been very useful in developing option pricing theory. By combining securities with claims on various portions of the ordered payoffs and by combining long and short positions, portfolios with an infinite variety of payoff characteristics can be created. From such portfolios various propositions with regard to option pricing relationships can be developed.[19]

---

[17] There are many examples of the usefulness of state-preference theory in the area of optimal capital structure or financing decisions; see, e.g., Stiglitz [1969], Mossin [1977], and DeAngelo and Masulis [1980a and 1980b].

[18] For applications of this approach see Kraus and Litzenberger [1973] and DeAngelo and Masulis [1980a].

[19] For some further applications of state-preference theory to option pricing theory see Merton [1973] and Ross [1976], and for application of both theories to investment and financing decision making see Appendixes B and C or Banz and Miller [1978].

SUMMARY

Wealth is held over periods of time, and the different future states of nature will change the value of a person's wealth position over time. Securities represent positions with regard to the relation between present and future wealth. Since securities involve taking a position over time, they inherently involve risk and uncertainty.

The states of nature capture a wide variety of factors that influence the future values of risky assets. Individuals must formulate judgments about payoffs under alternative future states of nature. From these state-contingent payoffs and market prices of securities, the prices of the underlying pure securities can be developed in a complete and perfect capital market. Given these pure security prices, the price of any other security can be determined from its state-contingent payoff vector. Conceptually, the equilibrium prices of the pure securities reflect the aggregate risk preferences of investors and investment opportunities of firms. Furthermore, the concept of a pure security facilitates analytical solutions to individuals' consumption/portfolio investment decisions under uncertainty.

The state-preference approach is a useful way of looking at firm investment decisions under uncertainty. In a perfect and complete capital market the net present value rule was shown to be an optimal firm investment decision rule. The property that firm decisions can be made independently of shareholder utility functions is termed the Fisher separation principle. State-preference theory also provides a conceptual basis for developing models for analyzing firm capital structure decisions and the pricing of option contracts. Thus the state-preference approach provides a useful way of thinking about finance problems both for the individual investor and for the corporate manager.

In summary the state-preference model has been shown to be very useful in a world of uncertainty. It can be used to develop optimal portfolio decisions for individuals and optimal investment rules for firms. We have found that in perfect and complete capital markets a set of equilibrium prices of all outstanding market securities can be derived. Further, these prices have been shown to be determined by (1) individual time preferences for consumption and the investment opportunities of firms, (2) probability beliefs concerning state-contingent payoffs, and (3) individual preferences toward risk and the level of nondiversifiable risk in the economy.

A number of important concepts developed in this chapter will be found to be very useful in the analysis to follow. In Chapter 6 we develop the fundamental properties of the mean-variance model, where the concept of diversifiable and nondiversifiable risk takes on added importance. In Chapter 7 the mean-variance framework is used to develop market equilibrium relationships that provide an alternative basis for pricing securities. Known as the capital asset pricing model, this model, like the state-preference model, has the property that securities having relatively high levels of nondiversifiable risk have relatively higher expected rates of return. The concept of arbitrage is fundamental to the development of arbitrage pricing theory (APT) in Chapter 7 and the option pricing model (OPM) in Chapter 8.

PROBLEM SET

5.1 Security A pays $30 if state 1 occurs and $10 if state 2 occurs. Security B pays $20 if state 1 occurs and $40 if state 2 occurs. The price of security A is $5 and the price of security B is $10.

a) Set up the payoff table for securities A and B.

b) Determine the prices of the two pure securities.

5.2 You are given the following information:

	Payoff		Security Prices
	State 1	*State 2*	
Security j	$12	$20	$p_j = \$22$
Security k	24	10	$p_k = \ 20$

a) What are the prices of pure security 1 and pure security 2?

b) What is the initial price of a third security i, for which the payoff in state 1 is $6 and the payoff in state 2 is $10?

5.3 Interplanetary starship captain José Ching has been pondering the investment of his recent pilot's bonus of 1000 stenglers. His choice is restricted to two securities: Galactic Steel, selling for 20 stenglers per share, and Nova Nutrients, at 10 stenglers per share. The future state of his solar system is uncertain. If there is a war with a nearby group of asteroids, Captain Ching expects Galactic Steel to be worth 36 stenglers per share. However, if peace prevails, Galactic Steel will be worth only 4 stenglers per share. Nova Nutrients should sell at a future price of 6 stenglers per share in either eventuality.

a) Construct the payoff table that summarizes the starship captain's assessment of future security prices, given the two possible future states of the solar system. What are the prices of the pure securities implicit in the payoff table?

b) If the captain buys only Nova Nutrients shares, how many can he buy? If he buys only Galactic Steel, how many shares can he buy? What would be his final wealth in both cases in peace? At war?

c) Suppose Captain Ching can issue (sell short) securities as well as buy them, but he must be able to meet all claims in the future. What is the maximum number of Nova Nutrients shares he could sell short to buy Galactic Steel? How many shares of Galactic Steel could he sell short to buy Nova Nutrients? What would be his final wealth in both cases and in each possible future state?

d) Suppose a third security, Astro Ammo, is available and should be worth 28 stenglers per share if peace continues and 36 stenglers per share if war breaks out. What would be the current price of Astro Ammo?

e) Summarize the results of (a) through (d) on a graph with axes W_1 and W_2.

f) Suppose the captain's utility function can be written $U = W_1^{.8} W_2^{.2}$. If his investment is restricted to Galactic Steel and/or Nova Nutrients, what is his optimal portfolio, i.e., how many shares of each security should he buy or sell?

5.4 Ms. Mary Kelley has initial wealth $W_0 = \$1200$ and faces an uncertain future that she partitions into two states, $s = 1$ and $s = 2$. She can invest in two securities, j and k, with initial prices of $p_j = \$10$ and $p_k = \$12$, and the following payoff table:

	Payoff	
Security	$s = 1$	$s = 2$
j	$10	$12
k	20	8

a) If she buys only security j, how many shares can she buy? If she buys only security k, how many can she buy? What would her final wealth, W_s, be in both cases and each state?

b) Suppose Ms. Kelley can issue as well as buy securities; however, she must be able to meet all claims under the occurrence of either state. What is the maximum number of shares of security j she could sell to buy security k? What is the maximum number of shares of security k she could sell to buy security j? What would her final wealth be in both cases and in each state?

c) What are the prices of the pure securities implicit in the payoff table?

d) What is the initial price of a third security i for which $Q_{i1} = \$5$ and $Q_{i2} = \$12$?

e) Summarize the results of (a) through (d) on a graph with axes W_1 and W_2.

f) Suppose Ms. Kelley has a utility function of the form $U = W_1^{.6} W_2^{.4}$. Find the optimal portfolio, assuming the issuance of securities is possible, if she restricts herself to a portfolio consisting only of j and k. How do you interpret your results?

5.5 Two securities have the following payoffs in two equally likely states of nature at the end of one year:

	Payoff	
Security	$s = 1$	$s = 2$
j	$10	$20
k	30	10

Security j costs $8 today, whereas k costs $9, and your total wealth is currently $720.

a) If you wanted to buy a completely risk-free portfolio (i.e., one that has the same payoff in both states of nature), how many shares of j and k would you buy? (You may buy fractions of shares.)

b) What is the one-period risk-free rate of interest?

c) If there were two securities and three states of nature, you would not be able to find a completely risk-free portfolio. Why not?

5.6 Suppose there are only two possible future states of the world, and the utility function is logarithmic. Let the probability of state 1, π_1, equal $\frac{2}{3}$, and the prices of the pure securities, p_1 and p_2, equal \$0.60 and \$0.40, respectively. An individual has an initial wealth or endowment, W_0, of \$50,000.

  a) What amounts will the risk-averse individual invest in pure securities 1 and 2?

  b) How will the individual divide his or her initial endowment between current and future consumption?

[*Hint:* Use the wealth constraint instead of the Lagrange multiplier technique.][20]

REFERENCES

Arrow, K. J., *Theory of Risk-Bearing.* Markham, Chicago, 1971.

————, "The Role of Securities in the Optimal Allocation of Risk-Bearing," *Review of Economic Studies*, 1964, 91–96.

Banz, R. W., and M. Miller, "Prices for State-Contingent Claims: Some Estimates and Applications," *Journal of Business*, October 1978, 653–672.

Breeden, D. T., and R. H. Litzenberger, "Prices of State-Contingent Claims Implicit in Option Prices," *Journal of Business*, October 1978, 621–651.

Brennan, M. J., and A. Kraus, "The Geometry of Separation and Myopia," *Journal of Financial and Quantitative Analysis*, June 1976, 171–193.

Cass, D., and J. E. Stiglitz, "The Structure of Investor Preferences and Asset Returns, and Separability in Portfolio Allocation: A Contribution to the Pure Theory of Mutual Funds," *Journal of Economic Theory*, June 1970, 122–160.

DeAngelo, H. C., "Competition and Unanimity," *American Economic Review*, March 1981, 18–28.

————, and R. W. Masulis, "Leverage and Dividend Irrelevance under Corporate and Personal Taxation," *Journal of Finance*, May 1980a, 453–464.

————, "Optimal Capital Structure under Corporate and Personal Taxation," *Journal of Financial Economics*, March 1980b, 3–29.

Debreu, G., *The Theory of Value.* Wiley, New York, 1959.

Dreze, J. H., "Market Allocation under Uncertainty," *European Economic Review*, Winter 1970–1971, 133–165.

Fama, E. F., and M. H. Miller, *The Theory of Finance.* Holt, Rinehart and Winston, New York, 1972.

Fisher, Irving, *The Theory of Interest.* Macmillan, London, 1930.

Garman, M., "The Pricing of Supershares," *Journal of Financial Economics*, March 1978, 3–10.

Hirshleifer, J., "Efficient Allocation of Capital in an Uncertain World," *American Economic Review*, May 1964, 77–85.

————, "Investment Decision under Uncertainty: Choice-Theoretic Approaches," *Quarterly Journal of Economics*, November 1965, 509–536.

---

[20] Problem 5.6 was suggested by Professor Herb Johnson of the University of California, Davis.

————, "Investment Decision under Uncertainty: Application of the State-Preference Approach," *Quarterly Journal of Economics*, May 1966, 252–277.

————, *Investment, Interest, and Capital*. Prentice-Hall, Englewood Cliffs, N.J., 1970, 215–276.

Kraus, A., and R. Litzenberger, "A State-Preference Model of Optimal Financial Leverage," *Journal of Finance*, September 1973, 911–922.

Krouse, C. G., *Capital Markets and Prices*. Elsevier Science Publishers B. V., Amsterdam, 1986.

Leland, H. E., "Production Theory and the Stock Market," *Bell Journal of Economics and Management Science*, 1974, 125–144.

Merton, R., "The Theory of Rational Option Pricing," *Bell Journal of Economics and Management Science*, Spring 1973, 141–183.

Mossin, J., *The Economic Efficiency of Financial Markets*. D. C. Heath, Lexington, 1977, 21–40.

Myers, S. C., "A Time-State Preference Model of Security Valuation," *Journal of Financial and Quantitative Analysis*, March 1968, 1–33.

Ross, S. A., "Options and Efficiency," *Quarterly Journal of Economics*, February 1976, 75–86.

————, "Return, Risk and Arbitrage," in Friend and Bicksler, eds., *Risk and Return in Finance, Volume 1*. Ballinger Publishing Company, Cambridge, Mass., 1977, 189–218.

————, "Mutual Fund Separation in Financial Theory—The Separating Distributions," *Journal of Economic Theory*, December 1978, 254–286.

Sharpe, W. F., *Portfolio Theory and Capital Markets*, Chapter 10, "State-Preference Theory." McGraw-Hill, New York, 1970, 202–222.

Stiglitz, J. E., "A Re-examination of the Modigliani-Miller Theorem," *American Economic Review*, December 1969, 784–793.

Appendix A to Chapter 5: Forming a Portfolio of Pure Securities

If we have n market securities and n states of the world, but we are not sure the n market securities are independent, we can find out by taking the determinant of the payoffs from the securities: a nonzero determinant implies independence. For example, the set of pure securities is independent since

$$\begin{vmatrix} 1 & 0 & 0 \\ 0 & 1 & 0 \\ 0 & 0 & 1 \end{vmatrix} = 1; \quad \text{but} \quad \begin{vmatrix} 1 & 0 & 0 \\ 0 & 1 & 1 \\ 1 & 1 & 1 \end{vmatrix} = \begin{vmatrix} 1 & 1 \\ 1 & 1 \end{vmatrix} = 0$$

implies that the security payoffs $(1, 0, 0)$, $(0, 1, 1)$, and $(1, 1, 1)$ are not linearly independent.

We can use Appendix B, "Matrix Algebra," found at the end of the book, to form a portfolio of pure securities from an arbitrary complete set of market securities. This involves computing the inverse of the payoff matrix for the actual securities. For example, if $(1, 0, 0)$, $(0, 1, 1)$, and $(0, 1, 3)$ are available, then define

$$A = \begin{pmatrix} 1 & 0 & 0 \\ 0 & 1 & 1 \\ 0 & 1 & 3 \end{pmatrix}$$

as the payoff matrix. Thus the determinant of A is

$$|A| = \begin{vmatrix} 1 & 0 & 0 \\ 0 & 1 & 1 \\ 0 & 1 & 3 \end{vmatrix} = \begin{vmatrix} 1 & 1 \\ 1 & 3 \end{vmatrix} = 2 \neq 0.$$

Let X_{ij} be the amount of the jth security one buys in forming the ith pure security, and let X be the matrix formed from the X_{ij}. Then we require that

$$XA = I \quad \text{where} \quad I = \begin{pmatrix} 1 & 0 & 0 \\ 0 & 1 & 0 \\ 0 & 0 & 1 \end{pmatrix}$$

is the identity matrix and also the matrix of payoffs from the pure securities. Hence $X = A^{-1}$. In the present example

$$A^{-1} = \tfrac{1}{2}\begin{pmatrix} 2 & 0 & 0 \\ 0 & 3 & -1 \\ 0 & -1 & 1 \end{pmatrix} = \begin{pmatrix} 1 & 0 & 0 \\ 0 & \tfrac{3}{2} & -\tfrac{1}{2} \\ 0 & -\tfrac{1}{2} & \tfrac{1}{2} \end{pmatrix}.$$

We then multiply X times A or equivalently $A^{-1}A$ to obtain a matrix of payoffs from the pure securities. We have:

$$\begin{pmatrix} 1 & 0 & 0 \\ 0 & \tfrac{3}{2} & -\tfrac{1}{2} \\ 0 & -\tfrac{1}{2} & \tfrac{1}{2} \end{pmatrix}\begin{pmatrix} 1 & 0 & 0 \\ 0 & 1 & 1 \\ 0 & 1 & 3 \end{pmatrix} = \begin{pmatrix} 1 & 0 & 0 \\ 0 & 1 & 0 \\ 0 & 0 & 1 \end{pmatrix}.$$

We can now see that the purpose of finding the inverse of A is to obtain directions for forming a portfolio that will yield a matrix of payoffs from the pure securities—the identity matrix. Recall that the three securities available are: $(1, 0, 0)$, $(0, 1, 1)$, and $(0, 1, 3)$. To obtain the pure security payoff $(1, 0, 0)$, we buy the security with that pattern of payoffs under the three states. To obtain $(0, 1, 0)$, we buy $\tfrac{3}{2}$ of $(0, 1, 1)$ and sell short $\tfrac{1}{2}$ of $(0, 1, 3)$. To obtain $(0, 0, 1)$, we sell short $\tfrac{1}{2}$ of $(0, 1, 1)$ and buy $\tfrac{1}{2}$ of $(0, 1, 3)$.

Appendix B to Chapter 5: Use of Prices for State-Contingent Claims in Capital Budgeting

Banz and Miller [1978] develop estimates of prices for state-contingent claims that can be applied in capital budgeting problems of the kind discussed in Chapter 12. They employ option pricing concepts discussed later in this book in Chapter 8. Similar methodologies were developed about the same time by Garman [1978] and by Breeden and Litzenberger [1978].

Banz and Miller note that a fundamental breakthrough was provided in Ross [1976], who demonstrated that by selling or buying options on a portfolio of existing securities, investors could obtain any desired pattern of returns—"investors could span the return space to any degree of fineness desired" [Banz and Miller, 1978, 658].

Banz and Miller present their estimates of state prices in a format similar to standard interest tables. Like other interest tables, the estimates of state prices can in principle be used by any firm in any industry or activity (subject to some important cautions and qualifications). Thus the reciprocals (minus one) of the state prices computed are analogous to single-period interest rates. Banz and Miller handle the multiperiod case by assuming stability in the relations between initial states and outcome states. Thus the two-period matrix is simply the square of the one-period matrix, the three-period matrix is the product of the one-period matrix and the two-period matrix, the four-period matrix is the product of the one-period matrix and the three-period matrix, and so on. In equation form,

$$V^n = V \cdot V^{n-1}. \tag{B5.1}$$

The perpetuity matrix is the one-period matrix times the inverse of the identity matrix minus the one-period matrix, or $V(I - V)^{-1}$.

Their computations for a V matrix of real discount factors for three states of the world is provided in Table B5.1. In the definition of states in Table B5.1 the state

Table B5.1   Three-State Matrix of State Prices and Matrix Powers

A. Definition of States		
State	State Boundaries*	Conditional Mean ($\bar{R}_{i,mr}$)
1	$-.8647-+.0006$	$-.1352$
2	$+.0006-+.2042$	$+.0972$
3	$+.2042-+1.7183^{\dagger}$	$+.3854$

B. State Prices

State	1	2	3	Row Sum	Implied Annual Real Riskless Rate
1 year (V):					
1	.5251	.2935	.1735	.9921	.0079
2	.5398	.2912	.1672	.9982	.0018
3	.5544	.2888	.1612	1.0044	$-.0044$
2 years (V^2):					
1	.5304	.2897	.1681	.9882	.0056
2	.5333	.2915	.1693	.9941	.0030
3	.5364	.2934	.1705	1.0003	$-.0001$
3 years (V^3):					
1	.5281	.2886	.1676	.9843	.0053
2	.5313	.2903	.1686	.9902	.0033
3	.5345	.2921	.1696	.9962	.0013
4 years (V^4):					
1	.5260	.2874	.1669	.9803	.0050
2	.5291	.2892	.1679	.9862	.0035
3	.5324	.2909	.1689	.9922	.0026
5 years (V^5):					
1	.5239	.2863	.1662	.9764	.0048
2	.5270	.2880	.1672	.9822	.0036
3	.5302	.2897	.1682	.9881	.0024
6 years (V^6):					
1	.5217	.2851	.1655	.9723	.0047
2	.5249	.2868	.1665	.9782	.0037
3	.5281	.2886	.1676	.9843	.0027
7 years (V^7):					
1	.5197	.2840	.1649	.9685	.0046
2	.5228	.2857	.1659	.9744	.0043
3	.5260	.2874	.1669	.9803	.0033

* Chosen to yield ranges of R_{mr} that are approximately equally probable.
† Arbitrary truncations.
Source: Banz and Miller [1978], 666.

Table B5.1, continued

					Implied Annual Real Riskless Rate
State	1	2	3	Row Sum	
8 years (V^8):					
1	.5176	.2828	.1642	.9646	.0045
2	.5207	.2845	.1652	.9704	.0038
3	.5239	.2863	.1662	.9764	.0030
9 years (V^9):					
1	.5155	.2817	.1636	.9608	.0045
2	.5186	.2834	.1645	.9665	.0038
3	.5218	.2851	.1655	.9724	.0031
10 years (V^{10}):					
1	.5134	.2806	.1629	.9569	.0044
2	.5165	.2823	.1639	.9627	.0038
3	.5197	.2840	.1649	.9686	.0032
Perpetuity $[V(I - V)^{-1}]$:					
1	132.50	72.41	42.05	246.96	.0040
2	133.31	72.85	42.30	248.46	.0040
3	134.14	73.29	42.55	249.98	.0040

B. State Prices

boundaries are defined over returns on the market. The conditional means are expected market returns under alternative states. The elements of any matrix V may be interpreted by use of the first group of data. The .5251 represents the outcome for state 1 when the initial state was also state 1. The .2935 represents the outcome for state 2 when state 1 was the initial state. The .1735 represents the outcome for state 3 when state 1 was the initial state. By analogy the .1612 represents an outcome for state 3 when state 3 was the initial state.

For equal probabilities the current price of a claim to funds in a state in which funds are scarce (a depression) will be higher than in a boom state when returns are more favorable. Thus a project with most of its payoffs contingent on a boom will have a lower value per dollar of expected returns than a project whose payoffs are relatively more favorable during a depression.

The vector of gross present values of the project, G_k will be

$$G_k = \sum_{t=1}^{p} V^t \bar{X}_k(t), \tag{B5.2}$$

where $\bar{X}_k(t)$ is a vector whose elements represent the expected real cash flows of project k in year t, assuming the economy is in state i. The summation is performed over time periods ending in p, the last period during which the project's cash flows are nonzero in any state.

Table B5.2 Cash Flow Patterns for an Investment

State of the Economy	Range of Rates of Return on the Market Portfolio	Cash Flow before Competition Enters $\bar{X}_m$	Steady-State Cash Flow after Competition Enters X_c
Depression	$-.8647-+.0006$	300	-20
Normal	$+.0006-+.2042$	400	20
Boom	$+.2042-+1.7183$	500	40

An example of how the "interest factors" in Table B5.1 can be applied is based on the illustration presented by Banz and Miller. The Omega Corporation is analyzing an investment project whose cash flow pattern in constant 1980 dollars (ignoring taxes and tax shields) is presented in Table B5.2.

The Banz-Miller example is sophisticated in illustrating that both the level and risk of the cash flows vary with the degree of competition. In our example we modify their estimates of the cumulative probabilities of competitive entry, using 0 in the year of introduction, .3 one year later, .6 two years later, and 1 three years later. The risk-adjusted gross present value vector for the project was set forth in Eq. (B5.2). For the assumptions of our example, the particular gross present value vector is $G_k = V\bar{X}_m + V^2(0.7\bar{X}_m + 0.3\bar{X}_c) + V^3(0.4\bar{X}_m + 0.6\bar{X}_c) + V^4[V(I - V)^{-1}]\bar{X}_c$. We use the values of V and its powers as presented in Table B5.1 to obtain the results shown in Table B5.3.

If the initial investment were \$1236 in every state of the economy, the project would not have a positive net present value if the economy were depressed or normal. However, the net present value would be positive if the economy were strong. If initial investment costs had cyclical behavior, particularly if supply bottlenecks developed during a boom, investment outlays might vary so strongly with states of the

Table B5.3 Calculation of Risk-Adjusted Present Values

$$
\begin{bmatrix} g_D \\ g_N \\ g_B \end{bmatrix} = \begin{bmatrix} .5251 & .2935 & .1735 \\ .5398 & .2912 & .1672 \\ .5544 & .2888 & .1612 \end{bmatrix} \begin{bmatrix} 300 \\ 400 \\ 500 \end{bmatrix}
$$

$$
+ \begin{bmatrix} .5304 & .2897 & .1681 \\ .5333 & .2915 & .1693 \\ .5364 & .2934 & .1705 \end{bmatrix} \begin{bmatrix} 204 \\ 286 \\ 362 \end{bmatrix} + \begin{bmatrix} .5281 & .2886 & .1676 \\ .5313 & .2903 & .1686 \\ .5345 & .2921 & .1696 \end{bmatrix} \begin{bmatrix} 108 \\ 172 \\ 224 \end{bmatrix}
$$

$$
+ \begin{bmatrix} .5260 & .2874 & .1669 \\ .5291 & .2892 & .1679 \\ .5324 & .2909 & .1689 \end{bmatrix} \begin{bmatrix} 132.50 & 72.41 & 42.05 \\ 133.31 & 72.85 & 42.30 \\ 134.14 & 73.29 & 42.55 \end{bmatrix} \begin{bmatrix} -20 \\ 20 \\ 40 \end{bmatrix}
$$

$$
= \begin{bmatrix} 1230.09 \\ 1235.68 \\ 1241.48 \end{bmatrix}
$$

world that net present values could be positive for a depressed economy and negative for a booming economy.

The Banz-Miller use of state prices in capital budgeting is a promising application of the state-preference model. Further applications will provide additional tests of the feasibility of their approach. More work in comparing the results under alternative approaches will provide increased understanding of the advantages and possible limitations of the use of state prices as discount factors in capital budgeting analysis.

Appendix C to Chapter 5: Application of the SPM in Capital Structure Decisions

The state-preference model (SPM) can also be used to analyze financing decisions if estimates of state prices as provided in the Banz-Miller paper are available. While capital structure decisions are discussed in Chapters 13 and 14, the following explanation is self-contained and provides an overview of some key aspects of the subject. In addition to the formal framework an illustrative numerical example will be developed.

The symbols that will be employed are listed and explained in Table C5.1. In the capital structure analysis three broad categories of alternative outcomes may take place. The outcomes are defined by the amount of net operating income achieved in relation to the amount of the debt obligations incurred. These three alternative

Table C5.1   Symbols Used in the SPM Analysis of Capital Structure Decisions

p_s = Market price of the primitive security that represents a claim on one dollar in state s and zero dollars in all other states

X_s = Earnings before interest and taxes that the firm will achieve in state s (EBIT)

B = Nominal payment to debt, representing a promise to pay fixed amount B, irrespective of the state that occurs

$S(B)$ = Market value of the firm's equity as a function of the amount of debt issued by the firm

$V(B)$ = Market value of the firm as a function of the amount of debt issued

f_s = Costs of failure in state s; $0 < f_s \leq X_s$

τ = Corporate tax rate = 40%.

Table C5.2   Amounts Received Under Alternative Outcomes

Outcome	Amount of X_s in Relation to B (1)	Debt Holders Receive (2)	Equity Holders Receive (3)
1	$X_s \geq B$	B	$(X_s - B)(1 - \tau)$
2	$0 \leq X_s < B$	$(X_s - f_s)$	0
3	$X_s < 0$	0	0

outcomes are specified by column (1) in Table C5.2. Under outcome 1 the state-dependent net operating income, X_s, is equal to or greater than the amount of the debt obligations, B. Debt holders will receive the total amount of promised payments, B. Equity holders will receive the after-tax income remaining after the debt payments. The amounts received by debt holders and equity holders are listed in columns (2) and (3) in Table C5.2.

Under outcome 2, the state-dependent net operating income is less than B but positive. Debt holders will receive the net operating income less bankruptcy costs that may be incurred. Equity holders will receive nothing. If the state-dependent income is negative, neither debt holders nor equity holders will receive anything.

In Table C5.3 the applicable state prices are multiplied times what the debt holders receive under alternative outcomes to determine the value of the debt holders' receipts in each state. Similarly, what the equity holders receive is multiplied by the state prices to give the value of equity. The value of the firm in each state is the sum of the market value of debt and the market value of equity.

This formal framework is next utilized in an illustrative numerical example. The basic data to be utilized are set forth in Table C5.4. In Table C5.5 the data are used to calculate the value of the firm under alternative debt levels. On the left-hand column labeled *Debt Levels* we begin by specifying the amount of debt and the resulting relationships between X_s, the EBIT under alternative states, and the promised debt payment. The applicable formulas for calculating the state-contingent value of the firm are specified for each level of debt. Utilizing the illustrative data from Table C5.4, we can then obtain the value of the firm's state payoff for alternative debt levels.

When the firm is unlevered ($B = 0$) its value is equal to the after-tax EBIT times the state price for each state, summed over all the states. The resulting value is $408.

When debt is $200 the value of the firm under state 1 is zero. For states 2, 3, and 4 both the debt and equity have value as shown in Table C5.5. When the value of debt is $500, again the firm has no value under state 1. Under states 2, 3, and 4 both debt and equity have value. The total value of the firm sums to $550.

Similarly, for a debt level of $800 the value of the firm is calculated as $386. For a value of debt of $2000 the value of the firm is $350.

The debt level that results in the highest indicated value of the firm as shown by Table C5.5 is $500. For alternative levels of debt the value of the firm is lower.

Table C5.3   Formulas for the Value of the Firm under Alternative Outcomes

Outcome	Amount of X_s in Relation to B (1)	Debt Holders Receive (2)	Value of Debt Holders' Receipts in State s (3)	Equity Holders Receive (4)	Value of Equity Holders' Receipts in State s (5)	Value of the Firm in State s (6)
1	$X_s \geq B$	B	Bp_s	$(X_s - B)(1 - \tau)$	$(X_s - B)(1 - \tau)p_s$	$Bp_s + (X_s - B)(1 - \tau)p_s$
2	$0 \leq X_s < B$	$(X_s - f_s)$	$(X_s - \tau_s)p_s$	0	0	$(X_s - f_s)p_s$
3	$X_s < 0$	0	0	0	0	0

Table C5.4   Data for SPM
Analysis of Capital Structure
Decisions

s (1)	X_s (2)	p_s (3)	f_s (4)
1	$ 100	$0.30	$ 100
2	500	0.50	400
3	1000	0.20	500
4	2000	0.10	1200

Table C5.5   Calculations of the Value of the Firm under
Alternative Debt Levels

Debt Levels	State	Value of Firm's State s Payoff
$B = 0,\ X_s > B$ for all s $V_s(0) = \sum_{s=1}^{4} X_s(1 - T)p_s$	1 2 3 4	$100(0.6)0.3 =\quad 18$ $500(0.6)0.5 =\quad 150$ $1000(0.6)0.2 =\quad 120$ $2000(0.6)0.1 =\quad 120$ $V(0) = \$408$
$B = 200,\ X_s < B$ for $s = 1$ $B = 200,\ X_s \geq B$ for $s = 2, 3, 4$ $V_s(200) = (X_s - f_s)p_s$ for $s = 1$ $V_s(200) = \sum_{s=2}^{4} Bp_s + \sum_{s=2}^{4} (X_s - B)(1 - T)p_s$	1 2 3 4	$(100 - 100)(0.6)0.3 =\quad 0$ $200(0.5) + (500 - 200)(0.6)0.5 =\quad 190$ $200(0.2) + (1000 - 200)(0.6)0.2 =\quad 136$ $200(0.1) + (2000 - 200)(0.6)0.1 =\quad 128$ $V(200) = \$454$
$B = 500,\ X_s < B$ for $s = 1$ $B = 500,\ X_s \geq B$ for $s = 2, 3, 4$ $V_s(500) = (X_s - f_s)p_s$ for $s = 1$ $V_s(500) = \sum_{s=2}^{4} Bp_s + \sum_{s=2}^{4} (X_s - B)(1 - T)p_s$	1 2 3 4	$(100 - 100)0.3 =\quad 0$ $500(0.5) + (500 - 500)(0.6)0.5 =\quad 250$ $500(0.2) + (1000 - 500)(0.6)0.2 =\quad 160$ $500(0.1) + (2000 - 500)(0.6)0.1 =\quad 140$ $V(500) = \$550$
$B = 800,\ X_s < B$ for $s = 1, 2$ $B = 800,\ X_s \geq B$ for $s = 3, 4$ $V_s(1000) = \sum_{s=1}^{2} (X_s - f_s)p_s$ $V_s(1000) = \sum_{s=3}^{4} Bp_s + \sum_{s=3}^{4} (X_s - B)(1 - T)p_s$	1 2 3 4	$(100 - 100)0.3 =\quad 0$ $(500 - 400)0.5 =\quad 50$ $800(0.2) + (1000 - 800)(0.6)0.2 =\quad 184$ $800(0.1) + (2000 - 800)(0.6)0.1 =\quad 152$ $V(800) = \$386$
$B = 2000,\ X_s < B$ for $s = 1, 2, 3$ $B = 2000,\ X_s \geq B$ for $s = 4$ $V_s(2000) = \sum_{s=1}^{3} (X_s - f_s)p_s$ $V_s(2000) = Bp_s + (X_s - B)(1 - T)p_s$ for $s = 4$	1 2 3 4	$(100 - 100)0.3 =\quad 0$ $(500 - 400)0.5 =\quad 50$ $(1000 - 500)0.2 =\quad 100$ $2000(0.1) + (2000 - 2000)(0.6)0.1 =\quad 200$ $V(2000) = \$350$

This result follows from the numerical values chosen for the illustration. The example illustrates the tax advantage of debt. Also, substantial bankruptcy costs are postulated. In addition, the bankruptcy costs are assumed to have a substantial fixed element as well as to rise with the amount of resources that may become available under each of the alternative states. Further aspects of capital structure decisions will be developed in Chapters 13 and 14.

6

The results of a portfolio analysis are no more than the logical consequence of its information concerning securities.
Harry Markowitz, *Portfolio Selection*, Yale University Press, New Haven, 1959, 205

Objects of Choice: Mean-Variance Uncertainty

Chapter 4 introduced the theory of how risk-averse investors make choices in a world with uncertainty. Chapter 5 used a state-preference framework to show that the fundamental objects of choice are payoffs offered in different states of nature. While this is a very general approach, it lacks empirical content. It would be difficult, if not impossible, to list all payoffs offered in different states of nature. To provide a framework for analysis where objects of choice are readily measurable, this chapter develops mean-variance objects of choice. Investors' indifference curves are assumed to be defined in terms of the mean and variance of asset returns. While much less general than state-preference theory, the mean-variance portfolio theory introduced here is statistical in nature and therefore lends itself to empirical testing. Some of the empirical tests of a mean-variance equilibrium pricing model are discussed in Chapter 7.

One of the most important developments in finance theory in the last few decades is the ability to talk about risk in a quantifiable fashion. If we know how to measure and price financial risk correctly, we can properly value risky assets. This in turn leads to better allocation of resources in the economy. Investors can do a better job of allocating their savings to various types of risky securities, and managers

145

can better allocate the funds provided by shareholders and creditors among scarce capital resources.

This chapter begins with simple measures of risk and return for a single asset and then complicates the discussion by moving to risk and return for a portfolio of many risky assets. Decision rules are then developed to show how individuals choose optimal portfolios that maximize their expected utility of wealth, first in a world without riskless borrowing and lending, then with such opportunities.

A. MEASURING RISK AND RETURN
FOR A SINGLE ASSET

Suppose the task at hand is to describe the relevant features of a common stock to a friend who is an investor. What are the really crucial facts that you should communicate? You could start off by giving the company's name, say Bayside Cigar Co. Then you would discuss the financial ratios of the company: its earnings per share, its inventory turnover, its financial leverage, its interest coverage, and so on. All these data are merely one way of getting at what is crucial—How will your friend's wealth position be affected if he or she invests in Bayside Cigar? Consequently, it is wise to talk about measures of the effect on relative wealth at the end of an investment period. The terminology used is *end-of-period wealth.*

The link between end-of-period wealth and an initial dollar investment is the *rate of return.* For the time being, we will not specify what calendar interval we are working with except to say that it is a single time period. If the initial investment is $\$I$ and the final wealth is $\$W$, then the investor's rate of return, R, is

$$R = \frac{W - I}{I}. \tag{6.1}$$

As you see, this is the same expression as that used for the present or future value formulas for one time period.

$$W = (1 + R)I, \qquad \text{future value formulation;} \tag{6.1a}$$

$$I = (1 + R)^{-1})W \qquad \text{present value formulation.} \tag{6.1b}$$

If end-of-period wealth is known with certainty, then so is the present value of the investment and the rate of return. However, this is seldom the case in the real world. Even short-term default-free bonds such as U.S. Treasury Bills are not completely risk free (although later on we shall use them as a close approximation to a risk-free security).

For risky assets often the best that can be done is to assign probabilities to various possible outcomes. Suppose the current price (P_0) of Bayside Cigar is $\$25$ per share and you tell your friend that after a careful analysis the best estimate of the price per share at the end of the time period is given in Table 6.1.

Table 6.1 Hypothetical Prices for Bayside Cigar Co.

$p_i = Probability$	End-of-Period Price per Share	$R_i = Return$
.1	$20.00	−20%
.2	22.50	−10
.4	25.00	0
.2	30.00	+20
.1	40.00	+60
1.0		

1. Measures of Location

It is desirable to develop some statistics that can summarize a wide set of possible outcomes. The most commonly used statistics are measures of location and dispersion. Measures of location are intended to describe the most likely outcome in a set of events. The most often used measure of location is the mean or expectation. It is defined as (the tilde, ~, is used to designate randomness)

$$E(\tilde{X}) = \sum_{i=1}^{N} p_i X_i, \tag{6.2}$$

where p_i is the probability of a random event, X_i, and N is the total number of possible events. Hence the mean weights each event by its probability, then sums all events. For Bayside Cigar the expected end-of-period price is

$$E(\tilde{P}) = .1(20) + .2(22.5) + .4(25) + .2(30) + .1(40) = \$26.50.$$

The expected or mean return is the expected price less the current price divided by the current price.

$$E(\tilde{R}) = \frac{E(\tilde{P}) - P_0}{P_0} = \frac{26.50 - 25}{25} = .06 \quad \text{or} \quad 6\%. \tag{6.3}$$

Implicitly, we have used two probability properties of the expected value operator to obtain Eq. (6.3).

Property 1. The expected value of a random variable $\tilde{X}$ plus a constant a is equal to the expected value of the random variable plus the constant:

$$E(\tilde{X} + a) = E(\tilde{X}) + a \tag{6.4}$$

Property 1 can be proved by using the definition of expected value. Since the random variable is $(\tilde{X} + a)$, we take its expectation by substituting $(X_i + a)$ for X_i in Eq. (6.2):

$$E(\tilde{X} + a) = \sum_{i=1}^{N} p_i(X_i + a).$$

Writing out all the terms in the sum, we have

$$E(\tilde{X} + a) = [p_1(X_1 + a) + p_2(X_2 + a) + \cdots + p_n(X_n + a)].$$

By simply collecting terms, we get

$$E(\tilde{X} + a) = \sum_{i=1}^{N} p_i X_i + a \sum_{i=1}^{N} p_i.$$

And since we know that the sum of the probabilities of all events must add to 1 ($\sum p_i \equiv 1$), we have proved Property 1:

$$E(\tilde{X} + a) = \sum_{i=1}^{N} p_i(X_i) + a,$$

$$E(\tilde{X} + a) = E(\tilde{X}) + a. \qquad \text{QED}$$

Property 2. The expected value of a random variable $\tilde{X}$ multiplied by a constant a is equal to the constant multiplied by the expected value of the random variable:

$$E(a\tilde{X}) = aE(\bar{X}). \tag{6.5}$$

Property 2 can also be proved by using the definition of the expected-value operator. Substituting aX_i for X_i in Eq. (6.2), we get

$$E(a\tilde{X}) = \sum_{i=1}^{N} p_i(aX_i).$$

Then by expanding the sum, we have

$$E(a\tilde{X}) = p_1 aX_1 + p_2 aX_2 + \cdots + p_n aX_n.$$

Next, a can be factored out:

$$E(a\tilde{X}) = a \sum_{i=1}^{N} p_i X_i.$$

And finally, recognizing that $\sum p_i X_i = E(\tilde{X})$, we have

$$E(a\tilde{X}) = aE(\tilde{X}). \qquad \text{QED}$$

When we used the definition of return and the expected end-of-period price to derive the expected return, we were using both properties of the expected-value operator described above. In the numerator of (6.3) the price of Bayside Cigar today, P_0, is known and is a constant. The end-of-period price is a random variable. Therefore, the right-hand side of Eq. (6.3) uses Property 1 in the numerator and Property 2 when the numerator is multiplied by $(1/P_0)$, a constant.

The expected outcome, or *the average*, is the most frequently used statistical measure of location, but it is not the only one. Before moving on to measures of dispersion, we should also mention the *median* and the *mode*, which are also measures of location. The median is defined as the outcome in the middle, often referred to as the 50th percentile. Consider the set of numbers (which are equally likely, i.e., $p_i = 1/N$) given in Table 6.2.

Table 6.2   Set of Numbers with Equal Probability

17	0	7	10	13	3
15	−4	6	−1	17	13
13	25	13	150	−1	6
−8	2	54	32	202	16
13	21	120	24	29	37

Figure 6.1 is a histogram for the set of numbers. Note that most of the probability (in fact 53.3%) lies between −1 and 20. However, the mean, which assigns equal weight to all observations in this case, gives 28.13 as the best measure of location. The median is 13. Clearly, in this case, where we have a distribution of outcomes that is skewed to the right, the median is a better measure of location than the mean is. Later on, when we actually look at empirical distributions of security returns, the choice of mean return as the best measure of central tendency will depend a great deal on whether or not the actual distributions are skewed.

The last measure of location to be considered is the mode. It is defined as the most frequent outcome. In the above example it is the number 13, which occurs five times, or the interval between 6 and 13, which contains 23.3% of the probability. The mode is not often used as a measure of location for empirical distributions of security returns because security returns are real numbers (i.e., they can take on any decimal value) and consequently do not repeat themselves frequently.

2. Measures of Dispersion

So far we have looked at statistical measures that can be used to best describe the most likely outcome when out friend invests in Bayside Cigar. An investment of $1000 can be expected to bring an end-of-period wealth of $1060. (Why?) But the question still remains—What risk is being taken? There are five measures of dispersion we could use: the range, the semiinterquartile range, the variance, the semivariance, and the mean absolute deviation. Each of these has slightly different implications for risk.

The *range* is the simplest statistic and is defined as the difference between the highest and lowest outcomes. For an investment in one share of Bayside Cigar (see

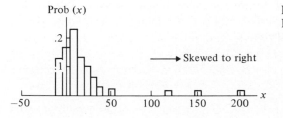

Prob (x)

Skewed to right

Figure 6.1
Histogram.

Table 6.1) the worst outcome is $20 and the best outcome is $40. Therefore the range is $20. However, the range is a very poor descriptive statistic because it becomes larger as sample size increases. Whenever the underlying probability distribution of investment outcomes is being estimated—e.g., by looking at observations of past performance—the estimated range will increase as more observations are included in the sample.

The *semiinterquartile range* is the difference between the observation of the 75th percentile, $X_{.75}$, and the 25th percentile, $X_{.25}$, divided by 2:

$$\text{Semiinterquartile range} = \frac{X_{.75} - X_{.25}}{2}. \tag{6.6}$$

Unlike the range, this statistic does not increase with sample size and is therefore much more reliable.[1] For the set of 30 numbers that we were using earlier (in Table 6.2) the semiinterquartile range is

$$\text{Semiinterquartile range} = \frac{27.0 - 4.5}{2} = 11.25.$$

This statistic is frequently used as a measure of dispersion when the variance of a distribution does not exist.

The *variance* is the statistic most frequently used to measure the dispersion of a distribution, and later on in this chapter it will be used as a measure of investment risk. It is defined as the expectation of the squared differences from the mean.

$$\text{VAR}(\tilde{X}) = E[(X_i - E(\tilde{X}))^2]. \tag{6.7a}$$

Recalling the definition of the mean as the sum of the probabilities of events times the value of the events, the definition of variance can be rewritten as

$$\text{VAR}(\tilde{X}) = \sum_{i=1}^{N} p_i(X_i - E(\tilde{X}))^2. \tag{6.7b}$$

Therefore for Bayside Cigar the variance of end-of-period prices is

$$\text{VAR}(\tilde{P}) = .1(20 - 26.5)^2 + .2(22.5 - 26.5)^2 + .4(25 - 26.5)^2$$

$$+ .2(30 - 26.5)^2 + .1(40 - 26.5)^2$$

$$= .1(42.25) + .2(16) + .4(2.25) + .2(12.25) + .1(182.25)$$

$$= 29.00, \quad \text{which represents dollars squared.}$$

Note that the variance is expressed in dollars squared. Since people do not usually think in these terms, the *standard deviation*, which is the positive square root of the variance, is often used to express dispersion:

$$\sigma(\tilde{P}) = \sqrt{\text{VAR}(\tilde{P})} = \$5.39.$$

---

[1] The interested reader is referred to Crámer [1961, 367–370] for proof that sample quantiles converge to consistent estimates as sample sizes increase.

The variance of the return from investing in Bayside Cigar is

$$\text{VAR}(\tilde{R}) = \frac{\text{VAR}(\tilde{P})}{P_0^2} = \frac{29}{(25)^2} = 4.64\%,$$

and the standard deviation is

$$\sigma(\tilde{R}) = \sqrt{\text{VAR}(\tilde{R})} = 21.54\%.$$

This result is derived by using two properties of the variance in much the same way as properties of the mean were used earlier.

Property 3. The variance of a random variable plus a constant is equal to the variance of the random variable.

It makes sense that adding a constant to a random variable would have no effect on the variance because the constant by itself has zero variance. This is demonstrated by using the definition of variance [Eq. (6.7)] and substituting $(X_i + a)$ for X_i as follows:

$$\text{VAR}(\tilde{X} + a) = E[((X_i + a) - E(\tilde{X} + a))^2].$$

From Property 1 of the expected-value operator, we know that

$$E(\tilde{X} + a) = E(\tilde{X}) + a;$$

therefore

$$\text{VAR}(\tilde{X} + a) = E[((X_i) + a - E(\tilde{X}) - a)^2].$$

Because the constant terms cancel out, we have

$$\text{VAR}(\tilde{X} + a) = E[(X_i - E(\tilde{X}))^2] = \text{VAR}(\tilde{X}). \qquad \text{QED} \qquad (6.8)$$

Property 4. The variance of a random variable multiplied by a constant is equal to the constant squared times the variance of the random variable.

For proof we again refer to the definition of variance and substitute of aX_i for X_i in Eq. (6.7):

$$\text{VAR}(a\tilde{X}) = E[(aX_i - aE(\tilde{X}))^2].$$

The constant term can be factored out as follows:

$$\text{VAR}(a\tilde{X}) = E[(a[X_i - E(\tilde{X})])^2]$$
$$= E[a^2(X_i - E(\tilde{X}))^2]$$
$$= a^2 E[(X_i - E(\tilde{X}))^2] = a^2\text{VAR}(X). \qquad \text{QED} \qquad (6.9)$$

Going back to the example where we computed the variance of return on Bayside Cigar directly from the variance of its price, we can readily see how Properties 3 and 4 were used. Let us recall that the definition of return is

$$R_i = \frac{P_i - P_0}{P_0},$$

and that the expected return is

$$E(\tilde{R}) = \frac{E(\tilde{P}) - P_0}{P_0}.$$

Therefore the variance of return is

$$VAR(\tilde{R}) = E[(R_i - E(\tilde{R}))^2]$$

$$= E\left[\left(\frac{P_i - P_0}{P_0} - \frac{E(\tilde{P}) - P_0}{P_0}\right)^2\right].$$

Because P_0 is a constant, we can use Property 4 to write

$$VAR(\tilde{R}) = \frac{1}{P_0^2} E[(P_i - E(\tilde{P}))^2]$$

$$= \frac{VAR(\tilde{P})}{P_0^2}.$$

And of course this is exactly the formula used earlier to compute the variance of return from our knowledge of the variance of prices.

The next section of this chapter uses the properties of the mean and variance that we have developed here in order to discuss the mean and variance of a portfolio of assets. At this point we could summarize the investment opportunity offered by Bayside Cigar by saying that the expected price is $26.50 with a standard deviation of $5.39. Or else we could say that the expected return on this investment is 6% with a standard deviation of 21.54%. However, before moving on, it will be useful to contrast the variance as a measure of risk with the *semivariance* and the *mean absolute deviation*.

One problem with the variance is that it gives equal weight to possibilities above as well as below the average. However, suppose that risk-averse investors are more concerned with downside risk. The semivariance is a statistic that relates to just that risk. It is defined as the expectation of the mean differences *below* the mean, squared. Mathematically, the definition is as follows. Let

$$X_i = \begin{cases} X_i - E(\tilde{X}) & \text{if} \quad X_i < E(\tilde{X}) \\ 0 & \text{if} \quad X_i \geq E(\tilde{X}), \end{cases}$$

then

$$SEMIVAR = E[(X_i)^2]. \tag{6.10}$$

If the semivariance is used as a measure of risk, an increase in the probability of events above the mean will change risk only slightly because the only effect would be to increase the mean slightly. For example, the semivariance of return for Bayside Cigar is

$$SEMIVAR = .1(-.20 - .06)^2 + .2(-.10 - .06)^2 + .4(0 - .06)^2$$

$$= 1.332\%.$$

But if the probability of a 60% return (in Table 6.1) were to increase to .2 while the probability of a 20% return fell to .1, the impact on semivariance would be slight. The new expected return would be 10% and the semivariance would increase to 2.1%. Given the same change in probabilities, the variance would increase from 4.64% to 7.2%.

Both the variance and the semivariance are sensitive to observations distant from the mean because the mean differences are squared. Squaring gives them greater weight. A statistic that avoids this difficulty is the *mean absolute deviation* (MAD), which is defined as the expectation of the absolute value of the differences from the mean:

$$\text{MAD} = E[|X_i - E(\tilde{X})|]. \tag{6.11}$$

For the Bayside Cigar example, the mean absolute deviation is

$$\text{MAD} = .1|(-.2 - .06)| + .2|(-.1 - .06)| + .4|(0 - .06)|$$
$$+ .2|(.2 - .06)| + .1|(.6 - .06)|$$
$$= 16.4\%.$$

Although for the most part we shall measure risk and return by using the variance (or standard deviation) and the mean return, it is useful to keep in mind that there are other statistics that, in some situations, may be more appropriate. An understanding of these statistics helps to put the mean and variance into proper perspective.

B. MEASURING PORTFOLIO RISK AND RETURN

From this point we assume that investors measure the expected utility of choices among risky assets by looking at the mean and variance provided by combinations of those assets. For a financial manager, the operating risk of the firm may be measured by estimating the mean and variance of returns provided by the portfolio of assets which the firm holds: its inventory, cash, accounts receivable, marketable securities, and physical plant. For a portfolio manager, the risk and return are the mean and variance of the weighted average of the assets in his or her portfolio. Therefore, in order to understand how to manage risk it becomes necessary to explore the risk and return provided by combinations of risky assets.

1. The Normal Distribution

By looking only at mean and variance, we are necessarily assuming that no other statistics are necessary to describe the distribution of end-of-period wealth. Unless investors have a special type of utility function (quadratic utility function), it is necessary to assume that returns have a normal distribution, which can be completely described by mean and variance. This is the bell-shaped probability distribution that many natural phenomena obey. For example, measures of intelligence quotients (IQs)

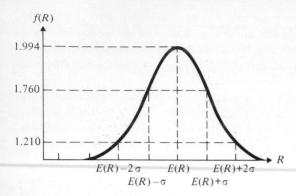

Figure 6.2
A normal distribution $[E(R) = .1, \sigma = .2]$.

follow this distribution. An example is given in Fig. 6.2. The frequency of a return is measured along the vertical axis, and the returns are measured along the horizontal axis. The normal distribution is perfectly symmetric, and 50% of the probability lies above the mean, 15.9% above a point one standard deviation above the mean, and 2.3% above a point two standard deviations above the mean. Because of its symmetry the variance and semivariance are equivalent measures of risk for the normal distribution. Furthermore, if you know the mean and standard deviation (or semivariance) of a normal distribution, you know the likelihood of every point in the distribution. This would not be true if the distribution were not symmetric. If it were skewed to the right, e.g., one would also need to know a measure of skewness in addition to the mean and standard deviation, and the variance and semivariance would not be equivalent.

The equation for the frequency of returns, R, which are normally distributed, is given below:[2]

$$f(R) = \frac{1}{\sigma\sqrt{2\pi}}\, e^{-(1/2)[(R-E(R))/\sigma]^2}. \tag{6.12}$$

If we know the mean, $E(R)$, and the standard deviation, σ, of the distribution, then we can plot the frequency of any return. For example, if $E(R) = 10\%$ and $\sigma = 20\%$, then the frequency of a 13% rate of return is

$$f(.13) = \frac{1}{.2\sqrt{2\pi}}\, e^{-(1/2)[(.13-.10)/.2]^2},$$

$$f(.13) = 1.972.$$

---

[2] Of course π is "pi," the ratio of the circumference and the diameter of a circle, and e is the base of natural logarithms.

Often a normal distribution is converted into a unit normal distribution that always has a mean of zero and a standard deviation of one. Most normal probability tables (like that given at the end of Chapter 8) are based on a unit normal distribution. To convert a return, R, into a unit normal variable, z, we subtract the mean, $E(R)$, and divide by the standard deviation, σ, as shown below:

$$z = \frac{R - E(R)}{\sigma}. \tag{6.13}$$

The frequency function for a unit normal variable is

$$f(z) = \frac{1}{\sqrt{2\pi}}\, e^{-(1/2)z^2}. \tag{6.14}$$

This could be plotted in Fig. 6.2. Of course the scales would change.

2. Calculating the Mean and Variance of a Two-Asset Portfolio

Consider a portfolio of two risky assets that are both normally distributed. How can we measure the mean and standard deviation of a portfolio with $a\%$ of our wealth invested in asset X, and $b\% = (1 - a\%)$ invested in asset Y? Mathematically, the portfolio return can be expressed as the weighted sum of two random variables:

$$\tilde{R}_p = a\tilde{X} + b\tilde{Y}.$$

By using the properties of mean and variance derived earlier we can derive the mean and variance of the portfolio. The mean return is the expected outcome

$$E(\tilde{R}_p) = E[a\tilde{X} + b\tilde{Y}].$$

Separating terms, we have

$$E(R_p) = E(a\tilde{X}) + E(b\tilde{Y}).$$

Using Property 2 [i.e., that $E(a\tilde{X}) = aE(\tilde{X})$], we have

$$E(\tilde{R}_p) = aE(\tilde{X}) + bE(\tilde{Y}). \tag{6.15}$$

Thus the portfolio mean return is seen to be simply the weighted average of returns on individual securities, where the weights are the percentage invested in those securities.

The variance of a portfolio return is expressed as

$$\text{VAR}(\tilde{R}_p) = E[\tilde{R}_p - E(\tilde{R}_p)]^2$$
$$= E[(a\tilde{X} + b\tilde{Y}) - E(a\tilde{X} + b\tilde{Y})]^2.$$

Again, using Property 2 and rearranging terms, we have

$$\text{VAR}(\tilde{R}_p) = E[(a\tilde{X} - aE(\tilde{X})) + (b\tilde{Y} - bE(\tilde{Y}))]^2.$$

By squaring the term in brackets and using Property 4, we have

$$\text{VAR}(\tilde{R}_p) = E[a^2(\tilde{X} - E(\tilde{X}))^2 + b^2(\tilde{Y} - E(\tilde{Y}))^2 + 2ab(\tilde{X} - E(\tilde{X}))(\tilde{Y} - E(\tilde{Y}))].$$

You will recall that from the definition of variance and by Property 4,

$$\text{VAR}(a\tilde{X}) = a^2 E[(\tilde{X} - E(\tilde{X}))^2] = a^2\text{VAR}(\tilde{X}).$$

Also,

$$\text{VAR}(b\tilde{Y}) = b^2 E[(\tilde{Y} - E(\tilde{Y}))^2] = b^2\text{VAR}(\tilde{Y}).$$

Therefore the portfolio variance is the sum of the variances of the individual securities multiplied by the square of their weights plus a third term, which includes the *covariance*, $\text{COV}(\tilde{X}, \tilde{Y})$:

$$\text{VAR}(\tilde{R}_p) = a^2\text{VAR}(\tilde{X}) + b^2\text{VAR}(\tilde{Y}) + 2abE[(\tilde{X} - E(\tilde{X}))(\tilde{Y} - E(\tilde{Y}))],$$

$$\text{COV}(\tilde{X}, \tilde{Y}) \equiv E[(\tilde{X} - E(\tilde{X}))(\tilde{Y} - E(\tilde{Y}))].$$

The covariance is a measure of the way in which the two random variables move in relation to each other. If the covariance is positive, the variables move in the same direction. If it is negative, they move in opposite directions. The covariance is an extremely important concept because it is the appropriate measure of the contribution of a single asset to portfolio risk. The variance of a random variable is really the same thing as its covariance with itself:[3]

$$\text{COV}(aX, aX) = a \cdot aE[(X - E(X))(X - E(X))]$$

$$= a^2 E[(X - E(X))^2] = a^2\text{VAR } X.$$

We now see that the variance for a portfolio of two assets is

$$\text{VAR}(R_p) = a^2\text{VAR}(X) + b^2\text{VAR}(Y) + 2ab\,\text{COV}(X, Y). \tag{6.16}$$

To provide a better intuitive feel for portfolio variance and for the meaning of covariance, consider the following set of returns for assets X and Y:

Probability	X_i	Y_i
.2	11%	−3%
.2	9	15
.2	25	2
.2	7	20
.2	−2	6

To simplify matters we have assumed that each pair of returns $[X_i, Y_i]$ has equal probability (Prob = .2). The expected value of X is 10%, and the expected value of Y is 8%. The variances are computed below.

---

[3] From this point on, the tilde, ~, will be used in the text to designate a random variable only when it is needed to prevent ambiguity.

$$\text{VAR}(X) = .2(.11 - .10)^2 + .2(.09 - .10)^2 + .2(.25 - .10)^2$$
$$+ .2(.07 - .10)^2 + .2(-.02 - .10)^2$$
$$= .0076.$$
$$\text{VAR}(Y) = .2(-.03 - .08)^2 + .2(.15 - .08)^2 + .2(.02 - .08)^2$$
$$+ .2(.20 - .08)^2 + .2(.06 - .08)^2$$
$$= .00708.$$

The covariance between X and Y is

$$\text{COV}(X, Y) = E[(X - E(X))(Y - E(Y))]$$
$$= .2(.11 - .10)(-.03 - .08) + .2(.09 - .10)(.15 - .08)$$
$$+ .2(.25 - .10)(.02 - .08) + .2(.07 - .10)(.20 - .08)$$
$$+ .2(-.02 - .10)(.06 - .08)$$
$$= -.0024.$$

Negative covariance implies that the returns on asset X and asset Y tend to move in opposite directions. If we invest in both securities at once the result is a portfolio that is less risky than holding either asset separately: while we are losing with asset X, we win with asset Y. Therefore our investment position is partially hedged, and risk is reduced.

As an illustration of the effect of diversification, suppose we invest half our assets in X and half in Y. By using Eqs. (6.15) and (6.16) we can compute portfolio return and risk directly.

$$E(R_p) = aE(X) + bE(Y) \tag{6.15}$$
$$= .5(.10) + .5(.08) = 9\%.$$

$$\text{VAR}(R_p) = a^2\text{VAR}(X) + b^2\text{VAR}(Y) + 2ab\,\text{COV}(X, Y) \tag{6.16}$$
$$= (.5)^2(.0076) + (.5)^2(.00708) + 2(.5)(.5)(-.0024)$$
$$= .00247 \quad \text{or} \quad \sigma(R_p) = 4.97\%.$$

The advantage of portfolio diversification becomes clear in this example. With half our assets in X and half in Y, the expected return is halfway between that offered by X and by Y, but the portfolio risk is considerably less than either $\text{VAR}(X)$ or $\text{VAR}(Y)$.

Of course, we may choose any combination of X and Y. Table 6.3 gives the mean and standard deviation of returns for some of the possibilities.

Figure 6.3(a) shows the relationship between (1) the expected return on the portfolio and (2) the percentage of the portfolio, a, that is invested in risky asset X. Note that the portfolio expected return is a linear function of the weight in asset X.

$$\frac{dE(R_p)}{da} = E(X) - E(Y) = 10.0\% - 8.0\% = 2\%.$$

Table 6.3   Mean and Standard Deviation of Returns

Percentage in X	Percentage in Y	$E(\tilde{R}_p)$	$\sigma(\tilde{R}_p)$
100	0	10.0%	8.72%
75	25	9.5	6.18
50	50	9.0	4.97
25	75	8.5	5.96
0	100	8.0	8.41

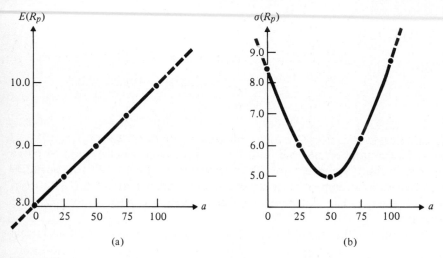

(a)   (b)

Figure 6.3
The portfolio return mean and standard deviation as a function of the percentage
invested in risky asset X.

For each 1% decline in "a" there will be a 2% decline in expected return. The relationship between the portfolio standard deviation, $\sigma(R_p)$, and the weight in asset X is non-
linear and reaches a minimum. Later on, we will show how to determine the portfolio
weights that will minimize portfolio risk.
     Figure 6.4 plots the portfolio mean and standard deviation on a single graph.
Each point represents a different weight in asset X. The solid portion of the line
represents all combinations where the weights in asset X range between 0% and 100%.

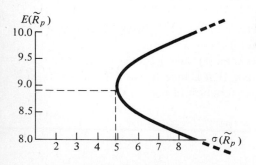

Figure 6.4
Trade-off between mean and standard
deviation.

If we can sell an asset short without restriction, then the dashed portions of the lines in Fig. 6.4 are feasible. Selling short means that you sell an asset that you do not already have. For example, it might be possible to sell short 50% of your wealth in asset X (even though you do not already own shares of asset X) and buy 150% of asset Y. If you sell X short, you should receive the proceeds, which you can then use to buy an extra 50% of Y. This is not possible in the real world because investors do not receive funds equal to the value of securities which they sell short. Nevertheless, for expositional purposes, we assume that short sales are not constrained. The mean and variance of the above short position are calculated below:

$$E(R_p) = -.5E(X) + 1.5E(Y)$$

$$= -.5(.10) + 1.5(.08) = 7.0\%.$$

$$\text{VAR}(R_p) = (-.5)^2\text{VAR}(X) + (1.5)^2\text{VAR}(Y) + 2(-.5)(1.5)\text{COV}(X, Y)$$

$$= .25(.0076) + (2.25)(.00708) + 2(-.75)(-.0024) = .02143.$$

$$\sigma(R_p) = \sqrt{\text{VAR}(R_p)} = 14.64\%.$$

Now that we have developed ways of measuring the risk (variance) and return (mean) for a portfolio of assets, there are several interesting questions to explore. For example, what happens if the covariance between X and Y is zero—i.e., what happens if the two securities are independent? On the other hand, what happens if they are perfectly correlated? How do we find the combination of X and Y that gives minimum variance?

3. The Correlation Coefficient

To answer some of these questions, it is useful to explain the concept of correlation, which is similar to covariance. The *correlation*, r_{xy}, between two random variables is defined as the covariance divided by the product of the standard deviations:

$$r_{xy} \equiv \frac{\text{COV}(X, Y)}{\sigma_x \sigma_y}. \tag{6.17}$$

Obviously, if returns on the two assets are independent, i.e., if the covariance between them is zero, then the correlation between them will be zero. Such a situation is shown in Fig. 6.5, which is a scatter diagram of two independent returns.

The opposite situation occurs when the returns are perfectly correlated, as in Fig. 6.6, in which the returns all fall on a straight line. Perfect correlation will result

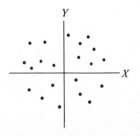

Figure 6.5
Independent returns.

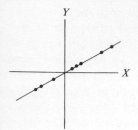

Figure 6.6
Perfectly correlated returns.

in a correlation coefficient equal to 1. To see that this is true we can use the fact that Y is a linear function of X. In other words, if we are given the value of X, we know for sure what the corresponding value of Y will be. This is expressed as a linear function:

$$Y = a + bX.$$

We also use the definition of the correlation coefficient. First, we derive the expected value and standard deviation of Y by using Properties 1 through 4:

$$E(Y) = a + bE(X),$$

$$\text{VAR}(Y) = b^2\text{VAR}(X),$$

$$\sigma_y = b\sigma_x.$$

The definition of the correlation coefficient is

$$r_{xy} = \frac{\text{COV}(X, Y)}{\sigma_x\sigma_y} = \frac{E[(X - E(X))(Y - E(Y))]}{\sigma_x\sigma_y}.$$

By substituting the mean and variance of Y, we obtain

$$r_{xy} = \frac{E[(X - E(X))(a + bX - a - bE(X))]}{\sigma_x b\sigma_x}$$

$$= \frac{E[(X - E(X))b(X - E(X))]}{b\sigma_x^2} = \frac{b\sigma_x^2}{b\sigma_x^2} = 1.$$

Therefore the correlation coefficient equals $+1$ if the returns are perfectly correlated, and it equals -1 if the returns are perfectly inversely correlated.[4] It is left as an exercise for the student to prove that the latter is true. The correlation coefficient ranges between $+1$ and -1:

$$-1 \leq r_{xy} \leq 1. \tag{6.18}$$

For the example we have been working with, the correlation between X and Y is

$$r_{xy} = \frac{\text{COV}(X, Y)}{\sigma_x\sigma_y} = \frac{-.0024}{(.0872)(.0841)} = -.33.$$

By rearranging the definition of the correlation coefficient [Eq. (6.17)] we get another definition of covariance whereby it is seen to be equal to the correlation

---

[4] The linear relationship between Y and X for perfect inverse correlation is $Y = a - bX$.

coefficient times the product of the standard deviations:

$$COV(X, Y) = r_{xy}\sigma_x\sigma_y. \tag{6.19}$$

This in turn can be substituted into the definition of the variance of a portfolio of two assets. Substituting (6.19) into (6.16), we have

$$VAR(R_p) = a^2 VAR(X) + b^2 VAR(Y) + 2abr_{xy}\sigma_x\sigma_y. \tag{6.20}$$

4. The Minimum Variance Portfolio

This reformulation of the variance definition is useful in a number of ways. First, it can be used to find the combination of random variables, X and Y, that provides the portfolio with minimum variance. This portfolio is the one where changes in variance (or standard deviation) with respect to changes in the percentage invested in X are zero.[5] First, recall that since the sum of weights must add to 1, $b = 1 - a$. Therefore the variance can be rewritten

$$VAR(R_p) = a^2\sigma_x^2 + (1 - a)^2\sigma_y^2 + 2a(1 - a)r_{xy}\sigma_x\sigma_y.$$

We can minimize portfolio variance by setting the first derivative equal to zero:

$$\frac{d\,VAR(R_p)}{da} = 2a\sigma_x^2 - 2\sigma_y^2 + 2a\sigma_y^2 + 2r_{xy}\sigma_x\sigma_y - 4ar_{xy}\sigma_x\sigma_y = 0$$

$$a(\sigma_x^2 + \sigma_y^2 - 2r_{xy}\sigma_x\sigma_y) + r_{xy}\sigma_x\sigma_y - \sigma_y^2 = 0.$$

Solving for the optimal percentage to invest in X in order to obtain the minimum variance portfolio, we get

$$a^* = \frac{\sigma_y^2 - r_{xy}\sigma_x\sigma_y}{\sigma_x^2 + \sigma_y^2 - 2r_{xy}\sigma_x\sigma_y}. \tag{6.21}$$

Continuing with the example used throughout this section, we see that the minimum variance portfolio is the one where

$$a^* = \frac{.00708 - (-.33)(.0872)(.0841)}{.0076 + .00708 - 2(-.33)(.0872)(.0841)} = .487.$$

The portfolio return and variance for the minimum variance portfolio are

$$E(R_p) = aE(X) + (1 - a)E(Y)$$

$$= .487(.10) + (.513)(.08) = 8.974\%.$$

$$VAR(R_p) = a^2 VAR(X) + (1 - a)^2 VAR(Y) + 2(a)(1 - a)r_{xy}\sigma_x\sigma_y$$

$$= (.487)^2(.0076) + (.513)^2(.00708) + 2(.487)(.513)(-.33)(.0872)(.0841)$$

$$= .0018025 + .0018632 - .0012092 = .0024565.$$

$$\sigma_p = 4.956\%.$$

---

[5] The student who wishes to review the mathematics of maximization is referred to Appendix D.

The minimum variance portfolio is represented by the intersection of the dashed lines in Fig. 6.4.

5. Perfectly Correlated Assets

Up to this point, we have considered an example where the returns of the two risky assets had a negative correlation. What happens if they are perfectly correlated? Suppose $r_{xy} = 1$. Table 6.4 gives an example of security returns where $X = 1.037Y + 1.703$. All combinations of X and Y lie along a straight line and hence are perfectly correlated.

Since we have used the same numbers for the returns on asset Y as were used in the previous example, its standard deviation is 8.41%. We can derive the standard deviation of X by using Property 4, and the covariance between X and Y by using the definition of covariance [Eq. (6.19)]. It is also interesting to look at the graph of mean versus variance (Fig. 6.7). Point A represents the risk and return for a portfolio consisting of 100% of our investment in X, and B represents 100% in Y. The dashed line represents the risk and return provided for all combinations of X and Y when they are perfectly correlated. To see that this trade-off is a straight line, in the mean-

Table 6.4 Perfectly Correlated Security Returns

Probability	X	Y
.2	-1.408%	-3%
.2	17.258	15
.2	3.777	2
.2	22.443	20
.2	7.925	6
	$\sigma_x = 1.037\sigma_y = 8.72\%,$	
	$\sigma_y = 8.41\%,$	
	$\text{COV}(X, Y) = r_{xy}\sigma_x\sigma_y = .007334.$	

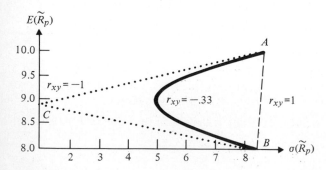

Figure 6.7
Risk-return trade-offs for two assets.

variance argument plane, we take a look at the definitions of mean and variance when $r_{xy} = 1$:

$$E(R_p) = aE(X) + (1 - a)E(Y),$$

$$VAR(R_p) = a^2\sigma_x^2 + (1 - a)^2\sigma_y^2 + 2a(1 - a)\sigma_x\sigma_y.$$

(6.22)

Note that the variance can be factored:

$$VAR(R_p) = [a\sigma_x + (1 - a)\sigma_y]^2;$$

therefore the standard deviation is

$$\sigma(R_p) = a\sigma_x + (1 - a)\sigma_y.$$

(6.23)

The easiest way to prove that the curve between A and B is a straight line is to show that its slope does not change as a, the proportion of the portfolio invested in X, changes. The slope of the line will be the derivative of expected value with respect to the weight in X divided by the derivative of standard deviation with respect to the weight in X:

$$\text{Slope} = \frac{dE(R_p)}{d\sigma(R_p)} = \frac{dE(R_p)/da}{d\sigma(R_p)/da}.$$

The derivative of the expected portfolio return with respect to a change in a is

$$\frac{dE(R_p)}{da} = E(X) - E(Y),$$

and the derivative of the standard deviation with respect to a is

$$\frac{d\sigma(R_p)}{da} = \sigma_x - \sigma_y.$$

Therefore the slope is

$$\frac{dE(R_p)}{d\sigma(R_p)} = \frac{E(X) - E(Y)}{\sigma_x - \sigma_y} = \frac{.10 - .08}{.0872 - .0841} = 6.45.$$

This proves that AB is a straight line because no matter what percentage of wealth, a, we choose to invest in X, the trade-off between expected value and standard deviation is constant.

Finally, suppose the returns on X and Y are perfectly inversely correlated; in other words, $r_{xy} = -1$. In this case the graph of the relationship between mean and standard deviation is the dotted line ACB in Fig. 6.7. We should expect that if the assets have perfect inverse correlation, it would be possible to construct a perfect hedge. That is, the appropriate choice of a will result in a portfolio with zero variance. The mean and variance for a portfolio with two perfectly inversely correlated assets are

$$E(R_p) = aE(X) + (1 - a)E(Y)$$

$$VAR(R_p) = a^2\sigma_x^2 + (1 - a)^2\sigma_y^2 - 2a(1 - a)\sigma_x\sigma_y, \quad \text{since} \quad r_{xy} = -1.$$

(6.24)

The variance can be factored as follows:

$$\text{VAR}(R_p) = [a\sigma_x - (1-a)\sigma_y]^2,$$

$$\sigma(R_p) = \pm[a\sigma_x - (1-a)\sigma_y]. \tag{6.25}$$

Note that Eq. (6.25) has both a positive and a negative root. The dotted line in Fig. 6.7 is really two line segments, one with a positive slope and the other with a negative slope. The following proofs show that the signs of the slopes of the line segments are determined by Eq. (6.25) and that they will always intersect the vertical axis in Fig. 6.7 at a point where the minimum variance portfolio has zero variance.

To show this result, we can use Eq. (6.21) to find the minimum variance portfolio:

$$a^* = \frac{\sigma_y^2 - r_{xy}\sigma_x\sigma_y}{\sigma_x^2 + \sigma_y^2 - 2r_{xy}\sigma_x\sigma_y}.$$

Because $r_{xy} = -1$, we have

$$a^* = \frac{\sigma_y^2 + \sigma_x\sigma_y}{\sigma_x^2 + \sigma_y^2 + 2\sigma_x\sigma_y} = \frac{\sigma_y}{\sigma_x + \sigma_y} = \frac{.0841}{.0872 + .0841} = 49.095\%.$$

By substituting this weight into the equations for mean and standard deviation we can demonstrate that the portfolio has zero variance:

$$E(R_p) = .49095(.10) + (1 - .49095)(.08) = 8.982\%,$$

$$\sigma(R_p) = .49095(.0872) - (1 - .49095)(.0841) = 0\%.$$

This result is represented by point C in Fig. 6.7.

Next, let us examine the properties of the line segments AC and CB in Fig. 6.7. To do so it is important to realize that the expression for the standard deviation [Eq. (6.25)] for a portfolio with two perfectly inversely correlated assets has both positive and negative roots. In our example, suppose that none of the portfolio is invested in X. Then $a = 0$, and the standard deviation is a negative number,

$$\sigma(R_p) = -(1-0)\sigma_y < 0.$$

Because standard deviations cannot be negative, the two roots of Eq. (6.25) need to be interpreted as follows. So long as the percentage invested in X is greater than or equal to 49.095% (which is a^*, the minimum variance portfolio), the standard deviation of the portfolio is

$$\sigma(R_p) = a\sigma_x - (1-a)\sigma_y, \quad \text{if} \quad a \geq \frac{\sigma_y}{\sigma_x + \sigma_y}. \tag{6.25a}$$

On the other hand, if less than 49.095% of the portfolio is invested in X, the standard deviation is

$$\sigma(R_p) = (1-a)\sigma_y - a\sigma_x, \quad \text{if} \quad a < \frac{\sigma_y}{\sigma_x + \sigma_y}. \tag{6.25b}$$

We can use these results to show that the line segments AC and CB are linear. The proof proceeds in precisely the same way that we were able to show that AB is linear if $r_{xy} = 1$. For the positively sloped line segment, AC, using Eq. (6.24), we have

$$\frac{dE(R_p)}{da} = E(X) - E(Y),$$

and using Eq. (6.25a), we have

$$\frac{d\sigma(R_p)}{da} = \sigma_x + \sigma_y \quad \text{if} \quad a \geq \frac{\sigma_y}{\sigma_x + \sigma_y}.$$

Therefore the slope of the line is

$$\frac{dE(R_p)}{d\sigma(R_p)} = \frac{dE(R_p)/da}{d\sigma(R_p)/da} = \frac{E(X) - E(Y)}{\sigma_x + \sigma_y} = \frac{.10 - .08}{.0872 + .0841} = .117 > 0.$$

The slope of AC is positive and AC is linear because the slope is invariant to changes in the percentage of an investor's portfolio invested in X.

For the negatively sloped line segment, CB, using Eq. (6.24), we have

$$\frac{dE(R_p)}{da} = E(X) - E(Y),$$

and using Eq. (6.25b), we have

$$\frac{d\sigma(R_p)}{da} = -\sigma_y - \sigma_x \quad \text{if} \quad a < \frac{\sigma_y}{\sigma_x + \sigma_y}.$$

Therefore the slope of the line is

$$\frac{dE(R_p)}{d\sigma(R_p)} = \frac{dE(R_p)/da}{d\sigma(R_p)/da} = \frac{E(X) - E(Y)}{-(\sigma_y + \sigma_x)} = \frac{.10 - .08}{-(.0872 + .0841)} = -.117 < 0.$$

The slope of CB is negative and CB is linear.

6. The Minimum Variance Opportunity Set

Line AB in Fig. 6.7 shows the risk-return trade-offs available to the investor if the two assets are perfectly correlated, and line segments AC and CB represent the trade-offs if the assets are perfectly inversely correlated. However, these are the two extreme cases. Usually assets are less than perfectly correlated, i.e., $-1 < r_{xy} < 1$. The general slope of the mean-variance opportunity set is the solid line in Fig. 6.7. The opportunity set can be defined as follows:

> *Minimum variance opportunity set.* The minimum variance opportunity set is the locus of risk and return combinations offered by portfolios of risky assets that yields the minimum variance for a given rate of return.

In general the minimum variance opportunity set will be convex (as represented by the solid line in Fig. 6.7). This property is rather obvious because the opportunity set is bounded by the triangle ACB. Intuitively, any set of portfolio combinations formed by two risky assets that are less than perfectly correlated must lie inside the triangle ACB and will be convex.

The concepts developed in this section can now be used to discuss the way we, as investors, are able to select portfolios that maximize our expected utility. The portfolio mean return and variance are the measures of return and risk. We choose the percentages of our wealth that we want to invest in each security in order to obtain the required risk and return. We have shown the choices that are possible if two risky assets are perfectly correlated, perfectly inversely correlated, and where their correlation lies between -1 and $+1$. We have also seen how we can find the minimum variance portfolio. Later in this chapter these results will be extended from the two-asset case to portfolios of many assets, and we will discuss an example wherein a corporate treasurer may use portfolio theory to reduce the risk (variability) of shareholders' wealth.

C. OPTIMAL PORTFOLIO CHOICE: THE EFFICIENT SET WITH TWO RISKY ASSETS (AND NO RISK-FREE ASSET)

The assumption of no risk-free asset is the same as saying that there are no borrowing or lending opportunities. In other words, this section shows how a single individual (Robinson Crusoe) will choose his optimal portfolio of risky assets in a world where there is no opportunity for exchange. As we shall see, the following discussion is analogous to the Robinson Crusoe economy described in Chapter 1 except that the objects of choice are risk and return rather than consumption and investment. The results are also similar. Robinson Crusoe's optimal portfolio will be that where his subjective marginal rate of substitution between risk and return is exactly equal to the objectively determined marginal rate of transformation (along his mean-variance opportunity set) between risk and return. At his optimal portfolio the equality between MRS and MRT determines his subjective price of risk. Later on, in section E.5, we shall introduce a marketplace with opportunities to exchange by borrowing and lending unlimited amounts of money at the risk-free rate. This exchange economy setting will show the existence of a single market-determined price of risk. All individuals and their agents (firms, for example) will use the market price of risk for optimal decisions in the face of uncertainty.

In the chapter on utility theory we saw that indifference curves for the risk-averse investor were convex in the mean-variance plane. Figure 6.8 shows a family of indifference curves as well as the convex set of portfolio choices offered by various percentages of investment in two risky assets. If we know our risk-return trade-off and also know the possibilities offered by combinations of risky assets, we will maximize our expected utility at point C in Fig. 6.8. This is where our indifference curve is tangent to the opportunity set offered by combinations of X and Y. Each indifference curve maps out all combinations of risk and return that provide us with the same total utility. Moving from right to left in Fig. 6.8, we know (from Chapter 4)

$E(\widetilde{R}_p)$

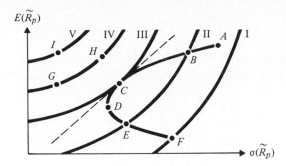

Figure 6.8
Optimal portfolio choice for a risk-averse investor
and two risky assets.

that indifference curve I has less total utility than indifference curve II, and so on. We could put all our money in one asset and receive the risk and return at point F, which is on indifference curve I, but of course we can do better at points B and E, and best at point C (on indifference curve III). Points G, H, and I have higher total utility than point C, but they are not feasible because the opportunity set offered by the risky assets does not extend that far.

An important feature of the optimal portfolio that we choose in order to maximize our utility is that the marginal rate of substitution between our preference for risk and return represented by our indifference curves must equal the marginal rate of transformation offered by the minimum variance opportunity set. The slope of the dashed line drawn tangent to our indifference curve at point C is our marginal rate of substitution between risk and return. This line is also tangent to the opportunity set at point C. Hence its slope also represents the trade-off between risk and return offered by the opportunity set. Therefore the way we can find a utility-maximizing portfolio is to try different portfolios along the opportunity set until we find the one where the marginal rate of transformation between risk and return along the minimum variance opportunity set just equals the marginal rate of substitution along our indifference curve:

$$\text{MRS}_{\sigma(R_p)}^{E(R_p)} = \text{MRT}_{\sigma(R_p)}^{E(R_p)}.$$

The fact that this point is unique is guaranteed by the convexity of our indifference curve and the convexity of the upper half of the minimum variance opportunity set.

Let us take a look at Fig. 6.9. Suppose we find ourselves endowed with a portfolio that has the mean-variance opportunities at point A. By changing the percentage of our wealth in each of the risky assets, we can reach any point along the minimum variance opportunity set. At point A the marginal rate of transformation between return and risk along the minimum variance opportunity set is equal to the slope of the line DAF. The low slope indicates that we will get rid of a lot of risk in exchange for giving up only a little return. On the other hand, the slope of our indifference curve, U_1, the slope of the line CAB at point A, indicates our subjective trade-off

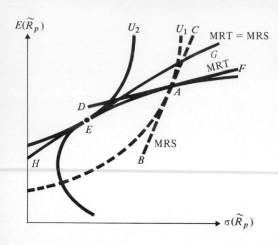

Figure 6.9
The utility maximizing choice equates the marginal rates of substitution and transformation.

between return and risk, i.e., our marginal rate of substitution. At point A, where we already have a relatively high level of risk, we are willing to give up a lot of return in order to get rid of a little risk. If we can move along the opportunity set toward point E without incurring any cost, we will clearly do so because the opportunity set at point A allows us to trade off return and risk at a more favorable rate than we require (according to our indifference curve). We will continue to move along the opportunity set until we reach point E. At this point we attain the highest possible expected utility on indifference curve U_2. Furthermore, the marginal rate of transformation between return and risk along the opportunity (the slope of line HEG) set is exactly equal to the marginal rate of substitution along the indifference curve (also, the slope of tangent line HEG). Thus we have shown that a necessary condition for expected utility maximization is that the marginal rate of substitution must equal the marginal rate of transformation. This also implies that at the optimum portfolio choice, we have a linear trade-off between return, $E(R_p)$, and risk, $\sigma(R_p)$.[6]

Even though different investors may have the same assessment of the return and risk offered by risky assets, they may hold different portfolios. Later we shall discover that when a riskless asset is introduced into the opportunity set, investors will hold identical combinations of risky assets even though they have different attitudes toward risk. However, in the current framework for analysis, we assume that investors have homogeneous beliefs about the opportunity set, that no risk-free asset exists, and that investors have different indifference curves, which reflect their differing attitudes toward risk.[7] Figure 6.10 shows three different indifference curves and the investment opportunity set. Investor III is more risk averse than investor II, who in turn is more risk averse than investor I. (Why is this true?) Consequently, they each will choose to invest a different percentage of their portfolio in the risky assets that make up the opportunity set.

---

[6] For an excellent mathematical development of this fact, see Fama and Miller [1972, Chapter 6].

[7] Homogeneous beliefs mean simply that everyone has exactly the same information so that they all perceive exactly the same opportunity set.

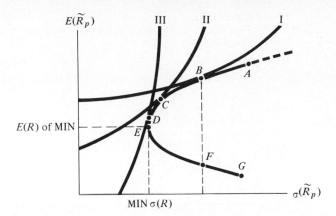

Figure 6.10
Choices by investors with different indifference curves.

Note that rational investors will never choose a portfolio below the minimum variance point. They can always attain higher expected utility along the positively sloped portion of the opportunity set represented by the line segment *EDCBA*. This concept leads to the definition of the efficient set.

> *Efficient set.* The efficient set is the set of mean-variance choices from the investment opportunity set where for a given variance (or standard deviation) no other investment opportunity offers a higher mean return.

The notion of an efficient set considerably narrows the number of portfolios from which an investor might choose. In Fig. 6.10, e.g., the portfolios at points *B* and *F* offer the same standard deviation, but *B* is on the efficient set because it offers a higher return for the same risk. Hence no rational investor would ever choose point *F* over point *B*, and we can ignore point *F*. Point *B* is stochastically dominant over point *F*. It is interesting to note, however, that investors will hold positions in an asset or portfolio at point *F*. No one will hold *F* by itself; rather it will be held as part of portfolios that lie along the efficient set.

Interesting special cases of the efficient set for two risky assets occur when their returns are perfectly correlated. Figure 6.11 shows perfect correlation, and Fig. 6.12

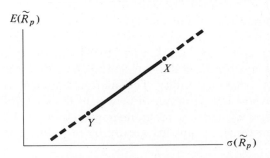

Figure 6.11
Two perfectly correlated assets.

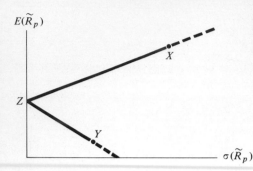

Figure 6.12
Two assets with perfect inverse correlation.

shows perfect inverse correlation. In both cases, the efficient set is linear. In Fig. 6.11 it is line XY and in Fig. 6.12 it is line XZ.

In general the locus of feasible mean-variance opportunities can be found by solving either of the following two mathematical programming problems. The first defines the minimum variance opportunity set, and the second defines the efficient set.

Programming Problem 1:

$$\text{MIN } \sigma^2(R_p) \quad \text{subject to} \quad E(R_p) = K. \tag{6.26a}$$

Programming Problem 2:

$$\text{MAX } E(R_p) \quad \text{subject to} \quad \sigma^2(R_p) = K. \tag{6.26b}$$

Note that the minimum variance opportunity set is found by finding all combinations that give the lowest risk for a given return. The efficient set is the locus of highest returns for a given risk. If we write out the first problem at greater length,

$$\text{MIN}\{\sigma^2(R_p) = [a^2\sigma_x^2 + (1-a)^2\sigma_y^2 + 2a(1-a)r_{xy}\sigma_x\sigma_y]\},$$

subject to

$$E(R_p) = aE(X) + (1-a)E(Y) = K,$$

we see that it is a quadratic programming problem because the objective function contains squared terms in the choice variable, a. The decision variable in either problem, of course, is to choose the percentage, a, to invest in asset X that minimizes variance subject to the expected return constraint. Markowitz [1959] was the first to define the investor's portfolio decision problem in this way and to show that it is equivalent to maximizing the investor's expected utility. The interested student is referred to his book for an excellent exposition. However, it is beyond the scope of the present text to explore the details of a quadratic programming solution to the efficient set. Furthermore, the problem can be simplified greatly by introducing a risk-free asset into the analysis.

D. THE EFFICIENT SET WITH ONE RISKY
AND ONE RISK-FREE ASSET

If one of the two assets, R_f, has zero variance, then the mean and variance of the portfolio become

$$E(R_p) = aE(X) + (1 - a)R_f,$$

$$\text{VAR}(R_p) = a^2\text{VAR}(X).$$

We have assumed that the risk-free asset is R_f. Its variance and its covariance with the risky asset are zero; therefore the second and third terms in the general expression for variance, Eq. (6.20), are equal to zero, and portfolio variance is simply the variance of the risky asset.

   Knowledge of the mean and variance of a portfolio with one risk-free and one risky asset allows us to plot the opportunity set in Fig. 6.13. It is linear. Proof of linearity proceeds in the same way as earlier proofs. All we need to do is show that the slope is independent of a, the percentage of the portfolio invested in the risky asset. The change in expected return with respect to the percentage invested in X is

$$\frac{dE(R_p)}{da} = E(X) - R_f,$$

and the change in standard deviation with respect to a is

$$\frac{d\sigma(R_p)}{da} = \sigma_x.$$

Therefore the slope of the line is

$$\frac{dE(R_p)}{d\sigma(R_p)} = \frac{dE(R_p)/da}{d\sigma(R_p)/da} = \frac{E(X) - R_f}{\sigma_x}.$$

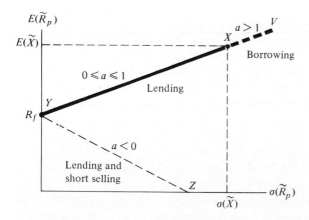

Figure 6.13
Opportunity set with one risky and one risk-free asset.

Consequently, the line VXY must be linear because its slope does not change with the percentage invested in X.

It is usually assumed that the rate of return on the risk-free asset is equal to the borrowing and lending rate in the economy. In the real world, of course, the borrowing and lending rates are not equal. One possible cause is transactions costs, i.e., frictions in the marketplace. However, like physicists who assume that friction does not exist in order to derive the laws of mechanics, economists assume that asset markets are frictionless in order to develop price theory. A frictionless world to an economist is one where all assets are infinitely divisible and where there are no transactions costs. In such a world, the borrowing rate would equal the lending rate for risk-free assets. We shall use this assumption to develop a theory for the equilibrium price of risk, then provide empirical evidence that indicates that in spite of several unrealistic assumptions, the theory describes reality surprisingly well.

Given the assumption that the borrowing rate equals the lending rate, YXV is a straight line. To reach portfolios along the line segment XV it is necessary to borrow in order to invest more than 100% of the portfolio in the risky asset. Note that borrowing is analogous to selling short the risk-free assets. Therefore along the line segment XV the percentage invested in X is greater than 1; in other words, $a > 1$. The mean and standard deviation of the portfolio along this portion of the line are

$$E(R_p) = aE(X) + (1 - a)R_f,$$

$$\sigma(R_p) = a\sigma_x.$$

On the other hand, when we decide to invest more than 100% of our portfolio in the risk-free asset, we must sell short the risky asset. Assuming no restrictions on short sales (another assumption necessary for frictionless markets), the mean and variance of the portfolio for $a < 0$ are

$$E(R_p) = (1 - a)R_f + aE(X),$$

$$\sigma(R_p) = |a|\sigma_x.$$

Note that because negative standard deviations are impossible, the absolute value of a is used to measure the standard deviation of the portfolio when the risky asset is sold short. The line segment YZ represents portfolio mean and variance in this case.

What about the efficient set for portfolios composed of one risk-free and one risky asset? Clearly no risk-averse investor would prefer line segment YZ in Fig. 6.13 because he or she can always do better along the positively sloped line segment YXV. Therefore the efficient set is composed of long positions in the risky asset combined with borrowing or lending. Why then do we observe short sales in the real world? The answer, of course, is that not all people hold the same probability beliefs about the distributions of returns provided by risky assets. Some investors may believe that the expected return on asset X is negative, in which case they would sell short. In equilibrium, however, we know that so long as investors are risk averse, the final price of the risky asset X must be adjusted so that its expected rate of return is greater than the risk-free rate. In equilibrium, assets of higher risk must have higher expected return.

E. OPTIMAL PORTFOLIO CHOICE: MANY ASSETS

Until now it has been convenient to discuss portfolios of only two assets. By generalizing the argument to many assets, we can discuss several important properties such as portfolio diversification, the separation principle, and the Capital Market Line. We can also provide a realistic example of how a corporate chief financial officer who views his or her firm as a portfolio can control the risk exposure of shareholders. We begin by developing the mean and variance for portfolios of many assets.

1. Portfolio Mean, Variance, and Covariance with N Risky Assets

Suppose we wish to talk about the mean and variance of portfolios of three assets instead of just two. Let w_1, w_2, and w_3 be the percentages of a portfolio invested in the three assets; let $E(R_1)$, $E(R_2)$, and $E(R_3)$ be the expected returns; let σ_1^2, σ_2^2, and σ_3^2 be the variances; and let σ_{12}, σ_{23}, and σ_{13} be the covariances. Finally, let R_1, R_2, R_3 be the random returns. The definition of the portfolio mean return is

$$E(R_p) = E[w_1 R_1 + w_2 R_2 + w_3 R_3],$$

and using Property 1, we have

$$E(R_p) = w_1 E(R_1) + w_2 E(R_2) + w_3 E(R_3).$$

As was the case for a portfolio with two assets, the expected portfolio return is simply a weighted average of the expected return on individual assets. This can be rewritten as

$$E(R_p) = \sum_{i=1}^{3} w_i E(R_i). \tag{6.27}$$

The definition of portfolio variance for three assets is the expectation of the sum of the mean differences squared:

$$
\begin{aligned}
\text{VAR}(R_p) &= E\{[(w_1 R_1 + w_2 R_2 + w_3 R_3) - (w_1 E(R_1) + w_2 E(R_2) + w_3 E(R_3))]^2\} \\
&= E\{[w_1(R_1 - E(R_1)) + w_2(R_2 - E(R_2)) + w_3(R_3 - E(R_3))]^2\} \\
&= E\{w_1^2(R_1 - E(R_1))^2 + w_2^2(R_2 - E(R_2))^2 + w_3^2(R_3 - E(R_3))^2 \\
&\quad + 2w_1 w_2(R_1 - E(R_1))(R_2 - E(R_2)) \\
&\quad + 2w_1 w_3(R_1 - E(R_1))(R_3 - E(R_3)) \\
&\quad + 2w_2 w_3(R_2 - E(R_2))(R_3 - E(R_3))\} \\
&= w_1^2 \text{VAR}(R_1) + w_2^2 \text{VAR}(R_2) + w_3^2 \text{VAR}(R_3) + 2w_1 w_2 \text{COV}(R_1, R_2) \\
&\quad + 2w_1 w_3 \text{COV}(R_1, R_3) + 2w_2 w_3 \text{COV}(R_2, R_3).
\end{aligned}
$$

The portfolio variance is a weighted sum of variance and covariance terms. It can be rewritten as

$$VAR(R_p) = \sum_{i=1}^{3} \sum_{j=1}^{3} w_i w_j \sigma_{ij}, \tag{6.28}$$

where w_i and w_j are the percentages invested in each asset, and σ_{ij} is the covariance of asset i with asset j. You will recall from the discussion of covariance earlier in the text that the variance is really a special case of covariance. The variance is the covariance of an asset with itself. For example, when $i = 2$ and $j = 2$, then we have $w_2 w_2 \sigma_{22}$, which is the same thing as $w_2^2 VAR(R_2)$. Therefore Eq. (6.28) contains three variance and six covariance terms.

If we replace the three assets with N, Eqs. (6.27) and (6.28) can be used as general representations of the mean and variance of a portfolio of N assets. We can also write Eqs. (6.27) and (6.28) in matrix form,[8] which for two assets looks like this:

$$E(R_p) = [E(R_1)E(R_2)] \begin{bmatrix} w_1 \\ w_2 \end{bmatrix} = \mathbf{R'W},$$

$$VAR(R_p) = [w_1 w_2] \begin{bmatrix} \sigma_{11} & \sigma_{12} \\ \sigma_{21} & \sigma_{22} \end{bmatrix} \begin{bmatrix} w_1 \\ w_2 \end{bmatrix} = \mathbf{W' \Sigma W}.$$

The expected portfolio return is the $(1 X N)$ row vector of expected returns, $[E(R_1), E(R_2)] = \mathbf{R'}$, postmultiplied by the $(N X 1)$ column vector of weights held in each asset, $[w_1 w_2] = \mathbf{W}$. The variance is the $(N X N)$ variance-covariance matrix, $\mathbf{\Sigma}$, premultiplied and postmultiplied by the vector of weights, $\mathbf{W}$. To see that the matrix definition of the variance is identical to Eq. (6.28), first postmultiply the variance-covariance matrix by the column vector of weights to get

$$VAR(R_p) = [w_1 w_2] \begin{bmatrix} w_1 \sigma_{11} + w_2 \sigma_{12} \\ w_1 \sigma_{21} + w_2 \sigma_{22} \end{bmatrix}.$$

Postmultiplying the second vector times the first, we have

$$VAR(R_p) = w_1^2 \sigma_{11} + w_1 w_2 \sigma_{12} + w_2 w_1 \sigma_{21} + w_2^2 \sigma_{22}.$$

Finally, collecting terms, we see that this is equal to

$$VAR(R_p) = \sum_{i=1}^{N} \sum_{j=1}^{N} w_i w_j \sigma_{ij}, \quad \text{where} \quad N = 2.$$

This shows that the matrix definition of variance is equivalent to Eq. (6.28).

Suppose we want to express the covariance between two portfolios, A and B, using matrix notation. This will prove to be an extremely powerful and useful tool later on. Let $\mathbf{W_1'}$ be the $(1 X N)$ row vector of weights held in portfolio A. For ex-

---

[8] The reader is referred to Appendix B for a review of matrix algebra.

ample, we might construct portfolio A by holding 50% of our wealth in asset X and the remaining 50% in asset Y. Next, let $\mathbf{W}_2$ be the $(NX1)$ column vector of weights used to construct portfolio B. For example, we might have 25% in X and 75% in Y. If $\mathbf{\mathfrak{L}}$ is the (NXN) variance-covariance matrix, then the covariance between the two portfolios is defined as

$$\text{COV}(R_A, R_B) \equiv \mathbf{W}'_1 \, \mathbf{\mathfrak{L}} \, \mathbf{W}_2$$

$$= \begin{bmatrix} w_{1a} & w_{2a} \end{bmatrix} \begin{bmatrix} \sigma_{11} & \sigma_{12} \\ \sigma_{21} & \sigma_{22} \end{bmatrix} \begin{bmatrix} w_{1b} \\ w_{2b} \end{bmatrix}, \tag{6.29}$$

Postmultiplying the variance-covariance matrix, $\mathbf{\mathfrak{L}}$, by the column vector, $\mathbf{W}_2$, we have

$$\text{COV}(R_A, R_B) = \begin{bmatrix} w_{1a} & w_{2a} \end{bmatrix} \begin{bmatrix} w_{1b}\sigma_{11} + w_{2b}\sigma_{12} \\ w_{1b}\sigma_{21} + w_{2b}\sigma_{22} \end{bmatrix},$$

and postmultiplying the row vector, $\mathbf{W}'_1$, by the column vector above, we obtain

$$\text{COV}(R_A, R_B) = w_{1a}w_{1b}\sigma_{11} + w_{1a}w_{2b}\sigma_{12} + w_{2a}w_{1b}\sigma_{21} + w_{2a}w_{2b}\sigma_{22}.$$

To show that this matrix result is indeed the same as the traditional definition, we begin with the usual covariance equation

$$\text{COV}(R_A, R_B) = E[(R_A - E(R_A))(R_B - E(R_B))].$$

We know that

$$R_A = w_{1a}R_x + w_{2a}R_y,$$

$$R_B = w_{1b}R_x + w_{2b}R_y.$$

Substituting these expressions as well as their expected values into the covariance definition, we have

$$\text{COV}(R_A, R_B) = E[(w_{1a}R_x + w_{2a}R_y - w_{1a}E(R_x) - w_{2a}E(R_y))$$

$$\times (w_{1b}R_x + w_{2b}R_y - w_{1b}E(R_x) - w_{2b}E(R_y))]$$

$$= E\{[w_{1a}(R_x - E(R_x)) + w_{2a}(R_y - E(R_y))]$$

$$\times [w_{1b}(R_x - E(R_x)) + w_{2b}(R_y - E(R_y))]\}$$

$$= w_{1a}w_{1b}\sigma_{11} + w_{1a}w_{2b}\sigma_{12} + w_{2a}w_{1b}\sigma_{21} + w_{2a}w_{2b}\sigma_{22}.$$

Note that this is exactly the same as the expanded covariance expression obtained from the matrix definition, Eq. (6.29).

The matrix definitions of portfolio mean, variance, and covariance are particularly powerful and useful because the size of the vectors and matrices can easily be expanded to handle any number of assets. The matrix form also lends itself naturally to computer programs.

2. An Application: Cross Hedging with Futures Contracts

Every corporation is really a portfolio. Take a look at the market value balance sheet in Table 6.5.

The assets of NR Inc. are primarily buildings and land, dispersed geographically, but with market values that are sensitive to changes in inflation. Long-term debt is Baa rated, with roughly 10 years before maturity. Its market value is sensitive to changes in interest rates. The shareholders' position may be conceptualized as portfolio that is long in the firm's assets and short in liabilities. It can be written as

$$\tilde{R}_S = W_{STA}\tilde{R}_{STA} + W_{LTA}\tilde{R}_{LTA} - W_{STL}\tilde{R}_{STL} - W_{LTD}\tilde{R}_{LTD}, \qquad (6.30)$$

where

$$\tilde{R}_S = \text{the risky return on shareholders' wealth,}$$
$$W_{STA}, \tilde{R}_{STA} = \text{the weight and return on short-term assets,}$$
$$W_{LTA}, \tilde{R}_{LTA} = \text{the weight and return on the firm's portfolio of long-term assets,}$$
$$W_{STL}, \tilde{R}_{STL} = \text{the weight and return on the firm's short-term liabilities,}$$
$$W_{LTD}, \tilde{R}_{LTD} = \text{the weight and return on the firm's long-term debt.}$$

Suppose that the firm's chief financial officer (CFO) is concerned that a tough anti-inflationary policy will cause a decline in inflation and in interest rates. The result would be a decline in the market value of the property held by the company (its major asset) and an increase in the market value of the firm's long-term debt. The net effect would be a dramatic rise in the firm's debt-to-assets ratio and a drop in the market value of equity. To hedge against this risk the CFO has decided to buy T-bond futures contracts (an investment that we shall assume, for the sake of convenience, requires no cash outlay).[9] A long position in T-bond futures is expected to be a hedge for two reasons. First, when inflation and interest rates fall the market value of the T-bond futures will rise to offset an expected decline in the market value of the firm's assets. Second, the T-bond position will hedge against an increase in the market value of the firm's debt liabilities.

Given that T-bond futures will provide a hedge, the CFO must determine the optimal number, N, of T-bond futures contracts to buy. Too few will not provide

Table 6.5   Market Value Balance Sheet for NR Inc.

Assets (in millions)		Liabilities (in millions)	
Short-term	239	Short-term	77
Long-term	200	Long-term debt	96
	439	Equity	266
			439

[9] Chapter 9 provides a complete description of futures contracts.

an adequate hedge. Too many will overhedge. If P_{TB} is the current price of a \$100,000 face-value T-bond contract, V is the market value of the firm, and $\tilde{R}_{TB}$ is the return on T-bond futures, then the return on equity, given the hedge position, becomes

$$\tilde{R}_S = W_{STA}\tilde{R}_{STA} + W_{LTA}\tilde{R}_{LTA} - W_{STL}\tilde{R}_{STL} - W_{LTD}\tilde{R}_{LTD} + \frac{NP_{TB}}{V}\tilde{R}_{TB}. \quad (6.31)$$

The variance of the equity return, expressed in matrix form, is

$$\text{VAR}(R_S) = \mathbf{W}' \mathbf{\Sigma} \mathbf{W}, \quad (6.32)$$

where

$$W' = \left[W_{STA}, W_{LTA}, -W_{STL}, -W_{LTD}, \frac{NP_{TB}}{V} \right],$$

$\mathbf{\Sigma}$ = the variance-covariance matrix of all assets and liabilities in the firm's hedge portfolio.

To find the optimal hedge portfolio, we can take the derivative of Eq. (6.32) with respect to N and set the result equal to zero:

$$\frac{d \text{ VAR}(R_S)}{dN} = \frac{2P_{TB}}{V} \sum_i w_i r_{i,TB}\sigma_i\sigma_{TB} + 2\frac{P_{TB}^2}{V^2}\sigma_{TB}^2 N = 0.$$

Note that $r_{i,TB}$ is the correlation between the ith portfolio asset (or liability) and T-bond futures contracts, σ_i is the standard deviation of the ith asset, and σ_{TB} is the standard deviation of the T-bond futures contract return. Solving for N, the optimal number of futures contracts, we have

$$N = -\sum_i \frac{V_i r_{i,TB}\sigma_i}{P_{TB}\sigma_{TB}}. \quad (6.33)$$

Equation (6.33) shows that the hedging asset, T-bond futures, affects shareholders' risk through the correlation betwen T-bond futures returns and the returns on the firm's other assets and liabilities, $r_{i,F}$.[10] The actual values for the parameters involved are

$$r_{STA,TB} = 0, \qquad\qquad r_{STL,TB} = 0,$$

$$r_{LTA,TB} = -.6725, \qquad r_{LTD,TB} = .7834,$$

$$\sigma_{LTD} = .0908, \qquad\qquad \sigma_{LTA} = .0482,$$

$$\sigma_{TB} = .0766, \qquad\qquad V_{TB} = \$70,250.$$

The correlations confirm the CFO's suspicion that T-bond futures will be a good hedge against changes in the market value of long-term assets and long-term debt.

---

[10] The expression $r_{i,TB}\sigma_i/\sigma_{TB}$ is equal to the slope in a linear regression of the returns on the ith asset or liability on T-bond futures.

T-bond futures returns are negatively correlated with assets and positively correlated with debt. Substituting the above values into Eq. (6.33) we have

$$N = \frac{-V_{LTA}r_{LTA,TB}\sigma_{LTA}}{P_{TB}\sigma_{TB}} + \frac{-V_{LTD}r_{LTD,TB}\sigma_{LTD}}{P_{TB}\sigma_{TB}},$$

$$N = \frac{-(200 \times 10^6)(-.6725)(.0482)}{(70.25 \times 10^3)(.0766)} + \frac{-(-96 \times 10^6)(.7834)(.0908)}{(70.25 \times 10^3)(.0766)},$$

$$N = 1205 \text{ contracts} + 1269 \text{ contracts}.$$

The numbers reveal that the CFO needs to buy 1205 contracts as a hedge against changes in the value of assets and 1269 contracts to hedge against changes in the value of long-term debt.

There are, of course, many ways a CFO might choose to reduce the risk of shareholders. This example shows that a total of 2474 T-bond contracts (i.e., $247.4 million worth) provides the optimal hedge. This example illustrates one way of conceptualizing the firm as a portfolio of risky assets. Whether or not the CFO should hedge in the first place and the set of other possible hedge techniques are topics that will be discussed later in the text.

3. The Opportunity Set with N Risky Assets

When considering portfolios with many assets, we can discover the opportunity set and efficient set if we know the expected returns and the variances of individual assets as well as the covariances between each pair of assets. There were not many assets to consider in the hedging example, but an investor can choose literally any combination of securities. This requires a great deal of information. The New York Stock Exchange alone lists at least 2000 securities. To determine the opportunity set it would be necessary to estimate 2000 mean returns, 2000 variances, and 1,999,000 covariances.[11] Fortunately, we shall soon see that there are ways around this computational nightmare.

The investment opportunity set has the same shape with many risky assets as it did with two.[12] The only difference is that with many assets to be considered some will fall in the interior of the opportunity set (Fig. 6.14). The opportunity set will be composed of various portfolios and of some individual assets that are mean-variance efficient by themselves. As long as there is no riskless asset, a risk-averse investor would maximize his or her expected utility in the same way as before—by finding the point of tangency between the efficient set and the highest indifference curve. But in order to do so, he or she would have to estimate all the means, variances, and covariances mentioned earlier.

---

[11] In general, if N securities are analyzed the variance-covariance matrix will have $\frac{1}{2}(N-1)N$ *different* covariance elements and N variance elements.

[12] For proof, see Merton [1972].

$E(\tilde{R}_p)$

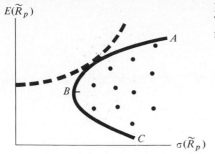

Figure 6.14
The investment opportunity set with
many risky assets.

4. The Efficient Set with N Risky Assets and One Risk-Free Asset

Once the risk-free asset is introduced into the analysis, the problem of portfolio selection is simplified. If, as before, we assume that the borrowing rate equals the lending rate, we can draw a straight line between any risky asset and the risk-free asset. Points along the line represent portfolios consisting of combinations of the risk-free and risky assets. Several possibilities are graphed in Fig. 6.15. Portfolios along any of the lines are possible, but only one line dominates. All investors will prefer combinations of the risk-free asset and portfolio M on the efficient set. (Why?) These combinations lie along the positively sloped portion of line NMR_fO. Therefore the efficient set (which is represented by line segment R_fMN) is linear in the presence of a risk-free asset. All an investor needs to know is the combination of assets that makes up portfolio M in Fig. 6.15 as well as the risk-free asset. This is true for any investor, regardless of his or her degree of risk aversion. Figure 6.16 clarifies this point. Investor III is the most risk averse of the three pictured in Fig. 6.16 and will choose to invest nearly all of his or her portfolio in the risk-free

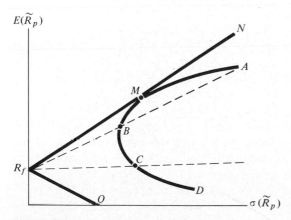

Figure 6.15
The efficient set with one risk-free and many risky assets.

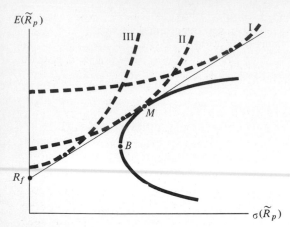

Figure 6.16
Dominance of the linear efficient set.

asset. Investor I, who is the least risk averse, will borrow (at the risk-free rate) to invest more than 100% of his or her portfolio in the risky portfolio M. However, no investor will choose to invest in any other risky portfolio except portfolio M. For example, all three could attain the minimum variance portfolio at point B, but none will choose this alternative because all can do better with some combination of the risk-free asset and portfolio M. Next we shall see that portfolio M can be identified as the market portfolio of all risky assets. All risky assets are held as part of risky portfolio M.

5. A Description of Equilibrium

In section C we analyzed a Robinson Crusoe economy where there was no opportunity for exchange. Robinson Crusoe's optimal portfolio resulted from maximizing his expected utility, given his risk preferences, subject to the feasible set of mean-variance trade-offs offered by a combination of two risky assets. In section D we saw how a linear efficient set could be formed from one risky and one risk-free asset. So far in section E, we have first described the opportunity set with risky assets, then with one risk-free asset and many risky assets.

The introduction of a risk-free asset may be thought of as creating an exchange or market economy where there are many individuals. Each of them may borrow or lend unlimited amounts at the risk-free rate. With the introduction of an exchange economy, we shall be able to describe a fundamental principle called two-fund separation. Analogous to Fisher separation found in Chapter 1 (where everyone used the market-determined time value of money to determine consumption/investment decisions), two-fund separation implies that there is a single market-determined equilibrium price of risk (which is used in portfolio decisions). This concept will prove extremely useful later on in the text when, e.g., we want to conceptualize the opportunity cost of capital for projects of different risk.

If—in addition to the earlier assumption of equality between the borrowing and lending rate that follows, given frictionless capital markets—we add the assumption that all investors have homogeneous (i.e., identical) beliefs about the expected distributions of returns offered by all assets, then all investors will perceive the same efficient set. Therefore they will all try to hold some combination of the risk-free asset, R_f, and portfolio M.

For the market to be in equilibrium, we require a set of market-clearing prices. All assets must be held. In other words the existence of an equilibrium requires that all prices be adjusted so that the excess demand for any asset will be zero. This market-clearing condition implies that an equilibrium is not attained until the single-tangency portfolio, M, which all investors (with homogeneous expectations) try to combine with risk-free borrowing or lending, is a portfolio in which all assets are held according to their market value weights. If V_i is the market value of the ith asset, then the percentage of wealth held in each asset is equal to the ratio of the market value of the asset to the market value of all assets. Mathematically,

$$w_i = \frac{V_i}{\sum_{i=1}^{N} V_i},$$

where w_i is the weight of the ith asset in the market portfolio and $\sum V_i$ is the total market value of all assets. Market equilibrium is not reached until the tangency portfolio, M, is the market portfolio. Also, the value of the risk-free rate must be such that aggregate borrowing and lending are equal.

The fact that the portfolios of all risk-averse investors will consist of different combinations of only two portfolios is an extremely powerful result. It has come to be known as the two-fund separation principle. Its definition is given below.

> *Two-fund separation.* Each investor will have a utility-maximizing portfolio that is a combination of the risk-free asset and a portfolio (or fund) of risky assets that is determined by the line drawn from the risk-free rate of return tangent to the investor's efficient set of risky assets.

The straight line in Fig. 6.16 will be the efficient set for all investors. This line has come to be known as the capital market line. It represents a linear relationship between portfolio risk and return.

> *Capital market line* (CML). If investors have homogeneous beliefs, then they all have the same linear efficient set called the capital market line.

Figure 6.17 is a graph of the capital market line. The intercept is the risk-free rate, R_f, and its slope is $[E(R_m) - R_f]/\sigma(R_m)$. Therefore the equation for the capital market line is

$$E(R_p) = R_f + \frac{E(R_m) - R_f}{\sigma(R_m)} \sigma(R_p). \tag{6.34}$$

It provides a simple linear relationship between the risk and return for *efficient portfolios* of assets. Having established the principle of two-fund separation and defined

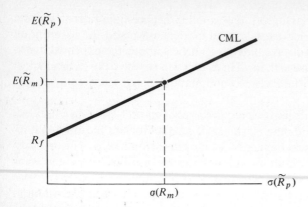

Figure 6.17
The capital market line.

the capital market line, we find it useful to describe the importance of capital market equilibrium from an individual's point of view.

We wish to compare expected utility-maximizing choices in a world without capital markets (as depicted in Fig. 6.9) with those in a world with capital markets (seen in Fig. 6.18). As in Chapter 1, a capital market is nothing more than the opportunity to borrow and lend at the risk-free rate. Chapter 1 emphasized that in a world with certainty everyone was better off, given that capital markets existed and Fisher separation obtained. Now we have extended this result to a world with mean-variance uncertainty. Everyone is better off with capital markets where two-fund separation obtains.

Figure 6.18 shows us endowed with the mean-variance combination at point A. With a capital market, we always have two choices available. We can move along the mean-variance opportunity set (by changing our portfolio of risky assets), or we can

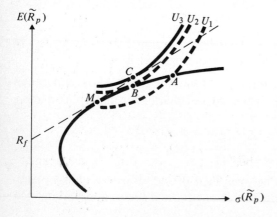

Figure 6.18
Individual expected utility maximization in a world with capital markets.

move along the Capital Market Line by borrowing or lending. Initially, at point A, the trade-off between return and risk is more favorable along the opportunity set than along the market line. Therefore we will move along the opportunity set toward point B where the marginal rate of transformation between return and risk on the opportunity set is equal to our subjective marginal rate of substitution along our indifference curve. In the absence of capital markets, we would have maximized our expected utility at point B. This would be the Robinson Crusoe solution, and our level of utility would have increased from U_1 to U_2. However, if we have the opportunity to move along the Capital Market Line, we can be even better off. By moving to point M, then borrowing to reach point C, we can increase our expected utility from U_2 to U_3. Therefore we have three important results. First, nearly everyone is better off in a world with capital markets (and no one is worse off). Second, two-fund separation obtains. This means that everyone, regardless of the shape of his or her indifference curve, will decide to hold various combinations of two funds: the market portfolio and the risk-free asset. And third, in equilibrium, the marginal rate of substitution (MRS) between return and risk is the same for all individuals, regardless of their subjective attitudes toward risk.

If the marginal rate of substitution between risk and return is the same for every individual in equilibrium, then the slope of the Capital Market Line is the equilibrium price of risk (EPR):

$$\text{EPR} = \text{MRS}_{\sigma(R_p)}^{E(R_p)} = \frac{E(R_m) - R_f}{\sigma(R_m)}. \tag{6.35}$$

The implication is that decision makers, e.g., managers of firms, can use the market-determined equilibrium price of risk to evaluate investment projects regardless of the tastes of shareholders. Every shareholder will unanimously agree on the price of risk even though different shareholders have different degrees of risk aversion. Also the marginal rates of substitution between risk and return for the ith and jth individuals in equilibrium will equal the marginal rate of transformation, and both will be equal to the equilibrium price of risk.

$$\text{MRS}_i = \text{MRS}_j = \frac{E(R_m) - R_f}{\sigma(R_m)} = \text{MRT}.$$

Next, and in Chapter 7, we turn our attention to the problem of measuring risk. We have already established that variance is an adequate measure of risk for portfolios of assets; however, it is not particularly useful when we wish to evaluate the risk of individual assets that do not lie on the efficient set. Nor is it possible, given our current development of the theory, to compare a single risky asset with a well-diversified portfolio. Therefore it is necessary to distinguish between portfolio risk and the contribution of a single asset to the riskiness of a well-diversified portfolio (such as the market portfolio).

To set the framework for the difference between portfolio risk and individual asset risk, we observe the average return and variance of return calculated for a single asset,

Bayside Cigar, and for a 100-stock portfolio of randomly selected common stocks. Return on the assets was defined as total return, i.e., dividends, Div_t, plus capital gains, $P_t - P_{t-1}$. The equation for a monthly return is given below:

$$R_t = \frac{P_t - P_{t-1} + \text{Div}_t}{P_{t-1}}.$$

Data were collected for the 306 months between January 1945 and June 1970.[13] The average monthly return on Bayside Cigar was .45%, which is approximately 5.4% per year, and the standard deviation was 7.26%. By comparison, the 100-stock portfolio had an average return of .91% per month or 10.9% per year. Its standard deviation was 4.45%. Normally, one would expect the standard deviation of a well-diversified portfolio to be lower than for a single asset, and the empirical results bear this out. But we also know that riskier assets should have higher returns. Therefore if standard deviation is the appropriate measure of risk for an individual asset, then Bayside Cigar should have a higher return. But it does not! We shall see in the next chapter that the resolution to this apparent paradox is that although the standard deviation is appropriate for measuring the risk of an efficient portfolio, it is not the appropriate measure of risk for individual assets or for comparing the riskiness of portfolios with the riskiness of assets.

F. PORTFOLIO DIVERSIFICATION AND INDIVIDUAL ASSET RISK

We begin by taking a look at what happens to portfolio variance as we increase the number of assets in a portfolio. Equation (6.28),

$$\text{VAR}(R_p) = \sum_{i=1}^{N} \sum_{j=1}^{N} w_i w_j \sigma_{ij},$$

provided an expression for the variance of a portfolio of many assets.

We shall see that as the number of assets in the portfolio increases, the portfolio variance decreases and approaches the average covariance. There are several ways to prove this. The easiest is simply to note that a two-asset portfolio has 2 variance and 2 covariance terms. A three-asset portfolio has 3 variance but 6 covariance terms. A four-asset portfolio has 4 variance terms and 12 covariance terms. In general the number of variance terms equals the number of assets in the portfolio, N, whereas the number of covariance terms equals $(N^2 - N)$ or $N(N - 1)$. Suppose that we have an equally weighted portfolio so that $w_i = w_j = 1/N$. Then the portfolio variance can be written from Eq. (6.28) as

$$\text{VAR}(R_p) = \sum_{i=1}^{N} \sum_{j=1}^{N} \frac{1}{N} \frac{1}{N} \sigma_{ij} = \frac{1}{N^2} \sum_{i=1}^{N} \sum_{j=1}^{N} \sigma_{ij}.$$

---

[13] See Modigliani and Pogue [1974].

This expression can be separated into variance and covariance terms as follows:

$$\text{VAR}(R_p) = \frac{1}{N^2} \sum_{i=1}^{N} \sigma_{ii} + \frac{1}{N^2} \sum_{i=1}^{N} \sum_{\substack{j=1 \\ i \neq j}}^{N} \sigma_{ij}. \tag{6.36}$$

Suppose that the largest individual asset variance is L. Then the first term, the variance term, is always less than or equal to

$$\frac{1}{N^2} \sum_{i=1}^{N} L = \frac{LN}{N^2} = \frac{L}{N},$$

and as the number of assets in the portfolio becomes large, this term approaches zero:

$$\lim_{N \to \infty} \frac{L}{N} = 0.$$

On the other hand, the covariance terms do not vanish. Let $\bar{\sigma}_{ij}$ be the average covariance. Then in the right-hand term in Eq. (6.36), there are $(N^2 - N)$ covariance terms, all equal to $\bar{\sigma}_{ij}$; therefore the right-hand term can be rewritten as

$$\frac{1}{N^2}(N^2 - N)\bar{\sigma}_{ij} = \frac{N^2}{N^2}\bar{\sigma}_{ij} - \frac{N}{N^2}\bar{\sigma}_{ij},$$

and the limit as N approaches infinity is

$$\lim_{N \to \infty} \left(\frac{N^2}{N^2}\bar{\sigma}_{ij} - \frac{N}{N^2}\bar{\sigma}_{ij} \right) = \bar{\sigma}_{ij}. \tag{6.37}$$

Consequently, as we form portfolios that have large numbers of assets and that are better diversified, the covariance terms become relatively more important.

Fama [1976] has illustrated this result empirically.[14] His results are shown in Fig. 6.19. He randomly selected 50 New York Stock Exchange (NYSE) listed securities and calculated their standard deviations using monthly data from July 1963 to June 1968. Then a single security was selected randomly. Its standard deviation of return was around 11%. Next, this security was combined with another (also randomly selected) to form an equally weighted portfolio of two securities. The standard deviation fell to around 7.2%. Step by step more securities were randomly added to the portfolio until all 50 securities were included. Almost all the diversification was obtained after the first 10 to 15 securities were randomly selected. In addition the portfolio standard deviation quickly approached a limit that is roughly equal to the average covariance of all securities. One of the practical implications is that most of the benefits of diversification (given a random portfolio selection strategy) can be achieved with fewer than 15 stocks.

Ibbotson and Sinquefield [1986], using monthly data between 1926 and 1985, have computed the geometric mean and standard deviation of returns for value-weighted portfolios of broad classes of assets, e.g., common stocks (the Standard and

---

[14] See Fama [1976, 253–254].

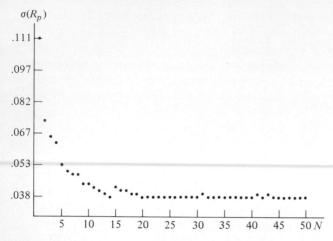

Figure 6.19
The standard deviation of portfolio return as a function of
the number of securities in the portfolio. (From Fama, E. F.,
Foundations of Finance, 1976, reprinted with permission of
the author.)

Poor's 500), small stocks (the smallest quintile on the New York Stock Exchange),
and bonds. Table 6.6 summarizes their results. Note that the standard deviation of
the portfolio of common stocks was 21.2% per year, whereas the standard deviation of small stocks (not a randomly selected portfolio) was about 70% larger at a
level of 36.0% per year. These data show the limits of diversification for different
classes of securities.

Still another way of looking at the risk of a single asset is to evaluate its contribution to total portfolio risk. This can be done by taking the partial derivative of
the expression for portfolio variance [Eq. (6.28)] with respect to w_i, the percentage
invested in the ith risky asset:

$$\frac{\partial \text{ VAR}(R_p)}{\partial w_i} = 2w_i\sigma_i^2 + 2\sum_{j=1}^{N} w_j\sigma_{ij}. \qquad (6.38)$$

Table 6.6   Annualized Returns Data 1926–1985

Portfolio	Geometric Mean	Standard Deviation
Value weighted common stocks	9.8%	21.2%
Smallest NYSE quintile stocks	12.6%	36.0%
High-grade long-term corporate bonds	4.8%	8.3%
Long-term U.S. government bonds	4.1%	8.2%
U.S. Treasury Bills	3.4%	3.4%
Consumer Price Index	3.1%	4.9%

Source: Ibbotson and Sinquefield [1986, 25].

Again, consider a portfolio where an equal percentage is invested in each asset, $w_i = 1/N$. As the number of assets in the portfolio increases, w_i approaches zero and $\sum w_j$ approaches one. Therefore for well-diversified portfolios the appropriate measure of the contribution of an asset to portfolio risk is its covariance with the other assets in the portfolio. In the marketplace for assets (e.g., the stock market) the number of risky assets is extremely large. We shall see (in Chapter 7) that the contribution of a single asset to market risk is its covariance with the market portfolio. Hence this is the measure of risk appropriate for a single asset even though individual investors may not, in reality, hold well-diversified portfolios. Relationships (6.37) and (6.38) help provide an intuitive appeal for covariance as the appropriate measure of risk for individual assets, but they are not proofs. For proof, we need to consider market equilibrium. In the next chapter we shall show that the covariance risk of an asset is the only portion of an asset's risk that an investor will pay to avoid. This important idea is embodied in what has come to be known as the *capital asset pricing model*. It is an equilibrium theory of risk and return, which is the main topic of Chapter 7.

But why can variance not be used as a measure of risk? After all, we know that expected utility-maximizing investors choose their optimal portfolios on the basis of mean and variance. The answer lies in Fig. 6.20. Asset I is inefficient because it does not lie on the capital market line. Consequently, even though we know the mean and variance of asset I, we cannot be sure what rate of return the market will require to hold the asset because it is not on the efficient frontier. Investors have available to them other opportunities that have the same expected return but lower variance. Therefore we cannot use our knowledge of the mean and variance of asset I to determine the rate of return that the market will require from asset I in order to hold it in equilibrium. In Chapter 7, given a market equilibrium setting, we shall see that only the portion of total variance that is correlated with the economy is relevant. Any portion of total risk that is not correlated with the economy is irrelevant and can be avoided at zero cost through diversification. Assets I, J, and K have the same expected return, $\bar{R}$, yet they all have different variances. If variance is the correct measure of the riskiness of an individual asset, then the implication is that these three assets, each with different "risk," all have the same expected return. This is nonsense. It would violate what has come to be known as the single-price law of securities.

The single-price law of securities. All securities or combinations of securities that have the same joint distributions of return will have the same price in equilibrium.

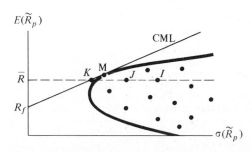

$E(\tilde{R}_p)$

Figure 6.20
The capital market line.

Since the three securities clearly have different distributions of return, they also have different prices. Even though we know the mean and variance of return offered by assets I, J, and K, we cannot be sure what prices they will have in equilibrium. The reason is that we do not know their joint distribution with all other assets. The missing information is the variance-covariance matrix of all assets. In Chapter 7 we shall see that variance is not the appropriate measure of risk for an individual asset. This was the point of Eqs. (6.37) and (6.38). As the number of assets in a portfolio increases, the risk that an asset contributes to a portfolio reduces to be exclusively the covariance risk. Therefore the portion of an asset's risk that is uncorrelated with the economy can be avoided at no cost. No rational investor will pay a premium to avoid diversifiable risk. On the other hand, because covariance risk cannot be diversified away, investors will pay a premium to escape it. Therefore covariance is the relevant measure of risk for an asset because it measures the contribution of an individual asset to the variance of a well-diversified portfolio.

SUMMARY

This chapter has combined our knowledge of the theory of investor choice (utility theory) with the objects of investor choice (the portfolio opportunity set) to show how risk-averse investors wishing to maximize expected utility will choose their optimal portfolios. We began with simple measures of risk and return (and simple probability theory) and ended with portfolio theory. Finally, we saw that when a risk-free asset exists, the opportunity set can be reduced to the simple, linear Capital Market Line. Given frictionless capital markets and homogeneous investor expectations, all individuals will choose to hold some combination of the risk-free asset and the market portfolio.

PROBLEM SET

6.1 Historically, the empirical distributions of stock prices on the NYSE have been skewed right. Why?

6.2 Given the following relationship between x and y,

$$y = a + bx, \qquad b < 0,$$

prove that x and y are perfectly negatively correlated.

6.3 Given the following hypothetical end-of-period prices for shares of the Drill-On Corporation,

Probability	*.15*	*.10*	*.30*	*20*	*.25*
End-of-period price per share	35.00	42.00	50.00	55.00	60.00

and assuming a current price of $50 per share:

a) Calculate the rate of return for each probability. What is the expected return? The variance of end-of-period returns? The range? The semiinterquartile range?

b) Suppose forecasting is refined such that probabilities of end-of-period prices can be broken down further, resulting in the following distribution:

Probability	.01	.05	.07	.02	.10	.30	.20	.15	.05	.05
End-of-period price per share	0	35.00	38.57	40.00	42.00	50.00	55.00	57.00	60.00	69.00

Calculate and explain the change in

a) The expected return;

b) The range of returns;

c) The semiinterquartile range of returns.

Calculate the semivariance of end-of-period returns. Why might some investors be concerned with semivariance as a measure of risk?

6.4 Derive an expression for the expectation of the product of two random variables:

$$E(\tilde{x}\tilde{y}) = ?$$

6.5 Using the definition of portfolio variance, prove that a perfectly hedged stock portfolio that is 100 shares long and 100 shares short is perfectly risk free.

6.6 Given the variance-covariance matrix

$$\begin{bmatrix} 24 & -10 & 25 \\ -10 & 75 & 32 \\ 25 & 32 & 12 \end{bmatrix}$$

a) Calculate the variance of an equally weighted portfolio.

b) Calculate the covariance of a portfolio that has 10% in asset 1, 80% in asset 2, and 10% in asset 3 with a second portfolio that has 125% in asset 1, -10% in asset 2, and -15% in asset 3.

6.7 Given two random variables, x and y,

Probability of State of Nature	State of Nature	Variable x	Variable y
.2	I	18	0
.2	II	5	-3
.2	III	12	15
.2	IV	4	12
.2	V	6	1

a) Calculate the mean and variance of each of these variables, and the covariance between them.

b) Suppose x and y represent the returns from two assets. Calculate the mean and variance for the following portfolios:

% in x	125	100	75	50	25	0	-25
% in y	-25	0	25	50	75	100	125

c) Find the portfolio that has the minimum variance.

d) Let portfolio A have 75% in x and portfolio B have 25% in x. Calculate the covariance between the two portfolios.

e) Calculate the covariance between the minimum variance portfolio and portfolio A, and the covariance between the minimum variance portfolio and portfolio B.

f) What is the covariance between the minimum variance portfolio and any other portfolio along the efficient set?

g) What is the relationship between the covariance of the minimum variance portfolio with other efficient portfolios, and the variance of the minimum variance portfolio?

6.8 Prove that for any securities $\tilde{X}$ and $\tilde{Y}$:

a) $E(a\tilde{X} + b\tilde{Y}) = aE(\tilde{X}) + bE(\tilde{Y})$.

b) $\text{VAR}(a\tilde{X} + b\tilde{Y}) = a^2\text{VAR}(\tilde{X}) + b^2\text{VAR}(\tilde{Y}) + 2ab\,\text{COV}(\tilde{X}, \tilde{Y})$.

c) $\text{COV}[(a\tilde{X} + b\tilde{Z}), \tilde{Y}] = a\,\text{COV}(\tilde{X}, \tilde{Y}) + b\,\text{COV}(\tilde{Z}, \tilde{Y})$.

d) $E(\tilde{X}^2) = (E(\tilde{X}))^2 + \text{VAR}(\tilde{X})$.

e) If $r_{xy} = 1$, then $\sigma(X + Y) = \sigma_x + \sigma_y$. If $r_{xy} = -1$, then $\sigma(\tilde{X} + \tilde{Y}) = \sigma_x - \sigma_y$.

6.9 Let R_1 and R_2 be the returns from two securities with $E(R_1) = .03$ and $E(R_2) = .08$, $\text{VAR}(R_1) = .02$, $\text{VAR}(R_2) = .05$, and $\text{COV}(R_1, R_2) = -.01$.

a) Plot the set of feasible mean-variance combinations of return, assuming that the two securities above are the only investment vehicles available.

b) If we want to minimize risk, how much of our portfolio will we invest in security 1?

c) Find the mean and standard deviation of a portfolio that is 50% in security 1.

6.10 (Our thanks to Nils Hakansson, University of California, Berkeley, for providing this problem.) Two securities have the following joint distribution of returns, r_1 and r_2:

$$P\{r_1 = -1.0 \text{ and } r_2 = .15\} = .1,$$
$$P\{r_1 = .5 \text{ and } r_2 = .15\} = .8,$$
$$P\{r_1 = .5 \text{ and } r_2 = 1.65\} = .1.$$

a) Compute the means, variances, and covariance of returns for the two securities.

b) Plot the feasible mean-standard deviation $[E(R), \sigma]$ combinations, assuming that the two securities are the only investment vehicles available.

c) Which portfolios belong to the mean-variance efficient set?

d) Show that security 2 is mean-variance dominated by security 1, yet enters all efficient portfolios but one. How do you explain this?

e) Suppose that the possibility of lending, but not borrowing, at 5% (without risk) is added to the previous opportunities. Draw the new set of $[E(R), \sigma]$ combinations. Which portfolios are now efficient?

6.11 Suppose a risk-averse investor can choose a portfolio from among N assets with independently distributed returns, all of which have identical means $[E(R_i) = E(R_j)]$ and identical variances $(\sigma_i^2 = \sigma_j^2)$. What will be the composition of his optimal portfolio?

6.12 Given decreasing marginal utility, it is possible to prove that in a mean-variance framework no individual will hold 100% of his or her wealth in the risk-free asset. Why? [*Hint:* The answer requires an understanding of the shape of investors' indifference curves as well as the capital market line.]

6.13 Given that assets X and Y are perfectly correlated such that $Y = 6 + .2X$ and the probability distribution for X is

Probability	X
.1	30%
.2	20
.4	15
.2	10
.1	−50

What is the percentage of your wealth to put into asset X to achieve zero variance? Graph the opportunity set and the zero variance point.

6.14 A market value balance sheet for the Carr Commercial Bank is given below in millions of dollars:

Assets		Liabilities	
Short-term	100	Short-term	50
U.S. government bonds	200	Deposits	850
Loans	700	Equity	100
	1000		1000

The standard deviations and correlations between returns on asset and liability categories (excepting equity) are as follows:

$$\sigma(STA) = .02, \quad r_{STA,US} = 0, \quad r_{STA,L} = 0, \quad r_{STA,STL} = 0,$$

$$r_{STA,D} = 0,$$

$$\sigma(US) = .04, \quad r_{US,L} = .8, \quad r_{US,STL} = 0, \quad r_{US,D} = .3,$$

$$\sigma(L) = .07, \quad r_{L,STL} = 0, \quad r_{L,D} = .2,$$

$$\sigma(STL) = .02, \quad r_{STL,D} = 0,$$

$$\sigma(D) = .03.$$

a) What is the standard deviation of the equity holder's position?

Suppose the bank decides to hedge by taking a position in T-bond futures contracts. You are given the following information:

$$V_{TB} = \$90,000 \text{ for a } \$100,000 \text{ face-value T-bond contract,}$$

$$\sigma_{TB} = .08, \quad r_{TB,STA} = 0, \quad r_{TB,US} = .9, \quad r_{TB,L} = .5, \quad r_{TB,STL} = 0, \quad r_{TB,D} = .3.$$

Should the bank take a long or short position in T-bond futures? How many futures contracts should they buy/sell? How much is the standard deviation of equity reduced?

REFERENCES

Crámer, H., *Mathematical Methods in Statistics*. Princeton University Press, Princeton, N.J., 1961.

Fama, E. F., *Foundations of Finance*. Basic Books, New York, 1976.

———, and M. Miller, *The Theory of Finance*. Holt, Rinehart and Winston, New York, 1972.

Ibbotson, R. G., and R. Sinquefield, *Stocks, Bonds, Bills and Inflation: 1986 Yearbook*. Ibbotson Associates, Inc., Chicago, Illinois, 1986.

Markowitz, H. M., *Portfolio Selection: Efficient Diversification of Investment* (Cowles Foundation Monograph 16). Yale University Press, New Haven, 1959.

Merton, R., "An Analytic Derivation of the Efficient Set," *Journal of Financial and Quantitative Analysis*, September 1972, 1851–1872.

Modigliani, F., and G. Pogue, "An Introduction to Risk and Return: Concepts and Evidence," *Financial Analysts Journal*, March–April and May–June, 1974, 68–80, 69–85.

Sharpe, W., "A Simplified Model for Portfolio Analysis," *Management Science*, January 1963, 277–293.

———, *Portfolio Theory and Capital Markets*. McGraw-Hill, New York, 1970.

Tobin, J., "Liquidity Preference as Behavior towards Risk," *Review of Economic Studies*, February 1958, 65–86.

7

Lucy: "I've just come up with the perfect theory. It's my theory that
Beethoven would have written even better music if he had been
married."
Schroeder: "What's so perfect about that theory?"
Lucy: "It can't be proved one way or the other!"

Charles Schulz, *Peanuts*, 1976

Market Equilibrium: CAPM *and* APT

A. INTRODUCTION

The greater portion of this chapter is devoted to extending the concept of market
equilibrium in order to determine the market price for risk and the appropriate measure of risk for a single asset. One economic model used to solve this problem was
developed almost simultaneously by Sharpe [1963, 1964], and Treynor [1961], while
Mossin [1966], Lintner [1965b, 1969], and Black [1972] developed it further. The first
model we will discuss is usually referred to as the *capital asset pricing model* (CAPM).
It will show that the equilibrium rates of return on all risky assets are a function of
their covariance with the market portfolio. A second important equilibrium pricing
model, called the *arbitrage pricing theory* (APT), was developed by Ross [1976]. It is
similar to the CAPM in that it is also an equilibrium asset pricing model. The return
on any risky asset is seen to be a linear combination of various common factors that
affect asset returns. It is more general than the CAPM because it allows numerous
factors to explain the equilibrium return on a risky asset. However, it is in the same
spirit as the CAPM. In fact, the CAPM can be shown to be a special case of the APT.

The organization of the chapter is to first develop the CAPM and its extensions,
then to summarize the empirical evidence relating to its validity. Thereafter the APT
will be developed and empirical evidence on it will be described. We begin with a list
of the assumptions that were first used to derive the CAPM.

The CAPM is developed in a hypothetical world where the following assumptions are made about investors and the opportunity set:

1. Investors are risk-averse individuals who maximize the expected utility of their end-of-period wealth.
2. Investors are price takers and have homogeneous expectations about asset returns that have a joint normal distribution.
3. There exists a risk-free asset such that investors may borrow or lend unlimited amounts at the risk-free rate.
4. The quantities of assets are fixed. Also, all assets are marketable and perfectly divisible.
5. Asset markets are frictionless and information is costless and simultaneously available to all investors.
6. There are no market imperfections such as taxes, regulations, or restrictions on short selling.

Many of these assumptions have been discussed earlier. However, it is worthwhile to discuss some of their implications. For example, if markets are frictionless, the borrowing rate equals the lending rate, and we are able to develop a linear efficient set called the Capital Market Line [Fig. 6.17 and Eq. (6.34)]. If all assets are divisible and marketable, we exclude the possibility of human capital as we usually think of it. In other words, slavery is allowed in the model. We are all able to sell (not rent for wages) various portions of our human capital (e.g., typing ability or reading ability) to other investors at market prices. Another important assumption is that investors have homogeneous beliefs. They all make decisions based on an identical opportunity set. In other words, no one can be fooled because everyone has the same information at the same time. Also, since all investors maximize the expected utility of their end-of-period wealth, the model is implicitly a one-period model.

Although not all these assumptions conform to reality, they are simplifications that permit the development of the CAPM, which is extremely useful for financial decision making because it quantifies and prices risk. Most of the restrictive assumptions will be relaxed later on.

B. THE EFFICIENCY OF THE MARKET PORTFOLIO

Proof of the CAPM requires that in equilibrium the market portfolio must be an efficient portfolio. It must lie on the upper half of the minimum variance opportunity set graphed in Fig. 7.1. One way to establish its efficiency is to argue that so long as investors have homogeneous expectations, they will all perceive the same minimum variance opportunity set.[1] Even without a risk-free asset, they will all select efficient portfolios regardless of their individual risk tolerances. As shown in Fig. 7.1, individ-

---

[1] For a more rigorous proof of the efficiency of the market portfolio see Fama [1976, Chapter 8].

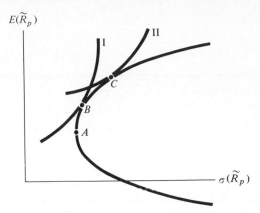

Figure 7.1
All investors select efficient portfolios.

ual I chooses efficient portfolio B, whereas individual II, who is less risk averse, chooses efficient portfolio C. Given that all individuals hold positive proportions of their wealth in efficient portfolios, then the market portfolio must be efficient because (1) the market is simply the sum of all individual holdings and (2) all individual holdings are efficient.

Thus, in theory, when all individuals have homogeneous expectations, the market portfolio must be efficient. Without homogeneous expectations the market portfolio is not necessarily efficient and the equilibrium model of capital markets that is derived in the next section does not necessarily hold. Thus the efficiency of the market portfolio and the capital asset pricing model are inseparable, joint hypotheses. It is not possible to test the validity of one without the other. We shall return to this important point when we discuss Roll's critique later in the chapter.

C. DERIVATION OF THE CAPM

Figure 7.2 shows the expected return and standard deviation of the market portfolio, M, the risk-free asset, R_f, and a risky asset, I. The straight line connecting the risk-free asset and the market portfolio is the capital market line. For example, see Fig. 6.17, in Chapter 6. We know that if a market equilibrium is to exist, the prices of all assets must adjust until all are held by investors. There can be no excess demand. In other words, prices must be established so that the supply of all assets equals the demand for holding them. Consequently, in equilibrium the market portfolio will consist of all marketable assets held in proportion to their value weights. The equilibrium proportion of each asset in the market portfolio must be

$$w_i = \frac{\text{Market value of individual asset}}{\text{Market value of all assets}}. \tag{7.1}$$

A portfolio consisting of $a\%$ invested in risky asset I and $(1 - a)\%$ in the market portfolio will have the following mean and standard deviation:

$$E(\tilde{R}_p) = aE(\tilde{R}_i) + (1 - a)E(\tilde{R}_m), \tag{7.2}$$

$$\sigma(\tilde{R}_p) = [a^2\sigma_i^2 + (1 - a)^2\sigma_m^2 + 2a(1 - a)\sigma_{im}]^{1/2}, \tag{7.3}$$

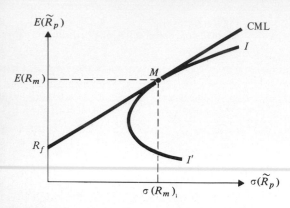

Figure 7.2
The opportunity set provided by combinations of
risky asset I and the market portfolio, M.

where

σ_i^2 = the variance of risky asset I,

σ_m^2 = the variance of the market portfolio,

σ_{im} = the covariance between asset I and the market portfolio.

We shall see shortly that the market portfolio already contains asset I held according to its market value weight. In fact the definition of the market portfolio is that it consists of all assets held according to their market value weights. The opportunity set provided by various combinations of the risky asset and the market portfolio is the line IMI' in Fig. 7.2. The change in the mean and standard deviation with respect to the percentage of the portfolio, a, invested in asset I is determined as follows:

$$\frac{\partial E(\tilde{R}_p)}{\partial a} = E(\tilde{R}_i) - E(\tilde{R}_m), \tag{7.4}$$

$$\frac{\partial \sigma(\tilde{R}_p)}{\partial a} = \tfrac{1}{2}[a^2\sigma_i^2 + (1-a)^2\sigma_m^2 + 2a(1-a)\sigma_{im}]^{-1/2}$$

$$\times [2a\sigma_i^2 - 2\sigma_m^2 + 2a\sigma_m^2 + 2\sigma_{im} - 4a\sigma_{im}]. \tag{7.5}$$

Sharpe's and Treynor's insight, which allowed them to use the above facts to determine a market equilibrium price for risk, was that in equilibrium the market portfolio already has the value weight, w_i percent, invested in the risky asset I. Therefore the percentage a in the above equations is the excess demand for an individual risky asset. But we know that in equilibrium the excess demand for any asset must be zero. Prices will adjust until all assets are held by someone. Therefore if Eqs. (7.4) and (7.5) are evaluated where excess demand, a, equals zero, then we can determine the equilibrium price relationships at point M in Fig. 7.2. This will provide the equilibrium price of risk. Evaluating Eqs. (7.4) and (7.5), where $a = 0$, we obtain

$$\left.\frac{\partial E(\tilde{R}_p)}{\partial a}\right|_{a=0} = E(\tilde{R}_i) - E(\tilde{R}_m), \tag{7.6}$$

$$\left.\frac{\partial \sigma(\tilde{R}_p)}{\partial a}\right|_{a=0} = \tfrac{1}{2}(\sigma_m^2)^{-1/2}(-2\sigma_m^2 + 2\sigma_{im}) = \frac{\sigma_{im} - \sigma_m^2}{\sigma_m}. \tag{7.7}$$

The slope of the risk-return trade-off evaluated at point M, in market equilibrium, is

$$\left.\frac{\partial E(\tilde{R}_p)/\partial a}{\partial \sigma(\tilde{R}_p)/\partial a}\right|_{a=0} = \frac{E(\tilde{R}_i) - E(\tilde{R}_m)}{(\sigma_{im} - \sigma_m^2)/\sigma_m}. \tag{7.8}$$

The final insight is to realize that the slope of the opportunity set IMI' provided by the relationship between the risky asset and the market portfolio at point M must also be equal to the slope of the capital market line, $R_f M$.

As established in Chapter 6, the capital market line is also an equilibrium relationship. Given market efficiency, the tangency portfolio, M, must be the market portfolio where all assets are held according to their market value weights. Recall that the slope of the capital market line in Eq. (6.34) is

$$\frac{E(\tilde{R}_m) - R_f}{\sigma_m},$$

where σ_m is the standard deviation of the market portfolio. Equating this with the slope of the opportunity set at point M, we have

$$\frac{E(\tilde{R}_m) - R_f}{\sigma_m} = \frac{E(\tilde{R}_i) - E(\tilde{R}_m)}{(\sigma_{im} - \sigma_m^2)/\sigma_m}.$$

This relationship can be arranged to solve for $E(\tilde{R}_i)$ as follows:

$$E(\tilde{R}_i) = R_f + [E(\tilde{R}_m) - R_f]\frac{\sigma_{im}}{\sigma_m^2}. \tag{7.9}$$

Equation (7.9) is known as the *capital asset pricing model*, CAPM. It is shown graphically in Fig. 7.3 where it is also called the *security market line*. The required rate of

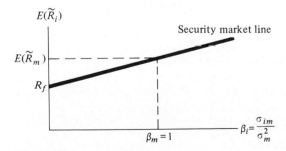

Figure 7.3
The capital asset pricing model.

return on *any* asset, $E(\tilde{R}_i)$ in Eq. (7.9), is equal to the risk-free rate of return plus a risk premium. The risk premium is the price of risk multiplied by the quantity of risk. In the terminology of the CAPM, the price of risk is the slope of the line, the difference between the expected rate of return on the market portfolio and the risk-free rate of return.[2] The quantity of risk is often called beta, β_i.

$$\beta_i = \frac{\sigma_{im}}{\sigma_m^2} = \frac{\text{COV}(R_i, R_m)}{\text{VAR}(R_m)}. \tag{7.10}$$

It is the covariance between returns on the risky asset, I, and market portfolio, M, divided by the variance of the market portfolio. The risk-free asset has a beta of zero because its covariance with the market portfolio is zero. The market portfolio has a beta of one because the covariance of the market portfolio with itself is identical to the variance of the market portfolio:

$$\beta_m = \frac{\text{COV}(R_m, R_m)}{\text{VAR}(R_m)} = \frac{\text{VAR}(R_m)}{\text{VAR}(R_m)} = 1.$$

D. PROPERTIES OF THE CAPM

There are several properties of the CAPM that are important. First, in equilibrium, every asset must be priced so that its risk-adjusted required rate of return falls exactly on the straight line in Fig. 7.3, which is called the *security market line*. This means, for example, that assets such as I and J in Fig. 6.20, which do not lie on the mean-variance efficient set, will lie exactly on the security market line in Fig. 7.3. This is true because not all the variance of an asset's return is of concern to risk-averse investors. As we saw in the previous chapter, investors can always diversify away all risk except the covariance of an asset with the market portfolio. In other words, they can diversify away all risk except the risk of the economy as a whole, which is inescapable (undiversifiable). Consequently, the only risk that investors will pay a premium to avoid is covariance risk. The total risk of any individual asset can be partitioned into two parts—systematic risk, which is a measure of how the asset covaries with the economy, and unsystematic risk, which is independent of the economy.

$$\text{Total risk} = \text{systematic risk} + \text{unsystematic risk}, \tag{7.11}$$

---

[2] Note that the CAPM terminology is somewhat different from that used in Chapter 6. Earlier, the equilibrium price of risk was seen to be the marginal rate of substitution between return and risk and was defined as

$$\frac{E(R_m) - R_f}{\sigma_m}.$$

Using this definition for the price of risk, the quantity of risk is

$$\frac{\text{COV}(R_i, R_m)}{\sigma_m}.$$

Because σ_m, the standard deviation of the market, is assumed to be constant, it does not make much difference which terminology we adopt. Hereafter, risk will be β and the price of risk will be $[E(R_m) - R_f]$.

Table 7.1 Risk and Return for Bayside Cigar and a 100-Stock Portfolio

	Annual Return	*Standard Deviation*	*Beta*
100-stock portfolio	10.9%	4.45%	1.11
Bayside Cigar	5.4	7.25	.71

Mathematical precision can be attached to this concept by noting that empirically the return on any asset is a linear function of market return plus a random error term $\tilde{\varepsilon}_j$, which is independent of the market:

$$\tilde{R}_j = a_j + b_j\tilde{R}_m + \tilde{\varepsilon}_j.$$

This equation contains three terms: a constant, a_j, which has no variance; a constant times a random variable, $b_j\tilde{R}_m$; and a second random variable, $\tilde{\varepsilon}_j$, which has zero covariance with $\tilde{R}_m$. Using Properties 3 and 4 of random variables (given in Chapter 6), we can immediately write the variance of this relationship as

$$\sigma_j^2 = b_j^2\sigma_m^2 + \sigma_\varepsilon^2. \tag{7.12}$$

The variance is total risk; it can be partitioned into systematic risk, $b_j^2\sigma_m^2$, and unsystematic risk, σ_ε^2. It turns out that b_j in the simple linear relationship between individual asset return and market return is exactly the same as β_j in the CAPM.[3]

If systematic risk is the only type of risk that investors will pay to avoid, and if the required rate of return for every asset in equilibrium must fall on the security market line, we should be able to go back to the example of Bayside Cigar Company and resolve the paradox introduced in Chapter 6. Table 7.1 summarizes the empirical findings. We know that if investors are risk averse, there should be a positive trade-off between risk and return. When we tried to use the standard deviation as a measure of risk for an individual asset, Bayside Cigar, in comparison with a well-diversified portfolio, we were forced to make the inappropriate observation that the asset with higher risk has a lower return. The difficulty was that we were using the wrong measure of risk. One cannot compare the variance of return on a single asset with the variance for a well-diversified portfolio. The variance of the portfolio will almost always be smaller. The appropriate measure of risk for a single asset is beta, its covariance with the market divided by the variance of the market. This risk is nondiversifiable and is linearly related to the rate of return [$E(R_i)$ in Eq. (7.9)] required in equilibrium. When we look at the appropriate measure of risk, we see that Bayside Cigar is *less risky* than the 100-stock portfolio, and we have the sensible result that lower risk is accompanied by lower return.

Table 7.2 shows the realized rates of return and the betas of many different assets between January 1945 and June 1970. The calculations are taken from an article by Modigliani and Pogue [1974] that used monthly observations. In most cases the risk-return relationships make sense. Consumer product companies such as Swift and Co.,

---

[3] The interested reader is referred to Appendix C on linear regression for proof that the slope coefficient, b_j, equals

$$b_j = \text{COV}(R_j, R_m)/\text{VAR}(R_m).$$

Table 7.2   Rates of Return and Betas for Selected Companies, 1945–1970

	Average Annual Return	*Standard Deviation*	*Beta*
City Investing Co.	17.4%	11.09%	1.67
Radio Corporation of America	11.4	8.30	1.35
Chrysler Corporation	7.0	7.73	1.21
Continental Steel Co.	11.9	7.50	1.12
100-stock portfolio	10.9	4.45	1.11
NYSE index	8.3	3.73	1.00
Swift and Co.	5.7	5.89	.81
Bayside Cigar	5.4	7.26	.71
American Snuff	6.5	4.77	.54
Homestake Mining Co.	4.0	6.55	.24

From F. Modigliani and G. Pogue, "An Introduction to Risk and Return," reprinted from *Financial Analysts Journal*, March–April 1974, 71.

Bayside Cigar, and American Snuff are all less risky than the market portfolio (represented here by the NYSE index). On the other hand, steel, electronics, and automobiles are riskier. Figure 7.4 plots the empirical relationship between risk (measured by beta) and return for the companies listed in Table 7.2. The linearity of the relationship appears to be reasonable, and the trade-off between risk and return is positive. A more thorough discussion of empirical tests of the CAPM will be given later in this chapter.

A second important property of the CAPM is that the measure of risk for individual assets is linearly additive when the assets are combined into portfolios. For example, if we put $a\%$ of our wealth into asset X, with systematic risk of β_x, and $b\%$ of our wealth into asset Y, with systematic risk of β_y, then the beta of the resulting portfolio, β_p, is simply the weighted average of the betas of the individual securities:

$$\beta_p = a\beta_x + b\beta_y. \tag{7.13}$$

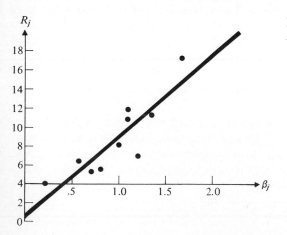

Figure 7.4
An empirical security market line.

Proof of this follows from the definition of covariance and the properties of the mean and variance. The definition of the portfolio beta is

$$\beta_p = \frac{E\{[aX + bY - aE(X) - bE(Y)][R_m - E(R_m)]\}}{VAR(R_m)}.$$

Rearranging terms, we have

$$\beta_p = \frac{E\{[a[X - E(X)] + b[Y - E(Y)]][R_m - E(R_m)]\}}{VAR(R_m)}.$$

Next, we factor out a and b:

$$\beta_p = a\frac{E[(X - E(X))(R_m - E(R_m))]}{VAR(R_m)} + b\frac{E[(Y - E(Y))(R_m - E(R_m))]}{VAR(R_m)}.$$

Finally, using the definition of β,

$$\beta_p = a\beta_x + b\beta_y. \qquad \text{QED}$$

The fact that portfolio betas are linearly weighted combinations of individual asset betas is an extremely useful tool. All that is needed to measure the systematic risk of portfolios is the betas of the individual assets. It is not necessary to solve a quadratic programming problem [see Eqs. (6.26a) and (6.26b)] to find the efficient set.

It is worth reiterating the relationship between individual asset risk and portfolio risk. The correct definition of an individual asset's risk is its contribution to portfolio risk. Referring to Eq. (6.28), we see that the variance of returns for a portfolio of assets is

$$VAR(\tilde{R}_p) = \sigma^2(\tilde{R}_p) = \sum_{i=1}^{N} \sum_{j=1}^{N} w_i w_j \sigma_{ij}, \tag{6.28}$$

which can be rewritten as[4]

$$\sigma^2(\tilde{R}_p) = \sum_{i=1}^{N} w_i \left(\sum_{j=1}^{N} w_j \sigma_{ij} \right) = \sum_{i=1}^{N} w_i COV(R_i, R_p). \tag{7.14}$$

---

[4] To see that $\sum w_i(\sum w_j \sigma_{ij}) = \sum w_i COV(R_i, R_p)$, consider a simple three-asset example. Rewriting the left-hand side, we have

$$\sum w_i(\sum w_j \sigma_{ij}) = w_1(w_1\sigma_{11} + w_2\sigma_{12} + w_3\sigma_{13})$$
$$+ w_2(w_1\sigma_{21} + w_2\sigma_{22} + w_3\sigma_{23})$$
$$+ w_3(w_1\sigma_{31} + w_2\sigma_{32} + w_3\sigma_{33}).$$

From the definition of covariance, we have

$$COV(R_1, R_p) = [1 \quad 0 \quad 0] \begin{bmatrix} \sigma_{11} & \sigma_{12} & \sigma_{13} \\ \sigma_{21} & \sigma_{22} & \sigma_{23} \\ \sigma_{31} & \sigma_{32} & \sigma_{33} \end{bmatrix} \begin{bmatrix} w_1 \\ w_2 \\ w_3 \end{bmatrix}$$

$$= w_1\sigma_{11} + w_2\sigma_{12} + w_3\sigma_{13}.$$

Then by multiplying by the weight in the first asset, we obtain

$$w_1 COV(R_1, R_p) = w_1(w_1\sigma_{11} + w_2\sigma_{12} + w_3\sigma_{13}).$$

Finally, by repeating this procedure for each of the three assets, we can demonstrate the equality in Eq. (7.14).

One could interpret

$$w_i \text{COV}(R_i, R_p) \tag{7.15}$$

as the risk of security i in portfolio p. However, at the margin, the change in the contribution of asset i to portfolio risk is simply

$$\text{COV}(R_i, R_p). \tag{7.16}$$

Therefore covariance risk is the appropriate definition of risk since it measures the change in portfolio risk as we change the weighting of an individual asset in the portfolio.

Although the use of *systematic risk* and *undiversifiable risk* have arisen in the literature as synonyms for *covariance risk*, they are somewhat misleading. They rely on the existence of costless diversification opportunities and on the existence of a large market portfolio. The definition of covariance risk given above does not. It continues to be relevant, even when the market portfolio under consideration has few assets.

E. USE OF THE CAPM FOR VALUATION: SINGLE-PERIOD MODELS, UNCERTAINTY

Because it provides a quantifiable measure of risk for individual assets, the CAPM is an extremely useful tool for valuing risky assets. For the time being, let us assume that we are dealing with a single time period. This assumption was built into the derivation of the CAPM. We want to value an asset that has a risky payoff at the end of the period. Call this $\tilde{P}_e$. It could represent the capital gain on a common stock or the capital gain plus a dividend. If the risky asset is a bond, it is the repayment of the principal plus the interest on the bond. The expected return on an investment in the risky asset is determined by the price we are willing to pay at the beginning of the time period for the right to the risky end-of-period payoff. If P_0 is the price we pay today, our risky return, $\tilde{R}_j$, is

$$\tilde{R}_j = \frac{\tilde{P}_e - P_0}{P_0}. \tag{7.17}$$

The CAPM can be used to determine what the current value of the asset, P_0, should be. The CAPM is

$$E(R_j) = R_f + [E(R_m) - R_f] \frac{\text{COV}(R_j, R_m)}{\text{VAR}(R_m)},$$

which can be rewritten as

$$E(R_j) = R_f + \lambda \, \text{COV}(R_j, R_m), \quad \text{where} \quad \lambda = \frac{E(R_m) - R_f}{\text{VAR}(R_m)}. \tag{7.18}$$

Note that λ can be described as the market price per unit risk. From Eq. (7.17) and the properties of the mean, we can equate the expected return from Eq. (7.17) with the expected return in Eq. (7.18):

$$\frac{E(\tilde{P}_e) - P_0}{P_0} = R_f + \lambda \, \text{COV}(\tilde{R}_j, \tilde{R}_m).$$

We can now interpret P_0 as the equilibrium price of the risky asset. Rearranging the above expression, we get

$$P_0 = \frac{E(\tilde{P}_e)}{1 + R_f + \lambda \, \text{COV}(\tilde{R}_j, \tilde{R}_m)}, \tag{7.19}$$

which is often referred to as the *risk-adjusted rate of return valuation formula*. The numerator is the expected end-of-period price for the risky asset, and the denominator can be thought of as a discount rate. If the asset has no risk, then its covariance with the market will be zero and the appropriate one-period discount rate is $(1 + R_f)$, i.e., $(1 + \text{the risk-free rate})$. For assets with positive systematic risk, a risk premium, $\lambda \, \text{COV}(\tilde{R}_j, \tilde{R}_m)$, is added to the risk-free rate so that the discount rate is risk adjusted.

An equivalent approach to valuation is to deduct a risk premium from $E(\tilde{P}_e)$ in the numerator, then discount at $(1 + R_f)$. The covariance between the risky asset and the market can be rewritten as

$$\text{COV}(\tilde{R}_j, \tilde{R}_m) = \text{COV}\left[\frac{\tilde{P}_e - P_0}{P_0}, \tilde{R}_m\right]$$

$$= E\left[\left(\frac{\tilde{P}_e - P_0}{P_0} - \frac{E(\tilde{P}_e) - P_0}{P_0}\right)(\tilde{R}_m - E(\tilde{R}_m))\right]$$

$$= \frac{1}{P_0} \text{COV}(\tilde{P}_e, \tilde{R}_m).$$

By substituting this into the risk-adjusted rate of return equation [Eq. (7.19)],

$$P_0 = \frac{E(\tilde{P}_e)}{1 + R_f + \lambda(1/P_0)\text{COV}(\tilde{P}_e, \tilde{R}_m)},$$

we can derive the *certainty equivalent valuation formula*:

$$P_0 = \frac{E(\tilde{P}_e) - \lambda \, \text{COV}(\tilde{P}_e, \tilde{R}_m)}{1 + R_f}. \tag{7.20}$$

The risk-adjusted rate of return and the certainty equivalent approaches are equivalent for one-period valuation models. It is important to realize that in both cases value does not depend on the utility preferences of individuals. All one needs to know in order to determine value is the expected end-of-period cash payoff, the quantity of risk provided by the asset, the risk-free rate, and the price of risk (which are market-determined variables). Consequently, individuals who perceive the same distribution of payoffs for a risky asset will price it in exactly the same way regardless of their individual utility functions. The separation of valuation from attitudes toward risk is a consequence of two-fund separation. This was discussed in Chapter 6, section E.5.

F. APPLICATIONS OF THE CAPM FOR CORPORATE POLICY

In Chapter 14 these one-period valuation models will be used to develop decision-making rules for the selection of investment projects by the firm, for measurement of the firm's cost of capital, and for capital structure (optimal debt/equity ratio) decisions. However, for the sake of curiosity, we shall take a quick look at the implications of the CAPM for some corporate policy decisions, assuming that our firm has no debt and that there are no corporate or personal taxes. The more complex results in a world with debt and taxes are left to Chapter 13.

The cost of equity capital for a firm is given directly by the CAPM. After all, the company's beta is measured by calculating the covariance between the return on its common stock and the market index. Consequently, the beta measures the systematic risk of the common stock, and if we know the systematic risk, we can use the CAPM to determine the required rate of return on equity. Equation (7.21) is the capital asset pricing model:

$$E(R_j) = R_f + [E(R_m) - R_f]\beta_j. \tag{7.21}$$

If it is possible to estimate the systematic risk of a company's equity as well as the market rate of return, then $E(R_j)$ is the required rate of return on equity, i.e., the cost of equity for the firm. If we designate the cost of equity as k_s, then

$$E(R_j) = k_s.$$

This is shown in Fig. 7.5. As long as all projects have the same risk as the firm, then k_s may also be interpreted as the minimum required rate of return on new capital projects.

But what if the project has a different risk from the firm as a whole? Then all that is necessary is to estimate the systematic risk of the project and use the CAPM to determine the appropriate required rate of return, $E(\tilde{R}_k)$. For example, in Fig. 7.5

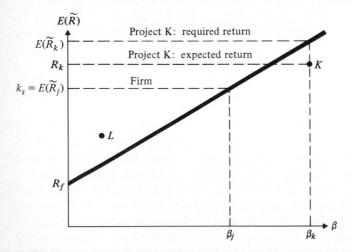

Figure 7.5
The cost of equity using the CAPM.

the projected rate of return on project K, R_k, is higher than the cost of equity for the firm, $E(R_j)$. But the project also is riskier than the firm because it has greater systematic risk. If the managers of the firm were to demand that it earn the same rate as the firm $[k_s = E(R_j)]$, the project would be accepted since its projected rate of return, R_k, is greater than the firm's cost of equity. However, this would be incorrect. The market requires a rate of return, $E(\tilde{R}_k)$, for a project with systematic risk of β_k, but the project will earn less. Therefore since $R_k < E(\tilde{R}_k)$ the project is clearly unacceptable. (Is project L acceptable? Why?)

Because the CAPM allows decision makers to estimate the required rate of return for projects of different risk, it is an extremely useful concept. Although we have assumed no debt or taxes in the above simple introduction, Chapter 13 will show how the model can be extended to properly conceptualize more realistic capital budgeting and cost of capital decisions.

G. EXTENSIONS OF THE CAPM

Virtually every one of the assumptions under which the CAPM is derived is violated in the real world. If so, then how good is the model? There are two parts to this question: (1) Is it possible to extend the model to relax the unrealistic assumptions without drastically changing it? (2) How well does the model stand up to empirical testing? The first part is the subject of this section of the chapter. Surprisingly, the model is fairly resilient to various extensions of it.

1. No Riskless Asset

First, how will the model change if investors cannot borrow and lend at the risk-free rate? In other words, how is the CAPM affected if there is no risk-free asset that has constant returns in every state of nature? This problem was solved by Black [1972]. His argument is illustrated in Fig. 7.6. Portfolio M is identified by the

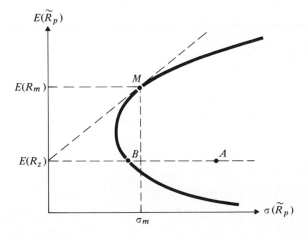

Figure 7.6
The capital market line with no risk-free rate.

investors as the market portfolio that lies on the efficient set.[5] Now, suppose that we can identify all portfolios that are uncorrelated with the true market portfolio.[6] This means that their returns have zero covariance with the market portfolio, and they have the same systematic risk (i.e., they have zero beta). Because they have the same systematic risk, each must have the same expected return. Portfolios A and B in Fig. 7.6 are both uncorrelated with the market portfolio M and have the same expected return, $E(R_z)$. However, only one of them, portfolio B, lies on the opportunity set. It is the minimum variance zero-beta portfolio and it is unique. Portfolio A also has zero beta, but it has a higher variance and therefore does not lie on the minimum variance opportunity set.

We can derive the slope of the line $E(R_z)M$ by forming a portfolio with $a\%$ in the market portfolio and $(1 - a)\%$ in the minimum variance zero-beta portfolio. The mean and standard deviation of such a portfolio can be written as follows:

$$E(R_p) = aE(R_m) + (1 - a)E(R_z),$$

$$\sigma(R_p) = [a^2\sigma_m^2 + (1 - a)^2\sigma_z^2 + 2a(1 - a)r_{zm}\sigma_z\sigma_m]^{1/2}.$$

But since the correlation, r_{zm}, between the zero-beta portfolio and the market portfolio is zero, the last term drops out. The slope of a line tangent to the efficient set at point M, where 100% of the investor's wealth is invested in the market portfolio, can be found by taking the partial derivatives of the above equations and evaluating them where $a = 1$. The partial derivative of the mean portfolio return is

$$\frac{\partial E(R_p)}{\partial a} = E(R_m) - E(R_z),$$

and the partial derivative of the standard deviation is

$$\frac{\partial \sigma(R_p)}{\partial a} = \tfrac{1}{2}[a^2\sigma_m^2 + (1 - a)^2\sigma_z^2]^{-1/2}[2a\sigma_m^2 - 2\sigma_z^2 + 2a\sigma_z^2].$$

---

[5] Note, however, that the extension of the CAPM that follows can be applied to *any* efficient portfolio, not just the market portfolio.

[6] As an example of how to calculate the vector of weights in a world with only two assets, see Problem 7.13. For portfolios with many assets, we are interested in identifying the portfolio that (a) has zero covariance with the market portfolio and (b) has the minimum variance. The solution will be the vector of weights that satisfies the following quadratic programming problem.

$$\text{MIN } \sigma_p^2 = W_1' \mathbf{\Sigma} W_1$$

$$\text{Subject to } W_1' \mathbf{\Sigma} W_m = \sigma_{1m} = 0$$

$$W_1'\mathbf{e} = 1,$$

where

σ_p^2 = the variance of the zero-beta portfolio,

W_1' = the row vector of weights in the minimum variance zero-beta portfolio (W_1 is a column vector with the same weights),

$\mathbf{\Sigma}$ = the variance/covariance matrix for all N assets in the market,

W_m = the vector of weights in the market portfolio,

σ_{1m} = the covariance between the zero-beta portfolio and the market—which must equal zero,

$\mathbf{e}$ = a column vector of ones.

Taking the ratio of these partials and evaluating where $a = 1$, we obtain the slope of the line $E(R_z)M$ in Fig. 7.6:

$$\frac{\partial E(R_p)/\partial a}{\partial \sigma(R_p)/\partial a} = \frac{E(R_m) - E(R_z)}{\sigma_m}. \tag{7.22}$$

Furthermore, since the line must pass through the point $[E(R_m), \sigma(R_m)]$, the intercept of the tangent line must be $E(R_z)$. Consequently, the equation of the line must be

$$E(R_p) = E(R_z) + \left[\frac{E(R_m) - E(R_z)}{\sigma_m}\right]\sigma_p. \tag{7.23}$$

This is exactly the same as the capital market line [Eq. (6.34)] except that the expected rate of return on the zero-beta portfolio, $E(R_z)$, has replaced the risk-free rate.

Given the above result, it is not hard to prove that the expected rate of return on *any* risky asset, whether or not it lies on the efficient set, must be a linear combination of the rate of return on the zero-beta portfolio and the market portfolio. To show this, recall that in equilibrium the slope of a line tangent to a portfolio composed of the market portfolio and any other asset at the point represented by the market portfolio must be equal to Eq. (7.8):

$$\left.\frac{\partial E(R_p)/\partial a}{\partial \sigma(R_p)/\partial a}\right|_{a=0} = \frac{E(R_i) - E(R_m)}{(\sigma_{im} - \sigma_m^2)/\sigma_m}. \tag{7.8}$$

If we equate the two definitions of the slope of a line tangent to point M [i.e., if we equate (7.8) and (7.22)], we have

$$\frac{E(R_m) - E(R_z)}{\sigma_m} = \frac{[E(R_i) - E(R_m)]\sigma_m}{\sigma_{im} - \sigma_m^2}.$$

Solving for the required rate of return on asset i, we have

$$E(R_i) = (1 - \beta_i)E(R_z) + \beta_i E(R_m), \tag{7.24}$$

where

$$\beta_i = \sigma_{im}/\sigma_m^2 = COV(R_i, R_m)/\sigma_m^2.$$

Equation (7.24) shows that the expected rate of return on any asset can be written as a linear combination of the expected rate of return of two assets—the market portfolio and the unique minimum variance zero-beta portfolio (which is chosen to be uncorrelated with the market portfolio). Interestingly, the weight to be invested in the market portfolio is the beta of the ith asset. If we rearrange (7.24), we see that it is exactly equal to the CAPM [Eqs. (7.9) and (7.21)] except that the expected rate of return on the zero-beta portfolio has replaced the rate of return on the risk-free asset:

$$E(R_i) = E(R_z) + [E(R_m) - E(R_z)]\beta_i. \tag{7.25}$$

The upshot of this proof is that the major results of the CAPM do not require the existence of a pure riskless asset. Beta is still the appropriate measure of systematic risk for an asset, and the linearity of the model still obtains. The version of the model given by Eq. (7.25) is usually called the *two-factor model*.

One limitation of the two-factor model is that it relies rather heavily on the assumption that there are no short sales constraints. In other words, investors are assumed to be able to sell shares that they do not already own, then use the proceeds to purchase other shares. Empirically, almost all asset returns have positive correlations. This makes it virtually impossible to construct a zero-beta portfolio composed of only long positions in securities. Therefore the unconstrained use of short sales is a practical necessity to obtain zero-beta portfolios. With short positions the correlation between asset returns is reversed. For example, if you have sold IBM short, you make positive returns when the asset price falls. In general, zero-beta portfolios would have to be composed of both long and short positions of risky assets. Ross [1977] has shown that in a world with short sales restrictions and no riskless asset the linear CAPM is invalid. Thus to obtain the CAPM in a linear form [Eqs. (7.9) and (7.25)] we require either (1) a risk-free asset that can be freely short sold or (2) no constraints on short sales.

2. Returns Not Jointly Normal

Obviously, returns on assets cannot be normally distributed because the largest negative return possible, given limited liability of the investor, is minus 100%. Unfortunately, the assumption of normally distributed returns implies that there is a finite possibility that returns will be less than minus 100% and that asset prices will be negative. However, as a practical matter, the probability of observing returns as low as minus 100% may be so small that it has no impact on the empirical validity of the CAPM.

Another implication of the normality assumption is that only two parameters are needed to completely describe the distribution: its mean and its variance. Fama [1965a] has investigated the empirical distribution of daily returns on New York Stock Exchange securities and discovered that they are distributed symmetrically but that the empirical distribution has "fat tails" and no finite variance.[7] In Fig. 7.7 the dashed line represents the empirical distribution of stock prices. The important ques-

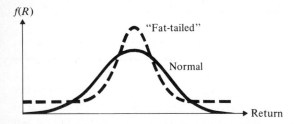

Figure 7.7
The empirical distribution of daily stock returns.

---

[7] There are various theories that explain the empirical distribution of daily returns. The interested reader is referred to Fama [1965a] for the stable Paretian hypothesis and to Clark [1973] for the subordinated stochastic process hypothesis.

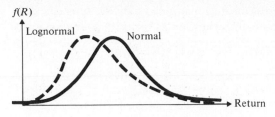

$f(R)$

Lognormal   Normal

Return

Figure 7.8
Over long intervals of time, security returns are lognormal.

tion that arises is, How can investors make choices based on mean and variance if the actual distribution of security prices is such that a variance does not exist? Fama [1965b] has shown that as long as the distribution is symmetric (and stable), investors can use measures of dispersion other than the variance (e.g., the semiinterquartile range) and the theory of portfolio choice is still valid.[8]

If security returns are measured over longer periods of time, their distribution is better approximated by a lognormal distribution that has positive skewness.[9] Figure 7.8 compares a normal with a lognormal distribution. There is no limit to the positive returns that may be realized on a successful investment, but the maximum negative return is minus 100%. This explains why the distribution of annual returns, e.g., tends to be lognormal. The CAPM makes no provision for investor preference for skewness; it is therefore an empirical question whether or not the model fits reality well enough to permit us to ignore the fact that the empirical distribution of returns is not normal. The empirical evidence is reviewed in the next section of this chapter.

3. The Existence of Nonmarketable Assets

Suppose that the cost of transacting in an asset is infinite or that by law or regulation the asset is not marketable. Perhaps the most important example of such an asset is human capital. You can rent your skills in return for wages, but you cannot sell yourself or buy anyone else. Slavery is forbidden. This has the effect of introducing a nondiversifiable asset into your portfolio—your human capital. Because you cannot divide up your skills and sell them to different investors, you are forced into making portfolio decisions where you are constrained to hold a large risky component of your wealth in the form of your own human capital. What impact does this have on portfolio decisions and the CAPM?

We saw earlier that if there are no transactions costs and if all assets are perfectly divisible, two-fund separation obtains (see Chapter 6). Every investor, regardless of the shape of his or her indifference curve, will hold one of two assets: the risk-free asset or the market portfolio. Of course, casual empiricism tells us that this is not what actually happens. People do hold different portfolios of risky assets. There are many reasons why this may be true, and the existence of nonmarketable assets is a good possibility.

---

[8] Usually we refer to distributions that are stable under addition. This means that the addition of two distributions (e.g., two normal distributions) will result in the same type of distribution.

[9] The natural logarithm of a lognormal distribution is normally distributed. See Eq. (6.12) for the equation of a normal distribution.

Mayers [1972] shows that when investors are constrained to hold nonmarketable assets that have risky (dollar) rates of return, R_H, the CAPM takes the following form:

$$E(R_j) = R_f + \lambda[V_m\text{COV}(R_j, R_m) + \text{COV}(R_j, R_H)], \tag{7.26}$$

where

$$\lambda = \frac{E(R_m) - R_f}{V_m\sigma_m^2 + \text{COV}(R_m, R_H)},$$

V_m = the current market value of all marketable assets,

R_H = the total dollar return on all nonmarketable assets.

In this version of the model, λ may be interpreted as the market price per unit risk where risk contains not only the market variance, σ_m^2, but also the covariance between the rate of return on marketable assets and the aggregate dollar return on non-marketable assets. This result is obtained by first deriving an individual's demand curves for holding marketable assets, then aggregating them to obtain Eq. (7.26), which is the return on a marketable asset required by the market equilibrium. There are three important implications. First, individuals will hold different portfolios of risky assets because their human capital has differing amounts of risk. Second, the market equilibrium price of a risky asset may still be determined independently of the shape of the individual's indifference curves. This implies that the separation principle still holds. There is still an objectively determined market price of risk that is independent of individual attitudes toward risk. No variable in Eq. (7.26) is sub-scripted for the preferences of the ith individual. Both the price of risk and the amount of risk depend only on properties of the jth asset, the portfolio of all marketable assets, and the portfolio of aggregated nonmarketable assets. Third, the appropriate measure of risk is still the covariance, but we must now consider the covariance between the jth risky asset and two portfolios, one composed of marketable and a second of nonmarketable assets.[10]

4. The Model in Continuous Time

Merton [1973] has derived a version of the CAPM that assumes (among other things) that trading takes place continuously over time, and that asset returns are distributed lognormally. If the risk-free rate of interest is nonstochastic over time, then (regardless of individual preferences, the distribution of individuals' wealth, or their time horizon), the equilibrium returns must satisfy

$$E(R_i) = r_f + [E(R_m) - r_f]\beta_i. \tag{7.27}$$

Equation (7.27) is the continuous-time analogy to the CAPM. In fact, it is exactly the same as the CAPM except that instantaneous rates of return have replaced rates of return over discrete intervals of time, and the distribution of returns is lognormal instead of normal.

---

[10] See Fama and Schwert [1977] for an empirical test of the model set forth by Mayers.

If the risk-free rate is stochastic, investors are exposed to another kind of risk, namely, the risk of unfavorable shifts in the investment opportunity set. Merton shows that investors will hold portfolios chosen from three funds: the riskless asset, the market portfolio, and a portfolio chosen so that its returns are perfectly negatively correlated with the riskless asset. This model exhibits three-fund separation. The third fund is necessary to hedge against unforeseen changes in the future risk-free rate. The required rate of return on the jth asset is

$$E(R_j) = r_f + \gamma_1 [E(R_m) - r_f] + \gamma_2 [E(R_N) - r_f], \tag{7.28}$$

where

R_N = the instantaneous rate of return on a portfolio that has perfect negative correlation with the riskless asset,

$$\gamma_1 = \frac{\beta_{jm} - \beta_{jN}\beta_{Nm}}{1 - \rho_{Nm}^2}, \qquad \gamma_2 = \frac{\beta_{jN} - \beta_{jm}\beta_{Nm}}{1 - \rho_{Nm}^2},$$

ρ_{Nm} = the correlation between portfolio N and the market portfolio, M,

$$\beta_{ik} = \frac{\text{COV}(R_i, R_k)}{\sigma_k^2}.$$

Merton argues that the sign of γ_2 will be negative for high beta assets and positive for low beta assets. As we shall see in the next section, which discusses the empirical tests of the CAPM, Merton's argument is consistent with the empirical evidence.

5. The Existence of Heterogeneous Expectations and Taxes

If investors do not have the same information about the distribution of future returns, they will perceive different opportunity sets and will obviously choose different portfolios. Lintner [1969] has shown that the existence of heterogeneous expectations does not critically alter the CAPM except that expected returns and covariances are expressed as complex weighted averages of investor expectations. However, if investors have heterogeneous expectations, the market portfolio is not necessarily efficient. This makes the CAPM nontestable. In fact, as we shall see when we discuss Roll's critique later in this chapter, the only legitimate test of the CAPM is a joint test to determine whether or not the market portfolio is efficient.

No one has investigated the equilibrium model in a world with personal as well as corporate taxes. However, Brennan [1970] has investigated the effect of differential tax rates on capital gains and dividends. Although he concludes that beta is the appropriate measure of risk, his model includes an extra term that causes the expected return on an asset to depend on dividend yield as well as systematic risk:

$$E(R_j) = \gamma_1 R_f + \gamma_2 \beta_j + \gamma_3 \text{DY}_j, \tag{7.29}$$

where

$$\text{DY}_j = \text{the dividend yield on asset } j.$$

We shall leave a complete discussion on the Brennan model to Chapters 15 and 16, which cover the theory and empirical evidence related to the corporate dividend policy decision. For now it is sufficient to note that Brennan's model predicts that higher rates of return will be required on assets with higher dividend yields. In other words, investors do not like dividends because they must pay ordinary income tax rates on dividends but only capital gains rates on stock price increases. (The 1986 tax code sets the capital gains rate equal to the ordinary income rate, but still allows capital gains to be realized at the option of the investor—a tax-timing option.)

H. EMPIRICAL TESTS OF THE CAPM

The CAPM is a simple linear model that is expressed in terms of expected returns and expected risk. In its *ex ante* form, we have

$$E(R_j) = R_f + [E(R_m) - R_f]\beta_j. \tag{7.30}$$

Although many of the aforementioned extensions of the model support this simple linear form, others suggest that it may not be linear, that factors other than beta are needed to explain $E(R_j)$, or that R_f is not the appropriate riskless rate. Therefore with so many alternative possibilities a great deal of energy has been devoted to the empirical question: How well does the model fit the data?

There have been numerous empirical tests of the CAPM, so many in fact that it would be fruitless to mention all of them. Also, the literature is interwoven with many serious and difficult econometric problems that must be confronted in order to provide the best empirical tests of the model.[11] Most of the econometric subtleties are beyond the scope of this text and are therefore ignored. However, in the opinion of the authors, the tests of the CAPM summarized below represent the best of the work that has been done to date.

The first step necessary to empirically test the theoretical CAPM is to transform it from expectations or *ex ante* form (expectations cannot be measured) into a form that uses observed data. This can be done by assuming that the rate of return on any asset is a *fair game*.[12] In other words, on average the realized rate of return on an asset is equal to the expected rate of return. We can write the fair game as follows:

$$R_{jt} = E(R_{jt}) + \beta_j \delta_{mt} + \varepsilon_{jt}, \tag{7.31}$$

where

$$\delta_{mt} = R_{mt} - E(R_{mt}),$$
$$E(\delta_{mt}) = 0,$$
$$\varepsilon_{jt} = \text{a random-error term,}$$

---

[11] For papers that discuss some of the econometric problems involved in testing the CAPM, the reader is referred to Miller and Scholes [1972], Roll [1977, 1981], Scholes and Williams [1977], Dimson [1979], and Gibbons [1982].

[12] Chapter 10 explains the theory of efficient capital markets that describes a fair game at length. Also, empirical evidence is presented that suggests that the market is in fact a fair game.

$$E(\varepsilon_{jt}) = 0$$

$$\text{COV}(\varepsilon_{jt}, \delta_{mt}) = 0,$$

$$\text{COV}(\varepsilon_{jt}, \varepsilon_{j,t-1}) = 0,$$

$$\beta_j = \text{COV}(R_{jt}, R_{mt})/\text{VAR}(R_{mt}).$$

Equation (7.31) is seen to be a fair game because if we take the expectation of both sides, the average realized return is equal to the expected return. In other words, on average you get the return you expected:

$$E(R_{jt}) = E(R_{jt}).$$

If we use the CAPM assumption that asset returns are jointly normal, then β_j in the fair game model is defined in exactly the same way as β_j in the CAPM. By substituting $E(R_j)$ from the CAPM into Eq. (7.31), we obtain

$$R_{jt} = R_{ft} + [E(R_{mt}) - R_{ft}]\beta_j + \beta_j[R_{mt} - E(R_{mt})] + \varepsilon_{jt}$$

$$= R_{ft} + (R_{mt} - R_{ft})\beta_j + \varepsilon_{jt}.$$

Finally, by subtracting R_{ft} from both sides, we have

$$R_{jt} - R_{ft} = (R_{mt} - R_{ft})\beta_j + \varepsilon_{jt}, \tag{7.32}$$

which is the *ex post* form of the CAPM. We derived it by simply assuming that returns are normally distributed and that capital markets are efficient in a fair game sense. Now we have an empirical version of the CAPM that is expressed in terms of *ex post* observations of return data instead of *ex ante* expectations.

One important difference between the *ex post* empirical model and the *ex ante* theoretical model is that the former can have a negative slope, whereas the latter cannot. After the fact we may have experienced a state of nature where the market rate of return was negative. When this happens the empirical security market line will slope downward as in Fig. 7.9(a). On the other hand, the theoretical CAPM always requires

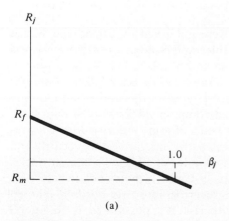 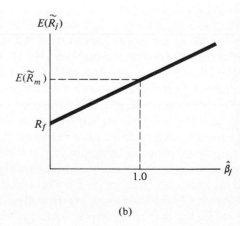

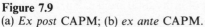

Figure 7.9
(a) *Ex post* CAPM; (b) *ex ante* CAPM.

the *ex ante* expected return on the market to be higher than the risk-free rate of return, as shown in Fig. 7.9(b). This is because prices must be established in such a way that riskier assets have higher expected rates of return. Of course, it may turn out that after the fact their return was low or negative, but that is what is meant by risk. If a risky asset has a beta of 2.0, it will lose roughly 20% when the market goes down by 10%.

When the CAPM is empirically tested it is usually written in the following form:

$$R'_{pt} = \gamma_0 + \gamma_1 \beta_p + \varepsilon_{pt}, \tag{7.33}$$

where

$\gamma_1 = R_{mt} - R_{ft}$,

R'_{pt}, = the excess return on portfolio p, $(R_{pt} - R_{ft})$.

This is the same as Eq. (7.32) except that a constant term, γ_0, has been added. Exactly what predictions made by the CAPM are tested in Eq. (7.33)? The predictions should meet the following criteria:

a) The intercept term, γ_0, should not be significantly different from zero. If it is different from zero, then there may be something "left out" of the CAPM that is captured in the empirically estimated intercept term.

b) Beta should be the only factor that explains the rate of return on a risky asset. If other terms such as residual variance, dividend yield, price/earnings ratios, firm size, or beta squared are included in an attempt to explain return, they should have no explanatory power.

c) The relationship should be linear in beta.

d) The coefficient of beta, γ_1, should be equal to $(R_{mt} - R_{ft})$.

e) When the equation is estimated over very long periods of time, the rate of return on the market portfolio should be greater than the risk-free rate. Because the market portfolio is riskier, on average it should have a higher rate of return.

The major empirical tests of the CAPM were published by Friend and Blume [1970], Black, Jensen, and Scholes [1972], Miller and Scholes [1972], Blume and Friend [1973], Blume and Husick [1973], Fama and Macbeth [1973], Basu [1977], Reinganum [1981b], Litzenberger and Ramaswamy [1979], Banz [1981], Gibbons [1982], Stambaugh [1982], and Shanken [1985b]. Most of the studies use monthly total returns (dividends are reinvested) on listed common stocks as their data base. A frequently used technique is to estimate the betas of every security during a five-year holding period, by computing the covariance between return on the security and a market index that is usually an equally weighted index of all listed common stocks. The securities are then ranked by beta and placed into N portfolios (where N is usually 10, 12, or 20). By grouping the individual securities into large portfolios chosen to provide the maximum dispersion in systematic risk, it is possible to avoid a good part of the measurement error in estimating betas of individual stocks. Next, the portfolio betas and returns are calculated over a second five-year period and a regression similar to Eq. (7.33) is run.

With few exceptions, the empirical studies agree on the following conclusions:

a) The intercept term, γ_0, *is* significantly different from zero, and the slope, γ_1, is less than the difference between the return on the market portfolio minus the risk-free rate.[13] The implication is that low beta securities earn more than the CAPM would predict and high beta securities earn less.

b) Versions of the model that include a squared beta term or unsystematic risk find that at best these explanatory factors are useful only in a small number of the time periods sampled. Beta dominates them as a measure of risk.

c) The simple linear empirical model [Eq. (7.33)] fits the data best. It is linear in beta. Also, over long periods of time the rate of return on the market portfolio is greater than the risk-free rate (i.e., $\gamma_1 > 0$).

d) Factors other than beta are successful in explaining that portion of security returns not captured by beta. Basu [1977] found that low price/earnings portfolios have rates of return higher than could be explained by the CAPM. Banz [1981] and Reinganum [1981b] found that the size of a firm is important. Smaller firms tend to have high abnormal rates of return. Litzenberger and Ramaswamy [1979] found that the market requires higher rates of return on equities with high dividend yields. Keim [1983, 1985] reports seasonality in stock returns—a January effect.

Figure 7.10 shows the average monthly returns on 10 portfolios vs. their systematic risk for the 35-year period 1931–1965 (taken from the Black-Jensen-Scholes study [1972]). The results shown here are typical. The empirical market line is linear with a positive trade-off between return and risk, but the intercept term is significantly different from zero. In fact, it is 9.79 standard deviations away. This forces us to reject the CAPM, given the empirical techniques of the previously mentioned studies. In addition, the ability of other variables such as price/earnings ratios to explain the portion of returns that are unexplained by the CAPM suggests either (1) that the CAPM is misspecified and requires the addition of factors other than beta to explain security returns or (2) that the problems in measuring beta are systematically related to variables such as firm size. Work that is consistent with this second point of view has been published by Rosenberg and Marathe [1977], who find that beta can be predicted much better if variables such as dividend yield, trading volume, and firm size are added to the predictive model. Roll [1981] suggests that infrequent trading of shares in small firms may explain much of the measurement error in estimating betas.

Gibbons [1982], Stambaugh [1982], and Shanken [1985b] test the CAPM by first assuming that the market model is true—i.e., that the return on the ith asset is a linear function of a market portfolio proxy such as an equally weighted market portfolio:

$$\tilde{R}_{it} = \alpha_i + \beta_i \tilde{R}_{mt} + \tilde{\varepsilon}_{it}. \tag{7.34}$$

---

[13] Empirical studies have used a 90-day Treasury bill as a proxy for the risk-free rate, and they have also laboriously calculated the return on the zero-beta portfolio. Either approach results in an intercept term significantly different from zero.

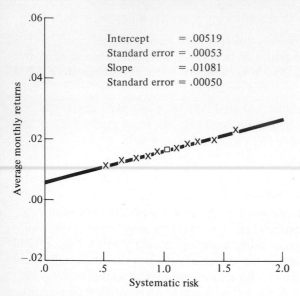

Figure 7.10
Average monthly returns vs. systematic risk for 10
portfolios, 1931–1965. (From *Studies in the Theory
of Capital Markets*, edited by Michael C. Jensen.
Copyright © 1972 by Praeger Publishers, Inc.
Reprinted by permission of Holt, Rinehart and
Winston.)

The market model, Eq. (7.34), is merely a statistical statement. It is not the CAPM.
The CAPM—e.g., Black's [1972] two-factor version—actually requires the intercept
term, $E(R_z)$ in Eq. (7.25), to be the same for all assets. The two-factor CAPM is true
across all assets at a point in time,

$$E(R_i) = E(R_z) + [E(R_m) - E(R_z)]\beta_i. \tag{7.25}$$

Gibbons [1982] points out that the two-factor CAPM implies the following constraint
on the intercept of the market model

$$\alpha_i = E(R_z)(1 - \beta_i) \tag{7.35}$$

for all securities during the same time interval. When he tests restriction (7.35), he
finds that it is violated and that the CAPM must be rejected.

The empirical evidence has led scholars to conclude that the pure theoretical form
of the CAPM does not agree well with reality. However, the empirical form of the
model, which has come to be known as the *empirical market line*,

$$R_{it} = \hat{\gamma}_{0t} + \hat{\gamma}_{1t}\beta_{it} + \varepsilon_{it}, \tag{7.36}$$

does provide an adequate model of security returns. The practitioner who wishes to
have unbiased estimates of the empirical market line parameters, $\hat{\gamma}_{0t}$ and $\hat{\gamma}_{1t}$, estimated

each month from January 1935 through June 1968, is referred to Fama [1976]. Obviously, if one can estimate a security's beta for a given period, then by knowing the empirical market line parameters, he can estimate the security's required rate of return from Eq. (7.36).

I. THE PROBLEM OF MEASURING PERFORMANCE: ROLL'S CRITIQUE

One of the potentially most useful applications of the securities market line in its *ex post* form [Eq. (7.32)] or the empirical market line [Eq. (7.36)] is that they might be used as benchmarks for security performance. The residual term, ε_{jt}, has been interpreted as abnormal because, as shown in Fig. 7.11, it represents return in excess of what is predicted by the security market line.

Roll [1977] takes exception to this interpretation of cross-section abnormal performance measures and to empirical tests of the CAPM in general. In brief, his major conclusions are:

1. The only legitimate test of the CAPM is whether or not the market portfolio (which includes *all* assets) is mean-variance efficient.

2. If performance is measured relative to an index that is *ex post* efficient, then from the mathematics of the efficient set no security will have abnormal performance when measured as a departure from the security market line.[14]

3. If performance is measured relative to an *ex post* inefficient index, then any ranking of portfolio performance is possible, depending on which inefficient index has been chosen.

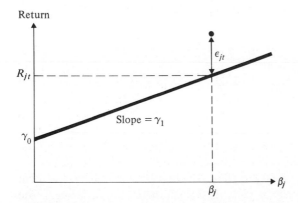

Figure 7.11
Abnormal return.

---

[14] It is important to note that Roll does not take exception to time series measures of abnormal performance such as those described by the market model in Chapter 11.

This is a startling statement. It implies that even if markets are efficient and the CAPM is valid, then the cross-section security market line cannot be used as a means of measuring the *ex post* performance of portfolio selection techniques. Furthermore, the efficiency of the market portfolio and the validity of the CAPM are joint hypotheses that are almost impossible to test because of the difficulty of measuring the true market portfolio.

To understand Roll's critique, we must go back to the derivation of the zero-beta portfolio. Recall that if there is no risk-free asset, it is still possible to write the security market line as a combination of the market portfolio and a zero-beta portfolio that is uncorrelated with the market index. Therefore the expected return on any asset could be written as a two-factor model:

$$E(R_i) = E(R_z) + [E(R_m) - E(R_z)]\beta_i. \tag{7.37}$$

Roll points out that there is nothing unique about the market portfolio. It is always possible to choose any efficient portfolio as an index, then find the minimum variance portfolio that is uncorrelated with the selected efficient index. This is shown in Fig. 7.12. Once this has been done, then Eq. (7.37) can be derived and written as

$$E(R_i) = E(R_{z,I}) + [E(R_I) - E(R_{z,I})]\beta_{i,I}. \tag{7.38}$$

Note that the market portfolio, R_m, has been replaced by any efficient index, R_I, and the beta is measured relative to the selected efficient index, $\beta_{i,I}$. Also, the zero-beta portfolio is measured relative to the index, $R_{z,I}$. Because the expected return on any asset can be written as a linear function of its beta measured relative to any efficient index, it is not necessary to know the market index. One only need know the composition of an efficient index in order to write Eq. (7.38). Furthermore, if the index turns out to be *ex post* efficient, then every asset will fall exactly on the security market line. There will be no abnormal returns. If there are systematic abnormal returns, it simply means that the index that has been chosen is not *ex post* efficient.

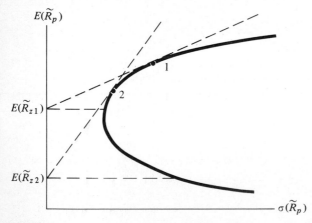

Figure 7.12
Two index portfolios with their respective orthogonal portfolios.

The Roll critique does not imply that the CAPM is an invalid theory. However, it does mean that tests of the CAPM must be interpreted with great caution. The fact that portfolio residuals exhibited no significant departures from linearity merely implies that the market index that was selected (usually an equally weighted index of all listed shares of common stock) was *ex post* efficient. In fact, the only way to test the CAPM directly is to see whether or not the true market portfolio is *ex post* efficient. Unfortunately, because the market portfolio contains all assets (marketable and nonmarketable, e.g., human capital, coins, houses, bonds, stocks, options, land, etc.), it is impossible to observe.

J. THE ARBITRAGE PRICING THEORY

1. The Theory

Formulated by Ross [1976], the arbitrage pricing theory (APT) offers a testable alternative to the capital asset pricing model. The CAPM predicts that security rates of return will be linearly related to a single common factor—the rate of return on the market portfolio. The APT is based on similar intuition but is much more general. It assumes that the rate of return on any security is a linear function of k factors as shown below:

$$\tilde{R}_i = E(\tilde{R}_i) + b_{i1}\tilde{F}_1 + \cdots + b_{ik}\tilde{F}_k + \tilde{\varepsilon}_i, \tag{7.39}$$

where

$\tilde{R}_i$ = the random rate of return on the ith asset,

$E(\tilde{R}_i)$ = the expected rate of return on the ith asset,

b_{ik} = the sensitivity of the ith asset's returns to the kth factor,

$\tilde{F}_k$ = the mean zero kth factor common to the returns of all assets under consideration,

$\tilde{\varepsilon}_i$ = a random zero mean noise term for the ith asset.

As we shall see later on, the CAPM may be viewed as a special case of the APT when the market rate of return is assumed to be the single relevant factor.

The APT is derived under the usual assumptions of perfectly competitive and frictionless capital markets. Furthermore, individuals are assumed to have homogeneous beliefs that the random returns for the set of assets being considered are governed by the linear k-factor model given in Eq. (7.39). The theory requires that the number of assets under consideration, n, be much larger than the number of factors, k, and that the noise term, $\tilde{\varepsilon}_i$, be the unsystematic risk component for the ith asset. It must be independent of all factors and all error terms for other assets.

The most important feature of the APT is reasonable and straightforward. In equilibrium all portfolios that can be selected from among the set of assets under consideration and that satisfy the conditions of (a) using no wealth and (b) having no risk must earn no return on average. These portfolios are called arbitrage portfolios. To see how they can be constructed, let w_i be the *change* in the dollar amount invested in the ith asset as a percentage of an individual's total invested wealth. To form an arbitrage portfolio that requires no change in wealth, the usual course of action would be to sell some assets and use the proceeds to buy others. Mathematically, the zero change in wealth is written as

$$\sum_{i=1}^{n} w_i = 0. \tag{7.40}$$

If there are n assets in the arbitrage portfolio, then the additional portfolio return gained is

$$\tilde{R}_p = \sum_{i=1}^{n} w_i \tilde{R}_i$$

$$= \sum_i w_i E(\tilde{R}_i) + \sum_i w_i b_{i1} \tilde{F}_1 + \cdots + \sum_i w_i b_{ik} \tilde{F}_k + \sum_i w_i \tilde{\varepsilon}_i. \tag{7.41}$$

To obtain a riskless arbitrage portfolio it is necessary to eliminate both diversifiable (i.e., unsystematic or idiosyncratic) and undiversifiable (i.e., systematic) risk. This can be done by meeting three conditions: (1) selecting percentage changes in investment ratios, w_i, that are small, (2) diversifying across a large number of assets, and (3) choosing changes, w_i, so that for each factor, k, the weighted sum of the systematic risk components, b_k, is zero. Mathematically, these conditions are

$$w_i \approx 1/n, \tag{7.42a}$$

$$n \text{ chosen to be a large number,} \tag{7.42b}$$

$$\sum_i w_i b_{ik} = 0 \quad \text{for each factor.} \tag{7.42c}$$

Because the error terms, $\tilde{\varepsilon}_i$, are independent the law of large numbers guarantees that a weighted average of many of them will approach zero in the limit as n becomes large. In other words, costless diversification eliminates the last term (the unsystematic or idiosyncratic risk) in Eq. (7.39). Thus we are left with

$$\tilde{R}_p = \sum_i w_i E(\tilde{R}_i) + \sum_i w_i b_{i1} \tilde{F}_1 + \cdots + \sum_i w_i b_{ik} \tilde{F}_k. \tag{7.43}$$

At first glance the return on our portfolio appears to be a random variable, but we have chosen the weighted average of the systematic risk components for each factor to be equal to zero ($\sum w_i b_{ik} = 0$). This eliminates all systematic risk. One might say that we have selected an arbitrage portfolio with zero beta in each factor. Consequently, the return on our arbitrage portfolio becomes a constant. Correct choice of the weights has eliminated all uncertainty, so that R_p is not a random variable. Therefore Eq. (7.41) becomes

$$R_p = \sum_i w_i E(\tilde{R}_i). \tag{7.43a}$$

Recall that the arbitrage portfolio, so constructed, has no risk (of any kind) and requires no new wealth. If the return on the arbitrage portfolio were not zero, then it would be possible to achieve an infinite rate of return with no capital requirements and no risk. Such an opportunity is clearly impossible if the market is to be in equilibrium. In fact, if the individual arbitrageur is in equilibrium (hence content with his or her current portfolio), then the return on any and all arbitrage portfolios must be zero. In other words,

$$R_p = \sum_i w_i E(\tilde{R}_i) = 0. \tag{7.44}$$

Eqs. (7.40), (7.42c), and (7.44) are really statements in linear algebra. Any vector that is orthogonal to the constant vector, i.e.,[15]

$$\left(\sum_i w_i\right) \cdot \mathbf{e} = 0, \tag{7.40}$$

and to each of the coefficient vectors, i.e.,

$$\sum_i w_i b_{ik} = 0 \quad \text{for each } k, \tag{7.42c}$$

must also be orthogonal to the vector of expected returns, i.e.,

$$\sum_i w_i E(\tilde{R}_i) = 0. \tag{7.44}$$

An algebraic consequence of this statement is that the expected return vector must be a linear combination of the constant vector and the coefficient vectors. Algebraically, there must exist a set of $k + 1$ coefficients, $\lambda_0, \lambda_1, \ldots, \lambda_k$ such that

$$E(\tilde{R}_i) = \lambda_0 + \lambda_1 b_{i1} + \cdots + \lambda_k b_{ik}. \tag{7.45}$$

Recall that the b_{ik} are the "sensitivities" of the returns on the ith security to the kth factor. If there is a riskless asset with a riskless rate of return, R_f, then $b_{0k} = 0$ and

$$R_f = \lambda_0.$$

Hence Eq. (7.45) can be rewritten in "excess returns form" as

$$E(R_i) - R_f = \lambda_1 b_{i1} + \cdots + \lambda_k b_{ik}. \tag{7.46}$$

Figure 7.13 illustrates the arbitrage pricing relationship (7.46) assuming that there is only a single stochastic factor, k. In equilibrium, all assets must fall on the *arbitrage pricing line*. A natural interpretation for λ is that it represents the risk premium (i.e., the price of risk), in equilibrium, for the kth factor. Because the arbitrage pricing relationship is linear we can use the slope-intercept definition of a straight line to rewrite Eq. (7.46) as

$$E(R_i) = R_f + [\bar{\delta}_k - R_f] b_{ik},$$

where $\bar{\delta}_k$ is the expected return on a portfolio with unit sensitivity to the kth factor and zero sensitivity to all other factors. Therefore the risk premium, λ_k, is equal to the difference between (1) the expectation of a portfolio that has unit response to the kth factor and zero response to the other factors and (2) the risk-free rate, R_f:

$$\lambda_k = \bar{\delta}_k - R_f.$$

---

[15] Note that Eq. (7.40) says that the sum of the investment weights equals zero. This is really a no-wealth constraint. No new wealth is required to take an arbitrage position. Recall that $\mathbf{e}$ is a column vector of ones.

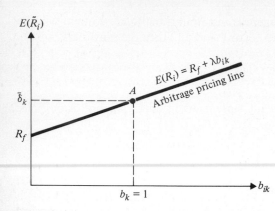

Figure 7.13
The arbitrage pricing line.

In general the arbitrage pricing theory can be rewritten as

$$E(R_i) - R_f = [\bar{\delta}_1 - R_f]b_{i1} + \cdots + [\bar{\delta}_k - R_f]b_{ik}. \tag{7.47}$$

If Eq. (7.47) is interpreted as a linear regression equation (assuming that the vectors of returns have a joint normal distribution and that the factors have been linearly transformed so that their transformed vectors are orthonormal), then the coefficients, b_{ik}, are defined in exactly the same way as beta in the capital asset pricing model, i.e.,

$$b_{ik} = \frac{\text{COV}(\tilde{R}_i, \tilde{\delta}_k)}{\text{VAR}(\tilde{\delta}_k)}, \tag{7.47a}$$

where

$\text{COV}(\tilde{R}_i, \tilde{\delta}_k)$ = the covariance between the ith asset's returns and the linear transformation of the kth factor,

$\text{VAR}(\tilde{\delta}_k)$ = the variance of the linear transformation of the kth factor.

Hence the CAPM is seen to be a special case of the APT (where asset returns are assumed to be joint normal).

The arbitrage pricing theory is much more robust than the capital asset pricing model for several reasons:

1. The APT makes no assumptions about the empirical distribution of asset returns.

2. The APT makes no strong assumptions about individuals' utility functions (at least nothing stronger than greed and risk aversion).

3. The APT allows the equilibrium returns of assets to be dependent on many factors, not just one (e.g., beta).

4. The APT yields a statement about the relative pricing of any subset of assets; hence one need not measure the entire universe of assets in order to test the theory.

5. There is no special role for the market portfolio in the APT, whereas the CAPM requires that the market portfolio be efficient.

6. The APT is easily extended to a multiperiod framework (see Ross [1976]).

Suppose that asset returns are determined by two underlying factors such as unanticipated changes in real output and unanticipated inflation. The arbitrage pricing theory can easily account for the effect of changes in both factors on asset returns. Because the capital asset pricing model relies on a single factor (the market index), it cannot do as well. Using the CAPM is a little like being lost in the clouds while piloting a private plane. You call the air controller and ask, "Where am I?" If the controller is using a unidimensional model like the CAPM, he or she is likely to respond, "Two hundred miles from New York City." Obviously, this is not a very helpful answer. A multidimensional model like the APT would be more useful. It would be nice to know latitude, longitude, and altitude.

Figure 7.14 illustrates the same point. The factor loadings (or factor sensitivities), b_{i1} and b_{i2}, for our two hypothetical factors—changes in unanticipated real output and changes in unanticipated inflation—are plotted on the axes. The origin represents the risk-free rate that is the rate of return received when an asset has zero beta in both factors. Points along the diagonal dashed lines have equal expected return but not the same risk. For example, all points along the line OJ have an expected rate of return equal to the risk-free rate but are not riskless portfolios. If the risk-free rate is 10%, one can obtain that rate either with a truly riskless portfolio that pays 10% in every state of nature or with a second portfolio that has positive sensitivity to one factor and negative sensitivity to the other factor.

Suppose the arbitrage pricing model, Eq. (7.47),

$$E(R_i) - R_f = [\bar{\delta}_1 - R_f]b_{i1} + [\bar{\delta}_2 - R_f]b_{i2},$$

is estimated to have the following numerical values: $R_f = 10\%$, $\bar{\delta}_1 = 20\%$, and $\bar{\delta}_2 = 15\%$. If b_{i1} is plotted on the vertical axis, then the vertical intercept for a given return $E(R_i)$ is

$$\alpha = \text{vertical intercept} = \frac{E(R_i) - R_f}{\delta_1 - R_f},$$

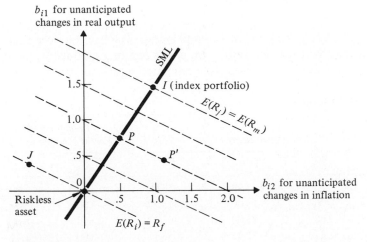

Figure 7.14
A graph of the CAPM and the APT.

and the slope of the equal return line is

$$m = \text{slope} = -\frac{\bar{\delta}_2 - R_f}{\bar{\delta}_1 - R_f}$$

where the equation for the equal return line is $b_{i1} = \alpha + mb_{i2}$.

Next, suppose that we know that a CAPM efficient index portfolio has been chosen, that its expected return is 30%, and that its sensitivities to changes in unanticipated real output and changes in unanticipated inflation are $b_{I1} = 1.5$ and $b_{I2} = 1.0$. The CAPM index portfolio is plotted at point I in Fig. 7.14. We know from the CAPM [Eq. (7.9)] that the security market line is represented by all linear combinations of the risk-free asset and the market index portfolio. Therefore the security market line is represented by the ray OI from the origin (which is the risk-free asset) to the efficient index portfolio (point I).

The CAPM measures risk only in one dimension, rather than two. If we are told that a portfolio's CAPM β is .5, then it will plot at point P in Fig. 7.14, halfway between the riskless asset and the index portfolio. However, according to the APT there are an infinite number of portfolios, all with the same expected return as portfolio P and each having a different sensitivity to the APT risk parameters b_{i1} and b_{i2}. If people are in fact sensitive to more than one type of risk when choosing among portfolios of equal return, then the APT is superior to the CAPM because the CAPM is unidimensional in risk. It is perfectly reasonable that portfolio P' might be preferred to portfolio P by some investors because it has the same return as portfolio P but a preferable combination of sensitivities to the underlying factors. For example, a public pension fund manager might not care much about the sensitivity of the value of the fund to industrial production but might be very concerned about hedging against unexpected changes in inflation. Later on we shall discuss some empirical work that provides evidence that more than one factor is significant in explaining security returns.

2. A Numerical Example

To illustrate how arbitrage pricing might be employed in practice, suppose that empirical work reveals that the expected returns on assets can be explained by two factors, F_1 and F_2. Table 7.3 shows the subjectively estimated returns on three assets

Table 7.3 Data for an APT Example

State of Nature	Prob.	Asset Returns (%)			Transformed Factor Changes (%)	
		$\tilde{X}$	$\tilde{Y}$	$\tilde{Z}$	$\tilde{\delta}_1$	$\tilde{\delta}_2$
Horrid	.2	−55.23	623.99	53.00	−10.00	−5.00
Bad	.2	70.70	10.00	413.37	−5.00	38.48
Average	.2	−9.00	25.00	−1493.12	25.00	8.00
Good	.2	−12.47	−3771.42	1058.75	40.00	−1.44
Great	.2	61.00	3237.44	83.00	50.00	0.00

$(X, Y,$ and $Z)$ and the changes in (orthogonal transformations of) the two factors for five equally likely states of nature. To make the problem tractable, assume that all factors and returns are normally distributed. In addition, suppose we know that the expected return on the risk-free asset, R_f, is 10%.

One of the requirements of the factor analysis program usually used to test the arbitrage pricing model is that we are working with linear transformations of the underlying factors. The transformations must be orthogonal, i.e., the product of their row and column vectors must equal zero. This is shown below for the transformed factors in Table 7.3:

$$[-10 \quad -5 \quad 25 \quad 40 \quad 50] \begin{bmatrix} -5.00 \\ 38.48 \\ 8.00 \\ -1.44 \\ 0 \end{bmatrix} = 0.$$

How can we tell from the bewildering set of numbers in Table 7.3 whether or not there are any arbitrage opportunities? And if there are, how can we take advantage of them by forming an arbitrage portfolio?

If there are only two factors that govern all returns, then the APT becomes

$$E(R_i) = R_f + [\bar{\delta}_1 - R_f]b_{i1} + [\bar{\delta}_2 - R_f]b_{i2}.$$

The data from Table 7.3 can be used to compute all the terms on the right-hand side of this equation. The factor loadings (or sensitivities) are the same as beta, Eq. (7.47a), given the assumption of normally distributed returns and orthogonal transformations of the factors. Using asset X as an example, we need to calculate

$$b_{x1} = \frac{\text{COV}(X, \delta_1)}{\text{VAR}(\delta_1)} = \frac{285.0}{570.0} = .5.$$

The computations are done in Table 7.4. Given that $b_{x1} = .5$ we know that a 1% increase in factor 1 will result in a .5% increase in the return on security X. We can think of the factor loadings (or sensitivities) in exactly the same way as we thought of beta (systematic risk) in the CAPM. The expectations of each asset and transformed factor and the factor loadings (sensitivities) are given in Table 7.5. By substituting these data into the APT equation, we can determine the market equilibrium rate of return, $E(R_i)$, for each of the three assets. This is done below:

$$E(R_x) = .10 + [.20 - .10].5 + [.08 - .10]2.0 = 11\%,$$
$$E(R_y) = .10 + [.20 - .10]1.0 + [.08 - .10]1.5 = 17\%,$$
$$E(R_z) = .10 + [.20 - .10]1.5 + [.08 - .10]1.0 = 23\%.$$

Note that the equilibrium return, $E(R_i)$, on assets X and Z is the same as the projected return, $\bar{R}_i$, computed from the data. Hence no arbitrage opportunities exist for trading in these two assets. On the other hand, the projected return on asset Y, $\bar{R}_y$, is 25% when computed from the data, and the market equilibrium return, $E(R_y)$, is only 17%.

Table 7.4   Calculating b_{x1} from the Data in Table 7.3

$p_i X_i$	$p_i \delta_{1i}$	$p_i(\delta_{1i} - \bar{\delta}_1)^2$
$.2(-55.23) = -11.046$	$.2(-10) = -2.0$	$.2(-10-20)^2 = 180$
$.2(70.70) = 14.140$	$.2(-5) = -1.0$	$.2(-5-20)^2 = 125$
$.2(-9.00) = -1.800$	$.2(25) = 5.0$	$.2(25-20)^2 = 5$
$.2(-12.47) = -2.494$	$.2(40) = 8.0$	$.2(40-20)^2 = 80$
$.2(61.00) = 12.200$	$.2(50) = 10.0$	$.2(50-20)^2 = 180$
$\bar{X} = 11.000$	$\bar{\delta}_1 = 20.0$	$\mathrm{VAR}(\delta_1) = 570$

$p_i(X_i - \bar{X})(\delta_i - \bar{\delta}_1)$	
$.2(-66.23)(-30) = 397.38$	
$.2(59.70)(-25) = -298.50$	
$.2(-20.00)(5) = -20.00$	$b_{x1} = \dfrac{285.00}{570.00} = .5$
$.2(-23.47)(20) = -93.88$	
$.2(50.00)(30) = 300.00$	
$\mathrm{COV}(X, \delta_1) = 285.00$	

Table 7.5   Statistics Computed from Table 7.3

Asset	R_i	Factor Loadings b_{i1}	Factor Loadings b_{i2}	Transformed Factor Expectations
X	11%	.5	2.0	$\bar{\delta}_1 = 20\%$
Y	25	1.0	1.5	$\bar{\delta}_2 = 8\%$
Z	23	1.5	1.0	

Therefore by selling the correct proportions of assets X and Z and buying asset Y, we can form an arbitrage portfolio that requires no new capital, has no change in risk, and earns a positive rate of return.

Suppose that we currently have one third of our wealth in each of the three assets. How should we change our portfolio to form a riskless arbitrage position? It turns out that so long as there are more assets than factors, there are virtually an infinite number of ways of forming arbitrage portfolios. But let us suppose that we desire to put the maximum investment into asset Y without actually selling short either X or Z. Our investment proportion in Y would go from one third to one; thus the *change* in holdings of asset Y would be $w_y = \frac{2}{3}$. We also require that the change portfolio have zero beta in each factor and that it need no net wealth. These conditions are stated in Eqs. (7.40) and (7.42c), which are repeated below:

$$\left(\sum_{i=1}^{3} w_i \right) \cdot \mathbf{e} = 0. \tag{7.40}$$

$$\sum_{i=1}^{3} w_i b_{ik} = 0 \quad \text{for each } k. \tag{7.42c}$$

Expanding these equations, we have

$$w_x + w_y + w_z = 0,$$

$$w_x b_{x1} + w_y b_{y1} + w_z b_{z1} = 0 \quad \text{for factor 1,}$$

$$w_x b_{x2} + w_y b_{y2} + w_z b_{z2} = 0 \quad \text{for factor 2.}$$

And substituting in the numbers of our problem, we get

$$w_x + \tfrac{2}{3} + w_z = 0,$$

$$w_x(.5) + \tfrac{2}{3}(1.0) + w_z(1.5) = 0,$$

$$w_x(2.0) + \tfrac{2}{3}(1.5) + w_z(1.0) = 0.$$

Solving, we find that

$$w_x = -\tfrac{1}{3}, \qquad w_y = \tfrac{2}{3}, \qquad w_z = -\tfrac{1}{3}.$$

Thus we would sell all our holdings in assets X and Z and invest the proceeds in asset Y. This strategy would require no new wealth and would have no change in risk. Note that our risk position before making the change was

$$\tfrac{1}{3}(.5) + \tfrac{1}{3}(1.0) + \tfrac{1}{3}(1.5) = 1.0 \quad \text{for factor 1,}$$

$$\tfrac{1}{3}(2) + \tfrac{1}{3}(1.5) + \tfrac{1}{3}(1.0) = 1.5 \quad \text{for factor 2.}$$

After undertaking the new investment strategy our risk will be

$$0(.5) + 1(1.0) + 0(1.5) = 1.0 \quad \text{for factor 1,}$$

$$0(2) + 1(1.5) + 0(1.0) = 1.5 \quad \text{for factor 2.}$$

Since our systematic risk has not changed, the extra systematic risk created by the arbitrage portfolio is zero.[16] Our originally projected portfolio return was

$$\tfrac{1}{3}(11\%) + \tfrac{1}{3}(25\%) + \tfrac{1}{3}(23\%) = 19.67\%.$$

But after investing in the arbitrage portfolio, we project a rate of return of

$$0(11\%) + 1(25\%) + 0(23\%) = 25\%.$$

Thus the arbitrage portfolio increases our return by 5.33% without changing our systematic risk.

Figure 7.15 provides a visual description of the example problem. Expected rates of return are plotted on the vertical axis, and asset betas in each of the two factors are plotted along the horizontal axes. Note that the expected returns for assets X and Z plot exactly on the arbitrage pricing plane. They are in equilibrium. But asset Y plots above the plane. Its return lies considerably above what the market requires

---

[16] Because there is idiosyncratic risk to contend with, total risk will in fact change. However, with well-diversified arbitrage portfolios this problem vanishes because diversification reduces idiosyncratic risk until it is negligible.

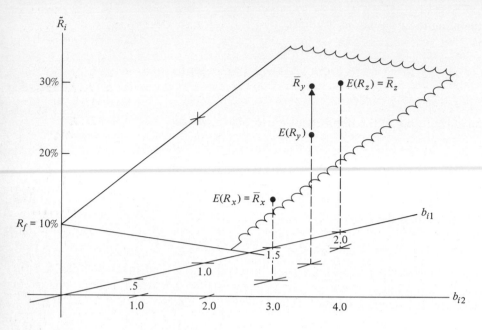

Figure 7.15
Arbitrage pricing plane for two factors.

for its factor loadings, b_{y1} and b_{y2}. Hence an arbitrage opportunity exists. If enough people take advantage of it the price of asset Y will rise, thereby forcing its rate of return down and back into equilibrium.

K. EMPIRICAL TESTS OF THE ARBITRAGE PRICING THEORY

Papers by Gehr [1975], Roll and Ross [1980], Reinganum [1981a], and Chen [1983] have tested the APT using data on equity daily rates of return for New York and American Stock Exchange listed stocks. The usual empirical procedure has the following steps:

1. Collect a time series of daily stock returns data for a group of stocks.

2. Compute the empirical variance-covariance matrix from the returns data.

3. Use a (maximum-likelihood) factor analysis procedure to identify the number of factors and their factor loadings, b_{ik}.

4. Use the estimated factor loadings, b_{ik}, to explain the cross-sectional variation of individual estimated expected returns and to measure the size and statistical significance of the estimated risk premia associated with each factor.

The Roll and Ross [1980] study used daily returns data for NYSE and AMEX companies listed on the exchanges on both July 3, 1962, and December 31, 1972.

There were a maximum of 2619 daily returns for each stock. The 1260 securities selected were divided alphabetically into groups of 30. For each group of 30 the procedure described above was carried out. The analysis showed that there are at least three and probably four "priced" factors. There may be other zero-priced factors, but this procedure cannot identify them because their regression coefficients in step 4 would be zero.

One of the frustrating things about using factor analysis to test the APT is that this procedure cannot tell us what the factors are. However, we can reject the APT if a specified alternative variable such as the total variance of individual returns, firm size, or the asset's last period return were to be significant in explaining the expected returns. Roll and Ross [1980], after correcting for the problem that positive skewness in lognormal returns can create dependence between the sample mean and the sample standard deviation, found that the total variance of security returns does not add any explanatory power for estimated expected returns. Therefore the APT could not be rejected on this basis. Although a different procedure was employed by Chen [1983], he was able to confirm this result. He also finds that the asset's last period return adds no explanatory power.

Currently there is a question whether or not firm size can be used to refute the APT because it adds explanatory power to the factor loadings. Reinganum [1981a] finds that it does. His test consisted of estimating the factor loadings in year $(t - 1)$ for all securities, then combining securities with similar loadings into control portfolios. In year t, excess security returns are computed by subtracting the daily control portfolio returns from the daily security returns. Finally, with excess returns in hand, the securities are ranked on the basis of the market value of all the firm's outstanding common stock at period $(t - 1)$. The APT predicts (if factor loadings are stationary across time) that all deciles of the market value ranked excess returns should have the same mean. Reinganum finds that there are significant differences between the mean excess returns and rejects the APT. Chen [1983], on the other hand, finds that firm size adds no explanatory power. His procedure uses Reinganum's data for the market value of each firm's equity. He divides the sample of firms into two groups—those with greater than the median market value and those with less. Then portfolios are formed from the high- and low-value firms so that the following conditions are satisfied: (1) each security in the portfolio has nonnegative weight and the weight should not be too far from $1/n$, where n is the number of securities in the portfolio; and (2) the resultant two portfolios have exactly the same factor loadings (arbitrage risk factors) in each factor. The factor loadings are determined by using returns data from odd days during each test period; the even-days returns from the same test period are used for measuring the average portfolio returns of the high- and low-valued portfolios. If the APT is correct the returns of the two portfolios should not be statistically different because they are selected to have the same "risk" as determined by the factor loadings. In only one of the four periods tested is the difference in returns statistically different at the 95% confidence level. Therefore Chen argues that firm size effects have insufficient explanatory power to reject the APT.

There is one parameter in the APT—namely, the intercept term $\lambda_0 = R_f$—that should be identical across groups of securities when the model is estimated separately for each group during a time period. Other factors need not be the same because the factor loadings are not unique from group to group. For example, factor 1 in group A might correspond to factor 3 in group B. The intercept term, λ_0, however, has the same meaning in each group because it is the return on an asset that has no sensitivity to the common factors. Roll and Ross [1980] tested for the equivalence of the λ_0 terms across 38 groups and found absolutely no evidence that the intercept terms were different. Again, the APT could not be rejected.

A direct comparison of the APT and the CAPM was performed by Chen [1983]. First, the APT model was fitted to the data as in the following equation:

$$\tilde{R}_i = \hat{\lambda}_0 + \hat{\lambda}_1 b_{i1} + \cdots + \hat{\lambda}_n b_{in} + \tilde{\varepsilon}_i. \qquad \text{(APT)}$$

Then the CAPM was fitted to the same data

$$\tilde{R}_i = \hat{\lambda}_0 + \hat{\lambda}_1 \hat{\beta}_i + \tilde{\eta}_i. \qquad \text{(CAPM)}$$

Next the CAPM residuals, η_i, were regressed on the arbitrage factor loadings, $\hat{\lambda}_k$, and the APT residuals, ε_i, were regressed on the CAPM coefficients. The results showed that the APT could explain a statistically significant portion of the CAPM residual variance, but the CAPM could not explain the APT residuals. This is strong evidence that the APT is a more reasonable model for explaining the cross-sectional variation in asset returns.

Although it is mathematically impossible to use factor analysis to unambiguously identify the underlying factors that drive security returns, Chen, Roll, and Ross [1983] have correlated various macroeconomic variables with returns on five portfolios that mimic the underlying factors. Their conclusions provide valuable insight into what the underlying factors might be. Four macroeconomic variables were significant:

1. An index of industrial production.
2. Changes in a default risk premium (measured by the differences in promised yields to maturity on AAA versus Baa corporate bonds).
3. Twists in the yield curve (measured by differences in promised yields to maturity on long- and short-term government bonds).
4. Unanticipated inflation.

The economic logic underlying these variables seems to make sense. Common stock prices are the present values of discounted cash flows. The industrial production index is obviously related to profitability. The remaining variables are related to the discount rate.

The intuition behind these factors is useful for portfolio management. For example, it has often been stated that common stocks are not a good hedge against inflation. Although it is true if one holds an equally weighted portfolio of all stocks, the logic of factor analysis suggests that there is a well-diversified subset of common stocks that is in fact a good hedge against inflation. Since the factors are mutually orthogonal, one can (at least in principle) choose a portfolio which is hedged against inflation risk without changing the portfolio sensitivity to any of the other three above-mentioned factors.

SUMMARY _____

This chapter has derived two theoretical models, the CAPM and the APT, that enable us to price risky assets in equilibrium. Within the CAPM framework the appropriate measure of risk is the covariance of returns between the risky asset in question and the market portfolio of all assets. The APT model is more general. Many factors (not just the market portfolio) may explain asset returns. For each factor the appropriate measure of risk is the sensitivity of asset returns to changes in the factor. For normally distributed returns the sensitivity is analogous to the beta (or systematic risk) of the CAPM.

The CAPM was shown to provide a useful conceptual framework for capital budgeting and the cost of capital. It is also reasonably unchanged by the relaxation of many of the unrealistic assumptions that made its derivation simpler. Finally, although the model is not perfectly validated by empirical tests, its main implications are upheld—namely, that systematic risk (beta) is a valid measure of risk, that the model is linear, and that the trade-off between return and risk is positive.

The APT can also be applied to cost of capital and capital budgeting problems. Chapter 12 will show how the APT can be used for capital budgeting in a multi-period framework. The earliest empirical tests of the APT have shown that asset returns are explained by three or possibly four factors and have ruled out the variance of an asset's own returns as one of the factors.

PROBLEM SET

7.1 Let us assume a normal distribution of returns and risk-averse utility functions. Under what conditions will all investors demand the same portfolio of risky assets?

7.2 The following data have been developed for the Donovan Company, the manufacturer of an advanced line of adhesives:

State	Probability	Market Return, R_m	Return for the Firm, R_j
1	.1	−.15	−.30
2	.3	.05	.00
3	.4	.15	.20
4	.2	.20	.50

The risk-free rate is 6%. Calculate the following:

a) The expected market return.

b) The variance of the market return.

c) The expected return for the Donovan Company.

d) The covariance of the return for the Donovan Company with the market return.

e) Write the equation of the security market line.

f) What is the required return for the Donovan Company? How does this compare with its expected return?

7.3 The following data have been developed for the Milliken Company:

Year	Market Return	Company Returns
1978	.27	.25
1977	.12	.05
1976	−.03	−.05
1975	.12	.15
1974	−.03	−.10
1973	.27	.30

The yield to maturity on Treasury Bills is .066 and is expected to remain at this point for the foreseeable future. Calculate the following:

a) The expected market return.

b) The variance of the market return.

c) The expected return for the Milliken Company.

d) The covariance of the return for the Milliken Company with the return on the market.

e) Write the equation of the security market line.

f) What is the required return for the Milliken Company?

7.4 For the data in Table Q7.4, perform the indicated calculations.

7.5 For the data in Table Q7.5, calculate the items indicated.

Table Q7.4   Estimates of Market Parameters

Year	S&P 500 Price Index	Percentage Change in Price	Dividend Yield	Percentage Return	Return Deviation	Market Variance	
	P_t	$\frac{P_t}{P_{t-1}} - 1$	$\frac{\text{Div}_t}{P_t}$	R_{mt} (3 + 4)	$(R_{mt} - \bar{R}_m)$ (5 − $\bar{R}_m$)	$(R_{mt} - \bar{R}_m)^2$ (6^2)	R_f
(1)	(2)	(3)	(4)	(5)	(6)	(7)	(8)
1960	55.85						
1961	66.27		.0298				.03
1962	62.38		.0337				.03
1963	69.87		.0317				.03
1964	81.37		.0301				.04
1965	88.17		.0300				.04
1966	85.26		.0340				.04
1967	91.93		.0320				.05
1968	98.70		.0307				.05
1969	97.84		.0324				.07
1970	83.22		.0383				.06

a) $\bar{R}_m = ?$ b) VAR(R_m) = ?   c) $\sigma(R_m) = ?$

Table Q7.5   Calculation of Beta for General Motors

Year	GM Price	Percentage Change in Price	Dividend Yield	Percentage Return	Deviation of Returns	Variance of Returns	Covariance with Market
	P_t	$\dfrac{P_t}{P_{t-1}} - 1$	$\dfrac{Div_t}{P_t}$	R_{jt} $(3+4)$	$(R_{jt} - \bar{R}_j)$ $(5 - \bar{R}_j)$	$(R_{jt} - \bar{R}_j)^2$ (6^2)	$(R_{jt} - \bar{R}_j)(R_{mt} - \bar{R}_m)$ (Col. 6 × Q7.4 Col. 6)
(1)	(2)	(3)	(4)	(5)	(6)	(7)	(8)
1960	48						
1961	49		.05				
1962	52		.06				
1963	74		.05				
1964	90		.05				
1965	102		.05				
1966	87		.05				
1967	78		.05				
1968	81		.05				
1969	74		.06				
1970	70		.05				

a) $\bar{R}_j = ?$ b) VAR$(R_j) = ?$ c) COV$(R_j, R_m) = ?$ d) $\beta_j = ?$

7.6 What are the assumptions sufficient to guarantee that the market portfolio is an efficient portfolio?

7.7 In the CAPM is there any way to identify the investors who are more risk averse? Explain. How would your answer change if there were not a riskless asset?

7.8 Given risk-free borrowing and lending, efficient portfolios have no unsystematic risk. True or false? Explain.

7.9 What is the beta of an efficient portfolio with $E(R_j) = 20\%$ if $R_f = 5\%$, $E(R_m) = 15\%$, and $\sigma_m = 20\%$? What is its σ_j? What is its correlation with the market?

7.10 Given the facts of Problem 7.9, and that the common stock of the Rapid Rolling Corporation has $E(R_k) = 25\%$ and $\sigma_k^2 = 52\%$, what is the systematic risk of the common stock? What is its unsystematic risk?

7.11

a) If the expected rate of return on the market portfolio is 14% and the risk-free rate is 6%, find the beta for a portfolio that has an expected rate of return of 10%. What assumptions concerning this portfolio and/or market conditions do you need to make to calculate the portfolio's beta?

b) What percentage of this portfolio must an individual put into the market portfolio in order to achieve an expected return of 10%?

7.12 You believe that the Beta Alpha Watch Company will be worth $100 per share one year from now. How much are you willing to pay for one share today if the risk-free rate is 8%, the expected rate of return on the market is 18%, and the company's beta is 2.0?

7.13 Given the following variance-covariance matrix and expected returns vector (for assets X and Y, respectively) for a two-asset world:

$$\Sigma = \begin{bmatrix} .01 & 0 \\ 0 & .0064 \end{bmatrix}, \quad \bar{R}_1' = [.2 \quad .1],$$

a) What is the expected return of a zero-beta portfolio, given that 50% of the index port-folio is invested in asset X and in asset Y?

b) What is the vector of weights in the global minimum variance portfolio?

c) What is the covariance between the global minimum variance portfolio and the zero-beta portfolio?

d) What is the equation of the market line?

7.14 Given the following variance-covariance matrix, calculate the covariance between portfolio A, which has 10% in asset 1 and 90% in asset 2, and portfolio B, which has 60% in asset 1 and 40% in asset 2:

$$\mathfrak{L} = \begin{bmatrix} .01 & -.02 \\ -.02 & .04 \end{bmatrix}.$$

7.15 Suppose that securities are priced as if they are traded in a two-parameter economy. You have forecast the correlation coefficient between the rate of return on Knowlode Mutual Fund and the market portfolio at .8. Your forecast of the standard deviations of the rates of return are .25 for Knowlode, and .20 for the market portfolio. How would you combine the Knowlode Fund and a riskless security to obtain a portfolio with a volatility (beta) of 1.6?

7.16 You currently have 50% of your wealth in a risk-free asset and 50% in the four assets below:

Asset	Expected Return on Asset i	β_i	Percentage Invested in Asset i
$i = 1$	7.6%	.2	10%
$i = 2$	12.4%	.8	10%
$i = 3$	15.6%	1.2	10%
$i = 4$	18.8%	1.6	20%

If you want an expected rate of return of 12%, you can obtain it by selling some of your holdings of the risk-free asset and using the proceeds to buy the equally weighted market portfolio. If this is the way you decide to revise your portfolio, what will the set of weights in your revised portfolio be? If you hold only the risk-free asset and the market portfolio, what set of weights would give you an expected 12% return?

7.17 The market price of a security is $40, the security's expected rate of return is 13%, the riskless rate of interest is 7%, and the market risk premium, $[E(R_m) - R_f]$, is 8%. What will be the security's current price if its expected future payoff remains the same but the covariance of its rate of return with the market portfolio doubles?

7.18 Suppose you are the manager of an investment fund in a two-parameter economy. Given the following forecast:

$$E(R_m) = .16, \qquad \sigma(R_m) = .20, \qquad R_f = .08,$$

a) Would you recommend investment in a security with $E(R_j) = .12$ and $COV(R_j, R_m) = .01$? [*Note:* Assume that this price change has no significant effect on the position of the security market line.]

b) Suppose that in the next period security R_j has earned only 5% over the preceding period. How would you explain this *ex post* return?

7.19 Why is the separation principle still valid in a world with

a) Nonmarketable assets?

b) A nonstochastic risk-free rate?

7.20 Assume that the mean-variance opportunity set is constructed from only two risky assets, A and B. Their variance-covariance matrix is given below:

$$\Sigma = \begin{bmatrix} .0081 & 0 \\ 0 & .0025 \end{bmatrix}.$$

Asset A has an expected return of 30%, and asset B has an expected return of 20%. Answer the following questions:

a) Suppose investor I chooses his "market portfolio" to consist of 75% in asset A and 25% in asset B, whereas investor J chooses a different "market portfolio" with 50% in asset A and 50% in asset B.

Weights chosen by I are: $[.75 \quad .25]$

Weights chosen by J are: $[.50 \quad .50]$

Given these facts, what β will each investor calculate for asset A?

b) Given your answer to part (a) above, which of the following is true and why?
1. Investor I will require a higher rate of return on asset A than will investor J.
2. They will both require the same return on asset A.
3. Investor J will require a higher rate of return on asset A than will investor I.

c) Compute the zero-beta portfolios and the equations for the security market line for each investor.

7.21 Ms. Bethel, manager of the Humongous Mutual Fund, knows that her fund currently is well diversified and that it has a CAPM beta of 1.0. The risk-free rate is 8% and the CAPM risk premium, $[E(R_m) - R_f]$, is 6.2%. She has been learning about APT measures of risk and knows that there are (at least) two factors: changes in the industrial production index, $\bar{\delta}_1$, and unexpected inflation, $\bar{\delta}_2$. The APT equation is

$$E(R_i) - R_f = [\bar{\delta}_1 - R_f]b_{i1} + [\bar{\delta}_2 - R_f]b_{i2},$$

$$E(R_i) = .08 + [.05]b_{i1} + [.11]b_{i2}.$$

a) If her portfolio currently has a sensitivity to the first factor of $b_{p1} = -.5$, what is its sensitivity to unexpected inflation?

b) If she rebalances her portfolio to keep the same expected return but reduce her exposure to inflation to zero (i.e., $b_{p2} = 0$), what will its sensitivity to the first factor become?

REFERENCES

Banz, R. W., "The Relationship between Return and Market Value of Common Stocks," *Journal of Financial Economics*, March 1981, 3–18.

Basu, S., "Investment Performance of Common Stocks in Relation to Their Price-Earnings Ratios: A Test of the Efficient Markets Hypothesis," *Journal of Finance*, June 1977, 663–682.

Black, F., "Capital Market Equilibrium with Restricted Borrowing," *Journal of Business*, July 1972, 444–455.

———, M. C. Jensen. and M. Scholes, "The Capital Asset Pricing Model: Some Empirical Tests," in Jensen, ed., *Studies in the Theory of Capital Markets*. Praeger, New York, 1972, 79–124.

Blume, M., "Portfolio Theory: A Step toward Its Practical Application," *Journal of Business*, April 1970, 152–173.

———, "On the Assessment of Risk," *Journal of Finance*, March 1971, 1–10.

———, and I. Friend, "A New Look at the Capital Asset Pricing Model," *Journal of Finance*, March 1973, 19–34.

———, and F. Husick, "Price, Beta and Exchange Listing," *Journal of Finance*, May 1973, 283–299.

———, and R. Stambaugh, "Biases in Computed Returns: An Application to the Size Effect," *Journal of Financial Economics*, November 1983, 387–404.

Bower, D.; R. Bower; and D. Logue, "Arbitrage Pricing Theory and Utility Stock Returns," *Journal of Finance*, September 1984, 1041–1054.

Breeden, D. T., "An Intertemporal Asset Pricing Model with Stochastic Consumption and Investment Opportunities," *Journal of Financial Economics*, September 1979, 265–296.

Brennan, M. J., "Taxes, Market Valuation and Corporation Financial Policy," *National Tax Journal*, December 1970, 417–427.

Chamberlain, G., and M. Rothschild, "Arbitrage, Factor Structure, and Mean-Variance Analysis on Large Asset Markets," *Econometrica*, September 1983, 1281–1304.

Chen, N. F., "Some Empirical Tests of the Theory of Arbitrage Pricing," *Journal of Finance*, December 1983, 1393–1414.

———, and J. Ingersoll, Jr., "Exact Pricing in Linear Factor Models with Finitely Many Assets," *Journal of Finance*, June 1983, 985–988.

———; R. Roll; and S. Ross, "Economic Forces and the Stock Market: Testing the APT and Alternative Asset Pricing Theories," Working Paper #20–83, UCLA, December 1983.

Clark, P. K., "A Subordinated Stochastic Process Model with Finite Variance for Speculative Prices," *Econometrica*, January 1973, 135–155.

Copeland, T. E., and D. Mayers, "The Value Line Enigma (1965–1978): A Case Study of Performance Evaluation Issues," *Journal of Financial Economics*, November 1982, 289–322.

Cornell, B., "Asymmetric Information and Portfolio Performance Measurement," *Journal of Financial Economics*, December 1979, 381–390.

Dhrymes, P.; I. Friend; and B. Gultekin, "A Critical Reexamination of the Empirical Evidence on the Arbitrage Pricing Theory," *Journal of Finance*, June 1984, 323–346.

Dimson, E., "Risk Measurement When Shares are Subject to Infrequent Trading," *Journal of Financial Economics*, June 1979, 197–226.

Dybvig, P., "An Explicit Bound on Individual Assets' Deviations from APT Pricing in a Finite Economy," *Journal of Financial Economics*, December 1983, 483–496.

———, and S. Ross, "Yes, the APT Is Testable," *Journal of Finance*, September 1985, 1173–1188.

Fama, E. F., "The Behavior of Stock Market Prices," *Journal of Business*, January 1965a, 34–105.

————, "Portfolio Analysis in a Stable Paretian Market," *Management Science*, January 1965b, 404–419.

————, "Risk, Return and Equilibrium: Some Clarifying Comments," *Journal of Finance*, March 1968, 29–40.

————, "Risk, Return and Equilibrium," *Journal of Political Economy*, January–February 1971, 30–55.

————, *Foundations of Finance*. Basic Books. New York, 1976.

————, and J. MacBeth, "Risk, Return and Equilibrium: Empirical Test," *Journal of Political Economy*, May–June 1973, 607–636.

————, and G. W. Schwert, "Human Capital and Capital Market Equilibrium," *Journal of Financial Economics*, January 1977, 95–125.

Friend, I., and M. Blume, "Measurement of Portfolio Performance under Uncertainty," *American Economic Review*, September 1970, 561–575.

Friend, I.; R. Westerfield; and M. Granito, "New Evidence on the Capital Asset Pricing Model," *Journal of Finance*, June 1978, 903–917.

Gehr, A., Jr., "Some Tests of the Arbitrage Pricing Theory," *Journal of the Midwest Finance Association*, 1975, 91–105.

Gibbons, M. R., "Multivariate Tests of Financial Models: A New Approach," *Journal of Financial Economics*, March 1982, 3–28.

————, and W. Ferson, "Testing Asset Pricing Models with Changing Expectations and an Unobservable Market Portfolio," *Journal of Financial Economics*, June 1985, 217–236.

Grinblatt, M., and S. Titman, "Factor Pricing in a Finite Economy," *Journal of Financial Economics*, December 1983, 497–507.

Hamada, R. S., "The Effect of the Firm's Capital Structure on the Systematic Risk of Common Stocks," *Journal of Finance*, May 1972, 435–452.

Huberman, G., "A Simple Approach to Arbitrage Pricing Theory," *Journal of Economic Theory*, 1982, 183–191.

Ibbotson, R., and R. Sinquefield, "Stocks, Bonds, Bills and Inflation: Year-by-year Historical Returns (1926–1974)," *Journal of Business*, January 1976, 11–47.

Jensen, M. C., "Capital Markets: Theory and Evidence," *Bell Journal of Economics and Management Science*, Autumn 1972a, 357–398.

————, ed., *Studies in the Theory of Capital Markets*. Praeger, New York, 1972b.

Keim, D., "Size-Related Anomalies and Stock-Market Seasonality: Further Empirical Evidence," *Journal of Financial Economics*, June 1983, 13–32.

————, "Dividend Yields and Stock Returns," *Journal of Financial Economics*, September 1985, 474–489.

Lawley, D. N., and A. E. Maxwell, *Factor Analysis as a Statistical Method*. Butterworths, London, 1963.

Lehmann, B., and D. Modest, "Mutual Fund Performance Evaluation: A Comparison of Benchmarks and Benchmark Comparisons," Working Paper, Columbia University, 1985.

Lintner, J., "Security Prices and Maximal Gains from Diversification," *Journal of Finance*, December 1965a, 587–616.

————, "The Valuation of Risk Assets and the Selection of Risky Investments in Stock Portfolios and Capital Budgets," *Review of Economics and Statistics*, February 1965b, 13–37.

————, "The Aggregation of Investor's Diverse Judgments and Preferences in Purely Competitive Security Markets," *Journal of Financial and Quantitative Analysis*, December 1969, 347–400.

Litzenberger, R., and K. Ramaswamy, "The Effect of Personal Taxes and Dividends and Capital Asset Prices: Theory and Empirical Evidence," *Journal of Financial Economics*, June 1979, 163–195.

Mayers, D., "Non-Marketable Assets and the Capital Market Equilibrium under Uncertainty," in Jensen, ed., *Studies in the Theory of Capital Markets*. Praeger, New York, 1972, 223–248.

————, and E. Rice, "Measuring Portfolio Performance and the Empirical Content of Asset Pricing Models," *Journal of Financial Economics*, March 1979, 3–28.

Merton, R., "An Intertemporal Capital Asset Pricing Model," *Econometrica*, September 1973, 867–888.

————, "On Estimating the Expected Return on the Market: An Exploratory Investigation," *Journal of Financial Economics*, December 1980, 323–361.

Miller, M., and M. Scholes, "Rates of Return in Relation to Risk: A Re-examination of Some Recent Findings," in Jensen, ed., *Studies in the Theory of Capital Markets*. Praeger, New York, 1972, 47–78.

Modigliani, F., and G. Pogue, "An Introduction to Risk and Return," *Financial Analysts Journal*, March–April 1974 and May–June 1974, 68–80, 69–85.

Mossin, J., "Equilibrium in a Capital Asset Market," *Econometrica*, October 1966, 768–783.

Oldfield, G., Jr., and R. Rogalski, "Treasury Bill Factors and Common Stock Returns," *Journal of Finance*, May 1981, 337–350.

Pettit, R. R., and R. Westerfield, "Using the Capital Asset Pricing Model and the Market Model to Predict Security Returns," *Journal of Financial and Quantitative Analysis*, September 1974, 579–605.

Reinganum, M. R., "The Arbitrage Pricing Theory: Some Empirical Results," *Journal of Finance*, May 1981a, 313–321.

————, "Misspecification of Capital Asset Pricing: Empirical Anomalies Based on Earnings Yields and Market Values," *Journal of Financial Economics*, March 1981b, 19–46.

Roll, R., "A Critique of the Asset Pricing Theory's Tests," *Journal of Financial Economics*, March 1977, 129–176.

————, "A Possible Explanation of the Small Firm Effect," *Journal of Finance*, September 1981, 879–888.

————, "A Note on the Geometry of Shanken's CSR T^2 Test for Mean/Variance Efficiency," *Journal of Financial Economics*, September 1985, 349–357.

————, and S. Ross, "An Empirical Investigation of the Arbitrage Pricing Theory," *Journal of Finance*, December 1980, 1073–1103.

————, "A Critical Reexamination of the Empirical Evidence on the Arbitrage Pricing Theory: A Reply," *Journal of Finance*, June 1984, 347–350.

Rosenberg, B., and V. Marathe, "Tests of Capital Asset Pricing Hypotheses," unpublished manuscript, University of California at Berkeley, 1977.

Ross, S. A., "Return, Risk and Arbitrage," in Friend and Bicksler, eds., *Risk and Return in Finance*, Heath Lexington, New York, 1974.

————, "The Arbitrage Theory of Capital Asset Pricing," *Journal of Economic Theory*, December 1976, 343–362.

————, "The Capital Asset Pricing Model (CAPM), Short Sales Restrictions and Related Issues," *Journal of Finance*, March 1977, 177–184.

————, "A Simple Approach to the Valuation of Risky Streams," *Journal of Business*, July 1978, 453–475.

Rubinstein, M. E., "A Mean-Variance Synthesis of Corporate Financial Theory," *Journal of Finance*, March 1973, 167–182.

Scholes, M., and J. Williams, "Estimating Betas from Non-synchronous Data," *Journal of Financial Economics*, December 1977, 309–327.

Shanken, J., "Multi-Beta CAPM or Equilibrium APT?: A Reply," *Journal of Finance*, September 1985a, 1189–1196.

————, "Multivariate Tests of the Zero-beta CAPM," *Journal of Financial Economics*, September 1985b, 327–348.

Sharpe, W. F., "A Simplified Model for Portfolio Analysis," *Management Science*, January 1963, 277–293.

————, "Capital Asset Prices: A Theory of Market Equilibrium under Conditions of Risk," *Journal of Finance*, September 1964, 425–442.

Stambaugh, R., "On the Exclusion of Assets from Tests of the Two-Parameter Model: A Sensitivity Analysis," *Journal of Financial Economics*, November 1982, 237–268.

Treynor, J., "Toward a Theory of the Market Value of Risky Assets," unpublished manuscript, 1961.

Vasicek, O. A., "Capital Market Equilibrium with No Riskless Borrowing," March 1971. Mimeograph available from the Wells Fargo Bank.

Verrecchia, R. E., "The Mayers-Rice Conjecture — A Counterexample," *Journal of Financial Economics*, March 1980, 87–100.

8

... option pricing theory is relevant to almost every area of finance. For example, virtually all corporate securities can be interpreted as portfolios of puts and calls on the firm.

J. C. Cox, S. A. Ross, and M. Rubinstein, "Option Pricing: A Simplified Approach," *Journal of Financial Economics*, September 1979, 230

Pricing Contingent Claims: Option Pricing Theory and Evidence

A. INTRODUCTION

The theory of option pricing has undergone rapid advances in recent years. Simultaneously, organized option markets have developed in the United States. On April 26, 1973, the Chicago Board of Options Exchange (CBOE) became the first organized exchange for trading standardized options contracts. By the end of 1974, in terms of share equivalents, volume on the CBOE was larger than that on the American Stock Exchange. By the end of 1976 there were 1337 registered CBOE exchange members, and the bid-ask price for a seat was $55,000 to $62,000.[1] This phenomenal growth in option trading has been catalyzed, at least in part, by the

---

[1] By comparison, during December 1976, nine seats on the New York Stock Exchange exchanged hands at prices ranging from $58,000 to $80,000.

standardization of contracts, which has had the effect of lowering the transaction costs of option trading.

There are many types of options, and at first the terminology is confusing with calls, puts, straps, strips, straddles, spreads, in-the-money options, out-of-the-money options, and so forth. This nomenclature can be greatly simplified if we recognize that all contracts are made up of four basic securities: puts, calls, stocks (the underlying asset), and default-free bonds. A *call option* is a contract that is contingent on the value of an underlying asset. For example, a call option on the CBOE allows its holder to purchase a share of stock in the underlying company at a fixed price, usually called the *exercise price* or the *striking price*, for a fixed length of time. Table 8.1 is a clipping from the *Wall Street Journal* of October 4, 1977. We see, for example, that three Bethlehem Steel call options were being traded based on the value of its common stock, which closed that day at $19\frac{7}{8}$ per share. The first option had an exercise price of $20 and three maturity dates, the third Friday in October 1977, January 1978, and April 1978.

Should the price of the common stock have climbed above $20 per share, a trader who held the call option with an exercise price of $20 could have exercised his or her option and kept the difference between the exercise price and the stock price. A *put* is exactly the opposite of a call option. The holder of a put has the right to sell the stock at the exercise price any time up to and including the maturity date of the put. For example, the holder of a January put option on Avon with the exercise price of $45 could have made a profit if the stock, which was then selling for $47 per share, fell below $45 before the third Friday in January.

B. A DESCRIPTION OF THE FACTORS THAT AFFECT PRICES OF EUROPEAN OPTIONS

To keep the theory simple for the time being, we assume that all options can be exercised only on their maturity date and that there are no cash payments (such as dividends) made by the underlying asset. Options of this type are called *European* options. They are considerably easier to price than their *American* option counterparts, which can be exercised at any date up to maturity.

A quick look at the option prices in Table 8.1 shows that at least three factors are important for the market value of an option. Since most of the options on the CBOE are call options, we shall, for the moment, confine our discussion to the determination of their value. Obviously, the higher the value of the underlying asset, S, the greater the value of an option written on it, ceteris paribus. Alcoa, American Express, Burlington Northern, Digital Equipment, and Walt Disney all have call options with an exercise price of $40 and a maturity date on the third Friday in January. Figure 8.1 clearly shows that the value of the call increases as a function of the value of the stock for a given exercise price and maturity date. Note also that the option still has a positive value even though the stock price is less than the exercise price. As long as investors believe that there is a chance that the stock price will

Table 8.1 CBOE Option Price Listing

Chicago Board

		– Oct –		– Jan –		– Apr –		N.Y.
Option &	price	Vol.	Last	Vol.	Last	Vol.	Last	Close
Alcoa	40	b	b	13	4¾	a	a	43¾
Alcoa	45	66	½	27	2	41	2¾	43¾
Alcoa	50	5	1-16	101	½	38	1	43¾
Am Exp	35	25	2¾	26	3⅜	1	4½	37⅛
Am Exp	40	166	1-16	6	¾	18	1½	37⅛
Am Tel	60	197	2	70	2½	76	2⅞	62
Am Tel	65	53	1-16	210	⅜	86	⅝	62
Atl R	50	276	2⅞	70	4¼	154	5⅛	52⅝
Atl R	60	32	1-16	62	⅝	33	1¼	52⅝
Avon	45	226	2⅛	105	3	216	3¾	47
Avon p	45	257	⅜	234	1 5-16	223	2 1-16	47
Avon	50	444	1-16	247	11-16	283	1 5-16	47
Avon p	50	44	3⅜	48	4⅛	186	5	47
BankAm	25	84	¼	32	¾	30	1¼	24¾
BankAm	30	25	1-16	a	a	b	b	24¾
Beth S	20	191	7-16	108	1 5-16	129	2⅛	19⅞
Beth S	25	3	1-16	161	¼	198	9-16	19⅞
Beth S	30	a	a	5	1-16	25	3-16	19⅞
Bruns	10	a	a	17	2⅜	14	2 11-16	12⅛
Bruns	15	4	1-16	93	3-16	69	7-16	12⅛
Burl N	40	2	3½	a	a	4	4⅞	43½
Burl ·'	45	57	¼	62	1⅜	41	2	43½
Burl N	50	a	a	9	5-16	25	11-16	43½
Burrgh	50	35	19	194	19	b	b	69
Burrgh	60	306	9	50	10⅜	27	11½	69
Burrgh	70	420	⅞	384	3¼	219	4⅞	69
Citicp	25	109	⅜	59	1¼	220	1¾	24⅝
Citicp	30	2	1-16	109	⅛	16	7-16	24⅝
Delta	30	55	3⅜	2	4¾	a	a	33⅜
Delta	35	88	¼	53	1⅜	a	a	33⅜
Dig Eq	35	186	11⅞	2	12⅞	b	b	46¾
Dig Eq	40	231	6⅞	32	8	b	b	46¾
Dig Eq	45	479	2 5-16	70	4¼	20	6	46¾
Dig Eq	50	210	¼	175	1¾	65	3	46¾
Disney	30	a	a	9	9	b	b	38⅝
Disney	35	60	3⅝	14	4⅜	6	5⅞	38⅝
Disney	40	177	¼	81	1⅝	54	2⅝	38⅝
Dow Ch	30	183	⅞	125	1 15-16	247	2⅞	30½
Dow Ch	35	64	1-16	251	⅜	63	⅞	30½
du Pnt	110	644	1¾	199	4¾	90	6⅝	110
du Pnt	120	108	1-16	241	1 5-16	100	2⅝	110
du Pnt	130	13	1-16	a	a	b	b	110
Eas Kd	50	252	10⅝	148	11	154	11⅝	60⅜
Eas Kd p	50	30	1-16		·-16	48	9-16	60⅜
Eas Kd	60	2006	1 9-·			148	5⅛	60⅜
Eas Kd p	60	1086				·1	3½	60⅜
·s Kd	70						1½	60·
·d p	70							

Listed Options Quotations

Tuesday, October 4, 1977

Closing prices of all options. Sales unit usually is 100 shares. Security description includes exercise price. Stock close is New York Stock Exchange final price. p-Put option. o-Old shares.

		– Oct –		– Jan –		– Apr –		N.Y.
Option &	price	Vol.	Last	Vol.	Last	Vol.	Last	Close
Xerox	45	268	8¾	282	8⅞	271	9⅝	53¾
Xerox	50	1306	3⅝	411	4⅞	203	5⅞	53¾
Xerox	60	130	1-16	545	⅝	578	1½	53¾
		– Nov –		– Feb –		– May –		
A E P	24⅞	67	3-16	15	5-16	b	b	24¼
A E P	25	b	b	b	b	10	½	24¼
Am Hos	20	5	4	a	a	a	a	24
Am Hos	25	18	⅜	20	1¼	a	a	24
A M P	25	1	3¾	a	a	a	a	28⅜
A M P	30	6	7-16	a	a	3	1⅞	28⅜
Bally	20	260	⅞	164	1 15-16	211	2⅝	20⅛
Bally	25	187	⅛	269	½	232	⅞	20⅛
Bally	30	10	1-16	b	b	b	b	20⅛
Baxter	30	58	5⅞	a	a	1	7	35⅝
Baxter	35	88	1½	31	2 5-16	7	3½	35⅝
Baxter	40	5	¼	b	b	b	b	35⅝
Blk Dk	15	122	1¼	11	1¾	13	2 1-16	16
Blk Dk	20	23	1-16	10	¼	32	½	16
Boeing o	20	29	4	b	b	b	b	23⅝
Boeing o	22½	87	2	b	b	b	b	23⅝
Boeing o	25	323	⅝	455	1⅜	178	2	23⅝
Boeing o	30	110	⅛	78	⅜	229	¾	23⅝
Bois C	25	168	1½	9	2¼	a	a	25¾
Bois C	30	63	⅛	7	7-16	16	¾	25¾
Bois C	·5	2	1-16	a	a	b	b	25¾
C B S		·a	a	a	a	15		·17⅞
C B S			1-16	1	½			
Co·			·⅝	5	5·			
				47				

		– Oct –		– Jan –		– Apr –		N.Y.
Option &	price	Vol.	Last	Vol.	Last	Vol.	Last	Close
Pfizer	25	11	1⅝	18	2⅛	a	a	26½
Pfizer	30	a	a	5	3-16	9	7-16	26½
Phelps	20	b	b	a	a	7	3¾	23⅜
Phelps	25	a	a	7	⅝	33	1¼	23⅜
Phelps	35	a	a	5	1-16	a	a	23⅜
Ph Mor	50	21	13¾	77	14⅛	2	14⅝	63¾
Ph Mor	60	482	3⅞	75	4⅝	459	5½	63¾
Pitney	15	3	1⅞	a	a	a	a	16¾
Pitney	20	1	1-16	20	¼	50	½	16¾
Proc G	70	15	13⅞	5	14½	b	b	83⅜
Proc G	80	74	3⅝	88	4⅞	10	6¼	83⅜
Proc G	90	5	1-16	80	11-16	79	1½	83⅜
Rite A	15	29	3⅝	21	3¾	23	4	18⅝
Rite A	20	41	⅛	63	¾	30	1 1-16	18⅝
St Cal	40	47	1⅝	21	2¼	20	2 11-16	41½
St Cal	45	5	1-16	41	7-16	24	⅞	41½
T R W	35	15	7-16	15	1 3-16	16	1¾	34¾
T R W	40	a	a	8	¼	2	7-16	34¾
Tandy	20	a	a	8	9⅞	a	a	29¼
Tandy	25	41	4½	35	5½	2	6¼	29¼
Tandy	30	201	7-16	160	2⅛	52	3	29¼
Tady	35	13	1-16	268	½	b	b	29¼
Texaco	25	15	3⅜	9	3½	7	4	28¼
Texaco	30	384	1-16	275	⅜	56	9-16	28¼
U Carb	45	83	⅜	67	1½	34	2⅜	43⅞
U Carb	50	4	1-16	73	5-16	84	¾	43⅞
U Carb	60	a	a	30	1-16	b	b	43⅞
U S St	25	b	b	73	4⅞	17	5	29⅜
U S St	30	456	5-16	804	1½	200	2 3-16	29⅜
U S St	35	a	a	183	5-16	103	⅝	29⅜
U S St	40	a	a	50	⅛	a	a	29⅜
U S St	45	a	a	105	1-16	b	b	29⅜
Wrn Lm	25	20	11-16	20	1½	10	2⅛	25⅝
Wrn Lm	30	a	a	a	a	3	7-16	25⅝
Westng	15	249	2½	109	2⅞	36	3¼	17⅜
Westng	20	320	1-16	274	½	204	⅞	17⅜
Westng	25	a	a	32	⅛	22	¼	17⅜
		– Nov –		– Feb –		– May –		
A M F	15	6	2 13-16	a	a	a	a	17½
A M F	20	28	1-16	a	a	8	9-16	17½
A S A	15	a	a	10	7¼	a	a	22
A S A	20	327	2⅜	183	3⅛	59	3½	22
A S A	25	144	¼	278	15-16	b	b	22
Avnet	15	55	2 3-16	13	2¾	2	3⅛	17¼
Avnet	20	26	⅛	83	7-16	15	1·	
Bally	·		15-16	91	1 15-16	73		
Bally			·	63	½			
Bally				·				

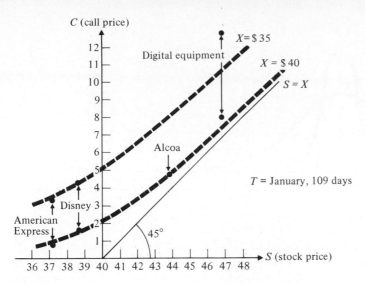

Figure 8.1
The relationship between the call price and the stock price.

exceed the exercise price before the option matures, the option will be valuable. Three of these companies, American Express, Digital Equipment, and Disney, have a second option with a lower exercise price of $35. Note that the relationship between the call price and the stock price has shifted upward. The lower the exercise price, the greater the value of a call option. The third obvious factor that affects call prices is the length of time to maturity. A quick look at any option in Table 8.1 shows that the longer the time to maturity, the higher the value of the option. The reason is that with more time to maturity there is a greater chance that the stock price will climb higher above the exercise price. Hence options with longer maturity have higher prices. In fact, a call option that has an infinite maturity date will have the same value as the stock, regardless of its exercise price. This is because the option will never be exercised. (Why not?)

In addition to the stock price, the exercise price, and the time to maturity, there are two other important (but less obvious) factors that affect the option's value: (1) the instantaneous variance of the rate of return on the underlying asset (common stock) and (2) the risk-free rate of return. The holder of a call option will prefer more variance in the price of the stock to less. The greater the variance, the greater the probability that the stock price will exceed the exercise price, and this is of value to the call holder. A call option is a type of contingent claim. In other words, the option holder gains only under the condition that the stock price exceeds the exercise price at the maturity date. Suppose we hold options and are faced with the two hypothetical stock price distributions shown in Fig. 8.2. Both distributions have identical means, but one has a larger variance. Which would we prefer if both have an identical exercise price, X? Recalling that option holders gain only when the stock price is greater than the exercise price, it becomes clear that we will prefer the option on the security that

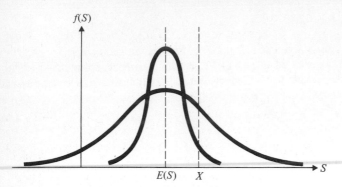

Figure 8.2
Hypothetical distributions of stock prices.

has the higher variance because the cumulative probability of receiving a gain is greater for a security of this sort.[2] This points out an important difference between the value of options and the value of the underlying asset. If we hold the asset, we receive payoffs offered by the entire probability distribution of outcomes. If we are risk averse, we will dislike higher variance, which means that we will require high returns along with high variance. On the other hand, if we hold an option, we receive payoffs only from the tail of the distribution. The contingent-claim feature of options makes higher variance desirable.

The value of higher variance is also illustrated in the following example. Suppose that a company has borrowed long-term debt with fixed interest payments of $8000 per year and that it finds itself with one of the two investment projects below:

Project 1		Project 2	
Probability	*Cash Flow*	*Probability*	*Cash Flow*
.2	4,000	.4	0
.6	5,000	.2	5,000
.2	6,000	.4	10,000

Both projects have identical expected cash flows of $5000. However, if the shareholders accept project 1, the firm will surely go bankrupt because all possible cash flows are less than the debt commitment of $8000. On the other hand, if they accept project 2, which has higher variance, there is a 40% chance that they will be able to pay off their debt obligation and have $2000 left over. Obviously they will choose the riskier project because it offers them a 40% chance of a positive value. This example further illustrates the fact that holders of contingent claims, i.e., holders of options, will prefer more variance to less. It also introduces the notion that the shareholders of a firm are really holders of call options on the market value of the firm.

---

[2] This example is given merely as an illustration. The example that follows is more accurate and more general.

If the value of the firm is less than the required debt payoff (the exercise price on the option), shareholders will allow their option to expire unexercised and turn over the assets of the firm to bondholders. If the value of the firm exceeds the debt payoff, they will exercise their option by paying off the debt holders and keeping any excess for themselves. In many of the chapters that follow we shall utilize option pricing theory for applications in corporate financial policy.

The final factor in determining the value of an option is the risk-free rate of interest. Of all the factors it is the least intuitive. Black and Scholes [1973] have shown that it is possible to create a risk-free hedged position consisting of a long position in the stock and a short position (where the investor writes a call) in the option. This insight allows them to argue that the rate of return on the equity in the hedged position is nonstochastic. Therefore the appropriate rate is the risk-free rate, and as it increases so does the rate of return on the hedged position. This implies that the value of the call option will increase as a function of the risk-free rate of return. The mechanics of forming the risk-free hedge, as well as a more precise exposition of the logic, will be given later in the chapter.

The preceding intuitive description shows that five factors are important in determining the value of a European option: the price of the underlying asset, S; the exercise price of the option, X; the instantaneous variance of the returns of the underlying asset, σ^2; the time to maturity of the option, T; and the risk-free rate, r_f. This may be written in functional form as

$$c = f(S, X, \sigma^2, T, r_f), \tag{8.1}$$

and the partial derivatives of the call price, c, with respect to its various arguments are:

$$\frac{\partial c}{\partial S} > 0, \qquad \frac{\partial c}{\partial X} < 0, \qquad \frac{\partial c}{\partial \sigma^2} > 0, \qquad \frac{\partial c}{\partial T} > 0, \qquad \frac{\partial c}{\partial r_f} > 0. \tag{8.2}$$

C. COMBINING OPTIONS, A GRAPHIC PRESENTATION

One of the most fascinating features of options is that they can be combined in many different ways to provide almost any desired pattern of payoffs. For the sake of simplicity, assume that European put and call options have the same maturity date and the same underlying asset, and that the exercise price is set equal to the asset price.[3] A graphic representation of the value of buying or selling a call option as a function of changes in the stock price is given in Fig. 8.3. When selling a call, we receive the call price now. If the stock price stays the same or falls, the option will mature unexpired, and we keep the future value of the sale price, $+e^{r_f T}C$. This is the horizontal portion of the dashed line in Fig. 8.3(a) with an intercept at $+e^{r_f T}C$. If the stock price rises, we lose a dollar for each dollar it rises. This is the portion of the dashed line with an intercept at $+e^{r_f T}C$ and a slope of -1. Buying a call is the opposite of

---

[3] We also assume that capital markets are frictionless and there are no taxes. This implies, among other things, that the risk-free borrowing rate equals the risk-free lending rate.

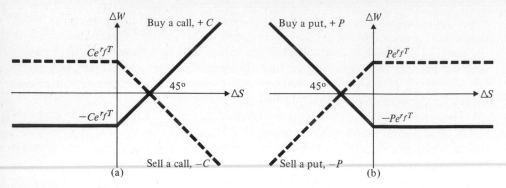

Figure 8.3
Payoffs from put and call options where $S = X$.

selling a call. If we sell a put, we receive $+P$ dollars now and lose a dollar for every dollar the stock price falls below the exercise price. This is represented by the dashed line in Fig. 8.3(b). The solid line, which represents buying a put, is just the opposite.

The payoffs for long and short positions for stocks and risk-free pure discount bonds are shown in Fig. 8.4. If we hold a long position in a stock, we gain or lose a dollar for every dollar the stock price changes. If we hold a bond, we receive the same payoff regardless of changes in the stock price because a risk-free bond is presumed to have identical payoffs irrespective of which state of the world obtains.

These elemental securities may be combined in various ways according to the following relationship:

$$S + P = B + C. \tag{8.3}$$

Buying a share of stock and buying a put written on that share yield the same payoff as holding a bond and buying a call. Alternatively, holding a portfolio made up of

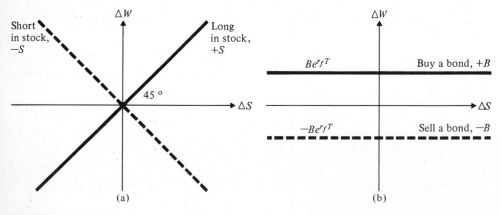

Figure 8.4
Payoffs from stock or bond.

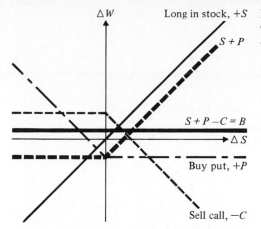

Figure 8.5
Grapical representation of
$S + P - C = B.$

long positions in the stock and the put and a short position in the call is equivalent to the perfectly risk-free payoff offered by holding the bond. This can be seen by simply rearranging Eq. (8.3) as follows:

$$S + P - C = B. \qquad (8.4)$$

Figure 8.5 shows how the payoffs can be combined graphically by adding the payoffs. The bold dashed line is the payoff from holding a put and a share of stock. On the graph it is the vertical sum of the payoffs of the two securities. Note that there is no risk if the stock price falls, because the put gains a dollar in value for every dollar the stock loses. In the terminology of Wall Street we say that the put insures against downside losses. If we also sell a call, any upside variability is eliminated, too, and the result is a perfectly risk-free payoff. Thus a portfolio composed of a long position in a stock, a put on the stock, and a short position in a call on the stock is completely risk free.

The reader may use the above graphic analysis to investigate the payoff patterns of many different securities. One often hears of straddles, spreads, straps, and strips. They are defined as follows:

- *Spread.* A combination of put and call options in a single contract, with the exercise price of the put usually less than the exercise price of the call. Because of the put-call parity relationship (discussed in the next section) the value of a spread is less than for a straddle.
- *Straddle.* A combination of put and call options in the same contract where the exercise price and maturity date are identical for both options. A straddle is graphed in Fig. 8.6.
- *Straps and strips.* Combinations of two calls and one put, and two puts and one call, respectively.

A straddle loses money for small changes in the stock price and gains money for large changes. This may seem to be "a good deal," but let us keep in mind that the

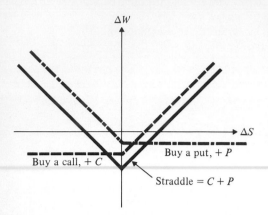

Figure 8.6
Payoff on a straddle.

market values of the put and call options are determined in a way that already incorporates the market's best estimate of the variance in the price of the underlying security. The greater the variance, the more we have to pay for the put and call options. Therefore greater price fluctuations will be needed to make a profit. In the final analysis the securities will always be priced to yield a fair return for their riskiness.

D. EQUITY AS A CALL OPTION

Option pricing theory has many applications in corporate finance. Black and Scholes [1973] were the first to point out that the equity in a levered firm is really a call option on the value of the firm. Later articles have shown how option pricing applies to many different corporate finance topics such as dividend policy, capital structure, mergers and acquisitions, investment policy, spinoffs, divestitures, convertible debt and warrants, and abandonment decisions. Needless to say, the more we know about option pricing theory, the better we shall understand corporate financial management.

To introduce equity as a call option on the assets of a levered firm, assume that the firm has only two sources of capital: equity and *risky* debt. The debt is a zero coupon bond, has a face value D, and matures T years from now. It is secured by the assets of the firm, but bondholders may not force the firm into bankruptcy until the maturity date of the bond. The firm pays no dividends.

We saw, in Eq. (8.3), that any risky portfolio can be constructed from the four basic building blocks

$$S + P = B + C. \tag{8.3}$$

For a CBOE call option the underlying asset is a share of stock, S. For our current discussion, it is the market value of the firm, V. The equity in a levered firm, S, is really a call option on the value of the firm. If, on the maturity date, the value of the firm, V, exceeds the face value of the bonds, D, the shareholders will exercise their call

Table 8.2 Stakeholders' Payoffs at Maturity

	Payoffs at Maturity	
	If $V \leq D$	*If $V > D$*
Shareholders' position:		
Call option, S	0	$(V - D)$
Bondholders' position:		
Risk-free bond	D	D
Put option, P	$-(D - V)$	0
Total for bondholders	V	D
Sum of stakeholder positions	$0 + V = V$	$V - D + D = V$

option by paying off the bonds and keeping the excess. On the other hand, if the value of the firm is less than the face value of the bonds, the shareholders will default on the debt by failing to exercise their option. Therefore at maturity the shareholders' wealth, S, is

$$S = \text{MAX}[0, V - D]. \tag{8.5}$$

If we substitute V for S and S for C in Eq. (8.3), we have

$$V = (B - P) + S. \tag{8.6}$$

Equation (8.6) tells us that the value of a risky asset, the levered firm, can be partitioned into two parts. The equity position, S, is a call option, and the risky debt position $(B - P)$, is equivalent to the present value of the risk-free debt, minus the value of a European put option, P. At maturity the bondholders receive

$$B - P = \text{MIN}[V, D]. \tag{8.7}$$

Table 8.2 shows how the payoffs to equity and risky debt add up to equal the value of the firm at maturity. We are assuming that there are no taxes and no bankruptcy costs paid to third parties (e.g., lawyers and the courts). At maturity the entire value of the firm is divided between bondholders and shareholders. If the firm is successful, i.e., if $V \geq D$, the bondholders receive the face value of the riskless bond, D, and their put option is worthless. If the firm is bankrupt, they still receive the face value of the riskless bond, but a put option has in effect been exercised against them because they lose the difference between the face value of the riskless debt, D, and the market value of the firm, V. They gain D but lose $(D - V)$; therefore their net position is V, the market value of the firm in bankruptcy.

The fact that the equity in a levered firm is really a call option on the value of the firm's assets will provide many insights throughout this chapter and in the remainder of the text. Now let us turn our attention to the problem of how to value a call option.

E. PUT-CALL PARITY

Table 8.1 shows some securities with both put and call options written against them. For example, Avon has puts and calls with exercise prices of $45 and $50. We show below that for European options there is a fixed relationship between the price of put and call options with the same maturity date that are written on a single underlying security. This relationship, derived by Stoll [1969], is called *put-call parity*. It implies that if we know the price of a European call on an asset, we can easily determine the price of a European put on the same asset.

Suppose we have a portfolio where we purchase one share of stock, one put option, and sell (write) one call option. Both options are written on the share of stock. Also, they have the same maturity date, T, and the same exercise price, X. At maturity all states of the world can be divided into those where the stock price is less than the exercise price, $S < X$, and those where it is greater than or equal to the exercise price, $S \geq X$. The payoffs from the portfolio in either state are listed below.

If $S < X$:

a) You hold the stock $\qquad\qquad$ S
b) The call option is worthless $\quad$ 0
c) The put option is worth $\qquad$ $X - S$
d) Therefore, your net position is $\quad$ X

If $S \geq X$:

a) You hold the stock $\qquad\qquad\qquad$ S
b) The call option is worth $\qquad\quad$ $-(S - X)$
c) And the put option is worthless $\quad$ 0
d) Therefore, your net position is $\qquad$ X

No matter what state of the world obtains at maturity, the portfolio will be worth X. Consequently, the payoff from the portfolio is completely risk free, and we can discount its value at the risk-free rate, r_f. Using discrete discounting, this is

$$S_0 + P_0 - c_0 = \frac{X}{1 + r_f}.$$

This can be rearranged to give the put-call parity formula

$$(c_0 - P_0) = \frac{(1 + r_f)S_0 - X}{1 + r_f}. \tag{8.8}$$

Note that the interest rate, r_f, is a one-period rate but that the time period need not equal a calendar year. For example, if the option expires in six months and r is an annual rate, then we can replace $(1 + r_f)$ in Eq. (8.8) with $(1 + r_f)^{1/2}$. Equation (8.8) is referred to as the *put-call parity* relationship for European options. A special case occurs when the exercise price, X, is set equal to the current stock price, S. When

$S = X$, we have

$$c_0 - P_0 = \frac{r_f S_0}{1 + r_f} > 0. \tag{8.9}$$

This shows that when all the valuation parameters are identical (the same stock price, instantaneous variance, exercise price, time to expiration, and risk-free rate) and the exercise price equals the stock price, the call option will have greater present value than the put option. It explains why the dashed call line in Fig. 8.6 lies below the put line.

An equivalent continuous compounding formula for put-call parity is

$$c_0 - P_0 = S_0 - Xe^{-r_f T}, \tag{8.10}$$

where r_f is the annual risk-free rate and T is the time to maturity (in years) of the put and call options. The put-call parity relationship is extremely useful for the valuation of European options because if we know the value of a European call, the put-call parity relationship also gives the value of a corresponding put.

F. SOME DOMINANCE THEOREMS THAT BOUND THE VALUE OF A CALL OPTION

The value of a call option has been described as a function of five parameters: the price of the underlying asset, S; the instantaneous variance of the asset returns, σ^2; the exercise price, X; the time to expiration, T; and the risk-free rate, r_f:

$$c = f(S, \sigma^2, X, T, r_f). \tag{8.1}$$

Perhaps even more interesting are some factors that do not affect the value of an option. For example, the option price does not depend on investor attitudes toward risk, nor does it depend on the expected rate of return of the underlying security. This section of the chapter provides a logical, rather than descriptive or intuitive, framework for understanding why these five parameters affect option value and why investor attitudes toward risk and the rate of return on the underlying security do not.

All the following discussion is based on the notion of stochastic dominance, which was introduced in Chapter 4. We shall use first-order stochastic dominance, which says that one asset will be preferred by all investors (be they risk averse, risk neutral, or risk loving) if the return that it offers is superior in every state of nature to the return offered by a second asset. If this is true, we say that the first asset is stochastically dominant over the second. Clearly, if all the following analysis is based on this simple notion, the value of a call option will not depend on individual risk preferences.

Before developing the analysis and some related theorems it is useful to spell out in detail the assumptions that have been used in developing valuation models for options:

- Frictionless capital markets with no transactions costs or taxes and with information simultaneously and costlessly available to all individuals.
- No restrictions on short sales.
- Continuous asset trading with all asset prices following continuous and stationary stochastic processes.[4]
- Nonstochastic risk-free rate (constant over time).[5]
- No dividends.[6]

Most of these assumptions are self-explanatory and are consistent with efficient capital markets. By *continuous stochastic processes* we mean that the price of the underlying asset can vary over time but does not have any discontinuities or jumps. In other words, we could graph the price movement over time without lifting our pen from the paper. A stationary stochastic process is one that is determined in the same way for all time periods of equal length. In particular the instantaneous price variance does not change over time. If the underlying asset is a common stock, we assume no dividend payments so that there are no jumps in the stock price. It is well known that the stock price falls by approximately the amount of the dividend on the ex-dividend date.

Our objectives are (1) to show the boundary conditions that limit the values a call option can take and (2) to prove that American calls on nondividend-paying stocks will optimally not be exercised prior to maturity. The reader who wishes to carefully study the theorems of option pricing is referred to the seminal work of Merton [1973b]. We shall adopt the convention that European calls that can be exercised only at maturity will be written with a lowercase c, whereas American calls that can be exercised any time will be written with an uppercase C.

The payoff to a call option at maturity is (1) the maximum of zero if the stock price is less than the exercise price or (2) the difference between the stock price and the exercise price if the stock price exceeds the exercise price, i.e.,

$$C \ge c = \text{MAX}[0, S - X] \ge 0. \tag{8.11}$$

Clearly, the call price must be nonnegative. Also, because the American call, C, can be exercised prior to maturity, its value must be greater than or equal to the European call value, c.

Equation (8.11) also tells us that the call price can never fall below $(S - X)$. Additionally, the option price will never exceed the price of the stock on which it is written. Even if the exercise price, X, is zero and the option never matures, it can be worth at most S. Even in this extreme case the option may be worth less than the stock because shareholders have voting rights, whereas option holders do not.

---

[4] Cox and Ross [1975] have relaxed this assumption.
[5] Merton [1976] has relaxed this assumption.
[6] Geske [1977] has relaxed this assumption.

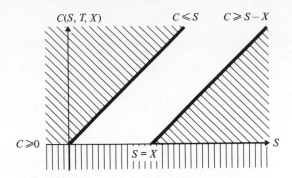

Figure 8.7
Boundaries for the value of a call option.

The preceding discussion serves to limit the possible values that option prices may take relative to the stock price. The results are illustrated in Fig. 8.7. The call option is a function of the stock price, S; the time to maturity, T; and the exercise price, $C(S, T, X)$. Its value is nonnegative, less than S, and greater than $S - X$. Note that the boundaries $C \leq S$ and $C \geq S - X$ are 45° lines.

Next, we shall prove that an American call option written on a nondividend-paying stock will not be exercised before the expiration date of the option. Along the way we will further bound the value that call options can take and we will see why the call value will increase when the risk-free rate does. The result we wish to prove is stated as Theorem 8.1.

Theorem 8.1. An American call on a nondividend-paying stock will not be exercised before the call expiration date.

To prove this, we first assume that $B(T)$ is the current price of a risk-free zero coupon bond. Given positive interest rates and assuming that the bond pays $1 upon maturity, we have[7]

$$B(T) = (\$1)e^{-r_f T}, \tag{8.12}$$

where r_f is the one-year risk-free rate and T is the number of years (or fraction of a year) to maturity. We shall adopt the convention that $T_1 > T_2 > \cdots > T_n$; therefore

$$0 = B(\infty) < B(T_1) < B(T_2) < \cdots < B(0) = \$1.$$

Now let us consider two portfolios. Portfolio A represents the purchase of one European call for $c(S, T, X)$ dollars and X bonds for $XB(T)$ dollars.[8] Portfolio B is the purchase of one share of stock for S dollars. Table 8.3 demonstrates the relationship between the terminal values for the two portfolios. If the stock price is less than

---

[7] This is the continuous discounting version of the more familiar discrete discounting formula

$$B(T) = \frac{\$1}{(1 + r_f)^T} = (\$1)(1 + r_f)^{-T}.$$

[8] In this proof we have defined T as the time to maturity for the call option.

Table 8.3   Relationship Between the Value of a Share of Stock and a Portfolio Made Up of a European Call and X Risk-Free Bonds

Portfolio	Current Value	Portfolio Value, Given Stock Price at T	
		$S < X$	$S \geq X$
A	$c(S, T, X) + XB(T)$	$0 + X$	$S - X + X$
B	S_0	S	S
Relationship between terminal values of A and B		$V_a > V_b$	$V_a = V_b$

the exercise price at the expiration date, the option will expire unexercised, with no value, and portfolio A will be worth X dollars. But since $X > S$, portfolio A will be worth more than portfolio B, which is one share of stock. On the other hand, when the stock price is greater than the exercise price, portfolios A and B have the same payoff. In any state of nature portfolio A pays an amount greater than or equal to portfolio B. Therefore, in order to prevent dominance, portfolio A must have a higher price than portfolio B:

$$c(S, T, X) + XB(T) \geq S.$$

This restriction may be rearranged to obtain

$$c(S, T, X) \geq \text{MAX}[0, S - XB(T)].$$

Finally, from (8.12) we have

$$c(S, T, X) \geq \text{MAX}[0, S - e^{-r_f T}X]. \tag{8.13}$$

Equation (8.13) applies to a European call, but we have already discussed the fact that an American call is always at least as valuable as an equivalent European call; therefore

$$C(S, T, X) \geq c(S, T, X) \geq \text{MAX}[0, S - e^{-r_f T}X]. \tag{8.14}$$

Furthermore, if exercised, the value of an American call is $\text{MAX}[0, S - X]$, which is less than $\text{MAX}[0, S - XB(T)]$, since $B(T) = e^{-r_f T}$, which is less than one, for positive r_f. Consequently, the holder of an American option can always do better by selling it in the marketplace rather than exercising it prior to expiration. This is an important result because European options are much simpler than American options.

Theorem 8.1 further limits the set of feasible prices for call options because the requirement that

$$c(S, T, X) \geq \text{MAX}[0, S - XB(T)]$$

is more restrictive than

$$c(S, T, X) \geq \text{MAX}[0, S - X].$$

This is shown in Fig. 8.8. Also, it is now possible to demonstrate, in a plausible fashion, that the call price will increase when the risk-free rate increases. Suppose

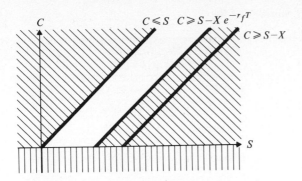

Figure 8.8
Further limitation of the feasible set of call prices.

the stock price is \$50, the exercise price is \$30, and the option expires in one year. If the risk-free rate is 5%, the lower bound on the option price will be \$21.46. If the risk-free rate changes to 10%, the lower bound increases to \$22.85. Intuitively, the call option is worth more because an investor has to pay less today to acquire the risk-free discount bond that guarantees \$1 at the end of the year. This makes portfolio A in Table 8.3 more valuable relative to portfolio B.

Theorem 8.2 introduces more realism into the analysis by showing what happens to the value of an American call option when the underlying stock pays a dividend. Since most firms pay dividends, investors who hold CBOE call options must be careful; the options are not protected against a drop in value when the underlying stock falls in price because it goes ex-dividend.

Theorem 8.2. Premature exercise of an American call may occur if the underlying security (common stock) pays dividends (and if the option is inadequately protected against the dividend payment).

In December 1976, General Motors stock was selling at around \$75 per share. Call options were outstanding with an exercise price of \$60. On the next day, the company was scheduled to go ex-dividend with a dividend of \$3 per share. This implied that the stock price would fall to approximately \$72 per share. CBOE call options provide no protection against dividend payments, and hence option holders found themselves with the following dilemma. Before the ex-dividend date the option price could not fall below $S - X$, or \$15. (Why?) On the following day, everyone knew the stock price would fall to around \$72 per share and that the option price would also fall (it fell to around \$12\frac{5}{8}). On one day their option was worth \$15 and on the next they knew it would have a lower price. Obviously, the rational thing to do was to exercise the option just before the stock went ex-dividend.

The rationality of the above example can be demonstrated by assuming that a security makes a certain dividend payment, Div, on the expiration date of an option. Consider two portfolios. Portfolio A is one European call and X + Div bonds. Portfolio B is one share of stock. Table 8.4 shows the terminal values of the two portfolios. The value of A is greater than that of B when the stock price is less than the exercise

Table 8.4   Options on Dividend-Paying Stocks May Be Exercised Prematurely

Portfolio	Current Value	Portfolio Value, Given Stock Price at T	
		$S < X$	$S \geq X$
A	$c(S, T, X) + (X + \text{Div})B(T)$	$0 + X + \text{Div}$	$S - X + X + \text{Div}$
B	S	$S + \text{Div}$	$S + \text{Div}$
Relationship between terminal values of A and B		$V_a > V_b$	$V_a = V_b$

price and equal to it otherwise. Therefore

$$c(S, T, X) + (X + \text{Div})B(T) \geq S.$$

By rearranging this and using Eq. (8.12), we obtain

$$c(S, T, X) \geq \text{MAX}[0, S - (X + \text{Div})e^{-r_f T}]. \tag{8.15}$$

Depending on the size of the dividend payment and the risk-free rate, it is possible to have the following situation:

$$(X + \text{Div})e^{-r_f T} > S,$$

in which case the value of the call in (8.15) is zero, at best. Therefore, in some cases it may be advantageous to exercise an American option prematurely.[9]

The preceding discussion has served to bound the possible values of call prices as shown in Fig. 8.8. This is done without any mention whatsoever of the risk preferences of different individuals. The dominance arguments used in the analysis are very robust. They require only that arbitrage opportunities in efficient capital markets do not result in dominated securities. Further, the theorems provide considerable insight into the relationship between option prices; the price of the underlying asset, S; the exercise price, X; the time to maturity, T; and the risk-free rate, r_f. In the next section we demonstrate the call valuation formula, which can be used to determine the price of a European call, given that we know the above four parameters and the instantaneous variance of the price of the underlying asset.

G. DERIVATION OF THE OPTION PRICING FORMULA—THE BINOMIAL APPROACH

We shall discuss two derivations of the (Black-Scholes) option pricing model (OPM). The first, a closed-form solution, was provided by Black and Scholes [1973]. They recognized that given the assumption of frictionless markets and continuous trading

---

[9] The reader who is interested in the valuation of call options written on dividend-paying stocks is referred to Roll [1977].

opportunities, it is possible to form a riskless hedge portfolio consisting of a long position in a stock and a short position in a European call written on that stock. As we shall see, this insight is critical for solving the option pricing problem. However, because their derivation requires the use of advanced mathematical tools such as stochastic differential equations, it is relegated to the appendix of this chapter. A somewhat more intuitive approach, which uses binomial distributions, was independently derived by Cox, Ross, and Rubinstein [1979] and Rendleman and Bartter [1979]. Besides being easier to understand, the binomial approach provides solutions, not only for a closed-form European option pricing model but also for the more difficult American option problem where numerical simulations must be employed.

1. The Simple Binomial Model for Pricing Call Options on Stock

In addition to the usual assumption of frictionless and competitive capital markets where no riskless arbitrage opportunities can exist, assume that the stock price, S, obeys a binomial generating process as shown in Fig. 8.9 where

$S = \$20.00 =$ the stock price,

$q = .5 =$ the probability the stock price will move upward,

$1 + r_f = 1.1 =$ one plus the risk free rate of interest,

$u = 1.2 =$ the multiplicative upward movement in the stock price
$\quad (u > 1 + r_f > 1)$,

$d = .67 =$ the multiplicative downward movement in the stock price
$\quad (d < 1 < 1 + r_f)$

At the end of one time period the stock price may increase to uS with probability q or decrease to dS with probability $1 - q$. Figure 8.9 provides a simple example where the current stock price is $20. There is a 50/50 chance (i.e., $q = .5$) it will increase to $24 or fall to $13.40 by the end of the period. Note that the downward multiplier for the stock price, d, must be less than one and greater than zero. This assumption ensures that the stock price will not fall below a value of $0, no matter how many time periods are eventually added. If there are n periods, then

$$\lim_{n \to \infty} d^n = 0 \quad \text{iff} \quad 0 \le d < 1.$$

Of course, there is no upper bound on the value that the stock price may take.

Next, denote $1 + r_f$ as one plus the riskless rate of interest over the single time period ($1 + r_f = 1.1$ in our example). The derivation requires that $u > 1 + r_f > d$. If

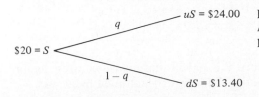

Figure 8.9
A one-period binomial generating process.

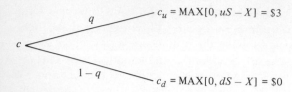

Figure 8.10
Payoffs for a one-period call option.

these inequalities did not hold, then riskless arbitrage opportunities would exist. Also, for convenience, we assume that $r_f > 0$.

Now, imagine a call option c, with an exercise price of $X = \$21$ written on the stock. The payoffs for the call are shown in Fig. 8.10. Given our numerical example, there is a 50/50 chance of ending up with $MAX[0, uS - X] = \$3$, or $MAX[0, dS - X] = \$0$. The question is, How much would we pay for the call right now?

To answer this question, we begin by constructing a risk-free hedge portfolio composed of one share of stock, S, and m shares of a call option written against the stock. Figure 8.11 shows the payoffs for the hedge portfolio. If the end-of-period payoffs are equal, the portfolio will be risk free. Equating the payoffs, we have

$$uS - mc_u = dS - mc_d,$$

and solving for m, the number of call options to be written against the share of stock, we have

$$m = \frac{S(u - d)}{c_u - c_d}. \qquad (8.16)$$

Substituting the numbers from our example problem, we see that the hedge ratio is

$$m = \frac{\$20(1.2 - .67)}{\$3 - \$0} = 3.53.$$

Thus the riskless hedge portfolio consists of buying one share of stock and writing 3.53 call options against it. The payoffs in the two states of nature are identical as shown below.

State of Nature	Portfolio	Payoff
Favorable	$uS - mc_u$	$1.2(\$20) - 3.53(\$3) = \$13.40$
Unfavorable	$dS - mc_d$	$.67(\$20) - 3.53(\ 0) = \$13.40$

Before we can determine what rate of return this payoff represents, we must figure out the call price, c, in order to know exactly what our original investment was.

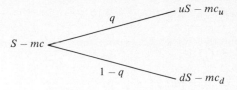

Figure 8.11
The payoffs for a risk-free hedge portfolio.

We also know that because the hedge portfolio is constructed to be riskless, the current value of the portfolio multiplied by one plus the risk-free rate must equal the end-of-period payoff. Mathematically, this is

$$(1 + r_f)(S - mc) = uS - mc_u,$$

$$c = \frac{S[(1 + r_f) - u] + mc_u}{m(1 + r_f)}. \tag{8.17}$$

Substituting the hedge ratio, m, into this equation and rearranging terms, we can solve for the value of the call option:

$$c = \left[c_u \left(\frac{(1 + r_f) - d}{u - d} \right) + c_d \left(\frac{u - (1 + r_f)}{u - d} \right) \right] \div (1 + r_f). \tag{8.18}$$

It can be simplified by letting

$$p = \frac{(1 + r_f) - d}{u - d} \quad \text{and} \quad 1 - p = \frac{u - (1 + r_f)}{u - d}.$$

Thus we have

$$c = [pc_u + (1 - p)c_d] \div (1 + r_f). \tag{8.19}$$

We shall call p the *hedging probability*. It is always greater than zero and less than one, so it has all the properties of a probability. In fact p is the value q would have in equilibrium if investors were risk neutral. Referring back to Fig. 8.9, a risk-neutral investor would require only the risk-free rate on an investment in the common stock; hence

$$(1 + r_f)S = quS + (1 - q)dS,$$

and solving for q, we have

$$q = \frac{(1 + r_f) - d}{u - d}.$$

Thus $p = q$ for a risk-neutral investor, and Eq. (8.18), which gives the value of a call, can be interpreted as the expectation of its discounted future value in a risk-neutral world. Of course, this does not imply that in equilibrium the required rate of return on a call is the risk-free rate. A call option has risk similar to that of buying the stock on margin.[10]

---

[10] *Buying on margin* means that part of the investment in the stock is borrowed. In fact the exact payoffs of the call option can be duplicated by buying $(c_u - c_d)/[(u - d)S]$ shares of stock and $[uc_d - dc_u]/(u - d)(1 + r_f)$ units of the risk-free bond. See Cox, Ross, and Rubinstein [1979].

Continuing with our numerical example, we can use Eq. (8.19) to solve for the value of the call option:

$$c = [pc_u + (1 - p)c_d] \div (1 + r_f)$$

$$= \left[\left(\frac{1.1 - .67}{1.2 - .67}\right)\$3 + \left(\frac{1.2 - 1.1}{1.2 - .67}\right)\$0\right] \div 1.1$$

$$= [(.8113)\$3 + (.1887)\$0] \div 1.1 = \$2.2126.$$

Referring back to Fig. 8.11, we can now compute the dollar investment required for our hedge portfolio and confirm that the payoff of $13.40 at the end of the period yields the risk-free rate of return. The hedge portfolio consists of one share of stock and 3.53 call options written against it; therefore the dollar investment is

$$S - mc = \$20.00 - 3.53(\$2.2126) = \$12.19$$

and the rate of return on investment is

$$\frac{\$13.40}{\$12.19} = 1.1 = 1 + r_f.$$

The preceding derivation of the value of a call option depends critically on the existence of a hedge portfolio and on the fact that the call option must be priced so that the risk-free hedge earns exactly the risk-free rate of return. If the call had a higher (or lower) price the hedge portfolio would earn more (or less) than the riskless rate, and opportunities to earn risk-free arbitrage profits would exist.

There are three interesting features of the call pricing formula:

- It does not depend on q, the probability of an upward movement in the stock price. Consequently, even though investors might have heterogeneous expectations about q, they will still agree on the call value relative to its other parameters, namely, u, S, X, and r_f (in the one-period model). The stock price itself aggregates investors' diverse opinions regarding q.

- Individuals' attitudes toward risk are irrelevant in deriving the call option formula. All that is required for our results is that people prefer more wealth to less so that arbitrage profits are eliminated.

- The only random variable on which the call value depends is the stock itself. It does not depend, e.g., on the market portfolio of all securities.

The next logical step is to extend the one-period model to many time periods in order to show how an option's time to maturity affects its value. First consider the two-period graphs of the stock prices and the call option payoffs as shown in Figs. 8.12 and 8.13. We assume that the two-period risk-free rate is simply $(1 + r_f)^2$.[11] Next, we can employ the one-period option pricing model, Eq. (8.19), to solve for c_u and

[11] This is equivalent to assuming a flat term structure of interest rates.

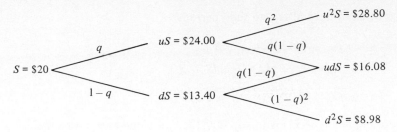

Figure 8.12
Stock prices with a two-period binomial process: $S = \$20$, $u = 1.2$, $d = .67$.

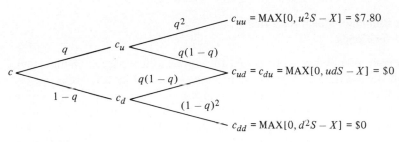

Figure 8.13
Two-period binomial call payoffs; $S = \$20$, $u = 1.2$, $d - .67$, $X = \$21$.

c_d, the values of the one-period options that started the end of the first period:

$$c_u = [pc_{uu} + (1 - p)c_{ud}] \div (1 + r_f),$$
$$c_d = [pc_{du} + (1 - p)c_{dd}] \div (1 + r_f). \quad (8.20)$$

As before, we can construct a riskless hedge during the first period to prevent riskless arbitrage opportunities. The result gives the following equation for the present value of the call:

$$c = [pc_u + (1 - p)c_d] \div (1 + r_f).$$

Substituting the values of c_u and c_d from Eq. (8.20), we have

$$c = [p^2 c_{uu} + p(1 - p)c_{ud} + (1 - p)pc_{du} + (1 - p)^2 c_{dd}] \div (1 + r_f)^2. \quad (8.21)$$

Equation (8.21) is the result of applying the one-period model twice.[12] The terms within the brackets of Eq. (8.21) are a binomial expansion of the terms within the brackets in Eq. (8.19), the one-period model. The terms c_{uu}, c_{ud}, and c_{dd} are the three

---

[12] One can easily imagine how this iterative technique lends itself easily to a computer program.

possible values the call can have after two time periods:

$$c_{uu} = \text{MAX}[0, u^2S - X],$$

$$c_{ud} = c_{du} = \text{MAX}[0, udS - X],$$

$$c_{dd} = \text{MAX}[0, d^2S - X].$$

Another way of looking at Eq. (8.21) is to say that the call value is equal to the expected two-period payoffs (where the expectation uses the hedging probabilities, p and $1 - p$) discounted at the risk-free rate.

2. A Simple Binomial Model for Pricing Call Options on Bonds

The time pattern for bond payouts is just the opposite from stock. While stock prices branch out across time to assume many values, as in Fig. 8.13, bond prices converge toward their face value at maturity. In addition, most bonds have coupon payments.[13] For our example we shall assume that the risk-free interest rate follows a binomial stochastic process as shown in Fig. 8.14. Assume that $r_f = 10\%$, that $u = 1.2$, that $d = .85$, and that there is a 50/50 chance of an up or down movement in interest rates, i.e., that $q = .5$. Next, assume a default-free bond that has a face value of $D = \$1000$, and that pays constant annual coupons of coup $= \$100$ at the end of each year during its three-year life. We assume that the bond price is the present value of the expected end-of-period payoffs, i.e.,

$$B_t = \frac{qB_{d,t+1} + (1 - q)B_{u,t+1} + \text{coup}}{1 + r_{ft}}. \tag{8.22}$$

Note that the bond price in the "up" state of nature when interest rates go down, B_u, is greater than when they go up, B_d. Figure 8.15 illustrates the bond valuation tree. The bond price is stochastic until its maturity because interest rates are.

Suppose we have a call option, with exercise price $X = \$1000$, written on the default-free bond. Let c_t be the market value of the call at period t. Its payoffs, if exercised, are illustrated in Fig. 8.16. Note that if the call had the same life as the default-free bond, the call would have the same payout in all final states of nature and would therefore be worthless. The call on a default-free bond must have a shorter life than the bond. Hence the call option illustrated in Fig. 8.16 has a two-period life, whereas the underlying bond matures after three periods.

To value the call option, we have to create a risk-free hedge of one bond minus the value of m calls written against it. A perfect hedge will give the same payoff in

---

[13] One of the problems with the analysis of options on bonds is that when interest rates change, the present values of all coupons shift in a correlated fashion not captured by our simple binomial process. Another problem is that the variance of the interest rate process is not stationary. The simple example given in the text ignores both these important problems.

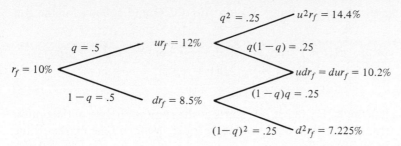

Figure 8.14
A binomial process for interest rates.

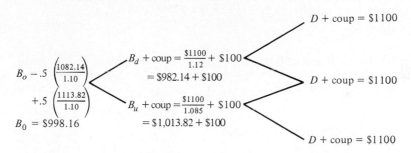

Figure 8.15
Expected bond prices.

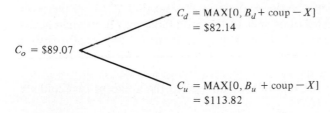

Figure 8.16
Payoffs for a call written on a default-free bond assuming the call is exercised at period t.

each state of nature (up or down); hence we may write

$$B_{d,t+1} + \text{coup} - mc_{d,t+1} = B_{u,t+1} + \text{coup} - mc_{u,t+1},$$

and the hedge ratio is

$$m = \frac{B_{d,t+1} - B_{u,t+1}}{c_{d,t+1} - c_{u,t+1}}. \tag{8.23}$$

We also know that the current value of the hedge portfolio, multiplied by $1 + r_{ft}$, will equal the end-of-period payoff,

$$(B_t - mc_t)(1 + r_{ft}) = B_{d,t+1} + \text{coup} - mc_{d,t+1}. \tag{8.24}$$

Substituting the value of m from Eq. (8.23) into Eq. (8.24) and solving for the call price, c_t, we have

$$c_t = \frac{[(B_{d,t+1} + \text{coup}) - B_t(1 + r_{ft})]c_{u,t+1} - [(B_{u,t+1} + \text{coup}) - B_t(1 + r_{ft})]c_{d,t+1}}{(B_{d,t+1} - B_{u,t+1})(1 + r_{ft})}.$$

(8.25)

To evaluate the call formula, Eq. (8.25), one starts at the expiration date of the option and works backward, step by step, until a value for c_0 is obtained. The market value of the call option in our example is

$$c_0 = \frac{[1082.14 - 998.16(1.10)]113.82 - [1113.82 - 998.16(1.10)]82.14}{(1082.14 - 1113.82)(1.10)},$$

$$c_0 = \$89.069.$$

Later on in the text, we shall use options on bonds to evaluate variable rate loans with CAPS, i.e., variable rate loans with an upper bound on the rate of interest. Many corporate loans and mortgage loans have this format.

3. A Digression on the Binomial Distribution

The reader who is already familiar with the binomial distribution can skip to part 4 of this section; otherwise a digression is in order. *Binomial trials*, as the name suggests, can take only two values, e.g., heads, h, or tails, t, in the flip of a coin. The coin flip need not be fair, so let p be the probability of a head and $(1 - p)$ the probability of a tail. A binomial distribution tells us the probability of observing n heads, given T flips of a coin. Designate this probability as $\Pr\{n|T\}$. A typical question might be, What is the probability, $\Pr\{2|3\}$, of observing two heads out of three coin flips? Useful for answering this question is Pascal's triangle, which is shown below. Each row is constructed from the sum of the numbers in the adjacent two columns in the row immediately above it.

Number of Trials	Pascal's Triangle
$T = 0$	1
$T = 1$	1 1
$T = 2$	1 2 1
$T = 3$	1 3 3 1
$T = 4$	1 4 6 4 1
Number of heads, $n =$	$T, T - 1, \ldots, T - T$

The numbers in the rows of Pascal's triangle are the coefficients for a binomial expansion, say $[p + (1 - p)]^T$. For example, if T is 3 and we want to know the coefficients in $[p + (1 - p)]^3$, they are 1, 3, 3, and 1 as in $1 \cdot p^3 + 3 \cdot p^2(1 - p) + 3 \cdot p(1 - p)^2 + 1 \cdot (1 - p)^3$. In general the probability of observing n heads in T trials is

$$\Pr\{n|Y\} = (\text{coef})p^n(1 - p)^{T - n},$$

where (coef) is the correct coefficient taken from Pascal's triangle. Thus the probability of observing two heads in three flips of a fair (i.e., $p = .5$) coin is

$$\Pr\{n = 2 \mid T = 3\} = 3(.5)^2(.5) = .375, \quad \text{where coef} = 3.$$

For large numbers Pascal's triangle is cumbersome. Another way of figuring out the coefficient is to use combinatorial notation as shown below:

$$\text{coef} = \binom{T}{n} = \frac{T!}{(T-n)!n!}.$$

The term in parentheses can be read "The number of combinations of T things chosen n at a time." For example, what are all the possible ways of getting two heads out of three coin flips? There should be three different ways of doing it, and they are: *hht, hth, thh.* The right-hand term uses factorial notation to compute the number of combinations. The term $T!$ (read T factorial) is the product of all the numbers from T down to 1. Thus if we want to compute the number of combinations of two heads in three coin flips, we have

$$\frac{T!}{(T-n)!n!} = \frac{3!}{(3-2)!2!} = \frac{3 \cdot 2 \cdot 1}{(1)2 \cdot 1} = 3.$$

By the way, 0! is always defined as being equal to 1.

The binomial probability of observing n heads out of T trials, given that the probability of a head is p, can be written

$$B(n \mid T, p) = \frac{T!}{(T-n)!n!} p^n(1-p)^{T-n} = \binom{T}{n} p^n(1-p)^{T-n}.$$

The mean, $E(n)$, of a binomial distribution is the expected number of heads in T trials. It is written

$$E(n) = Tp,$$

and the variance is $\text{VAR}(n) = Tp(1-p)$.[14]

4. The Complete Binomial Model for Pricing Call Options on Stock

The T-period generalization of the binomial call pricing formula is simply the probability of each final outcome multiplied by the value of that outcome and discounted at the risk-free rate for T time periods. Then the general form of the payoff is

$$\text{MAX}[0, u^n d^{T-n}S - X],$$

where T is the total number of time periods, and n is the number of upward movements in the stock price ($n = 0, 1, 2, \ldots, T$). The general form of the probabilities

---

[14] The reader who wants to read more on binomial trials is referred to Feller [1968, Chapter 6].

of each payoff is given by the binomial distribution

$$B(n \mid T, p) = \frac{T!}{(T-n)!n!} \, p^n (1-p)^{T-n}.$$

Multiplying the payoffs by the probabilities and summing across all possible payoffs, we have

$$c = \left\{ \sum_{n=0}^{T} \frac{T!}{(T-n)!n!} \, p^n (1-p)^{T-n} \mathrm{MAX}[0, u^n d^{T-n} S - X] \right\} \div (1 + r_f)^T. \quad (8.26)$$

Equation (8.26) is a complete expression for binomial option pricing. However, one of our objectives is to compare the binomial model, which is derived in discrete time, with the Black-Scholes model, which is a continuous time model. Therefore the following paragraphs show how to rewrite the binomial model so that it may be easily compared with the Black-Scholes model, which is given in the next section of this chapter.

First, let us make use of the fact that many of the final payoffs for a call option will be zero because the option finishes out-of-the-money. Denote a as the positive integer that bounds those states of nature where the option has a nonnegative value. Then Eq. (8.26) can be rewritten as

$$c = \left\{ \sum_{n=a}^{T} \frac{T!}{(T-n)!n!} \, p^n (1-p)^{T-n} [u^n d^{T-n} S - X] \right\} \div (1 + r_f)^T. \quad (8.27)$$

The summation in Eq. (8.26) was $n = 0 \ldots T$ and now it is $n = a \ldots T$. Also we are able to drop the notation $\mathrm{MAX}[0, u^n d^{T-n} S - X]$ because we are dealing only with nonnegative payoffs.

Next, separate Eq. (8.27) into two parts as follows:

$$c = S \left[\sum_{n=a}^{T} \frac{T!}{(T-n)!n!} \, p^n (1-p)^{T-n} \frac{u^n d^{T-n}}{(1+r_f)^T} \right]$$

$$- X(1 + r_f)^{-T} \left[\sum_{n=a}^{T} \frac{T!}{(T-n)!n!} \, p^n (1-p)^{T-n} \right]. \quad (8.28)$$

The second bracketed expression is the discounted value of the exercise price, $X(1 + r_f)^{-T}$ multiplied by a complementary binomial distribution $B(n \geq a \mid T, p)$. The complementary binomial probability is the cumulative probability of having in-the-money options (i.e., where $n \geq a$) where the probabilities are the hedging probabilities determined by the risk-free hedge portfolio. The first bracketed expression is the stock price, S, multiplied by a complementary binomial probability. It may be interpreted in the same way if we let

$$p' \equiv [u/(1 + r_f)]p \quad \text{and} \quad 1 - p' = [d/(1 + r_f)](1 - p).$$

We then have

$$p^n (1-p)^{T-n} \frac{u^n d^{T-n}}{(1+r_f)^T} = \left[\frac{u}{(1+r_f)} \, p \right]^n \left[\frac{d}{(1+r_f)} (1-p) \right]^{T-n} = (p')^n (1-p')^{T-n}.$$

The binomial model for the pricing of a European call option can be summarized as follows:

$$c = SB(n \geq a \,|\, T, p') - X(1 + r_f)^{-T} B(n \geq a \,|\, T, p), \qquad (8.29)$$

where

$$p \equiv \frac{(1 + r_f) - d}{u - d} \quad \text{and} \quad p' \equiv \left[\frac{u}{(1 + r_f)} \right] p,$$

$a \equiv$ the smallest nonnegative integer greater than $\ln(X/Sd^n)/\ln(u/d)$, and if $a > T$, then $c = 0$,

$B(n \geq a \,|\, T, p) = $ the complementary binomial probability that $n \geq a$.

The complementary binomial distribution function is the probability that the sum of n random variables, each of which can take on the value 1 with probability p and 0 with probability $(1 - p)$, will be greater than or equal to a. Mathematically, it is

$$B(n \geq a \,|\, T, p') = \sum_{n=a}^{T} \frac{T!}{(T - n)!n!} (p')^n (1 - p')^{T-n},$$

$T = $ the total number of time periods.

It is obvious from (8.29) that the call option increases in value when the stock price, S, rises, and decreases when the exercise price, X, rises. In addition, the risk-free rate, r_f, the number of time periods before the option matures, T, and the variance of the binomial distribution, $\sigma^2 = Tp(1 - p)$, affect the call value. When the risk-free rate increases, its main effect is to decrease the discounted value of the exercise price, $X(1 + r_f)^{-n}$, and this increases the call value (although there are secondary effects causing p and p' to decrease as r_f increases). An increase in the number of time periods to maturity clearly increases the call price. Recall that the call value is equivalent to the discounted value of the final payoffs multiplied by their hedging probabilities. The number of time periods does not change the hedging probabilities, p. However, it does increase the number of positive payoffs, because in Eq. (8.27) the integer, a, that bounds the positive payoffs will decrease as T increases. Also, the expected value of the binomial payoffs, $E(n) = pT$, increases with T. Finally, the call value will increase with increases in the binomial variance, $\text{VAR}(n) = Tp(1 - p)$. This happens because when the size of the stock price change, u, goes up, so does the variance of the binomial distribution. A greater variance increases the chances that the stock price will exceed the exercise price in the final payoffs, and therefore the call price goes up.

5. Extending the Binomial Model to Continuous Time—The Black-Scholes Option Pricing Mode

The binomial pricing model can be extended to derive a continuous time equivalent if we hold the amount of calendar time (say one year) constant and divide it into more and more binomial trials. We will define T as the life of the option expressed as a fraction of a year and will divide T into n smaller time intervals. As n

becomes larger, the calendar interval between binomial trials becomes shorter and shorter until, in the limit, we have a continuous stochastic process.[15] Note that in this section of the chapter we are interpreting T as one time interval—e.g., 1.6 years—where previously we used T as the number of periods until maturity. A continuous stochastic process has the stock price constantly changing, so its path can be drawn without ever lifting pen from paper.

Of particular concern is the way that the annual risk-free rate, r_f, the up and down movements, u and d, and the binomial process are to be handled as the number of time intervals, n, becomes infinite. If we define r_f as the rate of return for one year, and let j be the rate that is compounded n times in interval T (where T is a fraction of a year, e.g., six months), then in the limit we have[16]

$$\lim_{n \to \infty} \left(1 + \frac{j}{n/T}\right)^{n/T} = e^j = (1 + r_f).$$ (8.30)

Equation (8.30) shows how an annual rate of interest can be converted into the rate of interest for a binomial model with n binomial trials per year. Next, we need to know how the up and down movements, u and d, in a single binomial trial relate to the annual standard deviation of a stock's rate of return. Cox, Ross, and Rubinstein [1979] prove the following relationships:

$$u = e^{\sigma\sqrt{T/n}}$$

and (8.31)

$$d = e^{-\sigma\sqrt{T/n}}.$$

The relationships given in Eq. (8.31) are extremely useful for translating continuous time variables such as the annualized standard deviation, σ, into discrete variables such as u and d for use in the binomial option pricing model.

The continuous-time option pricing formula, derived by Black and Scholes [1973], is given below:[17]

$$c = SN(d_1) - Xe^{-r_fT}N(d_2),$$ (8.32)

where

$$d_1 = \frac{\ln(S/X) + r_fT}{\sigma\sqrt{T}} + \frac{1}{2}\sigma\sqrt{T},$$ (8.32a)

$$d_2 = d_1 - \sigma\sqrt{T}.$$ (8.32b)

---

[15] The binomial formula can also be used to model a jump stochastic process as a limiting case. See Cox, Ross, and Rubinstein [1979, 254–255] for the derivation. With a jump process the stock price will usually move in a smooth deterministic way but will occasionally experience sudden discontinuous jumps.

[16] For proof, see Appendix A at the end of the book.

[17] The appendix to this chapter gives the stochastic calculus derivation.

The terms $N(d_1)$ and $N(d_2)$ are the cumulative probabilities for a unit normal variable z where, e.g., $N(-\infty) = 0$, $N(0) = .5$, and $N(\infty) = 1.0$. Mathematically, this is

$$N(d_1) = \int_{-\infty}^{d_1} f(z)\, dz,$$

where $f(z)$ is distributed normally with mean zero and standard deviation one.

The binomial model is rewritten below so that it can be readily compared with the Black-Scholes model:

$$c = SB(n \geq a \,|\, T, p') - X(1 + r_f)^{-T} B(n \geq a \,|\, T, p). \tag{8.29}$$

The two equations look very similar. The variables S and X are exactly the same and Eq. (8.30) shows the relationship between $(1 + r_f)^{-T}$ and $e^{-r_f T}$. Cox, Ross, and Rubinstein [1979] have proved that as n, the number of binomial jumps per year, becomes large, the two formulas converge because

$$B(n \geq a \,|\, T, p') \rightarrow N(d_1) \quad \text{and} \quad B(n \geq a \,|\, T, p) \rightarrow N(d_2).$$

Thus the binomial option pricing formula contains the Black-Scholes formula as a limiting case.

Both formulas will be used throughout the remainder of the text, and the student should be familiar with how to use them. The next section gives a numerical example using both artificial data and data for Digital Equipment call options. Because Digital Equipment paid no dividends during the valuation period, the Black-Scholes and binomial pricing models can be used directly, without further modification.

H. VALUATION OF AN AMERICAN CALL WITH NO DIVIDEND PAYMENTS

1. An Example with Artificial Data

To understand the mechanics of using the OPM we can first use a simple example where all the parameters are given. Then we can proceed to a problem that uses real-world data.

Suppose that the current stock price is \$50, that the exercise price of an American call written on the stock is \$45, that the annual risk-free rate is $r_f = 6\%$, that the option matures in three months, and that the variance of the stock price is estimated to be 20% per year. Given these facts and the assumption that the stock will pay no dividends or undertake any other capital distributions, we can use the Black-Scholes OPM, Eq. (8.32), to value the call:

$$c = SN(d_1) - Xe^{-r_f T} N(d_2), \tag{8.32}$$

where

$$d_1 = \frac{\ln(S/X) + r_f T}{\sigma\sqrt{T}} + \frac{1}{2}\sigma\sqrt{T}, \tag{8.32a}$$

$$d_2 = d_1 - \sigma\sqrt{T}. \tag{8.32b}$$

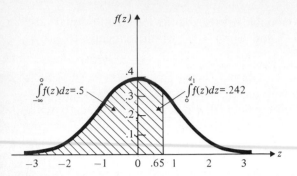

Figure 8.17
Illustration of $N(d_1)$.

To evaluate (8.32) we first calculate the value of d_1. The time to maturity, three months, must be expressed as a fraction of a year, i.e., one fourth of a year. Setting $T = .25$, and substituting in the values of the other parameters, we get

$$d_1 = \frac{\ln(50/45) + .06(.25)}{\sqrt{.2}\sqrt{.25}} + \frac{1}{2}(\sqrt{.2})\sqrt{.25}$$

$$= \frac{.12036}{.2236} + .1118 = .65.$$

Using (8.32b), we can solve for d_2:

$$d_2 = d_1 - \sigma\sqrt{T} = .65 - \sqrt{.2}\sqrt{.25} = .4264.$$

Substituting these values back into (8.32), we have

$$c = SN(.65) - e^{-r_f T}XN(.4264).$$

Recall that $N(\cdot)$ are cumulative probabilities for a unit normal variable. Therefore $N(d_1)$ is the cumulative probability from minus infinity to $+.65$ standard deviations above the mean (which is defined to be zero for a unit normal distribution). The probability contained in the shaded area of Fig. 8.17 will give us the value of $N(d_1)$. Table 8.7 ("Areas under the Normal Curve") (which appears at the end of the chapter) shows that if $d_1 = .65$, the cumulative probability from the mean ($\mu = 0$) to .65 is approximately .242. If we add this to the cumulative probability from minus infinity to zero (which equals .5), we get

$$N(d_1) = \int_{-\infty}^{0} f(z)\,dz + \int_{0}^{d_1} f(z)\,dz$$

$$= .5 + .242 = .742.$$

Repeating this procedure for $N(d_2)$, we get $N(d_2) = .6651$. Substituting these probabilities into the call valuation formula, we have

$$c = 50(.742) - e^{-.06(.25)}(45)(.6651)$$

$$= 37.10 - .9851(45)(.6651)$$

$$= 37.10 - 29.48 = \$7.62.$$

Table 8.5 $c(S, T, \sigma^2, X, r_f)$ for Different Stock Prices

Stock Price	d_1	$N(d_1)$	d_2	$N(d_2)$	Call Price	Given
$30	−1.63	.052	−1.85	.032	$ .14	
40	− .35	.363	− .57	.284	$ 1.93	$T = 3$ months
50	.65	.742	.43	.665	$ 7.62	$r_f = .06$
60	1.47	.929	1.24	.893	$16.15	$\sigma^2 = 20\%$
70	2.15	.984	1.93	.973	$25.75	$X = \$45$

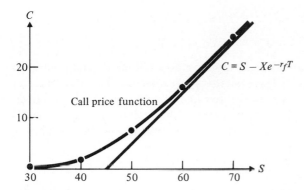

Figure 8.18
Call pricing example.

Table 8.5 gives the value of the call option for various stock prices and Fig. 8.18 plots the call price as a function of the stock price. Note that the call has little value until the stock price rises to the point where it is near the exercise price ($X = \$45$). When the stock price is well below the exercise price, the option is said to be "out-of-the-money," and the call will not be worth much. On the other hand, when the stock price is above the exercise price, the option is "in-the-money," and its value increases until in the limit it reaches $S - Xe^{-r_f T}$ for very high stock prices.

When pricing a real-world call it is important to keep in mind (1) that the Black-Scholes formula cannot be used if the common stock is expected to pay a dividend during the life of the option, (2) that a CBOE call option is not really a simple option but rather an option on an option, and (3) that the instantaneous variance is not stationary over time. If the common stock of a firm is really an option on the assets of the firm, then a call option written against the common stock is really an option on an option. The Black-Scholes formula tends to misprice deep out-of-the-money options and deep in-the-money options. One possible reason is that the simple OPM does not accurately price compound options, and that the bias increases as the stock price moves away from the exercise price.

It is also of interest to contrast the call prices obtained from the binomial model with those given by the Black-Scholes model. Suppose we assume there are only two time periods (each six weeks long). How closely does the binomial model with only two periods approximate the Black-Scholes continuous time call price of $7.62, given a $45 exercise price and three months to maturity?

First, we need to convert the annual effective risk-free rate, 6%, into a semi-quarterly rate, j. This is done below for T = three months, i.e., .25 years:[18]

$$\left(1 + \frac{j}{2/.25}\right)^{2/.25} = 1 + .06,$$

$$j/8 = .731\%.$$

Next, we need to convert the annualized standard deviation, $\sigma = \sqrt{.2} = .4472$, into the up and down variables of the option pricing formula. Using Eq. (8.31) we have

$$u = e^{\sigma\sqrt{T/n}} = e^{.4472\sqrt{.25/2}} = 1.1713,$$

$$d = e^{-\sigma\sqrt{T/n}} = e^{-.4472\sqrt{.25/2}} = .8538.$$

These numbers are needed to estimate the complementary binomial probabilities in the binomial option pricing formula. The easiest way to solve for the value of a call option is to use the iterative approach illustrated in Figs. 8.12 and 8.13 and given algebraically in Eq. (8.20). For the particular example at hand, the call option payoffs are given in Fig. 8.19. First solve for c_u, the option value at the end of the first period, given that the stock price moved up. Using Eq. (8.20) we have

$$c_u = [pc_{uu} + (1 - p)c_{ud}] \div (1 + r_f),$$

where

$$p = (1 + r_f - d)/(u - d)$$

$$= (1.00731 - .8538)/(1.1713 - .8538) = .4835$$

and

$$1 - p = .5165.$$

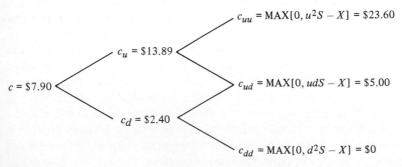

$$c_{uu} = \text{MAX}[0, u^2S - X] = \$23.60$$
$$c_u = \$13.89$$
$$c_{ud} = \text{MAX}[0, udS - X] = \$5.00$$
$$c = \$7.90$$
$$c_d = \$2.40$$
$$c_{dd} = \text{MAX}[0, d^2S - X] = \$0$$

Figure 8.19
Binomial call payoffs.

---

[18] See Eq. (8.30) or Appendix A at the back of the book.

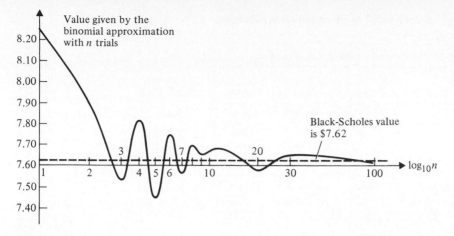

Figure 8.20
The binomial option pricing closely approximates the Black-Scholes result.

Therefore

$$c_u = [.4835(23.60) + .5165(5.00)] \div 1.00731 = \$13.8916.$$

A similar calculation reveals that

$$c_d = [pc_{du} + (1 - p)c_{dd}] \div (1 + r_f) = \$2.4000.$$

Now the above results for c_u and c_d can be used to solve for the current call value, c:

$$c = [pc_u + (1 - p)c_d] : (1 + r_f)$$

$$= [.4835(13.8916) + .5165(2.4000)] \div 1.00731$$

$$= \$7.90.$$

From the same data the Black-Scholes call value was computed to be $7.62. A two-period binomial approximation is reasonably accurate in this case. However, as the number of binomial trials is increased, the accuracy of the binomial approximation improves considerably. Figure 8.20 shows how the binomial approximation approaches the Black-Scholes answer as n increases. It is fairly easy to write a computer program to estimate the binomial pricing formula using either the iterative technique as illustrated above or Eq. (8.29).

2. An Example Using Real Data

Of the options listed in Table 8.1 only one, Digital Equipment, paid no dividend. For close-to-the-money calls on Digital Equipment the assumptions of the Black-Scholes model are closely approximated. Therefore we should be able to use it to give reasonable estimates of the price of the calls. Table 8.6 provides most of the information needed to value the call. The stock price, the exercise price, and the number of days to maturity are given for each option. The risk-free rate is estimated

Table 8.6 Data Needed to Price Digital Equipment Calls

	Call Price, Oct. 4			
Exercise Price	Oct.	Jan.	Apr.	Closing Stock Price
$35	11\frac{7}{8}$	12\frac{7}{8}$	n.a.	46\frac{3}{4}$
40	6$\frac{7}{8}$	8	n.a.	46$\frac{3}{4}$
45	2$\frac{15}{16}$	4$\frac{1}{4}$	6	46$\frac{3}{4}$
50	$\frac{1}{4}$	1$\frac{3}{4}$	3	46$\frac{3}{4}$
Maturity date	Oct. 21	Jan. 20	April 21	
Days to maturity	17	108	199	

Treasury Bill Rates on Oct. 4				
Maturity Date	Bid	Ask	Average	r_f
Oct. 20, 1977	$6.04	$5.70	$5.87	5.9%
Jan. 19, 1978	6.15	6.07	6.11	6.1
Apr. 4, 1978	6.29	6.21	6.25 ⎱	6.2
May 2, 1978	6.20	6.12	6.16 ⎰	

n.a. = not available.

by using the average of the bid and ask quotes on U.S. Treasury Bills of approximately the same maturity as the option. The only missing piece of information is the instantaneous variance of the stock rate of return. Several different techniques have been suggested for estimating it (e.g., see Latane and Rendleman [1976] or Parkinson [1977]). We shall use the implicit variance estimated from one call price in valuing the others. The implicit variance is calculated by simply using the actual call price and the four known exogenous parameters in the Black-Scholes formula, Eq. (8.32), to solve for an estimate of the instantaneous variance. We did this, using the January 45s on Digital Equipment, which were priced at 4\frac{1}{4}$ on October 4. The estimate of instantaneous variance was approximately 7.84% (this is a standard deviation of 28%).

Substituting our estimates of the five parameters into the Black-Scholes valuation equation, we can estimate the price of the April 45s as follows:

$$c = SN(d_1) - e^{-r_f T}XN(d_2),$$

where

$$r_f = .062, \quad T = 199/365, \quad S = \$46.75, \quad X = \$45, \quad \sigma = .28,$$

$$d_1 = \frac{\ln(S/X) + r_f T}{\sigma\sqrt{T}} + \frac{1}{2}\sigma\sqrt{T}, \quad d_2 = d_1 - \sigma\sqrt{T}.$$

The estimated call price turns out to be $5.58, whereas the actual call price is $6.00. If we repeat the procedure for the October 45s (now $r_f = .059$ and $T = 17/365$), the estimated call price is $2.28, whereas the actual price is $2.94. Since both the estimated prices are lower than the actual prices, our estimate of the instantaneous variance is probably too low.

The above examples show how the Black-Scholes valuation model may be used to price call options on nondividend-paying stocks. Roll [1977] and Geske [1979a] have solved the problem of valuing American calls when the common stock is assumed to make known dividend payments before the option matures.[19] However, the mathematics involved in the solution is beyond the level of this text.

3. Forming Hedge Portfolios

Suppose we wish to form a riskless hedge portfolio consisting of shares of Digital Equipment and call options written against them. If we own 100 shares, how many call options should be written? The answer is derived by noting that the Black-Scholes formula is

$$c = SN(d_1) - Xe^{-r_f T}N(d_2),$$

and its partial derivative with respect to a change in the stock price is[20]

$$\frac{\partial c}{\partial S} = N(d_1). \tag{8.33}$$

A riskless hedge portfolio will contain Q_S shares of stock and Q_c call options written against it. Its dollar return per unit time will be approximately

$$Q_S\left(\frac{dS}{dt}\right) - Q_c\left(\frac{dc}{dt}\right).$$

If we write $1/N(d_1)$ call options for each share of stock (i.e., $Q_S = 1$), the return on the hedge is approximately zero, as shown below:

$$1 \cdot \left(\frac{dS}{dt}\right) - \frac{1}{dc/dS}\left(\frac{dc}{dt}\right) = 0.$$

If we use the Digital Equipment April 45s to hedge against 100 shares of Digital Equipment common stock, then we would have to write 100 times $1/N(d_1)$ options. Computing $N(d_1)$ we have

$$d_1 = \frac{\ln(S/X) + r_f T}{\sigma\sqrt{T}} + \frac{1}{2}\sigma\sqrt{T}$$

$$= \frac{\ln(46.75/45) + .062(199/365)}{.28\sqrt{199/365}} + \frac{1}{2}(.28)\sqrt{199/365}$$

$$= .451409.$$

---

[19] Also see Whaley [1981].

[20] Equation (8.33) is the exact solution even though the derivative is complicated by the fact that $N(d_1)$ is a function of S. The curious reader is referred to Galai and Masulis [1976] for the math.

And referring to Table 8.7, we see that

$$N(d_1) = .5 + .1741 = .6741.$$

Therefore we want to write 100 times $1/N(d_1)$, or 148.3 call options.

It is important to bear in mind that this type of hedge is riskless only for small changes in the stock price. The hedge ratio must be adjusted whenever the stock price changes.

4. Intuitive Explanations of $N(d_1)$ and $N(d_2)$

The intuition of the call pricing formula is that the call is equal to the stock price, S, minus the discounted value of the exercise price, $Xe^{-r_f T}$. However, each component is weighted by a probability. The stock price is weighted by $N(d_1)$, which is the inverse of the hedge ratio. For each share of stock, a riskless hedge contains $1/N(d_1)$ call options written against the stock. On the other hand, the discounted value of the exercise price is multiplied by $N(d_2)$. We can interpret $N(d_2)$ as the probability that the option will finish in-the-money. The best way to see this is to go back to the binomial option model discussion, Eq. (8.29), and recall that there the discounted exercise price is multiplied by the complementary binomial probability, $B(n \geq a \mid T, p)$, which is the probability that the option will finish in-the-money, i.e., the probability that it will be exercised.

Thus the Black-Scholes model can be interpreted as the stock price multiplied by the inverse of the hedge ratio, minus the discounted exercise price multiplied by the probability that the option will be exercised.

I. PRICING AMERICAN PUT OPTIONS

Knowledge of put-call parity, Eq. (8.8), and the call option pricing formula is sufficient to value a European put option. Unfortunately, American put options can be exercised before maturity. Therefore put-call parity does not hold for them and they must be evaluated directly.

All known solutions to the American put valuation problem involve computerized numerical methods. Solutions have been provided by Parkinson [1977], Brennan and Schwartz [1977], and Cox, Ross, and Rubinstein [1979]. Because we have already made use of the binomial approach to option pricing in section G of this chapter, the easiest thing to do is to show how it may be employed to value American puts on nondividend-paying common stock.

To provide a concrete example, suppose we know the following facts for a two-period American put:

$u = 1.2 =$ the multiplicative upward movement in the stock price, $u > 1 + r_f > 1$,

$d = .6 =$ the multiplicative downward movement in the stock price, $d < 1 + r_f$,
$1 + r_f = 1.1 =$ one plus the risk-free rate,

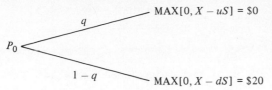

MAX[0, $X - uS$] = $0   **Figure 8.21**
Payoffs to the American put after one
period.

MAX[0, $X - dS$] = $20

$X = \$50 =$ the exercise price for the option,

$S = \$50 =$ the current value of the stock,

$P_0 =$ the present value of an American put.

Figure 8.21 shows the payoffs to the holder of an American put at the end of the
first of two time periods. A hedge portfolio can be formed by purchasing a fraction,
m, of the risky asset and simultaneously buying a put option written against it. The
hedge portfolio and its payoffs are given in Fig. 8.22. By equating the end-of-period
payoffs, we can solve for the hedging fraction, m, which gives a risk-free hedge:

$$muS + P_u = m\,dS + P_d,$$

$$m = \frac{P_d - P_u}{S(u - d)} = \frac{20 - 0}{50(1.2 - .6)} = .667. \tag{8.34}$$

The numerical payoffs from using a hedge consisting of (1) two thirds of a share of
stock and (2) one put option are given in Fig. 8.22. This risk-free hedge pays $40
regardless of whether the stock price moves up (to $60) or down (to $30). Also note
that the proper hedge does not depend on investors' subjective probabilities (q and
$1 - q$ in Fig. 8.21) of an upward or downward movement in the stock price.

Next, we can solve for the hedging probabilities (p and $1 - p$) by multiplying the
current price of the hedge portfolio by one plus the risk-free rate and equating this
to the end-of-period payoff

$$(1 + r_f)(mS + P_0) = muS + P_u.$$

Substituting the value of m [Eq. (8.34)] into this equation and solving for the current
put price, P_0, gives

$$P_0 = \left[\left(\frac{u - (1 + r_f)}{u - d} \right) P_d + \left(\frac{(1 + r_f) - d}{u - d} \right) P_u \right] \div (1 + r_f),$$

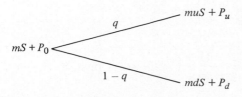

$muS + P_u$ **Figure 8.22**
One-period hedge portfolio payoffs.

$mS + P_0$

$mdS + P_d$

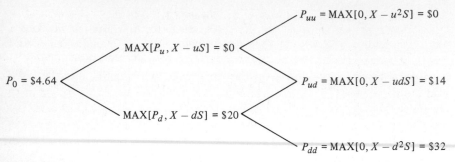

Figure 8.23
Payoffs for a two-period American put.

or

$$P_0 = [pP_d + (1 - p)P_u] \div (1 + r_f), \tag{8.35}$$

where p and $(1 - p)$ are the hedging probabilities:

$$p = \frac{u - (1 + r_f)}{u - d}, \qquad (1 - p) = \frac{(1 + r_f) - d}{u - d}. \tag{8.36}$$

This one-period put valuation equation can easily be extended recursively into a multiperiod framework to derive a binomial pricing equation for European puts similar to that for European calls (Eq. 8.29). However, our objective in this section is to price American puts that may be exercised before maturity. Figure 8.23 shows the payoffs for a two-period American put. Note that the problem is complicated by the fact that the put holder may decide to exercise his or her option at the end of the first period if the value from exercising, say, $X - dS$ is greater than the market value of the put, P_d. Given the numbers chosen for our example, this is exactly what will happen. For example, use the one-period put formula to evaluate P_u and P_d, the put values at the end of the first period. First, we know that the hedging probability is

$$p = \frac{u - (1 + r_f)}{u - d} = \frac{1.2 - 1.1}{1.2 - .6} = .167.$$

Substituting this into Eq. (8.35) we have

$$P_u = [pP_{ud} + (1 - p)P_{uu}] \div (1 + r_f)$$
$$= [.167(14) + .833(0)] \div 1.1 = 2.12$$

and

$$P_d = [pP_{dd} + (1 - p)P_{ud}] \div (1 + r_f)$$
$$= [.167(32) + .833(14)] \div 1.1 = 15.45.$$

Given that the stock price has fallen to $dS = \$30$ at the end of the first period, a rational investor can either exercise the option and receive $X - dS = \$50 - \$30 = \$20$ or hold it, in which case it is worth $15.45. Obviously it is better to exercise early and not hold the option to the end of the second period. This fact makes it difficult to come up with a closed-form solution to the American put valuation problem (see Geske and Johnson [1984]). However, a computer program that uses an iterative technique starting with the set of possible final payoffs in n periods and working backward, as illustrated in Fig. 8.23, can solve for the present value of American puts.

The opportunity to exercise early makes an American put option have a value equal to or greater than its European counterpart. For the numerical example we have been using, the put option is worth $4.64 if it is an American put and only $3.95 if it is a European put.

J. EXTENSIONS OF THE OPTION PRICING MODEL

All the models discussed so far have assumed that the stock price is generated by a continuous stochastic process with a constant variance. Changes in the assumptions about the distribution of stock prices that change the model are discussed in part 1 of this section. There are also various special circumstances (such as unusual types of contracts) that cause us to consider alterations in the model parameter definitions. For example, the exercise price might be a random variable or it may change in a predetermined fashion over the life of the option. Extensions of this type are discussed in part 2.

1. Changing the Distributional Assumptions

All changes in the distributional assumptions involve either the continuity assumption or the constant variance assumption. Black and Scholes assumed that stock prices are generated according to the following differential equation:

$$\frac{dS}{S} = \mu\,dt + \sigma\,dz, \tag{8.37}$$

where

μ = the instantaneous expected rate of return (measuring the drift on the random walk of the stock price through time),

σ = the instantaneous standard deviation of the rate of return, assumed constant,

dt = a small increment in time,

dz = a Wiener process.

If the stock price does not follow a continuous path through time, then it follows either a *pure jump process* or a *mixed diffusion-jump model*.

The pure jump model was introduced by Cox and Ross [1975]. The stock price path through time is described as a deterministic movement upon which are superimposed discrete jumps. It can be written as

$$\frac{dS}{S} = \mu \, dt + (k-1) \, d\pi$$

$$= \mu \, dt + \begin{array}{c} \lambda \, dt \\ \overline{1 - \lambda \, dt} \end{array} \begin{array}{c} k-1 \\ 0 \end{array}, \tag{8.38}$$

where

π = a continuous-time Poisson process,

λ = the intensity of the process,

$k-1$ = the jump amplitude.

Equation (8.38) says that the percentage jump on the stock price is composed of a drift term, $\mu \, dt$, and a term $d\pi$ that with probability $\lambda \, dt$ will jump the percentage stock change to $(k-1)$ and with probability $(1 - \lambda \, dt)$ will do nothing.

The mixed diffusion-jump model, developed by Merton [1976], is something of a mixture of the continuous and pure jump models. Its plausibility comes from the intuition that stock prices seem to have small, almost continuous movements most of the time but sometimes experience large discrete jumps when important new information arrives.

The next three models relax the Black-Scholes assumption that the instantaneous standard deviation is constant through time.

The *constant elasticity of variance model* was derived by Cox [1975] and Cox and Ross [1976]. Its mathematical statement is

$$dS = \mu S \, dt + \sigma S^{\alpha/2} \, dz, \tag{8.39}$$

where

α = the elasticity factor $(0 \leq \alpha < 2)$.

Note that if $\alpha = 2$, the constant elasticity of variance model reduces to the Black-Scholes model. For $\alpha < 2$ the standard deviation of the return distribution moves inversely with the level of the stock price. The intuitive appeal of such an argument is that every firm has fixed costs that have to be met regardless of the level of its income. A decrease in income will decrease the value of the firm and simultaneously increase its riskiness. Either operating or financial leverage may explain the inverse relationship between variance and stock price.

The *compound option model* of Geske [1977] shows how to price options on options. This may seem to be a complex abstraction until one considers that the equity in a levered firm is really an option on the assets of the firm. An example of this was given in section D of this chapter. A CBOE-listed call option is therefore an option on the firm's equity, which in turn is an option on the firm's assets. Thus a CBOE call option is really an option on an option. In Geske's model a compound call option is a function of seven variables instead of the usual five variables found in the Black-

Scholes model:

$$c = f(S, X, r_f, T, \sigma, D/V, t_B).$$

The two new variables are D/V, the ratio of the face value of debt to the market value of the firm, and t_B, the time to maturity of the firm's debt. Under certain conditions the compound option model can be made equal to the constant elasticity of variance model.

The *displaced diffusion model* by Rubinstein [1983] focuses on the assets side of a firm's balance sheet and divides it into a portfolio of riskless assets and risky assets. Like Geske's model it is a compound option formula and requires two parameters in addition to those of the Black-Scholes model. They are (1) the instantaneous volatility of the rate of return on the firm's risky assets and (2) the proportion of total assets invested in risky assets.

Section K of this chapter discusses the empirical evidence on option pricing formulas. Most of the research along these lines is very recent, and therefore the conclusions are tentative. Yet the evidence seems to provide support for the extensions of the Black-Scholes model over the original model.

2. Options to Value Special Situations

What happens to the value of an option if the exercise price is stochastic, if the stock price changes in a deterministic fashion, if the risk-free rate is stochastic, or if the payouts are truncated in unusual ways?

Fisher [1978] and Margrabe [1978] solve the problem of valuing an option when the exercise price is uncertain. An example of this problem is the option to exchange one asset for another. One example of this type of problem is a stock exchange offer between two unlevered firms.[21] Firm A tenders for the shares of firm B (a much smaller firm) by offering one of its own shares currently priced at, let us say, $S_A = \$50$ for one of firm B's shares priced at $S_B = \$30$. The offer might be good for 30 days. The shareholders of firm B have received an option to exchange one asset for another. The exercise price on the call option is the value of firm B's stock, a random variable.

Margrabe [1978] and Fisher [1978] show that the value of an option to exchange one asset for another depends on the standard deviations of the two assets and the correlation between them. Their formula is given below:

$$C(S_A, S_B, T) = S_A N(d_1) - S_B N(d_2),$$

where

$$d_1 = \frac{\ln(S_A/S_B) + V^2 T}{V\sqrt{T}},$$

$$d_2 = d_1 - V\sqrt{T},$$

$$V^2 = V_A^2 - 2\rho_{AB} V_A V_B + V_B^2.$$

---

[21] If the firms were levered the problem would be much the same except that we would have to deal with options on options.

Note that V^2 is the instantaneous proportional variance of the change in the ratio of the asset prices, S_A/S_B, and ρ_{AB} is the instantaneous correlation between them. The option is less (more) valuable if the assets are positively (negatively) correlated.

Another interesting option is the *truncated option* discussed by Johnson [1981]. Examples of a truncated option are an option on a firm consisting of two divisions, an option entitling the owner to a choice between two risky assets, and competing tender offers. Consider the case of an option on a firm with two risky divisions. Rubinstein's [1983] displaced diffusion model is a special case because it considers an option on a firm consisting of one riskless and one risky asset. Here we are examining the value of an option on a portfolio of two risky assets. If A_1 and A_2 are the lognormally distributed returns of the two divisions, the payoff to this type of truncated option at maturity is

$$C = \text{MAX}[0, A_1 + A_2 - X].$$

The actual solution is too complex for this text; however, the interested reader is referred to Johnson [1981] for the mathematics of this and three other truncated option cases. One of the implications is that an option on a portfolio of risky assets is less valuable than the corresponding portfolio of options.

Merton [1973b] solved the problem of pricing options when the value of the underlying asset and the risk-free rate are both stochastic. Option problems that as yet have no known solution are (1) options with stochastic variances and (2) options with random maturity dates.

K. EMPIRICAL EVIDENCE ON THE OPTION PRICING MODEL

Tests of the option pricing model (OPM), are different from those of the CAPM because options are contingent claims on an underlying asset, the stock price, that is directly observable. This fact, however, does not eliminate the problem that empirical tests of the OPM are joint tests of market efficiency and the validity of the model. In addition there are two practical problems: option prices must be recorded synchronously with prices of the underlying asset, and data must allow unbiased estimation of the OPM parameters.

There are three broad categories of OPM empirical tests. The most obvious are tests of the absolute price level of options to determine whether model prices are biased relative to market prices and to investigate the profitability of trading rules based on portfolios of mispriced options. One difficulty with these tests is that taxes and transactions costs must be taken into account in order to determine the net profit from any trading rule. A second form of test is based on violations of option pricing boundary conditions such as those implied by Theorems 8.1 and 8.2. Significant and persistent violations of these boundary conditions would imply either market inefficiency or that the OPM is incorrect. The third form of testing is based on the performance of hedge portfolios, i.e., combinations of options and other assets. Riskless hedge portfolios that earn returns above the risk-free rate are indications of a failure of either the OPM being tested or of market efficiency.

1. The Black-Scholes Study

The earliest empirical test of the Black-Scholes OPM was done by Black and Scholes themselves [1973]. They used price data from the over-the-counter option market (OTCOM) for contracts written on 545 securities between 1966 and 1969. Options traded on the OTCOM did not have standardized exercise prices or maturity dates; however, they were "dividend protected."[22] Whenever the common stock went ex-dividend, the exercise price on outstanding options was lowered by the amount of the dividend.

The secondary market in nonstandardized OTCOM options was virtually non-existent. Therefore Black and Scholes adopted a test procedure that used the OPM to generate the expected prices of each option on each trading day. By comparing the model prices with actual prices at the issuing date, they divided options into those "overvalued" and those "undervalued" by the market. For each option bought (if undervalued) or sold (if overvalued), a perfectly risk-free hedge portfolio was formed by selling or buying shares in the underlying stock. The excess dollar return on the hedge portfolio was defined as

$$\Delta V_H - V_H r_f \, \Delta t$$

$$\left(\Delta C - \frac{\partial C}{\partial S} \, \Delta S \right) - \left(C - \frac{\partial C}{\partial S} \, S \right) r_f \, \Delta t.$$

The first expression is the dollar return on the hedge portfolio, ΔV_H, where ΔC is the change in the value of a call option and where $\partial C/\partial S = N(d_1)$ is the number of shares multiplied by ΔS, the change in the price per share. The second expression, which is subtracted from the first in order to obtain *excess* returns, is the dollar return on a risk-free position. Theoretically, the difference between the two terms should be equal to zero because the portfolio is chosen to be a risk-free hedge. Therefore the portfolio should have zero beta and earn the risk-free rate.

The option position was maintained throughout the life of the option. The risk-free hedge was adjusted daily by buying or selling shares of stock in order to maintain the proportion $\partial C/\partial S = N(d_1)$. At the end of each day, the hedged position was assumed to be liquidated so that the daily dollar return could be calculated. The option position was then immediately reestablished and a new hedge position constructed.

Black and Scholes computed the systematic risk of the hedge portfolio by regressing its excess returns against a market index. The results verified that it has a beta not significantly different from zero (even though the hedge was not adjusted continuously).

---

[22] Of course, there is no such thing as perfect dividend protection. For example, if shareholders were to issue a liquidating dividend equal to the value of the firm's assets, the value of common stock would fall to zero, and no amount of dividend protection could keep the value of a call option from falling to zero.

Their results showed that (given *ex post* estimates of actual variances of the returns on the underlying stock over the holding period), in the absence of transactions costs, buying undervalued contracts and selling overvalued contracts at model prices produced insignificant average profits. However, when *ex ante* variances were estimated from past stock price histories, buying undervalued contracts and selling overvalued contracts at model prices resulted in significant negative excess portfolio returns. The same procedure, when repeated using market prices, yielded substantial positive excess returns. These results indicate that the market uses more than past price histories to estimate the *ex ante* instantaneous variance of stock returns. But when actual variances are used in the model, it matches actual option prices quite accurately.

When the transaction costs of trading in options were included, the implied profits vanished. Therefore even though the option market does not appear to be efficient before transaction costs are taken into account, there is no opportunity for traders to take advantage of this inefficiency.

2. The Galai Study

Galai [1977] used data from the Chicago Board of Options Exchange (CBOE) for each option traded between April 26, 1973, and November 30, 1973. Option contracts on the CBOE have standardized striking prices and expiration dates. Although the options are not dividend protected, the standardization of contracts has resulted in a substantial volume of trading and lower transaction costs.

The fact that option prices are listed every day allowed Galai to extend the Black-Scholes procedure. Black and Scholes established an initial option position and then maintained a hedge position by buying or selling shares of stock. They could not adjust the option position because they did not have market prices for the options. They were unable to exploit all the information available in the daily deviation of the option's actual prices from the model prices.

Galai duplicated the Black-Scholes tests and extended them by adjusting the option position each day. Undervalued options were bought and overvalued options were sold at the end of each day; in addition, the hedged position was maintained by buying or selling the appropriate number of shares of common stock. Galai used two tests: (1) an *ex post* test that assumed that traders can use the closing price on day t to determine whether the option is over- or undervalued and that they could transact at the closing prices on day t and (2) a more realistic *ex ante* test that assumed that the trading rule is determined from closing prices on day t but the transaction is not executed until the closing price at day $t + 1$. Both tests used various estimates of the variance of common stock rates of return that were based on data gathered *before* the trading rule was executed.

The main results of the test were:

1. Using *ex post* hedge returns, trading strategies (in the absence of transaction costs) that were based on the Black-Scholes model earned significant excess returns.

2. Given 1% transaction costs, the excess returns vanished.

3. The results were robust to changes in various parameters such as the risk-free rate or instantaneous variance.

4. The results are sensitive to dividend adjustment. Trading in options written on common stocks paying high dividends yielded lower profits than trading in options written on low-dividend stocks. This result, however, simply reflects the fact that the Black-Scholes formula assumes no dividend payments.

5. Deviations from the model's specifications led to worse performance.

6. Tests of spreading strategies yielded results similar to those produced by the hedging strategies described above.

Bhattacharya [1983] used CBOE transaction data from August 1976 to June 1977. He looked at three different boundary conditions. An immediate exercise test was composed of situations where the trader could earn more from exercising immediately than from keeping his or her option alive. For a sample of 86,137 transactions there were 1,120 immediate exercise opportunities assuming zero transactions costs. However, after transactions costs, even a member of the CBOE or NYSE would have realized negative average trading profits. Similar results were obtained for tests of dividend-adjusted lower bounds using the lower bound for European call options and for pseudo-American call options.

Taken together, the two studies mentioned above seem to indicate that the Black-Scholes OPM predicts option prices very well indeed. So well in fact, that excess returns can only be earned in the absence of transaction costs. However, once transaction costs are introduced into the trading strategies, excess profits vanish. This confirms the usual result that nonmember traders cannot beat the market. Prices are efficiently determined down to the level of transaction costs.

3. Klemkosky and Resnick on Put-Call Parity

Since June 1977, standardized put options have been offered on the CBOE. Klemkosky and Resnick [1979] collected continuous transactions data for put and call options for each of 15 companies for 12 days (one each month) during the July 1977 to June 1978 interval. A total of 606 long and short hedge portfolios were constructed. The put, call, and underlying stock had to have traded within one minute of each other. The hedge portfolios were based on the following inequalities:

$$(C - P - S)(1 + r_f) + X + \sum_{j=1}^{n} \text{Div}_j(1 + r_f)^{\delta_j} \leq 0 \qquad \text{long hedge,}$$

$$(S + P - C)(1 + r_f) - X - \sum_{j=1}^{n} \text{Div}_j(1 + r_f)^{\delta_j} \leq 0 \qquad \text{short hedge.}$$

These hedges are based on the gross terminal profit from engaging in a long or short hedge constructed from American options and the stock. The terms are as defined in the put-call parity equation (Eq. 8.8) where r_f is the risk-free rate of return covering the life of the option. The last term in each equation is the terminal value of the dividends where Div_j is assumed to be the known nonstochastic dividend paid during the life of the option, and δ_j is the length of time between the dividend and the expiration date of the options. The strongest assumption, of course, is that dividends were nonstochastic. However, the virtue of a test based on put-call parity is that it is not necessary to make any assumptions about which version of the option pricing model is best. If put-call parity holds, then there are no arbitrage profits and the market is efficient, regardless of how options are valued.

Klemkosky and Resnick find their results to be consistent with put-call parity and with efficiency for the registered options markets. If $20 is the minimum transactions cost for a member firm to take a hedge position, then only 27% of the hedges were profitable. If $60 is the minimum transactions cost for a nonmember investor, then only 7% of the hedges were profitable.

4. The Bhattacharya Study

If one is empirically testing the null hypothesis that observed market prices and the Black-Scholes (B-S) theoretical prices exhibit no systematic differences, the null hypothesis can be rejected for any of three reasons:

1. Inputs to the Black-Scholes model have been incorrectly measured or
2. The options market is inefficient or
3. The mathematical structure of the Black-Scholes model is incorrect.

Bhattacharya [1980] avoids difficulties (1) and (2) by creating hypothetical hedge portfolios based on simulated B-S option values. If a neutral hedge is adjusted daily (continuously would be even better), the excess return should be zero if the B-S formula is correct. The only observed data inputs are the stock price, the stock price variance estimated directly from stock data during the life of the hedge, and the risk-free rate. Bhattacharya's results show no operationally significant mispricing by the B-S formula except for at-the-money options very close to maturity where the B-S model overvalues options.

5. The MacBeth/Merville and Beckers Studies

Using CBOE daily closing prices between December 31, 1975, and December 31, 1976, for all call options listed for six major companies (AT&T, Avon, Kodak, Exxon, IBM, and Xerox), MacBeth and Merville [1979] tested the Black-Scholes model to see whether or not it over- or underpriced options. Also [1980], using the same data set, they tested the Black-Scholes model against an alternative constant elasticity of variance (CEV) model (derived by Cox [1975] and Cox and Ross [1976]).

In their first paper [1979], MacBeth and Merville estimate the implied standard deviation of the rate of return for the underlying common stock by employing the Black-Scholes model Eq. (8.32). Then, by assuming that the B-S model correctly prices at-the-money options with at least 90 days to expiration, they are able to estimate the percent deviation of observed call prices from B-S call prices. They conclude that:

1. The Black-Scholes model prices are on average less (greater) than market prices for in-the-money (out-of-the-money) options.

2. The extent to which the Black-Scholes model underprices (overprices) an in-the-money (out-of-the-money) option increases with the extent to which the option is in-the-money (out-of-the-money) and decreases as the time to expiration decreases.

3. The Black-Scholes model prices of out-of-the-money options with less than 90 days to expiration are, on the average, greater than market prices; but there does not appear to be any consistent relationship between the extent to which these options are overpriced by the B-S model and the degree to which these options are out-of-the-money or the time to expiration.

The second MacBeth and Merville paper [1980] compares the Black-Scholes model against the constant elasticity of variance (CEV) model. The primary difference between the two models is that the B-S model assumes the variance of returns on the underlying asset remains constant, whereas the constant elasticity of variance model assumes the variance changes when the stock price does. Empirical evidence on the relationship between the level of stock prices and the rate of return variance is somewhat mixed. Blattberg and Gonedes [1974] suggest that the variance may change randomly through time. Rosenberg [1973] finds that it follows an autoregressive scheme. And Black [1976] observes that the variance of returns varies inversely with stock prices. For the six securities that MacBeth and Merville studied the variance relative to the stock price seems to decrease as the stock price rises. Using their estimates of the constant elasticity of variance, they find that the Cox model fits the data better than the Black-Scholes model. Their empirical results are also consistent with the compound option model of Geske [1979b].

Beckers [1980] also compares the constant elasticity of variance model with the Black-Scholes model. First, however, he uses 1253 daily observations (September 18, 1972, to September 7, 1977) for 47 different stocks to test the Black-Scholes assumption that the stock variance is not a function of the stock price. The data reject this hypothesis. The variance was an inverse function of the stock price for 38 of the 47 stocks—a result consistent with the constant elasticity of variance model. This is sometimes called the volatility bias. When testing simulated Black-Scholes call prices against the constant elasticity of variance prices, Beckers found that the CEV model gives higher option prices than B-S for in-the-money options. This is consistent with the empirical work of MacBeth and Merville, who found that the B-S model undervalues in-the-money options.

Geske and Roll [1984a] use transactions data for all options traded at midday on August 24, 1976 (a sample of 667 different options on 85 stocks). A subsample of

119 options on 28 different stocks with zero scheduled dividends during their remaining life was identified within the main sample. Using regression analysis, Geske and Roll demonstrate that the original time, in versus out-of-the-money, and volatility biases are present in the entire sample. Next, they show that in the nondividend sample the time and "money" biases are significantly reduced but the volatility bias remains large. However, by correcting the volatility estimates of all stocks by using a "Stein shrinker" technique, the volatility bias is reduced. Geske and Roll conclude that the time and money biases may be related to improper model treatment of early exercise (the dividend problem), whereas the volatility bias problem may be more related to statistical errors in variance parameter estimates.

6 Rubinstein-Nonparametric Tests of Alternative Option Pricing Models

The five extensions of the option pricing model, discussed in section J, have been compared by Rubinstein [1985]. He used the MDR (market data report) data base of the Chicago Board of Options Exchange, which has been consolidated into the Berkeley Options Database. The data is a time-stamped record, to the nearest second, including option trade prices, quotes, and volume, coupled with the stock price at the corresponding time during the day.

Rubinstein's experimental design was to select matched pairs of options, e.g., all options belonging to the same stock, observed on the same day during the same constant stock price interval, having the same exercise price, and falling within a predetermined range of out-of-the-money values (e.g., $S/X = .75$ to .85). Pairing in this case was on the basis of different times to maturity. For example, one option might fall within the 71 to 120 day range and another on the 171 to 220 day range. There were actually 373 of these particular matched pairs (overall there were 19,094 pairs based on differences on time to expiration and 12,239 pairs based on equal time to maturity but different exercise prices). If the Black-Scholes formula is unbiased there should be a 50/50 chance that the implied option variance for the shorter maturity option is higher than for the longer maturity option. In fact, 94.1% of the shorter maturity options had higher variance. Thus in this case the Black-Scholes formula could be rejected.

Nonparametric tests of options paired either by differences in time to maturity or in exercise prices were performed for two time periods: (1) August 21, 1976, to October 21, 1977, and (2) October 24, 1977, to August 31, 1978. Two interesting conclusions were found. First, if the time to maturity is held constant, then the Black-Scholes model is biased, but the direction of the bias is different in the two time periods that were investigated. During the 1976–1977 interval in-the-money options were undervalued by the Black-Scholes formula. This confirms the work of MacBeth and Merville [1979]. The direction of the bias is reversed during the 1977–1978 period. No one knows why the bias should reverse. The second conclusion was that although some of the alternative option pricing models (e.g., the displaced diffusion model) were more compatible with the empirical results, none of them were superior in both time periods.

7. Summary of the Empirical Work

Studies that have used different versions of the option pricing model to try to find economically exploitable biases have been unsuccessful in doing so when transactions costs were deducted from trading rule profits. From this one can conclude that the option pricing models fit observed prices well in an economic sense. Also, the results are consistent with market efficiency.

On the other hand, there are statistically significant biases in the Black-Scholes model. This suggests that some alternative (perhaps composite) model can do better. Much work remains to be done in testing the OPM. Rubinstein's [1985] study suggests that none of the alternative models (the jump model, the mixed diffusion-jump model, the constant elasticity of variance model, the compound option model, or the displaced diffusion model) can explain all the biases all the time. Also, it remains unclear which of the observed biases are caused by model misspecification and which are due to statistical problems in estimating the model parameters.

SUMMARY _____

Closed-form solutions to the option pricing problem have been developed relatively recently. Yet their potential for application to problems in finance is tremendous. Almost all financial assets are really contingent claims. For example, common stock is really a call option on the value of the assets of a levered firm. Similarly, risky debt, insurance, warrants, and convertible debt may all be thought of as options. Also, option pricing theory has implications for the capital structure of the firm, for investment policy, for mergers and acquisitions, for spin-offs, and for dividend policy. Much of the rest of this book is devoted to exploring applications of the theories discussed so far: state-preference theory, the capital asset pricing model, arbitrage pricing theory, and option pricing. As we shall see, option pricing plays a major role in shaping our thinking.

We have established that option prices are functions of five parameters: the price of the underlying security, its instantaneous variance, the exercise price on the option, the time to maturity, and the risk-free rate. Only one of these variables, the instantaneous variance, is not directly observable. Even more interesting is the fact that the option price does not depend (1) on individual risk preferences or (2) on the expected rate of return on the underlying asset. Both results follow from the fact that option prices are determined from pure arbitrage conditions available to the investor who establishes perfectly hedged portfolios.

Much remains to be done to empirically test the validity of the option pricing model in general and of various versions of it such as the Black-Scholes model, the jump diffusion model, the constant elasticity of variance model, etc. The empirical results thus far tend to accept the option pricing model in the sense that differences between the prices it predicts and observed market prices are not economically significant. On the other hand, statistically significant departures from the Black-Scholes model have been discovered, but as yet no single superior model has been found.

Table 8.7   Areas under the Normal Curve

Areas under the Standard Normal Distribution Function $\int_0^z f(z)\,dz$

z	.00	.01	.02	.03	.04	.05	.06	.07	.08	.09
0.0	.0000	.0040	.0080	.0120	.0160	.0199	.0239	.0279	.0319	.0359
0.1	.0398	.0438	.0478	.0517	.0557	.0596	.0636	.0675	.0714	.0753
0.2	.0793	.0832	.0871	.0910	.0948	.0987	.1026	.1064	.1103	.1141
0.3	.1179	.1217	.1255	.1293	.1331	.1368	.1406	.1443	.1480	.1517
0.4	.1554	.1591	.1628	.1664	.1700	.1736	.1772	.1808	.1844	.1879
0.5	.1915	.1950	.1985	.2019	.2054	.2088	.2123	.2157	.2190	.2224
0.6	.2257	.2291	.2324	.2357	.2389	.2422	.2454	.2486	.2517	.2549
0.7	.2580	.2611	.2642	.2673	.2704	.2734	.2764	.2794	.2823	.2852
0.8	.2881	.2910	.2939	.2967	.2995	.3023	.3051	.3078	.3106	.3133
0.9	.3159	.3186	.3212	.3238	.3264	.3289	.3315	.3340	.3365	.3389
1.0	.3413	.3438	.3461	.3485	.3508	.3531	.3554	.3577	.3599	.3621
1.1	.3643	.3665	.3686	.3708	.3729	.3749	.3770	.3790	.3810	.3830
1.2	.3849	.3869	.3888	.3907	.3925	.3944	.3962	.3980	.3997	.4015
1.3	.4032	.4049	.4066	.4082	.4099	.4115	.4131	.4147	.4162	.4177
1.4	.4192	.4207	.4222	.4236	.4251	.4265	.4279	.4292	.4306	.4319
1.5	.4332	.4345	.4357	.4370	.4382	.4394	.4406	.4418	.4429	.4441
1.6	.4452	.4463	.4474	.4484	.4495	.4505	.4515	.4525	.4535	.4545
1.7	.4554	.4564	.4573	.4582	.4591	.4599	.4608	.4616	.4625	.4633
1.8	.4641	.4649	.4656	.4664	.4671	.4678	.4686	.4693	.4699	.4706
1.9	.4713	.4719	.4726	.4732	.4738	.4744	.4750	.4756	.4761	.4767
2.0	.4772	.4778	.4783	.4788	.4793	.4798	.4803	.4808	.4812	.4817
2.1	.4821	.4826	.4830	.4834	.4838	.4842	.4846	.4850	.4854	.4857
2.2	.4861	.4864	.4868	.4871	.4875	.4878	.4881	.4884	.4887	.4890
2.3	.4893	.4896	.4898	.4901	.4904	.4906	.4909	.4911	.4913	.4916
2.4	.4918	.4920	.4922	.4925	.4927	.4929	.4931	.4932	.4934	.4936
2.5	.4938	.4940	.4941	.4943	.4945	.4946	.4948	.4949	.4951	.4952
2.6	.4953	.4955	.4956	.4957	.4959	.4960	.4961	.4962	.4963	.4964
2.7	.4965	.4966	.4967	.4968	.4969	.4970	.4971	.4972	.4973	.4974
2.8	.4974	.4975	.4976	.4977	.4977	.4978	.4979	.4979	.4980	.4981
2.9	.4981	.4982	.4982	.4982	.4984	.4984	.4985	.4985	.4986	.4986
3.0	.4987	.4987	.4987	.4988	.4988	.4989	.4989	.4989	.4990	.4990

PROBLEM SET

8.1 What is the value of a European call option with an exercise price of $40 and a maturity date six months from now if the stock price is $28, the instantaneous variance of the stock price is .5, and the risk-free rate is 6%?

8.2 What is the price of a European put if the price of the underlying common stock is $20, the exercise price is $20, the risk-free rate is 8%, the variance of the price of the underlying stock is .36 (that is, $\sigma - .6$), and the option expires six months from now?

8.3

a) Graph changes in wealth, ΔW, vs. changes in the price of the underlying security, ΔS, for a portfolio where you sell one call option and sell one put option (both with the same X, T, σ, and r_f). Would this be a good strategy if you have inside information that leads you to expect the instantaneous variance of the underlying security will increase?

b) Graph ΔW against ΔS for a portfolio where you buy a call and sell a put. Would this be a good strategy if you expect an increase in the instantaneous variance?

8.4 Assume you are a senior financial analyst at Morgan Stanley. You are asked by a client to determine the maximum price he or she should be willing to pay to purchase Honeywell call options having an exercise price of $45 and expiring in 156 days. The current price of Honeywell stock is $44\frac{3}{8}$, the riskless interest rate is 7%, and the estimated rate of return variance of the stock is $\sigma^2 = .0961$. No dividends are expected to be declared over the next six months.

8.5 Given two European put options that are identical except that the exercise price of the first put, X_1, is greater than the exercise price of the second put, X_2, use first-order stochastic dominance and equilibrium in a perfect capital market to prove that one of the puts must have a higher price than the other. Which put option has the higher price? [*Hint:* Determine the relevant states of the world.]

8.6 Consider a firm with current value of $5,000,000 and outstanding debt of $4,000,000 that matures in 10 years. The firm's asset rate-of-return variance is .5. The interest on the debt is paid at maturity, and the firm has a policy of not paying cash dividends. Use the OPM to determine the change in the prices of the firm's debt and equity if there is an unanticipated rise in the rate of inflation of 5%, which raises the riskless nominal interest rate from 5% to 10%. Which class of security holders benefits from the rise in r_f?

8.7 Figure 8.3 graphs the value of a call option as a function of the value of the underlying stock. Graph the value of a call option (vertical axis) against

a) σ, the instantaneous standard deviation of the returns on the underlying asset;

b) r_f, the risk-free rate;

c) T, the time to maturity.

8.8 What are the conditions under which an American put would be exercised early on a stock that pays no dividends?

8.9 Consider the case of a firm with secured debt, subordinated debentures, and common stock, where the secured debt and subordinated debentures mature at the same time. Find the equations for the values of the three classes of securities using the OPM framework. Assume no dividends or interest payments prior to the debt's maturity and a lognormal distribution of the future value of the firm's assets, $\tilde{V}_t$, as shown in Fig. Q8.9, where V = market value of the firm, S = market value of the stock, B_S = market value of the senior debt, B_j = market value of the junior debt, D_S = face value of the senior debt, D_j = face value of the junior debt.

8.10 Why will the value of an American put always be greater than or equal to the value of a corresponding European put?

8.11 Options listed for Digital Equipment were used in the text as an example of option price estimation using implicit variance. The implicit variance from the January 45 option resulted in estimated call prices lower than actual call prices for the April 45 and October 45 options.

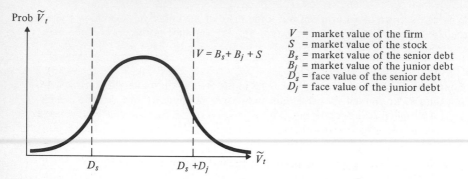

Prob $\tilde{V}_t$

$|V = B_s + B_j + S$

V = market value of the firm
S = market value of the stock
B_s = market value of the senior debt
B_j = market value of the junior debt
D_s = face value of the senior debt
D_j = face value of the junior debt

D_s $D_s + D_j$ $\tilde{V}_t$

Figure Q8.9

Assuming the Black-Scholes OPM is correct, and that all assumptions of the model are met in the marketplace: What hedge (i.e., riskless) portfolio can be formed to make arbitrage profits with Digital Equipment April 45 options?

8.12 The share price of Honeybear Inc. is $44.75. Call options written on Honeybear have an exercise price of $40 and mature in 71 days. The risk-free rate is $6\frac{1}{2}\%$, and the instantaneous price variance of Honeybear is 9.61% (i.e., $\sigma = .31$). What actions must you take in order to create a perfect hedge in the following situations:

a) If you own 100 shares of Honeybear stock, how many call options must you buy (sell)?

b) If you own five put option contracts, how many shares of stock do you need?

c) If you own one call contract, how many put contracts do you need?

8.13 After a call contract is created, the outcome must be a zero-sum game; i.e., the call writer may win or lose N, but the call buyer will experience an opposite return of exactly N and consequently their aggregate payoff is zero. Given this fact, can you explain how they could both enter into the contract anticipating a positive return?

8.14 Suppose that the government passes a usury law that prohibits lending at more than 5% interest, but normal market rates are much higher due to inflation. You have a customer, a Ms. Olsen, who wants to borrow at 20% and can put up her $100,000 store as collateral. Rather than refusing her request you decide to create a five-year contract with the following terms: You hold title to the store and receive the right to sell her the store for X at the end of five years. If you decide to sell she *must* buy. In return you give her $80,000 in cash (the amount she wants to borrow) and the right to buy the store from you for X at the end of five years. How can this contract provide you with a 20% annual rate of return on the $80,000?

REFERENCES

Ball, C. A., and W. N. Torous, "Bond Price Dynamics and Options," *Journal of Financial and Quantitative Analysis*, 1983, 517–531.

———, "On Jumps in Common Stock Prices and Their Impact on Call Option Pricing," *Journal of Finance*, March 1985, 155–173.

Beckers, S., "The Constant Elasticity of Variance Model and Its Implications for Option Pricing," *Journal of Finance*, June 1980, 661–673.

————, "A Note on Estimating the Parameters of the Diffusion-Jump Model of Stock Returns," *Journal of Financial and Quantitative Analysis*, March 1981, 127–139.

Bhattacharya, M., "Empirical Properties of the Black-Scholes Formula under Ideal Conditions," *Journal of Financial and Quantitative Analysis*, December 1980, 1081–1106.

————, "Transaction Data Tests on the Efficiency of the Chicago Board of Options Exchange," *Journal of Financial Economics*, August 1983, 161–185.

Black, F., "Studies of Stock Price Volatility Changes." Proceedings of the Meetings of the American Statistical Association, Business and Economics Statistics Section, Chicago, 1976.

————, and M. Scholes, "The Valuation of Option Contracts and a Test of Market Efficiency," *Journal of Finance*, May 1972, 399–418.

————, "The Pricing of Options and Corporate Liabilities," *Journal of Political Economy*, May–June 1973, 637–659.

Blattberg, R., and N. Gonedes, "A Comparison of the Stable and Student Distributions as Stochastic Models for Stock Prices," *Journal of Business*, 1974, 244–280.

Boyle, P., and D. Emmanuel, "Discretely Adjusted Option Hedges," *Journal of Financial Economics*, September 1980, 259–282.

Brennan, M., and E. Schwartz, "The Valuation of American Put Options," *Journal of Finance*, May 1977, 449–462.

Butler, J., and B. Schachter, "Unbiased Estimation of the Black-Scholes Formula," *Journal of Financial Economics*, March 1986, 341–357.

Chiras, D., and S. Manaster, "The Informational Content of Option Prices and a Test of Market Efficiency," *Journal of Financial Economics*, June–September 1978, 213–234.

Courtdon, G., "The Pricing of Options on Default-Free Bonds," *Journal of Financial and Quantitative Analysis*, March 1982, 75–100.

Cox, J., "Notes on Option Pricing I: Constant Elasticity of Diffusions," unpublished draft, Stanford University, September 1975.

————; J. Ingersoll; and S. Ross, "A Theory of the Term Structure of Interest Rates," *Econometrica*, March 1985, 385–407.

Cox, J., and S. Ross, "The Pricing of Options for Jump Processes," Working Paper No. 2–75, University of Pennsylvania, April 1975.

————, "The Valuation of Options for Alternative Stochastic Processes," *Journal of Financial Economics*, January–March 1976, 145–166.

————, and M. Rubinstein, "Option Pricing: A Simplified Approach," *Journal of Financial Economics*, September 1979, 229–263.

Cox, J., and M. Rubinstein, *Options Markets*. Prentice-Hall, Englewood Cliffs, N.J., 1985.

Feller, W., *An Introduction to Probability Theory and Its Applications*, Vol. I, 3rd ed. John Wiley and Sons, New York, 1968.

Finnerty, J., "The Chicago Board of Options Exchange and Market Efficiency," *Journal of Financial and Quantitative Analysis*, March 1978, 29–38.

Fisher, S., "Call Option Pricing When the Exercise Price Is Uncertain and the Valuation of Index Bonds," *Journal of Finance*, March 1978, 169–186.

Galai, D., "Tests of Market Efficiency of the Chicago Board of Options Exchange," *Journal of Business*, April 1977, 167–197.

————, "On the Boness and Black-Scholes Models for the Valuation of Call Options," *Journal of Financial and Quantitative Analysis*, March 1978, 15–27.

————, and R. Masulis, "The Option Pricing Model and the Risk Factor of Stock," *Journal of Financial Economics*, January–March 1976, 53–82.

Garman, M., "An Algebra for Evaluating Hedge Portfolios," *Journal of Financial Economics*, October 1976, 403–428.

Geske, R., "The Valuation of Corporate Liabilities as Compound Options," *Journal of Financial and Quantitative Analysis*, November 1977, 541–552.

————, "The Pricing of Options with Stochastic Dividend Yield," *Journal of Finance*, May 1978, 617–625.

————, "A Note on an Analytical Valuation Formula for Unprotected American Call Options on Stocks with Known Dividends," *Journal of Financial Economics*, December 1979a, 375–380.

————, "The Valuation of Compound Options," *Journal of Financial Economics*, March 1979b, 63–81.

————, and H. Johnson, "The American Put Option Valued Analytically," *Journal of Finance*, December 1984, 1511–1524.

Geske, R., and R. Roll, "Isolating the Obscured Biases in American Call Pricing: An Alternative Variance Estimator," UCLA Working Paper No. 4–84, February 1984a.

————, "On Valuing American Call Options with the Black-Scholes European Formula," *Journal of Finance*, 1984b, 443–455.

Gould, J., and D. Galai, "Transactions Costs and the Relationship between Put and Call Prices," *Journal of Financial Economics*, July 1974, 105–129.

Hsia, C., "Relationships among the Theories of MM, CAPM, and OPM," mimeograph, UCLA, 1978.

Johnson, H., "Three Topics in Option Pricing," Ph.D. dissertation, UCLA Graduate School of Management, 1981.

Klemkosky, R., and B. Resnick, "Put-Call Parity and Market Efficiency," *Journal of Finance*, December 1979, 1141–1155.

Kruizenga, R. J., "Introduction to the Option Contract," reprinted in Cootner, ed., *The Random Character of Stock Market Prices*. MIT Press, Cambridge, Mass., 1964, 377–391.

Latane, H., and R. J. Rendleman, Jr., "Standard Deviations of Stock Price Ratios Implied in Option Prices," *Journal of Finance*, May 1976, 369–382.

MacBeth, J., and L. Merville, "An Empirical Examination of the Black-Scholes Call Option Pricing Model," *Journal of Finance*, December 1979, 1173–1186.

————, "Tests of the Black-Scholes and Cox Call Option Valuation Models," *Journal of Finance*, May 1980, 285–300.

Margrabe, W., "The Value of an Option to Exchange One Asset for Another," *Journal of Finance*, March 1978, 177–186.

Merton, R., "An Intertemporal Capital Asset Pricing Model," *Econometrica*, September 1973a, 867–887.

————, "The Theory of Rational Option Pricing," *Bell Journal of Economics and Management Science*, Spring 1973b, 141–183.

————, "On the Pricing of Corporate Debt: The Risk Structure of Interest Rates," *Journal of Finance*, May 1974, 449–470.

————, "Option Pricing When Underlying Stock Returns Are Discontinuous," *Journal of Financial Economics*, January–March 1976, 125–144.

Parkinson, M., "Option Pricing: The American Put," *Journal of Business*, January 1977, 21–36.

————, "The Valuation of GNMA Options," *Financial Analysts Journal*, September–October 1982, 66–76.

Phillips, S., and C. Smith, "Trading Costs for Listed Options: The Implications for Market Efficiency," *Journal of Financial Economics*, 1980, 197–201.

Rendleman, R., Jr., and B. Bartter, "Two-State Option Pricing," *Journal of Finance*, December 1979, 1093–1110.

————, "The Pricing of Options on Debt Securities," *Journal of Financial and Quantitative Analysis*, March 1980, 11–24.

Roll, R., "An Analytic Valuation Formula for Unprotected American Call Options on Stocks with Known Dividends," *Journal of Financial Economics*, November 1977, 251–258.

Rosenberg, B., "The Behavior of Random Variables with Nonstationary Variance and the Distribution of Security Prices," manuscript, University of California, Berkeley, 1973.

Ross, S., "Options and Efficiency," *Quarterly Journal of Economics*, February 1976, 75–89.

Rubinstein, M., "The Valuation of Uncertain Income Streams and the Pricing of Options," *Bell Journal of Economics*, Autumn 1976, 407–425.

————, "Displaced Diffusion Option Pricing," *Journal of Finance*, March 1983, 213–265.

————, "Nonparametric Tests of Alternative Option Pricing Models," *Journal of Finance*, June 1985, 455–480.

Schmalensee, R., and R. Trippi, "Common Stock Volatility Expectations Implied by Option Premia," *Journal of Finance*, March 1978, 129–147.

Smith, C., "Option Pricing Review," *Journal of Financial Economics*, January–March 1976, 1–51.

Stoll, H. R., "The Relationship between Put and Call Option Prices," *Journal of Finance*, December 1969, 802–824.

Whaley, R., "On the Valuation of American Call Options on Stocks with Known Dividends," *Journal of Financial Economics*, June 1981, 207–212.

————, "Valuation of American Call Options on Dividend Paying Stocks: Empirical Tests," *Journal of Financial Economics*, 1982, 29–58.

Appendix to Chapter 8: Derivation of the Black-Scholes Option Pricing Model

Black and Scholes [1973] were the first to provide a closed-form solution for the valuation of European calls. They recognized that given the assumption of frictionless markets and continuous trading opportunities, it is possible to form a risk-free hedge portfolio consisting of a long position in the stock and a short position in the European call written on that stock. If the stock price changes over time, the risk-free hedge can be maintained by continuously readjusting the proportions of stock and calls. The value of the hedge portfolio, V_H, can be expressed as the number of shares of stock, Q_S, times the price per share, S, plus the quantity of calls, Q_c, times their price:

$$V_H = SQ_S + cQ_c. \tag{A8.1}$$

The change in the value of the hedge portfolio is the total derivative of (A8.1):

$$dV_H = Q_S \, dS + Q_c \, dc. \tag{A8.2}$$

Of course, the stock price moves randomly over time. We assume that it follows a geometric Brownian motion process. Its rate of return can be described as

$$\frac{dS}{S} = \mu \, dt + \sigma \, dz, \tag{A8.3}$$

where

μ = the instantaneous expected rate of return (it measures the drift in the random walk through time, dt),

σ = the instantaneous standard deviation of the rate of return,

dt = a small increment of time,

dz = a Wiener process.

296

Since the option's price is a function of the stock's price, its movement over time must be related to the stock's movement over time. Black and Scholes [1973] show that if the stock price follows a geometric Brownian motion process such as (A8.3), then using stochastic calculus (which is far beyond the mathematical capabilities assumed for this text) and employing a technique known as Ito's lemma, one can express the change in the option price by the following stochastic differential equation:

$$dc = \frac{\partial c}{\partial S} dS + \frac{\partial c}{\partial t} dt + \frac{1}{2} \frac{\partial^2 c}{\partial S^2} \sigma^2 S^2 dt. \tag{A8.4}$$

Note that the only stochastic term in the expression for dc is dS. The others are deterministic.

Substituting (A8.4) into (A8.2), we obtain

$$dV_H = Q_S dS + Q_c \left[\frac{\partial c}{\partial S} dS + \frac{\partial c}{\partial t} dt + \frac{1}{2} \frac{\partial^2 c}{\partial S^2} \sigma^2 S^2 dt \right]. \tag{A8.5}$$

As mentioned earlier, the insight that Black and Scholes provided was to notice that it is possible to continuously adjust the hedge portfolio, V_H, so that it becomes risk free. How this may be done is illustrated in Fig. A8.1. The curved line, labeled $c(S, T, X)$, represents the theoretical relationship between the call price and the stock price. If we buy one share of stock and sell a number of call options equal to the inverse of the slope of a line tangent to the curve $c(S, T, X)$, we can create a riskless hedge. For example, let us suppose that the current stock price is $15, and the option price is $5. We form a hedge portfolio by selling two calls (for which we receive $10) and by buying one share of stock for $15. Our net equity position would be $5. This is illustrated in Table A8.1. Next, for the sake of argument, let us assume that the stock price rises to $20 and the option price to $7\frac{7}{8}$. We gain $5 from the stock and lose $5\frac{3}{4}$ on the two call options. Our net equity has decreased by $.75. A similar small loss may be expected if the stock price falls by $5. Of course, for smaller changes in the stock price, our equity loss is even smaller. And if we continuously adjust our hedge portfolio to maintain a ratio of stock to call options of $1/(\partial_c/\partial S)$, the hedge will

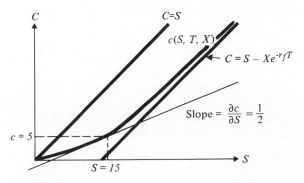

Figure A8.1
Forming a continually adjusted riskless hedge portfolio.

Table A8.1   An Example of a Riskless Hedge

	$\Delta S = -5$	*Initial*	$\Delta S = +5$
Stock price X	$10	$15	$20
Call price c	$2\frac{7}{8}$	5	$7\frac{7}{8}$
Short two calls	$5\frac{3}{4}$	10	$15\frac{3}{4}$
Equity position	$4\frac{1}{4}$	5	$4\frac{1}{4}$

be perfectly risk free. Therefore the risk-free hedge portfolio will earn the risk-free rate in equilibrium if capital markets are efficient. This is really the main insight. It is possible, given continuous trading, to form risk-free hedges with only two securities, the underlying asset and a call option. This equilibrium relationship is expressed as

$$\frac{dV_H}{V_H} = r_f \, dt. \tag{A8.6}$$

This fact and the fact that the riskless hedge is maintained by purchasing one share of stock and selling $1/(\partial c/\partial S)$ calls,

$$Q_S = 1, \qquad Q_c = -\frac{1}{(\partial c/\partial S)}, \tag{A8.7}$$

allows us to substitute (A8.6) and (A8.7) into (A8.5) in order to simplify it. This is done below:

$$dV_H = r_f \, dt V_H = (1) \, dS - \frac{\partial S}{\partial c}\left[\frac{\partial c}{\partial S}\, dS + \frac{\partial c}{\partial t}\, dt + \frac{1}{2}\frac{\partial^2 c}{\partial S^2}\, \sigma^2 S^2 \, dt\right],$$

$$\frac{\partial c}{\partial t} = r_f V_H\left(-\frac{\partial c}{\partial S}\right) - \frac{1}{2}\frac{\partial^2 c}{\partial S^2}\, \sigma^2 S^2.$$

Substituting (A8.1) for V_H and using (A8.7) again, we have

$$\frac{\partial c}{\partial t} = r_f(SQ_S + cQ_c)\left(-\frac{\partial c}{\partial S}\right) - \frac{1}{2}\frac{\partial^2 c}{\partial S^2}\, \sigma^2 S^2$$

$$= r_f c - r_f S \frac{\partial c}{\partial S} - \frac{1}{2}\frac{\partial^2 c}{\partial S^2}\, \sigma^2 S^2. \tag{A8.8}$$

Equation (A8.8) is a nonstochastic differential equation for the value of the option. By using the notion of a riskless hedge, Black and Scholes eliminate the only stochastic term, dS. Now the nonstochastic differential equation may be solved subject to the boundary conditions that at the terminal date the option price must be

$$c = \text{MAX}[0, S - X]$$

and that, for any date,

$$c(S = 0, T, X) = 0.$$

Black and Scholes [1973] transform the equation into the heat exchange equation from physics to find the following solution:[1]

$$c = S \cdot N \left\{ \frac{\ln(S/X) + [r_f + (\sigma^2/2)]T}{\sigma\sqrt{T}} \right\} - e^{-r_f T} X \cdot N \left\{ \frac{\ln(S/X) + [r_f - (\sigma^2/2)]T}{\sigma\sqrt{T}} \right\},$$

$$(A8.9)$$

where all variables are as defined previously except that

$N(\cdot)$ = the cumulative normal probability of a unit normal variable; where, e.g., $N(-\infty) = 0$, $N(0) = .5$, and $N(\infty) = 1.0$;

$N(\cdot) = \int_{-\infty}^{z} f(z) \, dz$, where $f(z)$ is distributed normally with mean zero and standard deviation one.

---

[1] Note that once we are given the call pricing solution [Eq. (A8.9)], we see that the hedge ratio in terms of the number of calls per share is

$$Q_c = -1/(\partial c/\partial S) = -1/N(d_1),$$

where $N(d_1)$ is the first term in braces in Eq. (A8.9). This fact is needed in order to continuously construct risk-free hedges.

9

Futures trading would seem to be one of those marvels that ought to be invented if it did not already exist. Yet the number of futures markets is surprisingly small: in the whole world there are probably not more than 60 or 70 ... and not more than 40 or 50 commodities traded on them.

H. S. Houthakker, "The Scope and Limits of Futures Trading," in Abramovitz, M., ed., *The Allocation of Economic Resources.* Stanford University Press, Stanford, 1959, 159

Futures Contracts and Markets

A. INTRODUCTION

In January 1987 the *Wall Street Journal* listed futures contracts on commodities (e.g., grains, livestock, food, fiber, metals, petroleum products, and wood), on foreign currencies (the British pound, Canadian dollar, Japanese yen, Swiss franc, German mark, and Eurodollar), on financial instruments (Treasury bonds, notes, and bills), and on stock indices (the Standard and Poor's 500, the NYSE Composite index, the Value Line index, and the Major Market index). Figure 9.1 shows a sampling of futures quotations. We can broadly divide futures contracts into three categories: commodities futures, financial futures, and futures on indices.

One chapter alone cannot cover all the details of every futures contract. Our objective is to describe the general features of futures contracts (such as standardization, delivery, clearing, open interest, and price limits) in section B, the theory of the pricing of futures contracts in section C, empirical evidence in section D, and synthetic futures and options on futures in section E.

B. GENERAL CHARACTERISTICS OF FUTURES CONTRACTS

1. Definition

When you buy a *forward contract*, you write a contract today at a stated price—but pay no cash—for promised future delivery of the underlying asset at a specified

FUTURES PRICES

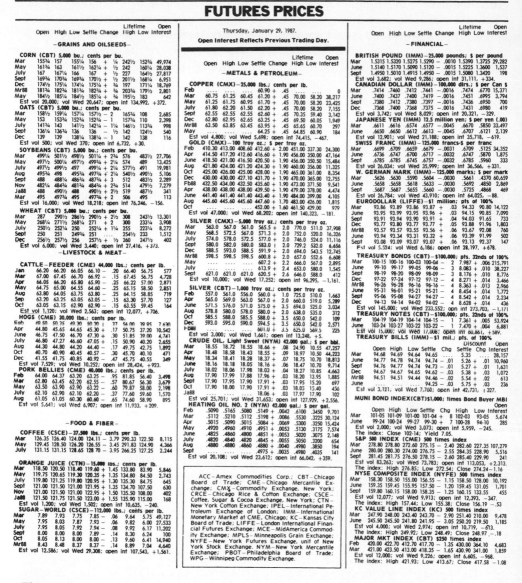

Figure 9.1
Selected futures contract prices, January 29, 1987. (Reprinted with permission from the Wall Street Journal © Dow Jones and Co. Inc., January 29, 1987. All rights reserved.)

time and place in the future. At the time of delivery you receive the asset you purchased and pay the contract price. Your profit (or loss) on the delivery date is the difference between the market value of the asset and the contract price. A *futures contract* is similar to a forward contract except that changes in the contract price are settled daily. There is nothing unusual about forward and futures contracts. In fact they are commonplace. For example, when you contract for purchase of a car that will be delivered six weeks from now (at the dealer's lot), you are buying a forward contract. If the future value of the car is known with certainty, the current value of the forward contract is easy to determine. For example, suppose you know the car will be worth $10,000 six weeks from now; then the current price of the contract, $_0F_T$, is

$$_0F_T = E(S_T), \tag{9.1}$$

where T is the time until delivery of the asset, and $E(S_T)$ is the expected price of the asset (the car) on the delivery date.[1] For our simple example, since there is no uncertainty, the contract price is $10,000. If there were a secondary market for futures contracts on cars, you could resell your contract for future delivery of the car, and the futures contract price would be $10,000.

Alternately, if you were able to purchase the car immediately, you would pay the *spot price*, which is the current market price of the commodity. The spot price today would be the expected spot price six weeks from now, discounted back to the present at the continuous annual risk-free rate, $r_f = 10\%$, since there is no uncertainty:

$$S_0 = E(S_T)e^{-r_fT}$$
$$= 10{,}000e^{-.10(6/52)}$$
$$= 10{,}000(.988528)$$
$$= \$9{,}885.28.$$

One pays the spot price for immediate delivery and the futures price at the time of future delivery.

When the forward/futures contract matures, six weeks from now, you receive a car worth $10,000 from the dealer and pay $10,000 in cash. Your net profit at delivery is zero because there was no uncertainty in our simple example. Had the future value of the car been uncertain, you could have gained or lost the difference between the market value of the car at the delivery date, T, and the $10,000 contract price that you must pay at T. In section C we shall examine some of the complications that arise in pricing futures contracts when the future commodity price is uncertain, when storage of the commodity is costly, and when taxes must be taken into consideration.

2. Standardization

Of course, if a secondary market existed, other buyers would like to know exactly what kind of car they would be buying (e.g., a blue four-cylinder Chevrolet with bucket seats and a four-speed manual transmission). The same is true of actual futures markets. The asset to be delivered must be standardized as much as is practical.

---

[1] Notation shall be standardized as follows: The T period futures (or forward) contract priced at time t will be written as $_tF_T$, and the spot price at time t as S_t. Whenever it is useful to subscript interest rates, the interest rate between t and T will be written as $_tr_T$.

Standardization helps to make the market large enough to attract active trading and to provide liquidity.

As an example of standardization the New York Mercantile Exchange (NYMEX) defines a contract in "light, sweet" crude oil as follows:[2]

1. The seller agrees to deliver 1,000 U.S. barrels (at 60°F. with a tolerance of $\pm 2\%$) of "light, sweet" crude oil meeting the following specifications:
   a) Sulfur—.50% or less by weight,
   b) Gravity—not less than 34° nor more than 45° API.
   Price adjustments can be made for oils departing from the aforementioned specifications.

2. Delivery shall be made FOB (free on board) at any pipeline or storage facility in Cushing, Oklahoma.

3. Delivery shall take place no earlier than the first calendar day and no later than the last calendar day of the delivery month. Delivery months are the six consecutive calender months following the current calendar month (in Fig. 9.1 these are the March through August 1987 contracts) as well as the following quarterly contracts (September, October, and January 1988 in Fig. 9.1) up to 18 months out.

4. Speculative position limits are imposed. No person shall own or control a net long or short position in all months combined of more than 5000 contracts and in the month preceding delivery no more than 750 contracts for the delivery month.

Although the definition of the commodity to be delivered seems very precise, to the extent that variations exist, the seller has an *implied delivery option* and will, if possible, deliver the lowest quality product at the latest possible date. The value of the implied delivery option varies from contract to contract and is implicit in the futures price.[3]

3. Clearing, Volume, and Open Interest

Both standardization of contracts and ease of clearing have helped to provide liquidity to futures markets. The futures *clearinghouse* stands between the buyer and seller in order to facilitate transactions. Think of the clearinghouse as an accounting system for long and short positions in futures contracts. Figure 9.2 illustrates a simple example.

At 11:15 A.M. Mr. A buys two contracts at a market price of $17.95 per barrel. He never knows the identity of the seller or sellers and probably does not care. The clearinghouse records his purchase along with the fact that one contract was sold at $17.95 per barrel by Mr. B and another by Mr. C. Next, at 1:20 P.M., Mr. A sells a contract at $17.98 per barrel (for a $0.03 gain), and Mr. D is on the buying side. Finally, Mr. C sells one contract for $17.96 a barrel to Mr. A at 2:10 P.M. There are

---

[2] Actual contract terms have been simplified for expositional purposes. Contact the NYMEX for full details.

[3] For research on the value of the implied delivery option see Hemmler [1987] or Gay and Manaster [1984].

Record of Transactions during the Trading Day:

Long Positions				Short Positions			
Buyer	Quantity	Price	Time	Seller	Quantity	Price	Time
Mr. A	2	$17.95	11:15A	Mr. B	1	$17.95	11:15A
Mr. D	1	17.98	1:20P	Mr. C	1	17.95	11:15A
Mr. A	1	17.96	2:10P	Mr. A	1	17.98	1:20P
				Mr. C	1	17.96	2:10P
	$\overline{4}$				$\overline{4}$		

Net Positions: (Market closing price = $17.96 per barrel)

Mr. A: 2 purchased at $17.95 = $-$$35,900
         1 purchased at $17.96 = $-$ 17,960
         1 sold   at $17.98 = $+$ 17,980
                                  $-$ 35,880
         2 long   at $17.96 = $+$ 35,920
         At settlement $+$ 40

Mr. B: 1 sold   at $17.95 = $+$ 17,950
         1 short   at $17.96 = $-$ 17,960
         At settlement $-$ 10

Mr. C: 1 sold   at $17.95 = $+$ 17,950
         1 sold   at $17.96 = $+$ 17,960
                                  $+$ 35,910
         2 short   at $17.96 = $-$ 35,920
         At settlement $-$ 10

Mr. D: 1 purchased at $17.98 = $-$ 17,980
         1 long   at $17.96 = $+$ 17,960
         At settlement $-$ 20

Figure 9.2
A clearinghouse illustration.

no further transactions and the market closes at $17.96 per barrel. The *Wall Street Journal* reports (see Fig. 9.1) that the market for August contracts opened at $17.90, the high was $17.99, the low was $17.88, and the closing price was $17.96. The price change from the previous day's close was $0.03.

At the end of the trading day, each trader's position is *marked to market* by the clearinghouse in its *daily settlement* operation. As shown in Fig. 9.2, Mr. A's net position for the day is a gain of $40. This amount of money is credited to his interest-bearing account at the clearinghouse. On the other hand, Mr. D lost $20 and he must pay the clearinghouse. In actuality, only brokers belong to the clearinghouse and it is their accounts that are settled daily. Each brokerage firm then acts as a clearinghouse for its clients.

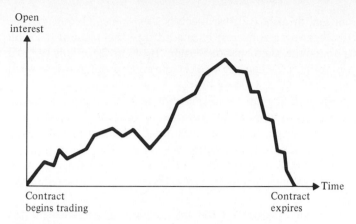

Figure 9.3
Typical pattern for open interest over the life of a futures contract.

Note that four contracts were traded during the day in our example. Actual trading volume in August contracts is not reported in the *Wall Street Journal*, but total trading volume for all oil contracts was estimated at 25,701. In addition to volume per day, the *Wall Street Journal* reports *open interest*, which is the total number of contracts outstanding as of the previous trading day. In most futures markets the open interest, as illustrated in Fig. 9.3, is relatively low during the early months of a contract, when it still has a long time before expiration. Then it rises as hedgers and speculators become more active in the market, and finally it falls rapidly as the contract expiration approaches. For example, in crude oil we see that the open interest in January 1988 contracts, which have almost two years to maturity, is only 102, whereas for the March 1987 contracts, open interest is 47,257. In some futures markets, e.g., stock index futures, there cannot be any open interest at the contract expiration date because it is not possible to actually deliver the underlying asset—the stock index. Even when the commodity can be delivered, relatively few of the futures positions (less than 3% on average) end in actual delivery of the commodity involved. Later on, in the theory section of the chapter, we shall discuss some reasons why open interest is so high relative to the number of contracts that result in delivery.

4. Margins

The example in Fig. 9.2 implicitly assumed that all traders invested an amount equal to the full value of the underlying commodity. This is rarely the case. Usually, the futures trader is required to put up only enough money to insure that the probability of reaching a negative equity position in one day is quite small. Each futures market has its own regulations, but the *initial margin* when a position is first opened is usually only 5% to 10% of the total value of the contract. The *maintenance margin* is the minimum amount of equity that the account may have and is usually set at 75% to 80% of the initial margin. If losses drive down the value of equity in the account below the maintenance margin, then the investor receives a *margin call* requiring that additional cash (or interest-bearing certificates) be placed into the account to bring the equity in the account above the maintenance margin. If the investor fails to meet the requirements of the margin call, then the broker may close out the investor's futures position.

There is, of course, nothing that requires an investor to use a margin account. The effect of trading on margin is to leverage any position so that the systematic and unsystematic risks are both greater per dollar of investment. High margin has given commodity futures markets the reputation of being very risky when in fact, as we shall see later on (in section D), 100% margin positions have about the same variance as common stock portfolios, although they have very different covariances with the market portfolio.

There are two commonly cited reasons for having margin requirements. First, a margin on a futures contract represents a performance bond, which serves to protect the integrity and reputation of the futures exchange and to protect the middleman (known as the futures commission merchant) from customer default. Second, it is often argued (by regulators) that higher margin requirements serve to reduce price volatility caused by speculative activity.

Hartzmark [1986] analyzes the effect of changes in margin requirements on futures markets and concludes (1) that when margin levels are raised (lowered) the number of open contracts falls (rises), (2) that there is weak evidence to support the conclusion that there is an inverse relationship between margin changes and trading volume, (3) that there are significant but unpredictable changes in the composition of traders in the market, and (4) that there is no systematic or significant relationship between margin changes and price volatility.

5. Price Limits

Another interesting feature of commodities markets is *price limits*. The U.S. Commodity Futures Trading Commission, which regulates trading on U.S. commodity exchanges, places limits on the extent to which futures prices are allowed to vary from day to day. For example, a simplified description of the price limits on frozen concentrated orange juice futures (after 1979) is that: (1) prices may move no more than $0.05 per pound ($750 per contract); (2) when three or more contract months have closed at the limit in the same direction for three successive business days, the limit is raised to $0.08 per pound; and (3) on the last three days before the near contract's expiration, its limit is $0.10 per pound. It is not unusual for the price to move up (or down) the limit (i.e., up or down by $0.10 per pound) for several days without any trading taking place.

There are arguments for and against price limits. For example, Roll [1984] notes that the orange juice futures price is rendered informationally inefficient by the imposition of price limits on price movements because prices respond to weather changes (especially freezes, which damage the crop) slower than they otherwise might in the absence of price limits. Brennan [1986b], however, provides an economic rationale for price limits. Against the clear costs on market participants imposed by prohibiting mutually beneficial trades at prices outside the price limits, he suggests that a benefit of price limits is that their imposition allows lower margin requirements than would otherwise prevail. Margin requirements and price limits are substitutes in ensuring contract performance without costly litigation. If margin requirements are costly, then having lower margin requirements is a benefit that results from price limits.

That margin requirements are costly is itself a debated proposition. Black [1976], e.g., argues that the opportunity cost of margins is zero with daily settlement because the value of the futures position goes to zero. This argument, however, fails to account for the costs associated with the initial margin. Others (e.g., Anderson [1981]) believe that margin positions have no opportunity cost because they can be satisfied with interest-bearing securities. However, Telser [1981a] provides a sensible argument for costly margin requirements, namely, that interest-bearing securities such as Treasury Bills are part of the holder's precautionary balance and if they are committed for use as margin, they are unavailable for other uses. Brennan [1986b] also points out that the bonding feature of margin requirements helps to avoid costly litigation that would otherwise be needed to enforce daily settlement on futures contracts.

Brennan [1986b] is also able to explain why some futures markets have price limits while others do not. A futures market with daily price limits helps to prevent default because the losing trader cannot be absolutely certain that defaulting is the best thing to do. For example, if the price moves down the limit, the trader may be subject to a maintenance margin call but will not necessarily be wiped out. Furthermore, the trader does not know what the futures price will be when the daily price limits no longer apply. Therefore he will tend to meet the maintenance margin rather than defaulting. An analogy (provided by Phil Dybvig of Yale) is that you take your aging car to the mechanic and ask him to fix it. The car is only worth $4000 and the mechanic knows it will take $4500 to complete all repairs. Rather than telling you the total cost of repair, and having you respond by junking the car instead of repairing it, the mechanic gives you a price limit. He says the first repair will cost $450. Once this is paid for, he announces that the second repair will cost $450. And so it goes. Of course, your ability to estimate the total cost of repairs is crucial. The reason the mechanic can fool you is that on average the total cost of the repair is, let's say, only $550. It pays you to pay $450 now because you are "saving" $100 on average. But occasionally you have bad luck and can be persuaded to pay up even when the eventual repair is much more. Similar, argues Brennan, is the investor's ability to estimate what the equilibrium futures price will be when the price limits are lifted. If there is an active spot market where spot prices are good predictors of futures prices (e.g., in interest rate, currency, stock index, and possibly metals futures) price limits will serve little use because investors can use the spot prices to learn the bad news. Also, price limits on short-term contracts should be larger or nonexistent because spot and futures prices are equal at maturity. Note that for orange juice futures the price limit is doubled for near-maturity contracts. For agricultural commodities futures with some time before delivery is due, there is usually no spot market (it's hard to trade orange juice when the crop is still in blossom) and price limits serve a useful role.

6. Taxation of Futures Contracts

The Internal Revenue Service distinguishes between *hedgers* and *speculators* for tax purposes. Hedgers are market participants whose positions are considered to be part of their normal commercial activities. Their profits and losses are treated as ordinary income for tax purposes. All other traders are defined as speculators and are considered to have a capital asset for tax purposes. The capital gain or loss is recorded when the position is closed out. The length of time that the position is maintained determines whether or not the capital gain is short- or long-term for tax purposes.

In 1982 Congress changed the capital gains treatment by stipulating that all futures positions must be marked to market at year's end. In addition, 40% of any gains or losses are treated as short-term capital gains or losses, with the remaining 60% as long term. The motivation for the change was the elimination of "tax straddles," which were being used for tax avoidance. A tax straddle was established by selling a contract in one commodity and buying a contract in a highly correlated commodity (e.g., corn and wheat). Gains in one contract would presumably offset losses in the other. Near year's end the losses in the declining contract were realized in order to shelter this year's income, and shortly after the end of the year, the winning position would be closed out but not taxed until next year. The only risk involved was the fact that the position was not hedged during the interval between the closing of the loss position and the closing of the gain position shortly thereafter.

Cornell and French [1983b] point out that the 1982 change in the tax code affected the pricing of stock index futures. The portfolio of stocks (e.g., the Standard and Poor's 500) from which the index is constructed does not have to be marked to market at year's end for tax purposes, but the stock futures contract on the index must be. Consequently, the index portfolio contains a valuable tax-timing option (see Constantinides [1983]) that the futures contract does not. A portfolio manager who holds the stock portfolio can hold his or her winning stocks to defer capital gains and sell the losing stocks to receive a tax shelter now. Hence the stock index futures contract should always sell for a discount relative to the stock index portfolio.

C. THE THEORY OF FUTURES MARKETS AND FUTURES CONTRACT PRICING

First, it is interesting to take a look at the fundamental question of why futures markets exist at all. What purpose do they serve, and why have some futures markets prospered while others have withered and failed? Next, how are futures contracts valued? Since there are so many different kinds of contracts, we will try to simplify matters by proceeding in three stages. Initially, we will discuss a generalized model of futures contracts (provided by Samuelson [1965]) to see how expected futures prices should be expected to vary randomly through time even though the variance of futures prices may increase, decrease, or remain constant as the contract life declines. Next we will turn to the pricing of financial futures contracts where arbitrage with the spot financial contracts helps to determine the market price. Finally, we will discuss commodities futures, where arbitrage in the spot contract is not always so easy.

1. Why Do Futures Markets Exist?

A quick look at the *Wall Street Journal* shows that there are no existing futures markets for many commodities. There are futures contracts for wheat, corn, and oats; but none for rye and barley (although rye futures were traded from 1869 to 1970, and barley futures between 1885 and 1940). There was also an active egg futures market at one time. Other commodities, which never had futures contracts, are tobacco, hay, and buckwheat. Why should some commodities have futures contracts while others do not?

There are probably three factors that contribute to the existence of a futures market. First, there must be enough of the underlying standardized commodity (or financial security) so that economies of scale lower transactions costs sufficiently to allow frequent trading. This point is emphasized by Telser [1981b]. Second, there must be sufficient price variability in the commodity to create a demand for risk sharing among hedgers and speculators. The theory of Keynes [1923] and Hicks [1946] is that producers are risk averse and are willing to offer a premium in order to sell futures contracts as a means of hedging against spot price fluctuations at harvest time. Speculators participate in the market in order to gain this premium by sharing risk. Without any price variability there would be no risk to share and no futures market. Finally, Working [1953] and Salmon [1985] extend the idea of risk sharing by recognizing that a "core" of trading activity among present and future commodity owners, trading futures contracts among themselves, must be present before speculators can be attracted. The incentive for commodity owners to trade among themselves is provided by uncorrelated production; using the terminology of Hirshleifer [1984], there must be diversity—something like "good-fair-weather farms," "average-market farms," and "good-poor-weather farms." Commodities supplied by farms with very different individual crop-outcome covariances with the market crop outcome will be more likely to have futures markets than commodities supplied by farms with very similar private crop-outcome covariances with the market.

Given that an active futures market exists, we now turn our attention to the pricing of futures contracts.

2. The Time Series Behavior of Futures Prices

In his classic paper entitled "Proof that Properly Anticipated Prices Fluctuate Randomly," Samuelson [1965] demonstrates that even though there may be a known seasonal pattern in spot (commodity) prices, the futures price will fluctuate randomly. He also shows the intuition for why the variance of futures prices may not be constant over the life of the contract.[4]

---

[4] The changing variance is important for those who wish to price options on futures contracts. Recall that the Black-Scholes option pricing model assumes a constant variance; hence it may not do well for pricing options on futures contracts. See section E of this chapter.

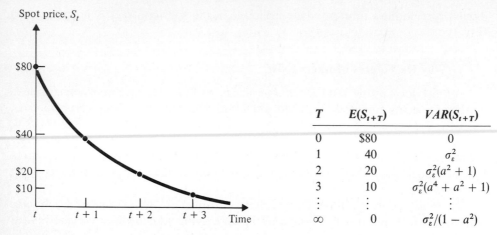

The table to the right of the figure:

T	$E(S_{t+T})$	$VAR(S_{t+T})$
0	$80	0
1	40	σ_ε^2
2	20	$\sigma_\varepsilon^2(a^2 + 1)$
3	10	$\sigma_\varepsilon^2(a^4 + a^2 + 1)$
$\vdots$	$\vdots$	$\vdots$
∞	0	$\sigma_\varepsilon^2/(1 - a^2)$

Figure 9.4
A hypothetical spot price that obeys
the autoregressive scheme in Eq. (9.2).

To replicate Samuelson's proof, assume that storage costs and interest rates are zero, and that the spot price, S_{t+1}, obeys the following stationary autoregressive scheme:

$$S_{t+1} = aS_t + \varepsilon_t, \qquad a < 1. \tag{9.2}$$

For the purposes of a numerical example, let the constant a equal $\frac{1}{2}$; the error term, ε_t, be distributed normally with mean zero and standard deviation, σ_ε; let the initial spot price be $80; and let the covariance between the error term and the spot price be zero, i.e., $COV(S_t, \varepsilon_t) = 0$. Given that $a = \frac{1}{2}$, the expected spot price one period ahead is one half of the previous period's spot price, as illustrated in Fig. 9.4. Needless to say, this is an aberrant example because the spot price does not behave randomly. However, as we shall soon see, the futures price will in fact be random even though the spot price is not.

Begin by deriving the mean and variance of the spot price. Today's spot price, S_t, is a constant with no variance. Next period's spot price, S_{t+1}, according to Eq. (9.2) is

$$S_{t+1} = aS_t + \varepsilon_t, \tag{9.3}$$

and using the properties of random variables (from Chapter 6) its mean and variance are

$$E(S_{t+1}) = aE(S_t) \quad \text{since} \quad E(\varepsilon_t) = 0 \tag{9.4}$$

and

$$VAR(S_{t+1}) = E[aS_t + \varepsilon_t - aE(S_t)]^2 \tag{9.5}$$
$$= E(\varepsilon_t)^2 = \sigma_\varepsilon^2.$$

The mean and variance of the spot price two periods hence can be derived by substituting Eq. (9.3) into the definition of S_{t+2}, namely,

$$S_{t+2} = aS_{t+1} + \varepsilon_{t+1}$$
$$= a(aS_t + \varepsilon_t) + \varepsilon_{t+1}$$
$$= a^2 S_t + a\varepsilon_t + \varepsilon_{t+1}.$$

The expected spot price for the second period is

$$E(S_{t+2}) = a^2 E(S_t) \quad \text{since} \quad E(\varepsilon_{t+1}) = E(\varepsilon_t) = 0, \tag{9.6}$$

and the variance is

$$VAR(S_{t+2}) = E[a^2 S_t + a\varepsilon_t + \varepsilon_{t+1} - a^2 E(S_t)]^2$$
$$= E[a^2 \varepsilon_t^2 + 2a\varepsilon_t \varepsilon_{t+1} + \varepsilon_{t+1}^2]$$
$$= a^2 \sigma_\varepsilon^2 + \sigma_\varepsilon^2$$
$$= \sigma_\varepsilon^2 (a^2 + 1) \tag{9.7}$$

since $E(\varepsilon_t \varepsilon_{t+1}) = COV(\varepsilon_t \varepsilon_{t+1}) = 0$ and $E(\varepsilon_t)^2 = E(\varepsilon_{t+1})^2 = \sigma_\varepsilon^2$.

The progression of expected spot prices and their variances is summarized below and in Fig. 9.4.[5]

T	$E(S_{t+T})$	$\sigma_\varepsilon^2(S_{t+T})$
0	S_t	0
1	$aE(S_t)$	σ_ε^2
2	$a^2 E(S_t)$	$\sigma_\varepsilon^2(a^2 + 1)$
3	$a^3 E(S_t)$	$\sigma_\varepsilon^2(a^4 + a^2 + 1)$
$\vdots$	$\vdots$	$\vdots$
∞	$a^T E(S_t)$	$\sigma_\varepsilon^2/(1 - a^2)$ (if $a < 1$)

Note that although the expected spot price declines across time, the variance of the expected spot price increases unless $a = 1$. If $a = 1$, the spot price follows a random walk with the expected spot price equal to the initial spot price, $S_t = E(S_{t+1}) = E(S_{t+2}) = \cdots = E(S_{t+T})$, and the variance is equal to $VAR(S_{t+T}) = T\sigma_\varepsilon^2$. In other words the standard deviation of the spot price is $\sigma_\varepsilon \sqrt{T}$. This is the standard square root relationship between the standard deviation of asset prices and time that we found in the Black-Scholes formula in Chapter 8.

---

[5] Note that for the third period

$$S_{t+3} = aS_{t+2} + \varepsilon_{t+2}$$
$$= a(a^2 S_t + a\varepsilon_t + \varepsilon_{t+1}) + \varepsilon_{t+2}$$
$$= a^3 S_t + a^2 \varepsilon_t + a\varepsilon_{t+1} + \varepsilon_{t+2}.$$

Having described the behavior of spot prices, we turn to the problem of pricing futures contracts. The price, $_tF_T$, of the futures contract at time t (today) on the commodity to be delivered at time T (e.g., three periods hence) in the absence of storage costs, interest rates, and a risk premium will be the expected spot price in period three. This may be written as

$$_tF_3 = E_t(S_{t+3})$$
$$= E_t(a^3S_t + a^2\varepsilon_{t+1} + a\varepsilon_{t+2} + \varepsilon_{t+3})$$
$$= a^3S_t \quad \text{since} \quad E_t(a^2\varepsilon_{t+1}) = E_t(a\varepsilon_{t+2}) = E_t(\varepsilon_{t+3}) = 0. \tag{9.8}$$

The futures price one period hence is still the expected spot price in period three, but the expectation must be made at $t + 1$; therefore

$$_{t+1}F_3 = E_{t+1}(S_{t+3})$$
$$= E_{t+1}(a^3S_t + a^2\varepsilon_{t+1} + a\varepsilon_{t+2} + \varepsilon_{t+3})$$
$$= a^3S_t + a^2\varepsilon_{t+1} \quad \text{since} \quad E_{t+1}(a\varepsilon_{t+2}) = E(\varepsilon_{t+3}) = 0. \tag{9.9}$$

Notice that the expectation, taken at $t + 1$, of the error term at $t + 1$ does not vanish because the error already exists at $t + 1$.

Next, Samuelson proves that the expected futures price does not change through time. The change in the futures price from t to $t + 1$ is

$$_{t+1}F_3 - {}_tF_3 = a^3S_t + a^2\varepsilon_{t+1} - a^3S_t, \tag{9.10}$$

and the expected futures price change, evaluated at time t, is zero since $E_t(a^2\varepsilon_{t+1}) = 0$. Thus even though the spot price changes in a known fashion, the futures price is not expected to change. Given no storage costs or interest rates, it is a random walk with no drift. The intuition is quite simple. Futures contracts are written for delivery at a single point in time. Hence the pattern of spot prices is irrelevant. All that counts is today's estimate of the expected spot price at maturity. For example, in Fig. 9.4 the futures price today for delivery in period $t + 2$ is \$20 even though today's spot price is \$80. Since expected information about the spot price at maturity is random and unbiased, $E(\varepsilon_{t+T}) = 0$, the futures price is a random walk with zero drift.

The variance of the futures price from t to $t + 1$ is taken from Eq. (9.10) as follows:

$$\text{VAR}[_{t+1}F_3 - {}_tF_3] = E_{t+1}[(a^2\varepsilon_{t+1})^2]$$
$$= a^4\sigma_\varepsilon^2, \tag{9.11}$$

and in general the futures price variance is

$$\text{VAR}[_{t+1}F_3 - {}_tF_3] = a^4\sigma_\varepsilon^2,$$
$$\text{VAR}[_{t+2}F_3 - {}_{t+1}F_3] = a^2\sigma_\varepsilon^2, \tag{9.12}$$
$$\text{VAR}[_{t+3}F_3 - {}_{t+2}F_3] = \sigma_\varepsilon^2.$$

Thus if $a < 1$, the variance of the futures price increases as we get closer to the maturity of the contract, but if $a = 1$, so that the spot price is a random walk, then the

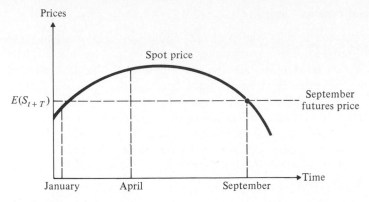

Figure 9.5
Hypothetical spot and futures prices.

standard deviation of the futures price is $\sigma_\varepsilon \sqrt{T}$, is constant across time, and is equal to the standard deviation of the spot price.

The basic intuition of Samuelson's model is that if we assume a stationary autoregressive process in spot prices, then the variance of futures prices will increase as the contract nears maturity. Far distant contracts will exhibit relatively lower variances because autoregressive prices will have a long interval to correct themselves. Near-maturity contracts will be more variable because prices have little time to correct. Of course, it may be too much to expect stationarity in the price-generating process. Many commodities, especially grains, have critical points in their growing seasons when weather dramatically affects the potential harvest. One might expect greater variance during these seasons than during other points in time.

Using daily data for 9 commodities between 1966 and 1980, Anderson [1985] finds evidence supporting both hypotheses—the Samuelson hypothesis that the futures price variance increases nearer maturity and the seasonal production hypothesis that variance is higher at critical information points. Milonas [1986] uses a slightly larger data base and, after removing seasonalities, finds a strong maturity effect on variance for 10 of 11 commodities tested—including financial futures (T-bills, T-bonds, and the GNMA, or Government National Mortgage Association) and metals (copper, gold, and silver).

The preceding analysis helps to make the point that there is no necessary relationship between today's spot price and today's futures price, which is the expectation of the spot price at the delivery date.[6] For example, the futures price for September contracts in Fig. 9.5 is the expected September spot price, $E(S_{t+T})$. The January spot price is below the expected September spot price (i.e., the futures price), and the April spot price is above it.

---

[6] In section E, we shall prove that, for financial futures at least, the current futures price must be a risk-adjusted expected spot price.

3. Pricing Financial Futures Contracts

Financial instruments are usually traded in very liquid spot markets, and there is virtually no cost of storage. This distinguishes them from commodity markets where the spot market may be thin and storage costs high. It also makes financial futures somewhat easier to price because arbitrage between the spot and futures markets helps to determine the futures price.

To see how riskless arbitrage determines prices of *interest rate futures* such as futures on T-bills and T-bonds, let $_tr_T$ be the riskless T-period interest rate observed at time t, let S_t be the current spot price, and let $_tF_T$ be the price at time t (today) of the T-period futures contract.[7] For riskless securities the futures price is the expectation of the future spot price:

$$_tF_T = E(S_{t+T}).\tag{9.13}$$

This implies that the futures price should be equal to the current spot price multiplied times a compounding factor:

$$_tF_T = S_t e^{_tr_T}.\tag{9.14}$$

Equation (9.13) is called the *expectations theory of futures prices*. Suppose Eq. (9.14) does not hold. In particular, suppose that the futures price is higher than the compounded spot price:

$$_tF_T > S_t e^{_tr_T}.$$

If this happens, a riskless arbitrage opportunity is available if investors short the futures contract and simultaneously buy the asset. At maturity the asset is then delivered to cover the short position in the futures contract. As more and more arbitrageurs sell the futures position, its price will fall. Simultaneously, buying pressure on the underlying asset will raise its price. Arbitrage will continue until the futures price just equals the compounded current spot price, as required by Eq. (9.14).

To make the concept of arbitrage more concrete, consider the following numerical example taken from the T-bill futures market. On January 5, 198X, you observe the following relationships:

	Life	Yield
Futures contract which requires delivery on March 22, 198X of a 90-day T-bill maturing on June 20, 198X	90 days	8.0%
T-bill maturing on June 20, 198X	167	12.0
T-bill maturing on March 22, 198X	77	14.0

What position should you take in order to earn an arbitrage profit? First, remember that the futures contract that matures on March 22 results in the delivery of a 90-day T-bill (maturing on June 20 with an expected yield of 8.0%). Therefore if you hold a portfolio consisting of the futures contract and the T-bill maturing on March 22,

---

[7] Later on, in section E, we shall return to the problem of pricing financial futures on risky assets.

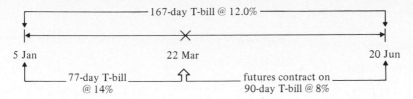

Figure 9.6
Time line for arbitrage example.

your position should be exactly equal to holding the June 20 T-bill, which matures in 167 days. This equivalence is illustrated in Fig. 9.6. In order for there to be no arbitrage, the product of the yields to maturity on the two shorter instruments should equal the yield to maturity on the longer instrument.[8] If there were no arbitrage, then

$$(1.14)^{77/360}(1.08)^{90/360} = (1.12)^{167/360},$$

$$(1.02842)(1.01943) = (1.05398),$$

$$1.04840 \neq 1.05398.$$

The 167-day yield is high relative to the product of the 77 and 90-day yields. Therefore the price of the 167-day T-bill is too low and it should be bought. If the face value on the 167-day T-bill is $1,000,000, today it is worth[9]

$$PV = 1,000,000(1.12)^{-167/360}$$

$$= 1,000,000(.94879)$$

$$= 948,786.08.$$

The cash necessary to purchase the T-bill can be raised by borrowing this amount for 77 days at 14%, which is the 77-day interest rate currently prevailing in the market.[10] Therefore in 77 days you will pay back a future value of

$$FV = 948,786.08(1.14)^{77/360}$$

$$= 948,786.08(1.02842)$$

$$= 975,752.39.$$

In addition to borrowing, you simultaneously sell short a T-bond futures contract with a $1,000,000 face value. On March 22 when the futures contract matures you will deliver the 167-day T-bill, which will have 90 days to maturity on March 22, in order to cover your short position in the futures contract, and you receive the following

---

[8] The convention in bond markets is to calculate the yield to maturity on the basis of a 360-day year.

[9] T-bills pay no interest and are sold on a discount basis.

[10] Capozza and Cornell [1979] have shown that the actual cost of borrowing in this case is approximately 50 basis points above the market yield. In our example this raises the cost of borrowing to 14.5% and the interest paid by $913.78. Profits will be reduced accordingly.

amount in cash:

$$PV = 1,000,000(1.08)^{-90/360}$$

$$= 1,000,000(.98094)$$

$$= 980,943.65.$$

This is more than enough to repay your loan that comes due on March 22. In fact, your net arbitrage profit on March 22 is

980,943.65	proceeds from the short position
−975,752.39	amount due on the loan
5,191.26	profit

Thus you earn a $5,191.26 arbitrage profit without taking any risk whatsoever and without investing any capital of your own. This is called a *self-financing riskless arbitrage*. There is no risk involved because you locked in the arbitrage by owning the 167-day T-bill and simultaneously borrowing and shorting the futures contract against it. No matter how prices changed in the interim before March 22, your profit was assured. When the loan came due, you received cash for delivering a T-bill that you owned. The deal was self-financing because you put up none of your own money.

Thus given the existence of arbitrage between spot and futures markets, financial futures contracts should be priced according to the expectations theory of Eq. (9.13). Empirical evidence by Rendleman and Carabini [1979] indicates that when brokerage costs, bid-ask spreads, and borrowing costs are taken into account, no pure arbitrage opportunities could be found. They conclude that "the inefficiencies in the Treasury bill futures market do not appear to be significant enough to offer attractive investment alternatives to the short-term portfolio manager" Capozza and Cornell [1979] concluded that near-term contracts were priced efficiently but that longer-term contracts tended to be underpriced; however, none of these discrepancies could have been arbitraged owing to the cost of shorting the spot bill necessary to establish the appropriate position.

Pricing *stock index futures* is more difficult than pricing interest rate futures for several reasons.[11] First, the market value of the stock index portfolio is affected by the fact that the portfolio of stocks pays dividends, but the index portfolio is only a weighted average of the stock prices. The index does not receive dividends. Therefore the stock index futures price must subtract the present value of expected dividends paid by the index stocks before the futures contract matures. Second, futures are taxed differently than the underlying stock index portfolio. All gains and losses are marked to market at year's end with 40% taxed at the short-term capital gains rate and 60% at the long-term capital gains rate. Hence capital gains taxes cannot be deferred on the futures contract, whereas they may on the underlying securities. Cornell and French [1983b] show how to price futures on stock indices and test their model on data taken from the first seven months of stock index futures trading.

---

[11] Stock index futures are traded on the Standard and Poor's 500 index, the New York Stock Exchange Composite index, and the Value Line index.

One of the interesting applications of stock index futures is to select a portfolio of securities that is expected to do better than a set of other companies from the same industries. Against this portfolio, one shorts a stock index futures contract in order to remove market risk. When this is done properly the selected portfolio will do well regardless of whether the market goes up or down, because changes in the value of the stock index futures contract offset the market risk in the selected portfolio. All that is left is the idiosyncratic component of returns.

4. Pricing Commodities Futures Contracts

The pricing of commodities futures contracts is complicated by the fact that storage is costly and that spot markets may be nonexistent or too thin for arbitrage. There are two general approaches for explaining returns on commodities futures, one based on convenience yields and storage costs, and the other on risk premia such as the CAPM beta.

A. FUTURES PRICES AND STORAGE. The traditional view explains the current futures price as the expected spot price, minus the cost of storage (interest foregone, warehousing, and shrinkage), and minus a convenience yield. Costs of storage are obvious, but *convenience yield* is much like a liquidity premium, usually being described as the convenience of holding inventories because many commodities (e.g., wheat) are inputs in the production process (e.g., bread making) or as the convenience of having inventory to meet unexpected demand. The theory of storage predicts low convenience yields when inventories are plentiful and high convenience yields when stockout is more likely. Telser [1958] and Brennan [1986a] have provided empirical estimates of the convenience yield that are consistent with the theory. Fama and French [1987] have provided evidence that marginal convenience yields vary seasonally for most agricultural and animal commodities but not for metals.

According to the storage theory, the futures price of a T-period contract observed at time t is given by

$$_tF_T = S_t e^{t'T} + {_tW_T} - {_tC_T},\qquad (9.15)$$

where $S_t e^{t'T}$ is the current spot price compounded by the interest rate between the current time, t, and the delivery date, T; where $_tW_T$ is the storage cost between now and delivery; and where $_tC_T$ is the convenience yield (in dollars) between now and delivery.

If storage costs and convenience yields are very low, then we would predict that prior to delivery the futures price is below the expected spot price,

$$_tF_T < E(S_T) = S_t e^{t'T}.\qquad (9.16)$$

This relationship, called *normal backwardation*, is graphed in Fig. 9.7. The origin of the idea is that producers (e.g., farmers) normally wish to hedge their risk by shorting the commodity. To attract speculators into the market, they have to sell futures contracts at a discount from the expected spot price. Consequently, futures contracts should yield a rate of return higher than the riskless interest rate, and their prices

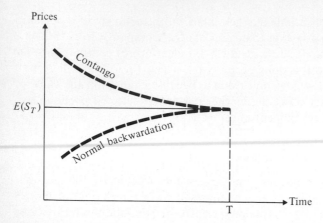

Figure 9.7
Normal backwardation and contango.

will rise (on average) through time until, at delivery, the futures price equals the spot price.

Also illustrated in Fig. 9.7 is a situation where the futures price is above the expected spot price:

$$_tF_T > E(S_T) = S_t e^{r_tT}.$$

Called *contango*, this is just the opposite of normal backwardation. If hedgers need to go long, or if the convenience yield is negative owing to oversupply, then they must pay a premium for futures contracts in order to induce speculators to go short.

B.   FUTURES PRICES AND THE CAPM.   A second way of explaining commodity futures prices posits that the futures price can be divided into the expected future spot price plus an expected risk premium based on the capital asset pricing model. For example, Dusak [1973] relates the CAPM to commodity futures in a one-period framework. Begin by writing out the CAPM:

$$E(R_i) = R_f + \left[\frac{E(R_m) - R_f}{\sigma(R_m)} \right] \frac{\text{COV}(R_i, R_m)}{\sigma(R_m)}, \qquad (9.17)$$

where

$\quad E(R_i) =$ the expected return on the ith asset,

$\quad\quad R_f =$ the risk-free rate, assumed to be constant over the life of the futures contract,

$\quad \sigma(R_m) =$ the standard deviation of return on a (single factor) market index portfolio,

$\text{COV}(R_i, R_m) =$ the expected covariance of returns between the ith asset and the market index portfolio.

Next, write down the definition of a one-period rate of return for an investor who holds the risky commodity. If S_{i0} is the current spot price of the ith commodity and $E(S_{iT})$ is the expected spot price at the time of delivery, T, we have

$$E(R_i) = \frac{E(S_{iT}) - S_{i0}}{S_{i0}}. \tag{9.18}$$

Combining Eq. (9.18) with Eq. (9.17), we have a certainty equivalent model for the spot price of the commodity:

$$S_{i0} = \frac{E(S_{iT}) - [E(R_m) - R_f]S_{i0}\beta_i}{1 + R_f}, \tag{9.19}$$

where

$$\beta_i = \frac{\text{COV}(R_i, R_m)}{\sigma^2(R_m)} = \text{the systematic risk of the } i\text{th commodity.}$$

Finally, a futures contract allows an investor to purchase an asset now but to defer payment for one period; therefore the current price of the futures contract, $_0F_{iT}$, must be the current spot price multiplied by a future value factor:[12]

$$_0F_{iT} = S_{i0}(1 + R_f). \tag{9.20}$$

Multiplying both sides of the certainty equivalent model, Eq. (9.19), by $(1 + R_f)$, and noting that the result is equivalent to Eq. (9.20), we have

$$_0F_{iT} = S_{i0}(1 + R_f) = E(S_{iT}) - [E(R_m) - R_f]S_{i0}\beta_i. \tag{9.21}$$

The futures price, $_0F_{iT}$, equals the expected spot price minus a risk premium based on the systematic risk of the commodity.

The CAPM approach, Eq. (9.21), argues that systematic risk should be important in the pricing of futures contracts but leaves out storage costs and convenience yields. On the other hand, the traditional approach, Eq. (9.15), ignores the possibility that systematic risk may affect the equilibrium prices of commodity futures contracts. We now turn to the empirical evidence, which is still in its infancy, to provide some clues to which theory is correct or whether some combination of them best describes commodities futures prices.

D. EMPIRICAL EVIDENCE

There are two interrelated lines of empirical research on futures contracts. One focuses on comparing models of futures prices to see which best explains the data. The other asks how well information is reflected in futures prices—Are they good forecasts of future spot prices? These ideas are interrelated because we need a good model to

---

[12] This is the same argument used in Eq. (9.14) for financial futures.

Table 9.1   Rate of Return Data, 1950–1976

Panel A: Comparison Rates of Return

	Nominal Returns		Real Returns	
	Mean	Std. Dev.	Mean	Std. Dev.
Common stock	13.05	18.95	9.58	19.65
Commodity futures	13.83	22.43	9.81	19.44
Long-term government bonds	2.84	6.53	−.51	6.81
T-bills	3.63	1.95	.22	1.80
Inflation	3.43	2.90	—	—

Panel B: Correlation Matrix of Nominal Returns

	Common	Futures	Bonds	T-bills	Inflation
Common	1.00	−.24	−.10	−.57	−.43
Futures		1.00	−.16	.34	.58
Bonds			1.00	.20	.03
T-bills				1.00	.76
Inflation					1.00

Adapted from Bodie Z and V. Rosansky, "Risk and Return in Commodities Futures," *Financial Analysts Journal*, May–June 1980, 27–39.

forecast future spot prices, and because the futures markets must be informationally efficient if the models are to have any hope of working.

Bodie and Rosansky [1980] provide a comprehensive analysis of rates of return on commodities futures prices between 1950 and 1976. Table 9.1 summarizes their results. Perhaps the most interesting fact is that an equally weighted portfolio of 23 commodities futures had roughly the same return and standard deviation as the equally weighted common stock portfolio.[13] Also, the correlation matrix (Panel B) indicates that stocks and futures are negatively correlated with each other. Furthermore, common stock returns are negatively correlated with inflation, whereas commodity futures are positively correlated. One interpretation of these facts is that different factors (in the arbitrage pricing model) affect commodities and stocks. A randomly chosen portfolio of common stock is a bad hedge against unexpected inflation, but a well-diversified commodity portfolio is a good hedge. Apparently, stocks have very different factor sensitivities to the factors in the arbitrage pricing model (APM) (especially unexpected inflation) than do commodities. If this interpretation is true, then it is not surprising that Bodie and Rosansky [1980] and Dusak [1973] both found that the CAPM does a poor job of explaining commodities returns. After all, a market portfolio of common stock is usually employed as the proxy for

---

[13] None of the futures positions were bought on margin.

the market portfolio (a single-factor model), and commodity returns are negatively correlated with common stock. Bodie and Rosansky found that 15 out of 23 commodities had negative betas and that the security market line, estimated using commodities data, had a negative slope. From these results we must conclude that the CAPM fails to explain (even approximately) the returns on commodities. We are waiting for someone to apply the APM to this problem.

On a more positive note, Bodie and Rosansky do find evidence of normal backwardation, where Dusak had not, because they used a longer time period. Mean returns in excess of the risk-free rate averaged 9.77% for commodity futures. Chang [1985] also finds evidence of normal backwardation for wheat, corn, and soybeans over the interval 1951 to 1980. Fama and French [1987] find marginal evidence of normal backwardation when commodities are combined into portfolios but conclude that the evidence is not strong enough to resolve the long-standing controversy about the existence of nonzero-risk premia. If there is a risk premium for commodity futures contracts, it is probably not related to the CAPM beta, and it may be time varying.

The second interesting question is whether or not futures prices are good forecasts of expected spot prices. The variability of spot prices will depend on seasonal supply and demand shocks, and on the availability of inventory to cushion them. One might expect that commodities with high inventory relative to production— e.g., precious metals (gold, silver, and platinum)—allow price shocks to be transmitted freely from one period to another. This implies that a demand shock today will affect both today's spot price and expected spot prices. If spot prices are linked in this fashion there is little left for futures prices to explain. French [1986] and Fama and French [1987] argue that futures prices cannot provide forecasts that are reliably better than the current spot price unless the variance in the expected spot price changes is a large fraction of the variance of the actual spot price changes. For metals this is not true, and they find that futures prices predict expected spot prices no better than do current spot prices. However, they find reliable evidence that futures prices are good forecasts for animal and agricultural commodity expected spot prices. This is consistent with the role of inventories because commodities are affected by relatively large storage costs and production seasonals.

Roll [1984] studied the orange juice futures market. Although the commodity is frozen and therefore not perishable, only a small amount (about 10%) is carried over in inventory from one year to the next. Almost all (98%) of U.S. production takes place in central Florida around Orlando. Short-term variations in supply due to planting decisions is low (because oranges grow on trees that require 5 to 15 years to mature) and short-term variations in demand are also low. All these facts imply that orange juice futures prices should be heavily influenced by weather, particularly by cold temperatures. Roll reports that the orange juice futures price is a statistically significant predictor of the forecast *error* of the U.S. National Weather Service. That is, futures prices predict the weather better than the weather service. Also, Roll finds (1) that price limits decrease the informational efficiency of the market and (2) that there is much more variability in futures prices than can be explained by the weather or any other measurable short-term supply or demand shock.

In sum, the existing empirical evidence indicates that inventories are important in explaining the ability of futures prices to predict expected spot prices. Also, there is weak evidence to support normal backwardation, but the risk premium may be time varying and is not related to a CAPM beta. In addition, it was reported earlier in the chapter that Brennan [1986a] and Fama and French [1987] have found evidence consistent with the existence of convenience yields that vary through time with inventory levels.

E. SYNTHETIC FUTURES AND OPTIONS ON FUTURES

1. Synthetic Futures

We can create a *synthetic forward contract* by buying a European call, C, on the underlying risky asset or commodity with time to maturity T and exercise price X, equal to the forward price, $_0F_T$, and simultaneously writing a European put, P, with the same time to maturity and exercise price. Table 9.2 shows that the end-of-period payoffs for the synthetic forward contract are equal to the payoffs on an actual forward contract. At maturity, if the price of the risky asset, S, is less than the exercise price, $X = _0F_T$, then the call is worthless and the put is exercised against us, creating a loss of $_0F_T - S_T$ dollars. Had we held the forward contract, we would have lost exactly the same dollar amount. Alternately, if the risky asset is worth more than the exercise price at maturity, the call pays the difference between the asset price and the delivery price, $S_T - _0F_T$, which is the same as the forward contract payout. Either way, the synthetic forward contract and the real forward contract have identical payouts.

The initial investments in the synthetic and real forward contracts must also be identical—they must both have zero initial outlay. This fact allows us to establish an interesting result, namely, the *expectations hypothesis for pricing financial futures*. We begin by writing down the formula for put-call parity from Chapter 8:

$$C_0 - P_0 = S_0 - Xe^{-r_f T}.$$

Next, our synthetic futures position has an exercise price, X, equal to the current forward price, $_0F_T$. Therefore

$$C_0 - P_0 = S_0 - _0F_T e^{-r_f T}. \tag{9.22}$$

Table 9.2   Payouts for a Synthetic Forward Contract

	Payouts at Delivery	
Portfolio	*If $S_T < X$*	*If $S_T \geq X$*
$V_A = C_0 - P_0$	$0 - (_0F_T - S_T)$	$S_T - _0F_T$
$V_B =$ forward contract	$S_T - _0F_T$	$S_T - _0F_T$
	$V_A = V_B$	$V_A = V_B$

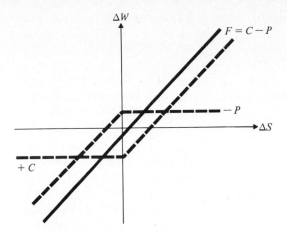

Figure 9.8
Constructing a synthetic future.

We also know that the synthetic forward contract requires zero cash outlay; therefore we can set Eq. (9.22) equal to zero:[14]

$$C_0 \quad P_0 - S_0 - {_0}F_T e^{-r_f T} - 0,$$

$$_0F_T = S_0 e^{r_f T}. \tag{9.23}$$

So the forward contract price must be equal to the current spot price multiplied by a riskless compounding factor. The forward price will always be less than the spot price. Furthermore, the expected spot price is the current spot price multiplied by a risk-adjusted compounding factor, based on the cost of equity, k_s:

$$E(S_T) = S_0 e^{k_s T}. \tag{9.24}$$

Solving Eq. (9.24) for S_0 and substituting the result into Eq. (9.23), we have

$$_0F_T = E(S_T)e^{-(k_s - r_f)T}. \tag{9.25}$$

Note that if the underlying asset is riskless, then $k_s = r_f$ and the forward price equals the expected spot price, as assumed in Eq. (9.13). Otherwise, if the underlying asset is risky, the forward price is the expected spot price discounted at a risk-adjusted rate, $e^{-(k_s - r_f)T}$.

Figure 9.8 graphs the end-of-period payoffs from our synthetic forward (or futures) contract. The solid line in Fig. 9.8 has the same end-of-period payouts as a futures contract, where delivery is accepted, and it requires no initial cash outlay. Hence when options on an asset or commodity are traded, but there is no futures market, it is always possible to construct a synthetic futures contract. There are problems, however. For example, the options are usually American options, which means the synthetic future can be disrupted if the American put is exercised early. Also, as we

---

[14] This is the same as Eq. (9.14).

have emphasized throughout, the synthetic future is really a forward contract since no daily marking to market is required.

2. Options on Futures

Options are traded on futures on stock market indices, on Treasury instruments, on foreign exchange rates, and on some metals. Since these options are merely contingent claims on the underlying risky assets, one would think that they could be priced using the Black-Scholes formula. Unfortunately, this is not quite true. Ramaswamy and Sundaresan [1985] have shown (1) that even with constant interest rates, premature exercise may be optimal and (2) that the fact that interest rates are stochastic is crucial for pricing options on futures.

To show why early exercise may be optimal, even with constant interest rates, it is useful to recognize that an option on a futures contract has the same payouts as an option on a portfolio with the same random price realizations as the futures contract but which pays a continuous dividend at the riskless rate of interest. Consider a generalization of Eq. (9.14), where the futures price was shown to be the spot price multiplied by a compounding factor:

$$_tF_T = S_t e^{_t r_T}. \tag{9.14}$$

The generalization is to define the rate of compounding as the risk-free rate plus (or minus) a risk premium, δ:

$$_t r_T = r_{f(T,t)} - \delta_{T,t}.$$

Thus the current futures price can be written as

$$_tF_T = S_t e^{(r_{f(T,t)} - \delta_{T,t})}. \tag{9.26}$$

If $r_f > \delta$, the futures price will be at a premium relative to the spot price throughout the contract's life (contango), and if $\delta > r_f$ the futures price will be at a discount (backwardation). Of course, as the contract approaches maturity the futures and spot prices will become equal. The dynamics of the futures price involve an "implicit dividend" flow, thereby suggesting that it may be optimal to exercise American calls (or puts) prematurely if the value of the exercise price reinvested at the riskless rate exceeds the value of the "implicit dividend" flow. Ramaswamy and Sundaresan [1985] have shown, under a reasonable set of parameters, that the value of early exercise is small.

Stochastic interest rates, however, can have a relatively important effect on the value of options on futures. If the riskless rate is expected to drift upward (because the term structure is upward sloping), then $r_{f(T,t)}$ in Eq. (9.26) will be expected to increase through time, thereby altering the expected implicit dividend and the option value. Numerical solution methods to simulate values for options on futures, employed by Ramaswamy and Sundaresan, show this effect to be relatively important.[15]

---

[15] Their model assumes the variance of the futures contract price is constant over the life of the contract but empirical evidence indicates that it increases.

SUMMARY

Futures contracts give one the right to receive delivery of a risky asset or commodity at a predetermined future date at a price agreed upon today. No cash changes hands at the time of purchase of the contract. Unlike forward contracts, which are usually bilateral contracts between two parties, futures contracts are marked to market each day via a clearinghouse. This procedure provides liquidity to the market and allows open interest to far exceed the quantity of the underlying asset to be delivered.

Most futures contracts are traded on margin, which has an opportunity cost to investors. Price limits on futures contracts are (imperfect) substitutes for margin levels, and therefore we can predict that contracts on assets with active spot markets will have low margins and no price limits, but when spot markets are thin (as with orange juice futures) price limits will play an important role.

Futures contract prices are determined by storage costs, by convenience yields, and probably by a risk premium, although the risk premium is not a function of the CAPM beta. The variance of futures prices appears to increase as the contract comes closer to maturity. Futures prices provide better forecasts of future spot prices than do current spot prices for those commodities where inventory levels are relatively low, e.g., for agricultural and animal commodities.

PROBLEM SET

9.1 Most futures contracts have fairly short lives, usually less than 18 months. Why are there not futures contracts with longer lives?

9.2 Suppose you observe the following yields on T-bills and T-bill futures contracts on January 5, 1991:

	Yield
March futures contract on a 90-day T-bill (futures contract matures in 77 days on March 22)	12.5%
167-day T-bill	10.0
77-day T-bill	6.0

a) What arbitrage position should you undertake in order to make a certain profit with no risk and no net investment?

b) How much profit do you expect to make from your arbitrage position?

9.3 Your team of agricultural experts has observed that spot prices of rutabagas show a definite pattern, rising from January through June, then falling toward a December low. You wish to buy contracts for May delivery.

a) What effect does the trend in spot prices have on the time pattern of the futures price for May contracts?

b) What effect does the trend in spot prices have on the variance of prices for May contracts sold in February?

9.4 Suppose you can buy or sell European puts and calls on the common stock of the XYZ Corporation, which has a current share price of $30, has a rate of return standard deviation of .3, and pays no dividends. The exercise price on six-month puts and calls is $35, and the risk-free rate is 7% per year. You believe the stock price will rise and wish to create a synthetic forward contract position for delivery of 100 shares six months hence.

a) How do you construct the synthetic futures position; how much must you borrow or lend?

b) What is your expected profit if you believe the share price will be $42 six months from now?

9.5 On January 29, 1987, you could buy a March 1987 silver contract for $5.610 per ounce and at the same time sell a March 1988 contract for $6.008 an ounce.

a) Exactly what would you have done had you taken these positions?

b) If the annual riskless rate of interest were 8%, would the position be profitable? Why or why not?

9.6 Suppose you believe your portfolio, which has a beta of 1.0, has been selected to outperform other portfolios of similar risk but you know you cannot predict which way the market will move. If it goes down, you will outperform the market but will still have a negative rate of return. What can you do to alleviate your timing risk?

9.7 Suppose you are convinced that the spread between long- and short-term rates will widen, whereas everyone else thinks it will remain constant. Unfortunately, you do not know whether the general level of interest rates will go up or down. What can you do?

9.8 Your bank is exploring the possibility of using T-bond futures to minimize the exposure of shareholders to changes in the interest rate. The market value of major assets and liabilities is given in the balance sheet below:

Market Value of Assets		Market Value of Liabilities	
Cash and reserves	$ 180MM	Demand deposits	$ 900MM
Loans	820MM	Equity	100MM
	$1,000MM		$1,000MM

The economics staff has used the rates of return on the asset and liability positions to compute the following long-run standard deviations and correlations:

	Standard Deviation	Correlation with T-Bond Futures
Cash and reserves	0	0
Loans	.06	+.30
Demand deposits	.02	+.15
T-bond futures	.08	1.00

If the current market value is $80,000 for a T-bond futures contract with a $100,000 face value, how many T-bond contracts will be needed to minimize shareholders' risk exposure to interest rate fluctuations?

REFERENCES

Anderson, R., "Comments on 'Margins and Futures Contracts,'" *Journal of Futures Markets*, Summer 1981, 259–264.

———, "Some Determinants of the Volatility of Futures Prices," *Journal of Futures Markets*, Fall 1985, 331–348.

————, and J. Danthine, "The Time Pattern of Hedging and the Volatility of Futures Prices," *Review of Economic Studies*, April 1983, 249–266.

Ball, C., and W. Torous, "Futures Options and the Volatility of Futures Prices," *Journal of Finance*, September 1986, 857–870.

Black, F., "The Pricing of Commodity Options," *Journal of Financial Economics*, March 1976, 167–179.

Bodie, Z., and V. Rosansky, "Risk and Return in Commodities Futures," *Financial Analysts Journal*, May-June 1980, 27–39.

Breeden, D., "Consumption Risk in Futures Markets," *Journal of Finance*, May 1980, 503–520.

Brennan, M. J., "The Supply of Storage," *American Economic Review*, March 1958, 50–72.

Brennan, M. "The Cost of Convenience and the Pricing of Commodity Contingent Claims," Working Paper, UCLA, 1986a.

————, "A Theory of Price Limits in Futures Markets," *Journal of Financial Economics*, June 1986b, 213–234.

Brenner, M.; G. Courtadon; and M. Subrahmanyam, "Options on the Spot and Options on Futures," *Journal of Finance*, December 1985, 1303–1317.

Capozza, D., and B. Cornell, "Treasury Bill Pricing in the Spot and Futures Markets," *Review of Economics and Statistics*, November 1979, 513–520.

Carlton, D., "Futures Markets: Their Purpose, Their History, Their Growth, Their Successes and Failures," *Journal of Futures Markets*, Fall 1984, 237–271.

Carter, C. A.; G. C. Rausser; and A. Schmitz, "Efficient Asset Portfolios and the Theory of Normal Backwardation," *Journal of Political Economy*, April 1983, 319–331.

Chang, E., "Returns to Speculators and the Theory of Normal Backwardation," *Journal of Finance*, March 1985, 193–208.

Constantinides, G. M., "Capital Market Equilibrium with Personal Tax," *Econometrica*, May 1983, 611–636.

Cootner, P., "Returns to Speculators: Telser vs. Keynes," *Journal of Political Economy*, August 1960, 396–414.

Cornell, B., and K. French, "The Pricing of Stock Index Futures," *Journal of Futures Markets*, Spring 1983a, 1–14.

————, "Taxes and the Pricing of Stock Index Futures," *Journal of Finance*, June 1983b, 675–694.

Cornell, B., and M. Reinganum, "Forward and Futures Prices: Evidence from the Foreign Exchange Markets," *Journal of Finance*, December 1981, 1035–1045.

Cox, J. C.; J. E. Ingersoll; and S. A. Ross, "The Relation between Forward Prices and Futures Prices," *Journal of Financial Economics*, December 1981, 321–346.

Dusak, K., "Futures Trading and Investor Returns: An Investigation of Commodity Market Risk Premiums," *Journal of Political Economy*, November–December 1973, 1387–1406.

Fama, E., and K. French, "Business Cycles and the Behavior of Metals Prices," Working Paper #31–86, UCLA, 1986.

————, "Commodity Futures Prices: Some Evidence on the Forecast Power, Premiums, and the Theory of Storage," *Journal of Business*, January 1987, 55–73.

Figlewski, S., "Margins and Market Integrity: Margin Setting for Stock Index Futures and Options," *Journal of Futures Markets*, Fall 1984, 385–416.

French, K., "Detecting Spot Price Forecasts in Futures Prices," *Journal of Business*, April 1986, 539–554.

Gay, G., and S. Manaster, "The Quality Option Implicit in Futures Contracts," *Journal of Financial Economics*, September 1984, 353–370.

Grauer, F., and R. Litzenberger, "The Pricing of Commodity Futures Contracts, Nominal Bonds and Other Assets under Commodity Price Uncertainty," *Journal of Finance*, March 1979, 69–83.

Hansen, L. P., and R. J. Hodrick, "Forward Exchange Rates as Optimal Predictors of Future Spot Rates: An Econometric Analysis," *Journal of Political Economy*, October 1980, 829–853.

Hartzmark, M. L., "The Effect of Changing Margin Levels on Futures Market Activity, the Composition of Traders in the Market, and Price Performance," *Journal of Business*, April 1986, S147–S180.

Hazuka, T., "Consumption Betas and Backwardation in Commodity Markets," *Journal of Finance*, July 1984, 647–655.

Hemmler, M., "The Quality Delivery Option in Treasury Bond Futures Contracts," Ph.D. dissertation, University of Chicago, 1987.

Hicks, J. R., *Value and Capital*, 2nd ed. Oxford University Press, Oxford, 1946.

Hirshleifer, D., "Risk, Equilibrium, and Futures Markets," Ph.D. dissertation, University of Chicago, 1984.

————, "Residual Risk, Trading Costs and Commodity Risk Premia," Working Paper, UCLA, 1986.

Houthakker, H. S., "The Scope and Limits of Futures Trading," in Abramovitz, ed., *The Allocation of Economic Resources*. Stanford University Press, Stanford, 1959.

Jagannathan, Ravi, "An Investigation of Commodity Futures Prices Using the Consumption-Based Intertemporal Capital Asset Pricing Model," *Journal of Finance*, March 1985, 175–191.

Kaldor, N., "Speculation and Economic Stability," *Review of Economic Studies*, October 1939, 1–27.

Keynes, J. M., "Some Aspects of Commodity Markets," *Manchester Guardian Commercial, European Reconstruction Series*, Section 13, March 29, 1923, 784–786.

Kolb, R., *Understanding Futures Markets*, Scott, Foresman and Company, Glenview, Ill. 1985.

————, and R. Chiang, "Improving Hedging Performance Using Interest Rate Futures," *Financial Management*, Autumn 1981, 72–79.

————, "Immunization and Hedging with Interest Rate Futures," *Journal of Financial Research*, Summer 1982, 161–170.

Kolb, R.; G. Gay; and J. Jordan, "Are There Arbitrage Opportunities in the Treasury-Bond Futures Market?" *Journal of Futures Markets*, Fall 1982, 217–230.

Milonas, N., "Price Variability and the Maturity Effect in Futures Markets," *Journal of Futures Markets*, Fall 1986, 443–460.

Modest, D., and M. Sundaresan, "The Relationship between Spot and Futures Prices in Stock Index Futures Markets: Some Preliminary Evidence," *Journal of Futures Markets*, Spring 1983, 15–41.

Oldfield, G., and C. Rovira, "Futures Contract Options," *Journal of Futures Markets*, Winter 1984, 479–490.

Pashigian, B. P., "The Political Economy of Futures Market Regulation," *Journal of Business*, April 1986, S55–S84.

Ramaswamy, K., and M. Sundaresan, "The Valuation of Options on Futures Contracts," *Journal of Finance*, December 1985, 1319–1340.

Rendleman, R., and C. Carabini, "The Efficiency of the Treasury Bill Futures Market," *Journal of Finance*, September 1979, 895–914.

Richard, S., and M. Sundaresan, "A Continuous Time Equilibrium Model of Forward Prices and Futures Prices in a Multigood Economy," *Journal of Financial Economics*, December 1981, 347–371.

Roll, R., "Orange Juice and Weather," *American Economic Review*, December 1984, 861–880.

Salmon, J. W., "The Emergence of Organized Futures Markets: The Distribution of Consumption Risk," Ph.D. dissertation, University of California at Los Angeles, 1985.

Samuelson, P., "Proof that Properly Anticipated Prices Fluctuate Randomly," *Industrial Management Review*, Spring 1965, 41–49.

———, "Proof that Properly Discounted Present Values of Assets Vibrate Randomly," in Nagatani and Crowley, eds., *Collected Scientific Papers of Paul A. Samuelson*, Vol. IV. MIT Press, Cambridge, Mass., 1977.

Shastri, K., and K. Tandon, "Options on Futures Contracts: A Comparison of European and American Pricing Models," *Journal of Futures Markets*, Winter 1986, 593–618.

Telser, L., "Futures Trading and the Storage of Cotton and Wheat," *Journal of Political Economy*, June 1958, 233–255.

———, "Margins and Futures Contracts," *Journal of Futures Markets*, Summer 1981a, 225–253.

———, "Why Are There Organized Futures Markets?" *Journal of Law and Economics*, April 1981b, 1–22.

Wolf, A., "Options on Futures: Pricing and the Effect of an Anticipated Price Change," *Journal of Futures Markets*, Winter 1984, 491–512.

Working, H., "Theory of the Price of Storage," *American Economic Review*, December 1949, 1254–1262.

———, "Futures Trading and Hedging," *American Economic Review*, June 1953, 312–343.

———, "Economic Functions of Futures Markets," in Peck, ed., *Selected Writings of Holbrook Working*. Board of Trade of the City of Chicago, 1977.

10

*In a world of uncertainty, information becomes a useful commodity—
acquisition of information to eliminate uncertainty should then be
considered as an alternative to productive investment subject to
uncertainty.*

J. Hirshleifer, *Investment, Interest, and Capital*, Prentice-Hall,
Englewood Cliffs, N.J., 1970, 311

Efficient Capital Markets: Theory

A. DEFINING CAPITAL MARKET EFFICIENCY

The purpose of capital markets is to transfer funds between lenders (savers) and borrowers (producers) efficiently. Individuals or firms may have an excess of productive investment opportunities with anticipated rates of return that exceed the market-determined borrowing rate but not enough funds to take advantage of all these opportunities. However, if capital markets exist, they can borrow the needed funds. Lenders, who have excess funds after exhausting all their productive opportunities with expected returns greater than the borrowing rate, will be willing to lend their excess funds because the borrowing/lending rate is higher than what they might otherwise earn. Therefore both borrowers and lenders are better off if efficient capital markets are used to facilitate fund transfers. The borrowing/lending rate is used as an important piece of information by each producer, who will accept projects until the rate of return on the least profitable project just equals the opportunity cost of external funds (the borrowing/lending rate). Thus a market is said to be *allocationally efficient* when prices are determined in a way that equates the *marginal* rates of return (adjusted for risk) for all producers and savers. In an allocationally efficient market, scarce savings are optimally allocated to productive investments in a way that benefits everyone.

To describe efficient capital markets it is useful, first of all, to contrast them with *perfect capital markets*. The following conditions are necessary for perfect capital markets:

- Markets are frictionless; i.e., there are no transactions costs or taxes, all assets are perfectly divisible and marketable, and there are no constraining regulations.
- There is perfect competition in product and securities markets. In product markets this means that all producers supply goods and services at minimum average cost, and in securities markets it means that all participants are price takers.
- Markets are informationally efficient; i.e., information is costless, and it is received simultaneously by all individuals.
- All individuals are rational expected utility maximizers.

Given these conditions both product and securities markets will be both allocationally and operationally efficient. *Allocational efficiency* has already been defined, but what about *operational efficiency*? Operational efficiency deals with the cost of transferring funds. In the idealized world of perfect capital markets, transactions costs are assumed to be zero; therefore we have perfect operational efficiency.[1] However, we shall see later, when we focus on empirical studies of real-world phenomena, that operational efficiency is indeed an important consideration.

Capital market efficiency is much less restrictive than the notion of perfect capital markets outlined above. In an efficient capital market, prices fully and instantaneously reflect all available relevant information. This means that when assets are traded, prices are accurate signals for capital allocation.

To show the difference between perfect markets and efficient capital markets we can relax some of the perfect market assumptions. For example, we can still have efficient capital markets if markets are not frictionless. Prices will still fully reflect all available information if, e.g., securities traders have to pay brokerage fees or if an individual's human capital (which, after all, is an asset) cannot be divided into a thousand parts and auctioned off. More important, there can be imperfect competition in product markets and we still have efficient capital markets. Hence if a firm can reap monopoly profits in the product market, the efficient capital market will determine a security price that fully reflects the present value of the anticipated stream of monopoly profits. Hence we can have allocative inefficiencies in product markets but still have efficient capital markets. Finally, it is not necessary to have costless information in efficient capital markets. This point is discussed in greater detail in section E of this chapter.

Still, in a somewhat limited sense, efficient capital markets imply operational efficiency as well as asset prices that are allocationally efficient. Asset prices are correct signals in the sense that they fully and instantaneously reflect all available relevant information and are useful for directing the flow of funds from savers to investment projects that yield the highest return (even though the return may reflect monopolistic practices in product markets). Capital markets are operationally efficient if intermediaries, who provide the service of channeling funds from savers to investors, do so at the minimum cost that provides them a fair return for their services.

---

[1] Note that even in perfect markets the minimum cost of transferring funds may not be zero if the transfer of funds also involves risk bearing.

Fama [1970, 1976] has done a great deal to operationalize the notion of capital market efficiency. He defines three types of efficiency, each of which is based on a different notion of exactly what type of information is understood to be relevant in the phrase "all prices fully reflect all *relevant* information."

1. *Weak-form efficiency.* No investor can earn excess returns by developing trading rules based on historical price or return information. In other words, the information in past prices or returns is not useful or relevant in achieving excess returns.

2. *Semistrong-form efficiency.* No investor can earn excess returns from trading rules based on any publicly available information. Examples of publicly available information are annual reports of companies, investment advisory data such as "Heard on the Street" in the *Wall Street Journal*, or ticker tape information.

3. *Strong-form efficiency.* No investor can earn excess returns using any information, whether publicly available or not.

Obviously, the last type of market efficiency is very strong indeed. If markets were efficient in their strong form, prices would fully reflect all information even though it might be held exclusively by a corporate insider. Suppose, e.g., we know that our company has just discovered how to control nuclear fusion. Even before we have a chance to trade based on the news, the strong form of market efficiency predicts that prices will have adjusted so that we cannot profit.

Rubinstein [1975] and Latham [1985] have extended the definition of market efficiency. The market is said to be efficient with regard to an information event if the information causes no portfolio changes. It is possible that people might disagree about the implications of a piece of information so that some buy an asset and others sell in such a way that the market price is unaffected. If the information does not change prices, then the market is said to be efficient with regard to the information in the Fama [1976] sense but not in the Rubinstein [1975] or Latham [1985] sense. The Rubinstein-Latham definition requires not only that there be no price change but also that there be no transactions. Hence it is a stronger form of market efficiency than even the Fama strong-form efficiency mentioned above.

B. A FORMAL DEFINITION OF THE VALUE OF INFORMATION

The notion of efficient capital markets depends on the precise definition of information and the value of information.[2] An *information structure* may be defined as a message about various events which may happen. For example, the message "There are no clouds in the sky" provides a probability distribution for the likelihood of rain within the next 24 hours. This message may have various values to different people depending on (1) whether or not they can take any actions based on the message and (2)

---

[2] For an excellent review of the economics of information, see Hirshleifer and Riley [1979].

what net benefits (gain in utility) will result from their actions. For example, a message related to rainfall can be of value to farmers, who can act on the information to increase their wealth. If there is to be no rain, the farmers might decide that it would be a good time to harvest hay. On the other hand, messages about rainfall have no value to deep-pit coal miners because such information probably will not alter the miners' actions at all.

A formal expression of the above concept defines the value of an information structure, $V(\eta)$, as

$$V(\eta) \equiv \sum_m q(m) \; \text{MAX}_a \sum_e p(e|m)U(a, e) - V(\eta_0), \qquad (10.1)$$

where

$q(m) = $ the marginal probability of receiving a message m;

$p(e|m) = $ the conditional probability of an event e, given a message m;

$U(a, e) = $ the utility resulting from an action a if an event e occurs; we shall call this a *benefit function*;

$V(\eta_0) = $ the expected utility of the decision maker without the information.

According to Eq. (10.1), a decision maker will evaluate an information structure (which, for the sake of generality, is defined as a set of messages) by choosing an action that will maximize his or her expected utility, given the arrival of a message. For example, if we receive a message (one of many that we could have received) that there is a 20% chance of rain, we may carry an umbrella because of the high "disutility" of getting drenched and the low cost of carrying it. For each possible message we can determine our optimal action. Mathematically, this is the solution to the problem:

$$\text{MAX}_a \sum_e p(e|m)U(a, e).$$

Finally, by weighting the expected utility of each optimal action (in response to all possible messages) by the probability, $q(m)$, of receiving the message that gives rise to the action, the decision maker knows the expected utility of the entire set of messages, which we call the *expected utility* (or *utility value*) of an information set, $V(\eta)$.

The following example applies the value-of-information concept to the theory of portfolio choice. We will choose our optimal portfolio as a combination of two funds: either the risk-free asset that yields 6%, or the market portfolio that may yield 16% or 10% or −5%.[3] Assume that we know the standard deviation of the market portfolio, σ_m, with certainty. Figure 10.1 shows the linear efficient set (the capital market line) for two of the three possible states of the world. As risk-averse investors, in this case, we will maximize our expected utility by choosing the portfolio where our indifference curve is tangent to the efficient set.

To calculate the value of an information set we need to know the payoff function $U(a, e)$, which tells us the utility of having taken a course of action, a, when an event

---

[3] A more general, but also more complicated, example would assign a continuous probability distribution to the possible returns offered by the market portfolio.

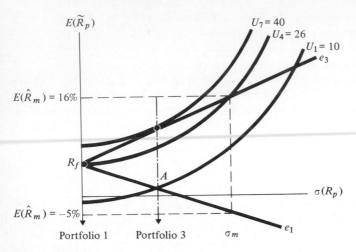

Figure 10.1
Optimal choices for two states of the world.

or state of the world, e, occurs. For the sake of convenience, we will label the three states of the world by their market returns: $e_3 = 16\%$, $e_2 = 10\%$, and $e_1 = -5\%$.

If the market return were 16%, we would choose portfolio 3 in Fig. 10.1, which is where indifference curve U_7 is tangent to the capital market line e_3. On the other hand, we would put all our portfolio in the risk-free asset (portfolio 1) if the market return were known to be -5%. This occurs where indifference curve U_4 passes through R_f. If we choose portfolio 3, and if the market rate of return really is 16%, then our payoff is $U_7 = 40$. But if we make a mistake and choose portfolio 3 when the market rate of return turns out to be -5%, our portfolio is suboptimal. After the fact, we would have been much better off with portfolio 1, the risk-free asset. Our utility for holding portfolio 3 when state 1 obtains (point A in Fig. 10.1) is $U_1 = 10$ less our regret, which is the difference between where we actually are and where we would like to be.[4] In this case our regret is the difference between U_4 and U_1. Therefore our net utility is $U_1 - (U_4 - U_1) = 2U_1 - U_4 = -6$. When we receive a message that provides estimates of the likelihood of future states of the world, we will choose an action (in our example this amounts to choosing a portfolio) that will maximize our expected utility, given that message. The utility provided by each portfolio choice (i.e., each action) in each state of the world can be taken from Fig. 10.2, which is similar to Fig. 10.1 except that it gives all possible portfolios and states of the world. The corresponding benefit function, $U(a, e)$, is given in Table 10.1.

In addition to a benefit matrix it is also necessary to have an information structure (a Markov matrix) that gives the probability that an event will actually occur, given that a particular message has been received. The two obvious polar cases are

---

[4] Needless to say, the computation of "regret" as suggested here is not necessarily accurate and is only for purposes of illustration. However, it is consistent with the fact that utilities may be state contingent. (See Chapter 5, "State-Preference Theory.")

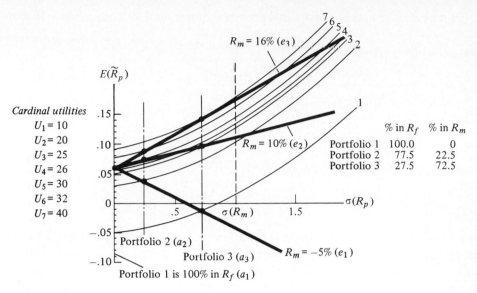

Figure 10.2
Optimal actions, given various states of the world.

perfect information and no information. Their matrices are given in Table 10.2. If the information structure is perfect, receipt of a message implies that a given state of the world will occur with certainty. This makes it easy to select a course of action that results in the highest utility. If you receive m_1, then the state of the world e_1 will obtain with certainty; therefore the best action is a_1, with expected utility $U_4 = 26$. Thus for each message it is possible to find the optimal action. Implicitly this procedure amounts to solving Eq. (10.1), which tells us the utility value of information.

Table 10.1   Benefit Function $U(a, e)$

Action	$e_1(R_m = -5\%)$	$e_2(R_m = 10\%)$	$e_3(R_m = 16\%)$
Portfolio 1 (action a_1)	$U_4 = 26$	$2U_4 - U_5 = 22$	$2U_4 - U_7 = 12$
Portfolio 2 (action a_2)	$2U_2 - U_4 = 14$	$U_5 = 30$	$2U_6 - U_7 = 24$
Portfolio 3 (action a_3)	$2U_1 - U_4 = -6$	$2U_3 - U_5 = 20$	$U_7 = 40$

Table 10.2   Information Structures

	η_2 = perfect information				η_0 = no information				η_1 = noisy information		
	m_1	m_2	m_3		m_1	m_2	m_3		m_1	m_2	m_3
e_1	1.0	0	0	e_1	$\frac{1}{3}$	$\frac{1}{3}$	$\frac{1}{3}$	e_1	.6	.3	.1
e_2	0	1.0	0	e_2	$\frac{1}{3}$	$\frac{1}{3}$	$\frac{1}{3}$	e_2	.2	.5	.3
e_3	0	0	1.0	e_3	$\frac{1}{3}$	$\frac{1}{3}$	$\frac{1}{3}$	e_3	.2	.2	.6

Given perfect information, the optimal action (and its utility) for each message is seen to be:

Message	Optimal Action	Utility
m_1	a_1 (invest in portfolio 1)	26
m_2	a_2 (invest in portfolio 2)	30
m_3	a_3 (invest in portfolio 3)	40

These actions represent the solution to one part of the value of information, i.e., Eq. (10.1):

$$\underset{a}{\text{MAX}} \sum_e p(e|m)U(a, e).$$

Finally, the utility of each action that results from a message is weighted by the probability of the message. In our example each of the three messages is assumed to be equally likely; therefore, using the notation of Eq. (10.1), we have $q(m_1) = \frac{1}{3}$, $q(m_2) = \frac{1}{3}$, and $q(m_3) = \frac{1}{3}$. The utility value of perfect information is

$$V(\eta_2) = \tfrac{1}{3}(26) + \tfrac{1}{3}(30) + \tfrac{1}{3}(40) = 32.$$

It is also useful to compute the dollar value of this information set to the ith individual. Of course, different individuals will have different utility functions and therefore different demand curves for a given information set. But for now we will focus only on the dollar value of information to one individual.[5] Suppose his utility function is

$$U(W) = 10 \ln(W - \$100).$$

Then if the expected utility of perfect information is 32 utiles, the corresponding dollar value is

$$32 = 10 \ln(W(\eta_2) - \$100),$$

$$3.2 = \ln(W(\eta_2) - \$100),$$

$$\$24.5325 = W(\eta_2) - \$100,$$

$$\$124.53 = W(\eta_2).$$

This is the increment to wealth that the ith individual would receive were he or she to acquire the information (at no cost).

Next, consider the value of no information. In Table 10.2 we see that no information means that all messages are identical. Each says the same thing: "All events are equally likely." For example, suppose a friend asks whether or not a movie was worth seeing. If we always reply yes, whether or not the movie is good, then the message contains no information. If we always say no, the result is the same—no information. In the example at hand, when asked about the probability of a state of the

---

[5] For more on this topic see Huang, Vertinsky, and Ziemba [1977].

world, we always answer, "One third." To compute the value of no information, we begin just as before, by selecting the optimal action for each message. For example, let us assume that we receive message 1:

If we take action	the expected utility is
a_1 (invest in portfolio 1)	$\frac{1}{3}(26) + \frac{1}{3}(22) + \frac{1}{3}(12) = 20$
a_2 (invest in portfolio 2)	$\frac{1}{3}(14) + \frac{1}{3}(30) + \frac{1}{3}(24) = 22.67$
a_3 (invest in portfolio 3)	$\frac{1}{3}(-6) + \frac{1}{3}(20) + \frac{1}{3}(40) = 18$

Suppose we receive message 2:

If we take action	the expected utility is
a_1 (invest in portfolio 1)	$\frac{1}{3}(26) + \frac{1}{3}(22) + \frac{1}{3}(12) = 20$
a_2 (invest in portfolio 2)	$\frac{1}{3}(14) + \frac{1}{3}(30) + \frac{1}{3}(24) = 22.67$
a_3 (invest in portfolio 3)	$\frac{1}{3}(-6) + \frac{1}{3}(20) + \frac{1}{3}(40) = 18$

And if we receive message 3 the expected utilities of our actions are the same (obviously, since the three messages are the same). Regardless of the message, our optimal action is always the same—invest in portfolio 2; and our expected utility is 22.67. As with perfect information the selection of optimal actions, given various messages, is the first part of the problem. The second part is to weight the expected utility of an action, given a message, by the probability of the message. The result is the utility value of information. The utility value of no information is

$$V(\eta_0) = \tfrac{1}{3}(22.67) + \tfrac{1}{3}(22.67) + \tfrac{1}{3}(22.67) = 22.67.$$

Using the same utility function as above, the dollar value of information in this case is $W(\eta_0) = \$109.65$. The difference between the dollar value of perfect information and no information is the maximum gain from information for the ith individual:

$$W(\eta_2) - W(\eta_0) = \$14.88.$$

Finally, consider the third information structure in Table 10.2. In this case the messages received are noisy. The first message says that there is a .6 probability that the first state of the world might obtain, but .4 of the time the message will err, with a .2 probability that e_2 will actually occur and a .2 probability that e_3 will obtain. To value the noisy information, we proceed as before. We choose the optimal action, given a message. For example, let us assume that m_1 is received.

If we take action	the expected utility is
a_1 (invest in portfolio 1)	$.6(26) + .2(22) + .2(12) = 22.4$
a_2 (invest in portfolio 2)	$.6(14) + .2(30) + .2(24) = 19.2$
a_3 (invest in portfolio 3)	$.6(-6) + .2(20) + .2(40) = 8.4$

Therefore the optimal action is to invest in portfolio 1 if message 1 is received. Similarly,

If we receive	the optimal action is	with expected utility
m_2	a_2	24.0
m_3	a_3	29.4

Finally, if we weight the utility of the optimal actions, given the three messages, by the probability of the messages, we have the utility value of the noisy information structure:

$$V(\eta_1) = \tfrac{1}{3}(22.4) + \tfrac{1}{3}(24) + \tfrac{1}{3}(29.4) = 25.27.$$

Its corresponding dollar value, for the ith individual, is $W(\eta_1) = \$112.52$.

C. THE RELATIONSHIP BETWEEN THE VALUE OF INFORMATION AND EFFICIENT CAPITAL MARKETS

Equation (10.1) can be used to evaluate any information structure. It also points out some ideas that are only implicit in the definition of *efficient markets*. Fama [1976] defines efficient capital markets as those where the joint distribution of security prices, $f_m(P_{1t}, P_{2t}, \ldots, P_{nt}|\eta_{t-1}^m)$, given the set of information that the *market uses* to determine security prices at $t-1$, is identical to the joint distribution of prices that would exist if *all relevant information* available at $t-1$ were used, $f(P_{1t}, P_{2t}, \ldots, P_{nt}|\eta_{t-1})$. Mathematically, this is

$$f_m(P_{1t}, \ldots, P_{nt}|\dot{\eta}_{t-1}^m) = f(P_{1t}, \ldots, P_{nt}|\eta_{t-1}). \qquad (10.2)$$

If an information structure is to have value, it must accurately tell us something we do not already know. If the distribution of prices in time period t (which was predicted in the previous time period $t-1$ and based on the information structure the market uses) is not different from the prices predicted by using all relevant information from the previous time period, then there must be no difference between the information the market uses and the set of all relevant information. This is the essence of an efficient capital market—it instantaneously and fully reflects all relevant information. Using information theory, this also means that *net of costs*, the utility value of the gain from information to the ith individual, must be zero:

$$V(\eta_i) - V(\eta_0) \equiv 0. \qquad (10.3)$$

For example, consider capital markets that are efficient in their weak form. The relevant information structure, η_i, is defined to be the set of historical prices on all assets. If capital markets are efficient, then Eq. (10.2) says that the distribution of security prices today has already incorporated past price histories. In other words, it is not possible to develop trading rules (courses of action) based on past prices that will allow anyone to beat the market. Equation (10.3) says that no one would pay anything for the information set of historical prices. The value of the information is zero. Empirical evidence on trading rules that use past price data is discussed in section F of this chapter.

It is important to emphasize that the value of information is determined net of costs. These include the cost of undertaking courses of action and the costs of transmitting and evaluating messages. Some of these costs in securities markets are transactions costs: e.g., brokerage fees, bid-ask spreads, costs involved in searching for the best price (if more than one price is quoted), and taxes, as well as data costs and analysts' fees. The capital market is efficient relative to a given information set only after consideration of the costs of acquiring messages and taking actions pursuant to a particular information structure.

D. RATIONAL EXPECTATIONS AND MARKET EFFICIENCY

The utility value of information has three parts: (1) the utilities of the payoffs, given an action; (2) the optimal actions, given receipt of a message; and (3) the probabilities of states of nature provided by the messages. We are interested in understanding how the individual's decision-making process, given the receipt of information, is reflected in the market prices of assets. This is not easy because it is impossible to observe the quantity and quality of information or the timing of its receipt in the real world. There is even disagreement among theorists about what information will be used by investors. For example, Forsythe, Palfrey, and Plott [1982] identify four different hypotheses. Each hypothesis assumes that investors know with certainty what their own payoffs will be across time, but they also know that different individuals may pay different prices because of differing preferences.

The first hypothesis is particularly nonsensical (call it the *naive hypothesis*) in that it asserts that asset prices are completely arbitrary and unrelated either to how much they will pay out in the future or to the probabilities of various payouts. The second hypothesis, call it the *speculative equilibrium hypothesis*, is captured in a quote taken from Keynes's *General Theory* [1936, 156]:

> *Professional investment may be likened to those newspaper competitions in which the competitors have to pick out the six prettiest faces from a hundred photographs, the prize being awarded to the competitor whose choice most nearly corresponds to the average preferences of the competitors as a whole; so that each competitor has to pick, not those faces which he himself finds the prettiest, but those which he thinks likeliest to catch the fancy of the other competitors, all of whom are looking at the problem from the same point of view. It is not a case of choosing those which, to the best of one's judgement, are really the prettiest, nor even those which average opinion genuinely thinks the prettiest. We have reached the third degree where we devote our intelligences to anticipating what average opinion expects the average opinion to be. And there are some, I believe, who practice the fourth, fifth and higher degrees.*

Table 10.3   Parameters for an Experimental Double Auction Spot Market

Investor Type	Initial Working Capital	Initial Shares Held	Fixed Cost	Dividends (francs)	
				Period A	Period B
I (3 people)	10,000 francs	2 shares	10,000 francs	300	50
II (3 people)	10,000 francs	2 shares	10,000 francs	50	300
III (3 people)	10,000 francs	2 shares	10,000 francs	150	250

We might debate about what Keynes really meant, but one interpretation is that all investors base their investment decisions entirely on their anticipation of other individuals' behavior without any necessary relationship to the actual payoffs that the assets are expected to provide. The third hypothesis is that asset prices are systematically related to their future payouts. Called the *intrinsic value hypothesis*, it says that prices will be determined by each individual's estimate of the payoffs of an asset without consideration of its resale value to other individuals. The fourth hypothesis may be called the *rational expectations hypothesis*. It predicts that prices are formed on the basis of the expected future payouts of the assets, including their resale value to third parties. Thus a rational expectations market is an efficient market because prices will reflect all information.

To make these hypotheses more concrete it is useful to review an experiment by Forsythe, Palfrey, and Plott [1982]. They set up an oral double auction market that had two time periods, one asset, and three "types" of individuals. An oral double auction market is one where individuals can call out both buying and selling prices for an asset. The largest market of this type is the New York Stock Exchange. All participants knew exactly how much the asset would pay them in each time period. They also knew that the asset would pay different amounts to the other market participants, but not how much. Thus the asset had different values to different individuals. Table 10.3 shows the experimental parameters. If you held an asset at the end of the first time period, you received 300, 50, or 150 "francs," depending on whether you were individual type I, II or III.[6] The differences in the franc payouts across individuals were designed to reflect differences among individual preferences and information sets at an instant in time. Each individual was endowed with 10,000 francs in working capital and two shares.[7] The 10,000 franc endowment was paid back at the end of the second time period (this is the fixed cost column in Table 10.3), but any dividends received and any trading profits were kept by the market participants.

The interesting question is, What will the market equilibrium prices be at the end of each of the two time periods? If either of the intrinsic value or rational expectations hypotheses are true, the period B price should be 300 francs (or very

---

[6] Each "franc" was worth $0.002.

[7] No short sales were allowed; thus the supply of assets was fixed.

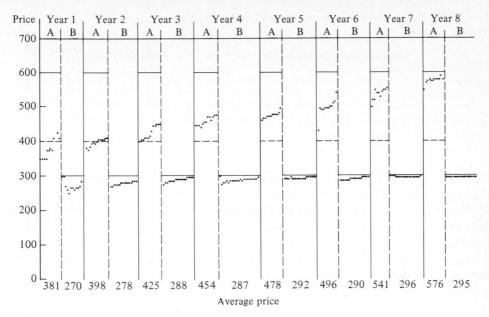

Figure 10.3
Spot price equilibria in an experimental market. (From R. Forsythe, T. Palfrey, and
C. R. Plott "Asset Valuation in an Experimental Market," reprinted from *Econometrica*,
May 1982, 550.)

close to it) because there are three people competing for that payoff. While the hypotheses agree about the second-period price, they make different predictions concerning the first-period price. The intrinsic value hypothesis predicts that people
will bid their own values. For example, if individual type III holds the asset for two
periods, he or she can collect 400 francs in dividends (150 in period *A* and 250 in
period *B*). This will also be the predicted first-period equilibrium price because it
represents the high bid. The rational expectations hypothesis predicts that the first-
period equilibrium price will be 600 francs because type I individuals can collect a
300 franc dividend in the first time period, then sell the asset for 300 francs to type
II individuals in the second time period.

Figure 10.3 shows the results of eight replications of the experiment for two
periods each. Note that the period *B* price quickly converges on the anticipated
equilibrium value of 300 francs. This result alone repudiates the naive value and the
speculative equilibrium hypotheses because the asset value is clearly based on its
actual second-period payout. The first-period price starts out at 400 francs, seemingly
verifying the intrinsic value hypothesis; but it then rises gradually until, by the eighth
replication of the experiment ("year" 8), it closes in on the rational expectations value.

The experiment seems to confirm the rational expectations hypothesis, but why
did it take so long to do so? The reason is that prices are determined in the first
period before second-period prices are known. In order for type I individuals to bid
the full 600 franc value, they need to have the information that the second-period

Table 10.4   Parameters for an Experimental Double Auction Futures Market

Investor Type	Initial Working Capital	Initial Shares Held	Fixed Cost	Dividends (francs) Period A	Dividends (francs) Period B
I	15,000 francs	2 shares	15,500 francs	403	146
II	15,000 francs	2 shares	15,500 francs	284	372
III	15,000 francs	2 shares	15,500 francs	110	442

value is really 300 francs. Obviously they do not know this during the first trial of the experiment, but they learn quickly.

If instead bidding had taken place in both period A and B markets simultaneously, perhaps the speed of adjustment to a rational expectations equilibrium would have been faster. In another experiment, Forsythe, Palfrey, and Plott [1982] opened a *futures market*. Everything remained the same as before except bidding for period B holdings was held concurrently with the period A spot market, and the payoffs were as shown in Table 10.4.

The rational expectations hypothesis predicts that the period A price will be 845 francs, whereas the intrinsic value hypothesis predicts 403 francs. They both predict a period B price of 442 francs. The results are shown in Fig. 10.4. Even in the first trial, the period A spot price closed at 742 francs, much closer to the rational expectations prediction. In subsequent trials ("years") the closing prices were even closer to the results predicted by the rational expectations hypothesis. Perhaps the

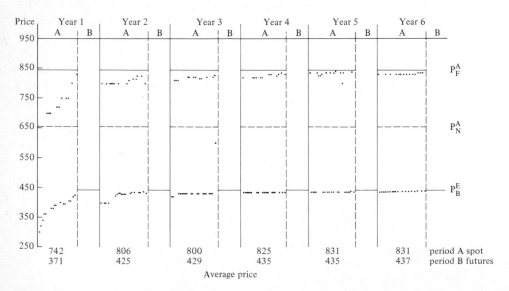

Figure 10.4
Rational expectations with a futures market. (From R. Forsythe, T. Palfrey, and C. R. Plott, "Asset Valuation in an Experimental Market," reprinted from *Econometrica*, May 1982, 554.)

most valuable implication of the experiment is that it clearly demonstrates the usefulness of futures markets. By allowing simultaneous trading in both markets, the speed with which information is made public is increased through price transactions. Information about the future value of assets is revealed today.

In the rational expectations equilibria described above, all traders knew with certainty what their own payoffs would be in each time period but did not know the asset clearing price because other individuals had different payoffs in the same state of nature. These different payoffs represent a form of heterogeneous expectations. In the above experiments all market participants were equally well informed. There is a different way of looking at heterogeneous expectations, however. Suppose that some traders are better informed about which states of nature will actually occur. Furthermore, suppose that different individuals have different information about which states will occur. For example, suppose investor I knows for sure that a Republican will be elected president but knows nothing else. Investor J, on the other hand, knows that both houses of Congress will be Democratic but knows nothing else. The question is this: Will market prices reflect the full impact of both pieces of information as though the market were fully informed, or will prices reflect only some average of the impact of both pieces of information? If prices reflect all information, the market is said to be *fully aggregating*; otherwise it is only *averaging* prices.

Very little is known about whether real-world capital markets fully aggregate information or merely average it. A fully aggregating market, however, would be consistent with Fama's [1970] definition of strong-form market efficiency. In a fully aggregating market even insiders who possess private information would not be able to profit by it. One mechanism for aggregation has been suggested by Grossman and Stiglitz [1976] and Grossman [1976].[8] In a market with two types of traders, "informed" and "uninformed," informed traders will acquire better estimates of future states of nature and take trading positions based on this information. When all informed traders do this, current prices are affected. Uninformed traders invest no resources in collecting information, but they can infer the information of informed traders by observing what happens to prices. Thus the market prices may aggregate information so that all traders (both informed and uninformed) become informed. In Chapter 11 we will suggest that capital markets do not instantaneously and fully aggregate information because empirical evidence on insider trading reveals that insiders can and do make abnormal returns.

E. MARKET EFFICIENCY WITH COSTLY INFORMATION

If capital markets are efficient, then no one can earn abnormal returns, but without abnormal returns there is no strong incentive to acquire information. Random selection of securities is just as effective. How, then, can prices reflect information if there

---

[8] Actually, this idea can be traced back to Hayek's classic article, "The Use of Knowledge in Society" [1945].

Table 10.5   Net Payoffs, Given Costly Information

		His Opponent Analyzes?	
		Yes	No
The Trader	Yes	$r - c_2 = -2\%$	$dr - c_2 = 4\%$
Analyzes?	No	$r/d - c_1 = -1\%$	$r - c_1 = 2\%$

$$r = \text{normal return} = 6\%$$
$$d = \text{competitive advantage} = 2\times$$
$$c_2 = \text{cost of analysis} = 8\%$$
$$c_1 = \text{cost with no analysis} = 4\%$$

is no incentive to search it out and use it for arbitrage? How can a securities analysis industry exist?

The above argument may have some merit in a world with costless information because all investors would have zero abnormal returns.[9] However, it is probably premature to predict the demise of the security analysis industry or to argue that prices are uninformative. Grossman and Stiglitz [1976, 1980] and Cornell and Roll [1981] have shown that a sensible asset market equilibrium must leave some room for analysis. Their articles make the more reasonable assumption that information acquisition is a costly activity. Because of its simplicity, the Cornell and Roll model is discussed below.

We want to analyze the rational behavior of individuals when information is useful—in the sense that having it will improve one's decisions—but also where information is costly. Imagine two simple strategies. The first is to pay a fee, say $c_2 = 8\%$, for acquiring valuable information. This is called the *analyst strategy*. The opposing strategy is to pay a minimal fee, say $c_1 = 4\%$, for the right to trade. Call this the *random selector's strategy*. Table 10.5 shows the net payoffs for various two-way trades involving all combinations of analysts and random selectors. Note that the "normal" rate of return, r, is 6% ($c_1 < r < c_2$).

The example in Table 10.5 assumes that the costly information doubles the competitive advantage, d, of an analyst whenever he or she trades with a random selector. The analyst, being better informed, grosses 12% and nets 4% after paying 8% for the information. Conversely, the random selector finds his or her gross return halved when trading with an analyst. He or she grosses only 3% and nets -1% after paying 4% on transactions costs. When an analyst trades with another analyst there is no competitive advantage because they possess the same information. Thus their gross return is only 6% and they net -2%.

A stable equilibrium can exist (1) if all trading is anonymous and (2) if the expected payoff to the analysis strategy equals the expected payoff to the random selection strategy.[10] If p is the probability of utilizing an analyst's strategy and

---

[9] Abnormal returns are returns in excess of what can be earned for a given level of risk.

[10] Anonymous trading is necessary so that uninformed random selectors will actually consummate a trade with an analyst with superior information. One service provided by brokers is to ensure the anonymity of their clients.

$1 - p$ is the probability of random selection, then the equilibrium condition is

$$E(\text{Payoff to analysis strategy}) = E(\text{Payoff to random selection})$$

$$p(r - c_2) + (1 - p)(dr - c_2) = p(r/d - c_1) + (1 - p)(r - c_1). \qquad (10.4)$$

The expected payoff to analysis [the left-hand side of Eq. (10.4)] is the probability that an analyst will confront another analyst multiplied by the net payoff given this event, plus the probability of confronting a random selector multiplied by the net payoff in that event. Similar logic produces the expected payoff for a random selector [the right-hand side of Eq. (10.4)]. Solving Eq. (10.4) for p, the probability of using analysis, we have

$$p = \frac{r(1 - d) + c_2 - c_1}{2r - rd - r/d}. \qquad (10.5)$$

A *mixed* stable strategy is one where $0 < p < 1$, that is, where analysts and random selectors will coexist in equilibrium. The necessary conditions for a mixed stable strategy are

$$r(d - 1) > c_2 - c_1 \quad \text{and} \quad r(1 - 1/d) < c_2 - c_1. \qquad (10.6)$$

These conditions can be derived from the definition of the equilibrium probability, p, Eq. (10.5). We know that the "normal" rate of return, r, is greater than zero and the competitive advantage, d, is greater than one. Therefore the denominator of Eq. (10.5), must be negative:

$$2r - rd - r/d < 0,$$

$$2d - d^2 - 1 < 0,$$

$$(d - 1)^2 > 0, \quad \text{since} \quad d > 1. \qquad \text{QED}$$

It follows that the numerator of Eq. (10.5) must also be negative if the probability, p, is to be positive. Therefore

$$r(1 - d) + c_2 - c_1 < 0,$$

$$r(d - 1) > c_2 - c_1,$$

and we have derived the first necessary condition in Eq. (10.6). Also, in order for $p < 1$ the numerator of Eq. (10.5) must be greater than the denominator (since both are negative numbers). This fact gives us the second necessary condition:

$$r(1 - d) + c_2 - c_1 > 2r - rd - r/d,$$

$$c_2 - c_1 > r(1 - 1/d).$$

If there is no net economic profit when the mixed stable strategy evolves, then there will be no incentive for new entrants to disturb the equilibrium. This zero profit condition is equivalent to setting both sides of Eq. (10.4), the expected payoff equation, equal to zero. This results in two equations, which when equated and simplified give the further result that

$$d = c_2/c_1 \quad \text{and} \quad p = (rd - c_2)/(rd - r)$$

for a stable mixed strategy where all net profits are zero.

Using the numbers in Table 10.5, we see that a stable mixed strategy with $p = \frac{2}{3}$ will exist. Thus with costly information we will observe the analyst strategy being used two thirds and the random selection strategy one third of the time. No one will be tempted to change strategies because there is no incentive to do so. Also, we will observe that the gross return for analysis is higher than for random selection. But once the cost of obtaining information is subtracted the net rate of return to both strategies is the same.

The simple model of Cornell and Roll [1981] shows that there is nothing inconsistent about having efficient markets and security analysis at the same time. The average individual who utilizes costly information to perform security analysis will outperform other individuals who use less information, but only in terms of gross returns. The net return to both strategies will be identical. Some empirical evidence consistent with this point of view is presented in Chapter 11 where mutual fund performance is discussed.

F. STATISTICAL TESTS UNADJUSTED FOR RISK

Historically it was possible to test certain predictions of the efficient markets hypothesis even before a theory of risk-bearing allowed comparison of risk-adjusted returns. For example, if the riskiness of an asset does not change over time or if its risk changes randomly over time, then there should be no pattern in the time series of security returns. If there were a recurring pattern of any type, investors who recognize it could use it to predict future returns and make excess profits. However, in their very efforts to use the patterns, they would eliminate them.

Three theories of the time series behavior of prices can be found in the literature: (1) the *fair-game model*, (2) the *martingale* or *submartingale*, and (3) the *random walk*. The fair game model is based on the behavior of average returns (not on the entire probability distribution). Its mathematical expression is

$$\varepsilon_{j,t+1} = \frac{P_{j,t+1} - P_{jt}}{P_{jt}} - \frac{E(P_{j,t+1}|\eta_t) - P_{jt}}{P_{jt}}$$

$$= \frac{P_{j,t+1} - E(P_{j,t+1}|\eta_t)}{P_{jt}}, \tag{10.7}$$

where

$P_{j,t+1}$ = the actual price of security j next period,

$E(P_{j,t+1}|\eta_t)$ = the predicted end-of-period price of security j given the current information structure, η_t,

$\varepsilon_{j,t+1}$ = the difference between actual and predicted returns.

Note that (10.7) is really written in returns form. If we let the one-period return be defined as

$$r_{j,t+1} = \frac{P_{j,t+1} - P_{jt}}{P_{jt}},$$

then (10.7) may be rewritten as

$$\varepsilon_{j,t+1} = r_{j,t+1} - E(r_{j,t+1}|\eta_t)$$

and

$$E(\varepsilon_{j,t+1}) = E[r_{j,t+1} - E(r_{j,t+1}|\eta_t)] = 0. \tag{10.8}$$

A fair game means that, on average, across a large number of samples the expected return on an asset equals its actual return. An example of a fair game would be games of chance in Las Vegas. Because of the house percentage, you should expect to lose, let us say, 10%; and sure enough, on the average that is what people actually lose. A fair game does not imply that you will earn a positive return; only that expectations are not biased.

Given the definition of a fair game in Eq. (10.7), a *submartingale* is a fair game where tomorrow's price is expected to be greater than today's price. Mathematically, a submartingale is

$$E(P_{j,t+1}|\eta_t) > P_{jt}.$$

In returns form this implies that expected returns are positive. This may be written as follows:

$$\frac{E(P_{j,t+1}|\eta_t) - P_{jt}}{P_{jt}} = E(r_{j,t+1}|\eta_t) > 0. \tag{10.9a}$$

A *martingale* is also a fair game. With a martingale, however, tomorrow's price is expected to be the same as today's price. Mathematically, this is

$$E(P_{j,t+1}|\eta_t) = P_{jt},$$

or in returns form, it is written as

$$\frac{E(P_{j,t+1}|\eta_t) - P_{jt}}{P_{jt}} = E(r_{j,t+1}|\eta_t) = 0. \tag{10.9b}$$

A submartingale has the following empirical implication: Because prices are expected to increase over time, any test of the abnormal return from an experimental portfolio must compare its return from a buy-and-hold strategy for a control portfolio of the same composition. If the market is an efficient submartingale, both portfolios will have a positive return, and the difference between their returns will be zero. In other words, we will observe a fair game with positive returns: a submartingale.

Finally, a *random walk* says that there is no difference between the distribution of returns conditional on a given information structure and the unconditional distribution of returns. Equation (10.2) is a random walk in prices. Equation (10.10) is a random walk in returns:

$$f(r_{1,t+1}, \ldots, r_{n,t+1}) = f(r_{1,t+1}, \ldots, r_{n,t+1}|\eta_t). \tag{10.10}$$

Random walks are much stronger conditions than fair games or martingales because they require all the parameters of a distribution (e.g., mean, variance, skewness, and kurtosis) to be the same with or without an information structure. Furthermore, successive drawings over time must (1) be independent and (2) be taken from the same distribution. If returns follow a random walk, then the mean of the underlying distribution does not change over time, and a fair game will result.

Most empirical evidence indicates that security returns do not follow a process that has all the properties of a random walk. This makes sense because the condition that the entire underlying probability distribution of returns remain stationary through time is simply too strong. It is reasonable to believe that because of changes in the risk of a firm, the variance of stock returns will change over time. This, in fact, appears to be the case. The fair-game model makes no statement about the variance of the distribution of security returns, and consequently, the nonstationarity of return variances is irrelevant to its validity.[11]

A statistical difference between fair games and random walks is that the latter hypothesis requires that all drawings be independently taken from the same distribution, whereas the former does not. This means that the random walk requires that serial covariances between returns for any lag must be zero. However, significant serial covariances of one-period returns are not inconsistent with a fair game. To see this, suppose that the relevant information structure consists of past returns. In other words, assume weak-form market efficiency. When Eq. (10.7) is written in returns form, we have

$$\varepsilon_{j,t+1} = r_{j,t+1} - E(r_{j,t+1} | r_{jt}, r_{j,t+1}, \ldots, r_{j,t-n}) \tag{10.11}$$

and

$$E(\varepsilon_{j,t+1}) = 0.$$

Note that the fair game variable, $\varepsilon_{j,t+1}$, is the deviation of the return in period $t+1$ from its conditional expectation, i.e., the residual. If the residual is a fair game, then it must have zero serial covariance for all lags. Yet even though the residual is a fair game variable, the conditional expectation of returns for $t+1$ can depend on the return observed for t. Therefore the serial covariances of *returns* need not be zero. The serial covariance for one-period returns is[12]

$$E[(r_{j,t+1} - E(r_{j,t+1}))(r_{jt} - E(r_{jt}))] = \text{COV}(r_{j,t+1}, r_{jt})$$

$$= \int_{r_{jt}} [r_{jt} - E(r_{jt})][r_{j,t+1} - E(r_{j,t+1})] f(r_{jt}) \, dr_{jt}. \tag{10.12}$$

---

[11] For example, consider a situation where random drawings are taken randomly from two normal distributions that have a mean return of zero but different return variances. The expected value of a large sample of alternative drawings would be zero; therefore we have a fair game. However, the experiment violates the random walk requirement that all drawings be taken from the same distribution.

[12] The reader who is unfamiliar with covariances is referred to Chapter 6. In general the covariance between two random variables, x and y, is

$$\text{COV}(x, y) = E[(x - E(x))(y - E(y))].$$

From (10.11) we know that $E[r_{j,t+1}|r_{jt}] = r_{j,t+1}$. Therefore

$$\text{COV}(r_{j,t+1}, r_{jt}) = \int_{r_{jt}} [r_{jt} - E(r_{jt})][E(r_{j,t+1}|r_{jt}) - E(r_{j,t+1})]f(r_{jt})\,dr_{jt}. \quad (10.13)$$

But the fair game in residuals, Eq. (10.11), does not imply that $E(r_{j,t+1}|r_{jt}) = E(r_{j,t+1})$. We have the result that the *deviation* of return for $t + 1$ from its conditional expectation is a fair game, but the conditional expectation of return itself can depend on the return observed for t. Therefore serial covariances of one-period returns are not inconsistent with a fair game model. However, they are inconsistent with a random walk because the latter requires that successive drawings be independent (a serial covariance of zero for all lags).

Fama [1965] has presented evidence to show that the serial correlations of one-day changes in the natural logarithm of price are significantly different from zero for 11 out of 30 of the Dow Jones Industrials.[13] Furthermore, 22 of the 30 estimated serial correlations are positive. This, as well as evidence collected by other authors, shows that security returns are not, strictly speaking, random walks. However, the evidence is not inconsistent with fair-game models or, in particular, the submartingale.

Direct tests of the fair-game model were provided by Alexander [1961] and Fama and Blume [1966]. They used a technical trading filter rule, which states: Using price history, buy a stock if the price rises $x\%$, hold it until the security falls $x\%$, then sell and go short. Maintain the short position until the price rises $x\%$, then cover the short position and establish a long position. This process is repeated for a fixed time interval, and the performance according to the filter rule is then compared with a buy-and-hold strategy in the same security. Because each security is compared with itself, there is no need to adjust for risk.

Filter rules are designed to make the investor a profit if there are any systematic patterns in the movement of prices over time. It is only a matter of trying enough different filters so that one of them picks up any serial dependencies in prices and makes a profit that exceeds the simple buy-and-hold strategy.

The filter rule tests have three important results. First, they show that even before subtracting transactions costs, filters greater than 1.5% cannot beat a simple buy-and-hold strategy. Second, filters below 1.5%, on the average, make very small profits that because of frequent trading can beat the market. This is evidence of a very short-term serial dependence in price changes. However, it is not necessarily evidence of capital market inefficiency. First one must subtract from gross profits the cost of taking action based on the filter rule. Fama and Blume [1966] show that even a floor trader (the owner of a seat on the NYSE) must pay at least .1% per transaction. Once these costs are deducted from the profits of filters that are less than 1.5%, the profits vanish. Therefore the capital market is allocationally efficient down to the

---

[13] To show that the logarithm of successive price changes is a good approximation of returns, assume one-period continuous compounding:

$$P_{t+1} = P_t e^{rt}, \quad \text{where} \quad t = 1,$$

$$\ln P_{t+1} - \ln P_t = \frac{P_{t+1} - P_t}{P_t}, \quad \text{where} \quad r = \frac{P_{t+1} - P_t}{P_t}.$$

level of transactions costs. The smaller the transactions costs are, the more operationally efficient the market is, and smaller price dependencies are eliminated by arbitrage trading. Capital markets are efficient in their weak form because the return on a portfolio managed with price-history information is the same as a buy-and-hold strategy that uses no information. Therefore the value of messages provided by filter rules is zero. Technical trading does not work.[14]

The third inference that can be drawn from filter tests is that the market appears to follow a submartingale. All the securities tested had average positive returns. This makes sense because risky assets are expected to yield positive returns to compensate investors for the risk they undertake.

G. THE JOINT HYPOTHESIS OF MARKET EFFICIENCY AND THE CAPM

Statistical tests and filter rules are interesting and present evidence of weak-form efficiency but are limited by the fact that they cannot compare assets of different risk. The CAPM provides a theory that allows the expected return of a fair-game model to be conditional on a relevant costless measure of risk.[15] If the CAPM is written as a fair game, we have

$$\varepsilon_{jt} = R_{jt} - E(R_{jt}|\hat{\beta}_{jt}),$$

$$E(R_{jt}|\hat{\beta}_{jt}) = R_{ft} + [E(R_{mt}|\hat{\beta}_{mt}) - R_{ft}]\hat{\beta}_{jt}, \tag{10.14}$$

$$E(\varepsilon_{jt}) = 0, \tag{10.15}$$

where

$E(R_{jt}|\hat{\beta}_{jt})$ = the expected rate of return on the jth asset during this time period, given a prediction of its systematic risk, $\hat{\beta}_{jt}$,

R_{ft} = the risk-free rate of return during this time period,

$E(R_{mt}|\hat{\beta}_{mt})$ = the expected market rate of return, given a prediction of its systematic risk, $\hat{\beta}_{mt}$,

$\hat{\beta}_{jt}$ = the estimated systematic risk of the jth security based on last time period's information structure η_{t-1}.

The CAPM is graphed in Fig. 10.5. According to the theory, the only relevant parameter necessary to evaluate the expected return for every security is its systematic risk.[16] Therefore if the CAPM is true *and* if markets are efficient, the expected return of every asset should fall exactly on the security market line. Any deviation from the

---

[14] See Ball [1978] for a discussion of filter rules and how to improve them as tests of market efficiency.

[15] Note that the discussion that follows also applies the arbitrage pricing theory if one allows the expected return to depend on multiple factor loadings (i.e., multiple betas).

[16] For a detailed explanation of the CAPM and empirical tests of it, see Chapter 7.

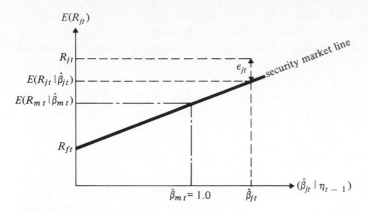

Figure 10.5
The CAPM as a fair game.

expected return is interpreted as an abnormal return, ε_{jt}, and can be taken as evidence of market inefficiency *if* the CAPM is correct.

The CAPM is derived from a set of assumptions that are very similar to those of market efficiency. For example, the Sharpe-Lintner-Mossin derivation of the CAPM assumes:

- All investors are single-period expected utility of wealth maximizers whose utility functions are based on the mean and variance of return.

- All investors can borrow or lend an indefinite amount at the risk-free rate, and there are no restrictions on short sales.

- All investors have homogeneous expectations of the end-of-period joint distributions of returns.

- Securities markets are frictionless and perfectly competitive.

In Chapter 11 we shall report the results of several empirical studies that use the CAPM as a tool for analyzing capital market efficiency. However, one should always keep in mind the fact that the CAPM and capital market efficiency are joint and inseparable hypotheses. If capital markets are inefficient, then the assumptions of the CAPM are invalid and a different model is required. And if the CAPM is inappropriate, even though capital markets are efficient, then the CAPM is the wrong tool to use in order to test for efficiency.

Various sophisticated empirical tests of the CAPM by Black, Jensen, and Scholes [1972], Black and Scholes [1974], and Fama and MacBeth [1973] show that the CAPM fits reality surprisingly well. However, because the theoretical CAPM assumes market efficiency, any empirical results that show that on the average there are no significant deviations from the model are merely consistent with market efficiency. They do not necessarily prove market efficiency because the model might be wrong. Therefore any test of market efficiency that uses the CAPM to adjust for risk is, as mentioned before, a joint test of the CAPM that assumes market efficiency for its derivation and of market efficiency itself.

One may also ask the question: "If I can accurately predict systematic risk, $\hat{\beta}_{jt}$, I can also predict the expected rate of return on an asset; doesn't this mean that I can beat the market?" The answer, of course, is: "Probably not." If the information necessary to estimate $\hat{\beta}_{jt}$ is publicly available and if markets are efficient in their semi-strong form, then prices will instantaneously and fully reflect all the information relevant for estimating $\hat{\beta}_{jt}$, the expected return of the security will fall exactly on the security line, and no abnormal returns will be observed.

Perhaps the most interesting use of the CAPM is to examine historical situations to see whether or not the market was efficient for a particular set of information. If the CAPM is valid (we shall assume it is, but keep in mind that it is a joint hypothesis with market efficiency), then any evidence of persistent deviations from the security market line can be interpreted as evidence of capital market inefficiency with regard to a particular information set. Chapter 11 is devoted to tests of market efficiency with regard to various information sets.

SUMMARY

The hypothesis of capital market efficiency has attracted a great deal of interest and critical comment. This is somewhat surprising because capital market efficiency is a fairly limited concept. It says that the prices of securities instantaneously and fully reflect all available relevant information. It does not imply that product markets are perfectly competitive or that information is costless.

Capital market efficiency relies on the ability of arbitrageurs to recognize that prices are out of line and to make a profit by driving them back to an equilibrium value consistent with available information. Given this type of behavioral paradigm, one often hears the following questions: If capital market efficiency implies that no one can beat the market (i.e., make an abnormal profit), then how can analysts be expected to exist since they, too, cannot beat the market? If capital markets are efficient, how can we explain the existence of a multibillion dollar security analysis industry? The answer, of course, is that neither of these questions is inconsistent with efficient capital markets. First, analysts can and do make profits. However, they compete with each other to do so. If the profit to analysis becomes abnormally large, then new individuals will enter the analysis business until, on average, the return from analysis equals the cost (which, by the way, includes a fair return to the resources that are employed). As shown by Cornell and Roll [1981], it is reasonable to have efficient markets where people earn different gross rates of return because they pay differing costs for information. However, net of costs their abnormal rates of return will be equal (to zero).

As we shall see in the next chapter, the concept of capital market efficiency is important in a wide range of applied topics, such as accounting information, new issues of securities, and portfolio performance measurement. By and large the evidence seems to indicate that capital markets are efficient in the weak and semistrong forms but not in the strong form.

PROBLEM SET

10.1 Suppose you know with certainty that the Clark Capital Corporation will pay a dividend of $10 per share on every January 1 forever. The continuously compounded risk-free rate is 5% (also forever).

a) Graph the price path of the Clark Capital common stock over time.

b) Is this (highly artificial) example a random walk? A martingale? A submartingale? (Why?)

10.2 Given the following situations, determine in each case whether or not the hypothesis of an efficient capital market (semistrong form) is contradicted.

a) Through the introduction of a complex computer program into the analysis of past stock price changes, a brokerage firm is able to predict price movements well enough to earn a consistent 3% profit, adjusted for risk, above normal market returns.

b) On the average, investors in the stock market this year are expected to earn a positive return (profit) on their investment. Some investors will earn considerably more than others.

c) You have discovered that the square root of any given stock price multiplied by the day of the month provides an indication of the direction in price movement of that particular stock with a probability of .7.

d) A Securities and Exchange Commission (SEC) suit was filed against Texas Gulf Sulphur Company in 1965 because its corporate employees had made unusually high profits on company stock that they had purchased after exploratory drilling had started in Ontario (in 1959) and before stock prices rose dramatically (in 1964) with the announcement of the discovery of large mineral deposits in Ontario.

10.3 The First National Bank has been losing money on automobile consumer loans and is considering the implementation of a new loan procedure that requires a credit check on loan applicants. Experience indicates that 82% of the loans were paid off, whereas the remainder defaulted. However, if the credit check is run, the probabilities can be revised as follows:

	Favorable Credit Check	Unfavorable Credit Check
Loan is paid	.9	.5
Loan is defaulted	.1	.5

An estimated 80% of the loan applicants receive a favorable credit check. Assume that the bank earns 18% on successful loans, loses 100% on defaulted loans, suffers an opportunity cost of 18% when the loan is not granted but would have been successful, and an opportunity cost of 0% when the loan is not granted and would have defaulted. If the cost of a credit check is 5% of the value of the loan and the bank is risk neutral, should the bank go ahead with the new policy?

10.4 Hearty Western Foods, one of the nation's largest consumer products firms, is trying to decide whether it should spend $5 million to test market a new ready-to-eat product (called Kidwich), to proceed directly to a nationwide marketing effort, or to cancel the product. The expected payoffs (in millions of dollars) from cancellation vs. nationwide marketing are given below:

| | Action | |
Market Conditions	Cancel	Go Nationwide
No acceptance	0	− 10
Marginal	0	10
Success	0	80

Prior experience with nationwide marketing efforts has been:

Market Conditions	Probability
No acceptance	.6
Marginal	.3
Success	.1

If the firm decides to test market the product, the following information will become available:

| | | Probability | | |
		No Acceptance	Marginal	Success
Outcome Predicted by the Test Market	No Acceptance	.9	.1	0
	Marginal	.1	.7	.2
	Success	.1	.3	.6

For example, if the test market results predict a success, there is a 60% chance that the nationwide marketing effort really will be a success but a 30% chance it will be marginal and a 10% chance it will have no acceptance.

a) If the firm is risk neutral, should it test market the product or not?

b) If the firm is risk averse with a utility function

$$U(W) = \ln(W + 11),$$

should it test market the product or not?

10.5 The efficient market hypothesis implies that abnormal returns are expected to be zero. Yet in order for markets to be efficient, arbitrageurs must be able to force prices back into equilibrium. If they earn profits in doing so, is this fact inconsistent with market efficiency?

10.6

a) In a poker game with six players, you can expect to lose 83% of the time. How can this still be a martingale?

b) In the options market, call options expire unexercised over 80% of the time.[17] Thus the option holders frequently lose all their investment. Does this imply that the options market is not a fair game? Not a martingale? Not a submartingale?

---

[17] See Chapter 8 for a description of call options.

10.7 If securities markets are efficient, what is the NPV of any security, regardless of its risk?

10.8 From time to time the federal government considers passing into law an excess profits tax on U.S. corporations. Given what you know about efficient markets and the CAPM, how would you define excess profits? What would be the effect of an excess profits tax on the investor?

10.9 State the assumptions inherent in this statement: A condition for market efficiency is that there be no second-order stochastic dominance.

REFERENCES

Alexander, S. S., "Price Movements in Speculative Markets: Trends or Random Walks," *Industrial Management Review*, May 1961, 7–26.

Ball, R., "Filter Rules: Interpretation of Market Efficiency, Experimental Problems and Australian Evidence," *Accounting Education*, November 1978, 1–17.

Black, F.; M. Jensen; and M. Scholes, "The Capital Asset Pricing Model: Some Empirical Tests," in Jensen, ed., *Studies in the Theory of Capital Markets*. Praeger, New York, 1972, 79–124.

Black, F., and M. Scholes, "The Effects of Dividend Yield and Dividend Policy on Common Stock Prices and Returns," *Journal of Financial Economics*, May 1974, 1–22.

Copeland, T. E., and D. Friedman, "The Market for Information: Some Experimental Results," Working Paper 5-87, UCLA Graduate School of Management, 1986.

Cornell, B., and R. Roll, "Strategies for Pairwise Competitions in Markets and Organizations," *Bell Journal of Economics*, Spring 1981, 201–213.

Fama, E. F., "The Behavior of Stock Market Prices," *Journal of Business*, January 1965, 34–105.

———, "Efficient Capital Markets: A Review of Theory and Empirical Work," *Journal of Finance*, May 1970, 383–417.

———, *Foundations of Finance*. Basic Books, New York, 1976.

———, and M. Blume, "Filter Rules and Stock Market Trading Profits," *Journal of Business*, January (spec. supp.) 1966, 226–241.

Fama, E. F., and J. MacBeth, "Risk, Return and Equilibrium: Empirical Test," *Journal of Political Economy*, May–June 1973, 607–636.

Finnerty, J. E., "Insiders and Market Efficiency," *Journal of Finance*, September 1976, 1141–1148.

Forsythe, R.; T. Palfrey; and C. R. Plott, "Asset Valuation in an Experimental Market," *Econometrica*, May 1982, 537–567.

Green, J. R., "Information, Efficiency and Equilibrium," Discussion Paper No. 284, Harvard Institute of Economic Research, March 1974.

Grossman, S. J., "On the Efficiency of Competitive Stock Markets Where Trades Have Diverse Information," *Journal of Finance*, May 1976, 573–586.

———, and J. Stiglitz, "Information and Competitive Price Systems," *American Economic Review*, May 1976, 246–253.

———, "The Impossibility of Informationally Efficient Markets," *American Economic Review*, June 1980, 393–408.

Harrison, J. M., and D. M. Kreps, "Speculative Investor Behavior in a Stock Market with Heterogeneous Expectations," *Quarterly Journal of Economics*, May 1978, 323–336.

Hayek, F. H., "The Use of Knowledge in Society," *American Economic Review*, September 1945.

Hirshleifer, J., *Investment, Interest, and Capital*. Prentice-Hall, Englewood Cliffs, N.J., 1970.

———, and J. Riley, "The Analytics of Uncertainty and Information—An Expository Survey," *Journal of Economic Literature*, December 1979, 1375–1421.

Huang, C. C.; I. Vertinsky; and W. T. Ziemba, "Sharp Bounds on the Value of Perfect Information," *Operations Research*, January–February 1977, 128–139.

Jaffe, J., "The Effect of Regulation Changes on Insider Trading," *Bell Journal of Economics and Management Science*, Spring 1974, 93–121.

Keynes, J. M., *The General Theory of Employment, Interest and Money*. Harcourt Brace, New York, 1936.

Latham, M., "Defining Capital Market Efficiency," Finance Working Paper 150, Institute for Business and Economic Research, University of California, Berkeley, April 1985.

Lucas, R. E., "Expectations and the Neutrality of Money," *Journal of Economic Theory*, April 1972, 103–124.

Marschak, J., *Economic Information, Decisions, and Predictions, Selected Essays*, Vol. 2. Reidel, Boston, 1974.

Miller, R. M.; C. R. Plott; and V. L. Smith, "Intertemporal Competitive Equilibrium: An Empirical Study of Speculation," *American Economic Review*, June 1981, 448–459.

Plott, C. R., and S. Sunder, "Efficiency of Experimental Security Markets with Insider Information: An Application of Rational Expectations Models," *Journal of Political Economy*, August 1982, 663–698.

Rubinstein, M., "Securities Market Efficiency in an Arrow-Debreu Economy," *American Economic Review*, December 1975, 812–824.

Samuelson, P. A., "Proof that Properly Anticipated Prices Fluctuate Randomly," *Industrial Management Review*, Spring 1965, 41–49.

Smith, V. L., "Experimental Economics: Induced Value Theory," *American Economic Review*, May 1976, 274–279.

Sunder, S., "Market for Information: Experimental Evidence," Working Paper, University of Minnesota, 1984.

PART II

Corporate Policy: Theory, Evidence, and Applications

T HE FIRST PART OF THE text covers most of what has come to be recognized as a unified theory of decision making under uncertainty as applied to the field of finance. The theory of finance, as presented in the first half of the text, is applicable to a wide range of finance topics. The theoretical foundations are prerequisite to almost any of the traditional subject areas in finance curricula; e.g., portfolio management, corporation finance, commercial banking, money and capital markets, financial institutions, security analysis, international finance, investment banking, speculative markets, insurance, and case studies in finance. Since all these topics require a thorough understanding of decision making under uncertainty, all use the theory of finance.

The second half of this text focuses, for the most part, on applications of the theory of finance to a corporate setting. The fundamental issues are: Does financing matter? Does the type of financing (debt or equity) have any real effect on the value of the firm? Does the form of financial payment (dividends or capital gains) have any effect on the value of claims held by various classes of security holders?

Because these issues are usually discussed in the context of corporate finance they may seem to be narrow. This is not the case. First of all, the definition of a corporation is very broad. The class of corporations includes not only manufacturing firms but also commercial banks, savings and loan associations, many brokerage houses, some investment banks, and even the major security exchanges. Second, the debt equity decision applies to all individuals as well as all corporations. Therefore although the language is narrow, the issues are very broad indeed. They affect almost every economic entity in the private sector of the economy.

As we shall see, the theoretical answer to the question "Does financing matter?" is often a loud and resounding "Maybe." Often the answer depends on the assumptions of the model employed to study the problem. Under different sets of assumptions, different and even opposite answers are possible. This is extremely disquieting to the student of finance. Therefore we have presented empirical evidence related to each of the theoretical hypotheses. Frequently, but not always, the preponderance of evidence supports a single conclusion.

It is important to keep in mind that hypotheses cannot be tested by the realism of the assumptions used to derive them. What counts for a positive science is the development of theories that yield valid and meaningful predictions about observed phenomena. On the first pass, what counts is whether or not the hypothesis is consistent with the evidence at hand. Further testing involves deducing new facts capable of being observed but not previously known, then checking those deduced facts against additional empirical evidence. As students of finance, which seeks to be a positive science, we must not only understand the theory, but also study the empirical evidence in order to determine which hypothesis is validated.

Chapter 11 is devoted to various empirical studies related to the efficient market hypothesis. Most of the evidence is consistent with the weak and semistrong forms of market efficiency but inconsistent with the strong form. In certain situations, individuals with inside information appear to be able to earn abnormal returns. In particular, corporate insiders can beat the market when trading in the securities of their firm. Also, block traders can earn abnormal returns when they trade at the block price, as can purchasers of new equity issues. The last two situations will surely lead to further research because current theory cannot explain why, in the absence of barriers to entry, there appear to be inexplicable abnormal rates of return. Chapter 12 returns to the theoretical problem of how to evaluate multiperiod investments in a world with uncertainty. It shows the set of assumptions necessary in order to extend the simple one-period CAPM rules into a multiperiod world. It also discusses two interesting applied issues: the abandonment problem, and the technique for discounting uncertain costs.

Chapter 13 explores the theory of capital structure and the cost of capital. This is the first of the corporate policy questions that relate to whether or not the value of the firm is affected by the type of financing it chooses. Also, we define a cost of capital that is consistent with the objective of maximizing the wealth of the current shareholders of the firm. This helps to complete, in a consistent fashion, the theory of project selection. Capital budgeting decisions that are consistent with shareholder wealth maximization require use of the correct technique (the NPV criterion), the correct definition of cash flows (operating cash flows after taxes), and the correct cost of capital definition.

Chapter 14 discusses empirical evidence on whether or not the debt-to-equity ratio (i.e., the type of financing) affects the value of the firm. This is one of the most difficult empirical issues in finance. Although not conclusive, the evidence is consistent with increases in the value of the firm resulting from increasing debt (up to some range) in the capital structure. However, much work remains to be done in this area. Chapter 14 also provides a short example of how to actually compute the cost of capital.

Chapter 15 looks at the relationship between dividend policy and the value of the firm. There are several competing theories. However, the dominant argument seems to be that the value of an all-equity firm depends on the expected returns from current and future investment and not on the form in which the returns are paid out. If investment is held constant, it makes no difference whether the firm pays out high or low dividends. On the other hand, a firm's announcement of increase in dividend payout may be interpreted as a signal by shareholders that the firm anticipates permanently higher levels of return from investment, and of course, higher returns on investment will result in higher share prices.

Chapter 16 presents empirical evidence on the relationship between dividend policy and the value of the firm that, for the most part, seems to be consistent with the theory—namely, that dividend policy does not affect shareholders' wealth. The chapter also applies the valuation models (presented in Chapter 15) to an example.

Chapter 17 uses the subject of leasing to bring together a number of further applications of capital structure and cost of capital issues. We also illustrate how option pricing can help clarify the nature of an operating lease under which the lessee may exercise a contractual right to cancel (with some notice and with moderate penalties). Chapter 18 discusses several applied topics of interest to chief financial officers—pension-fund management, executive compensation, leveraged buyouts, ESOP's and interest rate swaps.

Chapters 19 and 20 consider the widespread phenomenon of mergers. They begin with the proposition that without synergy, value additivity holds in mergers as it does in other types of capital budgeting analysis. Mergers do not affect value unless the underlying determinants of value—the patterns of future cash flows or the applicable capitalization factors—are changed by combining firms. Empirical tests of mergers indicate that the shareholders of acquired firms benefit, on the average, but the shareholders of acquiring firms experience neither significant benefit nor harm.

Chapters 21 and 22 conclude the book by placing finance in its increasingly important international setting. A framework for analyzing the international financial decisions of business firms is developed by summarizing the applicable fundamental propositions. The Fisher effect, which states that nominal interest rates reflect anticipated rates of inflation, is carried over to its international implications. This leads to the Interest Rate Parity Theorem, which states that the current forward exchange rate for a country's currency in relation to the currency of another country will reflect the present interest rate differentials between the two countries. The Purchasing Power Parity Theorem states that the difference between the current spot exchange rate and the future spot exchange rate of a country's currency in relation to the currency of another country will reflect the ratio of the rates of price changes of their internationally traded goods. We point out that exchange risk is a "myth" in the sense that departures from fundamental parity theorems reflect changes in underlying demand and supply conditions that would cause business risks even if international markets were not involved. The fundamental relations provide the principles to guide firms in adjusting their policies to the fluctuations in the exchange rate values of the currencies in which their business is conducted.

11

The only valid statement is that the current price embodies all knowledge, all expectations and all discounts that infringe upon the market.

C. W. J. Granger and O. Morgenstern, *Predictability of Stock Market Prices*, Heath Lexington Books, Lexington, Mass., 1970, 20

Efficient Capital Markets: Evidence

Empirical evidence for or against the hypothesis that capital markets are efficient takes many forms. This chapter is arranged in topical order rather than chronological order, degree of sophistication, or type of market efficiency being tested. Not all the articles mentioned completely support the efficient market hypothesis. However, most agree that capital markets are efficient in the weak and semistrong forms but not in the strong form. The majority of the studies are very recent, dating from the late 1960s and continuing up to the most recently published papers. Usually capital market efficiency has been tested in the large and sophisticated capital markets of developed countries. Therefore one must be careful to limit any conclusions to the appropriate arena from which they are drawn. Research into the efficiency of capital markets is an ongoing process, and the work is being extended to include assets other than common stock as well as smaller and less sophisticated marketplaces.

A. EMPIRICAL MODELS USED FOR RESIDUAL ANALYSIS

Before discussing the empirical tests of market efficiency it is useful to review the three basic types of empirical models that are frequently employed. The differences between them are important. The simplest model, called the *market model*, simply argues that

361

returns on security j are linearly related to returns on a "market" portfolio. Mathematically, the market model is described by

$$R_{jt} = a_j + b_j R_{mt} + \varepsilon_{jt}. \tag{11.1}$$

The market model is not supported by any theory. It assumes that the slope and intercept terms are constant over the time period during which the model is fit to the available data. This is a strong assumption, particularly if the time series is long.

The second model uses the capital asset pricing theory. It requires the intercept term to be equal to the risk-free rate, or the rate of return on the minimum variance zero-beta portfolio, both of which change over time. This CAPM-based methodology is written

$$R_{jt} = R_{ft} + [R_{mt} - R_{ft}]\beta_j + \varepsilon_{jt}. \tag{7.32}$$

Note, however, that systematic risk is assumed to remain constant over the interval of estimation. The use of the CAPM for residual analysis was explained at the end of Chapter 10.

Finally, we sometimes see the *empirical market line*, which was explained in Chapter 7 and is written as

$$R_{jt} = \hat{\gamma}_{0t} + \hat{\gamma}_{1t}\beta_{jt} + \varepsilon_{jt}. \tag{7.36}$$

Although related to the CAPM, it does not require the intercept term to equal the risk-free rate. Instead, both the intercept, $\hat{\gamma}_{0t}$, and the slope, $\hat{\gamma}_{1t}$, are the best linear estimates taken from cross-section data each time period (typically each month). Furthermore, it has the advantage that no parameters are assumed to be constant over time.

All three models use the residual term, ε_{jt}, as a measure of risk-adjusted abnormal performance. However, only one of the models, the second, relies exactly on the theoretical specification of the Sharpe-Lintner capital asset pricing model.

In each of the empirical studies discussed, we shall mention the empirical technique by name because the market model is not subject to Roll's critique (discussed in Chapter 7), whereas the CAPM and the empirical market line are. Thus residual analysis that employs the CAPM or the empirical market line may be subject to criticism.

B. ACCOUNTING INFORMATION

Market efficiency requires that security prices instantaneously and fully reflect all available relevant information. But what information is *relevant*? And how *fast* do security prices really react to new information? The answers to these questions are of particular interest to corporate officers who report the performance of their firm to the public; to the accounting profession, which audits these reports; and to the Securities and Exchange Commission, which regulates securities information.

The market value of assets is the present value of their cash flows discounted at the appropriate risk-adjusted rate. Investors should care only about the cash flow

Table 11.1   FIFO versus LIFO

	LIFO	FIFO	*Inventory at Cost*	
Revenue	100	100		
Cost of goods sold	90	25	Fourth item	90 → LIFO
Operating income	10	75	Third item	60
Taxes at 40%	4	30	Second item	40
Net income	6	45	First item	25 → FIFO
eps (100 shares)	.06	.45		
Cash flow per share	.96	.70		

implications of various corporate decisions. However, corporations report accounting definitions of earnings, not cash flow, and frequently the two are not related. Does an efficient market look at the effect of managerial decisions on earnings per share (eps) or cash flow? This is not an unimportant question, because frequently managers are observed to maximize eps rather than cash flow because they believe that the market value of the company depends on reported eps, when in fact (as we shall see) it does not.

Inventory accounting provides a good example of a situation where managerial decisions have opposite effects on eps and cash flow. During an inflationary economy the cost of producing the most recent inventory continues to rise. On the books, inventory is recorded at cost so that in the example given in Table 11.1 the fourth item added to the inventory costs more to produce than the first. If management elects to use first-in-first-out (FIFO) accounting, it will record a cost of goods sold of $25 against a revenue of $100 when an item is sold from inventory. This results in eps of $.45. On the other hand, if LIFO (last-in-first-out) is used, eps is $.06. The impact of the two accounting treatments on cash flow is in exactly the opposite direction. Because the goods were manufactured in past time periods, the actual costs of production are sunk costs and irrelevant to current decision making. Therefore current cash flows are revenues less taxes. The cost of goods sold is a noncash charge. Therefore, with FIFO, cash flow per share is $.70, whereas with LIFO it is $.96. LIFO provides more cash flow because taxes are lower.

If investors really value cash flow and not eps, we should expect to see stock prices rise when firms announce a switch from FIFO to LIFO accounting during inflationary periods. Sunder [1973, 1975] collected a sample of 110 firms that switched from FIFO to LIFO between 1946 and 1966 and 22 firms that switched from LIFO to FIFO. His procedure was to look at the pattern of cumulative average residuals from the CAPM. A residual return is the difference between the actual return and the return estimated by the model:

$$\varepsilon_{jt} = R_{jt} - E(R_{jt} | \hat{\beta}_{jt}).$$

The usual technique is to estimate ε_{jt} over an interval surrounding the economic event of interest. Taking monthly data, Sunder used all observations of returns except for those occurring plus or minus 12 months around the announcement of the inventory-accounting change. He then used the estimated $\hat{\beta}_{jt}$, the actual risk-free rate, and the actual market return during the 24-month period around the announcement date to predict the expected return.[1] Differences between estimated and actual returns were then averaged across all companies for each month. The average abnormal return in a given month is

$$AR_t = \frac{1}{N} \sum_{j=1}^{N} \varepsilon_{jt}, \quad \text{where} \quad N = \text{the number of companies.}$$

The cumulative average return (CAR) is the sum of average abnormal returns over all months from the start of the data up to and including the current month, T:

$$\text{CAR} = \sum_{t=1}^{T} AR_t,$$

where

T = the number of months being summed ($T = 1, 2, \ldots, M$),

M = the total number of months in the sample.

If there were no abnormal change in the value of the firm associated with the switch from FIFO to LIFO, we should observe no pattern in the residuals. They would fluctuate around zero and on the average would equal zero. In other words, we would have a fair game. Figure 11.1 shows Sunder's results. Assuming that risk does not change during the 24-month period, the cumulative average residuals for the firms switching to LIFO rise by 5.3% during the 12 months prior to the announcement of the accounting change. This is consistent with the fact that shareholders actually value cash flow, not eps. However, it does not necessarily mean that a switch to LIFO causes higher value. Almost all studies of this type, which focus on a particular phenomenon, suffer from what has come to be known as *postselection bias*. In this case, firms may decide to switch to LIFO because they are already doing well and their value may have risen for that reason, not because of the switch in accounting method. Either way, Sunder's results are inconsistent with the fact that shareholders look only at changes in eps in order to value common stock. He finds no evidence that the switch to LIFO lowered value even though it did lower eps.

More recently Ricks [1982] studied a set of 354 NYSE- and AMEX-listed firms that switched to LIFO in 1974. He computed their earnings "as if" they never switched and found that the firms that switched to LIFO had an average 47% increase in their as-if earnings, whereas a matched sample of no-change firms had an average 2% decrease. Ricks also found that the abnormal returns of the switching firms were significantly lower than the matched sample of no-change firms. These results are inconsistent with those reported by Sunder.

The studies above indicate that investors in efficient markets attempt to evaluate news about the effect of managerial decisions on cash flows—not on eps. This fact has

---

[1] Sunder used a moving-average beta technique in his second study [1975]. However, it did not substantially change his results.

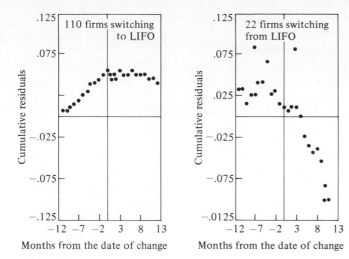

Figure 11.1
Cumulative average residuals for 24 months around the accounting change. (From S. Sunder, "Relationship between Accounting Changes and Stock Prices: Problems of Measurement and Some Empirical Evidence," reprinted from *Empirical Research in Accounting: Selected Studies*, 1973, 18.)

direct implications for the accounting treatment of mergers and acquisitions. Two types of accounting treatment are possible: pooling or purchase. In a pooling arrangement the income statements and balance sheets of the merging firms are simply added together. On the other hand, when one company purchases another, the assets of the acquired company are added to the acquiring company's balance sheet along with an item called *goodwill*. Goodwill is the difference between the purchase price and the book value of the acquired company's assets. Regulations require that goodwill be written off as a charge against earnings *after taxes* in a period not to exceed 40 years. Because the writeoff is after taxes, there is no effect on cash flows, but reported eps decline. The fact that there is no difference in cash flows between pooling and purchase and the fact that cash flows, not eps, are the relevant information used by investors to value the firm should convey to management the message that the accounting treatment of mergers and acquisitions is a matter of indifference.[2] Yet many managements prefer pooling, presumably because they do not like to see eps decline owing to the writeoff of goodwill. No economically rational basis for this type of behavior can be cited.

In a recent empirical study Hong, Kaplan, and Mandelker [1978] tested the effect of pooling and purchase techniques on stock prices of acquiring firms. Using monthly

---

[2] Prior to the 1986 Tax Reform Act, the Internal Revenue Service (IRS) allowed the book value of the assets of the acquired firm to be written up upon purchase. This reduced the amount of goodwill created, but even more important, it created a depreciation tax shield that did not exist in a pooling arrangement. Therefore cash flows for purchase were often higher than pooling. In these cases purchase was actually preferable to pooling, at least from the point of view of the acquiring firm.

data between 1954 and 1964, they compared a sample of 122 firms that used pooling and 37 that used purchase. The acquired firm had to be at least 3% of the net asset value of the acquiring firm. Mergers were excluded from the sample if another merger took place within 18 months, if the acquiring firm was not NYSE listed, or if the merger terms were not based on an exchange of shares. (This last criterion rules out taxable mergers.)

Using the simple time-series market model given below, they calculated cumulative abnormal residuals:

$$\ln R_{jt} = \alpha_j + \beta_j \ln R_{mt} + u_{jt},$$

where

R_{jt} = return on the jth security in time period t,

α_j = an intercept term assumed to be constant over the entire time period,

β_j = systematic risk assumed to be constant over the entire time period,

R_{mt} = market return in time period t,

u_{jt} = abnormal return for the jth security in time period t.

When the cumulative average residuals were centered around the month of the actual merger, the patterns revealed no evidence of abnormal performance for the sample of 122 poolings. This is shown in Fig. 11.2. Therefore there is no evidence that "dirty pooling" raises the stock prices of acquiring firms. Investors are not fooled by the accounting convention.

These results are just as important for acquiring firms that had to write off goodwill against their after-tax earnings because they used the purchase technique. As shown in Fig. 11.3, there is no evidence of negative abnormal returns, which is what we would expect if investors looked at eps. Instead, there is weak evidence that shareholders of acquiring firms experienced positive abnormal returns when the purchase technique was used. This is consistent with the hypothesis that investors value cash flows and that they disregard reported eps.

The empirical studies of Sunder [1973, 1975], and Hong, Kaplan, and Mandelker [1978] provide evidence on what is meant by *relevant* accounting information.

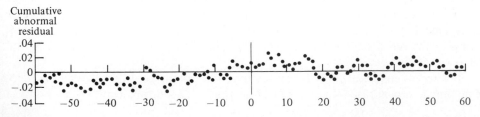

Figure 11.2
Cumulative abnormal residuals for 122 poolings with market value greater than book value in the month relative to merger. (From H. Hong, R. S. Kaplan, and G. Mandelker, "Pooling vs. Purchase: The Effects of Accounting for Mergers on Stock Prices," reprinted with permission of *Accounting Review*, January 1978, 42.)

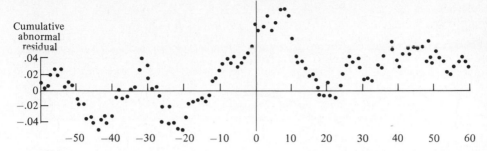

Figure 11.3
Thirty-seven purchases with market value greater than book value in the month relative
to merger. (From H. Hong, R. S. Kaplan, and G. Mandelker, "Pooling vs. Purchase:
The Effects of Accounting for Mergers on Stock Prices," reprinted with permission of
Accounting Review, January 1978, 42.)

By relevant we mean any information about the *expected distribution of future cash
flows*. Next, a study by Ball and Brown [1968] provides some evidence about the
speed of adjustment of efficient markets to new information.

Earnings data and cash flows are usually highly correlated. The examples discussed above merely serve to point out some situations where they are not related
and therefore allow empiricists to distinguish between the two. Ball and Brown used
monthly data for a sample of 261 firms between 1946 and 1965 to evaluate the usefulness of information in annual reports. First, they separated the sample into companies
that had earnings that were either higher or lower than those predicted by a naive
time series model. Their model for the change in earnings was

$$\Delta NI_{jt} = \hat{a} + \hat{b}_j \Delta m_t + \varepsilon_{jt}, \tag{11.2}$$

where

ΔNI_{jt} = the change in earnings per share for the jth firm,

Δm_t = the change in the average eps for all firms (other than firm j) in the market.

Next, this regression was used to predict next year's change in earnings, $\Delta \widehat{NI}_{j,t+1}$:

$$\Delta \widehat{NI}_{j,t+1} = \hat{a} + \hat{b}_j \Delta m_{t+1}, \tag{11.3}$$

where

$\hat{a}, \hat{b}$ = coefficients estimated from time series fits of Eq. (11.2) to the data,

Δm_{t+1} = the actual change in market average eps during the $(t + 1)$th time period.

Finally, estimated earnings changes were compared with actual earnings changes. If
the actual change was greater than estimated, the company was put into a portfolio
where returns were expected to be positive, and vice versa.

Figure 11.4 plots an abnormal performance index (API) that represents the value
of $1 invested in a portfolio 12 months before an annual report and held for T

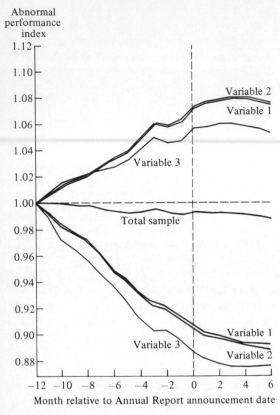

Figure 11.4
Abnormal performance index of portfolios chosen
on the basis of differences between actual and
predicted accounting income. (From R. Ball and
P. Brown, "An Empirical Evaluation of Accounting
Income Numbers," reprinted with permission of
Journal of Accounting Research, Autumn 1968, 169.)

months (where $T = 1, 2, \ldots, 12$). It is computed as follows:

$$\text{API} = \frac{1}{N} \sum_{j=1}^{N} \prod_{t=1}^{T} (1 + \varepsilon_{jt}),$$

where

N = the number of companies in a portfolio,

$T = 1, 2, \ldots, 12,$

ε_{jt} = abnormal performance measured by deviations from the market model.

A quick look at Fig. 11.4 shows that when earnings are higher than predicted, returns
are abnormally high. Furthermore, returns appear to adjust gradually until, by the
time of the annual report, almost all the adjustment has occurred. Most of the infor-

mation contained in the annual report is anticipated by the market *before* the annual report is released. In fact, anticipation is so accurate that the actual income number does not appear to cause any unusual jumps in the API in the announcement month. Most of the content of the annual report (about 85% to 90%) is captured by more timely sources of information. Apparently market prices adjust continuously to new information as it becomes publicly available throughout the year. The annual report has little new information to add.

These results suggest that prices in the marketplace continuously adjust in an unbiased manner to new information. Two implications for the corporate treasurers are: (1) significant new information, which will affect the future cash flows of the firm, should be announced as soon as it becomes available so that shareholders can use it without the (presumably greater) expense of discovering it from alternative sources; and (2) it probably does not make any difference whether cash flow effects are reported in the balance sheet, the income statement, or footnotes—the market can evaluate the news as long as it is publicly available, whatever form it may take.

The Ball and Brown study raised the question of whether or not annual reports contain any new information. More recent studies by Aharony and Swary [1980], Joy, Litzenberger and McEnally [1977], and Watts [1978] have focused on quarterly earnings reports where information revealed to the market is (perhaps) more timely than annual reports.[3] They typically use a time series model to predict quarterly earnings, then form two portfolios of equal risk, one consisting of firms with earnings higher than predicted and the other of firms with lower than expected earnings. The combined portfolio, which is long in the higher than expected earnings firms and short in the lower than expected earnings firms, is a zero-beta portfolio that (in perfect markets) requires no investment. It is an arbitrage portfolio and should have zero expected return. Watts [1978] finds a statistically significant return in the quarter of the announcement—a clear indication that quarterly earnings reports contain new information. However, he also finds a statistically significant return in the following quarter and concludes that "the existence of those abnormal returns is evidence that the market is inefficient."

Quarterly earnings reports are sometimes followed by announcements of dividend changes, which also affect the stock price. To study this problem, Aharony and Swary [1980] examine all dividend and earnings announcements within the same quarter that are at least 11 trading days apart. They conclude that both quarterly earnings announcements and dividend change announcements have statistically significant effects on the stock price. But more important they find no evidence of market inefficiency when the two types of announcement effects are separated. They used daily data and Watts [1978] used quarterly data, so we cannot be sure that the conclusions of the two studies regarding market inefficiency are inconsistent. All we can say is that unexpected changes in quarterly dividends and in quarterly earnings both have significant effects on the value of the firm and that more research needs to be done on possible market inefficiencies following the announcement of unexpected earnings changes.

---

[3] See also articles by Brown [1978], Griffin [1977], and Foster [1977].

Using intraday records of all transactions for the common stock returns of 96 (large) firms, Patell and Wolfson [1984] were able to estimate the speed of market reaction to disclosures of dividend and earnings information. In a simple trading rule, they bought (sold short) stocks whose dividend or earnings announcements exceeded (fell below) what had been forecast by Value Line Investor Service. The initial price reactions to earnings and dividend change announcements begin with the first pair of price changes following the appearance of the news release on the Broad Tape monitors. Although there was a hint of some activity in the hour or two preceding the Broad Tape news release, by far the largest portion of the price response occurs in the first 5 to 15 minutes after the disclosure. Thus, according to Patell and Wolfson, the market reacts to unexpected changes in earnings and dividends, and it reacts *very* quickly.

C. BLOCK TRADES

During a typical day for an actively traded security on a major stock exchange, thousands of shares will be traded, usually in round lots ranging between one hundred and several hundred shares. However, occasionally a large block, say 10,000 shares or more, is brought to the floor for trading. The behavior of the marketplace during the time interval around the trading of a large block provides a "laboratory" where the following questions can be investigated: (1) Does the block trade disrupt the market? (2) If the stock price falls when the block is sold, is the fall a liquidity effect, an information effect, or both? (3) Can anyone earn abnormal returns from the fall in price? (4) How fast does the market adjust to the effects of a block trade?

In perfect (rather than efficient) capital markets all securities of equal risk are perfect substitutes for each other. Because all individuals are assumed to possess the same information and because markets are assumed to be frictionless, the number of shares traded in a given security should have no effect on its price. If markets are less than perfect, the sale of a large block may have two effects (see Fig. 11.5). First, if it is believed to carry with it some new information about the security, the price will change (permanently) to reflect the new information. As illustrated in parts (c) and (d) of Fig. 11.5, the closing price is lower than the opening price and it remains low permanently.[4] Second, if buyers must incur extra costs when they accept the block, there may be a (temporary) decline in price to reflect what has been in various articles described as a price pressure, or distribution effect, or liquidity premium, as shown in parts (a) and (c). Figure 11.5 depicts how hypothesized information or price pressure effects can be expected to show up in continuous transactions data. For example, if the sale of a large block has both effects [Fig. 11.5(c)], we may expect the price to fall from the price before the trade $(-T)$ to the block price (BP) at the time of the block trade (BT), then to recover quickly from any price pressure effect by the time of

---

[4] The permanent decline in price is also tested by looking at the pattern of day-to-day closing prices. Evidence on this is reported in Fig. 11.6.

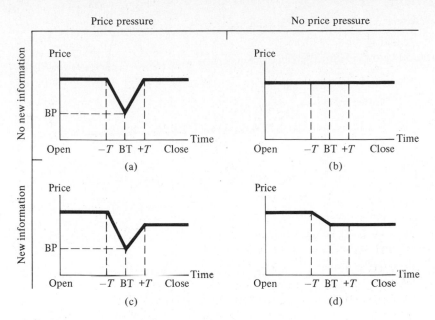

Figure 11.5
Competing hypotheses of price behavior around the sale of a large block.

the next trade $(+T)$ but to remain at a permanently lower level, which reflects the impact of new information on the value of the security.

Scholes [1972] and Kraus and Stoll [1972] provided the first empirical evidence about the price effects of block trading. Scholes used daily returns data to analyze 345 secondary distributions between July 1961 and December 1965. Secondary distributions, unlike primary distributions, are not initiated by the company but by shareholders who will receive the proceeds of the sale. The distributions are usually underwritten by an investment banking group that buys the entire block from the seller. The shares are then sold on a subscription basis *after* normal trading hours. The subscriber pays only the subscription price and not stock exchange or brokerage commissions. Figure 11.6 shows an abnormal performance index based on the market model and calculated for 40 trading days around the date of a secondary distribution. The abnormal performance index falls from an initial level of 1.0 to a final value of .977 just 14 days after the sale, a decline of 2.2%. On the day of the secondary distribution, the average abnormal performance was $-.5\%$. Because this study uses only close-to-close daily returns data, it focuses only on permanent price changes. We have characterized these as information effects [Fig. 11.5(c) and (d)]. Further evidence that the permanent decline in price is an information effect is revealed when the API is partitioned by vendor classification. These results appear in Table 11.2.

On the day of the offering the vendor is not usually known, but we may presume that the news becomes available soon thereafter. One may expect that an estate liquidation or portfolio rebalancing by a bank or insurance company would not be motivated by information about the performance of the firm. On the other hand, corporate

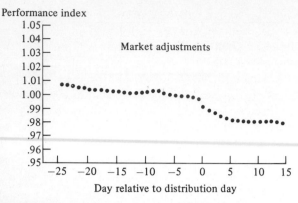

Figure 11.6
Abnormal performance index on days around a
secondary distribution. (From M. Scholes, "The Market
for Securities: Substitution vs. Price Pressure and the
Effects of Information on Share Prices," reprinted with
permission of *Journal of Business*, April 1972, 193.)
Copyright © 1972, The University of Chicago Press.

**Table 11.2   Abnormal Performance Index for Secondary
Distributions Partitioned by Vendor Category**

No. of Observations in Sample	Category	API	
		−10 to +10 Days	0 to +10 Days
192	Investment companies and mutual funds	−2.5%	−1.4%
31	Banks and insurance companies	−.3	−0.0
36	Individuals	−1.1	−.7
23	Corporations and officers	−2.9	−2.1
50	Estates and trusts	−.7	−.5

From M. Scholes, "The Market for Securities: Substitution vs. Price Pressure and the Effects of Information on Share Prices," reprinted with permission of *Journal of Business*, April 1972, 202. Copyright © 1972, The University of Chicago Press.

insiders as well as investment companies and mutual funds (with large research staffs) may be selling on the basis of adverse information. The data seem to support these suppositions. Greater price changes after the distribution are observed when the seller is presumed to have a knowledgeable reason for trading.[5]

Mikkelson and Partch [1985] studied a sample of 146 registered and 321 non-registered secondary offerings between 1972 and 1981. Using daily data, they find an

---

[5] A second test performed by Scholes showed that there was no relationship between the size of the distribution (as a percentage of the firm) and changes in the API on the distribution date. This would lead us to reject the hypothesis that investment companies and mutual funds may have had an impact because they sold larger blocks.

average statistically significant initial announcement price decline of -2.87% for registered secondaries and -1.96% for nonregistered secondaries. There was no significant price change at the actual offering date for registered distributions. The announcement date price declines are permanent, they are positively related to the size of the offering, and they are related to the identity of the seller (with the largest declines occurring when the vendors are directors or officers). These results are consistent with a permanent information effect. Mikkelson and Partch also find that the underwriting spread of secondaries is positively related to the relative size of the offering. This is consistent with the argument that the underwriting spread reflects compensation for the underwriter's selling effort or liquidity services. Therefore even though Mikkelson and Partch find no rebound in market prices following secondary offerings, they cannot conclude that the costs of liquidity are unimportant.

The data available to Kraus and Stoll [1972] pertain to open market block trades. They examined price effects for all block trades of 10,000 shares or more carried out on the NYSE between July 1, 1968, and September 30, 1969. They had prices for the close the day before the block trade, the price immediately prior to the transaction, the block price, and the closing price the day of the block trade. Abnormal performance indices based on daily data were consistent with Scholes' results. More interesting were intraday price effects, which are shown in Fig. 11.7. There is clear evidence of a price pressure or distribution effect. The stock price recovers substantially from the block price by the end of the trading day. The recovery averages .713%. For example, a stock that sold for $50.00 before the block transaction would

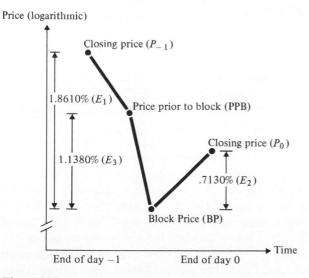

Figure 11.7
Intraday price impacts of block trading. (From A. Kraus and H. R. Stoll, "Price Impacts of Block Trading on the New York Stock Exchange," reprinted with permission of *Journal of Finance*, June 1972, 575.)

have a block price of $49.43, but by the end of the day the price would have recovered to $49.79.

The Scholes and Kraus-Stoll studies find evidence of a permanent price decline that is measured by price drops from the closing price the day before the block trade to the closing price the day of the block transaction. These negative returns seem to persist for at least a month after the block trade. In addition, Kraus and Stoll found evidence of temporary intraday price pressure effects. The implications of these findings are discussed by Dann, Mayers, and Raab [1977], who collected continuous transactions data during the day of a block trade for a sample of 298 blocks between July 1968 and December 1969. The open-to-block price decline was at least 4.56% for each block in the sample. The reason for restricting the sample to blocks with large price declines was to provide the strongest test of market efficiency. If an individual or a group of investors can establish a trading rule that allows them to buy a block whose open-to-block price change is at least 4.56%, then sell at the end of the day, they may be able to earn abnormal profits. This would be evidence of capital market inefficiency.

Testing a trading rule of this type takes great care. Normally, a block trade is not made publicly available until the trade has already been consummated and the transaction is recorded on the ticker. The semistrong form of market efficiency is based on the set of publicly available information. Therefore a critical issue is: Exactly how fast must we react after we observe that our -4.56% trading rule has been activated by the first publicly available announcement that occurs on the ticker tape? Figure 11.8 shows annualized rates of return using the -4.56% rule with the purchase made x minutes after the block and the stock then sold at the close. Returns are net of actual commissions and New York State transfer taxes. For both time periods that are reported, we would have to react in less than five minutes in order to earn a positive return. Such a rapid reaction is, for all practical purposes, impossible. It seems that no abnormal returns are available to individuals who trade on publicly available information about block trades because prices react so quickly. Fifteen minutes after the block trade, transaction prices have completely adjusted to unbiased estimates of closing prices. This gives some idea of how fast the market adjusts to new, unexpected information like a block trade.

What about people who can transact at the block price? Who are they and do they not earn an abnormal return? Usually, the specialist, the floor trader (a member of the NYSE), brokerage houses, and favored customers of the brokerage houses can participate at the block price. Dann, Mayers, and Raab show that with a -4.56% trading rule, an individual participating in every block with purchases of $100,000 or more could have earned a net annualized rate of return of 203% for the 173 blocks that activated the filter rule. Of course, this represents the maximum realizable rate of return. Nevertheless, it is clear that even after adjusting for risk, transactions costs, and taxes, it is possible to earn rates of return in excess of what any existing theory would call "normal." This may be interpreted as evidence that capital markets are inefficient in their strong form. Individuals who are notified of the pending block trade and who can participate at the block price before the information becomes publicly available do in fact appear to earn excess profits.

However, Dann, Mayers, and Raab caution us that we may not properly under-

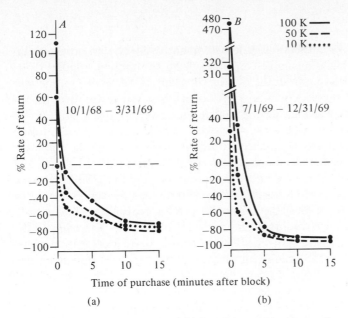

Annualized[a] rates of return on initial wealth, −4.56 percent rule; purchase at first price at least x minutes after block, sell at close[b] (using only first block per day). Gross returns less actual commissions and NY State transfer taxes (curves represent levels of initial wealth).

[a] Annualized rates of return are calculated by squaring the quantity one plus the respective six-month return.

[b] Blocks occurring within x minutes of the close were assumed not to have been acted upon.

Figure 11.8
Annualized rates of return on the −4.56% rule. (From L. Dann, D. Mayers, and R. Raab, "Trading Rules, Large Blocks, and the Speed of Adjustment," reprinted from *Journal of Financial Economics*, January 1977, 18.)

stand all the costs that a buyer faces in a block trade. One possibility is that the specialist (or anyone else) normally holds an optimal utility-maximizing portfolio. In order to accept part of a block trade, which forces the specialist away from that portfolio, he or she will charge a premium rate of return. In this way, what appear to be abnormal returns may actually be fair, competitively determined fees for a service rendered—the service of providing liquidity to a seller.

To date, the empirical research into the phenomenon of price changes around a block trade shows that block trades do not disrupt markets, that markets are efficient in the sense that they very quickly (less than 15 minutes) fully reflect all publicly available information. There is evidence of both a permanent effect and a (very) temporary liquidity or price pressure effect as illustrated in Fig. 11.5(c). The market is efficient in its semistrong form, but the fact that abnormal returns are earned by individuals who participate at the block price may indicate strong-form inefficiency.

D. INSIDER TRADING

A direct test of strong-form efficiency is whether or not insiders with access to information that is not publicly available can outperform the market.[6] Jaffe [1974] collected data on insider trading from the *Official Summary of Security Transactions and Holdings* published by the Securities and Exchange Commission. He then defined an intensive trading month as one during which there were at least three more insiders selling than buying, or vice versa. If a stock was intensively traded during a given month, it was included in an intensive-trading portfolio. Using the empirical market line, Jaffe then calculated cumulative average residuals. If the stock had intensive selling, its residual (which would presumably be negative) was multiplied by -1 and added to the portfolio returns, and conversely for intensive buying. For 861 observations during the 1960s, the residuals rose approximately 5% in eight months following the intensive-trading event, with 3% of the rise occurring in the last six months. These returns are statistically significant and are greater than transactions costs. A sample of insider trading during the 1950s produces similar results. These findings suggest that insiders do earn abnormal returns and that the strong-form hypothesis of market efficiency does not hold.

Jaffe also investigated the effect of regulation changes on insider trading. Two of the most significant changes in security regulation resulted from (1) the Cady-Roberts decision in November 1961, when the SEC first exercised its power to punish insider trading and thus established the precedent that corporate officials trading on insider information were liable for civil prosecution; and (2) the Texas Gulf Sulphur case in August 1966, when the courts upheld the earlier (April 1965) SEC indictment of company officials who had suppressed and traded on news about a vast mineral strike. After examining abnormal returns from intensive insider-trading samples around dates of these historic decisions, Jaffe was forced to the following conclusion: The data could not reject the null hypothesis that the enforcement of SEC regulations in these two cases had no effect on insider trading in general. At best the regulations prohibit only the most flagrant examples of speculation based on inside information.

A study by Finnerty [1976] corroborates Jaffe's conclusions. The major difference is that the Finnerty data sample was not restricted to an intensive trading group. By testing the entire population of insiders, the empirical findings allow an evaluation of the "average" insider returns. The data include over 30,000 individual insider transactions between January 1969 and December 1972. Abnormal returns computed from the market model indicate that insiders are able to "beat the market" on a risk-adjusted basis, both when selling and when buying.

A study by Givoly and Palmon [1985] correlates insider trading with subsequent news announcements to see if insiders trade in anticipation of news releases. The surprising result is that there is no relationship between insider trading and news events. Although insiders' transactions are associated with a strong price move-

---

[6] The Securities and Exchange Commission defines insiders as members of the board of directors, corporate officers, and any beneficial owner of more than 10% of any class of stock. They must disclose, on a monthly basis, any changes in their stock holdings.

ment in the direction of the trade during the month following the trade, these price movements occur independent of subsequent publication of news. This leads to the conjecture that outside investors accept (blindly) the superior knowledge and follow in the footsteps of insiders.

One of the interesting implications of the empirical work on insider trading is that it is consistent with the point of view that markets do *not* aggregate information. In Chapter 10, fully aggregating markets were described as those that reflect all available information even though it is not known to all market participants. In a fully aggregating market an insider should not be able to make abnormal returns because his trading activity would reveal his information to the market. The evidence on profitable insider trading shows that this is clearly not the case.

E. NEW ISSUES

There has been a long history of articles that have studied the pricing of the common stock of companies that is issued to the public for the first time. To mention a few, the list includes papers by the Securities and Exchange Commission [1963], Reilly and Hatfield [1969], Stickney [1970], McDonald and Fisher [1972], Logue [1973], Stigler [1964], and Shaw [1971]. They all faced a seemingly insoluble problem: How could returns on unseasoned issues be adjusted for risk if time series data on preissue prices were nonexistent? Any estimate of systematic risk, e.g., requires the computation of the covariance between time series returns for a given security and returns on a market portfolio. But new issues are not priced until they become public. An ingenious way around this problem was employed by Ibbotson [1975]. Portfolios of new issues with identical seasoning (defined as the number of months since issue) were formed. The monthly return on the XYZ Company in March 1964, say two months after its issue, was matched with the market return that month, resulting in one pair of returns for a portfolio of two months seasoning. By collecting a large number of return pairs for new issues that went public in different calendar months but that all had two months seasoning, it was possible to form a vector of returns of issues of two months seasoning for which Ibbotson could compute a covariance with the market. In this manner, he estimated the systematic risk of issues with various seasoning. Using the empirical market line, he was able to estimate abnormal performance indices in the month of initial issue (initial performance from the offering date price to the end of the first month) and in the aftermarket (months following the initial issue). From 2650 new issues between 1960 and 1969, Ibbotson randomly selected one new issue for each of the 120 calendar months.

The estimated systematic risk (beta) in the month of issue was 2.26, and the abnormal return was estimated to be 11.4%. Even after transactions costs, this represents a statistically significant positive abnormal return. Therefore either the offering price is set too low or investors systematically overvalue new issues at the end of the first month of seasoning. Later evidence shows that the aftermarket is efficient; therefore Ibbotson focused his attention on the possibility that offering prices determined by the investment banking firm are systematically set below the

Table 11.3   Gain and Loss Situations for a New Issue

	Situation	*Investors*	*Investment Banker*
I	Maximum offering price ≥ market price ≥ offering price	Gain	Parity
II	Maximum offering price ≥ offering price ≥ market price	Parity	Loss
III	Maximum offering price = offering price ≥ market price	Parity	Loss
IV	Market price ≥ maximum offering price = offering price	Gain	Parity

fair market value of the security. Regulations of the SEC require a maximum offering price for a new issue, which is usually filed two weeks in advance of the actual offering, although it can be adjusted in some cases.[7] The actual offering price is set immediately before the offering. The existence of a regulation that requires the actual offering price to be fixed creates the possibility of a "Heads I lose, tails you win" situation for the underwriter. Table 11.3 shows the four possibilities that can occur in a firm commitment offering (the underwriting syndicate buys the issue from the firm for the offering price less an underwriting spread, then sells the issue to the public at the fixed offering price). The best the underwriter can do is achieve a parity situation with no gain or loss. This happens whenever the market price turns out to be above the offering price (situations I and IV). Obviously, the investment banker does not want the market price to equal or exceed the *maximum* offering price (situations III and IV). This would infuriate the issuing firm and lead to a loss of future underwriting business. Therefore we usually observe situations I and II. But if the investment banking firm receives adequate compensation from its underwriting spread for the risk it undertakes, and if it cannot gain by setting the offer price lower than the market price, then why do we not observe offer prices (which, after all, are established only moments before the issues are sold to the public) set equal to the market value? Why can investors systematically earn an abnormal return of 11.4% during the first month of issue? This conundrum, like the difference between the block price and the closing price on the day of the block, cannot easily be explained by existing finance theory.

What about new issue performance in the aftermarket, i.e., for prices from the first market price onward? Figure 11.9 shows abnormal returns (based on the empirical market line) in the aftermarket for six-month holding periods and the significance tests (*t*-tests). The 9 periods other than the initial offering period include only 2 periods with results that are statistically different from zero (and returns in these 2 periods are negative). Ibbotson concludes that the evidence cannot allow us to reject the null hypothesis that aftermarkets are efficient, although it is interesting to note that returns in 7 out of 10 periods show negative returns.

Figure 11.10 shows plots of changes in systematic risk in the aftermarket; note the decline. The results show that the systematic risk of new issues is greater than

---

[7] In most cases the maximum offering price is set high enough to cause little concern that it may actually constrain the actual offering price.

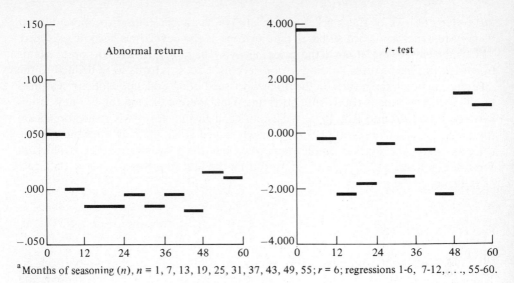

^{a}Months of seasoning (n), n = 1, 7, 13, 19, 25, 31, 37, 43, 49, 55; r = 6; regressions 1-6, 7-12, . . ., 55-60.

Figure 11.9
Abnormal returns for issues of different seasoning. (From R. Ibbotson, "Price Performance of Common Stock New Issues," reprinted from *Journal of Financial Economics*, September 1975, 254.)

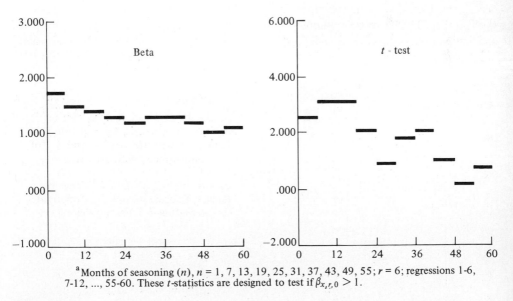

^{a}Months of seasoning (n), n = 1, 7, 13, 19, 25, 31, 37, 43, 49, 55; r = 6; regressions 1-6, 7-12, ..., 55-60. These t-statistics are designed to test if $\beta_{x,t,0} > 1$.

Figure 11.10
Systematic risk of issues with different seasoning. (From R. Ibbotson, "Price Performance of Common Stock New Issues," reprinted from *Journal of Financial Economics*, September 1975, 260.)

the systematic risk of the market (which always has a beta equal to one) and that their systematic risk is not stable in that it drops as the new issues become seasoned.

Weinstein [1978] studied the price behavior of newly issued corporate bonds by measuring their excess holding period returns. Excess returns were defined as the difference between the return on the ith newly issued bond and a portfolio of seasoned bonds with the same (Moody's) bond rating. Data were collected for 179 new issues between June 1962 and July 1974. Weinstein's conclusions for newly issued bonds are similar to those of Ibbotson [1975] for newly issued stock, namely, that the offering price is below the market equilibrium price but that the aftermarket is efficient. Weinstein found a .383% rate of return during the first month and only a .06% rate of return over the next six months.

F. STOCK SPLITS

Why do stocks split, and what effect, if any, do splits have on shareholder wealth? The best known study of stock splits was conducted by Fama, Fisher, Jensen, and Roll [1969]. Cumulative average residuals were calculated from the simple market model, using monthly data for an interval of 60 months around the split ex date for 940 splits between January 1927 and December 1959. Figure 11.11 shows the results. It plots the cumulative average return for the stock split sample. Positive abnormal returns are observed *before* the split but not afterward. This would seem to indicate that splits are the cause of the abnormal returns. But such a conclusion has no economic logic to it. The run-up in the cumulative average returns prior to the stock split in Fig. 11.11 can be explained by selection bias. Stocks split because their price has increased prior to the split date. Consequently, it should hardly be surprising that when we select a sample of split-up stocks, we observe that they have positive

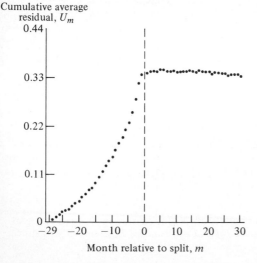

Figure 11.11
Cumulative average residuals for 60 months around stock splits. (From E. F. Fama, L. Fisher, M. Jensen, and R. Roll, "The Adjustment of Stock Prices to New Information," reprinted with permission of *International Economic Review*, February 1969, 13. Copyright © *International Economic Review*.)

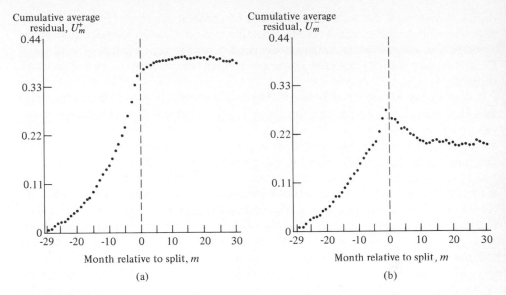

Figure 11.12
Cumulative average residuals for splits with (a) dividend increases and (b) decreases. (From
E. F. Fama, L. Fisher, M. Jensen, and R. Roll, "The Adjustment of Stock Prices to New
Information," reprinted with permission of *International Economic Review*, February 1969,
15. Copyright © *International Economic Review*.)

abnormal performance prior to the split date. Selection bias occurs because we are
studying a selected data set of stocks that have been observed to split.

Fama *et al.* [1969] speculated that stock splits might be interpreted by investors
as a message about future changes in the firm's expected cash flows. They hypothesized that stock splits might be interpreted as a message about dividend increases,
which in turn imply that the managers of the firm feel confident that it can maintain
a permanently higher level of cash flows. To test this hypothesis the sample was divided into those firms that increased their dividends beyond the average for the
market in the interval following the split and those that paid out lower dividends.
The results, shown in Fig. 11.12, reveal that stocks in the dividend "increased" class
have slightly positive returns following the split. This is consistent with the hypothesis
that splits are interpreted as messages about dividend increases.[8] Of course, a dividend increase does not always follow a split. Hence the slightly positive abnormal
return for the dividend-increase group reflects small price adjustments that occur
when the market is absolutely sure of the increase. On the other hand, the cumulative
average residuals of split-up stocks with poor dividend performance decline until
about a year after the split, by which time it must be very clear that the anticipated

---

[8] This does not imply that higher dividend payout per se causes an increase in the value of the firm. In
Chapter 15 "Dividend Policy" we shall see that higher dividends are interpreted as signals that the future
cash flows from the firm will increase.

dividend increase is not forthcoming. When we combine the results for the dividend increases and decreases, these results are consistent with the hypothesis that on the average the market makes unbiased dividend forecasts for split-up securities and these forecasts are fully reflected in the price of the security by the end of the split month.

A more recent study by Grinblatt, Masulis, and Titman [1984] used daily data and looked at shareholder returns on the split announcement date as well as the split ex date. They examined a special subsample of splits where no other announcements were made in the three-day period around the split announcement and where no cash dividends had been declared in the previous three years.[9] For this sample of 125 "pure" stock splits they found a statistically significant announcement return of 3.44%. They interpret stock split announcements as favorable signals about the firm's future cash flows. Surprisingly, they also find statistically significant returns (for their entire sample of 1360 stock splits) on the ex date. There is no good explanation for this result, and it is inconsistent with the earlier Fama et al. study that used monthly returns data.

In the same study, Grinblatt, Masulis, and Titman [1984] confirm earlier work on stock dividends by Foster and Vickrey [1978] and Woolridge [1983a, 1983b]. The announcement effects for stock dividends are large, 4.90% for a sample of 382 stock dividends and 5.89% for a smaller sample of 84 stock dividends with no other announcements in a three-day period around the stock dividend announcement. One possible reason for the larger announcement effect of a stock dividend is that retained earnings must be reduced by the dollar amount of the stock dividend. Only those companies that are confident they will not run afoul of debt restrictions that require minimum levels of retained earnings will willingly announce a stock dividend. Another reason is that convertible debt and warrant holders are not protected against dilution caused by stock dividends. As with stock splits, there was a significant positive return on the stock dividend ex date (and the day before). No explanation is offered for why the ex date effect is observed.

The results of Fama et al. [1969] are consistent with the semistrong form of market efficiency. Prices appear to fully reflect information about expected cash flows. The split per se has no effect on shareholder wealth. Rather, it merely serves as a message about the future prospects of the firm. Thus splits have benefits as signaling devices. There seems to be no way to use a split to increase one's expected returns, unless, of course, inside information concerning the split or subsequent dividend behavior is available.

One often hears that stocks split because there is an "optimal" price range for common stocks. Moving the security price into this range makes the market for trading in the security "wider" or "deeper"; hence there is more trading liquidity. Copeland [1979] reports that contrary to the above argument, market liquidity is actually lower following a stock split. Trading volume is proportionately lower than its presplit level, brokerage revenues (a major portion of transactions costs) are

---

[9] However, 11% of the pure samples declared a dividend within one year of the stock split.

proportionately higher, and bid-ask spreads are higher as a percentage of the bid price.[10] Taken together, these empirical results point to lower postsplit liquidity. Hence we can say that the market for split-up securities has lower operational efficiency relative to its presplit level. Ohlson and Penman [1985] report that the postsplit return standard deviation for split-up stocks exceeds the presplit return standard deviation by an average of 30%. Lower liquidity and higher return variance are both costs of splitting.

Brennan and Copeland [1987] provide a signaling theory explanation for stock splits and show that it is consistent with the data. The intuition can be explained as follows. Suppose that managers know the future prospects of their firm better than the market does. Furthermore, assume that there are two firms with a price of $60 per share which are alike in every way except that the managers of firm A know it has a bright future while the managers of firm B expect only average performance. Managers of both firms know that if they decide to announce a split, their shareholders will suffer from the higher transactions costs documented by Copeland [1979]. However, the successful firm A will bear these costs only temporarily, while firm B will bear them indefinitely. Hence firm A will signal its bright future with a stock split and the signal will not be mimicked by firm B. As a result, A's price will rise at the time of the announcement so as to reflect the present value of its future prospects. Furthermore, the lower the target price to which the firm splits, the greater confidence management has, and the larger will be the announcement residual. Empirical results by Brennan and Copeland [1987] confirm this prediction.

G. PERFORMANCE OF MANAGED PORTFOLIOS

1. Mutual Funds

Mutual funds allege that they can provide two types of service to their clients. First, they may minimize the amount of unsystematic risk an investor must face. This is done through efficient diversification in the face of transactions costs. Second, they may be able to use their professional expertise to earn abnormal returns through successful prediction of future security prices. This second claim is contradictory to the semistrong form of capital market efficiency unless, for some reason, mutual fund managers can consistently obtain information that is not publicly available.

A number of studies have focused their attention on the performance of mutual funds. A partial list includes Friend and Vickers [1965], Sharpe [1966], Treynor [1965], Farrar [1962], Friend, Blume, and Crockett [1970], Jensen [1968], Mains [1977], Henricksson [1984], and Grinblatt and Titman [1986]. Various performance

---

[10] The bid price is the price that a potential buyer offers, say $20, and the ask price is what the seller requires, suppose it is $20½. The bid-ask spread is the difference, specifically $½.

measures are used. Among them are:

$$\text{Reward to variability ratio} = \frac{R_{jt} - R_{ft}}{\sigma_j}, \tag{11.4}$$

$$\text{Treynor index} = \frac{R_{jt} - R_{ft}}{\hat{\beta}_j}, \tag{11.5}$$

$$\text{Abnormal performance} = \alpha_{jt} = (R_{jt} - R_{ft}) - [\hat{\beta}_j(R_{mt} - R_{ft})], \tag{11.6}$$

where

R_j = the return of the jth mutual fund,

R_f = the return on a risk-free asset (usually Treasury bills),

σ_j = the standard deviation of return on the jth mutual fund,

$\hat{\beta}_j$ = the estimated systematic risk of the jth mutual fund.

Of these, the abnormal performance measure [Eq. (11.6)] makes use of the CAPM. It was developed by Jensen [1968], who used it to test the abnormal performance of 115 mutual funds, using annual data between 1955 and 1964. If the performance index, α, is positive, then after adjusting for risk and for movements in the market index, the abnormal performance of a portfolio is also positive. The average α for returns measured net of costs (such as research costs, management fees, and brokerage commissions) was -1.1% per year over the 10-year period. This suggests that on the average the funds were not able to forecast future security prices well enough to cover their expenses. When returns were measured gross of expenses (excepting brokerage commissions), the average α was $-.4\%$ per year. Apparently the gross returns were not sufficient to recoup even brokerage commissions.

In sum, Jensen's study of mutual funds provides evidence that the 115 mutual funds, on the average, were not able to predict security prices well enough to outperform a buy-and-hold strategy. In addition, there was very little evidence that any individual fund was able to do better than what might be expected from mere random chance. These conclusions held even when fund returns were measured gross of management expenses and brokerage costs. Results obtained are consistent with the hypothesis of capital market efficiency in its semistrong form, because we may assume that, at the very least, mutual fund managers have access to publicly available information. However, they do not necessarily imply that mutual funds will not be held by rational investors. On the average the funds do an excellent job of diversification. This may by itself be a socially desirable service to investors.

More recently, Mains [1977] has reexamined the issue of mutual fund performance. He criticizes Jensen's work on two accounts. First, the rates of return were underestimated because dividends were assumed to be reinvested at year's end rather than during the quarter they were received and because when expenses were added back to obtain gross returns, they were added back at year's end instead of continuously throughout the year. By using monthly data instead of annual data, Mains is able to better estimate both net and gross returns. Second, Jensen assumed that mutual fund betas were stationary over long periods of time [note that $\hat{\beta}_j$ has no time subscript in Eq. (11.6)]. Using monthly data, Mains obtains lower estimates of $\hat{\beta}_j$ and argues that Jensen's estimates of risk were too high.

The abnormal performance results calculated for a sample of 70 mutual funds indicate that as a group the mutual funds had neutral risk-adjusted performance on a net return basis. On a gross return basis (i.e., before operating expenses and transactions costs), 80% of the funds sampled performed positively. This suggests that mutual funds are able to outperform the market well enough to earn back their operating expenses. It is also consistent with the theory of efficient markets given costly information. Recall from Chapter 10 that the theoretical work of Cornell and Roll [1981] and Grossman [1980] predicts a market equilibrium where investors who utilize costly information will have higher gross rates of return than their uninformed competitors. But because information is costly, the equilibrium net rates of return for informed and uninformed investors will be the same. This is just what Main's work shows. Mutual funds' gross rates of return are greater than the rate on a randomly selected portfolio of equivalent risk, but when costs (transactions costs and management fees) are subtracted, the net performance of mutual funds is the same as that for a naive investment strategy.

2. The Value Line Investor Survey

Hundreds of investment advisory services sell advice that predicts the performance of various types of assets. Perhaps the largest is the Value Line Investor Survey. Employing over 200 people, it ranks around 1700 securities each week. Securities are ranked 1 to 5 (with 1 being highest), based on their expected price performance relative to the other stocks covered in the survey. Security rankings result from a complex filter rule that utilizes four criteria: (1) the earnings and price rank of each security relative to all others, (2) a price momentum factor, (3) year-to-year relative changes in quarterly earnings, and (4) an earnings "surprise" factor. Roughly 53% of the securities are ranked third, 18% are ranked second or fourth, and 6% are ranked first or fifth.

The Value Line predictions have been the subject of many academic studies because they represent a clear attempt to use historical data in a complex computerized filter rule to try to predict future performance.[11] Figure Q11.8 (Problem 11.8 in the problem set at the end of this chapter) shows an 18-year price performance record assuming that all Value Line ranking changes had been followed between April 1965 and December 1983. Group 1 had price appreciation of 1295%, whereas Group 5 increased in price by only 35%. However, this is only the realized *price* appreciation. The rates of return reported in Fig. Q11.8 are not total returns because they do not include dividends. Furthermore, they are not adjusted for risk. The problem is how to measure the performance of a portfolio of securities assuming that the Value Line recommendations are used for portfolio formation.

---

[11] A partial list of Value Line–related studies is: Shelton [1967], Hausman [1969], Black [1971], Kaplan and Weil [1973], Brown and Rozeff [1978], Holloway [1981], and Copeland and Mayers [1982].

Black [1971] performed the first systematic study utilizing Jensen's abnormal performance measure as given in Eq. (11.6). Black's results indicate statistically significant abnormal performance for equally weighted portfolios formed from stocks ranked 1, 2, 4, and 5 by Value Line and rebalanced monthly. Before transactions costs, portfolios 1 and 5 had risk-adjusted rates of return of $+10\%$ and -10%, respectively. Even with round-trip transactions costs of 2%, the net rate of return for a long position in portfolio 1 would still have been positive, thereby indicating economically significant performance. One problem with these results is the Jensen methodology for measuring portfolio performance. It has been criticized by Roll [1977, 1978], who argues that any methodology based on the capital asset pricing model will measure either (1) no abnormal performance if the market index portfolio is *ex post* efficient or (2) a meaningless abnormal performance if the index portfolio is *ex post* inefficient.[12]

Copeland and Mayers [1982] and Chen, Copeland, and Mayers [1986] measured Value Line portfolio performance by using a *future benchmark technique* that avoids selection bias problems associated with using historic benchmarks as well as the known difficulties of using capital asset pricing model benchmarks.[13] The future benchmark technique uses the market model (described in section A of this chapter) fit using data after the test period where portfolio performance is being measured. The steps in the procedure are:

1. Using a sample from after the test period, calculate the market model equation for the portfolio being evaluated.

2. Use the parameters of the model as a benchmark for computing the portfolio's unexpected return during a test period.

3. Repeat the procedure and test to see whether the mean unexpected return is significantly different from zero.

In other words, rather than using a particular (perhaps suspect) model (such as the CAPM) of asset pricing as a benchmark, estimate the expected returns directly from the data. The future benchmark technique is not without its problems, however. It assumes that the portfolio characteristics (e.g., risk and dividend yield) remain essentially the same throughout the test and benchmark periods.

Copeland and Mayers find considerably less abnormal performance than Black, who used the Jensen methodology. Where Black reported (roughly) 20% per year for an investor who was long on portfolio 1 and short on portfolio 5, Copeland and Mayers find an annual rate of return of only 6.8%. Moreover, only portfolio 5 had statistically significant returns. Nevertheless, any significant performance is a potential violation of semistrong market efficiency. Thus Value Line remains an enigma.

---

[12] For a more complete discussion of Roll's critique, see Chapter 7.

[13] Using historic benchmarks creates a selection bias problem because Value Line uses a variant of the "relative strength" criterion to choose rankings. Portfolio 1 stocks tend to have abnormally high historic rates of return; thus subtracting these rates from test period returns would tend to bias the results against Value Line.

Stickel [1985] uses the future benchmark methodology to measure the abnormal performance resulting from *changes* in Value Line rankings. He finds statistically significant returns for reclassifications from rank 2 to rank 1 that are three times as large as the returns from reclassifications from 1 to 2. Upgradings from 5 to 4 were not associated with significant abnormal returns. He concludes that the market reacts to Value Line reclassifications as news events, that the price adjustment takes place over a multiple-day period, and that the size of the adjustment is larger for smaller firms.

3. Dual Purpose Funds

Dual-purpose funds are companies whose only assets are the securities of other companies. However, unlike open-end mutual funds, closed-end dual purpose funds neither issue new shares nor redeem outstanding ones. Investors who wish to own shares in a closed-end fund must purchase fund shares on the open market. The shares are divided into two types, both of which have claim on the same underlying assets. The *capital shares* of a dual fund pay no dividends and are redeemable at net asset value at the (predetermined) maturity date of the fund.[14] The *income shares* receive any dividends or income that the fund may earn, subject to a stated minimum cumulative dividend, and are redeemed at a fixed price at the fund's maturity date. Dual funds were established on the premise that some investors may wish to own a security providing only income, whereas other investors may desire only potential capital gains.

There are two very interesting issues that are raised when one observes the market price of closed-end shares. First, the market value of the fund's capital shares does not equal the *net asset value*.[15] Most often, the net asset value per share exceeds the actual price per share of the dual fund. In this case the dual fund is said to sell at a discount. Given that a speculator (especially a tax-exempt institution) could buy all of a fund's outstanding shares and liquidate the fund for its net asset value, it is a mystery why a discount (or premium) can persist. The second issue has to do with whether or not risk-adjusted abnormal rates of return accrue to investors who buy a dual fund when it is selling at a discount, then hold it for a period of time, possibly to maturity.

There have been several theories put forth to explain why dual fund shares should sell at a discount from their net asset value. Malkiel [1977] suggests that two of the important possibilities are (1) unrealized capital gains and (2) holdings of letter (un-registered) stock. If a fund is holding a portfolio of securities that have had substantial capital gains, then an investor who purchases shares in the fund automatically incurs a built-in capital gains liability that must be paid when the securities are sold by the

---

[14] The net asset value received at maturity is the market value of the securities in the fund at that date, less the promised repayment of capital to income shares.

[15] The net asset value is the value to shareholders measured as the market value of the securities held by the fund at a given point in time.

dual fund.[16] The same investor would incur no such tax liability by simply buying the same portfolio of securities on his or her own. One of the problems with this explanation, discussed by Thompson [1978], is that nontaxable institutions should be able to make a profit whenever a tax-induced discount occurs. They simply buy up all of a fund's outstanding shares, then liquidate the fund at its net asset value. In addition to capital gains tax liabilities, Malkiel finds that dual-fund holdings of letter stock helps to explain discounts. In most cases letter stock sells at a discount from market value, presumably because it is not marketable. The fund that buys letter stock is required to sign an "investment letter" pledging that the stock has been bought for investment purposes and indicating that the fund will hold the shares for a considerable period of time. Even though the stock is often purchased at discounts from the market price of the unrestricted shares of the company, the shares are recorded at market value on the dual fund's books. Hence for accounting reasons the net asset value may be overstated.

Ingersoll [1976] shows that the capital shares of a dual fund are analogous to call options written on the dividend-paying securities held by the fund. Holders of income shares are entitled to all income produced by the portfolio plus an amount equal to their initial investment payable when the fund matures. If S is the value of the fund at maturity and X is the promised payment to income shares, then capital shareowners receive the maximum of $(S - X)$ or zero, whichever is larger, at maturity. This payoff can be written as

$$MAX[S - X, 0]$$

and is exactly the same as the payoff to a call option.[17] We know, from option pricing theory, that the present value of a call option is bounded from below by $S - Xe^{-r_f T}$. However, dual funds are characterized by the fact that cash disbursements in the form of dividends and management fees are made over the life of the fund. If these disbursements are assumed to be continuous, then the present value of the fund is $Se^{-\gamma T}$, where γ is the rate of payment. Ingersoll shows that given the cash disbursements the lower bound on the value of the capital shares must be $Se^{-\gamma T} - Xe^{-r_f T}$, as shown in Fig. 11.13. The dashed line, $S - X$, is the net asset value of the capital shares.[18] When the fund value is above a critical level, S_c, the capital shares will sell at a discount. Below S_c they sell at a premium.

When Ingersoll used the option pricing model to estimate the market value of capital shares, he found that it tracked actual prices very well in spite of the fact that no tax effects were taken into account. The data consisted of prices for seven funds on a weekly basis between May 1967 and December 1973. Furthermore, he simulated

---

[16] Tax treatment of capital gains is not symmetrical. Although realized capital losses may be carried forward to offset future capital gains, the losses may not be distributed to a fund's shareholders as a tax shield. The tax argument, if valid, can also be used to explain dual fund premia. If a fund has unrealized losses, a taxable investor would prefer the fund over the alternative of investing in the underlying securities because expected future capital gains taxes would be lower with the dual fund.

[17] See, for example, Eq. (8.11).

[18] Figure 11.13 is very similar to Fig. 8.18 in the option pricing chapter. The valuation of dual fund capital shares is an application of option pricing theory.

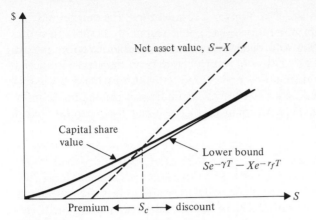

Figure 11.13
Capital share price as a function of asset value.
(From J. Ingersoll, Jr., "A Theoretical and Empirical
Investigation of Dual Purpose Funds," reprinted from
Journal of Financial Economics, January–March 1976,
87.)

a trading rule that bought (sold) capital shares when the option model price was
above (below) the market price and financed the investment by an opposite position
in the securities of the fund and borrowing or lending at the riskless rate. Thus a
hedged portfolio was created that required no investment and that had very low
risk.[19] The returns on the hedge portfolio were (almost always) insignificantly different from zero. This suggests that even though capital shares may sell for a discount
or premium, they are efficiently priced in a semistrong form sense.

Thompson [1978] measures the performance of closed-end dual funds by using
all three versions of the empirical models described at the beginning of this chapter.
He used monthly data for 23 closed-end funds. The longest-lived fund was in existence
from 1940 until 1975 (when the data set ended). A trading rule purchased shares in
each fund that was selling at a discount at the previous year's end, then held the
fund and reinvested all distributions until the end of the year. The procedure was
repeated for each year that data existed and abnormal returns were then calculated
for a portfolio based on this trading strategy. Thompson found that discounted
closed-end fund shares tend to outperform the market, adjusted for risk. By one
performance measure the annual abnormal return (i.e., the return above that earned
by NYSE stocks of equivalent risk) was in excess of 4%. It is interesting to note that
a trading strategy that purchased shares of funds selling at a premium would have
experienced a −7.9% per year abnormal return, although the results were not statistically significant.

---

[19] Not all risk could be eliminated because of (1) weekly rather than continuous adjustment of the hedge
position, (2) changes in the model deviation, and (3) improper hedge ratios if the option model of capital
shares is incorrect.

There are several explanations for Thompson's results. First, the market may be inefficient, at least for tax-exempt institutions that could seemingly be able to profit from the above-mentioned trading rule. Second, so long as taxable investors persist in holding closed-end shares the gross rates of return before taxes may have to exceed the market equilibrium rate of return in order to compensate for unrealized tax liabilities. Third, abnormal return measures based on the capital asset pricing model may be inappropriate for measuring the performance of closed-end fund capital shares that are call options.

An interesting paper by Brauer [1984] reports on the effects of open-ending 14 closed-end funds between 1960 and 1981. Funds that were open-ended had larger discounts from net asset value (23.6% versus 16.2%) and lower management fees (.78% versus 1.00%) than funds that were not open-ended. Large discounts provide shareholders with greater incentive to open-end their funds and lower management fees imply less management resistance. These two variables were actually able to predict which funds would be open-ended. In addition, Brauer reports that most of the (large) abnormal returns that resulted from the announcement of open-ending were realized by the end of the announcement month—a result consistent with semistrong-form market efficiency.

The problem of analyzing dual funds is not yet completely resolved. The observed discounts (premia) on capital shares may be attributable to (1) unrealized capital gains tax liabilities, (2) fund holdings of letter stock, (3) management and brokerage costs, or (4) the option nature of capital shares. The relative importance of these factors has not yet been completely resolved. There is no good explanation for why all funds selling at a discount have not been open-ended. In addition, there remains some question about whether or not abnormal returns can be earned by utilizing trading rules based on observed discounts (premia). Thompson's [1978] work suggests that abnormal returns are possible, whereas Ingersoll [1976] finds no evidence of abnormal returns.

H. WEEKEND AND YEAR-END EFFECTS

Any predictable pattern in asset returns may be exploitable and therefore judged as evidence against semistrong market efficiency. Even if the pattern cannot be employed directly in a trading rule because of prohibitive transactions costs, it may enable people who were going to trade anyway to increase their portfolio returns over what they otherwise may have received without knowledge of the pattern. Two statistically significant patterns in stock market returns are the weekend effect and the turn-of-the-year effect.

French [1980] studied daily returns on the Standard and Poor's composite portfolio of the 500 largest firms on the New York Stock Exchange over the period 1953 to 1977. Table 11.4 shows the summary statistics for returns by day of the week. The negative returns on Monday were highly significant. They were also significantly negative in each of the five-year subperiods that were studied.

Table 11.4   Summary Statistics for Daily Returns on the S&P 500 Stock Index, 1953–1977

Means, standard deviations, and t-statistics of the percent return from the close of the previous trading day to the close of the day indicated.[a]

		Monday	Tuesday	Wednesday	Thursday	Friday
1953–1977	Mean	−0.1681	0.0157	0.0967	0.0448	0.0873
	Standard deviation	0.8427	0.7267	0.7483	0.6857	0.6600
	t-statistic	−6.823[c]	0.746	4.534[c]	2.283[b]	4.599[c]
	observations	1170	1193	1231	1221	1209

[a] Returns for periods including a holiday are omitted. These returns are defined as $R_t = \ln(P_t/P_{t-1}) \cdot 100$.

[b] 5% significance level.

[c] 0.5% significance level.

From K. French, "Stock Returns and the Weekend Effect," reprinted from the *Journal of Financial Economics*, March 1980, 58.

An immediate natural reaction to explain this phenomenon is that firms wait until after the close of the market on Fridays to announce bad news. The problem is that soon people would anticipate such behavior and discount Friday prices to account for it. In this way negative returns over the weekend would soon be eliminated. Another explanation is that negative returns are caused by a general "market-closed" effect. French eliminated this possibility by showing that for days following holidays, only Tuesday returns were negative. All other days of the week that followed holidays had positive returns.

At present there is no satisfactory explanation for the weekend effect. It is not directly exploitable by a trading rule because transactions costs of even .25% eliminate all profits. However, it may be considered a form of market inefficiency because people who were going to trade anyway can delay purchases planned for Thursday or Friday until Monday and execute sales scheduled for Monday on the preceding Friday.

Another interesting pattern in stock prices is the so-called year-end effect, which has been documented by Dyl [1973], Branch [1977], Keim [1983], Reinganum [1983], Roll [1983], and Gultekin and Gultekin [1983]. Stock returns decline in December of each year, especially for small firms and for firms whose price had already declined during the year. Then the prices increase during the following January. Roll [1983] reported that for 18 consecutive years from 1963 to 1980, average returns of small firms have been larger than average returns of large firms on the first trading day of the calendar year. That day's difference in returns between equally weighted indices of AMEX- and NYSE-listed stocks averaged 1.16% over the 18 years. The t-statistic of the difference was 8.18.

Again quoting Roll [1983], "To put the turn-of-the-year period into perspective, the average annual return differential between equally-weighted and value-weighted indices of NYSE and AMEX stocks was 9.31% for calendar years 1963–1980 inclusive. During those same years, the average return for the five days of the turn-of-the-year (last day of December and first five days of January) was 3.45%. Thus, about 37% of the annual differential is due to just five trading days, 67% of the annual differential is due to the first twenty trading days of January plus the last day of December."

The most likely cause of the year-end effect is tax selling. At least there is a significant correlation between the realized rates of return during the year and the size of the turn-of-the-year price recovery. Whether or not this phenomenon is exploitable with a trading rule remains to be seen. However, an individual who was going to transact anyway can benefit by altering his or her timing to buy in late December or sell in early January.

SUMMARY

Most evidence suggests that capital markets are efficient in their weak and semistrong forms, that security prices conform to a fair-game model but not precisely to a random walk because of small first-order dependencies in prices and nonstationarities in the underlying price distribution over time, and that the strong-form hypothesis does not hold. However, any conclusions about the strong form of market efficiency need to be qualified by the fact that capital market efficiency must be considered jointly with competition and efficiency in markets for information. If insiders have monopolistic access to information, this fact may be considered an inefficiency in the market for information rather than in capital markets. Filter rules (described in Chapter 10) have shown that security prices exhibit no dependencies over time, at least down to the level of transactions costs. Thus capital markets are allocationally efficient up to the point of operational efficiency. If transactions costs amounted to a greater percentage of value traded, price dependencies for filter rules greater than 1.5% might have been found.

At least in two instances, special types of "abnormal" returns could not be explained. Block traders who can buy at the block price and sell at the market close could earn annual abnormal returns of over 200% per year even after transactions costs. Individuals who could buy new issues at the subscription price and sell at the end of the month could earn annual abnormal returns of 11.4% per month (this is over 350% per year). Although both these results may be interpreted as strong-form inefficiencies, the authors were quick to point out that they may simply represent fair returns for services by the block positioner or the investment banker. It is best to say at this point that we do not know.

Most of the studies reviewed in this chapter have used data from the stock market. However, there is evidence that other markets are also efficient. Roll [1970] showed that prices in the Treasury bill market obey a fair game model. Schwert [1977] concluded that the prices of New York Stock Exchange seats follow a multiplicative random walk. Stein [1977] examined the auction market for art and found it efficient. Larson [1964] looked at corn futures, and Mandelbrot [1964] investigated spot prices in cotton. In addition to these studies, we should mention in passing that there are many other topics related to the question of market efficiency that have not been discussed here.

PROBLEM SET

11.1 Roll's critique of tests of the CAPM shows that if the index portfolio is *ex post* efficient, it is mathematically impossible for abnormal returns, as measured by the empirical market line, to be statistically different from zero. Yet the Ibbotson study on new issues uses the cross-section empirical market line and finds significant abnormal returns in the month of issue and none in the following months. Given Roll's critique, this should have been impossible. How can the empirical results be reconciled with the theory?

11.2 In a study on corporate disclosure by a special committee of the Securities and Exchange Commission, we find the following statement (1977, D6):

> The "efficient market hypothesis"—which asserts that the current price of a security reflects all publicly available information—even if valid, does not negate the necessity of a mandatory disclosure system. This theory is concerned with how the market reacts to disclosed information and is silent as to the optimum amount of information required or whether that optimum should be achieved on a mandatory or voluntary basis; market forces alone are insufficient to cause all material information to be disclosed.

Two questions that arise are:

a) What is the difference between efficient markets for securities and efficient markets for information?

b) What criteria define "material information"?

11.3 In your own words, what does the empirical evidence on block trading tell us about market efficiency?

11.4 Which of the following types of information provides a likely opportunity to earn abnormal returns on the market?

a) The latest copy of a company's annual report.

b) News coming across the NYSE ticker tape that 100,000 shares of Lukens Steel Company were just traded in a single block.

c) Advance notice that the XYZ Company is going to split its common stock three for one but not increase dividend payout.

d) Advance notice that a large new issue of common stock in the ABC Company will be offered soon.

11.5 Mr. *A* has received, over the last three months, a solicitation to purchase a service that claims to be able to forecast movements in the Dow Jones Industrial index. Normally, he does not believe in such things, but the service provides evidence of amazing accuracy. In each of the last three months, it was always right in predicting whether or not the index would move up more than 10 points, stay within a 10-point range, or go down by more than 10 points. Would you advise him to purchase the service? Why or why not?

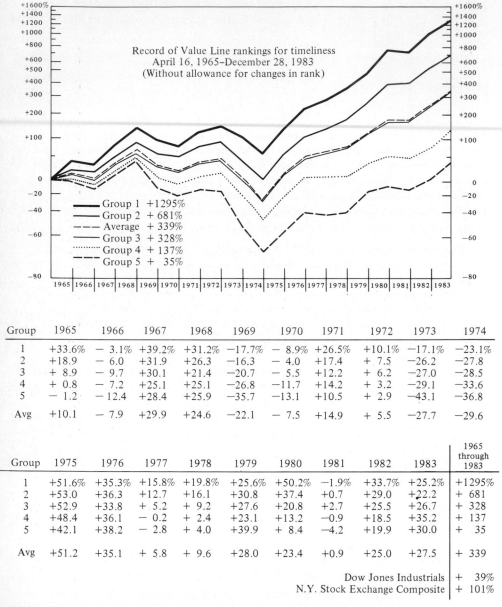

Group	1965	1966	1967	1968	1969	1970	1971	1972	1973	1974
1	+33.6%	− 3.1%	+39.2%	+31.2%	−17.7%	− 8.9%	+26.5%	+10.1%	−17.1%	−23.1%
2	+18.9	− 6.0	+31.9	+26.3	−16.3	− 4.0	+17.4	+ 7.5	−26.2	−27.8
3	+ 8.9	− 9.7	+30.1	+21.4	−20.7	− 5.5	+12.2	+ 6.2	−27.0	−28.5
4	+ 0.8	− 7.2	+25.1	+25.1	−26.8	−11.7	+14.2	+ 3.2	−29.1	−33.6
5	− 1.2	− 12.4	+28.4	+25.9	−35.7	−13.1	+10.5	+ 2.9	−43.1	−36.8
Avg	+10.1	− 7.9	+29.9	+24.6	−22.1	− 7.5	+14.9	+ 5.5	−27.7	−29.6

Group	1975	1976	1977	1978	1979	1980	1981	1982	1983	1965 through 1983
1	+51.6%	+35.3%	+15.8%	+19.8%	+25.6%	+50.2%	−1.9%	+33.7%	+25.2%	+1295%
2	+53.0	+36.3	+12.7	+16.1	+30.8	+37.4	+0.7	+29.0	+22.2	+ 681
3	+52.9	+33.8	+ 5.2	+ 9.2	+27.6	+20.8	+2.7	+25.5	+26.7	+ 328
4	+48.4	+36.1	− 0.2	+ 2.4	+23.1	+13.2	−0.9	+18.5	+35.2	+ 137
5	+42.1	+38.2	− 2.8	+ 4.0	+39.9	+ 8.4	−4.2	+19.9	+30.0	+ 35
Avg	+51.2	+35.1	+ 5.8	+ 9.6	+28.0	+23.4	+0.9	+25.0	+27.5	+ 339

Dow Jones Industrials + 39%

N.Y. Stock Exchange Composite + 101%

Figure Q11.8
Eighteen-year record of actual forecast assumes all rank changes have been followed. (From A. Bernhard, "The Value Line Investment Survey," *Investing in Common Stock*, Arnold Bernhard and Company, Inc. © Value Line, Inc. Reprinted with permission.)

11.6 The Ponzi Mutual Fund (which is not registered with the SEC) guarantees a 2% per month (24% per year) return on your money. You have looked into the matter and found that they have indeed been able to pay their shareholders the promised return for each of the 18 months they have been in operation. What implications does this have for capital markets? Should you invest?

11.7 Empirical evidence indicates that mutual funds that have abnormal returns in a given year are successful in attracting abnormally large numbers of new investors the following year. Is this inconsistent with capital market efficiency?

11.8 The Value Line Investment Survey publishes weekly stock performance forecasts. Stocks are grouped into five portfolios according to expected price performance, with Group 1 comprising the most highly recommended stocks. The chart of each portfolio's actual performance over an 18-year period (Fig. Q11.8) assumes that each of the five portfolios was adjusted on a weekly basis in accordance with Value Line's stock ratings. The chart shows that the portfolios' actual performances are consistent with Value Line's forecasts. Is this evidence against an efficient securities market?

11.9 In each of the following situations, explain the extent to which the empirical results offer reliable evidence for (or against) market efficiency.

a) A research study using data for firms continuously listed on the Compustat computer tapes from 1953 to 1973 finds no evidence of impending bankruptcy cost reflected in stock prices as a firm's debt/equity ratio increases.

b) One thousand stockbrokers are surveyed via questionnaire, and their stated investment preferences are classified according to industry groupings. The results can be used to explain rate of return differences across industries.

c) A study of the relationships between size of type in the *New York Times* headline and size of price change (in either direction) in the subsequent day's stock index reveals a significant positive correlation. Further, when independent subjects are asked to qualify the headline news as good, neutral, or bad, the direction of the following day's price change (up or down) is discovered to vary with the quality of news (good or bad).

d) Using 25 years of data in exhaustive regression analysis, a *Barron's* writer develops a statistical model that explains the 25-year period of stock returns (using 31 variables) with minuscule error.

REFERENCES

Aharony, J., and I. Swary, "Quarterly Dividend and Earnings Announcements and Stockholders' Returns: An Empirical Analysis," *Journal of Finance*, March 1980, 1–12.

Alexander, S. S., "Price Movements in Speculative Markets: Trends or Random Walks," *Industrial Management Review*, May 1961, 7–26.

Ball, R., and P. Brown, "An Empirical Evaluation of Accounting Income Numbers," *Journal of Accounting Research*, Autumn 1968, 159–178.

Barker, A., "Evaluation of Stock Dividends," *Harvard Business Review*, July–August 1958, 99–114.

Bernhard, A., *Investing in Common Stocks.* Arnold Bernhard & Co., Inc., New York, 1975.

———, *Value Line Methods of Evaluating Common Stocks.* Arnold Bernhard & Co., Inc., New York, 96 pp., 1975.

Black, F., "Yes, Virginia, There Is Hope: Tests of the Value Line Ranking System," Graduate School of Business, University of Chicago, May 1971.

———; M. Jensen; and M. Scholes, "The Capital Asset Pricing Model: Some Empirical Tests," in Jensen, ed., *Studies in the Theory of Capital Markets*. Praeger, New York, 1972, 79–121.

Black, F., and M. Scholes, "The Effects of Dividend Yield and Dividend Policy on Common Stock Prices and Returns," *Journal of Financial Economics*, May 1974, 1–22.

Boudreaux, K., "Discounts and Premiums on Closed-End Funds: A Study on Valuation," *Journal of Finance*, May 1973, 515–522.

Branch, B., "A Tax Loss Trading Rule," *Journal of Business*, April 1977, 198–207.

Brauer, G., "'Open-Ending' Closed-End Funds," *Journal of Financial Economics*, December 1984, 491–508.

Brennan, M., and T. Copeland, "A Signalling Model of Stock Split Behavior: Theory and Evidence," UCLA working paper, March 1987.

Brimmer, A., "Credit Conditions and Price Determination in the Corporate Bond Market," *Journal of Finance*, September 1960, 353–370.

Brown, L., and M. Rozeff, "The Superiority of Analyst Forecasts as Measures of Expectations: Evidence from Earnings," *Journal of Finance*, March 1978, 1–16.

Brown, S., "Earnings Changes, Stock Prices and Market Efficiency," *Journal of Finance*, March 1978, 17–28.

Chen, N. F.; T. Copeland; and D. Mayers, "A Comparison of Single and Multiple Factor Portfolio Performance Methodologies," Working Paper 2-86, UCLA, January 1986.

Chottiner, S., and A. Young, "A Test of the AICPA Differentiation between Stock Dividends and Stock Splits," *Journal of Accounting Research*, Autumn 1971, 367–374.

Copeland, T. E., "Liquidity Changes Following Stock Splits," *Journal of Finance*, March 1979, 115–141.

———, and D. Mayers, "The Value Line Enigma (1965–1978): A Case Study of Performance Evaluation Issues," *Journal of Financial Economics*, November 1982, 289–321.

Cornell, B., and R. Roll, "Strategies for Pairwise Competitions in Markets and Organizations," *Bell Journal of Economics*, Spring 1981, 201–213.

Dann, L.; D. Mayers; and R. Raab, "Trading Rules, Large Blocks and the Speed of Adjustment," *Journal of Financial Economics*, January 1977, 3–22.

Dyl, E., "The Effect of Capital Gains Taxation on the Stock Market," Ph.D. dissertation, Stanford University Graduate School of Business, August 1973.

Ederington, L., "The Yield Spread on New Issues of Corporate Bonds," *Journal of Finance*, December 1974, 1531–1543.

Fama, E. F., "The Behavior of Stock Market Prices," *Journal of Business*, January 1965, 34–105.

———, "Efficient Capital Markets: A Review of Theory and Empirical Work," *Journal of Finance*, May 1970, 383–417.

———, *Foundations of Finance*. Basic Books, New York, 1976.

Fama, E. F., and M. Blume, "Filter Rules and Stock Market Trading Profits," *Journal of Finance*, May 1970, 226–241.

Fama, E. F.; L. Fisher; M. Jensen; and R. Roll, "The Adjustment of Stock Prices to New Information," *International Economic Review*, February 1969, 1–21.

Fama, E. F., and J. MacBeth, "Risk, Return and Equilibrium: Empirical Test," *Journal of Political Economy*, May–June 1973, 607–635.

Farrar, D. E., *The Investment Decision under Uncertainty*. Prentice–Hall, Englewood Cliffs, N.J., 1962.

Finnerty, J. E., "Insiders and Market Efficiency," *Journal of Finance*, September 1976, 1141–1148.

Foster, G., "Quarterly Accounting Data: Time Series Properties and Predictive Ability Results," *Accounting Review*, January 1977, 1–21.

Foster, T., III, and D. Vickrey, "The Information Content of Stock Dividend Announcements," *Accounting Review*, April 1978, 360–370.

French, D., "The Weekend Effect on the Distribution of Stock Prices," *Journal of Financial Economics*, December 1984, 547–560.

French, K., "Stock Returns and the Weekend Effect," *Journal of Financial Economics*, March 1980, 55–69.

Friend, I.; M. Blume; and J. Crockett, *Mutual Funds and Other Institutional Investors*. McGraw-Hill, New York, 1970.

Friend, I.; F. E. Brown; E. S. Herman; and D. Vickers, *A Study of Mutual Funds*. U.S. Government Printing Office, Washington, D.C., 1962.

Friend, I., and D. Vickers, "Portfolio Selection and Investment Performance," *Journal of Finance*, September 1965, 391–415.

Gibbons, M., and P. Hess, "Day of the Week Effects and Asset Returns," *Journal of Business*, October 1981, 579–596.

Givoly, D., and D. Palmon, "Insider Trading and the Exploitation of Inside Information: Some Empirical Evidence," *Journal of Business*, January 1985, 69–87.

Granger, C. W. J., and O. Morgenstern, *Predictability of Stock Market Prices*. Heath Lexington Books, Lexington, Mass., 1970.

Griffin, P., "The Time-Series Behavior of Quarterly Earnings: Preliminary Evidence," *Journal of Accounting Research*, Spring 1977, 71–83.

Grinblatt, M.; R. Masulis; and S. Titman, "The Valuation Effects of Stock Splits and Stock Dividends," *Journal of Financial Economics*, December 1984, 461–490.

Grinblatt, M., and S. Titman, "A Comparison of Measures of Abnormal Performance on a Sample of Monthly Mutual Fund Returns," Working Paper 13-86, UCLA, 1986.

Grossman, S., "The Impossibility of Informationally Efficient Markets," *American Economic Review*, June 1980, 393–408.

Gultekin, M., and N. B. Gultekin, "Stock Market Seasonality: International Evidence," *Journal of Financial Economics*, December 1983, 469–481.

Hausman, W., "A Note on the Value Line Contest: A Test of the Predictability of Stock Price Changes," *Journal of Business*, July 1969, 317–320.

Henricksson, R., "Market Timing and Mutual Fund Performance: An Empirical Investigation," *Journal of Business*, January 1984, 73–96.

Holloway, C., "A Note on Testing in Aggressive Investment Strategy Using Value Line Ranks," *Journal of Finance*, June 1981, 711–719.

Hong, H.; R. S. Kaplan; and G. Mandelker, "Pooling vs. Purchase: The Effects of Accounting for Mergers on Stock Prices," *Accounting Review*, January 1978, 31–47.

Ibbotson, R., "Price Performance of Common Stock New Issues," *Journal of Financial Economics*, September 1975, 235–272.

Ingersoll, J., Jr., "A Theoretical and Empirical Investigation of the Dual Purpose Funds: An Application of Contingent Claims Analysis," *Journal of Financial Economics*, January–March 1976, 83–124.

Jaffe, J., "The Effect of Regulation Changes on Insider Trading," *Bell Journal of Economics and Management Science*, Spring 1974, 93–121.

Jensen, M., "The Performance of Mutual Funds in the Period 1945–64," *Journal of Finance*, May 1968, 389–416.

———, "Risk, the Pricing of Capital Assets, and the Evaluation of Investment Portfolios," *Journal of Business*, April 1969, 167–247.

———, "Capital Markets: Theory and Evidence," *Bell Journal of Economics and Management Science*, Autumn 1972, 357–398.

Joy, M.; R. Litzenberger; and R. McEnally, "The Adjustment of Stock Prices to Announcements of Unanticipated Changes in Quarterly Earnings," *Journal of Accounting Research*, Autumn 1977, 207–225.

Kaplan, R. S., and R. Roll, "Investor Evaluation of Accounting Information: Some Empirical Evidence," *Journal of Business*, April 1972, 225–257.

———, and R. Weil, "Risk and the Value Line Contest," *Financial Analysts Journal*, July–August 1973, 56–60.

Keim, D., "Size-Related Anomalies and Stock Return Seasonality: Further Empirical Evidence," *Journal of Financial Economics*, June 1983, 13–32.

Kraus, A., and H. R. Stoll, "Price Impacts of Block Trading on the New York Stock Exchange," *Journal of Finance*, June 1972, 569–588.

Larson, A. B., "Measurement of a Random Process in Futures Prices," in Cootner, ed., *The Random Character of Stock Market Prices*. MIT Press, Cambridge, Mass., 1964, 219–230.

Lindvall, J., "New Issue Corporate Bonds, Seasoned Market Efficiency, and Yield Spreads," *Journal of Finance*, September 1977, 1057–1067.

Lintner, J., "The Valuation of Risky Assets and the Selection of Risky Investments in Stock Portfolios and Capital Budgets," *Review of Economics and Statistics*, February 1965, 13–37.

Litzenberger, R., and H. Sosin, "The Structure and Management of Dual Purpose Funds," *Journal of Financial Economics*, March 1977, 203–230.

Logue, D. E., "On the Pricing of Unseasoned Equity Offerings: 1965–1969," *Journal of Financial and Quantitative Analysis*, January 1973, 91–104.

Mains, N. E., "Risk, the Pricing of Capital Assets, and the Evaluation of Investment Portfolios: Comment," *Journal of Business*, July 1977, 371–384.

Malkiel, B., "The Valuation of Closed-End Investment Company Shares," *Journal of Finance*, June 1977, 847–859.

Mandelbrot, B., "The Variation of Certain Speculative Prices," in Cootner, ed., *The Random Character of Stock Market Prices*. MIT Press, Cambridge, Mass., 1964, 307–332.

McDonald, J. G., and A. K. Fisher, "New Issue Stock Price Behavior," *Journal of Finance*, March 1972, 97–102.

Mikkelson, W., and M. Partch, "Stock Price Effects and the Costs of Secondary Distribution," *Journal of Financial Economics*, June 1985, 165–194.

Mossin, J., "Security Pricing and Investment Criteria in Competitive Markets," *American Economic Review*, December 1969, 749–756.

Ohlson, J., and S. Penman, "Volatility Increases Subsequent to Stock Splits: An Empirical Aberration," *Journal of Financial Economics*, June 1985, 251–266.

Patell, J., and M. Wolfson, "Anticipated Information Releases Reflected in Call Option Prices," *Journal of Accounting and Economics*, August 1979, 117–140.

———, "The Intraday Speed of Adjustment of Stock Prices to Earnings and Dividend Announcements," *Journal of Financial Economics*, June 1984, 223–252.

Pratt, E., "Myths Associated with Closed-End Investment Company Discounts," *Financial Analysts Journal*, July–August 1966, 79–82.

Reilly, F. K., and K. Hatfield, "Investor Experience with New Stock Issues," *Financial Analysts Journal*, September–October 1969, 73–80.

Reinganum, M., "The Anomalous Stock Market Behavior of Small Firms in January: Empirical Tests for Tax-Loss Selling Effects," *Journal of Financial Economics*, June 1983, 89–104.

Report of the Advisory Committee on Corporate Disclosure to the Securities and Exchange Commission. U.S. Government Printing Office, Washington, D.C., November 1977.

Ricks, W., "The Market's Responses to the 1974 LIFO Adoptions," *Journal of Accounting Research*, Autumn 1982, 367–387.

Roendfelt, R., and D. Tuttle, "An Examination of Discounts and Premiums of Closed-End Investment Companies," *Journal of Business Research*, Fall 1973, 129–140.

Roll, R. *The Behavior of Interest Rates*. Basic Books, New York, 1970.

———, "A Critique of the Asset Pricing Theory's Tests," *Journal of Financial Economics*, March 1977, 129–176.

———, "Ambiguity When Performance Is Measured by the Securities Market Line," *Journal of Finance*, September 1978, 1051–1069.

———, "The Turn-of-the-Year Effect and the Return Premia of Small Firms," *Journal of Portfolio Management*, Winter 1983, 18–28.

Scholes, M., "The Market for Securities: Substitution vs. Price Pressure and the Effects of Information on Share Prices," *Journal of Business*, April 1972, 179–211.

Schwert, W., "Stock Exchange Seats as Capital Assets," *Journal of Financial Economics*, January 1977, 51–78.

Securities and Exchange Commission, *Report of the Special Study on Securities Markets*. U.S. Government Printing Office, Washington, D.C., 1963.

Sharpe, W. F., "Mutual Fund Performance," *Journal of Business*, January 1966, 119–138.

Shaw, D., "The Performance of Primary Stock Offerings: A Canadian Comparison," *Journal of Finance*, December 1971, 1103–1113.

Shelton, J., "The Value Line Contest: A Test of the Predictability of Stock Price Changes," *Journal of Business*, July 1967, 251–269.

Stein, J. P., "The Monetary Appreciation of Paintings," *Journal of Political Economy*, October 1977, 1021–1036.

Stickel, S., "The Effect of Value Line Investment Survey Rank Changes on Common Stock Prices," *Journal of Financial Economics*, March 1985, 121–144.

Stickney, C. P., Jr., "A Study of the Relationships of Accounting Principles and Common Stock Prices of Firms Going Public," Ph.D. dissertation, Florida State University, Tallahassee, 1970.

Stigler, G., "Public Regulation of Security Markets," *Journal of Business*, April 1964, 117–142.

Sunder, S., "Relationship between Accounting Changes and Stock Prices: Problems of Measurement and Some Empirical Evidence," *Empirical Research in Accounting: Selected Studies*, 1973, 1–45.

———, "Stock Price and Risk Related Accounting Changes in Inventory Valuation," *Accounting Review*, April 1975, 305–315.

Thompson, R., "The Information Content of Discounts and Premiums on Closed-End Fund Shares," *Journal of Financial Economics*, June–September 1978, 151–186.

Treynor, J. L., "How to Rate Mutual Fund Performance," *Harvard Business Review*, January–February 1965, 63–75.

Watts, R., "Systematic 'Abnormal' Returns after Quarterly Earnings Announcements," *Journal of Financial Economics*, June–September 1978, 127–150.

Weinstein, M., "The Seasoning Process of New Corporate Bond Issues," *Journal of Finance*, December 1978, 1343–1354.

Woolridge, J. R., "Ex-date Stock Price Adjustment to Stock Dividends: A Note," *Journal of Finance*, March 1983a, 247–255.

———, "Stock Dividends as Signals," *Journal of Financial Research*, Spring 1983b, 1–12.

12

Former Student: Professor, this is the same examination you gave to my class when I was a student twenty years ago. Don't you ever change the questions?

Professor: The questions don't change—just the answers.

Capital Budgeting Under Uncertainty: The Multiperiod Case

A. INTRODUCTION

Chapters 2 and 3 discussed capital budgeting given the assumption that all future cash flows were known with certainty. The appropriate discount rate was assumed to be the risk-free rate, and the chapters focused on selection of discounting techniques consistent with the goal of maximizing the net present value of shareholders' wealth. Subsequent chapters introduced uncertainty in the context of a one-period equilibrium pricing model, the capital asset pricing model (CAPM).

In this chapter we introduce some of the difficulties implicit in the use of the CAPM to determine the appropriate multiperiod risk-adjusted discount rate for capital budgeting purposes. Given multiperiod uncertainty, under what conditions can one use the following formula to determine the NPV of risky projects?

$$\text{NPV}_j = \sum_{t=0}^{N} \frac{\text{NCF}_{jt}}{[1 + E(R_j)]^t}, \tag{12.1}$$

401

where

NPV_j = the net present value of project j,

NCF_{jt} = the net cash flow of project j in time t,

$E(R_j)$ = the risk-adjusted required rate of return for project j.

In particular, we are interested in the conditions under which the required rate of return on the project, frequently called the *weighted average cost of capital*, can be determined by the CAPM as written below:

$$E(R_j) = r_f + [E(R_m) - r_f]\beta_j. \tag{12.2}$$

Presumably, one would use *current* estimates of the risk-free rate, r_f, the expected rate of return on the market, $E(R_m)$, and the systematic risk of the project, β_j, in order to determine the multiperiod discount rate, $E(R_j)$.

In the first half of this chapter, which deals mainly with theoretical issues, we review the results of three articles. First, Bogue and Roll [1974] show that the problem may not be as simple as suggested in Eq. (12.1). They show that a much more complex procedure becomes necessary if we consider a world where the risk-free rate in future time periods is not known with certainty. Later Fama [1977] shows the set of assumptions necessary to use the risk-adjusted discounting procedure of Eq. (12.1), and Constantinides [1980] shows the minimum set of assumptions necessary for the multiperiod CAPM to be valid.

Section D of the chapter shows how to use the arbitrage pricing theory for capital budgeting purposes. While the technique is not easier to use in practice than the risk-adjusted discount rate, it has the advantage that it requires less stringent assumptions to be empirically valid.

Sections E and F deal with two applied issues. Both sections assume that the risk-adjusted discount rate may be used for multiperiod capital budgeting under uncertainty. The simpler of the two problems shows how to adjust the risk-adjusted discount rate when comparing cost (rather than total income) data for mutually exclusive projects. The second issue has come to be known as the *abandonment problem*. How should one evaluate the residual value of investment assets? We shall see how option pricing can be applied to this problem, then extend the analysis to discretionary temporary shutdown of operations, rather than permanent abandonment.

B. MULTIPERIOD CAPITAL BUDGETING WITH "IMPERFECT" MARKETS FOR PHYSICAL CAPITAL

Bogue and Roll [1974] analyze capital budgeting of risky projects in a multiperiod framework and conclude that it may be incorrect to discount cash flows by using the single-period risk-adjusted discount rate. However, under specified conditions, the investment decision for a multiperiod project can be made with a one-period forecast. If appropriate secondary markets exist for the project, only a one-period analysis is required for a decision. The firm makes a comparison between the current investment outlay and the value of the forecast of cash flows during the first period plus the forecast end-of-period secondary market price.

In addition, even with imperfect secondary markets for physical capital, some investment decisions can still be made with one-period forecasts. If the machine is acceptable on the basis of its one-period cash flow plus its net salvage value after the first period, the possibility of values in subsequent periods will only add to the acceptability of the project. Because the single-period analysis is important in its own right, and also because it will be used in a dynamic programming framework to solve the multiperiod problem, Bogue and Roll start the analysis with a single-period valuation model. They begin with the CAPM in value form. We derive their basic valuation expression by starting with the CAPM in return form as shown in Eq. (12.3):

$$E(\tilde{R}_1) = r_{f0} + [E(\tilde{R}_{m1}) - r_{f0}]\frac{\text{COV}(\tilde{R}_1, \tilde{R}_{m1})}{\sigma^2(\tilde{R}_{m1})}. \tag{12.3}$$

By definition,

$$\tilde{R}_{m1} = \frac{\tilde{V}_{m1} - V_{m0}}{V_{m0}} = \frac{\tilde{V}_{m1}}{V_{m0}} - 1, \qquad \tilde{R}_1 = \frac{\tilde{V}_1 - V_0}{V_0} = \frac{\tilde{V}_1}{V_0} - 1,$$

$$\sigma^2(\tilde{R}_{m1}) = \sigma^2\left(\frac{\tilde{V}_{m1}}{V_{m0}} - 1\right) = \sigma^2\left(\frac{\tilde{V}_{m1}}{V_{m0}}\right) = \frac{1}{(V_{m0})^2}\sigma^2(\tilde{V}_{m1}),$$

$$\text{COV}(\tilde{R}_1, \tilde{R}_{m1}) = \text{COV}\left(\frac{\tilde{V}_1}{V_0} - 1, \frac{\tilde{V}_{m1}}{V_{m0}} - 1\right) = \frac{1}{V_0 V_{m0}}\text{COV}(\tilde{V}_1, \tilde{V}_{m1}),$$

where

V_0 = the certain current value of the firm,

$\tilde{V}_1$ = the uncertain end-of-period value of the firm (including any dividends paid over the period),

$\tilde{V}_{m1}$ = the uncertain end-of-period value of the market portfolio,

r_{f0} = the risk-free rate of interest over the period.

Then the security market line (SML) is

$$\frac{E(\tilde{V}_1)}{V_0} - 1 = r_{f0} + \left[\frac{E(\tilde{V}_{m1})}{V_{m0}} - 1 - r_{f0}\right]\left(\frac{V_{m0}}{V_0}\right)\frac{\text{COV}(\tilde{V}_1, \tilde{V}_{m1})}{\sigma^2(\tilde{V}_{m1})}. \tag{12.4}$$

Substituting and rearranging, we can obtain a certainty equivalent value for the firm. First, we multiply both sides by V_0:

$$E(\tilde{V}_1) - V_0 = V_0 r_{f0} + [E(\tilde{V}_{m1}) - (1 + r_{f0})V_{m0}][\text{COV}(\tilde{V}_1, \tilde{V}_{m1})/\sigma^2(\tilde{V}_{m1})].$$

Next, we subtract $V_0 r_{f0}$ and $E(\tilde{V}_1)$ from both sides and change signs:

$$(1 + r_{f0})V_0 = E(\tilde{V}_1) - [E(\tilde{V}_{m1}) - (1 + r_{f0})V_{m0}][\text{COV}(\tilde{V}_1, \tilde{V}_{m1})/\sigma^2(\tilde{V}_{m1})].$$

Solving for V_0, we have

$$V_0 = \frac{E(\tilde{V}_1) - [E(\tilde{V}_{m1}) - (1 + r_{f0})V_{m0}][\text{COV}(\tilde{V}_1, \tilde{V}_{m1})/\sigma^2(\tilde{V}_{m1})]}{1 + r_{f0}}.$$

Using λ_0 (the market price per unit risk) to simplify, we obtain the certainty-equivalent value of the firm:

$$V_0 = \frac{E(\tilde{V}_1) - \lambda_0 \text{COV}(\tilde{V}_1, \tilde{V}_{m1})}{1 + r_{f0}}, \qquad (12.5)$$

where

$$\lambda_0 \equiv \frac{E(\tilde{V}_{m1}) - (1 + r_{f0})V_{m0}}{\sigma^2(\tilde{V}_{m1})} = \text{the market price per unit of risk.}$$

Now let $\tilde{X}_1$ be an incremental end-of-period net cash inflow from a project requiring current cash outlay of X_0. With the addition of the project, the end-of-period value of the firm will be $\tilde{V}_1 + \tilde{X}_1$. The new value of the firm is expressed by

$$V_0 + \Delta V_0 = \frac{E(\tilde{V}_1 + \tilde{X}_1) - \lambda_0 \text{COV}(\tilde{V}_1 + \tilde{X}_1, \tilde{V}_{m1})}{1 + r_{f0}}. \qquad (12.6)$$

When V_0 is subtracted from both sides of Eq. (12.6), we obtain

$$\Delta V_0 = \frac{E(\tilde{X}_1) - \lambda_0 \text{COV}(\tilde{X}_1, \tilde{V}_{m1})}{1 + r_{f0}}. \qquad (12.7)$$

which is the certainty-equivalent value of a project. If the left-hand side of Eq. (12.7) exceeds the right-hand side, the project is acceptable and should be undertaken. The methodology is to begin with an uncertain cash flow from which a certainty-equivalent value is constructed. The end-of-period certainty-equivalent value should be discounted at the risk-free rate to obtain its current value. This one-period result is used as the basis of generalization to the multiperiod case, which is considered next.

The firm is considering a project lasting over n periods. The net uncertain cash flows from the project are $\tilde{X}_t$, leading to increments to the value of the firm for each time period t of $\Delta \tilde{V}_t$. To solve the problem we start at the end where for the last period of the project we have[1]

$$\Delta \tilde{V}_n = \tilde{X}_n.$$

The next-to-last period represents a one-period valuation problem. Assuming that the capital market for equities is in equilibrium, the one-period valuation model can be used to find the value of the final cash flow at the end of the next-to-last period. This will enable us to obtain the discounted certainty equivalent of $\tilde{X}_n$ for period $n - 1$ expressed by

$$\frac{E(\tilde{X}_n | \tilde{\varepsilon}_{n-1}) - \tilde{\lambda}_{n-1} \widetilde{\text{COV}}(\tilde{X}_n, \tilde{V}_{mn} | \tilde{\varepsilon}_{n-1})}{1 + \tilde{r}_{f(n-1)}}, \qquad (12.8)$$

---

[1] Note that there is the implicit assumption that the project returns cash only in the nth time period.

where

$\tilde{\varepsilon}_{n-1}$ = state of the world at time $n-1$,

$\tilde{\lambda}_{n-1}$ = market price of risk at $n-1$,

$\tilde{r}_{f(n-1)}$ = risk-free rate at $n-1$ (assumed to be stochastic),

$E(\tilde{X}_n|\tilde{\varepsilon}_{n-1})$ = conditional expectation at $n-1$ of cash flows at n.

This enables us to obtain the incremental value at $n-1$:

$$\Delta V_{n-1} = X_{n-1} + \frac{\tilde{E}(\tilde{X}_n|\tilde{\varepsilon}_{n-1}) - \tilde{\lambda}_{n-1}\widetilde{\text{COV}}(\tilde{X}_n, \tilde{V}_{mn}|\tilde{\varepsilon}_{n-1})}{1 + \tilde{r}_{f(n-1)}}. \tag{12.9}$$

The result in Eq. (12.9) can be generalized to the recursive relationship for the incremental value at any time k:

$$\Delta \tilde{V}_k = \tilde{X}_k + \frac{\tilde{E}(\Delta \tilde{V}_{k+1}|\tilde{\varepsilon}_k) - \tilde{\lambda}_k\widetilde{\text{COV}}[\Delta \tilde{V}_{k+1}, \tilde{V}_{m(k+1)}|\tilde{\varepsilon}_k]}{1 + \tilde{r}_{fk}}. \tag{12.10}$$

From Eq. (12.10) we see that for an n-period project, an n-period infinite-state dynamic programming problem must be solved. Each step involves an application of the one-period valuation model with the parameters depending on the state of the world at the beginning of that particular period. Next, the nature of this solution is illustrated for the special case of a project with a single cash inflow two periods in the future. Using Eq. (12.10) with the risk-free interest rate expression placed on the left-hand side, we can obtain the incremental value for period 1 and period 0 as shown below:

$$\Delta \tilde{V}_1(1 + \tilde{r}_{f1}) = \tilde{E}(\tilde{X}_2|\tilde{\varepsilon}_1) - \tilde{\lambda}_1\widetilde{\text{COV}}(\tilde{X}_2, \tilde{V}_{m2}|\tilde{\varepsilon}_1), \tag{12.11}$$

$$\Delta V_0(1 + r_{f0}) = E(\Delta \tilde{V}_1) - \lambda_0\text{COV}(\Delta \tilde{V}_1, \tilde{V}_{m1}). \tag{12.12}$$

Note that the second-period risk-free rate, $\tilde{r}_{f1}$, is currently uncertain and will not be revealed until the end of the first period. Next, we take expectations of Eq. (12.11), and making use of the covariance identity,

$$\text{COV}(\tilde{X}, \tilde{Y}) = E(\tilde{X}, \tilde{Y}) - E(\tilde{X})E(\tilde{Y}),$$

we have[2]

$$E(\Delta \tilde{V}_1)E(1 + \tilde{r}_{f1}) + \text{COV}(\Delta \tilde{V}_1, \tilde{r}_{f1}) = E(\tilde{X}_2) - E[\tilde{\lambda}_1\widetilde{\text{COV}}(\tilde{X}_2, \tilde{V}_{m2}|\tilde{\varepsilon}_1)].$$

---

[2] The covariance identity follows directly from the definition of covariance:

$$\begin{aligned}\text{COV}(\tilde{X}, \tilde{Y}) &= E[(\tilde{X} - E(\tilde{X}))(\tilde{Y} - E(\tilde{Y}))] \\ &= E[(\tilde{X}\tilde{Y} - E(\tilde{X})\tilde{Y} - E(\tilde{Y})\tilde{X} + E(\tilde{X})E(\tilde{Y})] \\ &= E(\tilde{X}\tilde{Y}) - E(\tilde{X})E(\tilde{Y}) - E(\tilde{Y})E(\tilde{X}) + E(\tilde{X})E(\tilde{Y}) \\ &= E(\tilde{X}\tilde{Y}) - E(\tilde{X})E(\tilde{Y}).\end{aligned}$$

This result is applied to the left-hand side of Eq. (12.11) because it is the expectation of the product of two random variables.

We then solve Eq. (12.12) for $E(\Delta \tilde{V}_1)$ and substitute in the preceding expression and arrange terms. The result is

$$\Delta V_0 (1 + r_{f0}) E(1 + \tilde{r}_{f1}) = E(\tilde{X}_2) - E[\tilde{\lambda}_1 \widetilde{\text{COV}}(\tilde{X}_2, \tilde{V}_{m2} | \tilde{\varepsilon}_1)]$$
$$- \lambda_0 \text{COV}(\Delta \tilde{V}_1, \tilde{V}_{m1}) E(1 + \tilde{r}_{f1}) - \text{COV}(\Delta \tilde{V}_1, \tilde{r}_{f1}). \quad (12.13)$$

Equation (12.13) can also be written in the following form: ΔV_0, the present value of the single uncertain cash flow two periods in the future, is equal to

$$\Delta V_0 = \frac{E(\tilde{X}_2)}{(1 + r_{f0}) E(1 + \tilde{r}_{f1})} - \frac{E[\tilde{\lambda}_1 \widetilde{\text{COV}}(\tilde{X}_2, \tilde{V}_{m2} | \tilde{\varepsilon}_1)]}{(1 + r_{f0}) E(1 + \tilde{r}_{f1})} - \frac{\lambda_0 \text{COV}(\Delta \tilde{V}_1, \tilde{V}_{m1})}{(1 + r_{f0})}$$
$$- \frac{\text{COV}(\Delta \tilde{V}_1, \tilde{r}_{f1})}{(1 + r_{f0}) E(1 + \tilde{r}_{f1})}. \quad (12.14)$$

The first of the four terms on the right-hand side of (12.14) is the two-period discounted current expectation of the uncertain cash flow two periods in the future. Subtracted from it are three risk premiums: (1) covariation risk within the second period—i.e., beta risk; (2) covariation risk of the intermediate value of the project, which may be thought of as a reinvestment opportunity cost related to the sale of rights to the cash flow after one period has elapsed; and (3) the risk premium for interest rate fluctuations over the two time periods, which could cause changes in the project's value at intermediate periods.

In its rearranged form, Eq. (12.13) is in the same form and spirit as the single-period pricing model (Eq. 12.7). However, it contains two additional risk premia that have to be deducted from the two-period discounted current expectation of the single uncertain cash flow two periods in the future. The first is the covariation risk of the intermediate value of the project, and the second is the risk premium charged for the risk of interest fluctuations over the two time periods.

Bogue and Roll conclude by observing that if the errors in probability assessments of the cash flows over the multiple time periods are not systematically biased, stockholders can diversify away most of the error as the number of projects becomes large. Thus unbiased misassessments can be diversified in the personal portfolios of stockholders, whereas the use of a wrong capital budgeting criterion will result in aggregate errors that stockholders will not be able to reduce by diversification. In concept the multiperiod capital budgeting problem must utilize a valuation expression that includes two additional risk measures over and above the discounted current expectation of cash flows and the usual covariation of those flows with total market values.

C. AN EXAMINATION OF ADMISSIBLE
UNCERTAINTY IN A MULTIPERIOD
CAPITAL ASSET PRICING WORLD

In the previous section we presented Bogue and Roll's suggestion that in a two-period context the present value of the firm (Eq. 12.14) cannot be calculated by simply discounting the certainty equivalent cash flows at the end of the second time period back to the present. In addition, it is necessary to subtract two additional risk premia: (1) a term for the covariation risk of the intermediate value of the project and (2) a term for the risk of fluctuations in the risk-free rate over the two time periods.

Fama [1977] reexamines the multiperiod capital budgeting problem under uncertainty and clarifies the Bogue and Roll analysis by showing that within a CAPM world, certain types of uncertainty that are allowed by Bogue and Roll are inadmissible. He then shows that given the CAPM assumptions the last two terms of Eq. (12.14) vanish, and it is possible to use the risk-adjusted rate of return approach to capital budgeting as suggested in Eq. (12.1).

If we assume that the firm has net cash earnings, $\tilde{X}_t$, at time t and no cash flows at any other time, the recursive relationship for the value of the firm at $t - 1$ can be written in a form similar to Eq. (12.5):

$$V_{t-1} = \frac{E(\tilde{X}_t) - \phi_t \text{COV}(\tilde{X}_t, \tilde{R}_{mt})}{1 + r_{ft}}, \tag{12.15}$$

where $\phi_t = [E(\tilde{R}_{mt}) - r_{ft}]/\sigma^2(\tilde{R}_{mt})$. This is a certainty-equivalent expression for the value of the firm at $t - 1$. The firm's value at $t - 1$ can also be expressed using the risk-adjusted discount rate to compute the present value of the expected end-of-period cash flows:

$$V_{t-1} = \frac{E(\tilde{X}_t)}{1 + E(\tilde{R}_t)}, \tag{12.16}$$

where $E(\tilde{R}_t) = r_{ft} + [E(\tilde{R}_{mt}) - r_{ft}]\beta_t$.

So far all we have is a one-period expression for the value of cash flows at t, evaluated at $t - 1$. The way we write the value of the firm in a two-period context, at $t - 2$, depends on where we admit uncertainty into expression (12.16). Bogue and Roll allow uncertainty in the parameters of the market opportunity set, namely, (1) a stochastic risk-free rate, $\tilde{r}_{ft}$, and (2) uncertainty in the intermediate value of the firm, $\text{COV}(\Delta \tilde{V}_1, \tilde{V}_{m1})$. However, Fama points out that in a world where securities are priced according to the CAPM, relationships between uncertainty in the returns realized at $t - 1$ and the characteristics of the portfolio opportunity set are ruled out. Were such relationships to exist, they would provide initiative for investors to use their portfolio opportunities at $t - 2$ to hedge against uncertainty in portfolio opportunities at $t - 1$. The result is a pricing process different from the CAPM. The alternative pricing model that results has been discussed by Merton [1973] and Long [1974].[3] Therefore if we assume that the CAPM is the appropriate model, then any variation through time in the market parameters r_{ft} and ϕ_t is nonstochastic.

Having ruled out uncertainty about r_{ft} and ϕ_t, we can see from (12.15) that any uncertainty about V_{t-1} must arise from uncertainty about the values of $E(\tilde{X}_t)$ and $\text{COV}(\tilde{X}_t, \tilde{R}_{mt})$ assessed as of $t - 1$. The strongest assumption is that there is no intermediate uncertainty about $E(\tilde{X}_t)$ and $\text{COV}(\tilde{X}_t, \tilde{R}_{mt})$. If so, then the value in period $t - 2$ becomes

$$V_{t-2} = \frac{V_{t-1}}{1 + r_{f,t-1}},$$

---

[3] The Merton [1973] study is discussed briefly in Chapter 7.

and at $t = 0$ it is

$$V_0 = \prod_{k=1}^{t-1} \left(\frac{1}{1 + r_{fk}} \right) V_{t-1}.$$

Finally, using (12.16), we obtain

$$V_0 = \prod_{k=1}^{t-1} \left(\frac{1}{1 + r_{fk}} \right) \left(\frac{E(\tilde{X}_t)}{1 + E(\tilde{R}_t)} \right). \tag{12.17}$$

In this case the appropriate discount rates prior to period t are the risk-free rates because there is no uncertainty until period t. For period t the risk-adjusted rate is given by the CAPM relationships.

Of course the previous assumption is unreasonably strong. However, if V_{t-1} is to be uncertain prior to $t - 1$, the uncertainty must be introduced in a fashion consistent with the CAPM. Suppose that the cash flow in period t is estimated in an unbiased fashion in period $t - 1$ conditional on all information available at that time. This process can be expressed as

$$\tilde{X}_t = E_{t-1}(\tilde{X}_t)(1 + \tilde{\varepsilon}_t) = E_{t-1}(\tilde{X}_t) + E_{t-1}(\tilde{X}_t)\tilde{\varepsilon}_t, \tag{12.18}$$

where $E_{t-1}(\tilde{X}_t)$ is the expected value of $\tilde{X}_t$, and $\tilde{\varepsilon}_t$ is a random variable with expected value equal to zero. Prior to $t - 1$ the expected value itself is a random variable. This process evolves in the following fashion:

$$\tilde{E}_\tau(\tilde{X}_t) = E_{\tau-1}(\tilde{X}_t)(1 + \tilde{\varepsilon}_\tau) = E_{\tau-1}(\tilde{X}_t) + E_{\tau-1}(\tilde{X}_t)\tilde{\varepsilon}_\tau. \tag{12.19}$$

Again, the expected value of $\tilde{\varepsilon}_\tau$, conditional on the availability of information at $\tau - 1$, is equal to zero. Therefore, given rational expectations, the value of cash flow at time t, $\tilde{X}_t$, evolves as a martingale.[4] Note that $\tilde{\varepsilon}_\tau$ is the change in the expected value of $\tilde{X}_t$ per unit of $E_{\tau-1}(\tilde{X}_t)$:

$$\tilde{\varepsilon}_\tau = \frac{\tilde{E}_\tau(\tilde{X}_t) - E_{\tau-1}(\tilde{X}_t)}{E_{\tau-1}(\tilde{X}_t)} = \frac{\tilde{E}_\tau(\tilde{X}_t)}{E_{\tau-1}(\tilde{X}_t)} - 1. \tag{12.20}$$

Substituting (12.18) into (12.15), we have the value of the firm as of $t - 1$:

$$V_{t-1} = E_{t-1}(\tilde{X}_t) \left[\frac{1 - \phi_t \text{COV}(\tilde{\varepsilon}_t, \tilde{R}_{mt})}{1 + r_{ft}} \right] = E_{t-1}(\tilde{X}_t) \left[\frac{1}{1 + E(\tilde{R}_t)} \right]. \tag{12.21}$$

Note that because $\tilde{V}_t = \tilde{X}_t$, we have the following:

$$\frac{\text{COV}(\tilde{V}_t, \tilde{R}_{mt})}{E_{t-1}(\tilde{V}_t)} = \frac{\text{COV}(\tilde{X}_t, \tilde{R}_{mt})}{E_{t-1}(\tilde{X}_t)} = \text{COV}(\tilde{\varepsilon}_t, \tilde{R}_{mt}). \tag{12.22}$$

In (12.21) the return expected from the firm, $E(\tilde{R}_t)$, is part of the portfolio opportunity set perceived by investors at $t - 1$. Any stochastic change in this expected return

---

[4] See Chapter 10 for a discussion of martingales.

between $t - 2$ and $t - 1$ is likely to affect the value of the firm at $t - 1$. If such a stochastic relationship were to exist, the return realized at $t - 1$, $\tilde{R}_{t-1}$, would not be independent of the expected return, $E(\tilde{R}_t)$, from $t - 1$ to t, a result that would be inconsistent with the CAPM. Therefore uncertainty at $t - 2$ about the risk-adjusted discount rate, $E(\tilde{R}_t)$, in Eq. (12.21) is inadmissible in the multiperiod version of the CAPM. Since uncertainty about ϕ_t and r_{ft} have already been ruled out, the implication is that uncertainty about $\text{COV}(\tilde{\varepsilon}_t, \tilde{R}_{mt})$ in Eq. (12.21) is also inadmissible. Consequently, the expected earnings, $E_{t-1}(\tilde{X}_t)$, are the only parameter whose value can be uncertain at $t - 2$. This fact will allow us to simplify things considerably.

If $E(\tilde{R}_t)$ is certain, then by substituting (12.19) into (12.21) we have

$$\tilde{V}_{t-1} = \left[E_{t-2}(\tilde{X}_t) + E_{t-2}(\tilde{X}_t)\tilde{\varepsilon}_{t-1}\right]\left[\frac{1}{1 + E(\tilde{R}_t)}\right]. \tag{12.23}$$

The implication of (12.23) is that the value of the firm at $t - 1$ is perfectly correlated with $E_{t-1}(\tilde{X}_t)$, which is the assessment of the expected value of earnings turning up at $t - 1$.

Taking the expectation of (12.23), we see that the expected value of $\tilde{V}_{t-1}$ as of $t - 2$ is

$$E_{t-2}(\tilde{V}_{t-1}) = E_{t-2}(\tilde{X}_t)\left[\frac{1}{1 + E(\tilde{R}_t)}\right], \tag{12.24}$$

and using (12.22), we see that

$$\text{COV}(\tilde{V}_{t-1}, \tilde{R}_{m,t-1}) = E_{t-2}(\tilde{X}_t)\left[\frac{1}{1 + E(\tilde{R}_t)}\right]\text{COV}(\tilde{\varepsilon}_{t-1}, \tilde{R}_{m,t-1}). \tag{12.25}$$

Finally, taking the ratio of (12.24) and (12.25), we have

$$\frac{\text{COV}(\tilde{V}_{t-1}, \tilde{R}_{m,t-1})}{E_{t-2}(\tilde{V}_{t-1})} = \text{COV}(\tilde{\varepsilon}_{t-1}, \tilde{R}_{m,t-1}), \tag{12.26}$$

and from (12.20),

$$\frac{\text{COV}[\tilde{E}_{t-1}(\tilde{X}_t), \tilde{R}_{m,t-1}]}{E_{t-2}(\tilde{X}_t)} = \text{COV}(\tilde{\varepsilon}_{t-1}, \tilde{R}_{m,t-1}). \tag{12.27}$$

Therefore the covariance between the value of the firm at $t - 1$ and the market portfolio per unit of $E_{t-2}(\tilde{V}_{t-1})$ is identical to the covariance between the expected value of earnings and the market portfolio per unit of $E_{t-2}(\tilde{X}_t)$. Now the value of the firm as of $t - 2$ may be written as

$$V_{t-2} = \frac{E_{t-2}(\tilde{V}_{t-1}) - \phi_{t-1}\text{COV}(\tilde{V}_{t-1}, \tilde{R}_{m,t-1})}{1 + r_{f,t-1}}$$

$$= E_{t-2}(\tilde{V}_{t-1})\left[\frac{1 - \phi_{t-1}\text{COV}(\tilde{V}_{t-1}, \tilde{R}_{m,t-1})/E_{t-2}(\tilde{V}_{t-2})}{1 + r_{f,t-1}}\right],$$

and using (12.26), we have

$$V_{t-2} = E_{t-2}(\tilde{V}_{t-1})\left[\frac{1 - \phi_{t-1}\text{COV}(\tilde{\varepsilon}_{t-1}, \tilde{R}_{m,t-1})}{1 + r_{f,t-1}}\right]$$

$$= E_{t-2}(\tilde{V}_{t-1})\left[\frac{1}{1 + E(\tilde{R}_{t-1})}\right]. \qquad (12.28)$$

We can rewrite $E_{t-2}(\tilde{V}_{t-1})$ by using (12.24) to obtain

$$V_{t-2} = E_{t-2}(\tilde{X}_t)\left[\frac{1}{1 + E(\tilde{R}_t)}\right]\left[\frac{1}{1 + E(\tilde{R}_{t-1})}\right],$$

and in general, we obtain the recursive relationship

$$V_\tau = E_\tau(\tilde{X}_t)\left[\frac{1}{1 + E(\tilde{R}_{\tau+1})}\right]\cdots\left[\frac{1}{1 + E(\tilde{R}_t)}\right]. \qquad (12.29)$$

The market value of the firm at τ is the expected value at τ of the earnings to be realized at time t, discounted at the risk-adjusted discount rates for each of the periods between τ and t.

Fama points out that if the CAPM is assumed to hold, only uncertainty about $\tilde{E}_\tau(\tilde{X}_t)$ is admissible. Uncertainty about the risk-adjusted discount rates, $E(\tilde{R}_{\tau+1}), \ldots,$ $E(\tilde{R}_t)$, is not admissible. The risk adjustments in the discount rates arise because of the uncertain evolution through time of the expected value of cash flow.

If we are to obtain the usual solution to the multiperiod capital budgeting problem, we must also assume that the risk-free rate, r_{ft}, the covariance, $\text{COV}(\tilde{\varepsilon}_t, \tilde{R}_{mt})$, and the risk-adjusted rate, $E(\tilde{R}_t)$, are constant through time. If so, we obtain

$$V_0 = \frac{E_0(\tilde{X}_t)}{[1 + E(\tilde{R})]^t},$$

which, of course, is equal to Eq. (12.1) for an example with cash flow only in the last time period.

Bogue and Roll [1974] show that if the expected risk-free rate and therefore the expected portfolio opportunity set are stochastic, then the multiperiod capital budgeting problem is not easily solved. The investor must not only consider systematic risk in the usual CAPM sense but must also take into account two additional factors: (1) the risk of fluctuations in the risk-free rate and (2) the covariation risk of the intermediate value of the project. These results are consistent with various multiperiod versions of the CAPM (e.g., Merton [1973] and Long [1974]) that assume a stochastic risk-free rate.

Fama [1977] carefully examines the types of variability admissible under a stationary CAPM that assumes that the portfolio opportunity set is nonstochastic. In general the only admissible form of uncertainty is in the expected cash earnings in time t, assessed as of time $\tau < t$. The risk-adjusted discount rates in each future time period are known with certainty at time τ. Given the somewhat unpalatable assumptions of the stationary multiperiod CAPM, we have the result that the usual textbook treatment of multiperiod capital budgeting under uncertainty is reasonable.

Constantinides [1980] focuses on the minimum set of assumptions necessary for the CAPM to be valid in a multiperiod framework. In particular he utilizes the assumptions that (1) we have perfect markets, (2) investors all have homogeneous expectations, (3) investor utility functions are independent of the realized states of nature, and (4) there are competitive profit-maximizing firms whose output in period t is a function of input in period $t - 1$ and a random shock that is not dependent on the state of the economy in period $t - 1$. If the distribution of returns is normal or stable Paretian, then the multiperiod CAPM is valid. The important implication is that the multiperiod CAPM is valid even if the portfolio investment opportunity set is stochastic. Therefore Constantinides shows the CAPM to be valid under a less restrictive set of assumptions than Fama. Nonstationarity in the distribution of the market portfolio return, the return on the riskless asset, the security betas, and the market price of risk are all admissible in the context of the Sharpe, Lintner, Mossin CAPM. This is the good news. Unfortunately, the bad news, according to Constantinides, is that "the sequential application of the *SLM* model in the discounting of stochastic cash flows of multiperiod projects becomes computationally complex and of little practical use, unless one can produce convincing evidence to the effect that these nonstationarities are unimportant in practice."

Although the issues discussed in this chapter may seem exceedingly academic to the reader, they are no less important than the issue of whether to use the NPV or the IRR criterion as discussed in Chapter 2. Proper use of capital budgeting techniques is not a trivial issue. Until the question was posed by Bogue and Roll, little formal consideration had been given to the problems involved in the complex issue of multiperiod capital budgeting under uncertainty. Although the Fama article does much to clarify matters, we see that the standard solution to the problem requires a set of fairly restrictive assumptions.

D. USING THE ARBITRAGE PRICING THEORY FOR MULTIPERIOD CAPITAL BUDGETING

Recall, from Chapter 7, that the assumptions of the arbitrage pricing theory (APT) are less restrictive than those of the capital asset pricing model (CAPM), especially in its multiperiod form. The APT does not require that the market portfolio be observable, nor does it require intertemporal stationarity in the investment opportunity set. Rather, it requires only that at any instant in time there be no available arbitrage opportunities.

Ross [1979] shows how the APT can be used to value risky income streams, and Gehr [1981] shows how the idea can be applied specifically to the multiperiod capital budgeting problem. Gehr's example uses the APT to avoid the problems implicit in using a multiperiod risk-adjusted discount rate, but it is no panacea because it requires that we estimate a relationship between the future price of (some) publicly traded asset and future cash flows for a project.

Table 12.1   One Period APT Example

Period	Economic State	Subjective Probability	Project CF	r_f Risk-free Rate	S Comparison Stock
0	current	1.0	−8,000	NA	$ 9.00
1	bad	.3	8,000	10%	$ 8.00
1	good	.7	15,000	10%	$25.50

We begin by studying a simple one-period, two-state problem. Table 12.1 contains the data necessary to determine the net present value of a project that costs $8,000 today and that will return cash flows of $8,000 if economic conditions are bad or $15,000 otherwise. If we can create a *cash equivalent portfolio* from the risk-free asset and the comparison stock, then we can value the project. The cash equivalent portfolio will have exactly the same payoffs as the project in each state of nature. Because we know the prices of the risk-free asset and the comparison stock, the price of the cash equivalent portfolio will be the value of the project; otherwise arbitrage opportunities would exist.

How much should we invest in the risk-free asset and in the comparison stock to obtain exactly the same payoffs as the project? Let Q_r be the dollars invested in the risk-free asset and Q_s be the number of shares of the comparison stock (which costs $9.00 per share). The two equations below show the payoffs of the cash equivalent portfolio in each state of nature:[5]

Bad economic conditions $\quad 8.00Q_s + 1.10Q_r = 8,000,$

Good economic conditions $\quad 25.50Q_s + 1.10Q_r = 15,000.$

With two equations and two unknowns we can solve to find that $Q_s = 400$ shares and $Q_r = \$4363.64$. Therefore the current value of the cash equivalent portfolio, PV, is

$$\text{PV} = (400 \text{ shares})(\$9.00/\text{share}) + \$4363.64,$$

$$\text{PV} = \$3600 + \$4363.64 = \$7963.64.$$

This is also the present value of the project because the cash equivalent portfolio duplicates the project's payoffs in each state of nature. The NPV of the project is its present value minus the cash outlay needed to acquire it:

$$\text{NPV} = \text{PV} - I$$

$$= \$7964 - \$8000 = -\$36.$$

Because the NPV is negative the project should be rejected.

Note that it was never necessary to use the probability estimates of states of nature. The risk-adjusted discount rate was never computed, and nothing was known

---

[5] The price per share of the stock is $9, and implicitly the price per unit of the risk-free asset is $1.

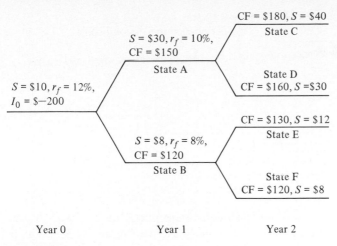

State C
CF = $180, S = $40

$S = \$30, r_f = 10\%,$
CF = $150

State A

State D
CF = $160, S = $30

$S = \$10, r_f = 12\%,$
$I_0 = \$-200$

State E
CF = $130, S = $12

$S = \$8, r_f = 8\%,$
CF = $120

State B

State F
CF = $120, S = $8

Year 0   Year 1   Year 2

Figure 12.1
Two-period APT example, first stage.

about the risk tolerances of the firm (or investors) that evaluated the project. All this information is implicitly included in the relative prices (across time and across states of nature) of the risk-free asset and the risky comparison stock. As long as their prices are true equilibrium prices, then the market information tells us all that we need to know.

The technique can readily be extended to a multiperiod economy, even one where the risk-free rate changes through time. Figure 12.1 gives data for a two-period example. The probabilities of states of nature are not given because they are not explicitly needed to solve the problem. Note that the risk-free rate is state contingent. If a favorable state of the economy prevails in year 1, then $r_f = 10\%$; otherwise it is 8%. Also, the correlation between the project and the comparison stock need not be stationary through time.

The project can be evaluated by finding the cash equivalent portfolios between years 1 and 2, then using this information to find the year 0 cash equivalent portfolio.[6] The two sets of simultaneous equations given below are used to determine the period 1 cash equivalent portfolios:

$$\text{State C} \quad 40Q_s + 1.10Q_r = 180 \left.\right\} \; Q_s = 2, \, Q_r = \$90.91$$
$$\text{State D} \quad 30Q_s + 1.10Q_r = 160 \left.\right\} \; V_A = \$150.91$$
$$\text{State E} \quad 12Q_s + 1.08Q_r = 130 \left.\right\} \; Q_s = 2.5, \, Q_r = \$92.59$$
$$\text{State F} \quad 8Q_s + 1.08Q_r = 120 \left.\right\} \; V_B = \$112.59.$$

---

[6] If this procedure sounds similar to the Cox, Ross, Rubinstein binomial model, derived in Chapter 8, it is. The arbitrage pricing theory, the option pricing model, and state-preference theory (even the CAPM) are all consistent with each other.

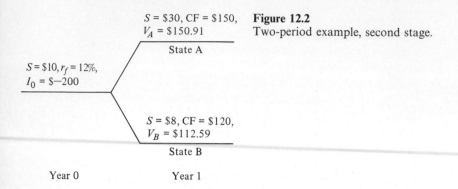

Figure 12.2
Two-period example, second stage.

As shown in Fig. 12.2, the values of the cash equivalent portfolios in States A and B are $150.91 and $112.59, respectively. The value of the project, in State A, e.g., is the cash flow that it provides in that state of nature, plus the cash equivalent value, V_A. This information can be used to write the appropriate set of payoffs for the period 1 cash equivalent portfolio as shown below:

$$\text{State A} \quad 30Q_s + 1.12Q_r = 150 + 150.91$$

$$\text{State B} \quad 8Q_s + 1.12Q_r = 120 + 112.59.$$

Solving, we find that $Q_s = 3.11$ shares and $Q_r = \$185.49$. Thus the value of the cash equivalent portfolio for the two-year project is

$$PV = (3.11 \text{ shares})(\$10.00/\text{share}) + \$185.49$$

$$= \$216.59,$$

and the net present value of the project is

$$NPV = PV - I = \$216.59 - \$200 = \$16.59.$$

Therefore the project should be accepted.

Despite the obvious theoretical advantages of using the arbitrage pricing theory for capital budgeting, there remains the practical problem of estimating the state-contingent prices of the comparison stock and the risk-free asset. Obviously this is no easy task. Whether or not decision makers will find this new technique of practical value remains to be seen. Who knows, maybe a decade from now, questionnaires on capital budgeting techniques will ask sophisticated firms whether or not they employ the APT capital budgeting technique. Only time can tell.

E. COMPARING RISKY COST STRUCTURES

Applied capital budgeting problems are almost always multiperiod, and frequently it is reasonable to assume that the revenues from two mutually exclusive projects will be identical. For example, this is the usual assumption in machine replacement problems. The revenues of the firm will be invariant to the choice of equipment. Therefore the usual capital budgeting process simply discounts the various incremental costs associated with the mutually exclusive alternatives and chooses the project with the lowest discounted cost.

Assuming that the multiperiod risk-adjusted rate of return is the appropriate technique for capital budgeting, how should it be used to compare cash outflows on a risk-adjusted basis? As we shall see, the correct approach discounts the expected costs at a lower rate when the cash outflows have greater variance. As long as the absolute value of the cash outflows is positively correlated with the market portfolio, greater variance in the outflows will imply lower overall project risk; i.e., there will be a lower project beta. To develop this result let us look at a simple one-period case. At the end of the period, the after-tax cash flows from operations may be written as follows:

$$\widetilde{CF} = (\widetilde{Rev} - \widetilde{VC})(1 - \tau_c) + \tau_c \text{dep},$$

where

$\widetilde{CF}$ = after-tax cash flows for capital budgeting purposes,

$\widetilde{Rev}$ = end-of-period revenues,

$\widetilde{VC}$ = end-of-period variable cash costs,

τ_c = the corporate tax rate,

dep = depreciation.

The rate of return, $\tilde{r}_j$, on the project is the return on investment (where investment is I_0):

$$\tilde{r}_j = \frac{(\widetilde{Rev} - \widetilde{VC})(1 - \tau_c) + \tau_c \text{dep} - I_0}{I_0}.$$

If we assume that the project is fully depreciated during the period, then $I_0 = $ dep, and we have

$$\tilde{r}_j = \frac{(\widetilde{Rev} - \widetilde{VC})(1 - \tau_c) - I_0(1 - \tau_c)}{I_0}$$

$$= \frac{(1 - \tau_c)}{I_0} \widetilde{Rev} - \frac{(1 - \tau_c)}{I_0} \widetilde{VC} - (1 - \tau_c).$$

Using the properties of random variables derived in Chapter 6, we can write the covariance between the return on the project and the return on the market portfolio as

$$\text{COV}(\tilde{r}_j, \tilde{r}_m) = \frac{(1 - \tau_c)}{I_0} \text{COV}(\widetilde{Rev}, \tilde{r}_m) - \frac{(1 - \tau_c)}{I_0} \text{COV}(\widetilde{VC}, \tilde{r}_m). \qquad (12.30)$$

Equation (12.30) shows that the covariance risk of a project can be partitioned into two parts: the covariance risk of its revenue stream and the covariance risk of its cost stream. Note that if the costs have positive covariance with the market in the sense that they are high when the market return is high, and vice versa, then their contribution to the project's covariance risk will be large and negative. This implies that the cost streams of riskier projects should be discounted at lower (and even negative) discount rates in order to properly adjust for risk. Note also that Eq. (12.30) can be rewritten in terms of systematic risk by dividing both sides by the variance of market return. This yields

$$\beta_j = \left(\frac{1 - \tau_c}{I_0}\right)\beta_{j\text{Rev}} - \left(\frac{1 - \tau_c}{I_0}\right)\beta_{j\text{VC}}, \tag{12.31}$$

where

β_j = the systematic risk of the project where $j = 1, 2$,

$\beta_{j\text{Rev}}$ = the systematic risk of the revenue stream,

$\beta_{j\text{VC}}$ = the systematic risk of the variable cost stream.

As an illustration, consider the following example. The two mutually exclusive projects given in Table 12.2 have identical revenue streams but different costs. In addition to the project cash flows, the table also provides the rate of return on the market portfolio, $\tilde{r}_m$, and the risk-free rate, r_f, in each of the three equally likely states of the world. The cost of the project, I_0, is \$100 and the corporate tax rate is 50%. The rate of return, $\tilde{r}_j$, on each project (columns 7 and 11) is calculated as follows:

$$\tilde{r}_j = \frac{\widetilde{CF}_j - I_0}{I_0}.$$

By inspecting the cash flows in Table 12.2, we see that the revenue streams are positively correlated with the market return, and so are the variable cost streams of the projects. However, the correlation between the variable cost stream of project 1 and the market return is such that it causes the project's net cash flow, CF, to be negatively correlated with the market. The higher variance and the positive correlation between (the absolute value of) the cash outflows of the first project and the market return require that its cash costs be discounted at a lower rate. Project 1 has a lower β than project 2.

Table 12.3 shows the results of computations of various statistics necessary for the calculation of the risk-adjusted rate of return. By using the CAPM and the statis-

Table 12.2 Projects with Different Risky Costs

	Probability	$\tilde{r}_m$	r_f	$\widetilde{Rev}_1$	$\widetilde{VC}_1$	$\widetilde{CF}_1$	$\tilde{r}_1$	$\widetilde{Rev}_2$	$\widetilde{VC}_2$	$\widetilde{CF}_2$	$\tilde{r}_2$
				Project 1				*Project 2*			
State 1	.33	.26	.04	610	500	105	.05	610	495	107.5	.075
State 2	.33	.14	.04	600	470	115	.15	600	500	100.0	0
State 3	.33	.20	.04	610	520	95	−.05	610	505	102.5	.025

Table 12.3   A List of Relevant Statistics

	Mean			Covariance with r_m			β		
	r	Rev	VC	r	Rev	VC	j	Rev	VC
Project 1	.050	606.67	496.67	−.0020	.20	.60	−.833	83.33	250.00
Project 2	.033	606.67	500.00	.0015	.20	−.10	.625	83.33	−41.67
Market return	.200	—	—	.0024	—	—	1.000	—	—

tics in Table 12.3, we can calculate the appropriate discount rates for the projects' net cash flow streams, or their cost streams. Using project 1 as an example, we employ the CAPM

$$E(\tilde{r}_j) = r_f + [E(\tilde{r}_m) - r_f]\beta_j,$$

and use Eq. (12.31) to compute the correct *adjusted betas*: for the project, β_j, its revenues, $\beta_{j\text{Rev}}$, and its costs, $\beta_{j\text{VC}}$:

$$\beta_j = \left(\frac{1 - \tau_c}{I_0}\right)\beta_{j\text{Rev}} - \left(\frac{1 - \tau_c}{I_0}\right)\beta_{j\text{VC}}.$$

Substituting data from Table 12.3, we see that the systematic risk for the project is a weighted average of the betas for the revenue and cost streams.[7]

$$-.833 = \left(\frac{1 - .5}{100}\right)(83.33) - \left(\frac{1 - .5}{100}\right)(250)$$

$$= .4167 - 1.25.$$

Now we have $\beta_1 = -.833$, $\beta_{1\text{Rev}} = .4167$, and $\beta_{1\text{VC}} = -1.25$.

Figure 12.3 graphs the security market line given by the CAPM and shows the betas and required rates of return for the project's cash flows, its revenue stream, and its cost stream.[8] Table 12.4 gives the appropriate discount rates and betas for the overall project cash flows and for the revenues and costs. Note that the cost stream should be discounted at −16%. Similar calculations show that for project 2 the cost stream should be discounted at 7.33%. Thus we have demonstrated the result that when (the absolute value of) cash outflows are positively correlated with the market, then cash outflows with greater variability should be discounted at lower rates. They have the effect of lowering project betas.

---

[7] Note that the beta for the cost stream is negative because the costs are outflows. The absolute value of the cost stream is positively correlated with the market, but the signed cash costs are negatively correlated with the market.

[8] It may seem unusual to discount cash flows at negative rates of return. Normally, this would not be the case because real-world projects are almost always positively correlated with the market. However, in the artificially constructed example above, it is perfectly consistent with the CAPM to require negative rates on projects with negative betas.

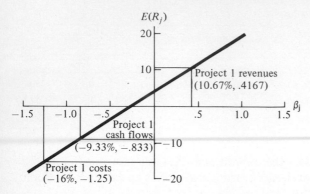

Figure 12.3
Systematic risk and required rate of return for project 1.

Suppose you are asked to compare the risk of two compensation schemes. In the first, salespeople are paid on a commission basis with no salary. The second scheme is straight salary with no commission. The expected revenues (annual sales figures) and expected sales costs (including compensation) are identical for both schemes. Which compensation plan has greater variance? Which has greater risk for shareholders? The intuition should be clear. The commission scheme has greater cost variance but results in less risk for shareholders because it smooths profits. When revenues are low, so are commissions, and vice versa. Hence profits have less variability than they otherwise might.

A word of caution to the practitioner is appropriate at this point. It is never advisable to totally ignore revenues or the riskiness of the revenue stream (even though this is frequent practice). In the above example the market required rate of return on project 2 is 14%, and the expected rate of return (the mean return in Table 12.3) is only 3.3%. Therefore project 2 is unacceptable under any circumstances. This could have been true for both projects. The practitioner who ignores revenues and chooses the project with the lower discounted cost may easily accept a project with negative NPV. Costs tell only half the story. Decision making on the basis of cost comparisons alone is inappropriate unless the decision maker is absolutely sure that the mutually exclusive projects all have positive net present value.

Given the results of Fama [1977] and Constantinides [1980], which were discussed in the previous section, it is possible to extend the one-period cost comparison

Table 12.4 Discount Rates and Adjusted Betas

	Discount Rates			Adjusted β		
	CF	Rev	VC	CF	Rev	VC
Project 1	−9.33%	10.67%	−16.00%	−.833	.4167	−1.2500
Project 2	14.00%	10.67%	7.33%	.625	.4167	.2083

procedure into a multiperiod framework. So long as the market parameters are assumed *ex ante* to be stationary over time, we still have the result that cost streams with higher variance should be discounted at lower rates.

F. ABANDONMENT VALUE

A critical multiperiod aspect of the capital budgeting decision is the consideration of the market value of the investment assets in alternative uses. At any time during the life of a project it may become advisable to sell it to someone else who can make better use of the assets for an alternative activity, to abandon it by scrapping it for its salvage value, or to shut it down temporarily until economic conditions improve. All these probabilities must be considered at the time of the initial capital budgeting decision. Even the simple ability to abandon a project has value.[9]

We analyze what has come to be called the *abandonment value* of a project in three parts. The easiest problem is simple abandonment. If you know that you can always sell your project for a minimum of X, how much does this add to the NPV of the project? Second, what if the project can be abandoned today at one price, but next year at a higher price? And finally, what if a project can be shut down temporarily, then restarted when economic conditions improve?

1. The Simple Abandonment Problem

When a project is abandoned (or sold), the expected liquidation (or resale) value sets a lower bound on the value of the project. This may be thought of as the exercise price of an American put option. When the present value of the asset falls below the liquidation value, the act of abandoning (or selling) the project is equivalent to exercising the put. Because the option to liquidate is valuable, a project that can be liquidated is worth more than the same project without the possibility of abandonment. To illustrate this principle, let us use a numerical example. First, we will solve the problem using decision trees, then using option pricing. This topic logically belongs in Chapter 3, "More Advanced Capital Budgeting Topics," but its treatment was deferred until option pricing theory was covered.

The Kirchner Corporation has invested $300 in new machinery with expected cash flows over two years. This is shown in Table 12.5. Two sets of probabilities are associated with the project. The initial probabilities should be interpreted as probabilities of particular cash flows from the first year only; the conditional probabilities are the probabilities of particular cash flows in the second year, given that a specific outcome has occurred in the first year. Thus the results in the second year are *conditional* upon the results of the first year. If high profits occur in the first year,

---

[9] For example, an accident at a nuclear power plant or a large chemical spill may leave management in the position where they wish they could simply walk away from the problem. *Ex ante* the NPV of such projects is reduced because, by law, they cannot be abandoned.

Table 12.5   Expected Cash Flows

Year 1		Year 2	
Initial Probability $p(1)$	Cash Flow	Conditional Probability $p(2\|1)$	Cash Flow
(0.3)	$200	(0.3)	$100
		(0.5)	200
		(0.2)	300
(0.4)	300	(0.3)	200
		(0.5)	300
		(0.2)	400
(0.3)	400	(0.3)	300
		(0.4)	400
		(0.3)	500

From J. F. Weston and T. E. Copeland, *Managerial Finance*, 8th edition, Hinsdale, Ill., Dryden Press, 1986, 514. © 1986 CBS Publishing.

chances are that the second year will also bring high profits. To obtain the probability that a particular first-year outcome and a particular second-year outcome will both occur, we must multiply the initial probability by the conditional probability to obtain what is termed the *joint probability*.

These concepts are applied to the data of Table 12.5 to construct Table 12.6. The project is not expected to have any returns after the second year. The cost of capital relevant to the project is assumed to be 12 percent. To indicate the role of abandonment value, we first calculate the expected net present value of the investment and the expected standard deviation of the project's internal rate of return without considering abandonment value. In the calculation made in Table 12.6, we find the expected NPV to be $201.

Next, in Table 12.7, we calculate the standard deviation of the project's rate of return, finding that $\sigma = 33.5\%$. Then, we can expand this analysis to take abandonment value into account. Suppose the abandonment value of the project at the end of the first year is estimated to be $250. This is the amount that can be obtained by liquidating the project after the first year, and the $250 is independent of actual first-year results.[10] If the project is abandoned after one year, then the $250 will replace any second-year returns. In other words, if the project is abandoned at the end of year 1, then year 1 returns will increase by $250 and year 2 returns will be zero. The present value of this estimated $250 abandonment value is, therefore, compared with the expected present values of the cash flows that would occur during the second

---

[10] In other words, we assume that the exercise price of the put option at the end of the first year is known with certainty. It is not a random variable.

Table 12.6 Calculation of Expected Net Present Value

Year 1			Year 2				Probability Analysis			
Cash Flow (1)	PV Factor (2)	Present Value: (1)×(2) (3)	Cash Flow (4)	PV Factor (5)	Present Value: (4)×(5) (6)	Present Value of Total Cash Flow: (3)+(6) (7)	Initial Probability (8)	Conditional Probability (9)	Joint Probability: (8)×(9) (10)	Expected Value: (7)×(10) (11)
$200	0.8929	179	$100	0.7972	80	$259	0.3	0.3	0.09	$ 23
			200	0.7972	159	338		0.5	0.15	51
			300	0.7972	239	418		0.2	0.06	25
300	0.8929	268	200	0.7972	159	427	0.4	0.3	0.12	51
			300	0.7972	239	507		0.5	0.20	101
			400	0.7972	319	587		0.2	0.08	47
400	0.8929	357	300	0.7972	239	596	0.3	0.3	0.09	54
			400	0.7972	319	676		0.4	0.12	81
			500	0.7972	399	756		0.3	0.09	68
									1.00	$501

Expected present value = $501

Expected net present value = $201

From J. F. Weston and T. E. Copeland, *Managerial Finance*, 8th edition, Hinsdale, Ill, Dryden Press, 1986, 515. © 1986 CBS Publishing.

Table 12.7 Calculation of Rate of Return Standard Deviation

Cash Flow		IRR	IRR − $\overline{\text{IRR}}$	(IRR − $\overline{\text{IRR}}$)²	×	Joint Probability	=	p_i(IRR − $\overline{\text{IRR}}$)²
Year 1	Year 2							
$200	$100	0.0%	−.594	.352		.09		.0318
200	200	21.5	−.379	.144		.15		.0215
200	300	38.7	−.207	.043		.06		.0026
300	200	45.7	−.137	.019		.12		.0023
300	300	61.8	.024	.001		.20		.0001
300	400	75.8	.164	.027		.08		.0022
400	300	86.9	.275	.076		.09		.0068
400	400	100.0	.406	.165		.12		.0198
400	500	112.0	.526	.277		.09		.0249
Sum						$\overline{1.00}$		VAR(IRR) = $\overline{.1120}$

Note: $\overline{\text{IRR}} = \sum p_i \text{IRR}_i$, where p_i = joint probability, $\overline{\text{IRR}}$ = 59.4%
[VAR(IRR)]$^{1/2}$ = σ(IRR) = .3347 or 33.47%.

From J. F. Weston and T. E. Copeland, *Managerial Finance*, 8th edition, Hinsdale, Ill., Dryden Press, 1986, 516. © 1986 CBS Publishing.

year if abandonment did not take place. To make the comparison valid, however, we must use the second-year flows based on the conditional probabilities only, rather than the joint probabilities that were used in the preceding analysis. This calculation is shown in Table 12.8.

We next compare the present value of the $250 abandonment value, $250 × 0.8929 = $223, with the branch expected present values for each of the three possible cash flow patterns (branches) depicted in Table 12.8. If the $223 present value of abandonment exceeds one or more of the expected present values of the possible branches of cash flows, taking abandonment value into account will improve the indicated returns from the project. The $223 does exceed the $152 expected PV shown in Table 12.8 for second-year cash flows when the first-year cash flow is $200. In Table 12.9, therefore, abandonment after year 1 is assumed for the $200 case and the new NPV is calculated; the $250 abandonment value is added to the $200 cash flow to obtain a $450 year 1 cash flow, and the year 2 cash flow becomes $0. The new calculation of the standard deviation of returns is shown in Table 12.10.

We may now compare the results when abandonment value is taken into account with the results when it is not considered. Including abandonment value in the calculations increases the expected net present value from $201 to $223, or by about 10%. It reduces the expected standard deviation of returns from 33.5% to 22.3%. Thus for this problem, abandonment value improves the attractiveness of the investment.

Abandonment value is important in another aspect of financial decision making: the reevaluation of projects in succeeding years after they have been undertaken. The decision to continue the project or to abandon it sometime during its life depends

Table 12.8   Expected Present Values of Cash Flow during the Second Year

Cash Flow	PV Factor	PV	Conditional Probability	Expected Present Value
$100	0.7972	80	0.3	$ 24
200	0.7972	159	0.5	80
300	0.7972	239	0.2	48
			Branch total	$152
200	0.7972	159	0.3	$ 48
300	0.7972	239	0.5	120
400	0.7972	319	0.2	64
			Branch total	$232
300	0.7972	239	0.3	$ 72
400	0.7972	319	0.4	128
500	0.7972	399	0.3	120
			Branch total	$320

From J. F. Weston and T. E. Copeland, *Managerial Finance*, 8th edition, Hinsdale, Ill., Dryden Press, 1986, 516. © 1986 CBS Publishing.

Table 12.9 Expected Net Present Value with Abandonment Value Included

Year 1 Cash Flow (1)	×	PV Factor (2)	=	PV (3)	×	Year 2 Cash Flow (4)	×	PV Factor (5)	=	PV (6)	Present Value of Total Cash Flow (7)	×	Joint Probability (8)	=	Expected Value (9)
$450		0.8929		$402		$ 0		0.7972		$ 0	$402		0.30		$121
300		0.8929		268		200		0.7972		159	427		0.12		51
						300		0.7972		239	507		0.20		101
						400		0.7972		319	587		0.08		47
400		0.8929		357		300		0.7972		239	596		0.09		54
						400		0.7972		319	676		0.12		81
						500		0.7972		399	756		0.09		68
													1.00		

Expected present value = $523

Expected net present value = $223

From J. F. Weston and T. E. Copeland, *Managerial Finance*, 8th edition, Hinsdale, Ill., Dryden Press, 1986, 517. © 1986 CBS Publishing.

Table 12.10 Calculation of Rate of Return Standard Deviation with Abandonment Value Included

| Cash Flow | | | | | | Joint | | |
Year 1	Year 2	IRR	IRR − $\overline{\text{IRR}}$	$(\text{IRR} − \overline{\text{IRR}})^2$	×	Probability	=	$p_i(\text{IRR} − \overline{\text{IRR}})^2$
$450	$ 0	50.0%	−.188	.035		.09		.0032
450	0	50.0	−.188	.035		.15		.0053
450	0	50.0	−.188	.035		.06		.0021
300	200	45.7	−.231	.053		.12		.0064
300	300	61.8	−.070	.005		.20		.0010
300	400	75.8	.070	.005		.08		.0004
400	300	86.9	.181	.033		.09		.0030
400	400	100.0	.312	.097		.12		.0116
400	500	112.0	.432	.187		.09		.0249
Sum						1.00		VAR(IRR) = .0498

Note: $\overline{\text{IRR}} = \sum p_i \text{IRR}_i$, where p_i = joint probability. $\overline{\text{IRR}}$ = 68.8%
$[\text{VAR}(\text{IRR})]^{1/2} = \sigma(\text{IRR})$ = .2232 or 22.32%.

From J. F. Weston and T. E. Copeland, *Managerial Finance*, 8th edition, Hinsdale, Ill., Dryden Press, 1986, 518. c 1986 CBS Publishing.

on which branch occurs during each time period. For example, suppose that during year 1 the cash flow actually obtained was $200. Then the three possibilities associated with year 2 are the three that were conditionally dependent upon a $200 outcome in year 1. The other six probabilities for year 2, which were considered in the initial evaluation, were conditional upon other first-year outcomes and are thus no longer relevant. A calculation (Table 12.11) is then made of the second-year net cash flows, discounted back one year.

At the end of the first year the abandonment value is $250. This is compared with the expected present value of the second-year net cash flow series discounted one year. This value is determined to be $171, so the abandonment value of $250 exceeds the net present value of returns for the second year. Therefore the project should be abandoned at the end of the first year.

In summary it is sometimes advantageous to abandon a project even though the net present value of continued operation is positive. The basic reason is that the present value of abandonment after a shorter time may actually be greater than the present value of continued operation.

Another, perhaps better, way to analyze the abandonment decision is to compute the NPV of the project without the option to abandon, then add to it the value of the abandonment put option. Thus we have

NPV (with abandonment) = NPV (without abandonment)

+ Value of abandonment put option.

The greater the variance of returns on the project, the greater will be the value of the abandonment option. In Table 12.7 we saw that the standard deviation of returns was 33.5% for the project without the abandonment option. This is the correct standard deviation to use in the Black-Scholes formula because it is an estimate of the standard deviation of returns on the underlying asset. The way our example has been structured, we also know that the put option may be exercised only at the end of the first year. Therefore it is a European put option with one year to maturity and an exercise price of $250. The present value of the underlying asset is the present value of the project without abandonment, i.e., $501. We assume the risk-free rate is 5%.

Table 12.11   Calculation of Expected Net Cash Flow for Second Period When $200 Was Earned During the First Year

Cash Flow	×	PV Factor	=	PV	×	Probability Factor	=	Discounted Expected Cash Flow
$100		0.8929		$ 89		0.3		$ 27
200		0.8929		179		0.5		90
300		0.8929		268		0.2		54
						Expected present value =		$171

From J. F. Weston and T. E. Copeland, *Managerial Finance*, 8th edition, Hinsdale, Ill., Dryden Press, 1986, 518. © 1986 CBS Publishing.

Table 12.12   Present Value of the Project Excluding First-Year Cash Flows

Year 2 Cash Flow	Joint Probability	PV Factor	PV
$100	.09	.7972	$ 7.17
200	.15	.7972	23.92
300	.06	.7972	14.35
200	.12	.7972	19.13
300	.20	.7972	47.83
400	.08	.7972	25.51
300	.09	.7972	21.52
400	.12	.7972	38.27
500	.09	.7972	35.87
Sum	1.00		233.57

From J. F. Weston and T. E. Copeland, *Managerial Finance*, 8th edition, Hinsdale, Ill., Dryden Press, 1986, 519. © 1986 CBS Publishing.

Note that if the project is abandoned at the end of the first year, we will abandon it only after receiving the first year's cash flows. Therefore we must compute the asset value *without* these cash flows in order to value the abandonment put option. The calculation is shown in Table 12.12.

The value of the abandonment put option can be found by using the Black-Scholes formula to value the corresponding call, then put-call parity to compute the put value. The Black-Scholes call value is

$$c = SN(d_1) - Xe^{-r_fT}N(d_2),$$

where

$$d_1 = \frac{\ln(S/X) + r_fT}{\sigma\sqrt{T}} + \frac{1}{2}\sigma\sqrt{T},$$

$$d_2 = d_1 - \sigma\sqrt{T}.$$

Substituting in the numbers from our example, we have

$$d_1 = \frac{\ln(233.57/250) + .05(1)}{.335\sqrt{1}} + \frac{1}{2}(.335)\sqrt{1}$$

$$= \frac{\ln(.9343) + .05}{.335} + .168$$

$$= \frac{-.068 + .05}{.335} + .168$$

$$= -.0537 + .168 = .1143$$

$$d_2 = .1143 - .335\sqrt{1} = -.2207.$$

Using the table of cumulative normal probabilities (Table 8.7) at the end of Chapter 8, we find that

$$N(d_1) = .5 + .0455 = .5455$$

and

$$N(d_2) = .5 - .0874 = .4126.$$

Thus the value of the call option is

$$c = 233.57(.5455) - 250(.4126)e^{-.05(1)}$$

$$= 127.41 - 250(.4126)(.9512)$$

$$= 127.41 - 98.12 = 29.29.$$

Finally, we can use Eq. (8.10), put-call parity, to find the value of the European put that is implied by the option to abandon:

$$c_0 - P_0 = S_0 - Xe^{-r_f T} \qquad\qquad (8.10)$$

$$P_0 = c_0 - S_0 + Xe^{-r_f T}$$

$$= 29.29 - 233.57 + 250e^{-.05(1)}$$

$$= 29.29 - 233.57 + 250(.9512)$$

$$= 29.29 - 233.57 + 237.80$$

$$= \$33.52.$$

The decision tree approach gave an abandonment value equal to $22 (i.e., $223, the value with abandonment, minus $201, the value without abandonment). The option pricing approach gave an abandonment value of $33.52. We obtained different answers because the assumptions of the Black-Scholes OPM and the decision tree approach are different. For example, Black-Scholes assumes a lognormal distribution of outcomes, whereas the decision tree only crudely approximates the continuum of possibilities. It is hard to say which assumption is more realistic for project abandonment decisions.

2. Deferred Abandonment

The traditional abandonment decision rule is that the project should be abandoned (or sold) in the first year that the abandonment value exceeds the present value of the remaining expected cash flows from continued operation. Unfortunately, abandonment at the first opportunity may not be optimal because deferred abandonment may result in an even greater net present value.[11] For example, consider a truck with two years of remaining useful life. The present value of continued use is, say, $900,

---

[11] See Dyl and Long [1969], Robichek and Van Horne [1967], and Joy [1976].

but the current market value of the truck is $1000. Clearly, if the proceeds from the sale can be invested to earn at least the applicable cost of capital, the better decision would be to sell the truck now. However, there is one option that has not been considered, which is to operate the truck for another year and collect the cash flow from one year's operations (which have a present value of $500) and then abandon it (assuming the present value of abandonment in a year is $600). Thus the present value of this alternative is $1100. In this case the truck should be used for one year and then sold.

The optimal abandonment decision rule is to determine the combination of remaining operating cash flows and future abandonment that has the maximum expected net present value. This decision rule is, unfortunately, difficult to implement, especially when the project life is long and there are numerous opportunities for abandonment over time. If a piece of equipment can be used for 20 years or abandoned at the end of any year, then 20 different net present value calculations might be required to determine the optimum pattern that will result in maximum expected net present value.

Option pricing is difficult to apply for two reasons. First, the resale price or abandonment value (analogous to the exercise price of the implied American put) is not constant across time and may be dependent on variables such as the state of the economy. Second, the underlying asset (the project) pays cash flows ("dividends") to those who hold the project and the implied American put on it.

At present the "best" solution to deferred abandonment decisions is to consider *n* different mutually exclusive alternatives for an *n* year project and choose from among them the one that has the greatest NPV.

3. Shutdown as an Alternative to Abandonment

Brennan and Schwartz [1985] point out that an obvious alternative to abandonment (or sale) is temporary shutdown. Consider a copper mine, for example. As copper prices fall it may become optimal to shut the mine down until they rise again. However, if they fall too far, then outright abandonment becomes the best decision. They are able to develop decision rules, based on the market price of copper, which enable managers to know when to open or shut down (or even abandon) the operation. The value of the option to shut down rises as the price of copper falls. Unfortunately, the mathematics employed is beyond the scope of this text.

4. Other Option Pricing Applications for Investment and Production Decisions

Mason and Merton [1985] summarize a variety of option pricing applications to investment and production decisions. The main theme is that flexibility has value. For example, a power plant that burns oil and coal is more expensive to build than one that burns only oil, but the greater flexibility may well be worth the extra cost. Option pricing provides an analytical tool for valuing flexibility. For example, Majd and Pindyck [1987] value the flexibility option to accelerate or delay the construction of a project. When uncertainty about the value of the completed project increases, so does the value of delaying. McDonald and Siegel [1986] model the value of waiting to invest in an irreversible project—a similar problem. It is likely that option pricing will provide a better way to think about research and development. Roberts and Weitzman [1981] have written an early paper on the topic. Paddock, Siegel, and Smith [1984] have applied the option pricing methodology to offshore oil leases.

The application of option pricing to the problem of modeling flexibility for strategic investment decisions is exciting because it is the first major advance in capital budgeting in decades. It shows great promise for solving a wide set of interesting and useful problems.

SUMMARY

By considering the relations between periods recursively, Bogue and Roll [1974] develop an equation for multiperiod capital budgeting. In addition to the usual beta risk, the resulting equation contains two additional risk premia: the covariation risk of the intermediate values of the project and the risk premium related to the risk of interest fluctuations. Fama [1977] points out that in a world in which securities are priced according to the CAPM, the only admissible form of uncertainty is the expected cash earnings in time t assessed one period earlier. The risk-free rate, the covariance, and the risk-adjusted rate are then constant through time, and the traditional capital budgeting model can be employed.

Gehr [1981] shows how the arbitrage pricing model can be employed to solve multiperiod capital budgeting problems. The technique avoids all the difficulties of the multiperiod CAPM but unfortunately requires estimates of state-contingent future security prices.

In most equipment replacement problems it is plausible that revenues from two mutually exclusive types of equipment will be identical. However, the riskiness of the cost streams may be different. We are accustomed to increasing the amount of risk adjustment in the capitalization factor applied to riskier net cash flow streams. This has the effect of penalizing riskier investments. When the streams under comparison are costs alone, we need to have higher present values for riskier cost streams. This is accomplished by lowering the discount rate, rather than increasing it.

Another important aspect of the assessment of risky investments is to estimate the abandonment value of an asset. The initial criterion proposed abandonment in the first year that abandonment value exceeded the present value of continued use of the asset. Later studies pointed out the necessity of consideration of abandonment possibilities in future years to obtain the maximum present value from the selection of the optimal time for abandonment. Finally, we saw that temporary shutdown is often a viable alternative to outright abandonment, and that option pricing may also be applied to the option to delay or accelerate investment and to research and development problems.

PROBLEM SET

12.1 Which of the following types of uncertainty are inadmissible in a multiperiod model if we are using the CAPM? Why?

a) $COV(\tilde{\varepsilon}_t, \tilde{R}_{mt})$

b) $\tilde{r}_{ft}$

c) $E_{t-1}(\tilde{X}_t)$

d) $COV(\tilde{V}_{t-1}, \tilde{R}_{m,t-1})$

e) $[E(\tilde{R}_{mt}) - r_{ft}]/\sigma^2(\tilde{R}_{mt})$

12.2 The Ramsden Company is installing 10 new forklift trucks. Electric trucks cost $8000 each, whereas gas-powered trucks cost $5000 each. The operating costs for the electric trucks would be $5200 per truck per year compared with $6000 per gas truck for the eight-year expected life of each vehicle. Expected salvage value is zero and straight-line depreciation is to be used. Ramsden will apply a 10% discount factor for analysis of the electric trucks and a 2% differential to the gas trucks owing to their higher operating risks. The applicable tax rate is 40%. Should electric or gas forklift trucks be purchased by Ramsden?

12.3 You are asked to perform a capital budgeting analysis of two projects. Both will require an immediate cash outlay of $1000. Both projects last one year and they both produce revenues at the end of the year amounting to $1500 with certainty. Cash outflows at the end of the year, however, are risky. They are given below, along with the market rate of return, R_m:

		End-of-Period Outflows		
State of Nature	Probability	Project A	Project B	R_m
Great	$\frac{1}{3}$	$500	$600	20%
Average	$\frac{1}{3}$	400	400	10%
Horrid	$\frac{1}{3}$	300	200	0%

Since you are given the cash flows, there is no need to worry about taxes, depreciation, or salvage value. Note that the cash outflows of Project B have higher variance than those of Project A. Which project has greater NPV? Show your work and explain your reasoning.

12.4 Your firm is trying to choose between two mutually exclusive projects. Both cost $10,000 and have a five-year life and no salvage value. The company uses straight-line depreciation and the corporate tax rate is 40%. Over the life of the project the annual expected rate of return on the market portfolio is 15% and the risk-free rate is 5%. The first project has expected revenues of $5,000 per year with an adjusted β_{Rev} of 1.5 and expected variable costs of $2,333 per year with an adjusted β_{VC} of -1.4 (i.e., both the revenues and variable costs are positively correlated with the market). The second project has expected revenues of $6,067 per year with an adjusted β_{Rev} of 1.3 and expected variable costs of $2,400 with an adjusted β_{VC} of .3 (i.e., revenues are positively correlated with the market, and variable costs are negatively correlated with the market). Which project should the firm accept? [*Note:* Adjusted βs are discussed in section E of Chapter 12.]

12.5 Figure Q12.5 gives the cash flows, CF, for a two-period project that requires a $300 initial outlay. Also shown are the state-contingent risk-free rates of return, r_f, and the state-contingent prices of a comparison risky asset. What is the NPV of the project?

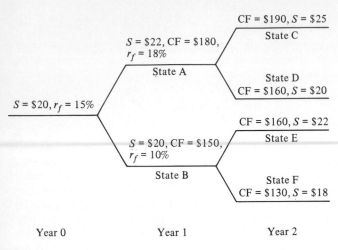

Year 0   Year 1   Year 2

Figure Q12.5

12.6 The following investment decision is being considered by Citrus Farms. For $7000 the company can acquire ownership of 10 acres of 15-year-old orange trees and a 15-year lease on the land. The productive life of an orange tree is divided into stages as follows:

State	Age of Trees, Years	Expected Annual Profit from 10 Acres, $
Peak	16–20	1000
Adult	21–25	900
Mature	26–30	800

There is a market for decorative orange trees. Suppliers will buy trees and remove them according to a schedule based on the age of the tree. Expected prices that can be obtained for the 10-acre harvest are: $9,000 at end of age 20, $12,000 at age 25, and $8,000 at age 30. Citrus Farms has a 10% cost of capital.

a) What is the present value of each alternative? Since the land and anything on it will belong to the lessor in 15 years, assume that once the trees are harvested the land will not be replanted by Citrus.

b) As an alternative to this investment, Citrus can use the $7,000 to buy a new orange-sorting machine. The machine would reduce sorting expenses by $1300 a year for 15 years. Which investment would you make? Why? Assume that all other investment opportunities for the next 15 years will earn the cost of capital.

c) In the tenth year Citrus discovers that everyone else with 25-year-old trees has sold them. As a consequence the price the firm can get for the trees is only $8000. Since so many trees have been sold for decoration, small orange crops are expected for the next 5 years. As a result the price of oranges will be higher. Your acreage will yield $1200 a year. The selling price of your trees in another 5 years is expected to be still depressed to $6000. What should you do?

d) Given the situation in (c), what was the NPV of your actual investment over the 15-year period?

e) What would the NPV be if the trees had been sold in year 10 for $8000?

12.7 *Southern Electric Power Company*[12]
The State Public Service Commission (PSC) is charged with the responsibility of regulating the two large public utility companies in the state. The PSC is composed of seven persons; four elected, one gubernatorial appointee, and one representative each from the two public utilities.

The PSC is currently considering a capacity expansion program submitted by Southern Electric Power (SE). SE operates three power plants, as shown in Table Q12.7a. The population in the area served by SE has been growing 2% per year. This trend is expected to continue for at least the next 10 years. Industrial growth is even more rapid—about 4% per year. As a result, demand for electricity is growing at approximately 3% per year. Peak-load demand is very near SE's capacity, so it is necessary to begin some expansion within the year.

Table Q12.7a   Operating Data for Three Power Plants

Type of Plant	Date Constructed	Percentage of Current Power Needs Supplied	Remaining Life, in Years
Coal	1946	25	30
Hydroelectric	1958	10	35
Natural gas generating	1963	65	45

Another problem the company is confronted with is the growing shortage of natural gas. Last year SE was unable to buy enough natural gas to meet the full electric power needs of the area. The company was able to buy electricity generated by a company in an adjoining state that has coal, but there is no assurance that this source of power can be relied on in the future.

Given the uncertainty of future natural gas supplies, and the fact that hydroelectric power is already being fully utilized, SE feels the only sensible course is to expand its own coal-generating capacity. This would be especially desirable since it would use the large soft-coal deposits in the northern part of the state.

There are two ways to increase the capacity for coal generation. For $40 million it would be possible to double the generating capacity of the existing plant. This would fully satisfy the growing demand for electricity for the next 6 to 8 years, after which time additional capacity would be needed. The expansion would have a useful life of 30 years. The existing plant is located 20 miles from the center of the largest city in the state. In 1946, when the plant was originally built, the location was selected specifically to be at a considerable distance from any populated area so that the smoke produced by burning coal would not be an environmental nuisance.

---

[12] This is really a short case, rather than a problem in the usual sense of the word. It does not necessarily have a simple, cut-and-dried solution.

In 30 years the city has grown considerably. Heavily populated suburbs are now located within four miles of the plant, and pollution created by SE is a growing political issue. The company believes it probable that within the next 5 years political pressure will require that smoke scrubbers be installed at the existing plant (Table Q12.7b). Scrubbers can be installed any time at the existing plant for $4 million. If plant capacity is doubled and scrubbers are installed at that time, the total cost would be $5.5 million. (This would be in addition to the base cost of the new plant discussed below.) If the installation of scrubbers is postponed, and carried out as a separate capital investment, the total cost is estimated to be $8 million, subject to the same probability that installation might never occur (see Table Q12.7b).

Table Q12.7b   Probability That Scrubbers Will Be Required

Time Frame	Probability
In year 2	0%
In year 3	10
In year 4	50
In year 5	40

The alternative to expanding the capacity of the old plant is to build an entirely new plant. Such a plant would cost $110 million and would have a maximum capacity of three times the existing coal plant. With the new capacity in addition to the existing plant, energy needs could be met for the next 18 to 20 years. The useful life of the plant would be 40 years. If desired, the capacity of the new plant could be increased to the point that the old plant could be abandoned and capacity would still be adequate for the same period. The additional cost of the extra capacity would be $22,082,000, which would be depreciated over the full life of the plant. If the old plant is abandoned, equipment worth $7 million could be used in the new plant, and sale of the land would provide additional capital of $3 million.

Annual operating costs of the old plant are $2 million. If its capacity is doubled, operating costs will rise by $1.5 million. Cost of operating the new plant will be $4 million per year. If the old plant is abandoned, operating costs of the new plant will increase by $450,000 per year for the remaining life of the old plant. SE uses straight-line depreciation to zero salvage value on all capital investments discussed here. The cost of scrubbers is amortized over the remaining life of the plant in which they are installed. Book value of the existing coal plant is $10 million.

SE has an effective tax rate of 40%. SE's weighted average cost of capital is 10%. Revenues and other costs will be the same under either alternative. Excess capacity can be sold outside the state at the same rate as within the state.

1. As a representative of the utility company, you are concerned with maximizing the present value of the project. Analyze the alternatives and indicate your recommendation.

2. Keeping in mind that you are working only with costs, how would you adjust the discount rate to account for: (a) the extra uncertainty for any alternative that includes delayed installation of smoke scrubbers; (b) the pollution that would result from operating the old plant without smoke scrubbers?

3. How would these factors affect your recommendation? As an elected member of the PSC, what factors would you include in your analysis of the project? How would each of these factors bear on your decision?

REFERENCES

Beedles, W., "Evaluating Negative Benefits," *Journal of Financial and Quantitative Analysis*, March 1978, 173–176.

Bogue, M. C., and R. R. Roll, "Capital Budgeting of Risky Projects with 'Imperfect' Markets for Physical Capital," *Journal of Finance*, May 1974, 601–613.

Booth, L., "Correct Procedures for the Evaluation of Risky Cash Outflows," *Journal of Financial and Quantitative Analysis*, June 1982, 287–300.

Breeden, D., "An Intertemporal Asset Pricing Model with Stochastic Investment Opportunities," *Journal of Financial Economics*, September 1979, 265–296.

Brennan, M., "An Approach to the Valuation of Uncertain Income Streams," *Journal of Finance*, June 1973, 661–674.

———, and E. Schwartz, "Evaluating Natural Resource Investments," *Journal of Business*, April 1985, 135–157.

Celec, S., and R. Pettway, "Some Observations on Risk-Adjusted Discount Rates: A Comment," *Journal of Finance*, September 1979, 1061–1063.

Constantinides, G., "Market Risk Adjustment in Project Valuation," *Journal of Finance*, May 1978, 603–616.

———, "Admissible Uncertainty in the Intertemporal Asset Pricing Model," *Journal of Financial Economics*, March 1980, 71–86.

Dyl, E. A., and H. W. Long, "Abandonment Value and Capital Budgeting: Comment," *Journal of Finance*, March 1969, 88–95.

Fama, E. F., "Multiperiod Consumption-Investment Decisions," *American Economic Review*, March 1970, 163–174.

———, "Risk-Adjusted Discount Rates and Capital Budgeting under Uncertainty," *Journal of Financial Economics*, August 1977, 3–24.

———, and J. D. MacBeth, "Tests of the Multiperiod Two-Parameter Model," *Journal of Financial Economics*, May 1974, 43–66.

Gehr, A., "Risk-Adjusted Capital Budgeting Using Arbitrage," *Financial Management*, Winter, 1981, 14–19.

Joy, O. M., "Abandonment Values and Abandonment Decisions: A Clarification," *Journal of Finance*, September 1976, 1225–1228.

Lewellen, W., "Some Observations on Risk-Adjusted Discount Rates," *Journal of Finance*, September 1977, 1331–1337.

———, "Reply to Pettway and Celec," *Journal of Finance*, September 1979, 1065–1066.

Long, J. B., Jr., "Stock Prices, Inflation and the Term Structure of Interest Rates," *Journal of Financial Economics*, July 1974, 131–170.

McDonald, R., and D. Siegel, "The Value of Waiting to Invest," *Quarterly Journal of Economics*, November 1986, 707–727.

Majd, S., and R. Pindyck, "Time to Build, Option Value, and Investment Decisions," *Journal of Financial Economics*, March 1987, 7–28.

Mason, S. P., and R. C. Merton, "The Role of Contingent Claims Analysis in Corporate Finance," in *Recent Advances in Corporate Finance*, E. I. Altman, and M. G. Subrahmanyam, eds., Richard D. Irwin, Homewood, Illinois, 1985, 7–54.

Merton, R. C., "An Intertemporal Capital Asset Pricing Model," *Econometrica*, September 1973, 867–887.

Miles, J., and D. Choi, "Comment: Evaluating Negative Benefits," *Journal of Financial and Quantitative Analysis*, December 1979, 1095–1099.

Miller, M., and C. Upton, "A Test of the Hotelling Valuation Principle," *Journal of Political Economy*, February 1985, 1–25.

Myers, S. C., "Procedures for Capital Budgeting under Uncertainty," *Industrial Management Review*, Spring 1968, 1–20.

———, and S. Majd, "Calculating Abandonment Value Using Option Pricing Theory," Working Paper, Sloan School of Management, MIT, 1983.

Myers, S. C., and S. M. Turnbull, "Capital Budgeting and the Capital Asset Pricing Model: Good News and Bad News," *Journal of Finance*, May 1977, 321–332.

Paddock, J., D. Siegel, and J. Smith, "Option Valuation of Claims and Physical Assets: The Case of Offshore Petroleum Leases," working paper, MIT Energy Laboratory, Cambridge Mass., 1984. September 1973, 867–887.

Roberts, K., and M. Weitzman, "Funding Criteria for Research, Development and Exploration Projects," *Econometrica*, September 1981, 1261–1288.

Robichek, A., and S. Myers, "Conceptual Problems in the Use of Risk-Adjusted Discount Rates," *Journal of Finance*, December 1966, 727–730.

Robichek, A., and J. C. Van Horne, "Abandonment Value and Capital Budgeting," *Journal of Finance*, December 1967, 577–590.

Ross, S., "A Simple Approach to the Valuation of Risky Streams," *Journal of Business*, July 1979, 254–286.

Stapleton, R., and M. Subrahmanyam, "A Multiperiod Equilibrium Asset Pricing Model," *Econometrica*, September 1978, 1077–1096.

———, "Multiperiod Equilibrium: Some Implications for Capital Budgeting," *TIMS Studies in the Management Sciences*, Vol. 11, 1979, 233–248.

Weitzman, M., W. Newey, and M. Robin, "Sequential R & D Strategy for Synfuels," *Bell Journal of Economics*, Autumn 1981, 574–590.

13

The average cost of capital to any firm is completely independent of its capital structure and is equal to the capitalization rate of a pure equity stream of its class.

F. Modigliani and M. H. Miller, "The Cost of Capital, Corporation Finance, and the Theory of Investment," *American Economic Review*, June 1958, 268

Capital Structure and the Cost of Capital: Theory

Funds for investment are provided to the firm by investors who hold various types of claims on the firm's cash flows. Debt holders have contracts (bonds) that promise to pay them fixed schedules of interest in the future in exchange for their cash now. Equity holders provide retained earnings (internal equity provided by *existing* shareholders) or purchase new shares (external equity provided by *new* shareholders). They do so in return for claims on the residual earnings of the firm in the future. Also, shareholders retain control of the investment decision, whereas bondholders have no direct control except for various types of indenture provisions in the bond that may constrain the decision making of shareholders. In addition to these two basic categories of claimants, there are others such as holders of convertible debentures, leases, preferred stock, nonvoting stock, and warrants.

Each investor category is confronted with a different type of risk, and therefore each requires a different expected rate of return in order to provide funds to the firm. The required rate of return is the opportunity cost to the investor of investing scarce resources elsewhere in opportunities with *equivalent risk*. As we shall see, the fact that shareholders are the ones who decide whether to accept or reject new projects is critical to understanding the cost of capital. They will accept only those projects that increase their expected utility of wealth. Each project must earn, on a risk-adjusted

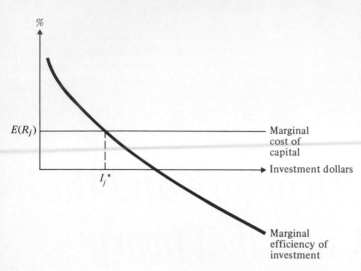

Figure 13.1
Demand and supply of investment for projects of equal risk.

basis, enough net cash flow to pay investors (bondholders and shareholders) their expected rates of return, to pay the principal amount that they originally provided, and to have something left over that will increase the wealth of existing shareholders. The cost of capital is the minimum risk-adjusted rate of return that a project must earn in order to be acceptable to shareholders.

The investment decision cannot be made without knowledge of the cost of capital. Consequently, many textbooks introduce the concept of the cost of capital before they discuss investment decisions. It probably does not matter which topic comes first. Both topics are important and they are interrelated. Figure 13.1 shows the investment decision as the intersection of the demand and supply of investment capital. All projects are assumed to have equivalent risk. Also, fund sources have equal risk (in other words, in Fig. 13.1 we make no distinction between equity and debt). Chapters 2, 3, and 12 discussed the ranking of projects assuming that the appropriate cost of capital was known. The schedule of projects with their rates of return is sometimes called the *marginal efficiency of investment schedule* and is shown as the demand curve in Fig. 13.1. The supply of capital, represented as the marginal cost of capital curve, is assumed to be infinitely elastic. Implicitly, the projects are assumed to have equal risk. Therefore the firm faces an infinite supply of capital at the rate $E(R_j)$ because it is assumed that the projects it offers are only a small portion of all investment in the economy. They affect neither the total risk of the economy nor the total supply of capital. The optimal amount of investment for the firm is I_j^*, and the marginally acceptable project must earn at least $E(R_j)$. All acceptable projects, of course, earn more than the marginal cost of capital.

Figure 13.1 is an oversimplified explanation of the relationship between the cost of capital and the amount of investment. However, it demonstrates the interrelatedness of the two concepts. For a given schedule of investments a rise in the cost of capital will result in less investment. This chapter shows how the firm's mix of debt and equity financing affects the cost of capital, explains how the cost of capital is related to shareholders' wealth, and shows how to extend the cost of capital concept to the situation where projects do not all have the same risk. If the cost of capital can be minimized via some judicious mixture of debt and equity financing, then the financing decision can maximize the value of the firm.

Whether or not an optimal capital structure exists is one of the most important issues in corporate finance—and one of the most complex. This chapter begins the discussion. It covers the effect of tax-deductible debt on the value of the firm, first in a world with only corporate taxes, then by adding personal taxes as well. There is also a discussion of the effect of risky debt, warrants, convertible bonds, and callable bonds.

Chapter 14 continues the discussion of optimal capital structure by introducing the effects of factors other than taxes. Bankruptcy costs, option pricing effects, agency costs, and signaling theory are all discussed along with empirical evidence bearing on their validity. Also, the optimal maturity structure of debt is presented. Corporate financial officers must decide not only how much debt to carry but also its duration. Should it be short-term or long-term debt?

A. THE VALUE OF THE FIRM GIVEN CORPORATE TAXES ONLY

1. The Value of the Levered Firm

Modigliani and Miller [1958, 1963] wrote the seminal paper on cost of capital, corporate valuation, and capital structure. They assumed either explicitly or implicitly that:

- Capital markets are frictionless.
- Individuals can borrow and lend at the risk-free rate.
- There are no costs to bankruptcy.
- Firms issue only two types of claims: risk-free debt and (risky) equity.
- All firms are assumed to be in the same risk class.
- Corporate taxes are the only form of government levy (i.e., there are no wealth taxes on corporations and no personal taxes).
- All cash flow streams are perpetuities (i.e., no growth).
- Corporate insiders and outsiders have the same information (i.e., no signaling opportunities).
- Managers always maximize shareholders' wealth (i.e., no agency costs).

It goes without saying that many of these assumptions are unrealistic, but later we can show that relaxing many of them does not really change the major conclusions of the model of firm behavior that Modigliani and Miller provide. Relaxing the assumption that corporate debt is risk free will not change the results (see section D). However, the assumptions of no bankruptcy costs (relaxed in Chapter 14) and no personal taxes (relaxed in section B of this chapter) are critical because they change the implications of the model. The last two assumptions rule out signaling behavior—because insiders and outsiders have the same information; and agency costs—because managers never seek to maximize their own wealth. These issues are discussed in Chapter 14.

One of the assumptions requires greater clarification. What is meant when we say that all firms have the same risk class? The implication is that the expected risky future net operating cash flows vary by, at most, a scale factor. Mathematically this is

$$\widetilde{CF}_i = \lambda \widetilde{CF}_j,$$

where

$\widetilde{CF}$ = the risky net cash flow from operations (cash flow before interest and taxes),

λ = a constant scale factor.

This implies that the expected future cash flows from the two firms (or projects) are perfectly correlated.

If, instead of focusing on the level of cash flow, we focus on the returns, the perfect correlation becomes obvious because the returns are identical, as shown below:

$$\tilde{R}_{i,t} = \frac{\widetilde{CF}_{i,t} - CF_{i,t-1}}{CF_{i,t-1}},$$

and because $\widetilde{CF}_{i,t} = \lambda \widetilde{CF}_{j,t}$, we have

$$\tilde{R}_{i,t} = \frac{\lambda \widetilde{CF}_{j,t} - \lambda CF_{j,t-1}}{\lambda CF_{j,t-1}} = \tilde{R}_{j,t}.$$

Therefore if two streams of cash flow differ by, at most, a scale factor, they will have the same distributions of returns, the same risk, and will require the same expected return.

Suppose the assets of a firm return the same distribution of net operating cash flows each time period for an infinite number of time periods. This is a no-growth situation because the average cash flow does not change over time. We can value this after-tax stream of cash flows by discounting its expected value at the appropriate risk-adjusted rate. The value of an unlevered firm, i.e., a firm with no debt, will be

$$V^U = \frac{E(\widetilde{FCF})}{\rho}, \tag{13.1}$$

where

V^U = the present value of an unlevered firm (i.e., all equity),

$E(\widetilde{FCF})$ = the perpetual free cash flow after taxes (to be explained in detail below),

ρ = the discount rate for an all-equity firm of equivalent risk.

This is the value of an unlevered firm because it represents the discounted value of a perpetual, nongrowing stream of free cash flows after taxes that would accrue to shareholders if the firm had no debt. To clarify this point, let us look at the following pro forma income statement:

Rev	Revenues
$-$VC	Variable costs of operations
$-$FCC	Fixed cash costs (e.g., administrative costs and real estate taxes)
$-$dep	Noncash charges (e.g., depreciation and deferred taxes)
NOI	Net operating income
$-k_dD$	Interest on debt (interest rate, times principal, D)
EBT	Earnings before taxes
$-T$	Taxes $= \tau_c$(EBT), where τ_c is the corporate tax rate
NI	Net income

It is extremely important to distinguish between cash flows and the accounting definition of profit. After-tax cash flows from operations may be calculated as follows. Net operating income less taxes is

$$\widetilde{NOI} - \tau_c(\widetilde{NOI}).$$

Rewriting this using the fact that $\widetilde{NOI} = \widetilde{Rev} - \widetilde{VC} - FCC - dep$, we have

$$(\widetilde{Rev} - \widetilde{VC} - FCC - dep)(1 - \tau_c).$$

This is operating income after taxes, but it is not yet a cash flow definition because a portion of total fixed costs are noncash expenses such as depreciation and deferred taxes. Total fixed costs are partitioned in two parts: FCC is the cash-fixed costs, and dep is the noncash-fixed costs.

To convert after-tax operating income into cash flows, we must add back depreciation and other noncash expenses. Doing this, we have

$$(\widetilde{Rev} - \widetilde{VC} - FCC - dep)(1 - \tau_c) + dep.$$

Finally, by assumption, we know that the firm has no growth; i.e., all cash flows are perpetuities. This implies that depreciation each year must be replaced by investment in order to keep the same amount of capital in place. Therefore dep $= I$, and the after-tax free cash flow available for payment to creditors and shareholders is

$$\widetilde{FCF} = (\widetilde{Rev} - \widetilde{VC} - FCC - dep)(1 - \tau_c) + dep - I,$$
$$\widetilde{FCF} = (\widetilde{Rev} - \widetilde{VC} - FCC - dep)(1 - \tau_c) \quad \text{since} \quad dep = I.$$

The interesting result is that when all cash flows are assumed to be perpetuities, free cash flow ($\widetilde{FCF}$) is the same thing as net operating income after taxes, i.e., the cash flow that the firm would have available if it had no debt at all. This is shown below:

$$\widetilde{NOI}(1 - \tau_c) = \widetilde{FCF} = (\widetilde{Rev} - \widetilde{VC} - FCC - dep)(1 - \tau_c).$$

Note also that this approach to cash flows is exactly the same as that used to define cash flows for capital budgeting purposes in Chapter 2. The reader should keep in mind that in order to determine the value of the firm correctly, the definition of cash flows and the definition of the discount rate, i.e., the weighted average cost of capital, must be consistent. The material that follows will prove that they are.

Given perpetual cash flows, Eq. (13.1), the value of an unlevered firm, can be written in either of two equivalent ways:[1]

$$V^U = \frac{E(\widetilde{FCF})}{\rho} \quad \text{or} \quad V^U = \frac{E(\widetilde{NOI})(1 - \tau_c)}{\rho}. \tag{13.1}$$

From this point forward we shall use the net operating income definition of cash flows in order to be consistent with the language originally employed by Modigliani and Miller.

Next assume that the firm issues debt. The after-tax cash flows must be split up between debt holders and shareholders. Shareholders receive $\widetilde{NI}$ + dep − I, net cash flows after interest, taxes, and replacement investment; and bondholders receive interest on debt, $k_d D$. Mathematically, this is equivalent to total cash flow available for payment to the private sector:[2]

$$\widetilde{NI} + \text{dep} - I + k_d D = (\widetilde{Rev} - \widetilde{VC} - \text{FCC} - \text{dep} - k_d D)(1 - \tau_c) + \text{dep} - I + k_d D.$$

Given that dep = I, for a nongrowing firm we can rearrange terms to obtain

$$\widetilde{NI} + k_d D = (\widetilde{Rev} - \widetilde{VC} - \text{FCC} - \text{dep})(1 - \tau_c) - k_d D + k_d D \tau_c + k_d D$$
$$= \widetilde{NOI}(1 - \tau_c) + k_d D \tau_c. \tag{13.2}$$

The first part of this stream, $\widetilde{NOI}(1 - \tau_c)$, is exactly the same as the cash flows for the unlevered firm [the numerator of (13.1)], with exactly the same risk. Therefore recalling that it is a perpetual stream, we can discount it at the rate appropriate for an unlevered firm, ρ. The second part of the stream, $k_d D \tau_c$, is assumed to be risk free. Therefore we shall discount it at the before-tax cost of risk-free debt, k_b. Consequently, the value of the levered firm is the sum of the discounted value of the two types of cash flow that it provides:

$$V^L = \frac{E(\widetilde{NOI})(1 - \tau_c)}{\rho} + \frac{k_d D \tau_c}{k_b}. \tag{13.3}$$

Note that $k_d D$ is the perpetual stream of risk-free payments to bondholders and that k_b is the current before-tax market-required rate of return for the risk-free stream. Therefore since the stream is perpetual, the market value of the bonds, B, is

$$B = k_d D / k_b. \tag{13.4}$$

---

[1] The present value of any constant perpetual stream of cash flows is simply the cash flow divided by the discount rate. See Appendix A at the end of the book, Eq. (A.5).
[2] The government receives all cash flows not included in Eq. (13.2); i.e., the government receives taxes (also a risky cash flow).

Table 13.1 Proposition I Arbitrage Example

	Company A	Company B
NOI	10,000	10,000
$-k_dD$	0	1,500
NI	10,000	8,500
k_s	10%	11%
S	100,000	77,272
B	0	30,000
$V = B + S$	100,000	107,272
WACC	10%	9.3%
B/S	0%	38.8%

Now we can rewrite Eq. (13.3) as

$$V^L = V^U + \tau_c B. \tag{13.5}$$

The value of the levered firm, V^L, is equal to the value of an unlevered firm, V^U, plus the present value of the tax shield provided by debt, $\tau_c B$. Later on we shall refer to the "extra" value created by the interest tax shield on debt as the *gain from leverage*. This is perhaps the single most important result in the theory of corporation finance obtained in the last 30 years. It says that in the absence of any market imperfections including corporate taxes (i.e., if $\tau_c = 0$), the value of the firm is completely independent of the type of financing used for its projects. Without taxes, we have

$$V^L = V^U, \quad \text{if} \quad \tau_c = 0. \tag{13.5a}$$

Equation (13.5a) is known as *Modigliani-Miller Proposition* I. "The market value of any firm is independent of its capital structure and is given by capitalizing its expected return at the rate ρ appropriate to its risk class."[3] In other words, the method of financing is irrelevant. Modigliani and Miller went on to support their position by using one of the very first arbitrage pricing arguments in finance theory. Consider the income statements of the two firms given in Table 13.1. Both companies have exactly the same perpetual cash flows from operations, NOI, but Company A has no debt, whereas Company B has $30,000 of debt paying 5% interest. The example reflects greater risk in holding the levered equity of Company B because the cost of equity, $k_s = \text{NI}/S$, for B is greater than that of Company A. The example has been constructed so that Company B has a greater market value than A and hence a lower weighted average cost of capital, $\text{WACC} = \text{NOI}/V$. The difference in values is a violation of Proposition I. However, the difference will not persist because if we, e.g., already own stock in B, we can earn a profit with no extra risk by borrowing (at

---

[3] Modigliani and Miller [1958, 268].

5%) and buying Company A. In effect, we create homemade leverage in the following way:

1. We sell our stock in B (say we own 1%, then we sell $772.72).
2. We borrow an amount equivalent to 1% of the debt in B, i.e., $300 at 5% interest.
3. We buy 1% of the shares in A.

Before arbitrage we held 1% of the equity of B and earned 11% on it, i.e., .11($772.72) = $85.00. After arbitrage we hold the following position:

$$1\% \text{ of A's equity and earn } 10\%, \text{ i.e., } .10(\$1000.00) = \$100.00$$
$$\text{pay interest on } \$300 \text{ of debt, i.e., } .05(\$300) = -15.00$$
$$\overline{85.00}$$

This gives us the same income as our levered position in Company B, but the amount of money we have available is $772.72 (from selling shares in B) plus $300 (from borrowing). So far, in the above calculation, we have used only $1000.00 to buy shares of A. Therefore we can invest another $72.72 in shares of A and earn 10%. This brings our total income up to $85 + $7.27 = $92.27, and we own $772.72 of *net* worth of equity in A (the bank "owns" $300). Therefore our return on equity is 11.94% (i.e., $92.27/$772.72). Furthermore, our personal leverage is the $300 in debt divided by the equity in A, $772.72. This is exactly the same leverage and therefore the same risk as we started with when we had an equity investment in B.

The upshot of the foregoing arbitrage argument is that we can use homemade leverage to invest in A. We earn a higher rate of return on equity without changing our risk at all. Consequently we will undertake the arbitrage operation by selling shares in B, borrowing, and buying shares in A. We will continue to do so until the market values of the two firms are identical. Therefore Modigliani-Miller Proposition I is a simple arbitrage argument. In a world without taxes the market values of the levered and unlevered firms must be identical.

However, as shown by Eq. (13.5), when the government "subsidizes" interest payments to providers of debt capital by allowing the corporation to deduct interest payments on debt as an expense, the market value of the corporation can increase as it takes on more and more (risk-free) debt. Ideally (given the assumptions of the model) the firm should take on 100% debt.[4]

2. The Weighted Average Cost of Capital

Next, we can determine the cost of capital by using the fact that shareholders will require the rate of return on new projects to be greater than the opportunity cost of the funds supplied by them and bondholders. This condition is equivalent to requiring

---

[4] We shall see later in this chapter that this result is modified when we consider a world with both corporate and personal taxes, or one where bankruptcy costs are nontrivial. Also, the Internal Revenue Service will disallow the tax deductibility of interest charges on debt if, in its judgment, the firm is using excessive debt financing as a tax shield.

that original shareholders' wealth increase. From Eq. (13.3) we see that the change in the value of the levered firm, ΔV^L, with respect to a new investment, ΔI, is[5]

$$\frac{\Delta V^L}{\Delta I} = \frac{(1 - \tau_c)}{\rho} \frac{\Delta E(\widetilde{NOI})}{\Delta I} + \tau_c \frac{\Delta B}{\Delta I}. \tag{13.6}$$

If we take the new project, the change in the value of the firm, ΔV^L, will also be equal to the change in the value of original shareholders' wealth, ΔS^o, plus the new equity required for the project, ΔS^n, plus the change in the value of bonds outstanding, ΔB^o, plus new bonds issued, ΔB^n:

$$\Delta V^L = \Delta S^o + \Delta S^n + \Delta B^o + \Delta B^n. \tag{13.7a}$$

Alternatively, the changes with respect to the new investment are

$$\frac{\Delta V^L}{\Delta I} = \frac{\Delta S^o}{\Delta I} + \frac{\Delta S^n}{\Delta I} + \frac{\Delta B^o}{\Delta I} + \frac{\Delta B^n}{\Delta I}. \tag{13.7b}$$

Because the old bondholders hold a contract that promises fixed payments of interest and principal, because the new project is assumed to be no riskier than those already outstanding, and especially because both old and new debt are assumed to be risk free, the change in the value of outstanding debt is zero ($\Delta B^o = 0$). Furthermore, the new project must be financed with either new debt, new equity, or both. This implies that[6]

$$\Delta I = \Delta S^n + \Delta B^n. \tag{13.8}$$

Using this fact (13.7b) can be rewritten as

$$\frac{\Delta V^L}{\Delta I} = \frac{\Delta S^o}{\Delta I} + \frac{\Delta S^n + \Delta B^n}{\Delta I} = \frac{\Delta S^o}{\Delta I} + 1. \tag{13.9}$$

For a project to be acceptable to original shareholders, it must increase their wealth. Therefore they will require that

$$\frac{\Delta S^o}{\Delta I} = \frac{\Delta V^L}{\Delta I} - 1 > 0, \tag{13.10}$$

which is equivalent to the requirement that $\Delta V^L/\Delta I > 1$. Note that the requirement that the change in original shareholders' wealth be positive, i.e., $\Delta S^o/\Delta I > 0$, is a behavioral assumption imposed by Modigliani and Miller. They were assuming (1) that managers always do exactly what shareholders wish and (2) that managers and shareholders always have the same information. The behavioral assumptions of Eq. (13.10) are essential for what follows.

---

[5] Note that τ_c and ρ do not change with ΔI. The cost of equity for an all-equity firm does not change because new projects are assumed to have the same risk as the old ones.

[6] Note that (13.8) does not require new issues of debt or equity to be positive. It is conceivable, e.g., that the firm might issue \$4000 in stock for a \$1000 project and repurchase \$3000 in debt.

When the assumptions of inequality [(13.10)] are imposed on Eq. (13.6) we are able to determine the cost of capital[7]

$$\frac{\Delta V^L}{\Delta I} = \frac{(1 - \tau_c)}{\rho} \frac{\Delta E(\widehat{NOI})}{\Delta I} + \tau_c \frac{\Delta B^n}{\Delta I} > 1,$$

or, by rearranging terms, we have

$$\frac{(1 - \tau_c) \Delta E(\widehat{NOI})}{\Delta I} > \rho \left(1 - \tau_c \frac{\Delta B}{\Delta I} \right). \tag{13.11}$$

The left-hand side of (13.11) is the after-tax change in net operating cash flows brought about by the new investment, i.e., the after-tax return on the project.[8] The right-hand side is the opportunity cost of capital applicable to the project. As long as the anticipated rate of return on investment is greater than the cost of capital, current shareholders' wealth will increase.

Note that if the corporate tax rate is zero, the cost of capital is independent of capital structure (the ratio of debt to total assets). This result is consistent with Eq. (13.5a), which says that the value of the firm is independent of capital structure. On the other hand, if corporate taxes are paid, the cost of capital declines steadily as the proportion of new investment financed with debt increases. The value of the levered firm reaches a maximum when there is 100% debt financing (so long as all of the debt is risk free).

3. Two Definitions of Market Value Weights

Equation (13.11) defines what has often been called the weighted average cost of capital, WACC, for the firm:

$$\text{WACC} = \rho \left(1 - \tau_c \frac{\Delta B}{\Delta I} \right). \tag{13.12}$$

An often debated question is the correct interpretation of $\Delta B/\Delta I$. Modigliani and Miller [1963, 441] interpret it by saying that

> If B^*/V^* denotes the firm's long run "target" debt ratio . . . then the firm can assume, to a first approximation at least, that for any particular investment $dB/dI = B^*/V^*$.

Two questions arise in the interpretation of the leverage ratio, $\Delta B/\Delta I$. First, is the leverage ratio marginal or average? Modigliani and Miller, in the above quote, set the marginal ratio equal to the average by assuming the firm sets a long-run target

---

[7] Note that ($\Delta B = \Delta B^n$) because ΔB^o is assumed to be zero.

[8] Chapter 2, the investment decision, stressed the point that the correct cash flows for capital budgeting purposes were always defined as net cash flows from operations after taxes. Equation (13.11) reiterates this point and shows that it is the *only* definition of cash flows that is consistent with the opportunity cost of capital for the firm. The numerator on the left-hand side, namely, $E(\widehat{NOI})(1 - \tau_c)$, is the after-tax cash flows from operations that the firm would have if it had no debt.

ratio, which is constant. Even if this is the case, we still must consider a second issue, namely: Is the ratio to be measured as *book value leverage, replacement value leverage,* or *reproduction value leverage*? The last two definitions, as we shall see, are both market values. At least one of these three measures, book value leverage, can be ruled out immediately as being meaningless. In particular, there is no relationship whatsoever between book value concepts, (e.g., retained earnings) and the economic value of equity.

The remaining two interpretations, replacement and reproduction value, make sense because they are both market value definitions. By replacement value, we mean the economic cost of putting a project in place. For capital projects a large part of this cost is usually the cost of purchasing plant, equipment, and working capital. In the Modigliani-Miller formulation, replacement cost is the market value of the investment in the project under consideration, ΔI. It is the denominator on both sides of the cost of capital inequality (13.11). On the other hand, reproduction value, ΔV, is the total present value of the stream of goods and services expected from the project. The two concepts can be compared by noting that the difference between them is the NPV of the project, that is,

$$\text{NPV} = \Delta V - \Delta I.$$

For a marginal project, where $\text{NPV} = 0$, replacement cost and reproduction value are equal.

Haley and Schall [1973, 306–311] introduce an alternative cost of capital definition where the "target" leverage is the ratio of debt to reproduction value, as shown below:

$$\text{WACC} = \rho\left(1 - \tau_c \frac{\Delta B}{\Delta V}\right). \tag{13.13}$$

If the firm uses a reproduction value concept for its "target" leverage, it will seek to maintain a constant ratio of the market value of debt to the market value of the firm.

With the foregoing as background, we can now reconcile the apparent conflict in the measurement of leverage applicable to the determination of the relevant cost of capital for a new investment project. Modigliani and Miller define the target L^* as the average, in the long run, of the debt-to-value ratio or B^*/V^*. Then regardless of how a particular investment is financed, the relevant leverage ratio is dB/dV. For example, a particular investment may be financed entirely by debt. But the cost of that particular increment of debt is not the relevant cost of capital for that investment. The debt would require an equity base. How much equity? This is answered by the long-run target B^*/V^*. So procedurally, we start with the actual amount of investment increment for the particular investment, dI. The L^* ratio then defines the amount of dB assigned to the investment. If the NPV from the investment is positive, then dV will be greater than dI. Hence the debt capacity of the firm will have been increased by more than dB. However, the relevant leverage for estimating the WACC will still be dB/dV, which will be equal to B^*/V^*. We emphasize that the latter is a policy target decision by the firm, based on relevant financial economic considerations. The dV is an amount assigned to the analysis to be consistent with L^*.

The issue is whether to use dB/dV or dB/dI as the weight in the cost of capital formula. The following example highlights the difference between the two approaches. Suppose a firm can undertake a new project that costs $1000 and has expected cash flows with a present value of $9000 when discounted at the cost of equity for an all-equity project of equivalent risk. If the ratio of the firm's target debt to value is 50% and if its tax rate is 40%, how much debt should it undertake? If it uses replacement value leverage, then $dB/dI = .5$ and $dB = \$500$; i.e., half of the $1000 investment is financed with debt. Using equation (13.5) the value of the levered firm is

$$dV^L = dV^U + \tau_c dB$$

$$= 9000 + .4(500)$$

$$= 9200.$$

The same formula can be used to compute the amount of debt if we use reproduction value leverage, i.e., $dB/dV^L = .5$, or $dV^L = 2\,dB$:

$$dV^L = 9000 + .4\,dB,$$

$$2\,dB = 9000 + .4\,dB \quad \text{since} \quad dV^L = 2\,dB,$$

$$dB = 5625.$$

If our target is set by using reproduction values, then we should issue $5625 of new debt for the $1000 project, and repurchase $4625 of equity. The change in the value of the firm will be

$$dV^L = dV^U + \tau_c dB$$

$$= 9000 + .4(5625)$$

$$= 11250.$$

Clearly, the value of the firm is higher if we use the reproduction value definition of leverage. But as a practical matter, what bank would lend $5625 on a project that has a $1000 replacement value of assets? If the bank and the firm have homogeneous expectations this is possible. If they do not, then it is likely that the firm is more optimistic than the bank about the project. In the case of heterogeneous expectations there is no clear solution to the problem. Hence we favor the original argument of Modigliani and Miller that the long-run target debt-to-value ratio will be close to dB/dI; i.e., use the replacement value definition.

4. The Cost of Equity

If Eqs. (13.12) and (13.13) are the weighted average cost of capital, how do we determine the cost of the two components, debt and equity? The cost of debt is the risk-free rate, at least given the assumptions of this model. (We shall discuss risky debt in section D.) The cost of equity capital is the change in the return to equity holders with respect to the change in their investment, $\Delta S^o + \Delta S^n$. The return to equity holders is the net cash flow after interest and taxes, NI. Therefore their rate of return is $\Delta \text{NI}/(\Delta S^o + \Delta S^n)$. To solve for this, we begin with identity (13.2),

$$\text{NI} + k_d D = \text{NOI}(1 - \tau_c) + k_d D \tau_c.$$

Next we divide by ΔI, the new investment, and obtain

$$\frac{\Delta \text{NI}}{\Delta I} + \frac{\Delta(k_d D)}{\Delta I} - \frac{\tau_c \Delta(k_d D)}{\Delta I} = (1 - \tau_c) \frac{\Delta \text{NOI}}{\Delta I}. \tag{13.14}$$

Substituting the left-hand side of (13.14) into (13.6), we get

$$\frac{\Delta V^L}{\Delta I} = \frac{\Delta \text{NI}/\Delta I + (1 - \tau_c)\Delta(k_d D)/\Delta I}{\rho} + \tau_c \frac{\Delta B}{\Delta I}. \tag{13.15}$$

From (13.7), we know that

$$\frac{\Delta V^L}{\Delta I} = \frac{\Delta S^o + \Delta S^n}{\Delta I} + \frac{\Delta B^n}{\Delta I}, \quad \text{since} \quad \Delta B^o \equiv 0. \tag{13.16}$$

Consequently, by equating (13.15) and (13.16) we get

$$\frac{\Delta V^L}{\Delta I} = \frac{\Delta S^o + \Delta S^n}{\Delta I} + \frac{\Delta B}{\Delta I} - \frac{\Delta \text{NI}/\Delta I + (1 - \tau_c)\,\Delta(k_d D)/\Delta I}{\rho} + \tau_c \frac{\Delta B}{\Delta I}.$$

Then, multiplying both sides by ΔI, we have

$$\Delta S^o + \Delta S^n + \Delta B = \frac{\Delta \text{NI} + (1 - \tau_c)\,\Delta(k_d D) + \rho \tau_c \,\Delta B}{\rho}.$$

Subtracting ΔB from both sides gives

$$\Delta S^o + \Delta S^n = \frac{\Delta \text{NI} + (1 - \tau_c)\,\Delta(k_d D) + \rho \tau_c \,\Delta B - \rho \,\Delta B}{\rho},$$

$$\rho(\Delta S^o + \Delta S^n) = \Delta \text{NI} - (1 - \tau_c)(\rho - k_b)\,\Delta B, \quad \text{since} \quad \Delta(k_d D) = k_b \,\Delta B.$$

And finally,

$$\frac{\Delta \text{NI}}{\Delta S^o + \Delta S^n} = \rho + (1 - \tau_c)(\rho - k_b)\frac{\Delta B}{\Delta S^o + \Delta S^n}. \tag{13.17}$$

The change in new equity plus old equity equals the change in the total equity of the firm ($\Delta S = \Delta S^o + \Delta S^n$). Therefore the cost of equity, $k_s = \Delta \text{NI}/\Delta S$, is written

$$k_s = \rho + (1 - \tau_c)(\rho - k_b)\frac{\Delta B}{\Delta S}. \tag{13.18}$$

The implication of Eq. (13.18) is that the opportunity cost of capital to shareholders increases linearly with changes in the market value ratio of debt to equity (assuming that $\Delta B/\Delta S = B/S$). If the firm has no debt in its capital structure, the levered cost of equity capital, k_s, is equal to the cost of equity for an all-equity firm, ρ.

5. A Graphical Presentation for the Cost of Capital

Figure 13.2 graphs the cost of capital and its components as a function of the ratio of debt to equity. The weighted average cost of capital is invariant to changes in capital structure in a world without corporate taxes; however, with taxes it declines as more and more debt is used in the firm's capital structure. In both cases the cost of equity capital increases with higher proportions of debt. This makes sense because increasing financial leverage implies a riskier position for shareholders as their residual claim on the firm becomes more variable. They require a higher rate of return to compensate them for the extra risk they take.

The careful reader will have noticed that in Fig. 13.2 B/S is on the horizontal axis, whereas Eqs. (13.13) and (13.18) are written in terms of $\Delta B/\Delta S$ or $\Delta B/\Delta V$, which are changes in debt with respect to changes in equity or value of the firm. The two are equal only when the firm's average debt-to-equity ratio is the same as its marginal debt-to-equity ratio. This will be true as long as the firm establishes a "target" debt-to-equity ratio equal to B/S and then finances all projects with the identical proportion of debt and equity so that $B/S = \Delta B/\Delta S$.

The usual definition of the weighted average cost of capital is to weight the after-tax cost of debt by the percentage of debt in the firm's capital structure and add the result to the cost of equity multiplied by the percentage of equity. The equation is

$$\text{WACC} = (1 - \tau_c)k_b \frac{B}{B + S} + k_s \frac{S}{B + S}. \tag{13.19}$$

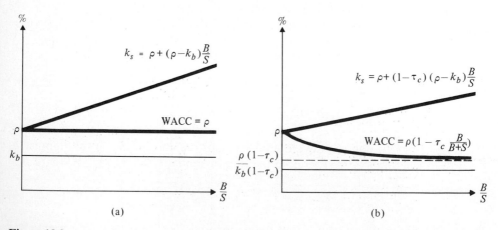

Figure 13.2
The cost of capital as a function of the ratio of debt to equity; (a) assuming $\tau_c = 0$; (b) assuming $\tau_c > 0$.

We can see that this is the same as the Modigliani-Miller definition, Eq. (13.12) by substituting (13.18) into (13.19) and assuming that $B/S = \Delta B/\Delta S$. This is done below:

$$\text{WACC} = (1 - \tau_c)k_b \frac{B}{B+S} + \left[\rho + (1 - \tau_c)(\rho - k_b)\frac{B}{S}\right]\frac{S}{B+S}$$

$$= (1 - \tau_c)k_b \frac{B}{B+S} + \rho \frac{S}{B+S} + (1 - \tau_c)\rho \frac{B}{S}\frac{S}{B+S} - (1 - \tau_c)k_b \frac{B}{S}\frac{S}{B+S}$$

$$= (1 - \tau_c)k_b \frac{B}{B+S} + \rho\left(\frac{S}{B+S} + \frac{B}{B+S}\right) - \rho\tau_c \frac{B}{B+S} - (1 - \tau_c)k_b \frac{B}{B+S}$$

$$= \rho\left(1 - \tau_c \frac{B}{B+S}\right). \qquad \text{QED}$$

There is no inconsistency between the traditional definition and the M-M definition of the cost of capital [Eqs. (13.12) and (13.19)]. They are identical.

B. THE VALUE OF THE FIRM IN A WORLD WITH BOTH PERSONAL AND CORPORATE TAXES

1. Assuming All Firms Have Identical Effective Tax Rates

In the original model the *gain from leverage*, G, is the difference between the value of the levered and unlevered firms, which is the product of the corporate tax rate and the market value of debt:

$$G = V^L - V^U = \tau_c B. \tag{13.20}$$

Miller [1977] modifies this result by introducing personal as well as corporate taxes into the model. In addition to making the model more realistic, the revised approach adds considerable insight into the effect of leverage on value in the real world. We do not, after all, observe firms with 100% debt in their capital structure as the original Modigliani-Miller model suggests.

Assume for the moment that there are only two types of personal tax rates: the rate on income received from holding shares, τ_{ps}, and the rate on income from bonds, τ_{pB}. The expected after-tax stream of cash flows to shareholders of an all-equity firm would be $(\text{NOI})(1 - \tau_c)(1 - \tau_{ps})$. By discounting this perpetual stream at the cost of equity for an all-equity firm we have the value of the unlevered firm:

$$V^U = \frac{E(\text{NOI})(1 - \tau_c)(1 - \tau_{ps})}{\rho}. \tag{13.21}$$

Alternatively, if the firm has both bonds and shares outstanding, the earnings stream is partitioned into two parts. Cash flows to shareholders after corporate and personal taxes are:

$$\text{Payments to shareholders} = (\text{NOI} - k_d D)(1 - \tau_c)(1 - \tau_{ps}),$$

and payments to bondholders, after personal taxes, are

$$\text{Payments to bondholders} = k_d D(1 - \tau_{pB}).$$

Adding these together and rearranging terms, we have

$$\frac{\text{Total cash payments}}{\text{to suppliers of capital}} = \text{NOI}(1 - \tau_c)(1 - \tau_{ps}) - k_d D(1 - \tau_c)(1 - \tau_{ps}) + k_d D(1 - \tau_{pB}).$$

$$(13.22)$$

The first term on the right-hand side of (13.22) is the same as the stream of cash flows to owners of the unlevered firm, and its expected value can be discounted at the cost of equity for an all-equity firm. The second and third terms are risk free and can be discounted at the risk-free rate, k_b. The sum of the discounted streams of cash flow is the value of the levered firm:

$$V^L = \frac{E(\text{NOI})(1 - \tau_c)(1 - \tau_{ps})}{\rho} + \frac{k_d D[(1 - \tau_{pB}) - (1 - \tau_c)(1 - \tau_{ps})]}{k_b}$$

$$= V^U + \left[1 - \frac{(1 - \tau_c)(1 - \tau_{ps})}{(1 - \tau_{pB})}\right]B, \qquad (13.23)$$

where $B = k_d D(1 - \tau_{pB})/k_b$, the market value of debt. Consequently, with the introduction of personal taxes, the gain from leverage is the second term in (13.23):

$$G = \left[1 - \frac{(1 - \tau_c)(1 - \tau_{ps})}{(1 - \tau_{pB})}\right]B. \qquad (13.24)$$

Note that when personal tax rates are set equal to zero, the gain from leverage in (13.24) equals the gain from leverage in (13.20), the earlier result. This finding also obtains when the personal tax rate on share income equals the rate on bond income. In the United States it is reasonable to assume that the effective tax rate on common stock is lower than that on bonds.[9] The implication is that the gain from leverage when personal taxes are considered [Eq. (13.24)] is lower than $\tau_c B$ [Eq. (13.20)].

If the personal income tax on stocks is less than the tax on income from bonds, then the before-tax return on bonds has to be high enough, other things being equal, to offset this disadvantage. Otherwise no investor would want to hold bonds. While it is true that owners of a levered corporation are subsidized by the interest deductibility of debt, this advantage is counterbalanced by the fact that the required interest payments have already been "grossed up" by any differential that bondholders must pay on their interest income. In this way the advantage of debt financing may be lost.

---

[9] The tax rate on stock is thought of as being lower than that on bonds because of a relatively higher capital gains component of return, and because capital gains are not taxed until the security is sold. Capital gains taxes can, therefore, be deferred indefinitely.

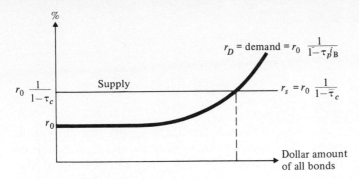

Figure 13.3
Aggregate supply and demand for corporate bonds (before tax rates).

In fact, whenever the following condition is met in Eq. (13.24),

$$(1 - \tau_{pB}) = (1 - \tau_c)(1 - \tau_{ps}),$$
(13.25)

the advantage of debt vanishes completely.

Suppose that the personal tax rate on income from common stock is zero. We may justify this by arguing that (1) no one has to realize a capital gain until after death; (2) gains and losses in well-diversified portfolios can offset each other, thereby eliminating the payment of capital gains taxes; (3) 80% of dividends received by taxable corporations can be excluded from taxable income; or (4) many types of investment funds pay no taxes at all (nonprofit organizations, pension funds, trust funds, etc.).[10] Figure 13.3 portrays the supply and demand for corporate bonds. The rate paid on the debt of tax-free institutions (municipal bonds, for example) is r_0. If all bonds paid only r_0, no one would hold them with the exception of tax-free institutions that are not affected by the tax disadvantage of holding debt when $\tau_{pB} > \tau_{ps}$. An individual with a marginal tax rate on income from bonds equal to τ_{pB}^i will not hold corporate bonds until they pay $r_0/(1 - \tau_{pB}^i)$, i.e., until their return is "grossed up." Since the personal income tax is progressive, the interest rate that is demanded has to keep rising to attract investors in higher and higher tax brackets.[11] The supply of corporate bonds is perfectly elastic, and bonds must pay a rate of $r_0/(1 - \tau_c)$ in equilibrium. To see that this is true, let us recall that the personal tax rate on stock is assumed to be zero ($\tau_{ps} = 0$) and rewrite the gain from leverage:

$$G = \left(1 - \frac{(1 - \tau_c)}{(1 - \tau_{pB})}\right) B.$$
(13.26)

If the rate of return on bonds supplied by corporations is $r_s = r_0/(1 - \tau_c)$, then the gain from leverage, in Eq. (13.26), will be zero. The supply rate of return equals the

---

[10] Also, as will be shown in Chapter 16, it is possible to shield up to $10,000 in dividend income from taxes.
[11] Keep in mind the fact that the tax rate on income from stock is assumed to be zero. Therefore the higher an individual's tax bracket becomes, the higher the before-tax rate on bonds must be in order for the after-tax rate on bonds to equal the rate of return on stock (after adjusting for risk).

demand rate of return in equilibrium:

$$r_s = \frac{r_0}{1 - \tau_c} = r_D = \frac{r_0}{1 - \tau_{pB}}.$$

Consequently,

$$(1 - \tau_c) = (1 - \tau_{pB}),$$

and the gain from leverage in (13.26) will equal zero. If the supply rate of return is less than $r_0/(1 - \tau_c)$, then the gain from leverage will be positive, and all corporations will try to have a capital structure containing 100% debt. They will rush out to issue new debt. On the other hand, if the supply rate of return is greater than $r_0/(1 - \tau_c)$, the gain from leverage will be negative and firms will take action to repay outstanding debt. Thus we see that in equilibrium, taxable debt must be supplied to the point where the before-tax cost of corporate debt must equal the rate that would be paid by tax-free institutions grossed up by the corporate tax rate.

Miller's argument has important implications for capital structure. First, the gain to leverage may be much smaller than previously thought. Consequently, optimal capital structure may be explained by a tradeoff between a small gain to leverage and relatively small costs such as expected bankruptcy costs. This tradeoff will be discussed at greater length in Chapter 14. Second, the observed market equilibrium interest rate is seen to be a before-tax rate that is "grossed up" so that most or all of the interest rate tax shield is lost. Finally, Miller's theory implies there is an equilibrium amount of aggregate debt outstanding in the economy that is determined by relative corporate and personal tax rates.

2. Assuming That Firms Have Different Marginal Effective Tax Rates

DeAngelo and Masulis [1980] extend Miller's work by analyzing the effect of tax shields other than interest payments on debt, e.g., noncash charges such as depreciation, oil depletion allowances, and investment tax credits. They are able to demonstrate the existence of an optimal (nonzero) corporate use of debt while still maintaining the assumption of zero bankruptcy (and zero agency) costs.

Their original argument is illustrated in Fig. 13.4. The corporate debt supply curve is downward sloping to reflect the fact that the expected marginal effective tax rate, τ_c^j, differs across corporate suppliers of debt. Investors with personal tax rates lower than the marginal individual earn a consumer surplus because they receive higher after-tax returns. Corporations with higher tax rates than the marginal firm receive a positive gain to leverage, a producer's surplus, in equilibrium because they pay what is for them a low pre-tax debt rate.

It is reasonable to expect depreciation expenses and investment tax credits to serve as tax shield substitutes for interest expenses. The DeAngelo and Masulis model predicts that firms will select a level of debt that is negatively related to the level of available tax shield substitutes such as depreciation, depletion, and investment tax credits. Also, as more and more debt is utilized, the probability of winding up with

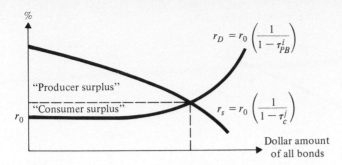

Figure 13.4
Aggregate debt equilibrium with heterogeneous corporate
and personal tax rates.

zero or negative earnings will increase, thereby causing the interest tax shield to
decline in expected value. They further show that if there are positive bankruptcy
costs, there will be an optimum tradeoff between the marginal expected benefit of
interest tax shields and the marginal expected cost of bankruptcy. This issue will be
further discussed in the next chapter.

C. INTRODUCING RISK –A SYNTHESIS OF M-M AND CAPM

The CAPM discussed in Chapter 7 provides a natural theory for the pricing of risk.
When combined with the cost of capital definitions derived by Modigliani and Miller
[1958, 1963], it provides a unified approach to the cost of capital. The work that we
shall describe was first published by Hamada [1969] and synthesized by Rubinstein
[1973].

The CAPM may be written as

$$E(R_j) = R_f + [E(R_m) - R_f]\beta_j, \tag{13.27}$$

where

$E(R_j)$ = the expected rate of return on asset j,

R_f = the (constant) risk-free rate,

$E(R_m)$ = the expected rate of return on the market portfolio,

$\beta_j = \text{COV}(R_j, R_m)/\text{VAR}(R_m)$.

Recall that all securities fall exactly on the security market line, which is illustrated
in Fig. 13.5. We can use this fact to discuss the implications for the cost of debt, the
cost of equity, and the weighted average cost of capital; and for capital budgeting
when projects have different risk.

Figure 13.5 illustrates the difference between the original Modigliani-Miller cost
of capital and the CAPM. Modigliani and Miller assumed that all projects within

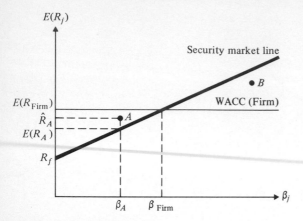

Figure 13.5
The security market line.

the firm had the same business or operating risk (mathematically, they assumed that $CF_i = \lambda CF_j$). This was expedient because in 1958, when the paper was written, there was no accepted theory that allowed adjustments for differences in systematic risk. Consequently, the Modigliani-Miller theory is represented by the horizontal line in Fig. 13.5. The WACC for the firm (implicitly) does not change as a function of systematic risk. This assumption, of course, must be modified because firms and projects differ in risk.

1. The Cost of Capital and Systematic Risk

Table 13.2 shows expressions for the cost of debt, k_b, unlevered equity, ρ, levered equity, k_s, and the weighted average cost of capital, WACC, in both the Modigliani-Miller and capital asset pricing model frameworks. It has already been demonstrated, in the proof following Eq. (13.19), that the traditional and M-M definitions of the weighted average cost of capital (the last line in Table 13.2) are identical. Modigliani and Miller assumed, for convenience, that corporate debt is risk free; i.e., that its price is insensitive to changes in interest rates and either that it has no default risk or that

Table 13.2 Comparison of M-M and CAPM Cost of Capital Equations

Type of Capital	CAPM Definition	M-M Definition
Debt	$k_b = R_f + [E(R_m) - R_f]\beta_b$	$k_b = R_f, \beta_b = 0$
Unlevered equity	$\rho = R_f + [E(R_m) - R_f]\beta_U$	$\rho = \rho$
Levered equity	$k_s = R_f + [E(R_m) - R_f]\beta_L$	$k_s = \rho + (\rho - k_b)(1 - \tau_c)\dfrac{B}{S}$
WACC for the firm	$\mathrm{WACC} = k_b(1 - \tau_c)\dfrac{B}{B + S} + k_s\dfrac{S}{B + S}$	$\mathrm{WACC} = \rho\left(1 - \tau_c\dfrac{B}{B + S}\right)$

default risk is completely diversifiable ($\beta_b = 0$). We shall temporarily maintain the assumption that $k_b = R_f$, then relax it a little later in the chapter.

The M-M definition of the cost of equity for the unlevered firm was tautological, i.e., $\rho = \rho$, because the concept of systematic risk had not been developed in 1958. We now know that it depends on the systematic risk of the firm's after-tax operating cash flows, β_U. Unfortunately for empirical work, the unlevered beta is not directly observable. We can, however, easily estimate the levered equity beta, β_L. (This has also been referred to as β_s elsewhere.) If there is a definable relationship between the two betas, there are many practical implications (as we shall demonstrate with a simple numerical example in the next section). To derive the relationship between the levered and unlevered betas, begin by equating the M-M and CAPM definitions of the cost of levered equity (line 3 in Table 13.2):

$$R_f + [E(R_m) - R_f]\beta_L = \rho + (\rho - k_b)(1 - \tau_c)\frac{B}{S}.$$

Next, use the simplifying assumption that $k_b = R_f$ to write

$$R_f + [E(R_m) - R_f]\beta_L = \rho + (\rho - R_f)(1 - \tau_c)\frac{B}{S}.$$

Then substitute into the right-hand side the CAPM definition of the cost of unlevered equity, ρ:

$$R_f + \lfloor E(R_m) - R_f]\beta_L = R_f + [E(R_m) - R_f]\beta_U$$

$$+ \{R_f + [E(R_m) - R_f]\beta_U - R_f\}(1 - \tau_c)\frac{B}{S}.$$

By canceling terms and rearranging the equation, we have

$$[E(R_m) - R_f]\beta_L = [E(R_m) - R_f]\left[1 + (1 - \tau_c)\frac{B}{S}\right]\beta_U,$$

$$\beta_L = \left[1 + (1 - \tau_c)\frac{B}{S}\right]\beta_U. \tag{13.28}$$

The implication of Eq. (13.28) is that if we can observe the levered beta by using observed rates of return on equity capital in the stock market, we can estimate the unlevered risk of the firm's operating cash flows.

2. A Simple Example

The usefulness of the theoretical results can be demonstrated by considering the following problem. The United Southern Construction Company currently has a market value capital structure of 20% debt to total assets. The company's treasurer believes that more debt can be taken on, up to a limit of 35% debt, without losing the firm's ability to borrow at 7%, the prime rate (also assumed to be the risk-free rate). The firm has a marginal tax rate of 50%. The expected return on the market next year is estimated to be 17%, and the systematic risk of the company's equity, β_L, is estimated to be .5.

- What is the company's current weighted average cost of capital? Its current cost of equity?
- What will the new weighted average cost of capital be if the "target" capital structure is changed to 35% debt?
- Should a project with a 9.25% expected rate of return be accepted if its systematic risk, β_L, is the same as that of the firm?

To calculate the company's current cost of equity capital we can use the CAPM:

$$k_s = R_f + [E(R_m) - R_f]\beta_L$$
$$= .07 + [.17 - .07].5 = .12.$$

Therefore the weighted average cost of capital is

$$\text{WACC} = (1 - \tau_c)R_f \frac{B}{B + S} + k_s \frac{S}{B + S}$$
$$= (1 - .5).07(.2) + .12(.8) = 10.3\%.$$

The weighted average cost of capital with the new capital structure is shown in Fig. 13.6.[12] Note that the cost of equity increases with increasing leverage. This simply reflects the fact that shareholders face more risk with higher financial leverage and that they require a higher return to compensate them for it. Therefore in order to calculate the new weighted average cost of capital we have to use the Modigliani-Miller definition to estimate the cost of equity for an all-equity firm:

$$\text{WACC} = \rho\left(1 - \tau_c \frac{B}{B + S}\right),$$

$$\rho = \frac{\text{WACC}}{1 - \tau_c[B/(B + S)]} = \frac{.103}{1 - .5(.2)} = 11.44\%.$$

As long as the firm does not change its business risk, its unlevered cost of equity capital, ρ, will not change. Therefore we can use ρ to estimate the weighted average cost of capital with the new capital structure:

$$\text{WACC} = .1144[1 - .5(.35)] = 9.438\%.$$

Therefore, the new project with its 9.25% rate of return will not be acceptable even if the firm increases its ratio of debt to total assets from 20% to 35%.

A common error made in this type of problem is to forget that the cost of equity capital will increase with higher leverage. Had we estimated the weighted average

---

[12] Note that if debt to total assets is 20%, then debt to equity is 25%. Also, 35% converts to 53.85% in Fig. 13.6.

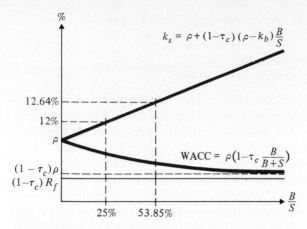

Figure 13.6
Changes in the cost of capital as leverage increases.

cost of capital, using 12% for the old cost of equity and 35% debt as the target capital structure, we would have obtained 9.03% as the estimated weighted average cost of capital and we would have accepted the project.

We can also use Eq. (13.28) to compute the unlevered beta for the firm. Before the capital structure change the levered beta was $\beta_L = .5$; therefore

$$\beta_L = \left[1 + (1 - \tau_c) \frac{B}{S} \right] \beta_U,$$

$$.5 = [1 + (1 - .5)(.25)]\beta_U,$$

$$\beta_U = .4444.$$

Note that the unlevered beta is consistent with the firm's unlevered cost of equity capital. Using the CAPM, we have

$$\rho = R_f + [E(R_m) - R_f]\beta_U$$

$$= .07 + [.17 - .07].4444$$

$$= 11.44\%.$$

Finally, we know that the unlevered beta will not change as long as the firm does not change its business risk, the risk of the portfolio of projects that it holds. Hence an increase in leverage will increase the levered beta, but the unlevered beta stays constant. Therefore we can use Eq. (13.28) to compute the new levered equity beta:

$$\beta_L = \left[1 + (1 - \tau_c) \frac{B}{S} \right] \beta_U$$

$$= [1 + (1 - .5).5385].4444$$

$$= .5641.$$

Hence the increase in leverage raises the levered equity beta from .5 to .5641, and the cost of levered equity increases from 12% to 12.64%.

3. The Cost of Capital for Projects of Differing Risk

A more difficult problem is to decide what to do if the project's risk is different from that of the firm. Suppose the new project would increase the replacement market value of the assets of the firm by 50% and that the systematic risk of the operating cash flows it provides is estimated to be $\beta_U = 1.2$. What rate of return must it earn in order to be profitable if the firm has (a) 20% or (b) 35% debt in its capital structure?

Figure 13.7 shows that the CAPM may be used to find the required rate of return given the beta of the project without leverage, $\beta_{U,p}$, which has been estimated to be 1.2. This is the beta for the *unlevered* project, because the beta is defined as the systematic risk of the operating cash flows. By definition this is the covariance between the cash flows *before* leverage and taxes and the market index. The required rate of return on the project, if it is an all-equity project, will be computed as shown below:

$$E(R_j) = R_f + [E(R_m) - R_f]\beta_{U,p}$$
$$= .07 + [.17 - .07]1.2 = 19\%.$$

Next we must "add in" the effect of the firm's leverage. If we recognize that 19% is the required rate if the project were all equity, we can find the required rate with 20% leverage by using the Modigliani-Miller weighted average cost of capital, Eq. (13.12):

$$\text{WACC} = \rho\left(1 - \tau_c\frac{B}{B + S}\right)$$
$$= .19[1 - .5(.2)] = 17.1\%.$$

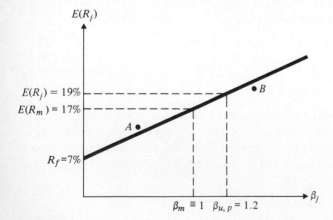

Figure 13.7
Using the CAPM to estimate the required rate of return on a project.

And if the leverage is increased to 35%, the required return falls to 15.675%:

$$\text{WACC} = .19[1 - .5(.35)] = 15.675\%.$$

Firms seek to find projects that earn more than the project's weighted average cost of capital. Suppose that, for the sake of argument, the WACC of our firm is 17%. Project B in Fig. 13.7 earns 20%, more than the firm's WACC, whereas project A in Fig. 13.7 earns only 15%, less than the firm's WACC. Does this mean that B should be accepted while A is rejected? Obviously not, because they have different risk (and possibly different optimal capital structures) than the firm as a whole. Project B is much riskier and must therefore earn a higher rate of return than the firm. In fact it must earn more than projects of equivalent risk. Since it falls below the security market line, it should be rejected. Alternately, project A should be accepted because its anticipated rate of return is higher than the rate that the market requires for projects of equivalent risk. It lies above the security market line in Fig. 13.7.

The examples above serve to illustrate the usefulness of the risk-adjusted cost of capital for capital budgeting purposes. Each project must be evaluated at a cost of capital that reflects the systematic risk of its operating cash flows as well as the financial leverage appropriate for the project. Estimates of the correct opportunity cost of capital are derived from a thorough understanding of the Modigliani-Miller cost of capital and the CAPM.

4. The Separability of Investment and Financing Decisions

The preceding example shows that the required rate of return on a new project is dependent on the project's weighted average cost of capital, which in turn may or may not be a function of the capital structure of the firm. What implications does this have for the relationship between investment and financing decisions; i.e., how independent is one of the other? The simplest possibility is that, after adjusting for project-specific risk, we can use the same capital structure—the capital structure of the entire firm—to estimate the cost of capital for all projects. However, this may not be the case. To clarify the issue we shall investigate two different suppositions.

1. If the weighted average cost of capital is invariant to changes in the firm's capital structure (i.e., if $\text{WACC} = \rho$ in Eq. (13.12) because $\tau_c - 0$), then the investment and financing decisions are completely separable. This might actually be the case if Miller's [1977] paper is empirically valid. The implication is that we can use NOI in Table 13.1 when estimating the appropriate cutoff rate for capital budgeting decisions. In other words, it is unnecessary to consider the financial leverage of the firm. Under the above assumptions, it is irrelevant.

2. If there really is gain from leverage, as would be suggested by the Modigliani-Miller theory if $\tau_c > 0$, or if the DeAngelo-Masulis [1980] extension of Miller's [1977] paper is empirically valid, then the value of a project is not independent of the capital structure assumed for it. In an earlier example we saw that the required rate of return on the project was 19% if the firm had no debt, 17.1% if it had 20% debt, and 15.675% if it had 35% debt in its capital structure. Therefore

the project has greater value as the financial leverage of the firm increases. As a practical matter, this problem is usually "handled" by assuming that the firm has decided on an "optimal" capital structure and that all projects are financed, at the margin, with the optimal ratio of debt to equity. The relevant factors that may be used to determine the optimal capital structure are discussed in the following chapter. However, assuming that an optimum does exist, and assuming that all projects are financed at the optimum, we may treat the investment decision *as if* it were separable from the financing decision. First the firm decides what optimal capital structure to use, then it applies the same capital structure to all projects. Under this set of assumptions the decision to accept or reject a particular project does not change the "optimal" capital structure. We could use Eq. (13.12) with $B/(B + S)$ set equal to the optimal capital structure in order to determine the appropriate cost of capital for a project. This is precisely what we did in the example.

But suppose projects carry with them the ability to change the optimal capital structure of the firm as a whole.[13] Suppose that some projects have more debt capacity than others. Then the investment and financing decisions cannot even be "handled" as if they were independent. There is very little in the accepted theory of finance that admits of this possibility, but it cannot be disregarded. One reason that projects may have separate debt capacities is the simple fact that they have different collateral values in bankruptcy. However, since the theory in this chapter has proceeded on the assumption that bankruptcy costs are zero, we shall refrain from further discussion of this point until the next chapter.

D. THE COST OF CAPITAL WITH RISKY DEBT

So far it has been convenient to assume that corporate debt is risk free. Obviously it is not. Consideration of risky debt raises several interesting questions. First, if debt is risky, how are the basic Modigliani-Miller propositions affected? We know that riskier debt will require higher rates of return. Does this reduce the tax gain from leverage? The answer is given in section D.1 below. The second question is, How can one estimate the required rate of return on risky debt? This is covered in section D.2.

1. The Effect of Risky Debt in the Absence of Bankruptcy Costs

The fundamental theorem set forth by Modigliani and Miller is that, given complete and perfect capital markets, it does not make any difference how one splits up the stream of operating cash flows. The percentage of debt or equity does not

---

[13] This may be particularly relevant when a firm is considering a conglomerate merger with another firm in a completely different line of business with a completely different optimal capital structure.

change the total value of the cash stream provided by the productive investments of the firm. Therefore so long as there are no costs of bankruptcy (paid to third parties like trustees and law firms), it should not make any difference whether debt is risk free or risky. The value of the firm should be equal to the value of the discounted cash flows from investment. A partition that divides these cash flows into risky debt and risky equity has no impact on value. Stiglitz [1969] first proved this result, using a state-preference framework, and Rubinstein [1973] provided a proof, using a mean-variance approach.

Risky debt, just like any other security, must be priced in equilibrium so that it falls on the security market line. Therefore if we designate the return on risky debt as $\tilde{R}_{bj}$, its expected return is

$$E(\tilde{R}_{bj}) = R_f + [E(\tilde{R}_m) - R_f]\beta_{bj}, \tag{13.29}$$

where $\beta_{bj} = \text{COV}(\tilde{R}_{bj}, \tilde{R}_m)/\sigma_m^2$. The return on the equity of a levered firm, k_s, can be written (for a perpetuity) as net income divided by the market value of equity:

$$k_s = \frac{(\widetilde{\text{NOI}} - \tilde{R}_{bj}B)(1 - \tau_c)}{S^L}. \tag{13.30}$$

Recall that $\widetilde{\text{NOI}}$ is net operating income, $\tilde{R}_{bj}B$ is the interest on debt, τ_c is the firm's tax rate, and S^L is the market value of the equity in a levered firm. Using the CAPM, we find that the expected return on equity will be[14]

$$E(k_s) = R_f + \lambda^* \text{COV}(k_s, R_m). \tag{13.31}$$

The covariance between the expected rate of return on equity and the market index is

$$\text{COV}(k_s, R_m) = E\left\{\left[\frac{(\text{NOI} - R_{bj}B)(1 - \tau_c)}{S^L} - E\left(\frac{(\text{NOI} - R_{bj}B)(1 - \tau_c)}{S^L}\right)\right]\right.$$
$$\left. \times [R_m - E(R_m)]\right\}$$
$$= \frac{1 - \tau_c}{S^L} \text{COV}(\text{NOI}, R_m) - \frac{(1 - \tau_c)B}{S^L} \text{COV}(R_{bj}, R_m). \tag{13.32}$$

Substituting this result into (13.31) and the combined result into (13.30), we have the following relationship for a levered firm:

$$R_f S^L + \lambda^*(1 - \tau_c)\text{COV}(\text{NOI}, R_m) - \lambda^*(1 - \tau_c)B[\text{COV}(R_{bj}, R_m)]$$
$$= E(\text{NOI})(1 - \tau_c) - E(R_{bj})B(1 - \tau_c). \tag{13.33}$$

By following a similar line of logic for the unlevered firm (where $B = 0$, and $S^L = V^U$) we have

$$R_f V^U + \lambda^*(1 - \tau_c)\text{COV}(\text{NOI}, R_m) = E(\text{NOI})(1 - \tau_c). \tag{13.34}$$

---

[14] In this instance $\lambda^* \equiv [E(R_m) - R_f]/\sigma_m^2$.

Substituting (13.34) for $E(\text{NOI})(1 - \tau_c)$ in the right-hand side of (13.33) and using the fact that $V^L = S^L + B$, we have

$$R_f S^L + \lambda^*(1 - \tau_c)\text{COV}(\text{NOI}, R_m) - \lambda^*(1 - \tau_c)B[\text{COV}(R_{bj}, R_m)]$$

$$= R_f V^U + \lambda^*(1 - \tau_c)\text{COV}(\text{NOI}, R_m) - E(R_{bj})B(1 - \tau_c),$$

$$R_f(V^L - B) - \lambda^*(1 - \tau_c)B[\text{COV}(R_{bj}, R_m)]$$

$$= R_f V^U - [R_f + \lambda^*\text{COV}(R_{bj}, R_m)]B(1 - \tau_c),$$

$$V^L = V^U + \tau_c B.$$

This is exactly the same Modigliani-Miller result that we obtained when the firm was assumed to issue only risk-free debt. Therefore the introduction of risky debt cannot, by itself, be used to explain the existence of an optimal capital structure. In Chapter 14 we shall see that direct bankruptcy costs such as losses to third parties (lawyers or the courts) or indirect bankruptcy costs (disruption of services to customers or disruption of the supply of skilled labor) are necessary in conjunction with risky debt and taxes in order to explain an optimal capital structure.

2. The Cost of Risky Debt—Using the Option Pricing Model

Even though risky debt without bankruptcy costs does not alter the basic Modigliani-Miller results, we are still interested in knowing how the cost of risky debt is affected by changes in capital structure. The simple algebraic approach that follows was proved by Hsia [1981], and it combines the option pricing model (OPM), the capital asset pricing model (CAPM), and the Modigliani-Miller theorems. They are all consistent with one another.

To present the issue in its simplest form, assume (1) that the firm issues zero coupon bonds[15] that prohibit any capital distributions (such as dividend payments) until after the bonds mature T time periods hence, (2) that there are no transactions costs or taxes, so that the value of the firm is unaffected by its capital structure (in other words, Modigliani-Miller Proposition I is assumed to be valid), (3) that there is a known nonstochastic risk-free rate of interest, and (4) that there are homogeneous expectations about the stochastic process that describes the value of the firm's assets. Given these assumptions, we can imagine a simple firm that issues only one class of bonds secured by the assets of the firm.

To illustrate the claims of debt and shareholders, let us use put-call parity from Chapter 8. The payoffs from the underlying risky asset (the value of the firm, V) plus a put written on it are identical to the payoffs from a default-free zero coupon bond plus a call (the value of shareholders' equity in a levered firm, S) on the risky asset.

---

[15] All accumulated interest on zero coupon bonds is paid at maturity; hence $B(T)$, the current market value of debt with maturity T, must be less than its face value, D, assuming a positive risk-free rate of discount.

Table 13.3   Stakeholders' Payoffs at Maturity

	Payoffs at Maturity	
Stakeholder Positions	*If $V \leq D$*	*If $V > D$*
Shareholders' position:		
Call option, S	0	$V - D$
Bondholders' position:		
Default-free bond, B	D	D
Minus a put option, P	$-(D - V)$	0
Value of the firm at maturity	V	V

Algebraically this is

$$V + P = B + S,$$

or rearranging,

$$V = (B - P) + S. \tag{13.35}$$

Equation (13.35) illustrates that the value of the firm can be partitioned into two claims. The low-risk claim is risky debt that is equivalent to default-free debt minus a put option, i.e., $(B - P)$. Thus, risky corporate debt is the same thing as default-free debt minus a put option. The exercise price for the put is the face value of debt, D, and the maturity of the put, T, is the same as the maturity of the risky debt. The higher-risk claim is shareholders' equity, which is equivalent to a call on the value of the firm with an exercise price D and a maturity T. The payoff to shareholders at maturity will be

$$S = \text{MAX}[0, V - D]. \tag{13.36}$$

Table 13.3 shows both stakeholders' payoffs at maturity. If the value of the firm is less than the face value of debt, shareholders file for bankruptcy and allow the bondholders to keep $V < D$. Alternately, if the value of the firm is greater than the face value of debt, shareholders will exercise their call option by paying its exercise price, D, the face value of debt to bondholders, and retain the excess value, $V - D$.

The realization that the equity and debt in a firm can be conceptualized as options allows us to use the insights of Chapter 8 on option pricing theory. For example, if the equity, S, in a levered firm is analogous to a call option then its value will increase with (1) an increase in the value of the firm's assets, V, (2) an increase in the variance of the value of the firm's assets, (3) an increase in the time to maturity of a given amount of debt with face value, D, and (4) an increase in the risk-free rate. The value of levered equity will decrease with a greater amount of debt, D, which is analogous to the exercise price on a call option.

Next, we wish to show the relationship between the CAPM measure of risk, i.e., β, and the option pricing model. First, however, it is useful to show how the CAPM and the OPM are related. Merton [1973] has derived a continuous-time version of the CAPM, which is given below:

$$E(r_i) = r_f + [E(r_m) - r_f]\beta_i, \tag{13.37}$$

where

$E(r_i)$ = the instantaneous expected rate of return on asset i,

β_i = the instantaneous systematic risk of the ith asset, $\beta_i = \text{COV}(r_i, r_m)/\text{VAR}(r_m)$,

$E(r_m)$ = the expected instantaneous rate of return on the market portfolio,

r_f = the nonstochastic instantaneous rate of return on the risk-free asset.

There appears to be no difference between the continuous-time version of the CAPM and the traditional one-period model derived in Chapter 7. However, it is important to prove that the CAPM also exists in continuous time because the Black-Scholes OPM requires continuous trading, and the assumptions underlying the two models must be consistent.

In order to relate the OPM to the CAPM it is easiest (believe it or not) to begin with the differential equation (A8.4) and to recognize that the call option is now the value of the common stock, S, which is written on the value of the levered firm, V. Therefore (A8.4) may be rewritten as

$$dS = \frac{\partial S}{\partial V} dV + \frac{\partial S}{\partial t} dt + \frac{1}{2} \frac{\partial^2 S}{\partial V^2} \sigma^2 V^2 dt. \tag{13.38}$$

This equation says that the change in the stock price is related to the change in the value of the firm, dV, movement of the stock price across time, dt, and the instantaneous variance of the firm's value, σ^2. Dividing by S, we have, in the limit as dt approaches zero,

$$\lim_{dt \to 0} \frac{dS}{S} = \frac{\partial S}{\partial V} \frac{dV}{S} = \frac{\partial S}{\partial V} \frac{dV}{V} \frac{V}{S}. \tag{13.39}$$

We recognize dS/S as the rate of return on the common stock, r_S, and dV/V as the rate of return on the firm's assets, r_V, therefore

$$r_S = \frac{\partial S}{\partial V} \frac{V}{S} r_V. \tag{13.40}$$

If the instantaneous systematic risk of common stock, β_S, and that of the firm's assets, β_V, are defined as

$$\beta_S \equiv \frac{\text{COV}(r_S, r_m)}{\text{VAR}(r_m)}, \qquad \beta_V \equiv \frac{\text{COV}(r_V, r_m)}{\text{VAR}(r_m)}, \tag{13.41}$$

then we can use (13.40) and (13.41) to rewrite the instantaneous covariance as

$$\beta_S = \frac{\partial S}{\partial V} \frac{V}{S} \frac{\text{COV}(r_V, r_m)}{\text{VAR}(r_m)} = \frac{\partial S}{\partial V} \frac{V}{S} \beta_V. \tag{13.42}$$

Now write the Black-Scholes OPM where the call option is the equity of the firm:

$$S = VN(d_1) - e^{-r_f T} DN(d_2), \tag{13.43}$$

where

S = the market value of equity,

V = the market value of the firm's assets,

r_f = the risk-free rate,

T = the time to maturity,

D = the face value of debt (book value),

$N(\cdot)$ = the cumulative normal probability of the unit normal variate, d_1,

$$d_1 = \frac{\ln(V/D) + r_f T}{\sigma\sqrt{T}} + \frac{1}{2}\sigma\sqrt{T}, \qquad d_2 = d_1 - \sigma\sqrt{T}.$$

Finally, the partial derivative of the equity value, S, with respect to the value of the underlying asset is

$$\frac{\partial S}{\partial V} = N(d_1), \quad \text{where} \quad 0 \le N(d_1) \le 1. \tag{13.44}$$

Substituting this into (13.42) we obtain

$$\beta_S = N(d_1)\frac{V}{S}\beta_V. \tag{13.45}$$

This tells us the relationship between the systematic risk of the equity, β_S, and the systematic risk of the firm's assets, β_V. The value of S is given by the OPM, Eq. (13.43); therefore we have

$$\beta_S = \frac{VN(d_1)}{VN(d_1) - De^{-r_f T}N(d_2)}\beta_V$$

$$= \frac{1}{1 - (D/V)e^{-r_f T}[N(d_2)/N(d_1)]}\beta_V. \tag{13.46}$$

We know that $D/V \le 1$, that $e^{-r_f T} < 1$, that $N(d_2) \le N(d_1)$, and hence that $\beta_S \ge \beta_V > 0$. This shows that the systematic risk of the equity of a levered firm is greater than the systematic risk of an unlevered firm, a result that is consistent with the results found elsewhere in the theory of finance. Note also that the beta of equity of the levered firm increases monotonically with leverage.

The OPM provides insight into the effect of its parameters on the systematic risk of equity. We may assume that the risk characteristics of the firm's assets, β_V, are constant over time. Therefore it can be shown that the partial derivatives of (13.46) have the following signs:

$$\frac{\partial \beta_S}{\partial V} < 0, \qquad \frac{\partial \beta_S}{\partial D} > 0, \qquad \frac{\partial \beta_S}{\partial r_f} < 0, \qquad \frac{\partial \beta_S}{\partial \sigma^2} < 0, \qquad \frac{\partial \beta_S}{\partial T} < 0.$$

Most of these have readily intuitive explanations. The systematic risk of equity falls as the market value of the firm increases, and it rises as the amount of debt issued increases. When the risk-free rate of return increases, the value of the equity option increases and its systematic risk decreases. The fourth partial derivative says that as the variance of the value of the firm's assets increases, the systematic risk of equity decreases. This result follows from the contingent claim nature of equity. The equity holders will prefer more variance to less because they profit from the probability that the value of the firm will exceed the face value of the debt. Therefore their risk actually decreases as the variance of the value of the firm's assets increases.[16] Finally, the fifth partial says that the systematic risk of equity declines as the maturity date of the debt becomes longer and longer. From the shareholders' point of view the best situation would be to never have to repay the face value of the debt. It is also possible to use Eq. (13.45) to view the cost of equity capital in an OPM framework and to compare it with the Modigliani-Miller results.

Substituting β_S from (13.45) into the CAPM, we obtain from Eq. (13.37) an expression for k_s, the cost of equity capital:

$$k_s = R_f + (R_m - R_f)N(d_1)\frac{V}{S}\beta_V. \tag{13.47}$$

Note that from Eq. (13.45), $\beta_S = N(d_1)(V/S)\beta_V$. Substituting this into (13.47) yields the familiar CAPM relationship $k_s = R_f + (R_m - R_f)\beta_S$. Furthermore, the CAPM can be rearranged to show that

$$\beta_V = \frac{R_V - R_f}{R_m - R_f},$$

which we substitute into (13.47) to obtain

$$k_s = R_f + N(d_1)(R_V - R_f)\frac{V}{S}. \tag{13.48}$$

Equation (13.48) shows that the cost of equity capital is an increasing function of financial leverage.

If we assume that debt is risky and assume that bankruptcy costs (i.e., losses to third parties other than creditors or shareholders) are zero, then the OPM, the CAPM, and the Modigliani-Miller propositions can be shown to be consistent. The simple algebraic approach given below was proved by Hsia [1981].

First, note that the systematic risk, β_B, of risky debt capital in a world without taxes can be written in an explanation similar to Eq. (13.42) as[17]

$$\beta_B = \beta_V \frac{\partial B}{\partial V}\frac{V}{B}. \tag{13.49}$$

We know that in a world without taxes the value of the firm is invariant to changes in its capital structure. Also, from Eq. (13.44), we know that if the common stock of a firm is thought of as a call option on the value of the firm, then

$$\frac{\partial S}{\partial V} = N(d_1).$$

---

[16] Note that since the value of the firm, V, and the debt equity ratio D/V are held constant, any change in total variance, σ^2, must be nonsystematic risk.

[17] See Galai and Masulis [1976, footnote 15].

These two facts imply that

$$\frac{\partial B}{\partial V} = N(-d_1) = 1 - N(d_1). \tag{13.50}$$

In other words, any change in the value of equity is offset by an equal and opposite change in the value of risky debt.

Next, the required rate of return on risky debt, k_b, can be expressed by using the CAPM, Eq. (13.37):

$$k_b = R_f + (R_m - R_f)\beta_B. \tag{13.51}$$

Substituting Eqs. (13.49) and (13.50) into (13.51), we have

$$k_b = R_f + (R_m - R_f)\beta_V N(-d_1)\frac{V}{B}.$$

From the CAPM, we know that

$$R_V - R_f = (R_m - R_f)\beta_V.$$

Therefore

$$k_b = R_f + (R_V - R_f)N(-d_1)\frac{V}{B}.$$

And since $R_V \equiv \rho$,

$$k_b = R_f + (\rho - R_f)N(-d_1)\frac{V}{B}. \tag{13.52}$$

Note that Eq. (13.52) expresses the cost of risky debt in terms of the OPM. The required rate of return on risky debt is equal to the risk-free rate, R_f, plus a risk premium, θ, where

$$\theta = (\rho - R_f)N(-d_1)\frac{V}{B}.$$

A numerical example can be used to illustrate how the cost of debt, in the absence of bankruptcy costs, increases with the firm's utilization of debt. Suppose the current value of a firm, V, is \$3 million; the face value of debt is \$1.5 million; and the debt will mature in $T = 8$ years. The variance of returns on the firm's assets, σ^2, is .09; its required return on assets is $\rho = .12$; and the riskless rate of interest, R_f, is 5%. From the Black-Scholes option pricing model, we know that

$$d_1 = \frac{\ln(V/D) + R_f T}{\sigma\sqrt{T}} + \frac{1}{2}\sigma\sqrt{T}$$

$$= \frac{\ln(3/1.5) + .05(8)}{.3\sqrt{8}} + .5(.3)\sqrt{8}$$

$$= \frac{.6931 + .4}{.8485} + .4243 = 1.7125.$$

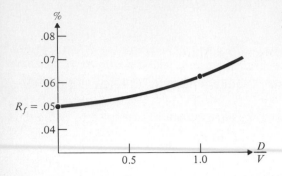

Figure 13.8
The cost of risky debt.

From the cumulative normal probability table (Table 8.7), the value of $N(-1.7125)$ is approximately .0434. Substituting into Eq. 13.52, we see that the cost of debt is increased from the risk-free rate, 5%, to

$$k_b = .05 + (.12 - .05)(.0434)\frac{3}{1.5}$$

$$= .05 + .0061 = .0561.$$

Figure 13.8 shows the relationship of the cost of debt and the ratio of the face value of debt to the current market value of the firm. For low levels of debt, bankruptcy risk is trivial and therefore the cost of debt is close to the riskless rate. It rises as D/V increases until k_b equals 6.3% when the face value of debt, due eight years from now, equals the current market value of the firm.

To arrive at a weighted average cost of capital, we multiply Eq. (13.52), the cost of debt, by the percentage of debt in the capital structure, B/V, then add this result to the cost of equity, Eq. (13.48) multiplied by S/V, the percentage of equity in the capital structure. The result is

$$k_b\frac{B}{V} + k_s\frac{S}{V} = \left[R_f + (\rho - R_f)N(-d_1)\frac{V}{B}\right]\frac{B}{V} + \left[R_f + N(d_1)(\rho - R_f)\frac{V}{S}\right]\frac{S}{V}$$

$$= R_f\left(\frac{B+S}{V}\right) + (\rho - R_f)[N(-d_1) + N(d_1)]$$

$$= R_f + (\rho - R_f)[1 - N(d_1) + N(d_1)]$$

$$= \rho. \tag{13.53}$$

Equation (13.53) is exactly the same as the Modigliani-Miller proposition that in a world without taxes the weighted average cost of capital is invariant to changes in the capital structure of the firm. Also, simply by rearranging terms, we have

$$k_s = \rho + (\rho - k_b)\frac{B}{S}. \tag{13.54}$$

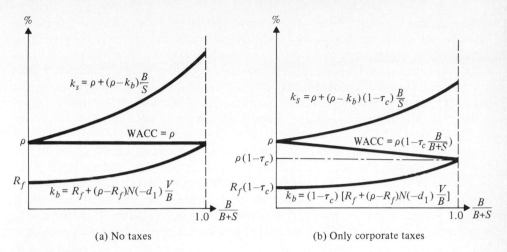

Figure 13.9
The cost of capital given risky debt.

This is exactly the same as Eq. (13.18), the Modigliani-Miller definition of the cost of equity capital in a world without taxes. Therefore if we assume that debt is risky, the OPM, the CAPM, and the Modigliani-Miller definition are all consistent with one another.

This result is shown graphically in Fig. 13.9(a). This figure is very similar to Fig. 13.2, which showed the cost of capital as a function of the debt to equity ratio, B/S, assuming riskless debt. The only differences between the two figures are that Fig. 13.9 has the debt to value ratio, $B/(B + S)$, on the horizontal axis and it assumes risky debt. Note that [in Fig. 13.9(a)] the cost of debt increases as more debt is used in the firm's capital structure. Also, if the firm were to become 100% debt (not a realistic alternative) then the cost of debt would equal the cost of capital for an all-equity firm, ρ. Figure 13.9(b) depicts the weighted average cost of capital in a world with corporate taxes only. The usual Modigliani-Miller result is shown, namely, that the weighted average cost of capital declines monotonically as more debt is employed in the capital structure of the firm. The fact that debt is risky does not change any of our previous results.

E. THE MATURITY STRUCTURE OF DEBT

Optimal capital structure refers not only to the ratio of debt to equity but also to the maturity structure of debt. What portion of total debt should be short term and what portion long term? Should the firm use variable rate or fixed rate debt? Should long-term bonds pay annual coupons with a balloon payment, or should they be fully amortized (equal periodic payments)?

There are three approaches to answering the maturity structure problem. The earliest, by Morris [1976], suggests that short-term debt or variable rate debt can reduce the risk to shareholders and thereby increase equity value if the covariance between net operating income and expected future interest rates is positive. This cross-hedging argument is based on the assumption that unexpected changes in interest rates are a priced (undiversifiable) factor in the arbitrage pricing model. It does not rely directly either on bankruptcy costs or on interest tax shields. However, the argument for cross-hedging is only strengthened if it increases debt capacity by reducing the risk of bankruptcy and thereby allowing a greater gain from leverage. Smith and Stulz [1985] support this point of view.

A second approach to optimal debt maturity is based on agency costs. Myers [1977] and Barnea, Haugen, and Senbet [1980] argue that if the shareholders' claim on the assets of a levered firm is similar to a call option, then shareholders have an incentive to undertake riskier (higher variance) projects because their call option value is greater when the assets of the firm have higher variance. If the firm with long-term risky debt outstanding undertakes positive net present value projects, shareholders will not be able to capture the full benefits because part of the value goes to debt holders in the form of a reduction in the probability of default. Short-term debt may alleviate this problem because the debt may come due before the firm decides to invest. Hence the theory suggests that firms with many investment opportunities may prefer to use short-term debt (or callable debt).

Brick and Ravid [1985] provide a tax-based explanation. Suppose the term structure of interest rates is not flat and there is a gain to leverage in the Miller [1977] sense. Then a long-term maturity is optimal because coupons on long-term bonds are currently higher than coupons on short-term bonds and the tax benefit of debt (the gain to leverage) is accelerated. If the gain to leverage is negative, then the result is reversed.

Although none of these theories has been adequately tested, each of them has some merit for potentially explaining cross-sectional regularities in the maturity structure of debt. This remains a fruitful area for further research.

F. THE EFFECT OF OTHER FINANCIAL INSTRUMENTS ON THE COST OF CAPITAL

Other than straight debt and equity, firms issue a variety of other securities and contingent claims. The number of different possibilities is limited only by your imagination. However, the actual number of alternative financial instruments is fairly small and their use is limited. A possible explanation for why corporations tend to use only straight debt and equity has been offered by Fama and Jensen [1982]. They argue that it makes sense to separate the financial claims on the firm into only two parts: a relatively low-risk component (i.e., debt capital) and a relatively high-risk residual claim (i.e., equity capital). Specialized risk bearing by residual claimants is an optimal form of contracting that has survival value because (1) it reduces contracting costs (i.e., the costs that would be incurred to monitor contract fulfillment) and (2) it lowers the cost of risk-bearing services.

For example, shareholders and bondholders do not have to monitor each other. It is necessary only for bondholders to monitor shareholders. This form of one-way monitoring reduces the total cost of contracting over what it might otherwise be. Thus it makes sense that most firms keep their capital structure fairly simple by using only debt and equity.

The theory of finance has no good explanation for why some firms use alternative financial instruments such as convertible debt, preferred stock, and warrants.

1. Warrants

A warrant is a security issued by the firm in return for cash. It promises to sell m shares (usually one share) of stock to an investor for a fixed exercise price at any time up to the maturity date. Therefore a warrant is very much like an American call option written by the firm. It is not exactly the same as a call because, when exercised, it increases the number of shares outstanding and thus dilutes the equity of the stockholders.

The problem of pricing warrants has been studied by Emanuel [1983], Schwartz [1977], Galai and Schneller [1978], and Constantinides [1984]. The simplest approach to the problem (Galai and Schneller [1978]) assumes a one-period model. The firm is assumed to be 100% equity financed, and its investment policy is not affected by its financing decisions. For example, the proceeds from issuing warrants are immediately distributed as dividends to the old shareholders. Also the firm pays no end-of-period dividends, and the warrants are assumed to be exercised as a block.[18] These somewhat restrictive assumptions facilitate the estimation of the warrant value and its equilibrium rate of return.

Galai and Schneller show, for the above-mentioned assumptions, that the returns on a warrant are perfectly correlated with those of a call option on the same firm *without* warrants. To obtain this result let V be the value of the firm's assets (without warrants) at the end of the time period, i.e., on the date when the warrants mature. Let n be the current number of shares outstanding and q be the ratio of warrants to shares outstanding.[19] Finally, let X be the exercise price of the warrant. If the firm had no warrants outstanding, the price per share at the end of the time period would be

$$S = \frac{V}{n}.$$

With warrants, the price per share, assuming that the warrants are exercised, will be

$$S = \frac{V + nqX}{n(1 + q)} = \frac{S + qX}{(1 + q)}.$$

---

[18] Block exercise is, perhaps, the most restrictive assumption.

[19] The amount of potential dilution can be significant. For example, in July 1977 there were 118 warrants outstanding. Of them 41% had a dilution factor of less than 10%, 25% had a dilution factor between 10 and 19%, 13% between 20 and 29%, and 21% a factor of over 50%.

Table 13.4   End-of-Period Payoffs for a Warrant and for a Call Option (Written on a Firm with No Warrants)

	End-of-Period Payoffs	
	If $S \leq X$	If $S > X$
Warrant on firm with warrants, W	0	$\dfrac{S + qX}{1 + q} - X = \dfrac{1}{1 + q}(S - X)$
Call on firm without warrants, C	0	$S - X$

Of course, nqX is the cash received and $n(1 + q)$ is the total number of shares outstanding if the warrants are exercised. The warrants will be exercised if their value when converted is greater than the exercise price, i.e., if

$$S = \frac{S + qX}{1 + q} > X.$$

This condition is exactly equivalent to $S > X$. In other words the warrant will be exercised whenever the firm's end-of-period share price *without* warrants exceeds the warrant exercise price. Therefore the warrant will be exercised in exactly the same states of nature as a call option with the same exercise price. Also, as shown in Table 13.4, the payoffs to the warrant are a constant fraction, $1/(1 + q)$, of the payoffs to the call written on the assets of the firm (without warrants).

Therefore the returns on the warrant are perfectly correlated with the dollar returns on a call option written on the firm without warrants. To prevent arbitrage the warrant price, W, will be a fraction of the call price, C, as shown below:

$$W = \frac{1}{1 + q} C. \tag{13.55}$$

Because the warrant and the call are perfectly correlated, they will have exactly the same systematic risk and therefore the same required rate of return.[20] This expected

---

[20] From Eq. (13.45) we know that the beta of an option is related to the beta of the underlying asset as follows:

$$\beta_c = N(d_1) \frac{S}{C} \beta_S.$$

From Eq. (13.55) we know that the warrant is perfectly correlated with a call option written on the shares of the company, *ex warrants*; therefore

$$\beta_W = \beta_c.$$

Consequently, it is not difficult to estimate the cost of capital for a warrant because we can estimate $\beta_c = \beta_W$ and then employ the CAPM.

return is the before-tax cost of capital for issuing warrants and can easily be estimated for a company that is contemplating a new issue of warrants.

One problem with the above approach is that warrants are not constrained to be exercised simultaneously in one large block. Emanuel [1983] demonstrated that if all the warrants were held by a single profit-maximizing monopolist, the warrants would be exercised sequentially. Constantinides [1984] has solved the warrant valuation problem for competitive warrant holders and shown that the warrant price, given a competitive equilibrium, is less than or equal to the value it would have given block exercise. Frequently the balance sheet of a firm has several contingent claim securities, e.g., warrants and convertible bonds, with different maturity dates. This means that the expiration and subsequent exercise (or conversion) of one security can result in equity dilution and therefore early exercise of the longer maturity contingent claim securities. Firms can also force early exercise or conversion by paying a large cash or stock dividend.

2. Convertible Bonds

As the name implies, convertible debt is a hybrid bond that allows its bearer to exchange it for a given number of shares of stock anytime up to and including the maturity date of the bond. Preferred stock is also frequently issued with a convertible provision and may be thought of as a convertible security (a bond) with an infinite maturity date.

A convertible bond is equivalent to a portfolio of two securities: straight debt with the same coupon rate and maturity as the convertible bond, and a warrant written on the value of the firm. The coupon rate on convertible bonds is usually lower than comparable straight debt because the right to convert is worth something. For example, in February 1982, the XYZ Company wanted to raise $50 million by using either straight debt or convertible bonds. An investment banking firm informed the company's treasurer that straight debt with a 25-year maturity would require a 17% coupon. Alternately, convertible debt with the same maturity would require only a 10% coupon. Both debt instruments would sell at par (i.e., $1000), and the convertible debt could be converted into 35.71 shares (i.e., an exercise price of $28 per share). The stock of the XYZ Company was selling for $25 per share at the time. Later on we will use these facts to compute the cost of capital for the convertible issue. But first, what do financial officers think of convertible debt?

Brigham [1966] received responses from the chief financial officers of 22 firms that had issued convertible debt. Of them, 68% said they used convertible debt because they believed their stock price would rise over time and that convertibles would provide a way of selling common stock at a price above the existing market. Another 27% said that their company wanted straight debt but found conditions to be such that a straight bond issue could not be sold at a reasonable rate of interest. The problem is that neither reason makes much sense. Convertible bonds are not "cheap debt." Because convertible bonds are riskier, their true cost of capital is greater (on a before-tax basis) than the cost of straight debt. Also, convertible bonds are not deferred sale of common stock at an attractive price.[21] The uncertain sale of shares for $28 each at some future date can hardly be compared directly with a current share price of $25.

Brennan and Schwartz [1977a] and Ingersoll [1977a] have analyzed the valuation of convertible bonds, assuming that the entire outstanding issue, if converted, will be converted as a block. Constantinides [1984] has extended their work to study the value of convertible debt if conversion does not occur all at once. The reader is referred to these articles for the derivations that show that the market value of convertible debt, CV, is equal to the market value of straight debt, B, and a warrant, W:

$$CV = B + W.$$

Suppose you want to compute the cost of capital for the convertible debt being considered by the XYZ Company as mentioned above. You already know that the maturity date is 25 years, similar straight debt yields 17% to maturity, the convertible bond coupon rate is 10% (with semiannual coupons), the conversion price (exercise price) is $28 per share, the bond will sell at par value, i.e., $1000, and the current stock price is $25. In addition you need to know that: (1) if converted the issue would increase the firm's outstanding shares by 5%, i.e., the dilution factor, q, is 5%; (2) the standard deviation of the firm's equity rate of return is $\sigma = .3$; (3) the risk-free rate is 14.5% for 25-year Treasury bonds; (4) the expected rate of return on the market portfolio is 20.6%; (5) the firm's equity beta is 1.5; and (6) the firm pays no dividends. Given these facts, it is possible to use the capital asset pricing model and the option pricing model to estimate the before-tax cost of capital, k_{CV}, on the firm's contemplated convertible bond issue as a weighted average of the cost of straight debt, k_b, and the cost of the warrant, k_w.[22]

$$k_{CV} = k_b \frac{B}{B + W} + k_w \frac{W}{B + W}.$$

The value of the straight debt, assuming semiannual coupons of $50, a principal payment of $1000 twenty-five years hence, and a 17% discount rate, is $B = \$619.91$. Therefore the remainder of the sale price—namely, $1000 - 619.91 = \$380.09$—is the value of the warrant to purchase 35.71 shares at $28 each. The cost of straight debt was given to be $k_b = 17\%$ before taxes. All that remains is to find the cost of the warrant. From section F.1 we know that the warrant implied in the convertible bond contract is perfectly correlated with a call option written on the firm (without warrants outstanding) and therefore has the same cost of capital. The cost of capital, k_c, for the call option can be estimated from the CAPM:

$$k_c = R_f + [E(R_m) - R_f]\beta_c,$$

---

[21] From the theory of option pricing we know that $S + P = B + C$; i.e., a bond plus a call option is the same thing as owning the stock and a put option. Thus one could think of a convertible bond as roughly equivalent to the stock plus a put.

[22] Throughout the analysis we assume that there is no tax gain to leverage. Therefore the conversion of the bond will decrease the firm's debt-to-equity ratio but not change the value of the firm.

where

k_c = the cost of capital for a call option with 25 years to maturity,[23]

R_f = the risk-free rate for a 25-year Treasury bond = 14.5%,

$E(R_m)$ = the expected rate of return on the market portfolio = 20.6%,

$\beta_c = N(d_1)(S/C)\beta_s$ = the systematic risk of the call option,

β_s = the systematic risk of the stock (without warrants) = 1.5,

$N(d_1)$ = the cumulative normal probability for option pricing in Chapter 8,

C = the value of a call option written on the stock, *ex warrants*.

$$d_1 = \frac{\ln(S/X) + R_f T}{\sigma \sqrt{T}} + \frac{1}{2}\sigma\sqrt{T}.$$

Substituting in the appropriate numbers, we find that $d_1 = 3.09114$ and $N(d_1) = .999$. And using the Black-Scholes version of the option pricing model, we find that $C = \$24.74$. Therefore

$$\beta_c = \frac{S}{C}N(d_1)\beta_s$$

$$= \frac{25.00}{24.74}(.999)(1.5) = 1.514,$$

and substituting into the CAPM we have

$$k_c = .145 + (.206 - .145)1.514$$

$$= 23.74\%.$$

The cost of capital for the warrant is slightly above the cost of equity for the firm. Actually, the warrant is not much riskier than the equity because its market value is almost equal to the market value of the firm's equity, given a 25-year life and only a \$3 difference between the exercise price and the stock price.

Taken together, these facts imply that the before-tax cost of capital for the convertible issue will be

$$k_{CV} = .17\,\frac{619.91}{1000.00} + .2374\,\frac{380.09}{1000.00}$$

$$= 19.56\%.$$

This answer is almost double the 10% coupon rate that the convertible promises to pay, and it shows that the higher risk of convertible debt requires a higher expected rate of return.

---

[23] If the firm pays dividends which are large enough, then the convertible debentures may be exercised if the implied warrants are in-the-money. Exercise would occur just prior to the ex dividend date(s). We are assuming, for the sake of simplicity, that the firm pays no dividends.

The final point of discussion is why convertible debt is used if financial officers understand its true cost. It certainly is not a cheap form of either debt or equity. Another irrational explanation is that until the accounting rules were changed to require reporting earnings per share on a fully diluted basis, it was possible for an aggressive firm to acquire another company via convertible debt financing. The lower interest charges of convertible debt meant that earnings of the merged company were often higher than the sum of premerger earnings of the separate entities. Also, the actual number of shares outstanding was lower than the number that would be reported if the conversion were to occur. Given all the evidence in Chapter 11 on the efficiency of markets, it is hard to believe that the market was fooled by the accounting conventions. A possible reason for issuing convertibles is that they are better tailored to the cash flow patterns of rapidly growing firms. The lower coupon rate during the early years keeps the probability of bankruptcy lower than straight debt; then, if the firm is successful, more cash for growth will be available after conversion takes place. Brennan and Schwartz [1986] suggest an alternative rationale—namely, that because of the relative insensitivity of convertible bonds to the risk of the issuing company, it is easier for the bond issuer and purchaser to agree on the value of the bond. This makes it easier for them to come to terms and requires no bonding or underwriting service by investment bankers. Green [1984] shows that agency costs between equity and bondholders are reduced by issuing convertible debt or straight debt with warrants. Bondholders are less concerned about the possibility that shareholders may undertake risky projects (thereby increasing the risk of bankruptcy) because their conversion privilege allows them to participate in the value created if riskier projects are undertaken. Finally, convertible debt may be preferred to straight debt with warrants attached because convertible debt often has a call provision built in that allows a firm to force conversion. The call feature is discussed in the next section.

3. Call Provisions

Many securities have call provisions that allow the firm to force redemption. Frequently, ordinary bonds may be redeemed at a *call premium* roughly equal to 1 year's interest. For example, the call premium on a 20-year $1000 face value bond with a 12% coupon might be $120 if the bond is called in the first year, $114 if called in the second year, and so on.

The call provision is equivalent to a call option written by the investors who buy the bonds from the firm. The bonds may be repurchased by the firm (at the exercise price, i.e., the call price) anytime during the life of the bond. If interest rates fall, the market price of the outstanding bonds may exceed the call price, thereby making it advantageous for the firm to exercise its option to call in the debt. Since the option is valuable to the firm, it must pay the bondholders by offering a higher interest rate on callable bonds than on similar ordinary bonds that do not have the call feature. New issues of callable bonds must often bear yields from one quarter to one half of a percent higher than the yields of noncallable bonds.

Brennan and Schwartz [1977a] show how to value callable bonds. If the objective of the firm is to maximize shareholders' wealth, then a call policy will be established to minimize the market value of callable debt. The value of the bonds will be minimized if they are called at the point where their uncalled value is equal to the call price. To call when the uncalled value is below the call price is to provide a needless gain to bondholders. To allow the uncalled bond value to rise above the call price is inconsistent with minimizing the bond value. Therefore the firm should call the bond when the market price first rises to reach the call price. Furthermore, we would never expect the market value of a callable bond to exceed the call price plus a small premium for the flotation costs the firm must bear in calling the issue.

Almost all corporate bonds are callable and none are puttable. Why? A plausible answer has been put forth by Boyce and Kalotay [1979]. Whenever the tax rate of the borrower exceeds the tax rate of the lender, there is a tax incentive for issuing callable debt. Since corporations have had marginal tax rates of around 50% while individuals have lower rates, corporations have had an incentive to issue callable bonds.[24] From the firm's point of view the coupons paid and the call premium are both deductible as interest expenses. The investor pays ordinary income taxes on interest received and capital gains taxes on the call premium. If the stream of payments on debt is even across time, then low and high tax bracket lenders and borrowers will value it equally. However, if it is decreasing across time, as it is expected to be with a callable bond, then low tax bracket lenders will assign a higher value because they discount at a higher after-tax rate. Near-term cash inflows are *relatively* more valuable to them. A high tax bracket borrower (i.e., the firm) will use a lower after-tax discount rate and will also prefer a decreasing cash flow pattern because the present value of the interest tax shield will be relatively higher. Even though the firm pays a higher gross rate, it prefers callable debt to ordinary debt because of the tax advantages for the net rate of return.

Brennan and Schwartz [1977a] and Ingersoll [1977a] both examined the effect of a call feature on convertible debt and preferred. Unlike simpler option securities, convertible bonds and preferred stocks contain dual options. The bondholder has the right to exchange a convertible for the company's common stock while the company retains the right to call the issue at the contracted call price. One interesting implication of the theory on call policies is that a convertible security should be called as soon as its conversion value (i.e., the value of the common stock that would be received in the conversion exchange) rises to equal the prevailing effective call price (i.e., the stated call price plus accrued interest). Ingersoll [1977b] collected data on 179 convertible issues that were called between 1968 and 1975. The calls on all but 9 were delayed beyond the time that the theory predicted. The median company waited until the conversion value of its debentures was 43.9% in excess of the call price.

---

[24] Interestingly, the opposite is true when the government is lending. The government has a zero tax rate and holders of government debt have positive rates. Consequently, the government has incentive to offer puttable debt and it does. Series E and H savings bonds are redeemable at the lender's option.

Mikkelson [1981] discovered that, on average, the common stock returns of companies announcing convertible debt calls fell by a statistically significant -1.065% per day over a two-day announcement period. These results are inconsistent with the idea that optimal calls of convertible debt are beneficial for shareholders.

Harris and Raviv [1985] provide a signaling model that simultaneously explains why calls are delayed far beyond what would seem to be a rational time and why stock returns are negative at the time of the call. Suppose that managers know the future prospects of their firm better than the marketplace—i.e., there is heterogeneous information. Also, assume that managers' compensation depends on the firm's stock price, both now and in future periods. If the managers suspect that the stock price will fall in the future, conversion will be forced now because what they receive now, given conversion, exceeds what they would otherwise receive in the future when the market learns of the bad news and does not convert. Conversely, managers' failure to convert now will be interpreted by the market as good news. There is incentive for managers not to force conversion early because the market views their stock favorably now, and it will also be viewed favorably in the future when the market is able to confirm the managers' good news. A paper of similar spirit by Robbins and Schatzberg [1986] explains the advantage of the call feature in nonconvertible long-term bonds.

4. Preferred Stock

Preferred stock is much like subordinated debt except that if the promised cash payments (i.e., the preferred coupons) are not paid on time, then preferred shareholders cannot force the firm into bankruptcy. All preferred stocks listed on the New York Stock Exchange must have voting rights in order to be listed. A high percentage of preferred stocks have no stated maturity date and also provide for cumulative dividend payments; i.e., all past preferred dividends must be paid before common stock dividends can be paid. Approximately 40% of new preferred stocks are convertible into common stock.

If preferred stock is not callable or convertible, and if its life is indefinite, then its market value is

$$P = \frac{\text{coupon}}{k_p},$$

where k_p is the before-tax cost of preferred. Of course, the before- and after-tax costs are the same for preferred stock because preferred dividends are not deductible as an expense before taxes. The nondeductibility of preferred dividends has led many companies to buy back their preferred stock and use subordinated debt instead. It is a puzzle why preferred stock is issued at all, especially if there is a gain to leverage from using debt capital as a substitute.

5. Committed Lines of Credit

A committed line of credit is still another form of contingent claim. It does not appear on the firm's balance sheet unless some of the committed line is actually used. Under the terms of the contract a commercial bank will agree to guarantee to supply up to a fixed limit of funds, e.g., up to $1 billion, at a variable rate of interest plus a fixed risk premium (e.g., LIBOR, the London interbank rate plus $\frac{3}{8}\%$). In return, the firm agrees to pay a fee, say $\frac{1}{4}\%$, on the unused balance. From the borrowing firm's point of view, a committed line may be thought of as the right to put callable debt to the bank. Embedded in this right is an option on the yield spread, i.e., on the difference between the rate paid by high- and low-grade debt. When the committed line is negotiated, the premium above the variable rate ($\frac{3}{8}\%$ in our example) reflects the current yield spread. If the economy or the fortunes of the firm worsen, the yield spread will probably increase, say to $\frac{5}{8}\%$. However, with a committed line the firm can still borrow and pay only $\frac{3}{8}\%$ yield spread—hence it has an in-the-money option because it is cheaper to borrow on the committed line than in the open market. For a paper analyzing committed lines, see Hawkins [1982].

SUMMARY

The cost of capital is seen to be a rate of return whose definition requires a project to improve the wealth position of the *current* shareholders of the firm. The original Modigliani-Miller work has been extended by using the CAPM so that a risk-adjusted cost of capital may be obtained for each project. When the expected cash flows of the project are discounted at the correct risk-adjusted rate, the result is the NPV of the project.

In a world without taxes the value of the firm is independent of its capital structure. However, there are several important extensions of the basic model. With the introduction of corporate taxes the optimal capital structure becomes 100% debt. Finally, when personal taxes are also introduced, the value of the firm is unaffected by the choice of financial leverage. Financing is irrelevant! The next chapter takes a more careful look at the question of optimal capital structure and summarizes some of the empirical work that has been done.

PROBLEM SET

13.1 The Modigliani-Miller theorem assumes that the firm has only two classes of securities, perpetual debt and equity. Suppose that the firm has issued a third class of securities—preferred stock—and that $X\%$ of preferred dividends may be written off as an expense ($0 \le X \le 1$).

a) What is the appropriate expression for the value of the levered firm?

b) What is the appropriate expression for the weighted average cost of capital?

13.2 The Acrosstown Company has an equity beta, β_L, of .5 and 50% debt in its capital structure. The company has risk-free debt that costs 6% before taxes, and the expected rate of return on the market is 18%. Acrosstown is considering the acquisition of a new project in the peanut-raising agribusiness that is expected to yield 25% on after-tax operating cash flows. The Carter-nut Company, which is the same product line (and risk class) as the project being considered, has an equity beta, β_L, of 2.0 and has 10% debt in its capital structure. If Acrosstown finances the new project with 50% debt, should it be accepted or rejected? Assume that the marginal tax rate, τ_c, for both companies is 50%.

13.3 The XYZ Company has a current market value of $1,000,000, half of which is debt. Its current weighted average cost of capital is 9%, and the corporate tax rate is 40%. The treasurer proposes to undertake a new project, which costs $500,000 and which can be financed completely with debt. The project is expected to have the same operating risk as the company and to earn 8.5% on its levered after-tax cash flows. The treasurer argues that the project is desirable because it earns more than 5%, which is the before-tax marginal cost of the debt used to finance it. What do you think?

13.4 Given a world with corporate taxes, τ_c, a personal tax rate paid on bonds, τ_{pB}, and a personal tax rate on income from equity, τ_{pS}, what would be the effect of a decrease in the corporate tax rate on

a) the aggregate amount of debt in the economy, and

b) the optimal capital structure of firms?

13.5 Congress has proposed to eliminate "double taxation" on dividends by reducing the personal tax on dividend income. At the same time, a compensating increase in taxes on capital gains (traditionally taxed at a much lower percentage than dividend income) has been proposed.

a) What effect would this joint proposal have on the optimal capital structure of a firm, according to the Miller model?

b) What effect would it have on the aggregate amount of corporate debt outstanding?

13.6 Consider firm B as an unlevered firm and firm C as a levered firm with target debt-to-equity ratio $(B/S)^* = 1$. Both firms have exactly the same perpetual net operating income, NOI = 180, before taxes. The before-tax cost of debt, k_b, is the same as the risk-free rate. The corporate tax rate = .5. Given the following market parameters,

$$E(R_m) = .12, \qquad \sigma_m^2 = .0144, \qquad R_f = .06, \qquad \beta_B = 1, \qquad \beta_C = 1.5,$$

a) Find the cost of capital and value for each firm. [Ignore any effect from personal income taxes.]

b) Evaluate the following four projects to determine their acceptance (or rejection) by firms B and C. What do the results of this evaluation tell you about leverage in a world with corporate taxes but no personal taxes? [*Note:* r_{jm} is the correlation between the unlevered free cash flows of each project and the market.]

$Project_j$	$Cost_j$	$E(\widetilde{NOI_j})$ (after-tax)	σ_j	r_{jm} Correlation of j with the Market
1	100	9	.10	.6
2	120	11	.11	.7
3	80	9	.12	.8
4	150	18	.20	.9

13.7 A firm with $1,000,000 in assets and 50% debt in its capital structure is considering a $250,000 project. The firm's after-tax weighted average cost of capital is 10.4%, the marginal

Table Q13.9

Income Statement	Before	After
Net operating income	100	100
Interest expense	80	40
Earnings before taxes	20	60
Taxes at 50%	10	30
Net income	10	30

Balance Sheet

	Before			After	
Assets	Liabilities		Assets	Liabilities	
	Debt	1000		Debt	500
	Equity	500		Equity	1000
Total = 1500	Total = 1500		Total = 1500	Total = 1500	

cost of debt is 8% (before taxes), and the marginal tax rate is 40%. If the project does not change the firm's operating risk and is financed exclusively with new equity, what rate of return must it earn to be acceptable?

13.8 The firm's cost of equity capital is 18%, the market value of the firm's equity is $8 million, the firm's cost of debt capital is 9%, and the market value of debt is $4 million. The firm is considering a new investment with an expected rate of return of 17%. This project is 30% riskier than the firm's average operations. The riskless rate of return is 5%; the variance of the market return is .08. Is the project profitable? [Assume a world without taxes.]

13.9 Susan Varhard, treasurer of the Gammamax Company, has proposed that the company should sell equity and buy back debt in order to maximize its value. As evidence, she presents the financial statements given in Table Q13.9. The company currently has a price/earnings ratio of 50. Before the change in capital structure it has 10 shares outstanding; therefore its earnings per share are $1.00, and the price per share is $50. If 10 new shares are issued at $50 each, $500 is collected and used to retire $500 of debt (which pays a coupon rate of 8%). After the capital structure change, earnings per share have increased to $1.50 (since there are now 20 shares outstanding); and with a price/earnings ratio of 50, presumably the price per share will increase from $50 before the capital structure change to $75 afterward. Given your understanding of modern finance theory, discuss the above proposal.

13.10 Community Bank must decide whether to open a new branch. The current market value of the bank is $2,500,000. According to company policy (and industry practice), the bank's capital structure is highly leveraged. The present (and optimal) ratio of debt to total assets is .9. Community Bank's debt is almost exclusively in the form of demand, savings, and time deposits. The average return on these deposits to the bank's clients has been 5% over the past five years. However, recently interest rates have climbed sharply, and as a result Community Bank presently pays an average annual rate of $6\frac{1}{4}\%$ on its accounts in order to remain competitive. In addition, the bank incurs a service cost of $2\frac{3}{4}\%$ per account. Because federal "Regulation Q" puts a ceiling on the amount of interest paid by banks on their accounts, the banking industry at large has been experiencing disintermediation—a loss of clients to the open money market (Treasury bills, etc.), where interest rates are higher. Largely because of the interest rate situation (which shows no sign of improving), Community Bank's president has stipulated that for the branch project to be acceptable its entire cost of $500,000 will have to be raised by 90% debt and 10% equity. The bank's cost of equity capital, k_s, is 11%. Community Bank's marginal tax rate is .48. Market analysis indicates that the new branch may be expected to return net cash flows according to the following schedule:

Year	0	1	2	3	4	5	6 to ∞
$	−500,000	25,000	35,000	45,000	45,000	50,000	50,000

Should Community Bank open the new branch?

13.11 A not-for-profit organization, such as a ballet company or a museum, usually carries no debt. Also, since there are no shareholders, there is no equity outstanding. How would you go about determining the appropriate weighted average cost of capital for not-for-profit organizations given that they have no debt or equity?

13.12 Firms A and B are each considering an unanticipated new investment opportunity that will marginally increase the value of the firm and will also increase the firm's level of diversification. Firm A is unlevered, and firm B has a capital structure of 50% debt. Assuming that the shareholders control the firm, will either firm make the investment?

13.13 In a world without taxes or transactions costs the Modigliani-Miller model predicts shareholders' wealth invariant to changes in capital structure, whereas the OPM predicts increased shareholder wealth with increased leverage. Given what you know about option pricing, is a 20% increase in the variance of return on the firm's assets more likely to benefit shareholders in a low-leverage or in a high-leverage firm?

13.14 The Sharpe version of the CAPM results in the principle of two-fund separation. Every individual holds the same portfolio of risky assets, namely, the market portfolio. Therefore individuals will be indifferent to redistribution effects caused by imperfect "me-first" rules. True or false? Why?

13.15 Consider a levered firm with $10 million face value of debt outstanding, maturing in one year. The riskless rate is 6% and the expected rate of return on the market is 12%. The systematic risk of the firm's assets is $\beta_V = 1.5$, the total risk of these assets is $\sigma_V = 1.3$, and their market value is $25 million.

a) Determine the market value of the firm's debt and equity.

b) Determine the cost of debt and equity capital (assuming a world without taxes).

13.16

a) True or false? The Modigliani-Miller model of cost of equity is equivalent to the OPM definition of cost of equity for an all-equity firm. Explain.

b) If we assume that $N(d_1) = 1$ in the OPM, what does this imply about $\partial S/\partial V$? About the firm's capital structure?

For Problems 13.17 and 13.18 assume the following:

a) We are dealing with a world where there are no taxes.

b) The changes in the parameters affecting value are unanticipated; therefore redistribution effects are possible.

c) Firms A and B initially have the following parameters:

$\sigma_A = \sigma_B = .2$	Instantaneous standard deviation
$T_A = T_B = 4$ years	Maturity of debt
$V_A = V_B = \$2000$	Value of the firm, $V = B + S$
$R_f = .06$	Risk-free rate
$D_A = D_B = \$1000$	Face value of debt

13.17 What is the initial market value of debt and equity for firms A and B?

13.18 Firm A decides to use some of its cash in order to purchase marketable securities. This has the effect of leaving its value, V_A, unchanged but increasing its instantaneous standard deviation from .2 to .3. What are the new values of debt and equity?

REFERENCES

Barnea, A.; R. Haugen; and L. Senbet, "A Rationale for Debt Maturity Structure and Call Provisions in the Agency Theory Framework," *Journal of Finance*, December 1980, 1223–1243.

Baxter, N. D., "Leverage, Risk of Ruin and the Cost of Capital," *Journal of Finance*, September 1967, 395–403.

Beranek, W., "The WACC Criterion and Shareholder Wealth Maximization," *Journal of Financial and Quantitative Analysis*, March 1977, 17–32.

Bierman, H., "The Cost of Warrants," *Journal of Financial and Quantitative Analysis*, June 1973, 499–503.

Black, F., and J. Cox, "Valuing Corporate Securities: Some Effects of Bond Indenture Provisions," *Journal of Finance*, May 1976, 351–367.

Boyce, W. M., and A. J. Kalotay, "Tax Differentials and Callable Bonds," *Journal of Finance*, September 1979, 825–838.

Brennan, M. J., and E. S. Schwartz, "Convertible Bonds: Valuation and Optimal Strategies for Call and Conversion," *Journal of Finance*, December 1977a, 1699–1715.

———, "Savings Bonds, Retractable Bonds and Callable Bonds," *Journal of Financial Economics*, August 1977b, 67–88.

———, "Corporate Income Taxes, Valuation, and the Problem of Optimal Capital Structure," *Journal of Business*, January 1978, 103–114.

———, "Analyzing Convertible Bonds," *Journal of Financial and Quantitative Analysis*, November 1980, 907–929.

———, "The Case for Convertibles," in Stern and Chew, eds., *The Revolution in Corporate Finance*. Basil Blackwell, Oxford, England, 1986.

Brick, I. E., and A. Ravid, "On the Relevance of Debt Maturity Structure," *Journal of Finance*, December 1985, 1423–1437.

Brigham, E. F., "An Analysis of Convertible Debentures," *Journal of Finance*, March 1966, 35–54.

Chen, A. H. Y., "A Model of Warrant Pricing in a Dynamic Market," *Journal of Finance*, December 1970, 1041–1060.

————, and H. Kim, "Theories of Corporate Debt Policy: A Synthesis," *Journal of Finance*, May 1979, 371–384.

Constantinides, G., "Warrant Exercise and Bond Conversion in Competitive Markets," *Journal of Financial Economics*, September 1984, 371–398.

DeAngelo, H., and R. Masulis, "Optimal Capital Structure under Corporate and Personal Taxation," *Journal of Financial Economics*, March 1980, 3–30.

Dunn, K. B., and C. S. Spatt, "A Strategic Analysis of Sinking Fund Bonds," *Journal of Financial Economics*, September 1984, 399–424.

Dyl, E., and M. Joehnk, "Sinking Funds and the Cost of Corporate Debt," *Journal of Finance*, September 1979, 887–893.

Emanuel, D. C., "Warrant Valuation and Exercise Strategy," *Journal of Financial Economics*, August 1983, 211–235.

Fama, E. F., and M. C. Jensen, "Agency Problems and Residual Claims," *Journal of Law and Economics*, June 1983, 327–349.

Fama, E. F., and M. H. Miller, *The Theory of Finance.* Holt, Rinehart and Winston, New York, 1972.

Farrar, D. E., and L. Selwyn, "Taxes, Corporate Financial Policies and Returns to Investors," *National Tax Journal*, December 1967, 444–454.

Galai, D., and R. W. Masulis, "The Option Pricing Model and the Risk Factor of Stock," *Journal of Financial Economics*, January–March 1976, 53–82.

Galai, D., and M. Schneller, "The Pricing of Warrants and the Value of the Firm," *Journal of Finance*, December 1978, 1333–1342.

Green, R., "Investment Incentives, Debt, and Warrants," *Journal of Financial Economics*, March 1984, 115–136.

Grove, M. A., "On Duration and the Optimal Maturity Structure of the Balance Sheet," *Bell Journal*, Autumn 1974, 696–709.

Haley, C. W., and L. D. Schall, *The Theory of Financial Decisions.* McGraw-Hill, New York, 1973.

Hamada, R. S., "Portfolio Analysis, Market Equilibrium, and Corporation Finance," *Journal of Finance*, March 1969, 13–31.

————, "The Effect of the Firm's Capital Structure on the Systematic Risk of Common Stocks," *Journal of Finance*, May 1972, 435–452.

Harris, M., and A. Raviv, "A Sequential Signalling Model of Convertible Debt Call Policy," *Journal of Finance*, December 1985, 1263–1282.

Hawkins, G. D., "An Analysis of Revolving Credit Agreements," *Journal of Financial Economics*, March 1982, 59–82.

Hsia, C. C., "Coherence of the Modern Theories of Finance," *Financial Review*, Winter 1981, 27–42.

Ingersoll, J., "A Contingent-Claims Valuation of Convertible Securities," *Journal of Financial Economics*, May 1977a, 289–322.

————, "An Examination of Corporate Call Policies on Convertible Securities," *Journal of Finance*, May 1977b, 463–478.

Jen, F. C., and J. E. Wert, "The Effects of Sinking Fund Provisions on Corporate Bond Yields," *Financial Analysts Journal*, March–April 1967, 125–133.

Jennings, E. H., "An Estimate of Convertible Bond Premiums," *Journal of Financial and Quantitative Analysis*, January 1974, 33–56.

Kim, H., "A Mean-Variance Theory of Optimal Capital Structure and Corporate Debt Capacity," *Journal of Finance*, March 1978, 45–64.

Kraus, A., and R. Litzenberger, "A State-Preference Model of Optimal Financial Leverage," *Journal of Finance*, September 1973, 911–922.

Marshall, W., and J. Yawitz, "Optimal Terms of the Call Provision on a Corporate Bond," *Journal of Financial Research*, Summer 1980, 202–211.

Mason, S. P., and S. Bhattacharya, "Risky Debt, Jump Processes, and Safety Covenants," *Journal of Financial Economics*, September 1981, 281–307.

Merton, R. C., "An Intertemporal Capital Asset Pricing Model," *Econometrica*, September 1973, 867–887.

Mikkelson, W. H., "Convertible Calls and Security Returns," *Journal of Financial Economics*, September 1981, 237–264.

Miller, M. H., "Debt and Taxes," *Journal of Finance*, May 1977, 261–275.

———, and F. Modigliani, "Some Estimates of the Cost of Capital to the Electric Utility Industry 1954–57," *American Economic Review*, June 1966, 333–348.

Modigliani, F., and M. H. Miller, "The Cost of Capital, Corporation Finance, and the Theory of Investment," *American Economic Review*, June 1958, 261–297.

———, "Corporate Income Taxes and the Cost of Capital," *American Economic Review*, June 1963, 433–443.

Morris, J. R., "On Corporate Debt Maturity Policies," *Journal of Finance*, March 1976a, 29–37.

———, "A Model for Corporate Debt Maturity Decisions," *Journal of Financial and Quantitative Analysis*, September 1976b, 339–357.

Myers, S. C., "Determinants of Corporate Borrowing," *Journal of Financial Economics*, November 1977, 147–176.

———, "The Capital Structure Puzzle," *Journal of Finance*, July 1984, 575–592.

Pye, G., "The Value of a Call Option on a Bond," *Journal of Political Economy*, April 1966, 200–205.

Robbins, E. H., and J. D. Schatzberg, "Callable Bonds: A Risk-Reducing Signalling Mechanism," *Journal of Finance*, September 1986, 935–949.

Robichek, A., and S. Myers, "Problems in the Theory of Optimal Capital Structure," *Journal of Financial and Quantitative Analysis*, June 1966, 1–35.

Rubinstein, M. E., "A Mean-Variance Synthesis of Corporate Financial Theory," *Journal of Finance*, March 1973, 167–181.

Samuelson, P. A., "Rational Theory of Warrant Pricing," *Industrial Management Review*, Spring 1965, 13–32.

Schneller, M., "Taxes and the Optimal Capital Structure of the Firm," *Journal of Finance*, March 1980, 119–127.

Schwartz, E. S., "The Valuation of Warrants: Implementing a New Approach," *Journal of Financial Economics*, January 1977, 79–93.

Smith, C., and R. Stulz, "The Determinants of a Firm's Hedging Policies," *Journal of Financial and Quantitative Analysis*, December 1985, 391–406.

Stiglitz, J. E., "A Re-examination of the Modigliani-Miller Theorem," *American Economic Review*, December 1969, 784–793.

———, "On the Irrelevance of Corporate Financial Policy," *American Economic Review*, December 1974, 851–866.

Stone, B. K., "Warrants Financing," *Journal of Financial and Quantitative Analysis*, March 1976, 143–153.

Taggert, R. A., Jr., "A Model of Corporate Financing Decisions," *Journal of Finance*, December 1977, 1467–1500.

Weil, R.; J. E. Segall; and D. Green, Jr., "Premiums on Convertible Bonds," *Journal of Finance*, 1968, 445–463.

Appendix to Chapter 13: Duration and Optimal Maturity Structure of the Balance Sheet

In Chapter 13, we analyzed several aspects of the cost and value of financial instruments. Another aspect of the valuation of securities is the sensitivity of their present values to unexpected changes in interest rates. We can conceptualize this relationship as the elasticity of the price of securities (particularly bonds) to interest rates. For bonds the elasticity is the ratio of percentage changes in prices to percentage changes in market rates of interest for a given coupon and face value.

A. DURATION

The "duration" of a payment stream is a measure of elasticity. Thus the duration of bond i can be expressed as follows:

$$D_i = -\frac{dB_i/B_i}{dr/r}, \tag{A13.1}$$

where

B_i = price of bond i,

r = market yield rate.

For measurement purposes the expression in Eq. (A13.1) would provide only an approximation since it holds strictly for only infinitely small changes in the market yield rate. We can derive a more operational measurement expression. We start with the value of a bond, B_0, as in Eq. (A13.2):

$$B_0 = \frac{I_1}{1+r} + \frac{I_2}{(1+r)^2} + \cdots + \frac{I_T}{(1+r)^T} + \frac{F}{(1+r)^T}, \qquad (A13.2)$$

where

I_t = dollar value of coupon payment in period t,

F = dollar value of maturity payment,

T = maturity period.

Next we take the derivative of the bond price to the change in the market yield rate:

$$\frac{dB_0}{d(1+r)} = -I(1+r)^{-2} - 2I(1+r)^{-3} - \cdots - TI(1+r)^{-(T+1)} - TF(1+r)^{-(T+1)}$$

$$= -\left[\frac{I}{(1+r)^2} + \frac{2I}{(1+r)^3} + \cdots + \frac{TI}{(1+r)^{T+1}} + \frac{TF}{(1+r)^{T+1}} \right].$$

Divide both sides by B_0 and $(1+r)$:

$$\frac{dB_0/B_0}{d(1+r)/(1+r)} = \frac{dB_0(1+r)}{d(1+r)B_0}$$

$$= -\frac{1}{B_0}\left[\frac{I}{1+r} + \frac{2I}{(1+r)^2} + \cdots + \frac{TI}{(1+r)^T} + \frac{TF}{(1+r)^T} \right].$$

Let C represent the appropriate cash flows, and express the result in summation form:

$$D_i = \frac{\displaystyle\sum_{t=1}^{T} \frac{tC_t}{(1+r)^t}}{B_0}. \qquad (A13.3)$$

This result can also be expressed as in Eq. (A13.3a):

$$D_i = \frac{\displaystyle\sum_{t=1}^{T} \frac{tI_t}{(1+r)^t} + \frac{TF}{(1+r)^T}}{\displaystyle\sum_{t=1}^{T} \frac{I_t}{(1+r)^t} + \frac{F}{(1+r)^T}}. \qquad (A13.3a)$$

From Eq. (A13.3a) we can see that duration is not the same as the time to maturity of the payment stream. Unlike maturity, duration considers all cash flows and gives some weight to their timing.

Thus duration is calculated as the weighted average of the lengths of time prior to the last cash flows, by using the ratios of the present values of each coupon payment to the present value of the bond as the weights. It identifies the "actual" weighted length of time needed to recover the current cost of the bond. For example, assume a five-year $1000 bond has a coupon payment of $25 each six months (5% coupon rate), pays $1000 at the end of the fifth year, and has a yield rate of 12%. The duration of the bond can be calculated as shown in Table A13.1.

**Table A13.1 $1000 Bond Issue, Five-Year, with
12% Yield Rate and 5% Coupon Rate Paid Semiannually**

(1) Period	(2) Cash Payments	(3) Discount Factor at 6% of Semiannual Yield Rate	(4) Present Value of Cash Payments (2) × (3)	(5) (4) × (1)
1	$ 25	.9434	$ 23.5850	$ 23.5850
2	25	.8900	22.2500	44.5000
3	25	.8396	20.9900	62.9700
4	25	.7921	19.8025	79.2100
5	25	.7473	18.6825	93.4125
6	25	.7050	17.6250	105.7500
7	25	.6651	16.6275	116.3925
8	25	.6274	15.6850	125.4800
9	25	.5919	14.7975	133.1775
10	1025	.5584	572.3600	5723.6000
		PV of bond =	$742.4050	$6508.0775

$$D = \frac{\$6{,}508.0775}{\$742.4050} = 8.7662 \text{ (semiannual)}$$

$$- 4.3831 \text{ years.}$$

A short-cut method of calculating duration as originally formulated by Macaulay [1938] is the following:

$$D = \frac{R}{R-1} - \frac{QR + T(1 + Q - QR)}{R^T - 1 - Q + QR}.$$ (A13.4)

The new terms in Eq. (A13.4) are

$R = (1 + r) = 1.06$,

$Q = (F/I_t) = \$1000/\$25 = 40$,

$T = 10$.

Only for zero coupon bonds is duration the same as maturity. For other payment streams, duration is shorter than maturity. For a given par value of a bond, the higher the coupon payments and the higher the yield to maturity, the shorter is duration.

The relationship between the bond price and its duration is more complicated. For bonds selling at or above par, the duration increases with maturity, but at a decreasing rate, and is bounded by $(r + p)/rp$ years, where r is the yield to maturity and p is the number of times per year interest is paid and compounded. For discount bonds, duration increases with maturity to a maximum point before it matures, and then declines. For shorter-term bonds, the differences between duration and maturity are small. However, as maturity increases, the differences will be substantially larger.

B. IMMUNIZATION

Immunization is a technique designed to achieve a specified return target in the face of changes in interest rates. The problem arises because with changing interest rates the reinvestment income will change. However, a bond or a bond portfolio can be immunized against this risk by selecting a maturity or group of maturities whose duration will be equal to the planning horizon of the decision maker. An illustration based on an example by Leibowitz [1981] will convey the ideas involved. The initial facts are these. We have a 9% par bond with a maturity of 6.7 years resulting in a 5-year duration related to the 5-year horizon of the decision maker. With semiannual compounding the bond maturity is 13.4 periods. The simple sum of the coupon income, based on the 9% rate over 5 years (10 periods), is $450.

To verify the relation between the maturity of 6.7 years and the duration of 5 years, we employ the Macaulay formulation. The key inputs are

$$R = 1 + r = 1.045,$$

$$Q = 1000/45 = 22.22,$$

$$T = 13.4.$$

We can now calculate duration, D, as

$$D = \frac{1.045}{.045} - \frac{22.22(1.045) + 13.4[23.22 - 22.22(1.045)]}{(1.045)^{13.4} - 23.22 + 22.22(1.045)}$$

$$= \frac{10.35}{2} = 5.17 \approx 5.$$

Suppose the market yield rate now changes from 9% to 10%. There will be a capital loss because of the rise in the yield rate, but the reinvestment income will be higher. We shall demonstrate that if the investor's planning horizon is 5 years, the yield will remain 9% and the capital gain or loss will be exactly balanced by the present value of the changed reinvestment income. We can demonstrate this by looking at the situation at the end of the fifth year or taking those results and discounting them back to the present. The income at 10% will be

$$= \$45 \times \text{FVIF}_a(5\%, 10 \text{ pds})$$

$$= (\$45 \times 12.5779)$$

$$= \$566.$$

However, the interest that would have been earned at a 9% rate would be

$$= \$45 \times \text{FVIF}_a(4\tfrac{1}{2}\%, 10 \text{ pds})$$

$$= (\$45 \times 12.2882)$$

$$= \$553.$$

Thus the gain in interest income is $13 as of the end of the fifth year.

Next we calculate the price that would be received when the bond is sold at the end of the five-year planning horizon. At the end of 5 years, or 10 periods, the bond had 1.7 years, or 3.4 periods, remaining. Its value and the capital gain (loss) at 10% are shown below:

$$V_b = \$45(3.0572) + \$1000(.8471)$$

$$= \$137.57 + \$847.10$$

$$= \$984.67$$

$$\text{Capital gain} = \$984.67 - \$1000 = -\$15.33.$$

Thus we see that the amount of the capital gain or loss is a negative $15. This is slightly different from the $13 gain on interest because we have used approximations for a duration of, e.g., 5 years when the exact duration was 5.17 years.

Next we can verify that a 9% yield will actually be achieved and that the current market value of $1000 is immunized against the rise in the required market yield. In the analysis we use

$$\text{FVIF}_a(4\tfrac{1}{2}\%, 10 \text{ pds}) = 7.9127, \text{ and PVIF}(4\tfrac{1}{2}\%, 10 \text{ pds}) = .6439.$$

So we have

Coupon interest @ 9%	$ 45 × 7.9127 = $356.07
Interest @ 10%	$566 × .6439 = 364.45
Capital gain	$985 × .6439 = 634.24
Less*	$553 × .6439 = (356.08)
	$998.70

* To adjust for the 9% interest rate implicit in the interest factor used to discount the present value of the coupon income.

The example illustrates that by choosing the duration of the payment stream to be equal to the length of the planning horizon, the present value of the payment stream is immunized against changes in the market rate of interest, and the initial yield on the stream is preserved.

Another example of immunization uses the total balance sheet position of a firm. Consider a bank portfolio manager with the following initial position:

	Initial Position	
	Assets	Liabilities
Portfolio value	$800,000	$800,000
Portfolio yield	12.0%	8.0%
Portfolio duration	8 yrs	3 yrs

With a 1% rise in yields, we can use Eq. (A13.1) to calculate the change in the equity position of the bank. For the assets side we have

$$dP_a = -D_a \left(\frac{dr}{r} \right) P_a$$

$$= -8 \frac{.01}{(1.12)} \$800,000$$

$$= -\$57,142.$$

For the liabilities (or claims on assets) side, we have

$$dP_c = -3 \frac{.01}{(1.08)} \$800,000$$

$$= -\$22,222.$$

So the decline in the value of assets exceeds the decline in the value of claims on assets by \$34,920. By changing the duration of the asset portfolio, the bank can be immunized against a change in the interest rate levels. The required duration for the asset portfolio is

$$dP_a = -D_a \frac{.01}{(1.12)} \$800,000 = -\$22,222.$$

Solving, we have D_a is 3.11, indicating the shorter duration required for immunization of the portfolio.

The examples above illustrate the mechanics of immunization procedures. In actual application immunization involves a wide range of assumptions in connection with its use in immunizing bond portfolios. One assumption is parallel shifts in the yield curve [Yawitz and Marshall, 1981]. The practical effects of this are small [Kolb and Gay, 1982, 83].

Also, there may be multiple rate changes during the planning horizon. This problem is dealt with by rebalancing the portfolio to maintain a duration matching the remaining life of the planning period. In addition, there are a wide variety of more aggressive approaches to managing the bond portfolio developed under the concept of contingent immunization [Leibowitz and Weinberger, 1981, 1982]. Contingent immunization is a form of active portfolio management. It generally involves some degree of rate anticipation reflecting the portfolio manager's judgments about the future direction of interest rates. The procedures are too detailed to be covered in this brief treatment.

C. APPLICATION OF DURATION TO DEBT MATURITY STRUCTURE

Redington [1952] applied the duration concept to the analysis of investment decisions made by insurance companies. He proposed an immunization rule under which the weighted durations of asset and liability streams are made equal so that the firm's net worth is hedged against interest rate movements. Redington noted that even for insurance companies the concept would be complex in its implementation. Grove [1974] analyzed immunization in a portfolio-choice model in a framework of uncertainty of income stream patterns and of interest rate changes.

Morris [1976a, 1976b] sought to apply the duration concept to the problem of corporate debt maturity strategies. Here the problem is even more complex than that faced by insurance companies. In theory insurance companies can formulate income and payment streams that are highly predictable by investing in fixed income securities, with payment streams related to the operation of life expectancy tables (which can be further hedged by combining death policies with annuity policies). For the industrial firm the liability structure can be fixed by its corporate debt maturity pattern. However, the income stream varies with the impact of the economy and competition on the firm's revenues and costs.

Morris observes that when the covariance of interest costs with the firm's net operating income is high, a short-term borrowing policy will reduce the variation of net income even though it increases the uncertainty of interest costs in future periods. Thus for a weighted asset life with long duration, immunization through the choice of the duration of the debt structure is not necessarily the least risky maturity policy because of the variability of the income streams from the assets. A shorter debt maturity policy may decrease the uncertainty of net income derived from the asset when there is a high covariance between net operating income and interest costs. If the duration of the asset structure is short, immunization calls for a weighted maturity of short-duration debt. But if long-term debt with a longer duration were employed, and if interest rates were negatively correlated with the firm's net operating income, a long-term borrowing policy could reduce the variance of net income. In addition, the level of interest costs would be fixed and certain over the life of the debt. Thus the concept of duration appears to have some potential for developing corporate debt maturity strategies. But the problem is more complex than that encountered in managing portfolios of financial assets and claims.

REFERENCES TO APPENDIX

Fisher, L., and R. L. Weil, "Coping with the Risk of Interest Rate Fluctuations: Returns to Bondholders from Naive and Optimal Strategies," *Journal of Business*, October 1971, 111–118.

Grove, M. A., "On 'Duration' and the Optimal Maturity Structure of the Balance Sheet," *Bell Journal*, Autumn 1974, 696–709.

Hicks, J. R., *Value and Capital*. Clarendon Press, Oxford, 1946.

Hopewell, M. H., and G. G. Kaufman, "Bond Price Volatility and Term to Maturity: A Generalized Respecification," *American Economic Review*, September 1973, 749–753.

Hsia, C. C., and J. F. Weston, "Price Behavior of Deep Discount Bonds," *Journal of Banking and Finance*, September 1981, 357–361.

Kolb, R. W., *Interest Rate Futures: A Comprehensive Introduction*. Dame, Richmond, Va., 1982.

————, and G. D. Gay, "Immunizing Bond Portfolios with Interest Rate Futures," *Financial Management*, Summer 1982, 81–89.

Leibowitz, M. L., "Specialized Fixed Income Security Strategies," in Altman, ed., *Financial Handbook*, 5th ed. Wiley, New York, 1981, section 19.

————, and A. Weinberger, *Contingent Immunization: A New Procedure for Structured Active Management*. Salomon, New York, 1981.

————, *Risk Control Procedures under Contingent Immunization*. Salomon, New York, 1982.

Macaulay, F. R., *Some Theoretical Problems Suggested by the Movements of Interest Rates, Bond Yields, and Stock Prices in the U.S. since 1856*. National Bureau of Economic Research, New York, 1938.

Morris, J. R., "On Corporate Debt Maturity Strategies," *Journal of Finance*, March 1976a, 29–37.

————, "A Model for Corporate Debt Maturity Decisions," *Journal of Financial and Quantitative Analysis*, September 1976b, 339–357.

Redington, F. M., "Review of the Principles of Life Office Valuations," *Journal of the Institute of Actuaries*, 1952 (vol. 78, part 3, no. 350), 286–340.

Samuelson, P. A., "The Effect of Interest Rate Increases on the Banking System," *American Economic Review*, March 1945, 16–27.

Weil, R. L., "Macaulay's Duration: An Appreciation," *Journal of Business*, October 1973, 589–592.

Yawitz, J. B., and W. J. Marshall, "The Shortcomings of Duration as a Risk Measure for Bonds," *Journal of Financial Research*, Summer 1981, 91–101.

14

One kind of evidence in favor of the traditional position is that companies in various industry groups appear to use leverage as if there is some optimal range appropriate to each group. While significant intercompany differences in debt ratios exist within each industry, the average use of leverage by broad industrial groups tends to follow a consistent pattern over time.

E. Solomon, *The Theory of Financial Management*, Columbia University Press, New York, 1963, p. 98.

Capital Structure: Empirical Evidence and Applications

A. INTRODUCTION

The theories presented in the previous chapter provide some fairly unsettling conclusions about capital structure. On one hand it is argued that capital structure has no effect on the value of the firm (Modigliani and Miller [1958] or Miller [1977]), and on the other hand it is suggested that the firm carry 100% debt (Modigliani and Miller [1963]). Neither result is consistent with what seem to be cross-sectional regularities in the observed capital structures of U.S. firms. For example, the electric utility and steel industries have high financial leverage, whereas service industries like accounting firms or brokerage houses have almost no long-term debt.

The first part of this chapter looks at some possible explanations for why there might be such a thing as an "optimal" capital structure that contains both debt and equity. Recall that in the previous chapter we examined the argument that risky debt (in a world without bankruptcy costs) may be the cause of an optimal capital structure and concluded that it has no effect. The first issue to be studied here is the effect of bankruptcy costs. It turns out that if they are nontrivial, then it is possible that an optimal capital structure can be obtained as the tax advantage of debt is traded off against the likelihood of incurring bankruptcy costs. Second, we consider the possibility that changes in financial structure may be interpreted by the market-place as signals of the future health (or sickness) of the firm. Based on the assumption that managers are better informed than outsiders, the signaling theories lead to a "pecking" order concept of capital structure where retained earnings is preferred to debt and debt is preferred to new equity. Third, we discuss the implications of option pricing theory for the capital structure of the firm and for the valuation of risky debt. Finally, we discuss agency costs as determinants of capital structure. Agency theory is novel because it can explain optimal capital structure without relying on taxes or bankruptcy costs.

Next, the discussion turns to the empirical evidence. The central issue is whether or not the value of the firm is affected by changes in its debt-equity ratio. Important related questions are: (1) Does the cost of equity increase as financial leverage does? (2) Are bankruptcy costs really nontrivial? (3) Which theory of optimal capital structure is best supported by the evidence? (4) How does the market interpret various leverage changing signals?

The third part of the chapter examines some practical issues dealing with changes in the liabilities side of the balance sheet. We discuss a wrong reason for carrying no debt, and how to make the debt refunding decision.

B. POSSIBLE REASONS FOR AN "OPTIMAL" MIX OF DEBT AND EQUITY

1. The Effect of Bankruptcy Costs

In Chapter 13 we discussed the effect of risky debt on the value of the firm. In a world without transactions costs there was no effect. When we consider bankruptcy costs the value of the firm in bankruptcy is reduced by the fact that payments must be made to third parties other than bond- or shareholders. Trustee fees, legal fees, and other costs of reorganization or bankruptcy are deducted from the net asset value of the bankrupt firm and from the proceeds that should go to bondholders. Consequently, the "dead weight" losses associated with bankruptcy may cause the value of the firm in bankruptcy to be less than the discounted value of the expected cash flows from operations. This fact can be used to explain the existence of an optimal capital structure. Baxter [1967] was one of the first to suggest this possibility. Since then more sophisticated treatments have been offered by Stiglitz [1972], Kraus and Litzenberger [1973], and Kim [1978]. The interested reader is referred to these papers for explicit mathematical treatment of optimal capital structure. Figure 14.1 summarizes the results: Fig. 14.1(a) shows the effects on various costs of capital. The dashed lines are the by now familiar Modigliani-Miller results, where the weighted average cost of capital (in a world with only corporate taxes) declines with leverage. The solid lines show what might happen if nontrivial bankruptcy costs are introduced. As the proportion of debt in the firm's capital structure is increased, the probability of bankruptcy also increases. Consequently, the rate of return required by

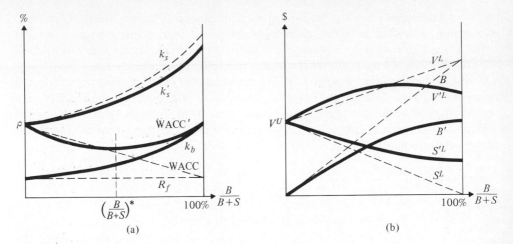

Figure 14.1
Optimal capital structure in the presence of bankruptcy costs: (a) the cost of capital; (b) the value of claims.

bondholders [the solid line, k_b, in Fig. 14.1(a)] increases with leverage. This in turn results in a "U-shaped" weighted average cost of capital (solid line WACC') and an optimal capital structure, $[B/(B + S)]^*$. The optimal ratio of debt to equity is determined by taking on increasing amounts of debt until the marginal gain from leverage is equal to the marginal expected loss from bankruptcy costs. The optimal capital structure minimizes the weighted average cost of capital and maximizes the value of the firm.

An important question for the existence of optimal capital structure brought about by the deadweight losses of bankruptcy is: Exactly how large are bankruptcy costs? If they are trivial, some other explanation for optimal capital structure is needed. Warner [1977b] collects data for 11 railroad bankruptcies that occurred between 1933 and 1955. He measures only direct costs, such as lawyers' and accountants' fees, other professional fees, and the value of managerial time spent in administering the bankruptcy. He does not estimate indirect costs to creditors, such as the opportunity cost of funds tied up during bankruptcy proceedings and losses in asset value due to forced capital structure changes, or indirect costs to shareholders, such as lost profits created by decreased sales in anticipation of bankruptcy or from disruptions in production during reorganization.[1] The evidence indicates that direct costs are trivial, averaging about 1% of the market value of the firm seven years prior to bankruptcy, and rising to 5.3% of the market value immediately prior to bankruptcy. Furthermore, direct costs as a percentage of value seem to decrease as a function of the size of the bankrupt firm. This would suggest that the direct

---

[1] Some of the agency costs that are discussed in section B.4 are closely related to bankruptcy and might also be considered indirect costs. For example, see Titman [1984].

costs of bankruptcy are less important for the capital structure decisions of large firms than of small firms. Although Warner's evidence is inconclusive because indirect costs are not measured, it does suggest that direct bankruptcy costs may not be sufficiently large to be important determinants of optimal leverage.

In a second paper, Warner [1977a] examines the effect of bankruptcy on the market returns of 73 defaulted bonds of 20 separate railroads, each of which was in bankruptcy at some time during the period from 1930 through 1955. None of the railroads was actually liquidated, although there were mergers, spinoffs, and abandonments of operations. The following effects were observed:

- The systematic risk of bonds increased prior to filing for bankruptcy. A reasonable explanation is that as the market value of equity, relative to bonds, falls prior to bankruptcy, the bondholders' claim becomes more like that of the shareholders of an all-equity firm, and hence their risk rises.

- After adjusting for risk, the performance of the bonds in the month of the bankruptcy petition was significantly negative.

- Investors who purchased a portfolio of bonds on the date of the bankruptcy petition appeared to earn significant risk-adjusted abnormal returns in the post-bankruptcy period. One possible explanation is that the courts approved capital structure simplifications that had been unanticipated and that benefited bondholders.

It is hard to argue that conclusions based on a study of the railroad industry can be generalized because federal regulations encourage the continued operation of railroad service even though the firm is in bankruptcy. Nevertheless, if one views the bondholders' position as being the residual claim at the time of bankruptcy, the significant negative return to bondholders on the date of the bankruptcy petition is evidence of nontrivial bankruptcy costs.

Evidence on indirect bankruptcy costs is provided by Altman [1984].[2] Admittedly, because indirect costs are opportunity costs (what might have happened in the absence of bankruptcy proceedings), they are difficult to estimate. Altman provides an estimate (for a sample of 19 firms, 12 retailers and 7 industrials, that went bankrupt between 1970 and 1978) that compares expected profits, computed from time series regressions, with actual profits. The arithmetic average indirect bankruptcy costs were 8.1% of firm value three years prior to bankruptcy and 10.5% the year of bankruptcy. A second method uses unexpected earnings from analysts' forecasts for a sample of 7 firms that went bankrupt in the 1980–1982 interval. Average indirect bankruptcy costs were 17.5% of value one year prior to bankruptcy. Although more research needs to be done on this topic, Altman's evidence suggests that total bankruptcy costs (direct and indirect) are sufficiently large to give credibility to a theory of optimal capital structure based on the trade-off between gains from leverage-induced tax shields and expected bankruptcy costs.

---

[2] Kalaba, Langetieg, Rasakhoo, and Weinstein [1984] discuss a potentially useful methodology for estimating the expected cost of bankruptcy from bond data but provide no empirical results.

2. Signaling Hypotheses

If we assume that financial markets are not fully aggregating in the sense that market prices do not reflect all information, especially that which is not publicly available, then it is possible that managers may elect to use financial policy decisions to convey information to the market. Changes in capital structure are an obvious candidate for a signaling device, and as we shall see in Chapter 15, so is dividend policy.

The first application of signaling to finance theory has been put forth by Ross [1977]. He suggests that implicit in the Miller-Modigliani irrelevancy proposition is the assumption that the market *knows* the (random) return stream of the firm and values this stream to set the value of the firm. What is valued in the market place, however, is the *perceived* stream of returns for the firm. Putting the issue this way raises the possibility that changes in the capital structure (or dividend payout) may alter the market's perception. In the terminology of Modigliani and Miller, by changing its financial structure (or dividend payout) the firm alters its perceived risk class even though the actual risk class remains unchanged.

Managers, as insiders who have monopolistic access to information about the firm's expected cash flows, will choose to establish unambiguous signals about the firm's future if they have the proper incentive to do so. To show how this incentive-signaling process works, let us assume that managers are prohibited (perhaps by SEC regulations) from trading in the securities of their own firm. This keeps them from profiting by issuing false signals, such as announcing bad news and selling short even though they know the firm will do well.

In a simple one-period model the manager's compensation, M, paid at the end of the period may be expressed as

$$M = (1 + r)\gamma_0 V_0 + \gamma_1 \begin{cases} V_1 & \text{if} \quad V_1 \geq D, \\ V_1 - C & \text{if} \quad V_1 < D, \end{cases} \tag{14.1}$$

where

γ_0, γ_1 = positive weights,

r = the one-period interest rate,

V_0, V_1 = the current and future value of the firm,

D = the face value of debt,

C = a penalty paid if bankruptcy occurs, i.e., if $V < D$.

This result can be used to establish a signaling equilibrium if we further assume that investors use D, the face value of debt, to tell them whether a firm is successful (type A) or unsuccessful (type B). Assume that D^* is the maximum amount of debt that an unsuccessful firm can carry without going bankrupt. If $D > D^*$, the market perceives the firm to be successful, and vice versa. For the signaling equilibrium to be established, (1) the signals must be unambiguous (i.e., when investors observe $D > D^*$, the firm is always type A), and (2) managers must have incentive to always give the appropriate signal. If the end-of-period value of a successful type-A firm is V_{1a} and is always greater than the value of an unsuccessful type-B firm, V_{1b}, then the compensation of the management of a type-A firm is

$$M_a = \begin{cases} \gamma_0(1+r)\dfrac{V_{1a}}{1+r} + \gamma_1 V_{1a} & \text{if } D^* < D \le V_{1a} \quad \text{(tell the truth),} \\ \gamma_0(1+r)\dfrac{V_{1b}}{1+r} + \gamma_1 V_{1a} & \text{if } D < D^* \qquad\qquad \text{(lie).} \end{cases} \tag{14.2}$$

Clearly, management of a type-A firm has incentive to establish a level of debt greater than D^* in order to earn maximum compensation. Therefore it will give the correct signal. But what about the management of a type-B firm? Does it not have incentive to lie by falsely signaling that its firm is type A? The answer is found by looking at the management-incentive scheme.

$$M_b = \begin{cases} \gamma_0(1+r)\dfrac{V_{1a}}{1+r} + \gamma_1(V_{1b} - C) & \text{if } D^* \le D < V_{1a} \quad \text{(lie),} \\ \gamma_0(1+r)\dfrac{V_{1b}}{1+r} + \gamma_1 V_{1b} & \text{if } D < D^* \qquad\qquad \text{(tell the truth).} \end{cases} \tag{14.3}$$

In order for management of a type-B firm to have incentive to signal that the firm will be unsuccessful, the payoff from telling the truth must be greater than that produced by telling lies. Mathematically,

$$\gamma_0 V_{1a} + \gamma_1(V_{1b} - C) < \gamma_0 V_{1b} + \gamma_1 V_{1b},$$

which can be rewritten as

$$\gamma_0(V_{1a} - V_{1b}) < \gamma_1 C. \tag{14.4}$$

This condition says that management will give the correct signal if the marginal gain from a false signal, $V_{1a} - V_{1b}$, weighted by management's share, γ_0, is less than the bankruptcy costs incurred by management, C, weighted by its share, γ_1.

The incentive-signaling approach suggests that management might choose real financial variables such as financial leverage or dividend policy as the means of sending unambiguous signals to the public about the future performance of the firm. These signals cannot be mimicked by unsuccessful firms because such firms do not have sufficient cash flow to back them up and because managers have incentives to tell the truth. Without management incentives to signal truthfully there would be no signaling equilibrium.

The concept is easily applied to dividend policy as well as to financial structure. A firm that increases dividend payout is signaling that it has expected future cash flows that are sufficiently large to meet debt payments and dividend payments without increasing the probability of bankruptcy. Therefore we may expect to find empirical evidence that the value of the firm increases, because dividends are taken as signals that the firm is expected to have permanently higher future cash flows. Chapter 16 reviews the empirical evidence relevant to dividend policy.

Ross's paper suggests that greater financial leverage can be used by managers to signal an optimistic future for the firm. Another signaling paper, by Leland and

Pyle [1977], focuses on owners instead of managers. They assume that entrepreneurs have better information about the expected value of their venture projects than do outsiders. The inside information held by an entrepreneur can be transferred to suppliers of capital because it is in the owner's interest to invest a greater fraction of his or her wealth in successful projects. Thus the owner's willingness to invest in his or her own projects can serve as a signal of project quality, and the value of the firm increases with the percentage of the equity held by the entrepreneur relative to what he or she otherwise would have held given a lower-quality project. An empirical implication of this signaling argument is that if the original founders of a company going public decide to keep a large fraction of the stock, then these firms should experience greater price earnings multiples. A second implication is that if the firm's value is positively related to the fraction of the owner's wealth held as equity in the firm, then the firm will have greater debt capacity and will use greater amounts of debt. Although debt is not a signal in this model, its use will be positively correlated with the firm's value.

Myers and Majluf [1984] present a signaling model that combines investment and financing decisions and that is rich in empirical implications. Managers, better than anyone else, are assumed to know the "true" future value of the firm and of any projects that it might undertake. Furthermore, they are assumed to act in the interest of "old" shareholders, i.e., those who hold shares in the firm at the time a decision is made. Finally, "old" shareholders are assumed to be passive in the sense that they do not actively change their personal portfolios to undo the decisions of management.[3] To keep things simple, assume that interest rates are zero and that there are no taxes, transactions costs, or other market imperfections.

To begin the analysis, consider a situation where there are two equally likely states of nature (good news and bad news). The firm has liquid assets, L_i, and tangible assets in place, A_i, that can take the values illustrated in Table 14.1. It has no positive net present value projects for the time being. (We shall examine the effect of positive NPV projects next.) Also, there is no debt (that will be the third case.) Information asymmetry is created by the fact that insiders are assumed to know which state, good or bad, will turn up for the firm. The market, however, knows nothing except what the value of the firm would be in each state of nature. If the firm does nothing, the market (i.e., outsiders) will compute the current value of the firm as the expected value of its payouts,

$$V_0 = \sum p_i(L_i + A_i) = .5(250) + .5(130) = 190.$$

This is equal to the value of the "old" shareholders' claim.

To establish a rational expectations signaling equilibrium let us look at the payoffs to "old" shareholders in each state of nature given each of two possible actions: (1) do nothing or (2) issue \$100 of new equity to new shareholders. We will see that although "old" shareholders have the incentive to issue new shares when the firm is overvalued—i.e., when they know the bad news is coming—the very fact that they try to issue shares will signal their information to the market and consequently destroy

---

[3] If shareholders systematically undertake personal portfolio changes to reverse management decisions, then managerial financial decisions become irrelevant.

Table 14.1   Issue Equity, No Positive NPV Projects

	Do Nothing		Issue Equity	
	Good	Bad	Good	Bad
Liquid assets, L_i	50	50	150	150
Assets in place, A_i	200	80	200	80
Value of firm, V_i	250	130	350	230

their informational advantage. If "old" shareholders know good news (state 1) will occur, their wealth conditional on doing nothing is

$$(V_0 | \text{good news, do nothing}) = L_1 + A_1 = 250.$$

Alternately, they can issue \$100 of new equity, E, and their value is

$$(V_0 | \text{good news, issue equity}) = \frac{V_0}{V_0 + E}(L_1 + A_1 + E) = \frac{190}{290}(350) = 229.31.$$

Their fraction of the firm if they issue new equity is their current value, 190, divided by 190 plus the cash received from the new equity issue, 100. If "old" shareholders know bad news (state 2) will occur, their payoff from doing nothing is

$$(V_0 | \text{bad news, do nothing}) = L_2 + A_2 = 130,$$

and if they issue new equity it is

$$(V_0 | \text{bad news, issue equity}) = \frac{V_0}{V_0 + E}(L_2 + A_2 + E) = \frac{190}{290}(230) = 150.69.$$

The payouts to original shareholders are summarized in Table 14.2. It seems that the optimal actions of the informed "old" shareholders (i.e., the payouts with asterisks) are to do nothing if they think the good news state will occur and to issue equity if the bad news state will occur, because the firm is currently overvalued. Outsiders, however, will not be fooled. When the firm issues new equity they know the firm believes the bad news state will occur, and they impute the bad news value, 130, to the firm. Therefore the expected payout to old shareholders, given that they issue new equity and that the outsiders infer bad news, is

$$(V_0 | \text{issue equity}) = \frac{V_2}{V_2 + E}(V_2 + E) = V_2 = 130.$$

**Table 14.2   "Old" Shareholder Payoffs—
Issue vs. Do Nothing**

	Do Nothing	Issue Equity
Good news	250.00*	229.31
Bad news	130.00	150.69*

Table 14.3   Positive NPV Project and New Equity

	Do Nothing		Invest and Issue Equity	
	Good	Bad	Good	Bad
Liquid assets, L_i	50	50	50	50
Assets in place, A_i	200	80	300	180
NPV of new project, b_i	0	0	20	10
Value of firm, V_i	250	130	370	240

The upshot of this argument is that original shareholders cannot take advantage of their inside information because the very act of issuing new shares (when they think the firm is overvalued) will reveal their information to the market. Hence they are indifferent between doing nothing and issuing new equity, and the market will attach no significance to new equity issues.

Next, let us complicate the model slightly by assuming that the firm has a positive net present value project that requires an initial cash outlay of \$100, and that has the state-dependent net present values, b_i, illustrated in Table 14.3. Going through the same type of computations as before, we first compute V_0, the unconditional value of original shareholders' wealth, assuming they do nothing.

$$V_0 = \sum p_i(L_i + A_i) = .5(250) + .5(130) = 190.$$

Alternately, if they issue and invest, their unconditional expected wealth is

$$V'_0 = \sum p_i(L_i + A_i + b_i) = .5(270) + .5(140) = 205.$$

Now let us examine their wealth, contingent on each state of nature. If they issue \$100 of new equity and invest the proceeds in the new positive NPV project, their wealth in the good news state is

$$(V_0 | \text{good news, invest and issue}) = \frac{V'_0}{V'_0 + E}(L_1 + A_1 + b_1 + E)$$

$$= \frac{205}{205 + 100}(370) = 248.69,$$

and if they do nothing, given good news, their wealth is 250. Given bad news, their payout if they issue and invest is

$$(V_0 | \text{bad news, invest and issue}) = \frac{V'_0}{V'_0 + E}(L_2 + A_2 + b_2 + E)$$

$$= \frac{205}{205 + 100}(240) = 161.31,$$

and if they do nothing, given bad news, their wealth is 130. Table 14.4 summarizes the payoffs from the "old" shareholders' point of view. As before, original shareholders

Table 14.4   "Old" Shareholder Payoffs—Issue and Invest vs. Nothing

	Do Nothing	Issue and Invest
Good news	250*	248.69
Bad news	130	161.31*

Table 14.5   Rational Expectations Equilibrium

	Do Nothing	Issue and Invest
Good news	250*	248.69
Bad news	130	140.00*

are better off doing nothing in the good state because the positive NPV of the project (given good news) is not large enough to offset the fraction of ownership that they must sacrifice by issuing new shares.[4] Hence they desire to issue new equity and invest only if they know the bad state will occur. As before, the market is not fooled. As soon as insiders announce their intention to issue and invest, the market learns that the bad state is forthcoming, and in the bad state the firm is worth only 240, with 100 going to outsiders and the remaining 140 going to original shareholders. The rational expectations equilibrium payoffs are illustrated in Table 14.5. In equilibrium, given the set of numbers we have chosen, the firm issues and invests in the bad news state but not in the good news state.[5] This surprising result implies that the value of the firm may fall when new equity issues are announced—an important empirical implication.

So far we have examined two cases. First, when the firm had no new projects and the market knew it, then issuing new equity was an unambiguous financial signal that the market could use to discover the inside information held by managers. Hence it was impossible for managers to benefit from issuing new equity when they knew the future prospects of the firm were dismal. Second, when positive NPV projects (good news) were financed with equity issues (bad news), the signal became mixed. The market could not separate information about new projects from information about whether the firm is under- or overvalued. If there were some way to provide two separate signals—one for investment decisions and another for financing decisions—the problem would vanish. If project outcomes were uncorrelated with states of nature (e.g., if the project had the same NPV in both states of nature), the problem would vanish. Or if the firm were to use financing that is not subject to the information asymmetry problem, the problem would vanish.

---

[4] It is important to realize that outsiders pay nothing for the expected NPV of the new project. The entire NPV accrues to "old" shareholders.

[5] It is puzzling to understand why old shareholders do not provide all investment funds if they know the good state will occur. These funds can come from cash (what Myers and Majluf call slack) or via a rights offering.

Myers and Majluf point out that if the firm uses its available liquid assets, L_i, to finance positive NPV projects, then all positive NPV projects would be undertaken because no new equity is issued and the information asymmetry problem is thereby resolved. They suggest that this may be a good reason for carrying excess liquid assets. They also suggest that debt financing, which has payoffs less correlated with future states of nature than equity, will be preferred to new equity as a means of financing. Myers [1984] suggests a *pecking order theory* for capital structure. Firms are said to prefer retained earnings (available liquid assets) as their main source of funds for investment. Next in order of preference is debt, and last comes external equity financing. Firms wish to avoid issuing common stock or other risky securities so that they do not run into the dilemma of either passing up positive NPV projects or issuing stock at a price they think is too low.

The pecking order theory is a dynamic story. The observed capital structure of each firm will depend on its history. For example, an unusually profitable firm in an industry with relatively slow growth (few investment opportunities) will end up with an unusually low debt-to-equity ratio. It has no incentive to issue debt and retire equity. An unprofitable firm in the same industry will end up with a high debt ratio.

3. Option Pricing Implications for Capital Structure— The Bondholder Wealth Expropriation Hypothesis

Black and Scholes [1973] suggest that the equity in a levered firm can be thought of as a call option. When shareholders issue bonds, it is equivalent to selling the assets of the firm (but not control over those assets) to the bondholders in return for cash (the proceeds of the bond issues) and a call option.

To reduce the analogy to its simplest form, assume that (1) the firm issues zero coupon bonds[6] that prohibit any capital disbursements (such as interest payments) until after the bonds mature T time periods hence, (2) there are no transactions costs or taxes so that the value of the firm is unaffected by its capital structure (in other words, Modigliani-Miller Proposition I is assumed to be valid), (3) there is a known nonstochastic risk-free rate of interest, and (4) there are homogeneous expectations about the stochastic process that describes the value of the firm's assets. Given these assumptions, we can imagine a simple firm that issues only one class of bonds secured by the assets of the firm. From the shareholders' point of view, cash is received from the sale of the bonds. The value of the shareholders' position is equal to the discounted value of the bonds and a call option. If, on the maturity date, the value of the firm, V, exceeds the face value of the bonds, D, the shareholders will exercise their call option by paying off the bonds and keeping the excess. On the other hand, if the value of the firm is less than the face value of the bonds, the shareholders will default on the debt by deciding not to exercise their option. Therefore at maturity the shareholders' wealth, S, has the same payouts as a European

---

[6] All accumulated interest on zero coupon bonds is paid at maturity; hence $B(T)$, the current market value of debt with maturity T, must be less than its face value, D, assuming a positive risk-free rate of discount.

call option,

$$S = \text{MAX}[0, V - D],$$

and bondholders' wealth is

$$B = \text{MIN}[V, D].$$

The option pricing model offers a great deal of insight into the way that capital structure changes may affect shareholders and bondholders. Although the arguments that follow are made intuitively, the reader who is interested in a mathematical presentation is referred to Galai and Masulis [1976].

In each of the following cases we rely on the Modigliani-Miller result that in the absence of transactions costs, information heterogeneity, or taxes the value of the firm remains constant regardless of the financial decisions made by management. Furthermore, we assume that any changes that affect the systematic risk of various securities, or their expected rate of return, are *unanticipated* changes. To the extent that changes in the value of securities are unanticipated, it is possible that there may be a redistribution of wealth from one class of security holders to another.

We also assume that two-fund separation does not apply. Two-fund separation implies, among other things, that all individuals hold the same portfolio of risky assets, namely, the market portfolio. For individuals holding both the equity and risky debt of a firm, any offsetting change in the market value of the debt and equity claims against the firm will not change their wealth position. Therefore they would be indifferent to the redistribution effects that we are about to discuss. It is necessary, then, to rule out two-fund separation and discuss the wealth of shareholders and bondholders as if they were separate and distinct. If shareholders are not constrained by the indenture provisions of debt from issuing new debt with an equal claim on the assets of the firm, then current bondholders will experience a loss of wealth when new debt is issued. It is possible to increase the book value debt-to-equity ratio by issuing new debt and using the proceeds to repurchase equity. In this way the assets of the firm remain unchanged. If the new debt has equal claim on those assets, then the current bondholders end up with only a partial claim to the assets of the firm, whereas before the new debt was issued, they had complete claim on the assets. Clearly, this approach puts current bondholders in a riskier position, and they are unable to charge more for the extra risk because the discounted value of their bonds has already been paid (i.e., they cannot raise their coupon payments once the bonds have been issued). Consequently, the market value of their bonds will fall. At the same time, the value of the firm remains unchanged, and new bondholders pay a fair market price for their position. Therefore the value that is expropriated from current bondholders must accrue to shareholders, who are the residual claimants of the firm. Their wealth increases. This is called the *bondholder wealth expropriation hypothesis*.

The theory of option pricing argues that in a world with no transactions costs or taxes the wealth of shareholders is increased by greater financial leverage. In Chapter 13, the Modigliani-Miller propositions argue that under the same set of assumptions the value of shareholders' wealth is unaffected by changes in capital structure. How can the seemingly contradictory conclusions of the two theories be explained? The crucial difference is that option pricing assumes that *unanticipated* redistributions of wealth are possible. To the extent that bondholders can appropriately assess the probability of shareholders' ability to expropriate their wealth, they can charge a rate of return that adequately compensates them for their risk or they can carefully write bond indenture provisions that restrict the actions of shareholders. Either way they can protect themselves against anticipated redistribution effects. Whether or not such protection is actually possible is an empirical question. Some of the empirical evidence will be discussed later on in this chapter.

4. The Effect of Agency Costs on Capital Structure

We saw, in section B.1., that if there is a gain from leverage because of the tax deductibility of interest expenses, and if bankruptcy costs are nontrivial, then it is possible to construct a theory of optimal capital structure. One troublesome aspect of this approach is that even before income taxes existed in the United States, firms used debt in their capital structure. Furthermore, the same cross-sectional regularities in financial leverage that exist today can also be observed in data prior to the introduction of corporate taxes. This suggests that optimal leverage (if it exists) may be explained by causes other than debt tax shields and bankruptcy costs.

Jensen and Meckling [1976] use agency costs to argue that the probability distribution of cash flows provided by the firm is not independent of its ownership structure and that this fact may be used to explain optimal leverage. First, there is an incentive problem associated with the issuance of new debt, an *agency cost of debt*. Consider an example where unbeknownst to lenders the firm has two different investment projects (see Table 14.6), both having the same systematic risk but different variances. The first has a 50/50 chance of yielding an end-of-period cash flow of $9,000 or $11,000. The second has a 50/50 chance of yielding $2,000 or $18,000. Both cost $8,000 and both have the same expected return. Suppose the firm shows only project 1 to lenders and asks to borrow $7,000. From the lenders' point of view this request seems reasonable because project 1 will always earn enough to pay off the loan. Of course, if creditors lend $7,000 and if the owners of the firm have the ability to switch to project 2, they will do so. (Why?) The result is the transfer of wealth from bondholders to shareholders. Hence bondholders may insist on various types of protective covenants and monitoring devices in order to protect their wealth from raids made on it by shareholders. However, the costs of writing and enforcing

Table 14.6   Two Investment Projects

Probability	Project 1	Project 2
.5	$ 9,000	$ 2,000
.5	11,000	18,000

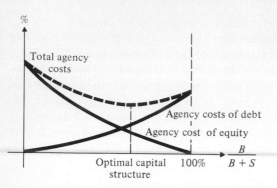

Figure 14.2
Optimal capital structure determined
by minimizing total agency costs.

such covenants may well be nontrivial. Debt holders must charge higher *ex ante* yields to compensate them for possible wealth expropriation by shareholders. Furthermore, these costs may increase with the percentage of financing supplied by bondholders as illustrated in Fig. 14.2.

On the other hand, there are *agency costs associated with external equity.* Suppose we begin with a firm owned exclusively by a single individual, the owner-manager (O-M). The O-M will obviously take every action possible to increase his or her own wealth. For example, if he or she decides to take Wednesday afternoon off, then as owner-manager he or she bears the full cost of doing so. However, if the O-M sells a portion of the ownership rights by selling external equity to new shareholders, there will arise conflicts in interest. Now the O-M is co-owner with the new shareholders. If the O-M can maximize his or her wealth at the expense of the new shareholders (e.g., by purchasing an executive jet and taking long vacations), then he or she will do so. Co-ownership of equity implies agency problems. The new shareholders will have to incur monitoring costs of one form or another in order to ensure that the original owner-manager acts in their interest. It is assumed, as illustrated in Fig. 14.2, that the agency costs of external equity increase as the percentage of financing supplied by external equity goes up. The agency costs of external equity may be reduced if the management and shareholders agree to hire an independent auditor. For an interesting exposition of this idea the reader is referred to an article by Watts and Zimmerman [1979].

Jensen and Meckling suggest that, given increasing agency costs with higher proportions of equity on the one hand and higher proportions of debt on the other, there is an optimum combination of outside debt and equity that will be chosen because it minimizes total agency costs. In this way it is possible to argue for the existence of an optimum capital structure even in a world without taxes or bankruptcy costs.

Figure 14.2 illustrates the Jensen-Meckling argument for an optimal capital structure based on the agency costs of external equity and debt (in a world without taxes). Agency costs of external equity are assumed to decrease as the percentage of external equity decreases, and the agency costs of debt are assumed to increase. Figure 14.2 illustrates a case where total agency costs are minimized with an optimal capital structure between 0% and 100%—an interior solution. If the agency costs of external equity are very low, as may be the case for a widely held firm, then optimal capital structure can result as a trade-off between the tax shelter benefit of debt and its agency cost.

The discussion of agency costs need not be limited to costs associated with providing debt and equity capital. For example, Titman [1984] suggests that agency costs are important for contracts (whether implied or explicit) between the firm and its customers or between the firm and its employees. Consider the relationship between a firm and its customers. If the firm's product is a durable good and requires future services such as parts and repair, the customer is paying not only for ownership of the product but also for the availability of an expected future stream of services. If the firm goes bankrupt, its customers lose their anticipated services without any hope of being compensated. Consequently, they must assess the probability of bankruptcy and weigh it in their decision to purchase durable goods. Firms that produce durable goods will have lower demand for their products if they increase their probability of bankruptcy by carrying more debt. This is an example of an indirect cost of bankruptcy. Ceteris paribus, we would expect durable goods producers to carry less debt.[7] Agency costs in labor contracts are also important. If a firm's labor force has acquired specialized skills that cannot easily be transferred to alternate employment, then laborers bear nontrivial costs if a firm goes bankrupt. They have to search for new jobs and learn new skills. There is no hope that the bankrupt firm will compensate them for their loss. Consequently, if labor markets are competitive, then laborers will charge lower wages to work for a firm that has a lower probability of bankruptcy. Thus we should expect to find that firms that use a larger percentage of job-specific human capital will also tend to carry less debt, ceteris paribus.

5. Contractual Methods for Reducing Agency Costs

There are many ways of avoiding agency costs. But that does not mean they are irrelevant. Perhaps a better way of thinking about agency costs is to recognize that they seem to explain the structure of a wide variety of contracts. In section B.6, e.g., we will discuss bond indenture provisions, commonly used by bondholders to protect themselves from shareholders, i.e., to reduce the agency costs of debt. And here we will focus on secured debt as a way to reduce agency costs.

Secured debt is collateralized by tangible assets owned by the firm. Scott [1976] shows that the optimal leverage may be related to the collateral value of the tangible assets held by the firm. If a firm goes bankrupt, the losses of bondholders are limited by the salvage value of the property held in the firm. If the corporate tax rate is zero, the optimal amount of debt in the capital structure is the discounted value of the liquidation price of the firm's assets in bankruptcy. This approach fits in with that of Jensen and Meckling if the bondholders simply require that the loan be tied to the salvage value of specific assets. Such a scheme considerably reduces

---

[7] An exception might be regulated firms. They can carry more debt because regulatory commissions are expected to "guarantee" a reasonable rate of return. Consequently, bankruptcy is very unlikely.

monitoring costs. For example, many bonds require periodic payments of both principal and interest and are fully amortized. This is a crude way of tying the market value of the debt to the projected liquidation (or resale) value of the underlying assets. An even more extreme method for reducing agency costs, one commonly employed by small firms, is leasing. Leased assets are fully secured because they are literally the property of the lessor and can be repossessed in the event of default on the lease payments.

Stulz and Johnson [1985] prove that secured debt actually increases the value of the firm, rather than merely redistributing wealth among various claim holders. There are two reasons. First, secured debt can decrease debt holders' monitoring costs because the firm cannot sell the collateral to pay dividends, because the collateral cannot be exchanged for a more risky asset, and because secured creditors are less likely to require restrictive covenants about what the firm can or cannot do later on. The second, and perhaps more important, reason is that secured debt makes it more advantageous for shareholders to undertake positive net present value projects. Thus secured debt will be generally preferred to unsecured debt, a result consistent with the Myers-Majluf [1984] story.

6. Bond Indenture Provisions and Bond Rating Agencies

To protect themselves from a wide variety of actions, it is necessary for bondholders to require protective covenants in their lending agreements with shareholders. Although no set of prearranged restrictions can cover every contingency, it is interesting to study the major types of covenants.

The riskiness of bonds, and therefore their required yield, is substantively affected by the bond covenants that are written into the bond contract. A good description of the multitude of specific provisions in debt contracts can be found in the American Bar Association compendium called *Commentaries on Model Debenture Indenture Provisions* [1971]. Bond covenants can be divided into four broad categories: (1) those restricting the issuance of new debt, (2) those with restrictions on dividend payments, (3) those with restrictions on merger activity, and (4) those with restrictions on the disposition of the firm's assets. Smith and Warner [1979] examined a random sample of 87 public issues of debt registered with the Securities and Exchange Commission between January 1974 and December 1975. They observed that fully 90.8% of the bonds restrict the issuance of additional debt, 23% restrict dividend payments, 39.1% restrict merger activity, and 35.6% constrain the firm's disposition of assets.

Bond covenants that restrict subsequent financing are by far the most common type. The provisions are usually stated in terms of accounting numbers and consequently are easy to monitor. The issuance of debt may carry restrictions that require all new debt to be subordinate to existing debt or prohibit the creation of new debt with a higher priority unless existing bonds are upgraded to have an equal priority. All these restrictions are designed to prevent the firm from increasing the riskiness of outstanding debt by issuing new debt with a superior or equal claim on the firm's assets. Alternate restrictions may prohibit the issuance of new debt unless the firm maintains minimum prescribed ratios between net tangible assets and funded (long-term) debt, capitalization and funded debt, tangible net worth and funded debt, income and interest charges, or current assets and current liabilities (working capital tests). There may also be "cleanup" provisions that require the company to be debt free for limited periods.

If there is any advantage to the firm that holds debt in its capital structure, bondholders can benefit by allowing new debt, but only under the condition that acquiring this obligation does not increase the riskiness of their position. Hence an outright prohibition of new debt under any condition is rare.

Other techniques that are used to protect bondholders against subsequent financing include restrictions on rentals, leases, and sale-leaseback agreements; sinking fund requirements (which roughly match the depreciation of the firm's tangible assets); required purchase of insurance; required financial reports and specification of accounting techniques; and required certifications of compliance by the officers of the firm.

Bond covenants that restrict dividend payments are necessary if for no other reason than to prohibit the extreme case of shareholders voting to pay themselves a liquidating dividend that would leave the bondholders holding an empty corporate shell. Kalay [1979] reported that in a random sample of 150 firms every firm had a dividend restriction in at least one of its debt instruments. Restrictions on dividend policy are relatively easy to monitor, and they protect debt holders against the unwarranted payout of the assets that serve as collateral. Appropriately, most indentures refer not only to cash dividends but to all distributions in respect to capital stock, whether they be dividends, redemptions, purchases, retirements, partial liquidations, or capital reductions, and whether in cash, in kind, or in the form of debt obligations to the company. Without such general provisions the firm could, e.g., use cash to repurchase its own shares. From the bondholders' point of view, the effect would be the same as payment of cash dividends.[8] No matter what the procedure is called, once cash is paid out to shareholders, it is no longer available for collateral in the event of reorganization or bankruptcy.

Most restrictions on the payout of the firm's assets require that dividends increase only if the firm's earnings are positive, if the firm issues new equity capital, or if dividends paid out since the bonds were issued have been kept below a predefined minimum level. Mathematically, the "inventory" of funds allowable for dividend payment, Div_T^*, in quarter T, can be expressed as

$$\text{Div}_T^* = K \sum_{t=0}^{T} \text{NI}_t + \sum_{t=0}^{T} S_t + F - \sum_{t=0}^{T-1} \text{Div}_t,$$

where,

NI = net earnings in quarter t,

K = predetermined constant, $0 \le K \le 1$,

S_t = net proceeds from issue of new equity,

F = number fixed over life of bonds, known as the "dip,"

Div_t = dividends paid out in quarter t.

---

[8] See Chapter 16 for empirical evidence regarding the effect of share repurchases on the wealth of bondholders and shareholders.

CAPITAL STRUCTURE: EMPIRICAL EVIDENCE AND APPLICATIONS

Thus the dividend covenant does not restrict dividends per se; rather, it restricts the financing of the payment of dividends with new debt or by sale of the firm's existing assets. This arrangement is in the interest of stockholders because it does not restrict the payment of earned income. It is also in the interest of bondholders because it prevents any dilution of their claim on the firm's assets.

Bond covenants that restrict merger activity prohibit many mergers. More often, though, they will allow mergers, provided certain conditions are met. The effect of a merger on bondholders can be beneficial if the cash flows of the merged firms are not perfectly correlated. Offsetting cash flow patterns can reduce the risk of default, thereby bettering the positions of the bondholders of both firms. Merger can also be detrimental to bondholders. For example, if firm A has much more debt in its capital structure than firm B, the bondholders of B will suffer increased risk after the merger.[9] Or if the maturity of debt in firm A is shorter than for firm B, the bondholders of B will (for all practical purposes) become subordinate to those of firm A after the merger.

To protect against the undesirable effects that can result from a merger, it is possible to require bond covenants that allow merger only if the net tangible assets of the firm, calculated on a postmerger basis, meet a certain dollar minimum or are at least a certain fraction of long-term debt. The merger can also be made contingent on the absence of default of any indenture provision after the transaction is completed.

Bond covenants that restrict production or investment policies are numerous. They are frequently difficult to enforce, however, given the impossibility of effectively monitoring the investment decisions that the managers of the firm decide not to undertake. Myers [1977] suggests that a substantial portion of the value of a firm is composed of intangible assets in the form of future investment opportunities. A firm with outstanding debt may have the incentive to reject projects that have a positive net present value if the benefit from accepting the project accrues to the bondholders without also increasing shareholders' wealth.

Direct restrictions on investment-disinvestment policy take the following forms: (1) restrictions on common stock investments, loans, extensions of credit, and advances that cause the firm to become a claim holder in another business enterprise, (2) restrictions on the disposition of assets, and (3) covenants requiring the maintenance of assets. Secured debt is an indirect restriction on investment policy. Assets that provide surety cannot be disposed of under the provisions of the indenture agreement. Collateralization also reduces foreclosure expenses because the lender already has established title via the bond covenant.

Even though covenants are designed to protect bondholders from various actions that can diminish the surety of their position, no set of covenants can eliminate all risk. Consequently, there is considerable interest in accurate information about changes in the riskiness of corporate debt on a firm-by-firm basis.

The usual method for determining the default risk of corporate long-term debt is to refer to the bond ratings supplied by various agencies. Major bond rating

---

[9] For a more complete exposition, see Shastri [1981].

Table 14.7   Sample of New Issues by Moody's Rating of Issue

Rating	Industrials	% of Total	Utilities	% of Total
Aaa	29	26.1	14	20.6
Aa	18	16.2	14	20.6
A	38	34.3	18	26.5
Baa	20	18.0	20	29.4
Ba	1	0.9	2	2.9
B	5	4.5	0	0
	111	100.0	68	100.0

Adapted from M. Weinstein, "The Effect of a Rating Change Announcement on Bond Price, *Journal of Financial Economics*, December 1977.

agencies are Moody's Investors Service, Inc., Standard & Poor's Corp., and Fitch Investor Service. Moody's bond rating has seven classifications, ranging from Aaa, which is the highest quality bond, down to Caa, the lowest quality. Weinstein [1977] collected data on 179 new bond issues between 1962 and 1964. Table 14.7 shows the distribution by risk class. About 40% of the new bonds qualified for the two highest quality ratings. Figure 14.3 shows the yields on bonds of different risk. Just as expected, the high-quality, low-risk bonds have lower promised yields than do the low-quality, high-risk bonds. A common-sense way of estimating the marginal cost of new debt for a firm (assuming that the new debt will not change the firm's bond rating) is to compute the yield to maturity on other bonds with maturities and bond ratings similar to the new issue.

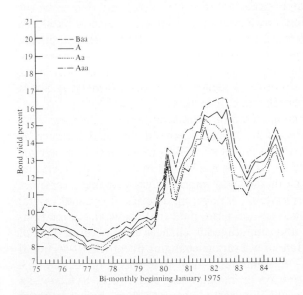

Figure 14.3
Comparison of bond yields for bonds of different risks. (From *Moody's Bond Record*, various issues.)

Of the roughly 2000 major corporations that are evaluated by the agencies, approximately 500 are rerated quarterly because they issue commercial paper, another 500 are rerated annually (most of the utilities), and the remaining 1000 have no established review date but are usually reviewed annually.

From an investor's point of view, one might ask the following question: Do the agencies determine the prices and interest rates paid for bonds or do investors in the capital markets? The evidence collected by Wakeman [1978] and Weinstein [1978] shows that changes in bond ratings are not treated as new information by capital markets. In fact, changes in ratings usually occur several months after the capital markets have already reacted to the fundamental change in the bond's quality. Changes in agency ratings do not cause changes in required yields to maturity. It is the other way around. However, this does not imply that bond ratings are without value. On average the ratings provide unbiased estimates of bond risk and are therefore a useful source of information.

C. EMPIRICAL EVIDENCE ON CAPITAL STRUCTURE

Capital structure is a difficult issue to test empirically. Often, changes in capital structure are made simultaneously with new investment decisions, thus making it nearly impossible to separate the financial impact on firm value from the effect of the investment decision. Additionally, capital structure is difficult to measure. It is hard enough to get good market value data for publicly held debt but nearly impossible to obtain data on privately held debt. Furthermore, the liabilities of the firm (including subsidiary obligations) include leasing contracts, pension liabilities, deferred compensation to management and employees, performance guarantees, lawsuits that are pending, warranties, and contingent securities such as warrants, convertible debt, and convertible preferred stock. Keeping these difficulties in mind, let us take a look at some of the empirical evidence that reveals something about the way that capital structure affects the value of the firm.

There are two broad approaches to empirical tests of capital structure. First are cross-sectional studies that attempt to explain observed financial leverage as a function of the firm's tax rate, its non-debt tax shields, its potential for agency costs (e.g., whether it produces durable goods or has specialized labor), its operating leverage, its systematic risk, etc. The incremental impact of each of these variables on financial leverage can help to separate the competing theories of optimal capital structure. The second broad approach is time series data that looks at the relationship between changes in leverage and simultaneous changes in the value of debt and equity on the announcement date of a leverage-changing event. Cross-sectional studies are discussed in section C.1 and announcement date effects in section C.3. Sandwiched between them is research on exchange offers and swaps. Evidence on the effects of exchange offers is extremely important because they change leverage without simultaneously changing the assets side of the balance sheet.

1. Cross-Sectional Studies

Modigliani and Miller [1958] use cross-section equations on data taken from 43 electric utilities during 1947–1948 and 42 oil companies during 1953. They estimate the weighted average cost of capital (WACC) as net operating cash flows after taxes divided by the market value of the firm.[10] When regressed against financial leverage (measured as the ratio of the market value of debt to the market value of the firm), the results were:[11]

$$\text{Electric utilities:} \quad \text{WACC} = 5.3 + .006d, \quad r = .12,$$
$$(.008)$$

$$\text{Oil companies:} \quad \text{WACC} = 8.5 + .006d, \quad r = .04,$$
$$(.024)$$

where d is the financial leverage of the firm and r is the correlation coefficient. These results suggest that the cost of capital is not affected by capital structure and therefore that there is no gain to leverage.

Weston [1963] criticizes the Modigliani-Miller results on two counts. First, the oil industry is not even approximately homogeneous in business risk (operating leverage); second, the valuation model from which the cost of capital is derived assumes that cash flows are perpetuities that do not grow. When growth is added to the cross-section regression, the result for electric utilities becomes

$$\text{WACC} = 5.91 - .0265d + .00A - .0822E, \quad r = .5268,$$
$$(.0079) \quad (.0001) \quad (.0024)$$

where A is the book value of assets (a proxy for firm size), and E is the compound growth in earnings per share (1949–1959). Since WACC decreases with leverage, Weston's results are consistent with the existence of a gain to leverage, i.e., that the tax shield on debt has value.

Later on, Miller and Modigliani [1966] also found results (based on a sample of 63 electric utility firms in 1954, 1956, and 1957) that were consistent with a gain from leverage. Table 14.8 summarizes their results. The value of the firm is attributed to the present value of the operating cash flows generated by assets in place, by the tax subsidy on debt, by growth potential, and by firm size. For our purposes the important result is that the empirical evidence indicates that the tax subsidy (i.e., the gain from leverage) on debt does contribute a significant amount to the value of the firm, about 26% on average. This is consistent with the notion that the firm's WACC falls as leverage increases.

---

[10] Net operating cash flows after taxes were actually estimated as net income after taxes plus interest payments on debt. This assumes that there is no growth in earnings and that replacement investment equals depreciation expense.

[11] Standard errors are in parentheses.

Table 14.8 Sources Contributing to the Value of the Firm

	Absolute Contribution			Percentage Contribution		
Source	1957	1956	1954	1957	1956	1954
1. Value of assets in place	.758	.808	.914	68.1	72.0	75.9
2. Tax subsidy on debt	.262	.254	.258	23.5	22.6	23.7
3. Growth potential	.112	.072	.028	10.0	6.4	2.3
4. Size of firm	−.019	−.008	−.021	−1.7	−.7	−1.7
Avg. (market/book) value	1.113	1.123	1.204	100.0	100.0	100.0

From M. Miller and F. Modigliani, "Some Estimates of the Cost of Capital to the Electric Utility Industry, 1954–57," *American Economic Review*, June 1966, 373. Reprinted by permission of the authors.

Cordes and Sheffrin [1983] use Treasury Department data to examine cross-sectional differences in effective tax rates that may be caused by tax carry-backs and carry-forwards, by foreign tax credits, by investment tax credits, by the alternate tax on capital gains, and by the minimum tax. They found significant differences across industries with the highest effective rate for tobacco manufacturing (45%) and the lowest rate (16%) for transportation and agriculture. This tends to support the DeAngelo-Masulis [1980] contention that the gain from leverage-induced tax shields can be positive.

An important part of the Modigliani-Miller theory is that the cost of equity capital increases with higher leverage. Hamada [1972] tests this proposition empirically by combining the Modigliani-Miller theory and the CAPM. He finds that on the average the systematic risk of the levered firm is greater than that for the unlevered firm:

$$\hat{\beta}^L = .91, \qquad \hat{\beta}^U = .70.$$

This, of course, is consistent with the increased risk associated with higher leverage. However, in order to construct the return on equity for an unlevered firm, Hamada had to assume that the Modigliani-Miller theory was correct. Suppose that it is not correct. Namely, what would happen if the return on equity (i.e., the cost of equity capital) did not increase with increasing leverage? We would expect that for a sample of firms with the same operating risk there would be no increase in systematic risk with higher financial leverage. Because it is almost impossible to find firms with identical operating risk, Hamada suggests that within an industry if the β^U-values of individual firms are closer or less scattered than their β^L-values, then the Modigliani-Miller theory would be supported. Greater variability in the β^L-values implies that the cost of equity changes with financial leverage. In nine industries examined, β^L was greater than β^U in all cases, and the standard deviation of the β^L-values was greater than eight out of nine of the β^U-values. This may be taken as indirect evidence that the cost of equity increases with higher financial leverage.

Recent cross-sectional work has been done by Bradley, Jarrell, and Kim [1984], Long and Malitz [1985], and Titman and Wessels [1985]. Bradley, Jarrell, and Kim regressed leverage against (1) earnings volatility as a proxy for bankruptcy risk, (2) the ratio of depreciation plus investment tax credits to earnings as a proxy for non-debt tax shields, and (3) the ratio of advertising plus research and development expenditures to net sales as a proxy for noncollateralizable assets. The first and third variables were significantly negative, supporting the importance of bankruptcy costs and collateral; but the second variable was significantly positive, seeming to be inconsistent with debt as a tax shield. Long and Malitz estimate a similar regression but add several additional variables. They obtain results similar to Bradley, Jarrell, and Kim but find non-debt tax shields to be negatively related to leverage (although not significant).

Titman and Wessels employ linear structural modeling to explicitly accommodate explanatory variables as proxies for their theoretical counterparts. Their results show that asset uniqueness and profitability were significantly negatively related to leverage. This result supports the Myers-Majluf [1984] pecking order theory, because more profitable firms will tend to use less external financing. It also supports the Titman [1984] idea that firms with unique assets can carry less debt owing to agency costs.

2. Evidence Based on Exchange Offers and Swaps

In an exchange offer or swap, one class of securities is exchanged for another in a deal that involves no cash. The most important feature is that with exchange offers there is no simultaneous change in the asset structure of the firm. Therefore they represent a relatively pure type of financial event that allows the researcher to isolate the effects of changes in capital structure on the firm. Consequently, exchange offers are one of the most intensively studied financial change phenomena.

For a sample containing 106 leverage-increasing and 57 leverage-decreasing exchange offers during the period 1962 through 1976, Masulis [1980] found highly significant announcement effects. For the *Wall Street Journal* announcement date and the following day, the announcement period return is 7.6% for leverage-increasing exchange offers and -5.4% for leverage-decreasing exchange offers.

These results are possibly consistent with three theories (1) that there is a valuable tax shield created when financial leverage is increased (and vice versa), (2) that debt holders' wealth is being expropriated by shareholders in leverage-increasing offers, and (3) that higher leverage is a signal of management's confidence in the future of the firm.

A leverage-increasing exchange offer can be damaging to original bondholders if they have imperfect protective covenants in the bond indentures. Masulis [1980] directly examines a sample of 18 nonconvertible debt issues without any covenants to protect against the issuance of new debt with equal seniority. The announcement period return is $-.84\%$ with a statistically significant t-test of 2.7. This result is consistent with expropriation of bondholder wealth. However, a larger sample of all nonconvertible debt issues (with and without protective covenants) experiences a negative .3% two-day announcement return. In general the empirical evidence does not strongly support the bondholder expropriation hypothesis.

Preferred-for-common exchange offers provide an indirect test of the interest tax shield hypothesis because preferred dividends are not tax deductible. Preferred-for-common exchange offers have no tax consequences. Masulis [1980] finds a statistically significant positive 3.3% common stock two-day announcement return for a sample of 43 preferred-for-common exchange offers and a significant positive 3.6% return for 43 debt-for-preferred exchange offers.[12] Pinegar and Lease [1986] find a statistically significant 4.05% positive common stock return for 15 leverage-increasing preferred-for-common exchange offers. The equity return for leverage-decreasing exchange offers is a significantly negative .73% (30 observations). These results favor the signaling hypothesis over the tax hypothesis but cannot be used to reject the tax hypothesis because it may still be relevant in those types of exchange offer where the interest tax shield is affected. Pinegar and Lease also find that preferred shareholders experience a significant 6.58% positive return during leverage-decreasing exchange offers, although total firm value (equity plus debt plus preferred) is estimated to decrease. They conclude that their results are consistent with the signaling hypothesis (firm value decreases) and with the expropriation hypothesis (preferred stock value increases).

Masulis [1980], in a cross-sectional study of the announcement returns of 133 exchange offers, finds evidence to support the conclusion that stock prices are positively related to leverage changes because of (1) a gain in value induced by tax shields on debt and (2) a positive signaling effect. Also, he concludes that leverage increases induce wealth transfers across security classes, with the greatest effect on unprotected nonconvertible debt.

Lee [1987] provides evidence that further strengthens the signaling interpretation of exchange offers. He notes that insiders typically do not sell their shares during the offer. Thus, for leverage-increasing exchanges, insiders' ownership in the firm increases when outsiders' shares are repurchased with debt. In support of the signaling hypothesis he finds (1) that 61 of 90 firms with leverage-increasing exchange offers experience decreases in systematic risk following the completion date and that 75 of 127 leverage-decreasing firms experience increases in systematic risk, (2) that earnings, sales, and capital expenditures per share (adjusted for the exchange offer) all increase following leverage-increasing exchange offers; and (3) that there were net insider purchases of stock prior to leverage-increasing exchange offer announcements for 36 of 40 events (where data were available) and net insider sales for 56 of 96 leverage-decreasing events.

On balance the empirical evidence from studying exchange offers is weakly consistent with tax effects (a gain to leverage) and with bondholder expropriation but is strongly consistent with management use of exchange offers to take advantage of superior information concerning the future prospects of the firm. The market interprets leverage-increasing offers as good news and leverage-decreasing offers as bad news.

---

[12] Returns for leverage-decreasing offers were multiplied by -1.0 and added to the returns of leverage-increasing offers.

Table 14.9 Announcement Effects of Corporate Events

Announcement	Security Issued	Security Retired	Average Sample Size	Two-day Return
Leverage-increasing:				
Stock repurchase	Debt	Common	45	21.9%
Exchange offer	Debt	Common	52	14.0
Exchange offer	Preferred	Common	9	8.3
Exchange offer	Debt	Preferred	24	2.2
Exchange offer	Income bonds	Preferred	24	2.2
Security sale (industrials)	Debt	None	248	−.3*
Security sale (utilities)	Debt	None	140	−1*
No−leverage change:				
Exchange offer	Debt	Debt	36	0.6*
Security sale	Debt	Debt	83	0.2*
Equity carve-out	Equity	Equity	76	0.7*
Security sale (dual offering)	Debt and equity	None	51	−2.6
Security sale	Convertible debt	None	132	−2.3
Security sale	Preferred	None	102	0.1*
Leverage-decreasing:				
Conversion-forcing call	Common	Convertible preferred	57	−0.4*
Conversion-forcing call	Common	Convertible bond	113	−2.1
Security sale	Convertible debt	Debt	15	−2.4
Exchange offer	Common	Preferred	30	−2.6
Exchange offer	Common	Debt	20	−9.9
Exchange offer	Preferred	Debt	9	−7.7
Security sale (industrials)	Common	None	388	−3.2
Security sale (utilities)	Common	None	584	−0.6
Investment				
Increases	None	None	510	1.0
Decreases	None	None	111	−1.1
Dividends				
Increases	None	None	280	0.9
Decreases	None	None	48	−3.6

* Interpreted as statistically insignificant.

3. Time Series Studies: Announcement Effects

Given the plausibility of the signaling hypothesis, it is interesting to take empirical results on dozens of different corporate events and compare them. Smith [1986] suggests that they be compared in two dimensions—events that increase financial leverage (a favorable signal) and those that imply favorable future cash flow changes.

Table 14.9 summarizes the two-day announcement effects for a wide variety of corporate events. We have already discussed exchange offers, which are purely financial changes. Generally speaking, leverage-increasing exchange offers have significant positive announcement effects. Exchanges of debt-for-debt, studied by Dietrich [1984], have no significant effect on shareholders' wealth, and leverage-decreasing exchange offers have a significant negative effect.

Stock repurchases and seasoned equity offerings are at the opposite end of the scale. Evidence by Masulis and Korwar [1986], Asquith and Mullins [1986], Kolodny and Suhler [1985], and Mikkelson and Partch [1986] indicates that issues of seasoned equity are interpreted as bad news by the marketplace, with significantly negative announcement date effects on equity prices. This result is consistent with the Myers-Majluf [1984] "pecking order" theory of capital structure. Firms will resort to equity issues only as a last resort. It is interesting to note that the negative announcement date residuals are large (-3.2%) for industrial firms that issue equity infrequently and small ($-.6\%$) for utilities that are frequent issuers. This result, too, seems to be consistent with the pecking order theory. Stock repurchases are at the opposite end of the spectrum. They increase leverage and they are interpreted as favorable signals about the future prospects of the firm. The announcement residuals are extremely large—positive 21.9% for repurchases where debt is issued to retire common and 14.0% for exchange offers of debt for common.

All leverage-decreasing events have negative announcement effects, and all leverage-increasing events, save one, have positive announcement effects. The exception

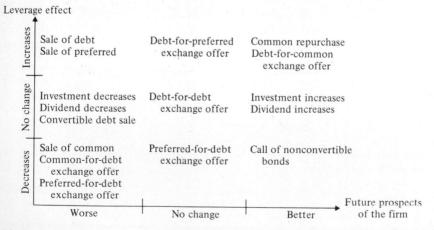

Figure 14.4
Two dimensions of announcement effects.

is the new issue of debt securities where Dann and Mikkelson [1984], Eckbo [1986], and Mikkelson and Partch [1986] found negative but insignificant announcement effects. This result is also consistent with the pecking order theory. The majority of events with no leverage change had insignificant announcement effects.

Announcements with favorable (unfavorable) implications for the future cash flows of the firm such as investment increases (decreases) and dividend increases (decreases) were accompanied by significant positive (negative) effects on shareholders' wealth.

With these results in mind, it is tempting to try to place each type of corporate event into the two dimensions of Fig. 14.4. Not all events fit neatly. Yet there does seem to be a convincing pattern. Events that both increase leverage and provide a favorable signal about the future prospects of the firm, common share repurchases, and debt-for-common exchange offers seem to have the largest positive announcement effects.

D. COST OF CAPITAL: APPLICATIONS

Even when one is very familiar with the theoretical concept of the cost of capital, it is not a straightforward or easy task to apply the theory to practice. Too often one is confronted with questions not made explicit because theoretical expositions are deliberately oversimplified. For example, how do unusual liabilities such as accruals, preferred debt, convertibles, or accounts payable affect the cost of capital? How should the market value weights of various sources of capital be estimated? How can one tell whether or not the firm is at its long-run target capital structure? This section further develops some of the cost of capital example calculations given in Chapter 13. First, however, a simple example shows how firms with high price/earnings ratios may choose to carry no debt—for the wrong reason. Second, a detailed cost of capital calculation is given for Bethlehem Steel. Third, the debt refunding and defeasance decisions are analyzed. And finally, the effect of flotation costs on the cost of capital is discussed.

1. The Wrong Reason for Carrying No Debt: An Example

Companies with high price/earnings ratios can increase their accounting earnings per share by issuing new equity and using the funds to buy back debt. Carried to the extreme, this process results in an optimal capital structure that contains zero debt. Much of the theory in Chapter 13 and the empirical evidence earlier in this chapter suggest that this idea is wrong. In fact, just the opposite is true. If there is a tax advantage to carrying debt, then shareholders' wealth will be increased if there is at least some debt. Nothing in the theory suggests that zero debt is optimal. Yet consider the following example and see whether you can identify the error in its logic.

Betamax currently has a price/earnings ratio of 50. Before the change in capital structure it has 10 shares outstanding; therefore its earnings per share is $1.00, and

Table 14.10   Higher Earnings per Share with Lower Leverage

Income Statement	Before	After
Net operating income	100	100
Interest expense	−80	−40
Earnings before taxes	20	60
Taxes at 50%	−10	−30
Net income	10	30
Earnings per share	$1.00	$1.50

Balance Sheet

Before				After			
Assets		Liabilities		Assets		Liabilities	
Current	200	Debt	1000	Current	200	Debt	500
Long-term	1300	Equity	500	Long-term	1300	Equity	1000
	1500		1500		1500		1500

the price per share is $50. If 10 new shares are issued at $50 each, $500 is collected and used to retire $500 of debt (which pays a coupon rate of 8%). After the capital structure change, earnings per share have increased to $1.50 per share (since there are now 20 shares outstanding), and with a price/earnings ratio of 50, presumably the price per share will increase from $50 before the capital structure change to $75 afterward. The pro forma income statements and balance sheets are shown in Table 14.10.

The above example shows that if a firm with a high price/earnings ratio seeks to maximize earnings per share, it will carry little or no debt. The problem of course is that shareholders care about net cash flows (and the gain from leverage), not earnings per share. In the above example, the change in operating cash flows is zero. Before debt is retired, cash flow (neglecting depreciation, which is not given anyway) is equal to net income, $10, plus interest on debt after taxes $(1 - \tau_c) \Delta(k_d D)$, $40, or a total of $50.[13] After the swap of stock for bonds the cash flow is still $50. If there were no gain from leverage, the value of the firm would be unchanged. However, because there is a leverage effect in a world with corporate taxes, the value of the firm will actually fall, because leverage declines.

Using the Modigliani-Miller valuation model, Eq. (13.3), we can calculate the decrease in the value of the firm. The value of the firm before the change is

$$V^L = \frac{E(\text{NOI})(1 - \tau_c)}{\rho} + \left(\frac{k_d D}{k_b}\right)\tau_c, \tag{13.3}$$

---

[13] This method for computing cash flows is covered in Chapter 2, footnote 15.

where

V^L = the market value of debt, B, plus the market value of equity, S,

$E(\text{NOI})$ = the expected operating income, \$100,

τ_c = the marginal corporate tax rate, 50%,

ρ = the cost of equity for an all-equity firm,

k_d = the coupon rate on bonds, 8%,

k_b = the market rate on new debt, 8%,

D = the book value of debt, \$1000.

Using the numbers in the Betamax example, we have

$$500 + 1000 = \frac{100(1 - .5)}{\rho} + \left[\frac{.08(1000)}{.08}\right].5.$$

Solving for ρ, the cost of equity for the unlevered firm, we have[14]

$$\rho = 5\%.$$

We can use the fact that ρ does not change when capital structure changes to determine the value of the firm after the repurchase of debt. Substituting the new, lower amount of debt into Eq. (13.3), we have

$$V^L = \frac{100(1 - .5)}{.05} + \left[\frac{.08(500)}{.08}\right].5 = \$1250.$$

Therefore the value of the firm has fallen from \$1500 to \$1250. Since $V^L = B + S$, the new value of equity is \$1250 - 500 = \$750.

We might also ask what the new price per share will be. It is common to assume that new shares can be issued at the preswap price of \$50. If this is the assumption, then 10 new shares are issued, bringing the total number of shares outstanding to 20 and the implied price per share to \$37.50.

Another (better) approach requires that we compute the new equilibrium price per share in order to determine the number of shares that must be issued in order to supply the \$500 needed for the proposed exchange offer. We know that the value of equity *after* the exchange, $S_0 + \Delta S$, is equal to the number of original shares, $n^0 = 10$, times the new price per share, P^n, plus the number of new shares n^n times the new price per share:

$$S_0 + \Delta S = n^0 P^n + n^n P^n = \$750.$$

We also know that the number of new shares times the price per share, $n^n P^n$, must equal the dollar amount of bonds repurchased, $\Delta B^n < 0$. Therefore

$$-\Delta B^n = n^n P^n = \$500.$$

---

[14] The astute reader will recognize that ρ, the cost of equity for the unlevered firm, is less than k_b, the before-tax cost of debt. This relationship is feasible in the presence of risky debt.

Combining these two expressions, we can solve for the price per share *after* the exchange offer:

$$S_0 + \Delta S = n^0 P^n + \Delta B^n,$$

$$\frac{S_0 + \Delta S - \Delta B^n}{n^0} = P^n,$$

$$\frac{\$750 - \$500}{10} = \$25 \text{ per share.}$$

Hence the firm will need to issue 20 new shares at $25 each in order to raise the $500 needed for the exchange. After the deal the total number of shares outstanding rises to 30, the price per share will fall from $50 to $25, earnings per share is $1, not $1.50, and the price/earnings ratio declines from 50 to 25.

2. The Cost of Capital: An Example Calculation (Bethlehem Steel)

From Chapter 13 we have two seemingly different, yet equivalent, definitions of the weighted average cost of capital. Equation (13.12), given below, is the Modigliani-Miller requirement that projects earn enough cash flow to increase the wealth of the original shareholders:

$$\text{WACC} = \rho\left(1 - \tau_c \frac{\Delta B}{\Delta I}\right), \tag{13.12}$$

where

ρ = the cost of equity for an all-equity firm,

τ_c = the marginal corporate tax rate,

ΔB = the market value of new debt,

ΔI = the replacement cost of new investment.

Given that the firm is at its long-run "optimal capital structure," we can say that an equivalent definition of the weighted average cost of capital is the weighted average of the marginal costs of various sources of capital, Eq. (13.19):

$$\text{WACC} = (1 - \tau_c)k_b \frac{B}{B + S} + k_s \frac{S}{B + S}. \tag{13.19}$$

To compute the weighted average cost of capital by means of Eq. (13.19), we must know (1) the marginal cost of debt and equity, k_b and k_s, and (2) the market value capital structure used by the firm.

Although we use the term *weighted average cost of capital* to mean the cost of a mixture of sources of funds, it is important to emphasize that the costs of these funds must be measured as *marginal* costs. Hence the weighted average cost of capital is a weighted average of the marginal costs of the firm's various sources of capital. In this context the word *marginal* has two meanings. Foremost is that marginal cost means

Table 14.11 Pro Forma Balance Sheet, Bethlehem Steel, December 1976 (in thousands of dollars)

Assets		Liabilities	
Cash	45,600	Accounts payable	274,800
Marketable securities	355,600	Notes payable	—
Receivables	421,500	Accruals	948,600
Inventories	834,100	Long-term debt[a]	1,023,100
Other assets	274,700	Common stock at par[b]	576,000
Long-term assets (net)	3,007,600	Less Treasury stock	69,300
Total assets	4,939,100	Retained earnings	2,185,900
		Total liabilities	4,939,100

[a] Long-term debt is detailed in Table 14.12.
[b] 43,665,578 shares outstanding with a market price of $40\frac{5}{8}$ per share on December 31, 1976.

the cost of *new* financing at current market equilibrium rates of return—not historical cost. Second, and implied in the rate of return required by the market, is the impact of new financing on the perceived capital structure of the firm. For example, if the percentage of debt is perceived to be rising, the marginal cost of debt must include its impact on the weighted average cost of capital. We shall ignore this second possibility by adopting the convention that the firm establishes a target capital structure and sticks with it. Given this assumption, Eqs. (13.12) and (13.19) are identical. Consequently, there are no changes in leverage to complicate matters.

Some of the complexities that arise while we estimate the cost of capital are illustrated by the following example, the cost of capital for Bethlehem Steel Corporation during December 1976. Because market-equilibrium conditions change from day to day, so does the cost of capital. Therefore, the estimate that is given below is only an historical number, valid at the end of 1976.

Bethlehem Steel is the second-largest producer of steel in the United States. It manufactures steel products for markets in construction, transportation, service centers, and machinery. It also produces minerals and plastic products for industrial uses. Table 14.11 provides a simplified pro forma balance sheet.[15] To estimate a weighted average cost of capital we need the marginal cost of each capital source and the appropriate weighting scheme.

A. THE COST OF LONG-TERM DEBT. The first problem is estimating the current market rate of return that would be required if the firm issued new long-term debt. (See Table 14.12.) Almost all of Bethlehem Steel's long-term debt has had a maturity of 25 to 30 years when first issued. Therefore we will assume that any new long-term debt will also be issued with a 30-year maturity and an Aa bond rating. What rate of return would the market require for a new issue with this risk? The "yield" provided by *Wall Street Journal* is not useful because it assumes an infinite maturity for the debt.

---

[15] Data taken from *Moody's Industrial Manual*.

Table 14.12   Composition of Long-term Debt (in thousands of dollars) in Table 14.11

Issue	Rating	Amount	Call Price	Recent Price	Yield	Year of Issue
Consol. Mtge. S.F. 3s, K, 1979	Aa	21,800	$100\frac{1}{8}$	NA	NA	1949
Debenture $3\frac{1}{4}$s, 1980	Aa	3,100	100	$89\frac{1}{2}$	3.6	1955
Debenture 5.40s, 1992	Aa	109,200	$102\frac{1}{2}$	$84\frac{3}{8}$	6.4	1967
Debenture $6\frac{7}{8}$s, 1999	Aa	85,800	$104\frac{1}{4}$	$94\frac{1}{4}$	6.6	1969
Debenture 9s, 2000	Aa	144,000	$105\frac{1}{2}$	$106\frac{1}{2}$	8.5	1970
Debenture 8.45s, 2005	Aa	250,000	107.45	$103\frac{1}{2}$	8.2	1975
Debenture $8\frac{3}{8}$s, 2001	Aa	200,000	106.63	$105\frac{1}{2}$	7.9	1976
Subord. Deb. $4\frac{1}{4}$s, 1990	A	94,500	102.40	$76\frac{1}{4}$	5.9	1965
Notes payable	—	30,000	—	NA	NA	NA
Subsidiary debt	—	3,200	—	NA	NA	NA
Revenue bonds $5\frac{1}{4}$s–6s, 2002	—	100,000	—	NA	NA	NA

NA = not applicable.

For example, take the $3\frac{1}{4}\%$ debentures that were due in 1980. The "yield" is the coupon divided by the market price:

$$\text{Yield} = \frac{32.50}{895.00} = 3.6\%.$$

This number is completely unrealistic. The required market rate of return is the rate that equates the discounted value of the expected future cash flows with the current market price of the security. We can find this rate by solving Eq. (14.5) for the before-tax cost of debt, k_b:

$$B_j = \sum_{t=1}^{T} \frac{E(\text{coupon})_t}{(1 + k_{bj})^t} + \frac{E(\text{face value})}{(1 + k_{bj})^T}, \tag{14.5}$$

where

$E(\text{coupon})$ = the expected coupon payment in year t (assumed to be \$32.50),

$E(\text{face value})$ = the expected face value (assumed to be \$1000),

$\qquad T$ = number of years to maturity,

$\qquad B_j$ = market value of the jth debt issue.

Note that we have assumed that the bond rated Aa will actually pay its full face value of \$1000 when it matures. This may not always be a valid assumption. If the bond is very risky, the expected payout may be less than \$1000. (Or if the bond is callable, the expected payout may be more than \$1000 and the time to maturity may be less than T if the bond is called early.) Given the above assumptions about the expected payout of the $3\frac{1}{4}\%$ debentures, the current required rate of return from them is approximately 8%. At the end of 1976, this was the appropriate interest rate for an

Table 14.13 Market Value Weights of Capital Sources

	Market Value (in thousands of dollars)	Percent	Cost (in percent)
Accounts payable and accruals	1,223,400	32.1	
Notes payable	0	0.0	4.9
Long-term debt	815,945	21.4	8.3
Equity	1,773,914	46.5	13.5
		100.0	

Aa-rated debenture due to mature in around four years.[16] Bonds with the same rating but longer maturities are slightly riskier and therefore yield higher rates. For example, the 8.45s maturing in the year 2005 yield approximately 8.3%. In our judgment, if Bethlehem Steel had decided to issue new long-term debt in December 1976 with an Aa bond rating and a maturity of between 25 and 30 years, the company would have had to pay approximately 8.3%. We shall use this as the before-tax cost, k_b, of long-term debt, because it is the best estimate of the marginal cost of *new* debt. Next we need an estimate of the percentage of long-term debt, $B/(B + S)$, used by Bethlehem in its target capital structure. Table 14.13 shows the market value weights of various capital sources.

B. MARKET VALUE WEIGHTS.   The market value weights of long-term debt and equity are obvious. For long-term debt we use the market values from Table 14.13, and when they are unavailable, we use book value. The market value of equity is simply the number of shares outstanding multiplied by the price per share. Short-term liabilities are calculated at book value. This is not an unreasonable assumption because, under normal circumstances, the market value of short-term debt rarely deviates much from its book value. We assume that the current market weights are a reasonable estimate of the firm's long-run "optimal" target capital structure. A quick, but somewhat unreliable, way of checking this assumption is to observe that the book value of long-term debt is currently 27.5% of total long-term debt plus equity. Its high between 1970 and 1976 was 27.5%, the average was 23.4%, and the low was 20.67%. Therefore the current capital structure is not too far from the normal pattern observed in recent years.

---

[16] Coupon payments of $16.25 per $1000 are made every May first and November first. The issue matured on May 1, 1980. Therefore the actual computation is more complicated than Eq. (14.5). Students familiar with the actuarial complexities of discounting formulas will find the exact calculation to be

$$\frac{895.00}{(1 + k_{bj})^{1/6}} = \left\{ \frac{32.50}{2} \left[\frac{1 - (1 + k_{bj}/2)^{-6}}{k_{bj}/2} \right] + \frac{1016.25}{(1 + k_{bj}/2)^7} \right\},$$

where $k_{bj}/2$ is a semiannual nominal rate. The solution to this problem provides an annual effective rate of approximately 8%.

C. THE COST OF SHORT-TERM LIABILITIES. The cost of short-term liabilities is an often-debated topic. One technique is to ignore it completely by arguing that payables and accruals may be thought of as "free" capital, because in the capital budgeting process such spontaneously generated funds may be netted out against the required investment outlay. There are two alternatives. One is to include short-term liabilities as one of the components of the weighted average cost of capital and to use a short-term interest rate, such as the commercial paper rate (which was 4.91% in December 1976) to approximate their cost. The problem with this approach is that the costs of noninterest-bearing short-term liabilities such as accruals and accounts payable is already implicitly accounted for in the cash flows from operations. For example, industries with generous trade credit terms on accounts payable will charge higher prices than they otherwise might in order to compensate for the cost of extending trade credit. Consequently, trade credit is implicitly included in the cost of goods sold for firms purchasing the products of those industries. The opportunity cost of accruals is more difficult to justify, but the lender, whether it be the government or an unpaid worker, almost surely has an opportunity cost that is accounted for in tax or wage rates. If the cost of trade credit and accruals are already deducted from cash flows from operations, then there is no need to adjust the cost of capital. Therefore we recommend a second alternative, namely, that one should include interest-bearing short-term liabilities (such as notes due) in the weighted average cost of capital but exclude noninterest-bearing items such as accounts payable and accruals.

Using the recommended approach, the market value weights, when expressed as a percentage of notes payable, long-term debt, and equity are given in Table 14.14.

D. THE COST OF EQUITY. We can use the CAPM to estimate the cost of equity, but two of the important parameters are judgmental. Equation (14.6) gives the CAPM equation for the cost of equity:

$$k_s = R_f + [E(R_m) - R_f]\beta_s. \tag{14.6}$$

The expected future rate of return on the market cannot be measured. However, a good way of guessing what it might be is to add three components: (1) the real rate of growth of the economy, 2% to 3%, (2) an adjustment for inflation next year (in December 1976 a good guess might have been 5% to 6%), and (3) a risk premium for

Table 14.14 Market Value Weights Excluding Noninterest-Bearing Liabilities

	Market Value (in thousands)	Percent	Cost
Notes due	0	0	4.9
Long-term debt	$ 815,945	31.5	8.3
Equity	1,773,914	68.5	13.5
		100.0	

the riskiness of the market portfolio (say 6% to 7%). Using the mean of each of these components, we estimate the expected rate of return as 14.5%. The risk-free rate may be approximated by the 90-day rate on U.S. government Treasury bills, which in December 1976 was 4.67%. Finally, we need an estimate of the systematic risk of the common stock of the company, which was .9.[17] This is really an estimate of the future systematic risk of Bethlehem Steel, and it is as much a guess as is the future rate of return on the market index. Substituting these parameter estimates into Eq. (14.6), we estimate the cost of equity capital to be 13.52%.

E. THE WEIGHTED AVERAGE COST OF CAPITAL.   Finally, by using the market value weights and capital costs in Table 14.14 we can estimate the weighted average cost of capital for Bethlehem Steel as of December 1976 by using Eq. (13.19) and a marginal corporate tax rate assumed to be 48%. The weighted average cost of capital is 10.61%. The calculation is given below:

$$\text{WACC} = (1 - \tau_c)k_{bj}\frac{B_j}{\Sigma B_j + S} + k_s\frac{S}{\Sigma B_j + S},$$

where

k_{bj} = the before-tax cost of the jth nonequity liability (e.g. k_{b1} is notes due and k_{b2} is long-term debt),

B_j = the market value of the jth nonequity liability,

k_s = the cost of equity,

S = the market value of equity.

Thus

$$\text{WACC} = (1 - .48)(0.0)(.049) + (1 - .48)(.083)(.315) + .135(.685) = 10.61\%.$$

3. Debt Refunding and Defeasance

In an era of falling interest rates a firm may find itself with bonds outstanding that pay a coupon rate higher than the prevailing market rate. A net present value analysis will reveal whether the outstanding bonds should be called or, if they are not callable, repurchased on the open market.[18] Almost all public bond issues have a call provision allowing the firm to force recall of the debt at a call premium.

---

[17] There are several companies that publish estimates of the systematic risk of individual firms. We used an estimate provided by Wilshire Associates, Santa Monica, California.

[18] The accounting treatment of bond repurchase when bonds are selling at a discount can cause extremely perverse behavior. Suppose that interest rates have risen, thereby causing fixed rate outstanding debt to sell at a discount. Repurchase of this debt at market value has no economic gain or loss before taxes because the firm is paying the fair market price. However, the accounting treatment allows the firm to record the difference between the face value and the market value as profit. Therefore firms that desire to increase their reported earnings per share may decide to repurchase discounted debt. Unfortunately, this is a negative present value decision because the firm has to pay (1) ordinary income taxes on its paper gain and (2) higher coupons on replacement debt.

To provide a focus for the analysis, consider the following facts. The L and S Company has a $10,000,000 bond issue outstanding with five years to maturity and a coupon rate of 16%, and with annual interest payments. The current market rate on debt of equivalent risk is 10%. The call price on the $1,000 face value debt is $1,050, and the firm has a 40% tax rate. What is the net present value of calling the outstanding bonds and replacing them with new bonds of equivalent maturity and risk? Assume no transactions costs.

This is a capital budgeting decision and the usual procedures apply. The changes in the after-tax cash flows should be discounted at the appropriate risk-adjusted after-tax discount rate. In this case the appropriate rate is the after-tax rate on debt of equivalent risk, i.e., $(1 - \tau_c)k_b = (1 - .4).10 = .06$. The after-tax cash flows have three components (in a world without transactions costs).

1. The *call premium* will cost $500,000. It is deductible as an expense; therefore its after-tax cost is $500,000(1 - .4) = $300,000.

2. The new debt issue will have to be $10,300,000, and it will pay a 10% coupon $(r_2 = 10\%)$; thus the new interest will be $1,030,000 per year. The old interest was 16% $(r_1 = 16\%)$ of $10,000,000, or $1,600,000 per year. Therefore the *after-tax interest saving* amounts to $(1 - \tau_c)(r_1 - r_2)B - (1 - \tau_c)r_2 \Delta B$, where B is the original book value and ΔB is the change in book value. Numerically the annual interest savings is

$$(1 - .4)(.16 - .10)(10,000,000) - (1 - .4)(.10)(300,000) = 342,000.$$

3. *Incremental principal* on the new debt, namely, $300,000, must be paid off at maturity.

The net present value of these components is

$$\text{NPV} = \sum_{t=1}^{N} \frac{(1 - \tau_c)(r_1 - r_2)B}{[1 + (1 - \tau_c)k_b]^t} - \sum_{t=1}^{N} \frac{(1 - \tau_c)r_2 \Delta B}{[1 + (1 - \tau_c)k_b]^t} - \frac{\Delta B}{[1 + (1 - \tau_c)k_b]^N}$$

$$= \sum_{t=1}^{5} \frac{(1 - .4)(.16 - .10)10,000,000}{[1 + (1 - .4)(.10)]^t} - \sum_{t=1}^{5} \frac{(1 - .4).10(300,000)}{[1 + (1 - .4)(.10)]^t}$$

$$- \frac{300,000}{[1 + (1 - .4)(.10)]^5}$$

$$= 1,516,464 - 75,823 - 224,190$$

$$= 1,216,451.$$

Therefore the debt should be refunded.

Two additional issues are pertinent. First, we should consider the fact that the debt refinancing will slightly alter the capital structure of the firm because the market value of the new debt issue exceeds the market value of the outstanding debt. This may create a tax gain from leverage. The second issue is that callable debt should never sell for more than the call price plus a small premium approximately equal to the flotation costs of exercising the call. No investor would rationally pay $1100 for a bond that might be called (any minute) at $1050.

Another method for refunding is called *debt defeasance*. It can be used to retire noncallable outstanding debt without actually purchasing the debt in the open market. The corporation purchases U.S. Treasury bonds (or other government-guaranteed obligations) with cash inflows that match the cash outflows of the debt to be defeased. The government securities are placed in an irrevocable trust, and the trustee is charged with making principal and interest payments on the corporate debt as they come due. The defeased debt may then be removed from the firm's balance sheet (and the government securities are not added).

In 1982 Exxon defeased six issues of long-term debt that had a total face value of $515 million and that had yields of 5.8 to 6.7%. To do the job, it purchased $312 million in U.S. Treasury bonds yielding 14%. The after-tax difference between the face value of the corporate bonds and the cost of the government bonds was about $132 million. Exxon added this amount to its second quarter income, increasing its per share earnings from about $0.87 to $1.02.[19]

Financial reporting for defeasance is governed by FASB No. 76, issued in 1983. The defeased debt is removed from the balance sheet and the U.S. government securities are not added. A footnote is required, giving the general terms of the defeasance and the amount being defeased. Only debt with specific maturities and fixed payment schedules may be defeased. Convertible securities, floating rate debt, and redeemable preferred stock cannot be defeased. Defeasance is nontaxable at the time it takes place. The difference between the face value of the corporate debt and the cost of the defeasance trust drops directly to the company's bottom line. The interest on the government securities in the defeasance trust is subject to an ordinary income tax. Finally, the difference between the cost of the government bonds (if they were bought at a discount) and their face value is subject to a capital gains tax when they mature.

Bierman [1985] and Peterson, Peterson, and Ang [1985] have analyzed the defeasance decision. Consider the following example. The XYZ Corporation has $500 million of low coupon debt outstanding that cannot be repurchased because it is a private placement. The debt has five years left before maturity and pays an (annual) coupon rate of 6%, with the face value due at maturity. You are considering defeasance with U.S. Treasury bonds that pay coupons on the same dates that your corporate debt payments come due. The T-bonds sell for par, yield 14%, and mature in five years. Your corporate tax rate is 40% (and the capital gains rate is half of the ordinary rate). How do you defease and what is the net present value of the defeasance decision?

To defease, it will be necessary to purchase two U.S. government bond issues. First, we need a five-year 14% bond that pays $30 million in interest each year. If D_1 is the face value of this bond, we know that

$$.14D_1 = \$30,000,000$$

$$D_1 = \$214,285,710.$$

This issue will provide cash flows to meet the scheduled coupon payments on our corporate debt, but it falls short of providing the full $500 million face value due

---

[19] The increase in earnings does not necessarily mean that this was a positive NPV decision. Remember, there is a difference between earnings and cash flows.

at maturity.[20] For this we need a second U.S. government bond, a zero coupon bond, with a face value of D_2, where

$$D_2 = \$500,000,000 - \$214,285,710$$

$$= \$285,714,290.$$

The present value of this bond is

$$B_2 = \frac{285,714,290}{(1.14)^5} = \$148,391,049.$$

The total cash outlay needed to build a defeasance trust is

$$B_1 + B_2 = 214,285,710 + 148,391,049$$

$$= 362,676,759$$

Note that this has exactly the same market value as the debt being defeased. Aside from tax consequences, we are using \$362.68 million of U.S. government debt to defease \$362.68 million of corporate debt.

The cash flows from the decision are (1) a current outlay of \$362.68 million that is used to retire \$362.68 million of debt, (2) interest saved of \$30 million per year and an equal amount of interest lost, (3) principal of \$500 million not paid in year 5 and an equal amount not received, and (4) capital gains tax on the zero coupon bond, paid in year 5. All cash flows, except for the last, net out. Therefore the NPV of the decision is

$$\text{NPV} = \frac{-(\text{capital gain on zero coupon bond})\,(\tau_c/2)}{[1 + k_b(1 - \tau_c)]^N}$$

$$= \frac{-(285,714,290 - 148,391,049)(.4/2)}{[1 + .14(1 - .4)]^5}$$

$$= -18,349,643.$$

This is a negative net present value decision because of the capital gains tax liability on the zero coupon government bonds. Note also that reported earnings would increase by the amount (\$500.0 million − \$362.68 million = \$137.32 million).

4. The Effect of Flotation Costs on the Cost of Capital

The flotation costs of issuing new debt or equity include cash expenses such as legal, accounting, engineering, trustee and listing fees, printing and engraving expenses, Securities and Exchange Commission registration fees, federal revenue stamps, and state taxes. Also an important part of many new issues is the compensation paid to investment bankers for underwriting services.[21] The method used by many

---

[20] Note that this bond yields the market rate exactly; therefore its present value is $B_1 = \$214,285,710$.

[21] For an excellent comparison of underwritten new issues versus rights issues, see Smith [1977].

managerial finance textbooks to include flotation costs in the cost of capital is not generally consistent with value maximization. The normally followed procedure has been to adjust the required rate of return for flotation costs, F. For example, if one were using the Gordon growth model to estimate the cost of equity, the incorrect formulation would be

$$k_s = \frac{\text{Div}_1}{\left(1 - \dfrac{F}{S}\right)S} + g,$$

where

Div_1 = the end-of-period expected dividends (aggregate dollar value),
  S = the current market value of equity,
  F = the dollar amount of flotation costs,
  g = the expected long-term growth in dividends.

The above approach is incorrect because it implicitly adjusts the opportunity cost of funds supplied to the firm. Yet the true market-determined opportunity cost is unaffected by the flotation costs of a particular firm.

The correct method is to begin with a definition of net present value that explicitly recognizes flotation costs. One approach, which uses reproduction cost leverage, has been provided by Ezzell and Porter [1976]. Another approach, which we prefer, uses replacement value leverage and is described below. Let F be the dollar amount of flotation costs for a project financed with ΔS dollars of equity and ΔB dollars of debt. Thus the firm's target leverage, L, is

$$L = \frac{\Delta B}{\Delta S + \Delta B}. \tag{14.7}$$

The total investment outlay for a project is ΔI dollars for capital invested and F dollars of flotation costs. Therefore we have

$$\Delta I + F = \Delta S + \Delta B = \Delta S + L(\Delta I + F). \tag{14.8}$$

If the firm's flotation costs are $\alpha\%$ of the new equity issued and $\gamma\%$ of new debt, then

$$F = \alpha\,\Delta S + \gamma\,\Delta B, \tag{14.9}$$

and the weighted percentage flotation cost, ε, is

$$\varepsilon = \alpha(1 - L) + \gamma L. \tag{14.10}$$

Substituting (14.7) and (14.8) into (14.9) yields

$$F = \alpha(\Delta I + F - L(\Delta I + F)) + \gamma L(\Delta I + F)$$
$$= \frac{\varepsilon\,\Delta I}{1 - \varepsilon}. \tag{14.11}$$

The NPV of the project will be

$$\text{NPV} = \sum_{t=1}^{N} \frac{\text{NCF}_t}{(1 + \text{WACC})^t} - \Delta I - F. \tag{14.12}$$

This definition explicitly recognizes that flotation costs are cash flows incurred at the present time, not stretched over the life of the project. Finally, substituting (14.11) into (14.12) we obtain

$$\text{NPV} = \sum_{t=1}^{N} \frac{\text{NCF}_t}{(1 + \text{WACC})^t} - \frac{1}{1 - \varepsilon} \Delta I. \tag{14.13}$$

Thus the correct procedure for the economic analysis of flotation costs does not alter the weighted average cost of capital, WACC. Rather, it grosses up the investment outlay by $[1/(1 - \epsilon)]$, a factor that considers the weighted average flotation costs of debt and equity.

SUMMARY

The cost of capital, the capital structure of the firm, and the capital budgeting decision are all inextricably linked. The theory of finance provides equations that may be applied to the solution of the weighted average cost of capital under a variety of assumptions. Although no completely satisfactory theory has yet been found to explain the existence of optimal capital structure, casual empiricism suggests that firms behave as though it does exist. Therefore, for the time being, suggested techniques for estimating the weighted average cost of capital usually assume that each firm has a target capital structure. This target is then applied to the cost of capital formulas.

A major empirical issue is the impact of capital structure on the value of the firm and on the weighted average cost of capital. Although the evidence is mixed, the articles that were summarized seem to indicate that there is in fact a gain from leverage that seems to be between 10% and 20%. Of course, this is less than the marginal corporate tax rate (34%), and we could have used a tax rate of 10% to 20% in estimating the cost of capital for Bethlehem Steel. If we had done so, the weighted average cost of capital would have been 11.34%.

PROBLEM SET

14.1 The puzzle of optimal capital structure is that there appear to be cross-sectional regularities in the observed ratios of debt to equity of U.S. firms. For example, the steel industry appears to carry a higher percentage of debt than the public accounting industry does. These same regularities appeared even before the existence of corporate income taxes. How can optimal leverage be explained without relying on the tax shield of debt or bankruptcy costs?

14.2 What are the empirical problems involved in testing for the effect of capital structure on the value of the firm?

14.3 Assume a world without taxes. How would the weighted average cost of capital vary with the ratio of debt to total assets, $B/(B + S)$, if the cost of equity remained constant, i.e., $k_s = \rho > k_b$?

14.4 During recent years your company has made considerable use of debt financing, to the extent that it is generally agreed that the percentage of debt in the firm's capital structure (either in book or market value terms) is too high. Further use of debt will likely lead to a drop in the firm's bond rating. You would like to recommend that the next major capital investment be financed with a new equity issue. Unfortunately, the firm has not been doing very well recently (nor has the market). In fact the rate of return on investment has been just equal to the cost of capital. As shown in the financial statement in Table Q14.4, the market value of the firm's equity is less than its book value. This means that even a profitable project will decrease earnings per share if it is financed with new equity. For example, the firm is considering a project that costs $400 but has a value of $500 (i.e., an NPV of $100), and that will increase total earnings by $60 per year. If it is financed with equity the $400 will require approximately 200 shares, thus bringing the total shares outstanding to 1200. The new earnings will be $660, and earnings per share will fall to $0.55. The president of the firm argues that the project should be delayed for three reasons.

a) It is too expensive for the firm to issue new debt.

b) Financing the project with new equity will reduce earnings per share because the market value of equity is less than book value.

c) Equity markets are currently depressed. If the firm waits until the market index improves, the market value of equity will exceed the book value and equity financing will no longer reduce earnings per share.

Critique the president's logic.

14.5 *Southwestern Electric Company.*[22] John Hatteras, the financial analyst for Southwestern Electric Company, is responsible for preliminary analysis of the company's investment projects.

Table Q14.4   Balance Sheet as of December 31, 19xx

Assets		Liabilities	
Short-term assets	2,000	Debt	6,000
Plant and equipment	8,000	Equity	4,000
	10,000	Total	10,000

Total market value of equity = $2,000.00
Number of shares outstanding = 1,000
Price per share = 2.00
Total earnings for the year 19xx = 600.00
Earnings per share = .60

[22] This problem is really a short case. It has a definite answer but requires knowledge of cash flows, discounting, the CAPM, and risky cost of capital.

Table Q14.5

Year	Outflows	Inflows	Interest
1	250	10	7.5
2	250	20	15.0
3	250	25	22.5
4	250	60	30.0
5–30	0	110	30.0
31–40	0	80	30.0
41	0	40	0

He is currently trying to evaluate two large projects that management has decided to consider as a single joint project, because it is felt that the geographical diversification the joint project provides would be advantageous.

Southwestern Electric was founded in the early 1930s and has operated profitably ever since. Growing at about the same rate as the population in its service areas, the company has usually been able to forecast its revenues with a great deal of accuracy. The stable pattern in revenues and a favorable regulatory environment have caused most investors to view Southwestern as an investment of very low risk.

Hatteras is concerned because one of the two projects uses a new technology that will be very profitable, assuming that demand is high in a booming economy, but will do poorly in a recessionary economy. However, the expected cash flows of the two projects, supplied by the engineering department, are identical. The expected after-tax cash flows on operating income for the joint project are given in Table Q14.5. Both projects are exactly the same size, so the cash flow for one is simply half the joint cash flow.

In order to better evaluate the project, Hatteras applies his knowledge of modern finance theory. He estimates that the beta of the riskier project is .75, whereas the beta for the less risky project is .4375. These betas, however, are based on the covariance between the return on after-tax operating income and the market. Hatteras vaguely recalls that any discount rate he decides to apply to the project should consider financial risk as well as operating (or business) risk. The beta for the equity of Southwestern is .5. The company has a ratio of debt to total assets of 50% and a marginal tax rate of 40%. Because the bonds of Southwestern are rated Aaa, Hatteras decides to assume that they are risk free. Finally, after consulting his investment banker, Hatteras believes that 18% is a reasonable estimate of the expected return on the market.

The joint project, if undertaken, will represent 10% of the corporation's assets. Southwestern intends to finance the joint project with 50% debt and 50% equity.

Hatteras wants to submit a report that answers the following questions:

a) What is the appropriate required rate of return for the new project?

b) What are the cost of equity capital and the weighted average cost of capital for Southwestern Electric before it takes the project?

c) Should the joint project be accepted?

d) What would the outcome be if the projects are considered separately?

e) If the joint project is accepted, what will the firm's new risk level be?

REFERENCES

Altman, E., "A Further Empirical Investigation of the Bankruptcy Cost Question," *Journal of Finance*, September 1984, 1067–1089.

American Bar Association, *Commentaries on Model Debenture Indenture Provisions*, ABA, Chicago, 1971.

Asquith, P., and D. Mullins, Jr., "Equity Issues and Offering Dilution," *Journal of Financial Economics*, January–February 1986, 61–90.

Barges, A., *The Effect of Capital Structure on the Cost of Capital*. Prentice-Hall, Englewood Cliffs, N.J., 1963.

Barnea, A.; R. Haugen; and L. Senbet, *Agency Problems and Financial Contracting*. Prentice-Hall, Englewood Cliffs, N.J., 1985.

Baron, D., and B. Holmström, "The Investment Banking Contract for New Issues under Asymmetric Information: Delegation and the Incentive Problem," *Journal of Finance*, December 1980, 1115–1138.

Baxter, N., "Leverage, Risk of Ruin and the Cost of Capital," *Journal of Finance*, September 1967, 395–403.

Beranek, W., *The Effect of Leverage on the Market Value of Common Stock*. Bureau of Business Research and Service, Madison, Wis., 1964.

Bhattacharya, S., "Imperfect Information, Dividend Policy, and 'The Bird in Hand' Fallacy," *Bell Journal of Economics*, Spring 1979, 259–270.

Bierman, H., "Defeasance Is Not a Free Lunch," *Journal of Corporate Finance*, Spring 1985, 13–16.

Black, F., and M. Scholes, "The Pricing of Options and Corporate Liabilities," *Journal of Political Economy*, May–June 1973, 637–654.

Boness, A. J., and G. M. Frankfurter, "Evidence of Non-Homogeneity of Capital Costs within 'Risk-Classes,'" *Journal of Finance*, June 1977, 775–787.

Booth, J., and R. Smith, "Capital Raising, Underwriting and the Certification Hypothesis," *Journal of Financial Economics*, January–February 1986.

Bradley, M.; G. Jarrell; and E. H. Kim, "On the Existence of an Optimal Capital Structure: Theory and Evidence," *Journal of Finance*, July 1984, 857–878.

Brennan, M., and E. Schwartz, "Savings Bonds, Retractable Bonds and Callable Bonds," *Journal of Financial Economics*, August 1977, 67–88.

———, "Optimal Financial Policy and Firm Valuation," *Journal of Finance*, July 1984, 593–607.

Cordes, J., and S. Sheffrin, "Estimating the Tax Advantage of Corporate Debt," *Journal of Finance*, March 1983, 95–105.

Dann, L., and W. Mikkelson, "Convertible Debt Issuance, Capital Structure Change and Financing-Related Information: Some New Evidence," *Journal of Financial Economics*, June 1984, 157–186.

Darrough, M., and N. Stoughton, "Moral Hazard and Adverse Selection: The Question of Financial Structure," *Journal of Finance*, June 1986, 501–513.

DeAngelo, H., and R. Masulis, "Optimal Capital Structure under Corporate and Personal Taxation," *Journal of Financial Economics*, March 1980, 3–30.

Dietrich, J. R., "Effects of Early Bond Refundings: An Empirical Investigation of Security Returns," *Journal of Accounting and Economics*, April 1984, 67–96.

Eckbo, B. E., "Valuation Effects of Corporate Debt Offerings," *Journal of Financial Economics*, January–February 1986, 119–152.

Ezzell, J., and B. Porter, "Flotation Costs and the Weighted Average Cost of Capital," *Journal of Financial and Quantitative Analysis*, September 1976, 403–413.

Finnerty, J., "Stock-for-Debt Swaps and Shareholder Returns," *Financial Management*, Autumn 1985, 5–17.

Fons, J., "The Default Premium and Corporate Bond Experience," *Journal of Finance*, March 1987, 81–97.

Galai, D., and R. W. Masulis, "The Option Pricing Model and the Risk Factor of Stock," *Journal of Financial Economics*, January–March 1976, 53–82.

Haley, C., and L. Schall, *The Theory of Financial Decisions*. McGraw-Hill, New York, 1973.

Hamada, R. S., "The Effect of the Firm's Capital Structure on the Systematic Risk of Common Stocks," *Journal of Finance*, May 1972, 435–452.

Haugen, R., and L. Senbet, "New Perspectives on Informational Asymmetry and Agency Relationships," *Journal of Financial and Quantitative Analysis*, November 1979, 671–694.

Ho, T., and R. Singer, "Bond Indenture Provisions and the Risk of Corporate Debt," *Journal of Financial Economics*, December 1982, 375–406.

Jensen, M., and W. Meckling, "Theory of the Firm: Managerial Behavior, Agency Costs, and Ownership Structure," *Journal of Financial Economics*, October 1976, 305–360.

Jones, E. P., S. Mason, and E. Rosenfeld, "Contingent Claims Analysis of Corporate Financial Structures: An Empirical Investigation," *Journal of Finance*, July 1984, 611–625.

Kalaba, R.; T. Langetieg; N. Rasakhoo; and M. Weinstein, "Estimation of Implicit Bankruptcy Costs," *Journal of Finance*, July 1984, 629–642.

Kalay, A., "Toward a Theory of Corporate Dividend Policy," Ph.D. dissertation, University of Rochester, 1979.

Kalotay, A., "On the Advanced Refunding of Discounted Debt," *Financial Management*, Summer 1978, 7–13.

Kane, A.; A. Marcus; and R. McDonald, "How Big Is the Tax Advantage to Debt?" *Journal of Finance*, July 1984, 841–853.

Kim, E. H., "A Mean Variance Theory of Optimal Capital Structure and Corporate Debt Capacity," *Journal of Finance*, March 1978, 45–64.

———; W. Lewellen; and J. McConnell, "Financial Leverage and Clienteles: Theory and Evidence," *Journal of Financial Economics*, March 1979, 83–110.

Kolodny, R., and D. Suhler, "Changes in Capital Structure, New Equity Issues, and Scale Effects," *Journal of Financial Research*, Summer 1985, 127–136.

Kraus, A., and R. Litzenberger, "A State-Preference Model of Optimal Financial Leverage," *Journal of Finance*, September 1973, 911–922.

Lee, W. H., "The Effect of Exchange Offers and Stock Swaps on Equity Risk and Shareholders' Wealth: A Signalling Model Approach," Ph.D. dissertation, UCLA, 1987.

Leland, H., and D. Pyle, "Informational Asymmetries, Financial Structure, and Financial Intermediation," *Journal of Finance*, May 1977, 371–388.

Linn, S., and J. M. Pinegar, "The Effect of Issuing Preferred Stock on Common and Preferred Stockholder Wealth," Working paper, University of Iowa, 1985.

Livingston, M., "Bond Refunding Reconsidered: Comment," *Journal of Finance*, March 1980, 191–196.

Long, M., and I. Malitz, "Investment Patterns and Financial Leverage," in Friedman, ed., *Corporate Capital Structure in the United States*. University of Chicago Press, Chicago, 1985.

Masulis, R., "The Effects of Capital Structure Change on Security Prices: A Study of Exchange Offers," *Journal of Financial Economics*, June 1980, 139–178.

———, "The Impact of Capital Structure Change on Firm Value, Some Estimates," *Journal of Finance*, March 1983, 107–126.

———, and A. Korwar, "Seasoned Equity Offerings: An Empirical Investigation," *Journal of Financial Economics*, January–February 1986, 91–118.

Mayor, T., and K. McCorn, "Bond Refunding: One or Two Faces?" *Journal of Finance*, March 1978, 349–353.

McConnell, J., and G. Schlarbaum, "Evidence on the Impact of Exchange Offers on Security Prices: The Case of Income Bonds," *Journal of Business*, January 1981, 65–85.

Mikkelson, W., and M. Partch, "Valuation Effects of Security Offerings and the Issuance Process," *Journal of Financial Economics*, January–February 1986, 31–60.

Miller, M., "Debt and Taxes," *Journal of Finance*, May 1977, 261–275.

———, and F. Modigliani, "Some Estimates of the Cost of Capital to the Electric Utility Industry, 1954–57," *American Economic Review*, June 1966, 333–391.

———, "Some Estimates of the Cost of Capital to the Electric Utility Industry, 1954–57: Reply," *American Economic Review*, December 1967, 1288–1300.

Modigliani, F., and M. Miller, "The Cost of Capital, Corporation Finance and the Theory of Investment," *American Economic Review*, June 1958, 261–297.

———, "Taxes and the Cost of Capital: A Correction," *American Economic Review*, June 1963, 433–443.

Myers, S. C., "Determinants of Corporate Borrowing," *Journal of Financial Economics*, November 1977, 147–176.

———, "The Capital Structure Puzzle," *Journal of Finance*, July 1984, 575–592.

———, and N. Majluf, "Corporate Financing and Investment Decisions When Firms Have Information That Investors Do Not Have," *Journal of Financial Economics*, June 1984, 187–221.

Ofer, A., and R. Taggart, Jr., "Bond Refunding: A Clarifying Analysis," *Journal of Finance*, March 1977, 21–30.

———, "Bond Refunding Reconsidered: Reply," *Journal of Finance*, March 1980, 197–200.

Peavy, J., and J. Scott, "The Effect of Stock-for-Debt Swaps on Security Returns," *Financial Review*, November 1985, 303–327.

Peterson, P.; D. Peterson; and J. Ang, "The Extinguishment of Debt through In-Substance Defeasance," *Financial Management*, Spring 1985, 59–67.

Pinegar, J., and R. Lease, "The Impact of Preferred-for-Common Exchange Offers on Firm Value," *Journal of Finance*, September 1986, 795–814.

Riley, J., "Competitive Signalling," *Journal of Economic Theory*, April 1975, 174–186.

Robichek, A.; J. McDonald; and R. Higgins, "Some Estimates of the Cost of Capital to the Electric Utility Industry, 1954–57: Comment," *American Economic Review*, December 1967, 1278–1288.

Rogers, R., and J. Owers, "Equity for Debt Exchanges and Shareholder Wealth," *Financial Management*, Autumn 1985, 18–26.

Ross, S. A., "The Determination of Financial Structure: The Incentive Signalling Approach," *Bell Journal of Economics*, Spring 1977, 23–40.

Rothschild, M., and J. Stiglitz, "Equilibrium in Competitive Insurance Markets," *Quarterly Journal of Economics*, November 1976, 629–650.

Rubinstein, M., "A Mean-Variance Synthesis of Corporate Financial Theory," *Journal of Finance*, March 1973, 167–181.

Schipper, K., and A. Smith, "A Comparison of Equity Carve-outs and Seasoned Equity Offerings: Share Price Effects and Corporate Restructuring," *Journal of Financial Economics*, January–February 1986, 153–186.

Scott, J. H., Jr., "A Theory of Optimal Capital Structure," *Bell Journal of Economics*, Spring 1976, 33–54.

———; G. H. Hempel; and J. Peavy III, "The Effect of Stock-for-Debt Swaps on Bank Holding Companies," *Journal of Banking and Finance*, June 1985, 233–251.

Shastri, K., "Two Essays Concerning the Effects of Firm Investment/Financing Decisions on Security Values: An Option Pricing Approach," Ph.D. dissertation, UCLA Graduate School of Management, 1981.

Smith, C., Jr., "Substitute Methods for Raising Additional Capital: Rights Offerings versus Underwritten Issues," *Journal of Financial Economics*, December 1977, 273–307.

———, "Investment Banking and the Capital Acquisition Process," *Journal of Financial Economics*, January–February 1986, 3–30.

———, and J. B. Warner, "On Financial Contracting: An Analysis of Bond Covenants," *Journal of Financial Economics*, June 1979, 117–161.

Solomon, E., *The Theory of Financial Management*. Columbia University Press, New York, 1963.

Spence, A. M., "Job Market Signaling," *Quarterly Journal of Economics*, August 1973, 355–379.

Stiglitz, J., "A Re-Examination of the Modigliani-Miller Theorem," *American Economic Review*, December 1969, 784–793.

———, "Some Aspects of the Pure Theory of Corporate Finance: Bankruptcies and Take-overs," *Bell Journal of Economics and Management Science*, Autumn 1972, 458–482.

———, "On the Irrelevance of Corporate Financial Policy," *American Economic Review*, December 1974, 851–866.

Stulz, R., and H. Johnson, "An Analysis of Secured Debt," *Journal of Financial Economics*, December 1985, 501–521.

Titman, S., "The Effect of Capital Structure on a Firm's Liquidation Decision," *Journal of Financial Economics*, March 1984, 137–151.

———, "Determinants of Capital Structure: An Empirical Analysis," Working paper, UCLA Graduate School of Management, 1982.

———, and R. Wessels, "The Determinants of Capital Structure Choice," Working paper, UCLA, 1985.

Wakeman, L. M., "Bond Rating Agencies and Capital Markets," Working paper, Graduate School of Management, University of Rochester, Rochester, N.Y., 1978.

Warner, J., "Bankruptcy, Absolute Priority, and the Pricing of Risky Debt Claims," *Journal of Financial Economics*, May 1977a, 239–276.

————, "Bankruptcy Costs: Some Evidence," *Journal of Finance*, May 1977b, 337–347.

Watts, R., and J. Zimmerman, "Towards a Positive Theory of the Determination of Accounting Standards," *Accounting Review*, January 1978, 112–134.

————, "The Demand for and Supply of Accounting Theories: The Market for Excuses," *Accounting Review*, April 1979, 273–305.

Weinstein, M. I., "The Effect of a Rating Change Announcement on Bond Price," *Journal of Financial Economics*, December 1977, 329–350.

————, "The Seasoning Process of New Corporate Bond Issues," *Journal of Finance*, December 1978, 1343–1354.

Weston, J. F., "A Test of Capital Propositions," *Southern Economic Journal*, October 1963, 105–112.

Williams, J., "Perquisites, Risk, and Capital Structure," *Journal of Finance*, March 1987, 29–48.

Yawitz, J.; K. Maloney; and L. Ederington, "Taxes Default Risk and Yield Spreads," *Journal of Finance*, September 1985, 1127–1140.

15

The one thing that shareholders cannot do through their purchase and sale transactions is negate the consequences of investment decisions by management.

J. E. Walter, "Dividend Policy: Its Influence on the Value of the Enterprise," *Journal of Finance*, May 1963, 284

Dividend Policy: Theory

Is the value of shareholders' wealth affected by the dividend policy of the firm? This is another variation on the basic question, Can any financing decision affect the value of the firm? The previous chapters looked at the relationship between capital structure and the value of the firm, using a fairly simple valuation model that assumed a non-growing stream of cash flows from investment. Capital structure theory shows that in a world without taxes, agency costs, or information asymmetry repackaging the firm's net operating cash flows into fixed cash flows for debt and residual cash flows for shareholders has no effect on the value of the firm. This chapter develops valuation models that include growth opportunities, thereby adding a greater element of realism. Even so, we shall show that, in a world without taxes, it makes no difference whether shareholders receive their cash flows as dividends or as capital gains. Thus in the absence of taxes, agency costs, or information asymmetry, dividend policy is irrelevant. It does not affect shareholders' wealth. The argument is then extended to a valuation model that includes growth and corporate taxes, but the result does not change. Dividend payout does not affect the value of the firm. However, in a world with personal as well as corporate taxes the possibility arises that dividends may affect value. Also, agency costs and information heterogeneity are proposed as possible explanations for dividend policy. Empirical tests of dividend policy and applications of corporate valuation are discussed in Chapter 16.

A. THE IRRELEVANCE OF DIVIDEND POLICY IN A WORLD WITHOUT TAXES

Miller and Modigliani [1961] present a cogent argument for the fact that the value of the firm is unaffected by dividend policy in a world without taxes or transactions costs. They begin by assuming that two firms are identical in every respect except for their dividend payout in the current time period. Their streams of future cash flows from operations are identical, their planned investment outlays are identical, and all future dividend payments from the second time period on are also identical. We can represent this mathematically as follows:

$$\widetilde{\text{NOI}}_1(t) = \widetilde{\text{NOI}}_2(t), \qquad t = 0, 1, \ldots, \infty,$$

$$\tilde{I}_1(t) = \tilde{I}_2(t), \qquad t = 0, 1, \ldots, \infty,$$

$$\widetilde{\text{Div}}_1(t) = \widetilde{\text{Div}}_2(t), \qquad t = 1, \ldots, \infty,$$

$$\text{Div}_1(0) \neq \text{Div}_2(0),$$

where

$\widetilde{\text{NOI}}_i(t) =$ the random future cash flows from operations for the ith firm in time period t,

$\tilde{I}_i(t) =$ the variable investment outlay for the ith firm in time period t,

$\widetilde{\text{Div}}_i(t) =$ the random dividend payout for firms in period t,

$\text{Div}_i(0) =$ the dividend payout for the ith firm during the current time period.

1. A Recursive Valuation Formula

The important question is whether or not the two firms will have different value if their current dividend payouts are different. To supply an answer we first need a simple valuation model. Let us begin by assuming that the market-required rates of return for firms in the same risk class are identical.[1] The two firms above obviously have the same risk because their streams of operating cash flows are identical. The rate of return is defined as dividends plus capital gains,

$$\rho(t + 1) = \frac{\text{div}_i(t + 1) + P_i(t + 1) - P_i(t)}{P_i(t)}, \qquad (15.1)$$

where

$\rho(t + 1) =$ the market-required rate of return during the time period t,

$\text{div}_i(t + 1) =$ dividends per share paid at the end of time period t,

$P_i(t + 1) =$ price per share at the end of time period t,

$P_i(t) =$ price per share at the beginning of time period t.

---

[1] For the sake of simplicity, we assume that both firms are 100% equity. This avoids the problem of confusing capital structure effects with possible dividend policy effects.

If the numerator and denominator of (15.1) are multiplied by the current number of shares outstanding, $n_i(t)$, then by rearranging terms, we have

$$V_i(t) = \frac{\text{Div}_i(t+1) + n_i(t)P_i(t+1)}{1 + \rho(t+1)}, \qquad (15.2)$$

where

$\text{Div}_i(t+1) = $ total dollar dividend payment $= n_i(t)\text{div}_i(t+1)$,

$\quad V_i(t) = $ the market value of the firm $= n_i(t)P_i(t)$.

Hence the value of the firm is seen to be equal to the discounted sum of two cash flows: any dividends paid out, $\text{Div}_i(t+1)$, and the end-of-period value of the firm. To show that the present value of the firm is independent of dividend payout, we shall examine the sources and uses of funds for the two firms in order to rewrite (15.2) in a way that is independent of dividends.

2. Sources and Uses of Funds

There are two major sources of funds for an all-equity firm. First, it receives cash from operations, $\widetilde{\text{NOI}}_i(t+1)$. Second, it may choose to issue new shares, $m_i(t+1)\widetilde{P}_i(t+1)$, where $m_i(t+1)$ is the number of new shares. There are also two major uses of funds: dividends paid out, $\widetilde{\text{Div}}_i(t+1)$, and planned cash outlays for investment, $\widetilde{I}_i(t+1)$.[2] By definition, sources and uses must be equal. Therefore we have the following identity:

$$\text{NOI}_i(t+1) + m_i(t+1)\widetilde{P}_i(t+1) \equiv \widetilde{I}_i(t+1) + \widetilde{\text{Div}}_i(t+1). \qquad (15.3)$$

We can use this fact to rewrite the numerator of the valuation equation (15.2). Calling the numerator of (15.2) the dollar return to shareholders, $\widetilde{R}_i(t+1)$, we have

$$\widetilde{R}_i(t+1) = \widetilde{\text{Div}}_i(t+1) + n_i(t)\widetilde{P}_i(t+1). \qquad (15.4)$$

We know that if new shares are issued, the total number of shares outstanding at the end of the period, $n(t+1)$, will be the sum of current shares, $n(t)$, and new shares, $m(t+1)$:

$$n_i(t+1) = n_i(t) + m_i(t+1). \qquad (15.5)$$

Using (15.5), we can rewrite (15.4) as

$$\widetilde{R}_i(t+1) = \widetilde{\text{Div}}_i(t+1) + n_i(t+1)\widetilde{P}_i(t+1) - m_i(t+1)\widetilde{P}_i(t+1). \qquad (15.6)$$

Finally, taking Eq. (15.3), which establishes the identity of the sources and uses of funds, to substitute for $m_i(t+1)\widetilde{P}_i(t+1)$ in the above equation, we obtain

$$\widetilde{R}_i(t+1) = \widetilde{\text{Div}}_i(t+1) + \widetilde{V}_i(t+1) - \widetilde{I}_i(t+1) + \widetilde{\text{NOI}}_i(t+1) - \widetilde{\text{Div}}_i(t+1)$$
$$= \widetilde{\text{NOI}}_i(t+1) - \widetilde{I}_i(t+1) + \widetilde{V}_i(t+1), \qquad (15.7)$$

---

[2] This argument assumes, for the sake of convenience, that sources and uses of funds from balance sheet items (e.g., changes in inventory or accounts receivable) are negligible.

where $\tilde{V}_i(t + 1) = n_i(t + 1)\tilde{P}_i(t + 1)$. Therefore the valuation equation (15.2) may be rewritten

$$\tilde{V}_i(t) = \frac{\widetilde{NOI}_i(t + 1) - \tilde{I}_i(t + 1) + \tilde{V}_i(t + 1)}{1 + \rho(t + 1)}. \tag{15.8}$$

3. Valuation and the Irrelevancy of Dividend Payout

It is no accident that dividends do not appear in the valuation equation (15.8). Given that there are no taxes, the firm can choose any dividend policy whatsoever without affecting the stream of cash flows received by shareholders. It could, e.g., elect to pay dividends in excess of cash flows from operations and still be able to undertake any planned investment. The extra funds needed are supplied by issuing new equity. On the other hand, it could decide to pay dividends less than the amount of cash left over from operations after making investments. The excess cash would be used to repurchase shares. It is the availability of external financing in a world without information asymmetry or transactions costs that makes the value of the firm independent of dividend policy.

We can use Eq. (15.8) to prove that two firms that are identical in every respect except for their current dividend payout must have the same value. The equation has four terms. First, the market-required rate of return, ρ, must be the same because both firms have identical risk, $\widetilde{NOI}_1(t) = \widetilde{NOI}_2(t)$, for all t. Second, current cash flows from operations and current investment outlays for the two firms have been assumed to be identical:

$$\widetilde{NOI}_1(1) = \widetilde{NOI}_2(1), \qquad \tilde{I}_1(1) = \tilde{I}_2(1).$$

Finally, the end-of-period values of the two firms depend only on *future* investments, dividends, and cash flows from operations, which also have been assumed to be identical. Therefore the end-of-period values of the two firms must be the same:

$$\tilde{V}_1(1) = \tilde{V}_2(1).$$

Consequently, the present values of the two firms must be identical regardless of their current dividend payout. Dividend policy is irrelevant because it has no effect on shareholders' wealth in a world without taxes, information asymmetry, or transactions costs.

Note that the proof of the irrelevancy of dividend policy was made using a multiperiod model whose returns were uncertain. Therefore it is an extremely general argument. In addition to providing insight into what does not affect the value of the firm, it provides considerable insight into what *does* affect value. The value of the firm depends only on the distribution of future cash flows provided by investment decisions. The key to the Miller-Modigliani argument is that investment decisions are completely independent of dividend policy. The firm can pay any level of dividends it wishes without affecting investment decisions. If dividends plus desired investment outlays use more cash flow than is provided from operations, the firm should seek external financing (e.g., equity). The desire to maintain a level of dividends need not ever affect the investment decision.

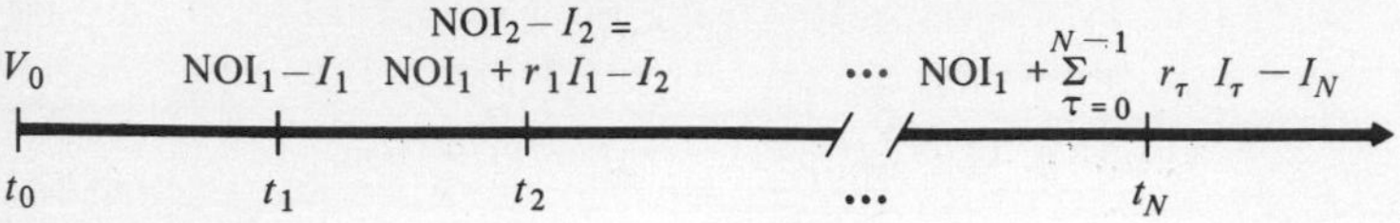

Figure 15.1
Time pattern of cash flows for a growing firm.

B. VALUATION, GROWTH, AND DIVIDEND POLICY

The Miller-Modigliani argument that the value of the firm is independent of dividend policy also extends into a world with corporate taxes but without personal taxes. In this section the valuation model [Eq. (15.8)] is extended to include corporate taxes and a growing stream of cash flows. The result is a valuation model that has realistic features and hence may be usefully applied to real-world valuation problems. Chapter 16 will expand on the usefulness of the valuation model by means of an example.

1. The Valuation of an All-Equity Firm with Growth

Figure 15.1 uses the time line as a graphic representation of the pattern of cash flows earned by a growing firm. Note that there is a current level of cash flow, NOI_1, that is assumed to be received at the end of each year forever. If the firm made no new investments and only maintained its current level of capital stock, it would receive cash flows each year equal to $\widetilde{NOI}_1$, but it would not be growing. Growth comes from new investment, not replacement investment. The value of new investment depends on the amount of investment, I_t, and its rate of return, r_t.

We can extend the valuation equation (15.8) by assuming that the discount rate, ρ, does not change from time period to time period. This is reasonable if all new projects have the same risk as those that the firm currently holds. Equation (15.8) is[3]

$$V_0 = \frac{NOI_1 - I_1}{1 + \rho} + \frac{V_1}{1 + \rho}. \tag{15.8}$$

Given a constant discount rate, ρ, the valuation model can be extended to N periods as follows:

$$V = \frac{NOI_1 - I_1}{1 + \rho} + \frac{NOI_2 - I_2}{(1 + \rho)^2} + \cdots + \frac{NOI_N - I_N}{(1 + \rho)^N} + \frac{V_N}{(1 + \rho)^N}. \tag{15.9}$$

A reasonable assumption is that in any time period the value of the firm, V_t, is finite.[4] Therefore, given a model with an infinite horizon, we have

$$V_0 = \lim_{N \to \infty} \sum_{t=1}^{N} \frac{NOI_t - I_t}{(1 + \rho)^t}. \tag{15.10}$$

---

[3] The tildes ($\sim$) are dropped for notational convenience. Also note that

$$NOI_2 = NOI_1 + r_1 I_1.$$

[4] After all, no one has observed a firm with infinite value as yet.

Table 15.1

Time Period	Cash Inflow	Cash Outflow	
1	NOI_1	$-I_1$	
2	$NOI_2 = NOI_1 + r_1 I_1$	$-I_2$	
3	$NOI_3 = NOI_1 + r_1 I_1 + r_2 I_2$	$-I_3$	(15.11)
$\vdots$	$\vdots$	$\vdots$	
N	$NOI_N = NOI_1 + \sum_{\tau=1}^{N-1} r_\tau I_\tau$	$-I_N$	

Equation (15.10) is the same formula used in Chapter 2 on capital budgeting. The present value of the firm is the sum of the discounted cash flows from operations less the new investment outlays necessary to undertake them.

Referring to Fig. 15.1, we can see that the average return on investment, r_t, is assumed to continue forever at a constant rate. This is a perfectly reasonable assumption because if the capital budgeting decision is made correctly, each project will return enough cash to cover payments to suppliers of capital and to recover the initial investment. Thus the cash flows are sufficient to provide any needed replacement investment to sustain the project at a constant level forever. The stream of cash flows for the growing firm in Fig. 15.1 is given in Table 15.1 [also Eq. (15.11)].

Substituting (15.11) into (15.10), we can express the present value of the growing firm as

$$V_0 = \frac{NOI_1 - I_1}{1+\rho} + \frac{NOI_1 + r_1 I_1 - I_2}{(1+\rho)^2} + \frac{NOI_1 + r_1 I_1 + r_2 I_2 - I_3}{(1+\rho)^3}$$

$$+ \cdots + \frac{NOI_1 + \sum_{\tau=1}^{N-1} r_\tau I_\tau - I_N}{(1+\rho)^N}. \tag{15.12}$$

This extended equation can be simplified greatly. First, rewrite it by rearranging terms as follows:

$$V_0 = \frac{NOI_1}{1+\rho} + \frac{NOI_1}{(1+\rho)^2} + \cdots + \frac{NOI_1}{(1+\rho)^N}$$

$$+ I_1 \left[\frac{r_1}{(1+\rho)^2} + \frac{r_1}{(1+\rho)^3} + \cdots + \frac{r_1}{(1+\rho)^N} - \frac{1}{1+\rho} \right]$$

$$+ I_2 \left[\frac{r_2}{(1+\rho)^3} + \frac{r_2}{(1+\rho)^4} + \cdots + \frac{r_2}{(1+\rho)^N} - \frac{1}{(1+\rho)^2} \right] + \cdots$$

This result can be generalized as

$$V_0 = \sum_{t=1}^{N} \frac{NOI_1}{(1+\rho)^t} + \sum_{t=1}^{N} I_t \left[\left(\sum_{\tau=t+1}^{N} \frac{r_t}{(1+\rho)^\tau} \right) - \frac{1}{(1+\rho)^t} \right]. \tag{15.13}$$

We can simplify Eq. (15.13) by recognizing that the first term is an infinite annuity with constant payments of NOI_1 per period. Therefore

$$\lim_{N \to \infty} \sum_{t=1}^{N} \frac{NOI_1}{(1 + \rho)^t} = \frac{NOI_1}{\rho}. \tag{15.14}$$

Next, the second term in (15.13) can be simplified as follows:

$$\sum_{\tau=t+1}^{N} \frac{r_t}{(1 + \rho)^\tau} = \frac{1}{(1 + \rho)^t} \sum_{\tau=1}^{N-t} \frac{r_t}{(1 + \rho)^\tau},$$

$$\frac{1}{(1 + \rho)^t} \lim_{N \to \infty} \frac{r_t}{(1 + \rho)^\tau} = \frac{1}{(1 + \rho)^t} \frac{r_t}{\rho}. \tag{15.15}$$

Substituting (15.14) and (15.15) back into (15.13), we obtain a simplified expression for the present value of the firm:

$$V_0 = \lim_{N \to \infty} \left\{ \frac{NOI_1}{\rho} + \sum_{t=1}^{N} I_t \left[\left(\frac{r_t}{\rho(1 + \rho)^t} \right) - \frac{1}{(1 + \rho)^t} \right] \right\}$$

$$= \frac{NOI_1}{\rho} + \sum_{t=1}^{\infty} \frac{I_t(r_t - \rho)}{\rho(1 + \rho)^t};$$

$$= \text{Value of assets in place} + \text{value of future growth}. \tag{15.16}$$

2. Why Earnings per Share Growth Maximization Is an Inappropriate Goal

This form of valuation equation provides important insights into the much abused term *growth stock*. The first term in Eq. (15.16) is the present value of a firm that makes no new investments. It is the present value of an infinite stream of constant cash flows. In other words it is the value of a firm that is not growing. It is the value of assets in place. But what about the firm that makes new investments? The present value of new investment is shown in the second term of Eq. (15.16). It is the present value of expected future growth. The *value* of new investment depends on two things: (1) the amount of investment made and (2) the difference between the average rate of return on the investment, r_t, and the market-required rate of return, ρ. The assets of a firm may grow, but they do not add anything to value unless they earn a rate of return greater than what the market requires for assets of equivalent risk. For example, supposing that the market requires a 10% rate of return (i.e., $\rho = 10\%$), consider the three situations given in Table 15.2.

Firm 3 has the greatest "growth" in earnings ($\Delta NOI = 5,000$). But which firm has the greatest increase in value? Obviously, firm 1 does. The reason is that it is the only firm that has new investments that earn more than the required market rate of return of 10%. Therefore the objective of a firm should *never* be to simply maximize growth in earnings or cash flows. The objective should be to maximize the market value of the firm, which is equivalent to maximizing wealth.

Table 15.2

	$\$\Delta I$	$\%r$	$\$\Delta$NOI	$\$\Delta V$
Firm 1	10,000	20	2,000	9,090
Firm 2	30,000	10	3,000	0
Firm 3	100,000	5	5.000	$-45,454$

Another feature of Eq. (15.16) is that it is derived directly from Eq. (15.8), and in both we have the result that dividend policy is irrelevant in a world without taxes, information asymmetry, or transactions costs. All that counts is cash flows from investment.

3. The Value of an All-Equity Firm that Grows at a Constant Rate Forever

Equation (15.16) is elegant but somewhat cumbersome to use.[5] It has two useful variations. The first, which is developed below, assumes that the firm experiences a constant rate of growth forever. We shall call it the *infinite constant growth model*. The second, developed later on, assumes that the firm can maintain a supernormal rate of growth (where $r_t > \rho$) for a finite period of time, T, and realizes a normal rate of growth thereafter. It is called the *finite supernormal growth model*.

The constant growth model can be derived from Eq. (15.16) if we assume that a constant fraction, K, of earnings is retained for investment and the average rate of return, r_t, on all projects is the same. The fraction of earnings to be retained for investment is usually called the retention ratio; however, there is no reason to restrict it to be less than 100% of cash flows from operations. Rather than calling K the retention rate, we shall call it the *investment rate*. As was mentioned in the first section of this chapter, the firm can invest more than cash flow from operations if it provides for the funds by issuing new equity. If investment is a constant proportion of cash flows, we have

$$I_t = K(\text{NOI}_t).\qquad(15.17)$$

And if the rate of return on investment, r_t, is the same for every project, then

$$\text{NOI}_t = \text{NOI}_{t-1} + rI_{t-1}$$
$$= \text{NOI}_{t-1} + rK\text{NOI}_{t-1}$$
$$= \text{NOI}_{t-1}(1 + rK).$$

By successive substitution, we have

$$\text{NOI}_t = \text{NOI}_1(1 + rK)^{t-1}.\qquad(15.18)$$

---

[5] However, do not underestimate the usefulness of Eq. (15.16). It is the basis for most commonly used valuation models, e.g., ALCAR, which is a personal computer–based model designed by Professor Al Rappaport of Northwestern.

Note that rK is the same as the rate of growth, g, for cash flows. In other words, NOI in the tth time period is the future value of NOI in the first time period, assuming that cash flows grow at a constant rate, g:

$$\text{NOI}_t = \text{NOI}_1(1 + g)^{t-1}.$$

By substituting (15.17) into (15.16) and maintaining the assumption that $r_t = r$, we have

$$V_0 = \frac{\text{NOI}_1}{\rho} + \sum_{t=1}^{\infty} \frac{K\text{NOI}_t(r - \rho)}{\rho(1 + \rho)^t}. \tag{15.19}$$

Then by using (15.18) in (15.19) we obtain

$$V_0 = \frac{\text{NOI}_1}{\rho} + K\text{NOI}_1\left(\frac{r - \rho}{\rho}\right) \sum_{t=1}^{\infty} \frac{(1 + rK)^{t-1}}{(1 + \rho)^t}$$

$$= \frac{\text{NOI}_1}{\rho}\left[1 + \frac{K(r - \rho)}{1 + rK} \sum_{t=1}^{\infty} \left(\frac{1 + rK}{1 + \rho}\right)^t\right]. \tag{15.20}$$

If $rK < \rho$, then the last term in (15.20) will have a finite limit:[6]

$$\lim_{N \to \infty} \sum_{t=1}^{N} \left(\frac{1 + rK}{1 + \rho}\right)^t = \frac{1 + rK}{\rho - rK} \quad \text{iff} \quad \rho > rK. \tag{15.20a}$$

Substituting (15.20a) into (15.20) and simplifying, we have an equation for the value of the firm, assuming infinite growth at a rate less than the market rate of return, ρ:

$$V_0 = \frac{\text{NOI}_1}{\rho}\left[1 + \frac{K(r - \rho)}{1 + Kr}\frac{1 + Kr}{\rho - rK}\right]$$

$$= \frac{\text{NOI}_1(1 - K)}{\rho - Kr}. \tag{15.21}$$

Equation (15.21), rewritten in a somewhat different form, is frequently referred to as the *Gordon growth model*. Note that since K is the investment rate (although K need not be less than one), the numerator of (15.21) is the same as dividends paid at the end of the first time period:

$$\text{NOI}_1(1 - K) = \text{Div}_1.$$

Also, as was shown earlier, the product of the investment rate and the average rate of return on investment is the same as the growth rate, g, in cash flows; therefore

$$Kr = g.$$

---

[6] For proof let $(1 + rK)/(1 + \rho) = U$. This can be written as

$$S - U + U^2 + \cdots + U^N.$$

Multiplying this by U and subtracting the result from the above, we have

$$S = U/(1 - U) - U^{N+1}/(1 - U).$$

The second term approaches zero in the limit as N approaches infinity. By substituting back the definition of U, we get (15.20a).

Given these facts and the necessary condition that $g < \rho$, the infinite growth model, Eq. (15.21), can be rewritten as

$$V_0 = \frac{\text{Div}_1}{\rho - g},$$ (15.21a)

which is the Gordon growth model.

4. Independence between Investment Plans and Dividend Payout

This form of the valuation model can be used to illustrate the relationship between the result that the value of the firm is independent of dividend policy and the assumption that investment decisions should never be affected by dividend payout. A commonly made error is to implicitly assume that there is some relationship between the amount of cash flow retained and the amount of investment the firm undertakes. Suppose we take the partial derivative of Eq. (15.21) with respect to changes in the investment rate, K:

$$\frac{\partial V_0}{\partial K} = \frac{\text{NOI}_1(r - \rho)}{(\rho - rK)^2} > 0.$$

This suggests that if the rate of return on investments, r, is greater than the market-required rate of return, ρ, the value of the firm will increase as more cash flow is retained, and presumably the increased amount of retained cash flow implies lower dividend payout. This line of reasoning is incorrect for two reasons. First, the amount of cash flow retained has nothing to do with dividend payout. As was shown in the sources and uses of funds, identity (15.3), the firm can arbitrarily set dividend payout at any level whatsoever, and if the sum of funds used for dividends and investment is greater than cash flows from operations, the firm will issue new equity. Second, the investment decision that maximizes shareholder wealth depends only on the market-required rate of return. The amount of cash flow retained could exceed the amount of investment, which would imply that shares would be repurchased. Therefore there is no relationship between the value of the firm and either dividend payout or cash flow retention.

5. The Bird-in-Hand Fallacy

A more sophisticated argument for a relationship between the value of the firm and dividend payout is that although the dividend decision cannot change the present value of cash payments to shareholders, it can affect the temporal pattern of payouts. Suppose that investors view distant dividend payments as riskier than current payments, might they not prefer a bird in the hand to two in the bush? We can represent this argument mathematically by assuming that higher investment rates mean lower current dividend payout, more risk, and therefore an increase in the market rate of return, ρ, as a function of the investment rate, K. A simple example would be to specify the relationship as

$$\rho = \alpha + \beta K^2, \qquad \beta > 0.$$

Then we would have

$$\frac{\partial V_0}{\partial K} = \frac{\text{NOI}_1(\beta K^2 - 2\beta K + r - \alpha)}{(\alpha + \beta K^2 - rK)^2}, \qquad \alpha + \beta K^2 - rK > 0.$$

This function will have a maximum where

$$\text{NOI}_1(\beta K^2 - 2\beta K + r - \alpha) = 0.$$

To see the error in this line of reasoning, we need only to return to our understanding of valuation under uncertainty. The risk of the firm is determined by the riskiness of the cash flows from its projects. An increase in dividend payout today will result in an equivalent drop in the ex-dividend price of the stock. It will not increase the value of the firm by reducing the riskiness of future cash flows.

6. Finite Supernormal Growth Model for an All-Equity Firm

Perhaps the most useful variation of the valuation equation is one that assumes that the rate of return on investment is greater than the market-required rate of return for a finite number of years, T, and from then on is equal to the market-required rate of return. In other words the firm experiences supernormal growth for a short period of time, then settles down and grows at a rate that is equal to the rate of growth in the economy. Obviously a firm cannot grow faster than the economy forever or it would soon be larger than the economy.

To derive the finite growth model we start with Eq. (15.20). Note that the summation is no longer infinite:

$$V_0 = \frac{\text{NOI}_1}{\rho}\left[1 + \frac{K(r - \rho)}{1 + rK}\sum_{t=1}^{T}\left(\frac{1 + rK}{1 + \rho}\right)^t\right]. \tag{15.20}$$

Instead, growth lasts for only T years. After year T, we assume that $r = \rho$, which means that the second term adds nothing to the present value of the firm. Whenever a firm is earning a rate of return just equal to its cost of capital, the net present value of investment is zero. The summation term in Eq. (15.20) can be evaluated as follows. Let

$$U = [(1 + rK)/(1 + \rho)].$$

We can then expand the sum:

$$S = U + U^2 + \cdots + U^T.$$

Multiplying this by U and subtracting the result, we have

$$S - US = U - U^{T+1}.$$

Solving for S and substituting back for U, we obtain

$$S = \frac{U - U^{T+1}}{1 - U} = \frac{[(1 + Kr)/(1 + \rho)] - [(1 + Kr)/(1 + \rho)]^{T+1}}{1 - [(1 + Kr)/(1 + \rho)]}$$

$$= \frac{(1 + Kr)\{1 - [(1 + Kr)/(1 + \rho)]^T\}}{\rho - Kr}. \tag{15.21b}$$

Substituting (15.21b) into (15.20) yields

$$V_0 = \frac{\text{NOI}_1}{\rho}\left\{1 + \frac{Kr - \rho K}{\rho - Kr}\left[1 - \left(\frac{1 + Kr}{1 + \rho}\right)^T\right]\right\}. \qquad (15.22)$$

As long as Kr is approximately equal to ρ, and T is small, we can approximate the last term as[7]

$$\left(\frac{1 + Kr}{1 + \rho}\right)^T \approx 1 - T\left(\frac{\rho - Kr}{1 + \rho}\right). \qquad (15.23)$$

By substituting the approximation (15.23) into the valuation equation (15.22), we have an approximate valuation formula for finite supernormal growth:[8]

$$V_0 = \frac{\text{NOI}_1}{\rho} + \frac{K(r - \rho)}{\rho - Kr}T\left(\frac{\rho - Kr}{1 + \rho}\right)\frac{\text{NOI}_1}{\rho}$$

$$= \frac{\text{NOI}_1}{\rho} + K(\text{NOI}_1)T\left[\frac{r - \rho}{\rho(1 + \rho)}\right]. \qquad (15.24)$$

---

[7] The binomial expansion can be used to derive the approximation in the following way. Let $(1 + Kr)/(1 + \rho) = 1 + \Delta$. Then, recalling that $Kr = g$, we have

$$\left(\frac{1 + g}{1 + \rho}\right)^T = (1 + \Delta)^T = \sum_{K=0}^{T}\binom{T}{K}(1)^{T-K}\Delta^K$$

$$= 1 + T\Delta + \sum_{K=2}^{T}\binom{T}{K}\Delta^K \approx 1 + T\Delta.$$

Solving for Δ, we have

$$\Delta = \frac{1 + Kr}{1 + \rho} - 1 = \frac{Kr - \rho}{1 + \rho}.$$

Therefore the correct approximation is

$$1 + T\Delta = 1 - T\left(\frac{\rho - Kr}{1 + \rho}\right).$$

[8] To simulate the validity of the approximation, assume that the investment rate, K, is 50%, the rate of return on investment, r, is 20%, and the market-required rate of return is 15%. Figure 15.A is a plot of $[(1 + Kr)/(1 + \rho)]$. We can see visually that the linear approximation is reasonable.

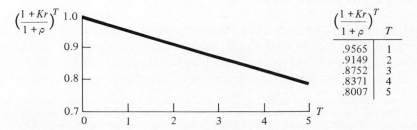

$\left(\frac{1+Kr}{1+\rho}\right)^T$	T
.9565	1
.9149	2
.8752	3
.8371	4
.8007	5

Figure 15.A
The linear approximation of the growth term.

7. Finite Supernormal Growth Model for a Firm with Debt and Taxes

Up to this point, we have maintained the assumption that we are dealing with an all-equity firm in a world without taxes. To extend the above valuation equation into a world where firms have debt as well as equity and where there are corporate taxes, we can rely on the results obtained in Chapter 13. The value of a levered firm with finite supernormal growth can be written as follows:

$$V = \frac{\text{NOI}_1(1 - \tau_c)}{\rho} + \tau_c B + K[\text{NOI}_1(1 - \tau_c)]T\left[\frac{r - \text{WACC}}{\text{WACC}(1 + \text{WACC})}\right], \quad (15.25)$$

where

   NOI = end-of-year net operating profits,

WACC = weighted average cost of capital = $\rho[1 - \tau_c B/(B + S)]$,

   B = market value of debt,

   K = investment rate,

   T = the number of years that $r > \text{WACC}$,

   r = the average rate of return on investment,

   ρ = the cost of equity capital for an all-equity firm.

The first two terms in (15.25) are the value of a levered firm with no growth, i.e., the value of assets in place. They are the same as Eq. (13.3), the Modigliani-Miller result that assumes that firms pay corporate taxes but are not growing. The third term in Eq. (15.25) is the value of growth for the levered firm. It depends on the amount of investment, $I_t = K(\text{NOI}_t)$, the difference between the expected average rate of return on investment and the weighted average cost of capital, $r - \text{WACC}$, and the length of time, T, that the new investment is expected to earn more than the weighted average cost of capital.

Equation (15.25) is used in Chapter 16 as the basis for the valuation of Bethlehem Steel. Note, however, that even in this model (which is the most realistic of those developed so far in this chapter) dividend payout is not relevant for determining the value of the firm.

C. DIVIDEND POLICY IN A WORLD WITH PERSONAL AND CORPORATE TAXES

Up to this point the models of firms that have been introduced assume a world with only corporate taxes. What happens when personal taxes are considered? In particular, how is dividend policy affected by the important fact that in the United States the capital gains tax is less than the personal income tax?[9] An answer to this question

---

[9] The 1986 tax code nominally makes the capital gains *rate* equal to the ordinary income rate. However, capital gains taxes are still less than ordinary taxes in effect, because capital gains can be deferred indefinitely, whereas taxes on ordinary income cannot.

is provided by Farrar and Selwyn [1967] and extended into a market equilibrium framework by Brennan [1970].[10]

Farrar and Selwyn use partial equilibrium analysis and assume that individuals attempt to maximize their after-tax income. Shareholders have two choices. They can own shares in an all-equity firm and borrow in order to provide personal leverage, or they can buy shares in a levered firm. Therefore the first choice is the amount of personal versus corporate leverage that is desired. The second choice is the form of payment to be made by the firm. It can pay out earnings as dividends, or it can retain earnings and allow shareholders to take their income in the form of capital gains. Shareholders must choose whether they want dividends or capital gains.

If the firm pays out all its cash flows as dividends, the ith shareholder will receive the following after-tax income, $\tilde{Y}_i^d$:

$$\tilde{Y}_i^d = [(\widetilde{\text{NOI}} - rD_c)(1 - \tau_c) - rD_{pi}](1 - \tau_{pi}), \tag{15.26}$$

where

$\tilde{Y}_i^d =$ the uncertain income to the ith individual if corporate income is received as dividends,

$\widetilde{\text{NOI}} =$ the uncertain cash flows from operations provided by the firm,

$r =$ the borrowing rate, which is assumed to be equal for individuals and firms,

$D_c =$ corporate debt,

$D_{pi} =$ personal debt held by the ith individual,

$\tau_c =$ the corporate tax rate,

$\tau_{pi} =$ the personal income tax rate of the ith individual.

The first term within the brackets is the after-tax cash flow of the firm, which is $(\widetilde{\text{NOI}} - rD)(1 - \tau_c)$. All of this is assumed to be paid out as dividends. The before-tax income to the shareholder is the dividends received minus the interest on debt used to buy shares. After subtracting income taxes on this income, we are left with Eq. (15.26).

Alternatively, the firm can decide to pay no dividends, in which case we assume that all gains are realized *immediately* by investors and taxed at the capital gains rate.[11] In this event the after-tax income of a shareholder is

$$\tilde{Y}_i^g = (\widetilde{\text{NOI}} - rD_c)(1 - \tau_c)(1 - \tau_{gi}) - rD_{pi}(1 - \tau_{pi}), \tag{15.27}$$

where

$\tilde{Y}_i^g =$ the uncertain income to the ith individual if corporate income is received as capital gains,

$\tau_{gi} =$ the capital gains rate for the ith individual.

---

[10] More recently Miller and Scholes [1978] have also considered a world with dividends and taxes. The implications of this paper are discussed later on in this chapter.

[11] Obviously there is the third possibility that earnings are translated into capital gains and the capital gains taxes are deferred to a later date. This possibility is considered in Farrar and Selwyn [1967]; it does not change their conclusions.

Now the individual pays a capital gains tax rate on the income from the firm and deducts after-tax interest expenses on personal debt. The corporation can implement the policy of translating cash flows into capital gains by simply repurchasing its shares in the open market.

We can rewrite Eq. (15.27) as follows:

$$\tilde{Y}_i^g = [(\widetilde{NOI} - rD_c)(1 - \tau_c) - rD_{pi}](1 - \tau_{gi}) + rD_{pi}(\tau_{pi} - \tau_{gi}). \qquad (15.28)$$

From Eqs. (15.26) and (15.28) the advantage to investors of receiving returns in the form of capital gains rather than dividends should be obvious. So long as the tax rate on capital gains is less than the personal tax rate ($\tau_{gi} < \tau_{pi}$), individuals will prefer capital gains to dividends for any positive operating cash flows, rate of interest, and level of debt (personal or corporate). The ratio of the two income streams,

$$\frac{\tilde{Y}_i^g}{\tilde{Y}_i^d} = \frac{[(\widetilde{NOI} - rD_c)(1 - \tau_c) - rD_{pi}](1 - \tau_{gi}) + rD_{pi}(\tau_{pi} - \tau_{gi})}{[(\widetilde{NOI} - rD_c)(1 - \tau_c) - rD_{pi}](1 - \tau_{pi})} > 1, \qquad (15.29)$$

is greater than one if $\tau_{gi} < \tau_{pi}$. In general the best form of payment is the one that is subject to least taxation. The implication, of course, is that corporations should never pay dividends. If payments are to be made to shareholders, they should always be made via share repurchase. This allows shareholders to avoid paying income tax rates on dividends. Instead, they receive their payments in the form of capital gains that are taxed at a lower rate.

What about debt policy? Again the same principle holds. The debt should be held by the party who can obtain the greatest tax shield from the deductible interest payments. This is the party with the greatest marginal tax rate. If the firm pays out all its cash flow in the form of dividends, the favorable tax treatment of capital gains is irrelevant. In this case we have the familiar Modigliani-Miller [1963] result that the value of the firm is maximized by taking on the maximum amount of debt (see Chapter 13). Proof is obtained by taking the partial derivative of Eq. (15.26) with respect to personal and corporate debt and comparing the results.

Debt policy becomes more complex when the corporation repurchases shares instead of paying dividends. Taking the partial derivatives of the capital gains income equation, (15.27), we obtain

$$\text{Corporate debt:} \quad \frac{\partial \tilde{Y}_i^g}{\partial D_c} = -r(1 - \tau_c)(1 - \tau_{gi}), \qquad (15.30)$$

$$\text{Personal debt:} \quad \frac{\partial \tilde{Y}_i^g}{\partial D_{pi}} = -r(1 - \tau_{pi}). \qquad (15.31)$$

If the effective tax rate on capital gains is zero (as Miller [1977] suggests), then personal debt will be preferred to corporate debt by those individuals who are in marginal tax brackets higher than the marginal tax bracket of the firm. This result allows the possibility of clientele effects where low-income investors prefer corporate debt and high-income investors prefer personal debt. Miller [1977] takes this argument even further. He shows that if the borrowing rate on debt is "grossed up" so that the after-tax rate on debt equals the after-tax rate on other sources of capital, the marginal investor will be indifferent between personal and corporate debt.[12]

Empirical evidence about the existence of debt clienteles is discussed in Chapter 16. Some clientele effects are obvious. For example, high tax bracket individuals hold tax-free municipal bonds, whereas low tax bracket investors like pension funds (which pay no taxes) prefer to invest in taxable corporate bonds. A much more subtle question, however, is whether investors discriminate among various corporate debt issues, i.e., do high tax bracket investors choose low-leverage firms?

Brennan [1970] extends the work of Farrar and Selwyn into a general equilibrium framework where investors are assumed to maximize their expected utility of wealth. Although this framework is more robust, Brennan's conclusions are not much different from those of Farrar and Selwyn. With regard to dividend payout Brennan concludes that "for a given level of risk, investors require a higher total return on a security the higher its prospective dividend yield is, because of the higher rate of tax levied on dividends than on capital gains." As we shall see in the next chapter, this statement has empirical implications for the CAPM. It suggests that dividend payout should be included as a second factor to explain the equilibrium rate of return on securities. If true, the empirical CAPM would become

$$R_{jt} - R_{ft} = \delta_0 + \delta_1\beta_{jt} + \delta_2[(\text{div}_{jt}/P_{jt} - R_{ft})] + \tilde{\varepsilon}_{jt}, \qquad (15.32)$$

where

δ_0 = a constant,

δ_1 = influence of systematic risk on R_{jt},

δ_2 = influence of dividend payout on R_{jt},

β_{jt} = the systematic risk of the jth security,

div_{jt}/P_{jt} = the dividend yield of the jth security,

$\tilde{\varepsilon}_{jt}$ = a random error term,

R_{ft} = the risk-free rate.

If the dividend yield factor turns out to be statistically significant, then we might conclude that dividend policy is not irrelevant. Direct empirical tests of the relationship between dividend yield and share value are discussed in Chapter 16.

A paper by Miller and Scholes [1978] shows that even if the tax on ordinary personal income is greater than the capital gains tax, many individuals need not pay more than the capital gains rate on dividends. The implication is that individuals will be indifferent between payments in the form of dividends or capital gains (if the firm decides to repurchase shares). Thus the firm's value may be unrelated to its dividend policy even in a world with personal and corporate taxes.

---

[12] The reader is referred to Chapter 13 for a complete discussion of this point.

Table 15.3

Opening Balance Sheet				*Closing Balance Sheet*			
Assets		Liabilities		Assets		Liabilities	
2,500 shares at $10	= 25,000	Loan	16,667	2,500 shares at $10.60	= 26,500	Loan	16,667
Insurance	16,667	Net worth	25,000	Accrued dividends	1,000	Accrued interest	1,000
	41,667		41,667	Insurance	16,667	Net worth	26,500
					44,167		44,167

Ordinary income		Capital gains	
Dividends received	$1,000	Sale of 2,500 shares at $10.60 = $26,500	
Less interest expense	1,000	Less original basis	25,000
	0		1,500
Nontaxable income	1,000		
	1,000		

To clarify their argument, Miller and Scholes provide the following simple example. Let us suppose we have an initial net worth of $25,000, which is represented wholly by an investment of 2500 shares worth $10 each in a company that earns $1.00 per share. At the end of the year the company pays $0.40 per share in dividends and retains $0.60. Consequently, its end-of-year price per share is $10.60. In order to neutralize our dividend income for tax purposes, we borrow $16,667 at 6% and invest the proceeds in a risk-free project (such as life insurance or a Keogh account) that pays 6% of tax-deferred interest. Our opening and closing balance sheets and our income statement are given in Table 15.3. Note that by investing in risk-free assets we have not increased the risk of our wealth position. The riskless cash inflows from insurance exactly match the required payments on debt. Our true economic income could be $1,500 in *unrealized* capital gains plus the $1,000 of tax-deferred interest from life insurance or our Keogh account.

Of course, federal tax laws are complex and these transactions cannot be carried out without some transactions costs.[13] Nevertheless, the above argument is a clever way to demonstrate the fact that ordinary income taxes on dividends can be avoided. The 1986 tax code eliminated interest deductions on all forms of personal debt except housing, where the amount of debt is limited to the original purchase price plus improvements. This shift in the tax code has caused a reorganization of the consumer debt market and made home equity loans a growth business.

---

[13] Also the maximum amount of dividends that can be sheltered in this way is $10,000. See Feenberg [1981].

D. TOWARD A THEORY OF OPTIMAL DIVIDEND POLICY

The Miller-Modigliani [1961] paper proved the irrelevance of dividend policy in a world where there were no taxes or transactions costs and where everyone was fully informed about the distribution of the firm's uncertain future cash flows. Once corporate and personal income taxes were introduced, then the theory (e.g., Farrar and Selwyn [1967] and Brennan [1970]) suggested that perhaps it would be optimal to pay no dividends at all because of the tax disadvantage of ordinary income over capital gains. This point of view was modified somewhat by Miller and Scholes [1978] who showed how dividend income could, to a large extent, be sheltered from taxation. The papers mentioned below go one step further. They provide theories to explain benefits as well as costs of dividend payout in an effort to move toward a theory of optimal dividend policy.

1. A Theory Based on Taxes and Investment Opportunities

The complex individual and corporate tax system in the United States may be an important part of the dividend puzzle. Masulis and Trueman [1986] model the investment and dividend decision under fairly realistic assumptions and show that the cost of deferring dividends may be large enough to induce firms to optimally pay cash dividends. The tax system that they model assumes:

1. Corporations all pay the same effective marginal tax rate, τ_c.
2. Personal tax rates on dividend income, τ_{di}, differ across individuals.
3. Capital gains taxes, τ_g, are effectively zero.
4. The IRS taxes regular corporate repurchases of equity in the same way as dividend payments.
5. There is an 80% dividend exclusion from taxes on all dividends paid by one corporation to another.[14]

In addition, to keep capital structure questions separate from dividend policy, they assume no debt.

Figure 15.2 illustrates the effect of taxes on the supply and demand for investment funds. Internal capital (retained earnings) and external equity capital (proceeds from new issues) have different costs to the firm. If retained earnings are not reinvested, then the ith shareholder receives the following after-tax return for each dollar paid out as dividends:

$$r_A(1 - \tau_c)(1 - \tau_{di}) = \text{Cost of internal funds}, \tag{15.33}$$

where r_A = the pretax return on investments in real assets.

---

[14] Prior to the 1986 tax code the dividend exclusion rate was 85%.

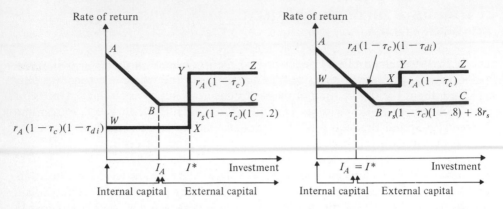

Figure 15.2
Corporate investment and dividend decisions with differing personal tax rates.

For example, if the pretax return required on investments of equal risk is $r_A = 15\%$, the corporate tax rate is $\tau_c = 50\%$, and the individual's tax rate is 40%, then the individual will be indifferent between (1) earning 9.0% before taxes on corporate investment and (2) receiving dividends.[15] If the individual's tax rate is 20%, a 12% before-tax rate on investment will be required. The higher an individual's tax bracket, the more likely he or she is to want the firm to invest cash flows internally instead of paying dividends, even when investment returns decline with more investment. The line segment WX in Fig. 15.2 represents the cost of capital to current shareholders in different tax brackets. In Fig. 15.2(a) it represents a high tax bracket shareholder, and in Fig. 15.2(b), a low tax bracket shareholder. At point Y are shareholders who pay no personal taxes at all (e.g., pension funds). They are indifferent between earnings retention and dividend payout because their opportunity cost is the same as the cost of external capital to the firm:

$$r_A = (1 - \tau_c) = \text{Cost of external funds.} \qquad (15.34)$$

External funds are more expensive to the firm because investors do not pay double taxes (corporate and personal) on funds put to other uses. It is assumed that alternative investments earn capital gains only and therefore are not taxed at the personal level. The cost of external equity capital is illustrated by the horizontal line segment YZ in Fig. 15.2 (both panels).

---

[15] Given an individual tax rate of 40%, and a 15% before-tax rate on investment, the after-tax rate on a dollar paid out as dividends should be

$$r_A(1 - \tau_c)(1 - \tau_{di}) = .15(1 - .5)(1 - .4) = .045.$$

If the money is kept in the firm, the before-tax return can fall to 9.0% and should give the same after-tax yield, assuming there is no capital gains tax:

$$r_A(1 - \tau_c) = .09(1 - .5) = .045.$$

See Eq. (15.34) for the cost of external equity capital.

The firm has two categories of investment opportunity. First are investments in real assets, represented by line segment AB and assumed to have diminishing returns to scale. Second are investments in securities of other firms. These securities investments have constant returns to scale as illustrated by line segment BC. The before-tax return on investments in securities of other firms is defined as r_s. There is a virtually infinite amount of security investment (in assets of equivalent risk), but their after-tax rate of return to the firm is affected by the fact that it must pay corporate taxes on 20% of the dividends it receives from ownership of other firms. Thus the after-tax return on security investments is

$$r_s(1 - \tau_c)(1 - .80) + .80r_s. \tag{15.35}$$

To reach its optimal investment/dividend decision the firm in Fig. 15.2(a) uses internal funds to undertake all investments in real assets, I_A, and then invests in securities of other firms up to the amount I^*. At this point it stops because the after-tax return on investing in securities is less than the opportunity cost of capital for externally supplied equity, and we see that the investment in real assets, I_A, is less than total investment, I^*. Since all internal funds have been used, dividends will not be paid out. The high tax bracket shareholders, in Fig. 15.2(a), prefer low (or zero) dividend payout.

In Fig. 15.2(b), which has the same investment schedule, low tax bracket shareholders have a higher opportunity cost for internally generated funds. They will want investment in real assets to stop at $I_A = I^*$. At this point, not all internally generated capital has been spent on real investment and dividends are paid out. For low tax bracket shareholders the cost of deferring dividends is sufficiently high that they prefer dividend payout.

One of the implications of this model is that shareholders with different tax rates, τ_{di}, will not unanimously agree on the firm's investment/dividend decision. High tax bracket shareholders would prefer the firm to invest more, whereas low tax bracket shareholders would prefer less investment and more dividend payout. This lack of unanimity can be diminished somewhat if investors self-select into clienteles with low tax bracket individuals purchasing shares of high-dividend firms and vice versa. Empirical evidence on dividend clienteles is reviewed in Chapter 16.

There are (at least) five other implications of the Masulis-Trueman model. (1) Firms are predicted not to externally finance security purchases for investment purposes. However, they are likely to purchase marketable securities with internally generated funds that remain after financing their own profitable production opportunities. (2) Firms with many profitable production opportunities (high-growth firms) will use up all their internally generated funds without paying dividends, but older, more mature firms will pay dividends because not all internally generated funds will be exhausted by investment opportunities. (3) Mergers are predicted between firms where one is internally financing its profitable investments and the other is externally financing. (4) While a decrease in current earnings should leave unchanged the investment expenditures of externally financed firms, it is likely to decrease investment expenditures of firms that initially planned to internally finance all their investments rather than to make up the shortfall of funds through external financing. (5) Shareholder disagreement over internally financed investment policy will be more likely the greater the amount of internally generated funds relative to the firm's investment opportunities. In these cases, firms are more likely to experience takeover attempts, proxy fights, and efforts to "go private." Given these tax-induced shareholder conflicts, diffuse ownership is more likely for externally financed firms than for internally financed firms.

2. Theories Based on the Informativeness of Dividend Payout

Ross [1977] suggests that implicit in the Miller-Modigliani dividend irrelevancy proposition is the assumption that the market *knows* the (random) return stream of the firm and values this stream to set the value of the firm. What is valued in the marketplace, however, is the *perceived* stream of returns for the firm. Putting the issue this way raises the possibility that changes in the capital structure (or dividend payout) may alter the market's perception. In the terminology of Modigliani and Miller, a change in the financial structure (or dividend payout) of the firm alters its perceived risk class even though the actual risk class remains unchanged.

Managers, as insiders who have monopolistic access to information about the firm's expected cash flows, will choose to establish unambiguous signals about the firm's future if they have the proper incentive to do so. We saw, in Chapter 14, that changes in the capital structure of the firm may be used as signals. In particular, Ross [1977] proved that an increase in the use of debt will represent an unambiguous signal to the marketplace that the firm's prospects have improved. Empirical evidence seems to confirm the theory.

The signaling concept is easily applied to dividend policy as well as to financial structure. We shall see that a possible benefit of dividends is that they provide valuable signals. This benefit can be balanced against the costs of paying dividends to establish a theory of optimal dividend policy.

A firm that increases dividend payout is signaling that it has expected future cash flows that are sufficiently large to meet debt payments and dividend payments without increasing the probability of bankruptcy. Therefore we may expect to find empirical evidence that shows that the value of the firm increases because dividends are taken as signals that the firm is expected to have permanently higher future cash flows. Chapter 16 reviews the empirical evidence on dividends as signals.

Bhattacharya [1979] develops a model closely related to that of Ross that can be used to explain why firms may pay dividends despite the tax disadvantage of doing so. If investors believe that firms that pay greater dividends per share have higher values, then an unexpected dividend increase will be taken as a favorable signal. Presumably dividends convey information about the value of the firm that cannot be fully communicated by other means such as annual reports, earnings forecasts, or presentations before security analysts. It is expensive for less successful firms to mimic the signal because they must incur extra costs associated with raising external funds in order to pay the cash dividend.[16] Hence the signaling value of dividends is positive and can be traded off against the tax loss associated with dividend income (as opposed to capital gains). Even firms that are closely held would prefer to pay dividends because the value induced by the signal is received by current owners only when the dividend message is communicated to outsiders. One of the important implications of this signaling argument is that it suggests the possibility of optimal dividend policy. The signaling benefits from paying dividends may be traded off against the tax disadvantages in order to achieve an optimal payout.

Hakansson [1982] has expanded the understanding of informative signaling to show that in addition to being informative at least one of three sufficient conditions must be met. Either investors must have different probability assessments of dividend payouts, or they must have differing attitudes about how they wish to allocate consumption expenditures over time, or the financial markets must be incomplete. All three of these effects may operate in a complementary fashion, and all three are reasonable.

Miller and Rock [1985] develop a financial signaling model founded on the concept of "net dividends." It is the first theory that explicitly combines dividends and external financing to show that they are merely two sides of the same coin. The announcement that "heads is up" also tells us that "tails is down." As was pointed out in the original Miller-Modigliani [1961] article, every firm is subject to a sources and uses of funds constraint:

$$\text{NOI} + mP + \Delta B = I + \text{Div}. \tag{15.36}$$

Recall that sources of funds are NOI, the firm's net operating income; mP, the proceeds from an issue of external equity (the number of new shares, m, times the price per share, P); and ΔB, the proceeds from new debt. Uses of funds are investment, I, and dividends, Div. The sources and uses constraint can be rearranged to have net cash flows from operations on the left-hand side and the firm's "net dividend" on the right-hand side:

$$\text{NOI} - I = \text{Div} - \Delta B - mP. \tag{15.37}$$

Now imagine a model where time 1 is the present, time 0 is the past, and time 2 is the future. The present value of the firm, cum dividend, is the value of the current dividend, Div_1, plus the discounted value of cash flows (discounted at the appropriate risk-adjusted rate, k):

$$V_1 = \text{Div}_1 + \frac{E(\text{NOI}_2)}{1 + k}. \tag{15.38}$$

---

[16] This suggests that dividend payout and debt level increases are interrelated signals. A firm that simultaneously pays dividends and borrows may be giving a different signal than if it had made the same dividend payment without borrowing.

Original shareholders' wealth is the value of the firm minus the market value of debt and new equity issued:

$$S_1 = V_1 - \Delta B_1 = \text{Div}_1 + \frac{E(\text{NOI}_2)}{1+k} - \Delta B_1 - mP_1. \qquad (15.39)$$

Using the sources and uses constraint, Eq. (15.37), we have

$$S_1 = \text{NOI}_1 - I_1 + \frac{E(\text{NOI}_2)}{1+k}. \qquad (15.40)$$

Without any information asymmetry, this is just the original Miller-Modigliani proposition that dividends are irrelevant. All that counts is the investment decision.

If there is information asymmetry, Eq. (15.40) must be rewritten to show how market expectations are formed. If future earnings depend on current investment, then we can write that net operating income is a function of the amount of investment plus a random error term,

$$\text{NOI}_1 = f(I_0) + \varepsilon_1,$$

$$\text{NOI}_2 = f(I_1) + \varepsilon_2,$$

where ε_1 and ε_2 are random error terms with zero mean, i.e., $E(\varepsilon_1) = E(\varepsilon_2) = 0$. We also adopt the special assumption that the expectation of ε_2 given ε_1 is not necessarily zero:

$$E(\varepsilon_2 | \varepsilon_1) = \gamma \varepsilon_1.$$

If γ is interpreted as a persistence coefficient, $0 < \gamma < 1$, the market is assumed to only partially adjust to new information (the first-period error). If we use the notation E_0 to remind us that the current value of the firm is based on preannouncement information, then the current expected value of shareholders' wealth is

$$E(S_1) = E_0(\text{NOI}_1) - E_0(I_1) + \frac{E_0[f(I_1)]}{1+k}$$

$$= f(I_0) - I_1 + \frac{f(I_1)}{1+k}. \qquad (15.41)$$

The corresponding postannouncement value of the firm is

$$S_1 = \text{NOI}_1 - I_1 + \frac{E_1(\text{NOI}_2)}{1+k}$$

$$= f(I_0) + \varepsilon_1 - I_1 + \frac{f(I_1) + \varepsilon_2}{1+k}$$

$$= f(I_0) + \varepsilon_1 - I_1 + \frac{f(I_1) + \gamma \varepsilon_1}{1+k}. \qquad (15.42)$$

Subtracting (15.41) from (15.42) gives the announcement effect

$$S_1 - E(S_1) = \varepsilon_1 \left[1 + \frac{\gamma}{1+k} \right]$$

$$= [\text{NOI}_1 - E_0(\text{NOI}_1)] \left[1 + \frac{\gamma}{1+k} \right]. \qquad (15.43)$$

Equation (15.43) says that the announcement effect on shareholders' wealth will depend on the "earnings surprise." Thus we would expect that unexpected changes in earnings will be correlated with share price changes on the announcement date.

Miller and Rock go on to show that the earnings, dividend, and financing announcements are closely related. Assuming that the expected and actual investment decisions are at an optimum level, and are therefore equal, then the difference between the actual and net dividends is

$$\text{Div}_1 - \Delta B_1 - m_1 P_1 - E_0(\text{Div}_1 - \Delta B_1 - m_1 P_1) = \text{NOI}_1 - I_1 - [E(\text{NOI}_1) - I_1]$$

$$= \text{NOI}_1 - E(\text{NOI}_1).$$

Thus the earnings surprise and the net dividend surprise can convey the same information. The financing announcement effect is merely the dividend announcement effect, but with the sign reversed. An unexpected increase in dividends will increase shareholders' wealth, and an unexpected issue of new equity or debt will be interpreted as bad news about the future prospects of the firm.

The Miller-Rock signaling approach shows that announcement effects (including earnings surprises, unexpected dividend changes, and unexpected external financing) emerge naturally as implications of the basic valuation model rather than as ad hoc appendages.

One problem that the above theories have in common is that although they explain how an optimal dividend policy may arise, none of them can successfully explain cross-sectional differences in dividend payouts across firms.[17]

3. Agency Costs, External Financing, and Optimal Dividend Payout

Rozeff [1982] suggests that optimal dividend policy may exist even though we ignore tax considerations. He suggests that cross-sectional regularities in corporate dividend payout ratios[18] may be explained by a trade-off between the flotation costs of raising external capital and the benefit of reduced agency costs when the firm increases its dividend payout. It is not hard to understand that owners prefer to avoid paying the transactions costs associated with external financing.

As discussed earlier (Chapter 14, section B.4), there are agency costs that arise when owner-managers sell portions of their stockholdings to so-called outside equity

---

[17] A possible exception is the work of Miller and Rock [1985], which suggests that the next theory shows better promise in this regard.

[18] The payout ratio is the ratio of dividends to net income.

owners. The outsiders will charge, *ex ante*, for the potential problem that owner-managers may increase their personal wealth at the expense of outsiders by means of more perquisites or shirking. To decrease the *ex ante* charge, owner-managers will find it in their own interest to agree to incur monitoring or bonding costs if such costs are less than the *ex ante* charge that outsiders would be forced to request. Thus a wealth-maximizing firm will adopt an optimal monitoring/bonding policy that minimizes agency costs.

Dividend payments may well serve as a means of monitoring or bonding management performance. Although greater dividend payout implies costly external financing, the very fact that the firm must go to the capital markets implies that it will come under greater scrutiny. For example, banks will require a careful analysis of the creditworthiness of the firm, and the Securities and Exchange Commission will require prospectus filings for new equity issues. Thus outside suppliers of capital help to monitor the owner-manager on behalf of outside equity owners. Of course, audited financial statements are a substitute means for supplying the same information, but they may not be a perfect substitute for the "adversary" relationship between the firm and suppliers of new capital.

Because of the transactions costs of external financing, Rozeff also argues that the variability of a firm's cash flows will affect its dividend payout. Consider two firms with the same average cash flows across time but different variability. The firm with greater volatility will borrow in bad years and repay in good. It will need to finance externally more often. Consequently, it will tend to have a lower dividend payout ratio.

Rozeff [1982] selected a sample of 1000 nonregulated firms in 64 different industries and examined their average dividend payout ratios during the 1974–1980 interval. Five proxy variables were chosen to test his theory. The results are shown in Table 15.4. The independent variables GROW1 and GROW2 are an attempt to measure the effect of costly external financing. Firms that grow faster can reduce their need to use external financing by paying lower dividends. GROW1 measures the growth rate in revenues between 1974 and 1979, whereas GROW2 is Value Line's forecast of the growth of sales revenue over the five-year period 1979–1984. Both variables are negatively related to dividend payout and are statistically significant. The variables INS and STOCK are proxies for the agency relationship. INS is the percentage of the firm held by insiders. Dividend payout is negatively related to the percentage of insiders because given a lower percentage of outsiders there is less need to pay dividends to reduce agency costs.[19] On the other hand, if the distribution of outsider holdings is diffuse, then agency costs will be higher; hence one would expect STOCK, the number of stockholders, to be positively related to dividend payout. Both INS and STOCK are statistically significant and of the predicted sign. Finally, the variable BETA measures the riskiness of the firm. The prediction that riskier firms have lower dividend payout is verified by the regression.

---

[19] This relationship is also consistent with the tax argument that assumes that high tax bracket insiders prefer to take their return in the form of capital gains rather than dividends.

Table 15.4   Cross-Sectional Dividend Payout Regressions

	CONSTANT	INS	GROW1	GROW2	BETA	STOCK	R^2	D.W.	F-statistic
(1)	47.81 (12.83)	−0.090 (−4.10)	−0.321 (−6.38)	−0.526 (−6.43)	−26.543 (−17.05)	2.584 (7.73)	0.48	1.88	185.47
(2)	24.73 (6.27)	−0.068 (−2.75)	−0.474 (−8.44)	−0.758 (−8.28)	—	2.517 (6.63)	0.33	1.79	123.23
(3)	70.63 (40.35)	—	−0.402 (−7.58)	−0.603 (−6.94)	−25.409 (−15.35)	—	0.41	1.88	231.46
(4)	39.56 (10.02)	−0.116 (−4.92)	—	—	−33.506 (−21.28)	3.151 (8.82)	0.39	1.80	218.10
(5)	1.03 (0.24)	−0.102 (−3.60)	—	—	—	3.429 (7.97)	0.12	1.60	69.33

t-statistics are shown in parentheses under estimated values of the regression coefficients. R^2 is adjusted for degrees of freedom. D.W. is Durbin-Watson statistic.

From M. Rozeff, "Growth, Beta, and Agency Costs as Determinants of Dividend Payout Ratios," *Journal of Financial Research*, Fall 1982, 249–259. Reprinted with permission.

The best regression in Table 15.4 explains 48% of the cross-sectional variability in dividend payout across individual firms. Although the results cannot be used to distinguish among various theories of optimal dividend policy, they are consistent with Rozeff's predictions. Furthermore, the very existence of strong cross-sectional regularities suggests that there is an optimal dividend policy.

E. OTHER DIVIDEND POLICY ISSUES

1. Dividends, Shares Repurchase, and Spinoffs from the Bondholders' Point of View

Debt contracts, particularly when long-term debt is involved, frequently restrict a firm's ability to pay cash dividends. Such restrictions usually state that (1) future dividends can be paid only out of earnings generated after the signing of the loan agreement (i.e., future dividends cannot be paid out of past retained earnings) and (2) dividends cannot be paid when net working capital (current assets minus current liabilities) is below a prespecified amount.

One need not restrict the argument to only dividend payout. When any of the assets of a corporation are paid out to shareholders in any type of capital distribution, the effect is to "steal away" a portion of the bondholders' collateral. In effect, some of the assets that bondholders could claim, in the event that shareholders decide to default, are paid out to shareholders. This diminishes the value of debt and increases the wealth of shareholders.

Of course, the most common type of capital distribution is a dividend payment. A portion of the firm's assets is paid out in the form of cash dividends to shareholders. The most extreme example of defrauding bondholders would be to simply liquidate the assets of the firm and pay out a single, final dividend to shareholders, thereby leaving bondholders with a claim to nothing. For this very reason, most bond indentures explicitly restrict the dividend policy of shareholders. Usually dividends cannot exceed the current earnings of the firm, and they cannot be paid out of retained earnings.

Other types of capital distributions are share repurchase and spinoffs. Share repurchase has exactly the same effect as dividend payment except that the form of payment is capital gains instead of dividend income. The conventional procedure for a spinoff is to take a portion of a firm's assets, often a division relatively unrelated to the rest of the firm, and create an independent firm with these assets. The important fact is that the shares of the new entity are distributed solely to the *shareholders* of the parent corporation. Therefore, like dividend payment or share repurchase, this may be used as a technique for taking collateral from bondholders. Empirical evidence on the effects of repurchases and spinoffs is covered in Chapter 16.

It is an interesting empirical question whether or not any dividend payment, no matter how large it is, will affect the market value of bonds. One would expect that the market price of bonds would reflect the risk that future dividend payments would lower the asset base that secures debt.[20] However, as changes in the dividend payments are actually realized, there may be changes in the expectations of the bondholders, which in turn would be reflected in the market price of bonds. All other things being equal, we may expect that higher dividend payments or share repurchases will be associated with a decline in the market value of debt. However, rarely do we have a situation where all other things are equal. For example, if announcements about dividend changes are interpreted as information about future cash flows, then a dividend increase means that current debt will be more secure because of the anticipated higher cash flows, and we would observe dividend increases to be positively correlated with increases in the market value of debt.

2. Stock Dividends and Share Repurchase

Stock dividends are often mentioned as part of the dividend policy of the firm. However, a stock dividend is nothing more than a small stock split. It simply increases the number of shares outstanding without changing any of the underlying risk or return characteristics of the firm. Therefore we might expect that it has little or no effect on shareholders' wealth except for the losses associated with the clerical and transactions costs that accompany the stock dividend. Recall, however, that the empirical evidence in Chapter 11 indicated that stock dividend announcements are in fact accompanied by statistically significant abnormal returns on the announcement date. So far, no adequate explanation has been provided for this fact, although Brennan and Copeland [1987] suggest that stock dividends may be used to force the early conversion of convertible debt, convertible preferred, or warrants, because these securities are frequently not protected against stock dividends.

---

[20] Dividend payments do not necessarily change the assets side of the balance sheet. When cash balances are reduced in order to pay dividends, there is an asset effect. However, it is not necessary. Dividends can also be paid by issuing new debt or equity. In this case, assets remain unaffected, and the dividend decision is purely financial in nature.

Another question that often arises is whether share repurchase is preferable to dividend payment as a means of distributing cash to shareholders. Share repurchase allows shareholders to receive the cash payment as a capital gain rather than as dividend income. Any shareholder who pays a higher tax rate on income than on capital gains would prefer share repurchase to dividend payment. But not all classes of shareholders have this preference. Some, like tax-free university endowment funds, are indifferent to income versus capital gains, whereas others, such as corporations with their dividend exclusions, would actually prefer dividends.

To see that share repurchase can result in the same benefit per share, consider the following example. The Universal Sourgum Company earns $4.4 million in 1981 and decides to pay out 50%, or $2.2 million, either as dividends or repurchase. The company has 1,100,000 shares outstanding with a market value of $22 per share. It can pay dividends of $2 per share or repurchase shares at $22 each. We know that the market price for repurchase is $22 rather than $20 because $22 will be the price per share after repurchase. To demonstrate this statement, we know that the current value of the (all-equity) firm is $24.2 million. For $2.2 million in cash it can repurchase 100,000 shares. Therefore after the repurchase the value of the firm falls to $24.2 − 2.2 = $22 million, and with 1,000,000 shares outstanding the price per share is $22. Thus, in theory, there is no price effect from repurchase.

A comparison of shareholders' wealth before taxes shows that it is the same with either payment technique. If dividends are paid, each shareholder receives a $2 dividend, and the ex-dividend price per share is $20 ($22 million ÷ 1.1 million shares). Alternately, as shown above, each share is worth $22 under repurchase, and a shareholder who needs cash can sell off a portion of his or her shares. The preferred form of payment (dividends versus repurchase) will depend on shareholders' tax rates.

In the example shown above there is no price effect from share repurchase. However, recent empirical studies of repurchases via tender offers have found a positive announcement effect. These studies are discussed in detail in Chapter 16.

SUMMARY

Several valuation models with or without growth and with or without corporate taxes have been developed. Dividend policy is irrelevant in all instances. It has no effect on shareholders' wealth. When personal taxes are introduced we have a result where dividends matter. For shareholders who pay higher taxes on dividends than on capital gains, the preferred dividend payout is zero; they would rather have the company distribute cash payments via the share repurchase mechanism. Yet corporations do pay dividends. The Rozeff [1982] paper suggests that there appear to be strong cross-sectional regularities in dividend payout. Thus there may be optimal dividend policies that result from a trade-off between the costs and benefits of paying dividends. The list of possible costs includes (1) tax disadvantages of receiving income in the form of dividends rather than capital gains, (2) the cost of raising external capital if dividends are paid out, and (3) the foregone use of funds for productive investment. The possible benefits of dividend payout are (1) higher perceived corporate value because of the signaling content of dividends, (2) lower agency costs of external equity, and (3) the ability of dividend payments to help complete the markets.

The next chapter presents empirical evidence that examines the relationship among the level of dividend payout, the value of the shares, and the amount of investment undertaken by the firm. Also, changes in dividend payout are studied in relation to their effect on share value. These studies provide greater insight into the empirical validity of the theories discussed here.

PROBLEM SET

15.1 The chairman of the board of Alphanull Corporation has announced that the corporation will change its dividend policy from paying a fixed dollar dividend per share. Instead, dividends will be paid out as a residual. That is, any cash flows left over after the firm has undertaken all profitable investments will be paid out to shareholders. This new policy will obviously increase the variability of dividends paid. How do you think it will affect the value of the firm?

15.2 The XYZ Company (an all-equity firm) currently has after-tax operating cash flows of $3.00 per share and pays out 50% of its earnings in dividends. If it expects to keep the same payout ratio, and to earn 20% on future investments forever, what will its current price per share be? Assume that the cost of capital is 15%.

15.3 The Highrise Investment Co. (an all-equity firm) currently pays a dividend of $2.00 per share, which is 75% of its after-tax cash flows from operations. It is currently selling for $16 a share and earns 40% on invested capital. Its equity β is 2.0, the expected market rate of return is 12.5%, and the risk-free rate is 5%. How long will its supernormal rate of growth last before it levels off to equal the normal rate for a company with its risk?

15.4 The balance sheet of the Universal Sour Candy Company is given in Table Q15.4. Assume that all balance sheet items are expressed in terms of market values. The company has decided to pay a $2000 dividend to shareholders. There are four ways to do it:

1) Pay a cash dividend.

2) Issue $2000 of new debt and equity in equal proportions ($1000 each) and use the proceeds to pay the dividend.

3) Issue $2000 of new equity and use the proceeds to pay the dividend.

4) Use the $2000 of cash to repurchase equity.

What impact will each of the four policies above have on the following?

a) The systematic risk of the portfolio of assets held by the firm,

b) The market value of original bondholders' wealth,

Table Q15.4   Balance Sheet as of December 31, 19xx

Assets		Liabilities	
Cash	$ 2,000	Debt	$ 5,000
Inventory	2,000	Equity	5,000
Property, plant, and equipment	6,000	Total liabilities	$10,000
Total assets	$10,000		

c) The market value ratio of debt to equity,

d) The market value of the firm in a world without taxes.

15.5 According to the valuation model [(15.25)] with finite supernormal growth and corporate taxes, there are six variables that affect the value of the firm.

a) What are they?

b) Why cannot the president of a firm cause the firm's market value to increase simply by reporting anticipated favorable changes in the six variables, e.g., an increase in expected return on investment?

15.6 Prove the following for a firm with no supernormal growth (in a world with only corporate taxes):

$$V^L = \frac{E(\text{NOI}_1)(1 - \tau_c)}{\text{WACC}} = V^U + \tau_c B.$$

15.7 Calculate the value of a company that earned $50,000 this year, has a 40% investment rate, K, and a tax rate of 40%; has $200,000 in debt outstanding and a weighted average cost of capital of 12%; and is expected to earn 40% on invested capital for the next five years, then 25% for the following five years, before the rate of return declines to a normal rate of growth.

15.8 How does an increase in the investment (retention) rate affect the anticipated stream of investments that a company will undertake?

15.9 It was suggested that if a firm announces its intention to increase its dividends (paid from cash), the price of common stock increases, presumably because the higher dividend payout represents an unambiguous signal to shareholders that anticipated cash flows from investment are permanently higher. A higher level of cash flows is also beneficial to bondholders because it diminishes the probability of default. If dividends are paid from cash, what does the OPM suggest will happen to the market value of debt? How does this contrast with the prediction in the above paragraph?

REFERENCES

Bar-Yosef, S., and R. Kolodny, "Dividend Policy and Market Theory," *Review of Economics and Statistics*, May 1976, 181–190.

Bhattacharya, S., "Imperfect Information, Dividend Policy, and 'The Bird in the Hand' Fallacy," *Bell Journal of Economics*, Spring 1979, 259–270.

Black, F., "The Dividend Puzzle," *Journal of Portfolio Management*, Winter 1976, 5–8.

———; M. Jensen; and M. Scholes, "The Capital Asset Pricing Model: Some Empirical Tests," in Jensen, ed., *Studies in the Theory of Capital Markets*. Praeger, New York, 1972, 79–124.

Black, F., and M. Scholes, "The Effects of Dividend Yield and Dividend Policy on Common Stock Prices and Returns," *Journal of Financial Economics*, May 1974, 1–22.

Brennan, M., "Taxes, Market Valuation and Corporate Financial Policy," *National Tax Journal*, December 1970, 417–427.

———, and T. Copeland, "A Model of Stock Split Behavior: Theory and Evidence," Working paper, Anderson Graduate School of Management, UCLA, April 1987.

Brittain, J. A., *Corporate Dividend Policy*. Brookings Institute, Washington, D.C., 1966.

Darling, P., "The Influence of Expectations and Liquidity on Dividend Policy," *Journal of Political Economy*, June 1957, 209–224.

Dobrovolsky, S., *The Economics of Corporation Finance*. McGraw-Hill, New York, 1971.

Fama, E., "The Empirical Relationships between the Dividend and Investment Decisions of Firms," *American Economic Review*, June 1974, 304–318.

———, and H. Babiak, "Dividend Policy: An Empirical Analysis," *Journal of the American Statistical Association*, December 1968, 1132–1161.

Fama, E., and M. H. Miller, *The Theory of Finance*. McGraw-Hill, New York, 1971.

Farrar, D., and L. Selwyn, "Taxes, Corporate Financial Policy and Return to Investors," *National Tax Journal*, December 1967, 444–454.

Feenberg, D., "Does the Investment Interest Limitation Explain the Existence of Dividends," *Journal of Financial Economics*, September 1981, 265–270.

Friend, I., and M. Puckett, "Dividends and Stock Prices," *American Economic Review*, September 1964, 656–682.

Gordon, M., "Dividends, Earnings, and Stock Prices," *Review of Economics and Statistics*, May 1959, 99–105.

———, "The Savings, Investment and Valuation of a Corporation," *Review of Economics and Statistics*, February 1962, 37–51.

Hakansson, N., "To Pay or Not to Pay Dividends," *Journal of Finance*, May 1982, 415–428.

John, K., and J. Williams, "Dividends, Dilution and Taxes: A Signalling Equilibrium," *Journal of Finance*, September 1985, 1053–1070.

Kaplanis, C., "Options, Taxes, and Ex-dividend Day Behavior," *Journal of Finance*, June 1986, 411–424.

Khoury, N., and K. Smith, "Dividend Policy and the Capital Gains Tax in Canada," *Journal of Business Administration*, Spring 1977.

Kim, E. H.; W. Lewellen; and J. McConnell, "Financial Leverage Clienteles: Theory and Evidence," *Journal of Financial Economics*, March 1979, 83–110.

Lintner, J., "Distribution of Incomes of Corporations among Dividends, Retained Earnings and Taxes," *American Economic Review*, May 1956, 97–113.

———, "Optimal Dividends and Corporate Growth under Uncertainty," *Quarterly Journal of Economics*, February 1964, 49–95.

———, "The Valuation of Risky Assets and the Selection of Risky Investments in Stock Portfolios and Capital Budgets," *Review of Economics and Statistics*, February 1965, 13–37.

Long, J., Jr., "Efficient Portfolio Choice with Differential Taxation of Dividends and Capital Gains," *Journal of Financial Economics*, August 1977, 25–54.

Masulis, R., and B. Trueman, "Corporate Investment and Dividend Decisions under Differential Personal Taxation," Working paper, Anderson Graduate School of Management, UCLA, 1986.

Miller, M., "Debt and Taxes," *The Journal of Finance*, May 1977, 261–275.

———, and F. Modigliani, "Dividend Policy, Growth and the Valuation of Shares," *Journal of Business*, October 1961, 411–433.

Miller, M. and K. Rock, "Dividend Policy Under Asymmetric Information," *Journal of Finance*, September 1985, 1031–1051.

Miller, M., and M. Scholes, "Dividends and Taxes," *Journal of Financial Economics*, December 1978, 333–364.

———, "Dividends and Taxes: Some Empirical Evidence," *Journal of Political Economy*, December 1982, 1118–1141.

Modigliani, F., and M. Miller, "Corporate Income Taxes and the Cost of Capital: A Correction," *American Economic Review*, June 1963, 433–442.

Pettit, R. R., "Dividend Announcements, Security Performance, and Capital Market Efficiency," *Journal of Finance*, December 1972, 993–1007.

Ross, S. A., "The Determination of Financial Structure: The Incentive-Signalling Approach," *Bell Journal of Economics*, Spring 1977, 23–40.

———, "Some Notes on Financial Incentive-Signalling Models, Activity Choice and Risk Preferences," *Journal of Finance*, June 1978, 777–792.

Rozeff, M., "Growth, Beta and Agency Costs as Determinants of Dividend Payout Ratios," *Journal of Financial Research*, Fall 1982, 249–259.

Sheffrin, H., and M. Statman, "Explaining Investor Preference for Cash Dividends," *Journal of Financial Economics*, June 1984, 253–282.

Walter, J. E., *Dividend Policy and Enterprise Valuation*. Wadsworth, Belmont, Calif., 1967.

Watts, R., "The Information Content of Dividends," *Journal of Business*, April 1973, 191–211.

16

. . . in the real world a change in the dividend rate is often followed by a change in the market price (sometimes spectacularly so). Such a phenomenon would not be incompatible with irrelevance to the extent that it was merely a reflection of what might be called the "informational content" of dividends . . .

M. Miller and F. Modigliani, "Dividend Policy, Growth, and the Valuation of Shares," *Journal of Business*, October 1961, 431.

Dividend Policy: Empirical Evidence and Applications

Our discussion first deals with models that simply explain the behavior of corporate dividend policy over time. Evidence indicates that U.S. corporations behave as if they had some target dividend payout in mind and that they move toward it with a lag. They also show reluctance to lower dividends.

Second, we look at the possibility of clientele effects. Do people in high tax brackets avoid investing in high-dividend companies in order to escape higher income taxes on dividend income? On this question, the empirical evidence is mixed, although it does lean toward the existence of a clientele effect.

Third, the information content of dividend increases is tested. There is reasonably strong evidence that leans toward validation of the signaling hypothesis.

Fourth, we focus on the relationship between dividend yield and the market value of equity. The best empirical evidence indicates that dividend yield is at most weakly related to the value of the firm. Several explanations are given for why this result is plausible, given our current tax system.

Fifth, the empirical literature relating to share repurchases via tender offer is reviewed. The announcement of share repurchases tends to be interpreted as unanticipated favorable news about the value of the company.

Finally, we apply the Miller-Modigliani valuation model to the case of Bethlehem Steel in order to demonstrate the relevance of the different factors that determine the value of a firm.

A. BEHAVIORAL MODELS OF DIVIDEND POLICY

Lintner [1956] conducted interviews with 28 carefully selected companies to investigate their thinking on the determination of dividend policy. His fieldwork suggested that (1) managers focused on the change in the existing rate of dividend payout, not on the amount of the newly established payout as such; (2) most managements sought to avoid making changes in their dividend rates that might have to be reversed within a year or so; (3) major changes in earnings "out of line" with existing dividend rates were the most important determinants of a company's dividend decisions; and (4) investment requirements generally had little effect on modifying the pattern of dividend behavior. Taken together, these observations suggest that most companies had somewhat flexible but nevertheless reasonably well-defined standards regarding the speed with which they would try to move toward a full adjustment of dividend payout to earnings. Lintner suggests that corporate dividend behavior can be described on the basis of the following equation:

$$\Delta \text{Div}_{it} = a_i + c_i(\text{Div}_{it}^* - \text{Div}_{i,t-1}) + U_{it}, \tag{16.1}$$

where

ΔDiv_{it} — the change in dividends,

$\quad c_i$ — the speed of adjustment to the difference between a target dividend payout and last year's payout,

Div_{it}^* = the target dividend payout,

$\text{Div}_{i,t-1}$ = last period's dividend payout,

$\quad a_i, U_{it}$ = a constant and a normally distributed random error term.

The target dividend payout, Div_{it}^*, is a fraction, r_i, of this period's earnings, NI_{it}. Upon fitting the equations to annual data from 1918 through 1941, Lintner finds that the model explains 85% of the changes in dividends for his sample of companies. The average speed of adjustment is approximately 30% per year, and the target payout is 50% of earnings.

Fama and Babiak [1968] investigate many different models for explaining dividend behavior. They use a sample of 201 firms with 17 years of data (1947–1964), then test each explanatory model by using it (1) to explain dividend policy for a holdout sample of 191 firms and (2) to predict dividend payments one year hence. Of the many models that they try, the two best are Lintner's model [Eq. (16.1)] and a similar model that suppresses the constant term and adds a term for the lagged level of earnings. The second model does slightly better than Lintner's.

One can conclude that U.S. corporations seem to increase dividends only after they are reasonably sure that they will be able to maintain them permanently at the new level. However, this does not help to answer the question of why corporations pay dividends in the first place.

B. CLIENTELE EFFECTS AND EX DATE EFFECTS

1. The Dividend Clientele Effect

The dividend clientele effect was originally suggested by Miller and Modigliani [1961]:

> If for example the frequency distribution of corporate payout ratios happened to correspond exactly with the distribution of investor preferences for payout ratios, then the existence of these preferences would clearly lead ultimately to a situation whose implications were different, in no fundamental respect, from the perfect market case. Each corporation would tend to attract to itself a "clientele" consisting of those preferring its particular payout ratio, but one clientele would be as good as another in terms of the valuation it would imply for firms.

The clientele effect is a possible explanation for management reluctance to alter established payout ratios because such changes might cause current shareholders to incur unwanted transactions costs.

Elton and Gruber [1970] attempt to measure clientele effects by observing the average price decline when a stock goes ex-dividend. If we were current shareholders and sold our stock the instant before it went ex-dividend, we would receive its price, P_B, and pay the capital gains rate, t_g, on the difference between the selling price and the price at which it was purchased, P_c. Alternatively, we could sell the stock after it went ex-dividend. In this case we would receive the dividend, div, and pay the ordinary tax rate, t_0, on it. In addition, we would pay a capital gains tax on the difference between its ex-dividend price, P_A, and the original purchase price P_c. To prevent arbitrage profits, our gain from either course of action must be the same, namely,

$$P_B - t_g(P_B - P_c) = P_A - t_g(P_A - P_c) + \text{div}(1 - t_0). \tag{16.2}$$

Rearranging (16.2), we get

$$\frac{P_B - P_A}{\text{div}} = \frac{1 - t_0}{1 - t_g}. \tag{16.3}$$

Therefore the ratio of the decline in stock price to the dividend paid becomes a means of estimating the marginal tax rate of the average investor, if we assume that the capital gains rate is half the ordinary tax rate, as it was during the time period used by Elton and Gruber for their empirical test.

Using 4148 observations between April 1, 1966, and March 31, 1967, Elton and Gruber discovered that the average price decline as a percentage of dividend paid was 77.7%. This implied that the marginal tax bracket of the average investor was 36.4%. They continued by arguing that

> ... the lower a firm's dividend yield the smaller the percentage of his total return that a stockholder expects to receive in the form of dividends and the larger the percentage he expects to receive in the form of capital gains. Therefore, investors who held stocks which have high dividend yields should be in low tax brackets relative to stockholders who hold stocks with low dividend yield. [Elton and Gruber, 1970]

Table 16.1 shows the dividend payout ranked from the lowest to highest deciles along with (1) the average drop in price as a percentage of dividends and (2) the implied tax bracket. Note that the implied tax bracket decreases when dividend payout increases. Elton and Gruber conclude that the evidence suggests that Miller and Modigliani were right in hypothesizing a clientele effect.

A possible counterargument to this interpretation, provided by Kalay [1977, 1982], is that arbitrage may also be carried out by traders who *do not own* the stock initially. They would not receive favored capital gains treatment but would have to pay ordinary income taxes on short-term gains. Their arbitrage profit, π, may be stated mathematically as

$$\pi = -P_B + \text{div} - t_0\text{div} + P_A + t_0(P_B - P_A). \tag{16.4}$$

Table 16.1   Dividend Yield Statistics Ranked by Decile

Decile	div/P Mean	$\frac{P_B - P_A*}{\text{div}}$ Mean	Standard Deviation	Z Value	Probability True Mean Is One or More	Implied Tax Bracket
1	.0124	.6690	.8054	.411	.341	.4974
2	.0216	.4873	.2080	2.465	.007	.6145
3	.0276	.5447	.1550	2.937	.002	.5915
4	.0328	.6246	.1216	3.087	.001	.5315
5	.0376	.7953	.1064	1.924	.027	.3398
6	.0416	.8679	.0712	1.855	.031	.2334
7	.0452	.9209	.0761	1.210	.113	.1465
8	.0496	.9054	.0691	1.369	.085	.1747
9	.0552	1.0123	.0538	.229	.591	†
10	.0708	1.1755	.0555	3.162	.999	†

* Spearman's rank correlation coefficient between div/P and $(P_B - P_A)$/div is .9152, which is significant at the 1% level.

† Indeterminant.

From E. J. Elton and M. J. Gruber, "Marginal Stockholders' Tax Rates and the Clientele Effect," reprinted with permission from *Review of Economics and Statistics*, February 1970, 72.

They spend P_B to acquire the stock before it goes ex-dividend, then receive the dividend and pay ordinary income taxes on it, and finally sell the stock after it goes ex-dividend (receiving P_A dollars) and receive a tax shield from their short-term loss. Rearranging (16.4), we see that their profit is

$$\pi = (1 - t_0)[P_A - P_B + \text{div}]. \tag{16.5}$$

To prevent arbitrage profits, the price decline must equal the amount of dividend payout, i.e., $P_B - P_A = \text{div}$.

The above condition is completely different from Eq. (16.3) proposed by Elton and Gruber. Of course neither model has taken transactions costs into account. Eades, Hess, and Kim [1984] replicate the Elton and Gruber work but report their results in the form of rates of return. If the price decline on the ex-date is less than the amount of the dividend, then the ex-date return,

$$R_t = \frac{P_{t+1} - P_t + \text{div}_t}{P_t},$$

will be positive. For the time period July 2, 1962, to April 30, 1975, they find the average ex-date excess return to be .176% (statistically significant). This time interval predates the era of negotiated commissions. On May 1, 1975, all brokerage commissions were competitively negotiated, and presumably transactions costs fell. For the time interval May 1, 1975, to December 31, 1980, Eades, Hess, and Kim found the ex-date return to be significantly lower—only .064%. This result suggests that, given lower transactions costs, it was easier for short-term traders to arbitrage, as was suggested by Kalay [Eq. (16.5)].

Eades, Hess, and Kim [1984] also examine ex-date dividend returns for a non-convertible preferred stock sample, characterized by a relatively large preferred dividend yield. During the sample period, January 1, 1974, to December 31, 1981, these securities had a total of 708 ex-days that occurred on 493 trading days. The average excess return was a significantly negative $-.141\%$. This implies that the stock price fell by more than the amount of the dividend. These results are consistent with tax-induced clienteles if the marginal purchasers are corporations. Corporations are able to exclude 85% of any dividends (80% following the 1986 tax code) received as taxable income, whereas capital gains are taxable at rates as high as 46% (less following the 1986 tax code) if they are short-term capital gains. To see how the price might fall by more than the dividend, suppose the preferred stock is worth $40 and it pays a $4 dividend. If the marginal purchaser is a corporation it receives the following returns:

$$[\text{div} - .46(.15)\text{div}] + (P_B - P_A)(1 - .46).$$

The first term is the dividend, minus the taxable portion (15% of the dividend times the tax rate); the second term is the tax shelter from the short-term capital loss (taxed at 46%). If we set this return equal to zero and solve, we have

$$\frac{P_B - P_A}{\text{div}} = \frac{-[1 - .46(.15)]}{1 - .46} = -172.4\%.$$

Table 16.2   Excess Rates of Return for Equally Weighted Ex-Date Portfolios, 1962–1980

Trading Day Relative to Ex-Day	Average Percent Excess Return	t-statistic
−5	.067	4.128
−4	.046	4.155
−3	.061	5.561
−2	.066	5.968
−1	.188	15.647
Ex-day	.142	11.741
+1	−.053	−4.355
+2	−.058	−4.911
+3	−.036	−2.707
+4	−.046	−4.195
+5	−.043	−3.700

K. Eades, P. Hess, and E. H. Kim, "On Interpreting Security Returns during the Ex-Dividend Period," reprinted with permission from *Journal of Financial Economics*, March 1984, 20. © North-Holland.

Thus the stock price could fall by as much as $4(1.724) = $6.90 in our example before the corporation would not profit. For large dividends and on preferred stock we tend to see security prices bid up prior to ex-dates.

Table 16.2 shows the pattern of excess returns, and *t*-statistics for all taxable distributions on NYSE common stocks. The puzzle here is that abnormal returns are not uniquely associated with the ex-day. No good explanation for this result has yet been proposed.

Finally, Eades, Hess, and Kim report on the ex-date behavior of nontaxable corporate distributions. They find significant positive returns for stock splits and stock dividends (later confirmed by Grinblatt, Masulis, and Titman [1984]) and significant negative returns for nontaxable cash dividends (primarily of high-yielding utilities). Although there is no explanation for the abnormally positive split ex-date returns, we may conjecture that tax arbitrage (short-term capital gains shelters) may explain the negative returns on nontaxable cash dividends.

Lakonishok and Vermaelen [1986] test the hypothesis of tax arbitrage by studying trading volume around the ex-date. If there is tax arbitrage, then volume should be abnormally high around ex-dates, and it should be positively related to dividend yield and negatively related to transactions costs. Their results show that trading volume does increase significantly around ex-dates and that it is more pronounced for high-yield, actively traded stocks and during the period following the introduction of negotiated trading commissions.

Pettit [1977] has tested for dividend clientele effects by examining the portfolio positions of approximately 914 individual accounts handled by a large retail brokerage house between 1964 and 1970. He argues that stocks with low dividend yields will be preferred by investors with high income, by younger investors, by investors whose ordinary and capital gains tax rates differ substantially, and by investors whose portfolios have high systematic risk. His model is

$$DY_i = a_1 + a_2\beta_i + a_3\text{AGE}_i + a_4\text{INC}_i + a_5\text{DTR}_i + \varepsilon_i, \qquad (16.6)$$

where

DY_i = dividend yield for the ith individual's portfolio in 1970,

β_i = the systematic risk of the ith individual's portfolio,

AGE_i = the age of the individual,

INC_i = the gross family income averaged over the last three years,

DTR_i = the difference between the income and capital gains tax rates for the ith individual,

ε_i = a normally distributed random error term.

He finds that[1]

$$DY_i = .042 - .021\beta_i + .031\text{AGE}_i - .037\text{INC}_i + .006\text{DTR}_i.$$

$$(11.01)(-16.03) \quad (6.15) \quad (-2.25) \quad (1.57)$$

The evidence suggests that there is a clientele effect because a significant portion of the observed cross-sectional variation in individual portfolio dividend yields can be explained. However, the study in no way suggests that the market price of a security is determined by the dividend policy followed by the firm.

A second study by Lewellen, Stanley, Lease, and Schlarbaum [1978] was drawn from the same data base as the Pettit study but reached different conclusions. They ran a multiple regression to explain the dividend yields of investor portfolios as a function of various investor characteristics. Although the tax rate variable was negatively related to dividend yield and was statistically significant, it implied that a 10% increase in an investor's marginal (imputed) tax bracket was associated with only a .1% decline in the yield of securities held. This suggests only a very weak dividend clientele effect.

2. Debt Clientele Effects

Investors can choose to borrow on their personal account or to invest in levered firms, thereby using the corporation's tax shelter on debt. In Chapter 15 we discussed the possibility of debt clientele effects. Personal debt will be preferred to corporate

---

[1] The numbers in parentheses are t-statistics. The r^2 was .3 for 914 observations.

Table 16.3 Regression Results: Corporate Total Debt to Total Capital Ratios vs. Shareholder Characteristics[a]

Independent Variable	Estimated Coefficient ($\times 10^{-2}$)	Standard Error ($\times 10^{-2}$)	t-statistic
Constant term	45.69	2.72	16.82[c]
Shareholder characteristics			
Sex	2.38	0.72	3.31[c]
Educational level	−0.31	0.08	−3.74[c]
Employment status	1.30	0.64	2.00[b]
Marginal tax rate	−6.81	2.19	−3.11[c]
Age	−0.07	0.03	−2.28[b]
Family size	−0.13	0.24	−0.56
Marital status	0.14	0.76	0.18

[a] Variables listed in stepwise entry order: $R^2 = 0.008$, $N = 6217$, F = 7.51.

[b] Denotes significance at the 0.05 level.

[c] Denotes significance at the 0.01 level.

From E. H. Kim, W. Lewellen, and J. McConnell, "Financial Leverage Clienteles: Theory and Evidence," reprinted with permission of *Journal of Financial Economics*, March 1979, 106. © North-Holland.

debt by individuals in high marginal personal tax brackets, and low-income investors will prefer to invest in firms with high leverage.

Kim, Lewellen, and McConnell [1979] and Harris, Roenfeldt, and Cooley [1983] tested for leverage-related clientele effects. The first study used a data set consisting of 1140 companies whose stock was owned by at least three investors from among a group of 887. Questionnaires provided demographic and income data for the investors during a three-year period from 1969 to 1971. From these data the marginal tax rates of the investors were determined. Table 16.3 shows the results of a multiple regression that explains the corporate total debt to total capital ratio as a function of various shareholder characteristics. The coefficients of five of the seven independent variables are statistically significant as is the overall significance of the regression (F = 7.51). The coefficient of the investor tax rate is of the correct sign and is statistically significant, but its magnitude indicates that an increase in an investor's personal tax rate from zero to 70% is associated with an increase of only 5% in the corporate leverage ratio. Kim, Lewellen, and McConnell [1979] suggest, "A relationship that slight has to be interpreted as somewhat less than strongly supportive of the financial leverage clientele hypothesis."

Harris, Roenfeldt, and Cooley [1983] estimate investor-implied tax rates by using the Elton and Gruber procedure, Eq. (16.3). They then examine a sample of large firms, 1968 to 1976, to see if firms with high leverage have investors with low tax rates, and vice versa. They find that implied tax rates are strongly negatively correlated with corporate financial leverage, thereby lending further support to the leverage clientele hypothesis.

C. DIVIDEND ANNOUNCEMENT EFFECTS ON THE VALUE OF THE FIRM: THE SIGNALING HYPOTHESIS

Most firms that pay dividends exhibit behavior that results in constant dividend payouts that are increased only when management is relatively certain that the higher dividend payout can be maintained indefinitely. Given this type of management behavior, it is likely that investors will interpret an increase in current dividend payout as a message that management anticipates permanently higher levels of cash flows from investment. We may therefore expect to observe an increase in share prices associated with public announcement of a dividend increase. The dividend per se does not affect the value of the firm. Instead it serves as a message from management that the firm is anticipated to do better. If dividend changes are to have an impact on share values, it is necessary that they convey information about future cash flows, but it is not sufficient. The same information may be provided to investors via other sources.[2] Therefore it becomes an empirical question whether or not announcements of dividend changes actually affect share value.

The first study to look at this issue was the stock split study of Fama, Fisher, Jensen, and Roll [1969], which was discussed in Chapter 11. They found that when splits were accompanied by dividend announcements, there was an increase in adjusted share prices for the group that announced dividend increases and a decline in share prices for the dividend decrease group. More recent studies of the effect of unexpected dividend changes on share prices have been made by Pettit [1972], Watts [1973], Kwan [1981], and Aharony and Swary [1980].

Watts finds a positive dividend announcement effect but concludes that the information content is of no economic significance because it would not enable a trader with monopolistic access to the information to earn abnormal returns after transactions costs. On the other hand, Pettit finds clear support for the proposition that the market uses dividend announcements as information for assessing security values. Their methodologies are also different. Watts proceeds in two stages. First, he develops a model to predict dividend changes. It is the same model that Fama and Babiak [1968] found to provide the best prediction of next period's dividends. It may be written as follows:

$$\Delta \text{Div}_t = \beta_1 \text{Div}_{t-1} + \beta_2 \text{NI}_t + \beta_3 \text{NI}_{t-1} + Z_t, \tag{16.7}$$

where

ΔDiv_t = the change in dividends in period t,

Div_{t-1} = the previous period's dividends,

NI_t = this period's earnings,

NI_{t-1} = last period's earnings,

Z_t = unanticipated dividend changes (the error term).

---

[2] Ross [1977] argues that an increase in dividend payout is an unambiguous message because (1) it cannot be mimicked by firms that do not anticipate higher earnings and (2) management has an incentive to "tell the truth."

Using this equation, we are able to estimate unanticipated dividend changes, Z_t. Next, an abnormal performance index that measures departures from the risk-adjusted rate of return can be constructed from the market model,

$$R_{jt} = \alpha + \beta_j R_{mt} + \varepsilon_{jt}, \tag{16.8}$$

where

R_{jt} = the total return (dividends and capital gains) on the common stock of the jth firm,

α = a constant term,

β_j = systematic risk,

R_{mt} = the rate of return on a market index,

ε_{jt} = the abnormal performance of the jth security

The abnormal performance index (API) for a security is computed as the product of its one-month abnormal returns:

$$\text{API} = \prod_{t=1}^{T} (1 + \varepsilon_{jt}), \qquad T = 1, \ldots, N.$$

Watts looked at the abnormal performance index averaged across 310 firms. The abnormal performance index for 24 months around the dividend announcement for the subsamples of firms that had unanticipated dividend increases or decreases is given in Table 16.4. The performance of firms with dividend increases is better than that of firms with dividend decreases, but the greatest difference between the two samples in the 6 months around the dividend change is only .7% in the month of the dividend. This is a trivial difference.

Pettit used both monthly and daily data to investigate the abnormal performance index of firms that had dividend changes of -1% to -99%, 1% to 10%, 10% to 25%, and over 25%. Figure 16.1 shows the cumulative abnormal performance index using daily data for 135 firms. Most of the price adjustment takes place very quickly either on the dividend announcement date or on the following day. Furthermore, the price changes appear to be significant. This leads Pettit to conclude that substantial information is conveyed by the announcement of dividend changes.

Pettit's results have been criticized because he used the observed dividend changes rather than the *unexpected* dividend changes. Kwan [1981] has improved on Pettit's design by forming portfolios based on unexpected dividend changes, and he finds statistically significant abnormal returns when firms announce unexpectedly large dividend changes. A study by Aharony and Swary [1980] separates the information content of quarterly earnings reports from that of unexpected quarterly dividend changes. They examine only those quarterly dividend and earnings announcements made public on different dates within any given quarter. Their findings strongly support the hypothesis that changes in quarterly cash dividends provide useful information beyond that provided by corresponding quarterly earnings numbers. Kane, Lee, and Marcus [1984] also select a set of firms whose quarterly dividend and earnings announcements are separated by at least 10 days, build models to predict expected

Table 16.4 Abnormal Performance Indices for Subsamples of Firms with Unanticipated Dividend Changes

Month Relative to Last Month of Fiscal Year	API		χ^2 Statistic for Sign of Stock Return Residual for Month and Dividend Residual for Year	Total API
	$\hat{z}_{i,t} > 0$	$\hat{z}_{i,t} < 0$		
−11	0.996	0.995	0.2	0.995
−10	0.998	0.997	0.3	0.998
−9	1.003	1.002	1.9	1.002
−8	1.002	1.002	4.0	1.002
−7	1.004	1.001	2.5	1.002
−6	1.004	0.999	2.6	1.001
−5	1.003	1.000	0.6	1.002
−4	1.001	0.999	0.3	1.000
−3	1.000	0.997	0.0	0.998
−2	1.003	1.001	2.6	1.002
−1	1.006	1.001	4.0	1.004
0	1.009	1.002	0.1	1.006
1	1.003	0.996	0.0	1.000
2	1.005	0.999	0.6	1.002
3	1.010	1.005	0.0	1.008
4	1.011	1.004	1.4	1.007
5	1.011	1.004	0.0	1.008
6	1.012	1.003	3.3	1.008
7	1.011	1.003	0.2	1.007
8	1.010	1.001	0.2	1.006
9	1.007	1.000	0.4	1.004
10	1.011	1.002	1.5	1.007
11	1.012	1.006	3.4	1.009
12	1.014	1.006	1.2	1.010

Probability $(\chi^2 > 3.84 | x^2 = 0) = .05$ for 1 df; probability $(\chi^2 > 6.64 | x^2 = 0) = .01$ for 1 df.

From R. Watts, "The Information Content of Dividends," reprinted from *Journal of Business*, April 1973, 206.

earnings and dividends, and then test to see if unexpected dividend and earnings announcements corroborate each other—in other words, is there an interaction effect? Their empirical results confirm the earlier studies that found that both earnings and dividend announcements have a significant effect on share price, and in addition they find a significant corroboration effect.

Woolridge [1983] studies the effect of dividend announcements on nonconvertible bonds and nonconvertible preferred stock in an attempt to separate expropriation effects from announcement effects. If dividend payouts to shareholders are viewed as payments of collateralizable assets, and if debt covenants are imperfect protection, then debt holders and preferred shareholders would view dividend increases as bad news and the market value of their claims on the firm would fall upon the an-

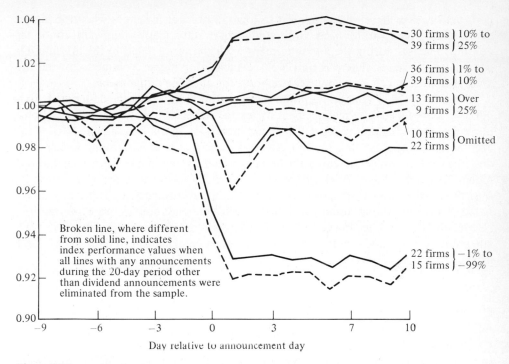

Figure 16.1
Abnormal performance index for dividend announcement effects, using daily data. (From
R. R. Pettit, "Dividend Announcements, Security Performance and Capital Market
Efficiency," reprinted with permission of *Journal of Finance*, December 1972, 1004.)

nouncement of dividend increases. On the other hand, if dividend increases are signals
about higher future cash flows, then bondholders and preferred stockholders should
feel more secure and the market value of their claims should increase. Woolridge's
empirical results support the signaling hypothesis (or at least the conclusion that the
signaling effect dominates any expropriation effect). Announcement date abnormal
returns are positive given unexpected dividend increases and negative given unexpected dividend decreases. Handjiinicolaou and Kalay [1984] find that for a sample
of 255 nonconvertible bonds, prices are unaffected by unexpected dividend increases
but react negatively to dividend reductions. They interpret this as evidence consistent
with the dividend signaling hypothesis.

   Asquith and Mullins [1983] and Richardson, Sefcik, and Thompson [1986] study
the effect on shareholder wealth of the initial dividend announcement—the firm's
first dividend (most firms had never paid a dividend, although a few had not paid a
dividend for 10 years). Both studies find large, statistically significant two-day announcement abnormal returns for initial dividend announcements, 3.7% to 4.0%. In
addition, Richardson, Sefcik, and Thompson (and Asquith and Krasker [1985]) study
trading volume around the announcement date, and between the announcement and
ex-dates. Unusual trading volume may be evidence of clientele changes induced when

high tax bracket shareholders sell out to low tax bracket investors when the higher dividend payout is announced. Both studies find statistically significant abnormal volume increases during the announcement week that are related to the information content of dividends. There is only weak evidence for higher volume following the announcement and hence only weak support for clientele adjustments.

Brickley [1983] studies the announcement effect of specially designated dividends—those labeled by management as "extra," "special," or "year-end," and compares them to surrounding regular dividend increases. Specially designated dividends are interesting because they are not intended to be a part of continuing higher dividend payout and may therefore not be interpreted by the market as a signal about higher future cash flows. Brickley's results support the opposite conclusion—namely, that the market does react positively to the information content of specially designated dividends but that dollar-for-dollar regular dividends convey more information.

In sum the evidence in support of the informational content of dividends is overwhelming. Unexpected dividend changes do convey information to the market about expected future cash flows.

D. THE RELATIONSHIP BETWEEN DIVIDENDS AND VALUE

In Chapter 15 we saw that in a world with only corporate taxes the Miller-Modigliani proposition suggests that dividend policy is irrelevant to value. However, when personal taxes are introduced with a capital gains rate that is less than the rate on ordinary income, the picture changes. Under this set of assumptions the firm should not pay any dividends. One way to test these theories is to look directly at the relationship between dividend payout and the price per share of equity.

Friend and Puckett [1964] use cross-section data to test the effect of dividend payout on share value. Prior to their work, most studies had related stock prices to current dividends and retained earnings, and reported that higher dividend payout was associated with higher price/earnings ratios. The "dividend multiplier" was found to be several times the "retained earnings multiplier." The usual cross-section equation was

$$P_{it} = a + b\text{Div}_{it} + cRE_{it} + \varepsilon_{it}, \tag{16.9}$$

where

P_{it} = the price per share,

Div_{it} = aggregate dividends paid out,

RE_{it} = retained earnings,

ε_{it} = the error term.

Friend and Puckett criticize the above approach on three major points. First, the equation is misspecified because it assumes that the riskiness of the firm is uncorrelated with dividend payout and price/earnings ratios. However, a look at the data suggests that riskier firms have both lower dividend payout and lower price/earnings ratios. Consequently, the omission of a risk variable may cause an upward bias in the dividend coefficient in Eq. (16.9). Second, there is almost no measurement error in dividends, but there is considerable measurement error in retained earnings. It is well known that accounting measures of income often imprecisely reflect the real economic earnings of the firm. The measurement error in retained earnings will cause its coefficient to be biased downward. Third, Friend and Puckett argue that even if dividends and earnings *do* have different impacts on share prices, we should expect their coefficients in (16.9) to be equal. In equilibrium, firms would change their dividend payout until the marginal effect of dividends is equal to the marginal effect of retained earnings. This will provide the optimum effect on their price per share.

No theory had been developed to allow the pricing of risk when they wrote their paper, but Friend and Puckett were able to eliminate the measurement error on retained earnings by calculating a normalized earnings variable based on a time series fit of the following equation:

$$\frac{(NI/P)_{it}}{(NI/P)_{kt}} = a_i + b_i t + \varepsilon_{it}, \tag{16.10}$$

where

$(NI/P)_{it}$ = the earnings/price ratio for the firm,

$(NI/P)_{kt}$ = the average earnings/price ratio for the industry,

$\quad t$ = a time index,

$\quad \varepsilon_{it}$ = the error term.

When normalized retained earnings were calculated by subtracting dividends from normalized earnings and then used in Eq. (16.9), the difference between the dividend and retained earnings coefficients was reduced. Unfortunately, no test was performed to see whether the differences between the impact of retained earnings and dividends were significant after Friend and Puckett had normalized earnings and controlled for firm effects.

A study by Black and Scholes [1974] uses capital asset pricing theory to control for risk.[3] Their conclusion is quite strong. "It is not possible to demonstrate, using the best empirical methods, that the expected returns on high yield common stock differ from the expected returns on low yield common stocks either before or after taxes." They begin by pointing out that the assumption that capital gains tax rates are lower than income tax rates does not apply to all classes of investors. Some classes of investors might logically prefer high dividend yields. They include: (a) corporations, because they usually pay higher taxes on realized capital gains than on dividend income (because of the 80% exclusion of dividends); (b) certain trust funds in which one beneficiary receives the dividend income and the other receives capital gains; (c) endowment funds from which only the dividend income may be spent; and (d) investors who are spending from wealth and may find it cheaper and easier to receive

---

[3] See Chapter 7 for a complete development of the capital asset pricing model.

dividends than to sell or borrow against their shares. Alternatively, investors who prefer low dividend yield will be those who pay higher taxes on dividend income than on capital gains. With all these diverse investors, it is possible that there are clientele effects that imply that if a firm changes its dividend payout, it may lose some shareholders, but they will be replaced by others who prefer the new policy. Thus dividend payout will have no effect on the value of an individual firm.[4]

The Black and Scholes [1974] study presents empirical evidence that the before-tax returns on common stock are unrelated to corporate dividend payout policy. They adjust for risk by using the CAPM.

The CAPM predicts that the expected return on any asset is a linear function of its systematic risk:

$$E(\tilde{R}_j) = R_f + [E(\tilde{R}_m) - R_f]\beta_j. \tag{16.11}$$

However, it is derived by assuming, among other things, that there are no differential tax effects that would affect investors' demands for different securities. Brennan [1970] has shown that if effective capital gains tax rates are lower than effective rates on dividend income, then investors will demand a higher rate of return on securities with higher dividend payout. Using annual data, Black and Scholes test this hypothesis by adding a dividend payout term to an empirical version of the CAPM:

$$\tilde{R}_j = \gamma_0 + [\tilde{R}_m - \gamma_0]\beta_j + \gamma_1(DY_j - DY_m)/DY_m + \varepsilon_j, \tag{16.21}$$

where

$\tilde{R}_j$ = the rate of return on the jth portfolio,

γ_0 = an intercept term that should be equal to the risk-free rate, R_f, according to the CAPM,

$\tilde{R}_m$ = the rate of return on the market portfolio,

β_j = the systematic risk of the jth portfolio,

γ_1 = the dividend impact coefficient,

DY_j = the dividend yield on the jth portfolio, measured as the sum of dividends paid during the previous year divided by the end-of-year stock price,

DY_m = the dividend yield on the market portfolio measured over the prior 12 months,

ε_j = the error term.

If the coefficient, γ_1, of the dividend yield is significantly different from zero, we would reject the null hypothesis that dividend payout has no impact on the required rate of return for securities. The results of Black and Scholes are summarized in Table 16.5. Note that the dividend impact coefficient, $\hat{\gamma}_1$, is not significantly different from

---

[4] This does not rule out the possibility that in aggregate there is a desired equilibrium amount of dividend payout. For example, in the United States there are obviously a far greater number of companies with generous dividend payout than without.

Table 16.5   Results of the Black-Scholes Test for Dividend Effects

The Portfolio Estimators for γ_1 (Part A) and γ_0 (Part B)

Period	$\alpha_1 = \hat{\gamma}_1$	t_α	$\hat{\beta}_1$	DY_1	DY_m
		Part A			
1936–66	0.0009	0.94	−0.01	0.044	0.048
1947–66	0.0009	0.90	0.08	0.047	0.049
1936–46	0.0011	0.54	−0.01	0.036	0.046
1947–56	0.0002	0.19	0.11	0.054	0.060
1957–66	0.0016	0.99	−0.14	0.040	0.038
1940–45	0.0018	0.34	0.15	0.051	0.052

Period	$\alpha_0 = \hat{\gamma}_0$	t_α	$\hat{\beta}_0$	DY_0	DY_m
		Part B			
1936–66	0.0060	3.02	0.02	0.048	0.048
1947–66	0.0073	3.93	0.03	0.049	0.049
1936–46	0.0033	0.72	−0.01	0.046	0.046
1947–56	0.0067	2.55	0.12	0.060	0.060
1957–66	0.0065	2.37	0.10	0.038	0.038

From F. Black and M. Scholes, "The Effects of Dividend Yield and Dividend Policy on Common Stock Prices and Returns," reprinted from *Journal of Financial Economics*, May 1974, 14. © 1974 North-Holland.

zero (since the *t*-test is less than the level required to make it significant at the 95% confidence level) across the entire time period, 1936 through 1966, or in any subperiod. This means that the expected returns on high-yield securities are not significantly different from the expected returns on low-yield securities, other things being equal.[5]

The Black-Scholes study has been criticized because their test is not very powerful. Had the null hypothesis been that dividend yield does matter, it could not have been rejected either. Their test is inefficient because they grouped stocks into portfolios instead of using individual stock returns and, perhaps, because they used annual data.

Litzenberger and Ramaswamy [1979] also test the relationship between dividends and security returns. They use the Brennan [1970] model, Eq. (16.13) below, with monthly data for individual securities:

$$E(\tilde{R}_{jt}) - R_{ft} = a_1 + a_2\beta_j + a_3(DY_{jt} - R_{ft}), \tag{16.13}$$

---

[5] The lower half of Table 16.5 shows that $\hat{\gamma}_0$ is significantly different from the risk-free rate. This is not important for the conclusions about dividend policy but is consistent with other empirical work (e.g., Black, Jensen, and Scholes [1972]) that shows that the intercept term in the CAPM is different from what theory would predict.

where

$E(\tilde{R}_{jt})$ = the expected before-tax return on the jth security,

R_{ft} = the before-tax return on the risk-free asset,

β_j = the systematic risk of the jth security,

a_1 = the constant term,

a_2 = the marginal effect of systematic risk,

a_3 = the marginal effective tax difference between ordinary income and capital gains rates,

DY_{jt} = the dividend yield, i.e., dividend divided by price, for the jth security.

Litzenberger and Ramaswamy conclude that risk-adjusted returns are higher for securities with higher dividend yields. The implication is that dividends are undesirable; hence higher returns are necessary to compensate investors in order to induce them to hold high dividend yield stocks.

There are (at least) three serious problems with testing for the dividend effect predicted by Eq. (16.13). The first is that investors use dividend announcements to estimate expected returns, $E(\tilde{R}_{jt})$; i.e., there is an information effect. The second is that measures of systematic risk, $\hat{\beta}_j$, are subject to a great deal of error. And the third is that individual security returns (rather than portfolio returns) are needed to obtain statistically powerful results. Litzenberger and Ramaswamy [1979] largely solved the second and third problems but have been criticized by Miller and Scholes [1982] for their handling of the information effect of dividend announcements. When using monthly data, about two thirds of the firms in the sample will have a zero yield because most firms pay dividends on a quarterly basis. Of the firms that pay their dividend (i.e., go ex-dividend) in month t, about 30% to 40% also announce the dividend in the same month. When the announcement date and the ex-dividend date occur in the same month, the monthly return will contain both the information effect and the tax effect (if any). To avoid confusing these effects, Litzenberger and Ramaswamy computed dividend yields in the following way:

- If a firm declared its dividend prior to month t and went ex-dividend in month t, then the dividend yield, DY_{jt}, was computed using the actual dividend paid in t divided by the share price at the end of month $t - 1$.

- If a firm both declared and went ex-dividend in month t, then the yield, DY_{jt}, was computed using the last regular dividend, going back as far as one year.

Table 16.6 shows the results of regressions run by Miller and Scholes [1982] using Eq. (16.13). Regressions using the actual dividend yield in month t show that the dividend variable has a coefficient of .317 and it is highly significant, but recall that the actual yield confuses announcement effects with dividend tax effects. When the Litzenberger-Ramaswamy measure of dividend yield (called the level-revised yield) was duplicated by Miller and Scholes, the dividend coefficient dropped from .317 to .179 and also dropped in significance.

Table 16.6   Cross-Sectional Estimates of the Dividend Yield Effect (Eq. 16.13), 1940–1978, *t*-statistics in Parentheses

Definition of Expected Dividend Yield	a_1	a_2	a_3
Actual dividend yield	.0059	.0024	.3173
	(4.5)	(1.6)	(10.2)
Level-revised monthly dividend yield	.0065	.0022	.1794
	(4.9)	(1.4)	(6.1)
Dividend yield of 12 months ago	.0038	.0019	.0376
	(2.9)	(1.3)	(1.3)
Only firms with dividends declared in advance	.0043	.0035	.0135
	(2.5)	(2.2)	(0.1)

From M. H. Miller and M. Scholes, "Dividends and Taxes: Some Empirical Evidence," *Journal of Political Economy*, December 1982, 1124, 1129.

The third regression in Table 16.6 corrects for a bias not contemplated in the two prior regressions. Namely, that some firms are expected to pay a dividend in month t, but for some reason, the board of directors suspends the dividend. Miller and Scholes call this the case of the "dog that didn't bark." Suppose that a $10 stock has a 50/50 chance of either announcing a $2 dividend (in which case the stock price doubles to $20) or suspending the dividend (thereby causing the stock price to fall to $5). The *ex ante* rate of return (and the average *ex post* return) is 35%, and the *ex ante* dividend yield is 10%.[6] However, if the level-revised measure of dividend yield is used, then if the firm actually pays the $2 dividend the yield is 20% and the return is 120%. But if the dividend is passed, the yield is 0% and a -50% return is recorded. Thus the regressions with the level-revised measure tend to show what appears to be a positive association between returns and dividend yields. However, the correlation is spurious. A simple way to correct for the problem is to use the dividend yield of 12 months ago. Shown in the third regression in Table 16.6, the results indicate a small, statistically insignificant relationship between dividend yields and returns.

Another approach, shown in the fourth regression in Table 16.6, is to drop from the sample all firms except those that both paid dividends in month t and announced them in advance. Again the dividend coefficient is insignificant.

Litzenberger and Ramaswamy [1982] have responded to the Miller-Scholes criticism by rerunning their regressions. Table 16.7 shows their results. The level-revised dividend yield gave the highest coefficient (a_3), and it is slightly higher than the Miller-Scholes estimate. Instead of using a dividend 12 months ago, Litzenberger

---

[6] The *ex ante* return is computed as

$$.5\left(\frac{20-10}{10} + \frac{2}{10}\right) + .5\left(\frac{5-10}{10}\right) = .35$$

and the *ex ante* dividend yield is

$$.5\left(\frac{2}{10}\right) + .5\left(\frac{0}{10}\right) = .10$$

Table 16.7   Pooled Time Series and Cross-Section Test of the Dividend Effect, 1940–1960

Definition of Expected Dividend Yield	a_1	a_2	a_3
Level-revised monthly dividend yield	.0031 (1.81)	.0048 (2.15)	.233 (8.79)
Predicted dividend yield	.0034 (1.95)	.0047 (2.08)	.151 (5.39)
Restricted subsample	.0010 (.052)	.0053 (2.33)	.135 (4.38)

t-statistics are in parentheses.

From R. Litzenberger and K. Ramaswamy, "The Effects of Dividends on Common Stock Prices: Tax Effects or Information Effects?" *Journal of Finance*, May 1982, 441. Reprinted with permission of the *Journal of Finance*.

and Ramaswamy built a more sophisticated model to predict dividends. Their "predicted dividend yield" model avoids the Miller-Scholes criticism and continues to give a statistically significant estimate of the dividend effect. So, too, does a restricted subsample designed to avoid the Miller-Scholes criticism. Thus the empirical evidence, at this point in time, points toward the conclusion that shareholders express their displeasure with corporate dividend payments by requiring a higher risk-adjusted return (i.e., by paying a lower price) for those stocks that have higher dividend yields.

The Friend and Puckett, Black and Scholes, and Miller and Scholes studies tend to support the conclusion that the value of the firm is independent of dividend yield. The Litzenberger and Ramaswamy study supports the conclusion that dividends are undesirable. The next study to be discussed concludes that dividends are desirable to shareholders; i.e., they will require a lower rate of return on shares that pay a high dividend yield.

Long [1978] provides a detailed analysis of two classes of shares issued by Citizens Utilities Company in 1956. They are virtually identical in all respects except for dividend payout. Series A shares pay only stock dividends that are not taxable as ordinary income (due to a special Internal Revenue Service ruling granted to Citizens Utilities). Series B shares pay only cash dividends. Series A shares are freely convertible into Series B shares (on a one-for-one basis) at any time. However, the opposite is not true. Series B shares may not be converted into Series A shares. Historically the directors of Citizens Utilities have semiannually declared stock dividends that (with a high degree of certainty) are 8% to 10% larger than the corresponding Series B cash dividends (paid on a quarterly basis).

Figure 16.2 shows the natural logarithm of the ratio of the prices of Series A to Series B shares on a monthly basis between 1956 and 1977. Note that the price of Series A shares, P_A, never falls significantly below the price of Series B shares, P_B. If it did, then Series A shareholders could immediately profit by converting to Series B. Figure 16.2 also shows, q, the ratio of Series A stock dividends to Series B cash dividends (illustrated by the circles). In a world without taxes the price per share of Series A "should" always equal q times the price per share of Series B stock, i.e.,

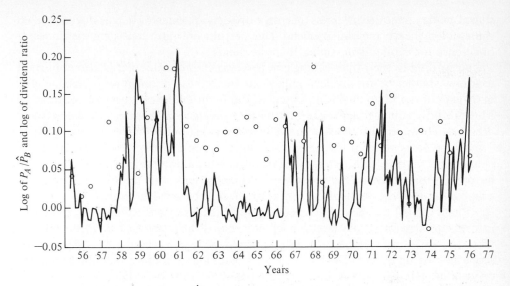

The natural log of $P_A/\hat{P}_B$ (the connected monthly observations) and the natural log of the semi-annual ratio of Series A to Series B dividends (the unconnected 0's) for the period 1956–1976. $\hat{P}_B$ is the price per share of Series B stock with dividends reinvested during each half-year prior to payment of the semi-annual Series A dividend. The unconnected points representing the log of the dividend ratio are placed in the figure at the end of the half-years to which they refer.

Figure 16.2
The natural log of $P_A/\hat{P}_B$ plotted monthly for the period April 1956 to December 1976. (From J. Long, Jr., "The Market Valuation of Cash Dividends: A Case to Consider," reprinted with permission from *Journal of Financial Economics*, June–September 1978, 254). © 1978 North-Holland.

$P_{At} = qP_{Bt}$ ($t = 0, 1, \ldots, N$). Figure 16.2 indicates that 80% of the dividend ratios, q, between 1962 and 1976 fall in the range 1.07 to 1.137. The ratio of stock prices, however, shows much more variability and is usually below the dividend ratio. How can this be explained?

In a world with taxes, cross-sectional heterogeneity in investor tax rates will cause the price ratio to differ from the dividend ratio. If very few investors face strictly higher taxes on stock dividends than on cash dividends, then the ratio of prices, P_A/P_B, should be greater than the dividend ratio, q. The equilibrium price ratio P_A/P_B will be less than q if there are sufficient numbers of investors who have a strict tax-induced preference for cash dividends over capital gains, and this is what is observed. Therefore Long [1978] concludes that "claims to cash dividends have, if anything, commanded a slight premium in the market to claims to equal amounts (before taxes) of capital gains." The Citizens Utilities case is anomalous because it is the only major study that indicates an investor preference for cash dividends. Furthermore, the strength of Long's conclusion has been weakened by Poterba [1986] who finds (1) that the relative price of the stock dividend shares has been higher since 1976 (the end of Long's sample); (2) that the ratio of stock dividend to cash dividend share prices averaged 1.134 during the 1976–1984 period; and (3) that the cash dividend shares' ex-day price decline is less than their dividend payment, whereas stock dividend shares fall by nearly their full dividend. These results are more consistent with investor preference for capital gains rather than dividends.

According to the Miller-Modigliani irrelevancy proposition, it is also important to know whether or not dividend policy can affect the investment decisions made by managers of the firm. This is a particularly difficult empirical question because the Miller-Modigliani theorem requires only that *dividend payout not affect investment decisions*. However, the opposite causality is not ruled out by Miller and Modigliani. That is, investment decisions can affect dividends. For example, the firm may simply choose to treat dividends as a residual payout after all profitable investment projects have been undertaken. This would not be inconsistent with the Miller-Modigliani proposition that the value of the firm is unaffected by dividend policy.

Fama [1974] uses a sophisticated two-stage least squares econometric technique in order to determine the direction of causality, if any, between dividend and investment decisions. Because a description of two-stage least squares is beyond the scope of this book, we refer the interested reader to Fama's article for a detailed exposition. His conclusion, however, is consistent with the Miller-Modigliani assumption that the period-by-period investment decisions of the firm are separable from its dividend decisions. There appears to be no causality in either direction. The data could not reject the hypothesis that investment and dividend decisions are completely independent from each other. Fama's conclusion that investment and dividend decisions are independent is supported by Smirlock and Marshall [1983] who employ causality tests using both firm-specific and aggregate data for 194 firms between 1958 and 1977.

Although the foregoing studies appear to support the Miller-Modigliani irrelevancy proposition from the point of view of an individual firm, they do not necessarily rule out the possibility that there may exist an aggregate equilibrium supply of dividends that will increase if the difference between the ordinary income rate and the capital gains rate declines. This type of situation is implicit in Miller's [1977] paper "Debt and Taxes," which was discussed at length in Chapter 13.

Some empirical evidence that is consistent with the thesis that the aggregate supply of dividends is sensitive to the differential between the ordinary income and capital gains rates is contained in a study by Khoury and Smith [1977]. They observed that Canadian corporations significantly increased their dividend payout after a capital gains tax was introduced for the first time in 1972. A more recent paper by Morgan [1980] finds that the change in the Canadian tax code in 1972 affected the cross-sectional relationship between dividends and capital gains. Prior to 1972 they were imperfect substitutes, but afterward they became more or less perfect substitutes.

E. CORPORATE EQUITY REPURCHASES VIA TENDER OFFER

Corporations can repurchase their own shares in either of two ways: on the open market or via tender offer. Open market repurchases usually (but not always) involve gradual programs to buy back shares over a period of time. In a tender offer the company usually specifies the number of shares it is offering to repurchase, a tender price, and a period of time during which the offer is in effect. If the number of shares actually tendered by shareholders exceeds the maximum number specified by the company, then purchases are usually made on a pro rata basis. Alternatively, if the tender offer is undersubscribed the firm may decide to cancel the offer or extend the expiration date. Shares tendered during the extension may be purchased on either a pro rata or first-come, first-served basis.

Tender offers are usually significant corporate events. Dann [1981] reports that for a sample of 143 cash tender offers by 122 different firms between 1962 and 1976, the average cash distributions proposed by the tender represented almost 20% of the market value of the company's pre-tender equity value. The announcement effects of tender offers on the market values of corporate securities have been studied by Masulis [1980], Dann [1981], and Vermaelen [1981].[7] Share repurchases are not just a simple alternative to cash dividends. Tender offers for repurchase are related to (at least) five separate, but not mutually exclusive, hypotheses:

1. *The information or signaling hypothesis.* The cash disbursed to shareholders in a tender offer may represent a signal that the firm is expected to have increased future cash flows, but it may also imply that the firm has exhausted profitable investment opportunities. Therefore the signal may be interpreted as either good or bad news by shareholders.

2. *The leverage tax shield hypothesis.* If the repurchase is financed by issuing debt rather than paying out cash, the leverage of the firm may increase, and if there is a gain to leverage as suggested by Modigliani and Miller [1963], then shareholders may benefit.

3. *The dividend tax avoidance hypothesis.* The tender for share repurchase will be taxed as a capital gain rather than a dividend if (according to Section 302 of the U.S. Internal Revenue Code) the redemption is "substantially disproportionate" to the extent that the individual shareholder must have sold more than 20% of his or her holdings in the tender.[8] This condition is rarely violated; consequently, there may be a tax incentive for repurchases as opposed to large extraordinary dividends.

4. *The bondholder expropriation hypothesis.* If the repurchase unexpectedly reduces the asset base of the company, then bondholders are worse off because they have less collateral. Of course, bond indentures serve to protect against this form of expropriation. A direct test of this hypothesis is to look at bond price changes on the repurchase announcement date.

5. *Wealth transfers among shareholders.* Wealth transfers between tendering and nontendering stockholders may occur when there are differential constraints and/or costs across groups of owners. Even when the tender price is substantially

---

[7] The reader is also referred to studies by Woods and Brigham [1966], Bierman and West [1966], Young [1967], Elton and Gruber [1968], Stewart [1976], Coates and Fredman [1976], and Lane [1976].

[8] According to Vermaelen [1981] only 3 out of 105 tender offers that he studied actually were subject to ordinary income taxes.

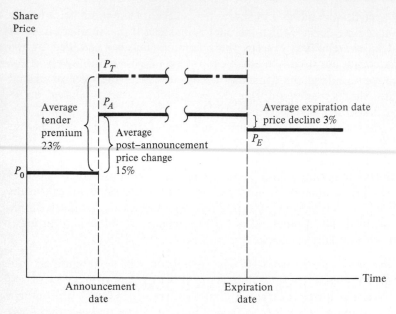

Figure 16.3
Schematic representation of average price changes surrounding tender offers for repurchase.

above the pre-tender stock price, some shareholders may voluntarily decide not to tender their shares.

A great deal can be learned about these hypotheses if we focus on the price effects on shares, bonds, and preferred stock. Figure 16.3 shows the average pattern of share price changes around the tender announcement date and the expiration date. More or less the same results were reported by Masulis [1980], Dann [1981], and Vermaelen [1981]. The average tender price, P_T, is roughly 23% above the preannouncement price, P_0. If all shares tendered were actually purchased by the firm, then the tender price, P_T, would equal the average postannouncement price, P_A. But because of pro rata repurchases given oversubscribed tenders, we observe that on average $P_A < P_T$. The postannouncement price, P_A, averages 15% above the preannouncement price, P_0. Finally, note that the average postexpiration price, P_E, is only 3% below the average postannouncement price, P_A, and is above the preannouncement price, P_0. This suggests that the tender offer may have increased the market value of the firm's equity.

Unfortunately, the difference between the preannouncement price and the post-expiration price does not measure the information effect of the tender offer. We have to look deeper. Begin by noting that the market value of the firm's equity after expiration, $P_E N_E$, is equal to the preannouncement value, $P_0 N_0$, minus the cash paid out in the tender, $P_T(N_0 - N_E)$, plus the tender offer effect, ΔW:

$$P_E N_E = P_0 N_0 - P_T(N_0 - N_E) + \Delta W, \qquad (16.14)$$

where

P_E = the postexpiration share price,

N_E = the number of shares outstanding after repurchase,

P_0 = the preannouncement share price,

N_0 = the preannouncement number of shares outstanding,

P_T = the tender price,

ΔW = the shareholder wealth effect attributable to the tender offer.

Note that the change in value attributable to the tender, ΔW, may be caused by (1) personal tax savings, (2) a leverage effect, (3) expropriation of bondholder wealth, or (4) the reassessment of the firm's earnings prospects.

If we define the fraction of shares repurchased, F_P, as

$$F_P = 1 - \frac{N_E}{N_0} \tag{16.15}$$

and divide Eq. (16.14) by N_0, we have

$$P_E(1 - F_P) = P_0 - P_T F_P + \frac{\Delta W}{N_0}. \tag{16.16}$$

Solving for $\Delta W/N_0$ and dividing by P_0 gives

$$\frac{\Delta W}{N_0 P_0} = (1 - F_P)\frac{P_E - P_0}{P_0} + F_P \frac{P_T - P_0}{P_0}. \tag{16.17}$$

Thus the rate of return created by the tender offer has two components. First is the rate of return received by nontendering shareholders weighted by the percentage of untendered shares, $1 - F_P$, and second is the rate of return received by tendering shareholders weighted by the percentage of shares purchased, F_P.

Vermaelen [1981] found that the average wealth effect, $\Delta W/N_0 P_0$, was 15.7% and that only 10.7% of the tender offers experienced a wealth decline. On average, both nontendered shares and tendered shares experienced a wealth increase, although not by equal amounts.

What causes the average 15.7% wealth gain from tender offers? Personal tax savings are a possibility but seem too small to explain the large wealth gain. For example, if 20% of the value of the firm is repurchased and if the marginal investor's tax rate is 40%, then the tax savings would imply a 4% rate of return. This is too small to explain the wealth gain.

The leverage hypothesis suggests that if the repurchase is financed with debt, and if there is a tax gain from leverage, then the shareholders will benefit. Both Masulis [1980] and Vermaelen [1981] find evidence consistent with a leverage effect. Masulis divided his sample into offers with more than 50% debt financing where the average announcement return was 21.9%, and offers with less than 50% debt where the average announcement return was only 17.1%. Vermaelen finds similar results and concludes that while it is not possible to reject the leverage hypothesis outright, it is possible to conclude that it is not the predominant explanation for the observed abnormal returns following the tender offer. Also, if leverage is a signal, then it is not possible to separate the leverage signaling effect from the leverage tax effect.[9]

The best explanation for the shareholder wealth gain from the tender offer is that the offer represents a favorable signal. Vermaelen [1981] finds that the per-share earnings of tendering firms are above what would have been predicted by a time series model using preannouncement data. Thus the tender offer may be interpreted as an announcement of favorable earnings prospects. Also, the size of the tender premium, the fraction of shares repurchased, and the fraction of insider holdings are all positively related to the wealth gain, ΔW, and explain roughly 60% of its variance. These results are also consistent with interpreting the tender offer as a signal.

Evidence on the bondholder wealth expropriation hypothesis is provided by looking at bond price changes around the announcement date. Dann [1981] found 122 publicly traded debt and preferred stock issues for 51 tender offers. There were 41 issues of straight debt, 34 issues of convertible debt, 9 issues of straight preferred stock, and 38 issues of convertible preferred stock. An analysis of abnormal returns around the announcement date revealed significant positive rates of return for the convertible securities and rates that were insignificantly different from zero for straight debt and preferred. Furthermore, the correlation between common stock returns and straight debt (and preferred) returns was positive. Thus the evidence seems to contradict bondholder expropriation as the dominant effect and seems to support the signaling hypothesis.

Repurchases via tender offer represent an interesting and significant corporate event. The empirical evidence, although not rejecting leverage effects or dividend tax avoidance effects, seems to most strongly support the hypothesis that the tender offer for repurchase is interpreted by the marketplace as favorable information regarding future prospects of the firm.

F. OVERVIEW OF EMPIRICAL EVIDENCE

The theory of finance clearly demonstrates that in the absence of taxes dividend policy has no effect on the value of the corporation. However, if taxes are introduced, then the firm can maximize the value of shareholders' wealth by paying no dividends so long as the personal tax rate on dividend income is higher than that on capital gains. However, this is not true for all types of shareholders; hence there exists the possibility of clientele effects with shareholders choosing the firm with the payout they prefer. The evidence supporting dividend clientele effects is much stronger than the evidence for capital structure clientele effects. Another issue is the relationship between dividend yield and equity values. The preponderance of empirical evidence seems to favor the conclusion that dividend yield has no strong effect on the required

---

[9] See the discussion of debt for common exchange offers in Chapter 14 for evidence consistent with the hypothesis that higher leverage (repurchases of equity with debt) is a favorable signal about the future prospects of the firm.

rate of return on equity; however, if there is any effect it is in favor of capital gains over dividends. The Litzenberger and Ramaswamy [1979, 1982] studies found that higher dividend yields required higher rates of return to compensate investors for the disadvantage of dividend payout. The only study that found that dividends were desirable was the Citizens Utilities case [Long, 1978], which has been questioned by Poterba [1986]. On the other hand, changes in dividends paid out are interpreted as new information about the future cash flows of the firm. There is strong evidence to support a dividend signaling effect. There appears to be no causal relationship between investment and dividend policy. Finally, empirical evidence on share repurchase via tender offer indicates that the announcement effect is predominantly viewed as favorable news regarding the firm's future cash flows. Little or no expropriation of bondholders' wealth was observed.

G. VALUATION AND CORPORATE POLICY

The valuation models developed in Chapter 15 have many useful applications. For example, fundamental analysis techniques use them as a tool for estimating the impact of various types of new information on the value of the firm. Although the valuation models cannot aid in attempts to "beat" the market, they do provide a useful framework for concentrating on relevant information. When a corporate president asks, "How much should we pay to acquire Company X?" the valuation model is a useful tool. When a company is going public for the first time or when it becomes necessary to value a privately held company, again the valuation model provides a relevant framework for analysis.

In the next section we continue the Bethlehem Steel example that was started in Chapter 14. The object is to see how to apply the Miller-Modigliani finite growth model. In so doing, it becomes possible to analyze six factors that affect corporate value.

1. Review of the Finite Growth Valuation Formula

The most complicated, and the most realistic, valuation model discussed in Chapter 15 assumed that the firm grows at a rate, g, for a finite number of years, T, and at the same rate as the economy thereafter.

The model is written below:[10]

$$V^L = \frac{E(\text{NOI}_1)(1 - \tau_c)}{\rho} + \tau_c B + K[E(\text{NOI}_1)(1 - \tau_c)]T\left[\frac{r - \text{WACC}}{\text{WACC}(1 + \text{WACC})}\right],$$

$$(16.18)$$

---

[10] Remember that we derive this version of the model by assuming, among other things, that corporate taxes are the only form of government levy. Personal taxes do not exist.

where

V^L = the market value of the levered firm, i.e., the market value of equity, S, plus the market value of debt, B,

$E(\text{NOI}_1)$ = the expected net cash flows from operations during the current year, net of capitalized maintenance,

ρ = the cost of equity for the firm if it had no debt, i.e., the cost of equity for an all-equity firm,

τ_c = the marginal effective corporate tax rate,

B = the market value of debt,

r = the expected rate of return on new projects,

K = the firm's investment rate,

WACC = the firm's weighted average cost of capital,

T = the number of years that r, the rate of return, is expected to be different from WACC, the market-determined weighted average cost of capital.

The first term in (16.18) is the capitalized value of the expected level of after-tax cash flows from investment that is currently in place. The second term is the value added by tax-deductible financial leverage. And the third term is the present value of the growth in cash flows from new investment.

Equation (16.18) can also be rewritten using only two terms, if the tax shield on debt is combined with the capitalized value of cash flows from assets in place:

$$V^L = \frac{E(\text{NOI}_1)(1 - \tau_c)}{\text{WACC}} + K[E(\text{NOI}_1)(1 - \tau_c)]T\left[\frac{r - \text{WACC}}{\text{WACC}(1 + \text{WACC})}\right].$$

The first of these two terms may also be thought of as the value of assets in place, whereas the second term is still the present value of the growth in cash flows from new investment.

It is also useful to recall a few of the relationships between the parameters of Eq. (16.18). For example, the rate of growth, g, in the firm's cash flows is equal to Kr, the product of the investment rate, K, and the rate of return on new projects, r. Also, the anticipated amount of new investment, I, is equal to the investment rate times the firm's expected after-tax cash flow, $E(\text{NOI}_1)$. In other words, then, $I = K[E(\text{NOI}_1)]$.

Equation (16.18) is a useful construct that uses modern finance theory for valuation. However, realistically it is at best only a crude tool. No one should be advised that it is the only approach to valuation or that it provides perfect answers. Yet it does point out precisely which pieces of information are relevant. Interestingly, none of them is provided in the annual report of the corporation. The only relevant parameters are forward looking. Although some can be estimated from historic accounting data, the most important information is hardly ever reported by corporate management to shareholders.

2. A Valuation Example: Bethlehem Steel

What are the six relevant valuation parameters? And how can they be estimated?

Table 16.8 Pro Forma Income Statements, Bethlehem Steel (in thousands of dollars)

	1976	1975	1974	1973
Net billings and other income	5,304,700	5,028,300	5,448,709	4,174,833
Cost of billings	4,082,100	3,854,300	4,052,478	3,138,048
Provisions for:				
Depreciation	275,600	234,200	210,912	196,086
Pensions	261,200	198,400	153,842	115,533
Misc. taxes	179,400	175,000	169,616	150,982
Selling and administrative expenses	234,700	220,000	210,842	178,641
Earnings before interest and taxes	271,700	346,400	660,019	395,543
Interest expense	77,700	63,400	43,985	38,934
Income taxes*	26,000	41,000	274,000	150,000
Net income	168,000	242,000	342,034	206,609
Dividends paid to common	87,400	120,000	100,172	72,431

* During 1976 this includes current taxes (federal, foreign, and state) of $-\$9,000,000$ and deferred taxes (federal and state) of $\$35,000,000$. Note that deferred taxes are a noncash charge.

A. EXPECTED AFTER-TAX CASH FLOWS FROM CURRENT OPERATIONS. Perhaps the most important factor is the level of cash flows earned on the projects that the firm has already undertaken. It is assumed that this level of cash flows will be maintained into perpetuity. Furthermore, it is assumed that depreciation allowances are sufficient to allow the current level of equipment to be maintained indefinitely.

Table 16.8 is a pro forma income statement for Bethlehem Steel for the years 1973–1976. We are attempting to estimate the value of the company as of December 31, 1976. (That is the date of our estimate of the cost of capital in Chapter 14.) The expected after-tax cash flows from operations during 1977, $E(\text{NOI}_1)(1 - \tau_c)$, can be estimated by computing 1976 cash flows and assuming that they will grow during 1977.

Cash flows for 1976 from operations, NOI_0, can be calculated from the income statement in one of two equivalent ways. For example, consider the pro forma income statement in Table 16.9. The equation for net income can be rearranged as follows:

$$(\text{Rev} - \text{VC} - F - k_d D)(1 - \tau_c) = \text{NI},$$

$$(\text{Rev} - \text{VC} - F)(1 - \tau_c) = \text{NI} + k_d D(1 - \tau_c). \tag{16.19}$$

By adding back noncash charges, such as depreciation expenses (and deferred income taxes), we have two definitions of cash flow from operations:[11]

$$(\text{Rev} - \text{VC})(1 - \tau_c) + \tau_c(\text{dep}) = \text{NI} + k_d D(1 - \tau_c) + \text{dep}. \tag{16.20}$$

The left-hand side starts at the top of the income statement in Table 16.9 and works down, whereas the right-hand side starts at the bottom and works up. In order

---

[11] Recall that we have assumed that $F = \text{dep}$.

Table 16.9   Pro Forma Income Statement

$100	Rev	Revenues
−60	−VC	−Cash costs of operations
−20	−F	−Noncash costs (depreciation)
20	EBIT	Earnings before interest and taxes
−10	−k_dD	−Interest expense
10	EBT	Earnings before taxes
−5	−T	−Taxes at 50%
5	NI	Net income

to obtain the correct definition of cash flows, one further adjustment must be made. Recall that the model assumes that depreciation is adequate to replace worn-out equipment. In other words, cash outflows used to replace equipment each year are exactly equivalent to depreciation. The two cancel each other. Therefore, because depreciation is used for replacement investment, it is not part of the *free cash flow* available to investors. Consequently, it is necessary to subtract depreciation from both sides of (16.20). The result is the correct definition of after-tax free cash flows from operations that can be maintained into perpetuity, $NOI_0(1 - \tau_c)$:

$$NOI_0(1 - \tau_c) = (Rev - VC)(1 - \tau_c) - dep(1 - \tau_c) = NI + k_dD(1 - \tau_c). \quad (16.21)$$

For the simple example above (if $\tau_c = .5$),

$$NOI_0(1 - \tau_c) = (100 - 60)(1 - .5) - 20(1 - .5) = 5 + 10(1 - .5) = 10.$$

For Bethlehem Steel the estimates are given in Table 16.10. Note that for 1976 estimates, we also have to add deferred taxes of $35 million, a noncash charge (discovered in the footnotes to the income statement). This makes our estimate of $NOI_0(1 - \tau_c)$ add up to be $243,404 instead of $208,404. Note that $\tau_c = .48$.

Table 16.10   Various Valuation Statistics for Bethlehem Steel ($ given in thousands)

	1976	1975	1974	1973
Net income	$168,000	$242,000	$342,034	$206,609
+$k_dD(1 - \tau_c)$	40,404	32,968	22,872	20,246
$NOI_0(1 - \tau_c)$	$208,404	$274,968	$364,906	$226,855
Dividends	$ 87,400	$120,100	$100,172	$ 72,431
Dividends/$NOI_0(1 - \tau_c)$	.419	.437	.275	.319
(Investment rate) = K	58.1%	56.3%	72.5%	68.1%
Book value of assets	4,939,100	4,591,500	4,512,617	3,919,264
$NOI_0(1 - \tau_c)$/BV = r	4.22%	5.99%	8.09%	5.79%
Growth = Kr	2.45%	3.37%	5.87%	3.94%

B. THE INVESTMENT RATE.   The reason for estimating the investment rate, K, is that it is useful in estimating two more fundamental parameters: (1) the expected dollar amount of new investment, $I = K(NOI_1)(1 - \tau_c)$ and (2) the expected rate of growth in the firm, $g = Kr$. There is no reason that the investment rate must be less than 100% of cash flows. A higher investment rate simply means that the firm will be issuing new equity in order to undertake new investment in excess of current cash flows. This is certainly feasible for a firm with $r > $ WACC.

From Table 16.10 we can estimate the investment rate by subtracting the dividend payout [dividends $\div NOI_0(1 - \tau_c)$] from 100%. Bethlehem did not issue new equity during the period 1973–1976. The average investment rate is 63.8%.

C. THE RATE OF RETURN ON NEW INVESTMENT.   It is very difficult to come up with a reasonable projection of the rate of return on new investment. In Table 16.10 it has been estimated as the ratio of after-tax cash flows to the book value of assets. But the book value of assets is a number with little meaning, particularly during an inflationary economy. Also, what is really needed is not an historic estimate of return on capital in place but rather an estimate of future return on investment. This information simply cannot be found in the accounting statements of the firm. The community of financial analysts make their living, at least in part, by trying to estimate the impact of future investment possibilities on the market value of the firm.

For lack of anything better to use, we have assumed that future growth is likely to be the same as that during the past four years. Estimated in Table 16.10, the average rate of return, r, on book value is 6.02%.

Once given the investment rate, $K = .638$, and the rate of return, $r = .0602$, we can estimate the rate of growth:

$$g = Kr = .0384.$$

D. THE TARGET CAPITAL STRUCTURE.   The target capital structure is useful for two purposes. First, as we saw in Chapter 14, it is needed in order to estimate the weighted average cost of capital. And second, when used in combination with the investment rate, it determines the extent to which the company will issue new equity.

In Chapter 14 we saw that Bethlehem Steel has had a fairly stable ratio of long-term debt to total assets of around 31.5% (see Table 14.11). Also, the market value of long-term debt, B, was estimated to be $815,945.

E. THE WEIGHTED AVERAGE COST OF CAPITAL.   Assuming that new projects undertaken by the firm will have the same risk as current projects, then the current estimate of the weighted average cost of capital represents the required rate of return on new investment. If the expected rate of return, r, is greater than the required rate, WACC, a quick glance at the third term in Eq. (16.18) reveals that new investment will add to the market value of the firm. If new investment does not meet this criterion, it cannot possibly increase value (although, as was shown in Chapter 15, if $0 < r < $ WACC it might cause growth in earnings per share).

We assume that Bethlehem Steel will take on new investments with approximately the same risk as its existing projects. Therefore we can use the weighted average cost of capital, estimated in Chapter 14. It was WACC = 10.61%. In addition, we need to know the cost of equity capital if Bethlehem Steel were an all-equity firm. This can be computed by using the Modigliani-Miller definition of cost of capital, Eq. (13.12):

$$\text{WACC} = \rho\left(1 - \tau_c \frac{B}{B+S}\right),$$

$$\rho = \frac{\text{WACC}}{\left(1 - \tau_c \dfrac{B}{B+S}\right)}, \tag{13.12}$$

where

ρ = the cost of equity for the all-equity firm,

τ_c = the corporate tax rate = .48,

$B/(B+S)$ = the percentage of debt in the capital structure of the firm = 31.5% (using market value weights),

WACC = the weighted average cost of capital = 10.61%.

Solving for ρ, we have

$$\rho = \frac{.1061}{1 - .48(.315)} = 12.50\%.$$

F. THE DURATION OF ABNORMAL GROWTH.   The final important question is how long the firm will be able to undertake new investment projects that earn abnormally high rates of return, i.e., projects that earn more than the rate required for investments of equal risk. How long will r be greater than WACC? Usually, the period of supernormal growth can be conceptualized as the length of time required for competition to enter the market and eliminate the firm's economic advantage.

In the case of Bethlehem Steel the estimated future rate of return, 6.02%, is less than the rate that the market requires, 10.61%. This means that we need to estimate the length of time it will take them to get out of trouble. This is a matter of judgment, and we have assumed that the current "growth" pattern shall persist for three years ($T = 3$).

G. THE VALUE OF BETHLEHEM STEEL.   All that remains is to use the estimates of the six valuation parameters in the valuation equation. For convenience it is rewritten below:

$$V = \frac{E(\text{NOI}_1)(1 - \tau_c)}{\rho} + \tau_c B + K[E(\text{NOI}_1)(1 - \tau_c)]T\left[\frac{r - \text{WACC}}{\text{WACC}(1 + \text{WACC})}\right]. \tag{16.18}$$

Note that the expected 1977 after-tax cash flows from operations, $E(\text{NOI}_1)(1 - \tau_c)$, equal the estimated 1976 figure multiplied by the estimated growth rate $(g = Kr)$:

$$E(\text{NOI}_1)(1 - \tau_c) = \text{NOI}_0(1 - \tau_c)(1 + Kr)$$

$$= 243{,}404[1 + .638(.0602)]$$

$$= 243{,}404(1.0384076) = \$252{,}753.$$

Substituting the values of the remaining parameters into (16.18), we have

$$V = \frac{252{,}753}{.125} + .48(815{,}945) + .638(252{,}753)3\left[\frac{.0602 - .1061}{.1061(1.1061)}\right]$$

$$= 2{,}022{,}024 + 391{,}653 - 189{,}209$$

$$= \$2{,}224{,}468 \text{ (thousands of dollars)}.$$

The actual market value of Bethlehem Steel at the end of December 1976 was \$2.590 billion.[12] Therefore the estimate provided by the valuation model is around \$0.366 billion too low, an error of around 14.1%. The discrepancy may be due to any number of reasons. Most likely our estimates of the anticipated operating cash flows and the rate of return on future investment (which were based on historical accounting data) were too low.

The valuation model does serve to point out the contribution of the three major components. Most of the market value of Bethlehem Steel comes from the stream of cash flows provided by investments that are already in place. Some extra value is provided by the tax shield from debt. And almost no value—or more accurately, negative value—results from the profitability of anticipated growth opportunities.

3. Implications for Accounting Information

The valuation example given above is useful for two reasons. First, it shows an investor how to evaluate the effect of new information on the market value of the firm. Second, it provides a shopping list of relevant information.

Investors gain little benefit from historic accounting data because they contain no new information. Therefore although the annual report may serve as a useful device for monitoring the performance of management, it has little value to the investment community. Relevant data are forward looking. Investors seek out information about the six parameters mentioned in section 2.

An interesting related issue is the behavior of the Securities and Exchange Commission. By charter, its chief function is to monitor the disclosure of information. Yet many of its rules are concerned with the quality of historic accounting data. For

---

[12] The market value of equity was \$40⅝ per share, and 43.665 million shares were outstanding. Thus the total value of equity was \$1.774 billion. Adding this to the \$0.816 billion of long-term debt, we obtain a market value of \$2.590 billion.

example, it supports the publication of segment-based revenue data. Companies are asked to break down their total sales by line of business. The justification is presumably that the line-of-business reporting improves the shareholder stewardship function and allows investors to better estimate future returns. As we have already argued, historic accounting data, whatever their form, are of little benefit to investors. Consequently, it is hard to understand why the SEC should ask companies to bear the added cost of meeting its requirement of reporting segmented sales revenue.

What investors would like to know is what the management estimates future performance to be. This kind of information can be supplied in the company president's letter in the annual report without legal liability in the event that things do not turn out as well as anticipated. In particular, investors would benefit from unbiased estimates of the rate of return on future investment, the dollar amount of new investment, the length of time supernormal growth is expected to persist, and the percentage of new capital that will be provided from equity sources.

Once again, it is important to keep in mind that the valuation model used in the above example is only as good as the assumptions used in its derivation. Also, it is limited by the inevitable inaccuracies in estimating future cash flows. At best, it is only a framework for analysis that is useful for structuring the way we conceptualize corporate valuation.

Not only is it useful to understand which parameters determine value; but it is also important to understand those that do not. For example, accounting conventions that do not affect cash flows are irrelevant.

PROBLEM SET

16.1 Under what conditions might dividend policy affect the value of the firm?

16.2 According to federal tax law, corporations need not pay taxes on 80% of dividends received from shares held in other corporations. In other words, only 20% of the dividends received by a corporate holder are taxable. Given this fact, how much must the price of a stock fall on the ex-dividend date in order to prevent a corporate holder from making arbitrage profits? Assume that the capital gains rate equals the corporate tax rate, $\tau_c = .5$.

16.3 Empirical evidence supports the existence of a clientele effect. This implies that every time a company revises its dividend policy to pay out a greater (or smaller) percentage of earnings, the characteristics of its shareholders also change. For example, a firm with a higher payout ratio may expect to have more shareholders in lower tax brackets. Suppose that lower-income people are also more risk averse. Would this have an effect on the value of the firm?

16.4 Miller and Scholes [1978] suggest that it is possible to shelter income from taxes in such a way that capital gains rates are paid on dividend income. Furthermore, since capital gains need never be realized, the effective tax rate will become zero. Why would this scheme not be used to shelter all income, instead of just dividend income? The implication would be that no one has to pay taxes—*ever*!

16.5 The Pettit study suggests an increase in the price per share of common stock commensurate with an increase in dividends. Can this be taken as evidence that the value of the firm is in fact affected by dividend policy?

16.6 Assume that the XYZ firm has the following parameters in a world with no taxes:

$$\sigma = .2 \qquad \text{instantaneous standard deviation,}$$

$$T = 4 \text{ years} \quad \text{maturity of debt,}$$

$$V = \$2000 \qquad \text{value of the firm; } V = B + S,$$

$$R_f = .06 \qquad \text{risk-free rate,}$$

$$D = \$1000 \qquad \text{face value of debt.}$$

a) What will be the market value of equity cum dividend (i.e., before any dividend is paid)?

b) If the shareholders decide to pay themselves a $500 dividend out of cash, what will be the ex-dividend wealth of shareholders? [*Note:* The dividend payment will have two effects. First, it will decrease the market value of the firm to $1500. Second, since cash has little or no risk, the instantaneous standard deviation of the firm's assets will increase to .25.]

REFERENCES

Aharony, J., and I. Swary, "Quarterly Dividend and Earnings Announcements and Stockholders' Returns: An Empirical Analysis," *Journal of Finance*, March 1980, 1–12.

Asquith, P., and W. Krasker, "Changes in Dividend Policy, and Stock Trading Volume," Working paper, Harvard Business School, Cambridge, Mass., October 1985.

Asquith, P., and D. Mullins, Jr., "The Impact of Initiating Dividend Payments on Shareholders' Wealth," *Journal of Business*, January 1983, 77–96.

Austin, D., "Treasury Stock Reacquisition by American Corporations 1961–1967," *Financial Executive*, May 1969, 40–61.

Bar-Yosef, S., and R. Kolodny, "Dividend Policy and Market Theory," *Review of Economics and Statistics*, May 1976, 181–190.

Bierman, H., and R. West, "The Acquisition of Common Stock by the Corporate Issuer," *Journal of Finance*, December 1966, 687–696.

Black, F.; M. Jensen; and M. Scholes, "The Capital Asset Pricing Model: Some Empirical Tests," in Jensen, ed., *Studies in the Theory of Capital Markets*. Praeger, New York, 1972, 79–124.

Black, F., and M. Scholes, "The Effects of Dividend Yield and Dividend Policy on Common Stock Prices and Returns," *Journal of Financial Economics*, May 1974, 1–22.

Blume, M., "Stock Returns and Dividend Yields: Some More Evidence," *Review of Economics and Statistics*, November 1980, 567–577.

Booth, L., and D. Johnston, "The Ex-Dividend Day Behavior of Canadian Stock Prices: Tax Changes and Clientele Effects," *Journal of Finance*, June 1984, 457–476.

Brennan, M., "Taxes, Market Valuation and Corporate Financial Policy," *National Tax Journal*, December 1970, 417–427.

Brickley, J., "Shareholder Wealth, Information Signaling and the Specially Designated Dividend," *Journal of Financial Economics*, August 1983, 187–210.

Brittain, J. A., *Corporate Dividend Policy.* Brookings Institution, Washington, D.C., 1966.

Charest, G., "Dividend Information, Stock Returns and Market Efficiency," *Journal of Financial Economics,* June–September 1978, 297–330.

Coates, C., and A. Fredman, "Price Behavior Associated with Tender Offers to Repurchase Common Stock," *Financial Executive,* April 1976, 40–44.

Dann, L., "Common Stock Repurchases: An Analysis of Returns to Bondholders and Stockholders," *Journal of Financial Economics,* June 1981, 113–138.

Darling, P., "The Influence of Expectations and Liquidity on Dividend Policy," *Journal of Political Economy,* June 1957, 209–224.

Dielman, T.; T. Nantell; and R. Wright, "Price Effects of Stock Repurchasing: A Random Coefficient Regression Approach," *Journal of Financial and Quantitative Analysis,* March 1980, 175–189.

Eades, K.; P. Hess; and E. H. Kim, "Market Rationality and Dividend Announcements," *Journal of Financial Economics,* December 1985, 581–604.

———, "On Interpreting Security Returns during the Ex-Dividend Period," *Journal of Financial Economics,* March 1984, 3–34.

Ellis, C., "Repurchase Stock to Revitalize Equity," *Harvard Business Review,* July–August 1965, 119–128.

Elton, E. J., and M. J. Gruber, "The Effect of Share Repurchase on the Value of the Firm," *Journal of Finance,* March 1968, 135–149.

———, "Marginal Stockholders' Tax Rates and the Clientele Effect," *Review of Economics and Statistics,* February 1970, 68–74.

Fama, E., "The Empirical Relationship between the Dividend and Investment Decisions of Firms," *American Economic Review,* June 1974, 304–318.

———, and H. Babiak, "Dividend Policy: An Empirical Analysis," *Journal of the American Statistical Association,* December 1968, 1132–1161.

Fama, E.; L. Fisher; M. Jensen; and R. Roll, "The Adjustment of Stock Prices to New Information," *International Economic Review,* February 1969, 1–21.

Farrar, D., and L. Selwyn, "Taxes, Corporate Financial Policy and Return to Investors," *National Tax Journal,* December 1967, 444–454.

Friend, I., and M. Puckett, "Dividends and Stock Prices," *American Economic Review,* September 1964, 656–682.

Gonedes, N., "Corporate Signaling, External Accounting, and Capital Market Equilibrium: Evidence on Dividends, Income, and Extraordinary Items," *Journal of Accounting Research,* Spring 1978, 26–79.

Gordon, M., "Dividends, Earnings, and Stock Prices," *Review of Economics and Statistics,* May 1959, 99–105.

———, "The Savings, Investment and Valuation of a Corporation," *Review of Economics and Statistics,* February 1962, 37–51.

Gordon, R., and D. Bradford, "Taxation and the Stock Market Valuation of Capital Gains and Dividends," *Journal of Public Economics,* October 1980, 103–136.

Griffin, P., "Competitive Information in the Stock Market: An Empirical Study of Earnings, Dividends and Analysts Forecasts," *Journal of Finance,* May 1976, 631–650.

Grinblatt, M.; R. Masulis, and S. Titman, "The Valuation Effects of Stock Splits and Stock Dividends," *Journal of Financial Economics,* December 1984, 461–490.

Guthart, L., "Why Companies Are Buying Their Own Stock," *Financial Analysts Journal*, March–April 1967, 105–110.

Handjiinicolaou, G., and A. Kalay, "Wealth Redistributions or Changes in Firm Value: An Analysis of Returns to Bondholders and Stockholders around Dividend Announcements," *Journal of Financial Economics*, March 1984, 35–64.

Harris J., Jr.; R. Roenfeldt; and P. Cooley, "Evidence of Financial Leverage Clienteles," *Journal of Finance*, September 1983, 1125–1132.

Hess, P., "The Ex-Dividend Behavior of Stock Returns: Further Evidence on Tax Effects," *Journal of Finance*, May 1982, 445–456.

Higgins, R., "The Corporate Dividend-Saving Decision," *Journal of Financial and Quantitative Analysis*, March 1972, 1527–1541.

Hite, G., and J. Owers, "Security Price Reactions around Corporate Spin-off Announcements," *Journal of Financial Economics*, December 1983, 409–436.

Kalay, A., "Essays in Dividend Policy," Ph.D. dissertation, University of Rochester, 1977.

———, "The Ex-Dividend Behavior of Stock Prices: A Re-examination of the Clientele Effect," *Journal of Finance*, September 1982, 1059–1070.

———, and U. Lowenstein, "Predictable Events and Excess Returns: The Case of Dividend Announcements," *Journal of Financial Economics*, September 1985, 423–450.

———, "The Informational Content of the Timing of Dividend Announcements," *Journal of Financial Economics*, July 1986, 373–388.

Kane, A.; Y. K. Lee; and A. Marcus, "Signaling, Information Content, and the Reluctance to Cut Dividends," *Journal of Financial and Quantitative Analysis*, November 1980, 855–870.

———, "Earnings and Dividend Announcements: Is There a Corroboration Effect?" *Journal of Finance*, September 1984, 1091–1099.

Keim, D., "Dividend Yields and Stock Returns: Implications of Abnormal January Returns," *Journal of Financial Economics*, September 1985, 473–490.

Khoury, N., and K. Smith, "Dividend Policy and the Capital Gains Tax in Canada," *Journal of Business Administration*, Spring 1977.

Kim, E. H.; W. Lewellen; and J. McConnell, "Financial Leverage Clienteles: Theory and Evidence," *Journal of Financial Economics*, March 1979, 83–110.

Kwan, C., "Efficient Market Tests of the Informational Content of Dividend Announcements: Critique and Extension," *Journal of Financial and Quantitative Analysis*, June 1981, 193–206.

Lakonishok, J., and T. Vermaelen, "Tax Reform and Ex-Dividend Day Behavior," *Journal of Finance*, September 1983, 1157–1179.

———, "Tax-induced Trading around Ex-Dividend Days," *Journal of Financial Economics*, July 1986, 287–320.

Lane, W., "Repurchase of Common Stock and Managerial Discretion," Ph.D. dissertation, University of North Carolina, 1976.

Laub, P. M., "On the Informational Content of Dividends," *Journal of Business*, January 1976, 73–80.

Lewellen, W.; K. Stanley; R. Lease; and G. Schlarbaum, "Some Direct Evidence on the Dividend Clientele Phenomenon," *Journal of Finance*, December 1978, 1385–1399.

Lintner, J., "Distribution of Incomes of Corporations among Dividends, Retained Earnings and Taxes," *American Economic Review*, May 1956, 97–113.

————, "Optimal Dividends and Corporate Growth under Uncertainty," *Quarterly Journal of Economics*, February 1964, 49–95.

————, "The Valuation of Risk Assets and the Selection of Risky Investments in Stock Portfolios and Capital Budgets," *Review of Economics and Statistics*, February 1965, 13–37.

Litzenberger, R., and K. Ramaswamy, "The Effect of Personal Taxes and Dividends on Capital Asset Prices: Theory and Empirical Evidence," *Journal of Financial Economics*, June 1979, 163–196.

————, "Dividends, Short-Selling Restrictions, Tax-Induced Investor Clienteles and Market Equilibrium," *Journal of Finance*, May 1980, 469–482.

————, "The Effects of Dividends on Common Stock Prices: Tax Effects or Information Effects?" *Journal of Finance*, May 1982, 429–444.

Long, J., Jr., "Efficient Portfolio Choice with Differential Taxation of Dividends and Capital Gains," *Journal of Financial Economics*, August 1977, 25–54.

————, "The Market Valuation of Cash Dividends: A Case to Consider," *Journal of Financial Economics*, June–September 1978, 235–264.

Masulis, R., "Stock Repurchase by Tender Offer: An Analysis of the Causes of Common Stock Price Changes," *Journal of Finance*, May 1980, 305–318.

McCabe, G., "The Empirical Relationship between Investment and Financing: A New Look," *Journal of Financial and Quantitative Analysis*, March 1979, 119–135.

Miller, M. H., "Debt and Taxes," *Journal of Finance*, May 1977, 261–275.

————, and F. Modigliani, "Dividend Policy, Growth, and the Valuation of Shares," *Journal of Business*, October 1961, 411–433.

Miller, M. H., and M. Scholes, "Dividends and Taxes," *Journal of Financial Economics*, December 1978, 333–364.

————, "Dividends and Taxes: Some Empirical Evidence," *Journal of Political Economy*, December 1982, 1118–1141.

Modigliani, F., and M. Miller, "Taxes and the Cost of Capital: A Correction," *American Economic Review*, June 1963, 433–443.

Morgan, I. G., "Dividends and Stock Price Behaviour in Canada," *Journal of Business Administration*, Fall 1980, 91–106.

Penman, S., "The Predictive Content of Earnings Forecasts and Dividends," *Journal of Finance*, September 1983, 1181–1199.

Pettit, R. R., "Dividend Announcements, Security Performance, and Capital Market Efficiency," *Journal of Finance*, December 1972, 993–1007.

————, "The Impact of Dividend and Earnings Announcements: A Reconciliation," *Journal of Business*, January 1976, 86–96.

————, "Taxes, Transactions Costs and Clientele Effects of Dividends," *Journal of Financial Economics*, December 1977, 419–436.

Poterba, J., "The Market Valuation of Cash Dividends: The Citizens Utilities Case Reconsidered," *Journal of Financial Economics*, March 1986, 395–406.

————, and L. Summers, "Taxes, Transactions Costs and Clientele Effects of Dividends," *Journal of Financial Economics*, December 1977, 419 436.

————, "New Evidence That Taxes Affect the Valuation of Dividends," *Journal of Finance*, December 1984, 1397–1415.

Richardson, G.; S. Sefcik; and R. Thompson, "A Test of Dividend Irrelevance Using Volume Reactions to a Change in Dividend Policy," *Journal of Financial Economics*, December 1986, 313–334.

Rosenberg, B., and V. Marathe, "Tests of the Capital Asset Pricing Hypothesis," *Research in Finance*, January 1979, 115–223.

Ross, S. A., "The Determination of Financial Structure: The Incentive-Signalling Approach," *Bell Journal of Economics*, Spring 1977, 23–40.

Smirlock, M., and W. Marshall, "An Examination of the Empirical Relationship between the Dividend and Investment Decisions: A Note," *Journal of Finance*, December 1983, 1659–1667.

Stewart, S., "Should a Corporation Repurchase Its Own Stock?" *Journal of Finance*, June 1976, 911–921.

Van Horne, J., and J. G. McDonald, "Dividend Policy and New Equity Financing," *Journal of Finance*, May 1971, 507–520.

Vermaelen, T., "Common Stock Repurchases and Market Signalling: An Empirical Study," *Journal of Financial Economics*, June 1981, 139–183.

Walter, J. E., *Dividend Policy and Enterprise Valuation*. Wadsworth, Belmont, Calif., 1967.

Watts, R., "The Information Content of Dividends," *Journal of Business*, April 1973, 191–211.

———, "Comments on 'The Impact of Dividend and Earnings Announcements: A Reconciliation,'" *Journal of Business*, January 1976a, 97–106.

———, "Comments on the Informational Content of Dividends," *Journal of Business*, January 1976b, 81–85.

Woods, D., and E. Brigham, "Stockholder Distribution Decisions: Share Repurchases or Dividends?" *Journal of Financial and Quantitative Analysis*, March 1966, 15–28.

Woolridge, J., "Dividend Changes and Security Prices," *Journal of Finance*, December 1983, 1607–1615.

Young, A., "The Performance of Common Stocks Subsequent to Repurchase," *Financial Analysts Journal*, September–October 1967, 117–121.

———, "Financial, Operating and Security Market Parameters of Repurchasing," *Financial Analysts Journal*, July–August 1969, 123–128.

17

It is estimated that from 15 to 20 percent of all new capital put in use by business each year is leased.

Peter Vanderwicken, "The Powerful Logic of the Leasing Boom," *Fortune*, November 1973, 136.

The Economics of Leasing

A. INTRODUCTION

Lease contracts have long been an important alternative to direct ownership of an asset. For example, one may choose to lease an automobile or rent a house, rather than owning them outright. For the student of finance, leasing is an important applied issue because the use of an asset and the methods of financing it are seemingly intertwined. However, this is an illusion. As we shall see, it is critical to keep the investment decision separate from the financing decision in the analysis. Failure to do so has led many decision makers to make the wrong comparisons between the lease/own decision and the lease/borrow decision.

For the purpose of consistency, we shall assume throughout most of the chapter that there are no transactions costs or economies of scale in financial contracts. Among other things, this implies that there are no flotation costs in issuing financial securities. Thus it would make no difference at all in the percentage of transactions costs whether one issues a bond for $100 or $100,000,000. Additionally, we shall assume (1) that firms possess optimal capital structures without specifying the the reason, (2) that firms may have different effective tax rates, and (3) that the Miller-Modigliani [1966] valuation framework is applicable. First, we review a detailed description of the legal and accounting treatment of different types of lease contracts. Then we analyze the economics of the lease/buy decision for noncancellable long-term leases, for cancellable leases, for leveraged leases, and for short-term leases. Finally, the scant empirical literature on leasing is reviewed.

614

B. THE LEGAL AND ACCOUNTING TREATMENT OF LEASES

1. Types of Leases

Leases take several different forms, the most important of which are sale and leaseback, service or operating leases, and straight financial leases. These three major types of leases are described below.

Under a *sale and leaseback arrangement*, a firm owning land, buildings, or equipment sells the property to a financial institution and simultaneously executes an agreement to lease the property back for a certain period under specific terms.

Note that the seller, or *lessee*, immediately receives the purchase price put up by the buyer, or *lessor*. At the same time, the seller-lessee retains the use of the property. This parallel is carried over to the lease payment schedule. Under a mortgage loan arrangement the financial institution receives a series of equal payments just sufficient to amortize the loan and to provide the lender with a specified rate of return on investment. Under a sale and leaseback arrangement the lease payments are set up in the same manner. The payments are sufficient to return the full purchase price to the financial institution in addition to providing it with some return on its investment.

Operating (or *service*) *leases* include both financing and maintenance services. IBM is one of the pioneers of the service lease contract. Computers and office copying machines, together with automobiles and trucks, are the primary types of equipment covered by operating leases. The leases ordinarily call for the lessor to maintain and service the leased equipment, and the costs of this maintenance are either built into the lease payments or contracted for separately.

Another important characteristic of the service lease is that it is frequently not fully amortized. In other words the payments required under the lease contract are *not* sufficient to recover the full cost of the equipment. Obviously, however, the lease contract is written for considerably less than the expected life of the leased equipment, and the lessor expects to recover the cost either in subsequent renewal payments or on disposal of the equipment.

A final feature of the service lease is that it frequently contains a cancellation clause giving the lessee the right to cancel the lease and return the equipment before the expiration of the basic agreement. This is an important consideration for the lessee, who can return the equipment if technological developments render it obsolete or if it simply is no longer needed.

A *strict financial lease* is one that does not provide for maintenance services, is not cancellable, and is fully amortized (i.e., the lessor contracts for rental payments equal to the full price of the leased equipment). The typical arrangement involves the following steps:

1. The user firm selects the specific equipment it requires and negotiates the price and delivery terms with the manufacturer or distributor.

2. Next, the user firm arranges with a bank or leasing company for the latter to buy the equipment from the manufacturer or distributor, simultaneously executing

an agreement to lease the equipment from the financial institution. The terms call for full amortization of the financial institution's cost, plus a rate of return on investment. The lessee generally has the option to renew the lease at a reduced rental on expiration of the basic lease but does not have the right to cancel the basic lease without completely paying off the financial institution.

Financial leases are almost the same as sale and leaseback arrangements, the main difference being that the leased equipment is new and the lessor buys it from a manufacturer or a distributor instead of from the user-lessee. A sale and leaseback can thus be thought of as a special type of financial lease.

2. Tax Treatment

The full amount of the annual lease payments is deductible for income tax purposes—provided the Internal Revenue Service (IRS) agrees that a particular contract is a genuine lease and not simply an installment loan called a lease. This makes it important that the lease contract be written in a form acceptable to the IRS. Following are the major requirements for bona fide lease transactions from the standpoint of the IRS:

1. The term must be less than 30 years; otherwise the lease is regarded as a form of sale.
2. The rent must represent a reasonable return to the lessor.
3. The renewal option must be bona fide, and this requirement can best be met by giving the lessee the first option to meet an equal bona fide outside offer.
4. There must be no repurchase option; if there is, the lessee should merely be given parity with an equal outside offer.

3. Accounting Treatment

In November 1976 the Financial Accounting Standards Board (FASB) issued its Statement of Financial Accounting Standards No. 13, *Accounting for Leases*. Like other FASB statements, the standards set forth must be followed by business firms if their financial statements are to receive certification by auditors. FASB Statement No. 13 has implications both for the utilization of leases and for their accounting treatment. Those elements of FASB Statement No. 13 that are most relevant for financial analysis of leases are summarized below.

For some types of leases, this FASB statement requires that the obligation be capitalized on the asset side of the balance sheet with a related lease obligation on the liability side. The accounting treatment depends on the type of lease. The classification is more detailed than the two categories of operating and financial leases described above.

From the lessee's point of view the two accounting categories are *capital leases* and *operating leases*. A lease is classified in Statement No. 13 as a capital lease if it meets one or more of four Paragraph 7 criteria:

1. The lease transfers ownership of the property to the lessee by the end of the lease term.

2. The lease gives the lessee the option to purchase the property at a price sufficiently below the expected fair value of the property that the exercise of the option is highly probable.

3. The lease term is equal to 75% or more of the estimated economic life of the property.

4. The present value of the minimum lease payments exceeds 90% of the fair value of the property at the inception of the lease. The discount factor to be used in calculating the present value is the implicit rate used by the lessor or the lessee's incremental borrowing rate, whichever is lower. (Note that the lower discount factor represents a higher present value factor and therefore a higher calculated present value for a given pattern of lease payments. It thus increases the likelihood that the 90% test will be met and that the lease will be classified as a capital lease.)

From the standpoint of the lessee, if a lease is not a capital lease, it is classified as an operating lease.

From the standpoint of the lessor, four types of leases are defined: (1) *sales-type leases*, (2) *direct financing leases*, (3) *leveraged leases*, and (4) *operating leases* representing all leases other than the first three types. Sales-type leases and direct financing leases meet one or more of the four Paragraph 7 criteria and both of the Paragraph 8 criteria, which are:

1. Collectability of the minimum lease payments is reasonably predictable.

2. No important uncertainties surround the amount of unreimbursable costs yet to be incurred by the lessor under the lease.

Sales-type leases give rise to profit (or loss) to the lessor—the fair value of the leased property at the inception of the lease is greater (or less) than its cost-of-carrying amount. Sales-type leases normally arise when manufacturers or dealers use leasing in marketing their products. Direct financing leases are leases other than leveraged leases for which the cost-of-carrying amount is equal to the fair value of the leased property at the inception of the lease. Leveraged leases are direct financing leases in which substantial financing is provided by a long-term creditor on a nonrecourse basis with respect to the general credit of the lessor.

The actual bookkeeping for lessees is set up in the following way. For operating leases, rentals must be charged to expense over the lease term, with disclosures of future rental obligations in total as well as by each of the following five years. For lessees, capital leases are to be capitalized and shown on the balance sheet both as a fixed asset and as a noncurrent obligation. Capitalization represents the present value of the minimum lease payments minus that portion of lease payments representing executory costs such as insurance, maintenance, and taxes to be paid by the lessor (including any profit return in such charges). The discount factor is [as described in Paragraph 7(4)] the lower of the implicit rates used by the lessor or the incremental borrowing rate of the lessee.

Table 17.1   Balance Sheet for Capitalized Leases

Assets	Liabilities
	Current:
Leased property under capital	Obligations under capital leases
leases less accumulated	Noncurrent:
amortization	Obligations under capital leases

The asset must be amortized in a manner consistent with the lessee's normal depreciation policy for owned assets. During the lease term, each lease payment is to be allocated between a reduction of the obligation and the interest expense to produce a constant rate of interest on the remaining balance of the obligation. Thus for capital leases the balance sheet includes the terms in Table 17.1.

In addition to the balance sheet capitalization of capital leases, substantial additional footnote disclosures are required for both capital and operating leases. These include a description of leasing arrangements, an analysis of leased property under capital leases by major classes of property, a schedule by years of future minimum lease payments (with executory and interest costs broken out for capital leases), and contingent rentals for operating leases.

FASB Statement No. 13 sets forth requirements for capitalizing capital leases and for standardizing disclosures by lessees for both capital leases and operating leases. Lease commitments therefore do not represent "off–balance sheet" financing for capital assets, and standard disclosure requirements make general the footnote reporting of information on operating leases. Hence the argument that leasing represents a form of financing that lenders may not take into account in their analysis of the financial position of firms seeking financing will be even less valid in the future than it is now.

It is unlikely that sophisticated lenders were ever fooled by off–balance sheet leasing obligations. However, the capitalization of capital leases and the standard disclosure requirements for operating leases will make it easier for general users of financial reports to obtain additional information on firms' leasing obligations. Hence the requirements of FASB Statement No. 13 are useful. Probably the extent to which leasing is used will remain substantially unaltered since the particular circumstances that have provided a basis for its use in the past are not likely to be greatly affected by the increased disclosure requirements.

C. THE THEORY OF LEASING

1. The Long-Term Lease from the Lessor's Point of View

The lessor is frequently a financial intermediary such as a commercial bank, an insurance company, or a leasing company. Also equipment manufacturers—e.g., GATX (railroad cars), IBM (computers and office equipment), and Xerox (copiers)— are among the largest lessors. However, the institutional arrangements are largely arbitrary. Anyone who owns an asset also may decide to lease it. For example, suppose one owns a car or a house. There is always the choice between owning it and using it for one's own purposes, thereby gaining a direct (nontaxable) stream of consumption of transportation or housing services. Or alternatively, one can lease the asset to a second party. In return one then receives a (taxable) stream of income that can be used for the consumption of transportation and housing (among other things). From the lessee's point of view, the choice to own the asset in the first place was an investment decision. At the same time, there is a separate decision to make—namely, the financing decision. Should use of the asset be financed with debt and equity, or should it be leased? How much of the lease financing can be considered to be debt? How much is equity?

In the analysis that follows it is convenient to divide lease contracts into major categories: (1) *strict financial leases* and (2) *operating leases.* Strict financial leases, along with sale and leaseback arrangements, will be characterized as perfect substitutes for debt capital; in other words, they have exactly the same risk.[1] A lessee may not cancel a strict financial lease, the failure to meet lease payments can force the lessee into bankruptcy (or reorganization), and the lease is fully amortized (i.e., the lessor receives lease payments that repay the full cost of the leased asset). Operating leases are riskier than financial leases. We assume that they may be cancelled at the option of the lessee, are usually not fully amortized, and require that the salvage value go to the lessor. Finally, either type of lease may involve a separable contract for various types of maintenance on the leased asset, e.g., automobile servicing. Because the maintenance contract is economically separable we shall not discuss it in this chapter.

Financial leases and operating leases involve very different risks to the lessor and must therefore be discussed separately. We shall defer a discussion of operating leases until later in the chapter and focus on the much simpler financial lease for the time being. Suppose that the lessor is a commercial bank. Recall that any commercial bank will hold a well-diversified portfolio of corporate debt as its major asset. Obviously it requires that this portfolio earn (at least) the bank's after-tax weighted average cost of capital. On the other hand, what we call the rate of return to the bank is also the cost of debt to the borrowing firm. Therefore if we designate the bank's after-tax weighted average cost of capital as $WACC_B$ and the firm's before-tax cost of debt as k_b, then

$$k_b = \frac{WACC_B}{(1 - \tau_c)},$$

where τ_c is the bank's marginal tax rate.

The Modigliani-Miller model may be employed to compute $WACC_B$, the lessor's after-tax weighted average cost of capital.[2] Designate ρ (lease) as the rate of return required on leasing projects, assuming that the lessor is 100% equity financed. Then, given that B and S are the market values of debt and equity, respectively, the M-M

---

[1] This means that debt capital lent to the ith firm and leased to the same firm have the *same* risk. Of course, lending to different firms may have different risks.

[2] See Chapter 13, Eq. 13.12.

cost of capital is

$$WACC_B = \rho(\text{lease})\left[1 - \tau_c \frac{B}{B+S}\right].$$

If the required rate of return on the lease project is 9.375% and the leasing firm (the bank) uses 90% debt in its optimal capital structure, and has a 40% marginal tax rate, then

$$WACC_B = .09375[1 - .4(.9)] = .06.$$

Thus from the lessor's point of view the lease project will have a 6% after-tax weighted average cost of capital. From the lessee's point of view the before-tax cost of leasing will be

$$k_b = \frac{WACC_B}{1 - \tau_c} = \frac{.06}{1 - .4} = 10\%.$$

As mentioned before, each dollar in a pure financial lease is a perfect substitute for one dollar of debt in the capital structure of the lessee firm. Thus if a lessee is at its optimal capital structure prior to signing a lease contract, and wishes to maintain that structure, then it must displace one dollar of debt for each dollar in the lease contract.

What lease fee should the lessor charge for a pure financial lease? Assume the cost of the leased asset is I, the lessor's tax rate is τ_c, and the annual (straight-line) depreciation write-off on the leased asset is dep_t.[3] Also, assume that there is no salvage value. If the lessor charges an annual lease payment of L_t, then the net present value of the lease to the lessor is[4]

$$NPV(\text{to lessor}) = -I + \sum_{t=1}^{N} \frac{L_t(1 - \tau_c) + \tau_c dep_t}{(1 + WACC_B)^t}. \tag{17.1}$$

The numerator of Eq. (17.1) is the standard definition of after-tax cash flows from an investment, including the depreciation tax shield.[5] To provide a numerical example, let $I = \$10,000$, $\tau_c = 40\%$, $WACC_B = 6\%$, and the life of the project, N, be 5 years. Given these facts and assuming that the lease fee is competitively determined so that NPV (to lessor) = 0, then the minimum lease fee, L_t, is

$$0 = -10,000 + \sum_{t=1}^{5} \frac{L_t(1 - .4) + .4(2000)}{(1 + .06)^t},$$

$$0 = -10,000 + L_t(.6)(4.212) + .4(2000)(4.212),$$

$$\frac{10,000 - .4(2000)(4.212)}{.6(4.212)} = L_t = \$2624.$$

---

[3] Although we have assumed straight-line depreciation for convenience, there is usually an optimal depreciation schedule that maximizes the present value of the depreciation tax shield. Our analysis will not change if, in practice, both the lessor and lessee use the same optimal depreciation schedule.

[4] For convenience, we have assumed that the stream of lease payments is an annuity with the first payment at the end of the first year. Most lease contracts require the first payment to be made immediately.

[5] If there were an investment tax credit it would also be counted as a cash inflow.

If the lessor charges \$2624, then it will earn a rate of return that just compensates it for taking a debt position in the lessee firm. A higher lease fee would result in a positive NPV.

2. The Investment Decision

Now suppose that, instead of leasing the asset, the *lessor* decides to own it and operate it. What rate of return would be required? Clearly, owning the asset exposes the lessor to more risk than a lending position of an equivalent dollar amount. Owning the project involves the total risk of its cash flows, not merely the risk of a debt position. Suppose we define the required rate of return on the unlevered cash flows from the project as $\rho(\text{project})$. We know that $\rho(\text{project}) > k_b(\text{lease}) \geq \text{WACC}_B$. Furthermore, if one borrows to undertake the investment, the Modigliani-Miller definition of the cost of capital can be applied. Then if the project's optimal capital structure is $B/(B + S)$, the appropriate weighted average cost of capital is

$$\text{WACC}(\text{project}) = \rho(\text{project})\left(1 - \tau_c \frac{B}{B + S}\right). \tag{17.2}$$

Note that this weighted average cost of capital for owning the project is the same no matter who owns it, so long as their marginal tax rates are the same. We assume that the optimal capital structure is project specific. For example, a commercial bank with 90–95% debt in its capital structure should not apply the same leverage to a wholly owned computer division. Presumably, the computer division has its own optimal leverage, different from (less than) the commercial bank's.

To continue with the numerical example, assume that the unlevered cost of capital, $\rho(\text{project})$, is 14% for the project and that its optimal capital structure is one third debt to total assets, i.e., $B/(B + S) = .33$. The required rate of return on the wholly owned project is

$$\text{WACC}(\text{project}) = .14[1 - .4(.33)] = 12.152\%.$$

If the project has a positive net present value when its after-tax operating cash flows are discounted at the appropriate WACC, then it is a good investment.

To add realism to the investment decision, assume that the investment project has expected annual sales revenues of $S_t = \$20,000$, and expected annual cash costs of $C_t = \$16,711$. Then the NPV of the investment project is

$$\text{NPV}(\text{investment}) = -I + \sum_{t=1}^{N} \frac{(S_t - C_t)(1 - \tau_c) + \tau_c \text{dep}_t}{(1 + \text{WACC})^t}$$

$$= -10,000 + \sum_{t=1}^{5} \frac{.6(20,000 - 16,711) + .4(2,000)}{(1.12152)^t}$$

$$= -10,000 + .6(20,000 - 16,711)(3.5912) + .4(2,000)(3.5912)$$

$$= -10,000 + 7,087 + 2,873$$

$$= -40.$$

Under these assumptions, the project should be rejected.

3. The Long-Term Lease Contract from the Lessee's Point of View

As before, we assume that the lease is a perfect substitute for debt because it is assumed to be a strict financial lease. Operating leases are riskier for the lessor and will be discussed later on.

Failure to remember that strict financial leases are perfect substitutes for debt causes much confusion about how to evaluate a lease contract. For example, one often hears the mistaken phrase that leases are 100% debt financing. The advertising of leasing companies invariably points out that lease payments are deductible in full, whereas owners deduct only the machine's depreciation plus that part of the capital costs represented by interest payments. This is nonsense. If all of a project is provided by lease financing, then the lessee firm's debt capacity is reduced by an equivalent dollar amount. Other projects can carry less debt financing. Hence an opportunity cost of leasing is the displacement of the firm's debt capacity, and the associated loss of the tax shield provided by that debt.

The lessee firm must make two decisions. First, is the project acceptable as an investment? Does it have a positive net present value if financed at its optimal capital structure? This analysis was described in section C.2 above. Second, should it be financed by leasing or borrowing? The user firm takes the lease-rental fee, L_t, as an input in making a comparison between the cost of leasing and the cost of borrowing. Myers, Dill, and Bautista [1976] have shown that the costs and benefits of leasing involve an analysis of the following cash flows:

1. A cash saving amounting to the dollar amount of the investment outlay, I, which the firm does not have to incur if it leases.

2. A cash outflow amounting to the present value of the after-tax lease payments, $PV[L_t(1 - \tau_c)]$.

3. The present value of the opportunity cost of the lost depreciation tax shield, $PV[\tau_c \text{dep}_t]$ (and lost investment tax credits, which were relevant prior to the 1986 tax code).

4. The present value of the *change* in the interest tax shield on debt that is displaced by the lease financing, $PV[\tau_c \triangle(k_d D_t)]$, where D_t is the remaining book value of debt outstanding in period t.

These four terms are summarized in Eq. (17.3) below:

$$\text{NPV(to lessee)} = I - PV[(1 - \tau_c)L_t] - PV[\tau_c \text{dep}_t] - PV[\tau_c \triangle(k_d D_t)]. \quad (17.3)$$

We have assumed for strict financial leases that debt and lease financing are perfect substitutes. Therefore the fourth term in Eq. (17.3) will reflect a dollar-for-dollar substitution of debt tax shield for leasing tax shield for the portion of the asset that would be debt financed at the project's optimal capital structure. Furthermore, because leasing and debt are perfect substitutes, the cash inflows to the lessor and the cash outflows from the lessee have the same risk. Therefore the appropriate before-tax discount rate for the cash flows in Eq. (17.3) is k_b, the borrowing rate. Eq. (17.3) may be rewritten as

$$\text{NPV(to lessee)} = I - \sum_{t=1}^{N} \frac{L_t(1 - \tau_c) + \tau_c\text{dep}_t + \tau_c \triangle(k_dD_t)}{(1 + k_b)^t}. \quad (17.4)$$

Table 17.2 illustrates how the cash flow definitions of Eq. (17.4) can be used to compute the present value of a lease contract. The example in Table 17.2 uses the same numbers we have developed in this chapter. The annual lease fee (assumed to be paid at the end of each year) is $2624. Except for a rounding error, the NPV of the lease is $0. This is to be expected in a competitive market where the tax rates of the lessor and lessee are identical. There is no advantage to leasing over borrowing in these circumstances.

One problem in applying Eq. (17.4) is that the remaining debt balance, D_t, declines each year as the lease fees amortize the principal. This makes computations more cumbersome than they need be. A much simpler way of looking at the problem was derived by Levy and Sarnat [1979]. Eq. (17.4) puts the tax effect of displaced debt in the numerator and discounts at the before-tax rate, k_b. However, it has been our practice throughout the text to account for the tax effect of financing costs by discounting at the after-tax rate in the denominator and writing the numerator in terms of after-tax cash flows net of financing effects. If this is done, Eq. (17.4) is equivalent to Eq. (17.5) below:

$$\text{NPV(to lessee)} = I - \sum_{t=1}^{N} \frac{L_t(1 - \tau_c) + \tau_c\text{dep}_t}{[1 + (1 - \tau_c)k_b]^t}. \quad (17.5)$$

Also, recall that $(1 - \tau_c)k_b = \text{WACC}_B$. Substituting the numbers from our previous example in order to determine the NPV of the lease, and assuming that the tax rate of the lessee is the same as the lessor, namely, 40%, we have

$$\text{NPV(to lessee)} = I - \sum_{t=1}^{N} \frac{L_t(1 - \tau_c) + \tau_c\text{dep}_t}{[1 + (1 - \tau_c)k_b]^t}$$

$$= 10,000 - \sum_{t=1}^{5} \frac{2,624(1 - .4) + .4(2,000)}{[1 + .6(.10)]^t}$$

$$= 10,000 - 2,624(.6)(4.212) - .4(2,000)(4.212)$$

$$= 10,000 - 6,631 - 3,369$$

$$= 0.$$

The numerical result shows very clearly that the risk and cash flows to the lessor and lessee are identical if they have the same marginal tax rates. There is an equilibrium between the lessor market and the user market. Each term in Eq. (17.5) is identical to the corresponding term in Eq. (17.1) except that the signs are reversed. In other words a cash outflow to the lessee is a cash inflow to the lessor, and vice versa.

Table 17.2 NPV (to lessee) Using Eq. (17.4)

(1) Year	(2) dep_t	(3) $\tau_c dep_t$	(4) $(1 - \tau_c)L_t$	(5) D_{t-1}	(6) $\Delta k_d D_t$	(7) $\tau_c \Delta k_d D_t$	(8) ΔD_t	(9) CF_t	(10) $(1 + k_b)^{-t}$	(11) $PV(CF_t)$
1	2,000	800	1574.4	10,000	1,000	400.0	1,638	2774.4	.909	2,521.93
2	2,000	800	1574.4	8,362	836	334.4	1,802	2708.8	.826	2,237.47
3	2,000	800	1574.4	6,560	656	262.4	1,982	2636.8	.751	1,980.24
4	2,000	800	1574.4	4,578	458	183.2	2,180	2557.6	.683	1,746.84
5	2,000	800	1574.4	2,398	240	96.0	2,398	2470.4	.621	1,534.12
							10,000			10,020.60

L_t = the annual lease fee on a fully amortized lease, i.e., no salvage value,

dep_t = the annual (straight-line) depreciation write-off,

τ_c = the lessee's marginal tax rate,

D_{t-1} = the face value of debt displaced by the lease in the previous time period,

k_d = the before-tax cost of the displaced debt capital

$\Delta k_d D_t$ = the change in the interest payments on debt displaced by the lease,

$\tau_c \Delta k_d D_t$ = the change in the interest tax shield displaced by the lease,

ΔD_t = the repayment of principal on debt,

CF_t = the cash flow for the lease contract = columns (3) + (4) + (7),

$(1 + k_b)^{-t}$ = the present value factor.

4. The Effect of Different Tax Rates on the Value of Leasing

Frequently the lessor and lessee have different marginal tax rates. If the lessor has a higher tax rate than the lessee, it may be possible to strike a bargain where the tax shield from owning the asset can be shared between the two. Suppose that we assume the lessor has a 40% marginal tax rate and charges a lease fee of $2624, as before, but that the marginal tax rate of the lessee is only 5%. What is the NPV of the lease contract to the lessee? Substituting into Eq. (17.5), we have

$$\text{NPV(to lessee)} = 10,000 - \sum_{t=1}^{5} \frac{2624(1 - .05) + .05(2000)}{[1 + (1 - .05).10]^t}$$

$$= 10,000 - 2624(.95)(3.8397) - .05(2000)(3.8397)$$

$$= 10,000 - 9571.59 - 383.97$$

$$= 44.44.$$

Now the lease contract has a positive net present value for the lessee.

Actually, the positive net present value created by the difference in the marginal tax rates can be shared between the lessor and lessee unless perfect competition among lessors results in giving the full value of the tax shield to the lessee. Also, note that any positive net present value from the lease contract that accrues to the lessee can be used to augment the net present value of the investment decision. It is conceivable that negative NPV projects might still be undertaken if the NPV of the lease contract is large enough. Consider the following example. The lease payments remain at $2,624 per year, but the operating costs (in the lessee's investment decision) are $17,060 rather than $16,711 per year. Given a 5% tax rate the lessee's weighted average cost of capital is

$$\text{WACC(project)} = .14[1 - .05(.33)] = 13.77\%,$$

and the NPV of the project becomes

$$\text{NPV} = -10,000 + \sum_{t=1}^{5} \frac{.95(20,000 - 17,060) + .05(2,000)}{(1 + .1377)^t}$$

$$= -10,000 + 2,893.00(3.4521)$$

$$= -10,000 + 9,986.93$$

$$= -13.07.$$

If the project is leased, rather than undertaken with debt financing, the NPV (to lessee) of the lease contract can offset the negative NPV of the investment, namely, $44.44 in our example. The NPV if the firm buys the project is $-13.07 but rises to ($-13.07 + $44.44 = $31.37) if leased.

Although the above numerical example shows a benefit to the lessee given that the lessor's tax rate is higher, this may not always be true. The tax effect can go either way. As pointed out by Lewellen, Long, and McConnell [1976] the net tax benefit will depend on the specific asset life (lease period), depreciation schedule, capitalization rates, and leverage policies involved.

5. Nontax Determinants of the Leasing Decision

While taxes provide strong incentives for leasing rather than owning, and can predict which firms will lease, they provide very little understanding of which assets will be leased. For example, why does a company lease some assets and own others when the company's tax rate applies equally to all projects? Smith and Wakeman [1985] provide a useful first look at this issue.[6] They point out, e.g., that since lessees have no right to the residual value of the asset, they have less incentive to take care of it. Thus the more sensitive the value of an asset to use and maintenance decisions, the higher is the probability that the asset will be purchased rather than leased. Most automobiles for personal use, for instance, are owned rather than leased. Another factor is the degree that an asset is specialized for use within a given firm. Organization-specific assets generate agency costs in the form of negotiation, administration, and enforcement costs due to conflicts between the lessor and lessee. According to Smith and Wakeman this may explain why corporations lease office facilities with greater frequency than production or research facilities.

The distinction between long-term leases and short-term leases is not trivial. At one end of the continuum are very short-term leases such as hotel room, automobile, truck, and tool rentals. For these contracts the differences in transactions costs between leasing and owning are likely to be more important than tax considerations. It is much easier to rent a room for a night than to buy it in the afternoon, then sell it back in the morning. On the other hand, for long-term leases, factors of this type are minimized, and consideration of the differences in tax rates is the major consideration. Since we have already discussed tax considerations at some length, it is appropriate to focus on transactions costs and economies of scale from specialization. For a reference on this point of view see Flath [1980].

Transactions costs may include clerical costs, search costs, and costs of assessing, assuring, and maintaining quality. Leasing transactions costs are different from owning because the set of rights being exchanged differs. A lessee obtains the right to use an asset for a fixed period of time. When this time interval is less than the economic life of the asset, transactions costs become relevant.

Suppose that an individual wishes to use an asset for only a fraction of its economic life. For example, suppose that tuxedos go out of style in five-year cycles, whether they are used or not, and that you plan to wear the tuxedo only one day per year. Then you would be willing to pay anything up to 99.73% ($= 364/365$) of the value of the asset to rent it. Of course, if other people also plan to use tuxedos and if the timing of their use is independent of yours, then it will pay someone else to own the tuxedo and rent it out. Thus if an individual wants to use an asset for an

---

[6] See their article for a more complete description of the many nontax determinants of leasing. Only a few are mentioned here.

interval considerably shorter than the asset's economic life, then a demand for short-term leasing will arise. If enough people have uncorrelated demand, then the volume of business will be sufficient for someone to specialize in renting the asset, thereby creating a supply.

It is conceivable that even though you want to use a tuxedo for one day, you could buy it at the beginning of the day and sell it at day's end. If so, why is leasing the preferred contract for obtaining short-term use of the asset? A supplier of short-term leases, e.g., a hotel owner, could arrange a one-day sale and buyback of a room rather than renting it out. There are, of course, some obvious transactions cost savings from short-term leasing. For example, the transactions demand for money is much less if people only have to exchange currency worth one day's use of an asset rather than its full value. Also, the need for the user to separately contract for insurance and financing is reduced.

Another consideration that favors short-term leasing over sale and buyback is the cost of evaluating the quality of the leased asset. A lease is a contract for the use of an asset, not its ownership. A potential owner of an asset, e.g., an automobile, will wish to have a detailed inspection of the car's quality. On the other hand, a lessee will only need to perform a less costly inspection because the potential loss from using a low-quality asset for one day is less than the loss from owning it. Also, from the owner's point of view the gain from deceiving a customer about an asset's quality is not as great for a short-term lease as for long-term ownership. Thus the lower cost of quality evaluation favors lease contracts over ownership. However, this advantage must be weighed against higher average usage costs. For example, a lessee has less incentive to take proper care of an asset than an owner. Lessors know this and include a "moral hazard" cost as part of the lease fee. Still, leasing will be preferred if the moral hazard cost is less than the cost of the frequent detailed inspections that would be necessary if ownership were exchanged.

Thus whenever the desired period of usage is less than the economic life of an asset, short-term leasing may be preferred to an ownership market such as a second-hand market.

6. Leveraged Leasing

A leveraged lease is one where the lessor borrows a substantial portion of the purchase price of the asset. Figure 17.1 is a schematic representation of the parties to a leveraged lease. The lender typically holds a first mortgage on the asset. Also, the lessor assigns the lease payments to the lender (or a trustee). The debt interest and principal are deducted by the lender, who then returns the balance of the lease payment which is kept by the equity holder. Equity may be supplied either directly by the lessor or indirectly by third parties. The loan arrangement is called a *non-recourse loan* because its effect is to indemnify the lessor in the event of default. The lessor benefits from the investment tax credit (if any) created when the asset is purchased, the depreciation tax shield, the residual value of the equipment (if any), the interest tax deduction, and the equity payments (if not turned over to third-party equity investors).

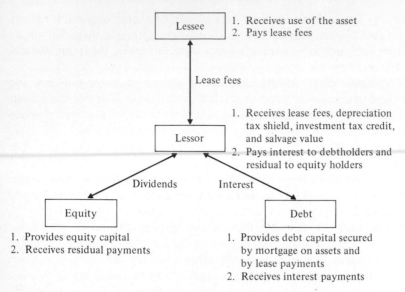

Figure 17.1
A schematic representation of a leveraged lease.

There is no real economic difference between the economics of leveraged lease contracts and strict financial lease contracts, which have already been discussed in detail.[7] In a strict financial lease, the lessor purchases the asset with a combination of debt and equity capital. The same is true in a leveraged lease with the possible exception that a different debt/equity mix may be used.

Leveraged leasing does, however, raise the issue of determining the opportunity cost of debt and equity funds employed in the lease. Suppose a lessor approaches your firm and asks that you lend funds or provide equity participation. What is your minimum acceptable rate of return?

To provide a concrete example we will use the same numerical example as employed earlier in the chapter. Also, as before, we will adopt the Modigliani-Miller valuation framework. Recall that the equipment cost $10,000 and had a five-year life with no salvage value, and there was no investment tax credit. The lease fee was determined to be $2,624. Both the lessor and lessee had marginal tax rates, τ_c, of 40%. The lessor earned 10% before taxes and had a 6% after-tax weighted average cost of capital.

The first question is, What is the cost of debt if it is lent by a third party? For straight financial leases the third party might be a depositor in a commercial bank or debt holders of an insurance company or a leasing company. For leveraged leases debt

---

[7] The existence of leveraged leases may be explained by various institutional considerations and agency costs. For example, for very large leveraged leases a single bank may be constrained from doing the deal because regulations prohibit it from lending more than a small percentage of its equity to a single firm. Also, leveraged leases match long-term borrowing against long-term lending (i.e., the lease), whereas most of a bank's other loans and deposits are short or intermediate term.

may be supplied, e.g., by an insurance company. We can get an idea of the rate of return that will be required on debt by noting that the lease payments must be riskier than the debt. In the event of default on a leveraged lease the debt holders are somewhat protected because they own the mortgage on the leased assets. By way of contrast the equity holders, being residual claimants, can lose everything. The lessor charges a 10% before-tax rate of return on the lease. This results in an 8% before-tax cost of borrowing, k_b, which is the rate at which the debt holders will supply capital to the leveraged lease.

The cost of equity depends on the amount of leverage used in the lease. For "blue-chip" leases the ratio of debt to total assets might be 90–95%. We assumed the ratio was 90%. Given these facts, we can employ the Modigliani-Miller cost of capital definitions (from Chapter 13) to compute the cost of equity in the leveraged lease. Recall that we assumed, earlier in the chapter, that the unlevered cost of equity, ρ, was 9.375%. The Modigliani-Miller definition of the cost of equity is

$$k_s = \rho + (\rho - k_b)(1 - \tau_c)\frac{B}{S},$$

where

ρ = the unlevered cost of equity = 9.375%,

k_b = the before-tax cost of borrowing = 8%,

τ_c = the marginal effective tax rate = 40%,

$\dfrac{B}{S}$ = the market value debt-to-equity ratio = 9.

Therefore the required rate of return on equity in the leveraged lease is

$$k_s = .09375 + (.09375 - .08)(1 - .4)9$$
$$= 16.8\%.$$

This is more than double the borrowing rate on the same project and reflects the greater risk accepted by the equity holders in a leveraged lease.

7. Cancellable Operating Leases

Unlike straight financial leases, operating leases may be cancelled at the option of the lessee. From the point of view of the lessee, capital employed under operating lease contracts becomes a variable cost (rather than a fixed cost) because the lease contract may be terminated (sometimes requiring a penalty to be paid) and the leased asset returned whenever economic conditions become unfavorable. It is like having equipment that can be laid off. From the lessor's point of view cancellable operating leases are riskier than straight financial leases. A straight lease, like a loan, is secured by all the assets in the firm. A cancellable operating lease is not.

The risk that the lessor must bear depends on the economic depreciation of the asset. There is always uncertainty about the ability of an asset to physically withstand

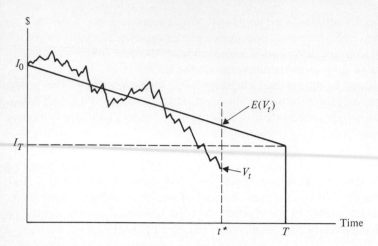

Figure 17.2
Changes in replacement value over time.

wear and tear. In addition, there is obsolescence caused by technological advances that cause the economic value of an asset to decline vis-à-vis newer assets. And finally, there is the risky end-of-period economic value of an asset, which is usually called its salvage value. All these concepts are different descriptions of economic depreciation, which henceforth we shall call *replacement cost* uncertainty.

To focus on replacement cost risk by itself, assume that we know with certainty the future revenue stream that the leased asset will produce as well as other costs unassociated with the economic value of the leased asset. Figure 17.2 shows an example of how the economic value of the asset might change over time. The downward-sloping line illustrates the expected decline in the asset's value due to anticipated wear and tear and obsolescence. Note that the value is expected to decline from I_0 to I_T over the life of the contract, T years. The expected salvage value is I_T.[8] It is reasonable to assume that the value of the asset never falls below zero. Given replacement cost uncertainty, the actual value of the asset at any time $t^* \leq T$ may be greater or less than expected. The particular situation that has been illustrated at t^* in Fig. 17.2 shows that if the value of the asset, V_t, falls far enough below the expected value, $E(V_t)$, it will pay the lessee to terminate the lease.

Thus the cancellation feature is really an option. In particular it is an American put held by the lessee. The present value of the relevant American put is derived by Copeland and Weston [1982], who utilize the binomial option pricing model. They use the following numerical example to illustrate the effect of the put option on leasing fees. Assume that a $10,000 asset is expected to have a three-year economic life and

---

[8] For a paper on how to deal with uncertain salvage values the reader is referred to Lee, Martin, and Senchack [1980] or to McConnell and Schallheim [1983].

depreciate an equal amount each year (i.e., the replacement value declines in a straight line at the rate of $1 - \theta$ each year, where $\theta = .667$). However, its value may be 50% higher or lower than expected at the end of a given year. Also, the lessor has a tax rate of 40% and will write a two-year lease. If the lease contract were a straight financial lease, it would require a 10% before-tax rate of return (i.e., $k_b = 10\%$). The salvage value is uncertain and requires a 16% risk-adjusted rate of return.[9] Using Eq. (17.1) we can write the competitive net present value of the lease, if it were non-cancelable, as follows:

$$0 = -I + \sum_{t=1}^{2} \frac{(1 - \tau_c)L_t + \tau_c \text{dep}_t}{[1 + (1 - \tau_c)k_b]^t} + \frac{E(MV)}{(1 + k_1)^2}, \qquad (17.6)$$

where

$E(MV)$ = the expected market value of the asset after two years,

k_1 = the risk-adjusted discount rate for the salvage value.

Substituting in the numbers, we have

$$0 = -10,000 + \sum_{t=1}^{2} \frac{(1 - .4)L_t + .4(3333)}{[1 + (1 - .4).10]^t} + \frac{3333}{(1.16)^2}.$$

Solving, we find that the competitive lease fee is $4617.

Next, we want to determine the competitive lease payments assuming that the above contract is a cancellable operating lease. Equation (17.6) must be modified by subtracting out the present value of the American put option, P. The new valuation equation is

$$0 = -I + \sum_{t=1}^{2} \frac{(1 - \tau_c)L_t + \tau_c \text{dep}_t}{[1 + (1 - \tau_c)k_b]^t} + \frac{E(MV)}{(1 + k_1)^2} - P.$$

The value of the put (see Copeland and Weston [1982]) is determined to be $850. Solving for the cancellable lease fee we find that it increases to $5392. The lease fee has increased substantially to reflect the extra risk of possible early cancellation of the operating lease.[10]

The example serves to illustrate that the replacement cost uncertainty borne by the lessor in a cancellable operating lease can have a profound impact on the competitive lease fee. In general the cancellation clause may be thought of as an American put purchased by the lessee. Its cost will increase with (1) greater uncertainty in the replacement value of the leased asset and (2) decreases in the risk-free discount rate.

---

[9] For simplicity we ignore capital gains taxation on the salvage value as well as investment tax credits.

[10] If a lessee takes the lease fee of $5392 as an input and tries to compute an internal rate of return on the contract using Eq. (17.6), the noncancellable lease formula, the IRR will be approximately 14%. However, the lessee would be mistaken to compare the 14% return on a cancellable lease with 10% on a straight financial lease (or comparable debt financing).

D. EMPIRICAL EVIDENCE ON LEASING

The empirical evidence on leasing-related issues is scant. There are (at least) four topics of interest. First is whether or not the theory of leasing is sufficiently rich to predict when a firm will use leasing instead of debt financing. Although debt and leasing are very similar, they are not necessarily perfect substitutes. Otherwise the form of financing being used would be randomly distributed across firms. Casual empiricism suggests that patterns of choice do exist. Factors such as tax shield utilization, economies of scale in service contracts, and comparative advantages in resale of equipment may explain the use of lease financing.

A second issue is the extent to which lease financing is a substitute for debt financing *within* a given firm. The theory of leasing logically assumes that each dollar of leasing utilized by the firm will replace one dollar of debt capacity; i.e., they are perfect substitutes. Whether or not firms actually behave in this manner is an empirical issue. Bowman [1980] collected a 1973 sample of 92 firms in seven different industries (according to the two-digit SIC code) where both lease and debt financing were reported. A second sample of 158 firms that did not use leasing was also collected. Bowman then ran a cross-section regression to explain the systematic risk of the nonlease sample as a function of the accounting beta and the debt-to-equity ratio. The results are given below, with t-statistics in parentheses:

$$\beta_i = 1.223 + 0.88\beta_i^A + .104(D/S)_i, \qquad (\bar{R}^2 = .29),$$
$$(2.51) \qquad (4.19)$$

where

β_i = the systematic risk of the ith firm estimated using the last 60 months of data,

β_i^A = an estimate of the accounting beta for the ith firm. Two versions were tested without obtaining different results. One version used the first difference of net income before extraordinary items and the second used EBIT.

$(D/S)_i$ = the book value of debt over the market value of equity.

The association between systematic risk and lease utilization was then tested by first adjusting the beta of the ith firm by using the above estimated coefficients, then regressing the result against a lease utilization variable as shown below:

$$\beta_i - 1.223 - .088\beta_i^A - .104(D/S)_i = \lambda(L/S)_i + \varepsilon_i,$$

where

$(L/S)_i$ = the book value of leasing over the market value of equity,

ε_i = the residual.

This research design controls for measurement error and multicollinearity. The relationship between systematic risk, β_i, and the use of leasing, $(L/S)_i$, was positive and statistically significant. This led Bowman to conclude that debt and lease financing both affected the market's estimate of the systematic risk of firms. Consequently, leasing and debt were recognized as close substitutes.

Ang and Peterson [1984] use cross-sectional data for approximately 600 nonregulated and nonfinancial firms each year between 1976 and 1981. The book value lease to equity ratio was explained as a function of the book value debt to equity ratio, operating leverage, the coefficient of variation of sales, return on net fixed plant, the price/earnings ratio, the book value of assets, and the current ratio. The results indicated a significant positive relationship between leasing and debt. The conclusion is that debt and leases appear to be complements, rather than perfect substitutes as assumed in the theory of leasing.

A third area of empirical interest is whether or not the mandated disclosure of off–balance sheet leasing had any measurable impact on the real decisions of firms. For example, in order to comply with the accounting disclosure changes, firms had to capitalize their lease obligations and report them on their balance sheets. When this was done, some firms found themselves in technical violation of their debt covenants. Ro [1978] tested whether the disclosure of lease information had an impact on security prices and concluded that it had an adverse impact. Abdel-Khalik, Thompson, and Taylor [1978] looked at the impact of lease disclosure on bond risk premia and found no impact on security prices. Thus the evidence is mixed. As more empirical research is reported we will obtain a better understanding of how the market reacts (if at all) to the initial disclosure of off–balance sheet financing.

Finally, studies by Sorensen and Johnson [1977], McGugan and Caves [1974], Gudikunst and Roberts [1975], and Crawford, Harper, and McConnell [1981] have empirically estimated the internal rates of return (i.e., the "yields") on commercial bank leases. They all report that the estimated yields were higher than debt of equivalent risk. If leases and debt are perfect substitutes in straight financial leases, this should not be so. Schallheim, Johnson, Lease, and McConnell [1986] provide a potential explanation for this puzzle. They find that the higher yields on financial leases are related to the discounted value of the leased asset's residual value covariance risk (or to the residual value itself). Franks and Hodges [1986] use a sample of English leasing data and conclude that low tax firms are lessees and high tax firms are lessors, but interestingly most of the tax shelter value was captured by the lessor rather than the lessee. Their result implies that the estimated yields on leases would be higher than the debt rate because taxable earnings (owned by lessors) was a scarce resource and lessees had to pay a premium for using it.

SUMMARY

We have examined the leasing problem from the point of view of the lessee and the lessor. If they have identical tax rates, then a competitive lease fee will have zero net present value to both parties. Yet if their leasing analysis inputs are different—e.g., the lessee may have a higher tax rate than the lessor—then it is possible that some negotiated lease fee can have a positive net present value to both parties. They can share the net present value of the tax shield from leasing (if any).

Strict financial leases are assumed to be perfect substitutes for debt capital. There is no such thing as 100% lease financing, just as there is no such thing as 100% debt financing. For each dollar of leasing employed by a firm, one dollar of debt capacity is displaced.

Leveraged leasing is really no different from straight financial leasing. Both employ debt and equity that are used by the lessor to purchase the asset for leasing. If one knows the financing mix that will be used by the lessor, the rate of return on the lease payments, and the (lower) rate of return received by debt holders in the contract, then it is possible to estimate the required rate of return on equity invested in leveraged leases.

Cancellable leases contain a put option sold to the lessee. Often valuable, this option may considerably raise the implied lease cost.

The character of short-term leases is quite different from that of long-term financial leases. In particular the transactions costs and agency costs of short-term leases are important in explaining why we rent hotel rooms instead of buying them for one day and then selling them back the next.

The empirical evidence on leasing is scant. What little there is provides mixed evidence on whether or not leasing is viewed by the market as a close substitute for debt financing.

PROBLEM SET

17.1 Your firm is considering lease financing for a computer that is expected to have a five-year life and no salvage value (it is a strict financial lease). You have the following facts:

- Your firm's tax rate is 30%. There is no investment tax credit.
- If purchased, the project would require a capital outlay of $100,000.
- The project will be depreciated using the straight-line method.
- Debt of equivalent risk costs 10% before taxes.
- The annual lease fee is $32,000 paid at the beginning of each year for five years.
- The optimal capital structure for the project is 50% debt to total assets.

Should you use lease financing or not?

17.2 Giveaway State Teacher's College is trying to decide whether to buy a new computer or to lease it from Readi Roller Leasing. The computer costs $500,000. Giveaway has a zero tax rate, whereas Readi Roller enjoys a 40% tax rate. There is no investment tax credit. The computer is expected to last five years and have no salvage value. It will be depreciated using the straight-line method. The college can borrow at a 15% interest rate. If the five annual lease fees are $147,577 paid at the end of each year,

a) What is the NPV of the lease for Readi Roller Leasing Co.?

b) What is the NPV of the lease for Giveaway State?

c) What do the results tell you about the lease/buy decision for tax-free institutions?

17.3 This question involves a more realistic set of facts and therefore requires a more detailed analysis of cash flows than contained in the chapter. Your company is going to negotiate a lease contract for manufacturing equipment. You have the following facts:

- The equipment cost $100,000 and is expected to have a five-year life with an expected salvage value of $10,000; however, it can be fully depreciated in four years using the sum-of-the-years digits method of accelerated depreciation.
- Whether leased or owned, the equipment will be sold for $1 at the end of the fifth year, and the owner will pay a capital gains tax equal to one half of the ordinary income tax rate on the difference between $1 and the book value.
- Your firm will pay no taxes for the next two years and then will return to its normal 48% tax rate.
- The leasing firm will require equal annual lease payments paid at the beginning of each year. The leasing firm's tax rate is 48%.
- Your firm can borrow at the prime rate plus 1%, i.e., at 17%.

a) What is the maximum lease payment that your firm can afford to offer in the negotiations?

b) What is the minimum lease payment that you think the leasing company can accept in the negotiations?

17.4 Your firm has been approached to become an equity participant in a leveraged leasing deal. You need to estimate the minimum rate of return on equity that is acceptable. You have collected the following facts:

- The asset to be leased will cost $100,000,000; 90% will be financed with debt and the remaining 10% with equity.
- The debt portion of the financing is to receive a 14% rate of return before taxes.
- Your tax rate is 40%. The lessor's tax rate is 48%.
- The before-tax rate of return that the lessee will be paying is 18%.

Use the Modigliani-Miller cost of capital assumptions to make your analysis (i.e., assume a world with corporate taxes only).

17.5 The Mortar Bored Company was considering whether to buy a new $100,000 reduction machine or to lease it. It was estimated that the machine would reduce variable costs by $31,000 per year and have an eight-year life with no salvage value. The machine will be depreciated on a straight-line basis, and there is no investment tax credit. The firm's optimal capital structure is 50% debt to total assets, its before-tax costs of debt and equity are 15% and 25%, respectively, and it has a 40% tax rate. If it were to lease, the fees would be $21,400 per year paid at the end of each year.

a) What is the NPV of the project if the firm owns the project?

b) What is the NPV of the lease to the company?

c) Should the company lease the project? Why or why not?

REFERENCES

Abdel-Khalik, A.; R. Thompson; and R. Taylor, "The Impact of Reporting Leases Off the Balance Sheet on Bond Risk Premiums: Two Explanatory Studies," Accounting Research Center Working Paper #78-2, University of Florida, February 1978.

Ang, J., and P. Peterson, "The Leasing Puzzle," *Journal of Finance*, September 1984, 1055–1065.

Athanosopoulos, P., and P. Bacon, "The Evaluation of Leveraged Leases," *Financial Management*, Spring 1980, 76–80.

Bower, R., "Issues in Lease Financing," *Financial Management*, Winter 1973, 25–33.

Bowman, R., "The Debt Equivalence of Leases: An Empirical Investigation," *Accounting Review*, April 1980, 237–253.

Brealey, R., and C. Young, "Debt, Taxes and Leasing—A Note," *Journal of Finance*, December 1980, 1245–1250.

Copeland, T., and J. F. Weston, "A Note on the Evaluation of Cancellable Operating Leases," *Financial Management*, Summer 1982, 60–67.

Cox, J.; S. Ross; and M. Rubinstein, "Option Pricing: A Simplified Approach," *Journal of Financial Economics*, September 1979, 229–264.

Crawford, P.; C. Harper; and J. McConnell, "Further Evidence on the Terms of Financial Leases," *Financial Management*, Autumn 1981, 7–14.

Dyl, E., and S. Martin, Jr., "Setting Terms for Leveraged Leases," *Financial Management*, Winter 1977, 20–27.

Elam, R., "The Effect of Lease Data on the Predictive Ability of Financial Ratios," *Accounting Review*, January 1975, 25–43.

Financial Accounting Standards Board, *Statement of Financial Accounting Standards no. 13*, Stamford, CT., 1976.

Flath, D., "The Economics of Short-Term Leasing," *Economic Inquiry*, April 1980, 247–259.

Franks, J., and S. Hodges, "Valuation of Financial Lease Contracts: A Note," *Journal of Finance*, May 1978, 647–669.

——— "Lease Valuation When Taxable Earnings Are a Scarce Resource," Working paper, London Business School, 1986.

Gudikunst, A., and G. Roberts, "Leasing: Analysis of a Theoretic-Pragmatic Dilemma," paper presented at the annual meeting of the Financial Management Association, Kansas City, October 1975.

Heaton, H., "Corporate Taxation and Leasing," *Journal of Financial and Quantitative Analysis*, September 1986, 351–359.

Idol, C., "A Note on Specifying Debt Displacement and Tax Shield Borrowing Opportunities in Financial Lease Valuation Models," *Financial Management*, Summer 1980, 24–29.

Johnson, R., and W. Lewellen, "Analysis of the Lease-or-Buy Decision," *Journal of Finance*, September 1972, 815–823.

Kim, E.; W. Lewellen; and J. McConnell, "Sale-and-Leaseback Agreements and Enterprise Valuation," *Journal of Financial and Quantitative Analysis*, December 1978, 871–883.

Lee, W.; J. Martin; and A. J. Senchack, "An Option Pricing Approach to the Evaluation of Salvage Values in Financial Lease Arrangements," Working paper, University of Texas at Austin, September 1980.

Levy, H., and M. Sarnat, "Leasing, Borrowing and Financial Risk," *Financial Management*, Winter 1979, 47–54.

Lewellen, W.; M. Long; and J. McConnell, "Asset Leasing in Competitive Capital Markets," *Journal of Finance*, June 1976, 787–798.

Long, M., "Leasing and the Cost of Capital," *Journal of Financial and Quantitative Analysis*, November 1977, 579–598.

McConnell, J., and J. Schallheim, "Valuation of Asset Leasing Contracts," *Journal of Financial Economics*, August 1983, 237–262.

McGugan, V., and R. Caves, "Integration and Competition in the Equipment Leasing Industry," *Journal of Business*, July 1974, 382–396.

Miller, M., and F. Modigliani, "Some Estimates of the Cost of Capital to the Electric Utility Industry, 1954–57," *American Economic Review*, June 1966, 333–391.

Miller, M., and C. Upton, "Leasing, Buying and the Cost of Capital Services," *Journal of Finance*, June 1976, 761–786.

Myers, S., "Interactions of Corporate Financing and Investment Decisions—Implications for Capital Budgeting," *Journal of Finance*, March 1974, 1–25.

———; D. Dill; and A. Bautista, "Valuation of Financial Lease Contracts," *Journal of Finance*, June 1976, 799–819.

Ofer, A., "The Evaluation of the Lease versus Purchase Alternatives," *Financial Management*, Summer 1976, 67–72.

Perg, W., "Leveraged Leasing: The Problem of Changing Leverage," *Financial Management*, Autumn 1978, 47–51.

Ro, B., "The Disclosure of Capitalized Lease Information and Stock Prices," *Journal of Accounting Research*, Autumn 1978, 315–340.

Roberts, G., and A. Gudikunst, "Equipment Financial Leasing Practices and Costs: Comment," *Financial Management*, Summer 1978, 79–81.

Schall, L., "Asset Valuation, Firm Investment, and Firm Diversification," *Journal of Business*, January 1972, 11–28.

———, "The Lease-or-Buy and Asset Acquisition Decisions," *Journal of Finance*, September 1974, 1203–1214.

Schallheim, J.; R. Johnson; R. Lease; and J. McConnell, "The Determinants of Yields on Financial Leasing Contracts," Working paper, University of Utah, 1986.

Smith, C. Jr., and L. Wakeman, "Determinants of Corporate Leasing Policy," *Journal of Finance*, July 1985, 896–908.

Snyder, N., "Financial Leases," in Weston and Goudzwaard, eds., *The Treasurer's Handbook*. Dow-Jones Irwin, Homewood, Ill., 1976, 783–822.

Sorensen, I., and R. Johnson, "Equipment Financial Leasing Practices and Costs: An Empirical Study," *Financial Management*, Spring 1977, 33–40.

Stickney, C.; R. Weil; and M. Wolfson, "Income Taxes and Tax Transfer Leases," *Accounting Review*, April 1983, 439–459.

Taylor, D., "Technological or Economic Obsolescence: Computer Purchase vs. Lease," *Management Accounting*, September 1968.

Vancil, R., "Lease or Borrow—New Method of Analysis," *Harvard Business Review*, September–October 1961.

Vanderwicken, P., "The Powerful Logic of the Leasing Boom," *Fortune*, November 1973, 136–140.

18

There is nothing on the label of a tool which says whether its intended use is harmful or beneficial, only how to use it, and sometimes that it should be used with caution.

Anonymous

Applied Issues in Corporate Finance

This chapter covers miscellaneous corporate finance topics that are (or should be) of particular interest to chief financial officers. We start with an analysis of pension fund management—a topic that requires prior knowledge of option pricing (Chapter 8), portfolio theory (Chapter 6), and Modigliani-Miller tax effects (Chapter 13). Then we focus on a variety of shorter topics. They include swaps of fixed for variable rate debt, going-private transactions, leveraged buyouts, and executive compensation schemes.

A. PENSION FUND MANAGEMENT

1. Overview: Historical Data and Financial Statements

Corporate pension plan liabilities have grown rapidly during the last three decades. For many companies, pension plan liabilities are larger than the book value of all long-term assets. We shall, in turn, discuss various types of pension plans, publicly accepted accounting principles that govern pension plan reporting, the regulation of pension plans by the Employment Retirement Income Security Act (ERISA), and management decision making about various pension plan problems, such as how to use pension fund assets to reduce the tax liabilities of the firm.

A pension plan is a promise by an employer to provide benefits to employees upon their retirement. Contractual pension fund commitments are a liability of the

Table 18.1 Distribution of Assets of Noninsured Pension Funds (percentage of the book value of total assets invested)

	1950	1960	1970	1980
U.S. government securities	30.5%	8.1%	3.1%	11.0%
Corporate bonds	43.8	47.4	30.6	24.9
Stocks	17.1	34.7	55.1	50.5
Mortgages	1.6	3.9	4.3	1.6
Cash, deposits, other	7.0	5.9	6.9	12.0
Total	100.0	100.0	100.0	100.0

From the U.S. Securities and Exchange Commission.

employer and must be disclosed in the firm's financial statements. A pension fund is established on behalf of employees and is managed by a trustee, who collects cash from the firm, manages the assets owned by the fund, and makes disbursements to retired employees. The firm is able to expense pension fund contributions for tax purposes. The fund pays no taxes on its earnings. However, beneficiaries must pay personal taxes upon receiving retirement payments from the fund. Hence pension funds are a tax-favored form of employee compensation because taxes are deferred until retirement.

The composition of pension fund assets is given in Table 18.1. Most pension funds hold their assets in the form of marketable securities: money market accounts, bonds, and stocks. Because pension fund earnings are not taxed, it never pays to hold municipal bonds because their low tax-exempt interest rates are always dominated by the higher interest paid by taxable bonds. Direct investment in real estate (with the possible exception of undeveloped land) is also not advisable because most real estate investments are priced such that the investor must be in a relatively high tax bracket in order to receive a positive after-tax return. Pension funds are in a zero tax bracket.

The most striking change in pension fund portfolio composition over the past four decades is the decline in the proportion invested in bonds from 74.3% in 1950 to 35.9% in 1980, and the increase in stocks (common and preferred) from 17.1% in 1950 to 50.5% in 1980.

Later on in the chapter we shall discuss some of the possible influences that may affect the composition of assets in pension fund portfolios. Although the pension fund can profitably hold taxable securities, it is not immediately clear what percentage should be held in the form of interest-bearing securities (money market funds and bonds) or common stock.

Table 18.2 gives the format for a typical pension fund income statement and balance sheet. Cash inflows to the fund are provided by corporate contributions, employee contributions, dividends and interest earned by the fund's stocks and bonds, and capital gains. Cash outflows are management fees, brokerage expenses, disbursements to beneficiaries, and capital losses. The change in the net fund balance is the difference between inflows and outflows. The fund's profit is not taxable. Marketable

Table 18.2 Format for a Pension Fund Income Statement and Balance Sheet

Pension Fund Income Statement	Pension Fund Balance Sheet
Funds received	Assets
From employer(s)	Marketable securities
From employees	cash
From dividends, interest, and	bonds
capital gains (losses)	stock
	PV of future contributions
Funds expended	Deficit (surplus)
Management fees and brokerage costs	
Disbursements to beneficiaries	Liabilities
	PV of benefits for past service
Change in net fund balance	PV of benefits for future service

securities is the only item in the pension fund balance sheet that is not the result of a present value calculation. The present value of future contributions to the fund is the other major asset. Contributions are received in two forms: cash from the firm and earnings on the fund's assets. A major issue is: What rate of return will be generated from the fund's assets? If the return is high, then the firm can reduce the amount of cash it puts into the fund. As we shall see, later in the chapter, the rate of return assumption is a tricky decision.

Liabilities are subdivided into two categories. The present value of benefits from past service is handled one of two ways. Some companies calculate the present value of vested benefits only. These are the benefits that would be paid if all employees left the firm immediately. However, it is typical that employees become vested in the pension plan only after accumulating a minimum period of seniority, say five years. If they leave prior to five years, they receive none of their promised pension benefits. An alternative procedure is to calculate the present value of all benefits accrued for past service whether employees are fully vested or not. Hence accrued benefits will usually be larger than vested benefits because not all employees are fully vested. Regardless of how the present value of benefits from past service is handled, total pension liabilities remain unchanged. If only vested benefits are included in the present value of benefits for past service, then unvested benefits are included in the second liability category.

The second major liability item is the present value (PV) of benefits for future service. Its computation is complex and depends on actuarial assumptions about the amount of employee turnover, the age and seniority of retiring employees, their life expectancy, and the choice of a discount rate for present value computations.

Of major concern to all parties is the size of the pension fund deficit or surplus. An unfunded deficit is an asset of the pension fund (as shown in Table 18.2) and a liability of the firm, and it can be enormous. For example, had the pension liabilities of Du Pont been included, its balance sheet for the end of its 1984 fiscal year would have looked like Table 18.3. The $7.6 billion pension liability represents the vested

**Table 18.3 Hypothetical 1984 Consolidated Year-End
Balance Sheet for Du Pont Showing Vested Pension Liabilities
(billions of dollars)**

Assets		Liabilities	
Pension fund	$ 8.4	Pension liability	$ 7.6
Plant and equipment	14.4	Long-term debt	3.4
Other long-term assets	1.0	Equity	13.0
Current assets	8.7	Other long-term liabilities	3.3
Total assets	$32.5	Current liabilities	5.2
		Total liabilities	$32.5

liabilities of Du Pont, i.e., the liability that would be incurred if all the employees left the firm at the end of 1984. Du Pont's pension was overfunded by $800 million. In principle, this money "belongs" to shareholders. Even though the pension was over-funded, the addition of pension assets and liabilities to the balance sheet raised Du Pont's debt-to-total-assets ratio from 49% to 60%.[1] Clearly, pension fund liabilities are important enough to require full disclosure.

2. Pension Fund Regulations: ERISA, FASB, and the IRS

With the rapid growth of pensions as a form of deferred compensation, it became more and more important than firms fully disclose their pension commitments in their financial statements and that various pension practices become regulated by law. The Financial Accounting Standards Board (FASB) has established the generally accepted accounting practices for reporting by pension funds and firms (FASB No. 35 and 36, issued in 1980). In September 1974, President Gerald Ford signed into law the Employment Retirement Income Security Act (ERISA), which regulates various aspects of pension plans, including eligibility, vesting, funding, fiduciary responsibility, reporting and disclosure, and plan termination insurance.

There are two types of pension plans. *Defined contribution plans* consist of funds built up over time via employee and employer contributions, but benefits are not predetermined. Employees are simply paid out the market value of their portion of the pension fund when they retire. The firm has no responsibilities other than paying its share of the contributions and prudent management of the pension fund assets. The second, and more common, type is a *defined benefit plan*. Corporations are required to pay a contractual benefit upon the retirement of a vested employee. When ERISA was signed, defined benefit pensions were converted from corporate promises to liabilities enforceable by law.

---

[1] The effect of the pension fund on the balance sheet is to increase assets by $8.4 billion, to increase pension liabilities by $7.6 billion, and to increase equity by $0.8 billion (the amount of overfunding). Note that Table 18.3 is purely hypothetical and does not conform to the generally accepted accounting practices that are discussed later in the chapter.

The provisions of ERISA are many. No employee older than 25 years and with more than 1 year of service with a company, or hired more than 5 years before normal retirement age, may be excluded from participation in that company's pension plan. Prior to ERISA, unusual vesting practices resulted in many injustices. For example, some plans required 20 or more years of uninterrupted service before an employee became vested. Sometimes workers would be fired in their nineteenth year simply to prevent vesting them in a pension plan. With the advent of ERISA and the passage of the 1986 tax code, all plans must choose from one of two minimum vesting schedules for the corporate portion of the contributions to the pension plan:

1. Cliff vesting: 100% vesting after 5 years of service.
2. Graded vesting: 20% vesting after 3 years of service and then increasing by 20% per year to 100% vesting after 7 years of service.

All employee contributions to a pension fund, and investment returns on such contributions, are fully vested from the beginning.

ERISA legislates the minimum funding of defined benefit plans, whereas the IRS (Internal Revenue Service) sets limits on the maximum corporate contribution. According to ERISA, the minimum contribution is determined as follows: (1) all normal costs attributable to benefit claims deriving from employee services in a given year must be paid that year; (2) any experience losses (caused by a decline in the value of the securities in the fund, by unexpected changes in employee turnover, or by changes in actuarial assumptions about the discount rate) must be amortized over a period not to exceed 15 years; and (3) supplemental liabilities resulting from increased benefits or unfunded past service costs must be amortized over a period not to exceed 30 years (40 years for companies with pre-ERISA supplemental liabilities). On the other hand, the IRS defines the maximum corporate pension contribution as the actuarially determined normal cost of the plan plus any amount necessary to amortize supplemental and experience losses over a 10-year period. The ERISA and IRS restrictions limit corporate discretion over the amount of funds contributed to a plan.

One of the most important provisions of ERISA was the creation of the Pension Benefit Guaranty Corporation (PBGC). It is a pension insurance fund operated under the supervision of the U.S. Department of Labor. Corporations must pay the PBGC a fixed annual premium (currently $16.00) for each employee in a pension plan.[1a] There is also a variable cost component for underfunded plans that can bring the premium up to a total of $50 per worker. This central fund is then used to guarantee pension benefits even if a plan fails. A pension plan may be terminated voluntarily by the corporation or involuntarily by the PBGC upon court order. The PBGC may terminate a plan (1) if the plan fails to meet minimum funding standards, (2) if the plan is unable to pay benefits when due, (3) if the plan is administered improperly, or (4) if the liability of the PBGC for fulfilling claims deriving from the plan is likely to increase unreasonably.

If a plan is terminated because it is underfunded, the company is liable for 100% of the deficit up to 30% of the company's net worth. Furthermore, the PBGC may

---

[1a] There is also a variable cost component for underfunded plans that can bring the premium up to a total of $50.00.

place a lien on corporate assets that has the same priority as federal taxes. Hence unfunded pension liabilities are equivalent to the most senior debt. A bankrupt firm may have few assets to pay to the PBGC; hence a worthy public policy question is whether the PBGC has enough resources of its own to adequately insure pensioners of major corporate bankruptcies. In July 1987 the PBGC had total assets of $3 billion and faced total obligations of $7 billion for people currently retired or who would retire under plans of which it was trustee. The agency also faced cash flow problems because the premium income that it collected from corporations and the dividends from its investments were less than the benefits that it had already undertaken to pay. These were the realized liabilities. The present value of the PBGC potential liabilities is much larger. Marcus [1985] estimates the present value of the PBGC insurance liability for a sample of 87 of the *Fortune* 100 companies based on their 1982 annual reports. His estimates range from $6.7 to $14.8 billion.

3. Managerial Decisions Regarding Pension Plans

Most of the foregoing discussion has been descriptive in nature. We have discussed the rapid growth of pension funds, their asset composition, the pension plan financial statements, and pension fund regulation by ERISA and the IRS. Now it is time to ask what types of pension fund decisions confront financial managers and how these decisions will affect the value of shareholders' wealth. Listed by order of presentation, the decisions are:

a) Which type of pension plan, defined contribution or defined benefit, should a firm choose?

b) What are the effects of changing the actuarial assumptions of a pension fund?

c) What is the optimal mix of pension fund assets?

d) When, if ever, is it optimal to voluntarily terminate a pension plan? How can termination be accomplished legally?

e) Should the firm manage its pension plan or enter into a contract with an insurance company?

These are common pension plan problems, and every chief financial officer should understand the impact that pension plan decisions will have on the corporation's shareholders.

A. CHOICE OF PLAN TYPE.   At first, it might seem that defined contribution plans are better than defined benefit plans because no promise of a predetermined retirement benefit is made to employees. With defined contribution plans they receive payments based on whatever is in the fund at retirement. However, there is a drawback to defined contribution plans, which from the corporation's point of view probably explains why most companies use defined benefit plans instead.

Defined benefit plans allow flexibility for the purpose of tax planning. With defined benefit plans the firm can slow its payments to the plan (down to the minimum allowed by ERISA) during years of low profitability when the cash is needed for other purposes; then, during years of high profitability, payment can be accelerated (up to the limits established by the IRS) as a way of sheltering cash flows from income taxes. Defined contribution plans do not allow similar flexibility because they are established as a fixed percentage of employee compensation. We might expect to see defined benefit plans used by corporations, especially those that can benefit from tax planning, and defined contribution plans are more likely to be used by nontaxable entities and by partnerships.

B. CHANGING THE ACTUARIAL ASSUMPTIONS.   In 1973, U.S. Steel increased its reported profits by $47 million by "reducing" its pension costs. This was accomplished by recognizing some appreciation in its $2 billion pension fund. Presumably, cash was then diverted from pension contributions to other uses. In the fourth quarter of 1980, Chrysler changed its assumed discount rate on its employee pension plan from 6% to 7%. Pension costs were reduced, and $50 million was added to profits. Also, in 1980, Bethlehem Steel changed the assumed discount rate for its pension benefits to 10% from 7%.[2] This 3% increase had the effect of decreasing the present value of accumulated pension plan benefits by $713 million (22.5% of total benefits). Before the change, pension plan net assets totaled $1.952 billion and the plan was underfunded by $1.215 billion. After the change, underfunding fell to $502 million, a 58.7% decline. *Accounting Trends and Techniques,* an annual survey of reporting practices of 600 companies, showed that roughly 30% of the companies sampled voluntarily changed their pension fund accounting assumptions at least once between 1975 and 1980.

The economic effect on shareholders' wealth depends on how the accounting changes revised shareholders' expectations about the level and riskiness of the future cash flows of the firm. The value of shareholders' wealth is equal to the market value of the firm, V, minus the market value of its liabilities. For convenience, we shall divide liabilities into pension fund liabilities, PFL, and other debt, B. When ERISA was signed, defined pension liabilities became senior debt of the firm. Equation (18.1) shows S, the value of shareholders' wealth:

$$S = V - \text{PFL} - B. \qquad (18.1)$$

We are interested in the market value of pension fund liabilities and how they are affected by accounting changes. The market value is the way the marketplace will view the true pension fund deficit and does not have any necessary relationship to the accounting or book value deficit. The market value of the pension fund deficit (or surplus) is given in Eq. (18.2):

PFL $= -$ Market value of pension fund assets

$\qquad - [\text{PV(expected contributions)}](1 - \tau_c)$

$\qquad + \text{PV(expected pension fund benefits from (past and future service).} \qquad (18.2)$

---

[2] FASB Statement No. 36 allows companies to use different interest rate assumptions for disclosure in the annual report and for funding purposes; for example, Bethlehem used 7% for funding and 10% for disclosure. See Regan [1982].

There are two major pension fund assets. First is the current market value of the stocks, bonds, mortgages, and so forth, held by the pension fund. Second is the present value of the expected pension fund contributions, which are multiplied by one minus the corporate tax rate $(1 - \tau_c)$ in order to reflect the fact that pension fund contributions are tax deductible by the firm. As long as the firm is making profits, then pension contributions are "shared" with the government because more contributions mean lower taxes.[3] Balancing the pension fund assets is the pension fund liability, the present value of expected pension fund benefits to be paid to employees.

The main difference between the book value of the pension fund deficit and its market value, or true economic value, PFL, is reflected in the rates of return (discount rates). Equation (18.3) further elaborates Eq. (18.2) by showing the present value of the pension fund along with the appropriate market-determined discount rates:

$$\text{PFL} = -\text{Market value of pension fund assets}$$

$$-\sum_{t=1}^{n} \frac{E(\text{contributions in year } t)(1 - \tau_c)}{[1 + k_b(1 - \tau_c)]^t}$$

$$+\sum_{t=1}^{n} \frac{E(\text{benefits in year } t)}{(1 + k_b)^t}. \tag{18.3}$$

The expected pension benefits are discounted at the pretax cost of senior debt, k_b, because ERISA has made the payment of pension benefits a senior obligation of the firm, second only to tax liabilities.[4] Pension contributions are also discounted at the rate k_b but on an after-tax basis. Prior to ERISA, the expected benefits would have been discounted at the cost of junior, or subordinated, debt, k_j, which is higher than k_b, the cost of senior debt. One of the major effects of ERISA was to transfer wealth from shareholders to pension beneficiaries by increasing the present value of pension deficits, PFL. The transfer was especially large for plans that were seriously underfunded.

The real effect of a change in pension plan actuarial assumptions depends on the cash flow consequences. If the *actuarial* discount rate assumption is raised, then the present value of accumulated benefits in book value terms decreases, as do the normal costs that have to be paid into the fund. This has the effect of decreasing the annual expected contributions into the fund and hence decreasing their present value in Eq. (18.3) because expected contributions decrease, whereas the *market-determined* discount rate, k_b, does not change. The present value of expected benefits, however,

---

[3] If one considers Social Security to be a pension plan, then recent changes in the Social Security tax law that require nonprofit organizations to pay Social Security for their employees are burdensome. Because nonprofit organizations have no tax shelter, they must bear the full cost of Social Security expenses.

[4] Some have argued that promised pension benefits are subordinated to other debt claims in spite of ERISA because other debt comes due before pension obligations. Pension beneficiaries cannot force the firm into bankruptcy, whereas debt holders can. The existence of large unfunded pension deficits will, in our opinion, cause debt holders to force bankruptcy sooner than they might if there were no pension obligations. Nevertheless, pension liabilities will still be senior claims at the time of bankruptcy.

remains unchanged. The net effect is to increase the market value of pension liabilities, PFL. There is usually no effect on the firm as a whole because the cash flow not put into pension fund contributions may be used either to decrease other liabilities or to increase assets. Either way, the increased pension liability is exactly offset.[5] Thus we see that, from the shareholders' point of view, changing the actuarial assumptions in order to change pension contributions is usually an exercise in futility. Even worse, if the funds generated by cutting pension contributions are used for a purpose that is not expensed (e.g., repaying the principal on debt), the effect is to increase taxable income and decrease net cash flows to shareholders. Accounting profits have increased, but the firm has sacrificed the pension contribution tax shield. The net effect (assuming the firm is paying taxes) is to benefit the IRS at the expense of shareholders. Finally, changing actuarial assumptions for disclosure in the annual report but not for funding purposes is chicanery at best and stupid at worst. If taxes are based on actual contributions, then, at best, managers think they can somehow fool the marketplace.

C. Choosing the Mix of Pension Plan Assets. As with any other portfolio decision, the choice of assets for a pension plan involves a selection of risk and return. Furthermore, tax considerations and pension fund insurance through ERISA are paramount.

Modeling pension plan payoffs. Before turning to the effect of ERISA and taxes on pension fund investments, let us build a more complete understanding of their risk and return characteristics. Prior to the passage of ERISA, corporate pension liabilities were analogous to risky debt, and the shareholders' position was equivalent to a call option on a leveraged firm.[6] To illustrate this, assume a one-period framework, an all-equity firm that has an uncertain end-of-period market value, V_1, and a world with no taxes. The pension fund holds some risky assets with an end-of-period value, A_1, and the pension beneficiaries have been promised an end-of-period benefit, B.

Figure 18.1 shows the end-of-period payoffs to the pension beneficiaries, assuming that the pension fund is uninsured. Along the horizontal axis, we have the market value of the firm plus the market value of the pension assets, $V + A$, whereas dollars of end-of-period payoff are graphed along the vertical axis. The pension beneficiaries will receive the full promised amount if the market value of total assets, $V + A$, exceeds the promised benefits, B. But if not, the pension beneficiaries receive $V + A < B$. The solid line OXB in Fig. 18.1 shows the pension beneficiaries' payoff. Because we have assumed the firm has no debt, the shareholders' payoff is simply the

---

[5] One sometimes hears that pension contributions can be legitimately cut if the funds are alternatively used to invest in positive net present value projects. This argument confuses the investment decision (take the profitable project) with the way it is financed (cut pension fund contributions). The project can be financed either by cutting pension contributions, which increases pension liabilities, or by borrowing, which increases debt liabilities. Either way, the effect on shareholders' wealth is the same.
[6] For a more complete presentation of pension fund liabilities as options, see Sharpe [1976] and Treynor, Priest, and Regan [1976].

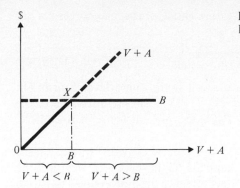

Figure 18.1
End-of-period pension fund payoffs.

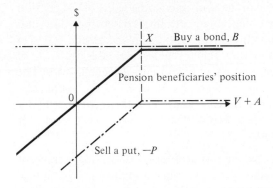

Figure 18.2
The pension beneficiaries' position is equivalent to risky debt (long in a riskless bond and short in a put option).

residual, as shown in the equation below:

$$\text{Shareholders' payoff} = \text{MAX}[0, (V + A) - B]. \tag{18.4}$$

Referring back to Chapter 8 on options on risky assets, we see that shareholders' payoff is identical to a call option on a levered firm. The pension beneficiaries' position is equivalent to owning a risk-free bond with an end-of-period value equal to the promised pension benefits, B, and selling a put option, P, on the assets of the firm.[7] In other words, they have a risky debt claim. Figure 18.2 shows that if we vertically sum the payoff from holding a riskless bond and selling a put option (at no cost to shareholders), we do indeed arrive at the pension beneficiaries' position.

The claims of all parties can be summarized by referring to the put-call parity equation (discussed in Chapter 8). Put-call parity said that the current market value of an underlying risky asset plus the value of a put option written on it (with maturity T periods hence and with an exercise price X) is equal to the value of a riskless bond plus a call option on the risky asset (with the same maturity and exercise price as

---

[7] Given that this is a one-period model and that pension benefits are not payable until employees retire at the end of the period, all options in the model are European options. They cannot be exercised before maturity.

the put). Using our current notation, the put-call parity expression becomes

$$(V_0 + A_0) + P_0 = B_0 + S_0,$$

$$S_0 = (V_0 + A_0) - (B_0 - P_0). \tag{18.5}$$

The shareholders' position, S_0, is equivalent to a call option on a levered firm. On the right-hand side of Eq. (18.5), we note that $(V_0 + A_0)$ is the present value of the firm and pension fund assets and that $(B_0 - P_0)$ is the present value of risky debt, i.e., the pension benefits.

Considerable insight into pension fund asset mix can be provided by this simple option pricing approach. For example, what happens to shareholders' wealth if the pension trustees change the mix of pension assets from a well-diversified portfolio of equity to being 100% invested in shares of the firm?[8] The effect would be to increase the correlation between V, the value of the firm, and A, the value of the pension assets. Consequently, the variance of the underlying portfolio of assets increases, and the value of shareholders' wealth, S_0, which is a call option on the assets, will also increase. Thus the effect of any decision that unexpectedly increases the risk of $(V + A)$ is to shift wealth to shareholders and away from pension beneficiaries. The only mitigating circumstance, which was pointed out by Sharpe [1976], is that employees may be able to demand higher wages to compensate them for the higher risk they must bear when pension assets are invested in the firm's own stock. Or they might require pension fund insurance.[9]

The effects of ERISA and the PBGC. Now let us look at the effect of government pension fund insurance on the pension fund asset mix but maintain our assumption that there are no taxes. As was mentioned earlier, the Pension Benefit Guaranty Corporation (PBGC) ensures pension fund liabilities. Corporations contribute into PBGC a fixed insurance premium per employee each year. In the event that an underfunded pension plan is terminated, the firm is liable up to 30% of its net worth, and the PBGC guarantees the remainder of the pension fund liability.

If the PBGC were a privately owned insurance company, it would charge premiums based on the probability of corporate default on a pension fund. However, as a government organization, it charges all firms exactly the same insurance premium regardless of the extent of pension plan underfunding or the likelihood of bankruptcy. One implication, of course, is that firms with overfunded pension funds are paying too much to the PBGC relative to those with badly underfunded pension plans. Another implication is that firms threatened with bankruptcy can decide to change their pension plan asset mix to maximize the value of the call option that represents their shareholders' wealth. If they go bankrupt, shareholders receive nothing, and although the PBGC can claim 30% of each firm's net worth, 30% of nothing is still nothing.

---

[8] This situation is not unusual. For example, at one time, the Sears pension fund had over 50% of its assets invested in its stock.

[9] For more on the economics of insuring portfolios of risky assets, see Gatto, Geske, Litzenberger, and Sosin [1980].

The PBGC claim on equity is worthless in both Chapter 7 bankruptcy and Chapter 11 reorganization. Consequently, the optimal strategy from the point of view of shareholders is to put all the pension assets into very risky stocks. If they are lucky the risky portfolio may do well and even result in overfunding of the pension fund. If they are unfortunate, then they end up with nothing, which is where they would have been anyway, and the PBGC has to pay off the pension beneficiaries.

Given that the PBGC undercharges for pension fund insurance for underfunded plans, then there is the distinct possibility that corporations facing potential bankruptcy can game the PBGC by shifting pension plan assets to being 100% invested in risky stocks.

An interesting case history of a company in trouble is International Harvester. In May 1982, the *Wall Street Journal* reported that International Harvester Company's pension fund abruptly switched at least $250 million of stock holdings into bonds, chiefly U.S. government issues. Pension industry executives suggested that the company was pursuing a strategy that would let it reduce pension contributions. As of October 31, 1981, Harvester's combined pension assets totaled $1.35 billion.

What are the real economic consequences of Harvester's decision? First, since the company had negative earnings, it is not likely that the tax consequences of the decision were important.[10] Second, by changing the actuarial assumptions of the plan either (1) by realizing gains on the stocks that were sold or (2) by raising the fund rate of return assumption due to the shift from stocks to bonds, Harvester could reduce its planned cash contributions to the fund. We have already seen (in the previous material in this chapter) that the change in actuarial assumptions has no effect on shareholders' wealth at best and a negative effect at worst. Finally, the analysis in this section of the chapter suggests that a shift from stock to bonds (in the absence of tax benefits) decreases shareholders' wealth and benefits pension beneficiaries (and debt holders) of the firm. Although we have insufficient information to draw a definite conclusion about the Harvester decision, it looks like the net effect was to diminish shareholders' wealth.

The effect of taxes. For most firms, pension fund contributions reduce taxes because they are immediately deductible. At the same time, the pension plan pays no taxes on its earnings. Hence the rapid growth of pensions is largely attributable to the fact that they are a form of tax-deferred compensation.

The pension assets should be invested in those securities that have the most favorable pretax rates of return. Obvious examples of securities that pension managers should *not* invest in are those that are used as tax shelters by investors with high marginal tax rates, such as municipal bonds or real estate with depreciable assets like buildings.

Perhaps the most interesting tax implication for the pension fund asset mix is that pension plans should be fully funded and invested totally in bonds as opposed

---

[10] The next section of this chapter provides the only rational tax explanation for why Harvester shareholders may have benefited from switching pension assets to bonds.

to equities.[11] The logic is developed in two parts. The first argument is that the return on debt held in a corporate pension fund is passed through the firm to its shareholders in the form of higher share prices because an overfunded pension plan is an asset of the firm.[12] The implication is that the return on debt held in the pension fund is ultimately taxed at the lower personal tax rate on equities. Shareholders will pay less tax than if the debt were held in their personal portfolios. Consequently, shareholders are better off if the pension funds of corporations are invested in bonds, whereas their personal portfolios are invested in equities. This conclusion is based on the fact that pension plan earnings are not taxed and that bond income is taxed at a higher rate than capital gains.[13] It does not depend on any theoretical gain to leverage (e.g., Chapter 13).

The second reason for investing pension assets in bonds is the potential value of the tax shelter involved when the firm borrows to invest pension assets in bonds. The following example compares two pension investment strategies, the first with all pension assets in stock and the second with all assets in bonds. For the sake of simplicity, we assume a one-period world with two equally likely states of nature. If the economy is good, stocks will yield a 100% rate of return, whereas bonds will yield 10%. If the economy is bad, stocks yield −50% and bonds yield 10%. The risk-free rate is 10%. Note that the expected (or average) return on stocks is 25%, whereas bonds are expected to yield only 10%. Even so, we will see that the bond investment strategy is better for shareholders.

Table 18.4 shows a beginning-of-period market value balance sheet that combines the firm and pension fund assets and liabilities for each of the two pension investment strategies: all stock and all bonds. The firm's defined benefit pension plan promises to pay $220 million at the end of the period. The present value of this liability is $200 million, and it appears on the liabilities side of the corporate balance sheet. On the assets side, the current market value of the pension assets is $200 million (either in stock or bonds). The pension plan is fully funded because the present value of its assets equals that of its liabilities.

If we employ the 100% stock investment strategy for our pension plan, the end-of-period payoffs are as shown in Table 18.5. Using the "good economy" as an example, we see that the pension fund stocks can be sold for $400 million at the end of the year. After paying the $220 million of pension benefits, shareholders are left with $180 million pretax and $90 million after taxes. In the "bad economy," they suffer a $60 million loss. The expected gain in shareholders' wealth is $15 million, but they are exposed to a great deal of risk. The alternate pension investment strategy is to invest $200 million in bonds. If that is all we did, the end-of-period payoff would be exactly $220 million in either economy, the pension benefits would be paid off, and

---

[11] For proof of this proposition, the reader is referred to Tepper and Affleck [1974], Black [1980], and especially to Tepper [1981].

[12] The next section of this chapter discusses ways that shareholders can gain access to the assets of over-funded pension plans.

[13] Even though the 1986 tax code makes the scheduled capital gains rate equal to the ordinary income rate, the effective capital gains rate is still lower because of the tax-timing option implicit in the realization of capital gains.

**Table 18.4   Beginning Balance Sheets for Two
Pension Investment Strategies**

*100% Stock Strategy
(millions of dollars)*

Assets		Liabilities	
Pension plan		Pension plan	
Bonds, B	0	PV of benefits, PFB	200
Stock, S	200	Corporate	
Corporate, A	800	Debt, D	300
	1000	Equity, E	500
			1000

*100% Bond Strategy
(millions of dollars)*

Assets		Liabilities	
Pension plan		Pension plan	
Bonds, B	200	PV of benefits, PFB	200
Stock, S	0	Corporate	
Corporate, A	800	Debt, D	400
	1000	Equity, E	400
			1000

**Table 18.5   Payoffs for the 100% Stock Pension Investment
Strategy (millions of dollars)**

	State of Nature	
	Good Economy	Bad Economy
Sell stock and receive	$400	$100
Pay off defined benefits	−220	−220
Cash to the firm	180	−120
Less taxes at 50%	−90	60
Net cash to shareholders	$ 90	−$ 60

there would be no gain or loss to shareholders. Their expected gain is zero, but they take no risk at all.

To present a valid comparison of the stock and bond strategies, we need to keep shareholders' risk constant. Then we can compare after-tax expected returns to see which strategy is better, given equivalent risk. Table 18.4 shows balance sheets that have the same risk for shareholders.[14] On the assets side, $200 million of bonds is less risky than $200 million of stock. Therefore to offset the decline in risk caused

---

[14] It really does not make any difference, in our example, how risk is measured. Shareholders' risk is equivalent whether one uses the range, the variance, or the beta to measure risk.

Table 18.6 Payoffs for the 100% Bond Pension Investment Strategy (millions of dollars)

	State of Nature	
	Good Economy	Bad Economy
Sell bonds and receive	$220	$220
Pay off defined benefits	−220	−220
	0	0
Sell stock (book value = $100)	200	50
Pay off extra bonds	−100	−100
	100	−50
Less interest on bonds	−10	−10
	90	−60
Plus tax shield on interest	5	5
Net cash to shareholders	$ 95	−$ 55

by the 100% bond strategy, we increase the firm's financial leverage by borrowing $100 million and using the proceeds to repurchase $100 million in equity.[15] The resulting payoffs are given in Table 18.6.

In the "good economy," the bonds are sold for $220 million and the proceeds are used to pay off the defined benefits. Next the $100 million of repurchased equity is reissued for $200 million (because the stock has appreciated by 100% in the good economy). Half of the $200 million is used to repay the $100 million of borrowing, and $10 million pays the required interest. Note that the interest payments are tax deductible. If the firm is in a 50% tax bracket, then taxes are reduced $5 million below what they otherwise would have been. Net cash available to shareholders in the favorable state of nature is $95 million with the 100% bond strategy but is only $90 million with the 100% equity strategy. The bond strategy also dominates the equity strategy in the unfavorable state of nature (−$55 million versus −$60 million). Hence our example demonstrates the superiority of the bond strategy from the shareholders' point of view. We have increased their return in both states of nature without changing their risk because the range of payoffs is $150 million in either case. Regardless of whether the actual return on stock investments is higher or lower than on bonds, the bond strategy is preferable.

Summarizing, we have seen that investing all pension fund assets in bonds benefits shareholders in two ways. First, the pretax bond rate of return is passed through the firm to its shareholders in the form of higher share prices, which are in turn taxed at the lower capital gains rate. This argument applies even if there is no gain to leverage. The second reason for favoring bonds over equity is that there may be a

---

[15] In practice, it is not necessary for corporations to actually repurchase shares in order to implement the 100% bond pension investment plan. What is important is that when pension assets are invested in bonds rather than stock, the risk of the corporate asset portfolio is lower. Hence, from the point of view of lenders, there is greater debt capacity. More borrowing provides a debt tax shield.

Value for shareholders

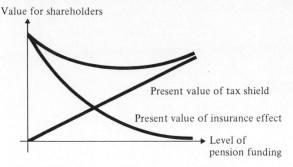

Figure 18.3
Corner solutions to the pension funding and asset
mix problem.

gain to firms that can carry more debt without increasing shareholders' risk—a gain
to leverage. We have seen that firms that choose to invest pension assets in bonds
actually experience lower total asset risk than firms that put pension assets into stock.
The lower risk means a greater debt capacity. If the firm uses this debt capacity and
if there is a valuable tax shield created by the deductibility of interest payments, then
there is a gain to leverage from investing pension assets in bonds while borrowing
to hold shareholders' risk constant.[16]

Empirical evidence by Landsman [1984] covering a large sample of firms for the
years 1979 through 1981 shows that on average each dollar contributed to the assets
of defined benefit pension funds results in a $1.12 increase in the value of shareholders'
equity, other things being held constant. That the increase is significantly greater
than $1 means that there may, in fact, be a clear tax advantage resulting from pension
assets held by the firm.

Combining the insurance and tax effects. The insurance and tax effects of pension
funding on shareholder wealth seem to suggest corner solutions for the choice of the
level of funding and the type of asset mix. If a firm is successful and is paying high
taxes, then it should make full use of the tax shield provided by pension plans—it
should overfund to the maximum extent permitted by law and invest primarily in
bonds. Alternatively, if it is losing money, or if it is not paying taxes for other reasons,
it cannot benefit from the pension fund tax shield and should therefore underfund to
the maximum extent permitted by law and put all the pension assets into risky equities.
This result is illustrated in Fig. 18.3. Note, however, that if the line representing the
present value of the tax shield were steeper, then the plan would be overfunded.

Bicksler and Chen [1985] and Westerfield and Marshall [1983] suggest that this
conclusion may be too strong. Rarely do firms actually go to either extreme. And
they usually have a mix of debt and equity in their pension fund portfolios. There

---

[16] The gain to leverage is most likely to be valuable for those firms that have higher effective tax rates
because their tax shelters from other sources (such as depreciation, research and development expenses,
or tax carryback and carryforward) are limited.

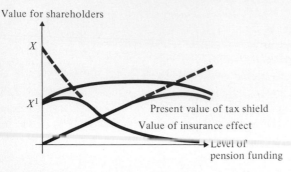

Figure 18.4
An interior solution for funding and the choice of
asset mix. (From J. Bicksler and A. Chen, "The
Integration of Insurance and Taxes in Corporate
Pension Strategy," *Journal of Finance*, July 1985,
951, reprinted with permission.)

are two reasons, and they are illustrated in Fig. 18.4. First, there are deadweight
losses associated with involuntary pension plan termination due to underfunding.
These costs have the effect of reducing the value of pension fund insurance provided
by the PBGC from point X to X'. Examples of such costs are legal expenses and
higher employee wage demands to offset the probability that their defined pension
benefits may not be paid. On the tax side, Bicksler and Chen suggest that the present
value of the tax shield diminishes because of the asymmetric structure of the U.S.
tax code. Firms pay taxes when their income is positive but cannot count on using
all tax credits from carryforwards and carrybacks if income is negative. As illustrated
in Fig. 18.4, the joint effects of termination deadweight losses and a diminishing tax
shelter result in an interior optimum. If the tax effect dominates, the level of pension
funding will be higher and more of the fund assets will be in bonds than stocks, and
vice versa.

  D. VOLUNTARY TERMINATION OF DEFINED BENEFIT PENSION PLANS.   In June
1983, Occidental Petroleum voluntarily terminated four defined benefit pension plans
for salaried employees in its oil and chemicals divisions, replacing them with defined
contribution plans. All employees covered by the terminated plans received a lump-
sum payment covering their vested benefits. Because the defined benefit plans were
overfunded by approximately $294 million (at the end of 1982), the voluntary termina-
tion boosted Occidental's after-tax net income by approximately $100 million, or 64%
of its 1982 earnings.

  Fortune magazine (December 26, 1983) reported that since 1980, 128 companies
have carried out 138 pension reversions where defined benefit plans were cancelled.
The excess assets, which reverted to use in operating and capital budgets, amounted
to $515 million. The Pension Benefit Guarantee Corporation (PBGC), which has to
approve any cancellations, was considering applications that would free up well over

$1 billion more in excess assets. Furthermore, an estimated $150 billion in excess assets sits untapped in other private pension plans.

These examples clearly demonstrate that if underfunded pension plans are liabilities of shareholders, then overfunded plans are assets. Although the firm owns the excess assets in the fund, it is restricted greatly in its ability to use them.[17] ERISA states that any residual assets in a terminated plan revert to the employer only if the pension plan explicitly provides for such a distribution upon termination. In many cases, the PBGC has contended that excess assets should go to plan beneficiaries. Consequently, firms must be careful about the process of terminating overfunded pension plans. It should also be noted that ERISA has made it more difficult to borrow against the assets in the pension fund, and that the IRS collects taxes plus a 10% surcharge when an overfunded plan is terminated (see the 1986 Tax Reform Act).

Usually, firms do not consider voluntary termination of underfunded plans because the PBGC can lay claim to 30% of their net worth. However, two questions arise. How is net worth to be measured? And, can a subsidiary with negative net worth terminate its pension plan and relinquish the unfunded liabilities to the PBGC? In answer to the second question, the PBGC has denied subsidiaries the right to terminate their plans so long as the parent company shows adequate net worth. Furthermore, the PBGC has argued that in determining net worth it can look beyond book value and use other information to establish the value of the firm as a going concern. Consequently, voluntary termination of underfunded plans is an unlikely strategy.

Most companies replace their defined benefit with defined contribution plans, thereby shifting the uncertainties of pension performance from themselves to their employees. The company simply promises to pay a fixed percentage of each employee's salary or wages into the defined contribution plan. Benefits upon retirement depend on the return on pension assets. Sometimes the defined contribution plans are coupled with the 401K tax-deferred savings plan authorized by the Internal Revenue Act of 1978. Employee contributions to the plan reduce their tax liabilities and earn tax-free returns until retirement. One drawback, from the company's perspective, is that its contribution to the 401K plan is vested immediately.

E. INSURANCE COMPANY CONTRACTS. About 39% of all nongovernment pension plans were invested with insurance companies. The usual insurance company contract provides "guaranteed" rates of return for a fixed period of time. For example, you may be guaranteed an 8% return for a 10-year period. The insurance companies can provide the guarantee because they invest your pension fund contributions in 10-year government bonds, which, if held to maturity, yield exactly 8%. The catch is that you cannot withdraw your pension plan assets if interest rates change. When market rates of interest rose rapidly during the late 1970s and early 1980s, many firms suddenly realized that a guaranteed rate of return was very different from a

---

[17] For a more complete exposition, the reader is referred to Bulow, Scholes, and Manell [1982].

riskless return. Market rates of interest of 14% on long-term bonds were not unusual, but those companies whose pension assets were committed to insurance company contracts found they were locked into an 8% return. This is the hard way to learn about opportunity cost (although it is still a fair game).

If your company is large enough to provide its own pension fund accounting for employees, then there is no difference between contributing pension funds to an insurance company plan and directly investing in 8% 10-year bonds yourself. Just bear in mind that long-term bonds are riskier than short-term bonds or money market assets. Some companies have decided to immunize their pension liabilities by purchasing long-term bonds that mature with the same pattern as employee retirements. They know for sure that maturing bonds will pay promised benefits.

4. Summary of Pension Fund Management

The rapid growth of pension funds in the last two decades has made their management one of the primary responsibilities of corporate chief financial officers (CFOs). CFOs must be familiar with accounting regulations governing pension fund reporting practices, with government regulation of defined benefit plans under ERISA, and with a wide range of managerial decisions. We discussed the economic implications of choosing between defined benefit and defined contribution plans, changing the pension fund actuarial assumptions, the choice of asset mix, the implications of voluntary termination of defined benefit plans, and the economics of investing pension plan assets with guaranteed insurance company plans.

There are still some as yet unanswered questions. For example, why were 50.5% of all noninsured pension fund assets invested in common stocks in 1980? The tax advantage of investing in bonds (at least for fully funded plans) seems obvious. Another question is, Why are actuarial changes so frequent when they have no impact on shareholder wealth (at best)?

B. INTEREST RATE SWAPS

It has been estimated that a total of at least $150 billion in interest rate swaps had been completed in the United States by the end of 1985. A fairly recent phenomenon, interest rate swaps are a rapidly growing activity.

An interest rate swap is a contract between firms in which interest payments are based on a notational principal amount that is itself never paid or received. Instead the parties agree to pay each other the interest that would be due on the notational principal. Swaps are usually between fixed and floating rate instruments, although floating for floating and fixed for fixed are also possible. The most common swap is where one interest stream, the floating payment, is tied to a short-term money market rate such as the U.S. Treasury bill rate or to LIBOR (the London Interbank Offer Rate). The other payment stream is fixed for the life of the swap. Both fixed and floating interest payments start accruing on the swap's effective date and cease on the swap's maturity date.

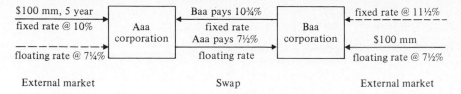

Figure 18.5
An interest rate swap.

Figure 18.5 illustrates a swap. Suppose that an Aaa-rated firm can borrow five-year fixed rate debt at 10% and floating rate debt at the T-bill rate, 7%, plus $\frac{1}{4}$%. At the same time, a Baa-rated firm can borrow five-year fixed rate debt at 11.5%, and floating rate debt at the T-bill rate plus $\frac{1}{2}$%. Thus the short-term quality premium is only $\frac{1}{4}$%, whereas the long-term premium is 1.5%.

Suppose the Aaa-rated firm has borrowed $100 million of five-year fixed rate debt at 10%. A swap can be arranged whereby the Baa-rated firm agrees to pay $10\frac{3}{4}$% on the five-year debt and the Aaa-rated firm pays the T-bill rate plus $\frac{1}{2}$% (i.e., $7\frac{1}{2}$%). The net position of the Aaa-rated firm is a gain of $\frac{1}{2}$%, the extra $\frac{3}{4}$% received on the five-year note less the extra $\frac{1}{4}$% paid on the variable rate loan. The Baa-rated firm borrows $100 million at the T-bill rate plus $\frac{1}{2}$%, receives the same rate from the Aaa-rated firm, and agrees to pay $10\frac{3}{4}$% on the fixed rate debt. Since the rate on the fixed debt is $\frac{3}{4}$% less than the Baa-rated firm would otherwise have to pay, it comes out $\frac{3}{4}$% ahead as a result of the swap. In this example the presumption is that both firms benefit by splitting the difference in the quality spread on short-term variable rate debt and longer-term fixed rate debt.

In the absence of market imperfections and comparative advantages among different classes of borrowers, there would be no reason for interest rate swaps. However, in less than perfect markets there are a number of possible motivations for engaging in a swap. Henderson and Price [1984], Bicksler and Chen [1985], and Smith, Smithson, and Wakeman [1986] discuss the more frequently mentioned reasons.

1. *Duration matching.* Firms with variable rate assets and fixed rate liabilities (or vice versa) are exposed to interest rate risk. If the rates that they receive on assets fall, but they continue to pay high fixed rates on their liabilities, they end up in a losing position. A swap of fixed rate for variable rate debt can help to match the duration of their assets and liabilities and to reduce their interest rate risk.

2. *Quality spread arbitrage.* When the quality spread between short- and long-term debt gets far enough out of line, it may be possible to engage in the quality spread arbitrage, as was illustrated in Fig. 18.5.[18]

---

[18] One of the reasons why the quality yield spread on short-term notes is less than the spread on long-term notes is that the probability of default on a low-quality bond is less in the short run than in the long run. Therefore parties who agree to lock into a long-term swap may be fooling themselves into thinking they are arbitraging the quality spread when in fact the spread on a one-year position rolled over N times should be the same as that on an N-year position.

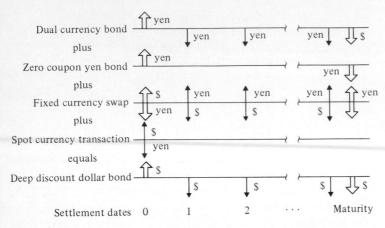

Figure 18.6
Creating a synthetic deep discount dollar–denominated bond. (From
C. Smith, Jr., C. Smithson, and L. Wakeman, "The Evolving Market for
Swaps," *Midland Corporate Finance Journal*, Winter 1986, 25, reprinted
with permission.)

3. *Refunding debt.* When debt is noncallable, or is privately held, swaps may be used
to refund the debt and to simultaneously convert fixed rates to variable.

4. *Tax and regulatory arbitrage.* The introduction of a swap allows an "unbundling"
of currency and interest rate exposure from regulation and tax rules in very cre-
ative ways. For example, until recently, zero coupon bonds in Japan were not
taxed until maturity and then only at the capital gains rate. Furthermore, the
Japanese Ministry of Finance limited the amount a pension fund could invest
in non-yen-denominated foreign issues to 10% of the fund's portfolio. U.S. firms
issued zero coupon yen bonds plus dual currency bonds (with interest payments
in yen and principal in dollars) and were able to capitalize on the superior tax
treatment of zero coupon bonds in Japan as well as the Japanese funds' desire
to diversify their funds internationally because the ministry qualified dual currency bonds as yen-denominated. To transfer their yen exposure back to a U.S.
dollar exposure, the U.S. firms used currency swaps in conjunction with spot
currency transactions. See Fig. 18.6 for an illustration of the cash flow pattern.

The economic evaluation of swap decisions requires that we compare the present
values of fixed and variable rate instruments—not an easy task because of differences
in default risk and the difficulty in modeling the term structure of interest rates. Cox,
Ingersoll, and Ross [1980], and Ramaswamy and Sundaresan [1986] have shown how
to value variable rate debt given various assumptions. The following example assumes
no default risk and a monotonic term structure of interest rates.

The first task, and by no means the easiest, is to model the term structure of interest
rates. To keep things simple, assume a three-period world where one-period risk-free

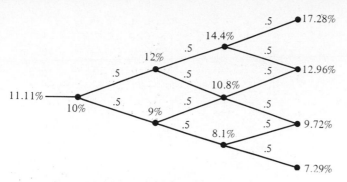

Figure 18.7
A binomial model of one-period riskless interest rates for three
time periods.

interest rates are modeled as binomial trials.[19] The interest rate can move up by a
factor of 1.2 or down by a factor of .9. Figure 18.7 shows the term structure assuming
that last period's rate was 11.11% and that this period's rate is 10%. Since the up
movements are larger than the down movements, the term structure is upward sloping in this example. Once one has an adequate model of the term structure, the next
step is to model the actual payouts on both instruments. If the floating rate bond
always paid the current one-period rate, it would adjust perfectly to changes in the
interest rate and would always sell for par. Unfortunately, this is not usually the case.
Suppose the floating rate bond promises to pay a coupon based on the arithmetic
average of the current one-period rate and last period's rate. Coupons based on moving average schemes of this type are common. Figure 18.8 illustrates the coupons that
would be paid, contingent on the path of one-period riskless rates. Since there is no
default risk involved, we can discount the coupon payments at the one-period riskless
rate. The iterative pricing formula is

$$B_{t,s} = \frac{q(\text{coupon}_{t,u}) + (1 - q)(\text{coupon}_{t,d})}{1 + r_{f,t,s}}, \tag{18.6}$$

where t is the time period; s is the state of nature (up or down); $\text{coupon}_{t,s}$ is the coupon
in period t and state s; q is the probability of an upward movement; and $r_{f,t,s}$ is the
riskless rate in period t and state s. To illustrate the use of Eq. (18.6) take the second
highest payoff (state 2) in the third time period (see Fig. 18.8). It was reached in one
of three ways: after two upward movements followed by one downward movement
in the interest rate, or after one downward and two upward movements, or via an up,
a down, and then an upward movement. With the first path, the coupon payment is
$136.80 and the face value is $1000, resulting in a total payment of $1136.80. Via the
second and third paths, the coupon is $118.80 and the face value is still $1000. Thus
the coupon payment is path dependent. To compute the value of the bond in state

---

[19] See Chapter 8 on option pricing for a complete exposition of the binomial model.

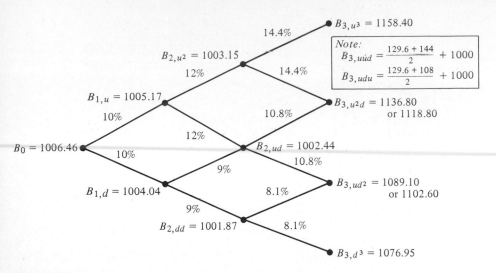

Figure 18.8
Payments on a floating rate bond where the coupon is an average of rates for the last two periods.

1 of period 2, one averages the payout in state 1 of period 3, $1158.40, with the payout in state 2 of period 3 which was reached via 2 upward and 1 downward movements, $1136.80; and discounts at 14.4%. The result is $B_{2,u^2} = 1003.15. The present value of the bond in state 1 of time period 2 is the average of the total payoffs (since they) are equally likely) discounted at the one-period rate, 14.4%. Given the numbers in our example, the present value of the floating rate bond (at time 0) is $1006.46.

Next, suppose that you are the treasurer of an Aaa-rated company that has $100 million of floating rate debt with exactly the same terms as the instrument we just valued. You are approached by a company that has the same default risk (assume no default risk at all for an Aaa-rated company). They want to swap their three-year fixed rate, which pays a 12% coupon, with your floating rate debt. What should you do? The solution of course is to analyze the fixed rate debt and compare its value with the value of your floating rate debt. If your debt is worth less than the fixed rate debt, you would take the offer.

Figure 18.9 shows how to use Eq. (18.6) to value the fixed rate debt. The procedure is much the same as before. The value of the bond cum coupon is discounted each period at the risk-free rate in the appropriate state of nature. The present value of the 12% fixed rate bond turns out to be $1038.41. Since it is worth more than your floating rate bond, you would be willing to undertake the proposed swap.

Interest rate and foreign exchange swaps are a rapidly growing business. There are many reasons. One is that there are capital market inefficiencies that allow arbitrage using swaps. But another is that the parties involved in the swaps are being fooled because they do not understand how to price the complex instruments involved in the deals—especially floating rate notes with default risk and with complex terms.

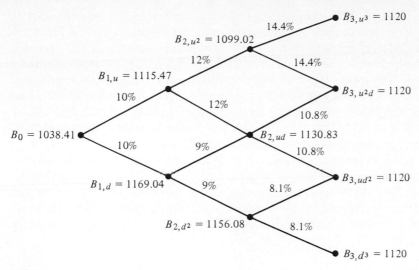

$B_0 = 1038.41$

$B_{1,u} = 1115.47$ — 10%

$B_{1,d} = 1169.04$ — 10%

$B_{2,u2} = 1099.02$ — 12%

$B_{2,ud} = 1130.83$ — 9%

$B_{2,d2} = 1156.08$ — 9%

$B_{3,u3} = 1120$ — 14.4%

$B_{3,u2d} = 1120$ — 14.4%

$B_{3,ud2} = 1120$ — 12%

$B_{3,d3} = 1120$

10.8%

10.8%

8.1%

8.1%

Figure 18.9
The valuation of three-year fixed rate debt paying a 12% coupon.

There is little empirical research yet to help answer the question of whether market inefficiencies are driving the growth in swaps. Partly this is so because of the lack of good data and partly because of the difficulty of theoretical models to predict yield premia. More research in both areas is needed.

C. LEVERAGED BUYOUTS AND GOING PRIVATE

Leveraged buyouts involve management purchase of the entire public stock interest of a firm, or division of a firm. If the shares are owned exclusively by management the transaction is called going private, and there is no market for trading its shares. If ownership in the subsequent private firm is shared with third-party investors and financed heavily with debt, the transaction is called a leveraged buyout. The issues raised by leveraged buyouts are many. Why do they happen in the first place? Are they motivated as an attempt by incumbent management to expropriate wealth from minority shareholders—a minority freezeout? Are they done for tax reasons? Who benefits? Who loses and why? How are the deals structured?

1. How to Go Private

There are four commonly used techniques for implementing the going-private transaction. Management may form a shell corporation that combines with the firm via *merger*. Usually merger approval is required by shareholders of the original firm, and the shell corporation may pay with cash or securities. *Asset sales* are similar in that a vote is required, and assets are purchased by a shell corporation owned by management. A *tender offer* does not require a vote and does not require minority shareholders to surrender their shares involuntarily. In a tender offer the firm buys back its own shares, either with cash, debt, or convertible securities. Least common among the methods is a *reverse stock split*. Holders of fractional shares are usually required to sell their ownership back to the corporation. DeAngelo, DeAngelo, and Rice [1984] found that of a sample of 81 going-private proposals between 1973 and 1980, 27 were mergers, 3 were sale of assets, 16 were tenders (or exchange offers), and 1 was a reverse split. The remaining 34 were either leveraged buyouts (LBOs) with third party participation (28) or unclassified acquisitions (6).

The distinction between a pure going-private transaction and a leveraged buyout with the involvement of third parties is important for leverage changes. DeAngelo, DeAngelo, and Rice [1984] report that for those firms where the proxy statement had a forecast of leverage changes, the leveraged buyout book ratio of debt to total assets increased from 11% to 86%, but for the pure going-private transactions it changed very little—26% versus 30%.

2. Gains from Going Private and LBOs

The most obvious gains from going private are the savings from reduced exchange registration and listing costs, and from the elimination of shareholder servicing costs. These savings, which have been estimated to range between $30,000 and $200,000 per annum, can be significant for smaller firms. If capitalized at 10%, the present value of the pretax savings is as high as $2 million—not a trivial number when compared with the median $2.8 million public capitalization of the DeAngelo, DeAngelo, and Rice sample of pure going-private firms.

Another frequently cited benefit is that management-shareholder agency costs are reduced. Following the transaction, management no longer shares the costs of perquisites or of shirking with outside owners. This may provide a strong incentive for better management performance and may therefore add value to the firm. Furthermore, in LBOs the greatly increased leverage may provide management with much stronger incentives to trim the fat from operating costs.

Along similar lines is the argument that agency costs arising from conflicts between debt and equity claims on the firm may be reduced. One reason is that third-party equity participants have a stronger incentive to monitor management than would diffuse ownership. And second, LBOs are often structured to use *strip financing*. Suppose an LBO creates several layers of nonequity financing such as senior debt, subordinated debt, convertible debt, and preferred stock. Securities between senior debt and equity are often called mezzanine level financing. Strip financing requires that a buyer who purchases X% of any mezzanine level security must purchase X% of all mezzanine level securities and some equity. Jensen [1987] points out that this LBO financing technique can be an advantage because as each level of financing senior to equity goes into default, the strip holder automatically receives new rights to intercede in the organization. As a result, it is quicker and less expensive to replace management in an LBO with strip financing. Strip financing also reduces (or even eliminates) conflicts between senior and junior claim holders. Figure 18.10 illustrates

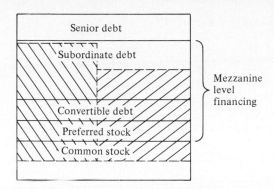

strip financing in an LBO. The senior claim is usually bank debt financing. Subordinate to it are the "mezzanine" securities including subordinate debt, convertible debt, and preferred stock. Third-party financiers typically hold strips of the mezzanine as well as equity. Venture capitalists may hold up to 80% of the equity, with management holding the remainder. Because venture capitalists are generally the largest shareholder and control the board of directors, they have both greater ability and stronger incentives to monitor managers than directors representing diffuse public shareholders in the typical public corporation.

LBO targets are frequently firms with relatively stable cash flows and unutilized debt capacity. It may be possible for management to benefit from the greater tax shield provided when the buyout is financed with debt. Thus the value gained from leverage may be an additional motivation for leveraged buyouts.

An example of how transactions might work out for a target company is shown in Table 18.7. Table 18.7 shows how the earnings before interest and taxes grow at 10% a year. The interest payments reflect the amortization of principal that takes place each year. A 40% tax rate is assumed. After deduction of taxes, net income is shown in row 5. Depreciation is added back to obtain the usual definition of cash flow shown in row 7. Row 8 illustrates an amortization schedule for the debt. This results in the cash flow cushion depicted in row 9. With the amortization schedule

Table 18.7   Pro Forma Cash Flows for a Leveraged Buyout

	Year 0	Year 1	Year 2	Year 3	Year 4	Year 5
1. EBIT	150.00	165.00	181.5	199.7	219.6	241.6
2. Interest		88.5	76.5	62.2	45.0	24.5
3. EBT		76.5	105.0	137.5	174.6	217.1
4. Taxes @ 40%		30.6	42.0	55.0	69.8	86.8
5. Net income		45.9	63.0	82.5	104.8	130.3
6. Depreciation		30.0	30.0	30.0	30.0	30.0
7. Cash flow		75.9	93.0	112.5	134.8	160.3
8. Amortization of loans		60.9	72.9	87.2	104.4	124.9
9. Cash flow cushion		15.0	20.1	25.3	30.4	35.4

Table 18.8   The Changing Debt Ratio in a Leveraged Buyout

	Year 0	Year 1	Year 2	Year 3	Year 4	Year 5
1. Equity	50.0	95.9	158.9	241.4	346.2	476.5
2. Debt	450.0	389.1	316.2	229.0	124.6	0
3. Total assets	500.0	485.0	475.1	469.7	470.1	476.5
4. Percent debt	90%	80%	67%	49%	26%	0%

shown in row 8, we can also indicate how the debt/equity position changes over time. This is illustrated by Table 18.8.

Table 18.8 reflects the amortization program agreed upon. Over the five-year period, debt is reduced from 90% to 0%. We then assume that the company is sold at its book value at the end of year 5. This is a conservative assumption because, with the record it has established, the firm might well sell for a premium over book value. The ratio of the price received to the initial equity investment is 476.5/50, which equals 953%. This represents a five-year annual compounded rate of return on the initial $50,000 investment of 57%. The plausibility of these results is indicated by some published statistics. A *Fortune* magazine article [Ross, 1984] stated that one of the leveraged buyout specialist companies, Kohlberg, Kravis, Roberts and Co., has earned an average annualized return of 62% on the equity it has invested in its transactions. Another buyout specialist, Carl Ferenbach, has stated that his firm expects an annual return of 50% on its equity investment [DeAngelo, DeAngelo, and Rice, 1984].

Much has been made of the conflict of interest that managers, as insiders, have when engaging in a buyout. If they obtain the best deal for themselves, it may be at the expense of minority shareholders. One would expect managers to try a buyout when they have inside information that indicates that the future of the firm is better than previously expected. Rational expectations theory, however, suggests that shareholders know that insiders have an informational advantage and are not fooled. Therefore they demand a higher price in order to sell their ownership claims. Furthermore, minority shareholders must approve the transaction and often have veto power. A countervailing force is that management frequently has a majority ownership position prior to the transaction. For example, DeAngelo, DeAngelo, and Rice [1984] report that the median management ownership was 51% of the stock in pure going-private transactions and 33% in LBOs with third-party participation. This makes it difficult for raiders to compete to bid away potential management gains. Therefore we might predict that gains from going private are shared between management and minority shareholders.

3. Empirical Evidence on the Announcement Effects

The empirical evidence is unable to separate the effect of favorable insider information from other benefits (e.g. reduced agency costs and reduced shareholder service costs). It can, however, tell us whether minority shareholders benefit and by how much.

DeAngelo, DeAngelo, and Rice (DDR) report a highly significant average 2-day abnormal return of 22.4% upon the initial announcement of a going-private or LBO transaction. If the announcement period is extended to include information leakage during the 40 trading days prior to the announcement, the cumulative abnormal return increases to 30.4%. DDR also report that the initial market reaction is well below the 56.3% average premium offered by management. The difference is explained by the relatively high percentage of offers that are withdrawn (18 firms). The 2-day abnormal return at the time of the withdrawal announcement was a significantly negative 8.9%. These facts clearly indicate that minority shareholders received significant gains from the transaction. They do not shed any light on what percentage of the total gain was received by management and by minority shareholders. For those buyouts that were consummated, both parties certainly believed they were gaining.

There are many unanswered questions regarding going-private and LBO transactions. For example, how does one evaluate the transaction on a net present value basis before actually taking action? What determines the best structure for the deal? And how does one estimate the required rates of return on the securities involved? Future research is needed to help answer these thorny problems.

D. EXECUTIVE COMPENSATION PLANS

The separation of ownership and control is commonplace in developed countries and is rarely questioned. You might decide to own a farm, e.g., but not operate it yourself because you know little about farming. Instead, you try to hire the best farmer possible and to motivate him or her to achieve the maximum production from the land. Separation of ownership and control makes sense, but it is not without problems. Among the most important are the agency problems that arise as owners attempt to motivate and monitor managers.

The objective of owners is to maximize the value of their residual claim on the firm, the market value of their equity. Managers may be assumed to maximize their personal wealth. Unfortunately, these objectives can be conflicting, and this makes the construction of optimal executive compensation plans a difficult task. There are (at least) six objectives of compensation plan design:

1. The plan should be easy to monitor because it is based on objective criteria, easily observed by all concerned parties, and incapable of being manipulated.

2. The plan should prevent excessive perquisites to management and should minimize shirking.

3. The plan should have a long horizon to match the perspective of shareholders.

4. The plan should attempt to match managers' risk to that of shareholders but should recognize that shareholders can diversify away from the idiosyncratic risk of the firm more easily than managers who have their human capital tied to the firm's future.

5. Management compensation should be tied to changes in shareholder wealth— and if possible, to management's specific contribution to changes in shareholders'

wealth. For example, it is conceivable that a firm can underperform relative to its competition but still experience an increase in share price simply because the market went up.

6. The tax efficiency of plans should be compared. If two plans are alike in most regards, but one is better designed to minimize the tax liabilities of the firm and its management, then its tax efficiency may become the decisive factor.

The popular press has often criticized management as overpaid. Owners worry that managers do not bear the full cost of shirking, or of excessive perquisites, and may choose to be more conservative in risk taking than owners would desire. Executive compensation schemes are a deliberate attempt to modify managerial behavior to more closely conform to shareholder objectives.

Empirical research into the relationship between the level of executive compensation and changes in shareholder wealth is just beginning. Murphy [1985] reports that a 10% change in the equity value of the firm is associated with only about a 2% increase in total executive compensation. Although the correlation is weak, it is statistically significant and positive. Coughlan and Schmidt [1985] also find a significant positive relationship between executive compensation and changes in shareholder wealth. These studies imply that executive compensation plans in the United States are not complete nonsense, but one can hardly infer that they are optimally designed.

1. Bonus Plans

Most executive compensation plans have three components: salary, stock options, and bonuses. The rough proportions for 1966, 1971, and 1981 are given in Brindisi [1985] (see Table 18.9). The proportion represented by option plans has been rising at the expense of bonus plans. Table 18.10 shows the measures that are typically used for bonuses. It is based on a sample of 80 firms reported by Brindisi [1985]. Most bonus plans are based on accounting data. Earnings per share, or the growth in earnings per share, is the most common measure. Earnings per share has been criticized because it is a short-term goal that can be easily manipulated and because it sometimes moves in the opposite direction from cash flows.

Table 18.9 Proportion of Executive Compensation from Various Sources

Source	1966	1971	1981
Salary	43%	58%	53%
Bonuses	22	19	6
Options	35	23	41

From L. Brindisi, Jr., "Creating Shareholder Value: A New Mission for Executive Compensation," *Midland Corporate Finance Journal*, Winter 1985, 62, reprinted with permission.

Table 18.10 Performance Measures Used for Chief Executive Officer Bonus Plans

Growth in income or earnings per share	85%
Return on investment	33
Individual objectives	17
Sales growth	3
Discretionary	27

From L. Brindisi, Jr., "Creating Shareholder Value: A New Mission for Executive Compensation," *Midland Corporate Finance Journal*, Winter 1985, 61, reprinted with permission.

Healy [1985] studied the relationship between year-end accounting changes and executive compensation plans. A typical funding formula for the yearly bonus pool establishes both a minimum threshold and a maximum payout. For example, no bonuses are paid unless net income exceeds 5% of total capital employed; and the maximum bonus cannot exceed some target percentage of executive salaries. Healy found that when firms had bonus plans, there was a tendency to defer the recognition of revenues and accelerate expenses when profits fell near the bonus threshold level. Although this behavior does not result in a bonus this year, it does increase the probability of receiving a bonus next year. When profits fell between the minimum and the ceiling, there was a tendency to accelerate the recognition of revenues and defer expenses. It is hard to believe that short-term behavior of this sort is intended to maximize shareholders' wealth.

Another problem with bonus plans based on earnings or earnings growth is that they can distort investment decisions. Many positive net present value projects lose money during their gestation phase. Managers who myopically pursue short-term profit objectives may decide to underinvest—to milk the firm for short-term profits. In an effort to modify bonus plans to provide incentives to adopt longer horizons, many firms have developed bonus plans based on a moving average of three to seven years of profits. This is an improvement, but it does not solve the problem that it is still based on accounting measures of income that may or may not have a direct correspondence with shareholder wealth creation. We shall also see, later on, that bonus plans are typically inferior from a tax point of view.

Another important dimension to executive compensation is risk. If all compensation were salary, unrelated to performance, then executives (as a group) would have more or less the same risk as bondholders in a levered firm. They could not do much to increase their income if the firm did well, and they would lose their salary only if the firm went bankrupt.[20] Consequently, many scholars of executive compensation believe that in order to encourage managers to take more risk, there must be option-like features to their compensation. As mentioned earlier, most bonus plans have this feature, especially if no bonus is earned unless a minimum threshold is exceeded and if there is no maximum. Executive stock options and stock appreciation rights (SARs) have exactly this type of payout.

2. Executive Stock Option Plans

An executive stock option plan is a form of long-term compensation contract that depends on market measures of corporate performance. It usually give managers the right to purchase a specified number of shares, for a specified period of time (called the *maturity date* of the plan), for a specified price (called the *exercise price*). Restricted stock options was the first stock option plan to receive favorable tax treatment with the Revenue Act of 1950. There have been many changes since then, but

---

[20] Fama [1980] presents an alternative point of view, arguing that the labor market for managers makes their salaries vary with their productivity, and that they do an excellent job of monitoring each other. Furthermore, salaries and bonuses can be adjusted *ex post* to eliminate the agency problem.

since 1981 the tax laws govern two types of plan: incentive stock options (ISOs) and stock appreciation rights (SARs).

Neither ISOs nor SARs have any tax consequences for either the firm or the executive at the time the options are issued. At the time of exercise, the ISO has no tax consequences; however, the SAR allows the firm to deduct the difference between the share price on the exercise date, S_e, and the exercise price, X, whereas the executive must pay ordinary income taxes on $S_e - X$. Finally, when the shares purchased by exercising the option are eventually sold, the executive can qualify for capital gains tax treatment. For ISOs the tax is on the difference between the sale price, S_t, and the exercise price, X; and for SARs it is on the difference between the sale price and the purchase price, $S_t - S_e$.

ISOs must be exercised sequentially, whereas SARs can be exercised in any order. There is a definite drawback to the sequential exercise requirement. Suppose the firm's share price was $50, fell to $30, then rose again to $40. If options were issued at each stage with the exercise price equal to the stock price, executives would be required to exercise the earlier $50 options (that are $10 out-of-the-money) before they could exercise the options issued at $30 (that are $10 in-the-money).

Both ISOs and SARs have a maximum life of 10 years from the date of issue. The exercise price of ISOs must be greater than or equal to the stock price at the time of issue, but SARs can have an exercise price as low as 50% of the stock price.

There is an increasing tendency to complement executive stock option plans with SARs. In 1970 none of the plans for the largest 100 companies in the United States had SARs, but according to Smith and Watts [1982], by 1980, 68 out of the top 100 firms had SARs.

Two reasons for using executive stock options at all are (1) that they augment salaries with a call option so that managers' total compensation pattern is more like that of shareholders and (2) that stock options are a more tax efficient form of compensation than straight salaries.

Miller and Scholes [1982] demonstrate that when compared with salaries SARs are tax neutral from the firm's point of view and tax dominant from the manager's point of view. To illustrate their argument, suppose that a firm expects $140 million of cash flows in a good state of nature before paying management salaries, and $120 million in a bad state. The firm's tax rate is 50%, and management salaries amount to $100 million. Table 18.11 shows their net payoffs after taxes and management salaries.

Table 18.11   Firm's Expected Cash Flows (millions of dollars)

	Good State	Bad State
Cash flow before salaries	$140	$120
Salaries	−100	−100
Cash flow before taxes	40	20
Taxes @ 50%	−20	−10
Net cash flow	$ 20	$ 10

Table 18.12   Call Option Payouts at Time 1

	Good State	Bad State
Share price	$2.00	$1.00
Less the exercise price	−1.50	−1.50
Payout	$0.50	$0.00

Table 18.13   The Subsidiary Balance Sheet (millions of dollars)

Beginning		Good State		Bad State	
Assets $15	Debt $12.5	Assets $15	Debt $15	Assets $10	Debt $10
	Equity 2.5		Equity 0		Equity 0
Total $15	Total $15.0	Total $15	Total $15	Total $10	Total $10

If the probability of the good state is .5 and if we assume the discount rate is zero, then the present value of the firm in this one-period example is $15 million. Assume that there are 10 million shares outstanding so that the price per share is $1.50. An at-the-money call option will sell for $0.25, the average of its good and bad state payouts, as shown in Table 18.12.

Now, suppose the company offers managers an SAR plan that is tax neutral from the company's point of view. What will it look like? The plan will have a present value of $2.5 million and will involve the issue of 10 million at-the-money options to management. In return, management agrees to reduce its salary by $2.5 million—an equal dollar amount.

It is assumed that the firm established a subsidiary to handle the potential liability created by the SAR plan. The subsidiary will have $2.5 million in equity (the salary expense reduction) and will borrow $12.5 million via a zero coupon bond with a face value of $15 million. The $15 million in cash is used to purchase 10 million shares of stock. Table 18.13 shows the current balance sheet of the subsidiary as well as its balance sheets given the good and bad states of nature. If the good state occurs, the options will be exercised whereupon the subsidiary receives $15 million in cash and delivers stock worth $20 million. The $15 million in cash is used to pay off the loan, and the equity in the subsidiary is worthless, leaving the parent firm with a $2.5 million tax-deductible loss. If the bad state occurs, the options will not be exercised, and the stock held by the subsidiary will be worth $10 million and turned over to the bank. The equity in the subsidiary will be worthless, once again leaving the parent with a $2.5 million tax-deductible loss. The bank lends $12.5 million, and its expected payoff is $12.5 million. The parent firm ends up with a $2.5 million loss either way.

Table 18.14 shows the firm's expected cash flows given the terms of the option plan, and its payoffs from the subsidiary. Comparing the net cash flow of Tables 18.14 and 18.11 we see that the firm is completely indifferent between the two alternatives.[21]

---

[21] Note that we have not argued that the firm will use the tax shelter created if it can write off the difference between the stock price and the exercise price in the good state of nature.

Table 18.14   The Firm's Cash Flow, Given the SAR Plan (millions of dollars)

	Good State	Bad State
Cash flow before salaries	$140.0	$120.0
Salaries	−97.5	−97.5
Cash flow after salaries	42.5	22.5
Investment loss	−2.5	−2.5
Cash flow before taxes	40.0	20.0
Taxes	−20.0	−10.0
Net cash flow	$ 20.0	$ 10.0

From the management perspective, after-tax salary could be invested in stock options in order to have the same pattern of future risky payoffs. The main advantage of the option plan is that taxes are deferred. Given that the plan is tax neutral from the firm's perspective and tax preferred by management, there is a strong incentive to adopt stock option plans.

Management whose compensation is based on straight salary cannot benefit from undertaking risky positive net present value projects unless their salaries are adjusted *ex post* to reflect good decisions. Stock option plans can help to correct this under-investment problem because the options, and the stock, are immediately more valuable when risky positive net present value projects are initiated. There are several possible drawbacks, however. Management cannot easily diversify the greater firm-specific risk imposed by stock option plans and may require a higher expected level of compensation. From the shareholders' point of view the cost of the higher expected compensation may offset the benefit of reducing the underinvestment problem. Furthermore, stock option plans are not protected against dividend payments. This produces reluctance in management to propose dividend increases when they may otherwise be warranted. Shareholders may view this as an additional cost. Finally, if the managers increase the firm's financial leverage, the resulting increase in the variability of the stock will increase the value of management's stock options.

Studies of the announcement effect of the inception of management stock option plans indicate that shareholders react favorably. They believe that the plans are a net benefit. Larcker [1983] finds a significantly positive return on the day following receipt of the first shareholder proxy statement. Brickley, Bhagat, and Lease [1985] find a significant positive 2.4% cumulative return between the board of directors meeting and the Security and Exchange Commission stamp date for the proxy statement. Lemgruber [1986] used monthly data for a sample of 119 firms with no other information in their proxy statements except for the election of board members. For the interval between the board meeting and the release of the proxy statement, he found a significant 2.7% abnormal return.

That the market reacts favorably to the inception of executive stock option compensation plans is consistent with the benefits of the plan exceeding its costs from the shareholders' point of view. Call this the *incentive hypotheses*. It is also consistent with a *signaling hypothesis*. If managers have superior information concerning the future prospects of the firm, they would want to initiate an executive stock option plan when they think the firm will be doing well. The market would respond favorably to their action. Positive announcement effects are also consistent with a *tax hypothesis*, namely, that the after-tax payoffs of a salary plus stock option plan dominate those for a salary and bonus plan. Consequently, the value of the firm will rise following the inception of a stock option plan because total costs fall.

It is not easy to separate the three aforementioned hypotheses. They all predict the observed positive market reaction to the inception of a stock option plan. They do, however, have differences in their predictions about management behavior. For example, the incentive hypothesis predicts greater investment, and higher leverage once the plan is started. The signaling and tax hypotheses predict greater earnings. All three hypotheses predict lower dividend payout after the plan begins. The empirical evidence seems to lend little support to the idea that there are strong incentive effects associated with the start of stock option plans. Lemgruber [1986] found no significant changes in the rate of investment, in financial leverage, or in the variance of the firm's stock price. Lambert and Larcker [1984] found the variance decreased. Lemgruber also found significant decreases in dividend payout following the beginning of stock option plans. Tehranian and Waegelein [1985] find that abnormal returns after the adoption of short-term compensation plans are associated with positive unexpected earnings. In sum, these results seem to suggest that stock option plans are adopted more for tax or signaling reasons than to reduce agency costs between owners and managers.

3. Plans Based on Relative Performance

Arguably, one drawback of plans tied to changes in the stock price is that not all stock price movements are attributable to management performance. For example, imagine an industry with 10 competitors and suppose that your company fell from third place to ninth place based on return on assets. Yet because of a strong bull market, your firm's share price increased 50%. Given a stock option plan, your managers would receive a positive reward for relatively poor performance. The stock price rose in spite of their efforts. The opposite scenario is also possible. Your firm may do extremely well in a depressed economy, but managers would not be rewarded because their options finished out of the money. Should management be rewarded on relative performance? It is hard to say. One argument against rewards based on relative performance is that resources should not be committed to losing situations. Managers with good relative performance in declining industries should not be encouraged to invest new capital in an effort to record good relative performance— especially if the investments have negative net present value.

Economic theory says that labor should be paid its marginal product. But as a practical matter, how is the marginal product of management to be measured? How does one separate value created by management decisions from value created (or destroyed) by movements in external factors such as interest rate changes, changes in tax rates, or changes in the foreign exchange rate? Were it possible to model the value of the firm as it is at a given point of time, then separate changes in the valuation parameters caused by management from those caused by external factors, it would be possible to measure the marginal product of management and reward management appropriately. Although there have been some attempts to accomplish this task, we still have no accurate guidelines.[22]

SUMMARY

This chapter has used the knowledge base provided earlier in the book to examine a number of topical issues. It was necessary to understand discounting, the risk-return trade-off, option pricing, and capital structure before tackling the practical issues covered here—pension fund management, interest rate swaps, going-private and leveraged buyout transactions, and executive compensation schemes. None of these topics has been completely researched, and therefore, all leave us with unanswered questions. However, they are all timely and of current interest to practitioners.

PROBLEM SET

18.1 Table 18.2 shows a pension fund income statement and balance sheet. Where in the balance sheet would you place the following items:

a) $500 million in U.S. government bonds that are held in trust for the members of the pension plan?

b) An amount of $200 per month that the firm plans to put aside to pay the pension of an existing employee?

c) A $15,000 per year pension that you expect to pay to an employee who is currently not vested?

d) A $10,000 per year pension that the plan is currently paying to a retired employee?

18.2 Suppose that your firm is Aaa-rated and can borrow five-year fixed rate debt at 12% and floating rate debt at the T-bill rate plus $\frac{1}{4}$%, i.e., at $9\frac{1}{4}$%. You are approached by a Baa-rated firm that can borrow five-year fixed rate debt at 13% and floating rate debt at the T-bill rate plus $\frac{3}{4}$%. The Baa firm wants to swap $100 million of its floating rate debt for an equivalent amount of your fixed rate debt. It is willing to pay $12\frac{1}{2}$% to you on the fixed rate debt and asks that you pay the T-bill rate plus $\frac{3}{4}$% on its floating rate debt. Should you do the deal?

18.3 Assume a binomial process for changes in the risk-free rate, with annual movements of $u = 1.3$ and $d = .7$. This period's rate is 8% and has just moved down from 11.4286%. What is the market value of a three-year variable rate loan where the variable rate is set as the arithmetic average of this period's rate and last period's rate? How would your answer change if the interest rate had just moved up from 6.1538% instead of down?

---

[22] For example, see Rappaport [1986, Chapter 8].

18.4 You are trying to structure a leveraged buyout (LBO) of an all-equity firm estimated to be worth $100 million. Its equity beta is .8 and the CAPM market risk premium is 6.2%. The deal is expected to be financed with 80% debt and will require a 50% premium above market. In other words, the firm will cost $150 million and you expect to borrow $120 million. The firm's tax rate is $41\frac{2}{3}\%$. The first $30 million is a five-year zero coupon loan designed to yield 10% to maturity. The next $90 million is zero coupon subordinated debt. If the standard deviation of return on the firm's assets is 34% per year, the five-year risk-free rate is 9%, and you expect zero dividend payout, what yield to maturity will be required on the subordinated debt if its face value is $267.065 million? What will the cost of equity be?

REFERENCES

American Institute of Certified Public Accountants, *Accounting Trends and Techniques*, N.Y.: AICPA, 1986.

Arnold, T., "How to Do Interest Rate Swaps," *Harvard Business Review*, September–October 1984, 96–101.

Bagehot, W. (pseud.), "Risk and Reward in Corporate Pension Funds," *Financial Analysts Journal*, January–February 1972, 80–84.

Bank Administration Institute, *Measuring the Investment Performance of Pension Plans*. BAI, Park Ridge, Ill., 1968.

Bicksler, J., and A. Chen, "The Integration of Insurance and Taxes in Corporate Pension Strategy," *Journal of Finance*, July 1985, 943–955.

———, "An Economic Analysis of Interest Rate Swaps," *Journal of Finance*, July 1986, 645–655.

Black, F. "The Tax Consequences of Long-run Pension Policy," *Financial Analysts Journal*, July–August 1980, 21–28.

Brickley, J.; S. Bhagat; and R. Lease, "The Impact of Long-range Managerial Compensation Plans on Shareholders' Wealth," *Journal of Accounting and Economics*, April 1985, 115–129.

Brindisi, L., Jr., "Creating Shareholder Value: A New Mission for Executive Compensation," *Midland Corporate Finance Journal*, Winter 1985, 56–66.

Bulow, J.; M. Scholes; and P. Manell, "Economic Implications of ERISA," Working paper, Graduate School of Business, University of Chicago, March 1982.

Copeland, T., "An Economic Approach to Pension Fund Management," *Midland Corporate Finance Journal*, Spring 1984, 26–39.

Cornell, B., "Pricing Interest Rate Swaps: Theory and Empirical Evidence," Working paper, Anderson Graduate School of Management, UCLA, April 1986.

Coughlan, A., and R. Schmidt, "Executive Compensation, Management Takeover, and Firm Performance: An Empirical Investigation," *Journal of Accounting and Economics*, April 1985, 43–66.

Cox, J.; J. Ingersoll; and S. Ross, "An Analysis of Variable Rate Loan Contracts," *Journal of Finance*, May 1980, 389–403.

Davidson, S.; C. Stickney; and R. Weil, *Intermediate Accounting*. Dryden Press, Hinsdale, Ill., 1980.

DeAngelo, H., and L. DeAngelo, "Management Buyouts of Publicly Traded Corporations," *Financial Analysts Journal*, May–June 1987, 38–48.

DeAngelo, H., L. De Angelo, and E. Rice, "Going Private: Minority Freezeouts and Stockholder Wealth," *Journal of Law and Economics*, October 1984, 367–401.

DeAngelo, L., "Accounting Numbers as Market Valuation Substitutes: A Study of Management Buyouts of Public Stockholders," *Accounting Review*, July 1986, 400–420.

Dreher, W., "Alternatives Available under APB No. 8: An Actuary's View," *Journal of Accountancy*, September 1967, 37–51.

Fama, E., "Agency Problems and the Theory of the Firm," *Journal of Political Economics*, April 1980, 288–307.

Feldstein, M., and S. Seligman, "Pension Funding, Share Prices and National Savings," *Journal of Finance*, September 1981, 801–824.

Gatto, M.; R. Geske; R. Litzenberger; and H. Sosin, "Mutual Fund Insurance," *Journal of Financial Economics*, September 1980, 283–317.

Haugen, R., and L. Senbet, "Resolving the Agency Costs of External Capital through Options," *Journal of Finance*, June 1981, 629–647.

Healy, P., "The Effect of Bonus Schemes on Accounting Decisions," *Journal of Accounting and Economics*, April 1985, 85–107.

Henderson, S., and J. Price, *Currency and Interest Rate Swaps*. Butterworths and Co. Ltd., London, 1984.

Hite, G., and M. Long, "Taxes and Executive Stock Options," *Journal of Accounting and Economics*," July 1982, 3–14.

Jay, W., "Long-term Incentives for Management, Part 2: What's New in Stock Option and Appreciation Right Plans," *Compensation Review*, Third Quarter 1980, 21–33.

Jensen, M., "Takeovers: Folklore and Science," *Harvard Business Review*, November–December 1984, 109–121.

———, "The Takeover Controversy: Analysis and Evidence," in Coffee, Lowenstein, and Rose-Ackerman, eds., *Takeovers and Contests for Corporate Control*. Oxford University Press, Oxford, 1987.

Korpprasch, R.; J. MacFarlane; D. Ross; and J. Showers, "The Interest Rate Swap Market: Yield Mathematics, Terminology and Conventions," Salomon Brothers Inc., June 1985.

Lambert, R., and D. Larcker, "Executive Compensation, Corporate Decision-making and Shareholder Wealth: A Review of the Evidence," *Midland Corporate Finance Journal*, Winter 1985, 6–22.

———, "Executive Compensation Effects of Large Corporate Acquisitions," Working paper, Northwestern University, 1984.

Landsman, W., "An Investigation of Pension Fund Property Rights," Ph.D. dissertation, Stanford University, 1984.

Larcker, D., "The Association between Performance Plan Adoption and Corporate Capital Investment," *Journal of Accounting and Economics*, April 1983, 3–30.

Lembgruber, E., "Stock Option Plans and Corporate Behavior," Ph.D. dissertation, University of California at Los Angeles, 1986.

Marcus, A., "Spinoff/Terminations and the Value of Pension Insurance," *Journal of Finance*, July 1985, 911–924.

Miller, M., and M. Scholes, "Executive Compensation, Taxes, and Incentives in Financial Economics," in *Financial Economics: Essays in Honor of Paul Cootner*. W. F. Sharpe and C. M. Cootner, eds., Englewood Cliffs, New Jersey: Prentice-Hall, 1982, 179–201.

Murphy, K., "Corporate Performance and Managerial Remuneration, *Journal of Accounting and Economics*," April 1985, 11–42.

Narayanan, M., "Managerial Incentives for Short-term Results," *Journal of Finance*, December 1985, 1469–1484.

Pesando, J., "The Usefulness of the Wind-up Measure of Pension Liabilities: A Labor Market Perspective," *Journal of Finance*, July 1985, 927–940.

Ramaswamy, K., and S. Sundaresan, "The Valuation of Floating Rate Instruments," *Journal of Financial Economics*, December 1986, 251–272

Rappaport, A., *Creating Shareholder Value*. Free Press, Macmillan Inc., New York, 1986.

Regan, P., "Reasons for the Improving Pension Fund Figures," *Financial Analysts Journal*, March–April 1982, 14–15.

Rich, J., and E. Bergsma, "Pay Executives to Create Wealth," *Chief Executive*, Autumn 1982.

Ross, I., "How the Champs Do Leveraged Buyouts," *Fortune*, January 23, 1984, 70–72, 74, 78.

Sharpe, W., "Corporate Pension Funding Policy," *Journal of Financial Economics*, June 1976, 183–194.

Smith, C., Jr., C. Smithson; and L. Wakeman, "The Evolving Market for Swaps," *Midland Corporate Finance Review*, Spring 1986, 16–31.

Smith, C., Jr., and R. Watts, "Incentive and Tax Effects of Executive Compensation Plans," *Australian Journal of Management*, 1982, 139–157.

Stowe, J., and M. Walker, "The Effect of Executive Stock Options on Corporate Financial Decisions," *Journal of Financial Research*, Spring 1980, 69–83.

Tehranian, H., and J. Waegelein, "Market Reaction to Short-term Executive Compensation Plan Adoption," *Journal of Accounting and Economics*, April 1985, 131–144.

Tepper, I., "Taxation and Corporate Pension Policy," *Journal of Finance*, March 1981, 1–13.

———, "The Future of Private Pension Funding," *Financial Analysts Journal*, 1982, 25–31.

———, and A. Affleck, "Pension Plan Liabilities and Corporate Financial Strategies," *Journal of Finance*, December 1974, 1549–1564.

Treynor, J., "The Principles of Corporate Pension Finance," *Journal of Finance*, May 1977, 627–638.

———; W. Priest; and Regan, P., *The Financial Reality of Funding under ERISA*, Dow Jones–Irwin Inc., Homewood, Ill., 1976.

Warner, J., "Stock Market Reaction to Management Incentive Plan Adoption: An Overview," *Journal of Accounting and Economics*, April 1985, 145–149.

Westerfield, R., and W. Marshall, "Pension Funding Decisions and Corporate Shareholder Value: A New Model and Some Empirical Results," mimeo, September 1983.

19

Corporate takeovers offer a field day for speculators and traders in our "Casino Society"; they strip away equity, build up shaky debt, and destabilize markets.

F. G. Rohatyn, "Needed: Restraints on the Takeover Mania," *Challenge*, May–June 1986, 30.

Mergers, Restructuring, and Corporate Control: Theory

A. INTRODUCTION

Takeovers and related activities in the 1980s are much broader in scope and raise more fundamental issues than previous merger movements. The daily newspapers are filled with a series of case studies of mergers and acquisitions (M&A's), tender offers (both friendly and hostile), spinoffs and divestitures, corporate restructuring, changes in ownership structures, and struggles for corporate control. In recent years, leverage ratios for some companies have increased, and newer forms of financing have proliferated, including an increase in the use of bonds with ratings below the first two levels of A and B (usually a C rating, referred to as *junk bonds*). Thus the traditional subject of M&A's has been expanded to include takeovers and related issues of corporate restructuring, corporate control, and changes in the ownership structure of firms, as suggested by the changed title of this chapter. An overview of the nature of the various activities will first be presented, then some will be analyzed in greater depth.

676

B. CORPORATE RESTRUCTURING AND CONTROL

Table 19.1 presents a listing of the many forms of corporate activities that have been filling the pages of both the popular and academic literature in recent years. The nature of each of the forms of activity will be briefly summarized to convey what is involved.

1. Expansion

Under expansion, we include mergers, tender offers, and joint ventures. Mergers and acquisitions have long played an important role in the growth of firms. Growth is generally viewed as vital to the well-being of a firm. Among other reasons, growth is needed for a firm to compete for the best managerial talent by offering rapid promotions and broadened responsibilities. Without a continued inflow of able executives, the firm is likely to decline in efficiency and value.

From a legal standpoint there are many distinctions between types of mergers and combinations. Most generally, *merger* means any transaction that forms one economic unit from two or more previous ones.

Table 19.1   Corporate Restructuring and Control

I. Expansion
   Mergers and acquisitions
   Tender offers
   Joint ventures

II. Sell-offs
   Spinoffs
      Splitoffs
      Splitups
   Divestitures
      Equity carve-outs

III. Corporate control
   Premium buybacks
   Standstill agreements
   Antitakeover amendments
   Proxy contests

IV. Changes in ownership structure
   Exchange offers
   Share repurchases
   Going private
   Leveraged buyouts

Several alternative forms of merger activity have been distinguished. A *horizontal merger* involves two firms operating in the same kind of business activity. Thus a merger between two steel firms would represent a horizontal merger. *Vertical mergers* involve different stages of production operations. In the oil industry distinctions are made between exploration and production activity, refining operations, and marketing to the ultimate consumer. In the pharmaceutical industry one could distinguish between research and the development of new drugs, the production of drugs, and the marketing of drug products through retail drugstores. *Conglomerate mergers* involve firms engaged in unrelated types of business activity. Thus the merger between Mobil Oil and Montgomery Ward was generally regarded as a conglomerate merger. Among conglomerate mergers three types have been distinguished. Product extension mergers broaden the product lines of firms. For example, in the Mobil-Ward merger some might view the retailing operations of Ward as an extension of the retail petroleum product marketing experience of Mobil. A geographic market extension merger involves two firms whose operations had been conducted in nonoverlapping geographic areas. Finally, a pure conglomerate merger involves unrelated business activities that would not qualify as either product extension or market extension mergers.

Another distinction, from an accounting standpoint, is between a *purchase* and a *pooling of interest*. A purchase generally refers to the acquisition of a much smaller entity, which is absorbed into the acquiring firm. The excess of the purchase price of the equity obtained over its book value is recorded as goodwill on the balance sheet of the acquiring company. A pooling of interest represents the joining of two firms of not greatly unequal size, followed by operations in which their identities are continued to a considerable degree. In pooling of interest accounting the total assets of the surviving firm is the sum of the total assets of the components. Any excess of market price paid over the book value of the equity acquired is reflected in adjustments to the net worth accounts of the surviving firm.

In a tender offer, one party takes the initiative in making a monetary offer directly to the shareholders of the target firm, with or without the approval of the board of directors. Thus the acquiring firm (the bidder) makes an offer to the stockholders of the firm it is seeking to control (the target) to submit or tender their shares in exchange for a specified price, expressed in cash or securities.

Joint ventures involve the intersection of only a small fraction of the activities of the companies involved and for limited duration of 10 to 15 years or less. They may represent a separate entity in which each of the parties makes cash and other forms of investments.

2. Selloffs

Several distinct types of selloffs should be distinguished. The two major types are (1) spinoffs and (2) divestitures. A spinoff creates a separate new legal entity; its shares are distributed on a pro rata basis to existing shareholders of the parent company. Thus existing stockholders have the same proportion of ownership in the new entity as in the original firm. There is, however, a separation of control, and over time, the new entity as a separate decision-making unit may develop policies and strategies different from those of the original parent. Note that no cash is received by the original parent. In some sense a spinoff represents a form of a dividend to existing shareholders. A variation of a spinoff is the splitoff, in which a portion of existing shareholders receive stock in a subsidiary in exchange for parent company stock. Still a different variation on the spinoff is a splitup, in which the entire firm is broken up into a series of spinoffs, so that the parent no longer exists and only the new offspring survive.

In contrast to the class of spinoffs in which only shares are transferred or exchanged is another group of transactions in which cash comes in to the firm—divestitures. Basically, a divestiture involves the sale of a portion of the firm to an outside third party. Cash or equivalent consideration is received by the divesting firm. Typically the buyer is an existing firm, so that no new legal entity results. It simply represents a form of expansion on the part of the buying firm. A variation on divestiture is the equity carve-out. An equity carve-out involves the sale of a portion of the firm via an equity offering to outsiders. In other words new shares of equity are sold to outsiders, which give them ownership of a portion of the previously existing firm. A new legal entity is created. The equity holders in the new entity need not be the same as the equity holders in the original seller. A new control group is immediately created.

The distinctions between these various forms of spinoffs are somewhat arbitrary, and some writers view them all as simply various forms of stock dividends, except for transactions that involve the sale of shares to parties other than existing shareholders.

3. Corporate Control

The third group of activities in Table 19.1 we have referred to as *corporate control*. Premium buybacks represent the repurchase of a substantial stockholder's ownership interest at a premium above the market price (called *greenmail*). Often in connection with such buybacks, a standstill agreement is written. These represent voluntary contracts in which the stockholder who is bought out agrees not to make further investments in the company in the future. When a standstill agreement is made without a buyback, the substantial stockholder simply agrees not to increase his or her ownership, which presumably would put that individual in an effective control position.

Antitakeover amendments are changes in the corporate bylaws to make an acquisition of the company more difficult or more expensive. These include (1) supermajority voting provisions, requiring a percentage (e.g., 80%) of stockholders to approve a merger; (2) staggered terms for directors, which can delay change of control for a number of years; (3) golden parachutes, which award large termination payments to existing management if control of the firm is changed and management is terminated; and (4) "poison pill" provisions, which give present stockholders the right to buy at a substantial discount the shares of a successor company formed by a stock takeover.

In a proxy contest an outside group seeks to obtain representation on the firm's board of directors. The outsiders are referred to as "dissidents" or "insurgents," who seek to reduce the control position of the "incumbents" or existing board of directors. Since the management of a firm often has effective control of the board of directors, proxy contests are often regarded as directed against the existing management.

4. Changes in Ownership Structure

Changes in ownership structure represent the fourth group of restructuring activities in Table 19.1. One form is through exchange offers, which may be the exchange of debt or preferred stock for common stock or, conversely, of common stock for the more senior claims. Exchanging debt for common stock increases leverage; exchanging common stock for debt decreases leverage.

A second form is share repurchase, which simply means that the corporation buys back some fraction of its outstanding shares of common stock, in some cases via "self-tender offers." The percentage of shares purchased may be small or substantial. If the latter the effect may be to change the control structure in the firm. For example, it has been said that the substantial share repurchase activity by Teledyne, Inc., has increased the effective control position of H. E. Singleton, the chairman and chief executive officer of the company. The company purchased shares from other shareholders, but Singleton did not reduce his already substantial holdings. The fixed holdings of Singleton thereby became a larger percentage of the new reduced company total.

In a "going-private" transaction, the entire equity interest in a previously public corporation is purchased by a small group of investors. The firm is no longer subject to the regulations of the Securities and Exchange Commission, whose purpose is to protect public investors. Going-private transactions typically include members of the incumbent management group, who obtain a substantial proportion of the equity ownership of the newly private company. Usually, a small group of outside investors provides funds and, typically, secures representation on the private company's board of directors. These outside investors also arrange other financing from third-party investors. When financing from third parties involves substantial borrowing by the private company, such transactions are referred to as *leveraged buyouts* (LBOs), discussed in Chapter 18.

Having described briefly each form of corporate restructuring and control, we now analyze some important forms in greater depth and explain the theory that seeks to provide a reason for the activity. We first take up the broad area of mergers and acquisitions (tender offers or takeover activity).

C. RECENT DEVELOPMENTS IN M&A ACTIVITY

Merger activity has been characterized by dramatic bidding wars involving tender offers and mergers of very substantial size. Notable was du Pont's November 1981 acquisition of Conoco for over $7.5 billion, in which du Pont outbid Seagram and Mobil. In November 1982 U.S. Steel outbid Mobil to obtain Marathon Oil for about $6.5 billion. Notable deals in 1984, some of which involved bidding contests, were the Chevron takeover of Gulf Oil for $13.2 billion and the Texaco acquisition of Getty Oil for $10.1 billion (the litigation with Pennzoil over this transaction had reached the U.S. Supreme Court in June 1986). Several notable transactions in 1984 did not involve oil companies. Nestlé (a Swiss company) acquired the Carnation Company for $2.9 billion. Beatrice bought Esmark for $2.5 billion and then itself was the subject of a leveraged buyout with a value of $5.4 billion by a group led by Kohlberg-Kravis. General Motors bought Electronic Data Systems in 1984 for $2.5 billion and Hughes Aircraft in 1985 for $5.0 billion. Other dramatic deals in 1985 included General Electric's purchase of RCA for $6.0 billion, Philip Morris of General Foods for $5.6 billion, R. J. Reynolds of Nabisco for $4.9 billion, Allied Chemical of Signal for $4.5 billion, and Baxter Travenol of American Hospital Supply for $3.7 billion.

Table 19.2 places these individual deals in broader perspective. Column (1) shows the total dollar value paid where a purchase price was disclosed; this would of course

Table 19.2   Merger Activity: The Grimm Series

	(1)	(2)	(3)	(4)	(5)	(6)
			Number of Transactions Valued at			1972
	Total Dollar Value Paid[a]		$100MM	$1,000MM	GNP Deflator	Constant Dollar
Year	($ billion)	Total[b]	or more	or more	(1972 = 100)	Consideration
1968	$ 43.6	4462	46	—	82.5	52.8
1969	23.7	6107	24	—	86.8	27.3
1970	16.4	5152	10	1	91.4	17.9
1971	12.6	4608	7	—	96.0	13.1
1972	16.7	4801	15	—	100.0	16.7
1973	16.7	4040	28	—	105.7	15.8
1974	12.4	2861	15	—	115.1	10.8
1975	11.8	2297	14	1	125.8	9.4
1976	20.0	2276	39	1	132.1	15.1
1977	21.9	2224	41	—	140.1	15.6
1978	34.2	2106	80	1	150.4	22.7
1979	43.5	2128	83	3	163.4	26.6
1980	44.3	1889	94	4	178.6	24.8
1981	82.6	2395	113	12	195.5	42.2
1982	53.8	2346	116	6	207.2	26.0
1983	73.1	2533	138	11	215.3	34.0
1984	122.2	2543	200	18	223.4	54.7
1985	179.6	3001	270	36	231.4	77.6

[a] Based on the number of transactions that disclosed a purchase price.

[b] Total: Net merger-acquisition announcements. The W. T. Grimm & Co. Research Department records publicly announced formal transfers of ownership of at least 10% of a company's assets or equity where the purchase price is at least $500,000, and where one of the parties is a U.S. company. These transactions are recorded as they are announced, not as they are completed. Canceled transactions are deducted from total announcements in the period in which the cancellation occurred, resulting in net merger-acquisition announcements for that period.

Columns (1–4): from W. T. Grimm & Co., *Mergerstat Review 1985*; column (5): from U.S. Department of Commerce; column (6): column (1) divided by column (5).

Table 19.3   Divestitures, 1966–1985

Year	Number	Percentage of All Transactions	Year	Number	Percentage of All Transactions
1966	264	11%	1975	1236	54%
1967	328	11	1976	1204	53
1968	557	12	1977	1002	45
1969	801	13	1978	820	39
1970	1401	27	1979	752	35
1971	1920	42	1980	666	35
1972	1770	37	1981	830	35
1973	1557	39	1982	875	37
1974	1331	47	1983	932	37
			1984	900	36
			1985	1237	41

From W. T. Grimm & Co., *Mergerstat Review 1985*, Chicago, 1986.

include all the large transactions. Column (2) shows that the net number of merger-acquisition announcements in 1985 was only about half the level of 1969. However, because the number of transactions valued at $100 million or more or $1 billion or more was much larger in later years, the constant dollar consideration involved in mergers was higher in 1985 than in 1968 or 1969, the previous high years. In fact it was not until 1984 that the constant dollar consideration in mergers exceeded the level that had been reached in 1968—and by a small margin at that. However, during 1985 the constant dollar consideration in mergers-acquisitions was almost 50% higher than the level of 1968. The year 1985 was truly a boom year in merger-acquisition activity.

Over the years, merger and acquisition activity has been highly correlated with plant and equipment expenditures averaging mostly between 16% and 20% of internal capital investments. In relation to total corporate assets, merger activity during an average year has represented under 1% of total corporate assets. Expressed in relation to the total market value of equities, merger and acquisition activity measured by the market value of acquired firms has been under 5% of the total market value of all equities. However, it has been estimated that 1984–1986 equity values that have disappeared as a consequence of merger activity totaled $110 billion per year. Beginning in the early 1970s, corporate divestitures or partial sales have represented from 40% to 50% of total merger and acquisition activities (see Table 19.3). This suggests that mergers and acquisitions perform a role in the reallocation of resources in the economy.

D. THEORIES OF M&A ACTIVITY

We have now viewed the various forms of corporate restructuring and control. We have also presented data on the amount of merger-acquisition activity. We will now seek to move on to understand the theories or rationale for mergers, tender offers, and joint ventures. We have grouped these theories into five major areas:

1. Efficiency,
2. Information,
3. Agency problems,
4. Market power, and
5. Taxes.

Each of these five groups of theories will be briefly discussed.

1. Efficiency Explanations

Efficiency theories are the most optimistic about the potential of mergers for social benefits. The most general theory involves differential efficiency. In theory, if the management of firm A is more efficient than the management of firm B, and if after firm A acquires firm B, the efficiency of firm B is brought up to the level of efficiency of firm A, efficiency is increased by merger. Note that this would be a social gain as well as a private gain. The level of efficiency in the economy would be raised by such mergers.

One difficulty in the differential efficiency theory is that if carried to its extreme, it would result in only one firm in the economy, indeed in the world—the firm with the greatest managerial efficiency. Clearly, problems of coordination in the firm would arise before that result was reached. Hence another formulation of the differential efficiency theory of mergers is that there are always many firms that exhibit below-average efficiency or that are not operating up to their potentials, however defined. It is further suggested that firms operating in similar kinds of business activity would be most likely to be the potential acquirers. They would have the background for detecting below-average or less-than-full-potential performance and have the managerial know-how for improving the performance of the acquired firm. The latter scenario is plausible, but in practice the acquiring firms may be overoptimistic in their judgments of their impact on the performance of the acquired firms. As a consequence, they may either pay too much for the acquired firm or fail to improve its performance to the degree reflected in the acquisition value placed upon it. (See Roll's [1986] hubris hypothesis under "Agency Problems" below.)

The inefficient management theory may be difficult to distinguish from the differential efficiency theory discussed above or the agency problem treated below. In one sense inefficient management is simply not performing up to its potential. Another control group might be able to manage the assets of this area of activity more effectively. Or inefficient management may simply represent management that is inept in some absolute sense. Almost anyone could do better. If so, this would provide a rationale for conglomerate mergers. The differential efficiency theory is more likely to involve management that is superior because it has experience in a particular line of business activity. The differential efficiency theory is more likely to be a basis for horizontal mergers. The inefficient management theory could be a basis for unrelated mergers.

Efficiency theories also include the possibility of achieving some form of synergy. If synergy occurs the value of the combined firm, V_{AB}, exceeds the value of the individual firms brought together by the mergers. With synergy,

$$V_{AB} > V_A + V_B.$$

Because much of the theoretical literature was stimulated in response to the dramatic conglomerate merger movement of the 1960s and because true social gains from conglomerate mergers were not readily perceived, much of the formal analysis in the scholarly literature assumed no synergy:

$$V_{AB} = V_A + V_B.$$

Myers [1968], Schall [1972], and Mossin [1973], in the spirit of the earlier Modigliani-Miller (M-M) [1958] formulation, have all argued that value is conserved (value additivity obtains) under addition of income streams (mergers). Nielsen [1974] pointed out that they utilized a partial equilibrium approach in which prices and other parameters are assumed to be constant. Nielsen also called attention to the underlying assumption that the capital markets are complete and perfect, and to the further assumption that the equilibrium allocation of income (hence also the marginal utilities of all investors) is invariant with respect to a change in the number of trading instruments due to merger. The conditions for value additivity are identical to those required for the M-M propositions. Thus at the theoretical level the conditions under which value is conserved (even assuming the absence of synergy) are more restrictive than generally acknowledged.

Nevertheless, the dominant theme in the theoretical literature is that the value-additivity principle holds in still another setting, the area of combining business entities through mergers or acquisitions. Much of the journal literature has sought to determine whether, in the absence of synergy, any theoretical justification for a merger could be found. However, the justification for mergers given by the executives engaging in mergers—and by some of the general literature as well—was that there were at least potential real gains from combining business firms. These arguments are stated in various forms, but implicitly they all depend on one condition—that operating economies of scale may be achieved. This theory is based on a number of major assumptions. It assumes that economies of scale do exist in the industry and that prior to the merger, the firms are operating at levels of activity that fall short of achieving the potentials for economies of scale.

Basically, economies of scale involve "indivisibilities," such as people, equipment, and overhead, which provide increasing returns if spread over a larger number of units of output. Thus in manufacturing operations, heavy investments in plant and equipment typically produce such economies. For example, costly machinery such as the large presses used to produce automobile bodies requires optimal utilization. Similarly, in the area of financing, data on flotation costs indicate that the cost of floating a larger issue amounts to a smaller percentage of the issue floated because the fixed costs of investigation and compliance with SEC regulations are spread over a larger dollar amount. (Financial synergy also encompasses the potential for achieving a lower cost of capital as a result of the reduced risk of bankruptcy when imperfectly correlated cash flow streams are joined.) And the same principle applies to the research and development (R & D) departments of chemical and pharmaceutical companies, which often have to have a large staff of highly competent scientists who, if given the opportunity, could develop and oversee a larger number of product areas. Finally, in marketing, having one organization cover the entire United States may yield economies of scale because of the increase in the ratio of calling-on-customer time to traveling time, which in turn is due to the higher density of customers who can be called on by the same number of salesmen.

One potential problem in merging firms with existing organizations is the question of how to combine and coordinate the good parts of the organizations and eliminate what is not required. Often the merger announcement will say that firm *A* is strong in research and development but weak in marketing, whereas firm *B* is strong in marketing but weak in R & D, and the two firms combined will complement each other. Analytically, this implies underutilization of some existing factors and inadequate investment in other factors of production. (Since the economies are jointly achieved, the assignment of the contributions of each firm to the merger is difficult both in theory and in practice.)

Economies in production, research, marketing, or finance are sometimes referred to as economies in the specific management functions. It has also been suggested that economies may be achieved in the generic management activity such as the planning and control functions of the firm. It is argued that firms of even moderate size need at least a minimum number of corporate officers. The corporate staff with capabilities for planning and control is therefore assumed to be underutilized to some degree. Acquisitions of firms just approaching the size where they need to add corporate staff would provide for fuller utilization of the corporate staff of the acquiring firm and avoid the necessity of adding such staff for the other firm.

A third area in which operating economies may be achieved is in vertical integration. Combining firms at different stages of an industry may achieve more efficient coordination of the different levels. The argument here is that costs of communication and various forms of bargaining can be avoided by vertical integration [Williamson, 1971; Arrow, 1975].

Efficiency theories provide a basis for mergers to achieve strategic planning goals in response to a rapidly changing environment. The literature on long-range strategic planning has exploded in recent years. This literature is related to diversification through mergers. The emphasis of strategic planning is on areas related to firms' environments and constituencies, not just operating decisions [Summer, 1980].

Earlier the emphasis of long-range strategic planning was on doing something about the so-called gap. When it is necessary to take action to close a prospective gap between the firm's objectives and its potential based on its present capabilities, some difficult choices must be made. For example, shall the firm attempt to change its environment or capabilities? What will be the costs of such changes? What are the risks and unknowns? What are the rewards if successful? What are the penalties of failure? Because the stakes are large, the iterative process is employed. A tentative decision is made. The process is repeated, perhaps from a different management function orientation, and at some point the total-enterprise point of view is brought to bear on the problem. Ultimately, decisions are made and must involve entrepreneurial judgments.

Alternatively, the emphasis may be on broader orientations to the effective alignment of the firm with its environments and constituencies. Different approaches may be emphasized. One approach seeks to choose products related to the needs or missions of the customer that will provide large markets. A second approach focuses on technological bottlenecks or barriers, the solution of which may create new markets. A third strategy chooses to be at the frontiers of technological capabilities on the theory that some attractive product fallout will result from such competence. A fourth approach emphasizes economic criteria including attractive growth prospects and appropriate stability.

Other things being equal, a preferred strategy is to move into a diversification program from the base of some existing capabilities or organizational strengths. Guidance may be obtained by answers to the following questions: Is there strength in the general management functions? Can the company provide staff expertise in a wide range of areas? Does the firm's financial planning and control effectiveness have a broad carryover? Are there specific capabilities such as research, marketing, and manufacturing that the firm is seeking to spread over a wider arena? [Chung and Weston, 1982].

It appears that the strategic planning approach to mergers implies either the possibilities of economies of scale or utilizing some unused capacity in the firm's present managerial capabilities. Another rationale is that by external diversification the firm acquires management skills for needed augmentation of its present capabilities. This still leaves some questions unanswered. New capabilities and new markets could be developed internally. It may be less risky to buy established organizations, but a competitive market for acquisitions implies that the net present value from such investments is likely to be zero. However, if these investments can be used as a base for still additional investments with positive net present values, the strategy may succeed.

2. Information Theories

The *information*, or *signaling*, *hypothesis* refers to the revaluation of the ownership shares of firms owing to new information that is generated during the merger negotiations, the tender offer process, or the joint venture planning. Alternative forms of the information hypothesis have been distinguished by Bradley, Desai, and Kim [1983]. One is the *kick-in-the-pants* explanation. Management is stimulated to implement a higher-valued operating strategy. A second is the *sitting-on-a-gold-mine hypothesis*. The negotiations or tendering activity may involve the dissemination of new information or lead the market to judge that the bidders have superior information. The market may then revalue previously "undervalued" shares.

Another aspect of the undervaluation theory is the difference in the position of a control group versus an individual investor. For example, in recent years the q-ratio has been running between .5 and .6. The q-ratio is the ratio of the market value of the firm's shares in relation to the replacement costs of the assets represented by these shares. Thus if a company wishes to obtain or add to capacity in producing a particular product, it can acquire the additional capacity more cheaply by buying a company that produces the product rather than building brick and mortar from scratch. If the q-ratio is .6 and if the average premium paid over market value is 50% (which is the average figure for recent years), the resulting purchase price is .6 times 1.5, which equals .9. This would mean that the average purchase price is still 10% below the current replacement costs of the assets acquired. This would provide a broad basis for the operation of the undervalued theory in recent years as the q-ratio has declined. Furthermore, for companies in natural resource industries, q-ratios have been as low as .2 because of the values of reserves in the ground. This provided a basis for even more substantial premiums where natural resource firms were involved in mergers. For example, although USX Corporation paid a substantial premium over market value in the Marathon merger, Marathon shareholders threatened suit because they stated that independent appraisals had estimated the current value of Marathon assets at more than double the price paid by USX Corporation. Of course, these appraisals were subject to considerable uncertainty.

3. Agency Problems

In their seminal paper, Jensen and Meckling [1976] formulated the implications of agency problems. An agency problem arises when managers own only a fraction of the ownership shares of the firm. This partial ownership may cause managers to work less vigorously than otherwise and/or to consume more perquisites (luxurious offices, company car, membership in clubs) because the majority owners bear most of the cost. Furthermore, the argument goes, in large corporations with widely dispersed ownership, there is not sufficient incentive for individual owners to expend the substantial resources required to monitor the behavior of managers. A number of compensation arrangements and the market for managers may mitigate the agency problem [Fama, 1980].

The agency problem theory of mergers has two aspects. On the one hand the threat of takeover may mitigate the agency problem by substituting for the need of individual shareholders to monitor the managers. The agency theory extends the previous work by Manne [1965]. Manne emphasized the market for corporate control and viewed mergers as a threat of takeover if a firm's management lagged in performance either because of inefficiency or because of agency problems.

On the other hand, mergers may be a manifestation of the agency problem rather than the solution. The "managerialism" explanation for mergers was set forth most fully by Mueller [1969]. Mueller hypothesizes that managers are motivated to increase the size of their firms further. He assumes that the compensation to managers is a function of the size of the firm, and he argues therefore that managers adopt a lower investment hurdle rate. But in a study critical of earlier evidence, Lewellen and Huntsman [1970] present findings that managers' compensation is significantly correlated with the firm's profit rate, not its level of sales. Thus the basic premise of the Mueller theory is doubtful.

Roll's [1986] *hubris hypothesis* also suggests that the agency problem is not checked by the control mechanisms above. *Hubris* is a Greek word meaning "animal spirits," with connotations of overexuberance and excess pride. Roll suggests that managers commit errors of overoptimism in evaluating potential merger candidates, thus bidding more than they should and transferring virtually all gains from the transaction to the target shareholders.

4. Market Power

One reason often given for a merger is that it will increase a firm's market share, but it is not clear how increasing the market share will achieve economies or synergies. If increasing the firm's market share simply means that the firm will be larger, then we are essentially talking about economies of scale, which we have already discussed. Increasing market share really means increasing the size of the firm *relative* to other firms in an industry. But it is not made clear why increasing the firm's relative size will provide economies or other social gains.

Indeed, this poses a challenge to the arguments for merger emphasizing economies of scale and vertical integration. These could also be achieved by the internal expansion of the firm. Why is the external acquisition of another firm necessary to achieve these economies if indeed they do exist? A number of possible explanations may be offered, such as acquiring a larger volume of operations sooner. But it is not clear whether the price required by the selling firm (the firm to be acquired) will really make the acquisition route the more economical method of expanding a firm's capacity either horizontally or vertically.

An objection that is often raised against permitting a firm to increase its market share by merger is that the result will be "undue concentration" in the industry. Indeed, public policy in the United States holds that when four or fewer firms account for 40% or more of the sales in a given market or line of business, an undesirable market structure or undue concentration exists. The argument in brief is that if four or fewer firms account for a substantial percentage of an industry's sales, these firms will recognize the impact of their actions and policies upon one another. This recognized interdependence will lead to a consideration of actions and reactions to changes in policy that will tend toward "tacit collusion." As a result, the prices and profits of the firms will contain monopoly elements. Thus if economies from mergers cannot be established, it is assumed that the resulting increases in concentration may lead to monopoly returns. If economies of scale can be demonstrated, then a comparison of efficiencies versus the effects of increased concentration must be made.

In 1982 and 1984, the Department of Justice announced new merger guidelines to supersede those that had been issued in May 1968. The new merger guidelines adopt the Herfindahl index (H index), which takes into consideration the market shares of all the firms in the industry. The theory behind the use of the Herfindahl index is that if one or more firms have relatively high market shares, this is of even greater concern than the share of the largest four firms. An example presented with the announcement of the new merger guidelines illustrates this point.

In one market four firms each hold a 15% market share and the remaining 40% is held by 40 firms, each with a 1% market share. Its H index would be

$$H = 4(15)^2 + 40(1)^2 = 940.$$

In another market one firm has a 57% market share and the remaining 43% is held by 43 firms, each with a 1% market share. Like the first market, the four-firm concentration ratio here would be the same 60%. However, the H index would be

$$H = (57)^2 + 43(1)^2 = 3292.$$

Thus the H index registers a concern about inequality as well as degree of concentration. The economic basis for either concern has not been well established.

The regulatory authorities also continue to give heavy weight to the percentage share of the market held by individual firms. It was on the basis of individual firm market shares that the Federal Trade Commission (FTC) raised objections in June 1986 to Coca-Cola's plan to buy Dr. Pepper and the offer of Philip Morris to sell its Seven-Up soft-drink unit to Pepsi. As a consequence of FTC objections Philip Morris withdrew its offer, but Coca-Cola and Dr. Pepper said they would challenge the FTC's attempt to block their merger. Similarly, in 1984 the FTC challenged a proposed merger between Warner Communications Inc. and Polygram Records Inc., principally owned by N. V. Philips, a Netherlands-based telecommunications and electronics concern. After some two years of legal maneuvering, in June 1986 both companies agreed to seek FTC approval before merging with, or acquiring a stake in, other large record companies. The basis for the original FTC challenge was that if Warner and Polygram were joined, it would become the largest recorded music distributor in the world, accounting for 26% of the U.S. market.

While some economists hold that high concentration, however measured, causes some degree of monopoly, other economists hold that increased concentration is generally the *result* of active and intense competition. They argue further that the intense competition continues among large firms in concentrated industries because the dimensions of decision making over prices, outputs, types of product, quality of product, service, etc., are so numerous and of so many gradations that collusion simply is not feasible. This is an area where the issues continue to be unresolved.

5. Tax Considerations

Tax considerations are also involved in mergers. One such tax consideration is to substitute capital gains taxes for ordinary income taxes by acquiring a growth firm with a small or no dividend payout and then selling it to realize capital gains. Also, when the growth of a firm has slowed so that earnings retention cannot be justified to the Internal Revenue Service, an incentive for sale to another firm is created. Rather than pay out future earnings as dividends subject to the ordinary personal income tax, an owner can capitalize future earnings in a sale to another firm. One often sees a small proprietor who develops an ongoing business (say, Company A) and begins to have a significant flow of net income. If he or she takes the net income as dividends, it is subject to a high personal income tax rate. Also, given potential competition from other firms, the ability of Company A to earn the income in the future is uncertain from the owner's standpoint. The certainty of that income flow would be increased if Company A were part of a larger firm that had the necessary full complement of management capabilities. The owner of Company A converts

a nonmarketable ownership claim to a marketable one. These considerations are reinforced by tax considerations for Company A's owner to sell out. By selling out, the
owner converts the uncertain future income into a capital gain. Usually the transaction is a tax-free exchange of securities. Company A's owner is not subject to taxes
until he or she sells off the securities received; it will be a capital gain, and the owner
can choose the time at which to recognize the gain.

Another tax factor is the sale of firms with accumulated tax losses. Although a
business purpose must also be demonstrated, a firm with tax losses can shelter the
positive earnings of another firm with which it is joined. The Economic Recovery
Tax Act of 1981 provided for the sale of tax credits from the use of accelerated
depreciation. These often involved sale and lease-back arrangements. This suggests
that whether tax considerations induce mergers depends on whether there are alternative methods of achieving equivalent tax benefits.

Still other tax effects are associated with inheritance taxes. A closely held firm
may be sold as the owners become older because of the uncertainty of the value
placed on the firm in connection with estate taxes. Or a sale may be made to provide
greater liquidity for the payment of estate taxes. A study of mergers in the newspaper
industry illustrates the effects of tax influences [Dertouzos and Thorpe, 1982]. The
stepped-up basis for depreciable assets leads to competition among bidding firms
that results in premiums paid for newspaper companies acquired. These high, demonstrated market values are then used by the income tax service in setting values on
newspaper companies for estate tax purposes. But the realization of the tax benefits
of the higher depreciable values requires actual transactions that stimulate the purchase of individual newspaper companies.

E. THEORIES OF RESTRUCTURING

The first group of activities in Table 19.1, expansion, involves combining assets. The
remaining groups involve uncombining assets (sell-offs); establishing and defending
rights to assets (corporate control); and altering the format of asset control (changes
in ownership structure).

Merger theories imply that $2 + 2$ can be greater than 4. The rationale for other
types of restructuring seems to be that $4 - 2$ can be more than 2; or that $3 + 1$ can
be more than $2 + 2$. Thus a new math has evolved to explain both mergers and other
restructuring activities.

The various forms of divestiture can be rationalized as transferring business assets
to a higher-valued use or to a more efficient user. A divestiture may create value by
slicing off a business that was a poor fit with the remaining operations. If so, good
divestiture programs may increase the market values of both the buying and selling
companies.

There is another aspect of the second to fourth categories of activities in Table
19.1 that deals with corporate control and rearranging the ownership structure. Here
the hypothesis is that improvements in managerial accountability and a strengthening
of incentives may be achieved by separating unrelated business activities. Spinoffs

may provide managers with greater decision-making authority. Better performance evaluation criteria and measurement may also be achieved. Having publicly traded stock that provides continuing market valuations is useful for performance evaluation. Improvements in profitability may also be achieved by linking managerial compensation more directly to performance tests, including those that track stock price behavior.

This still leaves some questions unanswered. New capabilities and new markets could be developed internally. It may be less risky to buy established organizations, but a competitive market for acquisitions implies that the net present value from such investments is likely to be zero. However, if these investments can be used as a base for still additional investments with positive net present values, the strategy may succeed.

F. CONGLOMERATE MERGERS

One reason for the study of conglomerate mergers is that after the tightening of the laws with respect to mergers that took place in 1950, most merger activity until the late 1970s was conglomerate because major horizontal and vertical mergers were subject to legal challenge. In addition the economic rationale for conglomerate mergers seemed to be the weakest. If by definition conglomerate mergers brought together unrelated activities, how could there be economic benefits? Some possible benefits of conglomerate mergers may be considered.

1. Financial Gains

Several financial gains from conglomerate mergers have been proposed. Arguments claiming financial gains from mergers other than the possible advantage of economies in financing are of dubious validity. As presented in most basic finance texts, it can readily be demonstrated that a differentially higher price/earnings ratio can achieve gains in earnings per share for acquiring firms. If merger terms represent a differentially higher price/earnings ratio for the acquiring firm, that firm's earnings per share after the acquisition will be higher and the earnings per share of the acquired firm will be lower. The acquiring firm achieves earnings accretion while the acquired firm suffers earnings dilution.

But it can be readily demonstrated that the higher price/earnings ratio must reflect differentially more favorable earnings growth prospects. The effect of acquiring firms with low price/earnings ratios and lower earnings growth prospects will be to depress the average rate of future growth in earnings of the combined firm. The new price/earnings ratio should reflect this change in the outlook for the growth in earnings of the merged firm so that there should be no gain in the value of the combined firm over the values of the two separate firms. Hence the differential price/earnings ratio theory and its immediate effects on earnings per share have no validity as a theory for measuring the potential gains of a merger, since it is valuation, not earnings per share, that is the relevant test.

2. Potential Sources of Synergy in Conglomerate Mergers

From the mid-1950s through 1968, economists and managers offered a number of reasons other than the ones discussed above to explain how economies might be achieved in conglomerate mergers. During this period, formal long-range enterprise planning developed, and computer technology began to be adapted to the management of the firm. Financial planning and control systems were extended with further improvements in the use of balanced, centralized-decentralized management control systems. Further, World War II and the Korean conflict had stimulated new technologies, resulting in an uneven diffusion of and wide variations in advanced technological capabilities among firms.

The major conceptual point here is that the role of the general management functions (planning, control, organizing, information systems) and functions centralized at top management levels (research, finance, legal) increased in importance in the management of enterprises. As a consequence the costs of managing large, diversified firms were substantially reduced relative to potential operating economies. This is the broader theoretical basis explaining the formation of conglomerates. However, there is considerable disagreement about whether synergy is achieved in conglomerate mergers from the sources just described. Most of the theoretical literature of finance has assumed no synergy in conglomerate mergers and has analyzed pure financial effects. For a theory of pure conglomerate mergers see Chung [1982].

3. Pure Financial Theories of Conglomerate Firms

The popular justification of conglomerate mergers was synergy—the $2 + 2 = 5$ effect. But other theories of conglomerate firms were set forth that did not require the assumption of synergy. Lewellen [1971], e.g., offered a purely financial rationale for conglomerate mergers. His theory may be summarized initially in terms of the numerical examples he provides, concluding with his general statement of conditions.

Let us consider two firms, A and B, whose annual cash flows are independent (correlation coefficient is zero) and each distributed as shown in columns (1) through (3) of Table 19.4.

Table 19.4*

(1) State (s_1)	(2) $P(s_1)$	(3) Y_1
1	.1	100
2	.2	250
3	.7	500

* *Note:* s_1 = alternative future state of the world; $P(s_1)$ = probability of alternative states; Y_1 = annual cash flow outcomes under alternative states.

It is assumed that each firm has incurred borrowings to the point that its annual cash contractual obligation amounts to $240. The probability, $P(D)$, that one or both firms will be unable to meet their debt service obligations of $240 each is shown below:

$$P(D) = P(Y_A < 240) + P(Y_B < 240) - P(Y_A < 240, Y_B < 240)$$
$$= .1 + .1 - (.1)(.1) = .19.$$

If the two firms merge, the distribution of their joint returns can be calculated as shown in the matrix in Table 19.5. The distribution of their joint returns would therefore become

Y_m	200	350	500	600	750	1,000
$P(Y_m)$	.01	.04	.04	.14	.28	.49

Since their aggregate debt burden would become $480 per annum, the probability of default now drops to .05 as compared with .19 before the merger.

The foregoing was based on the assumption of zero correlation between the two returns. If the correlation were -1, the gains from merger would be even greater. If the correlation were $+1$, reducing the probability of default would require other differences such as differences in the size of debt obligations. Thus if we assume the same distribution of returns for the two firms as before, but assume a correlation of $+1$ between the two and the debt obligations of A and B to be $255 and $240, respectively, the before-merger probability of default would be

$$P(D) = .3 + .1 - .1 = .3.$$

After merger the total debt obligations would be $495, and they would be related to the following combined cash flow pattern:

Y_m	200	500	1,000
$P(Y_m)$	.1	.2	.7

The probability of default would therefore fall to only 0.1.

Table 19.5

		.1	.2	.7
.1	Joint probability	.01	.02	.07
	Amount	200	350	600
.2	Joint probability	.02	.04	.14
	Amount	350	500	750
.7	Joint probability	.07	.14	.49
	Amount	600	750	1,000

Levy and Sarnat [1970, 801] set forth a similar argument. They state, "A somewhat stronger case can be made for conglomerate mergers when economies in capital costs are considered. . . . large firms have better access to the capital markets and also enjoy significant cost savings when securing their financing needs. . . . These cost savings presumably reflect, at least in part, the reduction in lenders' risk achieved through diversification."

Galai and Masulis [1976] point out the confusion involved between the value of the merged firm and the positions of the debt and equity holders. They argue that the value of the merged firm is the simple sum of the constituent firms. "This can be seen once one recognizes that investors in the marketplace could have created an identical financial position by purchasing equal proportions of the debt and equity of the two firms" [1976, 68]. The OPM establishes that the relative position of the creditors and the equity holders of the firms will be changed. If the correlation between the returns of the merging firms is less than 1, the variance in the rate of return of the merged firm will be lower than the variance of the rates of return of the merging firms (assumed to be equal). (For numerical illustrations see Problems 19.6 to 19.8.)

It follows from the OPM that the value of the equity of the merged firm will be less than the sum of the constituent equity values and the value of the debt will be higher. According to the OPM, increased variability increases the value of the option, and conversely. Since the equity is an option on the face value of the debt outstanding, its value will fall with a decrease in volatility. "What is taking place, as Rubinstein points out, is that the bondholders receive more protection since the stockholders of each firm have to back the claims of the bondholders of both companies. The stockholders are hurt since their limited liability is weakened" [Galai and Masulis, 1976, p. 68].

Thus a pure diversification rationale for conglomerate mergers would not seem valid. Reducing the risk to bondholders represents a redistribution of value from shareholders, leaving the total value of the firm unchanged.

However, a number of alternatives could be used to return the wealth of different classes of security holders to the original position they held prior to the merger. One solution would be to increase the amount of the face value of debt and use the proceeds to retire equity. This process is continued until the original bondholders' holdings have a market value equal to their constituent sum prior to the merger. The debt-to-equity ratio of the merged firm can be increased to offset the decrease in the volatility of the merged firm's rate of return. The increased amount of debt implies that the total value of the firm is increased through merger due to the tax deductibility of interest payments. Galai and Masulis suggest that this may explain some conglomerate mergers.

4. Shastri's Extension of the Analysis of the Effects of Mergers on Corporate Security Values

Shastri [1982] extends the Galai-Masulis (G-M) study by allowing the two firms to have different variances, different debt ratios, and different debt maturities. Shastri's results for the effects of mergers on shareholder values versus bondholders' positions

Table 19.6 The Effects of the Merger on Firm Security Values

		Bond A	Bond B	$S_c - (S_A + S_B)$ Common Stock*
Variance effect	$\sigma_A > \sigma_C > \sigma_B$	>0	<0	$\gtreqqless 0$
	$\sigma_A < \sigma_C < \sigma_B$	<0	>0	$\gtreqqless 0$
	$\sigma_{A,}\, \sigma_B > \sigma_C$	>0	>0	<0
Leverage effect	$M_A/V_A > M_B/V_B$	>0	<0	<0
	$M_A/V_A < M_B/V_B$	<0	>0	<0
Maturity effect		>0	$\gtreqqless 0$	<0

* The effect of the merger on each individual firm's stock would depend on the merger terms.

under these more general conditions are presented in Table 19.6. Because the correlation between the cash flow streams of the two firms can be either positive or negative, the resulting combined firm variance may be less than the variance of the individual firms or greater than one of the firms and less than the other firm. However, the leverage effects and maturity effects are simply weighted average effects. The combined firm will simply have a weighted average of the leverage or maturity pattern of the combining firms.

The other relationship that stands out in the table is that the value of the common stock of the combined firm may under some conditions be larger than the addition of the premerger stock values of the two firms even in a pure conglomerate merger, assuming no synergy. The reasons for Shastri's conclusions are reviewed next.

There are three possibilities under the variance effect. The variance of the combined firm may be less than the variance of either of the individual firms before the merger. This is the G-M result where the variance effect is positive for the bonds of both firm A and firm B and negative for both stocks. However, the variance of the combined firm may be greater than one of the firms and lower than the other. For example, when $\sigma_A > \sigma_C > \sigma_B$, the securities of firm B become riskier with the merger, conversely with firm A. So there is a positive impact on the bonds of A and the stock of B, negative on the bonds of B and the stock of A. The effects on the value of the stock of the combined firm compared with the sum of the premerger stock values is ambiguous depending on the relative magnitudes of the premerger stock A and stock B values.

Shastri defines the leverage ratio as the ratio of the face value of debt to firm value. If the leverage ratio of firm A is greater than the ratio for B, the combined firm has a leverage ratio less than that of firm A and greater than that of firm B. The merger results in a decrease in the leverage-ratio related risk for bond A, with the opposite result for bond B. This implies an increase in the value of bond A and a decrease in the value of bond B. When the leverage ratio of A is lower than that of

B, the opposite results follow. Because of an unambiguous increase in the bankruptcy-related risk for the combined equity, the leverage effect is always negative for the combined common stock.

The maturity effect has two components. Assume that the maturity of bond A is shorter than the maturity of bond B. The effect of a merger from the point of view of bond B is equivalent to having the firm issue new debt with a shorter maturity. Thus bond A is paid in full ahead of bond B and in some sense becomes "senior" to bond B. This seniority effect would be positive for bond A and negative for bond B.

The second effect is a bankruptcy effect. If bankruptcy occurs at bond A's maturity date, debt B also shares in the proceeds of the bankruptcy and so gains from the merger. Hence the bankruptcy component of the maturity effect is negative for debt A and positive for debt B.

The size of these two effects depends on both the probability of bankruptcy and the bankruptcy sharing rules. Shastri argues that the first effect will dominate the second for bond A so that it always gains in a merger. But the net effect on debt B is ambiguous. From the point of view of debt B, the "new debt issue" is always accompanied by a change in firm value by an amount generally greater than the face value of the "new issue." So the maturity effect on debt B value is ambiguous. The effect on the combined stock value is always negative. This is essentially because with a merger the option a shareholder of B had of buying out the debt of B is no longer available directly because debt A has to be paid off first. This loss of an option leads to a decline in the combined stock price.

Thus Shastri's extension of previous work yields some different empirical predictions. The value of the stock of the combined firm may, under certain conditions, exceed the combined premerger stock values of the combined firms. In addition, all three of the effects under certain conditions can be negative on at least one of the bonds, leading to a decline in value. So bonds do not necessarily gain in a merger. This explains why bond indentures may include covenants restricting the freedom of the firm to engage in mergers. Thus, in general, the extension by Shastri results in a generalization of predictions of the effects of mergers.

5. Scott's Model of Conglomerate Mergers

Scott [1977] formulates a model of conglomerate mergers in a state-preference framework with two dates. He considers the effects of (1) concontractual obligations such as damages awarded in lawsuits, etc., (2) bankruptcy costs, and (3) tax deductibility of debt and of losses.

The following notation is employed by Scott:

$Q_{aj} =$ firm A, state j cash flows;

$C_{aj} =$ noncontractual obligations such as sales taxes; these are junior to debt and fixed in amount;

$R_a =$ debt obligations;

$B_{aj} =$ bankruptcy costs.

For any firm A, then, the value of equity in state j is

$$S_{aj} = (1 - t)\text{MAX}[Q_{aj} - C_{aj} - R_a, 0].$$

The value of debt is

$$Y_{daj} = \begin{cases} R_a & \text{if } Q_{aj} \geq (R_a + C_{aj}) \\ \text{MIN}[R_a, Q_{aj} - B_{aj}] & \text{otherwise.} \end{cases}$$

This is using the fact that C is junior to debt.

Scott first analyzes the effects of merging all-equity firms. We have to assume that the merger does not affect the prices of the state-contingent claims (primitive state security prices), i.e., the merger does not diminish the "richness" of the market and cause spanning to break down. Scott obtains

$$S_{abj} = (1 - t)\text{MAX}[Q_{aj} - C_{aj} + Q_{bj} - C_{bj}, 0],$$

$$S_{abj} < (1 - t)\text{MAX}[Q_{aj} - C_{aj}, 0] + (1 - t)\text{MAX}[Q_{bj} - C_{bj}, 0].$$

Thus we obtain that

$$S_{ab} < S_a + S_b.$$

This states that a conglomerate merger of all-equity firms can never be profitable. The intuition is that the merger is unprofitable because the limited liability protection of a merged firm is weaker than that of two unmerged firms. This is a familiar result, but Scott's is the first paper to obtain this result so easily because of the state-preference approach he employs. Scott next analyzes the merger of levered firms. Evaluation relationships are as follows:

Mergers of Firms with Debt and Equity Outstanding

Y_{aj} represents the total value of A's outstanding securities in period 1:

$$Y_{aj} = \begin{cases} (1 - t)(Q_{aj} - C_{aj}) + tR_a & \text{if } Q_{aj} \geq (R_a + C_{aj}) \\ \text{MIN}[R_a, (Q_{aj} - B_{aj})] & \text{otherwise.} \end{cases}$$

Y_{abj} represents the period 1 value of debt plus equity of AB:

$$Y_{abj} = \begin{cases} [(1 - t)(Q_{aj} - C_{aj} + Q_{bj} - C_{bj}) + t(R_a + R_b)] = A & \text{if } A > (R_a + R_b) \\ \text{MIN}[(R_a + R_b), Q_{aj} + Q_{bj} - B_{abj}] & \text{otherwise.} \end{cases}$$

Using the valuation relationships above, Scott works out a table of the effects of pure conglomerate mergers. He explicitly considers all possible combinations of solvency and bankruptcy for the two merging firms and for the merged firm. He assumes economies of scale in bankruptcy costs. His table presents the incremental cash flows to security holders as a result of the conglomerate merger. His results are reproduced as our Table 19.7.

Table 19.7   Incremental Cash Flows in Period 1 to Security Holders as a Result of Conglomerate Merger

$$Z_j = (Y_{abj} - Y_{aj} - Y_{bj})$$

	AB Solvent	*AB Bankrupt*
A, B solvent*	0	
A solvent B bankrupt	$t(R_b + C_{bj} - Q_{bj}) - C_{bj}$ $+ \text{MAX}[B_{bj}, Q_{bj} - R_b]$	$t(Q_{aj} - C_{aj} - R_a) + C_{aj}$ $+ \text{MAX}[Q_{bj} - B_{abj}, R_a + R_b - Q_{aj}]$ $- \text{MIN}[Q_{bj} - B_{bj}, R_b]$
A bankrupt B solvent	$t(R_a + C_{aj} - Q_{aj}) - C_{aj}$ $+ \text{MAX}[B_{aj}, Q_{aj} - R_a]$	$t(Q_{bj} - C_{bj} - R_b) + C_{bj}$ $+ \text{MAX}[Q_{aj} - B_{abj}, R_a + R_b - Q_{bj}]$ $- \text{MIN}[Q_{aj} - B_{aj}, R_a]$
A, B bankrupt		$\text{MIN}[Q_{aj} + Q_{bj} - B_{abj}, R_a + R_b]$ $- \text{MIN}[Q_{aj} - B_{aj}, R_a]$ $- \text{MIN}[Q_{bj} - B_{bj}, R_b]$

* This should be interpreted as follows: If A and B had remained unmerged, these are the states in which neither would have gone bankrupt. The other entries are interpreted in a similar fashion.

From J. H. Scott, Jr., "On the Theory of Conglomerate Mergers," *Journal of Finance*, September 1977, 1244.

To aid in the interpretation of the table, consider the case where firm B would be bankrupt while firm A and the combined firm would remain solvent. The proof of his result is as follows:

B Bankrupt, whereas A and AB Solvent

$$Z_j = Y_{abj} - Y_{aj} - Y_{bj}$$

$$Z_j = [(1 - t)(Q_{aj} + Q_{bj} - C_{aj} - C_{bj})] + t(R_a + R_b) - (1 - t)(Q_{aj} - C_{aj}) - tR_a$$
$$- \text{MIN}[(Q_{bj} - B_{bj}), R_b]$$

$$Z_j = Q_{bj} - C_{bj} - tQ_{bj} + tC_{bj} + tR_b - \text{MIN}[(Q_{bj} - B_{bj}), R_b]$$

$$Z_j = t(R_b + C_{bj} - Q_{bj}) - C_{bj} + Q_{bj} - \text{MIN}[Q_{bj} - B_{bj}, R_b]$$

$$Z_j = t(R_b + C_{bj} - Q_{bj}) - C_{bj} + Q_{bj} + \text{MAX}[B_{bj} - Q_{bj}, -R_b]$$

$$Z_j = t(R_b + C_{bj} - Q_{bj}) - C_{bj} + \text{MAX}[B_{bj}, Q_{bj} - R_b] \lessgtr 0.$$

Some implications of his results may be noted. When one firm would have gone bankrupt by itself but the merged firm would not, the merged firm is able to use the loss of the component as a tax credit. Thus for Scott the corporate tax encourages mergers. Higgins and Schall [1975] assume that the bankrupt firm could have sold its tax credit to some other firm, so a merger is not needed to utilize the tax loss. Hence different assumptions about the use of tax credits give different results on the effects of a conglomerate merger.

Scott's introduction of noncontractual obligations (C) serves to decrease or increase the profitability of a conglomerate merger. A bankrupt firm could have defaulted on C because they are junior to debt. But the now-solvent merged firm cannot avoid paying C. On the other hand, if one firm by going bankrupt pulls the other one into bankruptcy when they are merged, the debt of the merged firm may be in a better position. In such states, payments that would have been made by the solvent (unmerged) firm to noncontractual creditors are diverted to pay the bondholders of the otherwise bankrupt (unmerged) firm. The practical importance of this case depends on the actual magnitudes of noncontractual obligations.

Bankruptcy costs play an important role in Scott's model. For some future states a merger may increase value by saving one of the firms from bankruptcy and its costs. But a merger may be unprofitable to the extent that there are future states in which the merger pulls an otherwise solvent firm into bankruptcy and its costs. Scott suggests that a merger between a large, stable firm and a small, profitable but unstable firm may reduce the present value of future bankruptcy costs and thus increase value. He suggests that a merger between a small, stable firm and a large, volatile one may reduce value by increasing the present value of future bankruptcy costs.

Finally, Scott illustrates the proposition that a merger may be unprofitable even though the cash flows are negatively correlated. He also illustrates how a profitable conglomerate merger need not increase debt capacity. His model is similar to that of Kraus and Litzenberger [1973], who demonstrated that the optimal level of debt is equal to one of the before-tax cash flows. Scott's numerical example assumes economies of scale in bankruptcy costs. The basic data for Scott's example are shown in Table 19.8.

Table 19.8   Data for Numerical Example

	Cash Flows of Solvent Firms			Bankruptcy Costs		
	Firm A	Firm B	Firm AB	Firm A	Firm B	Firm AB
State 1	$Q_{a1} = 20$	$Q_{b1} = 25$	$Q_{ab1} = 45$	$B_{a1} = 4$	$B_{b1} = 10$	$B_{ab1} = 13$
State 2	$Q_{a2} = 30$	$Q_{b2} = 20$	$Q_{ab2} = 50$	$B_{a2} = 10$	$B_{b2} = 2$	$B_{ab2} = 11$

From J. H. Scott, Jr., "On the Theory of Conglomerate Mergers," *Journal of Finance*, September 1977, 1248.

Scott assumes further that the tax rate is 50% and that the price of the state-contingent claims for either state is .4. The computations under alternative assumptions are as follows:

With no merger:

$$\text{If } R_a = Q_{a1} = 20$$

If State 1	$Y_{a1} = (1 - .5)(20) + .5(20)$	$20 \times .4 = 8$
If State 2	$Y_{a2} = (1 - .5)(30) + .5(20)$	$25 \times .4 = 10$
		$V_a^1 = \overline{18}$

If $R_a = Q_{a2} = 30$

If State 1	$Y_{a1} = \text{MIN}(30, 20 - 4)$	$16 \times .4 = 6.4$
If State 2	$Y_{a2} = (1 - .5)(30) + .5(30)$	$30 \times .4 = \underline{12.0}$
		$V_a^2 = \overline{18.4}$

So $R_a^* = Q_{a2} = 30$.

If $R_b = Q_{b1} = 25$

If State 1	$Y_{b1} = (1 - .5)(25) + .5(25)$	$25 \times .4 = 10.0$
If State 2	$Y_{b2} = \text{MIN}[25, (20 - 2)]$	$18 \times .4 = \underline{7.2}$
		$V_b^1 = \overline{17.2}$

If $R_b = Q_{b2} = 20$

If State 1	$Y_{b1} = (1 - .5)(25) + .5(20)$	$22.5 \times .4 = 9$
If State 2	$Y_{b2} = (1 - .5)(20) + .5(20)$	$20.0 \times .4 = \underline{8}$
		$V_b^2 = \overline{17}$

So $R_b^* = Q_{b1} = 25$.

With a merger:

If $R_{ab} = 55$

If State 1	$Y_{ab1} = \text{MIN}[55, (45 - 13)]$	$32 \times .4 = 12.8$
If State 2	$Y_{ab2} = \text{MIN}[55, (50 - 11)]$	$39 \times .4 = \underline{15.6}$
		$V_{ab} = \overline{28.4}$

If $R_{ab} = 45$

If State 1	$Y_{ab1} = (1 - .5)(45) + .5(45)$	$45.0 \times .4 = 18.0$
If State 2	$Y_{ab2} = (1 - .5)(50) + .5(45)$	$47.5 \times .4 = \underline{19.0}$
		$V_{ab}^1 = \overline{37.0}$

If $R_{ab} = 50$

If State 1	$Y_{ab1} = \text{MIN}[50, (45 - 13)]$	$32 \times .4 = 12.8$
If State 2	$Y_{ab2} = (1 - .5)(50) + .5(50)$	$50 \times .4 = \underline{20.0}$
		$V_{ab}^2 = \overline{32.8}$

So $R_{ab}^* = Q_{ab1} = 45$.

The numerical results above illustrate Scott's propositions. Like the Kraus and Litzenberger results they demonstrate that it is always profitable to increase the optimal level of debt, R^*, to equal one of the before-tax cash flows. This is because one can always increase the optimal debt level to the next highest cash flow, thereby decreasing the present value of future tax payments with no increase in the probability of incurring bankruptcy costs. To obtain the optimal capital structure we calculate the value of the firm when the debt level equals the pretax cash flow in state 1 and again when it equals the pretax cash flow in state 2. We then choose the debt level that results in the highest value of the firm. For the numerical example the optimal debt level is set equal to the cash flow of the firm that is highest for a given state.

However, after the merger the highest value of the firm is achieved with the state 1 cash flow of the merged firm that is lower than the assumed state 2 cash flow of the merged firm. If the merged firm were to maintain the capital structure of the unmerged firms at a level of 55, it would result in a value of the merged firm of 28.4. This is less than the value of the unmerged firms (18.4 + 17.2 = 35.6). Scott's example illustrates that optimal debt may be reduced, therefore, as a consequence of the pure conglomerate merger. Yet if the firm chooses an optimal level of debt after the merger, the value of the firm is increased to 37. This exceeds the sum of the components, which totaled 35.6.

These results are of course specific to the pattern of the numerical relationships chosen for Scott's example. They are general, however, to the extent that they are illustrative of the kind of possibilities that may conceivably occur. The general view is that conglomerate mergers may increase "debt capacity" (however defined) but may (or may not) increase firm value. Scott presents the possibility that the conglomerate merger may actually reduce the optimal level of debt. On the other hand, choosing an optimal level of debt after the merger may produce a value of the combined firm that is greater than the sum of the individual values of the components. Thus Scott concludes that the probability of bankruptcy is in general not an appropriate measure of the profitability of a conglomerate merger. He argues also that as a result of a conglomerate merger the resulting firm's optimal level of debt can either rise or fall.

These results illustrate a more general proposition about merger theory. Many possible motives for mergers can exist under various models and assumptions. Various types of complementarities may make mergers profitable. Alternative assumptions about tax rules can make mergers profitable or unprofitable under alternative assumptions. This makes modeling theories for testing mergers and approaching empirical data difficult to formulate.

6. The Option Pricing Model, Debt Capacity, and Mergers

Drawing on previous formulations by Brennan [1979] and by Cox, Ross, and Rubinstein [1979], Stapleton [1982] sets forth a framework for analyzing debt capacity without and with mergers, utilizing the option pricing model under alternative assumptions. In his formulation, debt capacity is defined as the maximum amount of debt that can be raised at a given interest rate.

First the analysis is made under risk neutrality. The value of a loan or debt as derived by Stapleton is shown in Eq. (19.1):

$$(1 + r)D_j = \mu_j F^*(Y_j) - \sigma_j f^*(Y_j) + Y_j[1 - F^*(Y_j)], \qquad (19.1)$$

where

$r =$ the risk-free interest rate,

$Y_j =$ the debt obligation due at the end of the period,

$X_j =$ cash flows at the end of the period (a one-period model is assumed), including the liquidation value of the assets,

μ_j = the mean of X_j,

σ_j = the standard deviation of X_j,

D_j = the market value of the promised debt obligations or, equivalently, the debt capacity,

f^* = the standard normal density function,

F^* = the cumulative standard normal distribution function.

With given values of the risk-free interest rate and the mean and standard deviation of X_j for a given level of debt obligations incurred, Y_j, Eq. (19.1) can be used with the additional constraint that $Y_j/D_j = (1 + i)$ to calculate debt capacity (i is equal to the effective yield to maturity on the debt).

To illustrate the calculation of debt capacity and some related relationships in the Stapleton formulation, let us use the following illustrative values:

$$\textit{For Firm A} \qquad \mu_A = 100, \quad \sigma_A = 25, \quad r = 10\%, \quad Y_A = 68.$$

The solution by iteration for debt capacity utilizing Eq. (19.1) plus the constraint with $i = .12$ is $D_A^* = 60.7$. Hence $Y_A = D_A^*(1 + i) = (60.7)(1.12) = 68$. The left-hand side (lhs) of Eq. (19.1) is 1.1 times D_A^* because the riskless rate is 10%. Thus the left-hand side of Eq. (19.1) is 1.1(60.7) = 66.77.

The right-hand side (rhs) of Eq. (19.1) is as follows:

$$\text{rhs} = 100F[(68 - 100)/25] - 25f[(68 - 100)/25] + 68(1 - F[(68 - 100)/25])$$

$$= 100(1 - F[(100 - 68)/25]) - 25f[(100 - 68)/25] + 68(F[(100 - 68)/25])$$

$$= 100(.1003) - 25(.1758) + 68(.8997)$$

$$= 10.03 - 4.395 + 61.18 = 66.81.$$

Therefore the equality of rhs to lhs is verified. Finally, the probability that X will be less than Y is just $F(Y) = F(68)$, which is $.1003 = 10.03\%$.

In a like manner, Stapleton calculates debt capacity for different firms with the same expected cash flow but increasing standard deviations of cash flows. The calculation is also performed for different required yields. The results are summarized in Table 19.9.

The data in Table 19.9 indicate that at any given required yield the amount of debt obtainable declines at an increasing rate as the risk of the underlying cash flows increases. Debt capacity increases at a diminishing rate as the promised coupon increases.

The analysis is next extended to an application to pure conglomerate mergers in which no synergy is assumed. The only influence is the effect on the standard deviation of the combined firm in relation to the component firms. The results in Table 19.10 depend on the correlation between cash flows of the merging firms. This, in turn, produces the magnitude of the standard deviation of returns for the combined firm.

The new sigma in Table 19.10 is obtained using the expression in Eq. (19.2):

$$\sigma_{BD}^2 = \sigma_B^2 + \sigma_D^2 + 2\rho_{BD}\sigma_B\sigma_D. \tag{19.2}$$

Table 19.9 Debt Values: Risk Neutrality

Cash Flow	Firm A				Firm B				Firm C				Firm D			
Mean μ	100				100				100				100			
Standard deviation σ	25				30				35				40			
	i percent	Y_A	D_A	$\frac{Y_A}{D_A}$	$P(X_A < Y_A)$	Y_B	D_B	$\frac{Y_B}{D_B}$	$P(X_B < Y_B)$	Y_C	D_C	$\frac{Y_C}{D_C}$	$P(X_C < Y_C)$	Y_D	D_D	$\frac{Y_D}{D_D}$	$P(X_D < Y_D)$
Debt level 1	12	68	60.7	1.12	.10	57	50.9	1.12	.08	42	38.4	1.12	.05	23	20.5	1.12	.03
Debt level 2	14	79	69.3	1.14	.20	70	61.4	1.14	.16	59	51.8	1.14	.12	45	39.5	1.14	.08
Debt level 3	16	86	74.1	1.16	.27	78	67.2	1.16	.23	70	60.3	1.16	.20	58	50.0	1.16	.15

From R. C. Stapleton, "Mergers, Debt Capacity and the Valuation of Corporate Loans," reprinted by permission of the publisher, from *Mergers and Acquisitions*, edited by Michael Keenan and Lawrence J. White, Lexington Books, D. C. Heath & Co., Lexington, Mass. Copyright © 1982, D. C. Heath & Co.

Table 19.10 Debt Capacity and Merger: Risk Neutrality

		Firm B	Firm D		Firm BD		
					$\rho = 0$	$\rho = 0.46$	$\rho = 1$
Mean μ		100	100		200	200	200
Standard deviation σ		30	40		50	60	70
	i percent	Y_B	Y_D	$Y_B + Y_D$	Y_{BD}	Y_{BD}	Y_{BD}
Debt capacity[a]	12	57	23	80	136	114	84
	14	70	45	115	158	140	118
	16	78	58	136	172	156	140
Debt capacity[b]		48.6	31.4	80	114.3	97.2	80
($\alpha = .043$)							

[a] Debt capacity is defined as in Table 19.9.

[b] Debt capacity defined, as in Lewellen (1971), as the level of promised payments such that $P(X_j < Y_j) \le \alpha$. Here, α is chosen so that the total debt of firms B and D is the same as that generated by a 12 percent interest-rate limit.

From R. C. Stapleton, "Mergers, Debt Capacity and the Valuation of Corporate Loans," reprinted by permission of the publisher, from *Mergers and Acquisitions*, edited by Michael Keenan and Lawrence J. White, Lexington Books, D. C. Heath & Co., Lexington, Mass. Copyright © 1982, D. C. Heath & Co.

The results in Table 19.10 follow directly from the application of Eq. (19.1) just as the computations were made for Table 19.9. For example, we simply verify that the left-hand side equals the right-hand side of Eq. (19.1) for the data in Table 19.10. At a yield of 12% the left-hand side is

$$\text{lhs} = 1.1 \times 57/1.12 = 55.98.$$

The right-hand side is calculated as in Table 19.9. The standardized variable is

$$(57 - 100)/30 = -1.43, \qquad F(-1.43) = 1 - .9236 = .0764.$$

Hence the right-hand side of the equation becomes

$$(100 \times .0764) - (30 \times .1435) + (57 \times .9236) = 7.64 - 4.30 + 52.65 = 55.99.$$

Thus, again, it is demonstrated that the values shown in Table 19.10 satisfy Eq. (19.1). The other results in Table 19.10 are calculated in a similar manner. The spread of results in Table 19.10 seeks to illustrate that the effect of merger on debt capacity is dependent on the relative risks of the merging firms as well as on the correlation between the earnings of the firms. The sum of the individual debt capacities of firms B and D at a required yield of 12% is $80. Table 19.10 then shows the effect on debt capacity of merging firms, assuming that the cash flows of the firm are uncorrelated, correlated, and perfectly correlated. Even in a perfect correlation case, debt capacity rises from $80 to $84. The specific numerical examples in Stapleton are special cases of the general propositions set forth by Shastri.

This contrasts with the results for Lewellen [1971] where debt capacity is defined as the level of promised payments such that the probability of X_j being less than Y_j

is less than α. In the example in Table 19.10, α is chosen so that the total debt of firms B and D is the same as that generated by a 12% interest yield requirement. Thus for the Lewellen formulation we have the requirement, using the data of Table 19.10, that

$$Pr(X_B < 48.6) = Pr(X_D < 31.4).$$

Now we can test the equality of the expression as follows:

$$\text{lhs} = 1 - F[(100 - 48.6)/30] = 1 - F(1.713) = 1 - .9564 = .0436,$$

$$\text{rhs} = 1 - F[(100 - 31.4)/40] = 1 - F(1.715).$$

Thus we have verified that lhs = rhs and that

$$Pr(X_B < 48.6) = Pr(X_D < 31.4) = .0436.$$

For the merged firm, when the correlation coefficient between the cash flows is zero, the standard deviation of the merged firm is 50. We then seek to verify that the debt capacity for the merged firm is 114.3. This is demonstrated by the following:

$$Pr(X_{BD} < 114.3) = 1 - F[(200 - 114.3)/50] = 1 - F(1.714) = .0436$$

as above.

The results for the calculations for correlation coefficients of .46 and 1.0 are also shown in the table. The results illustrate that debt capacity is higher under the OPM formulation than under the limited formulation of Lewellen. Indeed, with perfect correlation between the cash flows in the Lewellen formulation, debt capacity is not increased. However, in the OPM model, debt capacity is increased as long as the sigmas of the merging firms are different, even when the correlation coefficient between the returns is 1.

Similar calculations of the effects of mergers on debt capacity are also developed by Stapleton for the risk-averse case, using the results of Brennan [1979]. Here we do not have risk-neutral pricing; rather we have risk-averse pricing (greater covariances with the market lead to lower prices). Equation (19.1) is used again in Table 19.11; however, the location parameter for the distribution of cash flows (the mean return) has to be transformed to a certainty equivalent (rV). This can be calculated using the CAPM, since we assume exponential utility and a normal distribution. The determination of rV is given by Eq. (19.3):

$$rV = \mu_j - \lambda(\sigma_j \rho_{jm}). \tag{19.3}$$

Thus for a required yield of 12% and with $\lambda = \frac{1}{3}$ and a correlation coefficient with the market of 1 for firm B (whose $\sigma = 30$), the certainty equivalent $rV = 100 - [\frac{1}{3}(30 \times 1)] = 90$. This is substituted into Eq. (19.1) using rV instead of μ_j. Thus

$$\text{lhs} = 1.1 \times (44/1.12) = 43.21.$$

For the right-hand side we first calculate the standardized variable, which is

$$(44 - 90)/30 = -1.53, \qquad F(-1.53) = 1 - F(1.53) = 1 - .9370 = .0630.$$

Table 19.11   Debt Capacity: Risk Aversion

Cash Flow			Firm B			Firm C	Firm D
Mean μ			100			100	100
Standard deviation σ			30			35	40
Correlation with market ρ_m		1	0.75	0		0.75	0.75
	i percent	Y_B	Y_B	Y_B		Y_C	Y_D
Debt level 1	12	44	47	57		28	0
Debt level 2	14	56	60	70		46	22
Debt level 3	16	63	68	78		56	41

From R. C. Stapleton, "Mergers, Debt Capacity and the Valuation of Corporate Loans," reprinted by permission of the publisher, from *Mergers and Acquisitions*, edited by Michael Keenan and Lawrence J. White, Lexington Books, D. C. Heath & Co., Lexington, Mass. Copyright © 1982, D.C. Heath & Co.

We can now evaluate Eq. (19.1):

$$90(.063) - 30(.1238) + 44(.9370) = 5.67 - 3.71 + 41.23 = 43.19.$$

Thus lhs = rhs. The other debt capacity levels shown in Table 19.11 are calculated in a like manner.

Thus results in Table 19.11 illustrate that debt capacity declines as the correlation between the underlying cash flows in the market increases. If there is zero correlation between underlying cash flows in the market, debt capacities and debt values would be the same as they were under risk neutrality, since the underlying cash flows would be valued as if investors were risk neutral. In other words, the risk-adjustment factor in the CAPM drops out with the zero correlation term. Compared with the risk-neutral debt capacities of Table 19.9, the debt capacities under risk aversion in Table 19.11 are considerably lower.

Comparing Table 19.10 and Table 19.12 shows that under risk aversion the effect of mergers on debt capacity is much larger. Where the correlation coefficient, e.g., is

Table 19.12   Debt Capacity and Merger: Risk Aversion

					Firm BD	
		Firm B	Firm D		$\rho = 0.46$	$\rho = 1$
Mean μ		100	100		200	200
Standard deviation σ		30	40		60	70
Correlation with market ρ_m		0.75	0.75		0.875	0.75
	i percent	Y_B	Y_D	$Y_B + Y_D$	Y_{BD}	Y_{BD}
Debt capacity	12	47	0	47	91	56
Debt capacity	14	60	22	82	116	92
Debt capacity	16	68	41	109	133	112

From R. C. Stapleton, "Mergers, Debt Capacity and the Valuation of Corporate Loans," reprinted by permission of the publisher, from *Mergers and Acquisitions*, edited by Michael Keenan and Lawrence J. White, Lexington Books, D. C. Heath & Co., Lexington, Mass. Copyright © 1982, D. C. Heath & Co.

.46 the increase in debt capacity is larger in both absolute and relative terms, even though the initial debt capacities were smaller. This is a logical result because with risk aversion and the reduction in risk through merger, the impact on debt capacity is greater.

Thus the main results of the Stapleton formulation are quite strong. Using the OPM, the effects of merger on debt capacity are shown to be positive even when earnings of the component firms are perfectly correlated. By comparison, the Lewellen definition of debt capacity understates the effects of mergers.

Although debt capacity is increased, we should recall the results of Galai-Masulis and of Shastri. Their results suggest that in general the increase in debt capacity will benefit the creditors but have a negative effect on the value of the common stock. However, if the increase in debt capacity is utilized after merger, the value of the common stock may be increased owing to tax savings on interest payments.

7. Tests of the Performance of Conglomerate Firms

Empirical studies of conglomerate performance have been of two kinds. The first was a concern with their operating characteristics. In a study whose data ended in the early 1960s, Reid [1968] concluded that conglomerate mergers satisfied the desires of managers for larger firms but did not increase earnings or market prices. For a later period, 1958–1968, Weston and Mansinghka [1971] found that conglomerates as a group raised the depressed premerger rates of return on total assets up to the average for all firms. In the Melicher and Rush study [1974] for 1960–1969, conglomerates acquired more profitable firms than nonconglomerate acquirers and increased the utilization of latent debt capacity.

A second type of empirical study focused on conglomerate performance within the context of the CAPM. Weston, Smith, and Shrieves [1972] compared conglomerates with mutual funds (using annual data for 1960–1969), finding that conglomerates provided higher ratios of return to systematic risk. Melicher and Rush [1973] analyzed conglomerates against a matched sample of nonconglomerates. Operating comparisons were based on annual data, whereas market comparisons utilized monthly data over the period 1965–1971. Conglomerates exhibited higher levels of systematic risk but did not achieve significantly different rates of return or other performance measures. Joehnk and Nielsen [1974] compared levels of systematic risk and coefficients of determination for 21 conglomerates and 23 nonconglomerates (1962–1969). The market response for three years before and three years after each merger was not significantly different. Mason and Goudzwaard [1976] compared 22 conglomerates against randomly selected porfolios having similar asset structures for the years 1962–1967. They concluded that conglomerates performed statistically worse, on the basis of both return on assets and return on equity, compared with an unmanaged portfolio of similar industry investments.

In a later study, Smith and Weston [1977] retested their 1972 results, using monthly data and extending the coverage through 1973. Their research broadened the comparisons of Melicher and Rush [1973] by including mutual funds and closed-end investment companies as well as nonconglomerate firms. They studied a sample of 38 conglomerate firms. Conglomerates from their 1972 study were included for which complete data of monthly prices and dividends were available for the 10 years from 1964 through 1973. Similar data were available for 35 nonconglomerate firms that were part of a larger sample (matched by major industry) as developed by Melicher and Rush [1973]. Standard and Poor's Composite Stock Price Index was used as a surrogate for the overall stock market. For comparisons of managed portfolios, they compiled data for 104 mutual funds and also for 17 closed-end investment companies.

The risk-adjusted performance of conglomerates was found to be significantly better than that of the mutual funds. The higher-beta conglomerates performed better during the rising market but less well during the flat market. However, on theoretical grounds, the risk-adjusted performance measure should not show better performance for higher-risk securities during an up-market or worse performance during a down-market situation. As discussed by Friend and Blume [1970] and Black, Jensen, and Scholes [1972], a possible reason for the early differentially better performance of conglomerates is that the CAPM from which the risk-adjusted performance measures are derived is misspecified. An alternative explanation is expectation errors coupled with institutional changes. The attitudes toward conglomerates changed considerably over time, exhibiting overoptimism about their potential during 1964–1968. During the second period, 1969–1973, some unfavorable institutional changes took place. Accounting rules were changed, adverse tax treatment was legislated, and antitrust suits were filed by the Department of Justice. Also, the aerospace industry, which spawned many of the conglomerates as a form of defensive diversification, suffered from excess capacity and sharp product shifts with the escalation of the Vietnam war. Tests of operating effectiveness suggest an initial overoptimism about the potentials for management performance of conglomerates. Following 1969, conglomerates began to be viewed with considerable pessimism. These expectation changes are consistent with the risk-adjusted performance exhibited by the conglomerates.

As experience with conglomerates grew, investors were able to develop a more dependable basis for forming expectations with respect to their performance. We would expect conglomerates to continue to exhibit high betas because of the characteristics of the product markets of conglomerate firms. Risk-adjusted measures of conglomerate performance are not likely to be significantly different from those of other firms and portfolios. Further tests of merger performance, using residual analysis, are covered in the following chapter.

SUMMARY

Most generally mergers form one economic unit from two or more previous ones. In recent years increased use has been made of tender offers in which the bidder makes an offer directly to the stockholders of the firm it is seeking to control (the target). After obtaining control the bidder may merge the companies. Other recent developments include increased emphasis on so-called reverse mergers (selloffs), corporate control activities (takeover defenses), and changes in ownership structure.

Alternative theories of mergers have been formulated. Efficiency arguments include both the differential efficiency of acquiring firms over targets, and just plain inefficient management by the target. Another aspect of the efficiency rationale is synergy. The idea of synergy became almost a slogan during the conglomerate merger activity of the late 1960s. Most of the literature of financial economics has postulated the absence of synergy. If synergy is to have meaning, it represents the application of some economic concept. One possibility is economies of scale, which may be expressed in a number of ways, including complementarity between two merging organizations. In connection with vertical integration the economies may come from the more efficient flow of information or the more effective methods of conducting transactions. Of course, the "2 + 2 = 5" effect may also come from improving efficiency or dealing with agency problems as well.

Yet another approach emphasizes effective realignment of the firm to its changing environment. The emphasis here is that by external diversification the firm may more effectively acquire management skills for needed augmentation of its present capabilities.

The information or signaling hypothesis states that mergers take place because the target company is undervalued. A company may be undervalued for a number of reasons. One is because management is not operating up to its potential or other aspects of the inefficient management theories. Another possibility is that bidders have special inside information. Another aspect of the undervaluation theory relates to the difference between the replacement value of a target firm's assets and their current market value. Thus if a bidding company wishes to add to capacity in a particular line of business, it may be able to acquire the additional capacity more cheaply by buying a company that produces the product rather than constructing the new capacity itself.

The agency problem theory arises because managers own only a fraction of the ownership shares of the firm. This may lead managers to work less efficiently or to consume more perquisites because the majority owners bear most of the cost. In large corporations the individual shareholder with small holdings does not have sufficient incentive or resources to monitor effectively the behavior of managers. The threat of a takeover by a firm is a monitoring device that will cause the managers to identify more closely with the interest of shareholders. The market for corporate control may effectively deal with inefficiency or agency problems. Alternatively, the managerialism theory argues that mergers are the result of agency problems, not the solution. The managerialism theory states that mergers take place to increase the size of the firm for the sake of size alone or because the compensation of managers is based on the size of the firm.

Another motive for mergers may be to increase a firm's market share, but it is not clear how this will increase the value of the combined firm. If the increased size of a firm relative to other firms implies a firm of larger absolute size, then we must be talking about economies of scale again. An alternative theory is that increased market share implies increased market power and some elements of monopoly control.

A number of tax considerations may also be involved in mergers. One is the use of accumulated tax losses. Another is for owners of closely held firms to avoid paying taxes at personal income tax rates on ordinary income that would be earned over a number of years in the future by selling their companies at the capitalized values of those future incomes. Thus a capital gains tax may be substituted for a tax on ordinary income. In addition, if stock is received in payment, realization of the capital gain can be deferred to a time period selected by the sellers.

Other types of restructuring activities must also be assumed to have some rational explanation. Divestitures may create value by transferring assets to a higher-valued use. Corporate control and changes in structure may improve managerial efficiency by more directly linking accountability, performance evaluation measures, and compensation.

Conglomerate mergers have been an area of particular study because they were the only type of merger permitted after the tightening of the legal rules in 1950 until new theories and research findings influenced regulatory agencies and the courts in the 1970s to begin to depart from a strict concentration doctrine (market share is a measure of monopoly power) to consider international competition and industry dynamics in judging the effects of mergers. One potential source of synergy in conglomerate mergers was the application of the general management functions of planning and control to a wide range of companies, particularly those companies where these general functions had not been performed well. The pure financial theory of conglomerate mergers emphasized reduction in the probability of bankruptcy. If bankruptcy costs are large, debt capacity may be increased by conglomerate mergers. However, this simply transfers wealth from shareholders to debt holders in the firm.

Under alternative assumptions of the relative size of bankruptcy costs, the degree of interdependence or correlation between cash flows of the constituent companies, and different investor attitudes toward risk, a wide range of alternative models can be developed. These models predict the resulting effects on debt capacity.

In the option pricing model framework, the variance of the combined firm is decreased, which reduces the value of the combined stock and increases the value of the combined debt. Assuming that the value of the combined firm is still the sum of the individual constitutents, the transfer from owners to creditors can be redressed by increasing the debt ratio. These effects are more complex than originally set forth because of variations in the relationships among the variances and leverage ratios of the individual firms as well as in the maturity patterns of their debt structures.

Another explanation for conglomerate mergers is that they represent an outgrowth of the computer age. Improved information systems have expanded the generic managerial capabilities of some firms, leading them to view conglomerate mergers as a natural extension of their existing capabilities. Studies of market relationships have found that the performance of conglomerate firms is not significantly different from the performance of other firms on average over extended periods of time.

PROBLEM SET

19.1 Discuss the assumptions and implications of the proposition that value is conserved (value additivity obtains) under the addition of income streams (mergers).

19.2 Summarize the sources of synergy or operating gains from mergers that have been presented in the literature. Evaluate the validity of the arguments for synergy.

19.3 Explain and illustrate how differential price/earnings ratios reflected in the terms of mergers result in increases or decreases in earnings per share of the merging firms. Do such effects on price/earnings ratios also have effects on the valuation of the firms resulting from mergers?

19.4 Explain and evaluate the managerialism theory of conglomerate mergers set forth by Mueller.

19.5 Explain the pure financial theories of conglomerate firms and evaluate their validity.

For Problems 19.6 and 19.7 assume the following:

i) We are dealing with a world where there are no taxes.

ii) The changes in the parameters affecting value are unanticipated; therefore redistribution effects are possible.

iii) Firms A and B initially have the following parameters:

$$\sigma_A = \sigma_B = .2 \qquad \text{Instantaneous standard deviation}$$

$$T_A = T_B = 4 \text{ years} \qquad \text{Maturity of debt}$$

$$V_A = V_B = \$2000 \qquad \text{Value of the firm, } V = B + S$$

$$R_f = .06 \qquad \text{Risk-free rate}$$

$$D_A = D_B = \$1000 \qquad \text{Face value of debt}$$

19.6 The correlation between the cash flows of firms A and B is .6. If they merge, the resultant firm will be worth $\$4000 = V_A + V_B$, but its new instantaneous variance will be

$$\sigma_{AB}^2 = (\tfrac{1}{2})^2\sigma_A^2 + 2(\tfrac{1}{2})(\tfrac{1}{2})r_{AB}\sigma_A\sigma_B + (\tfrac{1}{2})^2\sigma_B^2$$

$$= (.25)(.2)^2 + 2(.5)(.5)(.6)(.2)(.2) + (.25)(.2)^2$$

$$= .01 + .012 + .01 = .032$$

$$\sigma_{AB} = .179.$$

What will the market value of debt and equity in the merged firm be? If there were no other merger effects, would shareholders agree to the merger?

19.7 Given the results of Problem 19.6, suppose that the merged firm has 1000 shares outstanding. Furthermore, suppose that the shareholders decide to issue $1000 of new debt (which is not subordinate to outstanding debt), maturing in four years, and invest the proceeds in marketable securities, so that the new value of the merged firm is $5000. What will be the new price per share? Assume the merged firm's instantaneous variance is unchanged by this investment.

19.8 You are given the following information:

	Firm A	Firm B
Value prior to merger	$1000	$1000
Face value of debt	500	500

In addition, the value of equity for firm A equals the value of equity for firm B, and the variance of returns for firm A and firm B are also equal. Using a risk-free rate of 8%, an appropriate time horizon of five years, and a variance for each firm of 10%, apply the OPM to calculate the value of equity of the two firms before the merger. Under the further assumption that the correlation between the percentage returns on firms A and B is zero, calculate the value of equity and the value of debt of the merged firm, using the OPM.

a) How does the new market value of equity and debt of the merged firm compare with the sum of the values of equity and debt of the constituent firms that combined in the merger?

b) How much additional debt would the merged firm have to issue to restore equity holders to their original position?

19.9 Empirical studies have established that the betas of conglomerate firms have been significantly above 1. What does this imply about diversification as a strong motive for conglomerate mergers?

19.10 Over a long period of time would you expect the risk-adjusted performance of conglomerate firms to be significantly different from the risk-adjusted performance of a broad market index? Explain.

19.11 Galai and Masulis argue that if two firms merge and thus decrease the probability of default on their debt along the lines of Lewellen's scenario, then the stockholders are actually hurt, since they have assumed some of the risk previously borne by the bondholders. Why might nonowner managers of a firm be motivated to transfer risk from bondholders to stockholders in this manner?

REFERENCES*

Alchian, A., and H. Demsetz, "Production, Information Costs, and Economic Organizations," *American Economic Review*, December 1972, 777–795.

Arrow, K. J., "Vertical Integration and Communication," *Bell Journal of Economics*, Spring 1975, 173–183.

Beckenstein, A. R., "Merger Activity and Merger Theories: An Empirical Investigation," *Antitrust Bulletin*, Spring 1979, 105–128.

Beman, L., "What We Learned from the Great Merger Frenzy," *Fortune*, April 1973, 70ff.

Black, F.; M. Jensen; and M. Scholes, "The Capital Asset Pricing Model: Some Empirical Tests," in Jensen, ed., *Studies in the Theory of Capital Markets*. Praeger, New York, 1972.

Blume, M., "Portfolio Theory: A Step toward Its Practical Application," *Journal of Business*, April 1970, 152–173.

Bock, B., *Statistical Games and the "200 Largest" Industrials: 1954 and 1968*. The Conference Board, Inc., New York, 1970.

Bradley, M.; A. Desai; and E. H. Kim, "The Rationale behind Interfirm Tender Offers: Information or Synergy?" *Journal of Financial Economics*, April 1983.

Brennan, M., "The Pricing of Contingent Claims in Discrete Time Models," *Journal of Finance*, March 1979, 53–68.

Celler, E., *Investigation of Conglomerate Corporations Hearings* before the Antitrust Subcommittee of the Committee on the Judiciary, House of Representatives, 1969–1970, Parts 1–7. U.S. Government Printing Office, Washington, D.C., 1971.

---

* Since Chapters 19 and 20 are closely related in subject matter, the reader is urged to consult the reference sections for both chapters.

Celler Committee Staff Report, *Investigation of Conglomerate Corporations*. U.S. Government Printing Office, Washington, D.C., June 1, 1971.

Chung, K. S., "Investment Opportunities, Synergies, and Conglomerate Mergers," Ph.D. dissertation, Graduate School of Management, University of California, Los Angeles, 1982.

———, and J. F. Weston, "Diversification and Mergers in a Strategic Long-Range-Planning Framework," in Keenan and White, eds., *Mergers and Acquisitions*. D. C. Heath, Lexington, Mass., 1982, Chapter 13.

Coase, R. H., "The Nature of the Firm," *Economica*, November 1937, 386–405.

Cox, J.; S. Ross; and M. Rubinstein, "Option Pricing: A Simplified Approach," *Journal of Financial Economics*, September 1979, 229–263.

DeAngelo, H.; L. DeAngelo; and E. M. Rice, "Going Private: The Effects of a Change in Corporate Ownership Structure," *Midland Corporate Finance Journal*, Summer 1984.

Dertouzos, J. N., and K. E. Thorpe, "Newspaper Groups: Economies of Scale, Tax Laws, and Merger Incentives," Santa Monica, California, Rand Corporation, R-2878-SBA, June 1982.

Dewing, A. S., "A Statistical Test of the Success of Consolidations," *Quarterly Journal of Economics*, November 1921, 84–101.

Fama, E., "Efficient Capital Markets: A Review of Theory and Empirical Work," *Journal of Finance*, May 1970, 383–417.

———, "Perfect Competition and Optimal Production Decisions under Uncertainty," *Bell Journal of Economics*, Autumn 1972, 509–530.

———, "Agency Problems and the Theory of the Firm," *Journal of Political Economy*, April 1980, 288–307.

Friend, I., and M. Blume, "Measurement of Portfolio Performance under Uncertainty," *American Economic Review*, September 1970, 561–575.

Galai, D., and R. W. Masulis, "The Option Pricing Model and the Risk Factor of Stock," *Journal of Financial Economics*, January–March 1976, 53–82.

Gort, M., "An Economic Disturbance Theory of Mergers," *Quarterly Journal of Economics*, November 1969, 624–642.

Grimm, W. T. and Co., *Mergerstat Review 1985*, Chicago, 1986.

Haugen, R. A., and J. G. Udell, "Rates of Return to Stockholders of Acquired Companies," *Journal of Financial and Quantitative Analysis*, January 1972, 1387–1398.

Higgins, R. C., "Discussion," *Journal of Finance*, May 1971, 543–545.

———, and L. D. Schall, "Corporate Bankruptcy and Conglomerate Merger," *Journal of Finance*, March 1975, 93–113.

Jensen, M., and J. Long, "Corporate Investment under Uncertainty and Pareto Optimality in the Capital Markets," *Bell Journal of Economics*, Spring 1972, 151–174.

Jensen, M., and W. Meckling, "Theory of the Firm: Managerial Behavior, Agency Costs and Ownership Structure," *Journal of Financial Economics*, October 1976, 305–360.

Joehnk, M. D., and J. F. Nielsen, "The Effects of Conglomerate Merger Activity on Systematic Risk," *Journal of Financial and Quantitative Analysis*, March 1974, 215–225.

Keenan, M., and L. J. White, *Mergers and Acquisitions*. D. C. Heath, Lexington, Mass., 1982.

Kraus, A., and R. Litzenberger, "A State-Preference Model of Optimal Financial Leverage," *Journal of Finance*, September 1973, 911–922.

Levy, H., and M. Sarnat, "Diversification, Portfolio Analysis and the Uneasy Case for Conglomerate Mergers," *Journal of Finance*, September 1970, 795–802.

Lewellen, W. G., "A Pure Financial Rationale for the Conglomerate Merger," *Journal of Finance*, May 1971, 521–545.

———, and B. Huntsman, "Managerial Pay and Corporate Performance," *American Economic Review*, September 1970, 710–720.

Lintner, J., "Conglomerate and Vertical Responses to Market Imperfection: Expectations, Mergers and Equilibrium in Purely Competitive Markets," *American Economic Review*, May 1971, 101–111.

Livermore, S., "The Success of Industrial Mergers," *Quarterly Journal of Economics*, November 1935, 63–96.

Lynch, H. H., *Financial Performance of Conglomerates*. Harvard Graduate School of Business Administration, Boston, 1971.

Manne, H. G., "Mergers and the Market for Corporate Control," *Journal of Political Economy*, April 1965, 110–120.

Markham, J. W., *Conglomerate Enterprises and Public Policy*. Harvard Graduate School of Business Administration, Boston, 1973a.

———, "Market Structure and Decision-Making in the Large Diversified Firm," in Weston and Ornstein, eds., *The Impact of Large Firms on the U.S. Economy*, Chapter 14. D. C. Heath, Lexington, Mass., 1973.

Mason, R. H., and M. B. Goudzwaard, "Performance of Conglomerate Firms: A Portfolio Approach," *Journal of Finance*, March 1976, 39–48.

Melicher, R. W., and T. H. Harter, "Stock Price Movements of Firms Engaged in Large Acquisition," *Journal of Financial and Quantitative Analysis*, March 1972, 1469–1475.

Melicher, R. W., and D. F. Rush, "The Performance of Conglomerate Firms: Recent Risk and Return Experience," *Journal of Finance*, May 1973, 381–388.

———, "Evidence on the Acquisition-Related Performance of Conglomerate Firms," *Journal of Finance*, March 1974, 141–149.

Merton, R., and M. Subrahmanyan, "The Optimality of a Competitive Stock Market," *Bell Journal of Economics*, Spring 1974, 145–170.

Modigliani, F., and M. H. Miller, "The Cost of Capital, Corporation Finance, and the Theory of Investment," *American Economic Review*, June 1958, 261–297.

Mossin, J., *Theory of Financial Markets*. Prentice-Hall, Englewood Cliffs, N.J., 1973.

Mueller, D. C., "A Theory of Conglomerate Mergers," *Quarterly Journal of Economics*, November 1969, 643–659. (See also comment by Dennis E. Logue and Philippe A. Naert, November 1970, 663–667; comment by David R. Kanerschen, 668–673; and reply by Dennis C. Mueller, 674–679.)

———, "The Effects of Conglomerate Mergers," *Journal of Banking and Finance*, 1977, 315–347.

Myers, S. C., "Procedures for Capital Budgeting under Uncertainty," *Industrial Management Review*, Spring 1968, 1–19.

Nielsen, N. C., "The Firm as an Intermediary between Consumers and Production Functions under Uncertainty," Ph.D. dissertation, Graduate School of Business, Stanford University, Palo Alto, Calif., 1974.

Reid, S. R., *Mergers, Managers and the Economy*. McGraw-Hill, New York, 1968.

Reinhardt, U. E., *Mergers and Consolidations: A Corporate Financial Approach*. General Learning Press, Morristown, N.J., 1972.

Rohatyn, F. G., "Needed: Restraints on the Takeover Mania," *Challenge*, May–June 1986, 30–34.

Schall, L. D., "Asset Valuation, Firm Investment, and Firm Diversification," *Journal of Business*, January 1972, 11–28.

Scott, J. H., Jr., "On the Theory of Conglomerate Mergers," *Journal of Finance*, September 1977, 1235–1250.

Shastri, K., "Valuing Corporate Securities: Some Effects of Mergers by Exchange Offers," Working Paper #S17, University of Pittsburgh, revised January 1982.

Shick, R. A., "The Analysis of Mergers and Acquisitions," *Journal of Finance*, May 1972, 495–502.

Smith, K. V., and J. F. Weston, "Further Evaluation of Conglomerate Performance," *Journal of Business Research*, March 1977, 5–14.

Stapleton, R. C., "Mergers, Debt Capacity, and the Valuation of Corporate Loans," in Keenan and White, eds., *Mergers and Acquisitions*, Chapter 2. D. C. Heath, Lexington, Mass., 1982.

Summer, C., *Strategic Behavior in Business and Government*. Little, Brown and Company, Boston, 1980.

U.S., Federal Trade Commission, Staff Report: *Economic Report on Conglomerate Merger Performance*. Government Printing Office, Washington, D.C., November 1972.

———, Staff Report: *Economic Report on Corporate Mergers*. Government Printing Office, Washington, D.C., August 28, 1969.

———, *Statistical Report on Mergers and Acquisitions*. Bureau of Economics, November 1977.

Westerfield, R., "A Note on the Measurement of Conglomerate Diversification," *Journal of Finance*, September 1970, 909–914.

Weston, J. F., "The Determination of Share Exchange Ratios," in Alberts and Segal, eds., *The Corporate Merger*, 117–138. University of Chicago Press, 1966.

———, "Discussion," *American Economic Review*, May 1971, 125–127.

———, "ROI Planning and Control," *Business Horizons*, August 1972, 35–42.

———, *Mergers and Economic Efficiency*, Proceedings of a Workshop and Supplementary Papers, Vol. 1. U.S. Government Printing Office, Washington, D.C., November 1980.

———, *Mergers and Economic Efficiency*, Industrial Concentration, Mergers and Growth, Vol. 2. U.S. Government Printing Office, Washington D.C., June 1981.

———, and S. K. Mansinghka, "Tests of the Efficiency Performance of Conglomerate Firms," *Journal of Finance*, September 1971, 919–936.

Weston, J. F., and E. M. Rice, "Discussion," *Journal of Finance*, May 1976, 743–747.

Weston, J. F.; K. V. Smith; and R. E. Shrieves, "Conglomerate Performance Using the Capital Asset Pricing Model," *Review of Economics and Statistics*, November 1972, 357–363.

Williamson, O. E., *Corporate Control and Business Behavior*. Prentice-Hall, Englewood Cliffs, N.J., 1970.

———, "The Vertical Integration of Production: Market Failure Considerations," *American Economic Review*, May 1971, 112–123.

20

Corporate takeovers are the logical outgrowth of competitive struggles in the free market. . . . Mergers and acquisitions make sense because they increase the value of the shares held in the target company. . . . The takeover market also provides a unique, powerful, and impersonal mechanism to accomplish the major restructuring and redeployment of assets continually required by changes in technology and consumer preferences. . . . Scientific evidence indicates that activities in the market for corporate control almost uniformly increase efficiency and shareholders' wealth. Yet there is an almost continuous flow of unfavorable publicity and calls for regulation and restriction of unfriendly takeovers. Many of these appeals arise from managers who want protection from competition for their jobs and others who desire more controls on corporations.

Reprinted by permission of the <u>Harvard Business Review</u>, "Takeovers: Folklore and Science" by Michael C. Jensen (Nov./Dec. 1984). Copyright © 1984 by the President and Fellows of Harvard College; all rights reserved.

Mergers and Restructuring: Tests and Applications

The preceding chapter dealt with theories of mergers and restructuring and described some empirical tests of conglomerate merger performance. In the first part of the present chapter we review tests of the theories by a consideration of empirical studies in four areas: (A) tests of merger and tender offer studies; (B) studies of antitrust cases; (C) studies of corporate governance; and (D) studies of other forms of restructuring. We then draw (E) generalizations from the studies. In the second part of the chapter we discuss managerial aspects of mergers, covering (F) terms of mergers and (G) managerial policies in a valuation framework.

Recall that in Chapter 11, describing tests of the efficient market hypothesis, three basic types of empirical models were employed. These were Eqs. (7.32), (7.36), and (11.1):

716

$$R_{jt} = R_{ft} + [R_{mt} - R_{ft}]\beta_j + \varepsilon_{jt}, \qquad (7.32)$$

$$R_{jt} = \hat{\gamma}_{0t} + \hat{\gamma}_{1t}\beta_{jt} + \varepsilon_{jt}, \qquad (7.36)$$

$$R_{jt} = a_j + b_j R_{mt} + \varepsilon_{jt}. \qquad (11.1)$$

Equation (7.32) uses the capital asset pricing theory. Equation (7.36) is the empirical market line derived from the CAPM. However, it does not require the intercept term to equal the risk-free rate. Equation (11.1) is the market model. Under appropriate definitions and assumptions, one can move from one model to another [Ellert, 1975, Appendix A]. However, as noted in Chapter 11, in empirical work the implications are different.

For example, the market model employs time series analysis, developing parameters for periods before and after a time interval influenced by the "event" under analysis. The meaning of the intercept term in the model is not defined, and the nature of the event may influence its measurement. Thus if firms that have not been "performing up to their potential" are the ones that become target or acquired firms, the intercept term will be negative. If firms that have had excellent and improving performance in managing assets become acquiring firms, their intercept term will be positive. In the calculation of the residuals, the intercept for the control period is deducted and hence this form of selection bias will influence the results.

The CAPM form of the model involves the use of a risk-free return. Empirical tests have yielded estimates of the intercept term that are systematically greater than the return on a riskless asset.

Since the implicit empirical assumptions of the alternative models differ, the results of studies using different models require interpretation related to the characteristics of the model employed. In Chapter 11 the three models were used to test for market efficiency. In the present chapter the models are used to test whether mergers or tender offers and other unique events produce temporary "abnormal" returns. Our discussion of the empirical studies of merger performance will take into account the implications of the particular statistical methodology employed.

A. TESTS OF MERGER AND TENDER OFFER RETURNS

Mergers and tender offers achieve similar ends; successful tender offers are followed by formal merger in more than two thirds of the cases. However, the means and motives may differ, resulting in unequal impacts on the shareholders of the firms involved. In tender offers, there is less likely to have been previous negotiations between the parties. In general there is likely to be less information leakage before the formal announcement. There is some plausibility also that synergy is more likely to be involved in mergers where previous discussions about fitting two companies together take place. In tender offers the likelihood is greater that the bidder sees an opportunity for improving the management of the target firm or that its shares are undervalued for one of a number of possible reasons.

1. Early Studies

Early empirical studies of mergers (pre-1973) used comparative studies of firm performance to test for synergy in mergers. Kelly [1967] was the first to study merger profitability using measures including security price changes. His sample consisted of 42 firms matched in 21 pairs of one merging and one nonmerging firm. He compared pre- and postmerger performance based on five measures of profitability (percentage changes in stock price, P/E ratio, EPS, sales per share, and profit margin) and concluded that mergers had little impact on acquiring firm shareholders.

Hogarty [1970] constructed indexes of investment performance based on changes in stock prices. His sample consisted of 43 acquiring firms whose indexes were compared with similarly constructed indexes of their respective industries. He concluded that mergers resulted in negative synergy; investment performance of acquiring firms was 5% less (significant at a 10% level) than their industries' performance.

Lev and Mandelker [1972] faced a similar problem of selecting a standard against which to compare merging firms' performance. Measuring profitability by the annual stock market return on each of 69 acquiring firms, they calculated the average return for the five premerger and five postmerger years for each firm; they then deducted the respective pre- and postmerger average returns of 69 matching firms to control for factors (other than the merger) presumed to identically affect each pair of firms. They found that the market value of acquiring firms rose an average of 5.6% (significant at the 10% level) more than that of the matching control firms.

To this point the evidence on security price changes resulting from mergers is conflicting and is confounded by legitimate criticisms of sample size, methodologies, and control devices used to screen out other influences. It is in this setting that the studies of Halpern [1973] and Mandelker [1974] appear. These two analyses begin the use of asset pricing models.

2. Halpern

Halpern [1973] attempts to directly measure buyer and seller premiums in mergers in a sample of approximately 75 acquisitions. Basically his method is to adjust the observed market prices of acquiring and acquired firms for general market variations during the period when merger information affects their share prices: the price change that remains unexplained by market variations is that attributable to the merger.

Two estimates are required to make the proposed share price adjustments and measurements. First, Halpern needs a base period, the interval before the announcement date during which merger information is reflected in the stock prices. To determine this, he employs the "residual technique" developed by Fama, Fisher, Jensen, and Roll and runs the following time series regression:

$$_jR_{i,t} = \alpha_i + \beta_{1j}R_{m,t*} + \beta_{2j}R_{I,t*} + \varepsilon_{i,t}, \tag{20.1}$$

where $_jR_{i,t}$ is the *price relative* for company i in industry j during the month t, $_jR_{I,t*}$ is the industry price relative, and $_jR_{m,t*}$, the market price relative. The regression yields estimates of $\hat{\alpha}_i$, $\hat{\beta}_1$, and $\hat{\beta}_2$. Substituting these, he rewrites the regression equation in the form

$$\varepsilon_{i,t} = {}_jR_{i,t} - \hat{\beta}_{1j}R_{m,t*}R_{I,t*} - \hat{\beta}_{2j} - \hat{\alpha}_i. \tag{20.2}$$

Halpern then notes that if all of company i's price relative in month t could be explained by industry or market price relatives, the value of the merger, as measured by $\varepsilon_{i,t}$, would be zero. Thus a nonzero $\varepsilon_{i,t}$ indicates that firm i's share price is not entirely accounted for by "normal" factors. Since mergers are unusual events, we would expect the estimated residuals to display unusual behavior during the merger adjustment period. A base date can then be chosen as that date before which "abnormal" residuals were observed. Because of extraneous influences, cross-sectional residuals (over merging firms) were calculated over time relative to the announcement date.

Halpern's analysis indicates that, on the average, merger information is available for seven months before the *announcement* date. From the twenty-third until the eighth month prior to announcements, the cumulative average residuals are randomly increasing and decreasing. From the seventh month onward, they increase steadily. Average residual values are small and vary in size until the large positive value is encountered in the seventh month. Also, a large proportion of positive residuals in the seventh month seems to strengthen this result.

The second element of Halpern's analysis is calculating adjusted security prices. Excluding data from the 12 months prior to the merger, Halpern runs the following equation for each firm using five years of monthly observations:

$$R_{k,t}^b = \alpha_k^b + \beta_1^b R_{m,t}^b + \beta_2^b R_{I,t}^b + \varepsilon. \tag{20.3}$$

From the estimates $\hat{\alpha}_k^b$, $\hat{\beta}_1^b$ and $\hat{\beta}_2^b$ and the actual price relative in the market and industry for the adjustment interval, Halpern calculates the unbiased estimates of the expected price relative for each firm. Multiplying this relative by the base period price and adjusting for dividends paid during the adjustment period, he then obtains an unbiased estimate of the adjusted price. After calculating the gains to "buyers" and "sellers," the firms were classified as "larger" or "smaller" on the basis of their equity value at the base date. Halpern finds that the mean gain prior to dividend adjustment of larger firms exceeded those of smaller firms by a factor of 4. After the dividend adjustment, the gains were smaller for both firm types and approximately equal in absolute amount. Adjustments also had a tendency to make negative gains less negative and at times turned negative "gains" into positive ones.

Subsequently Halpern calculates price premiums, the gain relative to a base price, for both acquiring and acquired firms. While the premium accruing to smaller firms was significantly greater than zero (at 5%), the premium accruing to larger firms was not. His results suggest synergy or improvement in the performance of the smaller firms that is reflected in prices paid by acquirers.

3. Mandelker

Mandelker [1974] used the Fama and MacBeth [1973] methodology to examine the testable implications of what we have termed the *empirical market line*,

$$R_{it} = \hat{\gamma}_{0t} + \hat{\gamma}_{1t}\beta_{it} + \varepsilon_{it}, \tag{7.36}$$

presented in Chapter 7.

First, Fama and MacBeth estimate betas with seven years of monthly data for individual securities using the regression analog of our Eq. (7.32):

$$R_{jt} - R_{ft} = (R_{mt} - R_{ft})\beta_j + \varepsilon_{jt}, \tag{7.32}$$

which is the *ex post* form of the CAPM equation. The individual betas are ranked and placed in 20 portfolios with maximum dispersion of systematic risk in the attempt to minimize the measurement error in the beta estimates.

Second, they use the next five years to recalculate the betas and average them to obtain the portfolio betas. The betas for individual securities are updated every 10 months on the basis of the return data for the preceding five years.

Third, using monthly data for the next four years, they run cross-sectional regressions for each month across the 20 portfolios utilizing Eq. (7.36), the empirical market line. These provide estimates of γ_0 and γ_1, which have been used as measures of the empirical market line parameters in a number of other studies.

Mandelker used the Fama and MacBeth procedures, adding two additional steps for his study of mergers.

Fourth, he estimated the betas for individual firms involved in mergers, using the *ex post* form of the asset pricing relation, Eq. (7.32). The time period measured covered months prior to the merger as well as months following it.

Fifth, he calculated residuals for each month, using the gamma values from Eq. (7.36) and utilizing the values of returns and betas calculated in the fourth step.

Mandelker tested two hypotheses. One was that acquisitions took place in a market under conditions of perfect competition. The other was the hypothesis of efficient capital markets with respect to information on acquisitions. The stockholders of the acquired firms received cumulative average residuals that were positive, indicating that they earned abnormal gains from the mergers. This suggests that the acquired firms may have had unique resources whose values are realized to a greater degree by mergers. Alternatively, the acquired firms may have been operating at below their optimal levels of efficiency, and the mergers were seen as increasing the effectiveness of their operations. The possible benefits to be derived from the acquired firms are apparently perceived by a number of potential acquirers. The competition in the market for acquisitions results in competitive prices for the acquired firms. The acquiring firms appear to operate in a competitive market so that the prices they pay for the acquired firm's stock result in normal returns on the acquisitions. The acquiring firms earn a rate of return equal to other investment or production activities of similar risks. The average residuals for the acquiring firms are generally positive but not statistically significant. This finding controverts the argument that acquiring firms overpay and lose from mergers.

With respect to the hypothesis of efficient capital markets, Mandelker's findings are consistent with the view that the stock market operates efficiently with respect to information on mergers. The price movements that take place at the time of the merger announcement and even before reflect all valuable information about the merger preceding the effective date of the transaction. The stock prices of the constituent firms at the date when the merger is consummated reflect the economic gains expected. The stock prices of the merged firms do not undergo postmerger adjustments.

While significant changes in betas were observed, the rates of return adjusted efficiently to the changes in risk. Stockholders were not misled by accounting manipulations in mergers or by the artificial increase in earnings per share resulting from the differential price/earnings ratio game played by acquiring firms. The views that mergers reflect the desires of managers to control larger firms and their emphasis on growth maximization imply losses to the acquiring stockholders. But the finding of positive average residuals for the acquiring firms is inconsistent with the managerialism hypothesis.

4. Ellert

Ellert [1975, 1976] also employs the Fama-MacBeth methodology, updating their estimates of γ_{0t}. Ellert's studies, like the earlier findings of Halpern [1973] and Mandelker [1974], indicate that the impact on the market prices of merging firms takes place 7 to 12 months prior to the actual merger. The announcement necessarily precedes the merger, and there are leaks even before the public announcement. For acquiring firms, his evidence indicates that while the cumulative average residual (CAR) is generally positive during this period, it is either not significant or the magnitude of the change in CAR during this period is small. This evidence is inconsistent with the managerial theory and its related growth maximization prediction. It is also inconsistent with the monopolistic exploitation theory, at least in providing monopoly gains to acquiring firms.

Both Mandelker and Ellert find that very substantial increases in the CAR of acquiring firms take place during the period from four to eight years prior to the merger activity. This is consistent with the hypothesis set forth by both Mandelker and Ellert that the differentially higher efficiency of acquiring firms prior to mergers leads to their subsequent expansion both externally and internally. With respect to acquired firms, both Mandelker and Ellert find that their CARs are significantly negative in the years and months running up to the period when information about their upcoming acquisition by others becomes available. In the subsequent 7 to 12 months through the actual merger date, the CARs turn strongly positive and are highly significant by statistical tests.

The finding of positive residuals for the acquired firms in the months preceding the merger is consistent with the theory of monopoly control with all the gains going to the acquired firms. However, the evidence of negative CARs in the period running up to the time information on the mergers becomes available is consistent with an alternative explanation. The inefficient utilization of economic resources by the management of the firms prior to the merger leads to their acquisition by firms with a record of above-average performance. Hence the evidence leans in the direction of efficiency and/or synergy as the explanation rather than the managerial or monopoly theories.

If differential efficiency between acquired and acquiring firms were the explanation for mergers, it is likely that there would be a number of acquiring firms bidding for an individual acquired firm. Competition among acquiring firms would, on the average, eliminate abnormal gains to the acquiring firm from the merger activity. This is consistent with the general findings of Mandelker and Ellert. If the acquiring firms had a unique synergistic relationship with an individual acquired firm, the gains from the merger would be attributable to both and could not be allocated individually. This is consistent with Halpern's finding that the absolute dollar amount of the gains is equally divided between acquiring and acquired firms. However, Halpern, Mandelker, and Ellert find that while the absolute gains of acquired firms were statistically significant, neither the percentage premium returns nor CARs for the acquiring firms were statistically significant.

5. Dodd and Ruback

The study by Dodd and Ruback [1977] analyzes tender offers of New York Stock Exchange companies covering the period 1958 through 1976. The market model expressed in our Eq. (11.1) is employed. The control period uses data from month -73 through month -14, and from month $+14$ through month $+73$, where month zero is the month of the first public announcement of the tender offer [Dodd and Ruback, 1977, 358]. Their study included unsuccessful as well as successful tender offers and included the following subsamples: (1) 172 bidding firms, of which 124 made successful tender offers and the remaining 48 made unsuccessful tender offers; (2) 172 target firms, of which 136 received successful tender offers and the remaining 36 received unsuccessful tender offers.

The highest t-values representing statistical significance pertained to the returns for the target firms in the month of the first public announcement of the tender offer. The favorable abnormal returns were about 21% for the successful offers and 19% for the unsuccessful offers. In addition, for the successful offers there was about a 9% positive residual for the period -12 to -1. For the bidding firms the residuals were a positive 12% for successful bids and about 8% for unsuccessful bids over the same period. There was a positive 3% cumulative average residual for successful bidders during the month of the first public announcement of the tender offer. The cumulative average residuals after the public announcement were not statistically significant for either bidding firms or target firms.

Dodd and Ruback were able to sharpen the empirical testing by analyzing a sample of unsuccessful tender offers. The period immediately following the time when the proposed merger or acquisition was supposed to have taken place, but for which the event does not occur in unsuccessful tenders, would carry alternative predictions. The monopoly power theory implies that shareholders of both acquiring and acquired firms would lose because the monopoly gains from the merger that did not take place will now be lost. The managerialism theory argues that shareholders of both the acquired and acquiring firms would benefit if the merger did not take place. Hence the CARs for aborted mergers would become positive. The internal efficiency and the undervalued asset theories imply that the shareholders of both acquiring and acquired firms would be unaffected. The shareholders of acquired firms would be unaffected because the announcement of a tender offer provides new information about the firm. It has some potentials for improvement in efficiency or because of the undervaluation of assets that will probably be recognized by other firms. Under the internal efficiency or undervalued asset theory, other firms will recognize that the assets of the firm that would have been acquired can be improved in value and there will be new suitors. Hence the near-term performance for both acquired and acquiring firms under the internal efficiency or undervalued assets theory would be unaffected by the unsuccessful tender offer. If the acquiring firm had spent substantial sums of money in the negotiations, this might cause a decline in the CARs because such investments in the effort to acquire other firms would not come to fruition. The Dodd-Ruback data for unsuccessful tenders in the near term following the event date show zero CARs for unsuccessful bidders as well as zero CARs for the target firms. This pattern is consistent with the internal efficiency or undervalued assets theory but not with the other theories.

Dodd and Ruback point out that a very substantial proportion of unsuccessful target firms merge within five years of the aborted tender offer [1977, 370]. This leads them to state that their conclusion that the results support the efficiency hypothesis is qualified by the possibility that the subsequent mergers may have been anticipated by the market. If so, the nondecline in the CAR after a tender is unsuccessful could be due to expectations of the future monopoly or synergistic gains from mergers [1977, 370]. However, since their sample period begins in 1958, and since most of the observations in their sample occur in the 1960s and 1970s, the monopoly explanation does not apply. The Celler-Kefauver Amendment, which greatly strengthened the Clayton Act of 1914, was enacted in 1950 and greatly reduced the relative number of horizontal and vertical mergers [Stigler, 1966]. Between 1950 and 1980, which encompasses the data for their study, the largest proportion of mergers had been conglomerate in nature where the issue has not been monopoly in individual markets [see also FTC Staff Report, 1972]. Therefore the Dodd and Ruback findings are consistent with the internal efficiency or undervalued asset theory as well as with the synergy theory but not with the monopoly power or managerialism theories.

6. Kummer and Hoffmeister

Kummer and Hoffmeister [1978] studied 88 New York Stock Exchange firms for whom cash tender offers were made during the period 1956–1974. Their sample was divided into three groups: 44 passive-successful takeovers, where the management of the target firm expressed agreement, neutrality, or no public opinion about the proposed takeover; 15 resist-unsuccessful targets, representing cases in which tender offers were resisted by management, the tender offer failed, and no subsequent tender offers were announced within 10 months of the offer under study; and 6 resist-successful targets, representing firms that were taken over in spite of resistance by the incumbent management.

Of target firms in all categories the cumulative abnormal residuals were negative for the period $(-40, -4)$ months. These negative residuals were statistically significant for all categories except the passive-successful targets. The negative residuals were large, ranging from 10 to 20%. During the four months before the tender offer announcement for each category, the shareholders of target firms received gains of 6% that were statistically significant. During the month of the announcement of the tender offer, the average abnormal return ranged from 16 to 20% for the three categories of target firms. These returns were all highly significant from a statistical standpoint.

For bidder firms the cumulative average residual rose to about 10% during the period $(-28, -11)$. Another gain of 6 percentage points was achieved by shareholders of bidder firms during the period $(-10, -1)$. An additional 5% abnormal gain was received during the month in which the tender offer was announced.

7. Langetieg

Langetieg [1978] reexamined 149 mergers using alternative performance indices as well as a matched nonmerging control group of firms and found that the results using alternative performance tests were generally consistent with the results of Mandelker. But the use of the control group changes the interpretation somewhat. For example, the acquired firms had a significantly negative cumulative average residual of 12.6% over the time interval $(-72, -19)$ months and a significantly positive stockholder gain of 10.6% over the time interval $(-6, -1)$. But the nonmerging control firms also exhibited negative excess returns in the time interval $(-72, -19)$. In two of the three paired-difference tests, Langetieg concludes that some external influence affected both the merging firms and the control firms in a similar way over the similar time periods. For the shareholders of acquiring firms, if the starting point is viewed as 18 months before the merger, the net benefit is 6.1%, which is statistically significant. But the stockholder gain for acquiring companies is substantially less than that for acquired firms.

Langetieg also found that the postmerger performance of a consolidated firm over the period (1, 24) was a negative 12.9 percent. However, in the paired-difference analysis, no significant cumulative difference existed. The postmerger performance of the consolidated companies reflected influences that affected similar nonmerging companies in the same way.

8. Firth

Firth's [1979] study of performance covers data for companies in the United Kingdom for the period 1972–1974. As in U.S. studies, the residuals for the acquired companies were slightly negative in the period $(-36, -12)$ months. The residuals had no strong movement until 1 month before the takeover announcement. Halpern and Mandelker reported that generally 7 months elapsed between the beginning of merger negotiations and the merger announcement. Tender offers, however, are less often associated with communications between the companies involved until very shortly before the public offer announcement.

The CARs in Firth's sample reached 38% for acquired firms within 2 months of the bid announcement. For the acquiring firms the CARs were slightly positive before the announcement but turned to a negative 4 to 5% within 24 months of the tender offer. In absolute amounts the shareholders of acquired firms gained about 650 million British pounds, whereas the shareholders of acquiring firms lost about the same amount. This contrasts with the earlier Halpern study for the United States in which there was a total gain of about $28 million that was split almost equally among the acquired and acquiring firms. Firth comments that previous research for the United Kingdom showed that acquired firms on average had poor profitability records but that the recovery potential was offset by the premiums paid by acquirers. He observes that the relative incidence of mergers in the United Kingdom has been higher than in the United States and suggests that acquired firms had the benefit of a stronger sellers' market for mergers. Also, Firth's data covered 1972–1974, whereas the U.S. studies covered longer periods starting in the 1950s. Analysis of mergers and tender offers in the United States for the years following 1970 might give results similar to those found by Firth for the United Kingdom.

9. Bradley

Bradley [1980] studied 258 cash tender offers that took place during the period July 1962 through December 1977. For calculating the residuals he uses the abnormal price indices compiled by the Center for Research in Security Prices (CRSP) of the University of Chicago. Their procedure is to group securities into 10 equal control portfolios according to their estimated risk. Using the CAPM, an estimate of the daily excess return for an individual security is the difference between the realized return to the security less its control portfolio's return.

For the 161 successful tender offers the mean premium is 49%. The postexecution market price of a target share is 36% higher than its preannouncement level. Hence there is a loss of 13% per target share to the acquirer, and target shareholders realized a significant 36% capital gain on the shares not purchased in the offer. Bradley comments that these data do not support a corporate raiding interpretation of tender offers. Despite the significant premium paid, the acquiring stockholders realize an excess capital gain of 5% within 40 days of the offer with an excess capital gain of 4% taking place within 5 trading days of the offer. Bradley comments that these results are consistent with synergistic gains but cannot distinguish whether they come from market power or cost reductions.

In 33 unsuccessful tender offers the postexecution price level of a target share is 67% above the preannouncement level. This increase in the value of the target shares is higher than the rejected offer premium by 15%. The foregoing results hold for tender offers where all shares were bid for. For fractional tender offers the target shareholders realized a 36% capital gain relative to the preannouncement price. This mean price index is 19% above the rejected tender offer. For the unsuccessful bidders the market price of their shares on the fortieth day after the offer is 4% below their preannouncement level. The negative returns for unsuccessful bidders are attributed by Bradley to the search and administrative costs of conducting a tender offer. Further analysis of unsuccessful takeovers in relation to single-bid versus multiple-bid situations would help sharpen the analysis. Our hypothesis is that positive returns are likely to be preserved with multiple bids but to fall in the single-bid cases. The more fundamental question is to explain the reasons for single bids versus multiple bids.

Bradley also calculates the results in absolute dollar terms. Over the period from two months before the announcement to two months after the announcement the average acquirer's equity increased by $7.7 million even though the average offer premium paid to tendering stockholders was also $7.7 million. Over the same period the value of the outstanding shares of target firms increased an average of $31 million.

10. Dodd

Dodd [1980] is the first of a number of studies of mergers, tenders, and other aspects of corporate governance to employ the market model expressed in our Eq. (11.1). Like Halpern, he uses the announcement date rather than the completion of the merger as the "event." However, studies indicate that there is leakage of information even before the public announcement date. Since Dodd seeks to point up the importance of the role of the announcement date, he uses daily returns rather than the monthly data employed in the previous merger studies.

Daily returns were studied for 151 merger proposals announced in the *Wall Street Journal* from 1971 to 1977. Of these, 71 were eventually completed, and 80 were canceled by either target or bidder management. The market reaction to the merger proposal over Day -1 and Day 0 was significantly positive for target firms (approximately 13%) and significantly negative (though smaller) for bidder firms (approximately -1%).

Dodd concludes that the gains from mergers go to target firms and not to bidders. Bidder CARs for the period 10 days before the proposal to 10 days after approval are negative (-7.22%); the bidder CAR is also negative for canceled mergers regardless of which firm terminates negotiations.

Target shareholders earn large significant positive returns at the proposal announcement (13.43%). For completed mergers the CAR from 10 days before the proposal to 10 days after approval is 33.96%. For canceled mergers the CAR from 10 days before the proposal to 10 days after cancellation is 3.68% for the entire 80 cancellations. For target-initiated cancellations the CAR is 10.95%. For bidder cancellations the target CAR over the same period is 0.18%; i.e., returns revert to their preproposal level. Dodd observes that since the net effect of target-canceled mergers is positive, it cannot be concluded that managers are necessarily acting against the best interests of shareholders when they veto a proposed merger. Our further judgment would be that cancellations by targets are taken as a signal by the market that the bidder has uncovered a profitable opportunity, or that there is a possibility of a return bid from someone else. Bidder cancellations may be taken as a signal that the target does not represent a profitable investment opportunity.

11. Jarrell and Bradley

Beginning with the Williams Act in 1968, increasing federal and state regulation of cash tender offers took place. The regulations provide for increased disclosure, a minimum tender period, and antifraud measures that facilitate defensive lawsuits by incumbent management.

Advocates of tender offer regulation support the view that shareholders need protection from undesirable takeovers, or corporate raiding, and that regulation provides more information and time for the shareholders' decision. Those opposed to regulation argue that it increases the information leakage in a takeover attempt, increasing competition for the target firm. The resulting higher premiums may benefit some target shareholders but amount to a kind of tax against the acquiring firm, decreasing the incentive to engage in acquisitions activity; also, potential target shareholders in combinations foregone will be left worse off by regulation. If, as is argued, corporate takeovers result in more efficient management of target resources, then foregone desirable combinations also impose social costs. Regulation is seen as providing an advantage to incumbent (possibly inept) management and mitigating the disciplinary effect of the market for corporate control.

The authors set out a theory of corporate acquisitions based on the production of knowledge (k) through innovative activity by highly skilled management teams. This knowledge must be combined with some other resource (x) in order to produce gains. If there is no market for the exchange of k, the only way to generate returns from its production is to acquire x, often through corporate takeovers. If k is specific to its producer, information leakage will not be a problem. But if k is specific to the target firm (i.e., k may be knowledge of target management inefficiency), information leakage may enable rival firms to appropriate the gains to k. At any rate, competition for the target will drive its price up. A sudden takeover reduces the leakage period, increasing returns to the producer of k; the delay and disclosure features of regulation increase leakage, reducing the returns to k and thus the incentive to produce it.

Jarrell and Bradley [1980] study the effects of such regulation. Their data included 161 tender offer targets between 1962 and 1977. Forty-seven of the takeovers were unregulated (pre-1968), 94 were subject to federal regulations alone, and 20 were subject to both state and federal regulations. Daily returns were calculated over the period from 40 days prior to the tender offer announcement to 80 days following.

The mean tender premium paid was increased from 32.4% (no regulations) to 52.8% (federal regulations only) to 73.1% (state and federal regulations). The percentage of target shares purchased was also increased by regulation from 42.1% to 71.8%. Cumulative abnormal returns to bidding firms were reduced by regulation.

Jarrell and Bradley conclude that the effect of regulation is to raise the purchase price of target firms, to decrease returns to bidder firms, and to reduce the volume and profitability of takeovers. This problem was reduced to some degree by the decision of the U.S. Supreme Court announced June 24, 1982. By a vote of 6:3 the Court ruled invalid the Illinois Business Takeover Act, which required a company to give state officials 20 days advance notice before offering to buy the shares of another firm. Illinois was one of 36 states that had passed laws regulating corporate acquisitions. The Supreme Court held that the Illinois law unconstitutionally interfered with interstate commerce. Later state statutes have been upheld.

12. Schipper and Thompson

Schipper and Thompson [1983] examine the market reaction to the announcement of a major acquisitions program. They propose that the stock price at the time of the announcement fully capitalizes the expected value of the program—the net benefits of anticipated mergers and the probability that they will occur.

Schipper and Thompson conclude that merger programs are capitalized as positive NPV projects. The positive premerger performance found in previous studies is viewed as a response to the merger program announcement. The small positive returns for acquirers at the merger event found in previous studies is consistent with the hypothesis that the initial capitalization of the acquisitions program is relatively accurate, with only a minor adjustment required at the actual merger, positive because of the resolution of uncertainty. Schipper and Thompson explain the negative postmerger performance found in some prior studies by the fact that many of the postmerger months in these studies fall in calendar time after the date of the regulatory changes.

13. Asquith and Coauthors

Asquith [1983] also finds that most of the gains from a merger go to stockholders of target firms. He finds that the cumulative residual for unsuccessful bidding firms is significantly negative between the announcement date and the outcome date. He hypothesizes that poorly managed merger attempts reflect negatively on the bidding firm.

A study by Asquith, Bruner, and Mullins [1983] tests the Schipper and Thompson hypothesis discussed above. Their more refined tests find that while some of the positive effects of a merger program are capitalized, subsequent mergers also yield positive residuals for bidder firms. They further find that there appear to be positive effects from leakage of information before the announcement date. In addition, when the relative size of bidder and target firms is taken into account, they conclude that bidding firm stockholders gain from merger activity, consistent with value-maximizing behavior.

Asquith and Kim [1982] test whether the gain to shareholders from mergers is at the expense of bondholders by increasing the firm's risk through merger, which they refer to as an agency "incentive effect." An alternative hypothesis is a "diversification effect," which reduces default risk, resulting in wealth transfers from stockholders to bondholders. They conduct a number of careful tests, concluding that mergers have no discernible impact on bondholders. They conclude that mergers are not motivated by the agency incentive effect. Nor do they find a diversification effect, but this may be because of the finding from other studies that leverage is increased after mergers, which would be offsetting.

14. Keown and Pinkerton

While the Keown and Pinkerton [1981] study is treated by its authors as an analysis of insider trading, it also provides a test of the announcement impact. Keown and Pinkerton's sample of 194 firms appears to include both mergers and tender offers. Average residuals and CARs were calculated over the period from 126 days before the announcement to 30 days after. Substantial insider trading begins one month before the announcement, and the activity is heightened in the 5–11 days preceding. For the entire sample, approximately one half of the total market reaction takes place prior to the announcement, with most of the remaining reaction taking place on the announcement day. There is also a significant increase in the trading volume in the three prior weeks. SEC records indicate that this increase is not caused by registered insiders; the implication is that trading is carried out through third parties. These results are consistent with other studies that also find evidence of leaks before the announcement date. But there is also support for semistrong-form market efficiency in that the market reaction is complete by the day after the announcement.

15. Malatesta

Malatesta [1983] uses the *ex post* form of the CAPM model expressed in our Eq. (7.32). However, he does not constrain the intercept term of the model to be zero. Rather, "it enters as a component of predicted *normal* returns" [21, emphasis in the original]. A distinctive variation in the Malatesta study is the calculation of the wealth effects of mergers by the abnormal dollar returns in addition to percentage returns. Malatesta also formulates a distinction between alternative definitions of "event" dates. He defines t_1 as the time when investors learn that the firm will invest resources in merger activity. A later time, t_2, is a resolution date at which a decision is made that the merger will take place or be abandoned. The announcement date is taken as a proxy for t_1, but Malatesta observes that for his sample in more than half the cases the first public announcement was that a merger had essentially been agreed upon. For t_2 his proxy is "substantial board/management approval of the merger" [20]. A problem here is that until stockholder approval takes place and the legal details completed, some risk remains that a merger will not actually take place. Some confounding of influences is involved for both reference dates.

Malatesta's findings based on percentage returns are generally consistent with those of previous studies. However, his results for dollar abnormal returns are different. Portfolios of firms experiencing an information event in the same month were formed both with equally weighted investments in each firm and with investments weighted in proportion to the market values of equity one month prior to the event. The dollar value cumulative excess return was calculated using the value-weighted portfolio forecast error and the total market value of equity of the firms in the portfolio at one month prior to the event. Monthly returns were studied over the period -24 to $+12$ months.

The first published reference to the merger in the *Wall Street Journal* was taken to be a proxy for t_1. For acquiring firms, percentage returns in the 24 months prior to t_1 were insignificantly different from zero, and postannouncement returns were significantly negative. For acquired firms, percentage returns in months -24 to -4 were negative but only marginally significant; then, however, they began to rise. The market reaction to the announcement was significantly positive, and postannouncement returns were also positive.

The first published announcement of substantial board approval was taken as a proxy for t_2. Acquiring firms exhibited inferior performance following t_2 (the cumulative average forecast error dropped 8% over months $+2$ to $+12$). Acquired firms experienced significant share price appreciation at t_2. (All the above results were essentially the same for both equally weighted and value-weighted portfolios.)

Dollar returns for acquiring firms (relative to the date of board approval) indicated cumulative excess negative returns of $49.3 million per firm in the 24 months prior to t_2, but this figure was only barely significant. Acquired firms had significant positive abnormal returns of $19.2 million in the 4 months prior to t_2. The effect of mergers seems to be a net reduction in shareholder wealth; the gain to acquired shareholders in the period -5 to t_2 is $5 million less than the loss to acquiring shareholders.

When Malatesta recalculates the postmerger results with a risk adjustment, the negative postmerger performance of large acquirers is eliminated. The overall result becomes insignificantly positive.

The statistical methodology takes on even greater significance for the Malatesta study. As noted at the beginning of this chapter, the use of the CAPM as expressed in Eq. (7.32) in excess return form implies no intercept term. The intercept term in Malatesta's model is taken as a component of the normal return. It may reflect problems of measuring the risk-free return as well as the behavior of the intercept term calculated for the prior control period. One possibility is that the acquired firms had negative intercept terms while acquiring firms had positive intercept terms for periods in years before the merger "event." If so, the net present value of merger activity adjusted could well be positive for Malatesta's study rather than negative.

B. STUDIES OF ANTITRUST CASES

Other studies that provide information on the role of mergers are those that analyze antitrust episodes. This was the major emphasis of the Ellert [1975, 1976] studies referred to above. Ellert analyzed the data for 205 defendants in antimerger complaints initiated by the Justice Department and Federal Trade Commission (FTC) under Section 7 of the Clayton Act for the period 1950–1972. Of the complaints, 121 were issued by the Justice Department and 84 by the FTC. Ellert observes that the government had not lost a single Supreme Court merger case after the 1950 revision to the Clayton Act. In 60% of the cases studied, defendants canceled merger plans or were ordered to divest part or all of the assets previously acquired. The average duration of litigation measured by the interval between the filing of the complaint and the entry of the last judicial order was 34 months.

Ellert analyzes the behavior of the data for the 205 defendants and also the two groups broken into 123 defendants ordered to divest acquired assets and 82 defendants not required to divest assets. For both groups of defendants for a period preceding the filing of a merger complaint by four years, the residual performance was positive and statistically significant for both groups. The cumulative average residual was over 18% for defendants ordered to divest and about 13% for defendants not required to divest. For the 48 months prior to the filing of the merger complaint, defendants required to divest achieved a further positive residual that was statistically significant. For the same 48 months proximate to the filing of the merger complaint, defendants not required to divest had returns that were not statistically different from the average for the market. In the 12 months preceding the merger complaint the residual performance was not statistically significant for either class of defendants.

On the filing of the merger complaint the average portfolio residual declines by 1.86% for defendants ordered to divest and 1.79% for defendants not required to divest. While these percentages are small, they represent substantial absolute amounts when applied to the large dollar amount of assets involved. In the postwar period these percentages translate into an average dollar loss per respondent of about $7.5 million.

Following the filing of the merger complaint the behavior of the residuals is not statistically significant. This is true for the period between the filing of the merger complaint and the settlement of the litigation. Also, in the 48-month period following the settlement of the litigation, the behavior of the returns to the companies is not statistically different from the market as a whole. It is of interest to note also that final settlements that resolve future uncertainties are typically followed by statistically insignificant behavior of the residuals. On the other hand, settlements such as nolo contendere, which are more likely to be followed by private triple damage suits, result in a persistence of negative residuals that are statistically significant.

It is somewhat surprising that the magnitude of the negative movement in the residuals upon the filing of a complaint is relatively small. The $7 million to $8 million involved is mainly accounted for by litigation costs. A possible explanation may be that there was no basis for bringing the complaint in the first place and that, therefore, nothing significant could be expected to be accomplished in the final action taken by the antitrust authorities. Ellert observes that these results "are also consistent with nonmonopolistic hypotheses of merger motivation. If merger is viewed as a means of expanding the operations of an efficient management group, a specific divestiture of assets would not be expected to constitute a large threat to stockholders, particularly if the firm may substitute internal expansion or external acquisitions in other markets in the future" [1976, 727].

A similar explanation is related to case selection by the FTC and the Department of Justice. Ellert [1975, 66–67] observed the following:

> *Observance of positive residuals in the pre-complaint stage is also consistent with a "harassment" hypothesis. The argument here is that the administrative procedures of the Commission lead it to select firms which, from a variety of competitive pursuits, have experienced abnormally good stock price performance. Whereas the FTC bears the entire financial burden for prosecuting a case, most of its investigations are prompted by complaints from competing firms. . . . The Commission does not disclose the identity of a complaining party. These arrangements create an incentive to invoke the administrative process as a means to harass competitors. If the objective of harassment is to increase the production costs of a rival, it is likely that the prime targets would be among the innovative and most profitable of firms. By their performance, these firms constitute the greatest threat to the complainants within a dynamic competitive framework.*

Thus acquiring firms had a record of effective management of assets in the years preceding their merger activity. Ellert also observes that companies acquired were typically those whose premerger performance was consistent with ineffective management of assets. This is consistent with the role of mergers as performing a useful economic function in reallocating resources from less efficient to more efficient users.

Both Stillman [1983] and Eckbo [1981] analyze the residuals of the rivals to firms participating in mergers. They sought to distinguish between the possible efficiency vs. monopolization effects of mergers. The problem is somewhat complex because at the theoretical level alternative hypotheses can be formulated. The complexity is illustrated by Table 20.1.

Table 20.1 Alternative Hypotheses of Merger Effects

	Participating Firms	*Rival Firms*
	I. Announcement of merger	
Collusion	+ Higher profits from colluding	+ Are part of the collusion
Efficiency	+ External investment with large positive NPV	+ Demonstrate how to achieve greater efficiency
		− Tougher competition
		0 Competition in marketplace unaffected by purchase of undervalued firm
	II. Announcement of challenge	
Collusion	− Collusion prevented	− Collusion prevented
Efficiency	− Prevents a positive NPV investment, also litigation costs	+ Threat of more efficient rivals reduced
		− Also prevented from mergers for efficiency
	0 Could do same thing internally	0 Can do internally
	III. Announcement of decision	
Collusion	− Collusion definitely prevented	− Collusion prevented
		+ Defendants prevented from being more efficient
	0 (1) Negative impact already, at challenge date	0 (1) Negative impact already, at challenge date
	(2) Leakage of likely judicial decision during trial	(2) Leakage of likely judicial decision during trial
	(3) Underlying economics of the industry not affected	(3) Underlying economics of the industry not affected
Efficiency	+ Increased efficiency	+ Can now legally merge for efficiency
		− Tougher competition
		0 Could have accomplished the same thing internally

In Table 20.1 three event dates are identified. They are announcement dates with respect to the merger, to its challenge by the antitrust authorities, and to the announcement of a government decision. For firms participating in the merger the second column of Table 20.1 indicates that the predicted signs of the CARs are the same for the collusion vs. efficiency hypotheses at the times of the announcements of the merger and its challenge. It was for the purpose of sharpening the analysis that the residuals for rival firms were analyzed. But as the final column of Table 20.1 indicates, there is considerable overlap in the predicted signs for the alternative collusion and efficiency hypotheses. Nevertheless, the pattern of these relationships is such that some judgments can be formulated.

Specifically, at the merger announcement date, if the sign of the effect on rivals is not positive, this is consistent with efficiency because efficiency can have a negative or zero sign. Similarly, at the date of the merger challenge, if the effect on the abnormal returns of rivals is not negative, this also is consistent with efficiency, which can also take on a positive or zero sign. In general, when the effect on the CARs is the same for both participants and rivals, it is not possible to distinguish between collusion and efficiency. If the signs differ, then the two groups are affected differently, which tends to rule out the collusion hypothesis. However, at the decision date the results are more difficult to interpret. This is because the effects on rivals can take any of the three possible signs for either outcome. In the light of the general framework presented, let us now look at the empirical results that have been compiled.

Stillman [1983] found that the effect of 30 major challenged horizontal mergers on the residuals of rivals was not statistically significant. The concentration-collusion theory argues that positive residuals should have been observed when the merger was in process and negative residuals when it was challenged. Lack of significance was observed both in relation to the original merger proposal and when it was challenged. Since the effect on rivals was not statistically significant, this casts doubt on the concentration-collusion theory that the mergers were in fact viewed as opportunities for increased possibilities of collusion among the firm's major rivals in the industry.

Eckbo [1981] extended the Stillman study, using a larger sample and a "control" sample of vertical mergers. Eckbo finds that on the announcement of the mergers there are positive residuals both for the participants and their major rivals. This appears to be consistent with the monopoly theory. It is not unambiguous though, because one could also argue that the announcement of the proposed merger conveys information to rivals of opportunities for increased efficiency by expanding scale. Eckbo further finds that at the announcement of the filing of a suit by the antitrust authorities, there is not much effect on the residuals of either the participants or their rivals; in fact, in cases brought by the Federal Trade Commission the effect on rivals is slightly positive. This is consistent with the explanation that the merger partners would have been more efficient and the rivals are protected from this increased efficiency by the Federal Trade Commission suit blocking the merger. Eckbo concludes that the positive performance of rivals of challenged mergers at the time of the original merger announcement reflects information conveyed by the proposed merger that efficiencies can be achieved by expanding scale either internally or externally.

In an extension of Eckbo's earlier work, Eckbo and Wier [1985] paid particular attention to mergers challenged after 1978—i.e., following passage of the Hart-Scott-Rodino Antitrust Improvements Act of 1976, which was intended to improve the likelihood that mergers selected for prosecution were truly anticompetitive. Eckbo and Wier found little evidence of improvement; the 17 post-1978 mergers in their study were "economically efficient" and "apparently would not have harmed competition" [139]. They lay the blame for this failure on the case selection criteria, i.e., inappropriate application of the Department of Justice Merger Guidelines of 1968 and 1982, including the Herfindahl-Hirschman index, which while representing an advance in economic thinking are still unduly dominated by the older "structural theory" of antitrust, which holds that the degree of concentration determines industry conduct and behavior.

The studies appear to support the efficiency basis for mergers. Ellert emphasized that acquiring firms had positive residuals in prior years and acquired firms had negative residuals in prior years. Stillman's evidence was that rival firms did not benefit from the announcement of proposed mergers, which is inconsistent with the concentration-collusion hypothesis. Eckbo, and Eckbo and Wier found positive residuals on the merger announcement but no negative effects on rivals when it appeared that the merger would be blocked by the antitrust authorities. He interprets this pattern of relationships as indicating that the main effect of the merger is to signal the possibility for achieving economies for the merging firms, providing information to rivals that such economies may also be available to them.

As Table 19.2 shows, the dollar values of mergers since 1984 have increased in magnitude even after deflating for higher price levels. Some hold that this is a temporary phenomenon reflecting the particular views of the Reagan administration and its new appointments to the regulatory and antitrust agencies. An alternative point of view is that the more permissive antitrust policies reflect changed economic circumstances such as increased international competition and new empirical research findings on the nature of industrial economics and competition. [Goldschmid, Mann, and Weston, 1974; 1982a, 1982b].[1]

C. CORPORATE GOVERNANCE

A number of other studies deal with corporate governance aspects of mergers and tender offer activity. In our judgment, the main significance of such studies is to emphasize the role of mergers and tender offers in dealing with agency problems. If the firm is not being managed in the best interests of shareholders, another group may see opportunities for increasing the value of the firm. The studies that will be treated next deal with this and related issues.

1. Grossman and Hart

Grossman and Hart [1980] deal with the problem that in a takeover bid individual shareholders, anticipating a rise in the share price, may refuse to tender their

---

[1] Concern has been expressed that older views of antitrust still unduly influence U.S. policy. A case in point is the offer by PPG Industries to acquire Swedlow Plastics, a specialized Defense Department–oriented glass manufacturer with advanced technology. Swedlow's founder was desirous of selling his firm because of his advancing age and the risks of further investments to stay abreast of rapidly advancing technology. PPG made an offer because it was willing to invest financial resources to maintain and perhaps advance Swedlow's technological leadership. But the Federal Trade Commission voted to subject the proposed merger to a lengthy administrative review and evaluation. Swedlow then accepted an offer from a major British glass firm because of the delays and uncertainties imposed by the U.S. antitrust regulatory agency, the FTC.

shares, thus "free-riding" on the value added by the bidder activity. The reduction in returns to bidder activity may cause underinvestment in acquisition activity. Grossman and Hart analyze how to deal with the free-rider problem. They seek to formulate a set of rules of the game so that if some of the shareholders do not tender, there will be some risk that they will have something to lose. The rules, it is hoped, will result in an optimal amount of acquisition activity.

Grossman and Hart observe that it is possible to avoid the free-rider problem by providing for a contract written into the charter of the firm itself that permits the bidder to "expropriate" the shareholders remaining after the takeover to the extent of a dilution factor they call ϕ. This expropriation may be accomplished by selling assets or output of the firm to another firm owned by the new control group at prices below market value.

What Grossman and Hart are seeking to achieve is best understood in the light of socially desirable mergers, acquisitions, and takeovers. From a social standpoint, they should have a positive NPV. For value to be created the bidding firm does something after the target firm is acquired. It changes the target firm in ways that will add value. Usually this involves the expenditure of resources by the bidding firm; at a minimum, it involves the expenditures required to research and to take over a company. The problem is that after the acquisition all shareholders share proportionately in any gains that are created. Because the old shareholders participate proportionately in the gains, this reduces the incentive to bidder firms to make investments that create additional value. From a social viewpoint this may lead to underinvestment in acquisition activity. The goal is to formulate rules of the game so that those who spend the resources are enabled to capture a portion of the gains commensurate with the resources they have committed and the risks they have incurred.

One of the implications of the Grossman and Hart model is the use of two-tier tender offers. A higher price and better terms, such as permitting a choice of cash or stock to fit the tax needs of the tendering shareholder, may be used on the first block of shares required for control. For the remaining shares the price is lower and the form of payment may be less attractive, such as the debt or preferred stock of the acquiring company. So shareholders have a strong incentive to tender in the first group rather than in the residual group. The first-tier offer is likely to be oversubscribed and therefore handled on a pro rata basis by the acquiring company. The real price realized by tendering shareholders is an average of the first-tier and second-tier arrangements. Thus differential prices can be used to increase the probability of success of the tender offer. The possibility of such an arrangement permits the dilution factor ϕ that will be set in the original charter to be much lower than otherwise.

An illustration of this two-tier bidding is provided in the U.S. Steel tender for Marathon Oil, which took place in early 1982. The first step was the bid by U.S. Steel on November 5, 1981, for 30 million Marathon common shares at a price of $125 per share. The second step was the provision that on the effective date of the merger each remaining shareholder of Marathon would be entitled to receive for each common share $100 principal amount of $12\frac{1}{2}$ percent guaranteed notes due 1994. Some dissatisfaction was expressed with the second step because the market value of the notes offered appeared to be in the $70 range. This offer represented an average value of $106 for Marathon shares. This was relatively close to Mobil's competing bid, which was valued at $108. When the U.S. Steel bid was approved by shareholders on March 11, 1982, the value of the notes was $76, and the tender was valued at $101 per Marathon share.

However, it is more appropriate to view the two steps as the components of a single price [Brudney and Chirelstein, 1978]. The two steps should be recognized as a useful social device for increasing the probability of success of tender offers. Thus it is a useful method of dealing with the managerial agency problem. Furthermore, competition among firms that make tender offers will push up the level of the average price in the two-part transaction. Grossman and Hart conclude that U.S. government policy on takeover bids from the Williams Act in 1968 to the present may have undesirable consequences. The disclosure provisions of the Williams Act require a bidder to make an announcement of intentions after buying 5% of the company. This encourages competition from other bidders but also aggravates the free-rider problem.

2. DeAngelo and Rice

Antitakeover amendments to corporate charters are studied by DeAngelo and Rice [1983]. Antitakeover amendments make the transfer of corporate control more difficult. DeAngelo and Rice analyzed a sample of 100 firms proposing amendments between 1974 and 1979. The main types of amendments found may be briefly described. (1) A staggered board typically requires that one third of the board would be elected each year for a three-year term, delaying the point at which a new majority shareholder could gain board control. In the DeAngelo-Rice sample 53% had this provision. (2) A supermajority rule would require more than 50% approval for a merger, typically 67% to 80%. (3) What they call a fair merger price is essentially an antidiscriminatory treatment provision. A typical stipulation is that remaining shareholders receive compensation at least as large as the maximum share price paid to acquire majority control. Other provisions strengthen the position of the board of directors (usually management controlled), further limiting stockholders (particularly a new control group.) Lockup provisions prevent circumvention of the antitakeover provisions and are typically adopted contemporaneously.

DeAngelo and Rice consider two hypotheses to explain antitakeover amendments. The managerial-entrenchment hypothesis states that incumbent management seeks job security at the expense of shareholders. It implies that the amendments increase the costs and weaken the disciplinary mechanisms in the stockholder/manager agency relationship. The managerial-entrenchment hypothesis predicts a negative share price reaction to proposed antitakeover amendments.

The stockholder-interests hypothesis holds that target shareholders may benefit from contractual mechanisms that enforce a cartelized response to an offer for control. The antitakeover amendments may place the target shareholders in a better bargaining position to obtain a higher price premium in a takeover. Subsidiary arguments might be that the provisions represent a type of long-term employment contract for managers, giving them incentives to pursue long-run maximization goals rather than short-term objectives.

In DeAngelo and Rice's empirical tests the mailing date of the proxy announcement is used as the best estimate of the date the amendments are compounded in the stock price. The analysis of daily returns indicates a weakly negative price impact, which is statistically insignificant. The methodology was varied in a number of ways without altering these results. DeAngelo and Rice observe that their tests may be biased against the managerial-entrenchment hypothesis because the proposal of anti-takeover amendments may signal an increased probability that the firm will be approached with a merger or tender offer. Since stockholders in acquired firms typically earn positive abnormal returns, such a signal should impart an upward bias to the announcement return. The signaling hypothesis would imply positive returns; the management-entrenchment hypothesis implies negative returns. The net effect of the two influences is uncertain. Their observance of nonsignificant negative returns implies that without the positive signaling influence the returns would be more strongly negative, consistent with the management-entrenchment motive for anti-takeover amendments.

3. Linn and McConnell

Linn and McConnell [1983] study a larger sample of 475 instances, proposed by 398 New York Stock Exchange corporations between January 1960 and December 1980. Most observations were clustered in the 1968–1970 and 1975–1978 years, with 97% appearing after January 1968. They investigated three alternative event dates: the date the amendments were ratified by the board of directors; the date of proxy mailing; and the date of the ratification vote at shareholder meetings. They also investigated intervals between these events.

Linn and McConnell generally find positive but insignificant effects of the anti-takeover amendment activity on stock prices. As a further check, they seek to measure the impact of the change in the Delaware corporation code in June 1969, which eliminated the supermajority approval requirement for mergers. The change in the Delaware law appeared to have a negative impact on stock prices. They also studied a small sample of antitakeover amendments that were rescinded. The results appeared to be negative but probably not significant. On a very small (10 firms) sample of defeated antitakeover amendments, the results are insignificantly positive.

The evidence and alternative hypotheses on the effects of antitakeover amendments on stock prices are conflicting. DeAngelo and Rice find a negative, but not significant, influence. Linn and McConnell find a positive effect of antitakeover amendments on share prices but predominantly insignificant. The conclusion suggested is that there is no effect of antitakeover amendments on share prices; but if there is no effect, why should a firm use resources to enact takeover amendments? One possible answer is that the absence of any effect of antitakeover amendments on stock prices is consistent with the operation of an efficient market for managerial services as well as for merger and takeover activity. But the results are also consistent with other hypotheses.

4. Dann and DeAngelo

Dann and DeAngelo [1983] analyze standstill agreements and negotiated premium buybacks. Standstill agreements limit a substantial shareholder's ownership to less than a controlling percentage for a specified number of years. Negotiated premium buybacks represent the repurchase of a substantial shareholder's block at a premium; the buyback may be a part of a standstill agreement. Like the antitakeover amendments, these mechanisms also reduce competition in the market for corporate control by reducing the threat of takeover by a substantial shareholder.

Two alternative hypotheses are considered. The management-entrenchment hypothesis argues that standstills and buybacks are used to reduce a takeover threat, thereby increasing the job security of managers and reducing the ability of the market for corporate control to deal with the agency problem or managerial inefficiency. Small individual shareholders do not have the incentives or resources to monitor managers effectively. However, the large block shareholder will gain substantially from an increase in efficiency and typically has the resources to take action. The alternative stockholder-interests hypothesis would argue that the market for managerial labor disciplines managerial efficiency under the threat of reduced compensation for ineffective performance. If the market for managerial labor is effective, then the actions of a shareholder who accumulates a large block of shares simply represent a power struggle between competing groups for corporate control. If only a power struggle is involved, the attendant costs will simply cause a reduction in the value of the stockholders' wealth. By avoiding the costs of a power struggle, the stockholders will benefit.

In their empirical tests of the competing hypotheses, Dann and DeAngelo take the first public announcement in the *Wall Street Journal* as the date when the standstill or buyback is compounded in the stock price. The sample included 81 firms with 19 pure standstills, 51 pure repurchases, and 11 standstills with repurchase. The average standstill period was five years, and the average maximum ownership interest permitted was 20% (in agreements without repurchase) and 0% (in standstills with repurchase). The average stake repurchased was 9.8% of outstanding stock, larger than the average open market repurchase (5%) but smaller than most tender offer repurchases (14–15%). The average premium in premium repurchases was 16.4% over the preannouncement price; this is similar to the average premium in tender offer repurchases.

The results indicated a significantly negative stock price impact at Day -1 and Day 0 for standstill agreements. The negative reaction was stronger for standstills with repurchase than for pure standstills. This reaction is consistent with the managerial-entrenchment hypothesis.

The results for negotiated buybacks were also negative but were not very significant. (Again, the negative reaction was reinforced if the buyback was accompanied by a standstill agreement.) This does not strongly support the managerial-entrenchment hypothesis, but it definitely does not support the stockholder-interests hypothesis, which predicts a positive price reaction. Despite the similarities with tender offer repurchases (or open market repurchases), negotiated buybacks do not have the same positive wealth impact (up to 16%).

5. Bradley and Wakeman

Bradley and Wakeman [1983] add several variations to the Dann-DeAngelo study. On single-block repurchases the effects on the repurchasing firm are negative, and significantly so. These effects are reinforced when the repurchase is associated with the termination of a prior takeover effort by the selling group. Bradley and Wakeman seek to separate the wealth transfer effect from information effects. For the nonmerger group (i.e., where the repurchase is not associated with a takeover termination), the information effects appear to be insignificant. Thus the wealth transfer implied by the repurchase premium is the dominant effect; however, while these effects are negative, they are not significant for the nonmerger group. For the merger group the information impact is negative for both firms, suggesting that the repurchase premium causes a positive NPV project to be abandoned.

Bradley and Wakeman also study repurchases from corporate officers. Scholes [1972] had found a negative reaction to insider sales, indicating that insiders possessed adverse information about the company. Bradley and Wakeman find a slight wealth gain, which they suggest is consistent with portfolio rebalancing by the insider, and the company's willingness to purchase their shares may signal the absence of adverse information. They suggest that secondary distributions (studied by Scholes) may reflect a decision by the company not to make the repurchase, thereby confirming a signal of adverse information.

The third area covered by Bradley and Wakeman is the repurchase of small share holdings. A rationale is to decrease shareholder servicing costs. They observe that the 1.25% gain is large in relation to estimates of savings, indicating that the repurchase also represents a positive information signal.

6. Dodd and Warner

Dodd and Warner [1983] study proxy contests, examining issues similar to those treated by Dann and DeAngelo in analyzing the role of block holders of shares. Dodd and Warner observe that for the sample analyzed in their study only 16 (about 15%) of the dissident groups were led by another firm. They say that this indicates a weak relationship between proxy contests and other takeover activity. An alternative view is that proxy contests may also be viewed as competing with other forms of takeover activity at the margin. At any rate, similar issues are involved.

One hypothesis is that proxy contests are motivated to deal with the agency problem. Since boards of directors are generally dominated by management, to the extent that the board does not act in the best interests of shareholders, a proxy contest may be viewed as a form of managerial labor market discipline. If so, proxy contests should result in higher share prices. An alternative hypothesis is that a proxy contest is simply a power struggle for the control of the firm. If so, share prices should not be affected or should fall because of the expenditure of company resources in defending incumbents.

The Dodd-Warner sample covered 96 proxy contests between 1962 and 1978; 71 were control contests (the dissidents sought 50% or more of board seats); and 25 were participation contests (the dissidents sought minority representation). Three events are pertinent: (1) the first announcement of the contest in the *Wall Street Journal*; (2) the stockholder meeting and election; and (3) the announcement of the election outcome.

Contrary to the improved-management hypothesis, there is little evidence of poor performance in the months and years preceding the contest. There is evidence of significant positive abnormal performance in the five months preceding the contest announcement. Daily returns show cumulative returns of +11.9 percent over the 60 days up to and including the announcement date. This is almost certainly related to the contest rather than to another simultaneous event: (1) the abnormal performance is concentrated in the days very close to the announcement; and (2) the *Wall Street Journal* announcement often comes relatively late in the proxy contest process, and preannouncement leakage is great. Positive performance persists in both control and participation contests (higher in control contests), and regardless of the eventual outcome (although it is higher for successful dissident groups).

Significant negative abnormal returns are observed in the period from the announcement through the election outcome; the mean cumulative residual is -4.3%. These returns are concentrated in control contests, but participation contests also exhibit insignificantly negative returns during this interim period. Again, these results persist in spite of outcome. Although these negative returns indicate that at least some of the preannouncement gains are not permanent, the net result over the entire period surrounding the contest remains positive for the entire sample.

Dodd and Warner conclude that proxy contests are associated with significant share price appreciation of an average magnitude of 5 to 10%, consistent with the improved management of corporate resources hypothesis. That the positive performance persists regardless of contest outcome indicates that it is the challenge per se that results in improved corporate performance. The erosion of early share price gains can be partly explained by the prior overvaluation caused by increased demand for the stock before the holder-of-record date.

7. Dann and DeAngelo

In a later study of antitakeover defenses, Dann and DeAngelo [1985] consider structural defensive measures—i.e., changes in asset or ownership structure in the face of anticipated or actual takeover threats. Anticipatory defenses in the absence of an explicit threat are difficult to detect or to distinguish from structural changes made for some other business motive. They may include having a very complex organizational structure or adhering to a highly technical line of business, both of which would make a firm less attractive to a broad spectrum of potential acquirers. Diversification into a regulated industry increases the scrutiny to which any future takeover would be subjected and thus might deter a less determined bidder. A third measure involves no more (and no less) than maintaining a balance sheet affording the financial flexibility to enhance the target's ability to respond to any threat that might arise.

Responsive structural defenses, on the other hand, include measures tailored to the goals and/or vulnerabilities of a specific hostile bidder. Examples would include divestiture of that portion of the target that the bidder most wanted to acquire, an acquisition by the target that would create an antitrust conflict with the bidder (or possibly an acquisition in a regulated industry). Defensive ownership restructurings include the private placement of a large block of voting stock in hands friendly to incumbent management, issuance of more equity to increase the cost of takeover, or repurchase of voting stock (financed by issuing debt), which both concentrates voting power in the target's management as well as leaving the target's financial structure highly levered and thus less attractive. The so-called Pac-man defense in which the target announces a plan to buy the bidder represents another type of responsive structural defense.

Dann and DeAngelo's sample consisted of 39 announcements (by 33 firms) of structural defenses to hostile takeover bids over the 1968–1983 period. The market model was applied to target common stock prices over the two-day trading period surrounding the announcement of the structural defense and resulted in a mean prediction error of -2.33%; i.e., the market's assessment was that target shareholders were harmed by the defense. Further analysis revealed that the proposed defenses were large both in terms of dollar value of assets involved (42.34% of the target's preoffer equity value) and in terms of voting rights (change of 27.62% in board votes). Roughly 37% of the defenses were closely related to bidder attributes (i.e., acquisition to raise an antitrust conflict, Pac-man defense, sale of assets the bidder wanted), whereas 63% represented attempts to create or enhance a consolidated voting block. Bidders' attempts to counter the proposed defensive changes (by, e.g., reducing the offer premium unless the plan were dropped or by litigation) were successful more than 25% of the time.

Finally, the sample was divided into three roughly equal subsamples, depending on contest outcome. (The evenly distributed outcomes lead Dann and DeAngelo to conclude that takeover battles occur when both sides see some possibility of success.) For subsample 1 (10 cases), the hostile bidder was successful in acquiring a majority or substantial minority interest in the target; target shareholders experienced significant abnormal returns of 42.97% over the period from 40 days prior to the contest initiation through its outcome. The second subsample included 11 cases in which the hostile bidder withdrew in the face of a third-party bid (typically a "white knight" more congenial to target management); target shareholder returns over the same period were 57.58%. The third group consisted of 12 cases where the hostile bidder withdrew, and there were no other offers outstanding for the target; in this case, target shareholders gained only 15.12% in the same -40 days-through-contest-outcome period (from the date of contest initiation through contest outcome, they suffered a loss of -3.81%). The decline at contest outcome—i.e., when the bidder withdrew with no other bids on the table—was greater than the decline upon announcement of the structural defense.

That the defenses were just that and not part of overall sound business strategy is supported by the fact that the plans were implemented more often when the incumbent or white knight prevailed than when the hostile bidder took control. The evidence is consistent with managerial self-interest influencing corporate structure, and there is some basis for policymakers' concerns about structural defenses; however, there is no indication that curbing such defenses would necessarily benefit shareholders. Instead, managers would rely more on less detectable anticipatory defenses which may be even more detrimental to shareholder interests. Further, such constraints on management's ability to resist control transfer would reduce the incentive to invest in firm-specific human capital inputs, with corresponding negative effects on shareholders.

8. Dual-Class Stock Studies

DeAngelo and DeAngelo [1985] examine the issue of management control over the board of directors, which would of course insulate management from the discipline of the corporate takeover market and the competition of rival management teams. Their sample consisted of 45 firms in 1980 with dual classes of common stock outstanding. The two classes of stock had identical residual cash flow rights but differed in voting rights in board elections. The authors found that a management coalition (consisting of corporate officers and their families) controlled a majority of the board of directors in 27 of the 45 firms. They further found that the management coalition concentrated its stockholdings in the superior-vote stock; i.e., the management group held a 56.9% median interest in voting rights versus only a 24% median interest in cash flow rights.

Dual-class firms are seen as an intermediate organizational form between privately held firms and dispersed-ownership public corporations necessitated by the personal wealth constraints of managers: they must sell external equity in order to take advantage of investment opportunities, but by using two classes of common stock, they can do so without relinquishing control. Among the benefits of dual-class stock are increased incentives for managers to invest in organization-specific human capital because of the reduced likelihood that returns to such investment will be expropriated. Because such dual-class arrangements are voluntary, and were typically of long standing, the authors conclude that they cannot, on average, be harmful to shareholders. They can be particularly useful in situations where it would be difficult and/or costly to communicate the information necessary to correctly evaluate management performance to outside shareholders. Disciplines other than the market for corporate control substitute for this mechanism to check managerial opportunism in dual-class firms. First, the external capital market reflects an assessment of management performance in the market prices of firms' debt and equity securities. Second, there are social sanctions arising out of the significant family involvement found in the sample firms. And finally, the management coalitions' not-insignificant holdings of cash flow rights mean that managers are not immune to the wealth effects of their decisions.

Lease, McConnell, and Mikkelson [1983] also studied dual-class stock firms. As in the DeAngelo and DeAngelo study, the two classes of common stock differed only in voting rights; however, the Lease et al. study required that both classes be actively publicly traded over the 1940–1978 period to test for differences in the market prices of the superior-vote versus inferior-vote stock. For 26 firms where only the common stock had voting rights, the mean price premium for the superior-vote stock was 5.44%; however, in 4 other firms that included a voting preferred stock issue in their capitalization in addition to the two classes of common stock, they found that the superior-vote common stock sold at a mean price discount of 1.25% relative to the inferior-vote common. Although the samples are small, statistical tests indicate that the results are significant and of economic importance in terms of dollar value. The authors conclude that superior voting rights must provide the potential for incremental benefits (of necessity indirect since explicit cash flow benefits are identical); one possibility is additional compensation and perquisites for employee/shareholders of the superior-vote stock. The incremental value of voting rights appears to be diluted when control is shared with voting preferred stock, indicating that control involves costs as well as benefits. The distribution of costs and benefits may, in part, be dependent on the complexity of the control structure. DeAngelo and DeAngelo confirmed, to some extent, the Lease *et al.* finding of a price premium for superior-vote stock in their analysis of four mergers in which the superior-vote common commanded a rare explicit price premium over inferior-vote common stock with an identical cash flow claim.

9. McDaniel

McDaniel [1986] emphasizes bondholder interests in his article. He examines the relationship between bondholders and shareholders overall, how bondholders are affected by mergers, spinoffs, etc., and the need for bondholder protection. While the traditional focus has been on shareholder wealth maximization and the differences between shareholder and bondholder claims, McDaniel suggests that the distinctions between the two securities are blurring. He holds that the average shareholder in a large public corporation with a nominal ownership interest is essentially a passive property owner not unlike the bondholder. (Junk bonds even have risk characteristics very similar to equity, and the changing nature of the bond markets has increased the risk volatility of all bonds.) Therefore, McDaniel suggests, the emphasis on shareholder wealth maximization may be misguided if such wealth comes at the expense of bondholders.

Firm value maximization is the preferred goal and is synonymous with shareholder wealth maximization only if bondholder interests are protected. There is some evidence that at least some of the shareholder gains in mergers and voluntary spinoffs are the result of bondholder expropriation; McDaniel argues that any degree of expropriation is unacceptable. With respect to voluntary spinoffs, e.g., Schipper and Smith [1983] indicate that bondholder expropriation is less likely under certain conditions (where parent debt is allocated to the spun-off subsidiary, or where the subsidiary has its own debt). But McDaniel suggests that bondholders are less protected than many previous authors have supposed.

Bond indentures with their protective covenants are regarded as a strong bulwark against expropriation. But McDaniel analyzes the indenture covenants of *Fortune* magazine's 1984 100 largest industrial corporations and finds virtually no restrictions on risk alteration or asset disposition (i.e., restrictions on investment risks and disinvestment), which can be damaging to bondholders. He feels that the trend over time has been toward fewer rather than more protective covenants. Perfect covenants require perfect foresight and costless contracting. If covenants are too lenient, shareholders may benefit at bondholder expense; if too strict, bondholders exercise virtual veto power over the firm's actions.

The bond trustee, another purported defender of bondholder interests, has almost no duties prior to default; his or her postdefault duties are of little help to bondholders since most of the damage has already occurred. State and federal statutory constraints do little more than restrict dividends and asset transfers that would result in outright insolvency, whereas alteration of investment risks can be very harmful to bondholders' positions well short of insolvency.

Stock exchange listing criteria are not very stringent, and in any case, bonds are increasingly unlisted; even listed bonds trade mostly on the over-the-counter market. Market forces that could discipline managers with higher interest rates for a reputation for harming bondholders are only effective if there is a "next time out." In merger contests the beleaguered target is in an "end-game" situation, which increases the incentive to exploit bondholders by, e.g., a scorched earth policy.

McDaniel argues that the costs and frictions in the market for corporate control reduce its disciplinary effectiveness. Bond market liquidity can protect bondholders against gradual deterioration in risk (by allowing bondholders the possibility of selling out quickly) but offers little protection against sudden changes in risk. Another possibility for bondholder protection is buying both stocks and bonds of the same firm (diversification in an all-bond portfolio would be ineffective, since the possibility of bondholder expropriation would be a systematic risk in that case).

McDaniel advocates applying the fiduciary duty principle of corporate law as a substitute for costly contracting to protect bondholder interests. This would give management a responsibility to look out for bondholders as well as shareholders. McDaniel would give bondholders the same right as shareholders to bring derivative suits (on behalf of the corporation) as well as direct suits (against the corporation), which is all that is permitted to bondholders under current law. He places great faith in the courts to decide whether management is acting according to its fiduciary duty and which type of lawsuit is appropriate in each case.

McDaniel also proposes a number of methods to protect bondholders in takeover contests, among them: (1) due-on-sale clauses, which would make debt payable upon sale of the firm; (2) requiring that bidders make tender offers for bonds as well as for shares, or enacting a conditional self-tender for bonds triggered by takeover; (3) higher interest rates and/or voting rights for bondholders triggered by takeover; (4) giving target bondholders a first mortgage on target assets, thus effectively subordinating all other debt.

D. STUDIES OF OTHER FORMS OF RESTRUCTURING

1. Alexander, Benson, and Kampmeyer

Alexander, Benson, and Kampmeyer [1984] investigate the valuation effects of voluntary corporate selloff announcements, i.e., when a firm sells a portion of its assets to outsiders, usually another firm. They hypothesize that voluntary selloffs (as opposed to forced or involuntary divestitures) are the result of positive net present value decisions, and thus their announcement should result in upward stock price movement. They use the mean-adjusted returns, or comparison period, technique for daily returns around the event date (the date of the *Wall Street Journal* in which the event is first announced). That is, the expected return on a security is assumed to be constant, and the analysis focuses on the error term, or the difference between the expected return and the actual observed return.

Three procedures for estimating the expected return and its standard deviation are discussed. The *pre-only procedure* uses data from a preevent estimation period; however, if either the expected return or its standard deviation or both shift to new levels following the event, the pre-only procedure will result in a biased estimator of postevent standardized residuals. A second procedure, the *both-combined method*, calculates estimates of expected return and standard deviation after combining pre-event and postevent estimation periods; the resulting standardized residual estimator may be biased for both pre- and postevent residuals. Alexander, Benson, and Kampmeyer propose a *both-but-separate technique* and calculate two separate standardized residual estimators; the preevent estimation period provides an unbiased estimator of preevent standardized residuals, and a postevent estimation period provides an unbiased estimator of postevent standardized residuals.

Three possible motives for voluntary selloffs are each associated with potentially unfavorable information: (1) firms seek to sell unprofitable ventures; (2) firms seek to become less diverse; and (3) firms seek to generate needed cash. Thus the selloff announcement itself may become part of a "bad news/good news" scenario. Since it is unlikely that a firm would release the good news before the bad news, the remaining alternatives are to release the bad news first or to release it simultaneously with the good news. Thus the expected stock price effects might follow a negative-normal-positive sequence or might be offsetting to some degree.

Alexander, Benson, and Kampmeyer's sample consisted of 53 voluntary selloff announcements by NYSE firms over 1964–1973; data consisted of 301 daily returns centered on the announcement date. Results were calculated using all three estimation procedures and using the market-adjusted returns technique as well as the mean-adjusted returns technique. The pattern and magnitude of cumulative average residuals (CARs) was found to be similar regardless of the estimation procedure, although there was some difference in significance of the results. Selloffs appear to be announced following a period of generally negative returns. The study found that voluntary selloff announcements had a very slight positive price impact; whether the size of the positive impact was offset by the simultaneous release of negative information, reflected a near-perfect market for selloffs, or was just indicative that the NPV of the selloff was small relative to all other cash flows of the firm is impossible to distinguish.

2. Jain

Jain [1985] also examines the effect of voluntary selloffs on shareholder wealth but extends the work of Alexander *et al.* by examining stock price reactions of both buying and selling firms. Jain identifies four possible motives for the selling firm: (1) unforeseen circumstances, such as poorer-than-expected earnings; (2) the selloff as a partial merger when certain parts of the firm may be more valuable to another user than to the current owners; (3) desire to specialize in a limited number of business activities, to become less diverse; and (4) desire to transfer wealth from bondholders to shareholders, the agency problem. Buyers are viewed as investors in new projects, and thus their shareholders are expected to experience zero or positive stock price effects since investors, on average, invest in at least nonnegative NPV projects.

Jain's sample consisted of 1062 event dates for sellers (date of first published information about a selloff in the *Wall Street Journal*, whether or not a buyer was identified) and 304 event dates for buyers (the date the possible buyer was initially identified in the *Wall Street Journal*—not necessarily the same as the seller's event date). The methodology consisted of estimating the expected return for a given security on a given date using beta-controlled portfolios of firms formed in event time, and a preevent estimation period.

Jain found that sellers earned significant positive excess returns of 0.70% over day -5 to day -1. Buyers were found to experience significant positive excess returns of 0.34% on day -1, although returns over days -5 to -1 were insignificantly different from zero. Thus selloff announcements appear to be good news for both buyers and sellers. The fact that abnormal returns to sellers are much smaller in absolute terms than those earned by target firms in mergers may reflect the relative importance of the two types of events or the fact that the selloff is initiated by the seller, whereas the merger is usually initiated by the buyer. The results may indicate that the selloff market is less than fully competitive—only rarely did more than one buyer come forward to competitively negotiate with the seller—or the seller's desire for a quick transaction for needed liquidity.

Examining the preevent period revealed significant negative abnormal returns for selling firms of -10.8% from day -360 to day -11. Thus selloffs may be one kind of action taken by managers in adversity to enhance their shareholders' welfare.

3. Miles and Rosenfeld

Spinoffs differ from the selloffs discussed above in that no money changes hands; ownership interests in the divested assets are distributed on a pro rata basis to the shareholders of the parent firm, and the former division or subsidiary becomes a separate entity rather than part of another firm.

Miles and Rosenfeld [1983] estimate the effect of voluntary spinoff announcements on shareholder wealth. They suggest three possible ways in which spinoffs might enhance parent firm value: (1) by eliminating negative synergies, which might increase future cash flows; (2) by expanding the opportunity set available to investors and providing investors with more flexibility in their choice between dividends and capital gains; and (3) by causing a wealth transfer from bondholders to stockholders, i.e., a manifestation of the agency problem.

They use the mean-adjusted returns technique on a sample of 55 spinoffs announced over 1963 through 1980 and find significant positive abnormal returns immediately surrounding the spinoff announcement. Day 1 abnormal returns were significantly positive, 2.5%, with a 3.3% positive abnormal return over a two-day announcement period.[2]

The authors test for the effect of spinoff size by splitting their sample into two subsamples: a large spinoff group for which the divested unit has an equity value of at least 10% as large as the parent's equity value, and a small spinoff group, consisting of 34 and 21 firms, respectively. The effect of minor spinoffs was, not surprisingly, significantly smaller relative to the effect of large spinoffs.

For the sample as a whole the abnormal return over the entire 181-day observation period (day −120 through day +60) was positive and significant at 22.1%, with more than half this total (13.6%) occurring over day −120 through day −20, leading Miles and Rosenfeld to conclude that spinoff announcements, on average, follow a period of abnormally positive returns, which is in marked contrast to the generally negative abnormal returns preceding selloff announcements. Thus while both spinoffs and selloffs are similar events and both result in positive share price effects, they appear to be motivated by very different underlying circumstances.

4. Schipper and Smith

Schipper and Smith [1983] also investigate shareholder wealth effects of voluntary spinoffs and go on to distinguish between alternative possible sources of shareholder gains. Their sample consists of 93 spinoff announcements between 1963 and 1981; they use the market model with a preevent estimation period to estimate abnormal returns. Their results over the two-day announcement period, day −1 and day 0 (corresponding to Miles and Rosenfeld's day 0 and day +1), were significant positive abnormal returns of 2.84%, consistent with the Miles and Rosenfeld results, but they found no evidence of abnormal share price behavior in the four months before (or in the two months after) the spinoff announcement.

Schipper and Smith split their sample into pre- and post-1970 subsamples to examine the effect of SEC regulations enacted in 1969–1970 requiring registration of spinoffs whenever future trading was intended in order to prevent the device from being used to circumvent disclosure requirements for "going public." However, it appeared that the regulatory changes had little impact on stock price reactions.

Potential sources of gains from spinoffs are classified in terms of "contract revisions." The bondholder expropriation theory involves a revision (or violation) of the contract between shareholders and bondholders. The authors examine a subsample of spinoffs with publicity traded bonds and find little evidence of a wealth transfer in the behavior of bond prices or bond ratings. They next investigate the possibility that spinoffs represent a revision of the contract between shareholders and regulators (including tax authorities and labor unions). In this hypothesis, shareholder gains could result from more favorable tax status (e.g., shifting some assets into a royalty

---

[2] Miles and Rosenfeld denote as day 0 the day *preceding* the *Wall Street Journal* publication date since this is the most likely date of the parent firm's press release announcing the spinoff; the significant positive returns on day 1 probably reflect the fact that press releases are often not issued until after the day's trading has closed.

trust); fewer government restrictions (e.g., spinning off a regulated utility or a foreign subsidiary); or relief from onerous labor union contracts (i.e., a spun-off subsidiary may not be obliged by collective bargaining obligations of its former parent). For 18 sample firms where the parent specifically stated regulatory or tax motives in its spin-off announcement, the two-day announcement period return was 5.07% (significant). Thus this type of contract revision is shown to be a source of shareholder wealth increase in cases where it is available. However, it cannot explain the gains for the entire sample.

Finally, Schipper and Smith consider the effect of spinoffs on the contract between shareholders and managers. Gains in this case could result from reducing the size and diversity of the asset base under a given management's control to eliminate or reduce diseconomies of scale and improve management incentives and productivity. The authors examine firm growth in the five years prior to the spinoff for evidence of possible diseconomies of size and find average annual sales growth, fixed asset growth, and number of employees growth of 20%, 30%, and 19%, respectively, for the sample as a whole. For a subsample of 30 firms with a stated motive of reducing size and diversity, some of this rapid growth was clearly the result of merger activity; 65 acquisitions were completed in the two years preceding the year of the spinoff, and 17 of the spinoffs were reversals of prior acquisitions.

The effect of diversity on diminishing returns to management is measured by the industry membership of parent and spun-off subsidiary. In 72 of 93 cases the subsidiary was classified in a different industry. A second measure of diversity seeks evidence of structural shifts in parent firm stock returns following the spinoffs. For a subsample of 62 firms for which sufficient data were available, 22 exhibited statistically significant shifts in stock returns, more than could be expected by chance, reinforcing the evidence of industry membership.

The authors conclude that spinoff announcements benefit parent firm shareholders and that the source of the gains is a combination of relaxed regulatory or tax constraints and increased productivity due to reduced size and diversity of assets under a single management. Bondholder expropriation was not judged to be a significant source of shareholder gain.

5. Hite and Owers

In their 1983 article on voluntary spinoffs, Hite and Owers investigate two hypotheses: that gains result from (1) effects on existing contracts, the possibility of bondholder expropriation in particular; or (2) effects on future contracting flexibility (i.e., the set of contracts that might be optimal for combined operations may not be identical to the optimal sets of contracts for the same activities carried out by independent entities). This includes the possibility that a subsidiary might have a different optimal leverage ratio from its parent firm, or that spinoffs may represent the types of contractual revisions discussed by Schipper and Smith above.

The authors studied a sample of 123 voluntary spinoffs by 116 firms over 1962–1981, identifying as the press date, day 0, the date of the first *Wall Street Journal* announcement that a spinoff might take place. Their event period begins 50 days prior to the press date and extends to a completion date, the date the spinoff dividend declaration is reported in the *Wall Street Journal*, an average of 62 days from the press date. They used the market model with a preevent estimation period, and their results are consistent with those of other studies—a significant abnormal two-day announcement period return of +3.3% for the sample as a whole. However, the results were not uniformly positive; 38 announcements resulted in a negative two-day return. Similarly, there was evidence of good price performance in the preannouncement period. For the entire sample the abnormal return over the event period is +7.7% (significant); postannouncement abnormal returns are insignificant here, as elsewhere, indicating semistrong market efficiency.

The expropriation hypothesis was tested on a subsample of 31 firms that had 53 publicly traded senior issues. Since infrequent trading can be a problem in analysis of senior security price changes, the authors used the period "around" the announcement date rather than a strict two-day announcement period return. However, there was no evidence of any significant price effect on senior security prices. Further, matching pairs of senior security price reactions and common stock price reactions resulted in price changes of the same sign in 29 of 53 cases. The authors reject the expropriation hypothesis.

Hite and Owers also tested for the effect of relative spinoff size, with results consistent with Miles and Rosenfeld. Large spinoffs led to a greater stock price reaction than small spinoffs (5.2% versus 0.8%, respectively, for the two-day announcement period return). They find that, overall, spinoffs generate gains roughly equal to the value of the divested unit; parent firm values were not significantly diminished by distributing assets to subsidiaries.

Finally, Hite and Owers break their sample into four subgroups according to the stated rationale for the spinoff. The first group consisted of 12 spinoffs designed to facilitate mergers (either the acquirer wanted only the subsidiary or only the parent) and resulted in event period excess returns of 11.6%. These so-called partial mergers thus produced shareholder gains analogous to the takeover premia paid to target firms in full mergers, but of a lesser magnitude.

For 27 spinoffs the stated motive was specialization, or "undiversification," to "get back to basics." This group showed the largest excess returns over the event period, 14.5%.

A third group of 19 spinoffs were undertaken as a defense against anticipated external interference, e.g., from regulators or antitrust authorities. Although the two-day announcement period return for this group was +3.4%, this barely overcame negative preannouncement performance of −3.2%, and the group experienced negative returns of −4.7% for the entire event period.

A catchall group of 63 spinoffs without explicitly stated motives not surprisingly showed price performance equivalent to a portfolio of the other three groups combined.

Reexamining their initial hypotheses, Hite and Owers conclude that there is little support for the expropriation hypothesis but also that the magnitude of abnormal returns is too large to be fully explained by unique optimal contracting for parent and subsidiary. Rather, they suggest that there must be some fundamental change in the underlying opportunity set facing parent and/or subsidiary that leads to the spinoff and is announced simultaneously. This is supported by the differences in abnormal returns for subsamples grouped by spinoff motive.

6. Schipper and Smith

In a 1986 study, Schipper and Smith turn their attention to equity carve-outs in which a parent firm offers the equity of a wholly owned subsidiary directly to the public. Their primary focus is distinguishing the stock price reaction to equity carve-outs from the stock price reaction to seasoned equity offerings of the parent, which typically result in abnormal losses. However, equity carve-outs are also similar to spinoffs in that they both initiate public trading of equity claims on subsidiary assets separate from the parent firm. They also parallel divestitures to the extent that they provide a cash inflow to the parent firm, although in divestitures there is no subsequent public trading of separate subsidiary stock. Also, in divestitures, and most spinoffs, the parent firm relinquishes control over the subsidiary; in equity carve-outs, however, the parent typically retains majority control.

The study sample consists of 76 announcements of equity carve-outs from 1965 to 1983. Day 0 is the date of the earliest announcement of intention in the *Wall Street Journal*, and the test period is focused on the five trading days ending on the announcement date. Abnormal returns (using the market model with a preevent estimation period) are compared with two benchmarks: (1) zero reaction and (2) the stock price reaction of the same parent firms to announcements of public offerings of their own common stock or convertible debt (a subsample of 26 matched pairs).

The results were consistent with significant positive average share price reaction to the equity carve-out announcement of 1.8% over the five-day announcement period. This is similar to results of spinoff studies but in marked contrast to the negative results found in this—and other studies—for seasoned equity offerings of the parent firm (-3.5% over the five-day announcement period). The average difference between the price reaction to the equity carve-out and parent equity offering announcements for the 26 matched pairs was $+5.5\%$ (significant) over the five-day period. Examination of individual returns in all cases indicated that average returns were not atypical; i.e., the results did not seem to be driven by a few outliers.

The negative share price reactions to seasoned equity offerings (and indeed to virtually all equity-increasing restructuring activities) have been explained in a number of ways. Two explanations involve information and signaling. First, the market interprets an increase in equity as having negative implications about management's assessment of stock value based on their superior private information. That is, managers issue equity when they believe it to be overvalued on the market. Second, the resulting decrease in the leverage ratio is taken to reflect management pessimism about future profitability. A third explanation suggests that underpricing of the new issue results in a wealth transfer from old to new shareholders.

The stated motives given for equity carve-outs were examined in an attempt to explain differences in results from those of seasoned offerings. In 19 cases, external capital was subsequently needed to finance the subsidiary's growth. This financing motive, which is not available in spinoffs, enables, e.g., a slow-to-moderate-growth parent firm to take advantage of opportunities facing a high-growth subsidiary while avoiding the negative information effects it might incur if it issued additional equity of its own. In support of this hypothesis the carved-out subsidiaries had higher P/E ratios, indicating higher growth, in 74% of the cases, a percentage higher than would be expected by chance.

Other carve-out motives and potential sources of gain are virtually identical to spinoff motives. In 14 carve-outs the stated motive included the hope that the increased exposure and disclosure requirements of the newly public firm would lead to increased understanding of the subsidiary by investors (sufficiently to offset the costs of providing the additional information). Asset restructuring and realignment of management responsibilities was also an important factor in many cases and was specifically stated in 10 cases. This plus managerial incentive contracts tied to market-determined assessments of performance via publicly traded stock prices tie equity carve-outs and their effects even more closely to spinoffs than to seasoned offerings.

On the negative side, equity carve-outs create a minority interest and the potential for conflicts of interest with the controlling parent firm. However, the minority interest can be and is eliminated if it becomes a problem without losing the benefits described above. Hence the equity carve-out can be viewed as an interim or temporary step in the restructuring process; 44 of the carve-outs in the sample studied here were subsequently reacquired by the parent, completely divested, spun off, or liquidated.

7. Copeland, Lemgruber, and Mayers

The spinoff study by Copeland, Lemgruber, and Mayers [1987] is distinctive in several respects. It avoids the post-selection bias by selecting a small sample based on announcements of spinoffs rather than on their completion (the "large sample"). They find that 11% of announced spinoffs are not completed. The first announcement abnormal return to shareholders of the small sample (unbiased) is 2.49% compared with 3.03% for the larger sample based on spinoff completions. The smaller return from the unbiased sample may reflect some probability that the announced spinoff will not be completed.

They also measure the effects of successive announcements of planned spinoffs, finding that they also result in positive gains for shareholders. Combining all these effects, they estimate the expected abnormal return for a completed spinoff as 5.02%. The spinoff ex-date abnormal returns are also significantly positive and significant; but since no new information is revealed, they exclude this element from their estimate of the abnormal return associated with a complete spinoff.

Consistent with previous studies, Copeland, Lemgruber, and Mayers find that the first announcement effects are positively related to the relative size of the spinoff. The returns from taxable spinoffs are not significantly different from zero. When the relative size of the spinoff is taken into account, the nontaxable spinoffs do not have higher returns than the average for the entire sample.

8. DeAngelo, DeAngelo, and Rice

DeAngelo, DeAngelo, and Rice [1984a,b] consider the wealth effects of going-private announcements on public shareholders. Going private entails replacing the entire public ownership with full equity ownership by incumbent management; leveraged buyouts (LBOs) are a subset of going private in which management shares equity ownership with third-party investors who help finance the transaction. Since going private merely restructures ownership, concerns have been raised that any gains that might result must come from the expropriation of public shareholders; these concerns have brought going-private transactions under SEC regulation requiring extensive disclosure with respect to purpose and fairness (to public shareholders) of the arrangements. In mergers and acquisitions, e.g., managers have a fiduciary duty to secure the maximum compensation per share for the firm's shareholders; in going private the incumbent management group has a conflicting incentive to minimize compensation paid to acquire control.

The authors investigate a sample of going-private proposals and find significant wealth increases for public shareholders. They suggest a number of sources of gains from going private and further argue that minority public shareholders have significant bargaining power (i.e., the right and ability to block, significantly delay, and/or greatly increase the costs of going private), which forces management to share these gains. Three sources of gain are cited. First, material cost reductions in registration, listing, disclosure, and shareholder servicing expenses can be achieved. Second, managerial incentives are improved. Greater rewards to discretionary effort can be made without the need to justify compensation to ill-informed outsiders. And third, in the case of LBOs effective monitoring of management is performed by highly motivated third-party investors, whose ties to institutional investors facilitate higher leverage and correspondingly higher interest tax shelter. The preoffer median debt-to-asset ratio in the leveraged buy-out sample was 11%; the forecast postoffer ratio was 86%. A potential drawback for the private firm is reduced access to public capital markets, but most LBOs contemplate a later public offering when value increases have been achieved.

DeAngelo, DeAngelo, and Rice investigated a sample of 81 going-private proposals by 72 firms (9 proposals were withdrawn and then revived) over the 1973–1980 period. Managers controlled the majority of stock in the typical transaction; transactions carried out as mergers into a shell corporation fully owned by management were successful 81% of the time, whereas the success rates for other institutional forms of carrying out the transaction (e.g., tender offers, asset sales, or leveraged buyouts) ranged from 40 to 43%. The authors applied a single-factor market model to test the gains-sharing hypothesis: a positive stock price reaction to the initial proposal with a negative reaction to its withdrawal would support the hypothesis. For the initial going-private announcement the two-day announcement period return was a significant +22.27%; the premium offered in 57 cash compensation proposals averaged 56.31% over the market price two months before the announcement. Thus the results strongly support the gains-sharing hypothesis. Further analysis to test whether the stock price reaction was biased upward by information (good news) regarding future profitability implicit in the going-private announcement indicated that the wealth increase could not be explained solely by this factor.

An 18-firm subsample of withdrawn offers exhibited a significant negative return of −8.88% over the 2-day announcement period, again corroborating the gains-sharing hypothesis. In spite of the negative response to the withdrawal announcement, the subsample showed a cumulative positive response of 21.89% from 40 days before the initial proposal through withdrawal, which was maintained through 40 days after withdrawal. This implies either (1) a permanent upward reappraisal of the firm's prospects as a public company or (2) the probability that management might revive the offer or (3) the possibility that another firm might offer to buy now that the potential for gains from restructuring had been revealed.

The authors conclude that public shareholder wealth effects to going-private announcements were similar to those experienced in such arm's length transactions as mergers and tender offers as were the premia offered by management. They find no indication of exploitation of minority shareholders and suggest a number of alternative possible sources of gain.

E. GENERALIZATIONS FROM THE STUDIES

While the numerous studies reviewed are not always in complete agreement, some generalizations can be formulated on the basis of the dominant patterns observed. These generalizations relate to an evaluation of the role of mergers and related restructuring activities on a number of important issues of corporate financial theory and policy. The empirical results are summarized in Table 20.2.

For acquired firms, from the period just before the merger announcement date, the shareholders achieve significant positive gains. In an earlier period the cumulative average residuals are negative, indicating that acquired firms had not been performing up to their potentials.

On average for the period just before the merger announcement date the shareholders of acquiring firms neither gained nor lost. But in tender offers where the negotiation period is shorter, gains for the shareholders of acquiring firms tend to be significantly positive. The conclusion indicated is that legislative enactments that have delayed the completion of tender offers have also reduced the gains for acquiring firms.

In earlier periods the CARs for acquiring firms are positive, indicating that acquiring firms have had a record of managing asset growth successfully. This leads to the further hypothesis that in pure conglomerate mergers the prospective depletion of internal investment opportunities leads acquiring firms to look to other industries where growth prospects are more attractive and to seek out firms that appear less capable of responding to these favorable prospects [Chung, 1982].

Some studies indicate that the CARs decline after the merger or tender offer. However, this appears to be accounted for by the nature of the industries in which the acquiring firms mainly operate. Netting out the industry effect, the CARs do not

**Table 20.2   Empirical Results from
Studies of Residuals**

Studies	Returns
A. Merger studies	
1. Acquired firms	20%
2. Acquiring firms	2–3[a]
B. Tender offer studies	
1. Acquired firms	35
2. Acquiring firms	3–5
C. Sell-offs	
1. Spinoffs	2–4
2. Divestitures	
Sellers	.5–1
Buyers	.34
3. Equity carve-outs	2
D. Premium buybacks	
1. Single blocks from outsiders	−2
2. From insiders or small shareholdings	1.2
3. Sellers of single blocks	1.5
E. Standstill agreements (nonparticipating stockholders)	−4
F. Antitakeover amendments	1.5
G. Proxy contests	10
H. Share repurchases	16
I. Going private	20
J. Leveraged buyouts	50

[a] Not statistically significant.

decline after the merger. These results contradict both the managerialism theory and the theory that mergers are not based on valid economic or business reasons.

Analysis of unsuccessful tender offers permits a further sharpening of the analysis among competing theories. The monopoly theory would hold that an unsuccessful tender offer should result in negative residuals for shareholders of both acquiring and acquired firms, since the gains from the monopoly rents will be lost. The managerialism theory predicts that shareholders of the acquiring firm would gain, since the proposed tender offer was uneconomic in the first place; aborting the combination therefore would be a blessing to shareholders of the acquiring firm. To the extent that these acquiring firms were ready to overpay the shareholders of the targets, the latter shareholders would lose if the tender offer does not succeed. An alternative theory would be that since the potentials for improving the management of the acquired firm or the possibilities of synergy between an acquiring and an acquired firm have been discovered and brought to light, no market reaction will occur when a particular tender offer is unsuccessful. The empirical results are that after unsuccessful tender offers there is no significant change in the CARs of the acquired firms. This is consistent with the new-information hypothesis. The effect on the bidding firms would be predicted to be negative because they have spent resources in search and costs of formulating the offer, and now these investments have no fruition. The data confirm that the residuals are negative, but they are not significant [Dodd and Ruback, 1977, 368]. One reason why the negative residuals are not significant is that the market may view bidder firms as engaged in a series of tender offer attempts, because they have a track record of managing assets effectively. Hence the market reacts negatively if search costs for specific tender offers fall through. But taking a longer view [à la Schipper and Thompson, 1983], the market judges that this experience will be put to good use in other tender and merger activities.

The differences in results obtained may be explained in part by the signaling effect of the type of compensation used in an acquisition [DeAngelo and DeAngelo, 1987]. If a firm uses stock in the acquisition, this may imply that it considers its stock to be overvalued. If a firm uses cash, this may reflect the firm's judgment that its own stock is too valuable to use—it is undervalued. (Cf. Myers and Majluf [1984] for a similar hypothesis with respect to internal investment decisions.) The empirical studies are consistent with this information hypothesis. The Bradley study is of cash tender offers, Dodd and Ruback study both cash and stock exchanges, and the Dodd study is on mergers with mainly stock swaps. Bradley found positive returns to acquiring firms, Dodd negative returns, and Dodd and Ruback no significant effects. When cash is used, this may signal that the stock of the acquiring firm is undervalued, and conversely when stock is used for the purchase. When both cash and stock are used, the two effects may be counterbalancing.

The studies of the effects of merger activity on rivals seek to distinguish between monopoly and efficiency motives for mergers. The concentration-collusion theory holds that there would be positive effects on rivals upon the announcement of major horizontal mergers. The evidence is somewhat conflicting on this point. The concentration-collusion theory also holds that when the government authorities make a final decision to prevent a merger, the effects should be negative residuals for the rivals as well as for the participant firms. However, there appear to be no significant effects on any of the groups. This is inconsistent with the monopoly hypothesis. It may be that, regardless of the actions taken by the antitrust authorities, the underlying economic forces of the industry have now been identified. It would appear that opportunities for efficiencies will be effectuated internally if they are not permitted to take place externally. If there are no monopoly effects from the horizontal mergers, and if the economic results are ultimately the same, then the antitrust activities represent extra costs in the economic resource allocation process that delay the achievement of potential improvements in efficiency.

The corporate governance studies portray an important role for merger and takeover activity (including proxy contests) in utilizing the market for corporate control to deal with agency problems. The literature is not in agreement on whether the market for managerial labor and various forms of settling up in compensation contracts are sufficient to deal with the agency problem. However, it would be plausible that the market for corporate control, the threat of takeovers, and the market for managers all operate to deal with the agency problem. Grossman and Hart treat the free-rider problem in the functioning of the market for takeovers. Charter provisions for dilution after the completion of a merger or two-tier merger proposal are among the mechanisms for dealing with the free-rider problem.

Some studies indicate that antitakeover provisions, standstill agreements, and buyback provisions may have a negative, but not significant, influence on share prices. Other tests find a positive but not significant influence. Structural defenses in response to hostile takeover bids had a negative effect on target share prices, although over the entire contest period, target shareholders were not harmed. Overall, the studies suggest no significant effect. This result could be consistent with an efficiently operating market for managers and a competitive market for corporate acquisitions. The Dodd-Warner study suggests that proxy contests represent an alternative at the margin for making the market for corporate control more effective. Their results are consistent with the hypothesis that proxy contests are not simply power struggles but are associated with changes that result in the improvement of share price performance of the firm. These studies highlight the importance of the agency problem introduced into the literature by Jensen and Meckling [1976].

Studies of takeover defenses and the extent of managerial vote control appear to indicate that the agency problem inherent in the shareholder-manager relationship is not a serious cause for concern. Rather, management's control over the board and its ability to resist takeover attempts may actually benefit shareholders by increasing manager's incentives to make firm-specific human capital investments and/or by driving up the price at which the firm ultimately sells.

The conflict between shareholders and bondholders may be more troublesome, since, as McDaniel [1986] points out, bond covenants offer bondholders very little protection against expropriation in takeovers. A 1986 study by Dennis and McConnell of senior security price reactions to merger announcements, however, finds little evidence of negative effects on bond prices.

Consistent with the above studies, analyses of various other forms of restructuring including selloffs, spinoffs, equity carve-outs, and going private were also found to benefit shareholders. Selloffs, which bring in additional funds, were found to follow periods of generally negative returns, whereas spinoffs, which generate no influx of cash to the parent firm, were found to follow periods of above-normal performance. Reasons for the positive stock price reaction to selloff and spinoff announcements include the elimination of negative synergies, improvements in managerial incentives and organizational design, and relaxation of regulatory or tax constraints. Expropriation of other security holders was ruled out as a primary source of gain.

In equity carve-outs the parent firm maintains control of the carved-out subsidiary while bringing in cash to finance its growth opportunities without the negative stock price effects generally associated with additional offerings of seasoned parent firm stock.

Going-private and leveraged buyout transactions resulted in gains to public shareholders almost as high as gains to target shareholders in tender offers, primarily owing to material reductions in shareholder communications, registration and disclosure costs, improved managerial incentives, and the ability of public shareholders to block the transactions, thus forcing management to share the gains with them.

We view mergers and corporate restructuring as a part of the general process of resource allocation in the economy. We would regard internal investments and external investments as alternatives that are not necessarily substitutable or mutually exclusive. Sometimes circumstances suggest the use of internal investments; other times they suggest external investments. Particularly in long-range strategic planning it may appear that it will be less risky and hence more likely to produce a positive net present value if management capabilities are augmented by combining with an existing ongoing investment—another firm. On the other hand, internal investments made in areas in which management has had historical experience may involve less risk in that unexpected events or surprises may be less likely. Buying another firm may involve less than complete information and characteristics that may have been hidden from outsiders. Particularly when an acquiring firm sees investment opportunities unattractive in familiar areas and seeks to augment its capabilities by combining with firms in completely different types of operations, the risk of making investment mistakes is increased. Merger activity from a capability base to achieve expansion into concentrically related areas appears to offer prospects of the greatest success [Rumelt, 1974].

We would expect that soundly conceived internal investments as well as soundly conceived external investments will, on average, have positive net present values. We see no theoretical basis for arguing that either form of investment would be superior in the long run. Both internal and external investments have appropriate roles to perform in the resource allocation processes of the economy and in the efforts of individual organizations to maximize their value.

In the first part of this chapter we dealt with tests of alternative restructuring theories. In the second part we deal with the managerial implications of the foregoing material. First, we consider terms of mergers, then we consider merger analysis in a valuation framework.

F. TERMS OF MERGERS

Larson and Gonedes [1969] set forth a model of exchange ratio determination. They reject the effect of mergers on earnings per share as a test and argue that the effects of mergers on market value would be an appropriate test. The market values of common stocks are used to determine the precombination wealth positions of the parties involved in a merger, and the result is compared with the postmerger wealth positions of the parties. Since the Larson-Gonedes decision horizon is the immediate postmerger market values, the postmerger price/earnings ratio of the merged firm receives their greatest emphasis. They observe that the earnings multiple of a combined firm will be a weighted average of the earnings multiples of the constituent firms if (1) the growth rate of the combined entity is a weighted average of its constituents' growth rates, and (2) the riskiness of earnings stream of the combined entity is a weighted average of the earnings streams [1969, 722]. The earnings multiple of a merged firm will exceed the average of its constituents' earnings multiples if the new growth rate exceeds the average of the constituents' growth rates. The earnings multiple of a combined entity will also be affected by its risk. The risk of the combined firm will be decreased, increased, or remain the same depending upon whether the covariance of the earnings stream with the market is decreased, increased, or remains the same.

The Larson-Gonedes model holds that the exchange ratio will be determined by each firm's assessment of the postmerger price/earnings multiple and postulates that each firm requires that its equivalent price per share be at least maintained as a result of the merger. Their model is summarized algebraically and graphically by Conn and Nielsen [1977], using the following symbols:

    ER = exchange ratio,
     P = price per share,
   EPS = earnings per share,
    PE = price/earnings multiple,
     E = earnings,
     S = number of common shares outstanding,
   AER = actual exchange ratio.

In the formulations that follow, subscripts 1, 2, and 12 are used to refer to the acquiring, acquired, and combined firms, respectively.

An exchange ratio is determined depending upon postmerger advantages expected from the combined firm subject to the stockholder wealth constraint. This is expressed as follows:

$$P_{12} \geq P_1. \tag{20.4}$$

We use the equality relationship. The market price per share for the combined firm is defined in terms of earnings and the price/earnings ratio as

$$P_{12} \equiv (PE_{12})(EPS_{12}) \equiv P_1. \tag{20.5}$$

The expression for the earnings per share of the combined firm is then detailed as follows:

$$EPS_{12} = \frac{E_1 + E_2}{S_1 + S_2(ER_1)}. \tag{20.6}$$

In this equation, ER_1 represents the exchange ratio of shares of firm 2 for shares of firm 1 from the perspective of firm 1. In Eq. (20.7), Eq. (20.6) is used to restate Eq. (20.5):

$$P_1 = \frac{(PE_{12})(E_1 + E_2)}{S_1 + S_2(ER_1)}. \tag{20.7}$$

Equation (20.7) is then solved for ER_1 to yield Eq. (20.8a):

$$ER_1 = -\frac{S_1}{S_2} + \frac{(E_1 + E_2)}{P_1 S_2} PE_{12}. \tag{20.8a}$$

Table 20.3

	Total Earnings, E	Number of Shares of Common Stock, S	Earnings per Share, EPS	Price/Earnings Ratio, PE	Market Price per Common Share, P
Firm 1	$200	100	$2.00	10	$20
Firm 2	200	100	2.00	20	40

An example will illustrate the nature of Eq. (20.8a) and some subsequent relationships. Let us assume that firm 1 and firm 2 are contemplating a merger in which
firm 1 will acquire firm 2. Table 20.3 contains the information gathered about the
two firms.

Using the data from Table 20.3 in Eq. (20.8a), we obtain

$$ER_1 = -\frac{100}{100} + \frac{400}{2000}PE_{12}, \tag{20.8b}$$

which is expressed in simplified form as

$$ER_1 = -1 + \tfrac{1}{5}PE_{12}. \tag{20.8c}$$

We then use some illustrative values of PE_{12} to indicate the required maximum
exchange ratio that firm 1 may offer the shareholders of firm 2 if the wealth constraint
for the shareholders of firm 1 is to be satisfied:

PE_{12}	0	7	10	11	12	15	20	30
Max ER_1	−1	0.4	1	1.2	1.4	2.0	3.0	5.0

These data, of course, plot on a straight line, as illustrated in Fig. 20.1. We have
discussed the maximum ER_1. Let us now consider the minimum ER_2 that may be

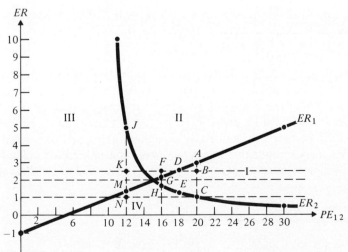

Figure 20.1
Influence of AER and PE_{12} on merger gains and losses.

accepted by the shareholders of firm 2 if their wealth constraint is to be satisfied. Their basic requirement is

$$P_{12} \geq P_2/ER_2. \tag{20.9}$$

Using the equality form of Eq. (20.9), we rewrite it utilizing the accounting determination of P_1. This is simply the price/earnings ratio times the earnings per share for the combined firm,

$$P_{12} = (PE_{12})(EPS_{12}) = \frac{P_2}{ER_2}, \tag{20.10a}$$

and substituting for the earnings per share from Eq. (20.6),

$$P_{12} = \frac{P_2}{ER_2} = \frac{(PE_{12})(E_1 + E_2)}{S_1 + S_2(ER_2)}. \tag{20.10b}$$

We then solve for ER_2:

$$\frac{P_2 S_1 + P_2 S_2(ER_2)}{ER_2} = (PE_{12})(E_1 + E_2),$$

$$ER_2 = \frac{P_2 S_1}{(PE_{12})(E_1 + E_2) - P_2 S_2}. \tag{20.11a}$$

Substituting the numerical values of our example, we obtain

$$ER_2 = \frac{4000}{400 PE_{12} - 4000} = \frac{10}{PE_{12} - 10}. \tag{20.11b}$$

Again, we show the nature of the relationship conveyed by Eq. (20.11b) by calculating values of ER_2 for a range of values of PE_{12}:

PE_{12}	11	12	15	20	30
Min ER_2	10	5	2	1	0.5

The above data are plotted in Fig. 20.1; as indicated, ER_2 is in the form of a hyperbola. Two relationships of significance are portrayed in the figure. One is the intersection of the two ER lines. The other is the four quadrants formed by the two lines. The two ER lines intersect at a PE_{12} of 15, and $ER_1 = ER_2 = 2$. Thus at an exchange ratio of 2 and a PE_{12} of 15, neither firm will have immediate gains or losses from the merger. The PE_{12} that brings about this result represents a weighted average of the two PE ratios. The weighted average can be expressed in two forms as shown below:

$$PE_{12}^* = \frac{P_1 S_1 + P_2 S_2}{E_1 + E_2} = \frac{2000 + 4000}{400} = 15 \tag{20.12a}$$

$$= \frac{(PE_1)S_1 + (PE_2)S_2}{S_1 + S_2} = \frac{1000 + 2000}{200} = 15. \tag{20.12b}$$

By the shareholder wealth constraint formulated by Larson-Gonedes, the actual exchange ratio (AER) should be bounded by quadrant I, in which the shareholders of both firms gain from the merger. In the other three quadrants, the shareholders of one or both firms will suffer a wealth loss. The calculation of merger premiums and discounts can be illustrated using the data of our example both numerically as shown in Table 20.4 and graphically as in Fig. 20.1. Four cases are presented in the table illustrating results for each of the four quadrants. For various combinations of the actual exchange ratio and illustrative values of PE_{12}, the resulting equivalent prices for the shareholders of firm 1 and firm 2 are shown in the columns headed by P_{12} and P_2^*, respectively. In the following two columns, the premium or discount for the shareholder of each firm is calculated. The corresponding merger premium in graphic terms as measured in Fig. 20.1 is then shown in the final two columns of Table 20.4.

Conn and Nielsen calculated the premium or discount combinations for major mergers defined as involving an acquired firm with assets of at least $10 million prior to the merger. The period covered was 1960 through 1969 for a sample of 131 mergers. To avoid premerger announcement effects, the variables P_1 and P_2 were calculated using an average of monthly high and low share prices during the period three to five months prior to the month of merger announcement. The postmerger results were calculated for the month following the consummation of the merger.

Table 20.4   Calculation of Merger Premiums or Discounts

Case	AER	PE_{12}	P_{12}	P_2^*	\multicolumn{2}{c}{Premium or (discount)}		\multicolumn{2}{c}{Merger Premium to}	
					$(P_{12} - P_1)/P_1$	$(P_2^* - P_2)/P_2$	1	2
1	2.5	20	22.86	57.15	+14.3%	+42.9%	AB	BC
2	2.5	16	18.29	45.72	− 8.6	+14.3	$-FG$	FH
3	2.5	12	13.71	34.28	−31.4	−14.3	$-KM$	$-JK$
4	1.0	12	24.00	24.00	+20.0	−40.0	MN	$-JN$

P_2^* = value of P_2 on the basis of the AER = P_{12}AER.

$$P_{12} = (PE_{12})(EPS_{12}) = \frac{(PE_{12})(E_1 + E_2)}{S_1 + S_2(ER)}.$$

$$\text{Case 1: } P_{12} = \frac{20(400)}{100 + 100(2.5)} = \frac{8000}{350} = \$22.86.$$

$$\text{Case 2: } P_{12} = \frac{16(400)}{350} = \frac{6400}{350} = \$18.29.$$

$$\text{Case 3: } P_{12} = \frac{12(400)}{350} = \frac{4800}{350} = \$13.71.$$

$$\text{Case 4: } P_{12} = \frac{12(400)}{100 + 100(1.0)} = \frac{4800}{200} = \$24.00.$$

Conn and Nielsen make the calculations with reference to announcement date, to merger consummation date, and for the month following the consummation of the merger. The results are summarized in Table 20.5.

Two statistical tests were employed by Conn and Nielsen. A nonparametric chi-square test of the hypothesis of equal likelihood that a merger will fall in any one of the four quadrants is rejected at the 1% level. A first-difference test of the Larson-Gonedes model was also statistically significant. Conn and Nielsen observed that the statistical tests supported the Larson-Gonedes model, but they also noted and were concerned about the relatively large 40% of the mergers that did not fall into quadrant I. But rarely did the stockholders of the acquiring firm gain while the acquired stockholders lost. In any event the pattern suggests a competitive market among acquiring firms in merger activity.

Conn and Nielsen noted that a large number of mergers fell into quadrant III; in these mergers the postmerger market valuation of the combined entity was less

Table 20.5 Number of Mergers by ex Post Quadrant and Changes in Quadrant Status from Month of Announcement to Month Following Merger Consummation

From Period of					*To Period of*							
	Announcement				Consummation				Month Following Consummation			
	I	II	III	IV*	I	II	III	IV	I	II	III	IV
Announcement												
I	78				66	8	3	1	60	14	3	1
II		36			4	25	7	0	5	23	8	0
III			12		0	3	8	1	1	3	5	3
IV				5	2	0	1	2	1	0	2	2
Consummation												
I					72				64	7	0	1
II						36			2	32	2	0
III							19		1	1	15	2
IV								4	0	0	1	3
Month following consummation												
I									67			
II										40		
III											18	
IV												6

* The roman numerals I, II, III, IV refer to the quadrants in which the *ex post* price/earnings ratios fall based on the prior decision rules.

From R. L. Conn and J. F. Nielsen, "An Empirical Test of the Larson-Gonedes Exchange Ratio Determination Model," *Journal of Finance*, June 1977, 754.

than the sum of the valuations of the acquiring and acquired firms prior to the merger announcement. However, Conn and Nielsen acknowledged that leakages of merger information might occur even earlier than the three to five months lead time they used in their study. They also recognized that analyzing the effects of the merger only one month after the consummation date might be too restrictive. It would be of interest to analyze the results over longer periods of time subsequent to the merger. Finally, Conn and Nielsen did not provide any numerical measures of possible changes in risk resulting from the merger.

G. MANAGERIAL POLICIES IN A VALUATION FRAMEWORK

In the perspective of alternative merger theories and empirical tests, the foundation has been provided for guides to managerial policies toward merger and acquisition decisions. From an operational standpoint, mergers and acquisitions should be related to a firm's general planning framework. These requirements have been set forth in detail in other studies [Weston, 1970]. Here we focus on merger policies in a valuation framework. We make the concepts explicit by using an illustrative case example to convey the ideas.

The Allison Corporation is a manufacturer of materials handling equipment with heavy emphasis on forklift trucks. Because of a low internal profitability rate and lack of favorable investment opportunities in its existing line of business, Allison is considering a merger to achieve more favorable growth and profitability opportunities. It has made an extensive search of a large number of corporations and has narrowed the candidates to two firms, for a number of considerations. The Connors Corporation is a manufacturer of agricultural equipment and is strong in research and marketing. It has had high internal profitability and substantial investment opportunities. The Dorden Company is a manufacturer of plastic toys. It has a better profitability record than Connors.

Some relevant data on the three firms are summarized in Table 20.6.

Additional information on market parameters includes a risk-free rate, r_f, of 6% and an expected return on the market, $E(R_m)$, of 11%. Each firm pays a 10% interest

Table 20.6 Comparative Statistics for the Year Ended 1978

	Book Value per Share	Price/ Earnings Ratio (P/E)	Number of Shares (millions)	Debt Ratio, % (B/S_A)	Beta for Existing Leverage	Internal Profit- ability Rate (r)	Invest- ment Rate (K)	Growth Rate (g)
Allison	$10.00	5.40	5	30	1.2	.04	0.1	.004
Connors	40.00	11.70	1	30	1.4	.12	1.5	.18
Dorden	40.00	9.88	1	30	1.6	.14	1.0	.14

Table 20.7 Accounting Balance Sheets (millions)

	Allison	*Connors*	*Dorden*
Debt	$15	$12	$12
Equity	50	40	40
Total assets	$65	$52	$52

rate on its debt. The tax rate, τ_c, of each is 50%. A period of 10 years is estimated for the duration of supernormal growth, T.

From the information provided we can first formulate the accounting balance sheets for the three firms (Table 20.7).

Dividing the internal profitability rate r by $(1 - \tau_c)$ and multiplying by total assets, we get the net operating income. From the net operating income we can obtain the market price per share and the total market value that would have to be paid for each of the three companies (Table 20.8).

We now have earnings per share, market values per share, and total market values of equity for use in the subsequent analysis.

One popular criterion for evaluating desirability of making acquisitions from the standpoint of the acquiring company is to determine the effect on its earnings per share. Table 20.9 illustrates these effects based on the data in the present example.

Table 20.8 Market Price per Share

	Allison	*Connors*	*Dorden*
1. Total assets (millions)	$65	$52	$52
2. Earning rate, $r \div (1 - \tau_c)$	.08	.24	.28
3. Net operating income (1) × (2) (millions)	$ 5.2	$12.48	$14.56
4. Interest on debt (millions)	1.5	1.20	1.20
5. Profit before tax (millions)	3.7	11.28	13.36
6. Taxes at 50% (millions)	1.85	5.64	6.68
7. Net income (millions)	1.85	5.64	6.68
8. Number of shares of common stock (millions)	5	1	1
9. Earnings per share of common stock, (7) ÷ (8)	$ .37	$ 5.64	$ 6.68
10. Price/earnings ratio (information provided)	5.4 ×	11.7 ×	9.88 ×
11. Market price per share, (9) × (10)	$ 2.00	$66.00	$66.00
12. Total market value of equity, (11) × (8) (millions)	$10	$66	$66

Table 20.9   EPS Analysis of Merger

	Effects on Allison's Earnings per Share If It Merges:	
	With Connors	*With Dorden*
1. Number of new shares* (millions)	33	33
2. Existing shares (millions)	5	5
3. Total new shares (millions)	38	38
4. Earnings after taxes (millions of dollars)	5.64	6.68
5. *Add* Allison's after-tax earnings (millions of dollars)	1.85	1.85
6. Total new earnings (millions of dollars)	7.490	8.530
7. New earnings per share, (6) ÷ (3), $	.197	.224
8. *Less* Allison's old earnings per share, $	.370	.370
9. Net effect	(.173)	(.146)
10. Percent dilution [(9 ÷ 8)100]	47%	39%

* Each share of Connors and Dorden has a market value 33 times that of Allison. Hence 33 shares times the 1 million existing shares of Connors and Dorden is the total number of new Allison shares required.

It can be seen that the merger effects on Allison's earnings per share is a substantial decline. The percentage dilution in Allison's earnings per share would be 47% if Connors were acquired, and 39% if Dorden were acquired. We believe that this widely used criterion is in error. It is the effect on market value that is relevant, not the effect on earnings per share.

In a valuation framework it is necessary to make a forecast of the key variables affecting value after the merger has taken place. This requires an in-depth business analysis of each proposed merger in terms of its impact on the key valuation factors. From the background provided, we observe that Allison is a manufacturer of materials handling equipment. Connors is a manufacturer of agricultural equipment with strength in research and marketing. Dorden is a manufacturer of plastic toys. While Dorden has a better profitability record than Connors, the toy industry is under the pressure of continuously creating new ideas and concepts if growth and profitability of a toy manufacturing firm are to continue. In addition, there seems to be less potential for favorable interaction of management capabilities in a merger between Allison and Dorden than there would be in a merger between Allison and Connors. Connors is known to have a strong research organization that may be able to develop new products in Allison's area of materials handling equipment. This merely sketches the kind of favorable carryover of capabilities that may be achieved in a merger between Allison and Connors. Reflecting these qualitative considerations, the following estimates are made of the new financial parameters of the combined firms:

	NOI	*r*	*K*	*g*
Allison/Connors (AC)	18	.14	1.0	.14
Allison/Dorden (AD)	16	.13	1.0	.13

We can now proceed to evaluate the two alternative acquisition prospects, using a valuation analysis. First we calculate the new beta for the merged company under the two alternatives. We assume the beta for the combined companies is a market value–weighted average of the betas of the constituent companies. We use the new betas in the security market line equation to obtain the cost of equity capital for each of the two combined firms:

$$\beta_{AC} = 1.2\left(\frac{10}{10 + 66}\right) + 1.4\left(\frac{66}{10 + 66}\right)$$

$$= .1579 + 1.2158 = 1.374 = 1.37.$$

$$k_s(AC) = R_f + [E(R_m) - R_f]\beta_{AC}$$

$$= .06 + [.05]1.37 = .1285 = 12.85\%.$$

$$\beta_{AD} = 1.2\left(\frac{10}{10 + 66}\right) + 1.6\left(\frac{66}{10 + 66}\right)$$

$$= .1579 + 1.3895 = 1.547 = 1.55.$$

$$k_s(AD) = .06 + .05(1.55)$$

$$= .1375 = 13.75\%.$$

Given the debt cost of 10% and the cost of equity capital as calculated, we can then proceed to determine the weighted average cost of capital for the two combined firms:

	AC	*AD*
Debt, *B*	27	27
Equity, *S*	76	76
Value, V^L	103	103

We now continue our calculations:

$$\text{WACC} = k_0 = k_s(S/V) + k_b(1 - \tau_c)(B/V).$$

$$k_0(AC) = .1285(\tfrac{76}{103}) + .05(\tfrac{27}{103})$$

$$= .0948 + .0131 = .1079 = 10.8\%.$$

$$k_0(AD) = .1375(\tfrac{76}{103}) + .05(\tfrac{27}{103})$$

$$= .1015 + .0131 = .1146 = 11.5\%.$$

We now have all the information required to calculate the valuation of the two alternative combinations. We will use the Modigliani-Miller valuation model in the expressions below:

$$V^L = \frac{[E(\widetilde{NOI})](1 - \tau_c)}{\rho} + \tau_c B + K[E(\widetilde{NOI})](1 - \tau_c)\left[\frac{r - \text{WACC}}{\text{WACC}(1 + \text{WACC})}\right]T,$$

where

K = the percentage of earnings invested in new assets, $K \gtrless 1$,

r = the tax-adjusted rate of return on new assets, $r >$ WACC,

T = the number of years during which $r >$ WACC (i.e., the number of years during which the firm experiences a rate of growth greater than the economy).

For ease of computation, we shall combine the first two terms in the equation. We can define V^L as

$$V^L = \frac{E(\widetilde{NOI})(1 - \tau_c)}{\rho} + \tau_c B$$

as

$$V^L = \frac{E(\widetilde{NOI})(1 - \tau_c)}{\text{WACC}} = \frac{E(\widetilde{NOI})(1 - \tau_c)}{k_0}.$$

The two are equivalent formulations of V^L, so we can use the simpler, latter equation. We can now insert the numerical values to determine the value of the combined firm if Allison merges with Connors (AC) or alternatively with Dorden (AD). The results are shown below:

Merger AC:

$$V^L = \frac{18(.5)}{.108} + 1[18(.5)]\left[\frac{.14 - .108}{.108(1 + .108)}\right]10$$

$$= 83.33 + 9\left(\frac{.032}{.119664}\right)10$$

$$= 83.33 + 90(.2674)$$

$$= 83.33 + 24.07$$

$$= 107.40 \approx 107.$$

Merger AD:

$$V^L = \frac{16(.5)}{.115} + 1[16(.5)]\left[\frac{.13 - .115}{.115(1 + .115)}\right]10$$

$$= 69.57 + 8\left(\frac{.015}{.128225}\right)10$$

$$= 69.57 + 80(.1170)$$

$$= 69.57 + 9.36$$

$$= 78.93 \approx 79.$$

Using the results obtained, we make a summary comparison of the gains or losses from the two alternative mergers. The data are summarized in Table 20.10.

Table 20.10 Comparison of Two Mergers

	Allison/Connors (millions)	Allison/Dorden (millions)
Postmerger value, V	$107	$79
Less amount of debt, B	− 27	27
Value of equity, S	80	52
Less Allison's premerger market value	10	10
Gain in equity value	70	42
Cost if acquired at market price	66	66
Gain in value (loss)	4	(24)

The data show that based on estimates of the key parameters a gain in value of $4 million would result from a merger between Allison and Connors. However, the merger between Allison and Dorden would result in a loss in valuation amounting to $24 million. We believe that comparing the effects on value represents the conceptually correct way of approaching merger analysis from a managerial standpoint. The results of this comparison permit some margin of error yet clearly indicate that a merger between Allison and Connors is preferable to a merger between Allison and Dorden. Indeed, the gain in value of $4 million could be divided between the shareholders of Allison and those of Connors. Allison could pay a premium over the current market price of Connors and still achieve a gain in net value that would go to its shareholders.

The foregoing illustrative case example provides a general methodology for the management analysis of merger activity, which utilizes a number of principles: The acquiring firm is considering other firms as alternative merger candidates. To come up with a rational basis for analysis, prospective returns and risk from alternative merger combinations must be estimated. While historical data may be used as inputs, a forecast or estimate must be made of the returns and risk that may arise after alternative merger combinations have taken place.

Thus the forecast of the variables that measure prospective returns and risk for alternative postmerger combinations is critical to a sound evaluation of merger alternatives. The estimates of net operating earnings and of their potential growth may or may not reflect synergy between the combining firms, depending on the nature and potential of the combined operations. Analysis in depth of the relevant product markets and the results of combining the organizations of the two firms is required. The resulting forecasts are subject to prediction errors that are sometimes of substantial magnitude.

We may obtain the measures of risk by market value–weighted averages of the betas (the systematic risk) of the combining firms. With the estimates of the new betas, along with a selection of market parameters, we can calculate the new relevant cost of capital for the merged firm, utilizing the security market line relationship. We must also estimate the effect of alternative merger combinations on the cost of debt. With estimates of the cost of equity capital and the cost of debt, we must formulate appropriate capital structure targets for the combined firm and use these to estimate a cost of capital.

Having obtained an estimate of the applicable cost of capital and the estimates of returns discussed earlier, we can apply valuation principles to formulate estimates of the value of alternative merger combinations. From these, we deduct the value of the acquiring firm in the absence of the merger to determine the total value remaining, which we next compare with the cost of acquiring the firm or firms with which a merger is being considered. If the value contributed by the merger exceeds the cost of the acquisition, the acquiring firm has a basis for making an offer that includes a premium to the shareholders of the acquired firm, yet still provides an increase in value for the shareholders of the acquiring firm.

Merger analysis thus involves the application of the same basic principles of cost of capital and valuation discussed in earlier chapters. However, the problems of application are more difficult. While merger analysis is fundamentally a form of capital budgeting analysis, the magnitudes of the alternative projects are usually quite large. Unlike standard capital budgeting projects in fields related to the firm's past experience, some mergers involve the analysis of industrial activities quite different from the firm's own experience. Prediction errors can therefore be substantial. Our emphasis has been to avoid compounding large potential errors of forecasting with unsound valuation procedures. What we have done in the foregoing illustration has been to utilize the predictions of the relevant return and risk data and apply sound valuation procedures to the process of determining whether the costs of a prospective acquisition result in commensurate increases in prospective values.

SUMMARY

The first part of this chapter was summarized in section E. Only the second part of the chapter will be covered here. Larson and Gonedes constructed a model specifying a region of mutually beneficial mergers. Conn and Nielsen used this model to measure market value changes in order to test the hypothesis that mergers were undertaken to increase values. They found some support for the hypothesis. They also observed that information about the intended merger appeared to be capitalized in the market well in advance of the actual merger announcement.

In the perspective of alternative merger theories and tests, we developed a framework for managerial analysis of prospective mergers. Basically, good forecasts of postmerger returns and risks are required as a starting point. Standard capital budgeting procedures, cost of capital analysis, and valuation principles presented in the preceding chapters are then applied. The aim is to determine whether the value of the merged firm exceeds the value of the constituent firms. If it does, the merger has a valid social and private justification.

PROBLEM SET

20.1 Firm 1 and firm 2 are contemplating a merger in which firm 1 will acquire firm 2. The information in Table Q20.1 has been developed on the two firms. In the questions and answers related to this case, let subscripts 1 and 2 refer to the individual firms. Let ER_1 stand for the

Table Q20.1

	Total Earnings, E	Number of Shares of Common Stock, S	Earnings per Share, EPS	Price/Earnings Ratio, PE	Market Price per Common Share, P
Firm 1	$400	100	$4.00	15	$60
Firm 2	200	400	0.50	30	15

exchange ratio from the standpoint of firm 1 and ER_2 stand for the exchange ratio from the standpoint of firm 2. AER is the actual exchange ratio. PE_{12} will be the price/earnings ratio for the merged firm, after the merger.

a) The managements of the two firms are negotiating the terms of the merger, specifically the number of shares of firm 1 that will be exchanged for one share of common stock of firm 2. Three alternative criteria are under consideration:

i) The effect on each firm's earnings per share after the merger.
ii) The expected market value of the merged firm's common stock per one original share immediately after the merger.
iii) The expected market value of the holdings per one original share after synergistic effects have been developed, e.g., three years after the merger.

Of the three criteria, which would it be most rational for the management and shareholders of the firms to emphasize?

b) Using the estimates of the following range of postmerger PE_{12} values, determine the ER_1 that will equate P_1 to P_{12}:

$$\text{Range of possible } PE_{12} \text{ values: } 12, 15, 20, 25, 30.$$

Make a graph on which ER_1 is plotted against PE_{12} and label the curve ER_1.

c) Calculate the ER_2 that will equate P_2 to P_{12} for the PE_{12} estimates given in part (b). Plot the curve ER_2 on the graph begun in part (b).

d) At what PE_{12} do the two curves intersect? What is the significance of this point of intersection?

e) For the following combinations, calculate and graph the premium or loss to each firm:

Actual exchange ratio (AER)	0.4	0.4	0.4	0.4	0.2	0.1
Postmerger price/earnings ratio (PE_{12})	30	26	22	18	16	18

20.2 The Watro Personal Computer Company is considering merger to achieve better growth and profitability. It has narrowed potential merger candidates to two firms. The Alber Company, a producer of PBXs, has a strong research department and a good record of internal profitability. The Saben Corporation operates a chain of variety stores and has a very high expansion rate. Data on all three firms are given below:

	Watro	Alber	Saben
Book value per share	$10	$10	$10
Number of shares (millions)	5	2.0	2.0
Debt/equity ratio	1	1	1
Internal profitability rate, r (after tax)	.09	.18	.15
Investment rate, K	1.0	1.0	1.5
Growth rate, $g = Kr$	.09	.18	.225
WACC	9%	11%	12%

Each firm pays 15% interest on its debt and has a 40% tax rate. Ten years of supernormal growth are forecast, followed by no growth.

a) What are the total assets of each firm?

b) What is each company's NOI if it earns its before-tax r on total assets?

c) What is the indicated market value of each firm?

d) Compare Watro's increase in value as a result of merger at market value with the cost of acquiring Alber or Saben if the combined firms have the following financial parameters:

	Watro-Alber	Watro-Saben
Net operating income	$30 million	$23 million
Internal profitability rate, r	20.09%	16%
WACC	11%	12%
Investment rate, K	1.1	1.0
Growth rate, $g = Kr$	.221	.16

20.3 The Jordan Corporation is a manufacturer of heavy-duty trucks. Because of a low internal profitability rate and lack of favorable investment opportunities in the existing line of business, Jordan is considering merger to achieve more favorable growth and profitability opportunities. It has made an extensive search of a large number of corporations and has narrowed the candidates to two firms. The Konrad Corporation is a manufacturer of materials handling equipment and is strong in research and marketing. It has had higher internal profitability than the other firm being considered and has substantial investment opportunities.

The Loomis Company is a manufacturer of food and candies. It has a better profitability record than Konrad. Data on all three firms are given in Table Q20.3. Additional information on market parameters includes a risk-free rate of 6% and an expected return on the market, $E(R_m)$, of 11%. Each firm pays a 10% interest rate on its debt. The tax rate, τ_c, of each is 40%. Ten years is estimated for the duration of supernormal growth.

a) Prepare the accounting balance sheets for the three firms.

b) If each company earns the before-tax r on total assets in the current year, what is the net operating income for each company?

Table Q20.3

	Book Value per Share, $	Price/ Earnings Ratio, PE	Number of Shares (millions)	Debt Ratio, B/S	β for Existing Leverage	Internal Profit- ability Rate, r	Invest- ment Rate, K	Growth Rate, g
Jordan	20.00	6	4	1	1.4	.06	0.5	.03
Konrad	20.00	15	2	1	1.2	.12	1.5	.18
Loomis	20.00	12	2	1	1.5	.15	1.0	.15

c) Given the indicated price/earnings ratios, what is the market price of the common stock for each company?

d) What will be the immediate effects on the earnings per share of Jordan if it acquires Konrad or Loomis at their current market prices by the exchange of stock based on the current market prices of each of the companies?

e) Compare Jordan's new beta and required return on equity if it merges with Konrad with the same parameters that would result from its merger with Loomis.

f) Calculate the new required cost of capital for a Jordan-Konrad combination and for a Jordan-Loomis combination, respectively.

g) Compare the increase in value of Jordan as a result of a merger at market values with the cost of acquiring either Konrad or Loomis if the combined firms have the following financial parameters:

	NOI	r	WACC	K	g
Jordan/Konrad	32	.16	9.3%	1.0	.16
Jordan/Loomis	36	.13	10.%	1.0	.13

20.4 The Sentry Company and the Wong Corporation have the same market value of $100 million. Both firms have the following identical parameters:

$$D_S = D_W = \$50 \text{ million} \qquad \text{Face value of debt}$$

$$T_S = T_W = 4 \text{ years} \qquad \text{Maturity of debt}$$

$$\sigma_S = \sigma_W = 0.4 \qquad \text{Instantaneous standard deviation}$$

$$r_f = 0.10 \qquad \text{Risk-free rate.}$$

a) What is the initial market value of debt and equity for Sentry and Wong?

b) The correlation between the two firms' cash flows is 0.5. If the two firms merge, the surviving firm will be worth $200 million. What will the market value of debt and equity in the merged firm be? If there were no other merger effects, would shareholders agree to the merger?

REFERENCES

Alexander, G. J.; P. G. Benson; and J. Kampmeyer, "Investigating the Valuation Effects of Voluntary Corporate Selloffs," *Journal of Finance*, June 1984, 503–517.

Asquith, P., "Merger Bids, Uncertainty and Stockholder Returns," *Journal of Financial Economics*, April 1983, 51–83.

———; R. F. Bruner; and D. W. Mullins, "The Gains to Bidding Firms from Merger," *Journal of Financial Economics*, April 1983, 121–139.

———, "Merger Returns and the Form of Financing," unpublished manuscript, Harvard Business School, October 1987.

Asquith, P., and E. H. Kim, "The Impact of Merger Bids on the Participating Firms' Security Returns," *Journal of Finance*, December 1982, 1209–1228.

Bradley, M., "Interfirm Tender Offers and the Market for Corporate Control," *Journal of Business*, October 1980, 345–376.

———; A. Desai; and E. H. Kim, "The Rationale behind Interfirm Tender Offers: Information or Synergy?" *Journal of Financial Economics*, April 1983, 183–206.

Bradley, M., and L. M. Wakeman, "The Wealth Effects of Targeted Share Repurchases," *Journal of Financial Economics*, April 1983, 302–328.

Brudney, V., and M. A. Chirelstein, "A Restatement of Corporate Freezeouts," *Yale Law Journal*, 1978, 1354–1376.

Chung, K. S., "Investment Opportunities, Synergies, and Conglomerate Mergers," Ph.D. dissertation, Graduate School of Management, University of California, Los Angeles, 1982.

———, and J. F. Weston, "Diversification and Mergers in a Strategic Long-Range-Planning Framework," in Keenan and White, eds., *Mergers and Acquisitions*, Chapter 13. D. C. Heath, Lexington, Mass., 1982.

Conn, R. L., and J. F. Nielsen, "An Empirical Test of the Larson-Gonedes Exchange Ratio Determination Model," *Journal of Finance*, June 1977, 749–759.

Copeland, T. E.; E. F. Lemgruber; and D. Mayers, "Corporate Spinoffs: Multiple Announcement and Ex-Date Abnormal Performance," in Copeland, ed., *Modern Finance and Industrial Economics*, Chapter 7. Basil Blackwell, New York, 1987.

Daems, H., *The Holding Company and Corporate Control.* H. E. Stenfert Kroese B. V., Leiden, The Netherlands, 1977.

Dann, L. Y., and H. DeAngelo, "Standstill Agreements, Privately Negotiated Stock Repurchases and the Market for Corporate Control," *Journal of Financial Economics*, April 1983, 275–300.

———, "Corporate Financial Policy and Corporate Control: A Study of Defensive Adjustments in Asset and Ownership Structure," ms., December 1985.

DeAngelo, H., and E. M. Rice, "Antitakeover Charter Amendments and Stockholder Wealth," *Journal of Financial Economics*, April 1983, 329–359.

DeAngelo, H., and L. DeAngelo, "Managerial Ownership of Voting Rights," *Journal of Financial Economics*, March 1985, 33–69.

———, "Management Buyouts of Publicly Traded Corporations," in Copeland, ed., *Modern Finance and Industrial Economics*, Chapter 6. Basil Blackwell, New York, 1987.

———, and E. M. Rice, "Going Private: The Effects of a Change in Corporate Ownership Structure," *Midland Corporate Finance Journal*, Summer 1984a, 35–43.

————, "Going Private: Minority Freezeouts and Stockholder Wealth," *Journal of Law and Economics*, October 1984b, 367–401.

Dennis, D., and J. McConnell, "Corporate Mergers and Security Returns," *Journal of Financial Economics*, June 1986, 143–187.

Dodd, P., "Merger Proposals, Management Discretion, and Stockholder Wealth," *Journal of Financial Economics*, June 1980, 105–137.

————, and R. Ruback, "Tender Offers and Stockholder Returns: An Empirical Analysis," *Journal of Financial Economics*, December 1977, 351–374.

Dodd, P., and J. B. Warner, "On Corporate Governance: A Study of Proxy Contests," *Journal of Financial Economics*, April 1983, 401–438.

Easterbrook, F. H., and D. R. Fischel, "Proper Role of a Target's Management in Responding to a Tender Offer," *Harvard Law Review*, April 1981, 1161–1204.

Eckbo, B. E., "Examining the Anti-Competitive Significance of Large Horizontal Mergers," Ph.D. dissertation, University of Rochester, 1981.

————, and P. Wier, "Antimerger Policy under the Hart-Scott-Rodino Act: A Reexamination of the Market Power Hypothesis," *Journal of Law and Economics*, April 1985, 119–149.

Ellert, J. C., "Mergers, Antitrust Law Enforcement and Stockholder Returns," *Journal of Finance*, May 1976, 715–732.

————, "Antitrust Enforcement and the Behavior of Stock Prices," Ph.D. dissertation, Graduate School of Business, University of Chicago, 1975.

Fama, E.; L. Fisher; M. Jensen; and R. Roll, "The Adjustment of Stock Prices to New Information," *International Economic Review*, February 1969, 1–21.

Fama, E., and J. MacBeth, "Risk, Return and Equilibrium," *Journal of Political Economy*, May 1973, 607–636.

Firth, M., "The Profitability of Takeovers and Mergers," *Economic Journal*, June 1979, 316–328.

Goldschmid, H. J.; H. M. Mann; and J. F. Weston, *Industrial Concentration: The New Learning*. Little, Brown and Company, Boston, Mass., 1974.

Grossman, S., and O. Hart, "Takeover Bids, the Free-Rider Problem and the Theory of the Corporation," *Bell Journal of Economics*, Spring 1980, 42–64.

————, "The Allocational Role of Takeover Bids in Situations of Asymmetric Information," *Journal of Finance*, May 1981, 253–270.

Halpern, P. J., "Empirical Estimates of the Amount and Distribution of Gains to Companies in Mergers," *Journal of Business*, October 1973, 554–575.

Hite, G. L., and J. E. Owers, "Security Price Reactions around Corporate Spin-off Announcements," *Journal of Financial Economics*, December 1983, 409–436.

Hogarty, T., "The Profitability of Corporate Mergers," *Journal of Business*, July 1970, 317–327.

Jain, P. C., "The Effect of Voluntary Sell-off Announcements on Shareholder Wealth," *Journal of Finance*, March 1985, 209–224.

Jarrell, G. A., and M. Bradley, "The Economic Effects of Federal and State Regulations of Cash Tender," *Journal of Law and Economics*, October 1980, 371–407.

Jensen, M. C., "Takeovers: Folklore and Science," *Harvard Business Review*, November–December 1984, 109–120.

————, and W. H. Meckling, "Theory of the Firm: Managerial Behavior, Agency Costs and Ownership Structure," *Journal of Financial Economics*, October 1976, 305–360.

Kelly, E. M., *The Profitability of Growth through Mergers*, Pennsylvania State University, University Park, Pa., 1967.

Keown, A. J., and J. M. Pinkerton, "Merger Announcements and Insider Trading Activity: An Empirical Investigation," *Journal of Finance*, September 1981, 855–870.

Krouse, C. G., "A Test of Competition in the Capital Market," manuscript of a presentation to UCLA, AT&T Seminar, August 13, 1975.

Kummer, D. R., and J. F. Hoffmeister, "Valuation Consequences of Cash Tender Offers," *Journal of Finance*, May 1978, 505–516.

Langetieg, T. C., "An Application of a Three-Factor Performance Index to Measure Stockholder Gains from Merger," *Journal of Financial Economics*, December 1978, 365–383.

Larson, K. D., and N. J. Gonedes, "Business Combinations: An Exchange Ratio Determination Model," *Accounting Review*, October 1969, 720–728.

Lease, R. C.; J. J. McConnell; and W. H. Mikkelson, "The Market Value of Control in Publicly Traded Corporations," *Journal of Financial Economics*, April 1983, 439–471.

Lev, B., and G. Mandelker, "The Microeconomic Consequences of Corporate Mergers," *Journal of Business*, January 1972, 85–104.

Linn, S. C., and J. J. McConnell, "An Empirical Investigation of the Impact of Antitakeover Amendments on Common Stock Prices," *Journal of Financial Economics*, April 1983, 361–399.

Malatesta, P. H., "The Wealth Effect of Merger Activity and the Objective Functions of Merging Firms," *Journal of Financial Economics*, April 1983, 155–181.

————, "Measuring Abnormal Performance: The Event Parameter Approach Using Joint Generalized Least Squares," *Journal of Financial and Quantitative Analysis*, March 1986, 27–38.

————, and R. Thompson, "Partially Anticipated Events," *Journal of Financial Economics*, June 1985, 237–250.

Mandelker, G., "Risk and Return: The Case of Merging Firms," *Journal of Financial Economics*, December 1974, 303–335.

Manne, H. G., "Mergers and the Market for Corporate Control," *Journal of Political Economy*, April 1965, 110–120.

McDaniel, M. W., "Bondholders and Corporate Governance," *Business Lawyer*, February 1986, 413–460.

Miles, J. A., and J. D. Rosenfeld, "The Effect of Voluntary Spin-off Announcements on Shareholder Wealth," *Journal of Finance*, December 1983, 1579–1606.

Myers, S. C., and N. S. Majluf, "Corporate Financing and Investment Decisions When Firms Have Information that Investors Do Not Have," *Journal of Financial Economics*, June 1984, 187–222.

Roll, R., "The Hubris Hypothesis of Corporate Takeovers," *Journal of Business*, April 1986, 197–216.

————, "Empirical Evidence on Takeover Activity and Shareholder Wealth," in Copeland, ed., *Modern Finance and Industrial Economics*, Chapter 5. Basil Blackwell, New York, 1987.

Rumelt, R. P., *Strategy, Structure, and Economic Performance*. Graduate School of Business Administration, Harvard University, Boston, Mass., 1974.

Schipper, K., and A. Smith, "Effects of Recontracting on Shareholder Wealth," *Journal of Financial Economics*, April 1983, 437–467.

————, "A Comparison of Equity Carve-outs and Seasoned Equity Offerings," *Journal of Financial Economics*, January/February 1986, 153–186.

Schipper K., and R. Thompson, "Evidence on the Capitalized Value of Merger Activity for Acquiring Firms," *Journal of Financial Economics*, April 1983, 85–119.

Scholes, M., "The Market for Securities: Substitution versus Price Pressure and the Effects of Information on Share Prices," *Journal of Business*, April 1972, 179–211.

Stigler, G. J., "The Economic Effects of Antitrust Laws," *Journal of Law and Economics*, October 1966, 225–258.

Stillman, R. S., "Examining Antitrust Policy towards Horizontal Mergers," *Journal of Financial Economics*, April 1983, 225–240.

Weston, J. F., "Mergers and Acquisitions in Business Planning," *Rivista Internazionale di Scienze Economiche e Commerciali*, April 1970, 309–320.

————, "Section 7 Enforcement: Implementation of Outmoded Theories," *Antitrust Law Journal*, 1982a, 1411–1450.

————, "Trends in Antitrust Policy," *Chase Financial Quarterly*, Spring 1982b, 66–87.

Williamson, O. E., *Corporate Control and Business Behavior*. Prentice-Hall, Englewood Cliffs, N.J., 1970.

21

Like the traffic lights in a city, the international monetary system is taken for granted until it begins to malfunction and to disrupt people's daily lives.

Robert Solomon, *The International Monetary System*, 1945–1976, *An Insider's View*, New York, Harper & Row, 1977, 1.

Exchange Rate Systems and Parity Conditions

A. THE IMPORTANCE OF INTERNATIONAL FINANCE

International finance in recent years has taken on great significance. Widely fluctuating exchange rates have affected not only profits and losses from changes in foreign currency values but also the ability to sell abroad and to meet import competition. For example, suppose that a Japanese auto producer needs to receive 1.2 million yen per car to cover costs plus a required return on equity. At an exchange rate of 200 yen to the dollar, a rate that existed in the late 1970s, the Japanese producer would have to receive $6000 for an automobile sold in the United States. When the exchange rate is 265 yen to the dollar, as existed in early 1985, dividing the 1.2 million yen by 265 tells us that the dollars required now are $4528. Thus the Japanese producer is in a position to either reduce his dollar price by approximately 25% and still receive the same number of yen or take higher profit margins on sales in the United States. By early 1987 the yen had moved to about 150 to the dollar. The Japanese car would then have to be priced at $8000, or profit margins (for the Japanese) would suffer. Of course, the success of Japanese auto companies in the United States has not been completely due to changes in foreign exchange rates alone. Auto producers in Japan have achieved improved production processes that have resulted in greater productivity and high-quality cars. But exchange rate movements have also been a factor, as the above example illustrates.

From the standpoint of U.S. companies selling products abroad, the rising value of the dollar in relation to foreign currencies has the opposite consequences. For example, suppose that an American producer is selling a product in the United Kingdom, and to meet competition, it has to be sold for 500 pounds. When the pound had a value of $2.25, as it did in the late 1970s, the dollar amount received by the U.S. seller would be $1125. By March 1985 the value of the pound had fallen to $1.07. If the U.S. producer continued to sell the product for 500 pounds, he or she would now receive $535. If the original $1125 represented a dollar price necessary to earn its cost of capital, the U.S. firm would find it difficult to survive with a price that had declined by more than 50 percent. Or alternatively, to continue to realize a dollar price of $1125 at the exchange rate of $1.07 to the pound would require a new selling price of 1051 pounds, a price increase of over 100% expressed in pounds. By early 1987 the British pound had risen to the $1.50 range—about midway between the two extremes. This moderated the unfavorable impact on U.S. sales in the United Kingdom.

From a general economic standpoint the main issues in international finance relate to efficient trading rules, the adjustment processes for achieving international equilibrium, and the issue of whether there are segmented international markets. Our emphasis in this book will be on the implications of adjustment processes for corporate financial policy. These in turn have implications for the activities of firms, such as sales, purchases, and investment policies.

The nature of risks in an international financial setting takes on new dimensions. We shall focus on corporate financial policies to manage these risks. In addition to the pattern of cash inflows and cash outflows that the firm develops, we shall examine the changes in its balance sheet in terms of monetary versus nonmonetary net positions. We shall also examine the use of the forward market for dealing with foreign exchange fluctuations and analyze the use of money and capital markets for managing foreign exchange risks. Issues here are whether outlays to limit the risks of exchange rate fluctuations are worth the cost. These activities will also be examined for their influence on keeping the international financial markets performing as efficient markets.

Our presentation will emphasize some basic propositions in international finance that are the key to measuring returns and costs in international financial activities. These basic relations are best understood after background material on the adjustment processes in international finance have been developed.

B. THE INTERNATIONAL FINANCIAL MECHANISM

The international financial markets as a part of a general system of financial intermediation perform the functions of increasing efficiency in the production and exchange of goods and services. Money and prices convey information about economic alternatives and guide the choices among the alternatives. International finance, like financial intermediation in general, provides for shifting patterns of investments and savings that increase productivity and provide opportunities for saving surplus units to postpone consumption and for deficit units to increase the output of real goods by utilizing these savings of (surplus) units willing to consume less now and more later.

1. The Economic Basis for International Transactions

The fundamental basis for international trade is the *principle of comparative advantage*. The law of comparative advantage states that trade will be mutually advantageous if one country is relatively more efficient in producing some products and other countries are relatively more efficient in producing other products. A classic illustration would be if you were a better typist than your secretary. Nevertheless, you hire your secretary to type your materials because your comparative advantage is your knowledge of international finance. To illustrate the opportunities for trade, consider the following example.

Let us postulate that opportunity costs in country A are reflected in prices of $3 for X and $1 for Y, whereas opportunity costs in country B result in prices of 12 marks for X and 6 marks for Y. The pattern is shown below:

	X	Y
Country A	$3	$1
Country B	M12	M6

At more than 6 marks per dollar, both goods X and Y would be cheaper in country B. Country B would export both X and Y and import neither. For example, at M8 = $1, B could sell X in A for $1.50 and Y in A for $0.75. On the other hand, a rate of less than 4 marks per dollar would make both goods cheaper in country A. Country A would export both and import neither. For example, at M2 = $1, A could sell X in B for M6 and Y in B for M2. To achieve equilibrium between the two countries, the exchange rate would have to fall somewhere between 6 and 4 marks per dollar. For example, at M5 = $1, B can sell X in A for $2.40, and A can sell Y in B for M5. A basis for cross trade would now exist.

In the example the relative prices of X and Y are 3:1 in country A and 2:1 in country B. With a large number of products the cheaper one country's currency is in relation to other currencies, the larger the range of that country's products that are underselling foreign products of the same type. As a result the importing country will need greater amounts per unit of time of the exporting country's currency in order to buy the latter's relatively cheap goods. Differences in the patterns of relative prices result from differences among countries in resources, skills, and tastes and in social and political conditions, which in turn lead to comparative advantages in different kinds of activities. As a consequence, there will be profit incentives for businesspeople to engage in trade. These private benefits will, in turn, lead to social gains as the theory describes. Exchange rates alone could bring the trade between countries to levels on which the exports and imports of individual countries will be in balance in their own currency.

However, the overall balance is affected by the existence of short- and long-term capital flows associated with borrowing and lending activities, shifts in the comparative rates of development of individual industries in different countries, and differences in the domestic economic development programs among individual countries. Possible imbalances in international activities can be restored to relative equilibrium by these adjustment processes. We discuss the adjustment processes for international disequilibrium under two alternative exchange mechanisms. One is a gold standard with fixed exchange rates. The other postulates flexible exchange rates.

2. Gold Standard and Fixed Exchange Rates

The mechanism governing the relationship of prices to the flow of gold was first formulated in the mideighteenth century. Country A runs an export balance surplus, whereas country B runs a deficit. Hence gold flows into A while it flows out of B. Domestic prices in A rise, the prices in B fall. Country A is an attractive market in which to increase sales from other countries, and A's imports increase. Country A's goods are more expensive in other countries, so its export sales decrease. Thus A's export surplus will be reduced or reversed until equilibrium between relative price relationships of the countries is restored. The flow of gold operates through prices to function as an adjustment mechanism for international balances of trade and payments as well as to regulate the price-change relationships between countries.

In addition to price changes, income and employment effects may also enter into the adjustment process. If the surplus country was not functioning at full employment, the export surplus increases its income and employment. Income and employment decline in the deficit country. Also, in the adjustment process, employment may decline in A and increase in B. The above pattern for the surplus country A can be summarized as follows:

Payments surplus and gold inflow

lead to

Increasing money supply,

which causes

Rising prices and increasing income,

which lead to

Worsening trade balance

which causes

End to surplus and gold inflow.

The reverse process takes place for country B, the deficit area.

Under the gold standard the exchange rates are said to remain "fixed" through this entire adjustment process, because of the inherent assumption that gold would flow to prevent exchange rates from moving beyond the "gold points." For example, let us suppose that the British pound contains four times as much gold as the U.S. dollar: the dollar contains .05 ounce of gold, whereas the British pound contains .2 ounce of gold. A U.S. trade deficit vis-à-vis the United Kingdom would increase the demand for pounds to pay for the imports from the United Kingdom, and the dollar price of pounds would therefore rise, say to $4.10. We could take $1000 to the U.S. Treasury and get 50 ounces of gold since $1 contains .05 ounce of gold. Next we could transport the 50 ounces of gold to the United Kingdom, where we would get £250 in exchange: $50 \div .2 = 250$. With the rate of exchange of $4.10 to £1 less the cost of transporting the gold amounting to $.02 for insurance and interest loss, we would net $4.08 for each pound. Multiplying $4.08 times £250 yields $1020, or a profit of $20. Thus at any rate of exchange above $4.02 or below $3.98, by the actions of the gold arbitrageurs, the rate of exchange would be checked from falling outside the gold points.

To the extent that a gold standard with fixed exchange rates worked, it was because maintaining two-way convertibility between a nation's monetary unit and a fixed amount of gold was a policy goal that received great emphasis and high priority. So long as it was recognized that convertibility was a major policy goal, speculative capital movements were likely to be stabilizing rather than destabilizing. In other words, the general expectation that the convertibility of the currency would be maintained was so strong that when a gold standard currency did weaken almost to its gold export points, one could reasonably assume that it would not drop much lower and indeed would probably rise. Speculators would then take positions based on the expectations that a rise in the value of the currency was imminent, and this would of course strengthen the currency.

During the post–World War II period the international monetary system was not a gold standard but rather a gold exchange standard. In addition to gold, nations held claims on the currency of other countries. Most countries simply related their exchange rates to one of the "key" or "reserve" currencies, holding part of their official reserves in that currency. Dollars and sterling were key currencies immediately after the end of World War II. The monetary authorities outside the United States had the assurance of the U.S. Treasury that the two-way convertibility between dollars and gold would be maintained.

Because the growing volume of international trade required an increase in the supply of international reserves, the initial balance of payments deficits of the United States during the 1950s performed the role of augmenting the supply of key currencies. The rate at which new gold was being produced was far too low to meet the rate of growth in demand for official reserves to support the growing volume of international trade. Problems developed with the gold exchange standard in the early 1970s, giving rise to a substantial shift to the use of flexible exchange rates. In the next section, we describe the nature of the adjustment process under flexible exchange rates. This provides a foundation for the discussion of the broader issues of achieving international equilibrium under current conditions in the international economy.

3. The Adjustment Process under Flexible Exchange Rates

Under a regime of flexible exchange rates no attempt is made to tie the value of a currency to gold or to any one foreign currency. The exchanges of currencies that take place in the international financial markets are based on the forces of demand and supply for the currencies. Exchange rates are likely to be roughly related to the purchasing powers over goods and services of the respective currencies.

To illustrate the operation of the adjustment process let us assume an initial relationship of 1 dollar to 4 deutsche marks: $1 = DM4.

Let us now assume that the volume of imports in the United States exceeds its exports in relationship to countries whose currency is the deutsche mark. The demand for deutsche marks relative to dollars increases. The value of the dollar falls. For purposes of illustration, let us assume $1 = DM2.

At the new exchange rate the prices of our imports and exports in dollars rise. For example, suppose that the Volkswagen sold in the United States for $2000 when the exchange rate was $1 to DM4. A sale at $2000 provided the German exporter with DM8000. At the new exchange rate the German exporter still seeks to receive DM8000. But at the new exchange rates the exporter needs $4000 for the VW.

Similarly, at the old exchange rate the price of wheat (a U.S. export good) was $4 per bushel. To obtain this price we needed to get DM16. At the new exchange rates, in order to receive $4 per bushel, we need get only DM8. Thus the prices of imports in dollars rise substantially at the new exchange rates. Conversely, the prices of exports in the foreign currency fall. The dollar price of exports could be increased and still represent substantially lower prices in the foreign currency.

In the United States at the new exchange rates, import purchases would have to be made at higher prices and export sales could be made under more favorable conditions than before. Conversely, foreign countries faced with lower prices in deutsche marks for both their imports and exports would be motivated to increase their purchases from us and reduce sales to us.

An argument for the use of flexible exchange rates is that the relations between the prices of domestic and foreign goods adjust through exchange rates. The prices of internationally traded goods carry most of the adjustment process. It is argued that under the gold standard with fixed exchange rates an incorrect exchange rate is adjusted not by changing exchange rates but by adjusting all other things. Under flexible exchange rates, when exchange rates are out of line the correction takes place in the exchange rates themselves. Since domestic wages and prices are relatively inflexible, they cannot in fact make the necessary adjustments. However, exchange rates do not have the same built-in institutional barriers to upward and downward flexibility and hence they are much more flexible tools of adjustment.

4. Consistent Foreign Exchange Rates

Equilibrating transactions take place when exchange rates are not in proper relationships with one another. This is illustrated by some examples with (unrealistically) rounded numbers to make the arithmetic of the calculations simple. The analysis will point in the right direction if the reader remembers the general maxim that arbitrageurs will seek to "sell high and buy low." First we discuss the consistency of spot rates. Let us suppose the dollar value of the pound sterling is $2 in New York City and $1.90 in London. The following adjustment actions would take place: In New York City, we sell £190 for $380. We sell the pounds in New York because this is where the pound value is high. In London, we sell $380 for £200. In London the dollar value is high in relation to the pound. Thus £190 sold in New York City for $380 can be used to buy £200 in London at a gain of £10. The sale of pounds in New York causes the value of the pound to decline, and the purchase of pounds in London causes their value to rise until no further arbitrage opportunities are left. Assuming minimal transportation costs, we postulate that the same foreign exchange prices obtain in all locations.

The relationship between the currencies of two individual localities can be generalized across all countries and is referred to as the *consistent cross rate*. It works in the following fashion: Assume that the equilibrium relation between the dollar and the pound is $2 to £1, and the dollar and the franc is $0.25 to Fr1. Now, suppose that in New York City, £.10 = Fr1. The following adjustment process will take place: We sell $200 for £100 and use these to obtain Fr1000, which in turn will buy $250. We thus make a profit of $50 over our initial $200. In general, then, we sell dollars for pounds and pounds for francs since the pound is overvalued with respect to the dollar-to-pound and dollar-to-franc relationships. The dollar will fall in relation to the pound, and the pound will fall in relation to the franc until consistent cross rates are reached. If the relation were Fr1 = £.125, the cross rates would be consistent. We check using the following relation:

$$\$1 = £.5, \qquad £1 = Fr8, \qquad Fr1 = \$.25.$$

The product of the right-hand sides of all three relationships must equal 1. *Check:* .5 × 8 × .25 = 1. We have thus established consistency between foreign exchange rates.

C. THE SHIFT FROM FIXED TO FLEXIBLE EXCHANGE RATES

We have described the adjustment processes under alternative types of mechanisms: fixed exchange rates and flexible exchange rates. Beginning in the eighteenth century and continuing through the early 1970s, the world adhered at least nominally to a gold exchange standard with fixed exchange rates. But recurrent international crises disturbed equilibrium and periodic devaluations took place. With the development of the Bretton Woods institutions after World War II, the International Monetary Fund and the World Bank, there was hope for improved stability. However, these expectations were not realized.

Particularly after the serious recession of the early 1930s, governments placed increased emphasis on full-employment policies and consequently were unwilling to accept the adjustment processes consistent with the gold standard or related systems

Table 21.1

U.S. Commercial Bank	U.S. Central Bank (FED)
Dr. Yen	Dr. Yen
Cr. Reserves with FED (Central Bank)	Cr. Gold certificates
Dr. Deposits, Mr. Smith	Dr. Member bank deposits
Cr. Yen	Cr. Yen

Commercial Bank, Japan	Central Bank, Japan
Dr. Yen	Dr. Gold certificates
Cr. Deposits, Mr. Toyama	Cr. Yen
Dr. Reserves with Central Bank	Dr. Yen
Cr. Yen	Cr. Member bank deposits

of fixed exchange rates, which call for shrinkage in the domestic money supplies and incomes of countries with external deficits. This shrinkage occurs through contraction in the reserves of member (of the Federal Reserve System) banks that must make payments to foreigners in foreign currency when the home country imports more than it exports. The process is readily summarized by a series of journal entries that would take place. For an excess of imports into the United States from Japan the journal entries are as shown in Table 21.1.

On the assumption that credit balances are not expanded, the journal entries reflect the demand of the Japanese exporter (Mr. Toyama) to be paid. The U.S. commercial bank obtains yen from the U.S. central bank (FED) by reducing its reserves with the Federal Reserve Bank (FED). The FED had purchased the yen by paying with gold certificates. The yen received by Mr. Toyama in Japan became primary deposits in a commercial bank in Japan. The reserves of the commercial banks in Japan increase and so do the holdings of gold certificates by the central bank of Japan.

The net result of the journal entries is a decrease in the deposits of the U.S. importer at that individual's commercial bank accompanied by a reduction in the commercial bank's reserves with the FED. For the U.S. central bank, member bank deposits decrease as does its gold certificate account. The opposite net transactions take place in Japan.

For a normal volume of transactions the exchange rate remains unchanged. However, there is a contraction in the effective money supply in the United States and an expansion in Japan. In utilizing its gold or other foreign exchange reserves, the central bank is covering the country's balance of payments deficits. The shrinkage of domestic bank reserves would bring about a deflationary adjustment of the classic gold standard kind. The resulting multiple contraction in the domestic money supply would deflate incomes and prices, reduce spending on imports, and stimulate efforts to achieve exports.

However, to counteract the deflationary tendency, the governmental authorities of the deficit country may engage in offsetting transactions. The central bank in the deficit country could buy domestic securities to replenish the reserve positions of its commercial banks. It could also lower reserve requirements and reduce the discount rate. Alternatively, in its domestic fiscal policy the deficit country could run internal deficits to offset the influences of its external deficits.

The reverse process may take place in a country with a balance of payments surplus. It could offset the expansion of the domestic reserves of its commercial banks by selling securities in the open market. Alternatively, it could run substantial governmental surpluses.

The adjustment processes under any exchange system can be neutralized by counteracting governmental policies. The practice of neutralizing the international adjustment process was particularly pronounced after World War II when greater emphasis was given to full-employment policies in individual national economies. The unwillingness to accept the automatic adjustment processes of an international financial system was also accompanied by efforts to intervene against freedom of trade and the free flow of capital between nations. A desire to control the adjustment process has led to tariff increases, the use of import quotas, and restrictions on lending and investing abroad.

Unwillingness to accept the international adjustment process resulted in increasing flows of international reserves away from deficit countries. In the case of the United States the early balance of payments deficits were welcomed. They had the positive benefit of mitigating the dollar shortage abroad and of increasing the rate of growth in international foreign exchange reserves. However, as the gold account of the United States shrank and as its balance of payments deficits increased rather than diminished, speculators began to become increasingly confident that the foreign exchange value of the dollar would not be maintained. Speculative sales of the dollar in favor of stronger currencies such as the German mark or Swiss franc further aggravated the drain on U.S. foreign exchange reserves. Finally these pressures built up to such a degree that the United States recognized the inevitable and in August 1971 suspended gold convertibility: de facto the dollar began to float in terms of its value in relation to other major currencies.

Other countries set their currencies afloat during the 1970s as well, a period during which the U.S. dollar was weak in foreign exchange markets. A system of floating exchange rates was legalized in 1978 in the second amendment of the charter of the International Monetary Fund (IMF). In October 1979 a strong program to curb inflation in the United States began to be credible. Beginning in late 1980 the dollar increased in strength, reaching its high point in February 1985. The dollar then continued to decline into early 1987 (the date of this writing). The magnitude of the rise and decline in the foreign currency price of the U.S. dollar is indicated by Fig. 21.1.

Some writers have argued that the exchange values of currencies have fluctuated excessively under the regime of flexible exchange rates [Triffin, 1986]. Others have argued that the variability of forecast errors of prices and output for some individual countries have been lower following the shift to fluctuating exchange rates [Meltzer,

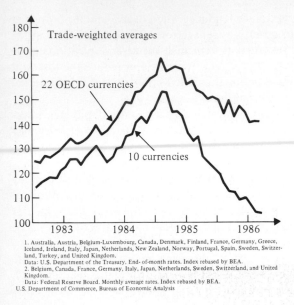

1. Australia, Austria, Belgium-Luxembourg, Canada, Denmark, Finland, France, Germany, Greece, Iceland, Ireland, Italy, Japan, Netherlands, New Zealand, Norway, Portugal, Spain, Sweden, Switzerland, Turkey, and United Kingdom.
Data: U.S. Department of the Treasury. End- of-month rates. Index rebased by BEA.
2. Belgium, Canada, France, Germany, Italy, Japan, Netherlands, Sweden, Switzerland, and United Kingdom.
Data: Federal Reserve Board. Monthly average rates. Index rebased by BEA.
U.S. Department of Commerce, Bureau of Economic Analysis

Figure 21.1
Indices of foreign currency price of the U.S. dollar (1977 = 100).
(From A. J. Dilullo, "U.S. International Transactions, Third
Quarter 1986," *Survey of Current Business*, December 1986, 25.)

1986]. It is the economic policies of individual countries that determine the variability of the exchange values of currencies. It is becoming recognized that it is the degree of coordination of economic policies among countries that determines the degree of fluctuations in foreign exchange rates rather than a fixed rate versus flexible exchange rate regime.

Nevertheless, proposals have been made to reduce the use of the U.S. dollar as an international reserve currency. Proposals have been made to extend the experience of the European monetary system more generally through the International Monetary Fund and the use of its Special Drawing Rights (SDRs). The nature of each of these will be briefly described.

1. The European Monetary System (EMS)

In the 1970s the European nations engaged in a joint float of their currencies referred to as the "European snake in a tunnel," indicating attempts at stabilizing fluctuations among the European currencies within a narrow band. The arrangement was formalized in the establishment of the European monetary system in March 1979 with the then nine-member countries of the European Community (EC). A European currency unit (ECU) was created, representing a currency market basket of the currencies of the participating countries plus the United Kingdom. The ECUs are used as reserves by participating central banks that borrow and lend them. Participating countries are required to maintain exchange rates within 2.25% on either side of a central par value (except Italy, which is allowed 6% deviations). An attempt is made to moderate fluctuations in the foreign exchange values of the currencies of the participating countries through intervention in the foreign exchange market. But periodically when the strains become large, revaluations of relative curency values formally take place.

These efforts have been viewed as successful by some, and it has been recommended that they be extended more generally under the aegis of the International Monetary Fund to the broader world economy [Triffin, 1986]. Fundamentally, this involves using the IMF as a kind of central bank. The beginning was made in 1970 when the IMF created Special Drawing Rights (SDRs).

Beginning July 1974 the value of the SDR is determined daily by the IMF on the basis of a basket of currencies, with each currency assigned a weight in the determination of that value. The currencies of the basket are valued at their market exchange rates for the U.S. dollar, and U.S. dollar equivalents of each of the currencies are summed to yield the rate of the SDR in terms of the U.S. dollar. Beginning January 1, 1986, the SDR valuation basket consists of the currencies of the five member countries having the largest exports of goods and services during the 1980–1984 period. The weights for the five currencies are: U.S. dollar, 42%; deutsche mark, 19%; Japanese yen, 15%; French franc and pound sterling, 12% each.

The SDRs are book entries that are credited to the accounts of IMF-member countries according to specified quotas. They can be used to help meet payments imbalances or to add to the stock of foreign exchange reserves of the individual countries. Interest is paid to the countries that hold SDRs and by those that draw on their SDRs, with the rate based on an average of money market interest rates in the United States, the United Kingdom, Japan, Germany, and France.

Thus the IMF operates as a kind of central bank to the countries of the world. It makes provision for the countries to have either balances or borrowings from the IMF. It is proposed that the central bank status of the IMF be extended so that it could moderate what some regard as unduly wild currency fluctuations under flexible exchange rates. The aim would be for "stable but flexible" exchange rate movements. It is recognized, however, that the basic cause of the fluctuations is lack of coordination among the policies of the individual countries. Nevertheless, a recent review of the European monetary system concludes that it has contributed toward economic convergence among EMS-member countries [Ungerer, Evans, Mayer, and Young, 1986]. In short, it is argued that increasing the use of the IMF as a central bank and as an international economic supervisory mechanism could potentially lead to better coordination among the monetary, fiscal, and other economic policies of the countries of the world.[1]

The previous analysis has used a balance of payments framework to appraise the need for international adjustment processes, including the devaluation or depreciation of the dollar. We next consider in somewhat more detail the role of a balance

---

[1] A full examination of these issues is made in a number of papers (with commentaries) originally presented at a meeting on exchange rates of the Royal Economic Society and published in the March 1987 issue of the *Economic Journal*.

of payments analysis in defining the kinds of policies and adjustments that may have to be made in corporate financial policy in order to deal with changes in the international financial environment.

D. BALANCE OF PAYMENTS ANALYSIS

In recent years the U.S. Department of Commerce has stopped using the term *balance of payments* in favor of the more general expression *U.S. international transactions*. However, the compilations are still a balance of payments analysis and will be discussed in those terms. The balance of payments of a nation is a double-entry accounting statement of its transactions with the rest of the world during a specified time period, usually one quarter or one year. Inflows are recorded as a plus. (Sometimes the words *receipts* and *credits* are used, but the terms *plus* and *minus* are preferred as being more neutral in their implications.) Outflows are a minus. (Sometimes called *debits* or *payments*, but again, *minus* is preferred.)

The basic entries in the balance of payments statement can be summarized into four categories of items as shown in Table 21.2. This summary indicates how the adjustment process can be complicated by a number of relationships going in different directions. Thus if a given country runs a deficit by having an excess of imports over exports, instead of settling the balance by payments in the foreign currency, a number of other offsets may take place. As shown in Table 21.2, the offsets can take the form of increasing liabilities to foreigners, decreasing claims on foreigners, liquidating assets, or decreasing other foreign investments. Consequently, there will be a lag in the pressures that would result if payments in foreign currencies had to be made immediately. This lag will postpone the contraction in the money supply or incomes of the deficit country.

Similarly, a country that is increasing its investments abroad will improve its investment position, but it will be creating minus entries in its current balance of payments statement. The long-run outlook for a country that is making substantial foreign investments, however, may be favorable as a result of the future income that may be generated from those investments.

The U.S. Department of Commerce follows the format for the balance of payments statement shown in Table 21.3. It has been modified to deemphasize individual balances.

Table 21.2   Effects on the Balance of Payments

Plus	*Minus*
Exports	Imports
Increase liabilities to foreigners	Decrease liabilities to foreigners
Decrease claims on foreigners	Increase claims on foreigners
Decrease investments; sell assets	Increase investments; buy assets

**Table 21.3   Summary of U.S. International Transactions
(billions of dollars)**

Line	Item	1985
1	Exports of goods and services	358
2	Merchandise, excluding military	214
3	Other goods and services	144
4	Imports of goods and services	−461
5	Merchandise, excluding military	−339
6	Other goods and services	−122
7	U.S. government grants (excluding military grants of goods and services)	−11
8	Remittances, pensions, and other transfers	−4
9	U.S. assets abroad, net [increase/capital outflow (−)]	−32
10	U.S. official reserve assets, net	−4
11	U.S. government assets, other than official reserve assets, net	−3
12	U.S. private assets, net	−26
13	Foreign assets in the United States, net [increase/capital inflow (+)]	127
14	Foreign official assets, net	−1
15	Other foreign assets, net	128
16	Allocations of special drawing rights	
17	Statistical discrepancy	23

From A. J. DiIullo, "U.S. International Transactions, Third Quarter 1986," *Survey of Current Business*, December 1986, 23.

In the traditional balance of payments statement, lines 1 and 4 give "the balance on goods and services." This is considered significant as an indicator of the basic trade position of the United States, which was a negative $103 billion in 1985.

Another balance also emphasized is the current account balance obtained by adding line 7 (U.S. government grants) and line 8 (remittances, pensions and other transfers). This was the negative $103 billion plus a negative $15 billion, giving a total of a negative $118 billion for 1985. This is the balance that will have to be offset by capital flows and changes in government official reserve assets. U.S. assets abroad also increased by $32 billion, so the total amount to be offset is $150 billion. This is exactly equal to the increase in foreign assets in the United States plus a statistical discrepancy. Basically, in 1985 (and in other recent years) a substantial current account deficit had to be offset by a substantial flow of foreign investment into the United States.

In summary, while government reports on U.S. international transactions avoid the concept of balance of payments, it is nevertheless there. The pattern in recent years for the United States has been a very substantial negative balance on current account. In terms of Table 21.2, the negative balance has been further aggravated by accumulating U.S. private assets abroad. However, a very substantial buildup of foreign private investments in the United States has taken place to offset the very large negative U.S. balance on trade and services.

The significance of alternative measures of "the balance of payments" depends on the circumstances of an individual country and the pattern of international economic developments taking place. To determine all contributing factors, one must analyze as many components of information as possible, including the more general economic developments taking place in individual countries. The balance of payments along with other information sources may be analyzed within a more general economic framework to develop judgments about adjustment processes taking place that will have implications for changes in foreign exchange rates as well. It is this kind of analysis that is required for formulating corporate financial policies of firms substantially affected by changes in foreign exchange rates. We next analyze some of the fundamental relationships that reflect the broad economic adjustment forces reflected in balance of payments statements.

E. FUNDAMENTAL EQUILIBRIUM RELATIONSHIPS

Foreign exchange management is a key aspect of applications discussed in the chapter that follows. Sound decision-making in managing foreign exchange risks requires an understanding of the key equilibrium relations involving international prices, interest rates, inflation rates, and spot versus forward exchange rates.

The analysis begins with assumptions required to establish the fundamental propositions, which can then be modified as applications require. The basic assumptions are those required for perfect markets.

A1. Financial markets are perfect. (Numerous buyers and sellers; no taxes, no information or transactions costs, no controls.)

A2. Goods markets are perfect. (Numerous buyers and sellers; no transportation costs or time, no barriers to trade.)

A3. There is a single consumption good common to all.

A4. The future is known with certainty.

A5. The competitive markets are in equilibrium.

The fundamental exchange relationships require one or more of the above assumptions. The following equilibrium relationships can then be established.

1. The purchasing power parity theorem (PPPT).
2. The international Fisher relation (IFR).
3. The interest rate parity theorem (IRPT).

4. The real rate of return relation (RRR).

5. The forward parity theorem (FPT).

As background for discussing each of these five relationships, we briefly present some basic definitions and conventions. International business transactions are conducted in many different currencies. However, a U.S. exporter selling to a foreigner expects to be paid in dollars. Conversely, a foreign importer buying from an American exporter may prefer to pay in his or her own currency. The existence of the foreign exchange markets allows buyers and sellers to deal in the currencies of their preference. The foreign exchange markets consist of individual brokers, the large international money banks, and many commercial banks that facilitate transactions on behalf of their customers. Payments may be made in one currency by an importer and received in another by the exporter.

Exchange rates may be expressed in dollars per foreign unit or in foreign currency (FC) units per dollar. An exchange rate of $0.50 to FC 1 shows the value of 1 foreign currency unit in terms of the dollar. We shall use E_0 to indicate the spot rate, E_f to indicate the forward rate at the present time, and E_1 to indicate the actual future spot rate corresponding to E_f. An exchange rate of FC 2 to $1 shows the value of the dollar in terms of the number of foreign currency units it will purchase. We will use the symbol X with corresponding subscripts to refer to the exchange rate expressed as the number of foreign currency units per dollar. We utilize these conventions in developing the five fundamental equilibrium relationships of international finance.

1. The Purchasing Power Parity Theorem (PPPT)

The purchasing power parity doctrine is an expression of the *law of one price*: In competitive markets the exchange-adjusted prices of identical tradable goods and financial assets must be equal worldwide (taking account of information and transaction costs). PPPT deals with the rates at which domestic goods are exchanged for foreign goods. Thus if I dollars buy a bushel of wheat in the United States, the I dollars should also buy a bushel of wheat in the United Kingdom.

Expressed equivalently, the purchasing power parity doctrine states that people will value currencies for what they will buy. If an American dollar buys the same basket of goods and services as five units of a foreign currency, we should have an exchange rate of five foreign currency units to the dollar, or each foreign currency unit should be worth $0.20. An attempt to compare price indices to computed purchasing power parity assumes that it is possible to compile comparable baskets of goods in different countries. As a practical matter, the parity rate is in general estimated from changes in the purchasing power of two currencies with reference to some past base period when the exchange rate was (theoretically) in equilibrium. Hence in using the PPPT our emphasis is on formulating it as a statement that *changes* in exchange rates reflect *changes* in the relative prices between two countries. In formal terms the PPPT may be stated as follows:

$$CX = \frac{X_1}{X_0} = \frac{P_{f1}/P_{f0}}{P_{d1}/P_{d0}} = RPC \tag{21.1}$$

where

$$\frac{X_1}{X_0} = \frac{E_0}{E_1}, \qquad \begin{aligned} X_0 &= \text{FC units per dollar now,} \\ X_1 &= \text{FC units per dollar one period later,} \end{aligned}$$

$$E_0 = \frac{1}{X_0} = \text{dollars per FC unit now,}$$

$$E_1 = \frac{1}{X_1} = \text{dollars per FC unit one period later,}$$

$$CX = \frac{X_1}{X_0} = \text{change in exchange rate,}$$

$$RPC = \frac{P_{f1}/P_{f0}}{P_{d1}/P_{d0}} = \text{change in relative prices} = \text{ratio of inflation rates,}$$

P_{f0} = initial price level in the foreign country,

P_{f1} = foreign country price level one period later,

T_f = foreign country inflation rate,

P_{d0} = initial domestic price level,

P_{d1} = domestic price level one period later,

T_d = domestic inflation rate.

Some numerical examples will illustrate some of the implications of the purchasing power parity doctrine. Let us assume that for a given time period foreign price levels have risen by 32%, whereas domestic price levels have risen by 20%. If the initial exchange rate is FC 10 to $1, the subsequent new exchange rate will be

$$\frac{1.32}{1.20} = \frac{X_1}{10}, \qquad X_1 = 1.1(10) = 11.$$

It will now take 10% more foreign currency units to equal $1 because the relative inflation rate has been higher in the foreign country. Alternatively, with an exchange rate of FC 10 to $1, let us assume that foreign prices have risen by 17% while domestic

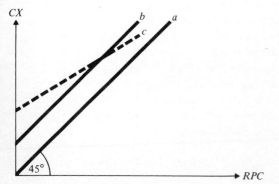

CX

45°

RPC

Figure 21.2
Alternative parity relationships.

prices have risen by 30%. The expected new exchange rate would be

$$\frac{1.17}{1.30} = \frac{X_1}{10}, \qquad X_1 = .9(10) = 9.$$

In the present instance the number of foreign currency units needed to buy $1 would drop by 10%. Thus the value of the foreign currency has increased by 10% due to the differential rates of inflation in domestic vs. foreign prices.

The approximation relationship is

$$T_f - T_d \cong \frac{X_1 - X_0}{X_0}.$$

Using the data from our above example, we would have

$$.32 - .20 \cong \frac{11 - 10}{10},$$

$$.12 \cong .10.$$

The nature of the relationships can vary from the precision suggested by the numerical examples. Some of the alternatives are suggested in Fig. 21.2. Line a implies that both the average and marginal relations are one to one. Line b implies that the marginal relation is one to one, but the average relation is not. Line c implies a relationship, but not a one-to-one relationship.

Empirical studies indicate that while the purchasing power parity relationship does not hold perfectly, it holds on average [Pippenger, 1986]. More fundamentally, the doctrine predicts that an equilibrium rate between two currencies will reflect market forces and that random deviations from the central tendency will tend to be self-correcting; i.e., it suggests the existence of some strong equilibrating forces. Furthermore, it argues that the relations between exchange rates will not be haphazard but will reflect underlying economic conditions and changes in these conditions. The relationships are not precise because of a number of factors. These include:

1. Differences in incomes or other endowments between the two countries.
2. Differences in tastes and/or market baskets consumed.
3. Changes in government policies.
4. Transportation costs.
5. Lags in market responses.
6. Differences between the two countries in the price ratios of internationally traded goods to domestically traded goods.
7. The addition of a risk premium influence.

2. The International Fisher Relation (IFR)

The neutrality of money implies that money should have no impact on real variables or on relative prices. If a 10% increase in the supply of money relative to the demand for money causes prices to rise by 10%, relative prices should remain unchanged. Although change in the quantity of money may affect prices and exchange rates, neutrality implies that the rate at which domestic goods are exchanged for foreign goods should not be changed (PPPT). Neither should there be an effect on the rate at which goods today are exchanged for goods in the future (the Fisher relation).

The Fisher relation states that nominal interest rates rise to reflect the anticipated rate of inflation. The Fisher relation can be stated in a number of forms, as shown below:

$$\frac{P_0}{P_1} = \frac{1+r}{1+R_n}, \tag{21.2a}$$

$$1+r = (1+R_n)\frac{P_0}{P_1}, \tag{21.2b}$$

$$r = \left[(1+R_n)\frac{P_0}{P_1}\right] - 1, \tag{21.2c}$$

$$R_n = \left[(1+r)\left(\frac{P_1}{P_0}\right)\right] - 1, \tag{21.2d}$$

where

P_0 = initial price level,

P_1 = subsequent price level,

P_1/P_0 = rate of inflation = T,

P_0/P_1 = relative purchasing power of the currency unit,

r = real rate of interest,

R_n = nominal rate of interest.

While the Fisher relation can be stated in a number of forms, its importance can be conveyed by a simple numerical example. Over a given period of time, if the price index is expected to rise 10% and the real rate of interest is 7%, then the current nominal rate of interest is

$$R_n = [(1.07)(1.10)] - 1 = 17.7\%.$$

Similarly, if the nominal rate of interest is 12% and the price index is expected to rise 10% over a given time period, the current real rate of interest is

$$r = [1.12(\tfrac{100}{110})] - 1 = 1.018 - 1 = .018 = 1.8\%.$$

An approximation of the relationship is

$$R_n \cong r + (T - 1).$$

For our data this would be

$$17.7\% \cong 7.0\% + 10\% \text{ for the first example.}$$

$$12.0\% \cong 1.8\% + 10\% \text{ for the second example.}$$

We shall also show how the Fisher relation in an international setting can be used to derive PPPT as well as the interest rate parity theorem presented next.

3. The Interest Rate Parity Theorem (IRPT)

The interest rate parity theorem holds that the ratio of the forward and spot exchange rates will equal the ratio of foreign and domestic nominal interest rates. The formal statement of the IRPT may be expressed as follows:

$$\frac{X_f}{X_0} = \frac{1 + R_{f0}}{1 + R_{d0}} = \frac{E_0}{E_f}, \tag{21.3}$$

where

X_f = current forward exchange rate expressed as FC units per \$1,

E_f = current forward exchange rate expressed as dollars per FC 1,

X_0 = current spot exchange rate expressed as FC units per \$1,

E_0 = current spot exchange rate expressed as dollars per FC 1,

R_{f0} = current foreign interest rate,

R_{d0} = current domestic interest rate.

Thus if the foreign interest rate is 15% while the domestic interest rate is 10% and the spot exchange rate is $X_0 = 10$, the predicted current forward exchange rate will be

$$X_f = \frac{1 + R_{f0}}{1 + R_{d0}} (X_0)$$

$$= \frac{1.15}{1.10} (10) = 10.45;$$

i.e., 10.45 units of foreign currency equal \$1. Thus, viewed on an annual basis, the foreign forward rate is seen to be at a discount of 4.5%. If we assume the time period of a transaction to be 90 days, we must rework the problem accordingly. The first step is to prorate the interest rates on a quarterly basis. Thus for 90 days,

$$X_f = \frac{1.0375}{1.025} (10)$$

$$= 10.122;$$

i.e., the 90-day forward rate is 10.122, and it follows that on the quarterly basis the discount on the 90-day forward rate is 1.22%.

The approximation for IRPT is

$$R_{fi} - R_{di} \cong \frac{X_f - X_0}{X_0}.$$

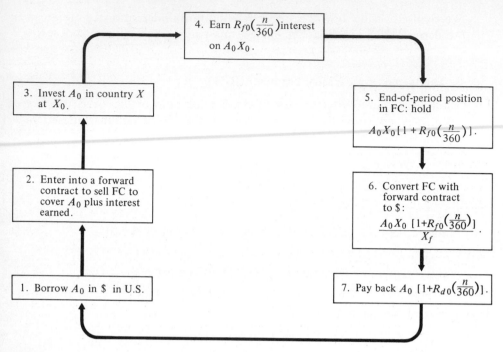

Figure 21.3
Covered interest arbitrage with investment outflows.

The data for the annual example are used to illustrate the approximation:

$$.15 - .10 \cong \frac{10.45 - 10}{10},$$

$$0.05 \cong .045.$$

The IRPT can also be used to illustrate another general proposition for international finance. In the absence of market imperfections, risk-adjusted expected real returns on financial assets will be the same in foreign markets as in domestic markets. Equilibrium among the current exchange rate, the forward exchange rate, the domestic interest rate, and the foreign interest rate is achieved through covered interest arbitrage. Assume that the forward contract is for n days and that R_{f0} and R_{d0} are annual rates. A sequence of seven transactions takes place when the interest rate differential in X exceeds the forward exchange discount on the currency of X (Fig. 21.3).

Equilibrium occurs when the principal + interest earned in country X equals the principal + interest paid in the United States, or when

$$\frac{A_0 X_0 [1 + R_{f0}(n/360)]}{X_f} = A_0 \left[1 + R_{d0}\left(\frac{n}{360}\right)\right], \quad \text{or} \quad \frac{X_f}{X_0} = \frac{1 + (n/360)R_{f0}}{1 + (n/360)R_{d0}}.$$

Alternatively, we would obtain the same equilibrium requirement if the interest rate differential in X were less than the forward exchange discount in the currency

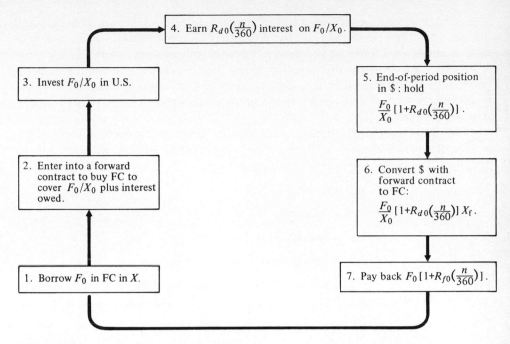

Figure 21.4
Covered interest arbitrage with investment inflows.

of X, by borrowing in the foreign country and buying FC to cover the amount borrowed plus interest owed (see Fig. 21.4).

Equilibrium occurs when the principal plus interest earned in the United States equals the principal plus interest paid in country X, or when

$$\left\{\frac{F_0}{X_0}\left[1 + R_{d0}\left(\frac{n}{360}\right)\right]\right\}X_f = F_0\left[1 + R_{f0}\left(\frac{n}{360}\right)\right], \quad \text{or} \quad \frac{X_f}{X_0} = \frac{1 + R_{f0}(n/360)}{1 + R_{d0}(n/360)}.$$

If the interest differentials are positive in the foreign country, the forward rate on the foreign currency will be negative. If negative, the forward rate on the foreign currency will be positive, as shown in Fig. 21.5.

		Interest rate differential (Foreign currency less U.S. $)	
		Plus	Minus
Forward market rates (in foreign currency units, X_f)	Discount	−1%, +2% IF −2%, +1% IH	
	Premium		+1%, −2% IH +2%, −1% IF

Figure 21.5
Covered interest arbitrage.

The pair of relations followed by "IF" indicate foreign investment in the covered interest arbitrage operation. The pair of relations followed by "IH" leads to investment in the United States in the covered interest arbitrage operation.

As we have demonstrated, whether or not the covered interest arbitrage operation results in investment in a foreign country in preference to investment in the United States, the resulting equilibrium interest and forward exchange parity relationship is the same.

The above general relationships can also be illustrated in some numerical examples of covered interest arbitrage. First, an arbitrage outflow situation will be described. The basic assumptions are as follows:

> U.S. interest rate 5%,
>
> German interest rate 7%,
>
> Spot exchange rate \$1 = DM4,
>
> Forward exchange rate discount 1% per annum.

The following arbitrage transaction will take place. In New York, we borrow \$100,000 for 90 days (one quarter) at 5%. The loan repayment at the end of 90 days is

$$\$100,000[1 + (5\% \times \tfrac{1}{4})] = \$101,250.$$

At the spot exchange rate, we convert the \$100,000 loan into DM400,000. In Germany, we invest the DM400,000 for 90 days at 7% and receive at the end of 90 days

$$DM400,000[1 + (7\% \times \tfrac{1}{4})] = DM407,000.$$

A covering transaction is also made. To ensure against adverse changes in the spot rate during the 90-day investment period, we sell the investment proceeds forward. Since the forward exchange rate discount is 1%, then

$$4[1 + (1\% \times \tfrac{1}{4})] = DM4.01$$

is required in exchange for \$1 in 90 days (forward). We sell the investment proceeds forward; i.e., we contract to receive DM407,000 ÷ 4.01 = \$101,496. The result of the two transactions is shown below:

> Arbitrage profits = investment receipts − loan payments
>
> = \$101,496 − 101,250
>
> = \$246.

The arbitrage transaction increases the *demand* for currency in New York and the *supply* of funds in Germany, which in turn raises the interest rate in New York and lowers it in Germany, thus narrowing the differential. The covering transaction increases the supply of German forward exchange, whereas the arbitrage investment action increases the demand for spot funds. Both forces tend to increase the forward exchange discount. The interest rate differential decreases and the forward rate discount increases until both are equalized, e.g., $[1 + (.068/4)]/[1 + (.052/4)] = (4.016/4)$.

An arbitrage inflow takes place when the forward exchange rate discount exceeds the interest rate differential. The basic facts are now:

U.S. interest rate 5%,

German interest rate 6%,

Spot exchange rate DM4 = $1,

Forward exchange rate discount 2% per annum.

The arbitrage transaction involves borrowing in the foreign country. In Germany, we borrow DM400,000 for 90 days at 6%. The loan repayment at the end of 90 days is

$$DM400,000[1 + (6\% \times \tfrac{1}{4})] = DM406,000.$$

At the spot exchange rate, we convert the DM400,000 loan into $100,000. In New York we invest the $100,000 for 90 days at 5% and receive at the end of 90 days

$$\$100,000[1 + (5\% \times \tfrac{1}{4})] = \$101,250.$$

Again, we would make a covering transaction. To ensure coverage for the loan repayment, we buy DM406,000 forward. At a 2% forward exchange rate discount, it costs $DM4[1 + (2\% \times \tfrac{1}{4})] = DM4.02$ to buy $1 forward. Thus repayment of principal plus interest requires

$$DM406,000 \div 4.02 = \$100,995.$$

Thus we have

$$\text{Arbitrage profits} = \text{investment receipts} - \text{loan repayments}$$

$$= \$101,250 - \$100,995$$

$$= \$255.$$

The arbitrage transaction increases the *demand* for deutsche marks and increases the supply of dollars. The U.S. interest rate decreases and the German rate rises; thus the differential increases. Covering transactions increase the demand for German forward exchange and increase the spot supply of deutsche marks, thus decreasing the discount on forward deutsche marks. The interest rate differential increases and the forward exchange rate discount decreases until both rates are equalized, e.g., $[1 + (.064/4)]/[1 + (.0481/4)] = (4.0158/4)$.

We can now show the relationships between the three fundamental equilibrium relationships thus far set forth. We begin with the international Fisher relation. The Fisher relation for country f can be written

1)
$$\frac{1 + R_f}{1 + r} = \frac{P_{f1}}{P_{f0}}.$$

And for country d it would be

2)
$$\frac{1 + R_d}{1 + r} = \frac{P_{d1}}{P_{d0}}.$$

Dividing (1) by (2) (and assuming the real rate of interest is equal across the two countries), we have

$$\frac{1 + R_f}{1 + R_d} = \frac{\dfrac{P_{f1}}{P_{f0}}}{\dfrac{P_{d1}}{P_{d0}}}.$$

The left-hand side is the IRPT $= \dfrac{1 + R_f}{1 + R_d} = \dfrac{X_f}{X_0}.$

The right-hand side is the PPPT $= \dfrac{P_{f1}/P_{f0}}{P_{d1}/P_{d0}} = \dfrac{X_1}{X_0}.$

The fundamental relations assumed are certainty, equal real rates of interest, and equilibrium. We can thus observe how the international Fisher relation can be used to derive both PPPT and IRPT. These relations are also utilized in measuring the real gains or losses in an international setting.

4. The Real Rate of Return Relation (RRR)

The real gain or loss from holding foreign currency units or net assets denominated in foreign currency units can be calculated by utilizing a number of the relationships set forth thus far. We begin with the end-of-period value of a foreign investment expressed in foreign currency. This is

1) $$F_0(1 + R_{f0}),$$

where F_0 is the value of the foreign investment expressed in foreign currency. If we multiply this expression by the value of a foreign currency unit expressed in dollars and also by the ratio of domestic prices to obtain real values in dollars, we have

2) $$E_1(P_0/P_1)[F_0(1 + R_{f0})].$$

This represents the end-of-period value in deflated dollars of a position taken in foreign currency units. The initial investment in dollars is

3) $$E_0F_0.$$

If this investment earns at the domestic real rate, its end-of-period value will be

4) $$E_0F_0(1 + r_d).$$

One plus the real return is the ratio of the end-of-period value of the position in foreign currency units to the end-of-period value of the domestic investment:

5) $$1 + r_1 = \frac{E_1(P_0/P_1)[F_0(1 + R_{f0})]}{E_0F_0(1 + r_d)}.$$

If the ratio on the right-hand side is equal to one, there is neither a benefit nor a loss from having a long position in foreign currency units as compared to having a long position in domestic currency units. We may next make use of the Fisher relation in the form

6) $$1 + r_d = (1 + R_{d0})(P_0/P_1).$$

We then substitute the right-hand side of the above expression for $(1 + r_d)$ in Eq. (5) and obtain Eq. (7a). The F_0's cancel, and

7a) $$1 + r_1 = \frac{(E_1/E_0)(P_0/P_1)(1 + R_{f0})}{(1 + R_{d0})(P_0/P_1)}.$$

The price ratios cancel to give us Eq. (7b):

7b) $$1 + r_1 = \frac{(E_1/E_0)(1 + R_{f0})}{1 + R_{d0}}.$$

The interest rate parity relationship is written as Eq. (8):

8) $$\frac{E_0}{E_f} = \frac{1 + R_{f0}}{1 + R_{d0}}.$$

The right-hand side of the equation is substituted in Eq. (7b), yielding Eq. (9).

9) $$1 + r_1 = \frac{E_1}{E_0}\frac{E_0}{E_f}.$$

Next we cancel the E_0 and solve for r_1:

$$r_1 = (E_1/E_f) - 1. \tag{21.4}$$

Thus the real return (gain or loss) from a long or short position in a foreign currency or net assets denominated in foreign currency units can be determined by a relatively simple expression. It is the ratio of the actual value of the foreign currency's future spot rate in relation to the expected value of its future spot rate reflected in its current forward rate.[2] We can illustrate the measurement of real gains or losses by a number of simple examples. First let us assume that we are long in foreign currency units and that the relative devaluation of the foreign currency units is more than anticipated in the current spot rate (E_f):

$$E_1 = \$.20, \qquad E_f = \$.25.$$

The real gain or loss can therefore be calculated as follows:

$$r_1 = (E_1/E_f) - 1 = (.20/.25) - 1 = -20\%.$$

Thus if we are long in foreign currency units and the forward value of the foreign currency unit was $.25 but its actual spot value at the end of the period is $.20, there has been a loss of 20%. On the other hand, if the spot rate one period later is $.30,

---

[2] The insight that the real return on an investment in foreign currency over the real domestic rate of interest can be calculated from the divergence between the anticipated and actual future spot rates of exchange is presented in Farber, Roll, and Solnik [1977].

we can calculate the real gain as follows:

$$r_1 - (.30/.25) - 1 = 1 \ 20\%.$$

If we have a short position in the foreign currency units, the signs of the above calculations will be reversed. Thus we have a powerful but simple measurement of gains or losses from long or short positions in foreign currency units or in assets denominated in foreign currency units. The practical implications are that a divergence between the current forward rate and the future spot rate will produce a real gain or loss. This means a violation of the forward parity theorem.

An issue raised with regard to the effect of the shift from fixed exchange rates to flexible exchange rates concerns the possibility of an increase in uncertainty under flexible exchange rates, which in turn could dampen the rate of growth in international trade. But if hedging can be used to limit risks from exchange rate fluctuations, increased fluctuations will be no problem unless the foreign exchange premium is increased. Furthermore, if there were an increase in uncertainty and if it were accompanied by an increase in expected returns, the reward-risk ratio could remain unchanged. The simple expression for measuring real gains or losses could thus be used to measure the extent to which net returns from unhedged positions were increased or decreased.

A similar model was formulated by Grauer, Litzenberger, and Stehle [1976]. Their model can be expressed as follows:

$$X_{f0} = E_1(X_1) + L_1, \tag{21.5}$$

where

X_{f0} = the current forward exchange rate,
X_1 = the future spot exchange rate,
E_1 = the expected value operator at time 1,
L_1 = the premium or discount resulting from systematic risk.

Now we can employ our measure of the real return (gain or loss) from a long or short position in a foreign currency or net assets denominated in foreign currency units, as a measure of the premium or discount in the relationship between the current forward rate and the future spot rate. We repeat Eq. (21.4) expressed in dollars per foreign currency unit or foreign currency units per dollar:

$$r_1 = (E_1/E_f) - 1 = (X_f/X_1) - 1. \tag{21.4}$$

In terms of our previous examples, if we are long in foreign currency units and the current forward value of the foreign currency unit *was* $0.25 but its actual spot value at the end of the period *is* $0.20, the future spot rate is at a discount from the current forward rate. This implies that the purchasing power uncertainty reflected in exchange rates is negatively correlated with world wealth so that the risk premium represents a reduction rather than an addition to the real rate of return. Conversely, if the future spot rate is higher than the current forward rate, we obtain a real gain.

If we are in a short position in the foreign currency units, the determination of premiums or discounts will be reversed.

5. The Forward Parity Theorem (FPT)

The examples we presented in describing the interest rate parity theorem illustrated that the forward exchange rate on the currency carrying a lower interest rate should be at a premium in relation to its spot value, where the exchange rates are expressed in the currency of the higher interest rate country. In our example the approximation for IRPT is

$$R_{fi} - R_{di} \cong \frac{X_f - X_0}{X_0}.$$

In our example we had

$$.15 - .10 \cong \frac{10.45 - 10}{10},$$

$$0.05 \cong .045.$$

This suggests that the interest differential should approximate the forward exchange rate differential percentage, measured as shown. The forward differential will therefore approximate the expected change in the exchange rate. Thus under the efficient market and perfect market assumptions postulated, forward exchange rates should be unbiased predictors of future spot rates.

SUMMARY

International financial markets direct savings flow into countries that can best employ the funds. The law of comparative advantage states that trade will be mutually advantageous since different countries have different relative efficiencies in producing different goods. A comparative advantage means that even though one country could produce some good more efficiently in absolute terms, it has other opportunities that are so superior that it is preferable for some other country—less efficient and with lower opportunity cost—to produce the good.

With a gold standard, countries with surplus exports receive gold in exchange. Domestic prices in the country receiving gold rise, and this price increase in turn stimulates imports to restore the trade balance. Income and employment may also be affected by the adjustment process. Convertibility of currencies to gold at fixed rates forces exchange rates to be fixed. With fixed exchange rates, disequilibrium forces all adjustments to be on prices of individual goods or capital flows.

Floating exchange rates were introduced to allow currency value adjustments based on the relative price changes of each country. The primary advantage is that the exchange rate is a market rate and is more flexible than wages and prices in general. But countries may establish programs to avoid or retard the automatic exchange rate adjustment processes. These include tariffs, duties, quotas, and domestic price controls. Typically the impact is to force the adjustment into another direction, such as changes in real output.

In balance of payments accounting, inflows are recorded as pluses and outflows as minuses. A trade imbalance may trigger a number of offsetting transactions. The subtotals of the balance of payments accounts provide much information about the short- and long-run developments for the economy of any country. Analysis of balance of payments trends can be useful for formulating corporate financial policy in managing exposure to exchange rate fluctuations and in the use of the international financial markets.

Foreign exchange markets enable buyers and sellers in different countries to deal in their own currencies. The foreign exchange rate is the price of one currency in terms of another and depends on the supply and demand relationships between the two currencies. There are strong forces linking spot, forward, future spot, and interest rates between countries. Arbitrage opportunities ensure these relationships against breakdowns. The consistency of cross rates means that given any three countries any one exchange rate will be determined by the other two exchange rates. If the relationship breaks down, an arbitrage opportunity will exist.

The purchasing power parity doctrine states that the change in exchange rates between countries depends on the relative changes in their prices for the same period. Thus the relative values of the currencies depend on what they will buy.

The Fisher relation holds that the nominal rate of interest is determined by the real rate of interest and the rate of inflation. The rate of inflation is also equal to the ratio of the expected future spot price to the current price. The current forward price is an estimate of what the future spot price will be.

The IRPT incorporates the Fisher relation by recognizing that between any two currencies the forward exchange rate should be the same as the spot exchange rate except for the anticipated effect of different rates of inflation. Since anticipated inflation rates are incorporated in the nominal interest rates of each country, there is a potential arbitrage possibility between current and forward exchange rates based on the relative interest rates of the countries. The process is known as covered interest arbitrage.

The real return from holding an investment denominated in a foreign currency (over and above the domestic real return) is a simple relationship of the future spot to the forward exchange rate. This relationship directs the international flow of investable funds. The forward parity theorem holds that the forward exchange rates should be unbiased predictors of future spot exchange rates.

The five fundamental equilibrium relationships imply the law of one price, which holds that under the assumptions set forth the exchange-adjusted prices of identical tradable goods and financial assets must be within transactions costs of equality throughout the world. Different rates of inflation and changing nominal interest rates should not affect the rates at which today's goods are exchanged for future goods or the rate at which domestic goods are exchanged for foreign goods. In the following chapter, we summarize empirical tests of the above propositions and discuss their implications for corporate international financial policies.

PROBLEM SET

21.1 You are given the prices of products in two countries as shown below:

	Product	
	X	Y
Country A	$3	$1
Country B	M12	M6

At an exchange rate of 5 marks per dollar, describe the pattern of exports and imports between countries A and B.

21.2 Country A and country B are each on a full gold standard with fixed exchange rates. Country A runs an export surplus, whereas country B runs an export balance deficit. Describe the adjustment process that will restore balance to the flow of trade between the two countries.

21.3 Country A and country B are on the gold standard. The currency of country A contains .1 ounce of gold, whereas the currency of country B contains .025 ounce of gold. What will be the par exchange rate between the two countries?

21.4 Consider two countries C and D operating in a world with complete flexible exchange rates. Country C runs a substantial export surplus to country D, which experiences a substantial trade deficit. Assuming no initial offsetting capital flows, explain the adjustment process to bring the trade between the two countries into balance.

21.5 Keep in mind Table Q21.5 listing the effects of individual transactions on the balance of payments.

Table Q21.5   Effects on the Balance of Payments, Country A

Plus (P)	Minus (M)
1. Exports	1. Imports
2. Increase liabilities to foreigners	2. Decrease liabilities to foreigners
3. Decrease claims on foreigners	3. Increase claims on foreigners
4. Decrease investments; sell assets	4. Increase investments; buy assets

Indicate the plus entry and the minus entry for the following transactions. For example, the country exports goods in the amount of $1000 paid for by the importer by a check on a foreign bank. The entry would be:

$$P1 \quad \$1000 \qquad M3 \quad \$1000$$

a) Country A exports $10,000 of goods to country I paid for by the importer by a check on his account with a bank in country A.

b) Country A imports $5000 worth of merchandise paid for by a check on a bank in country A.

c) Direct investment income of $2000 was received by a firm in country A from a foreign subsidiary, which paid by drawing a check on a bank in its own country F.

d) A multinational firm domiciled in country A made an investment of $1 million on a direct basis to establish a foreign subsidiary in country G. Payment was made by drawing on its bank account in country A.

e) A citizen of country A made a gift of $3000 to a friend in a foreign country who deposited the check drawn on a bank in country A in his own bank in country M.

f) A citizen in country A bought an airline ticket to Europe that he purchased from Lufthansa Airlines by a check for $500 drawn on a bank in country A.

21.6 In January 19X0 (when DM3 = $1) it was expected that by the end of 19X0 the price level in the United States would have risen by 10% and in West Germany by 5%. The real rate of interest in both countries is 4%.

a) Use the PPPT to project the expected DMs per $1 at the end of 19X0 (the expected future spot rate of DMs per $1).

b) Use the Fisher relation to estimate the nominal interest rates in each country that make it possible for investments in each country to earn their real rate of interest.

c) Use the IRPT to estimate the current one-year forward rate of DMs per $1.

d) Compare your estimate of the current forward rate in (c) with your estimate of the expected future spot rate in (a).

e) Prove analytically that the Fisher effect and the IRPT guarantee consistency with the PPPT relation when real interest rates in the different countries are equal. (Assume that all the fundamental relations hold.)

REFERENCES

Adler, M., and B. Dumas, "International Portfolio Choice and Corporation Finance: A Synthesis," *Journal of Finance*, June 1983, 925–984.

Adler, M., and B. Lehman, "Deviations from Purchasing Power Parity in the Long Run," *Journal of Finance*, December 1983, 1471–1487.

Aizenman, J., "Testing Deviations from Purchasing Power Parity," *Journal of International Money and Finance*, March 1986, 25–36.

Aliber, R. Z., *The International Money Game*, 3rd ed. Basic Books, New York, 1979.

Allsopp, C., "The Rise and Fall of the Dollar: A Comment," *Economic Journal*, March 1987, 44–48.

Barthold, T. A., and W. R. Dougan, "The Fisher Hypothesis under Different Monetary Regimes," *Review of Economics and Statistics*, November 1986, 674–679.

Batten, D. S., and D. L. Thornton, "Discount Rate Changes and the Foreign Exchange Market," *Journal of International Money and Finance*, December 1984, 279–292.

Calvo, G. A., "Temporary Stabilization: Predetermined Exchange Rates," *Journal of Political Economy*, December 1986, 1319–1337.

Caves, R. E., and R. W. Jones, *World Trade and Payments: An Introduction*, 2nd ed. Little, Brown, Boston, 1977.

Chacholiades, M., *International Trade Theory and Policy*, 2nd ed. McGraw-Hill, New York, 1978.

Chan, K. S., "The International Negotiation Game: Some Evidence from the Tokyo Round," *Review of Economics and Statistics*, August 1985, 456–464.

Cooper, R. N.; P. B. Kenen; J. Braga de Macedo; and J. van Ypersele, eds., *The International Monetary System under Flexible Exchange Rates*. Ballinger, Cambridge, Mass., 1982.

Corbo, V., "International Prices, Wages and Inflation in an Open Economy: A Chilean Model," *Review of Economics and Statistics*, November 1985, 564–573.

Cornell, B., and M. R. Reinganum, "Forward and Future Prices: Evidence from the Foreign Exchange Markets," *Journal of Finance*, December 1981, 1035–1045.

Dilullo, A. J., "U.S. International Transactions, Third Quarter 1986," *Survey of Current Business*, December 1986, 23–27.

Dornbusch, R., *Open Economy Macro-Economics*. Basic Books, New York, 1980.

———, "Exchange Rate Economics: 1986," *Economic Journal*, March 1987, 1–18.

Eiteman, D. K., and A. I. Stonehill, *Multinational Business Finance*, 4th ed. Addison-Wesley, Reading, Mass., 1986.

Errunza, V., and E. Losq, "International Asset Pricing under Mild Segmentation: Theory and Test," *Journal of Finance*, March 1985, 105–124.

Farber, A.; R. Roll; and B. Solnik, "An Empirical Study of Risk over Fixed and Flexible Exchange," *Journal of Monetary Economics*, Supplementary Series, 1977, 235–265.

Feige, E. L., and K. J. Singleton, "Multinational Inflation under Fixed Exchange Rates: Some Empirical Evidence from Latent Variable Models," *Review of Economics and Statistics*, February 1981, 11–19.

Frenkel, J. A., "The Implications of Mean-Variance Optimization for Four Questions in International Macroeconomics," *Journal of International Money and Finance*, March 1986, 853–876.

———, and H. G. Johnson, eds., *The Economics of Exchange Rates*. Addison-Wesley, Reading, Mass., 1978.

Goodhart, C., "Exchange Rate Economics 1986: A Comment," *Economic Journal*, March 1987, 19–22.

Grabbe, J. O., *International Financial Markets*. Elsevier, New York, 1986.

Grauer, F. L. A.; R. H. Litzenberger; and R. E. Stehle, "Sharing Rules and Equilibrium in an International Capital Market under Uncertainty," *Journal of Financial Economics*, June 1976, 233–256.

Grubel, H. G., *International Economics*. Richard D. Irwin, Homewood, Ill., 1977.

Haberler, G., "The International Monetary System," *Economist*, July 1986, 1–8.

Hakkio, C. S., "Interest Rates and Exchange Rates—What Is the Relationship?" Federal Reserve Bank of Kansas City, *Economic Review*, November 1986, 33–43.

Hartman, D. G., "The International Financial Market and U.S. Interest Rates," *Journal of International Money and Finance*, April 1984, 91–104.

Helpman, E., "A Simple Theory of International Trade with Multinational Corporations," *Journal of Political Economy*, June 1984, 451–471.

Huang, R. D., "The Monetary Approach to Exchange Rate in an Efficient Foreign Exchange Market: Tests Based on Volatility," *Journal of Finance*, March 1981, 31–41.

———, "Some Alternative Tests of Forward Exchange Rates as Predictors of Future Spot Rates," *Journal of International Money and Finance*, August 1984, 153–168.

Johannes, J. M., "Testing the Exogeneity Specification Underlying the Monetary Approach to the Balance of Payments," *Review of Economics and Statistics*, February 1981, 29–34.

Koromzay, V.; J. Llewellyn; and S. Potter, "The Rise and Fall of the Dollar: Some Explanations, Consequences and Lessons," *Economic Journal*, March 1987, 23–43.

Kreinin, M. E., *International Economics: A Policy Approach*, 3rd ed. Harcourt Brace Jovanovich, New York, 1979.

Lessard, D. R., *International Financial Management: Theory and Application*, 2nd ed. John Wiley & Sons, New York, 1985.

Levi, M., *International Finance*. McGraw-Hill, New York, 1983.

Lindert, P. H., and C. P. Kindleberger, *International Economics*, 7th ed. Richard D. Irwin, Homewood, Ill., 1982.

Mark, N. C., "Some Evidence on the International Inequality of Real Interest Rates," *Journal of International Money and Finance*, June 1985, 189–208.

Meltzer, H., "Monetary and Exchange Rate Regimes: A Comparison of Japan and the United States," *Cato Journal*, Fall 1986, 667–683.

Overturf, S. F., "Interest Rate Expectations and Interest Parity," *Journal of International Money and Finance*, March 1986, 91–98.

Pippenger, J., "Arbitrage and Efficient Markets Interpretations of Purchasing Power Parity: Theory and Evidence," Federal Reserve Bank of San Francisco, *Economic Review*, Winter 1986, 31–47.

Rodriguez, R. M., and E. E. Carter, *International Financial Management*, 2nd ed. Prentice-Hall, Englewood Cliffs, N.J., 1979.

Rolfe, S. E., and J. L. Burtle, *The Great Wheel: The World Monetary System*. Quadrangle/New York Times Book Company, New York, 1973.

Roll, R., "Violations of the Law of One Price and Their Implications for Differentially Denominated Assets," in Marshall Sarnat and George Szego, eds., *International Finance and Trade*, vol. 1, Ballinger, Cambridge, Mass., 1979.

Shapiro, A. C., *Multinational Financial Management*, 2nd ed. Allyn and Bacon, Boston, 1986.

Solnik, B. H., *European Capital Markets*. Lexington Books, Lexington, Mass., 1973.

———, "International Arbitrage Pricing Theory," *Journal of Finance*, May 1983, 449–457.

Solomon, R., *The International Monetary System, 1945–1976, An Insider's View*. Harper & Row, New York, 1977.

Takayama, A., *International Trade*. Holt, Rinehart and Winston, New York, 1972.

Triffin, R., "Correcting the World Monetary Scandal." *Challenge*, January–February 1986, 4–14.

Ungerer, H.; O. Evans; T. Mayer; and P. Young, "The European Monetary System: Recent Developments," International Monetary Fund Occasional Papers 48, International Monetary Fund, Washington, D.C., 1986.

Yeager, L. B., *International Monetary Mechanism*. Holt, Rinehart and Winston, New York, 1968.

———, *International Monetary Relations: Theory, History and Policy*, 2nd ed. Harper & Row, New York, 1976.

22

The exchanges between countries are at par only whilst they have precisely that quantity of currency, which in the actual situation of things, they should have to carry on the circulation of their commodities.

David Ricardo, *Principles of Political Economy and Taxation,*
Gonner Edition, G. Bell and Sons, Ltd., London, 1927, 213–214.

International Financial Management: Tests and Implications

A fundamental dimension of international investment is the existence of exchange risk and mechanisms providing inducements to investors to carry that risk. Intertemporal equilibrium models of international capital markets that take into account exchange risk, the existence of different interest rates, and different tastes across the world will be treated in this chapter. It will be demonstrated that changes in relative prices of goods due to supply or demand shifts induce changes in exchange rates and deviations from puchasing power parity. Although there are some difficulties in testing international asset pricing models, empirical studies show that an international market structure of price behavior appears to exist. Finally, techniques to minimize foreign exchange exposure and methods of foreign currency translation will be discussed.[1]

---

[1] A monograph-length treatment of the issues in this chapter is found in Shapiro [1986].

A. INTERNATIONAL DIVERSIFICATION

From the purely financial point of view, investors, whether they be firms or individuals, ought to consider the possibility of expanding their investments beyond the geographical limits of their own countries, if only because of the greater number and diversity of investment possibilities available. If the universe of assets available for investment is larger than just the assets in one country, even a country as large as the United States, our discussion in earlier chapters should suggest that investors may be able to reduce the risk of their investment portfolios by diversifying across countries. Solnik [1974b] has some empirical estimates for the risk of an internationally diversified portfolio compared with a diversified portfolio that is purely *domestic*. Using weekly data on stocks in eight major European countries and the United States, Solnik found that an internationally diversified portfolio would be one tenth as risky as a typical security and one half as risky as a well-diversified portfolio of U.S. stocks alone. He used the variance of returns as a measure of risk. He also found that inter*industry* diversification is inferior to intercountry diversification.

In a related study, Jacquillat and Solnik [1978] compared the performance of multinational corporations with that of an internationally diversified portfolio. By the same risk measure as above, a portfolio of U.S. multinational firms has about 90% of the standard deviation of a purely domestic U.S. portfolio. Internationally diversified portfolios have only about 30% to 50% of the risk of the U.S. domestic portfolio. This is suggestive evidence that the international dimension has not yet been fully exploited by multinational corporations (MNCs). A portfolio of MNC stocks is a poor substitute to the investor for a truly internationally diversified portfolio.

Two empirical studies relate to the above. Maldonado and Saunders [1983] concluded that their empirical evidence "supports capital market efficiency and the law of one price for internationally traded stocks" [23]. This casts doubt on the benefits of international diversification. But Philippatos, Christofi, and Christofi [1983] argue that the above study and an earlier one (Maldonado and Saunders [1981]) were influenced by methodologies and sample employed. They agree with other studies that find *ex ante* gains from international diversification.

B. ASSET PRICING MODELS

Asset pricing models, similar in form and spirit to the CAPM, have been derived for international financial assets. In a manner analogous to the standard CAPM derivations in continuous time, Solnik develops an international asset pricing model (IAPM) and tests it [1974a, 1974d]. A market portfolio, with properties similar to that in the CAPM, is specified by:

1. Market value–weighted stocks,
2. A pure exchange risk portfolio of risk-free assets of the various countries in the world. Relative weights in this portfolio depend on net foreign investment positions in each country and the relative risk aversions of citizens of each country.

A risk-pricing relationship similar in form to the standard CAPM is derived:

$$E(r_i) - R_i = \beta_i[E(r_m) - R_m],$$

where

r_i = the return on a security i,

R_i = the riskless rate in the country of security i in terms of the currency of country i,

R_m = an average riskless rate, with weights as in the market portfolio,

r_m = the return on the world market portfolio,

β_i = the *international* systematic risk coefficient of security i.

In his empirical tests, Solnik [1974a, 1974d] used daily data on stocks of eight European countries and of the United States. The results are weakly consistent with his IAPM. Solnik [1974d] also used the Solnik IAPM to test whether assets are best regarded as being traded in national (segmented) or in international (integrated) markets. This test is a simple extension of his IAPM tests. He found some evidence that markets are integrated, in that the IAPM performs better than a purely national specification.

Grauer, Litzenberger, and Stehle [1976] (GLS) also derive an international asset pricing model but under the assumptions of identical tastes across countries. Stehle [1977], building on GLS, improved upon Solnik's specification of the integration hypothesis and corrected some econometric problems with Solnik's methodology. He also found weak evidence in support of integration.

1. Use of Consumption Opportunity Sets

A new development in the field of international asset pricing parallels an advance in the standard domestic asset pricing theory. Breeden [1979] developed an asset pricing model that explicitly noted that individuals derive their utility from consumption. Maximizing lifetime utility from consumption, Breeden developed a more complete model for asset pricing, wherein pricing of an asset depended on covariances with aggregate consumption rather than any "market" index or portfolio. Such a model is more general than standard market models because, under certain conditions, a consumption-based model is equivalent to a multibeta model where an asset's pricing is allowed to depend on *many* state variables. In the field of international finance, Stulz [1981b] used Breeden's results to develop an asset pricing theory, much as Solnik [1974c] had followed Merton's [1973] lead.

Stulz extended Solnik's model essentially by allowing consumption opportunities to differ across countries, at least temporarily, until arbitrage through trade flows equalizes them. Stulz notes that Solnik's model requires the exchange rate to be perfectly correlated with the relative price of the two countries' imports (the terms of trade). The empirical evidence is that although a correlation exists, it is not perfect [Isard, 1978]. Stulz allows the consumption opportunity set to differ across countries. By "consumption opportunity set" is meant the set of goods available for consumption, current prices, and the distribution of future prices of these goods. It is assumed that prices of commodities and the exchange rate itself follow a stochastic Ito process. All assets are assumed to be traded, but all commodities are not. The law of one price (naive PPP) holds only for traded goods. A pricing relationship is derived, which states that

$$\mu - V_{aPm} = (T^W)^{-1}\{V_{aC} - V_{aP\alpha}C\}, \quad \text{where} \quad T^W = T^F + T^D. \tag{26}$$

Stulz [1981b, 396] comments on his Eq. (26) as follows:

> Here μ is the vector of expected excess returns for domestic investors. The excess return of an asset for a domestic investor is defined as the return in the domestic country of a portfolio with a long holding of that asset financed by selling the nominal safe bond of the home-country of the asset. T^W is a measure of world risk-tolerance. V_{aC} is the vector of covariances between home-country returns of risky assets and changes in world consumption in domestic currency. V_{aPm} and $V_{aP\alpha}$ are the vectors of covariances of home-country returns with $d \ln Pm$ and $d \ln P\alpha$. An increase in Pm means a decrease in the real value of a marginal dollar of consumption expenditures, whereas an increase in $P\alpha$ means a fall in the real value of total consumption expenditures. Eq. (26) is the fundamental pricing equation of this paper.

From his Eq. (26), a proposition is shown to follow: The expected excess real return of a risky asset is proportional to the covariance between the home currency rate of return of that asset and changes in world real consumption rate. Note that the return on an asset does not depend on unexpected changes in the exchange rate, so exchange rate risk is not rewarded.

As a further result, Stulz shows that the forward exchange rate is inversely proportional to the covariance between the changes in the exchange rate and changes in the real-world consumption rate. This is the first full model to permit the forward rate to change through time, always remaining in equilibrium. Stulz finally notes that this more general model of asset pricing in international financial markets may explain why some previous models seemed to find the international financial markets to be segmented: If changes in the world consumption rate are not perfectly correlated with the market indices used by previous researchers, spurious results may flow from the misspecification of the tested models. The Breeden and Stulz models have not been systematically tested to date.

2. Difficulties of Testing IAPM

The IAPM is subject to the same sort of problem in empirical testing that Roll [1977] has noted with the conventional CAPM. Strongly influenced by Roll's critique, Solnik [1977] pointed out that testing the IAPM in a satisfactory manner is an essentially impossible task. All the problems in testing methodology observed by Roll continue to plague the testing of the IAPM—after all, merely a variant of the CAPM.

In addition, the IAPM has its own problems. Solnik makes two points:

1. It is well documented that the covariance between national indices is quite low. In that case, even if markets were *completely* segmented and assets priced *entirely* in domestic markets, with no influence of the international financial markets,

an "optimal" portfolio, artificially constructed by the researcher without regard to actual feasibility, will always end up being well diversified internationally. Such a portfolio will be mean-variance efficient, and an IAPM-type test will "succeed," using this "optimal" portfolio as a proxy for the "world market portfolio." This is a direct consequence of Roll's insight about the role of the index. So the success of the test tells us nothing about how assets are actually priced.

2. Even if there were no conceptual problem as above, there is a practical problem. In Solnik's derivation of the IAPM, the world market portfolio turns out to include a portfolio he calls a "pure exchange risk asset." Weights of the nominally riskless securities of different countries in this portfolio are shown to be dependent on the net foreign investment positions in the different countries, and the relative risk aversions of citizens of the different countries. This specification would be difficult to implement in practice.

C. EXCHANGE RISK AND PURCHASING POWER PARITY

Fluctuating exchanges are often viewed as an additional source of risk facing the investor or trader importing and exporting goods. The prices of commodities, the yields on assets, are usually fixed in nominal terms, i.e., in fixed amounts of foreign currency at the time of transacting. An investor who buys a $100 pure discount bond, e.g., knows only that he or she will receive $100 at the maturity of the bond. But if the investor happens to be a German who needs marks for consumption, he or she does not know how many marks the dollars received will buy. That depends on the exchange rate between the dollar and the mark. With the highly fluctuating exchange rates of recent years, this seems to be a substantial source of risk.

Because the value of the investor's return at the end of the period is uncertain in terms of the investor's home currency, his or her consumption is uncertain. This is readily interpretable as the risk that the variations in exchange rates over a period will not exactly offset inflation differentials, which is another way of saying that PPP will not hold. Thus deviations from PPP acquire practical significance in terms of exchange risk.

The key to understanding departures from PPP, or equivalently, the phenomenon of exchange risk, is to recognize that there are many consumption goods. Further, people in different countries have different consumption baskets—they consume the goods in different proportions. For example, the Japanese consume more sake than wine and French consume more wine than sake. Such differences may be caused by a variety of factors: social, cultural, historical—everything subsumed under the expression "different tastes."

The relative prices of goods can fluctuate over time because of shifts in supply or demand conditions. Demand conditions may change with changes in tastes owing to shifts in the demographic composition of the population, for example. Supply conditions may change owing to bad weather or because of technological innovation.

We now proceed to distinguish between two phenomena: fluctuations in inflation rates and fluctuations in relative prices. When we say "fluctuations in inflation rates," we assume that everyone has the same consumption basket of goods, and that relative prices are unchanged. This is an assumption for simplication. In reality, both the overall price level and the relative prices of goods are likely to fluctuate simultaneously.

1. Inflation Risk

Suppose that we are investors in the United States who have a security in England whose return is fixed in pounds. Assuming that there is no inflation in the United States, but that the inflation rate in England is *uncertain*, the dollar value of our investment at the end of the period is uncertain and hence risky. Our position has "exchange risk." It is clear that this exchange risk is simply inflation risk. With no relative price fluctuations, arbitrage of physical goods will ensure that PPP holds, because now, in a sense, there is only one consumption good "composite" and PPP is the same as the law of one price, which always holds in perfect commodity markets. The change in exchange rate reflects exactly the change in inflation rates and nothing else.

However, the risk of our position is purely nominal. It can be eliminated by indexing all contracts, tying the quantity of pounds from the investment to the price index in England, for instance, or contracting in "real" terms. To the extent this is not feasible or not done, it reflects information costs or transations costs of doing so. In our present model of the world, it is perfectly feasible to eliminate nominal risk completely. In any case the point is that it is a mistake to attribute the "risk" to the exchange rate. It is caused by uncertainty about the foreign price level, not so much by the phenomenon of fluctuating exchange rates. If all contracts were written in real terms, all profits, all returns on investments of all kinds, would be independent of the geographical location of the investor or the investment, and the exchange rate would have no real role to play beyond the arithmetic of conversions. Grauer, Litzenberger, and Stehle [1976] have shown that, in the case where all individuals in the world have the same tastes, if a real riskless asset exists, all individuals face the same investment and consumption opportunity set—and so which country the investor happens to be in is irrelevant. The exchange risk is then merely some sort of white noise that has no effect on anything real, though it gives apparent fluctuations in prices in nominal terms. Under the assumption of identical homothetic tastes (equivalent to one consumption good when relative prices are constant), for the exchange risk to be irrelevant is for goods arbitrage to be instantaneous and costless, so that the real price of a good will be the same everywhere in the world.

2. "Real" Exchange Risk

Thus far we have assumed, explicitly, that relative prices are constant. But for exchange risk to matter to the investor, it must not be purely nominal. Such real risk is caused, we shall now see, by relative price fluctuations. The assumption of one consumption good is now dropped.

Solnik [1974c] was the first to explore formally the implications to financial markets of a world where individuals in different countries consume different baskets of goods. We shall use Solnik's [1978] example of Japanese who consume more sake than wine and French who consume more wine than sake. (We shall follow his notation for ease of reference to the original.) Wine and sake are the only goods in the world. It is not necessary for this story that the French produce wine and only wine, or that the Japanese produce sake and only sake.

Suppose, to begin with, the price of sake equals the price of wine—i.e., the relative price is 1, in both countries. The relative price must be the same in both countries, else there will be goods arbitrage, since the transportation of goods is perfect, instantaneous, and costless by the assumptions of the model. Suppose also that the exchange rate, which we shall define to be the price of yen in francs, is also 1. Next postulate an exogenous shock, e.g., something damages the wine crop. Then the relative prices of the two goods will change at once to reflect the reduced supply of wine. Wine will become more expensive. Again, because of the possibility of goods arbitrage, the relative price between wine and sake must be the same in both countries. The question we seek to answer is: What will be the new exchange rate? Assume the following relationships:

Before the shock

	Wine	Sake
French consumption	9 units	1 unit
Japanese consumption	1 unit	9 units

Price of wine = price of sake. The exchange rate is 1:1.

After the shock

	Wine	Sake
French consumption	8 units	$1\frac{1}{2}$ units
Japanese consumption	$\frac{1}{3}$ unit	$9\frac{1}{2}$ units

The price of wine = 1.5 × price of sake (assumed also).
The exchange rate is to be determined.

Note that the consumptions have adjusted to the changed relative price. Now, we need to separate the effect of a relative price change from that of an inflationary change. We next assume that there is no general rise in the price level in either country. The governments in both countries do whatever they have to do to ensure that the prices of the consumption baskets remain the same in terms of their respective local currencies: adjusting the money supply, etc.

Let the price of sake and wine in France be S_f^0 and W_f^0 and in Japan be S_j^0 and W_j^0 in francs and yen, respectively, before the shock. Let $W_f^1, S_f^1; W_j^1, S_j^1$ be the corresponding after-the-shock prices in nominal terms (i.e., in terms of the home currencies—francs in France and yen in Japan).

We know that

$$S_j^0 = W_j^0,$$

$$S_f^0 = W_f^0; \qquad \text{The relative price} = 1.$$

$$W_j^1 = 1.5\ S_j^1,$$

$$W_f^1 = 1.5\ S_f^1; \qquad \text{The new relative price} = 1.5.$$

In France. The consumption basket cost is $9\ W_f^0 + 1\ S_f^0 = 10\ S_f^0$ francs before the shock. The consumption bundle after the shock costs $8\ W_f^1 + 1.5\ S_f^1 = 12\ S_f^1 + 1.5\ S_f^1 = 13.5\ S_f^1$ francs. Because we are assuming no inflation, the price of the consumption basket in francs must be the same before and after the shock in nominal terms. Then $10\ S_f^0 = 13.5\ S_f^1$. So

$$S_f^1 = \frac{10}{13.5}\ S_f^0. \tag{22.1}$$

In Japan. The cost of the consumption bundle, in yen, is $9\ S_j^0 + 1\ W_j^0 = 10\ S_j^0$ before the shock. After the shock, it is $9.5\ S_j^1 + \frac{1}{3}\ W_j^1 = 9.5\ S_j^1 + \frac{1}{3} \times 1.5\ S_j^1 = 10\ S_j^1$. By the no-inflation condition, $10\ S_j^0 = 10\ S_j^1$ or

$$S_j^1 = S_j^0. \tag{22.2}$$

Now we note that by the law of one price the price of sake must be the same in both countries at a given time, after converting by the new exchange rate. Then after the shock, $\frac{10}{13.5}\ S_f^0$ francs must buy a unit of sake in both France and Japan, Eq. (22.1). Recall that $S_f^0 = S_j^0$ because the initial exchange rate was 1. By (22.2) we also have

$$S_f^0 = S_j^0 = S_j^1.$$

Hence we can substitute S_j^1 for S_f^0 in Eq. (22.1) to obtain

$$S_f^1 = \frac{10}{13.5}\ S_j^1.$$

This demonstrates that the new exchange rate will be .741 francs/yen. At the old exchange rate 1 yen was equal to 1 franc. At the new exchange rate, 1 yen is now worth only .741 francs.

Cornell [1980] provides a verbal explanation of the algebraic development. Because the cost of wine has risen, less wine will be consumed in both France and Japan. Because the French government was holding the inflation in France to 0, the price of the French basket could not rise in terms of francs. Japan also offset the rise in cost of its own basket. But that basket rose less than did the French, so the off-setting also had to be less. Hence the cost of the *French* basket must rise in *yen*. It cannot rise in francs, as we have seen. Yet the law of one price (no goods arbitrage) requires that the French basket cost the same, after conversion for the exchange rate, in both France and Japan. The only way this can happen is if the price of yen falls relative to the price of francs, which is what happened. Stockman [1980] makes the same general point.

In the Solnik example, the exchange rate fluctuation is a "real" risk because we cannot hedge it away merely by contracting in real terms. Those in France who have invested in Japan get only .741 of what they expected to get, in francs, and can only buy, in their own consumption baskets, .741 of what they had expected to buy if the shock had not occurred and the exchange rate had not changed.

In what sense is this an "exchange risk"? The risk was caused by a change in relative prices of goods. The risk did not come from the exchange rate directly. The exchange rate only reflected something more fundamental that changed. In fact, business firms always face the risk that there may be changes in the relative prices of their product relative to its substitutes, of the product relative to the inputs, etc. (So does any individual: a vegetarian, e.g., always faces the risk that the price of his or her food will change relative to the price of meat.) The point is that it is important to recognize that "exchange risk" is essentially the same as "business" risk. The fact that the firm may be operating in two different countries causes it only to be *manifested*, partly, through the exchange rate. To ascribe the investor's risk to the phenomenon of exchange rate fluctuations, or to the fact of flexible exchange rates, is to mistake the symptom for the malady.

To return this discussion to PPP, recall that in the extended example of the wine and sake there was no inflation in either country. PPP would require that the exchange rate remain the same. But it did not. Hence PPP was violated. Real exchange risk is to be found wherever PPP is violated.

3. Roll's Study of PPP Violations

In an efficient market's perspective, we would expect PPP to hold on an expected value basis, since the relative price fluctuations are random and not predictable, by their very nature. Observed violations of PPP should be uncorrelated over time.

Roll [1979] provided the first rigorous intertemporal specification of PPP and fused it with the notion of market efficiency. He set the *expected* return to intertemporal speculation conditional on information at the beginning of the period equal to zero. He found PPP to be valid in an average sense. However, the deviations from it attributable to relative price fluctuations dominated the effects of inflation on the exchange rates.

4. Empirical Investigation of Exchange Risk

We have established in theory that exchange risk, both nominal and real, may be substantial. Solnik [1974c] developed a model of exchange risk, as part of a larger theory of international asset pricing, which was empirically examined by Roll and Solnik [1977]. They used Solnik's formulation for exchange risk to test its magnitude and significance in asset pricing. Monthly data on six European countries, Canada, and the United States were used. The equilibrium relationship Solnik had derived showed that the difference between riskless nominal rates in two countries should be equal to the expected change in exchange rates plus a term depending on exchange rate covariances. Their findings indicate that exchange risk is substantial and significant.

D. MARKET EFFICIENCY

Having considered some fundamental ways in which the international financial markets may differ from domestic financial markets, we may now proceed to ask the sorts of questions we have been asking in our earlier studies of the domestic markets: To what degree are exchange markets efficient? What is the empirical magnitude and significance of exchange risk? Several possible approaches to the question of efficiency of the exchange markets are first examined.

1. Testing Arbitrage Relationships

The minimum requirement a market must satisfy if it is to be said to be efficient is that no arbitrage possibilities must exist. Recall that the interest rate parity theorem (IRPT) is one such arbitrage relationship that must hold in international financial markets. Consistent and systematic deviations from IRPT outside the bounds of transactions costs may be interpreted as evidence of inefficiency.

Frenkel and Levich [1977] study this question. They explicitly account for transactions costs and calculate a band around the interest rate parity line within which no arbitrage is profitable. Using weekly data for the period 1962–1975 and for three subperiods, they found that a very high percentage of observations are within the neutral band (more than 90% in most cases.) They conclude that—after allowing for transactions costs and ensuring that the arbitraged assets are comparable—covered interest arbitrage does not seem to entail unexploited opportunities for profit.

2. Equilibrium Pricing Models

Another approach to testing the efficiency of international financial markets, but without confining the test to arbitrage relationships between assets of "equal risk," is to develop a model for the pricing of risky assets and test whether financial markets price assets accordingly. In our study of domestic financial markets, for instance, we saw that tests of the CAPM can be construed to be joint tests of market efficiency and of the model itself. But a rejection of the model in empirical testing would be a rejection of the notion of efficiency of the market in which the assets are traded.

3. Trading Rule Tests

Another approach is to examine the profitability of simple trading rules like filters. One such study is by Cornell and Dietrich [1978]. Using daily exchange rates for the period March 1973 to September 1975, for a sample of currencies of major industrialized nations, they set up some simple filter rule–based trading strategies, taking transactions costs into account.

In the moving average filter, when the exchange rate moves $X\%$ above the moving average for a prespecified interval, the rule calls for the investor to move into the foreign currency; when it falls $X\%$ below the moving average, the investor moves back into dollars. Moving averages of 10, 25, and 50 days were tried. None of these filter rules produced a profit of more than 4% per annum for the British pound, Canadian dollar, or Japanese yen. However, the situation was quite different with the German mark, the Dutch guilder, and Swiss franc. The 25-day moving average rule consistently produced profits of more than 15% per annum for all three currencies, with filters ranging from 0.2% to 2.0%. The simple filter did not do quite as well, because of the larger transactions costs accruing to the larger number of transactions it triggered. Still, it did produce profits of more than 10% for some filters.

The three currencies with the high trading-rule profits were also the three with the highest variance. Hence the "profit" observed may well be merely compensation for the greater risk of trading in these currencies. Since variance alone is not systematic risk, Cornell and Dietrich attempted to separate the systematic from the unsystematic portion of the total variation. Exchange rate variations were correlated with the S&P 500 index as the "market." The result was to eliminate almost entirely the risk of these currencies, casting doubt on the proposition that the "excess profit" was a "risk premium."

As with all filter tests, the main problem in interpretation of the results seems to be that we do not know how to adjust for the different risks of the alternative strategies. Also, it does not appear that there is any way to determine, *ex ante*, the appropriate size of filter to test. They depend on historical relationships that are likely to be unstable over time.

4. Forward Speculation

A fourth approach to testing the efficiency of markets is to examine the returns to forward speculation. The basic assumption underlying the simpler versions of this class of efficiency tests is that the forward rate should be an unbiased forecaster of the future spot rate. But there may be good theoretical reasons for the forward rate to be systematically different from the expected (corresponding) future spot rate. For example, Stockman [1978] developed a simple model with only money supply uncertainty that shows that the forward rate may have a risk premium associated with it, which would lead it to be a biased estimator of the future spot rate. Another model that makes the same point is that of Grauer, Litzenberger, and Stehle [1976]. A forward bias can also come from the "real" exchange risk.

To turn to the empirical evidence itself, it appears that, on the whole, the forward rate is very close to the expected future spot rate. Stockman [1978] found that the risk premium is significant only for a couple of currencies (the British pound and the Swiss franc). He interpreted it to mean that the risk premium was not important. The risk premium, when significant, was not stable across subperiods. The question of exchange market efficiency was also studied by Cornell [1977]. Using monthly data on exchange rates for eight industrialized countries, Cornell finds:

1. There is some evidence of autocorrelation in the simple martingale model $E[X_t] = X_{t-1}$ where X is the spot exchange rate. Autoregressive models fit the data better.

2. He also tests the model $F_{t-1} = E_{t-1}[X_t] + L_t$ and $E_{t-1}[X_t] = X_t + u_t$,

where

X = the spot rate,

F = the forward rate,

L = a liquidity premium or risk premium,

u = the error term.

Cornell explicitly allows for the fact that a bias may exist in the forward rate as a predictor of the future spot rate.

The results are that the liquidity premium is positive but generally insignificant. Furthermore, autocorrelations are found in the residuals of $F_{t-1} - X_t$, suggesting that the liquidity premium is not stationary. A test is constructed for determining whether the forward rate incorporates all information in the history of spot rates. Since L_t (the liquidity premium) is not identically zero, it is necessary to assume that it is uncorrelated with past spot rates (a reasonable assumption), in which case equations of the form $F_{t-1} - X_t = a_0 + a_1[X_{t-1} - X_{t-2}]$ can be estimated. The behavior of the coefficients in this and other autoregressive models is very similar to that of the corresponding coefficients in the autoregressive models for the exchange rate changes alone (with no forward rate). This leads Cornell to conclude that the market prices forward exchange contracts as if the exchange rates are generated by a stochastic process with a constant term and a random noise term, since the autocorrelations in exchange rates changes are apparently ignored by the forward pricing market. Cornell suggests that the autocorrelations in the data could be caused by data problems and the (efficient) market correctly ignores them. He also found that the martingale model slightly outperforms the forward rate as a predictor of future exchange rates.

Empirical studies of the relation between forward exchange rates and expected future spot rates in the latter part of the 1970s gave support to the *unbiasedness hypothesis*. This holds that the forward rate is an unbiased predictor of the future spot rate, indicating market efficiency as well. Later empirical studies cast doubt on these findings. Hodrick and Srivastava [1984] examine these issues in depth. Using a variety of methodologies, they find that the empirical evidence does not support the unbiasedness hypothesis. They state that there are strong empirical and theoretical reasons for the existence of a risk premium. They observe considerable evidence of large differences in the average holding period returns on a variety of assets. The differences appear to reflect risk premia, and since many argue that exchange rates are determined in asset markets, one would expect to find a risk premium here as well. They observe that in intertemporal asset pricing theory, the covariation between intertemporal marginal rates of substitution on monies and the nominal returns on assets induces a risk premium on the asset. It can be argued that the risk premium on a forward contract depends on the same covariation, since forward contracts are risky nominal assets. But this position depends on the underlying theories of the relation between spot and future prices, as discussed in Chapter 9.

Huang [1984] reviews other studies that he argues use "more statistically powerful techniques" but are unable to confirm the hypothesis of forward rates as unbiased predictors of future spot rates. His own study of nine countries in relation to the United States yields results that "suggest support for the random walk model" [1984, 157]. He finds little evidence of a liquidity premium. When a second alternative hypothesis of excessive or inadequate volatility for market efficiency is considered, the evidence cannot reject the alternative hypothesis that forward rates are unbiased predictors of future spot rates.

Using an experimental market approach, Forsythe, Palfrey, and Plott [1984] find that the effect of a futures market is to increase the speed at which a rational expectation equilibrium is reached. The combination of the market process with each individual's learning process drives the market to a rational expectations equilibrium with a relatively small number of replications.

A careful analysis of the relation between forward rates and future spot rates, containing many insights, is due to Fama [1984]. We summarize his presentation.

The forward exchange rate, e_f, observed at time zero for an exchange at time 1 is the market-determined certainty equivalent of the future spot exchange rate, e_1.[2] We can split this certainty equivalent into an expected future spot rate and a premium:

$$\ln e_f = E(\ln e_1) + P_0. \tag{1}$$

From (1) the difference between the forward rate and the current spot rate is

$$\ln e_f - \ln e_0 = P_0 + E(\ln e_1 - \ln e_0). \tag{2}$$

Fama then considers the regressions of $(\ln e_f - \ln e_1)$ and $(\ln e_1 - \ln e_0)$, both observed at $t = 1$, on $(\ln e_f - \ln e_0)$, observed at $t = 0$:

$$(\ln e_f - \ln e_1) = \alpha_1 + \beta_1(\ln e_f - \ln e_0) + \varepsilon_1, \qquad t = 1, \tag{3}$$

$$(\ln e_1 - \ln e_0) = \alpha_2 + \beta_2(\ln e_f - \ln e_0) + \varepsilon_2, \qquad t = 1. \tag{4}$$

Since the dependent variables sum to the same independent variable in both (3) and (4), the sum of the intercepts in (3) and (4) must be 0, the sum of the slopes must be 1.0, and the disturbances, period by period, must sum to 0.0. Given an efficient or rational exchange market, the deviation of β_2 from 1.0 is a direct measure of the variation of the premium in the forward rate. The complementary of the regression coefficients in (3) and (4) help in the interpretation of the empirical results.

Since a major conclusion of his empirical findings is that variation in forward rates is mostly variation in premia, Fama examines the economics of premia. He shows that with three central conditions discussed in the previous chapter (PPP, IRP, and IFR), the premium in the forward rate expression [Eq. (1)] is the difference between the expected real returns on the nominal bonds of the two countries.

---

[2] Since Fama subsequently expresses all exchange rates in dollars per unit of foreign currency, we shall use our relatively simple notation but his equation numbering since he employs them in his explanations.

This is his Eq. (9):

$$\ln e_f = [E(r_{d,t+1}) - E(r_{f,t+1})] + E(\ln e_1). \tag{9}$$

In his regression tests, he finds that the coefficients in (3) are always greater than 1.0, and the coefficients in (4) are always negative. Negative covariation between the premium and $E(\ln e_1 - \ln e_0)$ attenuates the variability of $(\ln e_f - \ln e_0)$ and obscures the interpretation of the regression slope coefficients in (3) and (4). Both the premium and the expected changes in the spot rate $E(\ln e_1 - \ln e_0)$ in $(\ln e_f - \ln e_0)$ vary through time, and the variance in the premium is large relative to $\sigma^2[E(\ln e_1 - \ln e_0)]$.

Fama's Eq. (9) is similar in spirit to the Grauer, Litzenberger, and Stehle [1976] concept presented in Eq. (21.5) of the previous chapter. But in Fama's (9) the premium or discount between the current forward rate and the future spot rate is represented by the differences in real returns on domestic versus foreign bonds. The interpretation of Fama's results is also consistent with the Farber, Roll, Solnik [1977] measure of real gains or losses in (21.4).

Thus rewrite Fama's (9) as

$$e_f = E(\ln e_1) + P. \tag{9a}$$

If $e_f = \$0.25$ and e_1 ex post is \$0.20, the premium is positive, which implies that we would gain from investing in domestic bonds rather than in foreign bonds during that interval. But if e_1 is \$0.30, the premium is negative, which implies that we would gain from investing in foreign bonds rather than domestic bonds during that interval.

These results are consistent with previous empirical studies summarized by Fama. Fama [1982] found that variation in anticipated real activity and variation in expected inflation are negatively correlated. Fama and Gibbons [1982] observed that real returns on U.S. nominal bonds are driven by and positively correlated with anticipated real activity. Tobin [1965] and Mundell [1963] both show that the real and expected inflation components of nominal interest rates are negatively correlated. These findings together are consistent with higher real returns in U.S. bonds when U.S. inflation is low relative to foreign countries.

With respect to whether systematic gains could be made by explanatory relations between spot and futures foreign exchange markets, Fama finds that the variation in the *ex ante* forward spot differential is small relative to the variation of the *ex post* change in the spot rate. Hence gains are not likely from seeking to exploit movements between spot, forward, and future spot rates.

5. Performance of Forecasting Services

A final way to test for the efficiency of the exchange market is to study whether forecasting services can "beat" the market. This is a test of efficiency in semistrong form. Levich [1979] analyzes the currency forecasts made by a forecasting service. He found that the particular service studied yielded profits consistently and significantly for some currencies. For other currencies, it lost. The results of such studies have been mixed and generally hard to interpret. On the whole the picture that emerges from this literature on efficiency seems similar to the picture we have seen in earlier chapters of domestic financial markets. The evidence is consistent with weak-form and semistrong-form efficiency.

With the background of the general framework of Chapter 21 and the discussion of exchange risk, asset pricing models, and market efficiency in the present chapter, we next turn to the implications for management policy.

E. MANAGERIAL ASPECTS OF FOREIGN EXCHANGE RISKS

The first issue is whether the parity conditions described in Chapter 21 preclude the necessity of dealing with foreign exchange risk. Dufey and Srinivasulu [1983] address this question of whether the parity conditions make it unnecessary to attempt to manage foreign exchange risk. They point to a number of market imperfections that must be taken into account—incomplete securities markets, positive transactions and information costs, the deadweight costs of financial distress, and agency costs. Their existence makes it desirable for corporate management to seek to cope with exchange risk.

1. Empirical Studies of Foreign Exchange Exposure

A number of articles have dealt with the issue of how to measure foreign exchange exposure. Hekman [1985] develops a model of *foreign exchange exposure* defined as the sensitivity of an investment's value in reference currency to changes in exchange rate forecasts; this sensitivity is because some share of the cash flows from the investment are denominated in foreign currency. Also, a share of cash flows denominated in a reference currency affected by future exchange rates will also generate sensitivity.

Kaufold and Smirlock [1986] measure uncertainty about the domestic currency value of a corporation's net foreign exchange position as a function of the duration of the cash flows and unanticipated changes in foreign interest and exchange rates. They assert that despite the expanding opportunities for the use of interest rate swaps and currency swaps, it is often not possible to completely eliminate net foreign exposures of firms. It may not always be possible to find firms with exactly offsetting positions; also, the forward and futures currency markets may not be operative for the requisite maturities involved. They therefore develop illustrations of how to hedge a U.S. firm's foreign currency exposure using the domestic interest rate futures contract and the relevant currency futures contract. They observe that complete hedging requires that both domestic and foreign interest rates be related to the domestic risk-free rate without error.

Adler and Dumas [1984] take a market approach to exposure to currency risk. They reason that the exposure to exchange risk is essentially the same as exposure to market risk. They propose that a portfolio's average exposure to exchange risk measured on a historical basis can be measured by regressing its total dollar value on a vector of exchange rates. The resulting partial regression coefficients will represent the exposure to each currency. In principle, if the same relationships hold in the future, these exposures could be hedged. They recognize that as exposures vary over time, it would be necessary to seek to derive multiperiod hedging rules.

Johnson and Walther [1984] measure the effectiveness of portfolio hedges in currency forward markets. To hedge the exposed cash position using portfolio theory, the firm takes an offsetting position in the forward market. The portion of the spot market holding to be held in the forward market equals the variance-minimizing portfolio hedge ratio. This is the subjective covariance between the forward market price changes and the spot market price changes to the variance of the forward market price changes. The portfolio approach is compared with a naive hedge in which the exposure is offset completely in the forward market and the gain or loss is determined by the difference between the forward market rate and the future spot rate of the foreign currency. They conclude that the naive hedge is superior but that neither achieves complete elimination of foreign currency price risk.

2. Managing Foreign Exchange Exposure

With the background of empirical studies of a number of dimensions of foreign exchange exposure, we next turn to some managerial techniques for reducing or limiting such exposure. The exposure of a business firm to foreign exchange risks is determined by the pattern of its cash flow and asset stock positions, which in turn depend upon the pattern of flow of future receipts and payments and the pattern of the firm's net monetary position. Monetary assets are those assets denominated in a fixed number of units of money such as cash, marketable securities, accounts receivable, tax refunds receivable, notes receivable, and prepaid insurance. Monetary liabilities are those liabilities expressed in fixed monetary terms, such as accounts payable, notes payable, tax liability reserves, bonds, and preferred stock.

The effects of a net monetary position exposure can be formulated as follows:

$$C_p = [(\text{MA} - \text{ML})/X_0 - (\text{MA} - \text{ML})/X_1](1 - t_{\text{U.S.}})$$

$$= (E_0 - E_1)(\text{MA} - \text{ML})(1 - t_{\text{U.S.}})$$

$$= (E_0 - E_1)(\text{NMP})(1 - t_{\text{U.S.}}),$$

where

C_p = cost of net monetary position (NMP) due to exchange rate changes,

MA = monetary assets,

ML = monetary liabilities,

X_0 = exchange rate at the beginning = $1/E_0$,

X_1 = exchange rate a period later = $1/E_1$,

$t_{\text{U.S.}}$ = tax rate in the United States.

The effects of a decline in foreign currency value are:

a) Net monetary debtor gains.

b) Net monetary creditor loses.

Let us assume that

$$MA = FC\ 200{,}000; \qquad X_0 = 4, \qquad t_{U.S.} = .5;$$
$$ML = FC\ 100{,}000; \qquad X_1 = 5.$$

We calculate the net monetary position to which the effect of the exchange rate shift is applied:

1) $NMP = MA - ML = 200{,}000 - 100{,}000 = 100{,}000;$

$$C_p = NMP(E_0 - E_1)(1 - t_{U.S.}) = 100{,}000(.25 - .20)(.5)$$
$$= \$5000(.5) = \$2500.$$

Our calculations show a decrease in the dollar value of our asset position—i.e., a loss of $2500.

We now let $ML = FC\ 300{,}000$. Then

2) $NMP = MA - ML = 200{,}000 - 300{,}000 = -100{,}000;$

$$C_p = NMP(E_0 - E_1)(1 - t_{U.S.}) = -100{,}000(.25 - .20)(.5)$$
$$= -\$2500.$$

The net amount owed is decreased by $2500, representing a gain.

The effects of an increase in FC value are:

a) Net monetary debtor loses.

b) Net monetary creditor gains.

1) $\qquad MA = FC\ 10\ \text{million}, \qquad X_0 = 5, \qquad t_{U.S.} = 0;$

$\qquad\ ML = FC\ 8\ \text{million}, \qquad X_1 = 4,$

$\qquad NMP = 10{,}000{,}000 - 8{,}000{,}000 = 2{,}000{,}000,$

$$C_p = NMP(E_0 - E_1) = 2{,}000{,}000(.20 - .25) = -\$100{,}000.$$

The cost is a negative $100,000, representing a gain in the value of the net monetary position with revaluation upward in the FC currency.

2) Let $MA = FC\ 6\ \text{million}$. Then

$\qquad NMP = 6{,}000{,}000 - 8{,}000{,}000 = -2{,}000{,}000,$

$$C_p = NMP(E_0 - E_1) = -2{,}000{,}000(.20 - .25) = +\$100{,}000.$$

Both terms are negative, so their product is positive, indicating that revaluation upward results in a positive cost (or a *loss*) to a firm in a negative net monetary position (monetary liabilities exceed monetary assets). The FC values of its net obligations have increased.

The impact of an exposed position is similar if the exposure results from an excess of receipts over payments due to be paid in the foreign currency. A firm in this situation faces several combinations of patterns. We illustrate some of the alternatives:

1. The firm is exposed to a decline in the value of foreign currencies. Then

   a) Expected future receipts exceed expected future payments.

   b) The net monetary position is positive—monetary assets exceed monetary liabilities.

   A firm in such a position will lose from a devaluation (or decrease in value or depreciation in the value) of foreign currencies.

2. The firm is exposed to an increase in the value of foreign currencies. Then

   a) Expected future payments exceed expected future receipts.

   b) The net monetary position is negative.

A firm in such a position is concerned about upward revaluation of foreign currencies.

We can state as a general proposition that unless the payments and receipts in relation to the future net monetary position of the firm exactly balance, the firm is exposed to a decline or increase in the value of foreign currencies. Ordinarily, the normal pattern of operations will put the firm in an exposed position, that it can limit only by taking certain steps, all of which involve a cost. One strategy may be to rearrange the pattern of payments and the pattern of holdings of monetary assets and liabilities in foreign currencies to achieve perfect balance so that the net exposure is zero. But changes in the flow of receipts and payments or in the holdings of monetary assets and liabilities represent departures from the firm's normal operations. Such artificial changes from the firm's normal patterns will involve costs. To determine whether such adjustments are better than alternative methods of limiting exposure requires that management calculate the costs of altering the patterns of cash flows or of its net monetary position. This may be a rather complex undertaking for an individual firm but is nonetheless necessary if the firm is to make a rational choice among alternatives.

The next broad strategic analysis of alternatives that a firm may make is to gather and evaluate information about expected future rates of exchange. The development of an information bank providing data that permit the formulation of expected future exchange rates involves costs. The firm could purchase a forecasting service instead of developing its own information, but this also requires costs as well as outlays and efforts to appraise the service's qualifications and reliability.

In one perspective, if the foreign exchange markets are efficient and the interest rate parity relationship always holds, then the future expected exchange rates will be reflected in the current forward rate of exchange. However, given the dynamic changes that take place in the world economic environment (uncertainty), it is likely that future spot rates will be different from the levels forecast for them by the current forward rates. In theory, random changes in the relationship could be eliminated by forming portfolios so that the relationships would be subject only to systematic changes. The true minimum cost of protection against exposure to foreign exchange risk would then be measured by the covariance of the performance of such porfolios with changes in a world (market) portfolio, appropriately defined and measured. Recall the previous discussions of the difficulties presented in the literature on international asset pricing models (IAPM). In addition, transactions costs occur in the formation of such portfolios.

The behavior of firms will inherently involve a comparison of three alternatives. One is to develop information about and formulate expectations of the relation between expected future exchange rates and the current forward rate. A second alternative is to seek to hedge by using the forward market. A third alternative is to hedge by utilizing the money and capital markets. A continuous comparison of these three alternatives will lead to arbitrage operations by the firms that will tend to produce efficiency in the foreign exchange markets. We next discuss a format for calculating the net receipts or costs of utilizing the three alternative approaches.

Initially we assume that it would be very expensive for the firm to rearrange the pattern of receipts and payments along with its position in monetary assets and monetary liabilities to achieve zero exposure. Let us then first consider the firm that, on balance, expects future receipts to exceed future payments and/or has a net monetary position that is positive. The risk exposure faced by the firm is a decline in the value of the foreign currency. Hence the firm fears depreciation in the value of the foreign currency and will take action to deal with this possibility. We now set forth the framework for analyzing the cost of the three alternative protective policies the firm may follow.

Let us initially assume that the current spot price of the foreign currency expressed in dollars is $\$.30 = E_0$. The exposure is FC 100,000. The forward rate, E_f, is equal to $\$.25$. The action taken by the firm depends on its expectation of the future spot rate and the degree of confidence in that expectation. If the firm judges that the future spot rate will be $\$.23$ and does not hedge, it will incur a loss of $7000. However, if the firm expects the future spot rate to be $\$.27$, it will expect to incur a loss of only $3000. The current forward rate is the market's best judgment of what the future spot rate will be. If E_1 will actually be $\$.25$, it is a matter of indifference whether the firm hedges its long position in foreign currency or whether it does not purchase protection. There is an important consideration, however. If the firm enters into the forward market, it knows the cost of its foreign exchange risk exposure. This cost can be taken into account in the supply price of the goods and services sold. Therefore obtaining protection against the foreign exchange risk exposure limits the expected loss and removes uncertainty due to fluctuations between the current forward rate and the actual future spot rate.

The firm seeking protection against the foreign exchange risk exposure may employ two alternative methods.[3] One is the use of the forward market. The other is the use of the money and capital markets. If the interest rate parity relationship holds, it is a matter of indifference as to which of these two methods is employed. However, because temporary differences may develop, it is the arbitrage behavior, seeking to benefit from these divergences, that brings the markets back to interest rate parity.

---

[3] To simplify the discussion, we omit consideration of taxes here.

Let us suppose that interest rates in the foreign market are 32%, whereas interest rates in the domestic market are 10%. Then the expected ratio between the current spot rate and the current forward rate is 1.2. If the current spot rate is .3, the equilibrium forward rate is .25 ($1.32/1.10 = .30/E_f$).

If parity obtains, the cost of hedging in the forward market or of borrowing in foreign currency and investing in the United States is the same. For example, if the amount of foreign currency involved is 100,000 FC units, then the cost of hedging in the foreign market, C_f, is

$$C_f = (E_0 - E_f)F_0$$

$$= (.30 - .25)100,000$$

$$= \$5,000.$$

In the money and capital markets the situation is different from the covered interest arbitrage operation because an exposure of FC 100,000 already exists. If FC 100,000 is borrowed in the foreign country to neutralize the foreign exchange risk exposure, the principal is covered by the future net receipts or net monetary assets position of the firm. Hence the cost of using the money and capital markets by borrowing foreign currency and investing in the United States is

$$C_{bf} = \text{Cost of borrowing in foreign country}$$

$$= \bar{E}_1 F_0 R_f - E_0 F_0 R_{\text{U.S.}} = (\bar{E}_1 R_f - E_0 R_{\text{U.S.}})F_0$$

$$= [.32\bar{E}_1 - .30(.10)]100,000.$$

Now the cost of borrowing foreign currency depends on what the future spot rate will be, because interest on the foreign borrowing must be paid at the future spot rate. The firm can remove this uncertainty by buying the foreign currency in the amount of the required interest to be paid at the current forward rate. The cost of borrowing foreign now becomes

$$C_{bf} = \text{FC } 32,000E_f - \$3,000.$$

Next, we evaluate at the current forward rate:

$$C_{bf} = 32,000(.25) - \$3,000 = \$8,000 - \$3,000$$

$$= \$5,000.$$

The cost of borrowing foreign will now be $5,000, which is exactly the same as in the hedged case in which the foreign currency was sold in the forward exchange market. It should be emphasized that borrowing in the foreign market produces an interest obligation that will become due in the future. Hence to protect against this exposure, the action is to *buy* the foreign currency in the amount of the interest obligation in the forward market rather than *sell* it as in the hedging operation in the forward market. Because this strategy requires having foreign currency on hand in the future to pay the foreign interest, the effects on the position of the firm will be reversed if the firm does not cover its future interest payments to be made in foreign currency but permits matters to depend upon the future spot foreign exchange rate. For example, if the future spot foreign exchange rate is higher than the current forward rate, the cost of borrowing foreign will be higher:

$$C_{bf} = (\bar{E}_1 R_f - E_0 R_{U.S.})100,000$$

$$= [.27(.32) - .30(.10)]100,000$$

$$= (.0864 - .03)100,000 = .0564(100,000)$$

$$= \$5,640.$$

With the future expected spot rate being \$.27 rather than \$.25, costs of borrowing foreign are in excess of \$5,000. However, if the future spot rate falls below the current forward rate, the cost of borrowing foreign will be less than \$5,000. Hence if the firm does not immediately cover its future interest payments to be made in foreign currency, it continues to be exposed to foreign exchange risk.

We next consider the position of the firm that is in a negative net monetary position or that will be required, at some time in the future, to make net payments in excess of future receipts. The situation is the reverse of the firm in a positive monetary position. Instead of facing the risk of devaluation of FC units, the firm faces the risk of appreciation in the value of FC units. Hence its protective action in the forward market is to buy the FC units. If it does not obtain this protection, it will face an uncertain cost if the future spot rate is higher than the current forward rate. If it uses the money and capital markets, it will borrow in the United States and invest in the FC units in which it will have to make future payments.

This analysis demonstrates that if a firm is in an exposed foreign exchange position, it will incur some costs to obtain protection against that exposed position. Even rearranging the firm's pattern of payments and receipts or monetary assets and liabilities will represent a departure from normal operations and therefore involve some costs. If the firm uses the forward market or borrows, it incurs some costs, but it will know the exact amount of these costs.

F. INTEREST RATE AND CURRENCY SWAPS

Another important set of institutions has been developed to assist firms in managing risks arising from both interest rate and exchange rate volatility. These are interest rate and currency swaps that enable firms to lower financing costs and to provide hedges in foreign currencies. We begin with the discussion of interest rate swaps.[4]

1. Interest Rate Swaps (International Setting)

An interest rate swap is an agreement between two parties for the exchange of a series of cash payments, one on a fixed rate liability and the other on a floating rate liability. For example, a savings and loan association (S&L) has a portfolio of assets

---

[4] This presentation uses illustrations from Hutchison [1985]. See also Whittaker [1987].

consisting of long-term fixed rate mortgages. Its liabilities would be shorter-term deposits and money market certificates. It faces the risk of a rise in interest rates on its shorter duration liabilities.

An interest rate swap can reduce its risk exposure. The intermediary will typically be a European bank acting on behalf of a corporate customer seeking floating rate funding in dollars. The S&L agrees to make fixed interest payments to the intermediary, which in turn agrees to make variable interest payments to the S&L. The interest rates paid each other are negotiated. Although both parties swap net interest payments on their underlying liabilities, the principal amounts are not exchanged.

Another source of interest rate swaps results from different comparative advantages in generating funds in either the fixed or floating rate interest markets. An example would be that a low-rated company seeks fixed rate long-term credit but has access to variable interest rate funds at a margin of $1\frac{1}{2}\%$ over the London Interbank Offer Rate (LIBOR), whereas its direct borrowing costs in a fixed rate public market would be 13%. A high-rated company may have access to fixed rate funds in the Eurodollar bond market at 11% and variable rate funds at LIBOR $+ \frac{1}{2}\%$. Thus it has a relatively greater advantage in the fixed rate market. The high-rated company would borrow fixed rate funds at 11% in the Eurobond market while the low-rated company borrows an identical amount of variable rate funds at $1\frac{1}{2}\%$ over LIBOR. They swap the payment streams, negotiating the interest rate savings. A commercial bank or investment bank can act as the counterparty to each side of the transaction, often guaranteeing it and saving both parties interest costs on their preferred debt service flow. For their services the intermediary would receive compensation.

2. Currency Swaps

In currency swaps the two debt service flows are denominated in different currencies, and principal amounts may also be exchanged. A U.S. corporation may seek fixed rate funds in German marks (DM), whereas a German corporation may desire variable rate dollar financing. A bank intermediary may arrange a currency swap. The U.S. company borrows variable rate funds in dollars, whereas the German company borrows fixed rate funds in DM. The two companies swap both principal and interest payments. When the term of the swap matures, the principal amounts revert to the original holder. Both exchange rate and interest rate risks are thereby managed at cost savings to both parties because they borrow initially in the market where they have a comparative advantage, then swap for their preferred liability.

Currency swaps illustrate the basic principle of international transactions in that all parties benefit as a result of their differing comparative advantage. They then swap for the preferred liability. It enables firms to manage their portfolios at lowered transactions costs.

G. FOREIGN CURRENCY TRANSLATION

In December 1981 the Financial Accounting Standards Board (FASB) issued FASB No. 52, *Foreign Currency Translation*, superseding FASB No. 8, which had been issued in 1976. In general, translation gains or losses are carried directly to the equity account on the balance sheet and do not affect net income. Individual transactions gains or losses net of hedging costs and net of translation gains or losses do enter into the calculations that determine net income. Also, the method of translation is changed from the temporal method to the use of the current exchange rate for all balance sheet items and the use of the average exchange rate for the period for the income statement. However, the temporal method will continue to be applied to operations in highly inflationary economies, defined as those in which the price level doubles within a three-year period of time.

Since the temporal method of currency translation continues to be applied in the circumstances indicated, it will be useful to explain and illustrate both methods. The temporal method was essentially the monetary-nonmonetary method with one change. Under the monetary-nonmonetary method, the logic of defining exposure by the net monetary position was followed. Monetary assets and liabilities were translated at current exchange rates, whereas nonmonetary assets and liabilities were translated at the applicable historical exchange rates. Under the monetary-nonmonetary method of translation, inventories were treated as real assets to which the applicable historical exchange rate was applied. The temporal method recognizes that alternative inventory valuation methods may be used. For example, FIFO charges the income statement for the historical costs of inventory flows, resulting in balance sheet values that are closer to current values. The use of LIFO has the opposite effect. Thus if FIFO is used, the current exchange rate should be applied to the balance sheet inventory account; with LIFO an applicable historical rate should be used. This was the distinction recognized by the temporal method. The two methods are now illustrated by a numerical example.[5]

In this example the Canadian subsidiary of a U.S. company with a Canadian dollar functional currency started business and acquired fixed assets at the beginning of the year when the Canadian $/U.S. $ exchange rate was .95. The average exchange rate for the period was .90, the rate at the end of the period was .85, and the historical rate for inventory was .91. The LIFO inventory valuation method is employed.

The different methods are illustrated in Table 22.1. The temporal method used in FASB 8 and for inflationary economies in FASB 52 applies the current (end-of-period) rate to monetary assets and liabilities. It uses the applicable historical rates for the nonmonetary assets and liabilities. Since LIFO is used, the balance sheet inventory account reflects historical costs, and the historical rate for inventories is used. In the income statement the applicable average rates are applied to all items except cost of goods sold and depreciation. Depreciation expense in the income statement would employ the same rate as fixed assets on the balance sheet.

In contrast, FASB 52 applies the current rate to all balance sheet items except common stock to which the historical rate is applied. The average rate is applied to all income statement items. The net income figure that results is reflected in the translated retained earnings account. Total assets and claims are brought into balance by a translation adjustment account.

---

[5] Taken from Peat, Marwick, Mitchell & Co., *Statement of Financial Accounting Standards No. 52, Foreign Currency Translation*, 1981.

Table 22.1   Translation of Canadian Subsidiary Financial Statements—19x1

		FASB 8		FASB 52	
Balance Sheet	Canadian Dollars	Rates Used	U.S. Dollars	Rates Used	U.S. Dollars
Cash and receivables, net	100	.85	$ 85	.85	$ 85
Inventory	300	.91	273	.85	255
Fixed assets, net	600	.95	570	.85	510
	1000		$928		$850
Current liabilities	180	.85	$153	.85	$153
Long-term debt	700	.85	595	.85	595
Stockholders' equity:					
Common stock	100	.95	95	.95	95
Retained earnings	20		85		18
Equity adjustment from foreign currency translation	—		—		(11)
	1000		$928		$850
Income statement					
Revenue	130	.90	$117	.90	$117
Cost of goods sold	(60)	.93*	(56)	.90	(54)
Depreciation	(20)	.95*	(19)	.90	(18)
Other expenses, net	(10)	.90	(9)	.90	(9)
Foreign exchange gain	—		70		—
Income before taxes	40		$103		$36
Income taxes	(20)	.90	(18)	.90	(18)
Net income	20		$ 85		$ 18
Ratios					
Net income to revenue	.15		.73		.15
Gross profit	.54		.52		.54
Debt to equity	5.83		3.31		5.83

* Historical rates for cost of goods sold and depreciation of fixed assets.

From Peat, Marwick, Mitchell and Company, *Statement of Financial Accounting Standards, No. 52, Foreign Currency Translation*, December 1981, p. 52, reprinted with permission.

The use of the current method of FASB 52 results in financial ratios that are unchanged from their relationships in the foreign currency before translation. This is claimed to be an advantage of the new method. But if the underlying reality is a change in the ratios, preserving them is a distortion. The logic of the temporal method captures the underlying economic determinants of exposure as demonstrated in the previous discussion of the net monetary creditor or debtor position of the foreign subsidiary. It is difficult to discern the economic logic for the application of the current method prescribed by FASB 52.

SUMMARY

From the viewpoint of an individual or firm, investments in international portfolios offer greater diversification than purely domestic portfolios. Evidence establishes that internationally diversified portfolios are less risky (variance of returns is used as the measure of risk) than purely domestic portfolios and/or portfolios consisting of the securities of multinational companies.

Alternative forms of an international asset pricing model (IAPM) similar to the CAPM have been derived for international financial assets. The results of Solnik's tests are weakly consistent with his IAPM. In an extension of his IAPM, Solnik found that assets can be regarded as trading in international markets: i.e., the IAPM performs better than a purely domestic specification. Stehle [1977] has also found evidence of integration.

Stulz [1981b] developed an international asset pricing model that has individuals maximizing utility from consumption. Stulz extends Solnik's IAPM by allowing consumption opportunities to differ across countries, at least until arbitrage through trade flows equalizes them. All assets are assumed to be traded, but all commodities are not. Purchasing power parity holds *only* for those goods traded.

From his model Stulz derives the following proposition: The expected excess real return of a risky asset is proportional to the covariance between the home currency rate of return of that asset and changes in world real consumption. Since the return of an asset is not dependent on unexpected exchange rate changes, exchange rate risk is not rewarded. Also, if changes in world consumption rates are not perfectly correlated with market indices, tests of market integration will incorrectly accept the market segmentation hypothesis.

The IAPM is subject to the same criticisms in empirical tests as is the traditional CAPM. Solnik [1977] observed that the covariance between national stock market indices is quite low. If assets are priced entirely in domestic markets, with no international influence, an "optimal" portfolio can be artificially constructed that is internationally diversified. This portfolio will be mean-variance efficient, and an IAPM test will "succeed," using this proxy as the world market portfolio. This test, however, tells us nothing about the actual pricing of assets.

In Solnik's IAPM the world market portfolio contains a portfolio he calls a "pure exchange risk asset." The weights of the nominally riskless securities of different countries in this portfolio are shown to depend on net foreign investment positions in the different countries, and the relative risk aversions of citizens. This specification would be difficult to implement in practice.

To the individual agent dealing in goods or services in the international market, fluctuations in exchange rates appear to cause additional risk compared with purely domestic transactions. Most contracts are fixed in nominal terms in foreign currency units. Hence movements in exchange rates make consumption opportunities uncertain in terms of domestic currencies.

There are two types of phenomena to consider in the area of exchange risk: inflation risk and relative price risk. The risk to an agent in a world of pure inflation risk is purely nominal. This risk *can be* eliminated by the appropriate indexation of contracts in real terms. As GLS show, if a real riskless rate exists, and agents have identical homothetic tastes, this nominal exchange risk is irrelevant to real magnitudes.

As long as individuals consume different baskets of goods, relative prices will vary. This relative price risk is due to changes in underlying preferences of individuals and/or changes in supply conditions in various countries. Exchange rate changes due to relative price movements represent real risks that can be hedged only at a cost. As we demonstrated, exchange rate risk is a form of business risk resulting from changes in relative prices, which in turn reflect changes in demand and supply conditions.

In an efficient market we would expect PPP to hold on an expected value basis. Roll's [1979] study shows that PPP holds on average and that deviations from PPP are more attributable to relative price fluctuations than to inflation fluctuations. In examining other aspects of market efficiency, several different approaches have been used. We briefly describe the methods and results.

One requirement of market efficiency is that arbitrage profits after transactions costs do not exist. The preponderance of studies support this conclusion. Disagreement exists on whether the forward rate is an unbiased predictor of the spot rate. Some hold that a bias should exist as a premium for risk. But the empirical studies are not unanimous in this area.

A final test of market efficiency that has been used is to see if forecasting services can "beat" the market. Levich [1979] found that forecasting services may yield profits consistently for some currencies. On the whole the literature on market efficiency seems to suggest that international markets are weak-form and semistrong-form efficient.

The exposure of a business firm to exchange risks is defined by its cash flow and asset stock positions. These in turn depend on expected future receipts and payments and the firm's net monetary position. Unless payments and receipts in relation to the future net monetary position of the firm exactly balance, the firm is exposed to a decline or increase in the value of foreign currencies. If the net monetary position of a firm is positive and expected receipts exceed expected payments, the firm will suffer from a devaluation. The opposite will hold with respect to an appreciation if the firm has a negative net monetary position and expected payments exceed expected receipts.

There are three methods of managing exchange risk. One alternative is to develop information about and formulate expectations between expected future exchange rates and the current forward rate. A second is to hedge by using the forward market. A third is to use the money and capital markets. The firm will choose various combinations of these methods that will tend to produce efficiency in the foreign exchange markets. In comparing hedging versus money and capital markets it is important to note that IRPT will ensure agents are indifferent between the two. The benefit to the firm of using either the money and capital markets or hedging is that it knows what costs are involved.

PROBLEM SET

22.1 Agrimex, S.A., a Mexican corporation, borrowed $1,000,000 in dollars at a 15% interest rate when the exchange rate was 25 pesos per dollar. When the company repaid the loan plus interest one year later, the exchange rate was 40 pesos to the dollar.

a) What was the rate of interest on the loan based on the pesos received and paid back by Agrimex?

b) Use the interest rate parity theorem to illustrate this result.

22.2 An American manufacturing company has imported industrial machinery at a price of DM4.6 million. The machinery will be delivered and paid for in six months. For planning purposes, the American company wants to establish what the payment (in dollars) will be in six months. It decides to use the forward market to accomplish its objective. The company contacts its New York bank, which provides the quotations given in Table Q22.2. The bank states that it will charge a commission of $\frac{1}{4}\%$ on any transaction.

Table Q22.2

	DM	Swiss Franc	$
Six-month Eurocurrency rates (% p.a.) denominated in the following currencies	8	7	9
Spot exchange rates (currency/Swiss franc)	1.1648		.56

a) Does the American company enter the forward market to go long or short of forward DM?

b) What is the number of DM/$? What is the dollar value of the deutsche mark?

c) What is the equilibrium forward rate for the deutsche mark expressed as DM/$?

d) Does the commission increase or decrease the number of DM/$ in the transaction?

e) What price in dollars can the American company establish by using the forward market in deutsche marks?

22.3 A West German company buys industrial machinery from a U.S. company at a price of $10 million. The machinery will be delivered and paid for in six months. The German company seeks to establish its cost in deutsche marks. It decides to use the forward market to accomplish its objective. The company contacts its Bonn bank, which provides the quotations listed in Table Q22.3. The bank states that it will charge a commission of $\frac{1}{4}\%$ on any transaction.

a) Does the German company enter the forward market to go long or short of forward dollars?

Table Q22.3

	DM	£	$
Six-month Eurocurrency rates (% p.a.) denominated in the following currencies	8	9.5	9
Spot exchange rates (currency/U.K. £)	3.878		$1.90

b) What is the number of DM/$? What is the dollar value of the deutsche mark?

c) What is the equilibrium forward rate for the deutsche mark expressed as $/DM?

d) Does the commission increase or decrease the dollar value of the deutsche mark?

e) What price in deutsche marks can the German company establish by using the forward market in dollars?

22.4 Globalcorp makes a sale of goods to a foreign firm and will receive FC 380,000 three months later. Globalcorp has incurred costs in dollars and wishes to make definite the amount of dollars it will receive in three months. It plans to approach a foreign bank to borrow an amount of local currency such that the principal plus interest will equal the amount Globalcorp expects to receive. The interest rate it must pay on its loan is 28%. With the borrowed funds, Globalcorp purchases dollars at the current spot rate that are invested in the United States at an interest rate of 8%. When Globalcorp receives the FC 380,000 at the end of three months, it uses the funds to liquidate the loan at the foreign bank. The effective tax rate in both countries is 40%.

a) What is the net amount that Globalcorp will receive if the current spot rate is FC 1.90 to the dollar?

b) How much less is this than the amount Globalcorp would have received if the remittance had been made immediately instead of three months later?

c) At what forward rate of exchange would the amount received by Globalcorp have been the same as that it would have obtained using the capital markets? Would Globalcorp have sold the FC forward short or long to hedge its position?

d) If a speculator took the opposite position from Globalcorp in the forward market for FC, would the speculator sell long or short? If the speculator received a risk premium for holding this position, would this place the current forward rate in FC above or below the expected future spot rate in FC per dollar?

22.5 Transcorp has made a purchase of goods from a foreign firm that will require the payment of FC 380,000 six months later. Transcorp wishes to make definite the amount of dollars it will need to pay the FC 380,000 on the due date. The foreign firm is domiciled in a country whose currency has been rising in relation to the dollar in recent years. The tax rate in both countries is 40%. Transcorp plans to borrow an amount in dollars from a U.S. bank to immediately exchange into FCs to buy securities in the foreign country, which, with interest, will equal FC 380,000 six months later. The interest rate that will be paid in the United States is 12%; the interest rate that will be earned on the foreign securities is 8%. When at the end of six months Transcorp is required to make the payment in FC, it will use the funds from the maturing foreign securities in FC to meet its obligation in FC. At the same time it will pay off the loan plus interest in the United States in dollars.

a) What is the net amount that Transcorp pays to meet the obligation of FC 380,000 in six months if the current spot rate is FC 2.00 to the dollar?

b) How much more is this than the amount Transcorp would have paid if payment had been made immediately instead of six months later?

c) At what forward rate of exchange would the amount paid by Transcorp have been the same as that it would have paid using the capital markets? Would Transcorp have taken the long position in the forward FC or have sold the FC forward short to hedge its position?

d) If a speculator took the opposite position from Transcorp in the forward market for FCs, would the speculator be long or short? If the speculator received a risk premium for holding this position, would this place the current forward rate in FC above or below the expected future spot rate in FC per dollar?

REFERENCES

Adler, M., "The Cost of Capital and Valuation of a Two-Country Firm," *Journal of Finance*, March 1974, 119–132.

——, and B. Dumas, "Optimal International Acquisitions," *Journal of Finance*, March 1975, 1–20.

——, "Exposure to Currency Risk: Definition and Measurement," *Financial Management*, Summer 1984, 41–50.

Batten, S., and D. L. Thornton, "Discount Rate Changes and the Foreign Exchange Market," *Federal Reserve Bank of St. Louis Review*, December 1984, 279–292.

Black, F., "International Capital Market Equilibrium with Investment Barriers," *Journal of Financial Economics*, December 1974, 337–352.

Breeden, D. T., "An Intertemporal Asset Pricing Model with Stochastic Consumption and Investment Opportunities," *Journal of Financial Economics*, September 1979, 265–296.

Cho, D. C.; C. S. Eun; and L. Senbet, "International Arbitrage Pricing Theory: An Empirical Investigation," *Journal of Finance*, June 1986, 313–329.

Cornell, B., "Spot Rates, Forward Rates, and Exchange Market Efficiency," *Journal of Financial Economics*, August 1977, 55–65.

——, "Inflation, Relative Price Changes, and Exchange Risk," *Financial Management*, Autumn 1980, 30–34.

——, and K. Dietrich, "The Efficiency of the Market for Foreign Exchange under Floating Exchange Rates," *Review of Economics and Statistics*, February 1978, 111–121.

Dufey, G., and S. L. Srinivasulu, "The Case for Corporate Management of Foreign Exchange Risk," *Financial Management*, Winter 1983, 54–62.

Errunza, V. R., and L. W. Senbet, "The Effects of International Operations on the Market Value of the Firm: Theory and Evidence," *Journal of Finance*, May 1981, 401–419.

Fama, E. F., *Foundations of Finance*. Basic Books, New York, 1976.

——, "Inflation, Output and Money," *Journal of Business*, April 1982, 201–231.

——, "Forward and Spot Exchange Rates," *Journal of Monetary Economics*, 1984, 319–338.

——, and A. Farber, "Money Bonds and Foreign Exchange," *American Economic Review*, September 1979, 639–650.

Fama, E. F., and M. R. Gibbons, "Inflation, Real Returns, and Capital Investment," *Journal of Monetary Economics*, May 1982, 297–327.

Farber, A.; R. Roll; and B. Solnik, "An Empirical Study of Risk under Fixed and Flexible Exchange Rates," in Brunner and Meltzer, eds., *Stabilization of the Domestic and International Economy*. North Holland, Amsterdam, 1977, 235–275.

Fieleke, N. S., "Foreign-Currency Positioning by U.S. Firms: Some New Evidence," *Review of Economics and Statistics*, February 1981, 35–42.

Forsythe, R.; T. R. Palfrey; and C. R. Plott, "Futures Markets and Informational Efficiency: A Laboratory Examination," *Journal of Finance*, September 1984, 955–981.

Frenkel, J., and R. Levich, "Covered Interest Arbitrage: Unexploited Profits?" *Journal of Political Economy*, April 1975, 325–338.

———, "Transactions Costs and Interest Arbitrage: Tranquil versus Turbulent Periods," *Journal of Political Economy*, December 1977, 1209–1226.

Grauer, F. L. A.; R. H. Litzenberger; and R. E. Stehle, "Sharing Rules and Equilibrium in an International Capital Market under Uncertainty," *Journal of Financial Economics*, June 1976, 233–256.

Gregory, A. W., and T. H. McCurdy, "The Unbiasedness Hypothesis in the Forward Foreign Exchange Market," *European Economic Review*, 1986, 365–381.

Grubel, H. G., "Internationally Diversified Portfolios: Welfare Gains and Capital Flows," *American Economic Review*, December 1968, 1299–1314.

Hekman, C. R., "A Model of Foreign Exchange Exposure," *Journal of International Business Studies*, Summer 1985, 85–99.

Hodgson, J. S., and P. Phelps, "The Distributed Impact of Price-Level Variation on Floating Exchange Rates," *Review of Economics and Statistics*, February 1975, 58–64.

Hodrick, R. J., and S. Srivastava, "An Investigation of Risk and Return in Forward Foreign Exchange," *Journal of International Money and Finance*, April 1984, 5–30.

Huang, R. D., "Some Alternative Tests of Forward Exchange Rates as Predictors of Future Spot Rates," *Journal of International Money and Finance*, August 1984, 153–167.

Hutchison, M. M., "Swaps," *FRBSF Weekly Letter*, May 3, 1985.

Isard, P., "Exchange Rate Determination: A Survey of Popular Views and Recent Models." Princeton Studies in International Finance, No. 42, 1978.

Jacquillat, B., and B. Solnik, "Multinationals Are Poor Tools for Diversification," *Journal of Portfolio Management*, Winter 1978, 8–12.

Johnson, L. J., and C. H. Walther, "New Evidence of the Effectiveness of Portfolio Hedges in Currency Forward Markets," *Management International Review*, 1984, 15–23.

Kaufold, H., and M. Smirlock, "Managing Corporate Exchange and Interest Rate Exposure," *Financial Management*, Autumn 1986, 64–72.

Lee, C., "A Stock Adjustment Analysis of Capital Movements: The U.S. Canadian Case," *Journal of Political Economy*, July 1969, 512–523.

Lee, W. Y., and K. S. Sachdeva, "The Role of the Multinational Firm in the Integration of Segmented Capital Markets," *Journal of Finance*, May 1977, 479–492.

Lessard, D. R., "International Portfolio Diversification: A Multivariate Analysis for a Group of Latin-American Countries," *Journal of Finance*, June 1973, 619–633.

———, ed., *International Financial Management: Theory and Application*, 2nd ed. John Wiley and Sons, New York, 1985.

Levich, R., "The Efficiency of the Market for Foreign Exchange: A Review and Extension," in Lessard, ed., *International Financial Management*. Warren, Gorham and Lamont, Boston, 1979, 243–277.

Levy, H., and M. Sarnat, "International Diversification of Investment Portfolios," *American Economic Review*, September 1970, 668–675.

———, "Devaluation Risk and the Portfolio Analysis of International Investment," in Elton and Gruber, eds., *International Capital Markets*. North Holland, Amsterdam, 1975, 177–206.

Longworth, D., "Testing the Efficiency of the Canadian–U.S. Exchange Market under the Assumption of No Risk Premium," *Journal of Finance*, March 1981, 43–51.

Maldonado, R., and A. Saunders, "International Portfolio Diversification and the Inter-Temporal Stability of International Stock Market Relationships, 1957–78," *Financial Management*, Autumn 1981, 54–63.

———, "Foreign Exchange Restrictions and the Law of One Price," *Financial Management*, Spring 1983, 19–23.

Merton, R. C., "An Intertemporal Capital Asset Pricing Model," *Econometrica*, September 1973, 867–887.

Mundell, R., "Inflation and Real Interest," *Journal of Political Economy*, June 1963, 280–283.

Philippatos, G. C., and A. Christofi, "Liquid-Asset Management Modeling for Inter-Subsidiary Operations of Multinational Corporations," *Management International Review*, 1984, 4–14.

———, and P. Christofi, "The Inter-Temporal Stability of International Stock Market Relationships: Another View," *Financial Management*, Winter 1983, 63–69.

Robichek, A. A., and M. R. Eaker, "Foreign Exchange Hedging and the Capital Asset Pricing Model," *Journal of Finance*, June 1978, 1011–1018.

Rodriguez, R. M., "Corporate Exchange Risk Management: Theme and Aberrations," *Journal of Finance*, May 1981, 427–439.

Roll, R., "A Critique of the Asset Pricing Theory's Tests; Part I: On Past and Potential Testability of the Theory," *Journal of Financial Economics*, March 1977, 129–176.

———, "Violations of Purchasing Parity and their Implications for Efficient Markets," in Sarnat and Szego, eds., *International Finance and Trade*, Vol. 1. Ballinger, Cambridge, Mass., 1979, 133–176.

———, and B. Solnik, "A Pure Foreign Exchange Asset Pricing Model," *Journal of International Economics*, May 1977, 161–179.

Shapiro, A. C., *International Corporate Finance: A Survey and Synthesis*. Financial Management Association, Tampa, Fla., 1986.

Solnik, B., "The International Pricing of Risk: An Empirical Investigation of the World Capital Market Structure," *Journal of Finance*, May 1974a, 365–378.

———, "Why Not Diversify Internationally Rather Than Domestically?" *Financial Analysts Journal*, July–August 1974b, 48–54.

———, "An Equilibrium Model of the International Capital Market," *Journal of Economic Theory*, August 1974c, 500–525.

———, "An International Market Model of Security Price Behavior," *Journal of Financial and Quantitative Analysis*, September 1974d, 537–554.

———, "Testing International Asset Pricing: Some Pessimistic Views," *Journal of Finance*, May 1977, 503–512.

———, "International Parity Conditions and Exchange Risk," *Journal of Banking and Finance*, October 1978, 281–293.

Stehle, R., "An Empirical Test of the Alternate Hypotheses of National and International Pricing of Risky Assets," *Journal of Finance*, May 1977, 493–502.

Stockman, A., "Risk, Information, and Forward Exchange Rates," in Frenkel and Johnson, eds., *The Economics of Exchange Rates*. Addison-Wesley, Reading, Mass., 1978, 159–179.

———, "A Theory of Exchange Rate Determination," *Journal of Political Economy*, August 1980, 673–699.

Stulz, R., "On the Effects of Barriers to International Investment," *Journal of Finance*, September 1981a, 923–934.

————, "A Model of International Asset Pricing," *Journal of Financial Economics*, December 1981b, 383–406.

Tobin, J., "Money and Economic Growth," *Econometrica*, October 1965, 671–684.

Wallingford, B. A., "International Asset Pricing: A Comment," *Journal of Finance*, May 1974, 392–395.

Weston, J. F., and B. W. Sorge, *International Managerial Finance*. Richard D. Irwin, Homewood, Ill., 1972.

————, *Guide to International Financial Management*. McGraw-Hill, New York, 1977.

Whittaker, J. G., "Interest Rate Swaps: Risk and Regulation," *Economic Review*, Federal Reserve Bank of Kansas City, March 1987, 3–13.

Appendix A
Discounting

A. INTRODUCTION

In any economy, capitalist or socialist, we find positive rates of interest. This reflects two underlying influences: the productivity of economic goods and time preference. Capital goods are goods used in the production of other goods and services. Some capital goods are specialized machinery and others are materials—such as iron, copper, or textiles—used in the production of machinery to produce other goods. More basically, our productive efforts may be used to produce goods that we consume immediately or to produce goods that will produce other goods and services for future use. One reason to use some of our productive efforts to have goods that will produce future goods is that the postponement of current consumption will enable us to have more wealth in the future than we would otherwise have. This is true whether we think of the use of actual goods or financial spending power used on current consumption vs. goods that will produce future goods. For example, we can consume grains now or plant them to harvest future crops that will represent larger quantities than the seeds with which we started. Because of the productivity of goods, they have a time value. A bushel of seeds today will become several bushels of grain in the future. So productivity is one basis for the time value of money and positive rates of interest.

A second basis is time preference. Would we rather have the use of an automobile now or wait five years? Clearly, it is more advantageous to have the use of goods now than to wait for them.

B. THE TIME VALUE OF MONEY: DISCRETE COMPOUNDING

1. Compound Future Sums

Because of productivity and time preference, a positive rate of interest is a universal phenomenon. It is a necessary guide to present vs. future uses of goods and to the allocation of goods among alternative uses when time is involved. Since a positive rate of interest is a general phenomenon, future sums will be greater than present values. For example, assume that if a company received funds immediately, it could earn a 10% return on those funds. We could then state the problem as follows: Let

$$P = \text{principal, or beginning amount} \quad = \$1000,$$

$$r = \text{interest rate} \quad\quad\quad\quad\quad\quad\quad = 10\% = .10,$$

$$n = \text{number of years} \quad\quad\quad\quad\quad = 5,$$

$$S_n = \text{the value at the end of the year } n.$$

We can readily derive the applicable compound interest formula. The amount received at the end of the first year is $P(1 + r)$. This is again compounded to determine the amount received at the end of the second year, and so on.

	End of Year 1	End of Year 2	End of Year 3	$\cdots$	End of Year n
Amount Received	$P(1 + r)$ $P(1 + r)$	$P(1 + r)(1 + r)$ $P(1 + r)^2$	$P(1 + r)(1 + r)(1 + r)$ $P(1 + r)^3$	$\cdots$	$P(1 + r)^n$

The result is the compound interest formula. In general terms it may be stated as follows:

$$S_n = P(1 + r)^n. \tag{A.1}$$

We now have all the information needed to compute the value at the end of the fifth year, using a compound interest table[1] (Table A.1):

$$S_5 = \$1000(1.10)^5.$$

We then look in the compound interest table to find that at 10% a dollar over a five-year period grows to $1.611. Since the amount we have is $1000, it is multiplied times the interest factor:

$$S_5 = \$1000(1.611) = \$1611.$$

Therefore if the firm can earn 10% with the money, it is more worthwhile for it to receive the $1000 today rather than at the end of the fifth year.

2. Future Amounts and Their Present Values

A similar type of problem occurs when a company is offered an amount to be received in the future. It is desirable to compare that amount with the value of whatever amount could be received today. This requires the computation of the present value of the amount to be received in the future. The determination of present values involves the same formula except that it is solved for P, representing present value,

---

[1] All tables mentioned in Appendix A are located at the end of Appendix A.

instead of for S_n, which, in this situation, is known. By simple algebra the required formula would be:

$$P = \frac{S_n}{(1 + r)^n}.$$ (A.2)

Using our previous example, we determined S_n to be $1611. Since the appropriate interest rate is 10% and the number of years is five, this is what is required to determine P. This can be done by using our previous information and making a division. We would be dividing $1611 by 1.611 to obtain the result $1000. But we can also use a present value interest table (Table A.2), which is the reciprocal of a compound interest table. In this case the formula is

$$P = S_n(1 + r)^{-n}.$$ (A.2a)

We can now insert the illustrative numbers:

$$P = \$1611(0.621)$$

$$= \$1000.$$

The results of compound interest and present value computations are just two different ways of looking at the same relationship.

3. Constant Payment Annuities

An annuity is a series of periodic payments made over a span of time. This is a frequently encountered type of compound interest situation. For example, a firm may sell some goods that will be paid for in installments. A basic question is, What is the present value of those installment payments? Or the firm makes an investment from which it expects to receive a series of cash returns over a period of years. At an appropriate discount rate, what would the series of future income receipts be worth today? The firm needs this information in order to determine whether it is worthwhile to make the investment.

Some specific examples will further illustrate these ideas. The firm makes an investment. It is promised the payment of $1000 a year for 10 years with an interest rate of 10%. What is the present value of such a series of payments?

The basic formula involved is the present value of an annuity:

$$A_{n,r} = a\left[\frac{1 - (1 + r)^{-n}}{r}\right],$$ (A.3)

where

A = present value of an annuity,

a = amount of the periodic annuity payment,

r = interest factor,

n = number of annuity payments.

Equation (A.3) is derived by discounting the stream of payments, the first of which is made at the end of the first year. Mathematically, this is

$$A_{n,r} = \frac{a}{1+r} + \frac{a}{(1+r)^2} + \frac{a}{(1+r)^3} + \cdots + \frac{a}{(1+r)^n}.$$

If we let $u = [1/(1+r)]$ this becomes

$$A_{n,r} = au + au^2 + au^3 + \cdots + au^n. \tag{A.4}$$

Multiplying Eq. (A.4) by u and subtracting the result from Eq. (A.4) yields

$$A_{n,r} - uA_{n,r} = au - au^{n+1},$$

$$A_{n,r} = \frac{au(1-u^n)}{1-u}.$$

Substituting back the value of u we have:

$$A_{n,r} = \frac{a\left(\dfrac{1}{1+r}\right)\left[1 - \dfrac{1}{(1+r)^n}\right]}{\left(1 - \dfrac{1}{1+r}\right)}$$

$$= \frac{a[1 - (1+r)^{-n}]}{(1+r)\left(\dfrac{1+r-1}{1+r}\right)}$$

$$= a\left[\frac{1 - (1+r)^{-n}}{r}\right]. \tag{A.3}$$

Note that if the number of payments is infinite, then the present value of the annuity becomes

$$\lim_{n \to \infty} A_{n,r} = \frac{a}{r}, \tag{A.5}$$

since we know that when $r > 0$, then $\lim_{n \to \infty} (1+r)^{-n} = 0$. An example of an annuity with an infinite number of constant payments is a *consol* bond. It pays a coupon at the end of each time period (usually a year) and never matures.

The expression in brackets in Eq. (A.3) is rather cumbersome. For convenience, then, instead of the cumbersome expression set out above, we shall use the symbol $P_{n,r}$, where $P_{n,r}$ = present value of an annuity factor for n years at r percent. Equation (A.3) above can therefore be rewritten as

$$A_{n,r} = aP_{n,r}. \tag{A.3a}$$

Substituting actual numbers and using Table A.4 (the present value of an annuity interest table), we would have the following for 10 years at 10%:

$$\$6145 = \$1000(6.145).$$

In other words, applying an interest factor of 10% a series of payments of $1000 received for 10 years would be worth $6145 today. Hence if the amount of investment we were required to make were $8000, e.g., or any amount greater than $6145, we would be receiving a return of less than 10% on our investment. Conversely, if the investment necessary to earn annual payments of $1000 for 10 years at 10% were $5000 or any amount less than $6145, we would be earning a return greater than 10%.

A number of other questions can be answered using these same relationships. Suppose the decision facing the firm requires determining the rate of return on an investment. For example, suppose we would have $6145 to invest and that an investment opportunity promises an annual return of $1000 for 10 years. What is the indicated rate of return on our investment? Exactly the same relationship is involved, but we are now solving for the interest rate. We can therefore rewrite our equation as follows:

$$P_{10,10\%} = \frac{AP_{10,10\%}}{a}.$$

We can now substitute the appropriate figures:

$$P_{10,10\%} = \frac{\$6145}{\$1000} = 6.145.$$

In Table A.4, which shows the present value of periodic payments received annually, we look across the row for year 10 until we find the interest rate that corresponds to the interest factor 6.145. This is 10%. We are earning a 10% return on our investment.

Let us consider another situation. Suppose that we are going to receive a return of $2000 per year for five years from an investment of $8424. What is the return on our investment? This is generally referred to as the internal rate of return on the investment, or it is also sometimes referred to as the DCF—discounted cash flow—approach to valuing an investment.

We follow the same procedure as before:

$$P_{5,r} = \frac{\$8424}{\$2000}$$

$$= 4.212.$$

We look again in the present value of an annuity table (Table A.4) along the row for the year 5 to find the interest factor 4.212. We then look at the interest rate at the top of the column to find that it is 6%. Thus the return on that investment is 6%. If our required rate of return were 10% we would not find this investment attractive. On the other hand, if the required return on our investment were only 5%, we would consider the investment attractive.

These relationships can be used in still another way. Taking the facts of the preceding illustration, we may ask the following question: Given an investment that yields $2000 per year for five years, at an appropriate discount factor (or cost of capital) of

6%, what is that investment worth today? What is the present value of a series of future income flows? For example, if a firm were to make a sale of goods on an open account with a down payment of $1000 plus yearly payments of $2000 for five years, what would the present value of all the payments be at a 6% interest rate? From our previous calculations we know that the series of payments of $2000 for five years at a 6% interest rate are worth $8424 today. When we add the $1000 down payment to this figure we would have a total of $9424.

4. Compound Sum of an Annuity

We may need to know the future value or future sum to which a series of payments will accumulate. The reason may be to determine the amount of funds required to repay an obligation in the future. The sum of an annuity can be determined from the following basic relationship:[2]

$$S_{n,r} = a\left[\frac{(1 + r)^n - 1}{r}\right],\qquad\text{(A.6)}$$

where

$S_{n,r}$ = the future sum to which an annuity will accumulate in n years at rate r,

a = the amount of the annuity payment.

Suppose the firm were to receive annual payments of $1000 a year for 10 years and is earning an interest rate of 10%. What will be the amount that the firm will have at the end of 10 years? We can solve this problem by consulting Table A.3. Utilizing our equation, we would have

$$S_{n,r} = \$1,000(15.937)$$

$$= \$15,937.$$

The 10 payments of $1,000 with interest would amount to $15,937 by the end of the tenth year. Thus if we had to make a payment of $15,937 in 10 years, we would be able to do it by annual payments of $1,000 per year into a fund that earns interest at 10% per year.

---

[2] Note that the present value of an annuity can be obtained by discounting the expression back to the present:

$$A_{n,r} = a\left[\frac{(1 + r)^n - 1}{r(1 + r)^n}\right].$$

Now divide the numerator and the denominator by $(1 + r)^n$. We have

$$A_{n,r} = a\left[\frac{1 - (1 + r)^{-n}}{r}\right].$$

This is now in the form of Eq. (A.3), the present value of an annuity.

5. Calculations for a Series of Unequal Receipts or Payments

In all the previous illustrations we have assumed that the receipts flowing in or the payments to be made are of equal amounts. This simplifies the calculations. However, if unequal receipts or unequal payments are involved the principles are again the same, but the calculations must be somewhat extended. For example, suppose that the firm makes an investment from which it will receive the following amounts:

Year	Receipts	× Discount Factor (15%) =	Present Value
1	$100	.870	$ 87.00
2	200	.756	151.20
3	600	.658	394.80
4	300	.572	171.60
		PV of the investment =	$804.60

Using the present value interest table (Table A.2) at an interest rate of 15%, we obtain the amounts indicated above. The interest factor is multiplied by the receipts to provide the amounts in the present value column. The amounts for each year are then summed to provide the present value of the investment, which in this example is $804.60. What we are doing in this example is illustrating how an annuity of unequal payments that could not be computed directly from the present value of an annuity table (Table A.4) can be handled by breaking the problem into a series of one-year payments received at successively later time periods.

6. Annuities with Growing Payments

Previously we had assumed that annuity payments were constant through time. Now we consider the case where the payments are assumed to be growing at a constant rate, g. This is a more realistic assumption if, e.g., we are modeling the growing dividends paid out by a firm. Let d_0 be the current dividend per share and assume that it was paid just yesterday, so that it does not enter into the present value computations. The stream of growing dividends to be received starts with the first end-of-year dividend, $d_1 = d_0(1 + g)$. The dividend at the end of the second year is $d_2 = d_0(1 + g)^2$. The stream of payments is assumed to grow at a constant rate for n years; therefore its present value, PV, is

$$\text{PV} = \frac{d_1}{1 + r} + \frac{d_2}{(1 + r)^2} + \frac{d_3}{(1 + r)^3} + \cdots + \frac{d_n}{(1 + r)^n}$$

$$= \frac{d_0(1 + g)}{1 + r} + \frac{d_0(1 + g)^2}{(1 + r)^2} + \frac{d_0(1 + g)^3}{(1 + r)^3} + \cdots + \frac{d_0(1 + g)^n}{(1 + r)^n}.$$

If we let $u = (1 + g)/(1 + r)$ this can be rewritten as

$$\text{PV} = d_0 u + d_0 u^2 + d_0 u^3 + \cdots + d_0 u^n$$

$$= u d_0 (1 + u + u^2 + \cdots + u^{n-1}). \tag{A.7}$$

By multiplying Eq. (A.7) by u and subtracting the result from Eq. (A.7), we obtain

$$PV - uPV = ud_0(1 - u^n),$$

and solving for the present value of the growing annuity, we have

$$PV = \frac{ud_0(1 - u^n)}{1 - u}.$$

Substituting back the value of u gives us

$$PV = \frac{\left(\dfrac{1 + g}{1 + r}\right)d_0\left[1 - \left(\dfrac{1 + g}{1 + r}\right)^n\right]}{1 - \left(\dfrac{1 + g}{1 + r}\right)}.$$

By rearranging terms and recalling that $d_0(1 + g) = d_1$, we obtain

$$PV = \frac{d_1\left[1 - \left(\dfrac{1 + g}{1 + r}\right)^n\right]}{r - g}. \tag{A.8}$$

Equation (A.8) is the present value of n annuity payments that start at a level of d_0 and grow at a constant rate, g.

Note that if the number of payments is infinite, we can obtain a finite present value if we assume that the growth rate in dividends, g, is less than the time value of money, r. If $g < r$, then the fraction in the numerator of Eq. (A.8) goes to zero in the limit as n approaches infinity:

$$\lim_{n \to \infty} \left(\frac{1 + g}{1 + r}\right)^n = 0, \quad \text{iff} \quad g < r.$$

Therefore the present value of an infinite number of growing dividends is

$$\lim_{n \to \infty} PV = \frac{d_1}{r - g}. \tag{A.9}$$

Equation (A.9) is used frequently in the text, where it is called the *Gordon growth model*. It provides us with an estimate of the present value of a share of common stock where the stream of dividends received from it is assumed to grow at a constant rate that is assumed to be less than the discount rate (which in this case would be the cost of equity capital, k_s).

7. The Value-Additivity Principle and the NPV Criterion

It is worth emphasizing that in calculating present value (PV) relationships we have been drawing on the value-additivity principle. As the example from section B.5 illustrates, the present value of amounts $(A + B + C + D)$ is equal to the present value of A plus the present value of B plus the present value of C plus the present value of D. In this earlier example, we had four cash flows $(F_1 + F_2 + F_3 + F_4)$. They came in different time periods. We can obtain the present value of cash flows that occur in different years by applying the appropriate discount factor and adding:

$$PV = \frac{F_1}{(1+r)} + \frac{F_2}{(1+r)^2} + \frac{F_3}{(1+r)^3} + \frac{F_4}{(1+r)^4}. \tag{A.10}$$

Using the actual numbers, we have

$$PV = \frac{\$100}{(1.15)} + \frac{\$200}{(1.15)^2} + \frac{\$600}{(1.15)^3} + \frac{\$300}{(1.15)^4}.$$

This can also be written as

$$PV = \$100(.870) + \$200(.756) + \$600(.658) + \$300(.572) = \$804.60.$$

In general the present value calculations follow the principle of value additivity for any number of cash flows, simply involving addition of the individual flows. We can write

$$PV = \frac{F_1}{(1+r_1)} + \frac{F_2}{(1+r_2)^2} + \cdots + \frac{F_n}{(1+r_n)^n}. \tag{A.11}$$

The value-additivity relationship enables all types of computational operations to be performed. This makes possible the development of valuation relationships for a wide variety of cash flow patterns, as will be demonstrated in the subsequent materials.

Another general principle that flows from the preceding compound interest relationships is the net present value criterion. The net present value (NPV) is obtained by calculating the discounted value of the cash returns and subtracting the discounted value of the investments (or cash outflows) required to produce the positive cash flows. If a single investment is made, we add a single negative term to the present value calculations set forth above:

$$NPV = -I_0 + \frac{F_1}{(1+r)} + \frac{F_2}{(1+r)^2} + \cdots + \frac{F_n}{(1+r)^n}. \tag{A.12}$$

If investments over a period of years are required to produce the cash flows, their values are accumulated to the present:

$$NPV = -I_0 - I_1(1+r)^{-1} - I_2(1+r)^2 + \frac{F_1}{(1+r)} + \frac{F_2}{(1+r)^2} + \cdots + \frac{F_n}{(1+r)^n}. \tag{A.13}$$

The net present value represents the addition to value created by an investment project. The applicable discount factor is the rate of interest or cost of capital appropriate to the characteristics of a project. Hence the NPV criterion is a general rule for allocating resources. By following the NPV rule the financial markets produce the maximum amount of additions to the value of the economy. Individual investors can then buy and sell in the financial markets to obtain the use of funds for consumption in early years or to postpone consumption to later years. Nor do managers of individual firms need to consult the preferences of their shareholders or owners to determine whether they prefer investments that come to fruition in early years or later years. By following the NPV criterion, the maximum amount of additions to wealth will be achieved. The financial markets provide opportunities to the individual investors to arrange their consumption over time in years that they prefer. The NPV rule leads to the fundamental principles of valuation for flows of different kinds and different time patterns.

8. Compounding Periods within One Year

In the illustrations set forth thus far the examples have been for returns that were received once a year or annually. If the interest rates are calculated for periods of time within one year a simple relationship can be followed, utilizing the principles already set forth. For compounding within one year, we simply divide the interest rate by the number of compoundings within a year and multiply the annual periods by the same factor. For example, in our first equation for compound interest we had the following:

$$S_n = P(1 + r)^n.$$

This was for annual compounding. For semiannual compounding we would follow the rule just set forth. The equation would become

$$S_n = P\left(1 + \frac{r}{m}\right)^{nm}, \tag{A.14}$$

where m = the number of compoundings during a year.

We may apply this in a numerical illustration. Suppose the initial question is, "To how much would $1000 at a 6% interest rate accumulate over a five-year period?" The answer is $1338. Now we apply semiannual compounding. The equation would appear as follows:

$$S_{5/2} = \$1000\left(1 + \frac{.06}{2}\right)^{5(2)}.$$

Thus the new expression is equivalent to compounding the $1000 at 3% for 10 periods. The compound interest table (Table A.1) for 10 years shows that the interest factor would be 1.344. Our equation would therefore read:

$$S_{5/2} = \$1000(1 + .03)^{10},$$

$$= \$1344.$$

It will be noted that with semiannual compounding the future sum amounts to $1344 as compared with the $1338 we had before. Frequent compounding provides compound interest paid on compound interest, so the amount is higher. Thus we would expect that daily compounding, as some financial institutions advertise, or continuous compounding, as is employed under some assumptions, would give some-what larger amounts than annual or semiannual compounding. But the basic ideas are unchanged.

The same logic is equally applicable to all the categories of relationships we have described. For example, suppose a problem on the present value of an annuity was stated as the payment of $1000 a year for 10 years with an interest rate of 10% compounded annually. If the compounding is semiannual we would employ an interest rate of 5% and apply the compounding to a period of 20 years. When we compound semiannually we also have to divide the annual payment by the number of times the compounding takes place within the year. We would have the following expression:

$$A_{nm,r/m} = \$500(P_{nm,r/m})$$

$$= \$500[P_{10(2),10\%/2}]$$

$$= \$500(P_{20,5\%})$$

$$= \$500(12.462)$$

$$= \$6231.$$

It will be noted that with annual compounding the present value of the annuity was $6145. With semiannual compounding the present value is $6231. With more frequent compounding the resulting amounts will be somewhat higher because interest is compounded on interest more often.

C. THE TIME VALUE OF MONEY: CONTINUOUS COMPOUNDING

1. Compound Sums and Present Values

Continuous compounding simply extends the ideas involved in compounding periods within one year. Let us restate Eq. (A.14) in somewhat more general symbols:

$$V_t = P_0\left(1 + \frac{k}{q}\right)^{qt}. \tag{A.14a}$$

Since we can multiply qt by k/k, we can set $qt = (q/k)(kt)$ and rewrite Eq. (A.14a) as

$$V_t = P_0\left[\left(1 + \frac{k}{q}\right)^{(q/k)}\right]^{(kt)}. \tag{A.15}$$

Define $m = q/k$ and rewrite Eq. (A.15) as

$$V_t = P_0\left[\left(1 + \frac{1}{m}\right)^{m}\right]^{kt}. \tag{A.15a}$$

As the number of compounding periods, q, increases, m also increases; this causes the term in brackets in Eq. (A.15a) to increase. At the limit, when q and m approach infinity (and compounding is instantaneous, or continuous), the term in brackets approaches the value 2.718. ... The value e is defined as this limiting case:

$$e = \lim_{m \to \infty} \left(1 + \frac{1}{m}\right)^m = 2.718\ldots.$$

We may substitute e for the bracketed term:

$$V_t = P_0 e^{kt}. \tag{A.16}$$

Equation (A.16) is the expression for the case of continuous compounding (or continuous growth).

It is convenient to use natural logarithms to evaluate the formula for continuous compounding. We can rewrite Eq. (A.16) to express it as the relationship for $1 of initial principal. We obtain Eq. (A.17):

$$V_t = e^{kt}. \tag{A.17}$$

Next express Eq. (A.17) in log form, letting ln denote log to the base e:

$$\ln V_t = kt \ln e. \tag{A.18}$$

Since e is the base of the system of natural logarithms, ln e is equal to 1. Hence to use the table of natural logs, we have Eq. (A.19):

$$\ln V_t = kt. \tag{A.19}$$

For example, suppose our problem is to determine the future value of $1000 compounded continuously at 10% for eight years. Then $t = 8$ and $k = .10$, so $kt = .80$. We find .8 in the body of Table A.5 to be between .79751 and .80200. The first number corresponds to an interest factor of 2.22. We can then interpolate up to the .80000. This is the ratio .00249/.00449, which equals .555. Hence the interest factor is 2.22555. So the $1000 would compound to $2225.55 in eight years at 10%. This compares with $2144.00 with compounding on an annual basis.

Equation (A.16) can be transformed into Eq. (A.20) and used to determine present values under continuous compounding. Using k as the discount rate, we obtain

$$PV = \frac{V_t}{e^{kt}} = V_t e^{-kt}. \tag{A.20}$$

Thus if $2225 is due in eight years and if the appropriate continuous discount rate k is 10%, the present value of this future payment is

$$PV = \frac{\$2225}{2.225} = \$1000.$$

2. Constant Payment Annuities

If we assume that an asset pays a constant amount per unit time, then we can write that the payment at any point in time, a_t, is a constant, a_0:

$$a_t = a_0. \tag{A.21}$$

Using basic integral calculus (discussed in Appendix D), we can express the present value of a constant payment stream as the discounted value of the payment function given in Eq. (A.21):

$$PV = \int_0^n a_t e^{-kt}\, dt. \tag{A.22}$$

Note that we have employed Eq. (A.20) to discount each payment. The stream of payments is assumed to start immediately $(t = 0)$ and continue for n time periods. Hence the limits of integration in Eq. (A.22) are 0 to n. Following the applicable rules of integral calculus to evaluate the definite integral, we obtain

$$
\begin{aligned}
PV &= a_0 \int_0^n e^{-kt}\, dt \\
&= a_0 \left[\frac{-e^{-kt}}{k} \right]\Bigg|_0^n \\
&= a_0 \left[\frac{-e^{-kn}}{k} - \frac{-e^0}{k} \right] \\
&= a_0 \left[\frac{1 - e^{-kn}}{k} \right].
\end{aligned}
\tag{A.23}
$$

Equation (A.23) is the continuous-time analogue to Eq. (A.3), which was the discrete time version of the present value of an annuity of constant payments. Note that the continuous discount factor e^{-kn} in Eq. (A.23) is roughly equivalent to the discrete discount factor $(1 + r)^{-n}$ in Eq. (A.3).

If we want the present value of an infinite stream of constant, continuously compounded payments we take the limit of Eq. (A.23) as n becomes infinite:

$$\lim_{n \to \infty} PV = \frac{a_0}{k}. \tag{A.24}$$

Equation (A.24) is exactly equal to Eq. (A.5).

3. Annuities with Growing Payments

For a stream of growing payments we can see from Eq. (A.17) that the payment function is

$$a_t = a_0 e^{gt}. \tag{A.25}$$

The present value of such a stream is

$$
\begin{aligned}
PV &= \int_0^n a_t e^{-kt}\, dt \\
&= a_0 \int_0^n e^{gt} e^{-kt}\, dt.
\end{aligned}
$$

Combining terms, we have

$$PV = a_0 \int_0^n e^{-(k-g)t}\, dt.$$

Using the rules of integral calculus, the solution to this integral is

$$PV = a_0 \left[\frac{-e^{-(k-g)t}}{k-g} \right]\Big|_0^n$$

$$= a_0 \left[\frac{-e^{-(k-g)n}}{k-g} - \left(\frac{-e^0}{k-g} \right) \right]$$

$$= a_0 \left[\frac{1 - e^{-(k-g)n}}{k-g} \right]. \tag{A.26}$$

Equation (A.26) is analogous to Eq. (A.8), the discrete compounding version of the present value of an annuity of growing payments that lasts for n years.

As before, the present value of an infinite stream of payments is obtained by taking the limit of Eq. (A.26) as n approaches infinity:

$$\lim_{n \to \infty} PV = \frac{a_0}{k-g}, \quad \text{iff} \quad g < k. \tag{A.27}$$

SUMMARY

Consumption is allocated over time by "the" interest rate. Positive rates of interest induce people to postpone consumption and save part of their income. The pool of savings at any given time is used for investments that yield output in the form of goods that may be consumed at future dates.

The combined preferences of all members of society and the society's technology combine to determine the pattern of interest rates that will allocate consumption over time optimally. The structure of interest rates guides individuals into making investment decisions that are most desired by the society as a whole.

Present value or future value calculations at appropriately chosen interest rates, given the riskiness of the project, will tell an investor whether the future receipts are sufficient to justify the current investment. Since the pattern of interest rates is determined by the behavior of all members of society, a positive present value means not only that the project will yield a profit to the investor but also that no member of the society has a superior use for the resources being invested. If many other investment opportunities were to appear that were superior to the one in question, the interest rate appropriate for the present value calculation would rise, and the present value of the project might then appear to be negative.

To evaluate projects with cash flows distributed over time it is necessary to express all flows in terms of their value at one specific point in time. Expressing them in terms of value today is discounting to net present value; expressing them at their value on some future date is compounding to future value. There is conceptually no difference between the two approaches.

Interest rates are traditionally expressed per annum, but cash flows may occur at discrete periods during the year or may even be continuous. Again, there is no conceptual difference between discrete and continuous formulations. However, the continuous form expressions are often more convenient for complex valuation problems. For example, some models of option pricing assume that stock price behavior is continuous, and consequently most option valuation expressions are in continuous form.

Table A.1 Compound Sum of $1 $S_n = P(1 + r)^n$

Year	1%	2%	3%	4%	5%	6%	7%	8%	9%	10%	11%	12%	13%	14%	15%	16%
1	1.010	1.020	1.030	1.040	1.050	1.060	1.070	1.080	1.090	1.100	1.110	1.120	1.130	1.140	1.150	1.160
2	1.020	1.040	1.061	1.082	1.102	1.124	1.145	1.166	1.188	1.210	1.232	1.254	1.277	1.300	1.322	1.346
3	1.030	1.061	1.093	1.125	1.158	1.191	1.225	1.260	1.295	1.331	1.368	1.405	1.443	1.482	1.521	1.561
4	1.041	1.082	1.126	1.170	1.216	1.262	1.311	1.360	1.412	1.464	1.518	1.574	1.631	1.689	1.749	1.811
5	1.051	1.104	1.159	1.217	1.276	1.338	1.403	1.469	1.539	1.611	1.685	1.762	1.842	1.925	2.011	2.100
6	1.062	1.126	1.194	1.265	1.340	1.419	1.501	1.587	1.677	1.772	1.870	1.974	2.082	2.195	2.313	2.436
7	1.072	1.149	1.230	1.316	1.407	1.504	1.606	1.714	1.828	1.949	2.076	2.211	2.353	2.502	2.660	2.826
8	1.083	1.172	1.267	1.369	1.477	1.594	1.718	1.851	1.993	2.144	2.305	2.476	2.658	2.853	3.059	3.278
9	1.094	1.195	1.305	1.423	1.551	1.689	1.838	1.999	2.172	2.358	2.558	2.773	3.004	3.252	3.518	3.803
10	1.105	1.219	1.344	1.480	1.629	1.791	1.967	2.159	2.367	2.594	2.839	3.106	3.395	3.707	4.046	4.411
11	1.116	1.243	1.384	1.539	1.710	1.898	2.105	2.332	2.580	2.853	3.152	3.479	3.836	4.226	4.652	5.117
12	1.127	1.268	1.426	1.601	1.796	2.012	2.252	2.518	2.813	3.138	3.499	3.896	4.335	4.818	5.350	5.936
13	1.138	1.294	1.469	1.665	1.886	2.133	2.410	2.720	3.066	3.452	3.883	4.363	4.898	5.492	6.153	6.886
14	1.149	1.319	1.513	1.732	1.980	2.261	2.579	2.937	3.342	3.797	4.310	4.887	5.535	6.261	7.076	7.988
15	1.161	1.346	1.558	1.801	2.079	2.397	2.759	3.172	3.642	4.177	4.785	5.474	6.254	7.138	8.137	9.266
16	1.173	1.373	1.605	1.873	2.183	2.540	2.952	3.426	3.970	4.595	5.311	6.130	7.067	8.137	9.358	10.748
17	1.184	1.400	1.653	1.948	2.292	2.693	3.159	3.700	4.328	5.054	5.895	6.866	7.986	9.276	10.761	12.468
18	1.196	1.428	1.702	2.026	2.407	2.854	3.380	3.996	4.717	5.560	6.544	7.690	9.024	10.575	12.375	14.463
19	1.208	1.457	1.754	2.107	2.527	3.026	3.617	4.316	5.142	6.116	7.263	8.613	10.197	12.056	14.232	16.777
20	1.220	1.486	1.806	2.191	2.653	3.207	3.870	4.661	5.604	6.728	8.062	9.646	11.523	13.743	16.367	19.461

Table A.2 Present Value of $1 — $P = S_n(1 + r)^{-n}$

Years Hence	1%	2%	4%	6%	8%	10%	12%	14%	15%	16%	18%	20%	22%	24%	25%	26%	28%	30%	35%	40%	45%	50%
1	0.990	0.980	0.962	0.943	0.926	0.909	0.893	0.877	0.870	0.862	0.847	0.833	0.820	0.806	0.800	0.794	0.781	0.769	0.741	0.714	0.690	0.667
2	0.980	0.961	0.925	0.890	0.857	0.826	0.797	0.769	0.756	0.743	0.718	0.694	0.672	0.650	0.640	0.630	0.610	0.592	0.549	0.510	0.476	0.444
3	0.971	0.942	0.889	0.840	0.794	0.751	0.712	0.675	0.658	0.641	0.609	0.579	0.551	0.524	0.512	0.500	0.477	0.455	0.406	0.364	0.328	0.296
4	0.961	0.924	0.855	0.792	0.735	0.683	0.636	0.592	0.572	0.552	0.516	0.482	0.451	0.423	0.410	0.397	0.373	0.350	0.301	0.260	0.226	0.198
5	0.951	0.906	0.822	0.747	0.681	0.621	0.567	0.519	0.497	0.476	0.437	0.402	0.370	0.341	0.328	0.315	0.291	0.269	0.223	0.186	0.156	0.132
6	0.942	0.888	0.790	0.705	0.630	0.564	0.507	0.456	0.432	0.410	0.370	0.335	0.303	0.275	0.262	0.250	0.227	0.207	0.165	0.133	0.108	0.088
7	0.933	0.871	0.760	0.665	0.583	0.513	0.452	0.400	0.376	0.354	0.314	0.279	0.249	0.222	0.210	0.198	0.178	0.159	0.122	0.095	0.074	0.059
8	0.923	0.853	0.731	0.627	0.540	0.467	0.404	0.351	0.327	0.305	0.266	0.233	0.204	0.179	0.168	0.157	0.139	0.123	0.091	0.068	0.051	0.039
9	0.914	0.837	0.703	0.592	0.500	0.424	0.361	0.308	0.284	0.263	0.225	0.194	0.167	0.144	0.134	0.125	0.108	0.094	0.067	0.048	0.035	0.026
10	0.905	0.820	0.676	0.558	0.463	0.386	0.322	0.270	0.247	0.227	0.191	0.162	0.137	0.116	0.107	0.099	0.085	0.073	0.050	0.035	0.024	0.017
11	0.896	0.804	0.650	0.527	0.429	0.350	0.287	0.237	0.215	0.195	0.162	0.135	0.112	0.094	0.086	0.079	0.066	0.056	0.037	0.025	0.017	0.012
12	0.887	0.788	0.625	0.497	0.397	0.319	0.257	0.208	0.187	0.168	0.137	0.112	0.092	0.076	0.069	0.062	0.052	0.043	0.027	0.018	0.012	0.008
13	0.879	0.773	0.601	0.469	0.368	0.290	0.229	0.182	0.163	0.145	0.116	0.093	0.075	0.061	0.055	0.050	0.040	0.033	0.020	0.013	0.008	0.005
14	0.870	0.758	0.577	0.442	0.340	0.263	0.205	0.160	0.141	0.125	0.099	0.078	0.062	0.049	0.044	0.039	0.032	0.025	0.015	0.009	0.006	0.003
15	0.861	0.743	0.555	0.417	0.315	0.239	0.183	0.140	0.123	0.108	0.084	0.065	0.051	0.040	0.035	0.031	0.025	0.020	0.011	0.006	0.004	0.002
16	0.853	0.728	0.534	0.394	0.292	0.218	0.163	0.123	0.107	0.093	0.071	0.054	0.042	0.032	0.028	0.025	0.019	0.015	0.008	0.005	0.003	0.002
17	0.844	0.714	0.513	0.371	0.270	0.198	0.146	0.108	0.093	0.080	0.060	0.045	0.034	0.026	0.023	0.020	0.015	0.012	0.006	0.003	0.002	0.001
18	0.836	0.700	0.494	0.350	0.250	0.180	0.130	0.095	0.081	0.069	0.051	0.038	0.028	0.021	0.018	0.016	0.012	0.009	0.005	0.002	0.001	0.001
19	0.828	0.686	0.475	0.331	0.232	0.164	0.116	0.083	0.070	0.060	0.043	0.031	0.023	0.017	0.014	0.012	0.009	0.007	0.003	0.002	0.001	
20	0.820	0.673	0.456	0.312	0.215	0.149	0.104	0.073	0.061	0.051	0.037	0.026	0.019	0.014	0.012	0.010	0.007	0.005	0.002	0.001	0.001	
21	0.811	0.660	0.439	0.294	0.199	0.135	0.093	0.064	0.053	0.044	0.031	0.022	0.015	0.011	0.009	0.008	0.006	0.004	0.002	0.001		
22	0.803	0.647	0.422	0.278	0.184	0.123	0.083	0.056	0.046	0.038	0.026	0.018	0.013	0.009	0.007	0.006	0.004	0.003	0.001	0.001		
23	0.795	0.634	0.406	0.262	0.170	0.112	0.074	0.049	0.040	0.033	0.022	0.015	0.010	0.007	0.006	0.005	0.003	0.002	0.001			
24	0.788	0.622	0.390	0.247	0.158	0.102	0.066	0.043	0.035	0.028	0.019	0.013	0.008	0.006	0.005	0.004	0.003	0.002	0.001			
25	0.780	0.610	0.375	0.233	0.146	0.092	0.059	0.038	0.030	0.024	0.016	0.010	0.007	0.005	0.004	0.003	0.002	0.001				
26	0.772	0.598	0.361	0.220	0.135	0.084	0.053	0.033	0.026	0.021	0.014	0.009	0.006	0.004	0.003	0.002	0.002	0.001				
27	0.764	0.586	0.347	0.207	0.125	0.076	0.047	0.029	0.023	0.018	0.011	0.007	0.005	0.003	0.002	0.002	0.001	0.001				
28	0.757	0.574	0.333	0.196	0.116	0.069	0.042	0.026	0.020	0.016	0.010	0.006	0.004	0.002	0.002	0.002	0.001	0.001				
29	0.749	0.563	0.321	0.185	0.107	0.063	0.037	0.022	0.017	0.014	0.008	0.005	0.003	0.002	0.002	0.001	0.001	0.001				
30	0.742	0.552	0.308	0.174	0.099	0.057	0.033	0.020	0.015	0.012	0.007	0.004	0.003	0.002	0.001	0.001	0.001	0.001				
40	0.672	0.453	0.208	0.097	0.046	0.022	0.011	0.005	0.004	0.003	0.001	0.001										
50	0.608	0.372	0.141	0.054	0.021	0.009	0.003	0.001	0.001	0.001												

Table A.3 Sum of an Annuity for $1 for n Years $\quad S_{n,r} = \$1 \left[\dfrac{(1+r)^n - 1}{r} \right]$

Year	1%	2%	3%	4%	5%	6%	7%	8%	9%	10%	11%	12%	13%	14%	15%	16%
1	1.000	1.000	1.000	1.000	1.000	1.000	1.000	1.000	1.000	1.000	1.000	1.000	1.000	1.000	1.000	1.000
2	2.010	2.020	2.030	2.040	2.050	2.060	2.070	2.080	2.090	2.100	2.110	2.120	2.130	2.140	2.150	2.160
3	3.030	3.060	3.091	3.122	3.152	3.184	3.215	3.246	3.278	3.310	3.342	3.374	3.407	3.440	3.473	3.506
4	4.060	4.122	4.184	4.246	4.310	4.375	4.440	4.506	4.573	4.641	4.710	4.779	4.850	4.921	4.993	5.066
5	5.101	5.204	5.309	5.416	5.526	5.637	5.751	5.867	5.985	6.105	6.228	6.353	6.480	6.610	6.742	6.877
6	6.152	6.308	6.468	6.633	6.802	6.975	7.153	7.336	7.523	7.716	7.913	8.115	8.323	8.536	8.754	8.977
7	7.214	7.434	7.662	7.898	8.142	8.394	8.654	8.923	9.200	9.487	9.783	10.089	10.405	10.730	11.067	11.414
8	8.286	8.583	8.892	9.214	9.549	9.897	10.260	10.637	11.028	11.436	11.859	12.300	12.757	13.233	13.727	14.240
9	9.369	9.755	10.159	10.583	11.027	11.491	11.978	12.488	13.021	13.579	14.164	14.776	15.416	16.085	16.786	17.518
10	10.462	10.950	11.464	12.006	12.578	13.181	13.816	14.487	15.193	15.937	16.722	17.549	18.420	19.337	20.304	21.321
11	11.567	12.169	12.808	13.486	14.207	14.972	15.784	16.645	17.560	18.531	19.561	20.655	21.814	23.044	24.349	25.733
12	12.683	13.412	14.192	15.026	15.917	16.870	17.888	18.977	20.141	21.384	22.713	24.133	25.650	27.271	29.002	30.850
13	13.809	14.680	15.618	16.627	17.713	18.882	20.141	21.495	22.953	24.523	26.212	28.029	29.985	32.089	34.352	36.786
14	14.947	15.974	17.086	18.292	19.599	21.051	22.550	24.215	26.019	27.975	30.095	32.393	34.883	37.581	40.505	43.672
15	16.097	17.293	18.599	20.024	21.579	23.276	25.129	27.152	29.361	31.772	34.405	37.280	40.417	43.842	47.580	51.659

Table A.4 Present Value of $1 Received Annually $A_{n,r} = \$1\left[\dfrac{1-(1+r)^{-n}}{r}\right]$

Years (n)	1%	2%	4%	6%	8%	10%	12%	14%	15%	16%	18%	20%	22%	24%	25%	26%	28%	30%	35%	40%	45%	50%
1	0.990	0.980	0.962	0.943	0.926	0.909	0.893	0.877	0.870	0.862	0.847	0.833	0.820	0.806	0.800	0.794	0.781	0.769	0.741	0.714	0.690	0.667
2	1.970	1.942	1.886	1.833	1.783	1.736	1.690	1.647	1.626	1.605	1.566	1.528	1.492	1.457	1.440	1.424	1.392	1.361	1.289	1.224	1.165	1.111
3	2.941	2.884	2.775	2.673	2.577	2.487	2.402	2.322	2.283	2.246	2.174	2.106	2.042	1.981	1.952	1.923	1.868	1.816	1.696	1.589	1.493	1.407
4	3.902	3.808	3.630	3.465	3.312	3.170	3.037	2.914	2.855	2.798	2.690	2.589	2.494	2.404	2.362	2.320	2.241	2.166	1.997	1.849	1.720	1.605
5	4.853	4.713	4.452	4.212	3.993	3.791	3.605	3.433	3.352	3.274	3.127	2.991	2.864	2.745	2.689	2.635	2.532	2.436	2.220	2.035	1.876	1.737
6	5.795	5.601	5.242	4.917	4.623	4.355	4.111	3.889	3.784	3.685	3.498	3.326	3.167	3.020	2.951	2.885	2.759	2.643	2.385	2.168	1.983	1.824
7	6.728	6.472	6.002	5.582	5.206	4.868	4.564	4.288	4.160	4.039	3.812	3.605	3.416	3.242	3.161	3.083	2.937	2.802	2.508	2.263	2.057	1.883
8	7.652	7.325	6.733	6.210	5.747	5.335	4.968	4.639	4.487	4.344	4.078	3.837	3.619	3.421	3.329	3.241	3.076	2.925	2.598	2.331	2.108	1.922
9	8.566	8.162	7.435	6.802	6.247	5.759	5.328	4.946	4.772	4.607	4.303	4.031	3.786	3.566	3.463	3.366	3.184	3.019	2.665	2.379	2.144	1.948
10	9.471	8.983	8.111	7.360	6.710	6.145	5.650	5.216	5.019	4.833	4.494	4.192	3.923	3.682	3.571	3.465	3.269	3.092	2.715	2.414	2.168	1.965
11	10.368	9.787	8.760	7.887	7.139	6.495	5.937	5.453	5.234	5.029	4.656	4.327	4.035	3.776	3.656	3.544	3.335	3.147	2.752	2.438	2.185	1.977
12	11.255	10.575	9.385	8.384	7.536	6.814	6.194	5.660	5.421	5.197	4.793	4.439	4.127	3.851	3.725	3.606	3.387	3.190	2.779	2.456	2.196	1.985
13	12.134	11.343	9.986	8.853	7.904	7.103	6.424	5.842	5.583	5.342	4.910	4.533	4.203	3.912	3.780	3.656	3.427	3.223	2.799	2.468	2.204	1.990
14	13.004	12.106	10.563	9.295	8.244	7.367	6.628	6.002	5.724	5.468	5.008	4.611	4.265	3.962	3.824	3.695	3.459	3.249	2.814	2.477	2.210	1.993
15	13.865	12.849	11.118	9.712	8.559	7.606	6.811	6.142	5.847	5.575	5.092	4.675	4.315	4.001	3.859	3.726	3.483	3.268	2.825	2.484	2.214	1.995
16	14.718	13.578	11.652	10.106	8.851	7.824	6.974	6.265	5.954	5.669	5.162	4.730	4.357	4.033	3.887	3.751	3.503	3.283	2.834	2.489	2.216	1.997
17	15.562	14.292	12.166	10.477	9.122	8.022	7.120	6.373	6.047	5.749	5.222	4.775	4.391	4.059	3.910	3.771	3.518	3.295	2.840	2.492	2.218	1.998
18	16.398	14.992	12.659	10.828	9.372	8.201	7.250	6.467	6.128	5.818	5.273	4.812	4.419	4.080	3.928	3.786	3.529	3.304	2.844	2.494	2.219	1.999
19	17.226	15.678	13.134	11.158	9.604	8.365	7.366	6.550	6.198	5.877	5.316	4.844	4.442	4.097	3.942	3.799	3.539	3.311	2.848	2.496	2.220	1.999
20	18.046	16.351	13.590	11.470	9.818	8.514	7.469	6.623	6.259	5.929	5.353	4.870	4.460	4.110	3.954	3.808	3.546	3.316	2.850	2.497	2.221	1.999
21	18.857	17.011	14.029	11.764	10.017	8.649	7.562	6.687	6.312	5.973	5.384	4.891	4.476	4.121	3.963	3.816	3.551	3.320	2.852	2.498	2.221	2.000
22	19.660	17.658	14.451	12.042	10.201	8.772	7.645	6.743	6.359	6.011	5.410	4.909	4.488	4.130	3.970	3.822	3.556	3.323	2.853	2.498	2.222	2.000
23	20.456	18.292	14.857	12.303	10.371	8.883	7.718	6.792	6.399	6.044	5.432	4.925	4.499	4.137	3.976	3.827	3.559	3.325	2.854	2.499	2.222	2.000
24	21.243	18.914	15.247	12.550	10.529	8.985	7.784	6.835	6.434	6.073	5.451	4.937	4.507	4.143	3.981	3.831	3.562	3.327	2.855	2.499	2.222	2.000
25	22.023	19.523	15.622	12.783	10.675	9.077	7.843	6.873	6.464	6.097	5.467	4.948	4.514	4.147	3.985	3.834	3.564	3.329	2.856	2.499	2.222	2.000
26	22.795	20.121	15.983	13.003	10.810	9.161	7.896	6.906	6.491	6.118	5.480	4.956	4.520	4.151	3.988	3.837	3.566	3.330	2.856	2.500	2.222	2.000
27	23.560	20.707	16.330	13.211	10.935	9.237	7.943	6.935	6.514	6.136	5.492	4.964	4.524	4.154	3.990	3.839	3.567	3.331	2.856	2.500	2.222	2.000
28	24.316	21.281	16.663	13.406	11.051	9.307	7.984	6.961	6.534	6.152	5.502	4.970	4.528	4.157	3.992	3.840	3.568	3.331	2.857	2.500	2.222	2.000
29	25.066	21.844	16.984	13.591	11.158	9.370	8.022	6.983	6.551	6.166	5.510	4.975	4.531	4.159	3.994	3.841	3.569	3.332	2.857	2.500	2.222	2.000
30	25.808	22.396	17.292	13.765	11.258	9.427	8.055	7.003	6.566	6.177	5.517	4.979	4.534	4.160	3.995	3.842	3.569	3.332	2.857	2.500	2.222	2.000
40	32.835	27.355	19.793	15.046	11.925	9.779	8.244	7.105	6.642	6.234	5.548	4.997	4.544	4.166	3.999	3.846	3.571	3.333	2.857	2.500	2.222	2.000
50	39.196	31.424	21.482	15.762	12.234	9.915	8.304	7.133	6.661	6.246	5.554	4.999	4.545	4.167	4.000	3.846	3.571	3.333	2.857	2.500	2.222	2.000

860   DISCOUNTING

Table A.5   Natural Logarithms of Numbers between 1.0 and 4.99

N	0	1	2	3	4	5	6	7	8	9
1.0	0.00000	.00995	.01980	.02956	.03922	.04879	.05827	.06766	.07696	.08618
.1	.09531	.10436	.11333	.12222	.13103	.13976	.14842	.15700	.16551	.17395
.2	.18232	.19062	.19885	.20701	.21511	.22314	.23111	.23902	.24686	.25464
.3	.26236	.27003	.27763	.28518	.29267	.30010	.30748	.31481	.32208	.32930
.4	.33647	.34359	.35066	.35767	.36464	.37156	.37844	.38526	.39204	.39878
.5	.40547	.41211	.41871	.42527	.43178	.43825	.44469	.45108	.45742	.46373
.6	.47000	.47623	.48243	.48858	.49470	.50078	.50682	.51282	.51879	.52473
.7	.53063	.53649	.54232	.54812	.55389	.55962	.56531	.57098	.57661	.58222
.8	.58779	.59333	.59884	.60432	.60977	.61519	.62058	.62594	.63127	.63658
.9	.64185	.64710	.65233	.65752	.66269	.66783	.67294	.67803	.68310	.68813
2.0	0.69315	.69813	.70310	.70804	.71295	.71784	.72271	.72755	.73237	.73716
.1	.74194	.74669	.75142	.75612	.76081	.76547	.77011	.77473	.77932	.78390
.2	.78846	.79299	.79751	.80200	.80648	.81093	.81536	.81978	.82418	.82855
.3	.83291	.83725	.84157	.84587	.85015	.85442	.85866	.86289	.86710	.87129
.4	.87547	.87963	.88377	.88789	.89200	.89609	.90016	.90422	.90826	.91228
.5	.91629	.92028	.92426	.92822	.93216	.93609	.94001	.94391	.94779	.95166
.6	.95551	.95935	.96317	.96698	.97078	.97456	.97833	.98208	.98582	.98954
.7	.99325	.99695	.00063ᵃ	.00430ᵃ	.00796ᵃ	.01160ᵃ	.01523ᵃ	.01885ᵃ	.02245ᵃ	.02604ᵃ
.8	1.02962	.03318	.03674	.04028	.04380	.04732	.05082	.05431	.05779	.06126
.9	.06471	.06815	.07158	.07500	.07841	.08181	.08519	.08856	.09192	.09527
3.0	1.09861	.10194	.10526	.10856	.11186	.11514	.11841	.12168	.12493	.12817
.1	.13140	.13462	.13783	.14103	.14422	.14740	.15057	.15373	.15688	.16002
.2	.16315	.16627	.16938	.17248	.17557	.17865	.18173	.18479	.18784	.19089
.3	.19392	.19695	.19996	.20297	.20597	.20896	.21194	.21491	.21788	.22083
.4	.22378	.22671	.22964	.23256	.23547	.23837	.24127	.24415	.24703	.24990
.5	.25276	.25562	.25846	.26130	.26413	.26695	.26976	.27257	.27536	.27815
.6	.28093	.28371	.28647	.28923	.29198	.29473	.29746	.30019	.30291	.30563
.7	.30833	.31103	.31372	.31641	.31909	.32176	.32442	.32708	.32972	.33237
.8	.33500	.33763	.34025	.34286	.34547	.34807	.35067	.35325	.35584	.35841
.9	.36098	.36354	.36609	.36864	.37118	.37372	.37624	.37877	.38128	.38379
4.0	1.38629	.38879	.39128	.39377	.39624	.39872	.40118	.40364	.40610	.40854
.1	.41099	.41342	.41585	.41828	.42070	.42311	.42552	.42792	.43031	.43270
.2	.43508	.43746	.43984	.44220	.44456	.44692	.44927	.45161	.45395	.45629
.3	.45862	.46094	.46326	.46557	.46787	.47018	.47247	.47476	.47705	.47933
.4	.48160	.48387	.48614	.48840	.49065	.49290	.49515	.49739	.49962	.50185
.5	.50408	.50630	.50851	.51072	.51293	.51513	.51732	.51951	.52170	.52388
.6	.52606	.52823	.53039	.53256	.53471	.53687	.53902	.54116	.54330	.54543
.7	.54756	.54969	.55181	.55393	.55604	.55814	.56025	.56235	.56444	.56653
.8	.56862	.57070	.57277	.57485	.57691	.57898	.58104	.58309	.58515	.58719
.9	.58924	.59127	.59331	.59534	.59737	.59939	.60141	.60342	.60543	.60744

ᵃ Add 1.0 to indicated figure.

Appendix B
Matrix Algebra

A. MATRICES AND VECTORS

A matrix is a rectangular array of numbers. The following are examples of matrices:

$$\underset{(3 \times 2)}{A} = \begin{pmatrix} 1 & 2 \\ 0 & 1 \\ -1 & 4 \end{pmatrix},$$

$$\underset{(3 \times 4)}{B} = \begin{pmatrix} 2 & 3 & 1.5 & 0 \\ -1 & 4 & -1 & -1 \\ 3 & 1.1 & 2 & -5 \end{pmatrix},$$

$$\underset{(2 \times 2)}{C} = \begin{pmatrix} 2 & 1 \\ 1 & -2 \end{pmatrix}.$$

The matrix A is a 3×2 matrix because it has three rows and two columns. The matrix B is a 3×4 matrix because it has three rows and four columns. The matrix C is a 2×2 square matrix because it has two rows and two columns.

Each number in a matrix is called an element. The element on the ith row and jth column of the matrix A is designated by a_{ij}. For example, in the matrix A above, $a_{11} = 1$, $a_{12} = 2$, $a_{21} = 0$, and so on. Similarly, in the matrix B, $b_{12} = 3$, $b_{32} = 1.1$.

We say that two $m \times n$ matrices are equal if all their corresponding elements are identical. In other words, if both R and S are $m \times n$ matrices, then $R = S$ if and only if $r_{ij} = s_{ij}$ for all $i = 1, 2, \ldots, m$ and $j = 1, 2, \ldots, n$. For example,

$$\begin{pmatrix} 1 & 2 \\ -1 & 1 \end{pmatrix} = \begin{pmatrix} 1 & 2 \\ -1 & 1 \end{pmatrix} \quad \text{but} \quad \begin{pmatrix} 1 & 1 \\ 0 & 1 \end{pmatrix} \neq \begin{pmatrix} 1 & 0 \\ 1 & 1 \end{pmatrix}.$$

Vectors are matrices with only one row or one column. A $1 \times m$ matrix is called a row vector, and a $m \times 1$ matrix is called a column vector. For example,

$$\underset{(1 \times 3)}{a} = (1 \quad -1 \quad 1), \qquad \underset{(1 \times 4)}{b} = (1 \quad 2 \quad 0 \quad 1)$$

861

are row vectors and

$$c_{(2 \times 1)} = \begin{pmatrix} 1 \\ -1 \end{pmatrix}, \qquad d_{(3 \times 1)} = \begin{pmatrix} 1 \\ 3 \\ 2 \end{pmatrix}$$

are column vectors. Each number in a vector is called a component of that vector. The ith component of the vector a is designated by a_i. So, $a_1 = 1$, $a_2 = -1$, $a_3 = 1$ in the vector a above.

Two $1 \times n$ row vectors or two $m \times 1$ column vectors are equal if all the corresponding components are the same. For example,

$$\begin{pmatrix} 1 \\ 2 \end{pmatrix} = \begin{pmatrix} 1 \\ 2 \end{pmatrix}, \qquad (3 \quad 1 \quad 2) = (3 \quad 1 \quad 2),$$

but

$$\begin{pmatrix} 1 \\ 2 \end{pmatrix} \neq (1 \quad 2), \qquad \begin{pmatrix} 1 \\ 2 \end{pmatrix} \neq \begin{pmatrix} 2 \\ 1 \end{pmatrix}, \qquad \begin{pmatrix} 1 \\ 2 \end{pmatrix} \neq \begin{pmatrix} 1 \\ 2 \\ 3 \end{pmatrix}.$$

B. THE OPERATIONS OF MATRICES

Addition and subtraction of two matrices A and B can be performed if A and B have the same dimension—i.e., if the number of rows and the number of columns are the same. Addition and subtraction is carried out on each corresponding pair of elements. If $A + B = C$, then $a_{ij} + b_{ij} = c_{ij}$. For example,

$$\begin{pmatrix} 1 & 2 \\ 3 & 4 \end{pmatrix} + \begin{pmatrix} -1 & 1 \\ 2 & -1 \end{pmatrix} = \begin{pmatrix} 1-1 & 2+1 \\ 3+2 & 4-1 \end{pmatrix} = \begin{pmatrix} 0 & 3 \\ 5 & 3 \end{pmatrix},$$

$$\begin{pmatrix} 1 & 2 \\ 3 & 4 \end{pmatrix} - \begin{pmatrix} -1 & 1 \\ 2 & -1 \end{pmatrix} = \begin{pmatrix} 1-(-1) & 2-1 \\ 3-2 & 4-(-1) \end{pmatrix} = \begin{pmatrix} 2 & 1 \\ 1 & 5 \end{pmatrix},$$

$$\begin{pmatrix} 1 \\ 2 \end{pmatrix} - \begin{pmatrix} 1 \\ 1 \end{pmatrix} = \begin{pmatrix} 0 \\ 1 \end{pmatrix}, \qquad \begin{pmatrix} 1 \\ 2 \end{pmatrix} + \begin{pmatrix} 1 \\ 1 \end{pmatrix} = \begin{pmatrix} 2 \\ 3 \end{pmatrix}.$$

If we multiply a matrix A by a scalar, the resultant matrix is obtained by multiplying each element of A by that scalar. So if

$$A = \begin{pmatrix} 1 & 2 & 3 \\ -1 & 1 & 2 \end{pmatrix},$$

then

$$2A = \begin{pmatrix} 2 & 4 & 6 \\ -2 & 2 & 4 \end{pmatrix}, \qquad -3A = \begin{pmatrix} -3 & -6 & -9 \\ 3 & -3 & -6 \end{pmatrix}.$$

We can also multiply two matrices together provided that the number of columns in the first matrix is equal to the number of rows in the second matrix. To form the product AB of the two matrices A and B, the number of columns of A must be equal to the number of rows of B. If we designate the result of the matrix multiplication AB by C, then C is again a matrix and C has the same number of rows as A and the same number of columns as B. To summarize: if A is an $m \times n$ matrix and B a $p \times q$ matrix, then the product AB can be formed only if $n = p$; further, if $C = AB$, then C is an $m \times q$ matrix.

To complete our definition of matrix multiplication, we have to describe how the elements of C are obtained. The following rule specifies c_{ij}, the element in the ith row and jth column of the resultant matrix C, in terms of elements in A and B:

$$c_{ij} = a_{i1}b_{1j} + a_{i2}b_{2j} + \cdots + a_{in}b_{nj} = \sum_{k=1}^{n} a_{ik}b_{kj}, \tag{B.1}$$

where n = number of columns of A = number of rows of B.

Equation (B.1) tells us that c_{ij} is a sum of products. Each product consists of an element from the ith row of A and an element from the jth column of B. We multiply the first element in the ith row of A with the first element in the jth column of B, the second element in the ith row of A with the second element in the jth column of B—and so on until the last element in the ith row of A is multiplied with the last element in the jth column of B—and then sum all the products. Another way to look at this is: to obtain c_{ij}, we "multiply" the ith row of A with the jth column of B.

An example further clarifies Eq. (B.1). Consider $C = AB$, where

$$A = \begin{pmatrix} 1 & 2 & 3 \\ 1 & 0 & 1 \end{pmatrix}, \qquad B = \begin{pmatrix} -1 & 3 & 0 & 0 \\ 2 & 1 & 1 & 0 \\ 1 & 0 & 0 & 1 \end{pmatrix}.$$

Since A is 2×3 and B is 3×4, the product AB can be formed and C would be 2×4. According to Eq. (B.1),

$$c_{11} = a_{11}b_{11} + a_{12}b_{21} + a_{13}b_{31} = 1 \times (-1) + 2 \times 2 + 3 \times 1 = 6,$$

$$c_{12} = a_{11}b_{12} + a_{12}b_{22} + a_{13}b_{32} = 1 \times 3 + 2 \times 1 + 3 \times 0 = 5,$$

and so on. The result $AB = C$ is

$$\begin{pmatrix} \boxed{1 \quad 2 \quad 3} \\ 1 \quad 0 \quad 1 \end{pmatrix} \begin{pmatrix} -1 & \boxed{3} & 0 & 0 \\ 2 & 1 & 1 & 0 \\ 1 & \boxed{0} & 0 & 1 \end{pmatrix} = \begin{pmatrix} 6 & \boxed{5} & 2 & 3 \\ 0 & 3 & 0 & 1 \end{pmatrix}.$$

We should emphasize at this point that the product BA may not be defined even though AB is. We can take the above as an example. A is 2×3 and B is 3×4, so AB is defined, but BA is not, since $4 \neq 2$. In the event that BA is also defined, $BA \neq AB$ in general. For example, let

$$A = \begin{pmatrix} 1 & 1 \\ 0 & 1 \end{pmatrix}, \qquad B = \begin{pmatrix} 1 & 0 \\ 1 & 1 \end{pmatrix},$$

then

$$AB = \begin{pmatrix} 2 & 1 \\ 1 & 1 \end{pmatrix} \text{ but } BA = \begin{pmatrix} 1 & 1 \\ 1 & 2 \end{pmatrix}.$$

C. LINEAR EQUATIONS IN MATRIX FORM

A system of linear equations can be expressed in matrix form. First, let us consider one simple linear equation, say $X_1 - 2X_2 + 2X_3 = 4$. Using matrix multiplication, the equation can be expressed as

$$(1 \quad -2 \quad 2) \begin{pmatrix} X_1 \\ X_2 \\ X_3 \end{pmatrix} = 1X_1 + (-2)X_2 + 2X_3 = 4.$$

Suppose we now have the following system of three equations:

$$X_1 - 2X_2 + 2X_3 = 4,$$
$$X_1 + X_2 + X_3 = 5,$$
$$-X_1 + 5X_2 - 3X_3 = 1.$$

Using matrix multiplication, this is equivalent to

$$\begin{pmatrix} 1 & -2 & 2 \\ 1 & 1 & 1 \\ -1 & 5 & -3 \end{pmatrix} \begin{pmatrix} X_1 \\ X_2 \\ X_3 \end{pmatrix} = \begin{pmatrix} 1 \cdot X_1 - 2 \cdot X_2 + 2 \cdot X_3 \\ 1 \cdot X_1 + 1 \cdot X_2 + 1 \cdot X_3 \\ -1 \cdot X_1 + 5 \cdot X_2 - 3 \cdot X_3 \end{pmatrix} = \begin{pmatrix} 4 \\ 5 \\ 1 \end{pmatrix}$$

$$\begin{matrix} 3 \times 3 & \quad 3 \times 1 & \quad\quad\quad\quad\quad\quad 3 \times 1 \end{matrix}$$

And because of the equality definition of vectors, we must equate $(1 \cdot X_1 - 2 \cdot X_2 + 2 \cdot X_3)$ to 4 and $(1 \cdot X_1 + 1 \cdot X_2 + 1 \cdot X_3)$ to 5 and $(-1 \cdot X_1 + 5 \cdot X_2 - 3 \cdot X_3)$ to 1, which shows that the matrix formulation

$$\begin{pmatrix} 1 & -2 & 2 \\ 1 & 1 & 1 \\ -1 & 5 & -3 \end{pmatrix} \begin{pmatrix} X_1 \\ X_2 \\ X_3 \end{pmatrix} = \begin{pmatrix} 4 \\ 5 \\ 1 \end{pmatrix} \tag{B.2}$$

is equivalent to the system of linear equations. In general, Eq. (B.2) is written as $Ax = b$, where

$$A = \begin{pmatrix} 1 & -2 & 2 \\ 1 & 1 & 1 \\ -1 & 5 & -3 \end{pmatrix}, \quad x = \begin{pmatrix} X_1 \\ X_2 \\ X_3 \end{pmatrix}, \quad b = \begin{pmatrix} 4 \\ 5 \\ 1 \end{pmatrix}.$$

A is called the coefficient matrix, x is the vector of unknowns, and b is the vector of constants. Finding the solution to a system of linear equations is equivalent to solving for the unknown vector x in the matrix equation $Ax = b$. We will come back to solving $Ax = b$ in a later section.

D. SPECIAL MATRICES

There are several types of matrices that possess useful properties. Here we list some of the more important ones.

The zero (or null) matrix is a matrix with all elements (or components) being zero. For example,

$$\begin{pmatrix} 0 & 0 \\ 0 & 0 \end{pmatrix}, \qquad \begin{pmatrix} 0 & 0 & 0 & 0 \\ 0 & 0 & 0 & 0 \\ 0 & 0 & 0 & 0 \end{pmatrix}$$

are null matrices of dimensions 2×2 and 3×4. The zero matrix $\mathbf{0}$ possesses the property that

$$A + \mathbf{0} = \mathbf{0} + A = A$$

for any matrix A of the same dimension.

A diagonal matrix is a square matrix whose elements are all zeros except on the *main diagonal*—i.e., D is a diagonal matrix if $d_{ij} = 0$ for $i \neq j$. For example,

$$\begin{pmatrix} 1 & 0 \\ 0 & 2 \end{pmatrix}, \qquad \begin{pmatrix} 1 & 0 & 0 \\ 0 & 3 & 0 \\ 0 & 0 & 4 \end{pmatrix}$$

are diagonal matrices. The elements $d_{11}, d_{22}, \ldots, d_{nn}$ are called elements on the main diagonal. Note that all diagonal matrices are square by definition.

The identity matrix, I, is a diagonal matrix that has ones on the main diagonal and zeros everywhere else. For example,

$$\begin{pmatrix} 1 & 0 \\ 0 & 1 \end{pmatrix}, \qquad \begin{pmatrix} 1 & 0 & 0 \\ 0 & 1 & 0 \\ 0 & 0 & 1 \end{pmatrix}, \qquad \begin{pmatrix} 1 & 0 & 0 & 0 \\ 0 & 1 & 0 & 0 \\ 0 & 0 & 1 & 0 \\ 0 & 0 & 0 & 1 \end{pmatrix}$$

are identity matrices of dimensions 2×2, 3×3, 4×4. The identity matrix has the useful property that

$$AI = A, \qquad IB = B$$

for all matrices A and B provided the matrix multiplication is defined; i.e., A and B must be of appropriate dimensions.

E. MATRIX INVERSION DEFINED

Now, given a square matrix A, there may exist a matrix B, such that

$$AB = BA = I.$$

If such matrix B exists, then A is said to be nonsingular and the matrix B is called the multiplicative *inverse* of A. We usually write B as A^{-1} to denote inverse. A^{-1}

plays a very significant role in solving the matrix equation $Ax = b$. If A^{-1} is known, we can premultiply both sides of the matrix equation by A^{-1} to get

$$A^{-1}Ax = A^{-1}b.$$

Since $A^{-1}A = I$, the equation becomes

$$Ix = A^{-1}b.$$

But $Ix = x$ where x is an $(m \times 1)$ matrix; therefore

$$x = A^{-1}b.$$

The system can now be solved for the unknown vector, x, by carrying out the matrix multiplication, $A^{-1}b$.

F. MATRIX TRANSPOSITION

Before we describe how to compute A^{-1} we must first define the transpose of a matrix. For a given matrix A, the transpose of A, denoted by A', is obtained from A by writing the columns of A as rows of A'. Formally, we have $a'_{ij} = a_{ji}$. For example, if

$$A = \begin{pmatrix} 1 & 2 & 3 \\ 3 & 2 & 1 \\ 4 & 3 & 2 \end{pmatrix}, \quad \text{then} \quad A' = \begin{pmatrix} 1 & 3 & 4 \\ 2 & 2 & 3 \\ 3 & 1 & 2 \end{pmatrix}$$

Finally, if $A = A'$, then we say that A is a symmetric matrix. For example,

$$A = \begin{pmatrix} 1 & -1 & 4 \\ -1 & 2 & 5 \\ 4 & 5 & 3 \end{pmatrix}$$

is a symmetric matrix. Notice that the entries of A are symmetric across the main diagonal; hence all diagonal matrices are symmetric.

The class of symmetric matrices is very important and arises very often in many real-life problems. The covariance matrix in portfolio theory is a symmetric matrix. Furthermore, algebraic systems involving symmetric matrices are in general easier to solve.

G. DETERMINANTS

Given $x = A^{-1}b$, and A, the first step in finding A^{-1} is to first determine if A is non-singular. To do that, we make use of the determinant function that is defined for all square matrices.

The determinant of a square matrix A, denoted by $|A|$, is a unique number associated with that matrix. For a 2×2 matrix

$$A = \begin{pmatrix} a_{11} & a_{12} \\ a_{21} & a_{22} \end{pmatrix}, \quad |A| = a_{11}a_{22} - a_{12}a_{21}.$$

For example,

$$\begin{vmatrix} 2 & 1 \\ 3 & 4 \end{vmatrix} = (2 \times 4) - (1 \times 3) = 8 - 3 = 5.$$

So the determinant of the matrix is 5.

The definition of a determinant of a 3×3 or higher-order square matrix involves the notion of minors and cofactors of elements of the matrix. The minor of a_{ij}, denoted by $|M_{ij}|$, is the determinant of the *submatrix* of A obtained by deleting the ith row and jth column of A. Suppose

$$A = \begin{pmatrix} a_{11} & a_{12} & a_{13} \\ a_{21} & a_{22} & a_{23} \\ a_{31} & a_{32} & a_{33} \end{pmatrix};$$

then

$$|M_{11}| = \begin{vmatrix} a_{11} & a_{12} & a_{13} \\ a_{21} & a_{22} & a_{23} \\ a_{31} & a_{32} & a_{33} \end{vmatrix} = \begin{vmatrix} a_{22} & a_{23} \\ a_{32} & a_{33} \end{vmatrix} = a_{22}a_{33} - a_{23}a_{32},$$

$$|M_{21}| = \begin{vmatrix} a_{11} & a_{12} & a_{13} \\ a_{21} & a_{22} & a_{23} \\ a_{31} & a_{32} & a_{33} \end{vmatrix} = \begin{vmatrix} a_{12} & a_{13} \\ a_{32} & a_{33} \end{vmatrix} = a_{12}a_{33} - a_{13}a_{32},$$

and so on. The cofactor of a_{ij}, denoted by $|C_{ij}|$, is equal to $(-1)^{i+j}|M_{ij}|$. That is why sometimes cofactors are called signed minors. Whenever $i + j$ is even, $|C_{ij}| = |M_{ij}|$, and whenever $i + j$ is odd, $|C_{ij}| = -|M_{ij}|$. Take the 3×3 matrix, A,

$$A = \begin{pmatrix} 1 & 2 & 1 \\ 3 & 0 & 4 \\ 0 & 1 & 5 \end{pmatrix}, \quad \text{then} \quad |M_{11}| = \begin{vmatrix} 0 & 4 \\ 1 & 5 \end{vmatrix} = -4,$$

$$|M_{12}| = \begin{vmatrix} 3 & 4 \\ 0 & 5 \end{vmatrix} = 15, \quad |M_{13}| = \begin{vmatrix} 3 & 0 \\ 0 & 1 \end{vmatrix} = 3.$$

The reader may check that $|M_{21}| = 9$, $|M_{22}| = 5$, $|M_{23}| = 1$, $|M_{31}| = 8$, $|M_{32}| = 1$, $|M_{33}| = -6$. Hence $|C_{11}| = -4$, $|C_{12}| = -15$, $|C_{13}| = 3$, $|C_{21}| = -9$, $|C_{22}| = 5$, $|C_{23}| = -1$, $|C_{31}| = 8$, $|C_{32}| = -1$, $|C_{33}| = -6$.

The determinant of a general $n \times n$ matrix can now be defined in terms of minors, which are themselves determinants of $(n - 1) \times (n - 1)$ matrices. The rule is

$$|A| = a_{i1}(-1)^{i+1}|M_{i1}| + a_{i2}(-1)^{i+2}|M_{i2}| + \cdots + a_{in}(-1)^{i+n}|M_{in}|$$

$$= \sum_{j=1}^{n} a_{ij}(-1)^{i+j}|M_{ij}|. \tag{B.3a}$$

The operation described is known as finding the determinant by expansion by the ith row of A. It is possible to expand by any row or column in A to find $|A|$; hence, expanding by the jth column, we have

$$|A| = a_{1j}(-1)^{1+j}|M_{1j}| + a_{2j}(-1)^{2+j}|M_{2j}| + \cdots + a_{nj}(-1)^{n+j}|M_{nj}|$$

$$= \sum_{i=1}^{n} a_{ij}(-1)^{i+j}|M_{ij}|. \tag{B.3b}$$

Although Eq. (B.3a) and Eq. (B.3b) may look rather complicated at first glance, they are in fact quite simple. Each term of the sum in Eq. (B.3a) simply consists of an element in the ith row and its cofactor (signed minor). An example will clarify this further. Let

$$A = \begin{pmatrix} 1 & 2 & 1 \\ 3 & 0 & 4 \\ 0 & 1 & 5 \end{pmatrix}.$$

From Eq. (B.3a), taking $i = 1$, and expanding by the ith row,

$$|A| = a_{11}(-1)^{1+1}|M_{11}| + a_{12}(-1)^{1+2}|M_{12}| + a_{13}(-1)^{1+3}|M_{13}|$$

$$= 1 \cdot (-1)^2 \cdot \begin{vmatrix} 0 & 4 \\ 1 & 5 \end{vmatrix} + 2(-1)^3 \begin{vmatrix} 3 & 4 \\ 0 & 5 \end{vmatrix} + 1 \cdot (-1)^4 \begin{vmatrix} 3 & 0 \\ 0 & 1 \end{vmatrix}$$

$$= -4 + (-30) + 3 = -31.$$

In the above example $|A|$ was evaluated through expansion by the first row. According to Eq. (B.3b), we can also evaluate $|A|$ through expansion of the jth column. Let us take $j = 2$,

$$|A| = a_{12}(-1)^{1+2}|M_{12}| + a_{22}(-1)^{2+2}|M_{22}| + a_{32}(-1)^{3+2}|M_{32}|$$

$$= 2(-1)^3 \begin{vmatrix} 3 & 4 \\ 0 & 5 \end{vmatrix} + 0 \cdot (-1)^4 \begin{vmatrix} 1 & 1 \\ 0 & 5 \end{vmatrix} + 1(-1)^5 \begin{vmatrix} 1 & 1 \\ 3 & 4 \end{vmatrix}$$

$$= -30 + 0 + (-1) = -31,$$

which agrees with our previous result.

A key observation regarding the definition of the determinant of an $n \times n$ matrix is that we can express it in terms of determinants of $(n-1) \times (n-1)$ matrices (the minors). As in the above example, we reduce the determinant of a 3×3 matrix into a sum of terms involving determinants of 2×2 matrices. Since we know how to evaluate 2×2 determinants, the problem is solved. Now to evaluate a 4×4 determinant, we must first use Eq. (B.3a) or Eq. (B.3b) to reduce it in terms of 3×3 determinants, then use Eq. (B.3a) or Eq. (B.3b) again to reduce each 3×3 determinant to a sum of 2×2 determinants and then evaluate. So the reduction goes on, and we can now evaluate determinants of any size.

A well-known theorem in matrix algebra states that a square matrix A is nonsingular if and only if $|A| \neq 0$. So the matrix in the previous example has a multiplicative inverse because $|A| = -31 \neq 0$.

H. THE INVERSE OF A SQUARE MATRIX

Given a nonsingular square matrix A, construct a new matrix B of the same dimension with $b_{ij} = |C_{ij}|$, the cofactor of a_{ij}. Then transpose B and call the resultant matrix the adjoint of A, "adj A." That is, adj $A = B'$. It can be shown that

$$(\text{adj } A)(A) = |A| \cdot I.$$

Since the nonsingularity of A implies $|A| \neq 0$, we can divide both sides by the scalar $|A|$:

$$\frac{1}{|A|}(\text{adj } A)(A) = I;$$

since $A^{-1}A = I$, it is immediately evident that $(1/|A|)(\text{adj } A) = A^{-1}$.

As an example take the 3×3 matrix A from the previous section. We have already computed the determinant as well as all the cofactors, so

$$B = \begin{pmatrix} C_{11} & C_{12} & C_{13} \\ C_{21} & C_{22} & C_{23} \\ C_{31} & C_{32} & C_{33} \end{pmatrix} = \begin{pmatrix} -4 & -15 & 3 \\ -9 & 5 & -1 \\ 8 & -1 & -6 \end{pmatrix},$$

$$\text{adj } A = B' = \begin{pmatrix} -4 & -9 & 8 \\ -15 & 5 & -1 \\ 3 & -1 & -6 \end{pmatrix}.$$

Since $|A| = -31$, the inverse of A is simply

$$A^{-1} = \frac{1}{|A|}\text{adj } A = \begin{pmatrix} \dfrac{4}{31} & \dfrac{9}{31} & \dfrac{-8}{31} \\ \dfrac{15}{31} & \dfrac{-5}{31} & \dfrac{1}{31} \\ \dfrac{-3}{31} & \dfrac{1}{31} & \dfrac{6}{31} \end{pmatrix}.$$

The curious reader may verify that $A^{-1}A = I = AA^{-1}$, or

$$\begin{pmatrix} \dfrac{4}{31} & \dfrac{9}{31} & \dfrac{-8}{31} \\ \dfrac{15}{31} & \dfrac{-5}{31} & \dfrac{1}{31} \\ \dfrac{-3}{31} & \dfrac{1}{31} & \dfrac{6}{31} \end{pmatrix} \begin{pmatrix} 1 & 2 & 1 \\ 3 & 0 & 4 \\ 0 & 1 & 5 \end{pmatrix} = \begin{pmatrix} 1 & 0 & 0 \\ 0 & 1 & 0 \\ 0 & 0 & 1 \end{pmatrix} = \begin{pmatrix} 1 & 2 & 1 \\ 3 & 0 & 4 \\ 0 & 1 & 5 \end{pmatrix} \begin{pmatrix} \dfrac{4}{31} & \dfrac{9}{31} & \dfrac{-8}{31} \\ \dfrac{15}{31} & \dfrac{-5}{31} & \dfrac{1}{31} \\ \dfrac{-3}{31} & \dfrac{1}{31} & \dfrac{6}{31} \end{pmatrix}.$$

I. SOLVING LINEAR EQUATION SYSTEMS

Now suppose we have a system of linear equations:

$$X_1 + 2X_2 + X_3 = 1,$$
$$3X_1 \quad\quad + 4X_3 = -1,$$
$$X_2 + 5X_3 = 2.$$

The matrix formulation would look like $Ax = b$, or

$$\begin{pmatrix} 1 & 2 & 1 \\ 3 & 0 & 4 \\ 0 & 1 & 5 \end{pmatrix} \begin{pmatrix} X_1 \\ X_2 \\ X_3 \end{pmatrix} = \begin{pmatrix} 1 \\ -1 \\ 2 \end{pmatrix}.$$

We know what A^{-1} is, and we know that the solution of the system is $x = A^{-1}b$; therefore

$$\begin{pmatrix} X_1 \\ X_2 \\ X_3 \end{pmatrix} = \underset{3 \times 3}{\begin{pmatrix} \dfrac{4}{31} & \dfrac{9}{31} & \dfrac{-8}{31} \\ \dfrac{15}{31} & \dfrac{-5}{31} & \dfrac{1}{31} \\ \dfrac{-3}{31} & \dfrac{1}{31} & \dfrac{6}{31} \end{pmatrix}} \underset{3 \times 1}{\begin{pmatrix} 1 \\ -1 \\ 2 \end{pmatrix}} = \underset{3 \times 1}{\begin{pmatrix} \dfrac{-21}{31} \\ \dfrac{22}{31} \\ \dfrac{8}{31} \end{pmatrix}},$$

or

$$X_1 = \frac{-21}{31}, \quad X_2 = \frac{22}{31}, \quad X_3 = \frac{8}{31}.$$

As a check on the solution, we insert the values into the original equation system:

$$\frac{-21}{31} + \frac{44}{31} + \frac{8}{31} = 1,$$

$$\frac{-63}{31} + 0 + \frac{32}{31} = -1,$$

$$0 + \frac{22}{31} + \frac{40}{31} = 2.$$

J. CRAMER'S RULE

A direct but not obvious corollary to our derivation of A^{-1} is Cramer's rule for the solution of a linear equation. The rule states that

$$X_i = \frac{|\hat{A}_i|}{|A|},$$

where $\hat{A}_i$ is the matrix obtained from A by replacing the ith column with the *constant vector*. Using the same example and applying Cramer's rule, we first substitute the constant vector for the first column in the numerator and then expand by the first row. Recall that the sign changes are the result of converting minors to cofactors.

$$X_1 = \frac{\begin{vmatrix} 1 & 2 & 1 \\ -1 & 0 & 4 \\ 2 & 1 & 5 \end{vmatrix}}{|A|} = \frac{1 \cdot \begin{vmatrix} 0 & 4 \\ 1 & 5 \end{vmatrix} - 2 \cdot \begin{vmatrix} -1 & 4 \\ 2 & 5 \end{vmatrix} + 1 \cdot \begin{vmatrix} -1 & 0 \\ 2 & 1 \end{vmatrix}}{-31}$$

$$= \frac{-4 + 26 - 1}{-31} = -\frac{21}{31}.$$

Next we replace the second column of the original numerator by the constant vector and again expand by the first row:

$$X_2 = \frac{\begin{vmatrix} 1 & 1 & 1 \\ 3 & -1 & 4 \\ 0 & 2 & 5 \end{vmatrix}}{-31} = \frac{1 \cdot \begin{vmatrix} -1 & 4 \\ 2 & 5 \end{vmatrix} - 1 \cdot \begin{vmatrix} 3 & 4 \\ 0 & 5 \end{vmatrix} + 1 \cdot \begin{vmatrix} 3 & -1 \\ 0 & 2 \end{vmatrix}}{-31}$$

$$= \frac{-13 - 15 + 6}{-31} = \frac{22}{31},$$

and again for the third column,

$$X_3 = \frac{\begin{vmatrix} 1 & 2 & 1 \\ 3 & 0 & -1 \\ 0 & 1 & 2 \end{vmatrix}}{-31} = \frac{1 \cdot \begin{vmatrix} 0 & -1 \\ 1 & 2 \end{vmatrix} - 2 \cdot \begin{vmatrix} 3 & -1 \\ 0 & 2 \end{vmatrix} + 1 \cdot \begin{vmatrix} 3 & 0 \\ 0 & 1 \end{vmatrix}}{-31}$$

$$= \frac{1 - 12 + 3}{-31} = \frac{8}{31}.$$

This agrees with the previous result. All the determinants above were evaluated by expanding by the first row.

K. APPLICATIONS

In this section we present two applications of matrix algebra in the theory of finance.

1. Minimum Variance Portfolio

Suppose we are considering investing in three securities: X_1, X_2, and X_3, and we want to form the portfolio that minimizes the variance of return. Let $\sigma_1^2, \sigma_2^2, \sigma_3^2$ be individual variances of return, and x_1, x_2, x_3 be weights of investment in the portfolio of securities X_1, X_2, X_3, respectively. So $x_1 + x_2 + x_3 = 1$. Furthermore, let

$\sigma_{12} = \sigma_{21}$ be the covariance of return between X_1 and X_2, $\sigma_{13} = \sigma_{31}$ the covariance of return between X_1 and X_3, $\sigma_{23} = \sigma_{32}$ the covariance of return between X_2 and X_3. Constructing the covariance matrix A we wish to solve for the weight vector X that will minimize the variance. Let

$$
\underset{(3 \times 3)}{A} = \begin{pmatrix} \sigma_1^2 & \sigma_{12} & \sigma_{13} \\ \sigma_{21} & \sigma_2^2 & \sigma_{23} \\ \sigma_{31} & \sigma_{32} & \sigma_3^2 \end{pmatrix}, \qquad \underset{(3 \times 1)}{X} = \begin{pmatrix} x_1 \\ x_2 \\ x_3 \end{pmatrix}.
$$

The variance of the portfolio with x_1 of X_1, x_2 of X_2, x_3 of X_3 can be expressed in matrix form as $\sigma_p^2 = X'AX$. To minimize the variance of the portfolio is equivalent to minimizing σ_p^2 subject to the weight constraint $x_1 + x_2 + x_3 = 1$. This constrained optimization problem can be solved by the method of the Lagrange multiplier.[1] Let

$$
\begin{aligned}
g(x_1, x_2, x_3, \lambda') &= \sigma_p^2 + \lambda'(1 - x_1 - x_2 - x_3) \\
&= X'AX + \lambda'(1 - x_1 - x_2 - x_3),
\end{aligned}
$$

where $X'AX$ is the variance-covariance matrix of the portfolio and $(1 - x_1 - x_2 - x_3)$ is the implicit expression of the constraint that requires that the sum of the weights equal one. Then the first-order conditions for an extremum are attained by setting all the partial derivatives of g equal to zero:

$$
\frac{\partial g}{\partial x_1} = 0, \tag{B.4a}
$$

$$
\frac{\partial g}{\partial x_2} = 0, \tag{B.4b}
$$

$$
\frac{\partial g}{\partial x_3} = 0, \tag{B.4c}
$$

$$
\frac{\partial g}{\partial \lambda'} = 0. \tag{B.4d}
$$

The Eqs. (B.4a), (B.4b), and (B.4c) in matrix notation can be expressed as

$$
AX = \lambda e, \quad \text{where} \quad e = \begin{pmatrix} 1 \\ 1 \\ 1 \end{pmatrix} \quad \text{and} \quad \lambda = \lambda'/2, \tag{B.5}
$$

and (B.4d) is simply the reiteration of the constraint $x_1 + x_2 + x_3 = 1$. The solution to the matrix Eq. (B.5) will give us the answer in terms of λ, and the constraint condition will give us the value of λ, hence the complete solution.

---

[1] Readers unfamiliar with the method of solving constrained optimization problems using Lagrange multipliers should consult Appendix D.

As a numerical example, take

$$A = \begin{pmatrix} 2 & -1 & 0 \\ -1 & 2 & -1 \\ 0 & -1 & 2 \end{pmatrix}$$

as the covariance matrix for securities X_1, X_2, X_3. Then (B.5) becomes

$$\begin{pmatrix} 2 & -1 & 0 \\ -1 & 2 & -1 \\ 0 & -1 & 2 \end{pmatrix} \begin{pmatrix} X_1 \\ X_2 \\ X_3 \end{pmatrix} = \lambda \begin{pmatrix} 1 \\ 1 \\ 1 \end{pmatrix} = \begin{pmatrix} \lambda \\ \lambda \\ \lambda \end{pmatrix}.$$

Using Cramer's rule, substituting the λ vector for the first column, and expanding both numerator and denominator by the first column, we have

$$X_1 = \frac{\lambda \begin{vmatrix} 2 & -1 \\ -1 & 2 \end{vmatrix} - \lambda \begin{vmatrix} -1 & 0 \\ -1 & 2 \end{vmatrix} + \lambda \begin{vmatrix} -1 & 0 \\ 2 & -1 \end{vmatrix}}{2 \begin{vmatrix} 2 & -1 \\ -1 & 2 \end{vmatrix} + 1 \begin{vmatrix} -1 & 0 \\ -1 & 2 \end{vmatrix} + 0} = \frac{3\lambda + 2\lambda + \lambda}{6 - 2} = \frac{6\lambda}{4} = \frac{3}{2}\lambda.$$

Then substituting the vector λ in column 2 and expanding by column 1,

$$X_2 = \frac{2 \begin{vmatrix} \lambda & -1 \\ \lambda & 2 \end{vmatrix} + 1 \begin{vmatrix} \lambda & 0 \\ \lambda & 2 \end{vmatrix} + 0}{4} = \frac{6\lambda + 2\lambda}{4} = \frac{8\lambda}{4} = 2\lambda.$$

And finally substituting the vector λ in column 3,

$$X_3 = \frac{2 \begin{vmatrix} 2 & \lambda \\ -1 & \lambda \end{vmatrix} + 1 \begin{vmatrix} -1 & \lambda \\ -1 & \lambda \end{vmatrix} + 0}{4} = \frac{6\lambda + 0}{4} = \frac{6\lambda}{4} = \frac{3}{2}\lambda.$$

Since $1 = x_1 + x_2 + x_3 = \frac{3}{2}\lambda + 2\lambda + \frac{3}{2}\lambda = 5\lambda$, we have $\lambda = \frac{1}{5}$. Hence $x_1 = \frac{3}{10}$, $x_2 = \frac{2}{5}$, $x_3 = \frac{3}{10}$. In other words, if you have \$1000 to invest, you should put \$300 in X_1, \$400 in X_2, and \$300 in X_3 to form the minimum variance portfolio. Note that we have not actually established that this is the minimum variance portfolio. We have merely determined an extreme point that may be either a maximum or a minimum. To guarantee that this is the minimum variance portfolio, we would need to examine the second-order conditions. (For a discussion, see Appendix D.)

2. Linear Regression

Very often, when we consider a security, we like to know how its return varies as the market fluctuates. Suppose we have the data in Table B.1. Can we discern any pattern or simple relation between the return on security A and the market? First,

Table B.1

	Return (in %)					
Security A	9	9.5	10.5	10.5	11	12
Market	8	9	10	11	12	13
STATE	1	2	3	4	5	6

we put the data on a graph:

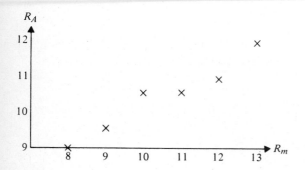

We can see that an approximately linear pattern exists. The following question naturally arises: What is the equation of the straight line that "best" fits the data points? In mathematical terms, this is equivalent to finding the values of two constants a and b such that whenever the return on the market is given, then the expression $[a + b \times \text{(return on market)}]$ will give the "best overall" predictive value of the return on security A. In symbols, let X_i, $i = 1, 2, 3, 4, 5, 6$, be the returns on the market given the various states of the world; let Y_i be the returns on security A; and let $\hat{Y}_i = a + bX_i$, the predicted return on security A using the best-fitting straight line. We call $e_i = Y_i - \hat{Y}_i$, which is the difference between the observed value and the predicted value of return on security A, the error term. These error terms can be positive or negative. To find the best-fitting straight line is equivalent to minimizing the magnitude of the error terms in a certain sense. The technique of minimizing the sum of the square of the error terms is called linear regression. In our example above with six different states, we have six error terms. Let

$$g(a, b) = \sum_{i=1}^{6} e_i^2 = \sum_{i=1}^{6} (Y_i - \hat{Y}_i)^2 = \sum_{i=1}^{6} (Y_i - a - bX_i)^2$$

be the sum of the squares of the error terms. The first-order conditions for minimizing $g(a, b)$ are

$$\frac{\partial g}{\partial a} = 0, \tag{B.6a}$$

$$\frac{\partial g}{\partial b} = 0. \tag{B.6b}$$

Equations (B.6a) and (B.6b) written in matrix form turn out to be

$$
\begin{pmatrix} 1 & 1 & 1 & 1 & 1 & 1 \\ X_1 & X_2 & X_3 & X_4 & X_5 & X_6 \end{pmatrix}
\begin{pmatrix} 1 & X_1 \\ 1 & X_2 \\ 1 & X_3 \\ 1 & X_4 \\ 1 & X_5 \\ 1 & X_6 \end{pmatrix}
\begin{pmatrix} a \\ b \end{pmatrix} =
\begin{pmatrix} 1 & 1 & 1 & 1 & 1 & 1 \\ X_1 & X_2 & X_3 & X_4 & X_5 & X_6 \end{pmatrix}
\begin{pmatrix} Y_1 \\ Y_2 \\ Y_3 \\ Y_4 \\ Y_5 \\ Y_6 \end{pmatrix}.
$$

Performing matrix multiplication, explained above, we get

$$
\begin{pmatrix} 6 & \sum_{i=1}^{6} X_i \\ \sum_{i=1}^{6} X_i & \sum_{i=1}^{6} X_i^2 \end{pmatrix}
\begin{pmatrix} a \\ b \end{pmatrix} =
\begin{pmatrix} \sum_{i=1}^{6} Y_i \\ \sum_{i=1}^{6} X_i Y_i \end{pmatrix}.
$$

This is equivalent to two equations and two unknowns (a and b). As a numerical example, let us take the data from Table B.1:

$$
\sum_{i=1}^{6} X_i = 8 + 9 + 10 + 11 + 12 + 13 = 63,
$$

$$
\sum_{i=1}^{6} X_i^2 = 8^2 + 9^2 + 10^2 + 11^2 + 12^2 + 13^2 = 679,
$$

$$
\sum_{i=1}^{6} Y_i = 9 + 9.5 + 10.5 + 10.5 + 11 + 12 = 62.5,
$$

$$
\sum_{i=1}^{6} X_i Y_i = 8 \times 9 + 9 \times 9.5 + 10 \times 10.5 + 11 \times 10.5 + 12 \times 11 + 13 \times 12 = 666,
$$

so

$$
\begin{pmatrix} 6 & 63 \\ 63 & 679 \end{pmatrix}
\begin{pmatrix} a \\ b \end{pmatrix} =
\begin{pmatrix} 62.5 \\ 666 \end{pmatrix}.
$$

By Cramer's rule, we have

$$
a = \frac{\begin{vmatrix} 62.5 & 63 \\ 666 & 679 \end{vmatrix}}{\begin{vmatrix} 6 & 63 \\ 63 & 679 \end{vmatrix}} = \frac{479.5}{105} = 4.57,
$$

$$
b = \frac{\begin{vmatrix} 6 & 62.5 \\ 63 & 666 \end{vmatrix}}{\begin{vmatrix} 6 & 63 \\ 63 & 679 \end{vmatrix}} = \frac{58.5}{105} = 0.56.
$$

Therefore the equation of the best-fitting straight line is $Y = 4.57 + 0.56X$. Note that b is the slope of the straight line. Both the sign and the magnitude of b contain important information. If b is positive, we would expect that the return on security A moves with the market, whereas a negative b implies that returns on security A and the market generally move in opposite directions. The magnitude of b measures the degree of volatility of security A. The larger the magnitude of b, the more volatile the return on security A.

Appendix C   An Introduction to Multiple Regression

Business students are frequently confronted with journal articles that are riddled with econometrics. On the other hand, econometrics courses assume prior knowledge of matrix algebra and calculus and therefore present a formidable barrier to the curious. This appendix is written to provide an overview of multiple regression techniques that assumes only the rudimentary knowledge of calculus and matrix algebra provided in the other appendixes. While not a substitute for a good econometrics course, this appendix enables the reader to understand and interpret the computer output from a typical multiple regression software package and to have an introductory level of understanding of some of the typical errors made in econometric studies.

A. ORDINARY LEAST SQUARES LINEAR ESTIMATION

If we are trying to explain the distribution of sales revenue for the XYZ Company given a forecast of gross national product, we might choose a linear model like

$$\tilde{Y}_t = a + bX_t + \tilde{\varepsilon}_t, \tag{C.1}$$

where

$\tilde{Y}_t$ = sales revenue in year t,

X_t = forecast of gross national product for year t,

$\tilde{\varepsilon}_t$ = error term (the difference between actual sales revenue and that predicted by the model).

Linear relationships have the virtue that they are simple and robust. Many natural phenomena are not linearly related, but linear approximations usually work very well within a limited range.

The object is to find the set of weights (a and b) in Eq. (C.1) that provide the best unbiased estimate of revenue given GNP. If GNP has any explanatory power

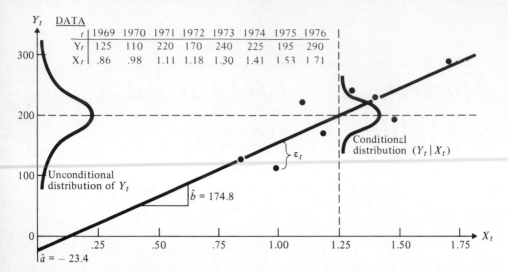

Figure C.1
Revenues vs. forecast GNP.

the conditional distribution of revenues, $\tilde{Y}_t | X_t$, will be different from their unconditional distribution. This is illustrated in Fig. C.1. The mean and standard deviation of the unconditional distribution of Y_t are $196.9 and $60.1. The unconditional probability distribution of revenues is plotted along the y-axis. The conditional distribution of $Y_t | X_t$ is the distribution of error terms, ε_t. For example, given that $X_t = $1.26 (its mean) then the estimated revenue is $196.9 (its mean) and the standard deviation of the estimate is $33.73. Notice that the conditional distribution has lower variance than the unconditional distribution. This is because knowledge of predicted GNP allows us to refine our estimate of sales revenue.

To obtain the best linear model to predict Y_t given X_t, we want to find the equation that minimizes the squared error terms. The error term is the difference between the actual revenue and the revenue predicted by the linear model. If we minimize the squared error terms, we are in effect minimizing the variance of the conditional distribution. To see how this is accomplished rewrite Eq. (C.1) as follows:

$$\varepsilon_t = Y_t - a - bX_t.$$

The variance of the error terms is[1]

$$\sigma_\varepsilon^2 = E[(Y_t - a - bX_t) - (\bar{Y} - a - b\bar{X})]^2, \tag{C.2}$$

$$\sigma_\varepsilon^2 = E[(Y_t - \bar{Y}) - b(X_t - \bar{X})]^2,$$

$$\sigma_\varepsilon^2 = \sigma_Y^2 - 2b\,\text{COV}(Y, X) + b^2\sigma_X^2.$$

We want to choose the slope, b, and the intercept, a, that minimize the squared error terms. To do this, take the derivative of σ_ε^2 with respect to b and set the result

---

[1] This result follows from the properties of random variables discussed in Chapter 6.

equal to zero:

$$\frac{d\sigma_\varepsilon^2}{db} = -2\,\text{COV}(Y, X) + 2b\sigma_X^2 = 0.$$

Solving for $\hat{b}$, the estimated slope term, we have

$$\hat{b} = \frac{\text{COV}(Y, X)}{\sigma_X^2}. \tag{C.3}$$

The intercept is determined by the fact that the line must pass through the mean values for both $\bar{Y}$ and $\bar{X}$. At that point, we have

$$\bar{Y} = \hat{a} + \hat{b}\bar{X}.$$

Therefore, solving for $\hat{a}$, we have

$$\hat{a} = \bar{Y} - \hat{b}\bar{X}.$$

The estimated slope and intercept terms are computed in Table C.1.

Having obtained estimates of the slope and intercept that minimize the squared error terms, we now have the following linear equation

$$\hat{Y}_t = -23.42 + 174.84X_t.$$

It can be used to predict sales revenue when given a forecast of GNP. The difference between predicted revenue and actual revenue in any given year is the error of estimate, often called the residual:

$$\varepsilon_t = Y_t - \hat{Y}_t.$$

Note that in Table C.1 the average error term $\bar{\varepsilon}_t$ (except for rounding error in the calculations) is zero. This implies that the linear estimate is unbiased. In other words, on average, there is no error of estimate.

In linear regression the residual errors indicate the extent of movement in the dependent variable (the variable on the left-hand side of the regression equation) that is not explained by the independent variable(s)—(the variable(s) on the right-hand side). If the residuals are small relative to the total movement in the dependent variable, then it follows that a major part of the movement has been explained. We define the summary statistic known as the squared multiple correlation coefficient, r^2, as the percentage of the total variation in the dependent variable that is explained by the regression equation. The square of the correlation coefficient is

$$r^2 = \frac{\text{Variation explained by the regression equation}}{\text{Total variation of the dependent variable}}$$

$$= \frac{\sum (Y - \bar{Y})^2 - \sum (\varepsilon - \bar{\varepsilon})^2}{\sum (Y - \bar{Y})^2}.$$

Note that $\sum (Y - \bar{Y})^2$ is the variance of the dependent variable, σ_Y^2, in our example. Note also that $\sum (\varepsilon - \bar{\varepsilon})^2$ is the variance of the residuals. Furthermore, the average

Table C.1   Simple Regression Computations

t	Y	Y − Ȳ	(Y − Ȳ)²	X	X − X̄	(X − X̄)²	(Y − Ȳ)(X − X̄)	ε = Ŷ − Y	ε²
1969	125	−71.875	5,166.01	.86	−.40	.1600	28.750	−1.94	3.7636
1970	110	−86.875	7,547.27	.98	−.28	.0784	24.325	−37.92	1437.9264
1971	220	23.125	534.76	1.11	−.15	.0225	−3.469	49.35	2435.4225
1972	170	−26.875	722.27	1.18	−.08	.0064	2.150	−12.89	166.1521
1973	240	43.125	1,859.76	1.30	.04	.0016	1.725	36.13	1305.3769
1974	225	28.125	791.02	1.41	.15	.0225	4.219	1.90	3.6100
1975	195	−1.875	3.52	1.53	.27	.0729	−.506	−49.09	2409.8281
1976	290	93.125	8,672.27	1.71	.45	.2025	41.906	14.44	208.5136
Sum	1575		25,296.89	10.08		.5668	99.100	−.02 ≈ 0	7970.5932

$$\bar{Y} = \frac{\sum Y}{N} = \frac{1575}{8} = 196.875$$

$$\sigma_Y^2 = \frac{\sum (Y - \bar{Y})^2}{N - 1} = \frac{25,296.89}{7} = 3613.84$$

$$\sigma_Y = \sqrt{\sigma_Y^2} = \sqrt{3613.84} = 60.12$$

$$COV(Y, X) = \frac{\sum (Y - \bar{Y})(X - \bar{X})}{N - 1} = \frac{99.10}{7} = 14.16$$

$$\hat{b} = \frac{COV(Y, X)}{\sigma_x^2} = \frac{14.16}{.0809714} = 174.88$$

$$\hat{a} = \bar{Y} - \hat{b}\bar{X} = 196.876 - 174.84(1.26) = -23.42$$

$$\bar{X} = \frac{\sum X}{N} = \frac{10.08}{8} = 1.26$$

$$\sigma_x^2 = \frac{\sum (X - \bar{X})^2}{N - 1} = \frac{.5668}{7} = .0809714$$

$$\sigma_x = \sqrt{\sigma_x^2} = .2846$$

Symbol Definitions:

$\bar{Y}, \bar{X}$ = the means of revenue and GNP, respectively,

N = the number of observations in the sample,

σ_Y^2, σ_x^2 = the variances of revenue and GNP, respectively,

$COV(Y, X)$ = the covariance between revenue and GNP,

$\hat{a}, \hat{b}$ = the intercept and slope estimates,

ε = the error term.

error term, $\bar{\varepsilon}$, is always zero; therefore we can rewrite the squared correlation coefficient as[2]

$$r^2 = \frac{\sum (Y - \bar{Y})^2 - \sum \varepsilon^2}{\sum (Y - \bar{Y})^2}. \tag{C.5}$$

Using the numbers from Table C.1,

$$r^2 = \frac{25{,}296.89 - 7970.5932}{25{,}296.89} = .6849.$$

This means that about 68.5% of the variance in the dependent variable, sales revenue, is explained by the independent variable, GNP. If all the variance were explained, then the sum of the squared residuals, $\sum \varepsilon^2$, would be zero and we would have $r^2 = 1$. At the opposite extreme the equation would not reduce the variance of the dependent variable at all, in which case we would have $r^2 = 0$.

B. SIMPLE HYPOTHESIS TESTING OF THE LINEAR REGRESSION ESTIMATES

Now that we know how to estimate the slope and the intercept, the next logical question is whether or not we can reject the null hypothesis that they are equal to

---

[2] An important relationship, which is used in Chapter 6, is that

$$r = \frac{\text{COV}(Y, X)}{\sigma_Y \sigma_X}.$$

Proof follows from the definition of r^2, of σ_ε^2, and of b. First, rewrite r^2 and the definition of b

$$r^2 = \frac{\sigma_Y^2 - \sigma_\varepsilon^2}{\sigma_Y^2}, \qquad b = \frac{\text{COV}(Y, X)}{\sigma_X^2}.$$

From Eq. (C.2), we have

$$\sigma_\varepsilon^2 = \sigma_y^2 - 2b\,\text{COV}(Y, X) + b^2 \sigma_x^2.$$

Substituting in the value of b, we have

$$\sigma_\varepsilon^2 = \sigma_y^2 - 2\left(\frac{\text{COV}(Y, X)}{\sigma_x^2}\right)\text{COV}(Y, X) + \left(\frac{\text{COV}(Y, X)}{\sigma_x^2}\right)^2 \sigma_x^2$$

$$= \sigma_y^2 - \frac{[\text{COV}(Y, X)]^2}{\sigma_x^2}.$$

Substituting this result into the definition of r^2 gives

$$r^2 = \frac{\sigma_y^2 - \sigma_y^2 + \dfrac{[\text{COV}(Y, X)]^2}{\sigma_x^2}}{\sigma_y^2}$$

$$= \frac{[\text{COV}(Y, X)]^2}{\sigma_x^2 \sigma_y^2}.$$

Therefore, taking the square root,

$$r = \frac{\text{COV}(Y, X)}{\sigma_x \sigma_y}. \qquad \text{QED}$$

zero. To do this we can calculate t-statistics in order to test the significance of the slope and intercept terms.

The t-statistics are defined as the estimates of the intercept, $\hat{a}$, or the slope, $\hat{b}$, divided by their respective standard errors of estimate:[3]

$$t_a = \frac{\hat{a}}{se(\hat{a})}, \qquad t_b = \frac{\hat{b}}{se(\hat{b})}. \tag{C.6}$$

We shall assume that the independent variable, X, can be treated as a constant in repeated samplings. In fact, this is where regression analysis derives its name. We say that Y is regressed on X. We also assume that the error terms are generated by random selection from a stationary statistical distribution with a mean of zero and a constant variance, σ_ε^2. Also, the error terms in successive samplings are independent. This specification of the error-generating process may be stated as

$$E(\varepsilon) = 0, \tag{C.7}$$

$$\text{VAR}(\varepsilon) = E[\varepsilon - E(\varepsilon)]^2 = E(\varepsilon)^2 = \sigma_\varepsilon^2, \tag{C.8}$$

$$\text{COV}(\varepsilon_t, \varepsilon_{t-1}) = 0. \tag{C.9}$$

To determine the standard error of estimate for $\hat{b}$, recall the definition given in Eq. (C.3):

$$\hat{b} = \frac{\text{COV}(Y, X)}{\sigma_X^2}. \tag{C.3}$$

We also know that the observed values of Y are

$$Y = a + bX + \varepsilon.$$

Rewriting Eq. (C.3), using the definitions of $\text{COV}(Y, X)$ and σ_X^2, we have

$$b = \frac{\sum [(X - \bar{X})(Y - \bar{Y})]}{\sum [(X - \bar{X})(X - \bar{X})]}.$$

Substituting in Y yields

$$\begin{aligned}
\hat{b} &= \frac{\sum [(X - \bar{X})(a + bX + \varepsilon - \bar{a} - \bar{b}X)]}{\sum [(X - \bar{X})(X - \bar{X})]} \\
&= \frac{\sum [(X - \bar{X})(Y - \bar{Y}) + (X - \bar{X})\varepsilon]}{\sum [(X - \bar{X})(X - \bar{X})]} \\
&= \frac{\sum [(X - \bar{X})(Y - \bar{Y})]}{\sum [(X - \bar{X})(X - \bar{X})]} + \frac{\sum [(X - \bar{X})\varepsilon]}{\sum [(X - \bar{X})(X - \bar{X})]} \\
&= b + \frac{\sum [(X - \bar{X})\varepsilon]}{\sum [(X - \bar{X})^2]}. \tag{C.10}
\end{aligned}$$

---

[3] A good reference to the t-distribution is Hoel [1954, 274–283].

Equation (C.10) tells us that the estimated slope, $\hat{b}$, is equal to the true slope, b, plus a term that depends on the variance of X (in the denominator) and the error terms (in the numerator). The expected value of $\hat{b}$ is

$$E(\hat{b}) = b, \quad \text{since} \quad E(\varepsilon) = 0. \tag{C.11}$$

Note that the expected value of the slope is equal to the true slope. Therefore we can say that the slope estimate is unbiased. The variance of $\hat{b}$ is

$$\mathrm{VAR}(\hat{b}) = E[\hat{b} - E(\hat{b})]^2$$

$$= E\left[b + \frac{\sum [(X_i - \bar{X})\varepsilon_i]}{\sum (X_i - \bar{X})^2} - b \right]^2$$

$$= E\left[\frac{\sum [(X_i - \bar{X})\varepsilon_i]}{\sum (X_i - \bar{X})^2} \right]^2,$$

and since X is assumed to be a constant, we have

$$\mathrm{VAR}(\hat{b}) = \left[\frac{1}{\sum (X_i - \bar{X})^2} \right]^2 E[\sum (X_i - \bar{X})\varepsilon_i]^2.$$

Expanding the second term yields

$$E[\sum (X_i - \bar{X})\varepsilon_i]^2 = E[(X_1 - \bar{X})^2\varepsilon_1^2 + (X_2 - \bar{X})^2\varepsilon_2^2 + \cdots$$

$$+ 2(X_1 - \bar{X})(X_2 - \bar{X})\varepsilon_1\varepsilon_2 + \cdots]$$

$$= (X_1 - \bar{X})^2 E(\varepsilon_1^2) + (X_2 - \bar{X})^2 E(\varepsilon_2^2) + \cdots$$

$$+ 2(X_1 - \bar{X})(X_2 - \bar{X})E(\varepsilon_1\varepsilon_2) + \cdots.$$

Using Eqs. (C.8) and (C.9), the above result can be reduced to

$$E[\sum (X_i - \bar{X})\varepsilon_i]^2 = [\sum (X_i - \bar{X})^2]\sigma_\varepsilon^2.$$

This means that the variance of the estimate of b can be written as

$$\mathrm{VAR}(\hat{b}) = \frac{\sum (X - \bar{X})^2}{[\sum (X - \bar{X})^2]^2} \sigma_\varepsilon^2$$

$$= \frac{\sigma_\varepsilon^2}{\sum (X - \bar{X})^2}. \tag{C.12}$$

We now have the result that the slope estimate, $\hat{b}$, is distributed normally with a mean of b and a variance of $\sigma_\varepsilon^2/\sigma_X^2$. The variance of the estimate of b provides a measure of the precision of the estimate. The larger the variance of the estimate, the more widespread the distribution and the smaller the precision of the estimate.

A similar derivation would show that the intercept estimate, $\hat{a}$, is also normally distributed with a mean of

$$E(\hat{a}) = a \tag{C.13}$$

and a variance of

$$\text{VAR}(\hat{a}) = \frac{(\sum X^2)/\sigma_\varepsilon^2}{N \sum (X - \bar{X})^2}, \qquad se(\hat{a}) = \sqrt{\text{VAR}(\hat{a})}, \tag{C.14}$$

where N is the number of observations in the sample.

Using Eqs. (C.12) and (C.14) for the sample problem of Table C.1, and given that the t-statistics defined in Eq. (C.6) have $N - m$ degrees of freedom (where $N = 8 =$ the number of observations and $m = 2 =$ the number of independent variables including the constant term), we can compute the appropriate significance tests for the slope and intercept. The standard error for the slope term is

$$se(\hat{b}) = \sqrt{\frac{\sigma_\varepsilon^2}{\sum (X - \bar{X})^2}} = \sqrt{\frac{7970.5932/(8 - 2)}{.5668}} = 48.41,$$

and the t-statistic for b is

$$t(\hat{b}) = \frac{\hat{b}}{se(\hat{b})} = \frac{174.84}{48.41} = 3.61.$$

We refer to the table of t-statistics (Table C.2) for $8 - 2 = 6$ degrees of freedom and a 95% confidence interval (in a two-tail t-test). That table shows that the t-statistic must be greater than 2.447 in order to reject the null hypothesis that the slope coefficient is not significantly different from zero. It is. Therefore we can say that predicted GNP, the independent variable, is a significant explanatory variable for sales revenue, given our sample data.

Next, compute the t-test to determine whether or not the intercept estimate, $\hat{a}$, is significantly different from zero. The standard error of $\hat{a}$ is

$$se(\hat{a}) = \left[\frac{(\sum X^2)\sigma_\varepsilon^2}{N \sum (X - \bar{X})^2} \right]^{1/2}$$

$$= \left[\frac{(13.2676)(7970.5932/6)}{8(.5668)} \right]^{1/2} = 62.35$$

and the t-statistic is

$$t(\hat{a}) = \frac{\hat{a}}{se(\hat{a})} = \frac{-23.42}{62.35} = -.375.$$

The t-statistic for $\hat{a}$ is less than 2.447, the required level for significance. Therefore we cannot conclude that the intercept term is significantly different from zero.

Summarizing, up to this point we can write the results of the regression analysis as follows:

$$Y_t = -23.42 + 174.84X_t \qquad r^2 = .6849$$
$$(-.38) \qquad (3.61) \qquad df = 6.$$

The numbers in parentheses are the appropriate t-statistics, and df designates the degrees of freedom.

Table C.2   Student's t Distribution

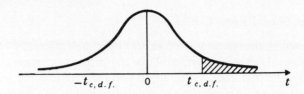

Degrees of Freedom	Probability of a Value Greater in Value than the Table Entry					
	0.005	*0.01*	*0.025*	*0.05*	*0.1*	*0.15*
1	63.657	31.821	12.706	6.314	3.078	1.963
2	9.925	6.965	4.303	2.920	1.886	1.386
3	5.841	4.541	3.182	2.353	1.638	1.250
4	4.604	3.747	2.776	2.132	1.533	1.190
5	4.032	3.365	2.571	2.015	1.476	1.156
6	3.707	3.143	2.447	1.943	1.440	1.134
7	3.499	2.998	2.365	1.895	1.415	1.119
8	3.355	2.896	2.306	1.860	1.397	1.108
9	3.250	2.821	2.262	1.833	1.383	1.100
10	3.169	2.764	2.228	1.812	1.372	1.093
11	3.106	2.718	2.201	1.796	1.363	1.088
12	3.055	2.681	2.179	1.782	1.356	1.083
13	3.012	2.650	2.160	1.771	1.350	1.079
14	2.977	2.624	2.145	1.761	1.345	1.076
15	2.947	2.602	2.131	1.753	1.341	1.074
16	2.921	2.583	2.120	1.746	1.337	1.071
17	2.898	2.567	2.110	1.740	1.333	1.069
18	2.878	2.552	2.101	1.734	1.330	1.067
19	2.861	2.539	2.093	1.729	1.328	1.066
20	2.845	2.528	2.086	1.725	1.325	1.064
21	2.831	2.518	2.080	1.721	1.323	1.063
22	2.819	2.508	2.074	1.717	1.321	1.061
23	2.807	2.500	2.069	1.714	1.319	1.060
24	2.797	2.492	2.064	1.711	1.318	1.059
25	2.787	2.485	2.060	1.708	1.316	1.058
26	2.779	2.479	2.056	1.706	1.315	1.058
27	2.771	2.473	2.052	1.703	1.314	1.057
28	2.763	2.467	2.048	1.701	1.313	1.056
29	2.756	2.462	2.045	1.699	1.311	1.055
30	2.750	2.457	2.042	1.697	1.310	1.055
∞	2.576	2.326	1.960	1.645	1.282	1.036

C. BIAS AND EFFICIENCY

1. The Mean Square Error Criterion

The researcher is always interested in the bias and efficiency of the estimated regression equations. Unbiased estimates have the property that on average the sample statistic equals the true value of the underlying population parameter. The most efficient estimate is the one with the lowest possible variance of estimation. Frequently there is a trade-off between bias and efficiency. One rule that weighs both of these aspects is the concept of "quadratic loss." The expected value of the distribution of quadratic loss is called the mean square error. It may be formally defined as

$$\text{MSE}(\hat{\theta}) = E(\hat{\theta} - \theta)^2, \tag{C.15}$$

where θ is the population parameter and $\hat{\theta}$ is the estimate of that parameter.

The mean square error can be expressed in terms of the variance and the bias of the estimate by first adding then subtracting $E(\hat{\theta})$ in Eq. (C.15). The result is

$$\text{MSE}(\hat{\theta}) = E[\hat{\theta} - E(\hat{\theta}) + E(\hat{\theta}) - \theta]^2$$
$$= E[\hat{\theta} - E(\hat{\theta})]^2 + [E(\hat{\theta}) - \theta]^2$$

because the cross-product term has a zero expected value. Therefore the mean square error can be written as

$$\text{MSE}(\hat{\theta}) = \text{Variance}(\hat{\theta}) + [\text{bias}(\hat{\theta})]^2. \tag{C.16}$$

Minimizing the MSE imposes an arbitrary judgment as to the relative importance of bias and variance. If it is thought that minimizing bias is of paramount importance, then the MSE may be inappropriate.

2. Sources of Bias

A. LEFT-OUT VARIABLES.   One of the most frequently encountered problems of regression analysis is that the empirical model is not founded on a sound theoretical footing. When this happens we say that the model is misspecified. If an important explanatory variable is left out of the regression equation, then the estimates of the coefficients for the variables included in the equations can be biased. This was one of the empirical difficulties in the early attempt to test for relationships between capital structure and value (see Chapter 14). The empirical work was done before a theoretical model of value had been derived. Therefore relevant variables were often left out and the empirical results were biased.

Suppose that the true theoretical relationship is

$$Y_t = a + b_1 X_{1t} + b_2 X_{2t} + \varepsilon_t \tag{C.17}$$

but that the researcher mistakenly estimates the following regression equation:

$$Y_t = a + \tilde{b}_1 X_{1t} + U_t. \tag{C.18}$$

From Eq. (C.3) the ordinary least squares estimate of $\tilde{b}_1$ is

$$\tilde{b}_1 = \frac{\sum (X_1 - \bar{X}_1)(Y - \bar{Y})}{\sum (X_1 - \bar{X}_1)(X_1 - \bar{X}_1)}. \tag{C.19}$$

By substituting the true relation [Eq. (C.17)] for Y into Eq. (C.19), we obtain

$$\tilde{b}_1 = \frac{\sum (X_1 - \bar{X}_1)(a + b_1 X_1 + b_2 X_2 + \varepsilon - a - b_1 \bar{X}_1 - b_2 \bar{X}_2)}{\sum (X_1 - \bar{X}_1)(X_1 - \bar{X}_1)}$$

$$= \frac{\sum (X_1 - \bar{X}_1)(a + b_1 X_1 - a - b_1 \bar{X}_1)}{\sum (X_1 - \bar{X}_1)^2}$$

$$+ \frac{\sum (X_1 - \bar{X}_1)(b_2 X_2 - b_2 \bar{X}_2)}{\sum (X_1 - \bar{X}_1)^2} + \frac{\sum (X_1 - \bar{X}_1)\varepsilon}{\sum (X_1 - \bar{X}_1)^2},$$

and because the error terms are assumed to follow Eqs. (C.7), (C.8), and (C.9), we have

$$\tilde{b}_1 = b_1 + b_2 \frac{\sum (X_1 - \bar{X}_1)(X_2 - \bar{X}_2)}{\sum (X_1 - \bar{X}_1)^2}. \tag{C.20}$$

Equation (C.20) shows that when a relevant variable is left out of the equation specification the slope estimate, $\tilde{b}$, is biased. The direction of the bias depends on the sign of b_2 (the relationship between Y and X_2) and on $\sum (X_1 - \bar{X}_1)(X_2 - \bar{X}_2)$ (the relationship between the independent variables, X_1 and X_2). If X_1, X_2, and Y are all positively related, then b will be biased upward. In general the only way to eliminate misspecification bias is to be sure that the empirical test is appropriately founded on sound theory, rather than going on an ad hoc "fishing trip."

B. ERRORS IN VARIABLES. There is almost always some measurement error involved when taking sample statistics. The degree of accuracy in estimating both independent and dependent variables can vary considerably, and unfortunately this problem also results in bias. For example, in Chapter 15, Friend and Puckett showed that measurement error is important when trying to estimate the relative effect of dividends and retained earnings on the price of common stock. The estimated equation was

$$P_{it} = a + bD_{it} + cR_{it} + \varepsilon_{it},$$

where

$P_{it} = $ the price per share,
$D_{it} = $ the aggregate dividends paid out,
$R_{it} = $ the retained earnings of the firm,
$\varepsilon_{it} = $ the error term.

Dividends can be measured without any error whatsoever, but retained earnings (the difference between accounting earnings and dividends paid) is only an estimate of true economic retained earnings on which value is based. Thus retained earnings possesses a great deal of measurement error. Consequently, the estimate of the effect of retained earnings on the price per share was biased downward. This led earlier researchers to incorrectly conclude that dividends had a greater effect on price per share than retained earnings.

To demonstrate the effect of measurement error, suppose that both the independent and dependent variables have sampling error. This may be written as

$$X = x + w, \tag{C.21}$$

$$Y = y + v, \tag{C.22}$$

where X and Y indicate the observations, x and y are the true values, and w and v are the measurement errors. Suppose, further, that the true variables have the following relationship:

$$y = a + bx. \tag{C.23}$$

We would like to have unbiased estimates of a and b.

Substituting Eqs. (C.21) and (C.22) into Eq. (C.23) gives

$$Y = a + bX + z,$$

where

$$z = v - bw.$$

From Eq. (C.3), the estimate of b is

$$\begin{aligned}
\hat{b} &= \frac{\sum (X - \bar{X})(Y - \bar{Y})}{\sum (X - \bar{X})(X - \bar{X})} \\
&= \frac{\sum (x + w - \bar{x} - \bar{w})(y + v - \bar{y} - \bar{v})}{\sum (x + w - \bar{x} - \bar{w})^2} \\
&= \frac{\sum (x - \bar{x})(y - \bar{y}) + \sum (x + \bar{x})(v - \bar{v}) + \sum (y - \bar{y})(w - \bar{w}) + \sum (w - \bar{w})(v - \bar{v})}{\sum (x - \bar{x})^2 + 2 \sum (x - \bar{x})(w - \bar{w}) + \sum (w - \bar{w})^2}.
\end{aligned}$$

Given that the measurement errors, w and v, are distributed independently of each other and of the true parameters, then the last three terms in the numerator and the middle term in the denominator vanish as the sample size becomes large. Therefore the limiting value of b is

$$\text{plim } \hat{b} = \frac{\sum (x - \bar{x})(y - \bar{y})}{\sum (x - \bar{x})^2 + \sum (w - \bar{w})^2}.$$

Dividing numerator and denominator by $\sum (x - \bar{x})^2$, we have

$$\hat{b} = \frac{b}{1 + [\sum (w - \bar{w})^2 / \sum (x - \bar{x})^2]}. \tag{C.24}$$

Equation (C.24) shows that even if the errors of measurement are assumed to be mutually independent, independent of the true values, and have constant variance, the estimate, b, will be biased downward. The greater the measurement error, the greater the downward bias.

There are two generally accepted techniques for overcoming the problem of errors in variables: (1) grouping and (2) instrumental variables. Grouping procedures can reduce measurement error because when grouped the errors of individual observations tend to be cancelled out by their mutual independence. Hence there is less measurement error in a group average than there would be if sample data were not grouped. An instrumental variable is one that is highly correlated with the independent variable but that is independent of the errors w and v [in Eqs. (C.21) and (C.22)]. This was the technique employed by Friend and Puckett in testing dividend policy. Instead of using the accounting measurement of earnings, they used normalized earnings (a time series estimate of predicted earnings) to eliminate most of the measurement error bias.

3. Loss of Efficiency

A. MULTICOLLINEARITY.   When two or more independent variables are highly correlated, it frequently becomes difficult to distinguish their separate effects on the dependent variable. In fact, if they are perfectly correlated it is impossible to distinguish. For example, consider the following equation:

$$S_t = a + b_1 R_t + b_2 L_t + b_3 O_t + \varepsilon_t,$$

where S_t is the sales revenue of a ski shop, R_t and L_t are the sales of left and right downhill skis, and O_t is the sales of other items. The estimated coefficient b_1 is supposed to measure the impact of the sale of the right skis, holding all other variables constant. Of course this is nonsense, since right and left skis are sold simultaneously.

The usual multicollinearity problem occurs when two independent variables are highly, but not perfectly, correlated. And usually the effect is to reduce the efficiency of estimates of b_1 and b_2 by increasing the standard error of estimate. The best remedy for the problem is larger sample sizes.

B. SERIAL CORRELATION.   One of the important assumptions for linear regression, Eq. (C.9), is that samplings are drawn *independently* from the same multivariate distribution. In other words, successive error terms should be independent. If this is not the case, we still obtain unbiased estimates of the slope and intercept terms, but there is a loss of efficiency because the sampling variances of these estimates may be unduly large. Consider the following two variable cases. Suppose that

$$Y_t = a + bX_t + \varepsilon_t$$

but that the error term follows a first-order autoregressive scheme such as

$$\varepsilon_t = K\varepsilon_{t-1} + U_t,$$

where $|K| < 1$ and U_t satisfies the assumptions

$$E(U_t) = 0,$$

$$E(U_t, U_{t-N}) = \begin{cases} \sigma_U^2 & \text{if } N = 0 \\ 0 & \text{if } N \neq 0 \end{cases}.$$

In general the tth error term can be written as

$$\varepsilon_t = K\varepsilon_{t-1} + U_t$$

$$= K(K\varepsilon_{t-2} + U_{t-1}) + U_t$$

$$= U_t + KU_{t-1} + K^2 U_{t-2} + \cdots + K^n U_{t-n}$$

$$= \sum_{\tau=0}^{\infty} K^\tau U_{t-\tau},$$

$$E(\varepsilon_t) = 0 \quad \text{since } E(U_t) = 0 \text{ for all } t.$$

The expected value of the squared error terms is

$$E(\varepsilon_t^2) = E(U_t^2) + K^2 E(U_{t-1}^2) + K^4 E(U_{t-2}^2) + \cdots,$$

since the error terms, U_t, are serially independent. Consequently,

$$E(\varepsilon_t^2) = (1 + K^2 + K^4 + \cdots)\sigma_U^2.$$

This is a geometric series that reduces to

$$E(\varepsilon_t^2) = \sigma_\varepsilon^2 = \frac{\sigma_U^2}{1 - K^2}. \tag{C.25}$$

Equation (C.25) shows that the closer the relationship between ε_t and ε_{t-1}, the closer K is to unity and the greater will be the estimated error term and the loss of efficiency.

We can test for serial correlation by using the Durbin-Watson d-statistic. If ε_t are the residuals from a fitted least squares equation, then d is defined as

$$d = \frac{\sum_{t=2}^{n} (\varepsilon_t - \varepsilon_{t-1})^2}{\sum_{t=1}^{n} \varepsilon_t^2}.$$

Durbin and Watson have tabulated upper and lower bounds d_u and d_l for various numbers of observations, n, and numbers of independent variables, K.

When the error terms are serially independent, the d-statistic has a theoretical distribution with a mean of 2, but sampling fluctuations may lead to a different estimate even when the errors are not autocorrelated. Table C.3 provides critical values for the d-statistic. If the computed d is smaller than the lower critical value, d_l, or above the critical value $(4 - d_l)$, then the null hypothesis of serial independence is rejected. When the statistic is larger than d_u but smaller than $(4 - d_u)$, then the null hypothesis is accepted. When neither of these two cases is true, then the test is inconclusive.

Table C.3   Critical Values for the Durbin-Watson Test:
5% Significance Points of d_l and d_u in Two-Tailed Tests

	$k' = 1$		$k' = 2$		$k' = 3$		$k' = 4$		$k' = 5$	
n	d_l	d_u	d_l	d_u	d_l	d_u	d_l	d_u	d_l	d_u
15	0.95	1.23	0.83	1.40	0.71	1.61	0.59	1.84	0.48	2.09
16	0.98	1.24	0.86	1.40	0.75	1.59	0.64	1.80	0.53	2.03
17	1.01	1.25	0.90	1.40	0.79	1.58	0.68	1.77	0.57	1.98
18	1.03	1.26	0.93	1.40	0.82	1.56	0.72	1.74	0.62	1.93
19	1.06	1.28	0.96	1.41	0.86	1.55	0.76	1.72	0.66	1.90
20	1.08	1.28	0.99	1.41	0.89	1.55	0.79	1.70	0.70	1.87
21	1.10	1.30	1.01	1.41	0.92	1.54	0.83	1.69	0.73	1.84
22	1.12	1.31	1.04	1.42	0.95	1.54	0.86	1.68	0.77	1.82
23	1.14	1.32	1.06	1.42	0.97	1.54	0.89	1.67	0.80	1.80
24	1.16	1.33	1.08	1.43	1.00	1.54	0.91	1.66	0.83	1.79
25	1.18	1.34	1.10	1.43	1.02	1.54	0.94	1.65	0.86	1.77
26	1.19	1.35	1.12	1.44	1.04	1.54	0.96	1.65	0.88	1.76
27	1.21	1.36	1.13	1.44	1.06	1.54	0.99	1.64	0.91	1.75
28	1.22	1.37	1.15	1.45	1.08	1.54	1.01	1.64	0.93	1.74
29	1.24	1.38	1.17	1.45	1.10	1.54	1.03	1.63	0.96	1.73
30	1.25	1.38	1.18	1.46	1.12	1.54	1.05	1.63	0.98	1.73
31	1.26	1.39	1.20	1.47	1.13	1.55	1.07	1.63	1.00	1.72
32	1.27	1.40	1.21	1.47	1.15	1.55	1.08	1.63	1.02	1.71
33	1.28	1.41	1.22	1.48	1.16	1.55	1.10	1.63	1.04	1.71
34	1.29	1.41	1.24	1.48	1.17	1.55	1.12	1.63	1.06	1.70
35	1.30	1.42	1.25	1.48	1.19	1.55	1.13	1.63	1.07	1.70
36	1.31	1.43	1.26	1.49	1.20	1.56	1.15	1.63	1.09	1.70
37	1.32	1.43	1.27	1.49	1.21	1.56	1.16	1.62	1.10	1.70
38	1.33	1.44	1.28	1.50	1.23	1.56	1.17	1.62	1.12	1.70
39	1.34	1.44	1.29	1.50	1.24	1.56	1.19	1.63	1.13	1.69
40	1.35	1.45	1.30	1.51	1.25	1.57	1.20	1.63	1.15	1.69
45	1.39	1.48	1.34	1.53	1.30	1.58	1.25	1.63	1.21	1.69
50	1.42	1.50	1.38	1.54	1.34	1.59	1.30	1.64	1.26	1.69
55	1.45	1.52	1.41	1.56	1.37	1.60	1.33	1.64	1.30	1.69
60	1.47	1.54	1.44	1.57	1.40	1.61	1.37	1.65	1.33	1.69
65	1.49	1.55	1.46	1.59	1.43	1.62	1.40	1.66	1.36	1.69
70	1.51	1.57	1.48	1.60	1.45	1.63	1.42	1.66	1.39	1.70
75	1.53	1.58	1.50	1.61	1.47	1.64	1.45	1.67	1.42	1.70
80	1.54	1.59	1.52	1.62	1.49	1.65	1.47	1.67	1.44	1.70
85	1.56	1.60	1.53	1.63	1.51	1.65	1.49	1.68	1.46	1.71
90	1.57	1.61	1.55	1.64	1.53	1.66	1.50	1.69	1.48	1.71
95	1.58	1.62	1.56	1.65	1.54	1.67	1.52	1.69	1.50	1.71
100	1.59	1.63	1.57	1.65	1.55	1.67	1.53	1.70	1.51	1.72

For the set of sample data in Table C.1, the estimated d-statistic is computed below:

t	ε_t	$\varepsilon_t - \varepsilon_{t-1}$	ε_t^2	$(\varepsilon_t - \varepsilon_{t-1})^2$
1976	14.44	63.53	208.5136	4036.0609
1975	−49.09	−50.99	2409.8281	2599.9801
1974	1.90	−34.23	3.6100	1171.6929
1973	36.13	49.02	1305.3769	2402.9604
1972	−12.89	−62.24	166.1521	3873.8176
1971	49.35	87.27	2435.4225	7616.0529
1970	−37.92	−35.98	1437.9264	1294.5604
1969	−1.94	—	3.7636	—
Sum			7970.5932	22995.1252

$$d = \frac{22{,}995.1252}{7{,}970.5932} = 2.88.$$

From Table C.3 the critical values for the Durbin-Watson test are $d_l = .95$ and $d_u = 1.23$. Since our computed value is neither below $d_l = .95$ nor above the critical value of $(4 - d_l) = 3.05$, the null hypothesis of serial independence cannot be rejected. However, because $d = 2.88$ is greater than $d_u = 1.23$ but not smaller than $(4 - d_u) = 2.77$, we cannot accept the null hypothesis. Because serial correlation cannot be either accepted or rejected, the test is inconclusive in this case.

SUMMARY

This has been an extremely brief overview of linear regression analysis. We have shown how to estimate the slope, the intercept, the standard errors of each, their t-statistics, and the correlation coefficient for a two-variable case. Multivariate estimates of the same variables in a multiple regression equation have the same interpretations and are provided by many different computer software packages. The summary statistics for the example problem of Table C.1 would appear in a computer printout in something like the following form:

$$Y_t = -23.42 + 174.84X_t \qquad r^2 = .6849 \qquad d = 2.88$$
$$(-.38) \qquad (3.61) \qquad df = 6$$

We can infer that sales revenue is significantly related to predicted GNP, with an intercept term insignificantly different from zero and a significant slope term. Because the Durbin-Watson test is inconclusive we cannot be sure whether or not serial correlation has reduced the efficiency of our estimates. Furthermore, additional testing would be necessary to determine whether or not left-out variables have caused a biased estimate of b_1.

The mean square error criterion is one way of trading off bias and loss of efficiency. It may be desirable, e.g., to accept a small bias in order to gain much greater efficiency. Although we have not discussed all the causes of bias or inefficiency, a few of the more important ones were covered. The interested reader should refer to an econometrics text for a more rigorous and detailed presentation.

REFERENCES

Christ, C. G., *Econometric Models and Methods*. Wiley, New York, 1966.

Dhrymes, P. J., *Econometrics: Statistical Foundations and Applications*. Harper & Row, New York, 1970.

Goldberger, A. S., *Econometric Theory*. Wiley, New York, 1964.

Hoel, P. G., *Introduction to Mathematical Statistics*, 3rd ed. Wiley, New York, 1954.

Johnston, J., *Econometric Methods*. McGraw-Hill, New York, 1963.

Rao, P., and L. Miller, *Applied Econometrics*. Wadsworth, Belmont, Calif., 1971.

Wonnacott, R. J., and T. H. Wonnacott, *Econometrics*. Wiley, New York, 1970.

Appendix D   Calculus and Optimization

Optimizing or maximizing are concepts basic to finance theory as well as to economics. In this brief review, we shall summarize the main concepts drawn on in the text. These include:

A. Functions

B. Differential Calculus

C. Optimization

D. Series

E. Integral Calculus

A. FUNCTIONS

A fundamental notion used in finance is the concept of a function. There are three ways to express functions: as (1) mathematical equations, (2) graphs, and (3) tables.

Example: Suppose a variable Y is related to a variable X by the following mathematical equation:

$$Y = 2X^2 - 3X + 6.$$

A shorthand way of expressing this relationship is to write $Y = f(X)$, which is read "Y is a function of the variable X" and where Y is the range and X is the domain of the function. X is also called the independent variable and Y the dependent variable, since Y's value $[f(X)]$ is *posited* to depend on X's value.

We can also express the function in a tabular and graphical manner. Thus the equation enables us to construct a range of Y values for a given table of X values. The data in the table can then be plotted in a graph as in Fig. D.1.

Definition: The *dimension* of a function is determined by the number of independent variables in the domain of the function.

Example: $Y = f(X, Z)$ is a two-dimensional function

$Y = f(X_1, X_2, \ldots, X_n)$ is an n-dimensional function.

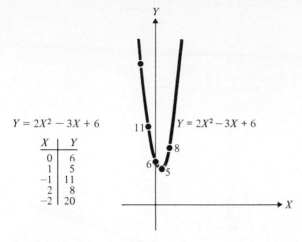

$Y = 2X^2 - 3X + 6$

X	Y
0	6
1	5
−1	11
2	8
−2	20

Figure D.1

Example: From basic capital budgeting concepts (see Chapter 2), we know that the net present value (NPV) of an investment project is equal to

$$\text{NPV} = \sum_{t=1}^{N} \frac{\text{NCF}_t}{(1 + k)^t} - I_0,$$

where

NCF_t = net cash flow in time period t,

I_0 = the project's initial cash outlay,

k = the firm's cost of capital,

N = the number of years in the project.

We can express this relationship functionally as

$$\text{NPV} = f(\text{NCF}_t, I_0, k, N) \qquad t = 1, \ldots, N.$$

Given values for the right-hand side independent variables we can determine the left-hand dependent variable, NPV. The functional relationship tells us that for every X that is in the domain of the function a unique value of Y can be determined.

1. Inverse Functions

How about going the other way? Given Y, can we determine X? Yes, we can.

Definition: The function that expresses the variable X in terms of the variable Y is called the *inverse function* and is denoted $X = f^{-1}(Y)$.

Example:

$$Y = f(X) = 2X - 5.$$

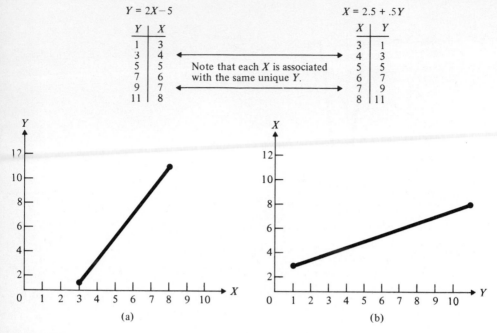

Figure D.2

Solving for X in terms of Y,

$$X = \frac{Y + 5}{2} = 2.5 + .5Y = f^{-1}(Y).$$

The inverse relationship can be seen more clearly if we graph the two functions (Fig. D.2). The inverse function, however, does not exist for all functions. But the inverse of a function always exists when we are dealing with one-to-one functions.

2. Linear Functions

An important type of function consists of *linear functions* of the form

$$Y = a_1 X_1 + a_2 X_2 + \cdots + a_n X_n.$$

These functions are used in regression and in the CAPM. In two dimensions a linear function is a straight line, usually written as $Y = a + bX$, where a is the intercept on the Y axis and b is the *slope* of the line:

$$\text{slope} = \frac{Y_1 - Y_2}{X_1 - X_2} = \frac{\Delta Y}{\Delta X}$$

$$= \frac{\text{change in } Y}{\text{change in } X} = \frac{\text{rise}}{\text{run}}.$$

The CAPM is of the form $Y = a + bX$, where $E(R_j) = R_f + \lambda \beta_j$. This equation plots like the relationship in Fig. D.3(a), as we see in Fig. D.3(b).

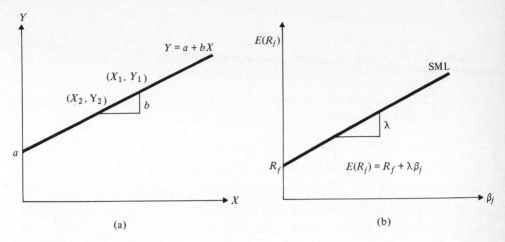

Figure D.3

The slope of the security market line in Fig. D.3(b) is $[E(R_m) - R_f]$, which is the market risk premium, λ.

The slope of a function is an important concept: it tells us the change in Y per unit change in X. The various types of slopes are pictured in Fig. D.4.

Example: Straight-line depreciation is a simple linear function:

$$BV = c - \left(\frac{c}{N}\right)X,$$

where

BV = book value of the asset,

c = original cost of the asset,

N = estimated economic life of the asset,

X = number of years that have elapsed,

so that the book value after two years is $BV = c - (c/N)2$.

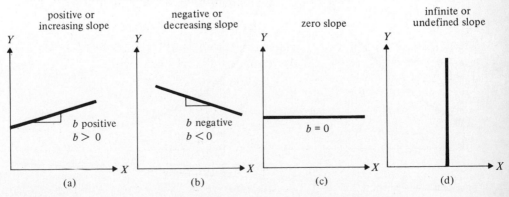

Figure D.4

3. Exponential Functions

As their names suggest, exponential functions are those in which the independent variable X appears as an exponent. They are useful for describing growth and compound interest. More formally:

Definition: The equation $Y = ma^X$ (a always > 0) is called an exponential function, and a is called the base.

Some properties of the exponential function are:

1. If $m > 0$, $a > 0$, then the function lies above the X-axis.
2. If $m < 0$, $a > 0$, then the function lies below the X-axis.
3. If $a > 1$, $m > 0$, then the curve rises to the right.
4. If $a < 1$, $m > 0$, then the curve rises to the left.

Example: An example of 3 and 4 above appears in Fig. D.5.

Example: Compound interest can be shown to be an exponential function. If you invest Z dollars in a bank that pays $r\%$ compound annual interest, then

$$Y_1 = Z + Zr = Z(1 + r)$$

= cumulative amount of money by the end of the first year,

$$Y_2 = Z(1 + r) + [Z(1 + r)]r = Z(1 + r)(1 + r)$$

$$= Z(1 + r)^2 = \text{cumulative amount of money by the end of the second year,}$$

$$\vdots$$

$$Y_n = Z(1 + r)^n = \text{amount at the end of } n \text{ years.}$$

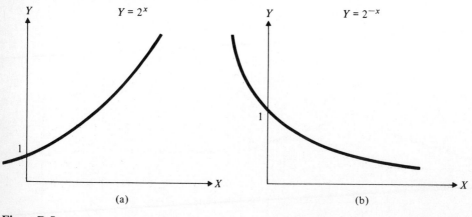

(a)   (b)

Figure D.5

This last expression is simply an exponential function

$$Y_n = Z(1 + r)^n$$

$$Y = ma^X, \quad \text{where the base is } (1 + r) \text{ and only } n \text{ can vary.}$$

Note that money grows exponentially [as in Fig. D.6(a)] when it is paid compound interest.

Example: Both compound value interest factors (CVIF) and present value interest factors (PVIF) are exponential functions. Consider the case of compounding and discounting $10 for five periods when the appropriate interest rate is 10%.

Compound sum	Present value
$Y = ma^X$	$Y = ma^{-X}$
$S = m(1 + r)^n$	$P = m(1 + r)^{-n}$
$a = (1 + r) > 1$	$a = (1 + r)^{-1} < 1$
$n = 1, 2, \ldots, N$	$n = 1, 2, \ldots, N$
For $r = 10\%$	For $r = 10\%$
$\quad m = \$10$	$\quad m = \$10$
$\quad n = 1, 2, \ldots, 5$	$\quad n = 1, 2, \ldots, 5$
$S = 10 \cdot (1 + r)^n$	$P = 10 \cdot (1 + r)^{-n}$
$\quad$ = compound value of $10 at the end of the nth period	$\quad$ = present value of $10 at the end of the nth period

S	n
11.00	1
12.10	2
13.31	3
14.64	4
16.11	5

P	n
9.09	1
8.26	2
7.51	3
6.83	4
6.21	5

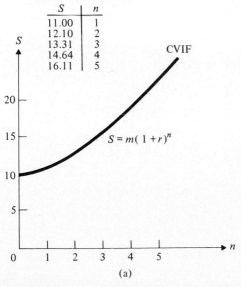

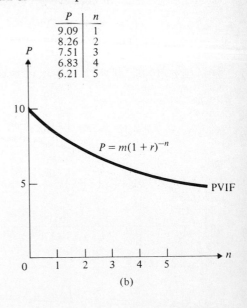

Figure D.6

4. Logarithmic Functions

Definition: If $N = b^r$, where both $n > 0$, $b > 0$, then we define $r = \log_b N$, which is read "r is the log to the base b of N."

In other words, $\log_b N$ is the number to which b has to be raised exponentially in order to equal N. So a log is simply an exponent.

Examples:

$$100 = 10^2$$

$$\text{so} \quad \log_{10} 100 = 2$$

$$\tfrac{1}{2} = 2^{-1}$$

$$\text{so} \quad \log_2 \tfrac{1}{2} = -1.$$

The two most widely used bases for logarithms are base 10 and base e, where e is an irrational number equal to 2.7182818....

Definition: The logarithm to the base 10 of N is called the "common logarithm of N." It is usually designated $\log N$.

Definition: The logarithm to the base e of N is called the "natural logarithm of N." To differentiate it from the common log, the natural log is usually designated: $\ln N$.

Definition: The function $Y = \log_b X$ is called a *logarithmic function*.

Since by definition $Y = \log_b X$ if and only if $X = b^Y$, we see that the exponential and logarithmic functions are inverse functions of each other:

$$X = 10^Y \Leftrightarrow Y = \log_{10} X$$

$$X = e^Y \Leftrightarrow Y = \ln X.$$

The logarithmic function $Y = \ln X$ is graphed in Fig. D.7.

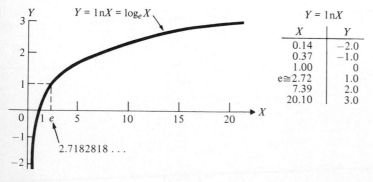

X	Y
0.14	−2.0
0.37	−1.0
1.00	0
$e \cong 2.72$	1.0
7.39	2.0
20.10	3.0

Figure D.7

Figure D.8

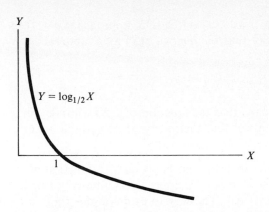

Some properties of the logarithmic function $Y = \log_b X$ are as follows:

1. The function equals zero when $X = 1$.
2. The function is an increasing function (i.e., it rises to the right) for all $b > 1$.
3. The function is a decreasing function (i.e., it falls to the right) for $0 < b < 1$. See Fig. D.8.
4. The function is negative when $0 < X < 1$ and $b > 1$.
5. The function is positive when $1 < X < \infty$.
6. The function is not defined when X is negative.

Example:

$$X = 2^{-Y} = \frac{1}{2^Y} = \left(\frac{1}{2}\right)^Y,$$

so $Y = \log_{1/2} X$.

Since logarithms are simply exponents, the rules of logs simply mirror the rules of exponents:

Exponents	*Logarithms*
$a^m \cdot a^n = a^{m+n}$	$\log_a(XY) = \log_a X + \log_a Y$
$\dfrac{a^m}{a^n} = a^{m-n}$ if $m > n$	$\log_a \dfrac{X}{Y} = \log_a X - \log_a Y$
$(a^m)^n = a^{mn}$	$\log_a(X^n) = n \log_a X$

B. DIFFERENTIAL CALCULUS

1. Limits

The central idea in calculus is the concept of the limit of a function. Often we want to know how the values of a function, $f(X)$, behave as the independent variable

X approaches some particular point, a. If as $X \to a$ (read "X approaches a"), $f(X)$ approaches some number L, then we say that *the limit* of $f(X)$ as X approaches a is L. This is written more compactly as

$$\lim_{X \to a} f(X) = L.$$

Intuitively, the existence of a limit L means that the function of $f(X)$ will take on a value as close to L as one may desire, given that the independent variable takes a value that is sufficiently close to a.

Example.   Many times we are interested in just what happens to a function as X increases without bound, i.e., when $X \to \infty$ (read "X approaches infinity"). For instance, what is lim as $X \to \infty$ of $[(X + 1)/X]$? The way to evaluate this limit is to observe the behavior of $f(X)$ as X gets larger and larger. From the table and the graph in Fig. D.9 we see that $f(X)$ approaches 1 as $X \to \infty$, so we can write lim as $X \to \infty$ of $[(X + 1)/X] = 1$.

Intuitively, as X gets very, very large, the fact that the numerator is greater by one than the denominator does not matter "much," so we have $X/X = 1$.

Example: As we will see next, we are often interested in what happens to $f(X)$ as X gets very, very small—i.e., when $X \to 0$. For instance, what is the lim as $X \to 0$ of $(3X/X^2)$? Again, to evaluate this limit we see what happens to $f(X)$ as $X \to 0$ (Fig. D.10).

Example: Generally we assume that compounding and discounting occur discretely in annual periods. If the compounding is more than once a year the compound value interest factor is changed from $(1 + r)^n$ to $[(1 + r/m)]^{nm}$, where m is the number of times per year compounding occurs. We can now see with limits what is the relationship between the continuous compounding rate and the discrete compounding rate. Continuous compounding means

$$\lim_{m \to \infty} \left[\left(1 + \frac{r}{m}\right)^{nm} \right] = e^{rn} \qquad \text{by definition of } e.$$

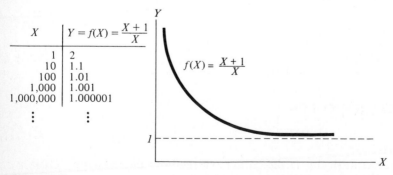

X	$Y = f(X) = \dfrac{X+1}{X}$
1	2
10	1.1
100	1.01
1,000	1.001
1,000,000	1.000001
⋮	⋮

Figure D.9

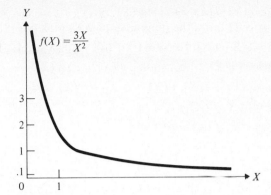

X	$Y=f(X)=\dfrac{3X}{X^2}$
1	3
.05	60
.01	300
.001	3,000
.0001	30,000
$\vdots$	$\vdots$

So we see that $\displaystyle\lim_{X\to 0}\frac{3X}{X^2}=\infty$

Figure D.10

If r_c = the continuous compounding rate and r_d = the discrete compounding rate, then $e^{r_c n} = (1 + r_d)^n$. Taking natural logs:

$$\ln\left[e^{r_c n}\right] = \ln(1 + r_d)^n,$$

$$r_c n \ln e = n \ln(1 + r_d),$$

$$r_c n = n \ln(1 + r_d) \qquad \text{since } \ln e \equiv 1,$$

$$r_c = \ln(1 + r_d).$$

So 5.25% continuously compounded is equal to 5.39% compounded annually. That is, if $r_c = 5.25\%$, then using $\ln(1 + r_d) = 5.25\%$, r_d must be 5.39%.

2. Derivatives

The rate of change of a function (the change in Y per unit change in X) is an important concept in mathematics. It is referred to as the *derivative* of Y with respect to X. In finance and economics the rate of change is called "marginal." For example, the marginal cost of capital (MCC) is the rate of change of the total cost of capital per change in new capital raised. Analytically, the marginal quantities are simply the *slopes* of the total quantities.

The derivative is usually denoted as dY/dX, or $f'(X)$. The advantage of the $f'(X)$ notation is that it reminds us that *the derivative is itself a function*: the value of the derivative depends on where it is evaluated. Fortunately there are special rules of differentiation that can be used to guide calculations.

3. Rules of Differentiation

1. $f(X) = c$ (c is a constant), $f'(X) = 0$. This rule states that the slope of a horizontal line is zero, since by definition Y does not change when X changes.
2. $f(X) = X^n$, $f'(X) = nX^{n-1}$. In order to differentiate X^n, reduce the exponent by one and multiply by n.

3. $f(X) = g(X) \cdot h(X)$, $f'(X) = g'(X) \cdot h(X) + h'(X) \cdot g(X)$. The derivative of $g(X) \cdot h(X)$ equals $h(X)$ times the derivative of $g(X)$ plus $g(X)$ times the derivative of $h(X)$.

4. $f(X) = g(X)/h(X)$, $[h(X) \neq 0]$, $f'(X) = [g'(X)h(X) - g(X)h'(X)]/[h(X)]^2$.

5. $f(X) = c \cdot g(X)$, $[c$ constant$]$, $f'(X) = c \cdot g'(X)$.

6. $f(X) = g(X) + h(X)$, $f'(X) = g'(X) + h'(X)$.

7. $f(X) = \ln X$, $f'(X) = 1/X$.

8. $f(X) = e^{g(X)}$, $f'(X) = g'(X)e^{g(X)}$.

9. $f(X) = X$, $f'(X) = 1$.

10. $f(X) = a^X$, $f'(X) = a^X \cdot \ln a$.

11. $f(X) = \log_b X$, $f'(X) = 1/(X \ln b)$.

12. $f(X) = \log[g(X)]$, $f'(X) = g'(X)/g(X)$.

Examples:

1) $Y = 6X^3 - 3X^2 + 4X + 7$,

$$\frac{dY}{dX} = 6 \cdot \frac{d}{dX}(X^3) - 3 \cdot \frac{d}{dX}(X^2) + 4 \cdot \frac{d}{dX}(X) + \frac{d}{dX}(7)$$

$$= 6(3X^2) - 3(2X) + 4(1) + 0$$

$$= 18X^2 - 6X + 4.$$

2) $Y = X^2(X + 3)$,

$$\frac{dY}{dX} = \left[\frac{d}{dX}(X^2)\right](X + 3) + \left[\frac{d}{dX}(X + 3)\right]X^2$$

$$= 2X(X + 3) + (1)X^2 = 3X^2 + 6X.$$

3) $Y = X^{-4}$,

$$\frac{dY}{dX} = -4X^{-5} = \frac{-4}{X^5}.$$

4) $Y = \frac{(2X^2 + 6)}{X^3}$,

$$\frac{dY}{dX} = \frac{4X(X^3) - (2X^2 + 6)(3X^2)}{(X^3)^2} = \frac{-2X^4 - 18X^2}{X^6}.$$

5) $Y = \frac{2}{\sqrt{X}} = 2X^{-1/2}$,

$$\frac{dY}{dX} = 2 \cdot -\frac{1}{2} \cdot X^{-3/2} = -X^{-3/2} = \frac{-1}{X^{3/2}} = \frac{-1}{\sqrt{X^3}}.$$

4. Chain Rule

An extremely useful and powerful tool in differential calculus is the chain rule, or the function of a function rule. Suppose Y is a function of a variable Z:

$$Y = f(Z),$$

but Z is in turn a function of another variable X:

$$Z = g(X).$$

Because Y depends on Z, and Z in turn depends on X, Y *is also a function of X*. We can express this fact by writing Y as a composite function (i.e., a function of a function) of $X : Y = f[g(X)]$.

To determine the change in Y from a change in X, the chain rule says:

$$\boxed{\frac{dY}{dX} = \frac{dY}{dZ}\frac{dZ}{dX} = f'(Z) \cdot g'(X) \qquad \text{Chain Rule}}$$

Intuitively the chain rule says, "Take the derivative of the outside (function) and multiply it by the derivative of the inside (function)." The reason behind the name "chain" rule is that there is a chain reaction relationship between X, Z, and Y:

$$\Delta X \xrightarrow{\text{via } g} \Delta Z \xrightarrow{\text{via } f} \Delta Y.$$

In words, a change in X has an ultimate impact on Y by causing a change in Z via function g, and this change in Z will in turn cause a change in Y by function f.

There is a temptation to look at the chain rule by canceling the intermediate dZ term:

$$\frac{dY}{dX} = \frac{dY}{dZ} \cdot \frac{dZ}{dX} = \frac{dY}{dX}.$$

This is incorrect! It is no more valid than canceling the 3s in

$$3 = \frac{39}{13} \neq \frac{9}{1} \neq 9.$$

The usefulness of the chain rule can best be seen by considering some examples in which it is used.

Examples:

Suppose we wanted to differentiate

$$Y = (3 + 6X^2)^{10}.$$

We could, by a considerable amount of work, expand $(3 + 6X^2)^{10}$ and differentiate term by term. Instead we can use the chain rule. Note that if we wanted to simply differentiate $Z = (3 + 6X^2)$, that would pose no problem:

$$\frac{dZ}{dX} = \frac{d}{dX}(3) + \frac{d(6X^2)}{dX}$$

$$= 0 + 12X,$$

$$\frac{dZ}{dX} = 12X.$$

Likewise, if we let

$$Y = (Z)^{10},$$

then we can differentiate easily

$$\frac{dY}{dZ} = \frac{d(Z)^{10}}{dZ} = 10Z^{10-1} = 10 \cdot Z^9.$$

The chain rule says to simply multiply these two results together to get dY/dX:

$$\frac{dY}{dX} = \frac{dY}{dZ} \cdot \frac{dZ}{dX}$$

$$= [10 \cdot Z^9]12X$$

$$= [10 \cdot (3 + 6X^2)^9]12X$$

$$= 120X(3 + 6X^2)^9.$$

Intuitively, the chain rule says to take the derivative of the function outside the parentheses—in this case, $10 \cdot (\ )^9$—and multiply it by the derivative of what is inside the parentheses—i.e., $12X$. So what seemed to be at first a rather forbidding problem turns out to be very easy to solve.

Two examples are given below:

$$\frac{d}{dX}(\sqrt[3]{5X + 7}) = \frac{d}{dX}(5X + 7)^{1/3}$$

$$= \frac{1}{3}(5X + 7)^{-2/3} \cdot 5$$

$$= \frac{5}{3}\frac{1}{(\sqrt[3]{5X + 7})^2}$$

$$= \frac{5}{3(5X + 7)^{2/3}}.$$

$$\frac{d}{dX}(e^{3X-4}) = e^{3X-4} \cdot 3$$

$$= 3e^{3X-4}.$$

5. Higher-Order Derivatives

In our development of derivatives we have emphasized that the derivative of a function is also a function. That is, the value of the derivative depends on the point X at which it is being evaluated. Like $f(X)$, $f'(X)$ is also a function of X.

Example: Consider the function

$$f(X) = -10X^2 + 2400X - 8500, \quad \text{then}$$

$$f'(X) = -20X + 2400.$$

The value of this derivative depends on the point at which it is being evaluated:

$$f'(120) = -20(120) + 2400 = 0,$$

$$f'(60) = -20(60) + 2400 = 1200.$$

Because it is also a function of X, we can take the derivative of $f'(X)$. This new function, $f''(X)$, is called the *second derivative* of the original function, $f(X)$. The *third derivative* is the derivative of the second derivative and is written $f'''(X)$. In principle we can go on forever and form derivatives of as high order as we like. Notationally these higher-order derivatives are symbolized in the same manner as the second derivative:

$$f'''(X), f^{(4)}(X), f^{(5)}(X), \ldots, f^{(n)}(X),$$

$$\frac{d^3Y}{dX^3}, \frac{d^4Y}{dX^4}, \frac{d^5Y}{dX^5}, \ldots, \frac{d^nY}{dX^n}.$$

Example:

$$Y = f(X) = X^3 - 7X^2 + 6X - 5,$$

$$f'(X) = 3X^2 - 14X + 6,$$

$$f''(X) = 6X - 14,$$

$$f'''(X) = 6,$$

$$f^{(4)}(X) = 0,$$

$$f^{(5)}(X) = 0,$$

$$\vdots$$

$$f^{(n)}(X) = 0.$$

As we shall see, higher-order derivatives play an important role in Taylor and Mac-Laurin series (see section D of this appendix). The most important of the higher-order derivatives is the second derivative. Understanding the meaning of the second derivative is crucial. We know that the first derivative of a function, $f'(X)$, is the slope of a function or the rate of change of Y as a result of a change in X. The second derivative, $f''(X)$, is the rate of change of the slope of $f(X)$; that is, it is the rate of

Table D.1

	$f'(X)$	$f''(X)$	$f(X)$ is
a)	> 0	> 0	Increasing at an increasing rate
b)	> 0	< 0	Increasing at a decreasing rate
c)	< 0	< 0	Decreasing at an increasing rate
d)	< 0	> 0	Decreasing at a decreasing rate

change of the rate of change of the original function, $f(X)$. Table D.1 and Fig. D.11 show various combinations of signs for $f'(X)$ and $f''(X)$ and the implied shape of the graph of $f(X)$.

Example: In developing the theory of investor choice under uncertainty, cardinal utility functions $[U(W)]$ are used. These utility functions should have the following

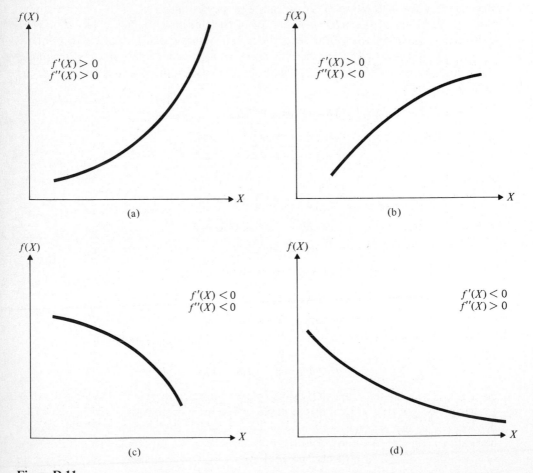

Figure D.11

property: $U'(W) > 0$, $U''(W) < 0$. That is, they should look like Fig. D.11(b). Check to see if and when the following four functions have this property.

1) $U(W) = aw - bw^2$ (quadratic utility function),

$\quad U'(W) = a - 2bw > 0$ when $a > 2bw$,

$\quad U''(W) = -2b < 0$ when $b > 0$.

2) $U(W) = \ln W$ (logarithmic utility function),

$\quad U'(W) = \dfrac{1}{W} > 0$ W always > 0 by definition of log function,

$\quad U''(W) = \dfrac{-1}{W^2} < 0$.

3) $U(W) = -e^{-aW}$ (exponential utility function),

$\quad U'(W) = -(-a)e^{-aW} = ae^{-aW} > 0$ if $a > 0$,

$\quad U''(W) = -a^2 e^{-aW} < 0$.

4) $U(W) = W^a$ (power utility function),

$\quad U'(W) = aW^{a-1} > 0$,

$\quad U''(W) = a(a-1)W^{a-2} < 0$ when $a < 1$.

Example: Given the following linear demand function

$$p = 100 - 10q,$$

where

p = price per unit sold (i.e., average revenue),

q = quantity sold,

(note that p is the dependent variable here).

We can obtain the total revenue function by multiplying through by q:

$$\text{TR} \equiv pq = 100q - 10q^2, \quad \text{which is a quadratic equation.}$$

The first derivative of total revenue tells us how total revenue responds to changes in the quantity sold. Economists call this function the marginal revenue:

$$\text{MR} \equiv \frac{d(\text{TR})}{dq} = 100 - 20q.$$

If we want to know by how much marginal revenue itself varies when quantity sold varies, we compute the slope of the marginal revenue. This is the second derivative of the total revenue function:

$$\frac{d(\text{MR})}{dq} = \frac{d^2(\text{TR})}{dq^2} = -20.$$

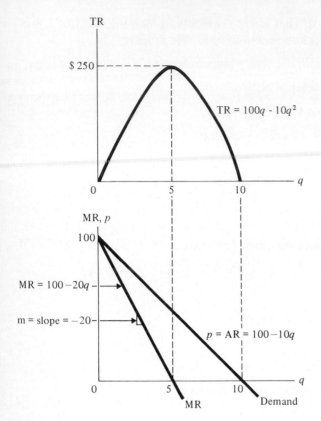

Figure D.12

So marginal revenue declines at a constant rate of -20 per unit increase in quantity sold. Graphically the relationship between total, average, and marginal revenue is shown in Fig. D.12.

> *Definition:* An important class of functions are those functions whose first derivative is positive for all values of the independent variable. Such functions are called *monotonically increasing* functions. Likewise, functions whose first derivative is negative for all values of the independent variable are *monotonically decreasing.*

6. Differentials

Let $Y = f(X)$; then the differential, dY, is defined as

$$dY = f'(X)\,dX.$$

If we regard $dX \equiv \Delta X$, a small increment in the independent variable X, then we can see that dY is an approximation to ΔY induced by ΔX because $f'(X) = \lim$ as $\Delta X \to 0$ of $(\Delta Y / \Delta X)$.

Example: Let $Y = 2X^2 + X + 2$, then $dY = (4X + 1)dX$. The concept of differentials is very useful when we consider integration later in section E.

7. Partial Differentiation

So far we have only considered differentiation of functions of one independent variable. In practice, functions of two or more independent variables do arise quite frequently. Since each independent variable influences the function differently, when we consider the instantaneous rate of change of the function, we have to isolate the effect of each of the independent variables. Let $W = f(X, Y, Z)$. When we consider how W changes as X changes, we want to hold the variables Y and Z constant. This gives rise to the concept of partial differentiation. Note that only the variable X is changing, while both Y and Z remain constant. The rules for partial differentiation and ordinary differentiation are exactly the same except that when we are taking partial derivative of one independent variable, we regard *all other independent variables as constants.*

Examples:

1) $W = XY + YZ + XZ$,

$$\frac{\partial W}{\partial X} = Y + 0 + Z = Y + Z,$$

$$\frac{\partial W}{\partial Y} = X + Z + 0 = X + Z,$$

$$\frac{\partial W}{\partial Z} = 0 + Y + X = Y + X.$$

2) $W = X^2YZ^3 + e^X + \ln YZ$,

$$\frac{\partial W}{\partial X} = 2XYZ^3 + e^X,$$

$$\frac{\partial W}{\partial Y} = X^2Z^3 + \frac{1}{YZ} \cdot Z = X^2Z^3 + \frac{1}{Y},$$

$$\frac{\partial W}{\partial Z} = 3X^2YZ^2 + \frac{1}{YZ} \cdot Y = 3X^2YZ^2 + \frac{1}{Z}.$$

C. OPTIMIZATION

A company seeks to maximize its profit. A production unit seeks to minimize its cost for a given level of output. An individual investor seeks to maximize his or her utility when choosing among investment alternatives. Indeed, we are all engaged in big and small optimization problems every day at work or at leisure. If we have a mathematical objective function, then we can solve our optimization problem using calculus.

Y

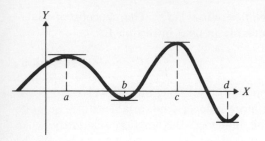

Figure D.13

The procedure is divided into two steps:

1. Locate all *relative* maxima and minima of the objective function.
2. Compare the function value at the relative maxima and minima and at the boundary points (to be explained later) to pick the highest (lowest) value to be the *global* maximum (minimum).

To accomplish step 1, let us first consider the graph of a function $f(X)$ that appears in Fig. D.13. At the point $X = a$, the function $f(X)$ is said to have a relative maximum because $f(a) > f(Z)$ for all Z sufficiently close to a. Similarly, $f(X)$ has a relative maximum at $X = c$, and $f(X)$ has relative minima at $X = b$ and $X = d$. One common characteristic those four points share is the slope of $f(X)$ at those points. If we draw tangent lines to $f(X)$ at $X = a, b, c, d$, then all the tangent lines must be perfectly horizontal. In other words the slopes $f'(a) = f'(b) = f'(c) = f'(d) = 0$. Thus we have the following theorem:

Theorem: If $f(X)$ has a relative maximum or minimum at $X = a$, then $f'(a) = 0$.

Note that the theorem does *not* say that if $f'(a) = 0$, then $X = a$ is a relative maximum or minimum. It says that if $f'(a) = 0$, then $X = a$ is a *candidate* for relative maximum or minimum. There exist points for which the derivative of $f(X)$ is zero, but the points are neither relative maxima nor minima. Nevertheless, to locate all relative maxima and minima, we differentiate $f(X)$, set the result to zero, and solve for X. That is, find all the solutions to the equation

$$f'(X) = 0.$$

The above equation is called the first-order condition. The solutions are candidates for relative maxima and minima. To determine which of these solutions are indeed relative maxima or minima, we need the so-called second-order conditions. Consider the relative maximum shown in Fig. D.14(a). The slope, $f'(X)$, is zero at the top, posi-

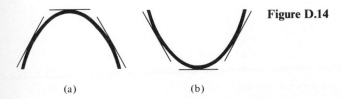

Figure D.14

(a)   (b)

tive to the left of the top, and negative to the right of the top. Therefore as X increases from left to right, the slope, $f'(X)$, is decreasing from positive to zero to negative. We know from the previous section that if $f'(X)$ is decreasing, then the derivative of $f'(X)$, $f''(X)$, is *negative*. The condition $f''(X) < 0$ is called the second-order condition for relative maxima. Similar reasoning would indicate that at a relative minimum, $f''(X) > 0$. We can now summarize step one: Find all the X such that $f'(X) = 0$; then for each of those X, if $f''(X) > 0$, it is a relative minimum; if $f''(X) < 0$, it is a relative maximum; if $f''(X) = 0$, we cannot tell (and have to use more sophisticated techniques.)

Step two requires us to compare function value at the relative maxima and minima and the boundary points to determine the global optimum. Boundary points exist because we generally wish to optimize $f(X)$ in some interval, say $a \leq X \leq b$, then a and b are boundary points. Sometimes the global maximum or minimum occurs at the boundary (see Fig. D.15). That is why we want to evaluate $f(X)$ at the boundary.

Example: A monopolist faces a downward-sloping demand curve given by $p(X) = 100 - 2X$, where X is the quantity and $p(X)$ is the price at that quantity. Suppose the fixed cost of production is 10 and variable cost is constant at 8 per unit. How many units should the monopolist produce to maximize profit?

$$\text{Profit} = \text{total revenue} - \text{total cost}$$

$$= \text{price} \times \text{quantity} - (\text{total variable cost} + \text{fixed cost}),$$

$$\pi(X) = (100 - 2X)X - (8X + 10)$$

$$= 100X - 2X^2 - 8X - 10$$

$$= 92X - 2X^2 - 10,$$

$$\pi'(X) = 92 - 4X = 0 \text{ (first-order condition)},$$

so

$$92 = 4X \quad \text{or} \quad X = 23,$$

$$\pi''(X) = -4;$$

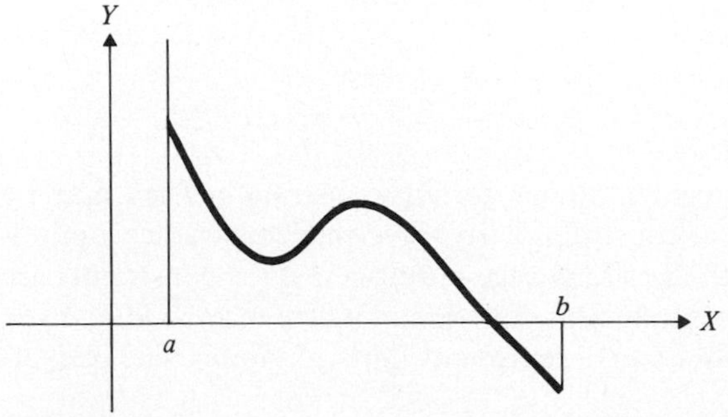

Figure D.15

hence

$$\pi''(X) < 0 \text{ (second-order condition)}.$$

Therefore $X = 23$ is a relative maximum. Implicit in this problem is the boundary $X \geq 0$. So $X = 0$ is a boundary. Obviously $\pi(0) = 0$ because this is the decision of not getting into the business at all. $\pi(23) = 92 \times 23 - 2 \times (23)^2 - 10 = 1048 > \pi(0)$. The solution to this problem is therefore $X = 23$. The monopolist should produce 23 units. If we change the original problem by making the fixed cost 1060 instead of 10, then $X = 23$ is still the only relative maximum. But now $\pi(23) = -2 < \pi(0)$. So the monopolist is better off not getting into the business at all. Here the optimum point occurs at the boundary.

If our objective function has two independent variables, then we have to resort to partial derivatives. Suppose $Z = f(X, Y)$, let

$$f_x = \frac{\partial Z}{\partial X}, \qquad f_y = \frac{\partial Z}{\partial Y}, \qquad f_{xx} = \frac{\partial}{\partial X}\left(\frac{\partial Z}{\partial X}\right)$$

(taking partial derivative twice with respect to X),

$$f_{yy} = \frac{\partial}{\partial Y}\left(\frac{\partial Z}{\partial Y}\right), \qquad f_{xy} = f_{yx} = \frac{\partial}{\partial X}\left(\frac{\partial Z}{\partial Y}\right)$$

(taking partial derivative twice, first with respect to Y, then with respect to X). The conditions for relative maxima and minima are

$$\left.\begin{array}{c} f_x = 0 \\ f_y = 0 \end{array}\right\} \text{ (first-order conditions)}.$$

In addition, if $f_{xx}f_{yy} > f_{xy}^2$, then the point is either a relative maximum or minimum. To distinguish relative maximum and minimum, we have

$$\left.\begin{array}{ll} f_{xx}, f_{yy} < 0 & \text{maximum} \\ f_{xx}, f_{yy} > 0 & \text{minimum} \end{array}\right\} \text{ (second-order conditions)}.$$

An example of using partial derivatives to find the optimum point is given in the application section of Appendix B.

1. Constrained Optimization

Very often, a business entity operates under certain constraints. They may be budgetary, technological, or physical constraints. To solve this constrained optimization problem, we can use the method of Lagrange multipliers if the constraints are given as equations. For example, the production function of a firm may be $F(X, Y) = 2XY$, where X represents units of labor and Y represents units of capital. The budgetary constraint may look like

$$g(X, Y) = 100 - 2X - 10Y = 0,$$

where 100 represents the maximum amount of money to be spent on this production and 2 and 10 represent unit costs of labor and capital, respectively. To use the method of Lagrange multipliers, we first construct a new function of three independent variables:

$$L(X, Y, \lambda) = f(X, Y) + \lambda g(X, Y)$$
$$= 2XY + \lambda(100 - 2X - 10Y),$$

where λ is a new variable that is called the Lagrange multiplier. The constrained optimum will appear as a solution to the first-order condition:

$$\left. \begin{array}{l} \dfrac{\partial L}{\partial X} = L_x = 0 \\[2ex] \dfrac{\partial L}{\partial Y} = L_y = 0 \\[2ex] \dfrac{\partial L}{\partial \lambda} - L_\lambda = 0 \end{array} \right\} \quad \text{(first-order conditions).}$$

Let

$$H = \begin{pmatrix} 0 & g_x & g_y \\ g_x & L_{xx} & L_{xy} \\ g_y & L_{yx} & L_{yy} \end{pmatrix} \quad \text{and} \quad |H| = \text{determinant of } H \text{ (defined in Appendix B);}$$

then

$$\left. \begin{array}{l} |H| < 0 \quad \text{relative minimum} \\[1ex] |H| > 0 \quad \text{relative maximum} \end{array} \right\} \quad \text{(second-order conditions).}$$

Example: Take the production function and the budgetary constraint above and find the optimal combination of labor and capital.

$$L(X, Y, \lambda) = 2XY + \lambda(100 - 2X - 10Y)$$

$$\left. \begin{array}{l} L_x = 2Y - 2\lambda = 0 \\ L_y = 2X - 10\lambda = 0 \\ L_\lambda = 100 - 2X - 10Y = 0 \end{array} \right\} \quad \text{(first-order conditions).}$$

Solving these equations simultaneously gives us $X = 25$, $Y = 5$, $\lambda = 5$. (For a discussion of methods of solving system of linear equations, see Appendix B.) Therefore under the budgetary constraint the maximum output level is $f(25, 5) = 2 \times 25 \times 5 = 250$ when we employ 25 units of labor and 5 units of capital. We know that this must be the maximum point before computing the second-order condition because a relative maximum is the only sensible solution. The interested reader may check that

$$|H| = \begin{vmatrix} 0 & -2 & -10 \\ -2 & 0 & 2 \\ -10 & 2 & 0 \end{vmatrix} = 80 > 0.$$

Another example of using the method of Lagrange multiplier can be found in the application section of Appendix B regarding the minimum variance porfolio.

2. The Meaning of λ

The solution of λ also has a meaning. The magnitude of λ measures how much the optimum changes as we relax the constraint. In the above example the solution of λ is 5. That means if we relax the budgetary constraint 1 unit from 100 to 101, the optimal level of output would increase approximately 5 units to 255.

If the solution to λ is equal to zero, then the constraint is not binding. That means the constrained optimum is equal to the unconstrained optimum.

D. TAYLOR AND MACLAURIN SERIES

The Taylor and MacLaurin series are widely used in economics and finance. Their most important use is to help evaluate the value of a function around a certain point. Suppose we are interested in evaluating the function $Y = f(X)$ around a point a in its domain. Then we can make use of Taylor's theorem:

Taylor's theorem. In the one-dimensional case we can evaluate the function $Y = f(X)$ around the point a in terms of its derivatives as follows:

$$f(X) = f(a) + f'(a)(X - a) + \frac{f''(a)(X - a)^2}{2!}$$

$$+ \frac{f'''(a)(X - a)^3}{3!} + \cdots + \frac{f^{(n)}(a)(X - a)^n}{n!}.$$

Alternatively, if we let $h = (X - a)$, then the Taylor series is

$$f(a + h) = f(a) + f'(a)h + \frac{f''(a)h^2}{2!}$$

$$+ \frac{f'''(a)h^3}{3!} + \cdots + \frac{f^{(n)}(a)h^n}{n!} \qquad \text{(Pratt [1964] uses this.)},$$

where $f(a)$ = value of the function at point a. This is called a *Taylor series.*

Definition: If we evaluate the function around zero (i.e., if $a = 0$ above), then we have what is called a *MacLaurin series:*

$$f(X) = f(0) + f'(0) \cdot X + \frac{f''(0)}{2!} \cdot X^2 + \frac{f'''(0)}{3!} \cdot X^3 + \cdots + \frac{f^{(n)}(0)}{n!} \cdot X^n.$$

Definition: The symbol $n!$ [read "n factorial"] represents the product of all positive integers from 1 to n (or vice versa). That is,

$$n! = n \cdot (n - 1) \cdot (n - 2) \cdot (n - 3) \cdot (n - 4) \cdots 4 \cdot 3 \cdot 2 \cdot 1.$$

Examples:

$$5! = 5 \cdot 4 \cdot 3 \cdot 2 \cdot 1 = 1 \cdot 2 \cdot 3 \cdot 4 \cdot 5 = 120,$$

$$10! = 10 \cdot 9 \cdot 8 \cdot 7 \cdot 6 \cdot 5 \cdot 4 \cdot 3 \cdot 2 \cdot 1 = 3{,}628{,}800,$$

$$(n - r)! = (n - r) \cdot (n - r - 1) \cdot (n - r - 2) \cdot (n - r - 3) \cdots 4 \cdot 3 \cdot 2 \cdot 1.$$

By definition $1! = 0! = 1$.

Intuitively, what the Taylor series is trying to do is to approximate the function $f(X)$ with the following polynomial:

1) $f(X) \approx T_0 + T_1(X - a) + T_2(X - a)^2 + T_3(X - a)^3 + \cdots$. The problem is to find the values of the coefficients (the Ts) of this polynomial. To find them, take the higher-order derivatives of (1):

2) $f'(X) = T_1 + T_2 \cdot 2(X - a) + T_3 \cdot 3(X - a)^2 + T_4 \cdot 4(X - a)^3 + \cdots$

3) $f''(X) = 2T_2 + T_3 \cdot 2 \cdot 3(X - a) + T_4 \cdot 4 \cdot 3(X - a)^2 + \cdots$

4) $f'''(X) = 2 \cdot 3T_3 + T_4 \cdot 4 \cdot 3 \cdot 2(X - a) + T_5 \cdot 5 \cdot 4 \cdot 3(X - a)^2 + \cdots$

$\quad\vdots\qquad\vdots$

If we evaluate (1) through (4) at $X = a$, then $(X - a) = 0$, so all terms involving $(X - a)$ will vanish:

$\left. \begin{array}{l} 1')\ f(X) = T_0 \\[4pt] 2')\ f'(X) = T_1 \\[10pt] 3')\ f''(X) = 2 \cdot T_2 \\[12pt] 4')\ f'''(X) = 2 \cdot 3T_3 \end{array} \right\}$ Solving for the Ts $\left\{ \begin{array}{l} T_0 = f(X) \\[4pt] T_1 = f'(X) \\[6pt] T_2 = \dfrac{f''(X)}{2} = \dfrac{f''(X)}{2 \cdot 1} = \dfrac{f''(X)}{2!} \\[12pt] T_3 = \dfrac{f'''(X)}{3 \cdot 2} = \dfrac{f'''(X)}{3 \cdot 2 \cdot 1} = \dfrac{f'''(X)}{3!} \\[10pt] \vdots \qquad \vdots \qquad \vdots \qquad \vdots \end{array} \right.$

Plugging these values of the Ts into (1) results in the Taylor series we stated earlier. The usefulness of Taylor series can best be seen with the help of a numerical example.

Example: Expand the function $f(X) = 1/X$ around 1, for $n = 0, 1, 2, 3$. Computing the derivatives:

$$f(X) = \frac{1}{X} \quad \text{so} \quad f(1) = \frac{1}{1} = 1,$$

$$f'(X) = \frac{-1}{X^2} \quad \text{so} \quad f'(1) = \frac{-1}{(1)^2} = -1,$$

$$f''(X) = \frac{2}{X^3} \quad \text{so} \quad f''(1) = \frac{2}{(1)^3} = 2,$$

$$f'''(X) = \frac{-6}{X^4} \quad \text{so} \quad f'''(1) = \frac{-6}{(1)^4} = -6.$$

a) The Taylor series approximation when $n = 0$ is

$$T_0(X) = f(a), \quad \text{since } a = 1 \quad \text{(we are expanding around 1)}$$
$$T_0(X) = f(1) = 1.$$

b) The Taylor approximation when $n = 1$ is

$$T_1(X) = f(a) + f'(a)(X - a)$$
$$= f(1) + (-1)(X - 1)$$
$$= 1 - (X - 1).$$

c) The approximation when $n = 2$ is

$$T_2(X) = f(a) + f'(a)(X - a) + \frac{f''(a)}{2!}(X - a)^2$$
$$= f(1) + (-1)(X - 1) + \frac{2}{2 \cdot 1}(X - 1)^2$$
$$= 1 - (X - 1) + (X - 1)^2.$$

d) The approximation when $n = 3$ is

$$T_3(X) = f(a) + f'(a)(X - a) + \frac{f''(a)}{2!}(X - a)^2 + \frac{f'''(a)}{3!}(X - a)^3$$
$$= 1 - (X - 1) + (X - 1)^2 + \frac{-6}{3 \cdot 2 \cdot 1}(X - 1)^3$$
$$= 1 - (X - 1) + (X - 1)^2 - (X - 1)^3.$$

Expanding and rearranging the polynomials:

$T_0(X) = 1$ (constant),

$T_1(X) = 1 - (X - 1) = -X + 2$ (straight line),

$T_2(X) = 1 - (X - 1) + (X - 1)^2 = X^2 - 3X + 3$ (parabola),

$T_3(X) = 1 - (X + 1) + (X - 1)^2 - (X - 1)^3 = -X^3 + 4X^2 - 6X + 4$ (cubic).

Figure D.16 graphs the function $f(X) = 1/X$ and each of the approximating polynomials:

$$\frac{dT_2(X)}{dX} = 2X - 3 = 0, \quad X = 1.5 = \min,$$

$$\frac{dT_3(X)}{dX} = -3X^2 + 8X - 6 = 0$$

$$(-3X + 2)(X - 3) \quad \text{inflection point} > 1.$$

From the graph we see that each successive Taylor series does a better job of approximating $f(X) = 1/X$ in the vicinity of 1; see Fig. D.17.

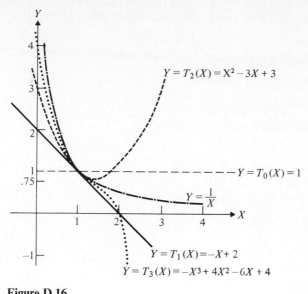

$Y = T_2(X) = X^2 - 3X + 3$

$Y = T_0(X) = 1$

$Y = \frac{1}{X}$

$Y = T_1(X) = -X + 2$

$Y = T_3(X) = -X^3 + 4X^2 - 6X + 4$

Figure D.16

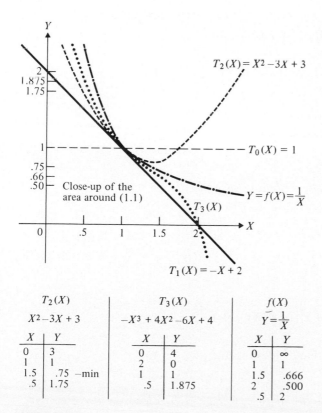

$T_2(X) = X^2 - 3X + 3$

$T_0(X) = 1$

$Y = f(X) = \frac{1}{X}$

$T_3(X)$

Close-up of the
area around (1.1)

$T_1(X) = -X + 2$

$T_2(X)$		$T_3(X)$		$f(X)$	
$X^2 - 3X + 3$		$-X^3 + 4X^2 - 6X + 4$		$Y = \frac{1}{X}$	
X	Y	X	Y	X	Y
0	3	0	4	0	∞
1	1	2	0	1	1
1.5	.75 −min	1	1	1.5	.666
.5	1.75	.5	1.875	2	.500
				.5	2

Figure D.17

Example: Pratt (1964) uses Taylor series to derive a measure of absolute relative risk aversion. Let

$$X = \text{amount of wealth,}$$

$$U = \text{acceptable utility function,}$$

$$\pi = \text{risk premium, } \pi \text{ is a function, } \pi(X, \tilde{Z}),$$

$$\tilde{Z} = \text{a gamble (and a random variable),}$$

$$\tilde{Z} \cdot E(\tilde{Z}) \quad \pi(X, \tilde{Z}).$$

1) $E\{U(X + \tilde{Z})\} = U[X + E(\tilde{Z}) - \pi(X, \tilde{Z})]$
   by choosing an actuarially neutral risk $E(\tilde{Z}) = 0$. So
1') $E\{U(X + \tilde{Z})\} = U[X - \pi(X, \tilde{Z})]$.

Expand the right-hand side of (1') using Taylor series:

$$U(X - \pi) = U(X) + \pi \cdot U'(X) - \frac{\pi^2}{2!} U''(X) - \cdots$$

Pratt assumes second-order and higher terms are insignificant.

Expand the left-hand side of (1') using Taylor series:

$$E\{U(X) + \tilde{Z}\} = E\{U(X) + \tilde{Z}U'(X) + \frac{\tilde{Z}^2}{2!} U''(X) + \cdots$$

$$\approx 0$$

$$= E\{U(X)\} + E\{\tilde{Z}\}U'(X) + \frac{E(\tilde{Z}^2)}{2!} U''(X).$$

But

$$E\{U(X)\} = U(X) \qquad \text{not a random variable,}$$

$$E\{\tilde{Z}\} = 0,$$

$$E\{\tilde{Z}^2\} = \sigma_Z^2 \quad \text{since} \quad \sigma_Z^2 = Z \, p_i[Z_i - E(Z_i)]^2 = \sum p_i Z_i^2 = E(Z_i^2).$$

$$0$$

So

$$E\{U(X) + \tilde{Z}\} = U(X) + 0 + \frac{\sigma_Z^2}{2} U''(X).$$

Putting the left-hand and right-hand sides together:

$$U(X) + \frac{\sigma_Z^2}{2} U''(X) = U(X) - \pi U'(X).$$

Solving for π, the risk premium:

$$\pi = \tfrac{1}{2}\sigma_{\tilde{Z}}^2\left\{-\frac{U''(X)}{U'(X)}\right]\right\} \qquad \text{a function of } \tilde{Z} \text{ and } X.$$

always positive ⟵ a measure of absolute
by definition of   risk aversion
variance

E. INTEGRAL CALCULUS

1. Indefinite Integrals

Integration is the reverse process to differentiation. Given a function $f(X)$, the indefinite integral of $f(X)$, denoted by $\int f(X)\,dX$, is a function whose derivative is $f(X)$. In other words,

$$\int f(X)\,dX = F(X) \quad \text{iff} \quad F'(X) = f(X).$$

A peculiar feature regarding the indefinite integral of $f(X)$ is that it is not unique. Observe the following fact: if $F'(X) = f(X)$, so is $[F(X) + C]' = F'(X) + 0 = f(X)$ where C is an arbitrary constant. Therefore both $F(X)$ and $F(X) + C$ can be an indefinite integral of $f(X)$. So, in general, we write

$$\int f(X)\,dX = F(X) + C$$

to indicate that an arbitrary constant may be added to the answer.

As in differentiation, we have rules of integration that correspond very closely with those of differentiation.

2. Rules of Integration

1. $\int X^n\,dX = \dfrac{1}{n+1}\,X^{n+1} + C. \qquad (n \neq -1)$

2. $\int \dfrac{1}{X}\,dX = \ln X + C. \qquad (X > 0)$

3. $\int e^X\,dX = e^X + C.$

4. $\int c \cdot g(X)\,dX = c \cdot \int g(X)\,dX. \qquad (c = \text{constant})$

5. $\int [g(X) + h(X)]\,dX = \int g(X)\,dX + \int h(X)\,dX.$

6. $\int a^X\,dX = \dfrac{1}{\ln a}\,a^X + C.$

7. Method of substitution (counterpart of chain rule in differentiation):

$$\int g(u) \frac{du}{dX} dX = \int g(u) \, du.$$

Example: $\int e^{2X} dX$. To compute this integral, we first substitute $u = 2X$, then $du = 2 \cdot dX$ (recall $du = (du/dX) \cdot dX$, the differential); therefore $dX = (du/2)$. Hence $\int e^{2X} dX = \int e^u (du/2)$, by substituting u for $2X$ and $(du/2)$ for dX. But $\int e^u (du/2) = \frac{1}{2} \int e^u du$ (by rule 4) $= \frac{1}{2} e^u + C$ (by rule 3) $= \frac{1}{2} e^{2X} + C$ (by substituting back $2X$ for u). This example shows the essence of the method of substitution. When it is not obvious how to integrate directly, we substitute u for part of the expression, we write everything in terms of u and du, and hopefully we come up with an expression in u that is easier to integrate (see also examples below).

Examples:

1) $\int 2X^2 + 3X + 1 \, dX = 2 \int X^2 \, dX + 3 \int X \, dX + \int 1 \, dX$

$$= 2 \cdot \frac{X^3}{3} + 3 \frac{X^2}{2} + X + C$$

$$= \tfrac{2}{3} X^3 + \tfrac{3}{2} X^2 + X + C.$$

2) $\int \dfrac{2X + 1}{X^2 + X} \, dX$. Here we have to use the method of substitution again.
   Let $u = X^2 + X$, then $du = (2X + 1) \, dX$.

$$\int \frac{2X + 1}{X^2 + X} \, dX = \int \frac{1}{u} \, du = \ln u + C = \ln(X^2 + X) + C.$$

3) $\int X \sqrt{X^2 + 1} \, dX$. Let $u = X^2 + 1$, then $du = 2X \, dX$ or $dX = (du/2X)$.

$$\int X \sqrt{X^2 + 1} \, dX = \int X \sqrt{u} \frac{du}{2X} = \int \frac{1}{2} \sqrt{u} \, du$$

$$= \frac{1}{2} \int u^{1/2} \, du = \frac{1}{2} \cdot \frac{1}{3/2} u^{3/2} + C$$

$$= \frac{1}{3} (X^2 + 1)^{3/2} + C.$$

3. Definite Integrals

A typical definite integral looks like $\int_a^b f(X) \, dX$ [read "integral of $f(X)$ from a to b"]. Here $f(X)$ is called the integrand, a is called the lower limit, and b is called the upper limit of integration. The main difference between an indefinite and a definite integral is that the result of indefinite integration is a function, whereas the result of definite integration is a number. The meaning of that number is as follows.

Let $\int_a^b f(X) \, dX = A$. If $f(X) \geq 0$, then A is simply the area under the curve $Y = f(X)$ from a to b, shown in Fig. D.18(a). That area is equal to $\int_a^b f(X) \, dX$. Suppose

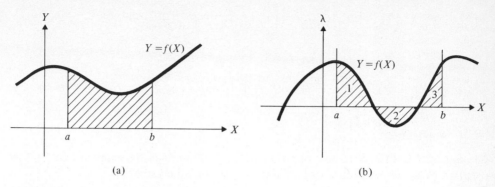

Figure D.18

now $f(X)$ is both positive and negative in the range of $a \leq X \leq b$, then A, the result of $\int_a^b f(X)\,dX$, is the *signed* area "under" $f(X)$ from a to b. By "signed area," we mean that the area above the X-axis is assigned a positive sign and the area below the X-axis is assigned a negative sign. Then A is the sum of all the positive and negative area [see Fig. D.18(b)]. If the curve of $f(X)$ is the one in Fig. D.18(b), then $\int_a^b f(X)\,dX = A = \text{area } 1 - \text{area } 2 + \text{area } 3$.

The link between the definite integral and the indefinite integral is given by the next theorem, which is called the Fundamental Theorem of Calculus.

Theorem: Let $F(X)$ be an indefinite integral of $f(X)$, then

$$\int_a^b f(X)\,dX = F(b) - F(a).$$

The theorem shows us a way to evaluate the definite integral. We need only to find the indefinite integral of the integrand and then substitute the upper and lower limits and find the difference. Although the indefinite integral of a function is not unique, the theorem says that any one will do, as long as it is the same one in which you substitute the upper and lower limits.

Examples:

1) $\displaystyle\int_1^2 (X + 2)\,dX = \left(\frac{X^2}{2} + 2X\right)\Big|_1^2 = \left[\frac{2^2}{2} + 2(2)\right] - \left[\frac{1^2}{2} + 2\cdot 1\right]$

$$= (2 + 4) - (\tfrac{1}{2} + 2) = 3\tfrac{1}{2},$$

2) $\displaystyle\int_0^1 e^X\,dX = e^X\Big|_0^1 = [e^1] - [e^0] = e - 1.$

PROPERTIES OF DEFINITE INTEGRALS

1. $\displaystyle\int_a^a f(X)\,dX = 0.$

2. $\displaystyle\int_a^b f(X)\,dX = -\int_b^a f(X)\,dX.$

3. If $a < c < b$, then $\int_a^b f(X)\,dX = \int_a^c f(X)\,dX + \int_c^b f(X)\,dX$.

4. $\int_a^b cf(X)\,dX = c\int_a^b f(X)\,dX$.

5. $\int_a^b [f(X) + g(X)]\,dX = \int_a^b f(X)\,dX + \int_a^b g(X)\,dX$.

4. Applications

Example 1:   Let the fixed cost of production be 100 and let marginal cost be $10/\sqrt{X}$ per unit. What is the total cost function for producing q units?

$$\text{Total cost} = \text{fixed cost} + \text{total variable cost}$$

$$= 100 + \int_0^q 10/\sqrt{X}\,dX$$

$$= 100 + \int_0^q 10X^{-1/2}\,dX$$

$$= 100 + 10\,\frac{1}{1/2} \cdot X^{1/2}\,\Big|_0^q$$

$$= 100 + [20\sqrt{q}] - [20\sqrt{0}]$$

$$= 100 + 20\sqrt{q}.$$

Example 2:   Suppose an income stream of 10,000/yr. is coming in continuously for the next 10 years. How much is it worth today if the discount rate is 5%?

$$\text{Present value} = \int_0^{10} 10{,}000e^{-0.5t}\,dt$$

$$= 10{,}000 \times \frac{-1}{.05}\,e^{-.05t}\,\Big|_0^{10}$$

$$= 10{,}000 \times \left(-\frac{1}{.05}\right)[e^{-.05 \times 10} - e^{-.05 \times 0}]$$

$$= -200{,}000[0.6065 - 1]$$

$$= 78{,}700.$$

Note that the formula for the present value of continuous discounting of a continuous flow is $\int_0^T (\text{CF})e^{-rt}\,dt$, where $\text{CF} = $ cash flow per time unit, $T = $ time when cash flow ends, and $r = $ discount rate.

5. Improper Integrals

Sometimes the limits of integration may be $-\infty$ or $+\infty$. Such a definite integral is called an improper integral. To evaluate an improper integral, we do not substitute $-\infty$ or $+\infty$ into the indefinite integral, but rather we substitute a variable b in place of $+\infty$ (or $-\infty$) and let $b \to \infty$ (or $-\infty$). In other words:

$$\int_a^\infty f(X)\,dX = \lim_{b \to \infty} \int_a^b f(X)\,dX,$$

$$\int_{-\infty}^a f(X)\,dX = \lim_{b \to -\infty} \int_b^a f(X)\,dX,$$

$$\int_{-\infty}^\infty f(X)\,dX = \lim_{\substack{a \to -\infty \\ b \to +\infty}} \int_b^a f(X)\,dX.$$

Example: Suppose the income stream in the previous example is perpetual; then the present value would be

$$PV = \int_0^\infty 10{,}000 e^{-.05t}\,dt$$

$$PV = \lim_{b \to \infty} \int_0^b 10{,}000 e^{-.05}\,dt$$

$$= \lim_{b \to \infty} 10{,}000 \left(-\frac{1}{.05}\right)[e^{-.05b} - e^{-.05 \times 0}]$$

$$= 10{,}000 \times (-20)[0 - 1], \quad \text{since } e^{-.05b} \to 0 \text{ as } b \to \infty,$$

$$PV = \$200{,}000.$$

Note that for a perpetual stream, we also have

$$PV = \frac{CF}{i} = \frac{10{,}000}{.05} = \$200{,}000 \qquad \text{where CF is the cash flow.}$$

This gives the same result as the integral calculus method.

REFERENCE

Pratt, J. W., "Risk Aversion in the Small and in the Large," *Econometrica*, January–April 1964, 122–136.

Author Index

927

Subject Index